Qur'an Revealed

A Christian Critique
Surah by Surah
Verse by Verse

ROBERT C. GREER, PH.D.

The Infancy Gospel of Pseudo-Matthew: Source: Translated by Alexander Walker, from Ante-Nicene Fathers, vol 8, eds.: Alexander Roberts, James Donaldson, A. Cleveland Coxe (Buffalo, NY: Christian Literature Publishing, Co., 1886).

The Book of Idols: Source: Hisham ibn-al-Kalbi, transl. Nabih Amin Faris. Princeton University Press, 1952; Used by Permission.

Image of the Mosque of Omar: Getty Images, license #10033029.

Gregory of Tours: Glory of the Martyrs: Source: Translated by Raymond Van Dam. Liverpool University Press, 1988. Used by Permission.

Believing and Obeying Jesus Christ: John R. W. Stott. Downers Grove: InterVarsity Press, Used by Permission.

Foundations of the Christian Faith: James Montgomery Boice. Downers Grove: InterVarsity Press, 1986, Used by Permission.

The Contemporary Christian: John R. W. Stott. Downers Grove: InterVarsity Press. 1992, Used by Permission.

The Message of the Sermon on the Mount: John R. W. Stott. InterVarsity Press, 1978, Used by Permission.

The Message of Galatians: John R. W. Stott. InterVarsity Press, 1968, Used by Permission.

The Cross of Christ: John R. W. Stott, InterVarsity Press, 1986, Used by Permission.

The Aramaic Bible, vol 18, The Two Targums of Esther: Translated by Bernard Grossfield. Liturgical Press, Collegeville, Minnesota, 1987. Used by Permission.

Hadiths: Sahih Bukhari, Sahih Muslim, Sahih Mwatta: Center for Muslim-Jewish Engagement. Los Angeles, Calif. 90089, Used by Permission.

New International Version of the Bible: Grand Rapids, Mich.: Zondervan Publishing House, 1995. Used by Permission.

Arabic Gospel of the Infancy of the Savior: Source: Translated by Alexander Walker, from Ante-Nicene Fathers, vol 8, eds.: Alexander Roberts, James Donaldson, A. Cleveland Coxe (Buffalo, NY: Christian Literature Publishing, Co., 1886).

Gospel of Thomas: Source: Translated by Alexander Walker, from Ante-Nicene Fathers, vol 8, eds.: Alexander Roberts, James Donaldson, A. Cleveland Coxe (Buffalo, NY: Christian Literature Publishing, Co., 1886).

The Qur'an by Edward Henry Palmer is in public domain.

The Apostles Creed is in the public domain.

The Definition of Chalcedon is in the public domain.

The Nicene-Constantinopolitan Creed is the in public domain.

Library of Congress Control Number: 2010940362

Cover design by Pat Theriault

Catagories:

1. Religion: Comparative Religion
2. Religion: Christian Theology—Apologetics
3. Religion: Islam: Koran and Sacred Writings

First Printing: March 2011
11 12 13 14 15 16 17 10 9 8 7 6 5 4 3 2 1
Printed in the United States of America

ACKNOWLEDGEMENTS

This book would have been impossible to complete without the continual support and consid-erable sacrifice of my beloved wife, Linda. Special friends also surrounded me, some with wise insights that made their way into the notes and commentary, and others with unending moral support and prayers. Special thanks are therefore due to Ron, Diane, Art, Theresa, Gray, Theresa, Doug, Karen, Gary, Carol, and Bill. Magda is also to be thanked for her artistic talents in several of the sketches. In addition, the people of Advantage Books have been a constant source of encouragement, along with their creativity, insights, and commitment to this project. The com-munity of Christian fellowship that surrounded me was such that I sensed the presence and power of God as I plodded forward, page after page. At times of discouragement, I sensed the divine Spirit nudge me to return to my computer keyboard, or pick up another book, or visit another library, or think hard about a difficult problem...and not give up.

The book is dedicated to my parents (now deceased), my beautiful wife, my two sons, their beautiful wives, and my two grandchildren. It is my prayer that the threat of Jihad and Shari'a Law that is pressing upon the West will be successfully resisted and that we will enjoy a season of peace.

The truth is not for all men, but only for those who seek it.

—Ayn Rand

All truths are easy to understand once they are discovered; the point is to discover them.

—Galileo Galilei

TABLE OF CONTENTS

v

Introduction

With its more than one and one half billion followers, Islam is the second largest religion in the world. It is second only to the Christian religion, which has an estimated two billion one hundred million followers. The earth's population currently stands at approximately six billion eight hundred million people. This means that slightly less than one in four people on the earth is a Muslim. Islam is therefore a serious force to be reckoned with, not only in respect to its understanding of spirituality but also in respect to the various Islamic cultures that have emerged out of its vast milieu.

For centuries, Islam was a military threat. Its empire reached across much of Asia, India, North Africa, and parts of Europe. Indeed, in three critical moments (the Battle of Tours in 732, the Siege of Vienna in 1529, and the Battle of Vienna in 1683), it threatened to overtake all of Europe. Turned back in these military engagements, it entered into a malaise, and became part of the third world—backwards, impoverished and underdeveloped. It was not until the advent of the industrial revolution in the West in the early twentieth century that all this changed. With the West's insatiable thirst for oil, the Muslim world awoke. Where it was once dirt poor, it became oil rich; and with its wealth came power. The Muslim world is now, once again, a major player on the world stage.

Five Forms of Islam

Broadly speaking, five forms of Islam exist in the world today. The first group is *traditional Islam*. Traditional Muslims read the Qur'an and study the life of Muhammad "without modification because they refuse to admit that the modern age mandates any reform whatsoever."[1] Practically speaking, the difference in their understanding of Islamic spirituality with that of their fundamentalist brethren is "so thin that the difference is often blurred."[2] Traditional Muslims tend to be peaceful people. They live isolated lives, wishing to live that which they believe is right, yet uninvolved in the non-Muslim world about them.

The second group is *folk Islam*. Born into Muslim families that are located in regions dominated by Islamic culture, this group of Muslims remain committed to Islam due to community expectations and requirements. Their knowledge of the Islamic faith is exceedingly limited, characteristically nothing more than a rudimentary understanding of Islamic dogma. Most are illiterate. For them, spirituality is a mixture of Islam with local superstitions, practices and convictions.[3] These superstitions, practices and convictions include a reliance on amulets, incantations, potions, and rituals—combined with words from the Qur'an.[4] It has been estimated that three-fourths of the Muslim world is characterized by folk Islam.[5]

The third group is *moderate Islam*. The dominant feature of moderate Islam is its commitment to the twin notions of world peace and moral purification. Moderate Muslims regard the Qur'an as containing a "canon within the canon"—specific verses believed to be the core of the Qur'an and therefore more authoritative than all the rest. This dominant inner canon (a) is characterized by peace and purity, and (b) pushes the verses characterized by violence and oppression to the margins of the Islamic faith. Moderate Muslims also perceive a compatibility of Western enlightenment and post-enlightenment values with this inner canon and are therefore in pursuit of a synthesis between the two. Islamic scholar Ali Minai explains: "The swamp that must be drained is not in the mountains of Afghanistan, but in the minds of hundreds of millions of Muslims. It is time for a new synthesis in Islam, and it can only be done from within by enlightened, informed, and faithful Muslims."[6] Accordingly, moderate Muslims condemn the oppressive treatment of women that exists in much of the Muslim world and the calculated training in hate and violence that typifies fundamentalist Islam. They also believe that the abject poverty and stagnation in most of the Muslim world is due, in large part, to a backwards and ossified reading of the Qur'an. Minai adds, "All Muslims believe that the words of the Qur'an are eternal, but that is no excuse to freeze the process of their interpretation. If the words are to provide guidance in an ever-changing world, they must speak in ever-changing ways."[7]

The fourth group is *fundamentalist Islam*. No aspect of the Islamic religion has so dominated the public eye throughout the world as has fundamentalist Islam. And this, of course, is due to the fanatical activism of Hamas, Hezbollah, al Qaeda, Lashkar-e-Taiba, Jaish-e-Mohammed, the Wahhabis, the Ayatollahs, the Jihadists and the suicide bombers. Ayaan Hirsi Ali writes: "Fundamentalists are on the rise everywhere, even among professionals with a high level of education (lawyers, doctors, and others). They are disappointed by secular ideologies such as liberal democracy, nationalism, and communism. Fundamentalists believe that all the social and economic miseries—'What went wrong'—are due to the widespread neglect of Islamic values and standards."[8] In contrast to moderate Islam, fundamentalist Muslims believe that the so-called "new inter-pretations" of the Qur'an are corruptions of a plain reading of the text, unduly influenced by Western values. They also proclaim the most dire consequences on all who refuse to submit to Allah, Muhammad, and the Qur'an.

The fifth group is *apostate Islam*. The defining characteristic of apostate Muslims is that they had at one time embraced the Islamic faith but have since turned away from it. Some have turned to the Christian faith, others to the Hindu faith, others still to Buddhism or one of the many other eastern religions. Another avenue of apostates is secularism, people with no apparent or defining religious interests. A final group of apostates are heterodox Muslims. They still think of themselves as Muslims, albeit in an unorthodox fashion due to their unorthodox beliefs. Apostate Muslims are sharp in their criticism of Islam. One such apostate Muslim has written, "To live under Islamic Shari'a law is to live in the world's largest maximum security prison, and I for one don't want to be incarcer-ated again."[9] Apostate Muslims are looked upon by fundamentalist Muslims as having committed treason against Allah and therefore worthy of death. It is because of this threat that many apostate Muslims keep their apostasy private. They maintain the out-ward appearance of faithfulness to the dogmas of Islam yet have quietly disavowed them.[10]

A further characteristic of Islam, one that encompasses all its groups, is that it has no priesthood. Since the Qur'an maintains that each person is responsible for his or her own salvation, Islam has no need of priests and their sacraments. Its clerics, called imams, are merely the dispensers of knowledge. Bernard Lewis explains, "In modern times there have been many changes, mainly under Western influences, and institutions and professions have developed which bear a suspicious resemblance to the churches and clerics of Christendom. But these represent a departure from classical Islam, not a return to it."[11]

The Spread of Religion

In his book *Inside the Revolution*, Joel C. Rosenberg has made the case that "behind the headlines of all the Middle Eastern wars and rumors of wars and revolutions and acts of terror, God is actually moving in an incredibly powerful way. People in the epicenter are coming to Christ in record numbers. Millions in Iran. Millions in Sudan. Millions in Pakistan. Millions in Egypt. And many more throughout the rest of the region. It is truly stunning to behold."[12] That which is happening is illustrative of what Jesus spoke long ago to his disciples: "I tell you, open your eyes and look at the fields! They are ripe for harvest" (Jn 4:35).

Yet the flip side of this phenomenon is that the world's fastest growing Muslim popu-lations (per capita) are now found in Europe and the United States of America. They are out-reproducing Christians and Jews almost seven to one. It is only a matter of a few generations before Muslims gain a demographic parity and then advantage in the West and begin enacting major cultural and religious changes. Some are already calling for recognition and respect for Shari'a Law.

The Question of Dialogue

In the West, Muslims and non-Muslims seem to rarely talk meaningfully of their differences. And when they do, neither side seems capable of listening. From the non-Muslim side, the reason for this impasse—in part—is a lack of understanding of the other side's most sacred literature: the Qur'an.

It is an odd curiosity that most non-Muslims—including Christians—have never read the Qur'an. This phenomenon has brought into existence a wall, the inability of Muslims and non-Muslims to dialogue intelligently and effectively with one another. Without an understanding of its foundational sacred literature, misunderstandings and voids of understanding are inevitable. The word *jihad* is a case in point. Does it mean a spiritual experience on the inside of the soul, something not unlike yoga, as moderate Muslims claim? Or does it have an aggressive outward side, a call to violence and Holy War, to bring the entire world into submission to Allah, as fundamentalist Muslims claim? Or is it perhaps both, intertwined into a singular vision? Another word is *islamification*. When Muslims speak of islamifying the world, what do they mean? How does the Islamic push for islamification affect cultures that have historically resisted Islam, such as cultures that possess a secular and Christian substructure? The Qur'an offers a way in to rightly understand these and other words...and the Muslim mind.

The first step in understanding Islam, then, is not to read books about Islam. Neither is it to engage in dialogue with Muslims, appealing as that may sound. Rather, the first step is to carefully read—and read with discrimination and discernment—the Qur'an. And, as just mentioned, this is the step most often skipped or overlooked by non-Muslims. Without a clear and working understanding of the Qur'an, an accurate assessment of the moderate Muslim mind, the history of Islam, Islamic fundamentalist terrorism, the Palestinian problem, the presence of Islam in the West, and so on, is an impossible task...and meaningful dialogue between Muslims and non-Muslims suffers accordingly.

The Purpose of *The Annotated Qur'an*

With this in mind, *Qur'an Revealed* has been written. Its intent is to equip the Christian believer with a working knowledge of the Qur'an. The notes are written to help the Christian better understand the qur'anic text and discern the doctrinal differences that divide the Islamic and Christian worldviews. The intent is to help Christians meet the current Islamic challenge in the West intelligently, meaningfully, and forcefully.

Muslims, of course, claim that the Qur'an is a sacred text and should be treated as such. *Qur'an Revealed* recognizes and is sensitive to this concern. Without question, the Qur'an should be treated with respect. But this does not mean that emotionally-charged and controversial topics should be avoided. They must be examined since, if left unaddressed, one has not rightly and fully considered the Qur'an. Anything less than a rigorous examination of these topics is to treat the Qur'an disrespectfully—to assume that it is a document that is indeed false and therefore in need of protection from the penetrating rays from the Light of Truth.

Moreover, the New Testament insists that we give the Qur'an a rigorous examination. We are mandated: "Do not treat prophecies with contempt. Test everything. Hold on to the good. Avoid every kind of evil" (1 Thess 5:20-22). And again: "Dear friends, do not believe every spirit, but test the spirits to see whether they are from God, because many false prophets have gone out into the world" (1 Jn 4:1).

The Annotated Qur'an: Its Four Features

1. Introductions. *Qur'an Revealed* contains six introductions to help the reader acquire an overall understanding of each of the six sections in the Qur'an. They are arranged chronologically, enabling the reader to place each section in its historical context. *The Annotated Qur'an* thereby rejects the mainstream Islamic notion that the Qur'an is an uncreated document existing eternally in the heavens and dictated to Muhammad one surah at a time. Rather, it is a wholly historical document and can only be rightly understood when its historical context and development are taken into consideration.

2. System of Notes. *Qur'an Revealed* is presented in a fashion similar to the annotated Bibles found in most evangelical Christian homes. The text of the Qur'an is located on the top portion of the page in two columns. On the bottom of each page are special notes that correspond to the text of the Qur'an located on the same page to help the reader better understand that which he or she is reading. Some of the notes provide helpful historical or cultural data. Others address figures of speech that the seventh century Arab would understand but are foreign to the modern reader. Because the Qur'an is a historical document, the historical-critical method is utilized in the examination of the one hundred fourteen surahs. Efforts are made to present mainstream Islamic interpretations of the Qur'an. When applicable, doctrinal issues are compared and contrasted with a biblical understanding of the same doctrine.

3. Essays. Mixed within each of the sections are a number of short essays that correspond to some theme mentioned in the Qur'an requiring further explanation. Included in these essays are archeological discoveries that impact one's reading of the text. Following the essays are an assortment of quotes from Islamic and non-Islamic scholars who have weighed in meaningfully on the topic of the essays. Their purpose is to expose the reader to a range of interpretations that exist in scholarship.

4. The Chronological Arrangement. In its standard and authorized arrangement, the one hundred fourteen surahs in the Qur'an are determined by length. With few exceptions, the longest surah comes first and the rest follow in descending order. This arrangement, then, has no thematic or chronological rationale. In *Qur'an Revealed,* the surahs are arranged in chronological order. This feature enables the reader to gain a sense of the historical context of each of the surahs and the development of the nascent Islamic faith.

The Qur'an was written over a twenty-two year period during the tumultuous early seventh century. Without an understanding of this historical period, two problems emerge when reading the Qur'an. First, interpretation and application become labored and tenuous, subject to a heightened degree of error. This is because surahs typically address problems faced by Muhammad as the early history of Islam unfolded. Without an understanding of the nature of these problems, it is difficult to correctly discern the intent of each of the surahs. Second, surahs are subject to the phenomenon of progressive revelation. Surahs written in an early period affirmed ideas that at times were set aside and replaced by surahs written in a latter period. The Qur'an itself acknowledges this phenomenon.[13] Without a knowledge of the chronology and historical development of the Qur'an, it is impossible to rightly interpret these conflicting passages.

Admittedly, not all scholars—Islamic and well as non-Islamic—are in agreement with the chronological ordering of the one hundred fourteen surahs. Some place certain surahs in the Meccan Period while others insist that they belong in the Medinan Period. And, the ordering of the surahs in each of the two periods differs among scholars. Nevertheless, a general consensus has emerged regarding most of the surahs. The differences that exist are minor and do not affect the overall sense of qur'anic development and chronology.

In *Qur'an Revealed,* I make use of Sir William Muir's chronological arrangement, adapted by Thomas Patrick Hughes as presented in the *Dictionary of Islam.* The Qur'an is divided into six periods, five composed in Mecca and one composed in Medinah. Their distinguishing characteristics are the following:

- **First Period.** These were the first surahs composed by Muhammad and constitute his initial presentation to the people of Mecca.

- **Second Period.** These were the surahs composed by Muhammad where he began to gain his theological footing and lay out the overall purpose of his ministry.

- **Third Period.** These were surahs composed during the time when the Meccan people, by in large, rejected Muhammad. It was a time when isolated episodes of persecution broke out against his small Muslim following.

- **Fourth Period.** The surahs of this period emphasized and brought clarity to Islamic doctrine. Included in this period was Muhammad's temporary compromise with idolatry, commonly known today as the Satanic Verses. It also includes the time in which a longstanding (two to three year) boycott took place with the intent of starving Muhammad and his followers into submission to the Meccan authorities.

- **Fifth Period.** The fifth period begins with the termination of the boycott and Muhammad's alleged encounter with *ginns* (genies). In this period, the Islamic theology is deepened and clarified. Also included in this period is Muhammad's alleged night trip to Temple Mount in Jerusalem and his brief ascension into heaven.

- **Sixth Period.** The final period took place following Muhammad's flight to Medinah. Here we see Muhammad as *prince*, laying down laws and precepts. He also gave a full development of Islam, as contrasted against Judaism and Christianity. Its major theme, however, is the development of the Doctrine of Jihad, providing the theological rationale for Islamic Holy War.

The chronological arrangement of the Qur'an, then, is admittedly an inexact science. Still, it is useful—indeed, necessary—for the reasons outlined above. And, as already mentioned, the differences between scholars involve only a few of the surahs. They have no effect in disturbing the established consensus in scholarship of the overall understanding of the Qur'an in its historical setting.

Hermeneutical Strategy

The strategy that I employed in the writing of notes was fivefold: (a) I emphasized mainstream Islamic scholarship in the interpretation of the overall presentation of each surah (chapter) and ayah (verse), (b) I supplemented this Islamic interpretation with canonical Hadiths that I believe to be relevant to the discussions at hand, (c) I made use of archeological evidence from accredited sources which, at times, challenged mainstream Islamic interpretations, (d) I interfaced each of the surahs with a Christian response—a response reflective of mainstream evangelicalism, and (e) I disregarded that form of historical-critical research which makes the case that the surahs were collected, edited, and published three decades after Muhammad's death. Though this research has some merit, it tends to disqualify the historicity of the Qur'an and Muhammad's role as Prophet. Consequently, I deliberately set aside this particular approach to historical-criticism, leaving it to other scholars to address the questions posed by the Qur'an's late editing.

The term "mainstream Islamic scholarship" is itself problematic. This is because varying strands exist that vie for the title *mainstream*—the two most prominent being moderate and fundamentalist Islam. The differences are stark and have generated much controversy within the Muslim world. Abdullah Al-Araby stands opposed to moderate Islam, describing it as inauthentic, a facelift to the original intent of the Qur'an and traditional Islamic values. That which drives moderate Islam, he maintains, is a desire to meld to Western values and be afforded a place at the table in Western culture. He comments:

> The "Islam" that Muslim activists introduce to the West these days is completely different from the Islam we knew and experienced in the Middle East. This is a new edition—revised, modified, expanded and abridged—of the real Islam. A major facelift operation has been taking place here.[14]

In contrast, Abou El Fadl, a major voice in moderate Islam, has written:

> Islam has become intimately associated with what can be described as ugliness—intolerance, persecution, oppression, and violence...For a Muslim who cares about his or her faith, this reality arouses intense feelings of hurt and anguish. More than a billion people find in Islam their emotional and spiritual sustenance and fulfillment. For those Muslims, Islam is their source of serenity and spiritual peace, and Islam offers moral and ethical guidance that, instead of ugliness, fills their lives with beauty.[15]

Which is the correct Islam, the one that rightly reflects its soul? Scholarship—both within and outside Islam—wrestles with this question. Moderate Muslims claim that dogma cannot be rightly understood in terms of a changelessly adequate embodiment of revealed eternal truths, for such abstracted embodiments do not exist. They say that meaning depends upon the situation in which abiding truths are found. To repeat an eternal truth in the same old ways in radically new circumstances is not to preserve but to betray it. Hence, they conclude that the only way to say the same thing in a new context is to say it differently. Yet, say traditional and fundamentalist Muslims, by saying it differently, is it not possible that one is no longer saying the same thing? Perhaps by saying it differently one is nudging Islam into something that it is not—morphing it with values that are Western, Hindu, or Eastern. And so the battle continues. The battle is not unlike the modernist-postmodernist war that has preoccupied much of Western scholarship in the last few decades.

The intent of *Qur'an Revealed* is not to enter into this battle and advance one side or the other. Rather, it is to help people—particularly Christians—acquire a working knowledge of the Qur'an. It is the foundation-stone of the faith and morality of Islam. The Qur'an will therefore be examined from within its own historical and grammatical context. This is ground zero. Hans Küng has rightly said that the Qur'an has "an amazing constancy in the changing and varied history of Islam from century to century, from land to land, from generation to generation, from person to person. What has been written remains written."[16] We will therefore strive to listen to the Qur'an, allowing it to speak to us on its own terms and within its own historical and cultural context.

Qur'an Revealed will then take the reader to the next level. Brief essays are intermingled in the pages, offering initial interpretations of the qur'anic material. They are theological reflections, a view of the Qur'an that attempts to make sense of its overall narrative. Though factual accuracy is sought in the essays, by their nature they are built upon a subjective substructure—that of the Christian worldview. In the final analysis, the question of the accuracy of the essays is left for the reader to determine. If they inspire the reader's own interpretation of the Qur'an, they will have achieved their purpose.

The English Translation

Qur'an Revealed makes use of the English translation of the Qur'an by Edward Henry Palmer (1840-1882), a professor of Arabic at Cambridge University. It is a widely accepted translation, written in 1880.

---

[1] Abou El Fadl, The Great Theft: Westling Islam from the Extemists, p. 106.

[2] Ibid.

[3] Hans Küng explains: "The more Islam spread, the less monolithic it became. It mixed with the practices and convictions of the popular cultures in which it found itself taking root. In this way it succeeded in penetrating groups of peoples, integrating them into states and often giving them a new social identity" (Islam: Past, Present & Future, p. 393).

[4] See Bill A. Musk, The Unseen Face of Islam and Rick Love, Muslims, Magic, and the Kingdom of God, two exposés of the occult in folk Islam; also see Christine A. Mallouhi, Waging Peace on Islam, p. 229.

[5] Rick Love, Muslims, Magic, and the Kingdom of God, p. 2.

[6] Ali Minai, "A Time for Renewal" in Taking Back Islam, p. 9. James Zogby claims that such moderate thinking also exists in the Muslim Mideast and North Africa (see Arab Voices, ch. 5).

[7] Ibid., pp. 9, 10.

[8] Ayaan Hirsi Ali, The Caged Virgin, p. 47.

[9] Nonie Darwish, Cruel and Usual Punishment, p. x.

[10] See Ibn Warraq, Leaving Islam: Apostates Speak Out.

[11] Bernard Lewis, The Crisis of Islam, pp. 9, 10.

[12] Joel Rosenberg, Inside the Revolution, p. 367.

[13] This is the famous Doctrine of Abrogation (see Q 2.106; 16.101 and 87.6-7).

[14] Abdullah Al-Araby, Islam: the Facade and the Facts.

[15] El Fadl, The Great Theft, pp. 3, 4.

[16] Küng, Islam: Past, Present & Future, p. 73.

Chronological Ordering of the Surahs

Surah	Page	Surah	Page	Surah	Page
First Period	19	**80**	73	**71**	202
103	22	**84**	78	**52**	203
100	23	**81**	79	**50**	206
99	23	**86**	84	**45**	209
91	26	**110**	85	**44**	214
106	30	**85**	86	**37**	217
1	31	**83**	90	**30**	225
101	35	**78**	98	**26**	232
95	36	**77**	99	**15**	242
102	36	**76**	101	**51**	250
104	37	**75**	104		
82	37	**70**	106	**Fifth Period**	254
92	40	**109**	113	**46**	256
105	41	**107**	113	**72**	261
89	42	**55**	114	**35**	268
90	44	**56**	120	**36**	273
93	51			**19**	280
94	52	**Fourth Period**	128	**18**	291
108	52	**67**	130	**27**	307
		53	132	**42**	321
Second Period	54	**32**	141	**40**	327
96	55	**39**	145	**38**	336
112	57	**73**	164	**25**	342
74	57	**79**	166	**20**	349
111	64	**54**	168	**43**	359
		34	175	**12**	366
Third Period	65	**31**	185	**11**	379
87	67	**69**	189	**10**	393
97	72	**68**	193	**14**	411
88	73	**41**	195	**6**	417

The 114 Surahs

Short Essays and Inserts

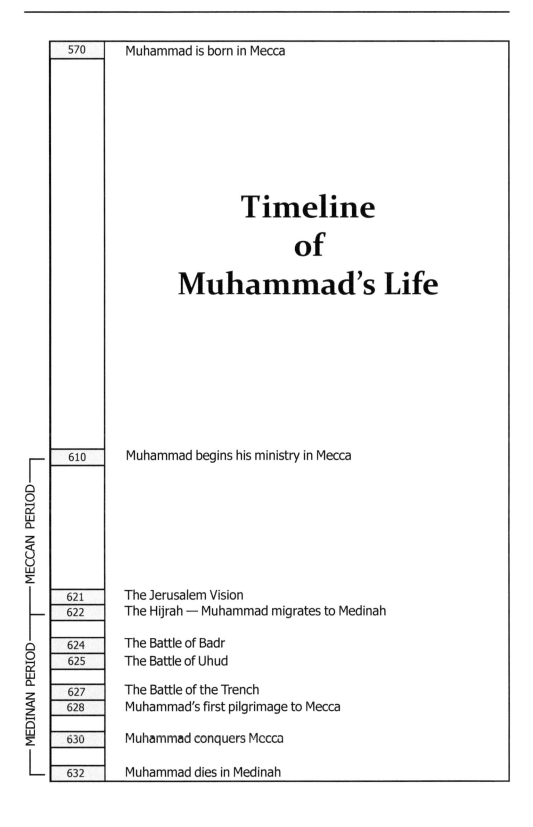

570	Muhammad is born in Mecca

Timeline
of
Muhammad's Life

610	Muhammad begins his ministry in Mecca
621	The Jerusalem Vision
622	The Hijrah — Muhammad migrates to Medinah
624	The Battle of Badr
625	The Battle of Uhud
627	The Battle of the Trench
628	Muhammad's first pilgrimage to Mecca
630	Muhammad conquers Mccca
632	Muhammad dies in Medinah

MECCAN PERIOD

MEDINAN PERIOD

ADVISORY

In the following pages, the Qur'an is annotated with information that makes it understandable to the reader:

- The Qur'an is divided into six periods, chronologically arranged, each with its own introduction to provide historical and thematic context.

- The upper portion of the pages is the Qur'an, the Palmer translation, written in 1880. Exceptions are the titles of each of the surahs and the captions at key transition points (written in italics) that provide helpful information in identifying the essence of the following qur'anic section.

- The lower portion of the pages are the notes that correspond to the verses in the Qur'an located on the same or adjacent page.

- Articles are interspersed in each of the six periods, designed to give a deeper understanding of the material being examined.

Accordingly, the Qur'an is carefully and respectfully presented.

INTRODUCTION

The First Period

Muhammad was born in Mecca in A.D. 570. This was a momentous year in the annals of Arabic lore, known as the legendary Year of the Elephant. An army from the southern tip of the Arabian Peninsula, equipped with elephants, threatened to attack and overcome Mecca. Miraculously, say those who recounted the legend, the invading army was defeated by birds who pelted the warriors with rocks (see Q 105 and corresponding note). Years later, Muhammad's followers would look at his birth falling precisely on the Year of the Elephant as a sign, an indication that he was destined for great things.

Muhammad was orphaned while an infant and raised by his uncle, Abu Talib. Since his uncle was one of the leaders of the dominant clans that made up Mecca (the Quraysh tribe), Muhammad was well cared for in his formative years. While a teen, he was assigned important activities associated with the pagan Ka'ba cult in Mecca. He also accompanied his uncle on caravans and thereby journeyed to distant lands. No doubt, while on these journeys he learned of the differing religions that made up the Middle East. In his twenties, he worked as a commercial agent for a rich widow, Khadijah, whom he later married.

A Collage of Religions. The Arabian Peninsula was a collage of competing religious interests. A belief in apparitions and daily encounters with the supernatural were commonplace. Prognosticators, spiritists, and self-proclaimed prophets, with their own small cult followings, came and went, each with a peculiar way of understanding the supernatural. Many were looked upon with suspicion by the general population, thought to be charlatans peddling a peculiar religion for their own particular advantage.

The dominant religion in the Arabian Peninsula was a peculiar version of astrology, rooted in the pagan Family Star religious system of the Sumerian culture of southeastern Iraq, centered in the city of Ur. Polytheistic in orientation, devotees of this religion looked to the stars as gods, all of which were interconnected in a vast and complex astral family—with gods procreating and giving birth to other gods. Virtually every physical item on earth was associated with one god or another. Superstitions were commonplace. Ka'ba altars were constructed in many of the cities in the Arabian Peninsula where devotees conducted their worship.

A lesser religion in Arabia was the occultic Religion of the Ginns (genies)—the black arts. Practitioners of ginn worship involved themselves in magic and sorceries. Reminiscent of the pagan religions practiced in Palestine prior and during the era when Israel occupied Palestine, they required the blood sacrifice of children as a way of showing their dedication to the ginns. The practice of ginn worship was deeply entrenched in Arabian culture, reaching back almost one thousand years.

Judaism was also found in northwest Arabia. Due to the Great Diaspora of the first century when the Roman Empire expelled the Jews from Palestine (c. A.D. 70), a number of Jews migrated south. Some settled in Hegra. Others settled in Yathrib (later called Medinah). Others still made their way further south and settled in Mecca. These Jews were steadfastly committed to the notion of monotheism and hence, stood opposed to the polytheism that was indigenous to the Arabian Peninsula.

And finally, a few Christian enclaves existed in Arabia. Some scholars, for example, believe that the Apostle Paul made Hegra his home during his three year sojourn in Arabia shortly after his conversion to the Christian faith (see Gal 1:17). A few Christians made Mecca their home. Similar to the Jews, the Christians too were committed to the notion of monotheism, albeit a peculiar form of monotheism—that which was called trinitarianism.

Muhammad's Early Spirituality. This collage of cultural and religious diversity shaped Muhammad's understanding of theology and spirituality. Rather than aligning himself with one of the established religions, he pursued a more eclectic approach. Influenced by the monotheisms of Judaism and Christianity, as well as the more indigenous religious ideas present in the Arabian Peninsula, he took that which he thought was correct and began the process of shaping his own brand of religion. Ernest Renan explains:

> His journeys to Syria, his contacts with Christian monks, and perhaps the personal influence of his uncle Waraqa, who was well versed in Jewish and Christian writings, would soon have introduced him to all the religious confusions of his century...The biblical stories had penetrated through to him by way of the narratives which had deeply impressed him, and which, having stayed in his mind in hazy recollections, gave his imagination free rein. To reproach Muhammad for having corrupted the biblical stories is totally misguided. Muhammad took these narratives as they were given to him; the narrative of the Koran is but the reproduction of the Talmudic traditions and the Apocrypha, above all the *Gospel of the Infancy*. This Gospel, which was translated into Arabic early on, and which has only survived in this language, had acquired a considerable reputation among Christians of the remote parts of the East, and had almost eclipsed the canonical texts. It is certain that these narratives were one of the most powerful sources of Muhammad's actions.[1]

With time, Muhammad wrote down his religious thoughts in the form of surahs—succinct poetical and rhetorical presentations—and recited them to anyone willing to listen, typically in the precinct of the Ka'ba altar. Thomas Patrick Hughes explained that the these eighteen surahs of this First Period are short rhapsodies that "may have been composed by Muhammad before he conceived the idea of a divine mission, none of which are in the form of message from the Deity."[2]

This, then, is the backdrop to the initial stage of Muhammad's career as Allah's alleged apostle and prophet. Some scholars believe that Muhammad was sincere in his efforts to reform the moral degeneracy of the Arabian culture. Others see him as an opportunist, seeking a political power base in Arabia and chose religion as his way to acquire such power. Still, others see him as a truly spiritual man who happened to have been misguided by hallucinations triggered by epileptic seizures that he falsely believed to be angelic visitations. Moreover, others see him as someone who was caught up in the occult (ginn/demonic worship) in the early years of his life; eventually, he made contact with such spirits who guided him in the founding of a new religion. And finally, many—indeed, the entire Muslim world—believe that Muhammad was Allah's chosen Prophet to communicate Allah's most complete and authoritative word to the world.

---

[1] Ernest Renan, "Muhammad and the Origins of Islam," in *The Quest for the Historical Muhammad*, p. 154.

[2] Thomas Patrick Hughes, *Dictionary of Islam*, p. 493.

Surah 103

In the name of the merciful and compassionate God

1   By the afternoon!

2   verily, man is in loss!
3   save those who believe and do right, and bid each other be true, and bid each other be patient.

Surah 103. The title of this surah, *The Afternoon,* comes from verse one. It is one of the smallest of surahs and its message is simple. It offers words of blessing for those who (a) believe, (b) do right, (c) are truthful, and (d) are patient. It therefore sets the overall theme for all the one hundred thirteen surahs that follow.

Surah 103 therefore parallels Psalm 1 in the Old Testament Psaltery, which carries a similar presentation of blessing for those who believe and seek to live a holy life.

103.3 *believe and do right* — These four words are often mentioned in the Qur'an and serve as a summary of the Islamic gospel (see Q 2.25, 62, 277; 3.57; 4.57, 122, 124, 146, 175; 5.93; 6.82; 10.4, 9; 11.23; 14.23; 16.97, 128; 18.30, 107; 19.60, 96; 22.14, 23, 50, 56; 24.5; 29.7, 9, 58; 30.15, 45; 31.8; 32.19; 34.4; 35.7; 38.24, 28; 40.58; 41.8; 42.22, 23, 26; 47.2, 12; 48.29; 64.9; 65.11; 84.25; 85.11; 95.6). Later in the Qur'an, Muhammad would fill in the details for what he meant. Salvation is a system of merit. A faithful Muslim was to place his or her faith in Allah (the Lord of the worlds) and Muhammad His Prophet. He or she was also to "do right," which meant unswerving obedience to the Five Pillars. Hence, belief and obedience are the roadmap to eternal life.

The Christian gospel stands opposed to the Islamic gospel. According to the New Testament, one does not work his or her way to salvation via the accumulation of good works. Rather, salvation is a question of placing one's faith in God who provides the blessing of eternal life via the death, burial, and resurrection of Jesus Christ. "He saved us, not because of righteous things we had done, but because of his mercy. He saved us through the washing of rebirth and renewal by the Holy Spirit, whom he poured out on us generously through Jesus Christ our Savior, so that, having been justified by his grace, we might become heirs having the hope of eternal life" (Titus 3:5-7).

One must think in terms of a courtroom to understand this spiritual process. We are acquitted on the grounds that Jesus Christ willingly stepped forward to be our substitute. That is, He paid the debt of sin on our behalf. God made Jesus Christ "who had no sin to be sin for us" (2 Cor 5:21).

Hence, salvation is not a system of merit, as it is in Islam. It cannot be earned. No matter how rightly lived our lives happen to be, sin is still present in each one of us. From God's perspective of absolute holiness, we all fall short—and grievously so. "For all have sinned and fall short of the glory of God" (Rom 3:23). Hence, our only option is to receive salvation as a gift—and this has been made available to us in Jesus Christ.

John R. W. Stott writes: "'Irresistible' is the word an Iranian student used when telling me of his conversion to Christ. Brought up to read the Qur'an, say his prayers and lead a good life, he nevertheless knew that he was separated from God by his sins.

Surah 100

In the name of the merciful and compassionate God.

1   By the snorting chargers!
2   And those who strike fire with their hoofs!
3   And those who make incursions in the morning,
4   And raise up dust therein,
5   And cleave through a host therein!
6   Verily, man is to his Lord ungrateful;
7   and, verily, he is a witness of that.
8   Verily, he is keen in his love of good.
9   Does he not know when the tombs are exposed,
10   and what is in the breasts is brought to light?
11   Verily, thy Lord upon that day indeed is well aware.

Surah 99

In the name of the merciful and compassionate God.

When Christian friends brought him to church and encouraged him to read the Bible, he learned that Jesus Christ had died for his forgiveness. 'For me the offer was irresistible and heaven-sent,' he said, and he cried to God to have mercy on him through Christ. Almost immediately 'the burden of my past life was lifted. I felt as if a huge weight...had gone. With the relief and sense of lightness came incredible joy. At last it happened. I was free of my past. I *knew* that God had forgiven me, and I felt clean. I wanted to shout, and tell everybody.' It was through the cross that the character of God came clearly into focus for him, and that he found Islam's missing dimension, 'the intimate fatherhood of God and the deep assurance of sins forgiven'" (*The Cross of Christ*, p. 42).
Surah 100. The title of this surah, *The Chargers*, comes from verse one. In this surah, Muhammad introduced the Doctrine of General Resurrection. This is the belief that all peoples will one day be raised from the dead and be held to account before a righteous God for the lives that they lived upon the earth. In this respect, the Doctrine of General Resurrection and the Doctrine of the Last Judgment are combined and cannot be rightly understood independently of one another. It is at this Last Judgment where that which "is in the breasts is brought to light" (v 10). This doctrine stood in contrast to the prevailing polytheism of the Arabian Peninsula, which denied a notion of a General Resurrection.

100.1-5 *by the snorting chargers! And those who strike fire with their hoofs! And those who make incursions in the morning...* The surah begins with the swearing of an oath. In contrast, Jesus admonished people to avoid speaking oaths: "But I tell you, do not swear at all...Simply let your Yes be Yes, and your No, No; anything beyond this comes from the evil one (see **Oaths in the Qur'an** on pp. 24-25).

100.6-8 Man remains ungrateful to the Lord, looking anywhere but to the Lord as the source of his many blessings. The Bible makes a similar claim (see Deut 8:11-18; Jer 2:31-32; Dan 5:4-5; Hos 2:8; 11:3-4; Rom 1:21; 2 Tim 3:2).

100.9-11 Man is unaware that he will one

Oaths in the Qur'an

In the Sermon on the Mount, Jesus spoke of the tradition of swearing, which was common in the Middle East. His point was for people not to swear at all and replace swearing with consistent display of integrity and honesty in their speech. He said: "Again, you have heard that it was said to the people long ago, 'Do not break your oath, but keep the oaths you have made to the Lord.' But I tell you, Do not swear at all: either by heaven, for it is God's throne; or by the earth, for it is his footstool; or by Jerusalem, for it is the city of the Great King. And do not swear by your head, for you cannot make even one hair white or black. Simply let your 'Yes' be 'Yes,' and your 'No,' 'No'; anything beyond this comes from the evil one" (Matt 5:33-37).

In contrast, Muhammad began a number of his surahs by swearing oaths. They were intended to give additional authority to what he was about to say. On a few occasions, he reversed himself, stating that the surah that he was about to recite did not require an oath.

By the snorting chargers! And those who strike fire with their hoofs! And those who make incursions in the morning, and raise up dust therein, and cleave through a host therein! (Q 100.1-5)

By the sun and its noonday brightness! And the moon when it follows him! And the day when it displays him! And the night when it covers him! And the heaven and what built it! And the earth and what spread it! (Q 91.1-6)

By the heaven and by the night star!   And what shall make thee know what the night star is?—The star of piercing brightness (Q 86.1-

3)

By the heaven with its zodiacal signs! And the promised day! And the witness and the witnessed! (Q 85.1-3)

By the dawn and ten nights! And the single and the double! And the night when it travels on! Is there in that an oath for a man of sense? (Q 89.1-5)

By the forenoon! And the night when it darkens... (Q 93.1-2)

By those sent in a series! And by those who speed swiftly! And by the dispensers abroad! And by the separators apart! And by those who instil the reminder, as an excuse or warning! (Q 77.1-6)

By the star when it falls, your comrade errs not, nor is he deluded! nor speaks he out of lust (Q 53.1-3)

By those who tear out violently! And by those who gaily release! And by those who float through the air! And the preceders who precede! And those who manage the affair! (Q 79.1-5)

By the pen, and what they write... (Q 68.1)

By the mount! by the Book inscribed upon an outstretched vellum! by the frequented house! by the elevated roof! by the swelling sea! (Q 52.1-6)

By the glorious Qur'an... (Q 50.1)

By the perspicuous Book! (Q 44.1)

By the (angels) ranged in ranks, and the drivers driving, and the reciters of the reminder (Q 37.1-3)

By the scatterers who scatter! and by those pregnant with their burden! and by those running on easily! and by the distributors of affairs! (Q 51.1-4)

By the wise Qur'an (Q 36.1)

I need not swear by the Lord of this land, and thou a dweller in this land! Nor by the begetter and what he begets! (Q 90.1-3)

I need not swear by the resurrection day! Nor need I swear by the self-accusing soul! (Q 75.1-2)

By the Qur'an with its reminder! (Q 38.1)

By the perspicuous Book... (Q 43.1)

1   When the earth shall quake with its quaking!
2   And the earth shall bring forth her burdens,
3   and man shall say, "What ails her!"
4   On that day she shall tell her tidings,
5   because thy Lord inspires her.
6   On the day when men shall come up in separate bands to show their works:
7   and he who does the weight of an

atom of good shall see it!
8   and he who does the weight of an atom of evil shall see it.

Surah 91

In the name of the merciful and compassionate God

1   By the sun and its noonday brightness!

day give an account to the Lord for his ungrateful spirit (see **The Last Judgment** on pp. 46-50).

Surah 99. The title of this surah, *The Quaking*, comes from verse one. According to Islamic tradition, Muhammad is believed to have said that whoever recites four times the surah beginning with the quake with its quaking will be rewarded just as much as one who recites the entire Qur'an. When a Muslim thinks in terms of the Last Judgment, recitations of this surah, then, is enormously useful since it avails one of a vast multiplication of good works.

Again, in this surah the Doctrine of General Resurrection is presented. Here Muhammad commented that the time of the general resurrection will confound people, since most people believe that no such a resurrection would take place.

99.7-8 *the weight of an atom of good —* At the Last Judgment, the smallest of deeds will be weighed and considered with the exactitude of the weight of an atom. With such precision, the implication is that the smallest deed could tip the balance towards either Paradise or Hell. Clearly, no one is capable of making such detailed assessments about the specific acts of one's life. Only Allah can. Al-

lah—and only Allah—knows with absolute precision (to an atom's weight) the measurement of the balance (see **The Last Judgment** on pp. 46-50).

In contrast, Christians can know with certainty their eternal destiny. The Apostle John wrote: "We know that we are children of God, and that the whole world is under the control of the evil one. We know also that the Son of God has come and has given us understanding, so that we may know him who is true. And we are in him who is true-even in his Son Jesus Christ. He is the true God and eternal life" (1 Jn 5:19-20; cf. Rom 8:16; 2 Cor 5:1; 2 Tim 1:12; 1 Jn 3:14; 24; 4:4-6).

Surah 91. The title of this surah, *The Sun*, comes from verse one. In this surah, Muhammad introduced the doctrine of the Apostles. He believed that divinely appointed apostles served Allah throughout history to the various peoples of the world. Those who heeded the warnings of the apostles would achieve eternal life. Those who did not, would be judged by Allah in this life as well at the Last Judgment (see **The Apostles** on pp. 396-398).

Muhammad highlighted the apostleship of Zali'h and those to whom he ministered:

the Thamudian people (also see Q 11.61-68; 14.9; 22.42; 25.38; 26.141-159; 27.45-53; 38.13; 41.17; 50.12; 51.43-45; 53.51; 54.22-31; 69.4-5; 85.18 89.9 and 91.11-14).

According to Q 7.73, the Thamudians were a people who came into being a generation after the people of Ad and inherited their land after the people of Ad were judged by Allah and utterly destroyed. Since Q 7.69 states that the people of Ad lived two generations after Noah and the Great Flood (Genesis 6-8), this places the Thamudian people as a truly ancient culture that existed *c.* 6000 B.C. or earlier. According to Q 15.80, they occupied the region of Hegra (also known as Hijr) in northwestern Arabia, southeast of the City of Petra in modern-day Jordan (see map on this page). They took for themselves "castles on its plains and hewed out mountains into houses" (Q 7.73).

It was at this time that Allah sent to the Thamudian people an apostle, Zali'h, to turn them from their false polytheistic religion and to the one true God. Some of the Thamudian people accepted Zali'h as a prophet but most did not and demanded a sign. They challenged him to produce a she-camel out of a rock. Zali'h prayed and the miracle took place. Later, the camel lived among them and gave birth to a calf. Because of this miracle, many people believed in Zali'h. Others, however, continued to reject him and his message. In their rebellion, they hamstrung his she-camel and ate it. As a form of divine judgment, the Thamudian people were then destroyed by an earthquake and volcanic eruption.

Yet the archeological record disputes these claims from the Qur'an. The Thamudian people were an Arabian tribe that did not appear before the eighth century, B.C. Towards the end of that century, they formed an allegiance with other Arabian tribes and attacked Sargon II and were quickly de-

feated. Many were then transported to Samaria where they continued as an organized tribe until the fifth century, A.D. They were dwellers in tents. No archeological evidence exists that they ever settled in Hegra. Rather, Hegra was built and occupied by the Nabatean people in the first century, B.C. (see **Hegra** on p. 28).

According to Umar ibn al-Khattah, in A.D. 630, while traveling to Tabuk (a small town in Saudi-Arabia: see map below) to fight a Byzantine army that Muhammad believed was traveling south to subdue him, Muhammad stopped at one of the abandoned houses in Hegra to draw water from a well. A Hadith comments that as the soldiers began to drink from its well and knead dough, Muhammad

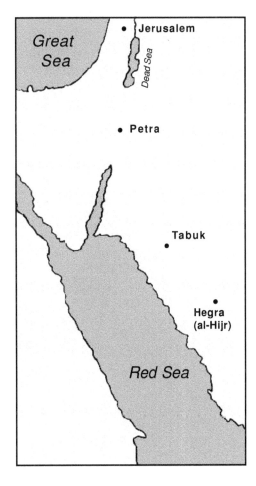

Hegra

Hegra (al-Hijr) is an archeological site that dates back to the second century, B.C. and extends to the second century, A.D. The site includes 131 tombs, walls, towers, water conduits, cisterns, and rooms for habitation, all excavated and carved into the stone walls. In this respect, Hegra is a small version of the City of Petra, located approximately two hundred twenty miles to the northwest. Ancient inscriptions on the walls are common. The Nabatean civilization constructed and dwelt at the site (see map on p. 27).

Hegra was situated on the caravan route that ran north and south in the Hejaz (the northwest region of the Arabian Peninsula, from the Gulf of Acaba to the city of Mecca). Hejaz literally means "'the ignorance,' but it also includes the notion of 'barbarism.' It is a term coined in Islamic times and is thus intended to discredit the idolatrous and licentious days of old, before the Islamic virtues and habits came to transform, to some extent, the life of Arabs."[1]

---

[1] Denny, *An Introduction to Islam*, p. 45

Early in the reign of Aretas IV—around the turn of the first millennium BC/AD—Hegra grew rapidly in size and importance. It was the most southerly of the Nabataean trading posts, offering protection and other services to caravans travelling along the rich trade route. There was also a strong military presence here, perhaps to defend the southerly border, and the traders, from raids by other Arab tribes. Here at Hegra incense-laden caravans from the south first entered Nabataean territory, and they remained in it all the way to Petra, and nearly as far as Gaza and the Mediterranean. With the rich pickings that protection offered, the provisioning of men and animals, the trade deals that were entered into and the tolls that were exacted on merchandise passing through their territory, the Hegra outpost soon became a large and prosperous settlement.

—Jane Taylor, *Petra and the Lost Kingdom of the Nabataeans*, p. 154

Hegra is an exceptionally attractive site, and there is much about its grandeur, even apart from the similarity of its tombs, that is reminiscent of the Nabataean capital. But while Petra is carved from a range of wild Nubian sandstone mountains of a predominantly russet tone, here at Hegra the Nabataeans chiseled their monuments into smaller and more orderly outcrops of gold Quweira sandstone that rise from a flat sandy floor. Higher mountains, some of them vast slabs of beige sandstone, ring the site and give the impression of enclosing a great lake of sand, with ships of rock moored here and there among spreading acacia trees.

—Jane Taylor, *Petra and the Lost Kingdom of the Nabataeans*, p. 154

The oldest tomb at Hegra can be dated to the year 1 B.C.E.; the most recent one to 75 C.E. Whereas the first has one of the most elaborate facades of the entire necropolis, both in type and style, others built many years later are capped with simple crenulations and have an unadorned facade.

—Maria Giulia Amadasi and Eugenia Equini Schneider, *Petra*, p. 139

Paul...naturally turned to the Jews and the God-fearers at Jerusalem's doors, in Damascus at first and later in Arabia [Gal 1:17]. Ministry in Nabatea was a natural extension of the ministry of other Christian workers in Palestine. The Nabateans were considered Ishmael's descendents and thus relatives—Semites. The same was true of the Idumeans. Paul's interest in them could have come from the prophetic promises to the "neighbours" (e.g. Jer 12:14-16). Hengel and Schwemer see Paul preaching all the way south, in Hegra.

—Ksenija Magda, *Paul's Territoriality and Mission Strategy*, p. 18

In Gal. 4:25...Hagar denotes the trading city of Hegra (Madain Salih), in South Nabatea, close to Petra...Paul had perhaps been there.

—Martin Hengel, *Paul and the Mosaic Law*, p. 38

2   And the moon when it follows
     him!

3   And the day when it displays him!

4   And the night when it covers him!

5   And the heaven and what built it!

6   And the earth and what spread it!

7   And the soul and what fashioned
     it,

8   and taught it its sin and its piety!

9   Prosperous is he who purifies it!

10   And disappointed is he who cor-
     rupts it!

11   Thamûd called the apostle a liar in
     their outrage,

12   when their wretch rose up

13   and the apostle of God said to
     them: "God's she-camel! so give
     her to drink."

14   But they called him a liar, and they
     ham-strung her; but their Lord
     destroyed them in their sins, and
     served them all alike;

15   and He fears not the result thereof!

Surah 106

*In the name of the merciful and compas-
sionate God*

---

rebuked them, poured the water to the ground, and fed the dough to the camels. His reasoning was that it was improper to take anything from Hegra since this city had been cursed by Allah for rejecting the ministry of Zali'h (*Sahih Bukhari* 4.55.562). In another Hadith, Muhammad added that the soldiers were not to enter the abandoned homes of the city of Hegra, unless they did so with weeping. Again, the reason was due to the curse that existed upon this site (*Sahih Bukhari* 4.55.563).

The Expedition to Tabuk, however, did not result in a battle against the Byzantines. According to the ninth surah, a military campaign was organized and a large Muslim army made its way to Tabuk, anticipating a battle with the Byzantines. Yet, the Byzantines failed to show up (see **The Expedition to Tabuk** on p. 862).

91.1-6 Muhammad introduced this surah with the swearing of an oath (see **Oaths in the Qur'an** on pp. 24-25). In this case, the swearing encompasses the day, night, heaven, earth, the soul, and Allah Himself.

91.7-8 In this passage, Muhammad hinted at the doctrine of double predestination. He explained that Allah teaches a soul to either sin or live piously (see the **Doctrine of al-Qadar** on pp. 264-266).

In contrast, Christians believe that God never "teaches" a soul to sin. It is God's will that none should perish (see 2 Pet 3:9) and that everyone embrace holiness (see Lev. 20:26; Matt 5:48; 1 Pet 1:16). The Book of Genesis states that God commanded Adam not to disobey Him. It is only because of Adam's disobedience that sin entered the world. He and his progeny have struggled with sin ever since (see Gen 2:16; Rom 5:12, 19; James 1:13-15).

91.13 *the apostle of God* — This refers to Zali'h, a legendary prophet of Allah who lived among the Thamudian people.

Surah 106. The title of this surah, *The Qurais*, comes from verse one. The Quraysh was the strongest of the tribal families in Mecca and therefore maintained control of its political, economic and religious life. Historians believe that this tribe was instrumen-

1 For the uniting of the Qurâis;	**Surah 1**
2 uniting them for the caravan of winter and summer.	
3 So let them serve the Lord of this house	1 In the name of the merciful and compassionate God
4 who feeds them against hunger and makes them safe against fear.	2 Praise belongs to God, the Lord of the worlds,
	3 the merciful, the compassionate,

tal in the founding of the city of Mecca sometime in the fourth century, A.D. Prior to this time, no evidence exists of Mecca (see **The City of Mecca** on pp. 32-34). Because of the rocky soil in the region surrounding Mecca, Mecca had little land suitable for agriculture. Its economy was therefore dependent upon the caravans that passed through its region and the revenue acquired by pilgrims who visited the Ka'ba altar.

106.1-2 *the caravans of winter and summer* — That is, the journeys of winter and summer. The Quraysh people of Mecca followed the tradition of forming pilgrimages to differing Ka'ba altars in Arabia, one in the summer and the other in the winter. In this surah, Muhammad called them to stop this practice and remain committed to exclusive worship at Mecca. This call suggests that worship at Mecca was initially not as esteemed as was worship at other Ka'ba altars in other cities in the Arabian Peninsula.

106.3 *the Lord of this house* — That is, the Lord of the Ka'ba altar. According to the qur'anic and hadithic literature, the Ka'ba altar was constructed by Hagar, Ishmael and the archangel Gabriel following Hagar's banishment from Abraham and Sarah (see Gen 21:15-18). Such an assertion, however, is contradicted by the records of ancient literature (see **The City of Mecca** on pp. 32-34).

106.3-4 Provided that the Quraysh tribe protected the Lord of the House (the Ka'ba

Altar), Muhammad explained, the Lord would care for the people of Mecca.

Surah 1. The title of this surah, *The Opening*, comes from the entire surah. This is the first of all the surahs and serves as the opening prayer for the Qur'an. It has been described by some Islamic scholars as the perfect prayer. It is recited by Muslims at funerals, memorial services, births, and during illnesses. Its overall theme is that of a doxology to Allah and an articulation of the two eternal paths: one path leads to Allah in eternal bliss, the other leads away from Allah in eternal torment. It also affirms the notion of absolute monotheism (the Doctrine of Tauhid).

Imam al Sadiq has written: "This is the path of knowledge of God, and there are two paths—one in this world and one in the hereafter. Whoever acknowledges him in this world and follows his guidance passes over that path which in the hereafter consists of the bridge over the hellfire. Whoever does not acknowledge him in this world, his foot will slip from the path in the hereafter, so that he falls into hellfire" (cited in Gätje, *The Qur'an and Its Exegesis*, p. 241).

1.2 *the Lord of the worlds* — That is, the Lord of all the worlds of the universe. It is a name for Allah that challenged the polytheists of his day who believed in the existence of many lords (gods) of the world (see **Polytheism in Seventh Century Arabia** on pp. 92-97). The term *the Lord of the worlds* is

The City of Mecca

According to the Qur'an and hadithic literature, the Ka'ba altar was constructed by Hagar, Ishmael and the archangel Gabriel following Hagar's
banishment from Abraham and Sarah in approximately 1900 B.C. (see
Gen 21:15-18). Later, Abraham visited Hagar and Ishmael and instituted
the annual pilgrimage to the altar.

Such an assertion, however, is contradicted by historical evidence,
specifically the literature of the ancients themselves. Ancient Greek
historians described the Arabian Peninsula in detail—yet made no mention of Mecca or its Ka'ba altar. This included Herodotus, Eratosthenes,
Agatharchides, Strabo, Artemidorus of Ephesus, and Pliny the Elder.[1] In
addition, a Roman expedition into Western Arabia in the first century,
B.C. traveled from the Gulf of Acaba to Yemen. One of the Roman
soldiers chronicled this journey down the west side of the Arabian Peninsula. He too made no mention of Mecca.[2] This lack of mention of
Mecca extended to questions related to the aromatic trade of the Arabian Peninsula. Patricia Crone, Ph.D., Princeton University, has written:

> It is obvious that if the Meccans had been middlemen in a long-distance trade
> of the kind described in (traditional Islamic) literature, there ought to have
> been some mention of this activity in the writings of their customers...who
> wrote extensively about the south Arabians who supplied them with aromat-
> ics. Despite the considerable attention paid to Arabian affairs, there is no
> mention at all of Quraysh (the tribe of Mohammad) and their trading center
> (Mecca) be it in the Greek, Latin, Syriac, Aramaic, Coptic, or other literature
> composed outside Arabia.[3]

It was not until the mid-fourth century, A.D. when records began to
appear of Mecca's existence.

The biblical record. The notion that Hagar and Ishmael constructed
the Ka'ba altar at Mecca also stands opposed to the biblical record. According to the Bible, following their banishment from Abraham, Hagar
and Ishmael wandered in the Desert of Beersheba (Gen 21:14) and
resided in the Desert of Paran (Gen 21:20). The deserts of Beersheba

and Paran are located in the northern regions of the Sinai Peninsula (Num 10:12). The implication is that Hagar and Ishmael dwelt in a region almost one thousand miles to the northwest of present day Mecca. Moreover, the land that existed in between was a vast barren waste-land. Caravan routes had not yet been established.

In addition, following the death of Abraham, both Isaac and Ishmael buried their father in the cave of Machpelah near Mamre, located in the southern regions of Canaan (see Gen 25:9). Since burial customs re-quired the dead to be buried the same day of the death, Ishmael had to have been living nearby (the Desert of Paran was not far from Mamre). In contrast, a journey from Mecca would have been clearly out of the question due to enormous distance required. Some Islamic scholars have attempted to solve this problem by speculating that Ishmael trav-eled to Mamre by means of a *buraq* (an angelic creature: half mule, half donkey, with wings). Yet this is a fanciful attempt to solve a clearly unsolvable problem.

The Ishmaelites. According to the Old Testament, Ishmael lived his entire adult life in the Desert of Paran in the Sinai Peninsula (Gen 21:21). His descendents "settled in the area from Havilah to Shur (see map on p. 38) near the border of Egypt" (Gen 25:18). Joseph was sold into slavery by a band of Ishmaelites traveling from the region of Havilah to Egypt (see Gen 37:36; 39:1; the terms *Ishmaelites* and *Midianites* were used interchangeably). In the days of King David, the Ishmaelites joined a confederacy with the Edomites, Moabites, Hagrites, Gebalites, Ammonites, Amalekites, Philistines, and the inhabitants of Tyre to op-pose Israel (Ps 83:5-8). Each of these kingdoms bordered Israel which placed them in the proximity of the land of Canaan. David was victorious in this war and subjugated these enemies, including the Ishmaelites (see 1 Chron 27:30). After the tenth century, B.C., the Ishmaelites lost their individual identity and were absorbed into other tribes.

The Legend. The legend that Hagar and Ishmael constructed the Ka'ba altar that was later dedicated by Abraham first emerged in the Qur'an itself. Along with this legend was the notion that Muhammad was a direct descendent of Abraham through the lineage of Ishmael. Accordingly, the Jewish-Arab animosity that has persisted for numerous centuries is believed to have been rooted to Abraham's unwise decision to have a child through Hagar. The rise of Islam in the mid-seventh century and the formation of its vast empire in the subsequent centuries ingrained this legend in the cultures of the Middle East, parts of Europe, North Africa, and much of Asia.

The legend has carried forward to the present day, illustrated with the often unchallenged assertion that the Arabic people are genealogically rooted to Ishmael. Yet, this is based upon a fanciful rewriting of history by Muhammad himself. The historical and archeological record points to the fact that Muhammad was from the Quraysh tribe which was rooted to the Sabaean civilization of South Arabia, in the region of Yemen.

---

[1] See Herodotus, *The Histories; The Geography of Strabo; Eratosthenes' Geography; The Periplus of the Erythraean Sea,* and Pliny the Elder, *Natural History;* also see Rafat Amari, *Islam: In Light of History,* pp. 104-246.

[2] See G. W. Bowersox, *Roman Arabia,* pp. 46-48.

[3] Patricia Crone, *Meccan Trade and the Rise of Islam,* p. 134.

From the fourth century, A.D., the city of Mecca had been a center of commerce. Foodstuffs and manufactured goods were imported there from the Byzantine and Persian domains, while precious stones, gold, odoriferous oils, tropical fruits and frankincense, all Arabian products, were exported, particularly from Yemen.

—Vahan M. Kurkjian, *A History of Armenia,* p. 141

In the mid-fourth century, when Christianity was spreading not only in the sedentary cultures of the Yemen and Abyssinia but also among the nomads in northern and eastern Arabia, an unmistakably pagan Mecca was still suffering the tribal strife that followed the accession of the sons and grandsons of Qusayy.

—Francis E. Peters, *Mecca: A Literary History of the Muslim Holy Land,* p. 25

In 440 CE, Kussai gathered the scattered members of the Quraysh tribe and settled them at Mecca. Its main function became the provision of food and water for the pilgrims. The religious observances of the Kaaba included the *umra* or lesser pilgrimage, the hasty passing to and fro seven times between the little hills of Safa and Marwa near the Kaaba...This examination by Muir of pre-Islamic religion suggests strongly that there was no Abrahamic element in the ceremonies of the Kaaba...Muslim sources...traced the Kaaba back to Abraham and Ishmael, but modern Western scholarship, unwilling to accept this view, interprets it as an attempt to provide the site with an Islamic legitimacy.

—Irving M. Zeitlin, *The Historical Muhammad,* pp. 43, 44, 49

4 the ruler of the day of judgment!	1 The smiting!
5 Thee we serve and Thee we ask for aid.	2 What is the smiting?
6 Guide us in the right path, the path	3 And what shall make thee know what the smiting is?
7 of those Thou art gracious to; not of those Thou art wroth with; nor of those who err.	4 The day when men shall be like scattered moths;
	5 and the mountains shall be like flocks of carded wool!
Surah 101	6 And as for him whose balance is heavy,
	7 he shall be in a well-pleasing life.
In the name of the merciful and compassionate God	8 But as for him whose balance is light

oft-repeated in the Qur'an (see Q 1.2; 6.45, 71, 162; 10.10, 37; 26.16, 23, 47, 77, 98, 109, 127, 145, 164, 180, 192; 27.8, 44; 28.30; 32.2; 37.182; 39.75; 40.64-66; 41.9; 43.46; 45.36; 56.80; 69.43; 81.29; 83.6).

1.6-7 *the right path* — The right path is that way of life that leads to eternal life (see Q 72.2, note). Those who err include the Jews, Christians, and polytheists—indeed, anyone who rejects Allah and Muhammad as his Prophet (see Q 3.32; 4.69, 79-80, 136; 5.80-81; 8.13, 20-23; 24.47, 48, 50-52, 54; 33.33, 71; 48.9-10; 57.19; 59.4; 72.22-23; and 46.16, note).

Surah 101. The title of this surah, *The Smiting,* comes from verse one. Its overall theme is that of divine judgment. It speaks of "the day"—the time when everyone will be summoned to appear at the Last Judgment. All sense of security and stability will be torn asunder. People will see themselves as scattered moths and mountains as flocks of flying wool. Also mentioned in this surah is the celestial balance, a devise to measure one's good and bad works. This balance is a major item in qur'anic theology since salvation is consistently presented in terms of merit—a life full of good works.

101.4-5 This is a description of the Last Days that will involve a major upheaval and transformation of the earth.

101.6, 8 *balance* — The imagery is that of a balance used in commercial transactions. The question to be answered at the Last Judgment is whether one's measure of good deeds is heavy or light. The outcome will determine whether one experiences the pleasures of Paradise or the torments of Hell (see Q 21.47; 42.17; 55.7-9, **The Last Judgment** on pp. 46-50, and the Second Great Creed—*Fikh Akbar II*—article twenty-one).

The New Testament also assesses a person's good and bad works (1 Cor 3:10-15), yet in a fashion that does not determines a person's eternal destiny. The imagery is that of a trial by fire that will either burn and destroy one's works (wood, hay, straw), or refine them (gold, silver, costly stones). The fire, then, reveals the quality of one's works and the corresponding rewards one will enjoy in Heaven. As such, the trial by fire has nothing to do with one's eternal salvation. Even if one's works are entire consumed by the fire, the Apostle Paul says that "he himself will be saved, but only

9 his dwelling shall be the pit of hell.	4 We have indeed created man in the best of symmetry.
10 And who shall make thee know what it is?	5 Then we will send him back the lowest of the low,
11 —a burning fire!	6 save those who believe and act aright; for theirs is a hire that is not grudged.
Surah 95	7 But what shall make thee call the judgment after this a lie!
In the name of the merciful and compassionate God	8 Is not God a most just of judges?
1 By the fig! And by the olive!	
2 And by Mount Sinai!	**Surah 102**
3 And by this safe land!	

as one escaping through the flames" (1 Cor 3:15). This is because the Bible presents salvation as a free gift offered to all who embrace Jesus Christ as the atoning sacrifice for sin (see Rom 5:1-10; Eph 2:8-10; and Titus 3:3-8).

Surah 95. The title of this surah, *The Fig*, comes from verse one. The theme of this surah is also the Last Judgment. The emphasis here, however, is the hope of eternal life. The Doctrine of Salvation by Works is mentioned, noting that "those who believe and act aright...is a hire that is not grudged" (see **The Last Judgment** on pp. 46-50, and Q 11.3, note).

95.1 Figs and olives existed in the eastern Mediterranean world, including Palestine. The reference to these foods and Mount Sinai are indicators that this surah is making a connection with the Hebrew prophets who dwelt in this land.

95.2 *Mount Sinai* — This is a reference to the ministry of Moses. Muhammad believed Moses was an apostle sent by Allah to proclaim the truths of Allah to Pharaoh and the Israelite people. Both rejected his message and were severely judged by Allah.

95.4-6a Muhammad maintained that Allah is sovereign over His entire creation, to the minutest detail. The universal presence of sin in the world, then, is also part of the divine plan. Accordingly, man was originally created perfect (the best of symmetry), but was made sinful (the lowest of the low) due to the sovereign will of Allah (see the **Doctrine of al-Qadar** on pp. 272-274).

Christians assert that man was made perfect (Gen 1:31). Because of the sin of Adam (Gen 3:1-6), the entire human race fell into sin. Salvation is offered to those who believe apart from works—that is, those who receive salvation as a free gift.

95.6b *believe and act aright* — This is a summary of the Islamic gospel (see Q 103.3, note).

95.8 According to Muhammad, Allah will serve as judge at the Last Judgment.

Surah 102. The title of this surah, *The Abundance of Wealth*, comes from verse one. The theme of this surah follows that of the previous two: a clarification of the Last Judgment. The particular emphasis of

In the name of the merciful and compassionate God

1 The contention about numbers deludes you
2 till ye visit the tombs!
3 Not so! In the end ye shall know!
4 And again not so! In the end ye shall know!
5 Not so! Did ye but know with certain knowledge!
6 Ye shall surely see hell!
7 And again ye shall surely see it with an eye of certainty.
8 Then ye shall surely be asked about pleasure!

Surah 104

In the name of the merciful and compassionate God

1 Woe to every slanderous backbiter,

2 who collects wealth and counts it.
3 He thinks that his wealth can immortalize him.
4 Not so! he shall be hurled into El 'Hutamah!
5 And what shall make thee understand what El 'Hutamah is?
6 —the fire of God kindled;
7 which rises above the hearts.
8 Verily, it is an archway over them
9 on long-drawn columns.

Surah 82

In the name of the merciful and compassionate God

1 When the heaven is cleft asunder,
2 And when the stars are scattered,
3 And when the seas gush together,
4 And when the tombs are turned upside down,
5 The soul shall know what it has

this surah, however, is on those who have many children and therefore have no time to think on themes pertaining to their eternal destiny. It is only when it is too late, on the day of their death, they will see it "with an eye of certainty" (v. 7).

102.1 *the contention about numbers —* That is, the contention about those who have many children.

102.8 At the Last Judgment, those who are rich will be questioned about their wealth. The question is whether their money was spent strictly on "pleasure" or in the giving of alms to the poor (see **The Last Judgment** on pp. 46-50).

Surah 104. The title of this surah, *The Slanderer*, comes from verse one. This surah begins with the word "woe," which sets its theme. It is a homily against those who amass riches in this life and yet are poor in regards to the life to come.

104.4-5 *El Hutamah —* Literally, that which crushes to pieces. According to Muhammad, Hell contains seven gates, each progressive in terms of heat and torment. According to Islamic tradition, *El Hutamah* is the third of the seven gates.

104.6 The threat of hellfire serves as a major motivation to turn to the Allah.

Surah 82. The title of this surah, *The Cleav-*

The Banishment
of Hagar and Ishmael

The Islamic and the Judeo-Christian traditions understand the location where Hagar and Ishmael lived subsequent to their banishment from Abraham differently. According to mainstream Islamic scholarship, Hagar and Ishmael traveled to the current site of Mecca. Abraham later journeyed to "Abraham brought her and her son Ishmael while she was suckling him, to a place near the Ka'ba under a tree on the spot of Zamzam, at the highest place in the mosque. During those days there was nobody in Mecca..." (*Sahih Bukhari* 4.55.583; also see *Sahih Bukhari* 4.55.584). Main-

stream Islamic scholarship asserts that it was during one of his visits to Mecca that Abraham was told by Allah to sacrifice his son Ishmael on Mt Mina, a few miles to the west of Mecca (see Q 37.99-113). At the last moment, Allah stopped Abraham from killing his son.

In contrast, the biblical text states that they wandered in the Desert of Beersheba (Gen 21:14) and then finally resided in the Desert of Paran (Gen. 21:20). Both these deserts are located in the northern region of the Sinai Peninsula, not far from Abraham, who remained in the land of Canaan with Sarah and Isaac. Abraham was later told to sacrifice his son

Isaac on Mt Moriah (thought to be Temple Mount in Jerusalem). At the last moment, the Lord stopped Abraham from killing his son.

———————•◦◆◦•———————

The Quran pays far greater attention than the Bible to the story of Abraham's "conversion" from his father's paganism to worship the One True God (6:74-79), but then it passes directly to the patriarch's activities in Mecca. There is no mention of Hagar or Sarah, nor of the Bible's elaborate stories of the births of Ishmael and Isaac. It was left for the later Muslim tradition to spell out the details of how Abraham and Ishmael got from Palestine to Mecca.

—Francis E. Peters, The Monotheists, p. 8

The first time Hagar left the household, she fled to the Wilderness of Shur. The Wilderness of Shur is on the border between Sinai and Egypt, and it appears that Hagar was trying to return to her homeland of Egypt...The angel specified that Ishmael was destined to live "in the presence of all his brethren" [Gen 16:12], which means "in the same area where the descendents of his brother, Isaac, were going to live."...Isaac's descendents were Jacob and Esau. Jacob lived in the land of Canaan, also known as Palestine, while Esau lived in southern Jordan. Ishmael lived in-between the two regions in the desert of Paran, exactly as the angel announced before Ishmael was born...Ishmael's descendents migrated into southern Jordan, into the rest of the Sinai, and even to the north towards Gilead and other areas in the Syro-Mesopotamian deserts, but they never migrated anywhere that was even near the area of Mecca.

—Rafat Amari, Islam: In Light of History, pp. 286, 287

The Arabs of the country call it Moilahhi Hadjar (Hagar). The Arabs from the neighborhood of Gaza called it Moilahhi Kadesah, but the former insisted upon its true name being Moilahhi Hadjar; and this, as they explained to me, not from the rocky mountains near, but from the name of a person called Hagar: and to confirm this statement of theirs, they conducted us to the *house* of Hagar (Beit Hajar), where they said such a person lived...Whether Ishmael may have constructed this as a refuge for his mother after her final expulsion from Abraham's house, or whether Ishmael himself passed any of his time here, it is very difficult of course now to say, though the Bedouins maintain the former. This is certainly true, that "the wilderness of Paran," where Ishmael is said to have dwelt (Gen xx.21) lies immediately to the south of this...This is *El-Paran*, or plain of Paran, alluded to in Gen. xiv. 6. This also is the country (excellent for pasture in some parts in the rainy season) where Abraham dwelt, *between* Kadesh and Shur...This is the Plain through which the Hebrews came from Sinai on their way to Kadesh.

—George Williams and Robert Willis, The Holy City, pp. 465, 466

sent on or kept back!

6   O man! what has seduced thee con-
      cerning thy generous Lord,

7   who created thee, and fashioned
      thee, and gave thee symmetry,

8   and in what form He pleased com-
      posed thee?

9   Nay, but ye call the judgment a lie!

10   but over you are guardians set

11   —noble, writing down!

12   they know what ye do!

Two eternal destinies

13   Verily, the righteous are in pleasure,

14   and, verily, the wicked are in hell;

15   they shall broil therein upon the
      judgment day;

16   nor shall they be absent therefrom!

17   And what shall make thee know
      what is the judgment day?

18   Again, what shall make thee know
      what is the judgment day?

19   a day when no soul shall control
      aught for another; and the bidding
      on that day belongs to God!

Surah 92

*In the name of the merciful and compas-
sionate God.*

1   By the night when it veils!

2   And the day when it is displayed!

3   And by what created male and fe-
      male!

4   Verily, your efforts are diverse!

---

ing, comes from verse one. Once again, the theme of the Last Judgment dominates this surah. The intended audience is the individual who has been beguiled from the Lord and therefore has no interest in pursuing an authentic spirituality.

82.6-9 This is a rhetorical question, pointing to the propensity within most people to deny the reality of the Last Judgment.

82.7 *gave thee symmetry* — Allah made the human being in balance: spiritual, emotional and intellectual characteristics in perfect equilibrium (see Q 95.4).

82.10-12 One of the responsibilities of angels is to write down the activities of people do in a book that will be opened and read at the Last Judgment. Similarly, the Bible notes that a book of works is being prepared for each soul who appears before the Lord at the Great White Throne (see Rev 20:11-15). The purpose of this book will deter-

mine the degree of suffering each unbeliever (see **The Last Judgment** on pp. 46-50).

82.13-15 Two reasons motivate people to repent and live righteous lives: (a) the threat of eternal hellfire, and (b) the anticipation of the pleasures of Paradise.

82.15 *broil* — Repeatedly, Muhammad described those in Hell as broiling (see Q 14.29; 17.18; 19.70; 36.64; 37.163; 38.56, 59; 52.16; 56.64, 94; 69.31; 74.26; 82.15; 83.16; 84.12; 87.12; 88.4; 92.15; 111.3).

Surah 92. The title of this surah, *The Night*, comes from verse one. It is a contrast between those who accept the best (Paradise) and those who reject the best and are cast into the flames of Hell (see **The Last Judgment** on pp. 46-50, **Paradise** on pp. 76-77, and **Hell** on pp. 80-82).

92.4 *your efforts are diverse* — The way in which we live our lives on earth is directed to two ends: a life of bliss in Paradise or

5 But as for him who gives alms and fears God,

6 And believes in the best,

7 We will send him easily to ease!

8 But as for him who is niggardly, and longs for wealth,

9 And calls the good a lie,

10 We will send him easily to difficulty!

11 And his wealth shall not avail him when he falls down (into hell)!

12 Verily, it is for us to guide;

13 And, verily, ours are the hereafter and the former life!

14 And I have warned you of a fire that flames!

15 None shall broil thereon, but the most wretched,

16 who says it is a lie and turns his back.

17 But the pious shall be kept away from it,

18 he who gives his wealth in alms,

19 and who gives no favour to any one for the sake of reward,

20 but only craving the face of his Lord most High;

21 in the end he shall be well pleased!

Surah 105

In the name of the merciful and compassionate God.

1 Hast thou not seen what thy Lord did with the fellows of the elephant?

2 Did He not make their stratagem lead them astray,

---

eternal torments in Hell.

92.11 One's wealth will not help in the Day of Judgment.

92.18 *gives his wealth in alms* — In the Qur'an, godliness is described in terms of giving away one's wealth without the hope of receiving a boon (a fortune) in recompense.

Surah 105. The title of this surah, *The Elephant*, comes from verse one. This surah has a curious history behind it. With the help of the Byzantine Empire, in 525 Abyssinia (modern-day Ethiopia) sent a military force across the Red Sea and conquered Yemen. The purpose of this military campaign was to punish the people of Mecca for their desecration of the temple in the city of Sana'a.

The newly installed viceroy on the Yemen side of the Red Sea, Abrahah, then built an elegant and costly Christian cathedral in the capital city of Sana'a. It was his hope to divert to his cathedral the many pilgrimages occurring annually throughout the Arabian Peninsula to various pagan Ka'ba altars. He wrote to the king, "I have built a church for you, O King, such as has not been built for any king before you. I shall not rest until I have diverted the Arabs' pilgrimage to it." As such, it was an intent to evangelize the Arabian Peninsula with the Christian gospel.

Throughout Arabia, Arabians were offended when they learned of this. A man from the town of Kinanah (near Mecca) and a member of the Quraysh clan (which was centered in Mecca), traveled to Sana'a and defecated on the floor of the cathedral as a way of showing his contempt.

When Abrahah heard of this sacrilege of the temple, he vowed revenge. A mili-

3   and send down on them birds in
     flocks,
4   to throw down on them stones of
     baked clay,
5   and make them like blades of herb-
     age eaten down?

Surah 89

*In the name of the merciful and compas-
sionate God.*

1   By the dawn
2   and ten nights!
3   And the single and the double!
4   And the night when it travels on!
5   Is there in that an oath for a man
     of sense?

*The people of Ad, Thamud,
and Pharaoh*

6   Hast thou not seen how thy Lord
     did with "Âd?"
7   —with Iram of the columns?
8   the like of which has not been cre-
     ated in the land?
9   And Thamûd when they hewed the
     stones in the valley?
10   And Pharaoh of the stakes?
11   Who were outrageous in the land,
12   and did multiply wickedness
     therein,
13   and thy Lord poured out upon them
     the scourge of torment.

The Lord is watching

---

tary expedition of 40,000 soldiers and eight elephants was organized. Abrahah then traveled north to conquer Mecca and put an end to the Ka'ba worship. As this Yemen military expedition approached Mecca, the leaders of Mecca prayed to the Ka'ba altar for protection. They then fled the city in fear.

Yet, when Abrahah's military force finally reached the outskirts of Mecca, the lead elephant inexplicability bowed to the ground and refused to enter the city. Then a dark cloud of small birds appeared from the Red Sea with large stones in their beaks and claws. They dropped the stones upon the invading army.

The army found itself in a state panic and chaos and fearful to enter Mecca, in spite of the fact that Mecca had been abandoned by the Meccan people. Morally defeated, Abrahah and his soldiers turned away from

Mecca and returned to Yemen. On the return trip, Abrahah fell ill and died (see Ibn Ishaq, *The Life of Muhammad*, pp. 21-28; Martin Lings, *Muhammad: His Life Based Upon the Earliest Sources,* pp. 19-22).

Surah 89. The title of this surah, *The Dawn,* comes from verse one. It makes the case that evil has its limits. Those who commit evil will eventually encounter a judgment that will bring an end to their evil (also see Gal 6:7-10 where a similar thought is expressed).

89.6 *Ad* — Ad is an ancient tribe that inhabited the region of northwest Arabia (see Q 54.17-21, note).

89.9 *Thamud* — The people who dwelt north of Medinah (see Q 91, note).

89.14-20 According to Muhammad, people are naively simplistic when thinking of the Lord and his ways in dealing with people. They look upon affluence as something that is owed to them by God, the absence of

14   Verily, thy Lord is on a watch tower!

15   and as for man, whenever his Lord tries him and honours him and grants him favour, then he says, "My Lord has honoured me;"

16   but whenever he tries him and doles out to him his subsistence, then he says, "My Lord despises me!"

17   Nay, but ye do not honour the orphan,

18   nor do ye urge each other to feed the poor,

19   and ye devour the inheritance (of the weak) with a general devouring,

20   and ye love wealth with a complete love!

The lamentation
of the unrighteous

21   Nay, when the earth is crushed to pieces,

22   and thy Lord comes with the angels, rank on rank,

23   and hell is brought on that day, — on that day shall man be reminded! but how shall he have a reminder?

24   He will say, "Would that I had sent something forward for my life!"

25   But on that day no one shall be tormented with a torment like his,

26   and none shall be bound with bonds like his!

Encouragement
for the faithful

27   O thou comforted soul!

28   return unto thy Lord, well pleased and well pleased with!

29   And enter amongst my servants,

affluence as a sign of God's injustice. They fail to take into consideration the question of good works—that the blessings of the Lord are commensurate with their lifestyles, whether they be righteous or unrighteous. **89.21** *when the earth is crushed to pieces* — the coming apocalypse. The Bible describes a similar future day, calling it the coming Day of the Lord. In the Book of Isaiah, for example, are the words: "See, the day of the Lord is coming—a cruel day, with wrath and fierce anger—to make the land desolate and destroy the sinners within it" (Isa 13:9ff; cf. Ezek 30:3; Joel 1:15; 2:1-18; Amos 5:18-20; Zeph 1:14-18). **89.24** *would that I had sent something forward for my life* — At the end of time, when the apocalyptic events come, followed by the Last Judgment, the unrighteous will

deeply regret that they had not lived righteous lives so that the celestial balance would tip to their favor at the Last Judgment (see **The Last Judgment** on pp. 46-50). This is an oft-repeated theme in the Qur'an: people are to preoccupy themselves with the afterlife by focusing their attention on the accumulation of acts of righteousness in this life. **89.27-30** These four verses are often used among Muslims to provide them with a sense of comfort and assurance as they anticipate the time when they will face Allah at the Last Judgment. They believe that they will pass over into Paradise, provided that they remain faithful. Less obedient Muslims will experience a period of time in Hell (an Islamic version of Purgatory), and then enter into Paradise (see Q 2.80 and 3.24; *Sahih*

30 and enter my Paradise!	1 I need not swear by the Lord of this land,
	2 and thou a dweller in this land!
Surah 90	3 Nor by the begetter and what he begets!
In the name of the merciful and compassionate God.	
	People of the Left Hand
Free from obligation	4 We have surely created man in

Bukhari 1.2.21; the Second Great Creed—*Fikh Akbar II*—article fourteen). The length of time in the Hell, however, is left unstated. Most likely, it is predicated upon the degree of disobedience during their lives on earth.

Apostate Muslims will suffer eternally in Hell for their profound disobedience. The avoidance of all forms of apostasy, then, has become a pressing concern for all Muslims.

In one Hadith, Muhammad stood at the gates of Hell in a vision and observed that the majority of its inhabitants were women. This is due to the fact that they had been "ungrateful to their husbands and are ungrateful for the favors and the good" (*Sahih Bukhari* 1.2.28). The Islamic scholar al-Ghazali added that Muhammad also said, "I peeped into Hell and found that the majority of its inmates are women...I peeped into Paradise and found that there are few women there" (*The Revival of Religious Learnings,* vol 2, Section 3).

Christians ask how and why Muslims can possess a confidence of Paradise since they believe that Allah will weigh each work with exceeding exactitude, to its atom's weight (Q 99.7-8), at the Last Judgment. Christians also ask about the spirituality of most women and their eternal destiny? To what extent does this fear of Hell drive the seriously minded Muslim to fanaticism in his or her faith? And, is it possible that this concern drives some Muslims to question the Islamic faith in its entirety and find a more satisfactory answer in the Gospel of Jesus Christ (Rom 10:9-13; 1 Jn 5:13)?

Surah 90. The title of this surah, *The City,* comes from verse one. The relationship between Muhammad and the people of Mecca had finally reached the point of final deterioration. According to Ibn Ishaq, Muhammad's most authoritative biographer, Muhammad's incessant preaching of his new religion agitated many people in Mecca. It caused the leaders and many of the people of the Quraysh tribe in Mecca to withdraw from him. They then went to his uncle, Abu Talib, and appealed to him to admonish Muhammad to cease and desist from his religious agitations. "By God," they said, "we cannot endure that our fathers should be reviled, our customs mocked and our gods insulted." If Abu Talib failed to stop his nephew, they added, they would hold him responsible and possibly bring violence upon them both. Though Abu Talib was not a Muslim convert, he told them that he could not desert his nephew (*The Life of Muhammad,* p. 119).

90.4 According to Muhammad, Allah created man "in trouble." This follows the Islamic belief of Allah's absolute sovereignty over the universe. If people are living in the midst of trouble, it is because Allah has ordained that they experience trouble.

trouble.

5 Does he think that none can do aught against him?

6 He says, "I have wasted wealth in plenty;"

7 does he think that no one sees him?

8 Have we not made for him two eyes

9 and a tongue, and two lips?

10 and guided him in the two high-ways?

11 but he will not attempt the steep!

People of the Right Hand

12 And what shall make thee know what the steep is?

13 It is freeing captives,

14 or feeding on the day of famine,

15 an orphan who is akin,

16 or a poor man who lies in the dust;

17 and again (it is) to be of these who

In contrast, the Christian believes that God created man to live in intimate relationship with Him in Paradise. It is only because of Adam's disobedience and fall into sin (Gen 3:1-6) that the world became chaotic, characterized by man in rebellion, separated from God. The death, burial, and resurrection of Jesus Christ not only redeems man from the penalty of sin, it will eventually result in a restoration of the world to its pre-fallen condition (see Rom 8:22-25; Rev 21:1).

90.5-11 Muhammad labeled those who had rejected his ministry: "fellows of the left" (v. 19), meaning "the left hand." They were the ones condemned to the fires of Hell.

90.10 *two highways* — That is, Allah guides people into either the ways of righteousness or the ways of unrighteousness. The first leads to Paradise. The second leads to Hell. The person of the Left Hand, however, will never choose the highway that is steep (the one that is difficult and requires effort to travel, the highway that leads to eternal life). Rather, he will always travel the easy highway (the one that leads to eternal damnation). This passage, then, hints at the Doctrine of Double Predestination which will be addressed in greater detail later in the Qur'an (see the **Doctrine of al-Qadar** on pp. 272-274).

90.11 *the steep* — The uphill road, the road to Paradise.

90.18 *the fellows of the right* — Muham-

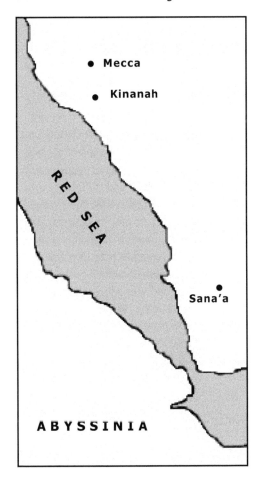

The Last Judgment

Of the three great monotheistic religions in the world—Judaism, Christianity, and Islam—all maintain the existence of a Last Judgment in the afterlife where his or her eternal destiny is determined. It is preceded by apocalyptic events on the earth and a general resurrection from the dead.

Islam understands the purpose of the Last Judgment as a repayment for good or evil deeds. A balance is understood to exist that will assess the quality of one's works done on the earth with the reward either being the eternal blisses of Paradise or the eternal torments of Hell (see Q 7.8; 17.35; 21.47; 42.17; 55.7-9; 57.25; 101.6-8). The *Fikh Akbar II*, article 21, states: "The weighing of works in the balance on the day of resurrection is a reality... Retaliation between litigants by means of good works on the day of resurrection is a reality. And if they do not possess good works, the wrongs, done by them to others, are thrown upon them; this is a real-

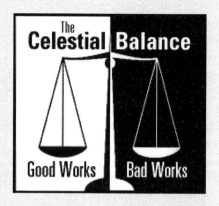

ity."[1] Islamic scholar Ibn Kathir commented: "When the people of Paradise enter Paradise, a caller will say: 'O people of Paradise, Allah has promised you something that he wishes to fulfill.'" The answer will be: "What is it? Has He not made our Scale heavy?" His point was that if one's good deeds are heavy, the person will enter the blisses of Paradise. But if one's good deeds are light, the person will enter the abyss of a burning fire.

Hence, foundational to Islamic theology is the Doctrine of Salvation by Works (a system of meritocracy). As it states in the Qur'an, "Every soul shall be paid what it has earned" (Q 16.111). Maulana Muhammad Ali writes, "Life after death takes two forms: a life in Paradise for those in whom the good preponderates over the evil, and a life in Hell for those in whom the evil preponderates over the good."[2] Ayaan Hirsi Ali adds, "Islamic morality demands that the individual subject himself completely to the will of Allah through the Shari'a, the code of law derived from the Koran, and to the religious community. The Muslim as an individual can do nothing individually: he even has to sit, eat, sleep, and travel according to strict rules; he cannot freely choose his own friends and is expected to have (and avoid) certain thoughts and feelings."[3] Part and parcel to this is the adherence to the Five Pillars of the Islamic Faith. The pillars are: (a) *Shahadah*—confession of the one true God and Muhammad as his prophet, (b) *al Salat*—dedication to daily prayer in the direction Mecca, (c) *al Zakat*—the giving of alms to the poor, (d) *Siyam*—observing the season of Ramadan each year, and (e) *Hajj*—going on a pilgrimage to Mecca to worship at the Ka'ba altar.

These good works are especially heavy when placed in the celestial balance. The first of the five pillars—*Shahadah*—is so heavy, in fact, that faithful Muslims are mindful to recite it often (daily) as a way of assuring them of a good outcome at the Last Judgment.

Without question, the most egregious bad work is the sin of *shirk*. This constitutes any form of idolatrous worship. According to the Qur'an, this includes the worship of the various gods at the Ka'ba altar, that was commonly practiced in Mecca and which Muhammad vehemently condemned. It also includes the worship of Jesus Christ as the Son of God. An oft-repeated statement in the Qur'an is that God has no Son. On one occasion, for example, the question was posed: "The inventor of the heavens and the earth! how can He have a son, when He has no female companion, and when He has created everything, and everything He knows?" (Q 6.101). The sin of *Shirk* is so heavy, in fact, that to have committed this sin guarantees a person's eternal destiny in the flames of Hell.

The Islamic version of the Doctrine of the Last Judgment leaves one with a troubling concern. It is impossible to know with certainty how one will fair at the Last Judgment since does not know with certainty the quality of one's works in this life. Moreover, one does not know whether he or she will fall into some grievous sin tomorrow. Muhammad noted that not all Muslims will enter Paradise. The esteemed Islamic scholar Sheikh Mohammed al-Ghazali has written, "No one knows what the future holds, but Muslims will have to continue to struggle on behalf of their religion and way of life, because divine justice will be done."[4]

For this reason, seriously minded Muslims are always on their guard pertaining to their own spirituality. To help Muslims not grow weary in well-doing, the Islamic faith has added incentives:

- "There are those from whom we accept the best of what they have done, and we pass over their offenses—amongst the fellows of Paradise, the prominent of truth which they have been promised." (Q 46.16)

- "Save he who turns again and believes and does a righteous work; for, as to those, God will change their evil deeds to good, for God is ever forgiving and merciful." (Q 25.70)

Muslims, however, do have one prospect to relieve their stress. Even if they are cast into Hell, their time in that dreadful abode is only temporary. They will eventually be released, once the divine retribution for the sins committed on the earth is satisfied. Apostate Muslims and infidels, however, have no such prospect. For them, Hell is a permanent abode.

Allah's attitude towards the unrighteous at the Last Judgment will be characterized by mockery, scorn, contempt, chiding, and rebukes (e.g., Q 32.20). When the unrighteous plead for mercy or for a second chance (an opportunity to return to the earth and re-live their lives in a fashion pleasing to Allah), all such requests will be chillingly disregarded. Then, without a second thought, the unrighteous will be cast into Hell.

Belief in this future divine judgment has given rise to a peculiar spirituality in Islam. Ayaan Hirsi Ali explains:

> Allah is almighty, and man is His slave and must obey His laws. Those who believe what is written in the Koran, who believe in Allah and accept Muhammad as His prophet, are superior to other religious peoples. Practicing Muslims are "tribes of the Scriptures" and are also superior to those whose beliefs have lapsed and to nonbelievers.[5]

In short, eternal life is predicated upon a system of individual merit. One's fate in the next life is a direct consequence of one's conduct in this life. And foundational to this is the question of submission (the Arabic word *islam* means submission).

Christian response. The Bible rejects this concept of meritocracy. It maintains that no matter how good we may live in this life, it is not sufficient to merit eternal life. This is because God demands perfection—not only in one's behavior, but also in one's thought life. The bar is raised so high, in fact, that everyone fails to reach it. The solution, however, is not to strive to merit eternal life, but to acknowledge that we are not worthy and plead for mercy and grace. Indeed, eternal life is embarrassingly that simple. Since Jesus Christ paid the penalty of the sins of the world with his death on the cross, we are to confess individual guilt and embrace Jesus Christ as the one who paid for our sins.

- "He who has the Son has life; he who does not have the Son of God does not have life." (1 Jn 5:12)

- "Many will say to me on that day, 'Lord, Lord, did we not prophesy in your name, and in your name drive out demons and perform many miracles?' Then I will tell them plainly, 'I never knew you. Away from me, you evildoers!'" (Matt 7:22-23)

- "He saved us, not because of righteous things we had done, but because of his mercy. He saved us through the washing of rebirth and renewal by the Holy Spirit, whom he poured out on us generously through Jesus Christ our Savior, so that, having been justified by his grace, we might become heirs having the hope of eternal life." (Titus 3:5-7)

- "You see, at just the right time, when we were still powerless, Christ died for the ungodly. Very rarely will anyone die for a righteous man, though for a good man someone might possibly dare to die. But God demonstrates his own love for us in this: While we were still sinners, Christ died for us. Since we have now been justified by his blood, how much more shall we be saved from God's wrath through him!" (Rom 5:6-9)

Still, at the Last Judgment our works will be examined. But the purpose of this examination is not to determine our eternal destiny. Rather, they are to determine the quantity and quality of the blessings we will enjoy while in Heaven (Matt 25:21, 23; 1 Cor 3:10-15).

What is more, prior to the coming of Jesus in the first century, A.D., the Old Testament peoples will be judged similarly. For them, faith in Jesus is pictured in the ritual sacrifices of animals of which they participated. Since these sacrifices pointed to Jesus Christ, the blood shed in these sacrifices was just as efficacious to them as it is for Christians who trust in the blood shed by Jesus at the cross (see Heb 9:11-14).

Hence, salvation from sin has always been a question of trusting in the atoning power of the blood of Jesus Christ. In the Old Testament, believers saw it obliquely via the animal sacrifices. In the New Testament, believers see it more clearly in Jesus Christ Himself. In neither case, is salvation a mixture of faith and works.

---

[1] Arent J. Wensinck, *The Muslim Creed,* p. 195. The *Fikh Akbar II* is also known as the Second Great Muslim Creed (eighth century) was written to clarify Islamic theology and pressed for a literal interpretation of the Qur'an.

[2] Maulana Muhammad Ali, *The Religion of Islam,* p. 218.

[3] Ayaan Hirsi Ali, *The Caged Virgin,* p. 133.

[4] Sheikh Mohammed al-Ghazali, *A Thematic Commentary on the Qur'an,* vol. 2, p. 145.

[5] *The Caged Virgin,* p. 28; cf. Q 2.159.

Islam shares with Christianity the beliefs of the Last Hour, the Resurrection of the Dead, the Last Judgment, and Heaven and Hell as man's recompense for his deeds on earth. There are, however, some differences regarding details.

—Ralph H. Salmi and Cesar Adib Majul, *Islam and Conflict Resolution,* p. 44

The Five Pillars of Faith are only the minimum requirements of Islam. In all things, true believers must seek to do the will of Allah as revealed in the Koran. They must also believe that God has predestined the ultimate fate of all humankind, to be revealed in the Last Judgment. Muhammad left vivid descriptions of hell and heaven. Unbelievers will burn eternally in a great pool of fire; believers who die in sin will also suffer there for a time but will finally be released. In the end, all Muslims (male and female)—who have accepted Allah—will enjoy the pleasures of paradise. Muhammad, drawing from Persian sources, pictured paradise in sensual terms as an oasis of delights, with sparkling beverages, luscious fruits, and dark-eyed beauties.

—Thomas H. Greer and Gavin Lewis, *A Brief History of the Western World,* p. 207

There will be brought forth at the last Judgment "the Book" containing an exact account of the smallest actions, together with "the Balance designed to weigh them". To this apparatus Muslim tradition adds the "bridge as sharp as a razor-edge across which the souls must pass". The *Mu'tazilites,* and in our day the progressives and modernists, see in "the bridge" and in "the torment of the tomb" which the "*aqidas*", professions of faith, have adopted, symbolic representation which it is better not to scrutinize too closely.

—Henri Lammens, *Islam: Beliefs and Institutions,* p. 54

believe and encourage each other to patience, and encourage each other to mercy,

18   —these are the fellows of the right!

Warning of Hell

19   But those who disbelieve in our signs, they are the fellows of the left,

20   for them is fire that closes in!

Surah 93

In the name of the merciful and compassionate God.

1   By the forenoon!

2   And the night when it darkens!

3   Thy Lord has not forsaken thee, nor hated thee!

4   and surely the hereafter is better for thee than the former;

5   and in the end thy Lord will give thee, and thou shalt be well pleased!

6   Did He not find thee an orphan, and give thee shelter?

7   and find thee erring, and guide thee?

8   and find thee poor with a family, and nourish thee?

9   But as for the orphan oppress him not;

10   and as for the beggar drive him not away;

mad labeled those who had embraced his ministry: "fellows of the right," meaning "the right hand." They were the ones whose lives were full of righteous deeds. They would enter Paradise.

Surah 93 The title of this surah, *The Forenoon,* comes from verse one. This is a surah of divine comfort for Muhammad. It was believed by Islamic scholars that following Surah 89, Allah did not provide any revelations to Muhammad for a period of time. His opponents took opportunity with this lapse of revelation to taunt him, saying: "Allah has forsaken you." Surah 93 is believed to be a response to those taunts.

93.3 *Thy Lord has not forsaken thee, nor hated thee!* — Since Muhammad had no recent visitations from the archangel Gabriel, he was mocked by the people of Mecca. One Hadith states that a woman from Mecca chided him, saying that Satan had deserted him (*Sahih Bukhari* 2.21.225).

93.6-8 This is a brief biographical sketch of

Muhammad's early life as a child. Muhammad's father died three months before Muhammad was born, and his mother died when he was approximately eight years old. It was then that his paternal uncle, Abu Talib, became his guardian.

93.10 We see here an early reference to Muhammad admonishing people to become almsgivers. Almsgiving is one of the Five Pillars of Islam (see ***al-Zakat*** on pp. 115-116).

The giving of alms is also a centerpiece of the Judeo-Christian tradition. Oswald Chambers wrote: "The law of the life of a disciple is give, give, give (e.g., Luke 6:38). As Christians our giving is to be proportionate to all we have received of the infinite giving of God. 'Freely ye have received, freely give.' Not how much we give, but what we do not give, is the test of our Christianity" (*Conformed to His Image,* p. 96).

Surah 94 The title of this surah, *The Expansion,* comes from verse one. This is a surah of encouragement for Muhammad. It

11   and as for the favour of thy Lord
      discourse thereof.

Surah 94

*In the name of merciful and compassion-
ate God.*

1   Have we not expanded for thee thy
     breast?
2   and set down from thee thy load
3   which galled thy back?
4   and exalted for thee thy renown?

5   Verily, with difficulty is ease!
6   verily, with difficulty is ease!
7   And when thou art at leisure then
     toil,
8   and for thy Lord do thou yearn!

Surah 108

*In the name of the merciful and compas-
sionate God.*

1   Verily, we have given thee *El
     KâuThar*;

is believed by some Islamic scholars that Surah 94 is a continuation of Surah 93 and that the two surahs were originally one.

94.1-3 Muhammad believed that Allah reached into his breast and took out the load of sin that had burdened his soul. This is referenced in a Hadith where it states that while a child an angel opened his chest, took out his heart and cleansed it in a golden bowl which removed the power of *sheitan* (the devil) over him (see *Sahih Bukhari* 1.8.345; 5.58.227).

This passage has given rise to the Doctrine of Isma, the belief that Muhammad was sinless. John Renard writes, "The opening of Muhammad's chest and the cleansing of his heart are part of an ancient purification legend, the general thrust of which finds parallels in other religious traditions as well, and it serves as a basis for the Islamic doctrine of *isma* or 'protection' of the Prophet Muhammad from sin" (*Windows on the House of Islam*, p. 337).

In contrast, Christians reject this account of Allah cleansing Muhammad's heart as fanciful fiction.

Surah 108. The title of this surah, *The Abundance of Good*, comes from verse one. The surah is addressed to Muhammad and makes the case that the Lord has given to him *El KâuThar* (a great abundance of spiritual gifts). He was instructed to pray, make a sacrifice to Allah, and believe that he has a posterity. This surah builds on the previous surah (Surah 94) inasmuch as it elevates Muhammad to an almost angelic status. Its implication is that he is to be unquestionably believed and respected.

In the years following his death, words of high praise have been given to Muhammad. The widely translated poem by al-Busiri, a thirteenth century Islamic scholar, wrote: "Muhammad, Lord of the two worlds ...surpassed the (other) prophets in physical and moral qualities, nor did they approach him in either knowledge or magnamity...In him the essence of goodness is undivided (al-Busari, *Burdah* 34, 38, 42-43 in *Muhammad and Jesus*, p. 193).

In the eleventh century, the esteemed Islamic scholar al-Ghazali wrote, "He (God) said: 'What the Apostle has brought you, receive; and what he has forbidden you, refrain from' (Q 59.7). So you must sit while

| 2 | So pray to thy Lord and slaughter (victims). | 3 | Verily, he who hates thee shall be childless. |

putting on trousers and stand while putting on a turban...When cutting your nails...you must begin with the little toe of the right foot and finish with the little toe of the left" (cited in *Muhammad and Jesus*, p. 192).

Moreover, in the Muslim world Muhammad has been elevated to the status of a saint, and treated accordingly. Maxime Rodinson explains: "A multitude of relics of him are preserved everywhere: hairs, teeth, sandals, his cloak, his prayer rug, a sword hilt, an arrow used by him. Constantinople, when it had become the capital of the Muslim world, boasted of the number of these relics to be found there. Two hairs from his beard were kept there in forty bags sewn one inside the other, and were solemnly shown to worshipers once a year" (*Muhammad: Prophet of Islam*, p. 308).

Yet, not to be outdone, within Church tradition Constantinople was also "home to an unrivalled collection of sacred relics, including Christ's crown of thorns, locks of the Virgin Mary's hair, at least two heads of John the Baptist and the bones of virtually all the Apostles" (Thomas Asbridge, *The Crusades*, p. 49).

Most Christian scholars, however, regard both collections of relics (Islamic as well as Christian) as not only false but as a form of idolatry. John Calvin, for example, described such relics as idolatrous paraphernalia and admonished that one would do well to keep away from them.

INTRODUCTION

The Second Period

Officially speaking, the era of Islam began with the first visitation of the archangel Gabriel to Muhammad in a cave on Mount Hira near Mecca. Faithful Muslims unwaveringly believe that such an angelic visitation indeed took place. Those in the rest of the world are of a different opinion. Some have their doubts. Many deny it altogether. Such is the case today, and such was the case among the people of seventh century Mecca.

This alleged visitation marked a fundamental transition in the Qur'an. Whereas previously Muhammad had been writing surahs in the attempt to better understand the spiritual life, a moment came when he believed the archangel Gabriel spoke to him and commissioned him to be a spokesman for Allah—to proclaim divinely inspired words that explained the straight and narrow way that leads to eternal life. Hence, it is here, with this alleged angelic visitation, that Islam began.

The surahs of this period were directed to his immediate family and close friends. He also reached out to a few social outcasts and slaves. It was his hope that they would repent from their idolatrous ways and turn to the one true God. David Cook explains: "The early *suras* (chapters) of the Qur'an proclaim this basic message: 'Say: He is Allah, the only One, Allah, the Everlasting. He did not beget and is not begotten, and none is His equal' (Qur'an 112). Initially, Muhammad was instructed merely to communicate this message to his immediate family and close friends, who, together with a number of social outcasts and slaves, formed the original community of Muslims."[1]

This new approach contained a heightened degree of authority since Muhammad now believed his surahs were divinely inspired. It was not a question of opinion or the force of logic. Allah Himself declared that all who lived idolatrous lives would suffer accordingly in the afterlife. Only those who worshipped Allah, and Him alone, would enjoy the blisses of Paradise.

---

[1] David Cook, *Understanding Jihad*, p. 5.

Surah 96

In the name of the merciful and compassionate God.

Muhammad's commission

1 Read, in the name of thy Lord!

2 Who created man from congealed blood!

3 Read, for thy Lord is most generous!

4 Who taught the pen!

5 Taught man what he did not know!

The nature of man

Surah 96. The title of this surah, *Congealed Blood,* comes from verse two. In this surah Muhammad began his public ministry as a divinely commissioned apostle. Prior to this time, in the first section of *Qur'an Revealed* (pp. 19-53), the surahs were impassioned utterances, efforts where Muhammad searched for a new and more correct way to understand the spiritual life and the nature of God. This changed, however, when the archangel Gabriel allegedly appeared to him and commissioned him to proclaim truths to the Meccan people.

Islamic scholars typically disagree with the chronological placement of this surah, maintaining that its position should be at the beginning, the first of all the surahs. Yet, even with mainstream Islamic scholarship differences exist. Some maintain that only the first half of this surah constitutes the beginning of the Qur'an, with the second half revealed to Muhammad sometime later. Esteemed Islamic scholar Muhammad Asad is representative of this opinion, commenting: "There is no doubt that the first five verses of this surah represent the very beginning of the revelation of the Qur'an...Verses 6-19 of this surah are of a somewhat later date" (*The Message of the Qur'an*, p. 1098).

Qur'an Revealed follows the chronological ordering of Thomas Patrick Hughes who insisted on preserving the integrity of this surah and thereby refused to divide it. With

this in mind, the entire surah is situated at the beginning of the Second Period.

96.1 *Read in the name of the Lord!* — This command represents Muhammad's inauguration as a divinely chosen Prophet from Allah. By reading in the name of Allah, his surahs were thereby the words of Allah, to be read to all who will listen.

96.2 Throughout the Qur'an, Muhammad referenced the creation of man. Clearly, he had a fascination with this topic, describing it in a variety of ways. In this verse, man is described as being formed from congealed blood. Elsewhere in the Qur'an, however, the creation of man is described otherwise. He came from (1) dust—Q 22.5, (2) spurting water coming from the kidneys, that is, the back and the ribs—Q 86.6-7, (3) contemptible water—Q 77.20, (4) a mingled clot—Q 76.2, (5) a morsel—Q 22.5, (6) a clot of blood—Q 18.37; 22.5; 80.19, (7) a single soul—Q 4.1, (8) clay—Q 6.2, (9) extract of despicable water—Q 32.8, crackling clay like the potters—Q 55.14, or (10) black mud—Q 15.26.

In contrast, the Bible maintains that "the Lord God formed the man from the dust of the ground and breathed into his nostrils the breath of life" (Gen 2:7). This corresponds to Muhammad's claim that man was made from dust (and roughly corresponds to the notion of clay and black mud). Yet, the Bible stands opposed to the other qur'anic asser-

6	Nay, verily, man is indeed outrageous		13	Hast thou considered if he said it was a lie, and turned his back?
7	at seeing himself get rich!		14	Did he not know that God can see?
8	Verily, unto thy Lord is the return!		15	Nay, surely, if he does not desist we will drag him by the forelock!
9	Hast thou considered him who forbids		16	—the lying sinful forelock!
10	a servant when he prays?		17	So let him call his counsel:
11	Hast thou considered if he were in guidance		18	we will call the guards of hell!
12	or bade piety?		19	Nay, obey him not, but adore and draw nigh!

tions.

Moreover, the Bible maintains that "God created man in his own image" (Gen 1:27). On this question, Islamic scholars are split. Al-Ghazali (Islam's most esteemed scholar), wrote: "Not only are man's attributes a reflection of God's attributes, but the mode of existence of man's soul affords some insight into God's mode of existence...From all this we see how true is the saying of the Prophet, 'God created man in His own likeness'" (*The Alchemy of Happiness*, p. 28). Another Islamic scholar, however, disagrees, stating: "The Christian argument is blasphemy according to Islam. Islam teaches that God breathed His spirit into all human beings, but we are not created in His divine image, nor do we share His likeness" (Abdullah Smith, *Genesis 1:26 Reinterpreted*).

96.6-19 This section of the surah is believed by many scholars (Islamic and non-Islamic) to have been composed at a time much later than that of the first section.

96.6 *man is indeed outrageous* — That is, man is indeed a sinner. Moreover, Allah sees all and will bring judgment on all evildoers ("we will drag him by the forelock...we will call the guards of hell!—vv. 15, 18). The only remedy of sin, said Muhammad, was for the sinner to "adore and draw nigh" (v. 19). In other words, that which is needed is a radi-

cal self-reformation.

The New Testament differs. It states that the individual is incapable of a sufficient self-reformation to make himself or herself acceptable before a holy and righteous God. This is because, no matter how hard we try, we all fall short of the glory of God. Accordingly, that which is required is (a) *divine forgiveness* for sins committed, and (b) *divine empowerment* to live a righteous life. Divine forgiveness occurs at the moment of salvation. Divine empowerment occurs as we yield moment by moment to the Holy Spirit, who entered the soul at the moment of salvation and began the lifelong process of an inner cleansing (see Rom 12:1-2; Gal 5:22-26; 1 Cor 2:6-16; 2 Cor 3:17-18; Eph 1:15-23; 3:14-21; Col 3:1-25).

Moreover, the New Testament adds that the cleansing of the human soul is evidenced by the emergence of the fruit of the Spirit. That fruit is love, joy, peace, patience, kindness, goodness, faithfulness, gentleness and self-control (see Gal 5:22-23). John R. W. Stott writes: "The Christian should resemble a fruit-tree, not a Christmas tree! For the gaudy decorations of a Christmas tree are only tied on, whereas fruit grows on a fruit-tree. In other words, Christian holiness is not an artificial human accretion, but a natural process of fruit-bearing by the power of

Surah 112	one!"
In the name of the merciful and compassionate God.	**Surah 74**
1 Say, "He is God alone!	*In the name of the merciful and compassionate God.*
2 God the Eternal!	
3 He begets not and is not begotten!	1 O thou who art covered!
4 Nor is there like unto Him any	

the Holy Spirit" (*Christ the Controversialist*, p. 143).

Surah 112. The title to this surah, *The Unity*, comes from verse one. The 112th Surah is one of the most celebrated surahs in the Qur'an, known as *Surat al Ikhlas* (the Pure Truth). In four concise verses, it presents the central doctrine of Islam: the supreme sovereignty and oneness of Allah, that which scholars call the Doctrine of Tauhid. The surah is often recited by faithful Muslims during their daily prayers. According to Kenneth Cragg, it "is held to be worth a third of the whole Qur'an and the seven heavens and the seven earths are founded upon it. To confess this verse, an Islamic tradition affirms, is to shed one's sins as a man might strip a tree in autumn of its leaves" (*The Call of the Minaret*, p. 39).

112.3 *He begets not* — According to Muhammad, Allah has no sons. With this statement, Muhammad assaulted one of the foundational theological pillars in the Star Family religious system that typified pagan Arabia.

The fundamental assumption of the Star Family Religion was that its many gods were members of a celestial family. Gods begat other gods (daughter and son gods), who in turn begat additional gods (see **Shahadah** on pp. 58-61 and **Polytheism in Seventh Century Arabia** on pp. 92-97).

The statement "He begets not" has also been used by Muslims as a central criticism of the Christian faith. The New Testament states that Jesus Christ is the "only begotten Son of God" (Jn 3:18, KJV; cf Jn 1:14, 18; 3:16; Acts 13:33; Heb 5:5; 1 Jn 4:9). Muslims regard this doctrine as blasphemy since, they say, it implies that God has sexual relations with someone in Paradise and thereby produced an offspring. Christian theologians counter, noting that the question of God begetting a Son is not to be understood in terms of celestial sex, as a begetting in a moment in time in the distant past. Rather, it is an eternal begetting, a Father-Son relationship that has always existed. Both have always existed since they are both eternal (see **The Doctrine of the Trinity** on pp. 735-736 and **The Nicene-Constantinopolitan Creed** on p. 740).

Surah 74. The title of this surah, *The One who is Covered*, comes from verse one. The occasion of the surah was the push-back from the Quraysh tribe of Mecca. The leaders of this tribe accused Muhammad of being a lunatic magician. Because his message was rejected by the leaders of Mecca who scoffed at the idea of resurrection and Final Judgment, he denounced them and warned of hellfire. With the exception of verse 31, an important characteristic of the surah is that it is written in short rhythmic sentences, enabling it to be easily set to Arabic music.

Shahadah

"I testify that there is no God but Allah,
and I testify that Muhammad is His prophet."

The *Shahadah* is Islam's most basic creed and presented as a confession. The creed affirms monotheism and declares that Muhammad is God's final prophet—or apostle. Its importance is testified by the fact that it is the gate, or entry point, into Islam. The word *shahadah* comes from the first word in the confession—I testify—as spoken in the Arabic language. The creed is also called the *Kalima*, which literally means "words." All who confess the creed enter into the Islamic faith.

Because the *Shahadah* stands opposed to polytheism—that is, the worship of multiple gods—all who are polytheists have fallen into the most grievous of sins: the sin of *Shirk.* They are labeled idolaters and condemned to the fires of Hell. The principal message of the many apostles that Allah has sent into the world, Muhammad explained, was to turn people away from polytheism and to a belief in the one true God.

In a canonical Hadith, Muhammad gave his own interpretation of the second half of the *Shahadah.* He reportedly said: "I have been given five things which were not given to anyone else before me. First, Allah made me victorious by awe, (by His frightening my enemies) for a distance of one month's journey. Second, the earth has been made for me (and for my followers) a place for praying and a thing to perform Tayammum, therefore anyone of my followers can pray wherever the time of prayer is due. Third, the booty has been made Halal (lawful) for me yet it was not lawful for anyone else before me. Fourth, I have been given the right of intercession (on the Day of Resurrection). Fifth, every Prophet used to be sent to his nation only but I have been sent to all mankind."[1]

Repetitively, the Qur'an affirms this unique status afforded Muhammad:

- "I swear by the glorious Qur'an (that Muhammad is the Apostle of Allah). Nay! They wonder that there has come to them a warner from among themselves, so the unbelievers say: This is a wonderful thing...Nay, they rejected the truth when it came to them, so they are (now) in a state of confusion." (Q 50.1-5)

- "But nay! I swear by that which you see, and that which you do not see. Most surely, it is the Word brought by an honored Apostle [Muhammad], and it is not the word of a poet; little is it that you believe; nor the word of a sooth-sayer; little is it that you mind. It is a revelation from the Lord of the worlds." (Q 69.38-43)

- "Most surely it [the Qur'an] is the Word of an honored messenger, the proces-sor of strength, having an honorable place with the Lord of the Dominion, one to be obeyed, and faithful in trust." (Q 81.19-21)

According to mainstream Islamic scholarship, a single honest recitation of the *Shahadah* is all that is required for a person to convert to Islam. Yet this honesty requires seven conditions in order to be efficacious. The first is *al-'Ilm*, which means that the contents of the creed must be understood. The second is the *al-Yaqueen*, which means that the creed must be be-lieved without reservation. The third is *al-Ikhlaas*, which means that the creed must be spoken with sincerity. The fourth is *al-Sidq*, which means that the creed must be understood as the essence of truth. The fifth is *al-Mahabbah*, which means that the creed is to be loved. The sixth is *al-Inquiad*, which means that the one speaking the creed will submit to all that it implies. The seventh is *al-Qubool*, which means that the creed must be fully and unreservedly believed.

Islam is not the only major religion with defining creeds. Both Judaism and Christianity are also grounded in creeds that give shape to its essential theology and conditions of genuine faith. They stand in contrast to the *Shahadah* that defines the Islamic faith.

Judaism. One of Judaism's most central creeds is the *Shema*. It states: "Hear, O Israel: the LORD our God, the LORD is one. Love the LORD your God with all your heart and with all your soul and with all your strength" (Deut 6:4-5). Its fundamental premise is twofold: (a) a confession of faith in Yahweh, the one and only God, and (b) a command to love Yahweh with all one's heart, soul, and strength. In this passage, the Hebrew word trans-lated LORD is Yahweh.

A second defining creed in Judaism is the *Arami Oved*, the Creed of the Wandering Aramean. It states: "Then you shall declare before the Lord your God: 'My father was a wandering Aramean, and he went down into

Egypt with a few people and lived there and became a great nation, powerful and numerous. But the Egyptians mistreated us and made us suffer, putting us to hard labor. Then we cried out to the LORD, the God of our fathers, and the LORD heard our voice and saw our misery, toil and oppression. So the LORD brought us out of Egypt with a mighty hand and an outstretched arm, with great terror and with miraculous signs and wonders. He brought us to this place and gave us this land, a land flowing with milk and honey'" (Deut 26:5-9). The crux of the Passover Haggadah, recited at every Passover Seder celebration, is the *Arami Oved*. The Mishah makes this point emphatically. It states that the leader of the Seder must expound "from A wandering Aramean was my father...until he finishes the whole section."[2] Rabbi Gamaliel said that anyone who did not recite the verses concerning the Creed of the Wandering Aramean at the Passover Seder "has not fulfilled his obligation."[3] In the *Laws of Chametz and Matza*, Maimonides added: "Anyone who draws out and expounds excessively on this *parasha* (story) is to be praised."[4] According to the Mishah, every Jew was required to not only recite the Arami Oved, but to also relive the experience, as if the exodus from slavery to freedom were taking place in the present.[5]

Christianity. The Christian creeds are centered on the nature of the Godhead and Jesus Christ. In regards to the first, the baptismal formula inaugurated by Jesus is a central Christian creed, affirmed by all who underwent baptism. Jesus said: "All authority in heaven and on earth has been given to me. Therefore go and make disciples of all nations, baptizing them in the name of the Father and of the Son and of the Holy Spirit, and teaching them to obey everything I have commanded you. And surely I am with you always, to the very end of the age" (Matt 28:18-20). The formula emphasized the Doctrine of the Trinity which was a belief in monotheism (God is one) who exists in Three Persons (Father, Son, and Holy Spirit).

A second creed is found in the writings of the Apostle Paul. He wrote: "For what I received I passed on to you as of first importance: that Christ died for our sins according to the Scriptures, that he was buried, that he was raised on the third day according to the Scriptures, and that he appeared to Peter, and then to the Twelve. After that, he appeared to more than five hundred of the brothers at the same time, most of whom are still living, though some have fallen asleep. Then he appeared to James, then to all the apostles" (1 Cor 15:3-7). By stating that it was "received" and then "passed on to you," Paul made the point that the early church was active in its transmission to all its members. It was part of the oral tradition in the early church.

A third creed is also found in the Apostle Paul's writings. In his epistle to the Philippians, he included a liturgical confession that was believed to be commonly used in the worship services of the early church. It begins in eternity past, addresses the incarnation of Jesus, then addresses the crucifixion and resurrection, and finally addresses the need for all people everywhere to confess Jesus as Lord. It states: "Who, being in very nature God, did not consider equality with God something to be grasped, but made himself nothing, taking the very nature of a servant, being made in human likeness. And being found in appearance as a man, he humbled himself and became obedient to death—even death on a cross! Therefore God exalted him to the highest place and gave him the name that is above every name, that at the name of Jesus every knee should bow, in heaven and on earth and under the earth, and every tongue confess that Jesus Christ is Lord, to the glory of God the Father" (Phil 2:6-11).

---

[1] *Sahih Bukhari* 1.7.331.
[2] *Mishna Pesahim* 10:4.
[3] *Mishna Pesahim* 10:5.
[4] *The Laws of Chametz and Matza*, in Mishah Torah by Maimonides, 7:4.
[5] *Mishna Pesahim* 10:5.

———•◆•———

The first and most important duty of every Muslim is to state their faith in Allah. Islam teaches that a person must speak of their faith in Allah with their lips and believe it in their heart...Saying these Arabic words is called *shahadah*, the statement of faith. The shahadah is said by Muslims at least twice every day, when they wake up and just before sleeping.

—Cesar E. Farah, *Islam: Beliefs and Observances*

Without [the Shahadah], a person is not a Muslim...The Shahadah has a fundamental importance for Islamic faith, since it expresses the first and second principles of faith in a nutshell.

—Sachiko Murata and William C. Chittick, *The Vision of Islam*, p. 45

Recitation of the Shahadah is used as the formal means of entry into Islam.

—Arshad Khan, *Islam 101: Principles and Practice*, p. 42

2   rise up and warn!
3   And thy Lord magnify!
4   And thy garments purify!
5   And abomination shun!
6   And grant not favours to gain increase!
7   And for thy Lord await!

The coming curse

8   And when the trump is blown,
9   —for that day is a difficult day!
10   for the misbelievers aught but easy!
11   Leave me alone with him I have created,
12   and for whom I have made extensive wealth,
13   and sons that he may look upon,
14   and for whom I have smoothed things down.
15   Then he desires that I should increase!
16   nay, verily, he is hostile to our signs!
17   I will drive him up a hill!
`18 Then he reflected and planned!
19   May he be killed,—how he planned!
20   Again, may he be killed,
21   —how he planned!

22   Then he looked; then he frowned and scowled;
23   then he retreated and was big with pride
24   and said, "This is only magic exhibited!
25   this is only mortal speech!"

The coming condemnation

26   —I will broil him in hell-fire!
27   and what shall make thee know what hell-fire is?
28   It will not leave and will not let alone.
29   It scorches the flesh;
30   over it are nineteen (angels).
31   We have made only angels guardians of the fire, and we have only made their number a trial to those who misbelieve; that those who have been given the Book may be certain, and that those who believe may be increased in faith; and that those who have been given the Book and the believers may not doubt; and that those in whose hearts is sickness, and the misbe-

74.1 *O thou who art covered* — Literally, O thou shrouded in thy mantle. The mantle (*maddaththir*) was worn over the undergarment and came in direct contact with the body. The point was that this garment was to remain pure. Besides prayer, personal hygiene was regarded as essential to the spiritual state of a Muslim.

74.8-31 The content of the surah is harsh, full of curses and condemnations upon the people of Mecca. Compare with Isa. 6:1-13 which is also a harsh denunciation of the evil people in the Prophet Isaiah's day.

74.30 *over it are nineteen* — Guarding over the gates of Hell are nineteen angels.

74.31 This is the longest verse in Section Two. Its purpose is to motivate people to avoid Hell in the afterlife and pursue a life of godliness in this life.

74.38 *Every soul is pledged for what it earns* — That is, salvation is a question of merit (see **The Last Judgment** on pp. 46-50 for a further discussion of this topic).

74.42 *What drove you into hell-fire?* —

lievers may say, "What does God mean by this as a parable?" Thus God leads astray whom He pleases, and guides him He pleases: and none knows the hosts of thy Lord save Himself; and it is only a reminder to mortals!

An oath

32 Nay, by the moon!
33 And the night when it retires!
34 And the morning when it brightly dawns!
35 Verily, it is one of the greatest misfortunes;
36 a warning to mortals;
37 for him amongst you who wishes to press forward or to tarry!
38 Every soul is pledged for what it earns;
39 except the fellows of the right:

40 in gardens shall they ask each other
41 about the sinners!
42 "—What drove you into hell-fire?"
43 They shall say, "We weren't of those who prayed;
44 we didn't feed the poor;
45 but we did plunge into discussion with those who plunged,
46 and we called the judgment day a lie
47 until the certainty did come to us!"
48 But there shall not profit them the intercession of the intercessors.
49 What ailed them that they turned away from the memorial
50 as though they were timid asses
51 fleeing from a lion?
52 Nay, every man of them wished that he might have given him books spread open!
53 Nay, but they did not fear the hereafter!

Again, the idea of salvation by good works is presented. When asked "What drove you into hell-fire, people will answer that they failed to pray and give alms to the poor (vv 43-44).

74.50-51 *timid asses fleeing from a lion* — The Last Judgment will be a disastrous time for the infidels, where judgment is fierce and unbending, as if they were timid asses fleeing from a ferocious lion.

The Bible speaks similarly. It refers to the Last Judgment as a place where the unbelievers "will not stand in the judgment" (Ps 1:5), will "lie fallen—thrown down, not able to rise!" (Ps 36:12). It is a place where they hang their heads in shame and confusion, with all their pleas and excuses overruled as frivolous and beside the point. More-

over, they will face an irreversible sentence, set for all eternity.

Nevertheless, a major difference exists between Islam and Christianity. The difference turns on the question of the nature of salvation. In the Qur'an, it is based upon *merit*—what one has earned (see Q 74.38). In the New Testament, it is based upon God *forgiveness*—what one has received. And that which has been received is a cleansing of sin by means of the blood of Jesus Christ (see Rom 3:25).

74.52 *books spread open!* — That is, divine revelation open and readily available (see **The Perspicuous Book** on pp. 178-179).

Surah 111. The title of this surah, *The Flame*, comes from verse three. Muhammad was preoccupied with the Doctrine of Hell

An admonition	*In the name of the merciful and compassionate God.*

An admonition

54   Nay, it is a memorial!
55   and let him who will remember it;
56   but none will remember it except
     God please. He is most worthy of
     fear; and he is most worthy to for-
     give!

Surah 111

In the name of the merciful and compassionate God.

1   Abu Laheb's two hands shall per-
    ish, and he shall perish!
2   His wealth shall not avail him, nor
    what he has earned!
3   He shall broil in a fire that flames,
4   and his wife carrying faggots!
5   —on her neck a cord of palm fi-
    bres.

and spent much time describing the nature of the torments and who it is who will occupy this horrific place. His most personalized example is located here in Surah 111, where his own uncle and aunt are cursed to Hell. This was because his uncle (Abu Lahab) and his uncle's wife (Umm Jamil) not only rejected his prophetic calling, they were leaders among those who opposed him.

According to Zayd ibn Ali, on one occasion Abu Lahab asked Muhammad how he would prosper if he converted to Islam. Muhammad answered that he would receive nothing more than what all other converts receive. Unimpressed, Abu Lahab then said: "May this religion perish in which I and all other people should be equal and alike!" Muham-

mad's aunt Umm Jamil responded similarly, cursing the Islamic religion (see Ibn Ishaq, *The Life of Muhammad*, p. 161).

111.1 In contrast to Abu Lahab, Abu Talib served as one of Muhammad's principal protectors. He also raised Muhammad from his early childhood. He too was one of the major leaders in Mecca. Oddly, though, Abu Talib never converted to Islam. Years later, at his funeral, Muhammad could not even bring himself to speak a prayer on his uncle's behalf. He merely said: "Perhaps my intercession will be helpful to him on the Day of Resurrection so that he may be put in a shallow fire reaching only up to his ankles. His brain will boil from it" (*Sahih Bukhari* 5.58.224; cf. *Sahih Muslim* 1.413).

INTRODUCTION

The Third Period

In the Third Period, Muhammad began the process of clarifying his message with powerful rhetorical presentations—surahs that were curt, grant, and sublime. Throughout, he offered glowing pictures of the happiness in store for those who embraced his message and frightful descriptions of the everlasting torments for all who remained in their polytheistic idolatries. His intent was to challenge and condemn the dominant religion in Mecca—the Arabic Star Family Religion—that was observed in the precinct of the Ka'ba altar. Polytheistic in orientation, he demanded that all people everywhere repent and worship the one true God—Allah.

Three Themes. Although a number of themes are presented in this series of surahs, three themes stand out as dominant. One addresses *eschatological issues.* He spoke of a coming resurrection of the dead and the Last Judgment when all the people of the earth would be judged. Two destinies followed this judgment: Paradise and Hell. He described both abodes with remarkable detail—descriptions that anticipated Dante's *Divine Comedy.* Paradise was characterized as the quintessential Arabian oasis with each occupant bequeathed his own private harem, with an unending supply of sensual and erotic delights, along with other comforts. Hell, in contrast, was a place of unending torment.

A second theme addresses *soteriological issues.* One's personal salvation, Muhammad explained, was a question of successfully walking the "uphill road" (Q 90.11); that is, a system of meritocracy. Over the course of a lifetime, one earns eternal life by amassing more good works than bad. The notion of good works included: (a) a singularly focused worship of Allah, (b) the recognition of Muhammad as Allah's prophet, and (c) faithful obedience of all the teachings in the Qur'an.

A third theme addresses *qur'anic textual issues.* Muhammad insisted that he did not author any of the surahs. Instead, they were already fully formed, existing in Paradise, guarded by Allah, and dictated one at a time to Muhammad by the archangel Gabriel. They are eternal, always having existed. Moreover, they are perfect and free from the influence of historical, cultural, or anything else existing inside of time. This afforded the surahs a sense of finality. They are authoritative and the determining norm in any culture and under any circumstances. Rather than cultural norms impacting the surahs and their interpretations, the surahs impact cultural norms and brings judgment upon their understandings of right and wrong.

The Response in Mecca. The chieftains of Mecca responded to Muhammad's ministry by appealing to his uncle, Abu Talib. They demanded that Muhammad desist with his surahs that insulted their gods, condemned their entire polytheistic understanding of religion, and mocked their way of life. They went to Abu Talib, Muhammad's uncle, and demanded that either he speak reason to his nephew or they would kill him. They noted that Abu Talib was a polytheist and, hence, not a follower of Muhammad's new religion. He should therefore be sympathetic to their point of view. Abu Talib offered a conciliatory soft reply to the chieftains, telling them that he would try to speak reason with his nephew. Abu Talib spoke to Muham-mad, but Muhammad refused to change his ways.[1]

An additional feature of this period was the first migration of Muslims from Mecca. Due to the threat of persecution, a large number of Muhammad's devotees migrated to Abyssinia. Abyssinia was a kingdom aligned with the Byzantine Empire, located on the western shores of the Red Sea south of Egypt (it extended into present day Ethiopia). According to Ibn Ishaq, the total number of emigrants to Abyssinia were eighty-three men, including an unknown number of women and children.[2]

---

[1] See Ibn Ishaq, *The Life of Muhammad*, pp. 118-119. Curiously Abu Talib was not, nor ever would be, a Muslim (see see *Sahih Bukhari* 6.60.295). On his deathbed, Abu Talib said that he remained committed to the religion of his own father, Abdul-Muttaleb, who had been a faithful devotee to ginn worship during his lifetime (see Ibn Ishaq, *The Life of Muhammad*, pp. 45, 66-68).

[2] Ibn Ishaq, *The Life of Muhammad*, p. 146.

Surah 87

In the name of the merciful and compassionate God.

1 Celebrated the name of thy Lord most High,
2 who created and fashioned,
3 and who decreed and guided,
4 and who brings forth the pasture,
5 and then makes it dusky stubble!

The command to recite

6 We will make thee recite, and thou shalt not forget,
7 save what God pleases. Verily, He knows the open and what is concealed;
8 and we will send thee easily to ease;
9 wherefore remind, for, verily, the reminder is useful.

Warning of Hell

10 But he who fears will be mindful;
11 but the wretch will avoid it;
12 he who will broil on the great fire,
13 and then therein shall neither die nor live!

Surah 87. The title of this surah, *The Most High*, comes from verse one. This surah was a response to the charge by his opponents in Mecca that Muhammad was a rogue charlatan prophet. These opponents, for the most part, were associated with the pagan Arabian Star Family Religion, a religion that boasted a longstanding tradition (anchored to the ancient Sumerian culture and its city of Ur). Muhammad's solution was to attach himself to an equally longstanding tradition: the monotheism of the Hebrew prophets. Accordingly, he wrapped himself around two of its most prominent patriarchs: Abraham and Moses (vv. 18-19). This move would eventually become the signature characteristic of his new religion.

A second feature in this surah is Muhammad's first mention of the Doctrine of Abrogation—a doctrine that legitimized contradictions within the Qur'an. Among the many doctrines mentioned in the Qur'an, this doctrine would become one of the most controversial and hotly debated.

87.6-7 *We will make thee recite, and thou shalt not forget, save what God pleases* — This is the Islamic Doctrine of Abrogation, a doctrine also mentioned in Q 2.106 and 13.39. Muhammad was allegedly instructed by Allah to forget specific verses in the Qur'an, and keep in his memory all the other verses (see **The Doctrine of Abrogation** on pp. 68-70).

Christian scholars find within the Doctrine of Abrogation an inherent inconsistency. If the Qur'an is an eternal document (see Q 85.21-22; *Second Great Creed*, third article), how is it possible that Allah would reveal to Muhammad truths that were later erased? Would not that make Allah to be neither omniscient nor infallible? Would not that cause the Qur'an to be less than perfect?

87.12-13 Two characteristics of Hell: (a) a great fire, and (b) those who enter are neither alive nor dead. Throughout the Qur'an, Muhammad provided vivid and gruesome descriptions of Hell. In contrast, the Bible is much more limited in its description of both Heaven and Hell. John R. W. Stott writes: "We may, and I think we should, preserve a

The Doctrine of Abrogation

The Doctrine of Abrogation addresses the question of contradictions within the Qur'an. It states that an earlier statement carrying legal or divine authority is abrogated (erased) by a later contradictory statement which also carries legal or divine authority. Maulana Muhammad Ali comments that some Islamic scholars place the number of abrogated verses in the Qur'an at five hundred. Other scholars, however, are more conservative, claiming a more correct number to be as few as twenty-one.[1]

Three passages in the Qur'an establish the doctrine:

- "Whatever verse we may annul or cause thee to forget, we will bring a better one than it, or one like it; dost thou not know that God is mighty over all?" (Q 2.106)

- "God blots out what He will, or He confirms; and with Him is the Mother of the Book." (Q 13.39)

- "We will make thee recite, and thou shalt not forget, save what God pleases." (Q 87.6-7)

The point is that statements made in earlier surahs are subject to abrogation if statements in later surahs teach differing concepts. In this respect, the doctrine employs the logic of chronology and progressive revelation. Proof-texting (that is, lifting a verse out of its context and chronological setting and thereby building a doctrine from it) is particularly problematic. Controversial topics—such as alcoholic beverages (wine), the nature of jihad, Muhammad's view of Jews and Christians—must be read in chronological order, since verses mentioned early in the Qur'an are not necessarily active in later surahs.

The Doctrine of Abrogation has proved to be troublesome for Islam. The problem is due to the fact that Muhammad insisted that the Qur'an is an eternal uncreated book—a book with no beginning, guarded in Paradise by Allah (see Q 85.21-22). Hence, Islamic scholars are left with no easy explanations to justify erasures and corrections within the Qur'an. Two common responses are the following:

- Many Islamic scholars deny the doctrine altogether. When rightly interpreted, they insist, apparent contradictions are understood to be no contradictions whatsoever.

- Other Islamic scholars argue against the notion of the Qur'an being an eternally uncreated book. The Qur'an could not be an eternal book without a beginning, as alleged, since the properties of change are necessarily connected to the properties of time. All such references in the Qur'an being an eternal document are therefore hyperboles—exaggerated speech—and not to be taken literally.

Moderate Islamic scholars lean towards the second response. Conservative Islamic scholars lean towards the first.

Christian response. The Doctrine of Abrogation demonstrates that the Qur'an is indeed a historical document. It was written in a specific time in history and within the interactions of a variety of cultures. Muhammad made changes to his developing theology due to changes in circumstances and his outlook on life. These changes affected specific teachings, such as his views on alcoholic beverages, Jihad, and Jews and Christians (see Q 2.106 and 13.39).

Christians have a similar understanding of the Bible. It too is a historical document, written in history within the competing interactions of differing cultures. God established covenants with His people in one historical moment that were later replaced or modified by other covenants in other historical moments. The Mosaic Covenant is a case in point. Established during the ministry of Moses, it was later replaced by the New Covenant (see Jer 31:30-34; Heb 8:13). In the Old Testament, a common teaching was that the blood of animals shed in ritual sacrifices provided divine forgiveness. In the New Testament, this teaching changed. It was the blood of Jesus Christ shed at the cross that provided divine forgiveness. The first was merely a prefiguring of the second (see Jn 1:17; Gal 3:24-25; Heb 9:12-14).

Hence, since Christians do not believe that the Bible is an eternal uncreated document, they have no problem with the Doctrine of Abrogation. In the Bible, God spoke within the context of culture and history, He made changes to His covenants, according to His divine will. In the Old Testament, people were instructed to place their faith in the efficacious work of animal sacrifices which covered their sins. In the New Testament, people were instructed to place their faith in the efficacious work of Jesus Christ, who died on the cross for their sins. The Apostle

Paul explained: "Before this faith came, we were held prisoners by the law, locked up until faith should be revealed. So the law was put in charge to lead us to Christ that we might be justified by faith. Now that faith has come, we are no longer under the supervision of the law" (Gal 3:23-25).

Moreover, the Bible is also understood to be a document with dual authorship, wholly written by God and wholly written by man. John R. W. Stott writes, "To say 'the Bible is the Word of God' is true, but it is only a half-truth, even a dangerous half-truth. For the Bible is also a human word and witness...Thus God spoke and men spoke. Both statements are true, and neither contradicts the other."[2]

It is in the human dimension that we see the presence of history and culture most forcefully in the Bible. Yet, the presence of history and culture does not negate its divine inspiration or authority. Indeed, Christians explain, this is how God always speaks to us—within the context of history and culture. This does not imply cultural and historical relativism. To the contrary, it makes the case that God challenges our cultural and historical predilections with a divinely inspired understanding of culture and history.

[1] See Maulana Muhammad Ali, *The Religion of Islam*, pp. 32, 33.
[2] John R. W. Stott, *Culture and the Bible*, p. 5.

The doctrine of abrogation was to Muhammad a doctrine of convenience. So when he claimed a revelation to be no longer suitable, he claimed that it was replaced by some new revelation. For example, initially in his mission Christians were friends and called the nearest and closest to Muslims, but later they were the enemies and the worst of Allah's creatures...Interestingly, the abrogated (nullified) verses are quoted to non-Muslims all the time, causing obfuscation and taking a Christian apologist by surprise!...It is not unusual for Muslim speakers to impress their Western audiences with these earlier "friendly" verses and to proclaim that there is hardly any difference between Islam and Christianity!

—Sam Solomon, *Beyond Opinion*, p. 74

Abrogation is a complex and controversial area within Islam. The number of abrogated verses ranges from five to five hundred. An additional problem deals with contradictions between the *Koran* and the *hadith* reports. Does the *Koran* abrogate contradictory passages in the *hadith* reports or do the *hadith* reports abrogate contradictory verses in the *Koran*? We also need to ask which prevails if there are contradictions among the *sunnah* (Muhammad's actions and behavior), the *hadith* reports, and the *Koran*. It would have been simpler if the Islamic god would have had Muslims "forget" the abrogated verses prior to their inclusion in the *Koran*.

—Richard Crandall, *Islam: the Enemy*, p. 52

In order to establish what verse or tradition abrogated which, it was, of course, essential to know which verse had been revealed first, or which tradition reported the earliest acts or sayings of the Prophet.

—Camilla Adang, *Muslim Writers on Judaism and the Hebrew Bible*, pp. 193, 194

The wine verses are a relatively clear instance of abrogation. Beyond that, there is wide disagreement among Muslim theologians as to precisely which verses have been abrogated and which others have replaced them...And generally, if a verse revealed at Mecca contradicts another revealed later at Medina, Muslim theologians will give great weight to the idea that the Meccan verse has been abrogated and replaced by the verse from Medina. This idea is crucial as a guide to the relationship of the Qur'an's peaceful passages to its violent ones.

—Robert Spencer, *Onward Muslim Soldiers*, pp. 135, 136

According to my views as expressed in my writings, the abrogation cannot be determined but in five verses only...The term abrogation has been used by almost all scholars in the sense of removal of the earlier verse by the incoming verse.

—Hamid Naseem Rafiabadi, *Challenges to Religions and Islam*, p. 332

The Qur'an can abrogate the Qur'an.

—Hamid Naseem Rafiabadi, *World Religions and Islam: A Critical Study*, vol. 1, p. 254

It is to be stressed that the greatest majority of jurists espoused the view that it is not the texts themselves that are actually abrogated, but rather the legal rulings comprised by these texts. The text *qua* text is not subject to repeal, for to argue that God revealed conflicting and even contradictory statements would entail that one of the statements is false, and this would in turn lead to the highly objectionable conclusion that God has revealed an untruth.

—Wael B. Hallaq, *A History of Islamic Legal Theories*, p. 69

14	Prosperous is he who purifies him-self,		**Surah 97**
15	and remembers the name of his Lord and prays!		*In the name of the merciful and compassionate God.*
16	Nay! but ye prefer the life of this world,	1	Verily, we sent it down on the Night of Power!
17	while the, hereafter is better and more lasting.	2	And what shall make thee know what the Night of Power is?
18	Verily, this was in the books of yore,	3	—the Night of Power is better than a thousand months!
19	—the books of Abraham and Moses.	4	The angels and the Spirit descend

certain reverent and humble agnosticism about the precise nature of hell, as about the precise nature of heaven. Both are beyond our understanding. But clear and definite we must be that hell is an awful, eternal reality. It is not dogmaticism that is unbecoming in speaking about the fact of hell; it is glibness and frivolity. How can we think about hell without tears?" (*Christian Mission in the Modern World*, p. 113).

87.18 *the books of yore* — The book of Moses is perhaps a reference to the Pentateuch. The book of Abraham is perhaps a reference to the *Testament of Abraham*. From a chronological perspective, this is the first mention of either Abraham or Moses in the Qur'an.

Surah 97. The title of this surah, *The Majesty*, based upon the events that occurred on "the Night of Power" mentioned in verse one. According to Muhammad, the Night of Power is the nocturnal event in which he first received a revelation via the archangel Gabriel. Though the exact day on the calendar is not known, it is believed by some Islamic scholars to have occurred sometime in the last ten nights of Ramadan. Other scholars maintain that it occurred on one of the odd nights in the last ten days of Ramadan.

Because of Muhammad's first encounter with the archangel Gabriel in the month of Ramadan, this month is especially celebrated and honored in the Muslim world.

97.1 *Night of Power* — According to this verse and Islamic lore, the first night in which Muhammad received a revelation from Allah via the archangel Gabriel was called the "Night of Power." It corresponds to that which Muhammad noted in Q 96.1-5 when he was told to "read (or recite) in the name of the Lord." Islamic scholars also refer to it as: the Blessed Night, the Night of Destiny, the Night of Innocence, the Night of Contact, and the Night of Mercy (see Q 44.3).

97.3 *a thousand months* — In the Muslim calendar, the Night of Power is considered a special night during the month of Ramadan, in which every act of worship or good deed is multiplied by a thousand. Since salvation is predicated upon a life rich in merit, Ramadan is therefore highly prized in the Muslim world.

Surah 88. The title of this surah, *The Overwhelming Event*, comes from verse one. Once again, in this surah Muhammad warned the people of Mecca of the existence of Hell and offered the hope of Paradise.

88.2-7 Five characteristics of Hell: (a) a place where people are humbled, (b) people

therein, by the permission of their Lord with every bidding.

5   Peace it is until rising of the dawn!

Surah 88

In the name of the merciful and compassionate God.

Warning of Hell

1   Has there come to thee the story of the overwhelming?
2   Faces on that day shall: be humble,
3   labouring, toiling,
4   —shall broil upon a burning fire;
5   shall be given to drink from a boiling spring!
6   no food shall they have save from the foul thorn,
7   which shall not fatten nor avail against hunger!

Hope of Paradise

8   Faces on that day shall be comfortable,
9   content with their past endeavours,
10   — in a lofty garden
11   wherein they shall hear no foolish word;

12   wherein is a flowing fountain;
13   wherein are couches raised on high,
14   and goblets set down,
15   and cushions arranged,
16   and carpets spread!
17   Do they not look then at the camel how she is created?
18   And at the heaven how it is reared?
19   And at the mountains how they are set up?
20   And at the earth how it is spread out?

Muhammad's ministry

21   But remind: thou art only one to remind;
22   thou art not in authority over them;
23   except such as turns his back and misbelieves, for him will
24   God torment with the greatest torment.
25   Verily, unto us is their return,
26   and, verily, for us is their account!

Surah 80

In the name of the merciful and compassionate God.

Muhammad rebuked by Allah

labor and toil, (c) a burning fire, (d) people made to drink from a boiling spring, and (e) people gripped by an unending hunger.
88.8-16 Five characteristics of Paradise: (a) contentment, (b) a lofty garden, (c) no vain talk, (d) much water, (e) raised couches situated on lush carpets, and (f) goblets.

88.21-22 Muhammad saw himself as a reminder. He believed that he had no authority or power to affect changes in people's hearts. All he could do was remind and warn.
88.23 *except such as turns his back and misbelieves* — That is, except the one who turns his back on Muhammad's message.

1 He frowned and turned his back,	9 fearing the while,
2 for that there came to him a blind man!	10 from him thou art diverted!
3 But what should make thee know whether haply he may be purified?	*The wealthy rebuked by Allah*
4 or may be mindful and the reminder profit him?	11 Nay! verily, it is a memorial;
5 But as for him who is wealthy,	12 and whoso pleases will remember it.
6 thou dost attend to him;	13 In honoured pages
7 and thou dost not care that he is not purified;	14 exalted, purified,
8 but as for him who comes to thee earnestly	15 in the hands of noble,
	16 righteous scribes!
	17 May man be killed! how ungrateful

Surah 80. The title of this surah, *He Frowned*, comes from verse one. Three themes are addressed in this short surah: wealth, the coming resurrection from the dead, the blessing of rain, and the Last Judgment. The most remarkable verses, however, address Allah's rebuke to Muhammad.

80.1-10 While engaged in a conversation with one of the chieftains of the Quraysh people of Mecca, Muhammad was approached by one of his blind followers—Abd Allah ibn Shurayh. Annoyed by this interruption, Muhammad "frowned and turned his back" (v. 1) on the blind man. As a result, Allah rebuked him for his deference to the wealthy (vv. 3-12).

The Doctrine of Isma, however, states that all prophets of Allah are sinless, since they are His representatives on earth (see Q 94.1-3, note). Adam Gaiser writes, "Muhammad was believed to have the quality of *isma*, a term defined by Schimmel as 'protection or freedom (from moral depravity)'" (*Muslim, Scholars, Soldiers*, p. 27). Yet, curiously, in this passage Muhammad sinned.

The famed Islamic treatise *The Second Great Creed* (eighth century)—also known

as *Fikh Akbar II*—attributed to Imam Abu Hanifah, attempted to resolve the problem presented in this surah. It stated: "All of the Prophets are exempt from sins, both grave and light, from unbelief and sordid deeds. Yet stumbling and mistakes may happen on their part" (article 8).

The Christian faith has a doctrine similar to the Islamic Doctrine of Isma. It is called the Doctrine of Impeccability, the absolute sinlessness and perfection of Jesus Christ (see Isa 53:9; 2 Cor 5:21; Heb 7:26; 1 Pet 2:22-24; 1 Jn 3:5). This sinlessness of Jesus Christ was absolute: He neither stumbled nor made mistakes.

80.13 *in honored pages* — That is, in the pages of divine revelation.

80.17 *how ungrateful he is* — Ungratefulness is a major sin in the Islamic hierarchy of sins. It is manifested by the refusal to surrender absolutely to the will of Allah. Since Allah provided many blessings to a person, for that individual to refuse to acknowledge the blessings as coming from Allah and respond with a surrendered and obedient heart is the height of insolence and arrogance.

In the Judeo-Christian tradition, ungrate-

he is!
18   Of what did He create him?
19   Of a clot. He created him and fated
      him;
20   then the path He did make easy for
      him;

The resurrection

21   then He killed him, and laid him in
      the tomb;
22   then when He pleases will He raise
      him up again.

The blessing of rain

23   Nay, he has not fulfilled his bidding!
24   But let man look unto his foods.

25   Verily, we have poured the water
      out in torrents:
26   then we have cleft the earth asun-
      der,
27   and made to grow therefrom the
      grain,
28   and the grape, and the hay,
29   and the olive, and the palm,
30   and gardens closely planted,
31   and fruits, and grass,
32   —a provision for you and for your
      cattle!

The Last Judgment

33   But when the stunning noise shall
      come,
34   on the day when man shall flee

---

fulness is also regarded as a major sin, and for the same fundamental reasons. "Come, let us sing for joy to the Lord; let us shout aloud to the Rock of our salvation. Let us come before him with thanksgiving and extol him with music and song. For the LORD is the great God, the great King above all gods. In his hand are the depths of the earth, and the mountain peaks belong to him. The sea is his, for he made it, and his hands formed the dry land" (Ps 95:1-5). Moreover, one of the cups at the Passover celebration is called the Cup of Thanksgiving—so called in remembrance of the Lord freeing the Hebrews from servitude in Egypt. In the New Testament are the words: "Give thanks in all circumstances, for this is God's will for you in Christ Jesus" (1 Thess 5:18).

80.19 *Of a clot* — Muhammad was fascinated with the origin of the human being. In this verse, he believed that man's origin came from a blood clot (see Q 96.2, note).

80.21-22 According to Muhammad, all people, both good and evil, will one day be raised from the grave and stand before Allah (cf. Job 19:25; Ps 49:15; 71:20; Lk 20:37; Jn 11:21-24; Acts 23:6; 24:15, 21).

80.23-32 Muhammad claimed that people should be grateful for Allah's blessings, but as a rule most are not. Understanding rain as a blessing from Allah is often overlooked by people (cf. 2 Chron 6:26-27; Job 5:10; 37:6-9; 38:25-28; Ps 147:8; Jer 14:22; Joel 2:23; Zech 10:1; Matt 5:45; Acts 14:17).

80.31 *grass* — In the Arabic language, the word is *abb*. In reference to this verse, Umar ibn al-Khattah (the second caliph and companion of Muhammad) once recited this verse and said: "We all know that. But what is *abb?*" Then he threw away a stick which he had in his hand and said: "By the eternal Allah! That is artificiality. What does it amount to for you, son of the mother of Umar, if you do not know what *abb* is?" Obey

Paradise

The way Paradise is presented in the Qur'an, it is first and foremost the abode of bliss in the afterlife. It is offered to the righteous as a reward for having lived in accord with divine revelation and having lived out that faith with good works and moral rectitude.

Having successfully passed the test of the Last Judgment, they hear the long awaited words: "Peace be upon you! enter ye into Paradise for that which ye have done" (Q 16.32). The righteous will then cross over *Sirat al-Jahim* (the Bridge of Hell), a bridge that is razor sharp, the width of a single hair, which all people must cross over after their time at the Last Judgment. It is an ominous bridge since below it are the fires of Hell. People who performed a sufficient number of good works during their liftetimes are transported across the bridge with speeds according to the quality and quantity of their works. Hence, only the righteous will pass over the bridge successfully.

What is Paradise? Paradise is characterized as the Gardens of Pleasure. More to the point, it is an oasis, rich with fruit, drink, shade, pools of water. Underneath are two well supplied rivers of water—aquifers—that keep the oasis perpetually green and fertile (see Q 16.31; 18.31; 20.76; 25.10; 39.20; 85.11). In addition, each righteous man is assigned a harem to care for his every sensual whim and need. Each of the young maidens who make up these harems possess "swelling breasts" (Q 78.33), a term which suggests that they are physiologically just beyond puberty. They also have wide lustrous eyes and modest glances. They recline on raised couches, situated on thick carpets awaiting the commands of their harem master. They are also attended by boys who remain eternally young (Q 52.24; 76.19). It is not clear where the righteous women go. Most Islamic scholars believe that they become members of harems, attending to the wishes and needs of the righteous man. In short, the imagery of Paradise is defined in terms of the culture of seventh century Arabian Sheikhs, a place of absolute and complete opulence.

Seven Heavens. Since Heaven is understood to contain seven tiers (Q 13.17; 41.12; 65.12; 67.3; 71.15; 78.12), the oases and harems to be enjoyed by the righteous people are situated on each one. Each tier is separated by a distance that calculates to a journey of five hundred years. Ranked from least to greatest, the Seven Heavens are: (a) Rafi, (b) Qaydum, (c) Marum, (d) Arfalun, (e) Hay'oun, (f) Arous, and (g) Ajma'. Allah occupies the Seventh Heaven and only those who achieved supreme righteousness are allowed entrance into this most restricted tier.

Christianity. In contrast, the Christian faith understands Heaven as a gracious gift—not as that which is earned by means of righteous living. Entrance into Heaven turns on the question of forgiveness. Moreover, this forgiveness is offered to any who embrace Jesus Christ, the one who died on the cross and rose from the dead as payment for the penalty of sin. The Apostle Paul wrote, "In him we have redemption through his blood, the forgiveness of sins, in accordance with the riches of God's grace" (Eph 1:7; cf. Matt 26:28; Lk 24:47; Acts 5:31; 10:43; 13:38; 26:18; Col 1:14; Heb 9:22).

In the New Testament, there is much about Heaven that we do not know. That which we do know includes the following:

- People will neither marry nor be given in marriage (Matt 22:30)

- People will occupy themselves with worship and various forms of service (Matt 25:14-23; Rev 22:3)

Hence, unlike Islam, Heaven is described as a place void of harems. No sexual activity will take place in Heaven of any kind.

Nobel laureate V. S. Naipaul, a non-Muslim who has traveled extensively in Muslim countries, thinks Paradise is the single biggest motivator of Muslims. "The idea in Islam, the most important thing, is paradise." For tough-minded Naipaul, Paradise makes fundamentalists of all Muslim governments.

—Edward Hotaling, *Islam without Illusions*, p. 62

A close reading of the Qur'an and Hadith clearly show that most references to Paradise feature perks that would not have been available in the desert landscape of Arabia.

—Michael McCullar, *A Christian's Guide to Islam*, p. 48

from his brother
35 and his mother and his father
36 and his spouse and his sons!
37 Every man among them on that day shall have a business to employ him.
38 Faces on that day shall be bright,
39 —laughing, joyous!
40 and faces shall have dust upon them,
41 —darkness shall cover them!
42 those are the wicked misbelievers!

Surah 84

In the name of the merciful and compassionate God.

Striving to Meet God

1 When the heaven is rent asunder
2 and gives ear unto its Lord, and is

dutiful!
3 And when the earth is stretched out
4 and casts forth what is in it, and is empty,
5 and gives ear unto its Lord, and is dutiful!
6 O man! verily, thou art toiling after thy Lord, toiling; wherefore shalt thou meet Him!

The two books

7 And as for him who is given his book in his right hand,
8 he shall be reckoned with by an easy reckoning;
9 and he shall go back to his family joyfully.
10 But as for him who is given his book behind his back,
11 he shall call out for destruction,
12 but he shall broil in a blaze!
13 Verily, he was amongst his family

what is clear to you in this Book and leave aside what is not clear!"

80.38-39 The faces of those who are righteous will be bright and joyous at the Last Judgment.

80.40 The faces of the infidels will be covered with dust and darkness at the Last Judgment.

Surah 84. The title of this surah, *The Bursting Asunder,* comes from verse one. In Mecca, resistance to Muhammad's message was beginning to mount. In this surah, evidence is presented of a growing sternness and hostility to Muhammad.

84.6 *thou art toiling after thy Lord —* Muhammad's point was that for the most part life is hard, full of strife and striving. The

difficult moments outweigh the pleasant ones. The Bible makes a similar claim (see Job 5:7; Ps 127:2; Eccl. 2:17, 22-23; 5:16-17; Matt 6:34; 11:28).

84.7 *his book —* The Book of Works, the book which contains all the works of an individual during his or her lifetime.

84.7-19 At the Last Judgment, Allah will hold two books, one in his right hand and one behind his back (presumably in his left hand). For those whose names are written in the book of Allah's right hand, they shall receive "an easy reckoning." For those whose names are written in the book held behind Allah's back, they shall be cast "into burning fire."

84.21 A central factor in determining the

joyful.

14 Verily, he thought that he should never return to God.

15 Yea, verily, his Lord on him did look!

16 I need not swear by the evening glow,

17 Or by the night, and what it drives together,

18 Or by the moon when it is at its full,

19 Ye shall be surely transferred from state to state!

Obeisance to the Qur'an

20 What ails them that they do not believe?

21 and, when the Qur'ân is read to them, do not adore?

22 Nay, those who misbelieve do say it is a lie,

23 but God knows best the (malice) that they hide.

24 So give them the glad tidings of grievous woe!

25 save those who believe and act aright, for them is hire that is not grudged!

Surah 81

In the name of the merciful and compassionate God.

The Last Judgment

1 When the sun is folded up,

2 And when the stars do fall,

book in which one's name is located is one's attitude toward the Qur'an. Did one humbly live in obeisance to the Qur'an? For those who did, their names are in the book of the right hand. For those who did not, their names are in the book behind Allah's back, held in his left hand. Hence, salvation based upon righteous deeds—a system of meritocracy.

In contrast, the New Testament makes the claim that our entrance into Heaven is predicated upon *forgiveness*, not *merit*. And this forgiveness is offered through Jesus Christ and his ministry of redemption at the cross. "In him we have redemption through his blood, the forgiveness of sins, in accordance with the riches of God's grace" (Eph 1:7; cf. Matt 26:28; Lk 1:77; 3:3; 24:47; Acts 2:38; 5:31; 10:43; 13:38; 26:18; Rom 3:24-25; Col 1:14; Heb 9:22). Moreover, Jesus Christ will

stand in judgment of people at the Last Judgment.

84.22 Muhammad believed that people, for the most part, will be unwilling to admit their sinfulness when before Allah.

84.25 *believe and act aright* — Salvation is presented in terms of faith and works, a system of meritocracy (see Q 103.3, note, and **The Last Judgment** on pp. 46-50).

Surah 81. This surah is another reminder of the coming Last Judgment and the coming threat of Hell. It is also a reminder that Muhammad is Allah's messenger and his words must be heeded, if one wishes to avoid eternal condemnation.

81.1-14 Muhammad believed that the General Resurrection from the dead, followed by the Last Judgment would be preceded by a time of apocalyptic events, such as those described in this passage.

Hell

In the Qur'an, Hell (*Jahannam*) is the place of eternal torment. It is the final abode for all the unrighteous, those who were pronounced cursed by Allah at the Last Judgment. In a Hadith, Muhammad noted that 99.9% of all humanity will be cast into Hell (*Sahih Bukhari* 4.55.567). Since Islam is the second largest world religion, with approximately one quarter of the world's population being Muslim, the mathematical implication of this percentage is that many Muslims will also be cast into Hell.

Similar to Paradise, which has seven paths, Hell has seven gates and seven levels (Q 39.71; 15.43). At the lowest level is the tree of Zaqqum and the cauldron of boiling pitch. One's placement in Hell depends upon the degree and volume of offenses committed while on earth. It is a place where scorched skins are replaced with new skins so that the torment can be experienced anew. Boiling water is poured over heads and forced down throats. Iron hooks grab inhabitants trying to escape, pulling them back. It is a place where people are forced to drink pus. The seven levels are:

1.	*Zamareer*	A place of extreme cold. This is reserved for Muslims who apostasized from the faith.
2.	*Laza*	"Nay, verily, it is a flame [*Laza*],—dragging by the scalp! it shall call those who retreated and turned their backs and who amassed and hoarded!" (Q 70.15-18)
3.	*El 'Hutamah*	"He shall be hurled into *El 'Hutamah!* And what shall make thee understand what *El 'Hutamah* is?—the fire of God kindled; which rises above the hearts." (Q 104.4-7)
4.	*Sa'ir*	"Verily, those who devour the property of orphans,

only devour into their bellies fire, and they shall broil in flames [*Sa'ir*]. Verily, it is an archway over them on long-drawn columns." (Q 4.10)

5.	***Saqar***	"Verily, the sinners are in error and excitement. On the day when they shall be dragged to the fire upon their faces!—'Taste ye the touch of hell [*Saqar*].'" (Q 54.47-48)
6.	***Al-Jahim***	"We have sent thee with the truth, a bearer of good things and of warning, and thou shalt not be questioned as to the fellows of hell [*Al-Jahim*]." (Q 2.113)
7.	***Hawiyah***	"But as for him whose balance is light his dwelling shall be the pit of hell [*Hawiyah*]." (Q 101.8-9)

The gates of each of the divisions in Hell are guarded by Maalik, one of the leaders of the angels. The angelic guards listen to those imprisoned yet respond by re-affirming the justice of Allah and the rightness of their eternal fate.

Christianity. Similar to Islam, the New Testament acknowledges the existence of Hell, though described with much less graphic detail. It is a place of torment, characterized by darkness and fire—the eternal abode of the damned. Its fundamental difference with Islam turns of the question: who goes there? Whereas Islam states that Hell is the destiny of the *unrighteous* (people whose lives were characterized by more bad than good works), the New Testament states that Hell is the destiny of the *unforgiven* (people who did not receive the forgiveness of sins through the atoning work of Jesus Christ on the cross). The Apostle Paul said, "Therefore, my brothers, I want you to know that through Jesus the forgiveness of sins is proclaimed to you" (Acts 13:38; cf. Matt 26:28; Lk 24:47; Eph 1:7; Col 1:14; Heb 9:22).

One of the biblical terms used for Hell is *Gehenna* (Matt 5:22, 29-30; 10:28; 18:9; 23:15, 33; Mk 9:43, 45, 47; and Lk 12:5). Several centuries prior to Jesus, the valley of Gehenna was the place where the depraved religious rites of Molech were observed—rites which included the burning of conscious babies and then offering them up to the god Molech in an act of worship. In first century Jerusalem, *Gehenna* had become the city garbage dump. It was located just beyond the city walls on its southwest side—a place of stench, decay, worms, and a constantly smoldering fire. Jesus called the place of torment in the afterlife *Gehenna* and described it in similar terms. He said that it is a place where the "worm does not die, and the fire is not quenched" (Mk 9:48).

Moreover, Hell possesses differing levels of torment. The intensity of torment is not based upon the degree of offenses committed on the earth, as it is in the Islamic faith. Rather, it is based upon the amount of spiritual light rejected. Jesus made this point during his description of three villages near the shores of the Sea of Galilee where he spent much time and performed many miracles, He said:

> Woe to you, Korazin! Woe to you, Bethsaida! If the miracles that were performed in you had been performed in Tyre and Sidon, they would have repented long ago in sackcloth and ashes. But I tell you, it will be more bearable for Tyre and Sidon on the day of judgment than for you. And you, Capernaum, will you be lifted up to the skies? No, you will go down to the depths. If the miracles that were performed in you had been performed in Sodom, it would have remained to this day. But I tell you that it will be more bearable for Sodom on the day of judgment than for you (Matt 11:21-24)

Dante gives a vivid and graphic picture of hell and chiefly he dwells on the furies of the Inferno...Now we find that all these descriptions are identical almost in minute details, with those of hell in the holy Quran...Miguel Asin Palacios, dealing at length with this subject, points out the influence of Islam on Dante.

—M. Q. Khan, *The Influence of Arabic Poetry on Dante's The Divine Comedy*, p. 25

Islam arose out of a form of revival preaching, the main argument of which concerned judgment and fear of hell.

—Tor Andræ, *In the Garden of Myrtles*, p. 100

One of the most significant aspects of the doctrine of everlasting punishment is the fact that Jesus himself defined this more specifically and in more instances than any New Testament prophet.

—John Walvoord, *Four Views on Hell*, pp. 19-20

3   And when the mountains are moved,

4   And when the she-camels ten months' gone with young shall be neglected,

5   And when the beasts shall be crowded together,

6   And when the seas shall surge up,

7   And when souls shall be paired with bodies,

8   And when the child who was buried alive shall be asked

9   for what sin she was slain,

10   And when the pages shall be spread out,

11   And when the heaven shall be flayed.

12   And when hell shall be set ablaze,

13   And when Paradise shall be brought nigh,

14   The soul shall know what it has produced!

The Honored Messenger

15   I need not swear by the stars that slink back,

16   moving swiftly, slinking into their dens!

17   Nor by the night when darkness draws on!

18   Nor by the morn when it first breathes up!

19   Verily, it is the speech of a noble apostle,

20   mighty, standing sure with the Lord of the throne,

21   obeyed and trusty too!

22   Your comrade is not mad;

23   he saw him on the plain horizon,

24   nor does he grudge to communicate the unseen.

81.8 *when the child who was buried alive* — A custom of pre-Islamic Arabia was to bury unwanted babies shortly after birth (infanticide). Typically, female babies were the ones buried. Muhammad was opposed to this practice (also see Q 6.137, 140). Though the practice of elective abortions is not mentioned in this verse, it is implied. Accordingly, current mainstream Islamic scholarship routinely condemns the practice of elective abortions that is widespread in the West.

81.19-21 Muhammad is the "noble apostle" with a "standing sure" with Allah. He is also "to be obeyed." Accordingly, in Islam it is required for one to confess faith in Allah and Muhammad, His Prophet (see Q 3.32; 4.69, 79-80, 136; 5.80-81; 8.13, 20-23; 24.47, 48, 50-52, 54; 33.33, 71; 48.9-10; 57.19; 59.4; 72.22-23, 81.19-21 and 46.16, note).

In contrast, Christianity looks to Jesus Christ as the Honored One (see Jn 14:6). The way in which C. S. Lewis explained it: "We must think of the Son always, so to speak, streaming forth from the Father, like light from a lamp, or heat from a fire, or thoughts from a mind. He is the self-expression of the Father" (*Mere Christianity*, pp. 173-174).

81.22 The Quraysh tribe in Mecca had accused Muhammad of madness (see Q 51.52; 68.2, 51; 51.52; 81.22).

81.25 The Quraysh tribe in Mecca also accused Muhammad as speaking the words of the devil.

81.28 *pleases to go straight* — That is, those who Allah has chosen to follow the straight path that leads to eternal life.

81.29 *the Lord of the world* — According

25 Nor is it the speech of a pelted devil.	**Surah 86**
26 Then whither do ye go?	
27 It is but a reminder to the worlds,	*In the name of the merciful and compassionate God.*
28 to whomsoever of you pleases to go straight:	
29 —but ye will not please, except God, the Lord of the world, should please.	*The Night Star*
	1 By the heaven and by the night star!

to this verse, Allah is "the Lord of the world." For the people of Mecca, this statement was a stern rebuke to their practice of polytheism (see **Polytheism in Seventh Century Arabia** on pp. 92-97).

Surah 86. The title of this surah, *The Comer by Night,* comes from verse one. The historical setting of this surah was that the Quraysh tribe in Mecca had begun to revile and ridicule Muhammad's message. In response, Muhammad noted that everyone would eventually appear before Allah at the Last Judgment and would give an account for their words of ridicule. Accordingly, in this life it behooved people to treat Muhammad with respect.

86.1 *the night star* — This star is Athtar, also known as Venus—the brightest celestial body in the night sky and also visible in the dawn sky. Muhammad described it as "the star of piercing brightness" (v. 3). See Mark S. Smith, *The Memoirs of God*, pp. 101-105.

In pre-Islamic Arabia, pagans believed that Allah and all other gods were celestial bodies—sun, moon, stars, and planets (known as wandering stars). According to some scholars, Allah was originally thought to be the moon and meteorites that impacted the earth were believed to be envoys sent from Allah. Among the pre-Islamic monotheists, Athtar (Venus) was understood to be the sole God. Those who worshipped Athtar "rejected the other gods who were

worshipped in Arabia" (Rafat Amarti, *Islam: In Light of History*, p. 276). Among the polytheists, the god "Al-Uzzah (the 'Strong One') was Venus, the Morning Star. She was the most important deity of the Quraysh tribe; human sacrifices were offered up to her" (Diane Morgan, *Essential Islam*, pp. xxvii, xxviii). Other Arabians in pre-Islamic Arabia identified Athtar (Venus) with Allah.

With an oath, Muhammad dedicated the entire surah to this "night star" and "the heaven" (the other celestial bodies). He also commented that "every soul has a guardian over it" (v. 4); that is, the gods (stars) serve as guardians over every person—a foundational facet in astrological dogma. Furthermore, in a Hadith Muhammad described Allah in astrological categories. He said that Allah "descends every night to the heaven of this world when the last third of the night is still to come" (*Sahih Mwatta* 15.8.30).

Muhammad's dabbling in astrology is evidence of his eclectic proclivities; that is, his drawing from a wide range of sources in the shaping of his new religion. Thomas Patrick Hughes observed that "Muhammad borrowed in several points from the doctrines of the Ebionites, Essenes, and Sabeites." Moreover, he included "oaths (by certain natural objects, as clouds, signs of the Zodiac, oil, the winds, etc.)...These points of contact with Islam, knowing as we do Muhammad's eclecticism, can hardly be accidental" (*Dictionary*

2   And what shall make thee know
      what the night star is?

3   —The star of piercing brightness.

4   Verily, every soul has a guardian
      over it.

5   Then let man look from what he is
      created:

6   he is created from water poured
      forth,

7   that comes out from between the
      loins and the breast bones.

8   Verily, He is able to send him back
      again,

9   on the day when the secrets shall
      be tried,

10   and he shall have no strength nor
      helper.

Muhammad's decisive word

11   By the heaven that sends back the
      rain!

12   And the earth with its sprouting!

13   Verily, it is indeed a distinguishing
      speech,

14   and it is no frivolity!

15   Verily, they do plot a plot!

16   But I plot my plot too!

17   let the misbelievers bide; do thou
      then let them bide awhile!

Surah 110

In the name of the merciful and compassionate God.

1   When there comes God's help and
      victory,

2   And thou shalt see men enter into
      God's religion by troops,

3   Then celebrate the praises of thy
      Lord, and ask forgiveness of Him,
      verily, He is relentant!

---

of Islam, p. 515).

Due to his eclectic propensities, then, Muhammad's repudiation of astrology proved to be a gradual process (see Q 25.61; 41.37-39; 53.4-12; 85.1-2).

86.5-7 In this passage, Muhammad made the claim that the origin of man came from water poured forth from between the loins and the breast bones (see Q 96.2, note).

86.14 *it is no frivolity!* — Muhammad defended his ministry against the Quraysh people of Mecca who ridiculed his message.

86.15-16 Plots and counterplots were beginning to take shape in Mecca between Muhammad and the leaders of Mecca.

Surah 110. The title of this surah, *The Help*, comes from verse one. This surah is a prophetic look into the future when the Muslim community would become an army and wage war on behalf of Allah. It is therefore the first reference to the Doctrine of Jihad in the Qur'an. Yet, not all Islamic scholars agree with this interpretation. Muhammad Asad notes that the term *troops* was meant figuratively and that Muhammad was referring to "the religion of self-surrender to God," a jihad of the soul (*The Message of the Qur'an*, p. 1121).

Surah 85. The title to this surah, *The Stars*, comes from verse one. The surah is a contrast between righteousness and unrighteousness, faith and infidelity, blessing and judgment.

85.1 *by the heaven with its zodiacal signs* — Muhammad dedicated this surah to the stars that comprise the zodiacal constellations.

Surah 85

In the name of the merciful and compassionate God.

The Oath

1   By the heaven with its zodiacal signs!
2   And the promised day!
3   And the witness and the witnessed!

The Pit

4   The fellows of the pit were slain;
5   And the fire with its kindling,
6   When they sat over it
7   And witnessed the while what they were doing with those who believed.
8   And they took not vengeance on them save for their belief in God, the mighty, the praiseworthy,
9   Whose is the kingdoms of the heavens and the earth; for God is witness over all!
10   Verily, those who make trial of the believers, men and women, and then do not repent, for them is the torment of hell, and for them is the torment of the burning!

The Blessing

11   Verily, those who believe and act aright, for them are gardens beneath which rivers flow, —that is

This parallels that which Muhammad said at the beginning of Surah 86 (see **Polytheism in Seventh Century Arabia** on pp. 92-97; also see Q 86.1-4).

85.3 *the witness and the witnessed —* Allah is the one who will bear witness at the Last Judgment.

85.4 *The fellows of the pit were slain —* Those who were put to death in the pit and burned are not identified. This is a possible reference to Muhammad's belief (later mentioned in the Qur'an) that while a teenager, Abraham was thrown into a pit, yet miraculously saved from harm by Allah (see Q 21.51-73; 29.24; 37.97-98). Another possibility is that the story is a reference to Shadrach, Meshach, and Abednego (three people mentioned in the Old Testament) when they were thrown into a fire (Dan 3:19-30). Still, others consider the story to be a parable and, hence, not to be taken literally. Islamic scholar Muhammad Asad is of this third opinion, believing that the story is not to be taken literally—that is, it is neither a legendary nor a historical event. The point of the parable is that idolaters will always look for ways in which to persecute the righteous (*The Message of the Qur'an*, pp. 1075-1076).

85.11a *those who believe and act aright —* Once again, salvation is presented in terms of faith and works—a system of meritocracy (see Q 103.3, note).

85.11b *beneath which rivers flow —* Repeatedly in the Qur'an is the imagery of Paradise as an oasis with well supplied aquifers (see **Paradise** on pp. 76-77).

85.12 *the violence of thy Lord is keen —* That is, Allah exhibits extreme violence on the infidel, not only in the afterlife (Hell) but in this life as well, with both the stories of Pharaoh and the people of Thamud serving as examples (vv. 17-18).

The Apostle's Creed

Second Century

I believe in God, the Father Almighty,
creator of heaven and earth;

I believe in Jesus Christ, His only Son, our Lord;
He was conceived by the power of the Holy Spirit,
and born of the Virgin Mary,
He suffered under Pontius Pilate,
was crucified, died, and was buried;
He descended to the dead.
On the third day He arose again.
He ascended into Heaven,
and is seated at the right hand of the Father.
He will come again to judge the living and the dead.

I believe in the Holy Spirit,
the holy catholic Church;
the communion of saints;
the forgiveness of sins;
the resurrection of the body;
and the life everlasting.

Amen.

———————————◆·◆·◆———————————

The Creed began as a profession or confession of faith made by converts at their baptism. Since then it has served other purposes—for example, as a test of orthodoxy for Christian leaders or as an act of praise in Christian worship...It attempts to give substance to a personal faith that already exists. You do not become a Christian by reciting a creed. Rather, the Creed provides a useful summary of the main points of your faith.

—Alister E. McGrath, *I Believe*, p. 14

The use of creeds to guard the church's teaching soon became almost as important as their use for new and old believers in the church. Looking at the form of words in the Apostles' Creed as an example, almost every phrase can be seen to protect the church against heretical teaching...Although these creeds did not originally arise as fences against heretical teaching, they soon came to fill that important function.

—Mark A. Noll, *Turning Points*, p. 44

The creed does have a legitimate claim to its title on the basis of the fact that all of its articles are to be found in the theological formulas that were current around A.D. 100.

—John H. Leith, *Creeds of the Churches*, p. 22

The [Islamic] Creed begins with an affirmation of God: "There is no god but God." This simple and austere affirmation of monotheism further establishes Islam within the Abrahamic tradition. It is reminiscent of the opening sentence of Genesis, "In the beginning God..." (Gen 1:1), and of the opening of the Apostles' Creed, "I believe in God..." With a single brief phrase, Islam wipes out a host of heresies that have tormented the Christian faith—atheism (there is no God), agnosticism (whether God exists cannot be ascertained), materialism and naturalism (the material world is the only reality), pantheism (God is identical with the world), deism (God does not intervene in human affairs, and polytheism (there are many gods). The Islamic Confession asserts theism in its boldest sense: there is a God, the Creator, the Merciful, the Provider, the Judge, the Revealer of himself. Jews and Christians could utter this part of the Shahada with a clear conscience.

—Keith E. Swartley, *Encountering the World of Islam*, p. 89

The creed was "the earliest existing summary of the essentials of Christian belief as transmitted by the Apostles," writes H. W. Crocker III...But Muhammad, while glorifying God as the Creator, rejected the notion that Christ was God's son, even while accepting Jesus as a prophet.

—Edward Hotaling, *Islam without Illusions*, p. 16

	the great bliss!		the hosts
12	Verily, the violence of thy Lord is keen!	18	of Pharaoh and Thamûd?
13	Verily, He produces and returns,	19	Nay, those who misbelieve do say it is a lie;
14	and He is the forgiving, the loving,	20	but God is behind them—encompassing!
15	the Lord of the glorious throne;		
16	the doer of what He will!	21	Nay, it is a glorious Qur'ân
17	Has there come to thee the story of	22	in a preserved tablet.

85.18 *Pharaoh and Thamud* — Just as the mighty people of Egypt and Thamud were destroyed by God because of their wickedness, so too will those who persecute the Muslim people.

85.21-22 *It is a glorious Qur'an in a preserved tablet* — According to Muhammad, the Qur'an exists in Paradise as a fully formed document, guarded by Allah. This is supported by the third article of the *Second Great Creed*, which states: "Our pronouncing, writing and reciting the Kuran [Qur'an] is created, whereas the Kuran [Qur'an] is uncreated..."

Four implications follow from this. *First,* Muhammad made the case that the Qur'an was not the product of some soothsayer or evil spirit, as the people of Mecca were claiming. Rather, the Qur'an existed eternally with Allah. *Second,* nobody is able to tamper with its contents since it is guarded by Allah in Paradise. *Third,* the Qur'an was transmitted to earth in the seventh century by means of dictation (see Q 76.23, note)—that is, the archangel Gabriel repeated the contents of the Qur'an to Muhammad verbatim, word by word, surah by surah. Muhammad did not participate either consciously or subconsciously in its authorship. In Q 12.2, a *fourth insight* is that the Qur'an exists in Paradise in the Arabic language (see **The Perspicuous Book** on pp. 178-179).

Still, not all Islamic scholars interpret these two verses (vv 21-22) literally. Muhammad Asad, a moderate Islamic scholar, commented that the phrase ("a preserved tablet") has a metaphorical meaning. Rather than the Qur'an existing eternally in Paradise and then repeated piecemeal to Muhammad via the archangel Gabriel, the idea of its eternality is merely an allusion to the imperishableness of the Qur'an, that it will remain uncorrupted —free of additions or subtractions (see *The Message of the Qur'an,* p. 1077).

Yet, the metaphorical interpretation has problems. Multiple Qur'ans exist. The authoritative text is the Cairo edition (1923-1924), also known as the Egyptian Version. By the ninth century, several alternate Qur'ans were in circulation. Though most of the variances were inconsequential, Islamic scholar Alfred Guillaume notes that they are "not always trifling and insignificant" (*Islam,* p. 189). Claude Gilliot adds: "There exist no copies of these early codices, either primary or secondary, but some of their features and variants are known through later sources like qur'anic commentaries" (*Cambridge Companion to the Qur'an,* p. 47).

Furthermore, early texts of the Qur'an were written *scripto defectiva,* which means that they are unpointed—without dots, dashes, and commas. This is because the seventh century Arabic language did not include these lexiconical additions. Since then, dots, dashes and commas have been added,

Surah 83

In the name of the merciful and compassionate God.

Denunciation of False Weights

1   Woe to those
2   who give short weight!
3   who when they measure against others take full measure; but when they measure to them or weigh to them, diminish!
4   Do not these think that they shall be raised again
5   at the mighty day?
6   the day when men shall stand before the Lord of the worlds!
7   Nay, verily, the book of the wicked is in Siggîn;
8   and what shall make thee know what Siggîn is?
9   —a book inscribed!

The Last Judgment

10   Woe on that day for those who say it is a lie!

causing the edited texts to become *scripto plena*. Yet, scholars are not in agreement with this editing process. This process has thereby resulted in fourteen alternate renderings of the Qur'an; that is, fourteen different arrangements of dots, dashes, and commas. The Cairo edition, with its arrangement of dots, dashes, and commas, has been chosen to be the authorized version (see **The Qur'an** on pp. 150-153).

Surah 83. The title to this surah, *Default in Duty*, comes from verse three. Islamic scholars are divided on this historical location of this surah—some placing it at the end of the Meccan period, others at the beginning of the Medinan period, and a third group placing it early in the Meccan period. The problem with the surah is that its content addresses issues that existed throughout Muhammad's ministry and could therefore have been written at almost any time.

In the surah, Muhammad denounced the people of Mecca, especially the Quraysh tribe, for their use of false weights in commercial activities. He described it as a form of thievery and dishonesty, and people will be held to account for such activities at the Last Judg-

ment. Later in the surah, Muhammad also encouraged his small Muslim community with words of divine blessings.

83.1-6 Muhammad pronounced a woe on those who steal by means of false balances (cf. Deut 25:13-16; Prov 11:1; 16:11; 20:10, 23; Hos 12:7; Amos 8:5-6; Mic 6:10-11).

83.7 *the book of the wicked* — Islamic scholars claim that this book is a listing of the names of those who are wicked. Moreover, these names are sealed and not subject to change. Accordingly, the Book of the Wicked gives evidence to the doctrine of double predestination (see **The Doctrine of al-Qadar** on pp. 264-266).

83.7-8 *Siggin* — Prison or a deep pit.

83.13 *Old folks' tales* — That is, unsubstantiated legends. The deriding of the surahs as "old folks' tales" would be repeated multiple times in the Qur'an (see Q 6.25; 16.24; 23.83; 25.5; 26.137; 27.68; 46.17; 68.15).

83.17 *what ye once did call a lie* — Throughout the Qur'an, Muhammad said that it is a serious sin to call the Qur'an a collection of lies (see Q 55.43; 56.51, 82, 92; 75.32; 77.15, 19, 24, 28, 29, 34, 37, 40, 45, 47, 49; 78.28).

11 Who call the judgment day a lie!

12 but none shall call it a lie except every sinful transgressor,

13 who, when our signs are read to him, says, "Old folks' tales!"

14 Nay, but that which they have gained has settled upon their hearts.

15 Nay, verily, from their Lord on that day are they veiled;

16 and then, verily, they shall broil in hell;

17 then it shall be said, "This is what ye once did call a lie!"

*Blessings
for the Righteous*

18 Nay, verily, the book of the righteous is in 'Illiyûn;

19 and what shall make thee know what 'Illiyûn is?

20 —a book inscribed!

21 those nigh to God shall witness it.

22 Verily, the righteous shall be in pleasure;

23 upon couches shall they gaze;

24 thou mayest recognise in their faces the brightness of pleasure;

25 they shall be given to drink wine that is sealed,

26 whose seal is musk; for that then let the aspirants aspire!

27 —and it shall be tempered with Tasnîm,

28 —a spring from which those nigh to God shall drink.

*Judgment will come to
those who mock*

29 Verily, those who sin do laugh at those who believe;

30 and when they pass by they wink at one another,

31 and when they return to their family they return ridiculing them;

32 and when they see them they say, "Verily, these do go astray!"

33 —but they are not sent as guardians over them!

34 But today those who believe shall at the misbelievers laugh!

35 Upon couches shall they gaze;

36 are the misbelievers rewarded for what they have done?

83.18 *the book of the righteous* — Similar to Q 83.7, the names written in this book are sealed and unchangeable, suggesting that the names in this celestial book are foreordained (see **The Doctrine of al-Qadar** on pp. 264-266).

83.18-19 *Illiyun* — A book in Paradise with the blessings of people's righteous deeds written down (cf. Ps 56:8 and Mal 3:16).

83.27-28 *Tasnim* — A legendary spring in Paradise.

83.29-33 This passage offers a snapshot into the attitudes and responses of the Quraysh people in Mecca to Muhammad and his ministry. They (a) laughed, (b) winked to one another, (c) walked away exulting, and (d) commented that Muhammad and his small following had gone astray from the truth.

83.35 *Upon couches shall they gaze* — This is an allusion to Paradise when the believers will recline on couches and gaze from a dis-

Polytheism
in Seventh Century Arabia

In the ancient Near East, religion and spirituality were rooted in the culture of the Sumerian civilization, centered at the city of Ur near the mouths of the Tigris and Euphrates Rivers. The worldview of this culture was not only polytheistic, it was committed to star worship in a scheme that united the heavens, earth, and a subterranean netherworld into an interconnected system. It became "the basic creed and dogma of much of the ancient Near East,"[1] including Arabia, situated directly to the south of Ur.

In this scheme, the earth was understood to be a flat disk. Above it was the atmosphere, which included the clouds, sun, moon, stars, and planets (wandering stars). Beneath the surface of the earth was a vast subterranean nether-world where many of the gods dwelt, along with the spirits of deceased human beings. Surrounding this three-tiered cosmos was a boundless sea—on all sides, top as well as bottom. The stars and other heavenly bodies (understood to be gods) made their appearance in the sky on a daily basis, then retreated into the netherworld, only to reappear once again on a twenty-four hour cycle.

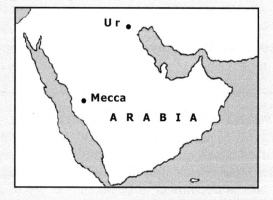

The gods were part of a vast pantheon of beings—manlike, superhuman and immortal. They were identified with an array of objects found in nature: astral bodies, the wind, storms, seas, rivers, mountains, plains, ditches, cultivated fields, pickaxes, brick molds, plows cities, and so on. They conducted themselves with a general sense of harmony, following specific rules and regulations. They also procreated, giving birth to new gods and goddesses. The supreme ruler of the pantheon was An, yet over the course of time another god, Enlil, took An's place. Enlil was called "the father of the gods." Yet, with time, even Enlil fell into disrepute and replaced by others. People maintained a general reverence for all the gods, since this was their best assurance that the cosmos would run effectively. Each city was identified with a specific god. Also each family had its own particular god. "The Sumerian thinkers contrived and evolved the notion of a personal god, a kind of good angel to each particular individual and family head, his divine father who had begot him, as it were. It was to him, to his personal deity, that the individual sufferer bared his heart in prayer and supplication, and it was through him that he found his salvation."[2]

Human beings were believed to have been fashioned from clay. Their chief purpose was to serve the gods by supplying them with food, drink, and other offerings at the temples. When misfortune befell a person, he was to "continually glorify his god and keep wailing and lamenting before him until he turns a favorable ear to his prayers."[3] At the time of death, the spirit of the human being entered the subterranean netherworld, never to return. This was a continuing source of anxiety and perplexity since the netherworld "was beset with enigmas, paradoxes and dilemmas...it is no wonder that the Sumerian ideas pertaining to them were neither precise nor consistent."[4]

Pilgrimages (Hajjs) to sacred sites were a common occurrence. People traveled to particular sites to pay homage and seek divine favor. Gifts were left at the Ka'ba altars as a form of worship. Since some sites were deemed more powerful than others, certain cities were the beneficiaries of more religious pilgrimages than others. A central feature of the Ka'ba altars were the revered black stones—stones that had fallen from the sky. They were believed to contain magical powers—able to heal the sick, bring about monetary fortune, or resolve some other perplexing problem. Thought to be especially associated with the gods (stars) who sent them down, these stones are now believed to be nothing more than meteorite fragments. Spiritual harmony extended to the Ka'ba altars themselves, which were quite similar in appearance. The Ka'ba altar in the city of Taif, for example, was called Ka'ba of Ellat—or the *Temple of the Sun*. It was identical in appearance to the Ka'ba altar in Mecca—both were the same dimensions, had a well in which to put gifts, and had a dress which covered the sacred stones. It was also similar in size, shape, and decoration to the Ka'ba altar in Yemen.

Allah was believed to have had a wife, the goddess Lilith, who gave birth to three other goddesses: Allat, Uzza, and Manat. With time, however, a group of Arabs opposed these polytheistic beliefs. They became monotheistic, devoting themselves to a single god, whom they identified with Athtar (Venus). Rafat Amari writes: "Venus worship endeavored to overshadow the worship of other deities of Arabia, willing to impose itself as the monotheistic worship of northern Arabia."[5] These monotheists identified Allah with Venus. Amari adds, "The worshippers of Allah, the biggest star, considered other deities of the Star Family as subordinate to Allah, and maintained that he was the most important in the Star Family."[6]

It was this clash between polytheism and monotheism in seventh century Arabia that formed the religious backdrop to the one hundred fourteen surahs that comprise the Qur'an. Muhammad acquiesced the importance of the "night star" (Venus) in one of his early surahs (86.1-10); nevertheless, such attention to this star remained in the margins of his thinking. That which dominated his thinking was the condemnation of polytheism and the elevation of monotheism. To marshal strength to this developing theology, he made the case that his religion was rooted in Judaism and Christianity, two established monotheistic religions in the Middle East. Yet, rather than embracing either Judaism or Christianity *in toto*, he attempted "to synthesize the Arabian legacy" with both of them. Hence, the Ka'ba altar in Mecca "was retained as a place of worship but was henceforth identified as a site built by Abraham."[7]

The Book of Idols

Much of what we know of the paganism of pre-Islamic Mecca comes from Ibn al-Kalbi (A.D. 737-819), an Arab historian. His work on seventh century Arabic culture, specifically the gods and rites of the pre-Islamic Arab religion, is regarded as a reliable source of this historical period. Below are a number of citations from his *The Book of Idols* that lay out the nature of this paganism and the gods that were worshipped. Muhammad would later incorporate several of these pagan practices into his Islamic religion.

Isif and Ni'ilah idols. Isif (man) and Ni'ilah (woman) were two lovers who entered the Ka'ba altar at Mecca. Taking advantage of the absence of anyone else and of the privacy of the Sacred House, committed adultery inside the sanctuary. According to legend, "thereupon they were transformed into stone, becoming two *miskhs* (statutes). They were then taken out and placed in their respective places (next to the Ka'ba). Later on, the Khuza'ah and Quraysh (the two dominant tribes of Mecca), as well as everyone who came on pilgrimage to the Sacred House, worshipped them."[8]

The Manah idol. The most ancient of the idols in the region of Mecca was called Manah. "The Arabs used to name their children 'Abd-Manah and Zayd-Manah. Manah was erected on the seashore in the vicinity of the al-Mushallal in Qudayd, between Medina and Mecca. All the Arabs used to venerate her and sacrifice before her. In particular the Aws and the Khazraj, as well as the inhabitants of Medina and Mecca and their vicinities, used to venerate Manah, sacrifice before her, and bring unto her their offerings." The people of Yathrib (Medinah) "were wont to go on pilgrimage and observe the vigil at all the appointed places, but not shave their heads. At the end of the pilgrimage, however, when they were about to return home, they would set to the place where Manah stood, shave their heads, and stay there a while. They did not consider their pilgrimage completed until they visited Manah."[9]

The Allat Idol. The people of Mecca also adopted Allat as one of their goddesses. The Allat idol "stood in al-Ta'if, and was more recent than Manah. She was a cubic rock beside which a certain Jew used to prepare his barley porridge. Her custody was in the hands of the banu-'Attab ibn-Malik of the Thaqif, who built an edifice over her. The Quraysh, as well as all the Arabs, were wont to venerate Allat. They also used to name their children after her, calling them Zayd-Allat and Taym-Allat."[10]

The Uzza idol. The Meccan people also adopted Uzza as one of their goddesses. "She is, in point in time, more recent than either Allat or Manah, since I have heard that the Arabs named their children after the latter two before they named them after al-'Uzza...The person who introduced al-'Uzza was Zalim ibn-As'ad. Her idol was situated in a valley in Nakhlat al-Sha'miyah called Hurad, alongside al-Ghumayr' to the right of the road from Mecca to al-'Iraq, above Dhat-Irq and nine miles from al-Bustin." Over the Uzza idol, Zalim "built a house called Buss in which the people used to receive oracular communications. The Arabs as well as the Quraysh were wont to name their children 'Abd-al-Uzza. Further-more, al-'Uzza was the greatest idol among the Quraysh. They used to journey to her, offer gifts unto her, and seek her favours through sacrifice...The Quraysh were wont to circumambulate the Ka'ba and say: 'By Allat and al-'Uzza, and Manah, the third idol besides,, verily they are the most exalted females whose intercession is to be sought.' They were also called the daughters of Allah and were supposed to intercede before God."[11]

The Dhu-al-Khalasah idol. "Among those idols, too, was Dhu-al-Khalasah. It was a carved piece of white quartz with something in the form of a crown upon its head. It stood in Tahalah, between Mecca and San'a, at a distance of seven nights' journey from Mecca."[12]

The 'Amm-Anas idol. "The Khawlin had in the land of Khawlan an idol called 'Amm-Anas. They were wont to set apart a portion of their livestock property and land products and give one part of it to it and the other to God. Whatever portion of the part allotted to 'Amm-Anas made its way to the part set aside for God they would restore to the idol; but whatever portion of the part consecrated to God made its way to the part allotted to the idol they would leave to the idol."[13]

General Behavior. "The Arabs were passionately fond of worshipping idols. Some of them took unto themselves a temple around which they centered their worship, while others adopted an idol to which they offered their adoration. The person who was unable to build himself a temple or adopt an idol would erect a stone in front of the Sacred House or in front of any other temple which he might prefer, and them circumambulate it in the same manner in which he would circumambulate the Sacred House. The Arabs called these stones *baetyls*. Whenever these stones resembled a living form they called them idols (*ansam*) and images (*awthan*). The act of circumambulating them they called circumrotation (*dawar*). Whenever a traveler stopped at a place or station in order to rest or spend the night, he would select for himself four stones, pick out the finest among them and adopt it as his god, and use the remaining three as supports for his cooking pot. On his departure, he would leave them behind, and would do the same on his other stops. The Arabs were wont to offer sacrifices before all these idols, *baetyls*, and stones. Nevertheless, they were aware of the excellence and superiority of the Ka'ba, to which they went on pilgrimage and visitation. What they did on their travels was a perpetuation of what they did at the Ka'ba, because of their devotion to it."[14]

---

[1] Samuel Noah Kramer, *The Sumerians: Their History, Culture, and Character*, p. 112.

[2] Ibid., 126.

[3] Ibid.

4   Ibid., p. 129.
5   Rafat Amari, *Islam: In Light of History*, p. 273.
6   Ibid., 274.
7   David Pinault, *The Shiites*, p. 24.
8   Kitab al-Asnam, *The Book of Idols*, p. 51.
9   Ibid., p. 134.
10 Ibid., p. 14.
11 Ibid., pp. 16, 17.
12 Ibid., pp. 29, 30.
13 Ibid., p. 37.
14 Ibid., pp. 28, 29.

If there is no hereafter, and no cosmic accountability for one's deeds, what prevents society from collapsing into full-blown chaos? It would be a great injustice to assume that pre-Islamic society was simply bereft of any code of ethics. As we have seen, codes of honor, nobility, tribal loyalty, and generosity were well known. Instead, what pre-Islamic Arabs found baffling was the Qur'anic notion of cosmic and individual accountability before a singular God.

—Omid Safi, *Memories of Muhammad*, pp. 70-71

The religious beliefs of the pre-Islamic Arabs of the Hejaz include the veneration of stones, wells, trees, and sacred precincts connected with the tribe's origins. Many deities were recognized, and on the eve of Islam, the Ka'ba, Mecca's very archaic sanctuary, contained representations of 360 of them.

—Frederick Mathewson Denny, *An Introduction to Islam*, p. 52

We should be wary of exaggerating the gulf between pre-Islamic and Islamic religiosity...It is abundantly clear from the Qur'an, for example, that Muhammad felt no need to introduce Allah to his Arabian audience. Allah was already known to them. Thus, for instance, when an early revelation given to him called on the people of Mecca to "worship the Lord of this House"—i.e., the Ka'ba—no need was felt to explain who the "Lord of the House" was. Still, Allah was what historians of religion have sometimes termed a *deus otiosus*—a deity so distant and transcendent that he was of little practical relevance to the lives of the people. Their attentions seem to have been focused more on his three purported daughters—Manat, Allat, and al-Uzza—and on the quasi-divine beings known collectively as the jinn, than on Allah...These deities and demigods lived in or were represented by trees, fountains, and most particularly certain sacred stones.

—David Freedman and Michael McClymond, *The Rivers of Paradise*, p. 475

Surah 78

In the name of the merciful and compassionate God.

1   Of what do they ask each other?
2   —Of the mighty information
3   whereon they do dispute?
4   nay, they shall know too well! Again,
5   nay, they shall know too well!
6   Have we not set the earth as a couch,
7   and the mountains as stakes,
8   and created you in pairs,
9   and made your sleep for rest,
10 and made the night a garment,
11 and made the day for livelihood,
12 and built above you seven solid (heavens)
13 and set a burning lamp,
14 and, sent down from the rain-expressing clouds water pouring

15 to bring out thereby the grain and herb
16 and gardens thickly planted?

The Day of Decision

17 Verily, the day of decision is an appointed time;
18 and the day when the trumpet shall be blown, and ye shall come in troops,
19 and the heavens shall be opened, and shall be all doors,
20 and the mountains shall be moved, and shall be like a mirage!

Hell

21 Verily, hell is an ambuscade;
22 a reward for the outrageous,
23 to tarry therein for ages.
24 They shall not taste therein cool nor

tance upon the fate of the infidels.

Surah 78. The title of this surah, *The Mighty Information*, comes from verse two. The purpose of this surah is to affirm the resurrection of the dead. The final destiny of all people will either be Paradise or Hell. This surah provides details of both abodes.

78.12 *seven solid (heavens)* — Muhammad believed Heaven (Paradise) to be divided into seven levels. When righteous people die they enter the layer of Heaven that corresponds to the quality of their works (see Q 13.17 note, and Q 41.12).

78.17 *the day of decision* — The Last Judgment. The event will take place on earth. The heavens will open so that the spiritual realm will be visible to those on earth and the mountains will be flattened (cf. Ps 9:7; 96:10-13; Eccl 3:17; 11:9; Matt 11:20-24; Heb 9:27; 10:26; and Rev 20:11-15, and *The Last Judgment* on pp. 46-50).

78.18 *the trumpet shall be blown* — The Day of Decision will commence with the sounding of a trumpet. In the Judeo-Christian tradition, the Last Trumpet is that which will inaugurate end-time apocalyptic prophecies (see 1 Cor 15:52 and 1 Thess 4:16).

78.22-25 Three characteristics of Hell: (a) those who enter will live there for ages, (b) they shall not taste cool drink, and (c) they will drink boiling and intensely cold water.

78.29 *everything have we remembered in a book* — This is the book in Paradise that recounts everything that ever occurred.

drink,

25   but only boiling water and pus;

26   —a fit reward!

27   Verily, they did not hope for the account;

28   but they ever said our signs were lies.

29   Everything have we remembered in a book.

30   "Then taste, for we will only increase your torment!"

Paradise

31   Verily, for the pious is a blissful place,

32   —gardens and vineyards,

33   and girls with swelling breasts of the same age as themselves,

34   and a brimming cup;

35   they shall hear therein no folly and no lie;

36   —a reward from thy Lord, a sufficient gift!

37   The Lord of the heavens and the earth, and what is between them

both—the Merciful—they cannot obtain audience of Him!

38   The day when the Spirit and the angels shall stand in ranks, they shall not speak save to whom the Merciful permits, and who speaks aright.

39   That is the true day; and whoso pleases let him take to a resort unto his Lord!

Warning

40   Verily, we have warned you of a torment that is nigh: on a day when man shall see what his two hands have sent forward; and the misbeliever shall say, "Would that I were dust!"

Surah 77

In the name of the merciful and compassionate God.

78.31-39 Four characteristics of Paradise: (a) a place of gardens and vineyards, (b) everyone will remain in the freshness of youth, equal in age, (c) people will drink from a pure cup, and (d) no vain words will be spoken.
78.33 *girls with swelling breasts* — Chronologically speaking, this is the first reference in the Qur'an of the virgins in Paradise. They are described as having "swelling breasts" (that is, young women just beyond puberty). The virgins and the men whom they serve will remain physiologically as young adults (see Q 55 and 56 where the description of the virgins and harems is given more detail, and **The**

Virgins on pp. 107-109).

In contrast, Jesus taught that in Heaven there is neither marriage nor the giving of marriage, implying that sexual activity will be non-existent (see Mk 12:25; Lk 20:34-36).
78.40 *his two hands* — On the Day of Decision, God will hold two books in his hands. In his right hand will be the book which includes the names of those who will enter Paradise. In his left hand (which is also held behind his back) will be the book which includes the names of those who will enter Hell (see Q 74.39; 84.7-19; and 90.4-20).
Surah 77. The title of this surah, *Those Sent*

Apocalyptic events

1   By those sent in a series!
2   And by those who speed swiftly!
3   And by the dispensers abroad!
4   And by the separators apart!
5   And by those who instill the re-
      minder,
6   as an excuse or warning!
7   Verily, what ye are threatened with
      shall surely happen!
8   And when the stars shall be erased!
9   And when the heaven shall be cleft!
10   And when the mountains shall be
      winnowed!
11   And when the apostles shall have a
      time appointed for them!

Seven woes

12   For what day is the appointment
      made?
13   For the day of decision!
14   and what shall make thee know
      what the decision is?
15   Woe on that day for those who say

      it is a lie!
16   Have we not destroyed those of
      yore,
17   and then followed them up with
      those of the latter day?
18   Thus do we with the sinners.
19   Woe on that day for those who say
      it is a lie!
20   Did we not create you from con-
      temptible water,
21   and place it in a sure depository
22   unto a certain decreed term?
23   for we are able and well able too!
24   Woe on that day for those who say
      it is a lie!
25   Have we not made for them the
      earth to hold
26   the living and the dead?
27   and set thereon firm mountains
      reared aloft? and given you to drink
      water in streams?
28   Woe on that day for those who say
      it is a lie!
29   Go off to that which ye did call a
      lie!
30   Go off to the shadow of three col-

in a Series, comes from verse one. The purpose of this surah is to affirm the resurrection of the dead and explain the fate of all people, especially on those who reject Muhammad's message and ministry. To drive this point home, Muhammad mentioned seven woes upon the infidels.

77.8 *when the stars shall be erased* — This is a subtle disparagement of the many gods worshipped in Arabia (see **Polytheism in Seventh Century Arabia** on pp. 92-97).

77.8-11 Muhammad stated that these are apocalyptic events that will take place just

prior to the Day of Decision. Two noteworthy events are the following: (a) the stars will lose their lights, and (b) the mountains will be flattened.

77.15-40 *Woe on that day for those who say it is a lie!* — Seven woes are spoken by Allah to the rejecters of righteousness (vv. 15, 19, 24, 28, 34, 37, 40). On the Day of Decision (the Last Judgment), the unrighteous will not be given opportunity to offer excuses to ward off their impending eternal judgment in Hell. In each case, they will have falsely called God a liar.

umns,

31 that shall not shade nor avail against the flame!

32 Verily, it throws off sparks like towers,

33 —as though they were yellow camels!

34 Woe on that day for those who say it is a lie!

35 This is the day when they may not speak,

36 —when they are not permitted to excuse themselves!

37 Woe on that day for those who say it is a lie!

38 This is the day of decision! We have assembled you with those of yore;

39 if ye have any stratagem employ it now!

40 Woe on that day for those who say it is a lie!

Blessing for the Righteous

41 Verily, the pious are amid shades and springs

42 and fruit such as they love.

43 —"Eat and drink with good digestion, for that which ye have done!"

44 Verily, thus do we reward those

who do well.

Three additional woes

45 Woe on that day for those who say it is a lie!

46 "Eat and enjoy yourselves for a little; verily, ye are sinners!"

47 Woe on that day for those who say it is a lie!

48 And when it is said to them bow down, they bow not down.

49 Woe on that day for those who say it is a lie!

50 And in what new discourse after it will they believe?

Surah 76

In the name of the merciful and compassionate God.

Every person tested by Allah

1 Does there not come on man a portion of time when he is nothing worth mentioning?

2 Verily, we created man from a mingled clot, to try him; and we

77.41-44 Three characteristics of Paradise: (a) people shall dwell amid shades and fountains, (b) people shall eat fruit such as they desire, and (c) people will drink pleasantly.
77.45-50 Three additional woes are spoken to all who say that the Last Judgment is a lie. On that day, the sins of each person will be presented in stark detail.
Surah 76. The title of this surah, *The Man*,

comes from verse one. The purpose of this surah is to affirm the resurrection and explain the fate of all people—especially those who reject Muhammad's message. Their final destiny will either be Paradise or Hell. This surah provides details of both abodes.
76.1-2 In his description of the creation of man, Muhammad noted that man has "nothing worth mentioning." In contrast, the Bible

gave him hearing and sight.

3   Verily, we guided him in the way, whether he be grateful or ungrateful.

Hell

4   Verily, we have prepared for those who misbelieve chains and fetters and a blaze!

Paradise

5   Verily, the righteous shall drink of a cup tempered with Kâfûr,
6   a spring from which God's servants shall drink and make it gush out as they please!

*Alms for the
poor and orphans*

7   They who fulfil their vows, and fear a day, the evil which shall fly abroad,
8   and who give food for His love to the poor and the orphan and the captive.

9   "We only feed you for God's sake; we desire not from you either reward or thanks;
10   we fear from our Lord a frowning, calamitous day!"

Paradise

11   And God will guard them from the evil of that day and will cast on them brightness and joy;
12   and their reward for their patience shall be Paradise and silk!
13   reclining therein upon couches they shall neither see therein sun nor piercing cold;
14   and close down upon them shall be its shadows; and lowered over them its fruits to cull;
15   and they shall be served round with vessels of silver and goblets that are as flagons
16   —flagons of silver which they shall mete out!

---

describes the creation of man as "very good" (Gen 1:31) and that man was made in "the image of God" (Gen 1:27)—a status that is indeed high and exalted.

76.3 *Grateful* — The question of thankfulness is a major theme in the Qur'an.

76.4 Two characteristics of Hell: (a) chains and shackles, and (b) a burning fire.

76.5-6 *Kafur* — camphor.

76.7-10 Three characteristics of the righteous: they (a) fulfill their vows, (b) fear the day of evil, and (c) give food out of love for God to the poor, the orphan.

76.11-21 According to Muhammad, a celestial oasis awaits each righteous Muslim who makes it to Paradise. Its characteristics include: (a) being guarded from evil, (b) people adorned in silk garments, (c) people reclining on raised couches in temperate climates, (d) abundant fruit, (e) drinking vessels of silver, (f) beverages that include ginger, (g) personal harems. The virgins in the harems never alter in age. They are dressed in garments of fine green silk interwoven with gold, adorned with bracelets of silver, and drink pure drink (nonalcoholic beverages).

17 and they shall drink therein a cup tempered with Zingabîl,	*A Reminder*
18 a spring therein named Silsabîl!	22 Verily, this is a reward for you, and your efforts are thanked.
19 and there shall go round about them eternal boys; when thou seest them thou wilt think them scattered pearls;	23 Verily, we have sent down upon thee the Qur'ân.
20 and when thou seest them thou shalt see pleasure and a great estate!	24 Wherefore wait patiently for the judgment of thy Lord, and obey not any sinner or misbeliever amongst them.
21 On them shall be garments of green embroidered satin and brocade; and they shall be adorned with bracelets of silver; and their Lord shall give them to drink pure drink!	25 But remember the name of thy Lord morning, and evening,
	26 and through the night, and adore Him, and celebrate His praises the

76.17 *Zingabil* — A herb similar to ginger.

76.18 *Silsabil* — According to Islamic lore, Salsabil is a river in Paradise.

76.19 *eternal boys* — This is one of the more troubling verses in the Qur'an. The problem turns on this question: what are young boys doing in harems where extensive and continuous sexual activity is the norm?

Some scholars have suggested that their presence points to homosexual pedophilia in Paradise. This interpretation is furthered by the similarity of the phrase "scattered pearls" in this verse which applies to the eternal boys, with the phrases "pearls" (Q 55.58) and "hidden pearls" (Q 56.23), which apply to the maidens of the celestial harems Later in the Qur'an, these same boys are called "hidden pearls" (Q 52.24). Peter Lamborn Wilson affirms this interpretation, describing the activity of the boys as "sacred pedophilia" (see *Scandal: Essays in Islamic Heresy*, pp. 93-122).

Other scholars disagree, insisting that the role of the boys in the harems is non-sexual. Khaled el-Rouayheb comments, "The domi-

nant interpretation...was that the boys were specially created by God, like the *houris*, to serve the believers. In the case of the boys, the service was...usually not thought to be of a sexual nature. Yet the commentators did not shy from the fact that the verses seem to present the physical beauty of the boys as one of the attractions of paradise" (*Before Homosexuality in the Arab-Islamic World*, p. 124).

76.23 According to this verse, the Qur'an was sent down from Paradise (see Q 2.285; 3.3; 10.94; 14.1; 15.6, 9; 16.30, 44, 64, 89; 18.1; 20.2; 21.10, 50; 22.16; 25.1, 32; 28.87; 34.6; 38.29; 39.41; 42.15, 17; 43.31; 46.30; 64.8).

In a Hadith, Muhammad explained the nature of this revelation. He said that on occasion the archangel Gabriel appeared to him with "the ringing of a bell." On other occasions, the angel appeared to him "in the form of a man" and talked to him (see *Sahih Bukhari* 1.1.2).

76.24-31 Three pillars for the faithful: (a) wait patiently for the command of the Lord, (b) do not obey the words of sinners or the

whole night long.

27　Verily, these love the transitory life, and leave behind them a heavy day!

28　We created them and strengthened their joints; and if we please we can exchange for the likes of them in their stead.

29　Verily, this is a memorial, and whoso will, let him take unto his Lord a way.

30　But ye will not please except God please! Verily, God is knowing, wise.

31　He makes whomsoever He pleases to enter into His mercy; but the unjust He has prepared for them a grievous woe!

Surah 75

In the name of the merciful and compassionate God.

The Day of Resurrection

1　I need not swear by the resurrection day!

2　Nor need I swear by the self-ac-cusing soul!

3　Does man think that we shall not collect his bones?

4　Able are we to arrange his finger tips!

5　Nay, but man wishes to be wicked henceforward!

Apocalyptic events

6　He asks, When is the resurrection day?

7　But when the sight shall be dazed,

8　and the moon be eclipsed,

9　and the sun and the moon be to-gether,

Day of Decision

10　and man shall say upon that day, "Where is a place to flee to?"

11　—nay, no refuge!

12　and to thy Lord that day is the sure settlement:

13　He will inform man on that day of what He has sent forward or de-layed!

14　Nay, man is an evidence against himself,

ungrateful, and (c) glorify the name of the Lord morning, evening, and during the night. **Surah 75.** The title of this surah, *The Resurrection Day*, comes from verse one. This surah is a warning about the coming resurrection. Since it is followed by the Day of Decision (the Last Judgment), it will be a time of the eternal condemnation to all infidels. **75.2** Muhammad believed that each human being is aware of his or her moral failures.

75.3 *Does man think that we shall not collect his bones?* — This is a vivid picture of that which will take place at the general resurrection from the dead.
75.5 Muhammad associated the general resurrection from the dead with the Last Judgment. Because the wicked did not believe in the resurrection, neither did they believe in the Last Judgment where their sins will be held to account.

15   and even if he thrusts forward his excuses—.

Parenthesis

16   Do not move thy tongue thereby to hasten it.
17   It is for us to collect it and to read it;
18   and when we read it then follow its reading.
19   And again it is for us to explain it.

Words of condemnation

20   Nay, indeed, but ye love the transient life,
21   and ye neglect the hereafter!
22   Faces on that day shall be bright,
23   gazing on their Lord!

24   And faces on that day shall be dismal!
25   Thou wilt think that a back-breaking calamity has happened to them!
26   Nay, but when the (soul) comes up into the throat,
27   and it is said, "Who will charm it back?"
28   and he will think that it is his parting (hour).
29   And leg shall be pressed on leg;
30   unto thy Lord on that day shall the driving be.
31   For he did not believe and did not pray;
32   but he said it was a lie, and turned his back!
33   Then he went to his people haughtily
34   —woe to thee, and woe to thee!

75.16-19 These are words directed specifically to Muhammad. Muhammad believed that Allah encouraged him to slow down in his oral recitation of the surahs to the people of Mecca.

75.19 This verse makes the point that the Qur'an is itself its own best commentary. As it is recited, Allah illuminates the listener to rightly understand its spiritual message.

75.20 *ye love the transient life* — That is, the focus of infidels was the current life, with little concern with the afterlife. Muhammad wanted them to stretch their mental horizons and consider the events of the Last Judgment where Allah would be their judge. Regrettably, their polytheistic beliefs left them with a false sense of security that their star deities would care for them in the afterlife, just as they cared for them in this life.

The Christian faith also admonishes people not to be overly preoccupied with this world and the worldly gains that they acquire. One verse states, "Do not love the world or anything in the world. If anyone loves the world, the love of the Father is not in him. For everything in the world—the cravings of sinful man, the lust of his eyes and the boasting of what he has and does—comes not from the Father but from the world. The world and its desires pass away, but the man who does the will of God lives forever" (1 Jn 2:15-17; cf. Rom 12:2; Col.3:1-2; James 4:4).

75.22-23 When people see Allah in Paradise, their faces will brighten with a divine glow. The Bible makes a similar claim (see 2 Cor 3:7-18).

75.29 *leg shall be pressed on leg* — This is an idiomatic expression meaning difficulty pressed upon with more difficulty, an increased hardship and burden.

35 again woe to thee, and woe to thee!	must befall,
36 Does man think that he shall be left to himself?	2 for the unbelievers; there is no repelling it;
37 Wasn't he a clot of emitted seed?	3 from God the Lord of the ascents,
38 Then he was congealed blood, and (God) created him, and fashioned him,	4 whereby ascend the angels and the Spirit unto Him in a day whose length is fifty thousand years.
39 and made of him pairs, male and female.	5 Wherefore be patient with fair patience; verily,
40 Is not He able to quicken the dead?	6 they see it as afar off,
	7 but we see it nigh!
	8 The day when the heaven shall be as molten brass,

Surah 70

In the name of the merciful and compassionate God.

The coming Apocalypse

1   An asker asked for torment that

9   and the mountains shall be like flocks of wool;

10 when no warm friend shall question friend;

11 they shall gaze on each other, and the sinner would fain give as a ransom from the torment of that day

75.34, 35 *woe to thee* — This phrase is mentioned four times, suggesting that the infidel will face an enormously dire fate in the afterlife.

75.37-38 Once again, Muhammad speculated on the creation of man. Here man is described as "a clot of emitted seed...then he was congealed blood" (see Q 96.2, note).

Surah 70. The title of this surah, *The Ways of Ascent,* comes from verse three. An apocalyptic day is approaching, a day of calamity and utter destruction. Since only the righteous will be spared, the surah serves as a threat to all infidels of their impending doom.

70.3 *the Lord of the ascents* — This is also known as the Lord of the ascending stairways. Paradise is upward—one ascends to Paradise by way of a life full of good works (see Q 90.11).

70.4 The final day when all people will be resurrected and summoned to the Last Judgment is more correctly understood as an age: an age that will last fifty thousand years. That is, the Day of Judgment is a period of time that will take fifty thousand years to complete.

70.8 *heaven shall be as molten brass* — This is an apocalyptic description that will take place just prior to the general resurrection and the Last Judgment. The beautiful blue sky will be transformed and likened to that of molten brass (the dregs of oil)—an appearance that is ominous and threatening.

70.9 *mountains shall be like flocks of wool* — That is, mountains shall come apart similar to flocks of wool.

70.11 Muhammad envisioned that at the Last Judgment, the infidels will be so desperate to avoid the torments of Hell that they would willingly sacrifice their own family

The Virgins

Repeatedly in the Qur'an, Muhammad stated that Allah will bequeath the righteous in heaven with their own private oases, fully furnished with all kinds of food and drink—and virgins. More to the point, each righteous Muslim will be bequeathed with his own private harem, women called *houris*.

In the *Jamil' at-Tirmidhi*, Abu al-Tirmidhi wrote: "Anas narrated the Prophet said, 'The believer shall be given in Paradise such and such strength in intercourse.' It was said, 'O Messenger of Allah! And will he be able to do that? He said, 'He will be given the strength of a hundred." He then added, "All the bounties bestowed upon the people in Paradise will be endless with no fear of their dwindling or diminishing. No weakness, therefore, shall occur for the male partners after having conjugal relations umpteen times with their consorts"[1]

Centuries later, Suyuti (*c.* 1445-1505) added: "Each time we sleep with a Houri we find her virgin. Besides, the penis of the Elected never softens. The erection is eternal; the sensation that you feel each time you make love is utterly delicious and out of this world...All [Houris] will have appetizing vaginas."[2]

These virgins are eternally young, never pregnant, and not subject to menstruations. In addition, according to the Qur'an, they are...

1.   Darlings with swelling breasts

"darlings of equal age (with their spouses)" (Q 56.37)

"for the pious is a blissful place,—gardens and vineyards, and girls with swelling breasts of the same age as themselves" (Q 78.31-33)

"And one of His signs is that He created mates for you from yourselves that you may find rest in them, and He put between you love and compassion, most surely there are signs in this for a people who reflect" (Q 30.21)

2. **Women who are chaste and restrained in their glances**

And with them shall be those who restrain the eyes, having beautiful eyes (Q 37.48)

"Therein are maids of modest glances whom no man no ginn has deflowered before" (Q 55.56)

"Bright and large-eyed maids kept in their tents" (Q 55.72)

"and beside them maidens of modest glance" (Q 38.52)

3. **Women with wide, beautiful and lustrous eyes**

"Reclining on thrones set in lines, and We will unite them to large-eyed beautiful ones" (Q 52.20)

"Bright and large-eyed maids (Q 56.22)

"And with them shall be those who restrain the eyes, having beautiful eyes; as if they were eggs carefully protected" (Q 37.48-49)

4. **Women likened unto rubies, coral, and pearls**

"As though they were rubies and pearls" (Q 55.58)

"like hidden pearls" (Q 56.23)

5. **Virgins**

"and made them virgins" (Q 56.36)

"Therein are maids of modest glances whom no man nor ginn has deflowered before" (Q 55.56; 3.15)

6. **Women reclining on cushions and carpets**

"Reclining on green cushions and beautiful carpets" (Q 55.76)

7. **Women who are pure and beautiful**

"Thus (shall it be), and We will wed them with Houris pure, beautiful ones" (Q 44.54)

[1] *Jamil' at-Tirmidhi*, vol. 4, ch. 6, no. 2536.
[2] Suyuti, *Perfect Guide to the Sciences of the Qur'an (Al-Itqan fi 'Ulum Al-Qur'an)*, p. 351. Lucidly written and exhaustive in its use of sources, this book is regarded in the Islamic world as key in qur'anic studies and research.

The Islamic vision of a heaven complete with "seventy virgins" became familiar in the United States the month before 9/11 attacks when CBS aired an interview with Hamas activist Muhammad Abu Wardeh, who recruited terrorists for suicide bombings in Israel. Abu Wardeh told CBS that he recruited his suicide bombers by describing to them how God would compensate a martyr for sacrificing his life for the expulsion of the Jews from Palestine. Abu Wardeh's vision of heaven for martyrs was a vision of a place where each martyr for Allah would be given seventy virgin wives and "everlasting happiness."

—Brian R. Farmer, *Understanding Radical Islam*, p. 55

It's strange how all you infidels have such a voyeur-like fascination with virgins. But, since you asked, yes, it is true that Muslims believe that every shaheed [martyr] gets 72 dark-eyed houris or virgins in Paradise. While there is no mention in the Koran itself of the exact number of virgins, it is specified in the hadiths or records of the Prophet's utterances that have been passed down from generation to generation. Equally important, but not of as much prurient interest to infidels, is that Muslims believe that every shaheed [martyr] gets the privilege of bringing 70 of his family and friends along to Paradise with him. That's why many Muslim mothers rejoice when their sons become shaheeds [martyrs]. Mohammed himself said that most women end up in hell for not obeying their husbands (*Sahih Bukhari* 1.022.028). Some women may take this seriously and see having a son as a shaheed [martyr] as their only hope of entering Paradise.

—Patrick Grady, *Royal Canadian Jihad*, pp, 41-42

Paradise also seems to feature sensual delights that are patently male-dominated. The Qur'anic description of *houris*, dark-eyed, young, and chaste beauties, is now infamous; but is it accurate? Do men actually spend time with specially created perfect females in Paradise, and if so, what do Muslim women experience in the afterlife? There is great debate over these questions in Muslim theology, and no clear consensus exists. It is widely taught that righteous Muslim women will also enter into Paradise, There are no Qur'anic verses that state otherwise, but neither are there any that feature women exclusively. In most cases the inclusive, plural nouns "servants" or "believers" are employed, signifying both genders. There seems to be virtually no doubt that both men and women are eligible for Paradise. The exact role and status of women in Paradise is the larger question. A follow-up query would focus on the nature of Paradise: Is it sensual or is it spiritual? Once again, there is no consensus among Muslim scholars and specialists.

—Michael McCullar, *A Christian's Guide to Islam*, p. 48

The misconceived notion that a Muslim male who dies as a martyr is rewarded in the hereafter with seventy-two virgins has brought Islam into disrepute and ridicule, and proved a source of much amusement and mockery for those unaware of the teachings of Islam regarding the hereafter.

—Zahid Aziz, *Islam, Peace and Tolerance*, p. 52

It is also time to put the "72 virgins" to rest; this is a quaint, lurid, provocative interpretation of an obscure passage in the Qur'an, avidly seized upon by Westerners who find it amusing and use it repeatedly to ridicule Islamic belief. Typical is an article in *The Washington Post* that opened, "He was promised a straight shot to heaven and 72 maidens to wait on him once he got there, but Hoshir Sabir Hasan was not ready to die." A brochure from the Institute of Islamic Education states, "The promise of '70 or 72 virgins' is fiction written by some anti-Islam bigots." The belief is to mainstream Muslims as the belief that we will one day be issued wings and a harp, and walk on clouds, is to mainstream Christians.

—Margaret Kleffner Nydell, *Understanding Arabs*, p. 109

How can any normal person believe in Islam with such a pagan Paradise?...Estimates vary as to the number of virgins (2 to 72) per male Muslim in heaven (Sahih Bukahri 4.54.476, Al-Tirmidhi 2562). Actually the Tirmidhi Hadith states that 72 wives is the minimum, perhaps for the not so devout Muslims in the 7th heaven. Muhammad said: "The least reward for the people of paradise is 80,000 servants and 72 wives"—Al-Timrmidhi 2562, 2687.

—Jake Neuman, *God of Moral Perfection*, p. 175

Does the woman homicide bomber likewise acquire seventy-two celestial virgins (perhaps males) as a prize for martyrdom in the name of Allah? Or does she become one of the virgins?...Islamic heaven is designed, at the popular level at least, to appeal to the Muslim's animal nature.

—John A. Rush, *Failed God*, pp. 377, 378

Islam, according to Ait Sabbah, is in essence a pyramidal relationship with God at the top, the woman at the bottom, and the male believer situated between the two. Women's submission is central to upholding the edifice...She writes that the houri [virgin in Paradise] does not think; she is an object of male pleasure.

—Raja Rhouni, *Secular and Islamic Feminist Critiques*, p. 186

his sons

12 and his mate, and his brother

13 and his kin who stand by him,

14 and all who are in the earth, that yet it might rescue him!

15 Nay, verily, it is a flame,

16 —dragging by the scalp!

17 it shall call those who retreated and turned their backs

18 and who amassed and hoarded!

19 Verily, man is by nature rash!

20 when evil touches him,

21 very impatient; when good touches him, niggardly;

Protection for the Righteous

22 all save those who pray,

23 who remain at their prayers,

24 and in whose wealth is a reasonable due (set aside)

25 for him who asks and him who is kept from asking,

26 and those who believe in a day of judgment,

27 and those who shrink in terror from the torment of their Lord;

28 —verily, the torment of their Lord is not safe;

29 —and those who guard their private parts,

30 except for their wives or the (slave girls) whom their right hands possess, for they are not to be blamed;

31 but whoso craves beyond this, they are the transgressors;

members. But this, said Muhammad, is not possible since nobody can serve as a ransom for another person.

The Bible, however, makes an opposing claim. It states that such a ransom is indeed offered to all people. That ransom is Jesus Christ. He sacrificed Himself on the cross as a substitute for the sins of all peoples. "God made him [Jesus Christ] who had no sin to be sin for us, so that in him we might become the righteousness of God" (2 Cor 5:21), and "Very rarely will anyone die for a righteous man, though for a good man someone might possibly dare to die. But God demonstrates his own love for us in this: While we were still sinners, Christ died for us" (Rom 5:7-8), and "My command is this: Love each other as I have loved you. Greater love has no one than this, that he lay down his life for his friends" (Jn 15:12-14; cf. Isa 53:4-6; Rom 8:3; Gal 3:13; Eph 5:2; 1 Pet 3:18; and 1 Jn 2:1-2).

The way C. S. Lewis put it: "The central Christian belief is that Christ's death has somehow put us right with God and given us a fresh start...We are told that Christ was killed for us, that His death has washed out our sins, and that by dying He disabled death itself. That is the formula. That is Christianity. That is what has to be believed" (*Mere Christianity*, pp. 57-58).

70.16 *dragging by the scalp* — See Q 55.41.

70.22-35 Five righteous works that builds towards one's eternal salvation: (a) devotedness to prayer, (b) the giving of alms to the poor, (c) the preservation of one's chastity, (d) the respect for one's trusts, covenants, and testimonies, and (e) faithfulness in worship. These verses make the case for the Islamic Doctrine of Salvation by Works that we have seen in previous surahs (see Q 101.6-11, note).

70.29-30 *guard their private parts* — That is, guard their chastity. According to this pas-

32   and those who observe their trusts
      and their compacts,

33   and those who are upright in their
      testimonies,

34   and those who keep their prayers,

35   these shall dwell in gardens
      honoured.

Fate of the Unrighteous

36   What ails the misbelievers that they
      hurry on before thee,

37   crowding together on the right and
      on the left?

38   Does every man of them wish to
      enter the garden of pleasure?

39   Nay, we created them of what they

      know!

40   And I need not swear by the Lord
      of the easts and the wests;

41   verily, we are able to change them
      for others better, nor are we pre-
      vented!

42   So leave them to plunge in discus-
      sion, and to play until they meet
      that day of theirs which they are
      threatened with,

43   the day when they shall come forth
      in haste from the graves, as though
      they flock to a standard!

44   with their looks abashed; meanness
      shall cover then! That is the day
      which they were promised!

sage, sexual activity is to be limited to one's wives (polygamy is permitted) and one's slaves "whom their right hands possess." In the *Tafsir al-Jalalayn*, it is stated: "Except from their spouses, that is, to their spouses, and what their right hands possess, that is, con-cubines, for them they are not blamewor-thy, in having sexual intercourse with them." Also see Q 23.6 where the same concept is presented.

70.31 *whoso craves beyond this* — That is, whosoever seeks sexual relations beyond one's wives and slaves (concubines) has fallen into a transgression.

70.35 Those who will enter Paradise are those who fulfill the requirements of the pre-vious twelve verses (vv. 22-34). Once again, this is an affirmation of the Doctrine of Salva-tion by Works (see Q 101.6-11, note).

70.36-37 According to these two verses, the road leading to perdition is crowded with many travelers. The New Testament makes a similar claim: "Enter through the narrow

gate. For wide is the gate and broad is the road that leads to destruction, and many enter through it. But small is the gate and narrow the road that leads to life, and only a few find it" (Matt 7:13-14; cf. Gen 6:5, 11-12; 1 Jn 5:19).

70.39-44 This passage promotes the Doc-trine of al-Qadar—double predestination. The infidel rejected the ministry of Muhammad and his message of warning because Allah chose for them not to respond. The way Muhammad explained it: Allah was "able to change them for others better" (v. 41). Mu-hammad was therefore admonished to leave them alone and allow them to play (in their sinfulness) until the day upon which they will meet Allah should come upon them. On that day, "they shall come forth in haste from the graves, as though they flock to a standard" (v 43). For further discussion on this topic, see **The Doctrine of al-Qadar** on pp. 264-266.

70.42 *So leave them to plunge in discus-*

Surah 109

In the name of the merciful compassionate God.

1   Say, "O ye misbelievers!
2   I do not serve what ye serve;
3   nor will ye serve what I serve;
4   nor will I serve what ye serve;
5   nor will ye serve what I serve;
6   —ye have your religion, and I have my religion!"

Surah 107

In the name of the merciful and compassionate God.

1   Hast thou considered him who calls the judgment a lie?
2   He it is who pushes the orphan away;
3   and urges not (others) to feed the poor.
4   But we to those who pray

---

sion — That is, leave them in their false beliefs.

Surah 109. The title of this surah, *The Misbelievers*, comes from verse one. The surah follows the theme of the previous surah (Q 70). The infidels are left to their fate: "Ye shall have your religion, and I have my religion!"

Moderate Muslims claim that the surah teaches religious tolerance. Hence, it stands opposed to the use of threats or coercion in the conversion of infidels to the Islamic faith (see **Islamification** on pp. 851-852).

Yet, most Islamic scholars disagree. In his commentary on this surah, Syed Maududi writes: "One finds that it was not revealed to preach religious tolerance as some people of today seem to think, but it was revealed in order to exonerate the Muslims from the disbelievers' religion, their rites of worship, and their gods, and to express their total disgust and unconcern with them and to tell them that Islam and *kufr* (unbelief) had nothing in common and there was no possibility of their being combined and mixed into one entity" (see Q 2.256a, note, Q 3.84, note, Q 3.85, note; and Jane Dammen McAuliffe, *The Cambridge Companion to the Qur'an*, pp. 200-203).

Surah 107. The title of this surah, *The Acts of Kindness*, comes from verse seven. This surah draws attention to the hypocrisy and absence of rightness in those who call the coming Last Judgment a lie.

107.2 *He it is who pushes the orphan away* — a refusal to care for the poor or orphans is a great sin. For this reason, caring for such people is one of the Five Pillars of Islam (see **al-Zakat** on pp. 115-116).

107.4-6 Muhammad criticized the infidels, noting that their prayers were insincere. He described their prayers as careless, and the infidels themselves as pretenders who withhold the fundamentals of prayer (that is, the necessaries).

Christians agree with this general assessment. The prayers of many people are ineffective. They are mere formalities that lack true sincerity. Prayers of faith that are effective and powerful are characterized by the following: (a) grounded in a right relationship with God through Jesus Christ, (b) not harboring sin in one's life, and (c) full of faith. John R. W. Stott adds, "Prevailing Christian prayer is wonderfully comprehensive. It has four universals, indicated in Ephesians 6:18 by the fourfold use of 'all.' We are to pray *at all times* (both regularly and constantly), *with*

5   and who are careless in their prayers,

6   Who pretend

7   and withhold necessaries.

Surah 55

In the name of the merciful and compassionate God.

1   The Merciful

2   taught the Qur'ân;

3   He created man,

4   taught him plain speech.

Life on the Earth

5   The sun and the moon have their appointed time;

6   The herbs and the trees adore;

7   And the heavens, He raised them and set the balance,

8   that ye should not be outrageous in the balance;

9   But weigh ye aright, and stint not the balance.

10   And the earth He has set it for liv-

all prayer and supplication (for it takes many and varied forms), *with all perseverance* (because we need like good soldiers to keep alert, and neither give up nor fall asleep), *making supplication for all the saints* (since the unity of God's new society, which has been the preoccupation of this whole letter, must be reflected in our prayers)" (*The Message of Ephesians*, p. 283).

Surah 55. The title of this surah, *The Merciful One*, comes from verse one. It is characterized by a repeating refrain: "Which of the bounties of your Lord will you deny?" The point is that the infidels in Mecca were ungrateful to Allah. The surah also describes the cataclysmic times of apocalypse, to the Last Judgment, and then to the flames of Hell. In the final section of the surah, a description of Paradise is presented. It is a place where virgins (maidens) serve the righteous in harems and attend to all their erotic and fanciful desires.

55.7-9 *the balance* —The balance is mentioned three times in three consecutive verses. At the Last Judgment, a celestial balance will determine one's eternal fate (see

The Last Judgment on pp. 46-50). Christian author John R. W. Stott writes: "The repeated promises in the Qur'an of the forgiveness of a compassionate and merciful Allah are all made to the meritorious, whose merits have been weighed in Allah's scales, whereas the gospel is good news of mercy to the undeserving. The symbol of the religion of Jesus is the cross, not the scales (*Christian Mission in the Modern World*, p. 51).

55.13 *Then which of your Lord's bounties will ye twain deny?* — This is a refrain repeated thirty-one times (vv. 13, 16, 18, 21, 23, 25, 28, 30, 32, 34, 36, 38, 40, 42, 45, 47, 49, 51, 53, 55, 57, 59, 61, 63, 65, 67, 69, 71, 73, 75, and 77). The point of this passage is that Allah has bestowed upon man numerous blessings, beginning with creation and concluding with the blessings of Paradise.

55.14 *he made men of crackling clay like the potters* — Once again, Muhammad speculated on the creation of man. He claimed that man was made from "crackling clay like the potters" (see Q 96.2, note).

55.15, 33, 39, 56, 74 *ginn* — genie (see

al-Zakat

The Giving of Alms

Al-Zakat, derived from *zaka'* (thrive, increase, to be pure in heart, righteous, good) is the practice of alms-giving to the poor. Depending on the Islamic sect, Muslims are required to give anywhere from 2.5 percent to 10 percent of their income as alms for the poor.

The Qur'an repeatedly admonishes the faithful to perform *zakat*.

- "Verily, those who believe, and act righteously, and are steadfast in prayer, and giving alms, theirs is their hire with their Lord; there is no fear on them, nor shall they grieve" (Q 2.277)

- "Alms are only for the poor and needy, and those who work for them, and those whose hearts are reconciled, and those in captivity, and those in debt, and those who are on God's path, and for the warfarer—an ordinance this from God, for God is knowing, wise" (Q 9.60)

- "And in whose wealth is a reasonable due (set aside) for him who asks and him who is kept from asking, and those who shrink in terror from the torment of their Lord" (Q 70.24-27)

- "...then read what is easy of it and be steadfast in prayer, and give alms, and lend to God a goodly loan, for what ye send forward for yourselves of good ye will find it with God. It is better and a greater hire; and ask ye pardon of God; verily, God is forgiving, merciful!" (Q 73.20b)

In his book *Inner Dimensions of Islamic Worship*, al-Ghazali noted eight insights related to the practice of almsgiving. First, he noted that the giver of alms should be mindful of its fundamental purpose and significance. That, he explained, was to test the degree of devotion and love one has for Allah. Since wealth is held dear to a Muslim, the degree of love for Allah "is tested by separating the lover from other things he loves."[1] He added:

> Worldly goods are an object of love in everybody's eyes, being the means by which they enjoy the benefits of this world; because of them they become attached to life and shy away from death, even though death leads to meet-

ing the Beloved. The truth of our claim to love God is therefore put to the test, and we are asked to give up the wealth which is the darling apple of our eye.[2]

Second, the giver of alms should make payment in the proper time. The proper time is the month of Muharram, since it is the first of the Sacred Months in the Islamic calendar.

Third, the giving of alms should be done in secret. This is to remove the temptation of hypocrisy and reputation-seeking in one's act of piety.

Fourth, the giving of alms can be given openly, if the intent is "to encourage others to follow suit."[3]

Fifth, the giver of alms should avoid taunting and hurting the ones who are the recipients of the gift. That is, one is not to remind a person of the favor given, or to scold and rebuke the beggar.

Sixth, the giver of alms should adopt the posture of humility by thinking "little of one's donation."[4] When this occurs, the gift is magnified in the eyes of Allah.

Seventh, the giver of alms is to select the best and dearest from his or her wealth.

Eighth, the giver of alms is to seek out a truly worthy recipient of one's gift. Special attention is to be given to those who are pious in their Muslim faith, who are intent to better know the Qur'an and the ways of Allah. With this in mind, non-Muslims are excluded, since they are not deemed worthy of Allah's gifts.

---

[1] *Inner Dimensions of Islamic Worship*, p. 54.
[2] Ibid.
[3] Ibid., p. 60.
[4] Ibid., p. 65.

The institution of prescribed alms-giving is literally a "purification" intended to attenuate or wipe out the attachment to material goods which tarnishes the heart, engages it in the accumulation of ephemeral riches, and engenders what Islam condemns as one of the most unforgivable of faults, namely: that of "associating" (*shirk*) other divinities with God, or as the most profound Islamic thinkers have understood it, of treating Truth and illusion on an equal footing, even preferring illusion to truth.

—Jean-Louis Michon, *Introduction to Traditional Islam*, p. 26

In both Islam and Judaism laws that express both theology and public policy govern activities usually classed as "almsgiving" or as "charity." These are not merely encouraged, they represent an absolute obligation. And that means, in both instances, that "beggars" are not treated disdainfully but with respect, fully part of the social order and legitimately so...Both religious legal systems lay heavy stress on support for the poor.

—Jacob Neusner, Tamara Sonn, and Jonathan Brockopp,
Judaism and Islam in Practice, p. 129

The giving of charity is considered an extremely meritorious act in Islam. Just as in the case of prayer, a particular kind of alms-giving is differentiated from others because it is done ritually. Known as *zakat*, it consists of giving away a certain percentage of one's wealth in charity. The percentage given away varies by sect, ranging from 2.5 percent among Sunnis to 10 percent in some Shi'a groups. There is also a great deal of variation in what forms of wealth and income are considered taxable for *zakat:* for example, whether or not income (as opposed to assets) is taxable, and in how one calculates the tax for agricultural products.

—Jamal J. Elias, *Islam*, pp. 67, 68

In some Muslim nations *zakat* is a required tax, and *zakat* stamps may be purchased from post offices. However, much giving is voluntary, and mosques and the poor are supported by gifts.

—George W. Braswell, *What You Need to Know about Islam and Muslims*, p. 34

The Koran gives specific instructions as to whom Muslims are expected to give charity—namely, the poor, the captive, those in debt, those who fight jihad, and to travelers who do not have access to personal funds...Moreover, the Koran does not just encourage Muslims to perform their obligation of alms-giving, rather it warns them that serious consequences will follow if they do not spend their money in the "Way of Allah." Specifically, they are told that they should expect "a painful torment" on Judgment Day and that any gold or silver they may have hoarded will be used as a branding iron to negatively mark their foreheads, flanks, and backs on Judgment Day.

—Jalil Rawshandil and Sharon Chadha, *Jihad and International Security*, p. 137

The number of charities that have supported Islamist jihadists and their terrorist activities will never be known, but they were surely a small percentage of the total number of Islamic charities worldwide...Islam does not distinguish between church and state. Muslims who are obligated to perform *zakat*, and individual donors, make no distinction between the secular and religious uses to which their donations may be employed.

—J, Millard Burr and Robert O. Collins, *Alms for Jihad*, pp. 1, 7

ing creatures;

11 therein are fruits and palms, with sheaths;

12 and grain with chaff and frequent shoots;

13 Then which of your Lord's bounties will ye twain deny?

14 He created men of crackling clay like the potters.

15 And He created the ginn from smokeless fire.

16 Then which of your Lord's bounties will ye twain deny?

17 The Lord of the two easts and the Lord of the two wests!

18 Then which of your Lord's bounties will ye twain deny?

19 He has let loose the two seas that meet together;

20 between them is a barrier they cannot pass!

21 Then which of your Lord's bounties will ye twain deny?

22 He brings forth from each pearls both large and small!

23 Then which of your Lord's bounties will ye twain deny?

24 His are the ships which rear aloft in the sea like mountains.

25 Then which of your Lord's bounties will ye twain deny?

26 Every one upon it is transient, but the face of thy

27 Lord endowed with majesty and

honour shall endure.

28 Then which of your Lord's bounties will ye twain deny?

29 Of Him whosoever is in the heaven and the earth does beg; every day He is in (some fresh) business!

30 Then which of your Lord's bounties will ye twain deny?

Apocalypse

31 We shall be at leisure for you, O ye two weighty ones!

32 Then which of your Lord's bounties will ye twain deny?

33 O assembly of ginns and mankind! if ye are able to pass through the confines of heaven and earth then pass through them!—ye cannot pass through save by authority!

34 Then which of your Lord's bounties will ye twain deny?

35 There shall be sent against you a flash of fire, and molten copper, and ye shall not be helped!

36 Then which of your Lord's bounties will ye twain deny?

37 And when the heaven is rent asunder and become rosy red — (melting) like grease!

38 Then which of your Lord's bounties will ye twain deny?

Day of Judgment

Occultism in Seventh Century Arabia on pp. 123-125).
55.39-41 According to these verses, at the Last Judgment the wicked will be not confronted with their sins. Rather, their bodies will manifest marks that identify them as sinners. They will then be seized by their forelocks and feet and cast into boiling water.
55.41 *seized by the forelock and the feet* — See Q 70.16.

39 On that day neither man nor ginn shall be asked about his crime!	trees.
40 Then which of your Lord's bounties will ye twain deny?	49 Then which of your Lord's bounties will ye twain deny?
41 The sinners shall be known by their marks, and shall be seized by the forelock and the feet!	50 In each are flowing springs.
42 Then which of your Lord's bounties will ye twain deny?	51 Then which of your Lord's bounties will ye twain deny?
	52 In each are, of every fruit, two kinds.
Hell	53 Then which of your Lord's bounties will ye twain deny?
43 "This is hell, which the sinners did call a lie!	54 Reclining on beds the linings of which are of brocade, and the fruit of the two gardens within reach to cull.
44 they shall circulate between it and water boiling quite!"	55 Then which of your Lord's bounties will ye twain deny?
45 Then which of your Lord's bounties will ye twain deny?	56 Therein are maids of modest glances whom no man nor ginn has deflowered before.
Paradise	57 Then which of your Lord's bounties will ye twain deny?
46 But for him who fears the station of his Lord are gardens twain!	58 As though they were rubies and pearls.
47 Then which of your Lord's bounties will ye twain deny?	59 Then which of your Lord's bounties will ye twain deny?
48 Both furnished with branching	60 Is the reward of goodness aught

55.43-45 The infidels typically deny the existence of Hell. Nevertheless, said Muhammad, it is a place where the water boils.

55.46-61 This image of Paradise is that of a Bedouin tribal leader living in a lush oasis (two gardens) with his own private harem. Four characteristics of Paradise are: (a) two gardens in both of which are two flowing fountains, (b) in the gardens are two pairs of every fruit, (c) people will recline on carpets lined with rich brocade with fruit readily accessible, and (d) inhabited by chaste maidens with restraining glances.

This imagery of Paradise being a garden is oft-repeated in the Qur'an (see Q 10.9; 14.23; 15.45; 16.31; 18.31, 107; 19.61; 20.76; 22.14; 25.10, 15; 30.15; 31.8; 32.19; 34.16; 35.33; 37.43; 38.50; 40.8; 44.52; 51.15; 52.17; 53.15; 54.54; 55.46, 54, 62; 56.12, 89; 64.9; 68.34; 69.22; 70.35, 38; 71.12; 78.32; 85.11; 88.10).

55.54 *the linings of which are brocade —* embossed cloth, richly decorated, often made with silk and lined with silver and gold thread.

55.56 *no man nor ginn has deflowered before —* That is, these young women are vir-

but goodness?

61   Then which of your Lord's boun-
      ties will ye twain deny?

Two additional gardens

62   And besides these, are gardens
      twain,
63   Then which of your Lord's boun-
      ties will ye twain deny?
64   With dark green foliage.
65   Then which of your Lord's boun-
      ties will ye twain deny?
66   In each two gushing springs.
67   Then which of your Lord's boun-
      ties will ye twain deny?
68   In each fruit and palms and pome-
      granates.
69   Then which of your Lord's boun-
      ties will ye twain deny?
70   In them maidens best and fairest!
71   Then which of your Lord's boun-
      ties will ye twain deny?
72   Bright and large-eyed maids kept
      in their tents.
73   Then which of your Lord's boun-
      ties will ye twain deny?
74   Whom no man nor ginn has de-
      flowered before them.

75   Then which of your Lord's boun-
      ties will ye twain deny?
76   Reclining. on green cushions and
      beautiful carpets.
77   Then which of your Lord's boun-
      ties will ye twain deny?
78   Blessed be the name of thy Lord
      possessed of majesty and honour!

Surah 56

*In the name of merciful and compassionate
God.*

The coming Apocalypse

1   When the inevitable happens;
2   none shall call its happening a lie!
3   —abasing—exalting!
4   When the earth shall quake, quak-
     ing!
5   and the mountains shall crumble,
     crumbling,
6   and become like motes dispersed!

Three classes of people

7   And ye shall be three sorts;

---

gins (also see v. 74; cf. Q 56.36).

55.62-78 In addition to the previous two gardens (oases) mentioned above, Paradise is likened to two additional gardens. They (a) will be dark green in color due to plentiful watering, (b) contain two springs pouring forth water in abundance, (c) have fruits, dates, and pomegranates, and (d) will be inhabited by beautiful chaste maidens in pavilions, reclining on green cushions and beauti-

ful carpets. Again, the image is that of a Bedouin tribal leader living in a lush oasis with his own private harem.

55.74 *no man nor ginn has deflowered before them* — That is, these young women are virgins (also see v. 56; cf. Q 56.36).

Surah 56. The title of this surah, *The Event*, comes from verse one. This surah describes the eternal state of three classes of people: the foremost in faith, the people of the right

8 And the fellows of the right hand— what right lucky fellows!	22 And bright and large-eyed maids
9 And the fellows of the left hand— what unlucky fellows!	23 like hidden pearls;
10 And the foremost foremost!	24 A reward for that which they have done!
	25 They shall hear no folly there and no sin;
Foremost in faith	26 Only the speech, "Peace, Peace!"
11 These are they who are brought nigh,	*People of the Right Hand*
12 In gardens of pleasure!	27 And the fellows of the right—what right lucky fellows!
13 A crowd of those of yore,	28 Amid thornless lote trees.
14 And a few of those of the latter day!	29 And tal'h trees with piles of fruit;
15 And gold-weft couches,	30 And outspread shade,
16 reclining on them face to face.	31 And water out-poured;
17 Around them shall go eternal youths,	32 And fruit in abundance,
18 with goblets and ewers and a cup of flowing wine;	33 neither failing nor forbidden;
19 no headache shall they feel therefrom, nor shall their wits be dimmed!	34 And beds upraised!
	35 Verily, we have produced them a production.
20 And fruits such as they deem the best;	36 And made them virgins,
21 And flesh of fowl as they desire;	37 darlings of equal age (with their spouses)
	38 for the fellows of the right!

hand, and the people of the left hand.

56.11-26 Five characteristics of Paradise for the foremost in faith: (a) it is likened to a lush oasis, (b) people will recline on couches with gold and precious stones, (c) they will be served by a harem of eternally youthful maidens, (d) they will eat fruit and the flesh of fowls, and (e) a place of peace. In short, Islamic Paradise is described as a place of great sensual delight. It consists of one's choice of food, drink and sex—without limits and without negative side effects. This Islamic description of Paradise, of course, is restricted to the male perspective.

This description stands in contrast to the biblical depiction of Heaven. Jesus said that in Heaven people will "neither marry nor be given in marriage; they will be like the angels in heaven" (Matt 22:30).

56.12 Gardens of sensual and erotic delights (also see Q 10.9; 22.56; 31.8; 37.40-50; and 68.34).

56.13-14 Muhammad believed that the majority of people in Paradise are those who were faithful to Allah prior to those of the latter day (that is, people of yore: before the seventh century, A.D.).

56.27-40 Three characteristics of Paradise:

39   A crowd of those of yore,
40   and a crowd of those of the latter
     day!

People of the Left Hand

41   And the fellows of the left—what
     unlucky fellows!
42   In hot blasts and boiling water;
43   And a shade of pitchy smoke,
44   Neither cool nor generous!
45   Verily, they were affluent ere this,
46   and did persist in mighty crime;

Regrets

47   and used to say, "What, when we

die and have become dust and
bones, shall we then indeed be
raised?
48   or our fathers of yore?"
49   Say, "Verily, those of yore and those
     of the latter day
50   shall surely be gathered together
     unto the tryst of the well-known
     day."
51   Then ye, O ye who err! who say it
     is a lie!
52   shall eat of the Zaqqûm tree!
53   and fill your bellies with it!
54   and drink thereon of boiling water!
55   and drink as drinks the thirsty
     camel.
56   This is their entertainment on the

(a) Paradise contains lote and tal'h trees and an abundance of water, (b) people will recline on couches, and (c) they will be served by a harem—maidens full of love for their mates. In short, similar to Q 56.39, Islamic Paradise is described as a place of great sensual delight. It consists of one's choice of food, drink and sex—without limits and without negative side effects. This Islamic description of Paradise, of course, is limited to the male perspective.

56.28 *thornless lote trees* — These are mystical Islamic trees not found on earth. In Islamic lore, lote trees are located in Paradise. They serve as a barrier, preventing a person from getting too close to God (see Q 53.10-18).

56.29 *tal'h trees* — Acacia trees. On earth, talh trees have wide leafs that offer much shade. They do not, however, bear fruit. In Islamic lore, tal'h trees exist in Paradise and also bear fruit.

56.36 *made them virgins* — Islamic scholarship is in general agreement that the women in Paradise will remain virgins eternally. Yet, this does not mean that they will abstain from sexual activity. Rather, following a sexual encounter, the hymen will reform. Hence, each sexual encounter will be a virginal encounter.

56.37 *darlings of equal age* — That is, maidens full of erotic love.

56.39 *a crowd of those of yore* — That is, a crowd of the righteous who lived prior to Muhammad (see vv. 13-14).

56.40 *a crowd of those of the latter day* — That is, a crowd of the righteous who lived during or after Muhammad (see vv. 13-14).

56.41-46 Three characteristics of Hell: (a) people will enter the blast of fire (b) people will be forced to drink boiling water, and (c) people will reside in shades of black smoke.

56.52 *Zaqqum tree* — A mythical Islamic tree that exists in Hell. Its fruit is the food of sinners. It is poisonous and likened to the taste of boiling oil (see Q 17.60 and 44.43).

Occultism in
the Seventh Century Arabia

Alongside the Star Family religion in seventh century Arabia was the practice of Ginn-Devil Worship. *Ginn* was the name given to malevolent spirit
beings who wrought havoc in people's lives when not venerated. They
are roughly the same beings with that which the Judeo-Christian tradition describes as *demons* and *unclean spirits*. Greek historians, starting
with Herodotus in the fifth century, B.C., referenced such occultic activity in Arabia.

Ginn-Devil priests and priestesses administered the worship activities
of the numerous Ka'ba altars, blending ginn worship with Star Family
astrology. Typical worship rites included devotees circumambulating around
the altars and offer gifts to the ginn statutes.

An important feature of ginn worship was the practice of human
sacrifice. According to Ibn Ishaq, the author of the oldest and most
authoritative biography on Muhammad, Muttaleb (Muhammad's grandfather) was a committed ginn devotee. In a vision, he was told by a ginn
to dig a well at Zam-zam (in Mecca) between two ginn idols, Isaf and
Na'ila. Having done so, he was then told to sacrifice one of his ten sons
to the ginn. Lots were cast and the son chosen was Abdullah, the
future father of Muhammad. Alarmed, people of Mecca intervened and
beckoned him not to carry out the deed. They told him to instead go
the city of Khaybar where a ginn sorceress lived. Perhaps, they reasoned, the sorceress would suggest an alternate sacrifice. He followed
their advise. After a series of incantations, the sorceress told him to
sacrifice a number of camels in the place of his son.[1]

Muhammad grew up in the midst of this occultic environment. His
uncle Abu Talib, who raised him, was a devotee to ginn worship.[2] His
first wife, Khadijah, was a widow who had been previously married to
Nabash bin Zarareh bin Wakdan, a ginn visionary. She was a woman of
stature in Mecca since, being the wife of this visionary, Arabians traveled

great distances to their home with the hope of acquiring prognostications and related occultic information.[3] Following the death of Nabash,
Muhammad married her.

Muhammad attempted to break free of ginn-worship, condemning
it repeatedly in his early surahs. Yet, just prior to leaving Mecca, he
embraced a middle ground, noting that even some of the ginns had
begun responding positively to the "glad tidings" of his message of Islam. He claimed to have encountered several ginns, saw them with his
own eyes, spoke with them, and was pleased that they affirmed the
message that he had been preaching to the people of Mecca (Q 72.1-
19).

Muhammad in Prayer. According to the hadithic literature,
Muhammad encountered ginns in his prayer life. Abu Darda' reported:

> Allah's messenger...stood up (to pray) and we heard him say, "I seek refuge
> in Allah from thee." Then said: "Curse thee with Allah's curse" three times,
> then stretched out his hand as though he was taking hold of something.
> When he finished the prayer, we said: "Messenger of Allah, we have not
> heard you say before, and we saw you stretch out your hand. He replied:
> "Allah's enemy Iblis [Satan] came with a flame of fire to put it in my face, so I
> said three times: "I seek refuge in Allah from thee." Then I said three times:
> "I curse thee with Allah's full curse." But he did not retreat (on any one of
> these) three occasions. Thereafter I meant to seize him. I swear by Allah
> that had it not been for the supplication of my brother Sulaiman he would have
> been bound, and made an object of sport for the children of Medina."[4]

The phrase "my brother Sulaiman" is a reference to King Solomon, who
was allegedly there without being seen by anyone except Muhammad.

Characteristics of Ginns. In pre-Islamic Arabic lore, ginns were
believed to be a race of spirit beings that roamed the earth. They were
similar to angels since their bodies were of an spiritual (immaterial) substance. They were invisible to the human eye, yet had the ability to
manifest themselves to human beings as apparitions. The word "genie"
is the English term for these spirit beings.

In the Qur'an, they are described as simpletons, easily beguiled, and
prone to sin. In addition, the Qur'an notes that:

- Ginns are created from smokeless fire (Q 55.15)
- Ginns can have sexual relations with human females (Q 55.56,
  74)
- Ginns are prone to telling lies (Q 34.8)

- Most polytheists are worshippers of ginns (Q 34.41)
- Solomon's army included ginns (Q 27.17)
- Hell is populated by both human beings and ginns (Q 32.13; 41.25; 46.18)
- Some ginns affirmed Muhammad's Islamic message (Q 46.29; Q 72)

---

[1] Ibn Ishaq, *The Life of Muhammad,* pp. 45, 66-68.

[2] See *Sahih Bukhari* 6.60.295.

[3] Ibn Duraid, *Al-Ishtiqaq,* pp. 88-89; cited by Rafat Amari in *Islam in Light of History,* p. 409.

[4] *Sahih Muslim* 4.1106.

———•◆•———

Gottfried Simon has shown conclusively that Islam cannot uproot pagan practices or remove the terror of spirits and demon-worship in Sumatra and Java. This is true everywhere. In its conflict with Animism Islam has not been the victor but the vanquished. Christianity on the contrary, as Harnack has shown, did win in its conflict with demon-worship and is winning today.

—Samuel Marinus Zwemer, *The Influence of Animism on Islam,* p. 18

One Baahithiin shaman told me that he received his supernatural powers while on the ritual pilgrimage in Mecca. His experience shows that folk Islam touches even Saudi Arabia, which takes pride in being the heartland of formal Islam.

—Rick Love, *Muslims, Magic and the Kingdom of God,* p. 23

Muslims also look for help through harnessing the spiritual powers to work for them. This includes the quasi-Islamic magical practices of folk-Islam, like sheikhs writing charms, and the activities of the mediums dealing in the occult.

—Christine A. Mallouhi, *Waging Peace on Islam,* p. 229

Shamanistic practices...are now expressed within the framework of Islam and in the persons of mendicants and mystics.

—Peter J, Claus, Sarah Diamond, Margaret Ann Mills, *South Asian Folklore,* p. 545

judgment day!

A final appeal

57   We created you, then why do ye
      not credit?
58   Have ye considered what ye emit?
`59   Do we create it, or are we the cre-
      ators?
60   We have decreed amongst you
      death; but we are not forestalled
61   from making the likes of you in
      exchange, or producing you as ye
      know not of.
62   Ye do know the first production—
      why then do ye not mind?
63   Have ye considered what ye till?
64   Do ye make it bear seed, or do we
      make it bear seed?
65   If we pleased we could make it
      mere grit, so that ye would pause
      to marvel:
66   "Verily, we have got into debt
67   and we are excluded."
68   Have ye considered the water
      which ye drink?
69   Do ye make it come down from
      the clouds, or do we make it come
      down?
70   If we pleased we could make it
      pungent—why then do ye not give

      thanks?
71   Have ye considered the fire which
      ye strike?
72   Do ye produce the tree that gives
      it, or do we produce it?
73   We have made it a memorial and a
      chattel for the traveller of the
      waste?
74   Then celebrate the grand name of
      thy Lord!

Those who reject the Qur'an

75   So I will not swear by the posi-
      tions of the stars;
76   and, verily, it is a grand oath if ye
      did but know
77   —that, verily, this is the honourable
      Qur'ân
78   —in the laid-up Book!
79   Let none touch it but the purified!
80   A revelation from the Lord of the
      worlds.
81   What! this new discourse will ye
      despise?
82   And make for your provision, that
      you call it a lie?
83   Why then—when it comes up to
      the throat,
84   and ye at that time look on,
85   though we are nearer to him than

56.58 *Have ye considered...?* — Four times this question is asked in this section of this surah (vv. 58, 63, 68, and 71). Have ye considered what ye emit, what ye till, the water which ye drink, and the fire which ye strike? Muhammad's point was that even in every day events, it is Allah—and not the person—who makes it all possible.

56.78 *the laid-up Book* — the Book of Allah that resides eternally in Paradise.
56.79 *none shall touch but those who are clean* — Two interpretations exist within Islamic scholarship: (a) only those who are pure in heart can rightly understand the Qur'an, and (b) only those who are pure in heart are permitted to touch the book.

you are, but ye cannot see,
86 —why, if ye are not to be judged,
87 do ye not send it back, if ye do tell the truth?

Conclusion

88 But either, if he be of those brought nigh to God,
89 —then rest and fragrance and the garden of pleasure!
90 Or, if he be of the fellows of the right!
91 then "Peace to thee!" from the fellows of the right!
92 Or, if he be of those who say it is a lie —who err!
93 then an entertainment of boiling water!
94 and broiling in hell!
95 Verily, this is surely certain truth!
96 So celebrate the grand name of thy Lord!

56.89 *garden of pleasure* — That is, garden of erotic pleasures.

56.93 *entertainment of boiling water* — This is a horrific description of Hell.

INTRODUCTION

INTRODUCTION

The Fourth Period

As the years past, Muhammad refused to yield to the demands of the leaders of Mecca. With regularity, he recited one surah after another in the precinct of the Ka'ba altar before audiences, large and small. Many of the surahs were critical of the established religious culture of Mecca. Not only were the surahs irritating since they mocked the religion of the Meccan people, they threatened one of the major sources of the city's income: the cult of the Ka'ba altar. Pilgrims came to Mecca to offer prayers to their particular god or gods and leave financial offerings. Muhammad's loud and repeated denunciations of this practice was having an effect on these pilgrimages and the money they left behind.

The Boycott. It was inevitable that the conflict between Muhammad and the leaders of Mecca would escalate and come to a head. The Meccan leaders organized a boycott against Muhammad, his small Muslim community, and the Bani Hashim (the small Meccan clan of which Muhammad was a member and which offered him protection). A document was drawn up that stated that (a) people were prohibited from marrying anyone of the Bani Hashim, and (b) people were prohibited from engaging in commerce with Muhammad, his Muslim followers, and the people of the Bani Hashim. The boycott was to continue until the Bani Hashim had enough and banished Muhammad. Forty of the Meccan leaders signed their names to the document. The document was then placed inside the Ka'ba altar. This act demonstrated that the leaders of Mecca were beseeching the many gods of the Ka'ba altar to bless the document and aid them in the eradication of the Muslim menace.

The boycott was not rigorously enforced. Since intermarriage between the clans of Mecca had already taken place, the wives of their husbands' clan were still regarded as members of their original birth clans. Accordingly, the boycott did not specifically apply to them; they received supplies and then passed them on to the others. In addition, the boycott did not apply to caravans passing through Mecca. Furthermore, many people of Mecca empathized with the plight of those being boycotted and secretly sent supplies to them in the dead of night. Still, the boycott had its moments of success, which placed a strain upon Muhammad, the Muslim community, and the Bani Hashim clan.

The Aftermath. The boycott continued for two years, more or less. The leaders of Mecca finally lifted the boycott when they came to the realization that the boycott was not serving their purposes. Not only did it not eradicate the Muslim problem in Mecca, it had resulted in the unintended effect of "causing the new religion to be talked about more than ever throughout Arabia,"[1] and engendering sympathy for the Muslim cause.

---

[1] Martin Lings, *Muhammad: Life Based Upon the Earliest Sources,* p. 92.

Surah 67

In the name of the merciful and compassionate God.

Allah is blessed

1   Blessed be He in whose hand is the kingdom, for He is mighty over all!
2   Who created death and life, to try you, which of you does best; for He is the mighty, the forgiving!
3   Who created seven heavens in stories; thou canst not see any discordance in the creation of the Merciful!

Hell

4   Why, look again! canst thou see a flaw? Then look again twice!—thy look shall return to thee driven back and dulled!
5   And we have adorned the lower heaven with lamps; and set them to pelt the devils with; and we have prepared for them the torment of the blaze!
6   And for those who disbelieve in their Lord is the torment of hell, and an evil journey shall it be!
7   When they shall be cast therein they shall hear its braying as it boils—it will well-nigh burst for rage!
8   Whenever a troop of them is thrown in, its treasurers shall ask them, "Did not a warner come to

Surah 67. The title of this surah, *The Kingdom*, comes from verse one. The two central ideas in the surah address the mighty power of Allah and man's complete dependence on divine revelation to understand spiritual realities. These ideas find their vortex with Muhammad, Allah's duly called prophet. He explained the nature of Allah's power and the content of divine revelation. Those who rejected his claim, he warned, would be cast into Hell.

67.2 *created death and life* — Muhammad claimed that Allah "created death and life." Both were within the divine plan—foreordained and thereby inevitable. All the other gods worshipped at Mecca, then, were puny and insignificant in comparison.

In contrast, the Bible is more nuanced in its discussion of death. Though God is indeed sovereign over His universe, death is nevertheless described as an enemy (1 Cor 15:26). It is a fact of life that was never originally intended by God. It came about due to sin and will someday be vanquished by God Himself. The Apostle Paul stated: "The last enemy to be destroyed is death" (1 Cor 15:26).

67.3 *seven heavens in stories* — Paradise is arranged in seven layers of increasing excellence (see Q 13.1; 23.86; 41.12; 65.12; 78.12; **Paradise** on pp. 76-77).

67.5 *lamps* — According to this verse, lamps in the lower heavens (meteorites) pelt (torment) the devils when they hit the earth.

67.8-9 *a warner* — In the Qur'an, one of Muhammad's favorite descriptions of his ministry was that of "a warner." Similar to the ministry of all of Allah's apostles, his mission was to warn people of a coming judgment in this life as well as the afterlife if they did not heed his message of monotheism and turn to Allah in complete submission. Implied in the warning, then, was the threat of violence and destruction.

you?"

9   They shall say, "Yea! a warner came to us, and we called him liar, and said, 'God has not sent down aught; ye are but in great error!'"

10   And they shall say, "Had we but listened or had sense we had not been amongst the fellows of the blaze!"

11   And they will confess their sins; but "Avaunt [forward] to the fellows of the blaze!"

*Blessings on those
who fear the Lord*

12   Verily, those who fear their Lord in secret, for them is forgiveness and a great hire!

13   Speak ye secretly or openly, verily, He knows the nature of men's breasts!

14   Ay! He knows who created! for He is the subtle, the well-aware!

15   He it is who made the earth flat for you; so walk in the spacious sides thereof and eat of His provision; for unto Him the resurrection is!

Seven Questions

16   Are ye sure that He who is in the heaven will not cleave the earth with you, and that it then shall quake?

17   Or are ye sure that He who is in the heaven will not send against you a heavy sand storm, and that ye then shall know how the warning was?

18   But those before them did call the apostles liars, and what a change it was!

19   Or have they not looked at the birds above them expanding their wings or closing them?—none holds them in except the Merciful One; for He on everything doth look.

20   Or who is this who will be a host for you, to help you against the Merciful?—the misbelievers are only in delusion!

21   Or who is this who will provide you if He hold back His provision?—Nay, but they persist in perverseness and aversion!

22   Is he who walks prone upon his

67.10 According to this verse, avoiding the fires of Hell required people to *listen* to divine revelation and have the *sense of mind* to heed its message.

67.13 *he knows the nature of men's breasts* — This is consistent with Allah's sovereignty is His omniscience. He knows all things, including the thoughts of each person. The Judeo-Christian tradition is in agreement with this assertion (see Gen 6:5; Ex 3:7; 1 Kings 8:39; 2 Chron 16:9; Job 28:12-

28; Ps 7:9; 94:11; 139:1-10; Acts 1:24; Rom 11:33; Heb 4:13; and 1 Jn 3:19-20).

67.16-22 These seven questions are reminiscent of the series of questions asked by God to Job (see Job 38 and 39). The purpose of each was to magnify Allah's wisdom and minimize human wisdom.

67.20 *the misbelievers are only in delusion* — This theme is constant throughout the Qur'an. The Bible makes a similar claim about unbelievers (see 2 Cor 4:4 and 2 Thess 2:9-

face more guided than he who walks upright upon a straight path?

Seven statements

23   Say, "It is He who produced you and made for you hearing and sight and hearts"—little is it that ye give thanks.

24   Say, "It is He who sowed you in the earth, and unto Him shall ye be gathered!"

25   They say, "When shall this threat be, if ye do speak the truth?"

26   Say, "The knowledge is only with God; and I am but a plain warner!"

27   And when they see it nigh, sorry shall be the faces of those who misbelieve; and it shall be said, "This is that for which ye used to call!"

28   Say, "Have ye considered, whether God destroy me and those with me, or whether we obtain mercy, yet who will protect the misbelievers from grievous torment?"

29   Say, "He is the Merciful; we believe in Him, and upon Him do we rely; and ye shall shortly know who it is that is in obvious error!"

30   Say, "Have ye considered if your waters on the morrow should have sunk, who is to bring you flowing water?"

Surah 53

In the name of the merciful and compassionate God.

1   By the star when it falls,

2   your comrade errs not, nor is he deluded!

---

10).

67.23 When listing sins in order of most to least severe, the Qur'an places the sin of unthankfulness as one of the most severe. The Bible makes a similar claim (see Rom 1:21 and 2 Tim 3:2).

67.30 *Have ye considered if your waters on the morrow should have sunk* — In the Arabian desert, life was dependent upon underground aquifers. They reached the surface and formed oases, or near the surface of the ground where its water was accessed with wells. If the aquifers were to drop to a much deeper level so that oases and wells became dry, then all life would cease. Muhammad's point was that he was challenging his opponents to consider that it was Allah who kept the aquifers sufficiently close

to the surface of the ground.

Surah 53. The title of this surah, *The Star,* comes from verse one. Known for the so-called *Satanic Verses Controversy* located in this surah, Surah 53 is the most theologically contentious of all the surahs in the Qur'an. Apart from this controversy, the surah is a challenge to infidels to turn from their polytheism and worship Allah, and Allah alone.

53.1 *the star when it falls* — Islamic scholars differ in their interpretation of this phrase. Some maintain that it refers to a star moving under the horizon on the western horizon when the sun rises in the east. Others maintain that it refers to a falling star (meteorite) thrown at Satan.

53.2 *your comrade errs not* — That is, Muhammad's surahs were without error. Muham-

3	nor speaks he out of lust!	7	and appeared, he being in the loftiest tract.
	Two Visions of Allah	8	Then drew he near and hovered o'er!
4	It is but an inspiration inspired!	9	until he was two bows' length off or nigher still!
5	One mighty in power taught him,	10	Then he inspired his servant what he inspired him;
6	endowed with sound understanding,		

mad was neither deluded nor speaks lustfully (v. 3). Most likely, the charges of delusion and lust were spoken by his opponents as a way of discrediting his ministry.

53.4 *an inspiration inspired* — Muhammad understood himself to be inspired of Allah. The words in his surahs, then, were the very Words of God (see Q 2.2-5; 136-137; 3.32; 6.19, 50; 10.2, 15; 12.3; 18.27, 110; 20.13; 21.7, 45, 73, 108; 24.1; 33.2; 34.50; 35.31; 38.70; 39.1-2; 65; 41.6; 42.3, 13, 51-52; 43.43; 46.9; 53.4, 10 and 72.1). Muhammad understood himself to be a conduit, a channel, that Allah had chosen to communicate His eternal book to the people of Mecca— and by extension, the people of the world (see **The Qur'an** on pp. 150-153).

Yet this doctrine has posed a problem for many within mainstream Islamic scholarship. Islamic scholars claim that only the words spoken by Allah are inspired. How then do they explain the many words in the Qur'an spoken by Muhammad, other people, genies (ginns), and even angels? Some scholars have suggested that the word *say* should be inserted in front of the sayings attributed to others, causing them to become dictations from God. Yet this answer is unsatisfactory since the Qur'an is understood to be perfect, not requiring the insertion of any additional words.

Hence, a consistent application of the doctrine of inspiration, as understood by Islamic scholarship, demands that not all of the Qur'an is inspired—only those passages within the Qur'an where Allah is the one speaking. All the other speakers (Muhammad, other people, genies, and angels) are not inspired.

In contrast, the Christian faith has no such problem with its understanding of inspiration. Its divinely inspired Scriptures are believed to be the joint product of God and the human author. That is, it is a combined effort with the finished product being the divine Word of God. This is true, no matter who the actual speaker in Scripture happens to be (see Q 36-36-38, note).

53.9 *two bows' length off* — That is, approximately ten feet off.

53.4-18 *One mighty in power* — The being described in this passage is Allah. The phrase "he appeared in the loftiest tract" is a reference to the tract that the stars follow each night, suggesting that Allah manifested Himself as a star. Muhammad believes that on a particular night, Allah drew "near and hovered o'er" until he was "two bows' length off" or quite close to Muhammad (see Q 86.1, note). On a second occasion, at *The Night Journey* (the Mi'raj) when Muhammad traveled to Jerusalem and then to the Seventh Heaven, Muhammad claims that he saw Allah from beyond the lote tree (see Q 17.1, note).

In contrast, Christians are warned not to be deceived by supernatural apparitions.

11 the heart belies not what he saw!

12 What, will ye dispute with him on what he saw?

13 And he saw him another time,

14 by the lote tree none may pass;

15 near which is the garden of the Abode!

16 When there covered the lote tree what did cover it!

17 The sight swerved not nor wandered.

18 He saw then the greatest of the signs of his Lord.

Allat, Al 'Huzza, and Manat

19 Have ye considered Allât and Al 'Huzzâ,

20 and Manât the other third?

21 Shall there be male offspring for Him and female for you?

22 That were an unfair division!

The error of polytheism

23 They are but names which ye have named, ye and your fathers! God has sent down no authority for them! They do but follow suspicion and what their souls lust after!—And yet there has come to

The deciding question is not whether an apparition manifested itself, but the nature of the information communicated by the apparition. The Apostle Paul wrote: "But even if we or an angel from heaven should preach a gospel other than the one we preached to you, let him be eternally condemned! As we have already said, so now I say again: If anybody is preaching to you a gospel other than what you accepted, let him be eternally condemned!" (Gal 1:8-9), and "And no wonder, for Satan himself masquerades as an angel of light. It is not surprising, then, if his servants masquerade as servants of righteousness. Their end will be what their actions deserve" (2 Cor 11:14-15).

53.14 *lote tree* — The tree in the seventh heaven that resides near Allah.

53.19-22 Without question, this is the most controversial of all the passages in the Qur'an. In this passage, Muhammad drew attention to three of the gods worshipped by the polytheists in Arabia: Allat, Al 'Huzza, and Manat. Each was worshipped at the Ka'ba altar in Mecca. All three were understood to be

goddesses. The question posed was this: "Shall there be male offspring for Him [Allah] and female for you?" The question was a challenge to the Star Family religious system (gods procreating other gods).

Yet an early biographer of Muhammad, Ibn Ishaq, attests that this passage had been altered, not part of the original surah. Rather, while Muhammad was in Mecca he briefly lapsed into polytheism by affirming the goddesses of Allat, Al 'Huzza, and Manat. Afterwards, he became aware of his error, returned to the people who had heard his first presentation of the surah in the precinct of the Ka'ba altar, and confessed that he had been temporarily beguiled by Satan. He then rewrote the surah with words that affirmed monotheism. These revised words are found in the authorized version of the Qur'an (see **The Satanic Verses Controversy** on pp. 135-137 for a fuller presentation of this controversy).

53.23 *God has sent down no authority for them* — That is, the previously mentioned goddesses, Allat, Al 'Huzza, and Manat, are

The Satanic Verses Controversy

VERSION A	VERSION B
19 Have ye considered Allât and Al 'Huzzâ,	19 Have you then con- sidrered Allât and Al 'Huzzâ,
20 and Manât the other third?	20 and Manât, the third, the last?
21 Shall there be male offspring for Him and female for you?	21 These are high flying cranes (interces- sors);
22 That were an unfair division!	22 verily their interces- sion is accepted with approval.

The controversy surrounding the Satanic Verses is centered in Surah 53.19-22. Two versions exist, one officially sanctioned by Islamic schol-ars and leaders and the other unsanctioned, yet carrying historical weight.

The first version (Version A) makes the case that three of the goddesses worshipped by the polytheists of Arabia—Allat, Al 'Huzza, and Manat—would have offsprings of their own. It was based upon the esteemed Sumerian culture (centered in the city of Ur) where gods were believed to procreate and give birth to other gods. Muhammad rejected this idea of gods and goddesses procreating.

The second version (Version B) makes the case that Muhammad acquiesced to the demands of the polytheists of Mecca and brought honor to three of their goddesses by claiming that their intercession was accepted with approval by Allah. Afterwards, Muhammad saw the error of his ways, came back to the Ka'ba altar, and amended the surah with the words of Version A. This reversal enflamed the tensions with the people of Mecca with the pledge of increased hostilities against

Muhammad and his followers. Ibn Ishaq, the first biographer of Muhammad attests to the accuracy of this second version.

The fundamental problem with the account of the Satanic Verses is that it stands in contradiction to the Doctrine of Isma (the moral and spiritual perfections of Muhammad). Hence, the story is a source of much embarrassment. Salman Rushdie's novel *The Satanic Verses* (1989), which highlighted this story about Muhammad, offended many in the Islamic world. The *fatwa* calling for Rushdie's death by the Ayatollah Khomeini is an example of the degree of sensitivity many Muslims still have in reference to this subject.

Ibn Ishaq's account

When considering Muhammad's alleged temporary lapse into polytheism (the Satanic Verses), scholarship looks to the biography by Ibn Ishaq on Muhammad, entitled *The Life of Muhammad*. It was the earliest of all the biographies on Muhammad, written in the mid-eighth century. All biographies on Muhammad written hence are dependent upon Ishaq's work.[1]

According to Ishaq, Muhammad's temporary lapse into polytheism was centered in his efforts to find common ground with the Quraysh people in Mecca, to offer a theological compromise that would hopefully eliminate the contentiousness that had so badly divided the city and prompted the first *Hijrah* (re-settlement) when a number of Muslims emigrated to Abyssinia on the western shores of the Red Sea to avoid the impending persecution. Since the principal bone of contention between Muhammad and his opponents turned on the question of monotheism versus pantheism, he sought a way to reduce the heat in this debate. His solution was to soften his opinion and attitude of three of the principal goddesses worshipped by the Quraysh people: Allat, al-Huzza and Manat. In the proximity of the Ka'ba altar in Mecca, he recited his newest surah, which included the words: "Have you considered Allat, al-Huzza, and Manat, the third, the last? These are high flying cranes (intercessors); verily their intercession is accepted with approval." He then prostrated himself to the ground. The people, delighted with his words that validated their goddesses, responded in kind by prostrating themselves to the ground.

Everyone in the mosque, believer and unbeliever prostrated, except al-Walid bin al-Mughira who was an old man who could not do so, so he took a handful of dirt from the valley and bent over it. Then the people dispersed and Quraysh went out, delighted at what had been said about their gods, saying, "Muhammad has spoken of our gods in splendid fashion. He alleged in what he read that they are the exalted Gharaniq whose intercession is approved."[2]

News of this reconciliation between Muhammad and his opponents in Mecca reached across the Red Sea to the exiled Muslims living in Abyssinia. Assuming that the conflict had ended and that it was now safe to return, they gathered their possessions and began to journey back to Mecca.

Yet, according to Ishaq, the archangel Gabriel was displeased with Muhammad. He reappeared to Muhammad and rebuked him. "What have you done? You have read to these people something I did not bring you from God"[3] In his attempt to reach out to the idolaters in Mecca and seek a compromise that would put an end to the animosity and contempt, Muhammad had stumbled into the sin of *Shirk*—idolatry. Alarmed by the rebuke, Muhammad quickly repented and became fearful that he would now face divine retribution—in this life as well as the next. Yet, remarkably, rather than visiting him with divine judgment, Allah offered to him mercy by sending down a new surah that corrected the old.

Muhammad then returned to the Ka'ba altar and recanted the previous surah with the presentation of a new surah. As he spoke, he abrogated his previous confirmation of the three Arabic goddesses. He also confessed that the origin of the words (verses) were from Satan. Hence, they were—in so many words—Satanic words (verses). The Meccan people were understandably insulted by this turn of events. In their anger, they pledged increased opposition and hostility to Muhammad and his nascent Muslim community. Moreover, when news of this reversal reached the Muslims who were now in route to Mecca, many aborted their journey and return to Abyssinia. A few continued to Mecca and stood in solidarity with Muhammad.

The net result of the episode was fourfold: (a) Muhammad was relieved of his failure and restored to his relationship with Allah, (b) the doctrine of Tauhid (absolute monotheism) was reaffirmed and polytheism resolutely rejected, (c) the faith of some of the Muslim believers was troubled, with some abandoning Muhammad altogether, and (d)

Muhammad's opponents in Mecca refused to forget the affair.

---

[1] See Hans Küng, *Islam: Past, Present & Future*, pp. 100-103. Küng's account provides a useful summary of this controversy.
[2] Ibn Ishaq, *The Life of Muhammad*, p. 166.
[3] Ibid.

———•◆•———

The "Satanic Verses" *do not now* appear in the Qur'an, and whether they were ever there is a matter of controversy. Most Muslims believe they never existed. Things are complicated by the fact that Tabari included two different and conflicting accounts of these verses, so it is hard to know which (if either) is correct. One story suggests that members of the Quraysh tried to make a deal with Muhammad about accepting the goddesses; in the other version, the impression is given that Muhammad himself was searching to find a way to combine his revelation with the received tradition. Tabari may simply have been recounting alternate versions of the history and allowing his readers to choose which if either they wished to accept. The whole controversy heated up enormously in 1988 with the publication of Salman Rushdie's *Satanic Verses*, which Muslims believe to be an attack on the Qur'an and which earned Rushdie a notorious *fatwa* calling for his death.

—Diane Morgan, *Essential Islam*, pp. 116, 117

The Satanic verses incident has naturally caused Muslims acute embarrassment for centuries. Indeed, it casts a shadow over the veracity of Muhammad's entire claim to be a prophet.

—Robert Spencer, *The Truth About Muhammad*, p. 82

The affair of *The Satanic Verses*, culminating in the *fatwa* pronounced by the Ayatollah Khomeini against its author, Salman Rushdie, has reverberated round the world. It has been a dramatic demonstration of globalization. Islamists have been mobilized in response to the threat that the price of inclusion in a global system dominated by non-Islamic cultures is surrender of the core belief in the immutable sacredness of the Qur'an. Islamists are seeking not to reverse globalization but to shape the global reality (Beyer 1994)...The story of the satanic verses is dangerous because it threatens both the integrity of the Qur'an and the character of the Prophet...The *fatwa* pronounced by the Ayatollah...was addressed to "all intrepid Muslims in the world," calling them to act against the author and his accomplices "wherever they may be" (Kepel 1997:137-140).

—Alan Aldridge,*Religion in the Contemporary World*, p. 135

them guidance from their Lord.

24 Shall man have what he desires?

25 But God's is the hereafter and the present!

26 How many an angel in the heaven!—their intercession avails not at all, save after God has given permission to whomsoever He will and is pleased with!

27 Verily, those who believe not in the hereafter do surely name the angels with female names!

28 —but they have no knowledge thereof; they do but follow suspicion, and, verily, suspicion shall not avail against the truth at all!

Turning aside

29 But turn aside from him who turns

his back upon our remembrance and desires naught but this world's life!

30 This is their sum of knowledge; verily, thy Lord knows best who has erred from His way, and He knows best who is guided!

31 God's is what is in the heavens and what is in the earth, that He may reward those who do evil for what they have done; and may reward those who do good with good!

32 those who shun great sins and iniquities,—all but venial faults,— verily, thy Lord is of ample forgiveness; He knows best about you, when He produced you from the earth, and when ye were embryos in the wombs of your mothers. Make not yourselves out,

not genuine goddesses. Those who worshipped them, Muhammad explained, were lusting after them.

53.26 Even angels in Paradise, said Muhammad, have no intercessory effect upon Allah, apart from those whom Allah "has given permission" (see **Divine Forgiveness in Islam** on pp. 158-161).

53.29-30 Muhammad said that people were not to turn their back upon "our remembrance" (divine revelation). Since Allah is all-knowing, one must guard his or her mind and thoughts diligently to avoid lapses into polytheism.

53.31 *He rewards those* — A major theme in the Qur'an is that one's salvation is based upon one's merits. That is, Allah rewards evil people with evil and good people with good (see Q 103.3, note).

53.32a *shun great sins and iniquities* —

Since one's salvation was believed to be based upon a meritoriously lived life, people were duly warned to "shun great sins and iniquities," the greatest of which is the sin of Shirk—idolatry.

53.32b *venial faults* — In the Islamic faith, a venial fault is a lesser sin that will not bear significant weight at the Last Judgment; that is, it will have little effect in tipping the celestial balance away from Paradise. Moreover, Allah is willing to forgive venial faults.

53.32c *Make not yourselves out, then, to be pure* — That is, do not deceive yourselves into thinking that you have never sinned. Christians agree with this sentiment. Sinless perfection is not possible in this life. Those who think otherwise, said John Calvin, are "Cyclopes and monsters in heresy...who speak so much of perfection in holiness" (*Commentary on the Book of*

then, to be pure; He knows best
who it is that fears.

Three Questions

33　Hast thou considered him who
　　turns his back?
34　who gives but little and then stops?
35　Has he then the knowledge of the
　　unseen, so that he can see?
36　Has he not been informed of what
　　is in the pages of Moses
37　and Abraham who fulfilled his
　　word?
38　—that no burdened soul shall bear
　　the burden of another?
39　and that man shall have only that
　　for which he strives;
40　and that his striving shall at length
　　be seen?

*The wicked will be rewarded
with destruction*

41　Then shall he be rewarded for it
　　with the most full reward;
42　and that unto thy Lord is the limit;
43　and that it is He who makes men
　　laugh and weep;
44　and that it is He who kills and
　　makes alive;
45　and that He created pairs, male and
　　female,
46　from a clot when it is emitted;
47　and that for Him is the next pro-
　　duction;
48　and that he enriches and gives pos-
　　session:
49　and that He is the Lord of the Dog-
　　star,
50　and that He it was who destroyed
　　'Âd of yore,
51　and Thamûd, and left none of them;
52　and the people of Noah before
　　them,—verily, they were most un-
　　just and outrageous!
53　And the overthrown (cities) He

Psalms, 5:250).
53.33-37 Muhammad encouraged his listeners to consider three questions: (a) Have
you considered him who has turned his back
on Allah and lives only for this world? (b)
Does the one who has rejected Allah have a
genuine awareness of spiritual truth...the
unseen? (c) Does such an individual know
what is in the writings of Moses and Abraham? With each question, Muhammad made
the point that nobody shall bear the burdens of another. Each person will stand before Allah alone and the Last Judgment (see
Q 35.18; cf. Gal 6:7-9).
53.41-54 Allah is sovereign over His entire
creation. Nothing occurs without His permission or enablement.

53.46 Here Muhammad claimed that people
are made from "a clot when it is emitted"
(see Q 96.2, note).
53.49 *He is the Lord of the Dog-star* —
That is, Allah is the Lord of the star Sirius, a
star of the first magnitude, belonging to the
constellation Canis Major (the Big Dog Constellation). The star was widely worshipped
and believed to possess enormous astrological power. The term "The Dog Days of Summer," for example, is associated with this star.
It was believed to generate the hot and
sultry weather patterns in summer. Also, the
summer flooding of the Nile was associated
with this star. Muhammad's point is that Allah is Lord even of Sirius, and by extension
sovereign over those who worship Sirius.

threw down;

54   and there covered them what did cover them!

Final Appeal

55   Which then of your Lord's benefits do ye dispute?
56   This is a warner, one of the warners of yore!
57   The approaching day approaches;
58   there is none to discover it but God.
59   At this new discourse then do ye wonder?
60   and do ye laugh and not weep?
61   and ye divert yourselves the while!

62   But adore God and serve (Him).

Surah 32

In the name of the merciful and compassionate God.

1   A. L. M.

Qur'an

2   The revelation of the Book, there is no doubt therein, from the Lord of the worlds.
3   Do they say, "He has forged it"?

53.50-54 *Ad, Thamud, and the people of Noah* — Muhammad's point was that all these peoples were unjust and were therefore overthrown by Allah (see Q 17. 15b, note; **The Apostles** on pp. 396-398).

53.57 *the approaching day approaches* — That is, the day of the Last Judgment is approaching.

53.61 *and divert yourselves the while* — That is, while you are indulging in a variety of diversions and entertainments, you fail to weep because of the approaching day of the Last Judgment.

In the New Testament, Jesus made a similar observation of the attitudes of the unrighteous. He said: "As it was in the days of Noah, so it will be at the coming of the Son of Man. For in the days before the flood, people were eating and drinking, marrying and giving in marriage, up to the day Noah entered the ark; and they knew nothing about what would happen until the flood came and took them all away. That is how it will be at the coming of the Son of Man"

(Matt 24:37-39). John Calvin observed: "Nothing is more abominable in the sight of God than the contempt of divine truth" (*Commentary on Jeremiah* 1:345).

Surah 32. The title of this surah, *The Adoration*, comes from verse 15. Its main thought is that the Qur'an is consistent with the message of the prophets found in the Old Testament. Just as Allah judged the children of Israel for their disobedience, the people of Mecca would be judged similarly by Allah for their disobedience.

32.1 Literally, *Alif Lam Mim.* About a quarter of the surahs are preceded by mysterious Arabic letters such as the ones in this verse. Of the twenty-eight letters in the Arabic alphabet, exactly one half are found in these prefaces. Some scholars have suggested that they are the initials of the scribes of those who originally wrote down the surahs. Others have suggested that they are oblique references to Allah. Most scholars, however, affirm that no explanation is compelling or even marginally satisfactory.

Nay! it is the truth from thy Lord, that thou mayest warn a people, to whom no warner has come before thee, haply they may be guided.

The Creation Story

4   God it is who created the heavens and the earth and what is between the two in six days; then He made for the throne! ye have no patron beside Him and no intercessor; are ye not then mindful?

5   He governs the affair from the heaven unto the earth; then shall it ascend to him in a day, the measure of which is as a thousand years of what ye number.

6   That is He who knows the unseen and the visible; the mighty, the merciful,

7   who has made the best of the creation of everything, and produced the creation of man from clay;

8   then He made his stock from an extract of despicable water;

9   then He fashioned him and breathed into him of His spirit, and made for you hearing and eyesight and hearts;—little is it that ye give thanks!

General Resurrection

10   And they say, "When we are lost in the earth, shall we then become a new creation?" Nay! in the meeting of their Lord they disbelieve.

The letters remain a mystery.

32.2 *the Book* — divine revelation. In this case, the eternal Book of God that resides in Paradise and was revealed piecemeal in the various surahs of the Qur'an (see **The Perspicuous Book** on pp. 178-179).

32.3 *He has forged it* — A common complaint of the people of Mecca was that Muhammad wrote his own surahs. He then falsified their origin by declaring to the people of Mecca that they came to him via the archangel Gabriel who, in turn, received them from Allah.

In the centuries since Muhammad, this accusation that the Qur'an is not inspired of God has persisted, up to and including the present age. Indeed, one of the fundamental issues separating Jews and Christians from Muslims turns on this question: are the qur'anic surahs of human or divine origin?

32.4-9 This passage in based upon Gen 1:1 to Gen 2:7, the classic passage in the Bible that describes the creation of the heavens and the earth.

32.5 *a thousand years* — Muhammad's point is that a thousand years on the earth is regarded as merely the passing of a single day in Paradise. The Bible makes a similar claim: "For a thousand years in your sight are like a day that has just gone by, or like a watch in the night" (Ps 90:4; cf. 2 Pet 3:8).

32.7-8 *the creation of man from clay, then he made his stock from an extract of despicable water* — Again, Muhammad explained the way in which God fashioned man (see Q 96.2, note). In this case, man came from an extract of sewer water.

32.11 *angel of death* — An angel whose charge is to cause one to die at an appointed time. In the Roman Catholic Church, the

11   Say, "The angel of death shall take you away, he who is given charge of you; then unto your Lord shall ye be returned."

12   And couldst thou see when the sinners hang down their heads before their Lord, "O Lord! we have seen and we have heard; send us back then and we will do right. Verily, we are sure!"

Hell

13   Had we pleased we would have given to everything its guidance; but the sentence was due from me—I will surely fill hell with the ginns and with men all together:

14   So taste ye, for that ye forgat the meeting of this day of yours—verily, we have forgotten you! and taste ye the torment of eternity for that which ye have done!

Paradise

15   They only believe in our signs who when they are reminded of them fall down adoring and celebrate the praises of their Lord, and are not too big with pride.

16   As their sides forsake their beds, they call upon their Lord with fear and hope; and of what we have bestowed upon them do they give alms.

17   No soul knows what is reserved for them of cheerfulness for eye, as a reward for that which they have done!

18   Is he who is a believer like him who is a sinner? they shall not be held equal.

19   As for those who believe and do right, for them are the gardens of resort, an entertainment for that which they have done!

---

archangel Michael is called the Death Angel. At the time of death, Michael transports the spirits of the deceased into the arms of God.
32.13 Muhammad believed that if Allah so willed, He could have filled Hell with "the ginns and with men all together"—and have done so without empathy or compassion.

In contrast, the Bible presents God as burdened and saddened by the sinfulness of people, finding no pleasure in damnation of those who refuse the Gospel of Jesus Christ. "The Lord is not slow in keeping his promise, as some understand slowness. He is patient with you, not wanting anyone to perish, but everyone to come to repentance" (2 Pet 3:9; cf. 1 Tim 2:4).
32.14 Those who are cast into Hell will be

known as the Forgotten Ones.
32.15 *our signs* — That is, divine revelation, the message of the Qur'an. According to Islam, true believers are called upon to listen to the Qur'an, fall down, make obeisance and celebrate the praise of the Lord (see **al-Salat** on pp. 169-170).
32.16 *forsake their beds* — Faithful Muslims are called upon to perform nightly rituals of prayer and worship (see **al-Salat** on pp. 169-170).
32.19a *believe and do right* — These words are repeated often in the Qur'an and serve as a brief summary of the Islamic gospel (see Q 103.3 note).
32.19b *gardens of resort* — The righteous will enter Paradise, which is described as "the

Hell (cont'd)

20   But as for those who commit abomination their resort is the Fire. Every time that they desire to go forth therefrom, we will send them back therein, and it will be said to them, "Taste ye the torment of the fire which ye did call a lie!"

21   and we will surely make them taste of the torment of the nearer torment beside the greater torment— haply they may yet return.

22   Who is more unjust than he who is reminded of the signs of his Lord, and then turns away from them? Verily, we will take vengeance on the sinners!

Jews will be judged

23   And we did give Moses the Book; be not then in doubt concerning the meeting with him; and we made it a guidance to the children of Israel.

24   And we made amongst them high priests who guided by our bidding, since they were patient and were sure of our signs.

25   Verily, thy Lord, he shall decide between them on the resurrection day concerning that whereon they do dispute.

26   Is it not conspicuous to them how many generations we have destroyed before them? they walk over their dwellings! verily, in that are signs: do they not then hear?

27   Have they not seen that we drive the water to the sterile land, and bring forth thereby corn from which their cattle and themselves do eat? do they not then see?

28   And they say, "When shall this decision come if ye do tell the truth?"

---

gardens," where they will enjoy "entertainment for that which they have done." One Hadith records words allegedly spoken by Muhammad: "I establish their honour with My own hand and then set a seal over it...which no eye has seen, no ear has heard and no human mind has perceived and this is substantiated by the Book of Allah, exalted and great" (*Sahih Muslim* 1.83.0363; also see Q 55.46-78 and 56.11-46).

32.20 In addition to casting them into the Fire, Allah will mock the infidels: "Taste the torment of the fire which ye did call a lie."

32.22a *signs of his Lord* — That is, the message of the Qur'an. People in Hell had heard the Qur'an yet turned away from it.

32.22b *we will take vengeance on the sin-* ners — This theme of vengeance is repeated multiple times in the Qur'an, almost endlessly.

32.23 *the Book* — divine revelation. In this case, the eternal Book of God that resides in Paradise and was partially revealed to Moses (see *The Perspicuous Book* on pp. 178-179).

32.23-30 Within the Pentateuch (the first five Books in the Old Testament) are repeated episodes of the "children of Israel" hearing the Word of the Lord, yet turning away from it in disobedience. The implication is that the people of Mecca were disobedient to Allah, similar to the disobedience seen in the children of Israel.

32.29 *the day of the decision* — That is, the day of the Last Judgment.

29   Say, "On the day of the decision
      their faith shall not profit those who
      misbe-lieved, nor shall they be re-
      spited;"
30   turn then from them and wait; ver-
      ily, they are waiting too!

Surah 39

*In the name of the merciful and compas-
sionate God.*

Qur'an

1   The sending down of the Book from
      God, the mighty, the wise.
2   Verily, we have sent down to thee
      the Book in truth, then serve God,
      being sincere in religion unto Him.

The nature of God

3   Aye! God's is the sincere religion:
      and those who take beside Him
      patrons,"We do not serve them
      save that they may bring us near

to God." Verily, God will judge between them concerning that
whereon they do dispute. Verily,
God guides not him who is a
misbelieving liar.
4   Had God wished to take to Him-
      self a child, He would have cho-
      sen what He pleased from what He
      creates;—celebrated be His
      praises! He is God, the one, the
      victorious.
5   He created the heavens and the
      earth in truth! It is He who clothes
      the day with night; and clothes the
      night with day; and subjects the
      sun and the moon, each one runs
      on to an appointed time; aye! He is
      the mighty, the forgiving!
6   He created you from one soul; then
      He made from it its mate; and He
      sent down upon you of the cattle
      four pairs! He creates you in the
      bellies of your mothers,—creation
      after creation, in three darknesses.
      That is God for you! His is the
      kingdom, there is no god but He;
      how then can ye be turned away?

Surah 39. The title of this surah, *The
Troops*, comes from verse 71. Similar to the
previous surah, in this surah Muhammad affirmed the Qur'an as divine revelation and
demanded obedience to Allah, and Allah
alone. The words spoken in v. 53 set the
theme of the surah: "Say, 'O my servants!
who have been extravagant against their own
souls!' Be not in despair of the mercy of God;
verily, God forgives sins, all of them, verily,
He is forgiving, merciful."

39.1-2 *the Book* — divine revelation. In

this case, the eternal Book of Allah that resides in Paradise and was revealed piecemeal
in the various surahs that comprise the
Qur'an (see **The Perspicuous Book** on pp.
178-179).

39.4 Muhammad attacked the polytheism
of his day, the Star Family religious system.
This understanding of religion claimed that
the gods were a large celestial family that
gave birth to new deities (see **Polytheism
in Seventh Century Arabia** on pp. 92-97).

39.7 *if ye be thankless* — A common theme

Ingratitude

7   If ye be thankless, yet is God in-
     dependent of you. He is not
     pleased with ingratitude in His ser-
     vants; but if ye give thanks, He is
     pleased with that in you. But no
     burdened soul shall bear the bur-
     den of another; then unto your
     Lord is your return, and He will
     inform you of that which ye have
     done. Verily, He knows the natures
     of men's breasts!

8   And when distress touches a man
     he calls his Lord, turning repen-
     tant to Him; then when He con-
     fers on him a favour from Him-
     self he forgets what he had called
     upon Him for before, and makes
     peers for God to lead astray from
     His way! Say, "Enjoy thyself in thy
     misbelief a little, verily, thou art of
     the fellows of the Fire."

Submission

9   Shall he who is devout throughout

the night, adoring and standing,
cautious concerning the hereafter,
and hoping for the mercy of his
Lord...? Say, "Shall those who
know be deemed equal with those
who know not? only those will remember, who are endowed with
minds!"

10   Say, "O my servants who believe!
     fear your Lord! for those who do
     well in this world is good, and
     God's earth is spacious; verily, the
     patient shall be paid their hire with-
     out count!"

11   Say, "Verily, I am bidden to serve
     God, being sincere in religion to
     Him;

12   and I am bidden that I be the first
     of those resigned."

13   Say, "Verily, I fear, if I rebel against
     my Lord, the torment of a mighty
     day."

14   Say, "God do I serve, being sin-
     cere in my religion to Him;

15   serve then what ye will beside
     Him!" Say, "Verily, the losers are
     those who lose themselves and

in the Qur'an is that the infidel is a thankless being, especially in regards to his or her relationship to Allah. Yet, said Muhammad, Allah is independent of people, having no need for them. Hence, the ingratitude of people has no direct impact upon Allah. Such individuals only hurt themselves since ingratitude is a sin severely judged at the Last Judgment.

39:9-20 Submission is the primary response of Muslims to Allah, a life of obedience that neither questions nor challenges the Qur'an.

Accordingly, while in prayer, Muslims were instructed to say: "I fear, if I rebel against my Lord, the torment of a mighty day" (Q 39.13; cf. Q 39.20).

The Christian faith defines a believer's relationship with God in terms three distinct attitudes: submission, love, and fear (Jn 13:34-35; 15:17; 1 Jn 4:7; 5:2; cf. Gal 5:22-23; 1 Jn 2:3-6; 4:21). When either of the three takes preeminence over the other two, practical Christian living becomes imbalanced and drifts into error.

their families on the resurrection day. Aye, that is the obvious loss."

16 They shall have over them shades of fire, and under them shades; with that does God frighten His servants: O my servants! then fear me.

17 But those who avoid Tâghût and serve them not, but turn repentant unto God, for them shall be glad tidings.

18 Then give glad tidings to my servants who listen to the word and follow the best thereof; they it is whom God guides, and they it is

who are endowed with minds.

19 Him against whom the word of torment is due,—canst thou rescue him from the fire?

20 But for those who fear their Lord for them are upper chambers, and upper chambers above them built, beneath which rivers flow; God's promise! God does not fail in His promise.

Softness of heart

21 Hast thou not seen that God sends down from the heaven water, and

The notion of fear, however, is not a fear of Hell. That concern had been settled at the time when the Christian embraced the Gospel of Jesus Christ and was pardoned of all sin. The Christian's only fear is in disappointing the One who loved him and made the provision of such a great salvation. John R. W. Stott explains: "Salvation is a big and comprehensive word. It embraces the totality of God's saving work, from beginning to end. In fact salvation has three tenses, past, present, and future. I am myself always grateful to the good man who led me to Christ over forty years ago that he taught me, raw and brash young convert that I was, to keep saying: 'I have been saved (in the past) from the penalty of sin by a crucified Saviour. I am being saved (in the present) from the power of sin by a living Saviour. And I shall be saved (in the future) from the verse presence of sin by a coming Saviour...If therefore you were to ask me, 'Are you saved?' There is only one correct biblical answer which I could give you: 'yes and no.' Yes, in the sense that by the sheer

grace and mercy of God through the death of Jesus Christ my Saviour he has forgiven my sins, justified me and reconciled me to himself. But no, in the sense that I still have a fallen nature and live in a fallen world and have a corruptible body, and I am longing for my salvation to be brought to its triumphant completion" (*Believing and Obeying Jesus Christ*, p. 103).

39.12 *I be the first of those resigned —* That is, I am the first Muslim. The word "Muslim" is an Arabic word that means in submission or resigned. It serves as the central theme in Islam, that which defines the nature of true spirituality.

39.17 *Taghut* — an Arabic word that means idolatry and religious impurity. Anyone who claims to be holy outside of Islam's definition of holiness is *Taghut* (see Q 16.36).

39.20 *beneath which rivers flow* — Repeatedly in the Qur'an is the imagery of Paradise as that of an oasis with well supplied aquifers, an underground river system sufficiently close to the surface to keep the oasis fertile and green (see Q 16.31; 18.31; 20.76;

conducts it into springs in the earth? then He brings forth therewith corn varied in kind, then it dries up, and ye see it grow yellow; then He makes it grit;—verily, in that is a reminder for those endowed with minds.

22   Is he whose breast God has expanded for Islâm, and who is in light from his Lord ...? And woe to those whose hearts are hardened against a remembrance of God! those are in obvious error.

Qur'an

23   God has sent down the best of legends, a book uniform and repeating; whereat the skins of those who fear their Lord do creep! then their skins and their hearts soften at the remembrance of God. That is the guidance of God! He guides therewith whom He will. But he whom God leads astray there is no guide for him.

24   Shall he who must screen himself with his own face from the evil torment on the resurrection day...? And it shall be said of those who do wrong, taste what ye have earned.

25   Those before them called the (prophets) liars, and the torment came to them from whence they perceived it not;

26   and God made them taste disgrace in the life of this world. But surely the torment of the hereafter is greater, if they did but know.

27   We have struck out for men in this Qur'ân every sort of parable, haply they may be mindful.

28   An Arabic Qur'ân with no crookedness therein; haply they may fear!

25.10; 85.11).

39.21 The cycle of vegetation: rain fills the springs on the earth, which brings forth herbage of various colors, which then eventually withers and becomes yellow, and which then is finally crushed and broken into pieces.

39.23a *a book* — divine revelation. In this case, the eternal Book of God that resides in Paradise and was revealed to the various apostles sent from God to the peoples of the world (see **The Perspicuous Book** on pp. 178-179).

39.23b *uniform and repeating* — Muhammad believed that his many surahs were consistent (uniform and repeating). Yet, the abrogated verses speak otherwise (see **The Doctrine of Abrogation** on pp. 68-70).

39.23c *guides therewith whom He will. But he whom God leads astray there is no guide for him* — Allah has predestinated those who will believe and those who will not. Allah leads astray whosoever He wishes. Accordingly, the person has no choice in his or her eternal destiny. This is the Islamic doctrine of double predestination (see **Doctrine of al-Qadar** on pp. 264-266).

39.28 *Arabic Qur'an with no crookedness* — It is commonly believed in the Muslim world that only an Arabic Qur'an possesses no crookedness (deviations, falseness).

All translations of the Qur'an are therefore crooked; that is, they are subject to error and not to be trusted. Curiously, though, the Qur'an contains many non-Ara-

The Parable of the Two Slaves

29   God has struck out a parable, a man
      who has partners who oppose
      each other; and a man who is
      wholly given up to another; shall
      they be deemed equal in similitude?
      praise be to God! nay, but most
      of them know not!
30   Verily, thou shalt die, and, verily,
      they shall die; then, verily,
31   on the resurrection day before your
      Lord shall ye dispute.
32   And who is more unjust than he
      who lies against God, and calls the
      truth a lie when it comes to him?

      Is there not in hell a resort for those
      who misbelieve?
33   but whoso brings the truth and be-
      lieves in it, these are they who fear.
34   For them is what they please with
      their Lord, that is the reward of
      those who do well;
35   that God may cover for them their
      offences which they have done,
      and may reward them with their
      hire for the best of that which they
      have done.

Catachism

36   Is not God sufficient for His ser-

bic words, one being the word "Qur'an" which is of Syrian origin. Some Islamic scholars have attempted to reconcile this discrepancy by claiming that the Qur'an arabicized foreign words found in its pages. Moreover, the Arabic language of the seventh century is different from modern Arabic, since the ancient language did not include the dots, dashes, and commas in its written form. Most modern Arabs cannot read the Qur'an as originally composed, in the seventh century Arabic dialect. This calls into question the requirement for Muslims to read the Qur'an in the Arabic language (see **The Qur'an** on pp. 150-153).

In contrast, the Christian faith encourages people to read the Bible in the common languages of the world. This is not to say that the original languages of the Bible—Hebrew and Greek—do not offer a most precise reading. Rather, the point is that translations of the Bible offer a sufficient understanding of the biblical text, provided that the translations are done with scholarship and

care. They also make available sacred Scripture to people who would have no other way in which to read and understand it.

A case in point is the Septuagint, a Greek translation of the Hebrew Old Testament. In first century Palestine, only a few people spoke and/or read Hebrew. The prevailing language was Aramaic and the *lengua franca* of the Mediterranean world was Greek. Consequently, the Septuagint became the standardized translation of the Old Testament for the early Christians, with the apostles using it in their own writings when citing Old Testament verses.

39.29-35 In the parable, a man has multiple partners, all of whom oppose one another. A second man has only one partner. Which relationship is more equitable and functional? The first relationship is analogous to polytheism whereas the second is analogous to monotheism. At the Last Judgment, Allah will reward those who do well and cast into hell "those who misbelieve."

39.36-66 This catechismal instruction is de-

The Qur'an

The sacred Scripture of the Islamic religion is the Qur'an. It is believed to be of divinely inspired and wholly authoritative, Allah's final and most definitive word for mankind. All Shari'a Law is anchored to the Qur'an. In the following, we will consider six characteristics of the Qur'an.

1. Eternal and uncreated. The Qur'an presents itself as a literal revelation, communicated *verbatim* to Muhammad in the Arabic language. Its sole authorship, then, is Allah. Muhammad neither added to nor paraphrased this revelation in the one hundred fourteen surahs that constitute the Qur'an. The third article of the *Second Great Creed* states: "The Qur'an is the speech of Allah, written in the copies, pre-served in the memories, recited by the tongues, revealed to the Prophet. Our pronouncing, writing and reciting the Qur'an is created, whereas the Qur'an is uncreated."[1] It therefore exists outside of time and his-tory, frozen in its own eternality, and therefore stands as the final word and critique of all cultures in all historical epochs. Moreover, to deface the Qur'an is to deface Allah.

2. Multiple Qur'ans. For orthodox Muslims, the only legitimate Qur'an is the one established under Uthman ibn 'Affan (third caliph) in the seventh century. According to Islamic tradition, Umar ibn al-Khattah (second caliph) was worried that many Muslims who had memorized the Qur'an were killed in the Battle of Yamama in Central Arabia. This was problematic since not all of the Qur'an had been written down. Abu Bakr, the first caliph (successor) ordered that all the pieces of the Qur'anic revelations (those that had been written down and those that had been committed to memory) be gathered and assembled into a single book. His concern was that if this project were not quickly completed, those who had memorized large portions of a number of surahs would die and a knowledge of these surahs would permanently disappear. The project was completed in two years.

Yet, other Muslims in other provinces were engaged in the same activity. They gathered revelations and produced alternate Qur'ans.

The back story to these alternate Qur'ans is that Muslims in distant provinces rejected the authority of a centralized caliphate. They wished to remain Muslim, yet with no political ties to the caliph. When Uthman (the third caliph) learned of the existence of alternate Qur'ans, he sent copies of his Qur'an to Kufa, Basra, Damascus, and kept his copy in Mecca. He also ordered all other versions to be destroyed.

   3. Not the pure Word of God. Since Islam insists that the Qur'an was dictated word-for-word by the angel Gabriel to Muhammad, some Islamic scholars do not view the Qur'an as the pure word of God. When Allah speaks, it is the word of God. When the speaker in the text is Muhammad or angels, it is not (e.g., Q 19.64-65; 36.36-38). The *Second Great Creed* makes this point in article three. It states:

> Whatever Allah quotes in the Kuran [Qur'an] from Moses or other Prophets, from Pharaoh or from Satan, is the speech of Allah in relation to theirs. The speech of Allah is uncreated, but the speech of Moses and the other creatures is created. The Kuran [Qur'an] is the speech of Allah and as such from eternity, not theirs.[2]

This observation, however, is troublesome to some Muslims. They have tried to overcome this problem by adding the word "say" in front of the statements attributed to Muhammad or the angels. With this addition, Allah is understood to be commanding Muhammad or the angels to speak certain words—causing those passages to also be the word of Allah. Still, this requires a tampering with the Qur'an which is not permitted by Islamic law.

   4. The Qur'an includes non-Arabic words. Repeatedly in the Qur'an, it is stated that it is written in the Arabic language (Q 12.2; 20.113; 26.195; 39.28; 41.3, 44; 43.3). In addition, the original Qur'an is said to be in Heaven, eternal (no beginning or end), and written in the sacred Arabic tongue—the *lingua sacra*. To assert that within the Qur'an are non-Arabic words, then, is to assault the very foundation of the Islamic faith. Abu 'Ubaida, companion to Muhammad, wrote: "Whoever pretends that there is in the Qur'an anything other than the Arabic tongue has made a serious charge against God."[3]

   Nevertheless, both Islamic and non-Islamic scholars have identified a large quantity of non-Arabic words in the Qur'an. Islamic scholar al-Suyuti, for example, has identified 107 foreign words in the Qur'an—Aramaic, Hebrew, Syriac, Ethiopic, Persian, and Greek. Remarkably, the word *Qur'an* itself is a Syriac word.

   Another Islamic scholar, ath-Tha'alibi, seemingly solved this dilemma by admitting the foreign words are found in the Qur'an but that "the Arabs made use of them and Arabicized them, so from this point of view they are Arabic."[4]

5. The Qur'an possesses variant readings. A singular interpretation of the Qur'an is not possible. This is because, say Islamic scholars, the Qur'an was originally *scripto defectiva*.

- The Qur'an was originally unpointed—that is, without dots. It was impossible to distinguish a "b" from a "t" or "th." This created the problem of confusing one word for another.

- The Qur'an originally lacked dashes and commas. Without dashes and commas, the reader had no way of knowing which vowels were intended for each word. This further confused the reader since different vowels resulted in different words.

With time, dots, dashes and commas were added to overcome this confusion. It became, what Islamic scholars call, *scripto plena*. Still, not everyone was in agreement with which dots, dashes and commas were the correct choices. Currently, the Islamic faith recognizes seven alternate readings of the Qur'an (that is, seven different arrangements of dots, dashes and commas; some Islamic traditions recognize fourteen different arrangements). The authorized text of the Qur'an is the Cairo version, also known as the Egyptian version (compiled in 1923-1924). Still, during the recitations of the Qur'an in mosques, all recognized variants can be recited. "Muslims interpreted this variety of possible readings as a blessing, not a curse for the community, and all accepted readings were deemed to have come ultimately from Muhammad himself."[5]

6. The Qur'an contains internal contradictions. Islamic scholars acknowledge that certain words revealed to Muhammad on one occasion were contradicted by words revealed to him at a later date. The Qur'an anticipated this problem and solved it by stating: "Whatever verses we cancel or cause you to forget, we bring a better or its like" (Q 2.105). Verses that are cancelled are called *mansukh* and those that replace them are called *nasikh*.

This is the famous Doctrine of Abrogation. It employs the logic of chronology and progressive revelation. This doctrine has resulted in Islamic scholarship spending much time attempting to determine which *surahs* (chapters) were of the Meccan period and which were of the Medinan period. Also, in each of the periods, which verses come before others? That is another question scholars are attempting to answer.

---

[1] See Arent J. Wensinck, *The Muslim Creed*, p. 189. Curiously, during the caliphates of al-Ma'mun, al-Mu'tasim, and al-Watiq (813-847), an inquisition took place in the Islamic world where all who claimed that the Qur'an was *uncreated* were charged with the sin of idolatry (that is, they were accused of ascribing an attribute to the Qur'an that was reserved for Allah alone). Such people were tortured and put to death. Most Muslims, however, grit their teeth and acquiesced the caliph's view, hoping that eventually the inquisition would cease and the doctrine of the uncreatedness of the Qur'an would be embraced once again. In 847, the doctrine of the uncreatedness of the Qur'an was reinstated throughout the Islamic empire.

If the doctrine of the createdness of the Qur'an would have persisted, it could have been the basis for a textual-critical Islamic theology, which in turn could have opened the Islamic world to a fully considered historical-critical analysis of the Qur'an. Again, in turn, this could have blunted the duration and imperiousness of Shari'a Law in the Muslim world. Yet, regrettably, this did not happen.

[2] Ibid.

[3] Cited in Anwar G. Chejne, *The Arabic Language: Its Role in History*, p. 9.

[4] Cited in Arthur Jeffery, *The Foreign Vocabulary of the Qur'an*, p. 10; also see Hans Küng, *Islam: Past, Present & Future*, pp. 35, 36.

[5] William A. Graham and Navid Kermani, *The Cambridge Companion to the Qur'an*, p. 117; also see Küng, *Islam: Past, Present & Future*, pp. 69, 70.

Considered by Muslim and Western scholars alike to be the finest work of Classical Arabic rhymed prose, the Qur'an still forms the bedrock of all Islamic learning because it is usually held to be the Word of God. With the exception of the opening verses and a few passages where Muhammad or Gabriel is the speaker, the speaker is God Himself, who speaks in the *pluralis majestatis* ("We"), the first person singular ("I") or the third person singular ("He"). Along with the Torah and the Bible, it can legitimately claim to be one of the most influential books of all time.

—Hunt Janin, *The Pursuit of Learning in the Islamic World*, p. 31

Most of the cultural vocabulary of the Qur'an is of non-Arabic origin...Quite early in the history of Islam, Muslims themselves were confronted with the perplexing problem of these foreign words...It is clear that in the earliest circle of exegetes it was fully recognized and frankly admitted that there were numerous foreign words in the Qur'an. Only a little later, however, when the dogma of the eternal nature of the Qur'an was being elaborated, this was strenuously denied.

—Arthur Jeffery, *The Foreign Vocabulary of the Qur'an*, pp. 2, 5

Muslims believe that the Qur'an contains the exact words revealed by God to the PropheMuhammad.

—Randa A. Kayyali, *The Arab Americans*, p. 13

All Muslims, regardless of their native language, memorize and recite the Qur'an in Arabic, the language in which it was revealed, whether they fully understand this language or not. So too, all over the world, regardless of their local language, when Muslims pray they do so in Arabic. Until modern times, the Qur'an was printed in Arabic only. Even now, in translations, which more correctly are viewed by Muslims as "interpretations," the Arabic text is often printed alongside.

—John L. Esposito, *What Everyone Needs to Know About Islam*, p. 10

From this discussion the meaning of the outward and inward aspects of the Qur'an has become clear. It has also become evident that the inner meaning of the Qur'an does not eradicate or invalidate its outward meaning. Rather, it is like the soul which gives life to the body.

—Muhammad Husayn Tabataba'i, *Shi'ite Islam*, p. 98

A Muslim who believes in the Qur'an as the word of Allah cannot dare to differ with the Qur'an. If you do not see eye to eye with the Divine book, you are free to differ but only after denouncing faith in Islam...But the difficulty with our learned writer and the like, brought up in west-oriented institutions, is that they do not have the courage to adopt the first course [belief in the Qur'an] and feel ashamed of taking to the second course [denouncing faith in Islam]. They have, there-fore, taken to a middle course, which is quite illogical. They insist on being accepted as Muslims, claim to be desirous of the name and fame of Islam, and express great concern for Islam and Muslims, yet they speak and work against Islam...They do not spare even the holy Qur'an from their criticism, and hit at the very foundations of Islam.

—Syed Maududi, *Modernist and Fundamentalist Debates in Islam*, pp. 211, 212

Historical-critical study of the Qur'an is difficult to reconcile with the foundational principles of Islamic faith. This study has therefore been conducted almost exclusively by scholars outside the Islamic community—and often with polemical as well as academic aims.

—Maria Massi Dakake, *Crisis, Call, and Leadership in the Abrahamic Traditions*, p. 191

The Qur'an, like the Jewish Torah and the Christian Bible, has inspired a vast library of exegesis, exposition, and commentary. Only recently have some scholars begun to apply the methods of historical-critical analysis to the text of the Qur'an. Most Muslims regard this enterprise with disdain and see it as an example of unbelief and spiritual imperialism.

—Timothy George, *Is the Father of Jesus the God of Muhammad?*, p. 44

vants? and yet they would frighten thee with those beside Him.

37   But he whom God leads astray there is no guide for him; and he whom God guides there is none to lead him astray: is not God mighty, the Lord of vengeance?

38   And if thou shouldst ask them who created the heavens and the earth, they will surely say, "God!" Say, "Have ye considered what ye call on beside God? If God wished me harm, could they remove His harm? or did He wish me mercy, could they withhold His mercy?" Say, "God is enough for me, and on Him rely those who rely."

39   Say, "O my people! act according to your power; I too am going to act; and ye shall know."

40   He to whom the torment comes it shall disgrace him, and there shall alight upon him lasting torment.

41   Verily, we have sent down to thee the Book for men in truth; and whosoever is guided it is for his own soul: but whoso goes astray it is against them, and thou art not a guardian for them.

42   God takes to Himself souls at the time of their death; and those which do not die (He takes) in their sleep; and He holds back those on whom He has decreed death, and

signed to help the Muslim believer understand the basic arguments related to the monotheist-polytheist controversy. Rather than being divided into distinct questions and answers, an approach which characterizes most catechisms, this catechism is less structured with questions and answers blending into a less regimented discussion. The catechism begins with the question: "Is not God [Allah] sufficient for His servants?" (v. 36). The implied answer is yes. Seven reasons follow: (a) Allah is sovereign over all creation, His kingdom extends over Paradise and earth, (b) the gods worshipped by the polytheists have no control over anything, (c) the gods cannot affect the will of Allah, (d) Allah alone is the intercessor for mankind, (e) Allah alone possesses the keys to both Paradise and Hell, (f) Allah alone determines who receives blessings and who do not, and (g) Allah will extend forgiveness and mercy to those who have served lesser gods and have repented and turned to Him.

39.37 Due to the sovereignty of Allah, one's eternal destiny is foreordained (see **The Doctrine of al-Qadar** on pp. 264-266).

39.41a *the Book* — divine revelation. In this case, this is the eternal Book of Allah in Paradise that was revealed piecemeal in the various surahs that comprise the Qur'an. According to the Qur'an, it is "the Book of truth for men." Each person is responsible to believe and embrace the Qur'an (see **The Perspicuous Book** on pp. 178-179).

39.41b *thou art not a guardian for them* — That is, Muhammad is not responsible for the eternal destiny of those to whom he ministered. The attitude is that of a cold disinterest. The New Testament speaks otherwise of its ministers. The Apostle Paul was deeply burdened for the spiritual destiny of others (Rom 9:1-3; cf. see Jer 9:1; Lk 19:41-44; Rom 10:1; Phil 3:8).

39.42 *sends others back till their appointed time* — That is, Allah restores to life some who have entered into a death-like coma.

sends others back till their appointed time—verily, in that are signs unto a people who reflect.

43 Do they take besides God intercessors? Say, "What! though they have no control over anything and have no sense."

44 Say, "God's is the intercession, all of it; His is the kingdom of the heavens and the earth; then unto Him shall ye be sent back."

45 And when Allah alone is mentioned, the hearts of those who do not believe in the hereafter shrink, and when those besides Him are mentioned, lo! they are joyful.

46 Say, "O God! originator of the heavens and the earth, who knowest the unseen and the vis-

ible, thou wilt judge between thy servants concerning that whereon they do dispute!"

47 And had those who do wrong all that is in the earth, and the like thereof with it, they would ransom themselves therewith from the evil of the torment on the resurrection day! but there shall appear to them from God that which they had not reckoned on;

48 and the evils of what they have earned shall appear to them; but that shall close in on them at which they mocked!

49 And when harm touches man he calls on us; then, when we grant him favour from us, he says, "Verily, I am given it through knowl-

39.43 *Do they take besides God intercessors?* — The pagan polytheists of Arabia pleaded with their gods to intercede on their behalf; e.g., to restore their health and/or wealth. Muhammad insisted that these gods have no such power (see **Divine Forgiveness in Islam** on pp. 158-161).

39.44 *God's is the intercession, all of it* — That is, Allah intercedes on the earth performing His perfect will. Islamic scholar Muhammad Asad asserts that the Qur'an rejects the popular teaching that was developing within the Church of the seventh century of the unqualified intercession by dead saints. Rather, as is presented elsewhere in the Qur'an (e.g., in Q 20.109; 21.28; 34.23), Allah will grant to His prophets on Judgment Day the permission to offer a symbolic prayer of intercession. Being symbolic, it will have no effectual bearing on the fate of the person that will receive the prayer (*The Mes-

sage of the Qur'an* p. 325; and **Divine Forgiveness in Islam** on pp. 158-161).

The prayer is a symbolic exercise since (a) such intercessions were already included in Allah's sovereign will, and (b) Allah foreordained the eternal destiny of the person in question (see **The Doctrine of al-Qadar** on pp. 264-266).

39.46-56 According to Muhammad, infidels will offer all their wealth as a ransom to Allah at the Last Judgment, not knowing that Allah has no interest in their wealth.

In contrast, that which is required of infidels is the following: (a) repentance, (b) embracing the forgiveness of Allah, and (c) obedience to the teachings found in the Qur'an—"follow the best of what has been sent down to you from your Lord" (Q 39.55), lest a soul should say: "O my sighing! for what I have neglected towards God!" (Q 39.56).

edge!" nay, it is a trial,—but most of them do not know!

50 Those before them said it too, but that availed them not which they had earned,

51 and there befell them the evil deeds of what they had earned: and those who do wrong of these (Meccans), there shall befall them too the evil deeds of what they had earned, nor shall they frustrate Him.

52 Have they not known that God extends His provision to whom He pleases, or doles it out? verily, in that are signs unto a people who believe.

53 Say, "O my servants! who have been extravagant against their own souls!" be not in despair of the mercy of God; verily, God forgives sins, all of them; verily, He is forgiving, merciful.

54 But turn repentant unto your Lord, and resign yourselves to Him, before there comes on you torment! then ye shall not be helped:

55 and follow the best of what has been sent down to you from your Lord, before there come on you the torment suddenly, ere ye can perceive!

56 Lest a soul should say, "O my sighing! for what I have neglected towards God! for, verily, I was amongst those who did jest!"

57 or lest it should say, "If God had but guided me, I should surely have been of those who fear!"

58 or lest it should say, when it sees the torment, "Had I another turn I should be of those who do well!"

39.53 *God forgives sins, all of them* — This statement does not contradict the dominant teaching in the Qur'an of salvation by personal merit: "believe and do right" (that is, the Doctrine of Salvation by Works). The grace of divine forgiveness is only given to those who have earned forgiveness with lives full of righteous deeds (see **Divine Forgiveness in Islam** on pp. 158-161, and **The Last Judgment** on pp. 46-50).

This understanding of divine forgiveness, then, precludes the possibility of deathbed conversions. Repentance "is not for those who do evil, until, when death comes before one of them, he says, 'Now I turn again;' nor yet for those who die in misbelief. For such as these have we prepared a grievous woe" (Q 4.18).

39.54 *resign yourselves to Him* — surren-

der completely to do the will of Allah and "follow the best of what has been sent down to you from your Lord" in the form of divine revelation (the Qur'an). Otherwise, "there will come upon you torment."

In contrast, the Christian faith asserts that a Christian need not fear divine torment. Salvation is a divine gift procured through the work of Jesus Christ. Oswald Chambers wrote: "The one thing Satan tries to shake is our confidence in God...Satan may shake that as much as he likes, but he cannot shake the fact that God remains faithful (see 2 Tim 2:13) and we must not cast away our confidence in Him" (*The Pilgrim's Song Book*, p. 28).

39.58 *Had I another turn* — That is, had I another opportunity to live my life over again.

Divine Forgiveness
in Islam

Similar to both Judaism and Christianity, Islam is also a religion that makes the case that with God the notion of divine forgiveness exists. Yet, it stands apart since Islam also insists upon the notion of individual merit. That is, in Islam eternal salvation is still a matter of one's righteous behavior. It is the blending of the two that makes Islam's understanding of divine forgiveness unique concept among the religions of the world.

The first, and most dominant of the two, is that a person's eternal fate is determined by the level of righteousness displayed while alive on the earth (Q 6.3; 16.111; 39.70; 45.22; 74.38). Repeatedly, the Qur'an mentions a balance present at the Last Judgment which measures the quantity and quality of one's deeds. Dependent upon the outcome of this judgment, a person will be sent into either Paradise or Hell.

The second, and less dominant, is that Allah will forgive a person's sins. He offers and withholds forgiveness according to his own sovereign will. On what basis, then, is divine forgiveness granted? In short, it too must be earned. Divine forgiveness is offered only to those who have shown themselves worthy of divine forgiveness. It is not bequeathed to those who are fundamentally unrighteous and thereby unworthy. Daniel C. Peterson explains, "He forgives those who sin ignorantly, but repent quickly (Q 4.17). He does not, however, forgive those who reject faith and persist in evildoing, and is unlikely to forgive repeated apostasy."[1] The Qur'an, Ian Markham and Ibrahim Özdemi add, "takes into consideration and allows for the reality of human failure by urging believers to return to God in repentance, seeking forgiveness, and starting over."[2]

The one exception is intercessory prayer. Provided that the one interceding on behalf of another is exceedingly righteous, Allah may listen and respond positively. More will be said of this in the section below.

Moderate Islam follows the above scheme, yet differs on the question of one's worthiness. Forgiveness is offered liberally, with little concern on questions related to striving to live righteously. In her book, *The Pure and Powerful: Studies in Contemporary Muslim Society*, Nadia Abu-Zahra adds, "Islamic discourse on mortuary rites in Egypt centres on the subject of divine forgiveness. It includes belief in the creed of Islam, which promises that those who believe in Islam will be forgiven their sins on the Day of Judgement, for belief in Islam is the key to Paradise."[3] Conspicuously absent, however, is the requirement of a righteous lifestyle.

Intercessory Prayer. The Qur'an also encourages intercessory prayer. Both angels (Q 40.7-9) and people (Q 4.85) are said to be able to intercede with Allah to cause Him to do their bidding. People are encouraged to pray for themselves, that they will live faithful lives before Allah. Muhammad wrote, "O my Lord! make me enter with a just entry; and make me come forth with a just coming forth, and grant me from Thee authority to aid" (Q 17.80; cf. Q 2.152, 186; 40.60). Moreover, in a Hadith, it is stated: "O Allah! We used to ask our Prophet to invoke You for rain, and You would bless us with rain, and now we ask his uncle to invoke You for rain. O Allah! Bless us with rain. And so it would rain."[4]

Yet it is in the afterlife, when at the Last Judgment, that intercession has the most lasting and profound effect. People who have lived godly lives, yet not sufficiently godly to merit Paradise, may receive the intercession of angels and Muhammad with the intent of encouraging Allah to allow them entrance into Paradise.

The Doctrine of Intercessory Prayer in Islam, however, has posed a problem for Islamic theologians. The problem turns on two questions: (a) how does this doctrine harmonize with the view of divine election, where Allah has chosen a person's eternal fate in eternity past? and (b) how does this doctrine harmonize with the teaching of meritocracy—that is, salvation via individual righteous deeds?

- Some Islamic scholars believe that both prayer and the outcome of prayer have been planned by Allah in eternity past. They neither compete with His sovereign plan nor alter His predetermined will. Other scholars understand intercessory prayer to be a mere symbolic gesture that has no meaningful role in determining an individual's fate in the afterlife.

- Some Islamic scholars believe that intercessory prayer is efficacious, provided that the beneficiaries of the petition are already fundamentally righteous people. Other scholars, however, are more aggressive in their response and deny any role of intercessory prayer within Islam. The practice is looked upon as a form of idol worship that typifies other religions, such as Christianity, and therefore to be shunned altogether.

- In the popular world of folk Islam, however, intercessory prayer is looked upon as efficacious. Provided that the one offering the prayer is a righteous individual, Allah is predisposed to respond approvingly to the petition.

Hence, when it comes to the purpose and value of intercessory prayer, Islam is divided. It has no singular authoritative voice on the matter. This, I believe, is because the Qur'an itself did not clarify the relationship of intercessory prayer with the sovereign will of Allah.

Christian response. Christianity rejects the Islamic understanding of divine forgiveness. In the early centuries of the church, the notion of salvation being a combination of faith and good works with divine pardon granted to only those who have attained to a life of righteousness emerged. It was called Pelagianism. Pelagianism was condemned at the Council of Carthage in 418 and then ratified as a heresy at the Council of Ephesus in 431.

The premise of Pelagianism is that man must earn divine forgiveness by means of righteous behavior. Yet, this is not a difficult endeavor, said Pelagius, since (a) God "so designed and ordered things that there is a natural tendency towards good and away from evil," (b) Jesus Christ is Savior inasmuch as He is the perfect guide, encouraging people to obey "his commands without question," and (c) people have within themselves "the freedom and power to choose between good and evil."[5] The onus of salvation, then, resides with the individual and is awarded to only those whose lives were well lived. In Pelagianism, then, the Cross of Jesus Christ is nothing more than an example of self-sacrifice for a righteous cause. The blood of Jesus has no essential efficacy in the atoning of one's sins.

Augustine of Hippo (354-430) was one of the major Christian theologians who refuted Pelagianism. He taught:

- Because of universal sin, man was so hopelessly corrupted by the effects of sin to be unable to achieve a life of righteousness.

- Since man was hopelessly corrupted, salvation must come from another source: God Himself. God the Son died on the cross to pay the penalty of sin. God the Father opened the spiritual eyes so that man could rightly understand the purpose of the cross. God the Spirit indwelt and empowered man to act on these beliefs.

Hence, in contrast to Pelagianism, true spirituality is centered on the greatness of God who has redeemed sinful man. It has nothing to do with man either earning salvation via a life of good works or of somehow becoming worthy of divine forgiveness. Our relationship to God is strictly an act of grace, rooted in the Cross of Jesus Christ.

In that context, intercessory prayer emerges. Like everything else in the Christian life, its foundation is the Cross of Jesus Christ. Since God has reached down and made redemption from sin possible via the Cross, we can now reach up in prayer. It should not surprise us, then, that illustrations of intercessory prayer abound in Scripture (e.g., Ex 32:31-32; 1 Kings 18:36-37; Jn 17:20-22; Acts 7:60; Eph 1:15-23; 3:14-20; James 5:13-16). Christians do not pray that people will live lives worthy of eternal life. Intercessory prayer addresses other issues; specifically, temporal needs, spiritual growth, and that God would open the eyes of the non-Christian whereby he or she would embrace the gospel.

---

[1] Daniel C. Peterson, "Forgiveness" in *The Encyclopedia of the Qur'an*, vol. 2, p. 245.

[2] Ian Markham and Ibrahim Özdemir, *Globalization: Ethics and Islam*, p. 40.

[3] Nadia Abu-Zahra, *The Pure and Powerful: Studies in Contemporary Muslim Society*, p. 51.

[4] *Sahih Bukhari* 2.17.123.

[5] *Letter of Pelagius to Demetrias*, from the book *Letters of Pelagius*, ed. Robert Van der Weyer.

Wahhabism bars prayers supererogatory or supplemental to the standard ritual as illegitimate and rejects intercessory prayer through prophets, saints, and other pious figures, dead or alive, as a form of idol worship. Wahhabism rejects any reverence to the dead, including honors to the Prophet Muhammad, so that, until very recently, pilgrims to Mecca during the hajj were forbidden to visit the Prophet's shrine for religious purposes. With the deepening of the crisis that followed September 11, 2001, concessions to popular feelings have included permission to pray at the shrine but not inside it. Touching the shrine as an act of devotion is still punished by arrests and beatings.

—Paul A. Marshall, *Radical Islam's Rules*, p. 22

Muslims are taught that God is very forgiving and merciful because He realizes that human beings make mistakes all the time. Therefore, if they repent sincerely, they can expect God to forgive any sin with the exception of the gravest sin—shirk. Hence, Muslims are also encouraged to be forgiving of the wrongs that others commit against them.

—Arshad Khan, *Islam, Muslims, and America*, p. 201

59   "Yea! there came to thee my signs and thou didst call them lies, and wert too big with pride, and wert of those who misbelieved!"

60   And on the resurrection day thou shalt see those who lied against God, with their faces blackened. Is there not in hell a resort for those who are too big with pride?

61   And God shall rescue those who fear Him, into their safe place; no evil shall touch them, nor shall they be grieved.

62   God is the creator of everything, and He is guardian over everything;

63   His are the keys of the heavens and the earth; and those who misbelieve in the signs of God, they it is who lose!

64   Say, "What! other than God would you bid me serve, O ye ignorant ones?"

65   When He has inspired thee and those before thee that, "If thou dost associate aught with Him, thy work will surely be in vain, and thou shalt surely be of those who lose!"

66   "Nay, but God do thou serve, and be of those who do give thanks!"

The Last Judgment

67   And they do not value God at His true value; while the earth all of it is but a handful for Him on the resurrection day, and the heavens shall be rolled up in His right hand! Celebrated be His praise! and exalted be He above what they associate with Him!

68   And the trumpet shall be blown, and those who are in the heavens and in the earth shall swoon, save whom God pleases. Then it shall be blown again, and, lo! they shall

39.59, 63 *to thee my signs ...misbelieve in the signs of God* — the Qur'an. According to the Qur'an, those who reject the Qur'an are infidels, and all infidels will be cast into the fires of Hell.

39.60 *with their faces blackened* — At the Last Judgment, the faces of the unrighteous will turn black. No racial overtones are intended in this description. The color black is symbolic of sin (see Q 10.26-27; 43.17). The Bible uses a similar metaphor (see Prov. 2:13 and Jn 3:19-20; 12:35; Rom 1:21; 1 Thess 5:5-7).

39.63 *His are the keys of the heavens and the earth* — Allah holds the keys of heaven and earth. In contrast, according to the New Testament, Jesus Christ holds the keys

to death and Hades (Rev 1:18).

39.64 In the Qur'an, the unrighteous are sometimes called "the ignorant ones." Their ignorance is both willful and predetermined by the sovereign will of Allah (see Q 6.35, 111; 11.29, 46; 12.33; 25.63; 27.55; 28.55; 46.23).

39.67 *while the earth all of it is but a handful for Him on the resurrection day* — On the day of resurrection Allah will show himself to be sovereign over the earth.

39.68 *the trumpet shall be blown* — That is, the trumpet that will inaugurate the events of the general resurrection and Last Judgment (see Q 78.18, note).

39.69 *the Book* — This is the book of the Last Judgment. In previous surahs, it is de-

stand up and look on.

69 And the earth shall beam with the light of its Lord, and the Book shall be set forth, and the prophets and martyrs shall be brought; and it shall be decreed between them in truth, and they shall not be wronged!

70 And every soul shall be paid for what it has done, and He knows best that which they do;

Hell

71 and those who misbelieve shall be driven to hell in troops; and when they come there, its doors shall be opened, and its keepers shall say to them, "Did not apostles from amongst yourselves come to you to recite to you the signs of your Lord, and to warn you of the meeting of this day of yours?" They shall say, "Yea, but the sentence of torment was due against the misbelievers!"

72 It shall be said, "Enter ye the gates

of hell, to dwell therein for aye! Hell is the resort of those who are too big with pride!"

Paradise

73 But those who fear their Lord shall be driven to Paradise in troops; until they come there, its doors shall be opened, and its keepers shall say to them, "Peace be upon you, ye have done well! so enter in to dwell for aye!"

74 and they shall say, "Praise be to God, who hath made good His promise to us, and hath given us the earth to inherit! We establish ourselves in Paradise wherever we please; and goodly is the reward of those who work!"

75 And thou shalt see the angels circling round about the throne, celebrating the praise of their Lord; and it shall be decided between them in truth; and it shall be said, "Praise be to God, the Lord of the worlds!"

---

scribed as two books: the book of the right hand (with the names of the believers written down) and the book of the left hand (with the names of the infidels written down). It roughly corresponds to "the book" mentioned in the Bible (Rev. 20:11-12).

39.70 *every soul shall be paid for what it has done* — That is, Allah rewards people based upon what they have done, whether good or evil. Accordingly, their placement in either Paradise or Hell is determined by the quality of their lives as they were lived on

earth (see **The Last Judgment** on pp. 46-50; **The Doctrine of al-Qadar** on pp. 264-266).

39.71-72 Those who enter Hell will be mocked by the keepers of the gate. In contrast, the New Testament presents a deep remorse for all who fail to embrace salvation (see Matt 23;37; Rom 9:1-3).

39.73 *ye have done well!* — According to the Qur'an, salvation is a question of merit—Doctrine of Salvation by Works (see **The Last Judgment** on pp. 46-50).

Surah 73

In the name of the merciful and compassionate God.

Night Prayers

1   O thou who art enwrapped!
2   rise by night except a little
3   —the half, or deduct therefrom a little,
4   or add thereto, and chant the Qur'ân chanting.
5   Verily, we will cast on thee a heavy speech.
6   Verily, the early part of the night is stronger in impressions and more upright In speech!

Complete devotion

7   Verily, thou hast by day a long em-ployment;
8   but mention the name of thy Lord and devote thyself thoroughly to Him,
9   the Lord of the east and the west; there is no god but He; then take Him for a guardian!
10   And endure patiently what they say, and flee from them with a decorous flight.
11   And leave me and those who say it is a lie, who are possessed of comfort; and let them bide for a while.

Coming judgment

12   Verily, with us are heavy fetters and hell-fire,
13   and food that chokes, and mighty woe!
14   On the day when the earth and the mountains shall tremble and the

---

39.74 *the earth to inherit* — Islamic scholars understand the word *earth* (*ard*) in this verse to be a poetic metaphor. That which is intended is Paradise. Also, the word *inherit* means: a rightful due.

Surah 73. The title of this surah, *The One Who is Enwrapped*, comes from verse one. Muslim believers were called upon to demonstrate their devotion to Allah with the practice of night prayers. Their purpose is to acquire additional good works so that in the Day of Judgment they would not be cast into the fires of Hell. Again, in this surah the believers are reminded that Muhammad is their apostle sent from God. They are to remain patient while living in a world full of infidels. A day will come when Allah will reward the righteous and punish the infidel.

73.3-6 The recommended length of night prayers is half of the night. Prayer should be characterized by recitations of the Qur'an. This is believed to be the "firmest way to tread and the best corrective of speech"; in other words, it is the best way in which to acquire a life that is pleasing to Allah and thereby enter into Paradise and avoid the "heavy fetters and flaming fire" of Hell (Q 73.12).

73.4 *chant the Qur'an chanting* — Night prayers recitations of various passages in the Qur'an, chanted in a solemn and measured rhythm.

73.9 *there is no god but He* — As part of the prayers, Muslims were to recite the Doctrine of Tauhid (see Q 112).

73.10a *endure patiently what they say* —

earth shall be as a crumbling sand-hill!

15 Verily, we have sent unto you an apostle bearing witness against you, as we sent an apostle unto Pharaoh.

16 But Pharaoh rebelled against the apostle, and we seized him with an overpowering punishment.

17 Then how will ye shield yourselves if ye misbelieve from the day which shall make children grey-headed,

18 whereon the heaven cleaves —its promise shall be fulfilled!

19 Verily, this is a memorial, and whoso will, let him take unto his Lord a way.

A reminder

20 Verily, thy Lord knows that thou dost stand up to pray nearly two-thirds of the night, or the half of it or the third of it, as do part of those who are with thee; for God measures the night and the day; He knows that ye cannot calculate it, and He turns relentant towards you. So read what is easy of the Qur'ân. He knows that there will be of you some who are sick and others who beat about in the earth craving the grace of God, and others who are fighting in the cause of God. Then read what is easy of it and be steadfast in prayer, and give alms, and lend to God a goodly loan, for what ye send forward for yourselves of good ye will find it with God. It is better and a greater

Muslims are instructed to deafen themselves to any doctrines that oppose Islam.

73.10b *flee from them with a decorous flight* — Muslims were instructed to flee from those who proclaim doctrines that oppose Islam in a decorous (culturally proper) manner.

73.12-13 A description of Hell: people are bound in heavy fetters in the midst of hell-fire. They will also be fed food that chokes.

73.15-17 The apostle that Allah sent to Pharaoh was Moses. Muhammad is reckoned as a Moses-like figure.

73.19 *this is a memorial* — That is, the imagery of Hell should be a constant reminder of people to live their lives in complete submission to Allah.

73.20a Some believers pass two-thirds of the night in prayer, others half, and others a third. For those who cannot accomplish this

task due to illness, business responsibilities, or warfare on behalf of Allah, Allah offers alternate duties: (a) pray as much as possible, (b) pay the poor-rate (alms), (c) give donations for the work of Allah, and (d) ask forgiveness from Allah (see **al-Salat** on pp. 169-170).

The Christian tradition is divided in regards to prayer. Those within liturgical traditions tend to favor rote and regimented prayers, such as those practiced in monasteries. In less liturgical traditions, a more extemporaneous approach is emphasized.

In defense of the less regimented approach to prayer, C. S. Lewis has written: "No one in his senses, if he has any power of ordering his own day, would reserve his chief prayers for bedtime—obviously the worst possible hour for any action which needs concentration. The trouble is that thousands

hire; and ask ye pardon of God: verily, God is forgiving, merciful!

Surah 79

In the name of the merciful and compassionate God.

The work of angels

1   By those who tear out violently!
2   And by those who gaily release!
3   And by those who float through the air!

4   And the preceders who precede!
5   And those who manage the affair!

Lamentations

6   On the day when the quaking quakes
7   which the following one shall succeed!
8   Hearts on that day shall tremble;
9   eyes thereon be humbled!
10   They say, "Shall we be sent back to our old course?
11   —What! when we are rotten bones?"

---

of unfortunate people can hardly find any other. Even for us, who are the lucky ones, it is not always easy. My own plan, when hard pressed, is to seize any time, and place, however unsuitable, in preference to the last waking moment. On a day of traveling—with, perhaps, some ghastly meeting at the end of it—I'd rather pray sitting in a crowded train than put it off till midnight when one reaches a hotel bedroom with aching head and dry throat and one's mind partly in a stupor and partly in a whirl. On other, and slightly less crowded, days a bench in a park, or a back street where one can pace up and down, will do" (*Letters to Malcolm: Chiefly on Prayer*, pp. 16-17).

73.20b *others who are fighting in the cause of God* — This phrase may have been edited into this surah during the Medinah period since warfare among the Muslims did not take place during the Meccan period.

Surah 79. The title of this surah, *Those Who Tear Out Violently*, comes from verse one. Those violently torn out include Satan, demons, and infidels. Following a dis-

cussion of Moses and Pharaoh, Muhammad described the coming judgment on all who failed to heed his message.

79.1-5 At the time of death, the wicked will be violently pulled from the earth by angels. In contrast, the blessed ones will be gently drawn out.

79.6-14 This is a prophetic look into the future. Infidels will be smitten with deep regret for their failure to heed the message of the Qur'an when they had the opportunity.

79.11 *rotten bones* — The unrighteous dead will be resurrected with rotten bones.

79.15-26 Drawing upon the story of the exodus from the book of Exodus (Ex 3-14), Muhammad made the case that when Pharaoh rejected the message of Moses, Allah seized him with punishment in both the hereafter and the former life (v. 25). The implication is that a similar situation would occur with Muhammad and the people of Mecca.

79.16 *the holy valley of Tuva* — This is the valley where Moses encountered the burning bush. The word *Tuva* in the Arabic lan-

12   they say, "That then were a losing
      return!"
13   But it will only be one scare,
14   and lo! they will be on the surface!

Moses and Pharaoh

15   Has the story of Moses come to
      you?
16   when his Lord addressed him in the
      holy valley of Tuvâ,
17   "Go unto Pharaoh, verily, he is
      outrageous;
18   and say, 'Hast thou a wish to pu-
      rify thyself,
19   and that I may guide thee to thy
      Lord, and thou mayest fear?'"
20   So he showed him the greatest
      signs;
21   but he called him a liar and rebelled.
22   Then he re-treated hastily,
23   and gathered, and proclaimed,
24   and said, "I am your Lord most
      High!"
25   but God seized him with the pun-
      ishment of the future life and of
      the former.
26   Verily, in that is a lesson to him who
      fears!

Two ways, two destinies

27   Are ye harder to create or the
      heaven that He has built?
28   He raised its height and fashioned
      it;
29   and made its night to cover it, and
      brought forth its noonday light;
30   and the earth after that He did
      stretch out.
31   He brings forth from it its water
      and its pasture.
32   And the mountains He did firmly
      set,
33   a provision for you and for your
      cattle.
34   And when the great predominant
      calamity shall come,
35   on the day when man shall remem-
      ber what he strove after,
36   and hell shall be brought out for
      him who sees!
37   And as for him who was outra-
      geous
38   and preferred the life of this world,
39   verily, hell is the resort!
40   But as for him who feared the sta-
      tion of his Lord, and prohibited his
      soul from lust,

guage means "twice." Scholars typically understand this to mean a valley that is twice
hallowed—meaning an intensely holy valley.
In contrast, the Book of Exodus states that
Moses encountered the burning bush on the
side of a mountain (see Q 20.12; Ex 3:1-2).
79.20 *great signs* — divine revelations.
79.34 *the great predominant calamity* —
This is a reference to the apocalyptic events
immediately preceding the general resurrection of the dead, which immediately pre-
cedes the day of the Last Judgment.
79.38-41 The fundamental difference between the wicked and righteous is described
in this passage. The wicked one "prefers
the life of this world." The righteous "forbids the soul from low desires." The destiny
of the first is Hell. The destiny of the second is Paradise.
79.42 *the Hour* — This is the time when

			Surah 54
41	verily, Paradise is the resort!		*In the name of the merciful and compassionate God.*
	Muhammad: the warner		
42	They shall ask thee about the Hour, for when it is set.		*The moon split asunder*
43	Whereby canst thou mention it?	1	The Hour draws nigh, and the moon is split asunder.
44	Unto thy Lord its period belongs.		
45	Thou art only a warner to him who fears it.	2	But if they see a sign they turn aside and say, "Magic, continuous!"
46	On the day they see it, it will be as though they had only tarried an evening or the noon thereof.	3	And they call it a lie and follow their

people will be summoned to the Last Judgment. Prior to this time, the souls of the dead will be consciously awaiting their final destiny (see Q 12.107; 15.85; 18.21; 19.75; 21.49; 22.1, 7, 55; 25.11; 30.12, 14, 55; 31.34; 34.3; 40.46, 59; 41.47, 50; 42.17-18; 43.61, 66, 85; 45.27, 32; 54.1, 46).

In a Hadith, Muhammad clarified that which will take place during the waiting period in the afterlife. "When anyone of you dies, he is shown his place both in the morning and in the evening. If he is one of the people of Paradise, he is shown his place in it, and if he is from the people of the Hell Fire, he is shown his place therein. Then it is said to him, 'This is your place till Allah resurrect you on the Day of Resurrection'" (*Sahih Bukhari* 2.23.461).

Surah 54. The title of this surah, *The Moon*, comes from verse one. This surah is a lesson from history of how God had brought destruction upon different civilizations for their resistance of the messages of divinely appointed apostles. The civilizations mentioned in the surah are the antediluvian people of Noah's time, the peoples of Ad, Thamud, Sodom and Gomorrah, and Egypt. The surah is also bookended with two short

presentations of Muhammad as a true prophet of Allah. Moreover, a phrase is repeated four times in the surah: "We have made the Qur'an easy as a reminder—but is there anyone who will mind?" (vv. 17, 22, 32, and 40). The phrase countered the claim that the Qur'an was unclear and diffuse.

54.1a *The Hour* —The Hour is the moment in time when people will be summoned to the Last Judgment (see Q 79.42, note).

54.1b *the moon is split asunder* — Repeatedly in the Qur'an, Muhammad was criticized by his opponents for the absence of miracles. Without miracles, they said, his prophetic credentials remained inauthentic and therefore invalid. In this verse, Muhammad claimed to have performed miracle with the hope that it would silence his critics. That which he did was split the moon into two halves.

According to a Hadith, "The demand of the pagans to the Prophet to show them a miracle. The Prophet showed them the splitting of the moon. Narrated 'Abdullah ibn Mas'ud: During the lifetime of the Prophet the moon was split into two parts and on that the Prophet said: 'Bear witness (to this)'" (*Sahih Bukhari* 4.26.830; also see 4.26.831, 832; and Q 15.6-7, note).

al-Salat

Daily Prayer

Al-Salat is the regime of prayers required by all faithful Muslims. For those committed to the "uphill road" (Q 90.11)—that is, desirous of entering Paradise and avoiding Hell in the afterlife—a daily observance of the *Salat* is indispensable. It is to be performed five times a day (before dawn, at noon, at mid-afternoon, after sunset, and sometime around midnight), facing towards Mecca. Shi'ite Muslims are required to pray in the direction of Mecca three times a day (see Al-Ghazali, *Inner Dimension of Islamic Worship*, pp. 19-52 for a further discussion of *al-Salat*.

Preparation

Cleanliness is a central requirement for the *Salat*. This includes one's personal hygiene, clothing, and the place where prayers are being recited. If water is not available in one's cleansing, fine sand is permitted as a substitute (*tayammum*). The Qur'an sanctions this practice (Q 5.6).

Typical Prayer Regime

Throughout the prayer regime, the person faces towards Mecca

1. Stand straight
2. Recite the *Takbeeratul-Ihram*   "God is the greatest"
3. Recite the *al-Fatiha*   Surah 1
4. Recite a second surah   choice of surah varies
5. Bow
6. Stand straight
7. Prostration
8. Rising from prostration

9. Second Prostration
10. Kneels
11. Recite the *Tashahhud*
12. Salam   Salutatiion

Tashahhud

All worships are for Allah. Allah's peace be upon you, O Prophet, and His mercy and blessings. Peace be on us and on all righteous servants of Allah. I bear witness that there is none worthy of worship except Allah, and I bear witness that Muhammad is His servant and messenger.

The Du'a

Alongside the *al-Salat*, which is a formalized prayer full of ritual, is the *du'a*. The *du'a* is informal communication between the Muslim and Allah. Where *al-Salat* is obligatory, *du'a* is optional. For many Muslims, it is the *du'a* that is more highly prized since it is less burdensome and can be offered anytime and apart from ritual requirements. Moreover, whereas *al-Salat* emphasizes an acknowledgement of the lordship of Allah and a surrender to do his will, that which characterizes the *du'a* are words of thanksgiving and supplications. They include:

*   private thanksgiving for some blessing received (e.g., recoveries from sickness, the birth of a child, release from worry)
*   cries for help
*   pleas for forgiveness
*   general requests for God's guidance and blessing.[1]

These prayers are spoken extemporaneously—from the heart, without preparation, and without rehearsal. Accordingly, for most Muslims the *du'a* are offered with more passion than are the *al-Salat*.

---

[1] Ruqaiyyah Waris Maqsood, *Islam*, p. 60.

Although the Koran repeatedly commands Muslims to perform the *salat*, it says little about what the *salat* actually involves. How to perform the *salat* was taught by the Prophet, and thus Muslims today, wherever they live, pray in essentially the same way that Muhammad prayed and taught them to pray.

—Sachiko Murata and William C. Chittick, *The Vision of Islam*, p. 12

It is folly to be satisfied with the outward performance of *Salat*. Most people observe the *Salat* only formally and get through it quickly as if it were a burdensome tax which should be got rid of speedily...You should seek to make your *Salat* delicious like food and cold water. *Salat* is an obligation due to God. It should be carried out in an excellent manner.

—Ghulam Amad and Munawar Ahmed Saeed, *The Essence of Islam*, p. 303

The first Pillar, and first distinctly Muslim practice enacted by Muhammad in Mecca, is *salat*, or ritual prayer. There are two kinds of prayer in Islam: *du'a*, which refers to individual, informal communication between the believer and God; and *salat*, which is the ritualized, obligatory prayer performed five times a day: sunrise, noon, afternoon, sunset, and evening. *Salat*, which means "to bow, bend, or stretch," is composed of a series of yogic movements that include standing, bowing, rising, sitting, turning east and west, and falling prostrate, all repeated in cycles, and accompanied by specific verses from the Quran. As with all Muslim rituals, *salat* can begin only after the intention to pray is voiced, and only while the Muslim faces toward Mecca, the direction of prayer, or *qiblah*.

—Reza Aslan, *No god but God*, p. 146

The prayer act consists of obligatory prayers performed five times per day within the Sunni world. The actual occasions of prayer are announced by a special call in Arabic proclaimed by the *muezzin* (the one who makes the public call to prayer) from a *minaret* (a tower) that is part of a mosque. In many places, especially larger towns in Muslim countries, this call may be broadcast through speaker systems within a mosque and often to the world outside. The call to prayer (*adzran*) includes the uttering of the shahada within it.

—Douglas Pratt, *The Challenge of Islam*, p. 84

The Arabic word *masjid* (mosque) means "place of prostrations" (bowing down), and *salat* involves a particular ritual of movements and words that is performed on the floor.

—Nicola Barber, *Islamic Empires*, p. 38

lusts; but every matter is settled!

4   There has come to them some information with restraint in it

5   —wisdom far-reaching—but warners avail not!

A difficult day

6   But turn thy back on them! The day when the caller shall call to an awkward thing.

7   Humbly casting down their looks shall they come forth from their graves, as though they were locusts scattered abroad!

8   Hurrying forwards to the caller! the misbelievers shall say, "This is a difficult day!"

Divine punishment upon the people of Noah's day

9   Noah's people before them called (the apostles) liars; they called our servant a liar; and they said, "Mad!" and he was rejected.

10   And he called upon his Lord, "Verily, I am overcome, come then to my help!"

11   And we opened the gates of heaven with water pouring down!

12   And we made the earth burst forth in springs, and the waters met at a bidding already decreed.

To the present day, the splitting of the moon in two has remained an abiding symbol within Islam of the authenticity of Muhammad's prophetic calling and ministry. Detractors maintain that the event is either a fable invented to fill the need for miracles in Muhammad's life or that it was an eclipse of the moon that Muhammad used to his personal advantage (see Uri Rubin, *The Cambridge Companion to Muhammad*, pp. 47-50).

54.2-5 According to Muhammad, his opponents continued in their disbelief, claiming that he had performed magic—and was therefore a mere magician and not a true spokesperson for Allah.

54.6 *turn they back on them* — Muslims were instructed to become detached from the infidels.

54.9-15 The point of this passage is that just as the people in Noah's day rejected Noah's message and were destroyed in the flood, so too will be the people of Mecca if they continued in their opposition to him.

54.16-21 Ad was an ancient tribe that inhabited the region of northwest Arabia that was eventually absorbed by other tribes in the region. It was first mentioned by Claudius Ptolemy of Alexandria (A.D. 90-168) in one of his maps that detailed northwest Arabia. He called Ad the Oaditæ people (see Charles Forster, *The Historical Geography of Arabia*, pp. 32, 33, 374; Syed Muzaffar Uddin Nadvi, *A Geographical History of the Qur'an*, p. 126).

Muhammad claimed that the Ad civilization had its beginnings in the second generation following Noah (Q 7.69). Moreover, he commented that the people of Ad were "increased...in length of stature" (Q 7.69)—that is, people of considerable height. He did not specify their exact height, but the Book of First Enoch offers a clue. It notes that just prior to the Great Flood giants roamed the earth, devilish human hybrid creatures that reached the height of four

13   But we bore him on the thing of
      planks and nails;
14   sailing on beneath our eyes, a re-
      ward for him who had been dis-
      believed!
15   And we left it a sign;—but is there
      any one who will mind?

Divine punishment
upon Ad

16   'Âd called the apostles liars, and
      how was my punishment and my
      warning?
17   We have made the Qur'ân easy as
      a reminder—but is there any one
      who will mind?

18   Ad treated (the truth) as a lie, so
      how (great) was My punishment
      and My warning!
19   Verily, we sent on them a cold
      storm wind on a day of continu-
      ous ill-luck!
20   It reft men away as though they
      had been palm stumps torn up!
21   How (great) was then My punish-
      ment and My warning!

Divine punishment
upon Thamud

22   We have made the Qur'ân easy as
      a reminder—but is there any one
      who will mind?

hundred fifty feet (1 Enoch 7:2). Another clue comes from a Hadith, where Muhammad reportedly said of Adam: "Allah created Adam, making him 60 cubits tall [ninety feet] ...Any person who will enter Paradise will resemble Adam (in appearance and figure). People have been decreasing in stature since Adam's creation" (*Sahih Bukhari* 4.55.543).

Muhammad also claimed that the Ad people lived in "castles on its plains and hewed out mountains into houses" (Q 7.73) —that is, the city of Hegra (see **Hegra** on p. 28).

According to Muhammad, the people of Ad had forgotten the spiritual teachings of Noah. Hud (a warner) came to the people and told them to turn away from idolatry (Q 46.22). Since they refused to do so, Allah sent a wind storm and covered their city with sand over a course of seven nights and eight days (see Q 69.7 and 89.6-8). The desolate city was then inhabited by the people of Thamud (Q 15.80 and 7.73).

This problem of dating the Ad civilization to the era of Noah has not gone unnoticed by Islamic scholarship. Some scholars have stated that two Ad civilizations existed, one in Hegra of the second century, A.D. and the other dating back to the second generation following the Great Flood on the southern coast of Arabia, west of Yemen. The problem with this solution, however, is that no evidence exists for this second location for Ad. It is neither in the archeological record nor mentioned in ancient literature.

54.22-31 The people of Thamud were destroyed by Allah since they rejected the message of Zali'h, who was an apostle sent to them. Allah caused a she-camel to emerge from the dust of the ground as a bona-fide miracle as a means of convincing the Thamud people that Zali'h was indeed a prophet of Allah. The people, however, responded by killing the she-camel (see Q 91, note). Therefore, Allah destroyed the Thamud people by sending to them a singular "noise"

23   Thamûd called the warnings lies,
24   and said, "A mortal, one of us, alone, shall we follow him? then indeed were we in error and excitement!"
25   Is the warning cast on him alone among us? nay, he is an insolent liar!
26   "They shall know tomorrow about the insolent liar!"
27   "Verily, we are about to send the she-camel as a trial for them, then watch them and have patience!
28   and inform them that the water is shared between them (and her); each draught shall be sought by turns."
29   Then they called their companion, and he plied (a knife) and hamstrung her.
30   Then how was my punishment and my warning?
31   Verily, we sent against them one noise, and they were like the dry sticks of him who builds a fold.

*Divine punishment upon
Sodom and Gomorrah*

32   We have made the Qur'ân easy as a reminder—but is there any one who will mind?
33   Lot's people called the apostles liars;
34   verily, we sent against them a heavy sand storm; all, save Lot's family, we saved them at the dawn.
35   As a favour from us; so do we reward him who gives thanks!
36   He indeed had warned them of our assault, but they doubted of the warning.
37   And they desired his guest, and we put out their eyes. "So taste ye my torment and warning!"
38   And there overtook them on the morning a settled punishment!
39   "So taste ye my torment and warning!"

*Divine punishment
upon Egypt*

40   We have made the Qur'ân easy as a reminder—but is there any one who will mind?
41   The warning came to Pharaoh's

(v. 31).
54.31 *one noise* — This mysterious *one noise* is mentioned elsewhere in the Qur'an as a divine judgment that destroyed a number of civilizations (see Q 11.67, 94; 15.73, 83; 23.41; 29.40; 36.29, 49, 53; 38.15; 51.44).
54.32-39 This passage describes the events mentioned in Gen 19. Muhammad explained that Lot was the divinely appointed apostle to the people of Sodom and Gomorrah. Because they rejected his message, divine judg-

ment fell upon them.
54.34 *a heavy sand storm* — According to Muhammad, the judgment that destroyed Sodom and Gomorrah was a heavy sand storm. The Bible, however, speaks otherwise. According to Gen. 19:23, a burning sulphur rained down from heaven and destroyed the two cities.
54.37 *we blinded their eyes* — This refers to the blinding of the eyes of the men of Sodom who wished to have sexual relations with the angels who had entered Lot's home

people;

42 they called our signs all lies, and we seized on them with the seizing of a mighty powerful one.

The people of Mecca

43 Are your misbelievers better than they? or have ye an exemption in the Scriptures?

44 Or do they say we are a victorious company?

45 The whole shall be routed and shall turn their backs in flight.

46 Nay, the Hour is their promised time! and the Hour is most severe and bitter!

47 Verily, the sinners are in error and excitement.

48 On the day when they shall be dragged to the fire upon their faces!— "Taste ye the touch of hell."

49 Verily, everything have we created

by decree,

50 and our bidding is but one (word), like the twinkling of an eye!

51 We have destroyed the like of you—but is there any who will mind?

52 And everything they do is in the books,

53 and everything small and great is written down.

Final Blessing

54 Verily, the pious shall be amid gardens and rivers,

55 in the seat of truth, with the powerful king.

Surah 34

In the name of the merciful and compassionate God.

to warn him to flee the city (Gen 19:4-10).
54.40-42 This passage is a brief reference to the Ten Plagues that brought destruction upon the land of Egypt and the drowning of the Egyptian army in the Red (Reed) Sea (Ex 7-14).
54.43-53 Muhammad then turned his attention to the Quraysh tribe of Mecca. He imagined that they saw themselves as exceptions from history, that somehow they would be spared divine judgment. He also imagined that they saw themselves as sufficiently strong to withstand divine judgment and that somehow they would defeat Allah. Yet, in both cases, he maintained, the Meccan people were mistaken. In "the twin-

kling of an eye," said Muhammad, they will be destroyed (v. 50). This "one word" may be synonymous with the "one noise" mentioned elsewhere in the Qur'an (see Q 54.22-31, note).
The phrase "the twinkling of an eye" is also mentioned in the New Testament, yet in an entirely different context (see 1 Cor 15:52).
54.46 *the Hour* — This is the time when all people will be summoned to the Last Judgment (see Q 79.42, note). In this verse, it is called: "the promised time."
Surah 34. The title of this surah, *The Seba*, comes from verse 15. This surah is an extended catechism for the Muslim people: a

Allah:

omniscient and gracious

1   Praise belongs to God, whose is whatsoever is in the heavens and whatsoever is in the earth; His is the praise in the next world, and He is the wise and well aware!

2   He knows what goes into the earth, and what comes forth therefrom, and what comes down from the sky, and what ascends thereto; for He is the merciful, forgiving.

First rebuttal

3   Those who misbelieve say, "The Hour shall not come to us;" say, "Yea, by my Lord it shall surely come to you! by Him who knows the unseen! nor shall there escape from it the weight of an atom, in the heavens or in the earth, or even less than that, or greater, save in

the perspicuous Book;"

4   and that He may reward those who believe and do right; these—for them is forgiveness and a noble provision.

5   But those who strive concerning our signs to frustrate them; these,—for them is the torment of a grievous plague.

6   And those to whom knowledge has been given see that what is sent down to thee from thy Lord is the truth, and guides unto the way of the mighty, the praiseworthy.

Second rebuttal

7   And those who misbelieve say, "Shall we guide you to a man who will inform you that when ye are torn all to pieces, then ye shall be a new creation?

8   he has forged against God a lie, or there is a ginn in him;"—nay, those

---

series of seventeen rebuttals to be used when conversing with infidels. In the middle of the surah is a parenthesis where two historical events are mentioned: (a) the ministries of David and Solomon, and (b) the people of Sheba who turned away from God in disobedience and suffered divine judgment. Also included in this surah are the twin notions that only Allah is to be worshipped. Moreover, Muhammad (his prophet) is not mad.

34.1-2 In this doxology, three attributes of Allah are presented: (a) omnipresence, (b) omniscience, and (c) compassion. It is similar to the biblical doxology located in Rom 11:33-36.

34.3 *the perspicuous Book* — That is, a clear Book. According to Muhammad, this is the eternal Book in Paradise that Allah reveals to his apostles on earth; the Qur'an is allegedly the most complete representation of the perspicuous Book (see *The Perspicuous Book* on pp. 178-179).

34.3-6 The infidels say: "The hour (of the Last Judgment) shall not come upon us." Muhammad's answer: "It shall certainly come upon you."

34.4 *believe and do right* — These words are repeated often in the Qur'an and serve as a brief summary of the Islamic gospel (see Q 103.3 note).

34.7-9 The infidels say: Following death,

who believe not in the hereafter are in the torment and in the remote error!

9   Have they not looked at what is before them and what is behind them of the heaven and the earth? if we pleased we would cleave the earth open with them, or we would make to fall upon them a portion of the heaven; verily, in that is a sign to every repentant servant.

Blessings given to
David and Solomon

10   And we did give David grace from us, "O ye mountains! echo (God's praises) with him, and ye birds!" and we softened for him iron:

11   "Make thou coats of mail and adapt the rings thereof, and do right; verily, I at what ye do do look."

12   And to Solomon the wind; its morning journey was a month, and its evening journey was a month;

and we made to flow for him a fountain of molten brass; and of the ginns some to work before him by the permission of his Lord; and whoso swerves amongst them from our bidding we will give him to taste the torment and the blaze;

13   and they made for him what he pleased of chambers, and images, and dishes like troughs, and firm pots;—work, O ye family of David! thankfully; few is it of my servants who are thankful.

14   And when we decreed for him death, naught guided them to his death save a reptile of the earth that ate his staff; and when he fell down it was made manifest to the ginns that, had they but known the unseen, they need not have tarried in the shameful torment.

Seba suffered
divine judgment

one's body decomposes to an "utmost scattering." How then can one's body be reconstituted and resurrected? Muhammad's answer: Consider the vastness of the heavens and the earth. Allah has the power to do whatever He pleases.

34.10-14 *Parenthesis: David and Solomon.* Allah blessed David and Solomon with material abundance. The abundance was to such an extent that the Queen of Sheba saw it as a sign from God (see Q 27.22-44).

34.10 *we softened for him iron* — That is, we made bronze for him. Bronze is an alloy of copper and tin (and sometimes phosphorus or aluminum). It was particularly useful

in ship fittings prior to the invention of stainless steel. It was also used as the principal material in statues and musical instruments. The process of making bronze was such a significant invention that it gave rise to the Bronze Age in antiquity.

34.12 *molten brass* — An alloy of copper and zinc. It is a soft metal useful in decorative designs and functional items, such a door handles.

34.14 *we decreed for him death* — According to this passage, when Allah decreed the moment of Solomon's death, he was standing and leaning upon his staff. Since his corpse remained standing, the ginns

The Perspicuous Book

A central premise within Islamic theology, that which sets it apart from other world religions, is the notion of the Perspicuous Book.

The word *perspicuous* means clear and, as such, refers to a book that is lucid and understandable. The Perspicuous Book exists eternally in Paradise (see *The Second Great Creed*, article three). It clarifies the nature of God, the nature of salvation, the nature of good and evil and how they differ from one another, the nature of humankind, and so on. The book was sent down to earth to various apostles (see Q 10.94; 14.1; 15.6, 9; 16.30, 44, 64, 89; 18.1; 20.2; 21.10, 50; 22.16; 25.1, 32; 28.87; 34.41; 42.15, 17; 43.31; 46.30; 64.8; 76.23).

Muhammad believed that this book was supernaturally revealed to apostles commissioned by Allah to the peoples of the world throughout time (Q 13.38). Some apostles received more of the book than others, yet all received a sufficient amount of the book to make a clear presentation to the communities in which they lived about Allah and how to avoid the eternal torments of Hell. These apostles included Adam, Enoch, Noah, Abraham, Lot, Joseph, Moses, Aaron, David, Solomon, Jonah, and Jesus (biblical characters) and Hud, Zali'h, Sho'haib and Loqman (nonbiblical characters). "Has not the story come to you of those who were before you," Muhammad asked, "of the people of Noah, and Ad, and Thamud, and those who came after them?" (Q 14.9).

Muhammad claimed that he was one such apostle, with the sole distinction being that, unlike the apostles who had come before him, he was the benefactor of the *entire* Perspicuous Book. The book was dictated to him in the Arabic language. This notion elevates the Islamic religion above all other religions since the revelation given to Muhammad was complete. In addition, since the revelations given to those before him—such as those who received the New Testament—had been corrupted by those who copied the texts, the Qur'an is the only pure and uncorrupted revelation still on earth. This further elevates the Islamic religion above all other religions on earth. It, and it alone, is the uncorrupted Word of God. It is the "Mother of the Book" (Q 43.4), high and wise. Ihn Kathir described the Qur'an as "the most honored Book, that Allah sent down from heaven to the most honored Messenger of Allah sent to all the people of the earth, Arabs and non-Arabs alike."

Christian response. In contrast, Christianity understands sacred literature differently. No such eternal book is believed to exist in heaven. Its sacred literature (Old and New Testaments) came into being in a cooperative venture between the Holy Spirit and holy men (and possibly some women). "Above all, you must understand that no prophecy of Scripture came about by the prophet's own interpretation. For prophecy never had its origin in the will of man, but men spoke from God as they were carried along by the Holy Spirit" (2 Pet 2:20-21).

In addition, the Judeo-Christian tradition insists that only its sacred literature is inspired of God. The notion that God sent apostles to other peoples in other times and places in history and equipped them with their own inspired literature is wholly absent from the Judeo-Christian tradition. Instead, God sent missionaries to all parts of the world to present its sacred literature (Old and New Testaments) and preach the gospel message (see Matt 28:18-20; Acts 1:6-8). This, of course, excludes Muhammad as an apostle sent from God and the Qur'an as a divinely inspired text.

The Koran [Qur'an] does describe itself as a "perspicuous book. The English word "perspicuous" is a translation of the Arabic word *mubin*. The idea is that the message is "plain and clear." In other words, imams, ayatollahs, and other privileged adherents of Islam are not necessary for a reader to understand the words of Allah recorded in the Koran [Qur'an].

—Marvin W. Heyboer,
Journeys into the Heart and Heartland of Islam, p. 57

Although the Koran describes itself as perspicuous, it is imperative (already declared in eleventh century hadiths) that readers connect the messages to the appropriate corresponding events. Because the messages are not presented in chronological order, in the Koran, the accurate dating of word with event does become a more difficult task.

—Marvin W. Heyboer, *Journeys into the Heart and Heartland of Islam*, p. 57

The Muslim understanding of the Qur'an as the Word of God is the basis of the Islamic view of revelation. The Arabic word for revelation is *wahy*. As a revelation from God, *wahy* carries the sense of otherness—that is, it is an objective phenomenon. In other words, *wahy* is not the product of a Prophet's mind but is transmitted by a prophet from God without any alteration of form or meaning. On this view, the Qur'an is the Word of God, not the Word of Muhammad.

—Vincent J. Cornell, *Voices of Islam*, p. 49

The perspicuous Book is a witness that We sent it down on a night of blessing—so that We could warn—on which all affairs are sorted out and divided as commands from Us (Qur'an 44.2-5)...If one were to ask what is the significance of the sending down of the Qur'an on this night, I would respond: It is said that God first sent it down in its entirety from the seventh heaven to the lowest heaven. Then He commanded excellent writers to transcribe it on the Night of Destiny. Gabriel subsequently revealed it piece by piece to the Messenger of God.

—Francis E. Peters, *A Reader on Classical Islam*, p. 170

Whereas in Christianity in the beginning was the Word and the Word became flesh, in Islam in the beginning was the Word and the Word became a Book!

—Norman Geisler and Abdul Saleeb, *Answering Islam*, p. 100

If the heavenly Qur'an was, indeed, eternal and uncreated, then the book that Muslims held in their hands was, in some sense, a manifestation of an eternal aspect of God. Accordingly, some theologians went so far as to argue that every syllable, sound, and written character of the Qur'an is pre-existing and eternal. If, on the other hand, God's speech was a created thing, might the Qur'an not be seen as a mere book, subject to the limiting and shaping effects of time and environment?

—Daniel W. Brown, *A New Introduction to Islam*, p. 177

The Qur'an does not seem to be an eternal book, as Muslims claim. Indeed, if the Qur'an is eternal, why does it allocate so many words to temporal issues that existed among Muhammad's own family and fellow Muslims? The Suras include a curse against Muhammad's uncle (Sura 111), an admonition to Muhammad's wives to remain subject to him (Sura 33), and words against the elephant brigade of Abraha, the Christian ruler of Abyssinia, who had come up against the Muslims in Mecca (Sura 105). Gleason Archer suggests that the fact that the Qur'an "is so focused on the lifetime of Muhammad himself strongly suggests that it was actually Muhammad who composed the book himself, rather than it being dictated to him by some angelic spokesman of Allah."

—Ron Rhodes, *The 10 Things You Need to Know About Islam*, p. 32

15   Sebâ had in their dwellings a sign; two gardens, on the right hand and on the left, "Eat from the provision of your Lord; and give thanks to Him! a good country and a forgiving Lord!"

16   But they turned away, and we sent against them the flood of the dyke; and we changed for them their two gardens into two gardens that grew bitter fruit and tamarisk, and some few lote trees.

17   This did we reward them with, for that they misbelieved; and do we so reward any but misbelievers?

18   And we made between them and the cities which we had blessed (other) cities which were evident; and we measured out the journey: "Journey ye thereto nights and days in safety!"

19   And they said, "Our Lord! make a greater distance between our journeys;" and they wronged themselves, and we made them legends; and we tore them all to pieces; verily, in that are signs to every patient, grateful person,

20   And Iblîs verified his suspicion concerning them, and they followed him, save a party of the believers.

21   Yet had he no authority over them, save that we might know who it was that believed in the hereafter from him who amongst them was in doubt; for thy Lord guards everything.

Third rebuttal

22   Say, "Call on those whom ye pretend beside God;" they cannot control the weight of an atom in the heavens or in the earth; nor have they any partnership in either; nor has He amongst them any supporter;

thought that he was still alive and continued to serve him, until a reptile ate his staff. When the staff finally snapped in two, Solomon's corpse fell to the floor, making clear to the ginns that he was indeed dead (see **Occultism in Seventh Century Arabia** on pp. 123-125).

34.15a *Seba* — This is the nation that the Bible describes as Sheba, located near present-day Yemen on the southwestern horn of southern Arabia.

34.15b The sign for Seba: the nation acquired two well provisioned gardens. It was a sign of the blessings of Allah.

34.16a *the flood of the dyke* — According to this verse, Allah brought judgment upon Sheba (Seba) for turning away in unbelief. A dyke (dam) broke free and flooded the land. The date of this catastrophe cannot be established since no historical records exist of any such breakage of a dyke in Sheba.

34.16b *tamarisk* — A deciduous shrub or tree that grows to eighteen meters in height forming dense thickets.

34.16c *lote trees* — Trees in Paradise that exist near the abode of God.

34.20 *Iblis* — Satan.

34.22-23 The infidels claim that their saints or gods are able to intercede on their behalf. Muhammad's answer: All such intercession "will not avail aught with Him save of whom He permits" (see **Divine Forgiveness**

23 nor is intercession of any avail with Him, except for him whom He permits; so that when fright is removed from their hearts they say, "What is it that your Lord says?" they say, "The truth; for He is the high, the great."

Fourth rebuttal

24 Say, "Who provides from the heavens and the earth?" Say, "God." And, verily, we or ye are surely in guidance or in an obvious error.

Fifth rebuttal

25 Say, "Ye shall not be asked about what we have sent, nor shall we be asked about what ye do."

Sixth rebuttal

26 "Our Lord shall assemble us together; then He shall open between us in truth, for He is the opener who knows."

Seventh rebuttal

27 Say, "Show me those whom ye have added to Him as partners; not so! nay, but He is God, the mighty, the wise!"

28 We have only sent thee to men generally as a herald of glad tidings and a warner; but most men do not know.

Eighth rebuttal

29 And they say, "When shall this promise be, if ye do speak the truth?"

30 say, "For you is the appointment of a day of which ye shall not keep back an hour, nor shall ye bring it on!"

Ninth rebuttal

31 And those who misbelieve say, "We will never believe in this Qur'ân or in what is before it;" but couldst thou see when the unjust are set before their Lord, they shall rebut each other in speech.

32 Those who were thought weak shall say to those who were big

in Islam on pp. 158-161).

34.23b *He is the high, the great* — This phrase, in the Muslim world, is called *Takbir* (*Allahu akbar*). The phrase frequently occurs in daily prayer. It is also used as a slogan and as a chant in political rallies, religious events, and jihadic battles. In addition, the *Takbir* is the national anthem of Libya (also see Q 2.185; 22.62; 31.30; 40.12 where the phrase is mentioned).

34.24 Everyone is in "manifest error" if they

think that their sustenance does not come from Allah.

34.25 Each person will be questioned by Allah for his or her own deeds, not the deeds of someone else.

34.26 Everyone will be gathered together at the Last Judgment where they will be judged by the all-knowing Allah.

34.27-28 Allah has no associates. This is a condemnation of the Arabian polytheism that characterized pre-Islamic Arabia (see **Poly-**

with pride, "Had it not been for you we should have been believers." Those who were big with pride shall say to those who were thought weak, "Was it we who turned you away from the guidance after it came to you? nay, ye were sinners."

33 And those who were thought weak shall say to those who were, big with pride, "Nay, but it was the plotting by night and day, when ye did bid us to disbelieve in God, and to make peers for Him!" and they shall display repentance when they see the torment; and we will put fetters on the necks of those who misbelieved. Shall they be rewarded except for that which they have done?

34 We have not sent to any city a warner but the opulent thereof said, "We, in what ye are sent with, disbelieve."

Tenth rebuttal

35 And they say, "We have more wealth and children, and we shall not be tormented."

36 Say, "Verily, my Lord extends provision to whom He pleases or doles it out, but most men do not know;

37 but neither your wealth nor your children is that which will bring you to a near approach to us, save him who believes and does right; these, for them is a double reward for what they have done, and they in upper rooms shall be secure."

Eleventh rebuttal

38 And those who strive concerning our signs to frustrate them, these in the torment shall be arraigned.

39 Verily, my Lord extends provision to whomsoever He will of His servants, or doles it out to him. And what ye expend in alms at all, He will repay it; for He is the best of providers.

40 And on the day He will gather them all together, then He will say to the angels, "Are these those who used to worship you?"

41 They shall say, "Celebrated be thy praises! thou art our patron instead of them. Nay, they used to worship the ginns, most of them be-

theism in Seventh Century Arabia on pp. 92-97).

34.29-30 The infidels ask of the timing of the general resurrection and the Last Judgment. Answer: Allah has an appointed day that cannot be adjusted. It will neither move forwards or backwards in time.

34.31-34 The infidels say that by no means will they believe in the Qur'an. Muhammad's answer: At the Last Judgment they will re-

gret that they disbelieved in Allah and refused to listen to him when they had opportunity.

34.35-37 The infidels claim that their wealth and progeny will keep them from divine judgment. Muhammad's answer: Neither wealth nor children draws one close to Allah.

34.38-42 At the Last Judgment it will be made manifest that these infidels were worshippers of the *ginn* (devilish spirits) and will

lieve in them.

42   But today they cannot control for each other, either profit or harm;" and we will say to those who have done wrong, "Taste ye the torment of the fire wherein ye did disbelieve!"

Twelfth rebuttal

43   And when our signs are recited to them they say, "This is only a man who wishes to turn you from what your fathers served;" and they say, 'This is only a lie forged,' and those who misbelieve will say of the truth when it comes to them, 'It is only obvious sorcery!'"

44   But we have not brought them any book which they may study, and we have not sent to them before thee a warner.

45   Those before them said it was a lie, and these have not reached a tithe of what we had given them. And they said my apostles were

liars, and how great a change was then!

46   Say, "I only admonish you of one thing, that ye should stand up before God in twos or singly, and then that ye reflect that there is no ginn in your companion. He is only a warner to you before the keen torment."

Thirteenth rebuttal

47   Say, "I do not ask you for it a hire; that is for yourselves; my hire is only from God, and He is witness over all."

Fourteenth rebuttal

48   Say, "Verily, my Lord hurls forth the truth; and He well knows the unseen."

Fifteenth rebuttal

49   Say, "The truth has come, and

then be cast into Hell.

34.43 The infidels oppose the Qur'an, claiming that it is merely the writings of a man who wishes to turn the hearts of the people of Mecca away from that which their fathers rightly worshipped. Answer: Allah has spoken the truth to them.

34.44a Muhammad claimed that prior to his surahs, God had not brought to the Meccan people a divinely inspired Scriptures with which to know the way to eternal life. Yet, portions of the Old and New Testaments were readily available throughout the Arabian Peninsula and Muhammad made re-

peated references to them (see Q 2.44, 121; 3.3-4, 48; 4.46-47; 6.90-92, 114, 154-155; 7.169; 10.94; 17.4; 19.12, 16; 29.46; 32.23; 35.25; 40.53; 45.16).

34.44b Muhammad believed that he was the first divinely appointed warner (apostle) to the people of Mecca.

34.47 Muhammad claimed that his reward for his ministry is to serve Allah. He had no interest in worldly gain.

34.48 Allah speaks the truth.

34.49 Muhammad believed that the truth is found in the Qur'an. It will eventually take hold and cause all falsehood to vanish.

falsehood shall vanish and shall not come back."

Sixteenth rebuttal

50 Say, "If I err I only err against myself; and if I am guided it is all what my Lord inspires me: verily, He is the hearing, the nigh!"

Seventeenth rebuttal

51 And couldst thou see when they are scared, and there shall be no escape, and they shall be taken from a place that is nigh.
52 And they say, "We believe in it." But how can they partake of it from a distant place?
53 They misbelieved before, and conjectured about the unseen from a distant place.
54 And there shall be a barrier between

them and that which they lust after; as we did with their fellow sectaries before; verily, they were in hesitating doubt.

Surah 31

In the name of the merciful and compassionate God.

1 A. L. M.

Two Ways, Two Destinies

2 These are the signs of the wise Book,
3 a guidance and a mercy to those who do well,
4 who are steadfast in prayer and give alms and who of the hereafter are sure;
5 these are in guidance from their

34.50 Muhammad believed that Allah always shows the right direction. If a follower in Allah errs in word or deed, it does not reflect on Allah.
34.51-54 All infidels will eventually believe the truth about Allah when they are in "a near place" (standing before Allah at the Last Judgment). Yet this last minute conversion to the truth will not benefit them. Since they disbelieved in Allah when they were in "a distant place" (on earth), it will be too late to receive the benefits of belief in "a near place." A barrier shall be placed between them and their desires of Paradise.
Surah 31. The title of this surah, *Loqman*, comes from verse 12. This surah is an admonition to remain true to Allah in a world where

disbelief abounds, even among people of one's own family. Those who remain faithful will be rewarded with the joys of Paradise.
31.1 Literally, *Alif Lam Mim.* See Q 32.1, note.
31.2 *the wise Book* — Divine revelations from the eternal Book in Paradise (see **The Perspicuous Book** on pp. 178-179).
31.2-9 The two ways contrasted. The way of goodness is traveled by those who (a) listen to the Qur'an, (b) keep up prayer, and (c) pay the poor-rate. The way of wickedness is traveled by those who (a) engage in frivolous discourse, (b) mocks the way of Allah, and (c) reject the recitations from the Qur'an. The Old Testament also presents a

Lord, and these are the prosperous.

6 And amongst men is one who buys sportive legends, to lead astray from God's path, without knowledge, and to make a jest of it; these, for them is shameful woe!

7 And when our signs are recited to him, he turns his back, too big with pride, as though he heard them not,—as if in his two ears were dulness. But give to him glad tidings of grievous woe!

8 Verily, those who believe and do right, for them are gardens of pleasure,

9 to dwell therein for aye;—God's promise in truth, and He is mighty, wise.

Allah: the creator of the heavens and the earth

10 He created the heavens without pillars that ye can see, and He threw upon the earth firm mountains lest it should move with you; and He dispersed thereon every sort of beast; and we send down from the heavens water, and we caused to grow therein of every noble kind.

11 This is God's creation; show me what others beside Him have created;—nay, the unjust are in obvious error!

The wisdom of Loqman

12 We did give unto Loqmân wisdom,

contrast of the two ways in the First Psalm.
31.6 *sportive legends* —That is, false legends from the polytheists.
31.8a *believe and do right* — These words are repeated often in the Qur'an and serve as a brief summary of the Islamic gospel (see Q 103.3 note).

Those who "believe and do right" are promised "the gardens of pleasure." In an earlier surah, this phrase is used in relationship to the harems of maidens that will be assigned to the righteous in Paradise (see Q 56.12-26). With this in mind, the word "pleasure" is a reference to eroticism (see Q 10.9; 22.56; 31.8; 37.40-50; and 68.34; **The Last Judgment** on pp. 46-50, and **Paradise** on pp. 76-77).
31.10-11 Allah is the creator of the heavens and the earth. The mockers of Allah, however, have created nothing. Hence, their mockery is "manifest error."

31.12-22 Loqman is a legendary figure. He is the prototype of the sage who lived approximately 1100, B.C. He disdained worldly ambition and strived for inner perfection. He had become a character in legends, stories, and parables whose point is the acquisition of a deepened wisdom and spiritual maturity. He was also believed to be able to understand the language of flowers and grass, who told him the secret of eternal life, which was an elixir made by one of the plants. He wrote down the recipe, then lost it as it fell into the wild waters of the Ceyhan River in present-day eastern Turkey.

The only surviving ancient literature that mentions Loqman is the Qur'an. In this passage, the Qur'an made use of the Loqmanian legend to further advance the message of Muhammad. In Muhammad's re-telling, Loqman and Muhammad offered the same essential understanding of wisdom and spiritu-

saying, "Thank God; for he who thanks God is only thankful for his own soul; and he who is ungrateful—verily, God is independent, worthy of praise!"

13 And when Loqmân said to his son while admonishing him, "O my boy! associate none with God, for, verily, such association is a mighty wrong."

14 For we have commended his parents to man; his mother bore him with weakness upon weakness; and his weaning is in two years;—"Be thankful to me and to thy parents; for unto me shall your journey be.

15 But if they strive with thee that thou shouldst associate with me that which thou hast no knowledge of, then obey them not. But associate with them in the world with kindness, and follow the way of him who turns repentant unto me; then unto me is your return, and I will inform you of that which ye have done!

16 O my son! verily, if there were the weight of a grain of mustard seed

and it were (hidden) in the rock, or in the heaven, or in the earth, God would bring it (to light). Verily, God is subtle, well aware!"

17 "O my son! be steadfast in prayer, and bid what is reasonable and forbid what is wrong; be patient of what befalls thee, verily, that is one of the determined affairs."

18 "And twist not thy cheek proudly, nor walk in the land haughtily; verily, God loves not every arrogant boaster:

19 but be moderate in thy walk, and lower thy voice; verily, the most disagreeable of voices is the voice of asses!"

20 Have ye not seen that God has subjected to you what is in the heavens and what is in the earth, and has poured down upon you His favours, outwardly and inwardly? but amongst men are those who wrangle about God, without knowledge, and without guidance, and without an illuminating book!

21 And when it is said to them, "Follow what God has sent down;" they say, "Nay! we will follow

ality. Polytheism is wrong and the singular devotion to Allah is the not only right, it is the beginning of true wisdom. One is also to remain faithful in prayer and humble. Moreover, one is to avoid those who speak disrespectfully of Allah. If one's parents should perchance discourage this approach to spirituality and wisdom, a child was to reject their teachings and remain true to Allah.

31.19 *the voice of asses* — In the Islamic faith, true spirituality is manifested with a display of humility in one's personal life. Those who speak boastfully are described as possessing "voices of asses."

31.21 A common complaint from Muhammad was that the Meccan people were committed to the religion of their fathers—that is, the Arabic Star Family religion. He believed that they were satanically motivated

what we found our fathers agreed upon;"—what! though Satan calls them to the torment of the blaze?

22 But he who resigns his face unto God, and does good, he has grasped the firm handle; unto God is the issue of affairs.

Spiritual contentment
in a world of disbelief

23 But he who misbelieves, let not his misbelief grieve thee; to us is their return, and we will inform them of what they do;—for, verily, God knows the nature of men's breasts!

24 We will let them enjoy themselves a little; then we will force them to rigorous woe!

25 And if thou shouldst ask them who created the heavens and the earth, they will surely say, "God." Say, "Praise be to God!" but most of them do not know.

26 God's is what is in the heavens and what is in the earth; verily, God, He is the independent, worthy of praise.

27 And were the trees that are in the earth pens, and the sea (ink) with seven more seas to swell its tide, the words of God would not be spent; verily, God is mighty, wise!

28 Your creation and your rising again are but as that of one soul; verily, God both hears and sees!

Illustration:
Day and Night

29 Dost thou not see that God joins on the night to the day, and joins on the day to the night, and has subjected the sun and the moon,— each of them runs on unto an appointed time? and that God of what ye do is well aware?

30 That is because God, He is true, and because what ye call on beside Him is falsehood, and because

---

to remain committed to it.

31.23 *God knows the nature of men's breasts* — The Bible makes a similar claim (see 1 Sam 16:7; 1 Chron 28:9; Ps 139:23-24; Matt 9:4; Jn 2:24; 5:42; 16:30; Acts 1:24; Heb 4:13).

31.24 According to Muhammad, Allah remained coldly disinterested and detached from infidels. He allowed them momentary pleasures and then would rain down upon them His judgment. In contrast, God (as presented in the Bible) and His people possess deep burdens for those who have not embraced the Gospel (see 1 Sam 15:35; Ps 119:136; Jer 9:1; 13:17; Ezek 9:4; Lk 19:41-

44; Rom 9:1-5; Phil 3:18; 2 Pet 3:9).

31.27 With poetic flare, this verse states that if the trees were pens and the seas were ink, the words of Allah could not be exhausted. Compare John 20:25 where a similar sentiment is expressed in reference to the ministry of Jesus Christ.

31.29 All of creation operates in submission to the all-powerful Allah.

31.30 *God, He is the high, the great* — This phrase, in the Muslim world, is called Takbir (*Allahu akbar*). See Q 34.23, note.

31.31 Navigation and the telling of direction through a knowledge of the stars (His signs) is possible because creation remains

God, He is the high, the great!

Illustration:
Allah's care on the high seas

31   Dost thou not see that the ship
      rides on in the sea by the favour
      of God, that He may show you of
      His signs? verily, in that are signs
      to every grateful person.
32   And when a wave like shadows
      covers them, they call on God,
      being sincere in their religion; and
      when He saves them to the shore,
      then amongst them are some who
      halt between two opinions. But
      none gainsays our signs save ev-
      ery perfidious misbeliever.

Conclusion

33   O ye folk! fear your Lord and dread
      the day when the father shall not

atone for his son, nor shall the child
atone aught for its parent. Verily,
the promise of God is true! Say,
"Let not the life of this world beguile you; and let not the beguiler
beguile you concerning God."
34   Verily, God, with Him is the knowl-
      edge of the Hour; and He sends
      down the rain; and He knows what
      is in the wombs; and no soul
      knows what it is that it shall earn
      to-morrow; and no soul knows in
      what land it shall die; verily, God
      is knowing, well aware!

Surah 69

In the name of the compassionate and mer-
ciful God.

The Infallible

submissive to the will of Allah.
31.32a *gainsays our signs* — That is, declares divine revelation to be false.
31.32b *perfidious misbeliever* — That is,
faithless infidel.
31.33 At the Last Judgment, each person
will face his or her own sins. Nobody will be
allowed to atone for another's sins (cf. Ezek
18:19-20). The New Testament, of course,
claims otherwise, that Jesus Christ is the
atonement for the sins of the world. "God
made him who had no sin to be sin for us, so
that in him we might become the righteousness of God" (2 Cor 5:21; also see Rom 5:6-
8; 1 Cor 15:3; Gal 3:13; Titus 2:14; 1 Pet
2:24; 3:18).
31.33-34 People are admonished to (a)

guard themselves against the possibilities of
being cast into Hell, (b) not allow worldly life
deceive them, (c) not allow the arch deceiver (Satan) deceive them, and (d) remember that Allah knows all things.
31.34 *the Hour* — This is the moment of
time when the Last Judgment will occur (see
Q 79.42, note).
Surah 69. The title of this surah, *The Sure*
Truth, comes from verse 41. The theme of
this surah is the Last Judgment. Just as Allah had severely punished civilizations of a
bye-gone era, Allah will also judge those of
the present era. The surah is a reminder of
ideas mentioned in previous surahs: the book
of the left hand, the book of the right hand,
the rewards of Paradise and Hell, and

1   The Infallible,

2   what is the Infallible?

3   and what should make thee know what the Infallible is?

Two Illustrations:
Thamud and Ad

4   Thamûd and 'Âd called the Striking Day a lie;

5   but as for Thamûd they perished by the shock;

6   and as for 'Âd they perished with the violent cold blast of wind,

7   which He subjected against them for seven nights and eight days consecutively. Thou mightest see the people therein prostrate as though they were palm stumps thrown down,

8   and canst thou see any of them left?

Third Illustration:
Pharaoh

9   And Pharaoh and those before him of the overturned cities committed sins,

10   and they rebelled against the apostle of their Lord, and He seized them with an excessive punishment.

Fourth Illustration:
storms on the high seas

11   Verily, we, when the water surged, bore you on it in a sailing ship,

12   to make it a memorial for you, and that the retentive ear might hold it.

The Last Judgment

13   And when the trumpet shall be blown with one blast,

14   and the earth shall be borne away, and the mountains too, and both be crushed with one crushing;

15   on that day shall the inevitable happen;

Muhammad as the prophet who will be esteemed as the faithful warner of all that will come to pass.

69.1 *the infallible* — That is, the Qur'an. Muhammad understood his surahs to be without error. All divine revelations are, by definition, infallible. Yet, Muhammad maintained that only the Qur'an has been preserved infallible. The rest, including both the Old and New Testaments, have been corrupted by scribes who altered the original texts. Accordingly, Islamic scholars believe that only the Qur'an is a reliable divinely revealed document. Yet, this doctrine of infallibility collides against the opposing doctrine of abrogation (see **The Doctrine of Abrogation** on pp. 68-70).

69.4 *Thamud and Ad* — These are two ancient civilizations that were destroyed because they failed to heed the message of the apostles sent to them from God, warning of judgment to come if they did not repent (see Q 91, note, and Q 54.17-21, note).

69.11-12 The Red Sea was known for terrifying storms that would arrive in a moment's time. It is because of this that goods were typically transported by caravans across the desert rather than by ships on the sea.

69.13 According to Muhammad, at the blowing the trumpet at the Hour of the resurrection and summoning to the Last Judgment, the earth will be reduced to dust that is blown away in a moment of time. The

16   and the heaven on that day shall be
      cleft asunder, for on that day shall
      it wane!

17   and the angels upon the sides
      thereof; and above them on that
      day shall eight bear the throne of
      thy Lord!

18   On the day when ye shall be set
      forth no hidden thing of yours shall
      be concealed.

The book in the right hand

19   And as for him who is given his
      book in his right hand, he shall say,
      "Here! take and read my book.

20   Verily, I thought that I should meet
      my reckoning;"

21   and he shall be in a pleasing life,

22   in a lofty garden,

23   whose fruits are nigh to cull

24   —"Eat ye and drink with good di-
      gestion, for what ye did aforetime
      in the days that have gone by!"

The book in the left hand

25   But as for him who is given his
      book in his left hand he shall say,
      "O, would that I had not received
      my book!

26   I did not know what my account
      would be.

27   O, would that it had been an end
      of me!

28   my wealth availed me not!

29   my authority has perished from
      me!"

30   "Take him and fetter him,

31   then in hell broil him!

32   then into a chain whose length is
      seventy cubits force him!

33   verily, he believed not in the mighty
      God,

34   nor was he particular to feed the
      poor:

35   therefore he has not here to-day
      any warm friend,

36   nor any food except foul ichor,

Bible comments that at the blowing of the final trumpet, the earth will suffer a series of profound apocalyptic devastations (see Rev. 8:1ff). The earth, however, will not be reduced to dust and blown away.

69.18 *on that day when ye shall be set forth no hidden thing of you shall be concealed* — That is, all secret sins and all hidden acts of righteousness will be revealed (cf. Ps 130:3; 143:2; Matt 10:42; 12:36; Mk 9:41; Rom 2:16; 1 Cor 3:12-15; Gal 6:7-9; Eph 6:8; and Heb 6:10).

69.19 *his book in his right hand* — That is, the book full of good works of those destined for eternal life (see Q 56.7-10, 27-40; 84.7-8).

69.22 In the Qur'an, Paradise is often described as a garden, or oasis (see Q 55.46-61, note, and **Paradise** on pp. 76-77).

69.25 *his book in his left hand* — That is, the book of evil works of those destined for Hell (see Q 56.9, 41-46).

69.31 Repeatedly, Muhammad described people in Hell as being broiled (see Q 82.15, note).

69.33-35 The criteria for having one's name mentioned in the Book in the Left Hand is: (a) not believing in Allah, and (b) not participating in the feeding of the poor.

69.38-52 According to this passage, at the Last Judgment Muhammad will be called the "noble apostle" (v. 40) and the Qur'an "the

37	which none save sinners shall eat."	44	Why if he had invented against us any sayings,
	Muhammad:	45	we would have seized him by the right hand,
	the Apostle of Allah	46	then we would have cut his jugular vein;
38	I need not swear by what ye see	47	nor could any one of you have kept us off from him.
39	or what ye do not see,	48	Verily, it is a memorial to the pious;
40	verily, it is the speech of a noble apostle;	49	and, verily, we know that there are amongst you those who say it is a lie;
41	and it is not the speech of a poet:— little is it ye believe!	50	and, verily, it is a source of sighing to the misbelievers;
42	And it is not the speech of a sooth-sayer—little is it that ye mind!	51	and, verily, it is certain truth!
43	—a revelation from the Lord of the worlds.		

revelation from the Lord of the worlds" (v. 43).

69.44-47 According to this passage, one of the signs that Muhammad is a true prophet of Allah is that if he were not, then Allah "would certainly have seized him by the right hand" and "cut his jugular vein." Since this did not happen, this is a proof that Muhammad is a true prophet of Allah.

The Bible, in contrast, teaches that false prophets are typically not judged in such an obvious fashion. Rather, it will be at the Last Judgment when all such pretenders will be revealed and condemned (Matt 7:15, 21-23; cf. Jer 14:14; 27:15).

John R. W. Stott comments: "In telling people to beware of *false prophets* (Matt 7:15), Jesus obviously assumed that there were such. There is no sense in putting on your garden gate the notice 'Beware of the dog' if all you have at home is a couple of cats and budgerigar! No. Jesus warned his followers of false prophets because they already existed. We come across them on numerous occasions in the Old Testament,

and Jesus seems to have regarded the Pharisees and Sadducees in the same light. 'Blind leaders of the blind,' he called them. He also implied that they would increase, and that the period preceding the end would be characterized not only by the worldwide spread of the gospel but also by the rise of false teachers who would lead many astray. We hear them in nearly every New Testament letter. They are called either 'pseudo-prophets' as here ('prophets' presumably because they claimed divine inspiration), or 'pseudo-apostles' (because they claimed apostolic authority) or 'pseudo-teachers' or even 'pseudo-Christs' (because they made messianic pretensions or denied that Jesus was the Christ come in the flesh. But each was 'pseudo', and *pseudos* is the Greek word for a lie. The history of the Christian church has been a long and dreary story of controversy with false teachers. Their value, in the overruling providence of God, is that they have presented the church with a challenge to think out and define the truth, but they have caused much damage. I fear there are

52   Therefore celebrate the name of thy mighty Lord!

Surah 68

In the name of the merciful and compassionate God.

1   N.

A defense for Muhammad

By the pen, and what they write,

2   thou art not, by God's grace, mad!
3   and, verily, thine is a hire that is not grudged!
4   and, verily, thou art of a grand nature!
5   But thou shalt see and they shall see
6   which of you is the infatuated.

7   Verily, thy Lord He knows best who errs from His way; and He knows best those who are guided.
8   Then obey not those who call thee liar;

Strategy of the infidels

9   they would fain that thou shouldst be smooth with them, then would they be smooth with thee!
10   And obey not any mean swearer, a backbiter,
11   a walker about with slander;
12   a forbidder of good, a transgressor, a sinner;
13   rude, and base-born too;
14   though he have wealth and sons!
15   When our signs are recited to him he says, "Old folks' tales!"
16   We will brand him on the snout!

still many in today's church" (*The Message of the Sermon on the Mount,* p. 197).

Surah 68. The title to this surah, *The Pen,* comes from verse one. This surah addresses the question of madness. Was Muhammad mad, as the polytheists insist, or were they the ones who were mad? Muhammad believed that he was admonished by Allah to remain steadfast in his beliefs in Allah and Islamic doctrine.

68.1 Literally, *Nun.* See Surah 32.1 note.

68.2 The Meccan people accused Muhammad of madness (see Q 17.47; 26.27; 44.14; 51.52; 52.29, 68.51). Allah, in contrast, reassured Muhammad that he was sane.

68.4 *thou art of a grand nature* — That is, Muhammad believed that he was a man of outstanding morality and wisdom. In con-

trast, Christians look to Jesus as the Perfect Man. "Let us fix our eyes on Jesus, the author and perfecter of our faith, who for the joy set before him endured the cross, scorning its shame, and sat down at the right hand of the throne of God. Consider him who endured such opposition from sinful men, so that you will not grow weary and lose heart" (Heb 12:2-3).

68.9-16 Seven characteristics of the polytheists: (a) full of slander, (b) forbidders of good, (c) step beyond the limits, (d) sinful, (e) ignoble, (f) base born, and (g) claim that the Qur'an is false.

68.16 *brand him on the snout* — This is an idiomatic Arabic phrase that means to stigmatize Muhammad with disgrace.

68.17 *cut off the produce in the morning*

Story of the selfish farmers

17   Verily, we have tried them as we tried the fellows of the garden when they swore, "We will cut its fruit at morn!"

18   But they made not the exception;

19   and there came round about it an encompassing calamity from thy Lord the while they slept;

20   and on the morrow it was as one the fruit of which is cut.

21   And they cried to each other in the morning,

22   "Go early to your tilth if ye would cut it!"

23   So they set off, saying privily to each other,

24   "There shall surely enter it today unto you no poor person!"

25   And they went early deciding to be stingy.

26   And when they saw it they said, "Verily, we have erred!

27   Nay, we are forbidden (its fruit)!"

28   Said the most moderate of them, "Said I not to you, 'unless ye celebrate God's praises!'"

29   Said they, "Celebrated be the praises of our Lord! verily, we

were unjust!"

30   And they approached each other with mutual blame.

31   Said they, "O woe to us! verily, we have been outrageous!

32   Haply our Lord may give us instead a better than it; verily, we unto our Lord do yearn,"

33   Thus is the torment, but, verily, the torment of the hereafter is greater, if ye did but know!

*A coming calamity
upon the infidels*

34   Verily, for the pious with their Lord are gardens of pleasure!

35   Shall we then make the Muslims like the sinners?

36   What ails you? how ye judge!

37   Or have ye a book in which ye can study,

38   that ye are surely to have what ye may choose?

39   Or have ye oaths binding on us until the judgment day that ye are surely to have what ye may judge?

40   Ask them, which of them will vouch for this?

41   Or have they partners, then let

— That is, harvest the fruit in the morning.

68.18 A custom of the ancient Middle East was that the poor were permitted to glean leftover harvested foods. Many farmers, however, did not follow this custom (cf. Lev 19:9-10; 23:22; Deut 24:19-22; and Ruth 2:2).

68.22 *tilth* — cultivated land.

68.33 The moral of the story is that selfish-

ness invites judgment from Allah—in this life as well as the afterlife. The judgment in the afterlife, however, is far worse.

68.34 At the Last Judgment, the pious are promised "the gardens of pleasure." The word "pleasure" more than likely refers to erotic pleasure (see **The Last Judgment** on pp. 46-50 and **Paradise** on pp. 76-77).

68.39-41 Muhammad's point was that no-

them bring their partners if they do speak the truth?

42 On the day when the leg shall be bared; and they shall be called to adore and shall not be able!

43 Lowering their looks, abasement shall attack them, for they were called to adore while yet they were safe!

44 But let me alone with him who calls this new discourse a lie. We will surely bring them down by degrees from whence they do not know.

45 And I will let them have their way! for my device is sure.

46 Or dost thou ask them a hire for it while they are burdened with debts?

47 Or have they the knowledge of the unseen, so that they write?

Example of Jonah

48 But wait patiently for the judgment

of thy Lord, and be not like the fellow of the fish, when he cried out as he was choking with rage.

49 Had it not been that grace from his Lord reached him, he would have been cast out on the naked (shore) and blamed the while!

50 But his Lord elected him, and made him of the pious.

51 The misbelievers well-nigh upset thee with their looks when they hear the reminder, and they say, "Surely he is mad!"

52 And yet it is but a reminder to the worlds!

Surah 41

In the name of the compassionate and merciful God.

1 H. M.

In Praise of the Qur'an

---

body has the right to demand entrance into Paradise.

68.42-43 According to Muhammad, the time to make obeisance to Allah is in this life. For those who wait until the Last Judgment, it will be too late (cf. Matt 7:21-23).

68.44 *We will overtake them by degrees* — Allah will bring the wicked down, step by step, without their knowledge.

68.48 *the fellow of the fish* — This is a reference to the story of Jonah. He cried out in distress to the Lord while in the belly of the great fish. Jonah refused to "wait patiently" for the judgment of the Lord, took matters into his own hands, fled from the

Lord, and suffered for it.

68.51 Again, Muhammad was accused of madness (see Q 51.52; 81.22; 68.2).

Surah 41. The title of this surah, *Ha Mim*, comes from verse one. Presented as a catechism, it addresses the question of reasoned acceptance or willful rejection of the Qur'an. The surah begins with four rebuttals of those who reject the Qur'an, and then transitions into a series of warnings. The surah concludes with a warning to those who remained obstinate in their unbelief of Muhammad's message.

41.1 Literally, *Ha Mim*. See Q 32.1, note.

41.2-4a According to this passage, the

2   A revelation from the merciful, the compassionate;

3   a book whose signs are detailed; an Arabic Qur'ân for a people who do know;

4   a herald of glad tidings and a warning.

First rebuttal

But most of them turn aside and do not hear,

5   and say, "Our hearts are veiled from what thou dost call us to, and in our ears is dullness, and between us and thee there is a veil. Act thou; verily, we are acting too!"

6   Say, "I am but a mortal like yourselves, I am inspired that your God is one God; then go straight to Him, and ask forgiveness of Him; and woe to the idolaters, who give not alms, and in the hereafter disbelieve!"

8   Verily, those who believe and do right, for them is a hire that is not grudged.

Second rebuttal

9   Say, "What! do ye really misbelieve in Him who created the earth in two days, and do ye make peers for Him?—that is the Lord of the worlds!"

10   And He placed thereon firm mountains above it and blessed it, and apportioned therein its foods in four days alike for those who ask.

11   Then He made for the heaven and it was but smoke, and He said to it and to the earth, "Come, ye two, whether ye will or no!" They said, "We come willingly!"

12   And He decreed them seven heavens in two days, and inspired every heaven with its bidding: and we adorned the lower heaven with

Qur'an is: (a) is a revelation from Allah, (b) plainly written, (c) written in Arabic, (d) a herald of good news, and (e) a warning. The Qur'an, as noted in Q 39.28, note, contains non-Arabic words (see **The Qur'an** on pp. 150-153).

41.4b-8 According to Muhammad, the hearts of infidels are heavy and cannot understand the Qur'an. Those who believe and do good will have a reward that will never cease (see **Divine Forgiveness in Islam** on pp. 158-161).

41.6 *I am but a mortal like yourselves* — Muhammad sensed a need to clarify that he was a mere mortal—and not a god. Perhaps rumors were forming in Mecca that he

thought of himself as a god. In contrast, Jesus Christ had no qualms making the claim of deity (see John 8:58; 10:30; 14:9; 17:21; also see the **Definition of Chalcedon** on pp. 785-786).

41.8 *believe and do right* — These words are repeated often in the Qur'an and serve as a brief summary of the Islamic gospel (see Q 103.3 note and **The Last Judgment** on pp. 46-50).

41.9-12 According to Muhammad, infidels should be ashamed of themselves for their lack of belief and their substitution of other gods for the one true God. Muhammad also believed that the earth was made in two days and then apportioned food in the fol-

lamps and guardian angels; that is the decree of the mighty, the knowing One.

Third rebuttal

13   But if they turn aside, then say, "I have warned you of a thunder-clap like the thunder-clap of 'Âd and Thamûd;

14   when their apostles came to them from before them and from behind them (saying), 'Serve ye none but God.'" They said, "If our Lord pleased He would send down angels; so we in what ye are sent with disbelieve."

15   And as for 'Âd, they were big with pride in the land, without right, and said, "Who is stronger than us in might?" Did they not see that God who created them He was stronger than they in might? But they did gainsay our signs.

16   And we sent upon them a cold blast in unfortunate days, that we might make them taste the torment of disgrace in the life of this world;— but the torment of the hereafter is more disgraceful, and they shall not be helped.

17   And as for Thamûd we guided them; but they preferred blindness to guidance, and the thunder-clap of the torment of abasement caught them for what they had earned;

18   but we saved those who believed and who did fear.

Fourth rebuttal

19   And the day when the enemies of God shall be gathered together into the fire, marshalled along;

20   until when they come to it, their hearing and their eyesight and their skins shall bear witness against

---

lowing four days. The first chapter of Genesis states otherwise (see Gen 1:1-31).

41.11 In this passage, the creation of the earth is used as a simile of obedience expected by Allah. Just as the mountains, the heavens and the vapor (smoke) were called into existence, and they willingly obeyed, so too people are to be in submission to the will of Allah.

41.12 *seven heavens* — The Qur'an divides Paradise into seven layers (see Q 13.17 note, 23.86, note, 65.12, note, 78.12, and **Paradise** on pp. 76-77).

41.13-18 *Third Rebuttal.* If infidels turn aside, tell them that they have been duly warned. Their judgment will be like that of

Ad and Thamud (see Q 91, note, and Q 55.17-21).

41.19-29 *Fourth Rebuttal.* Infidels say that people should not listen to the Qur'an. Muhammad's answer: the fires of Hell await all infidels. Six characteristics of Hell: (a) one's ears, eyes, and skin will bear witness against him or her, (b) those in Hell are known as "the lost ones," (c) people will not be granted good will, (d) people in Hell are known as the losers, (e) the reward for denying the Qur'an, and (f) a yearning to trample under their feet all those who led them astray from the truth of Allah.

41.21 *they shall say to their skins* — The meaning of this phrase is unclear.

them of that which they have done.

21   And they shall say to their skins, "Why have ye borne witness against us?" they shall say, "God gave us speech who has given speech to everything; He created you at first, and unto Him shall ye be returned;

22   and ye could not conceal yourselves that your hearing and your eyesight should not be witness against you, nor your skins; but ye thought that God did not know much. of what ye do.

23   And that thought of yours which ye thought concerning your Lord has destroyed you, and ye have now become of those who lose!"

24   And if they are patient, still the fire is a resort for them; and if they ask for favour again, they shall not be taken into favour.

25   We will allot to them mates, for they have made seemly to them what was before them and what was behind them; and due against them was the sentence on the nations who passed away before them; both of ginns and of mankind; verily, they were the losers!

26   Those who misbelieve say, "Listen not to this Qur'ân, but talk

foolishly about it, haply ye may gain the upper hand."

27   But we will make those who misbelieve taste keen torment; and we will recompense them with the worst of that which they have done.

28   That is, the recompense of the enemies of God,—the fire! for them is an eternal abode therein: a recom-pence for that they did gainsay our signs.

29   And those who misbelieved say, "Our Lord, show us those who have led us astray amongst the ginns and mankind; we will place them beneath our feet, and they shall both be amongst those who are put down!"

An appeal to stay true
to the Qur'an

30   Verily, those who say, "Our Lord is—God," and then go straight, the angels descend upon them—"fear not and be not grieved, but receive the glad tidings of Paradise which ye were promised;

31   we are your patrons in the life of this world and in the next, and ye shall have therein what your souls

---

41.25, 29 *ginns* — genies (see **Occultism in Seventh Century Arabia** on pp. 123-125).

41.26-28 *Listen not to this Qur'an* — Apparently, this was a refrain common in Mecca by those who opposed Muhammad's ministry. According to Muhammad, all who ridi-

culed the Qur'an were destined for the fires of Hell.

41.30 *glad tidings of Paradise* — That is, the Islamic gospel.

41.30-36 Two characteristics of Paradise: (a) People will enter the garden that they were promised, and (b) they will enjoy all

desire, and ye shall have therein what ye call for,

32   —an entertainment from the forgiving, the merciful!"

33   And who speaks better than he who calls to God and does right, and says, "Verily, I am of those resigned?"

34   Good and evil shall not be deemed alike; repel (evil) with what is best, and lo! He between whom and thyself was enmity is as though he were a warm patron.

35   But none shall meet with it save those who are patient; and none shall meet with it save those who are endowed with mighty good fortune.

36   And if an incitement from the devil incites you, then seek refuge in God; verily, He both hears and knows.

First warning:
Avoid star worship

37   And of His signs are the night and the day, and the sun and the moon. Adore ye not the sun, neither the moon; but adore God who created you, if it be Him ye serve.

38   But if they be too big with pride— yet those who are with thy Lord celebrate His praises by night and day, and they are never weary.

39   And of His signs (is this), that thou mayest see the earth drooping, and when we send down water upon it it stirs and swells; verily, He who quickens it will surely quicken the dead; verily, He is mighty over all.

Second warning:
Avoid disbelief in the Qur'an

40   Verily, those who are inclined to oppose our signs are not hidden from us. Is he who is cast into the fire better, or he who comes safe on the resurrection day? Do what ye will: verily, He on what ye do

their souls' desire.

41.33 *I am of those resigned* — That is, "I am of those in *islam*, in full submission to the will of Allah." The Christian gospel also admonishes people to be surrendered to the will of God (e.g., Rom 12:1, 2) yet it does not equate the obedience to God with the gospel itself. The gospel is a free gift, apart from good works and therefore cannot be earned (see Eph 2:8, 9). Obedience to God (that is, a surrendered life to God's will) is our way of being thankful to the gift of eternal life and is, therefore, a natural outgrowth of the gospel.

41.36 According to this verse, the devil

can cause interference in keeping one from belief in Allah and the practice of good works (cf. 1 Kings 22:22; Matt 13:19; and 2 Cor 4:4).

41.37-39 The first warning was directed at the devotees of the Star Family religion. Throughout Arabia, the sun, moon, and other stars were worshipped (see **Polytheism in Seventh Century Arabia** on pp. 92-97). In its place, Muhammad admonished that people were to worship Allah—and Allah alone.

41.40-43 The second warning was directed at all who reject the Qur'an. According to Muhammad, all such people will be cast into

doth look.

41 Verily, those who misbelieve in the reminder when it comes to them— and, verily, it is a glorious Book!

42 falsehood shall not come to it, from before it, nor from behind it—a revelation from the wise, the praiseworthy One.

43 Naught is said to thee but what was said to the apostles before thee, "Verily, thy Lord is Lord of forgiveness and Lord of grievous torment!"

*The Qur'an is a clear
and correct communication*

44 And had we made it a foreign Qur'ân, they would have said, "Unless its signs be detailed... What! foreign and Arabic?" Say,

"It is, for those who believe, a guidance and a healing. But those who believe not, in their ears is dullness, and it is blindness to them; these are called to from a far-off place."

45 And we gave Moses the Book, and it was disputed about; but had it not been for thy Lord's word already passed it would have been decided between them, for., verily, they were in hesitating doubt thereon.

Warning to the polytheists

46 Whoso does right it is for his soul, and whoso does evil it is against it, for thy Lord is not unjust towards His servants.

47 To Him is referred the knowledge

the fires of Hell. This is because the Qur'an is "a glorious Book"—a book with no falsehood. Christians, of course, reject this assertion, claiming that the Qur'an is not divinely inspired.

41.44a *a foreign Qur'an* — According to Muhammad, all versions of the Qur'an not written in the Arabic language is "a foreign Qur'an." Only when read in the Arabic language, is the Qur'an "a guidance and a healing." This is a curious statement since the Arabic Qur'an itself contains foreign non-Arabic words (see **The Qur'an** on pp. 150-153; also see Q 12.2; 13.37; 20.113; 26.195; 39.28; 42.7; and 43.3).

In contrast, Christianity makes no such provincial or linguistic restrictions on its sacred literature. Though originally written in Hebrew (with a few passages in the Chaldean

language), the Old Testament was eventually translated into Greek (second century, B.C.) since Greek had become the *lengua franca* of the east Mediterranean world. The New Testament writers made use of the Greek translation of the Old Testament, the Septuagint, when including OT citations in their sacred documents. Though Jesus knew Hebrew, He spoke Aramaic since that was the *lengua franca* of the native inhabitants of Palestine. Today the Bible has been translated into most of the languages of the world, with the full blessings of the Church in this endeavor.

41.44b *guidance and a healing* — Muhammad believed that belief in the Qur'an results in (a) spiritual guidance, and (b) a healing of sickness and disease.

41.45 As was the case with the Qur'an in

of the Hour: and no fruits come forth from their husks, and no female conceives, or is delivered, save with His knowledge. And the day when He shall call to them, "Where are the partners ye did join with me?" they shall say, "We do own to thee there is no witness amongst us!"

48   and that on which they used to call before shall stray away from them, and they shall think there is no escape for them.

Warning to the infidels

49   Man is never tired of praying for good, but if evil touch him, then he is despairing and hopeless.

50   But if we make him taste mercy from us after distress has touched him he will surely say, "This is for me, and I do not think the Hour is imminent; and if I be brought back to my Lord, verily, I shall surely have good with Him;" but we will inform those who misbelieve of what they have done, and we will surely make them taste wretched torment.

51   And when we have been gracious to man, he turns away and goes aside; but when evil touches him he is one of copious prayer.

52   Say, "Let us see now! if it be from God and ye disbelieve in it, who is more in error than he who is in a remote schism?"

53   We will show them our signs in the regions and in themselves, until it is plain to them that it is the truth. Is it not enough for thy Lord that He is witness over all?

54   Ay, verily, they are in doubt about

Muhammad's day, some people accepted the book of Moses (the Pentateuch) and some rejected it.

41.47a *the Hour* — This is the moment when all people will be summoned to appear at the Last Judgment (see Q 79.24, note).

41.47b *the partners*— That is, the many gods worshipped in the Star Family religion. According to this religious system, all the gods (stars) are of the same celestial family. It is in this sense that they were *partners*. Proselytization was therefore strongly discouraged since it disrupted the inherent ecumenical logic of within this religious system. Muhammad's insistence in the worship of Allah—and Allah alone—was therefore a direct assault on the Arabic Star Family religion.

41.49-54 Muhammad's point was that unbelief and unthankfulness are twin sins—where one is the other is often near at hand. In spite of the many blessings that Allah bestows upon people, if they should turn away and refuse to submit to Allah, it is a sign of both an ungrateful and an unbelieving heart.

41.50 *the Hour* — The moment in time when all people will be summoned to appear at the Last Judgment (see Q 79.24, note).

41.53 *we will show them our signs* — Muhammad believed that Allah reveals the truths of the Qur'an in "the regions" (that is, round about people) and "in themselves" (that is, deep within their hearts).

The Bible makes a similar claim about the

the meeting of their Lord! Ay, verily, He encompasses all!

Surah 71

In the name of the compassionate and merciful God.

The story of Noah

1   Verily, we sent Noah to his people, "Warn thy people before there come to them a grievous torment!"

2   Said he, "O my people! verily, I am to you an obvious warner,

3   that ye serve God and fear Him and obey me.

4   He will pardon you your sins, and will defer you unto an appointed time; verily, God's appointed time when it comes will not be deferred, did ye but know!"

5   Said he, "My Lord! verily, I have called my people by night and day,

6   and my call did but increase them in flight;

7   and, verily, every time I called them, that Thou mightest pardon them, they placed their fingers in their ears and tried to cover themselves with their garments and persisted, and were very big with pride.

8   Then I called them openly;

9   then I published to them and I spoke to them in secret,

10   and I said, 'Ask forgiveness of your Lord, verily, He is very forgiving.

11   He will send the rain upon you in torrents,

12   and will extend to you wealth and children, and will make for you gardens, and will make for you rivers.

13   What ails you that ye hope not for something serious from God,

14   when He has created you by steps?

15   Do ye not see how God has created the seven heavens in stories,

---

Old and New Testaments. External evidence (that is, archeological and historical verifications) and internal evidence (that is, the assertions within the biblical text itself) makes a case for its claim of divine inspiration. In addition to this, the Holy Spirit speaks to the heart and confirms the divine origin of the biblical text (see Jn 14:26; 15:26; 16:8-15; 1 Cor 2:6-16).

Surah 71. The title to this surah, *Noah*, comes from verse one. The surah draws on the oft-repeated theme in the Qur'an: that Allah has sent many apostles to the peoples of the world to warn them of judgment to come (in this life as well as the life to come)

and therefore to repent and turn back to Allah. Most people, however, reject this message. This surah draws attention to Noah to illustrate this message.

71.2 *an obvious warner* — This phrase, which Muhammad used repeatedly of himself, was intended as a source of comparison between himself and Noah. In this respect, this surah presents Muhammad as a Noah-like figure.

71.7 *fingers in their ears* — The reaction of the people of Noah's day to his message of repentance was meant to be a parallel with that of Muhammad's ministry to the Meccan people. In both cases, people had "placed

16 and has set the moon therein for a light, and set the sun for a lamp?

17 and God has made you grow out of the earth,

18 and then He will make you return thereto, and will make you come forth therefrom;

19 and God has made for you the earth a carpet

20 that ye may walk therein in broad paths.'"

21 Said Noah, "My Lord! verily, they have rebelled against me, and followed him whose wealth and children have but added to his loss,

22 and they have plotted a great plot,

23 and said, 'Ye shall surely not leave your gods: ye shall surely neither leave Wadd, nor Suwâ'h, nor Yaghûth, nor Ya'ûq, nor Nasr.

24 and they led astray many.'" And thou (Mohammed) wilt only increase the unjust in their error

25 —because of their sins they were drowned and made to enter into the fire, and they found no helpers against God!

26 And Noah said, "My Lord! leave not upon the earth one dweller of the misbelievers.

27 Verily, Thou, if Thou shouldst leave them, they will lead astray Thy servants, and they will only bear for children sinners and misbelievers.

28 My Lord! pardon me and my two parents, and whomsoever enters my house believing, and (pardon) the believers men and women— but Thou shalt only increase the unjust in loss."

Surah 52

In the name of merciful and compassionate God.

Oaths

1 By the mount!

2 by the Book inscribed

3 upon an outstretched vellum!

4 by the frequented house!

5 by the elevated roof!

---

their fingers in their ears" and ignored the messages.

71.14 *He has created you by steps* — That is, Allah created man from fertilized egg, to fetus, and finally to baby.

71.21-23 This quote is not found in the Genesis account of Noah. It is apparently Muhammad's own invention.

71.23 According to this passage, the antediluvian people of Noah's age worshipped a number of differing false gods: Wadd, Suwa'h, Yaghuth, Ya'uq and Nasr. Curiously, these were the same gods worshipped by people of Muhammad's day in western Arabia. Muhammad's point, of course, was that the people of his day were following the precise error of the people of Noah's day, and will suffer divine chastisement just as did the people of Noah's day.

Since no documentary evidence exists of the names of the gods worshipped in the antediluvian world, it is likely that Muhammad took the names of gods worshipped in western Arabia of his day and interpolated them backwards in time, making the connection between the idolatry of a bye-gone era with

6   by the swelling sea!

The Last Judgment

7   verily, the torment of thy Lord will come to pass;
8   —there is none to avert it!
9   The day when the heavens shall reel about,
10   and the mountains shall move about,
11   —then woe upon that day to those who call (the apostles) liars,
12   who plunge into discussion for a sport!
13   On the day when they shall be thrust away into the fire of hell,
14   — "This is the fire, the which ye used to call a lie!
15   —Is it magic, this? or can ye not

see?
16   —broil ye therein, and be patient thereof or be not patient, it is the same to you: ye are but rewarded for that which ye did do!"

The coming blessing
for those who guard against evil

17   Verily, the pious (shall be) in gardens and pleasure,
18   enjoying what their Lord has given them; for their Lord will save them from the torment of hell.
19   "Eat and drink with good digestion, for that which ye have done!"
20   Reclining on couches in rows; and we will wed them to large-eyed maids.
21   And those who believe and whose

the idolatry of his own. In Muhammad's day (seventh century Arabia), the Arabian tribe of Kalb worshipped Wadd, the tribe of Hamdan worshipped Suwa'h, the tribe of Madhhij worshipped Yaghuth, the tribe of Murad worshipped Ya'uq, and the tribe of Himyan worshipped Nasr.

71.25 Muhammad surmised that the infidels of Noah's day were cast into Hell following their deaths by drowning.

Surah 52. The title to this surah, *The Mount*, comes from verse one. It is a polemical argument directed against Muhammad's opponents. The intended audience was the Muslim community with the intent of strengthening their resolve and stand firm against the infidels who had been speaking ill of Muhammad.

52.1 *the mount* — That is, Mount Sinai.
52.2 *the Book inscribed* — That is, the eter-

nal Book in Paradise (see **The Perspicuous Book** on pp. 178-177).
52.4 *the frequented house* — That is, the Ka'ba altar.
52.5 *the elevated roof* — That is, Paradise.
52.6 *the swelling sea* — This is a reference to the immensity of the waters in the ocean.
52.7-16 Woe is pronounced on all who rejected Muhammad's message. On the last day, the mountains and the heavens will be disturbed and all the infidels will be cast into the fires of Hell.
52.17-27 In contrast, all the blessed ones will enter into the gardens of pleasure. In this passage, Paradise is described as a place of sensual delights: (a) people will enjoy their own private harems, (b) people will be united with their offspring, provided that they too lived righteous lives, (c) people will eat fruit and meat, and drink beverages, such as they

seed follows them in the faith, we
will unite their seed with them; and
we will not cheat them of their
work at all;—every man is pledged
for what he earns.

22 And we will extend to them fruit
and flesh such as they like.

23 They shall pass to and fro therein
a cup in which is neither folly nor
sin.

24 And round them shall go boys of
theirs, as though they were hidden pearls.

25 And they shall accost each other
and ask questions,

26 and shall say, "Verily, we were before amidst our families shrinking
with terror,

27 but God has been gracious to us
and saved us from the torment of
the hot blast.

28 Verily, we used to call on Him before; verily, He is the righteous, the
compassionate!"

Muhammad's opponents

29 Wherefore do thou remind them:
for thou art, by the favour of thy
Lord, neither a soothsayer nor
mad!

30 Will they say, "A poet; we wait for
him the sad accidents of fate?"

31 Say, "Wait ye then; for I too am
of those who wait!"

32 Do their dreams bid them this? or
are they an outrageous people?

33 Or will they say, "He has invented
it?"—nay, but they do not believe!

34 But let them bring a discourse like
it, if they tell the truth!

Ten questions
for Muhammad's opponents

35 Or were they created of nothing,
or were they the creators?

36 Or did they create the heavens and
the earth?—nay, but they are not

---

desire, and (d) people will be attended by
boys, "as if they were hidden pearls" (see
Paradise on pp. 76-77).

52.24 *hidden pearls* — This phrase refers
to boys who will be attentive to the righteous in their gardens of bliss (harems). Since
this metaphor is also consistently used of the
celestial harem maidens (Q 55.58; 56.23;
76.19), this verse and Q 76.19 have caused
some scholars to surmise that pedophilic homosexuality is what Muhammad had in mind.
As such, it is problematic since other passages in the Qur'an condemn homosexuality
(see Q 4.16; 7.80-81; 26.165-166; and
27.55; George Braswell, *What You Need to*

Know about Islam and Muslims, pp. 83-84;
and Q 76.19 note). Pedophilia, however, is
not condemned since Muhammad took a girl
at the age of nine (A'isha) to be his wife.

The above concerns notwithstanding,
the role of these boys in these celestial harems is commonly understood within mainstream Islamic scholarship to be nonsexual—
they are mere attendants to those in the
harems and observers to all that takes place
there.

52.29 According to Muhammad, he was
told by Allah to remind people that he was
not a soothsayer (false prophet) or a madman (see Q 68.2, note).

sure!

37　Or have they the treasures of thy Lord? or are they the governors supreme?

38　Or have they a ladder whereon they can listen?—then let their listener bring obvious authority.

39　Has He daughters, while ye have sons?

40　Or dost thou ask them a hire, while they are borne down by debt?

41　Or have they the unseen, so that they write it down?

42　Or do they desire a plot?—but those who misbelieve it is who are plotted against!

43　Or have they a god beside God? celebrated be God's praises above what they join with Him!

*The dismissal
of Muhammad's opponents*

44　But if they should see a fragment of the sky falling down, they would say, "Clouds in masses!"

45　But leave them till they meet that day of theirs whereon they shall swoon;

46　the day when their plotting shall avail them naught, and they shall not be helped!

47　And, verily, there is a torment beside that for those who do wrong; but most of them do not know!

48　But wait thou patiently for the judgment of thy Lord, for thou art in our eyes. And celebrate the praises of thy Lord what time thou risest,

49　and in the night, and at the fading of the stars!

Surah 50

In the name of merciful and compassionate God.

1　Q.

*Muhammad:
the Apostle of Allah*

By the glorious Qur'ân!

52.35-43 These questions were intended to put Muhammad's opponents on the defensive and strengthen the confidence to his small Muslim community (cf. Job 38, 39). **52.45** Muhammad's opponents were summarily dismissed. The impression is that Muhammad had rejected them in the same way that they had rejected him. **52.49** *the fading of the stars* — This is a subtle condemnation of the Family Star religion. **Surah 50.** The title of this surah, *Qaf,* comes from verse one. The surah is a reinforce-

ment of the fundamentals already presented in earlier surahs: (a) Muhammad is the apostle of Allah, following in the line of other prophets of God, (b) Allah is the Almighty One and the source of all blessings, (c) the Last Judgment is an event to be feared, (d) the wicked will be cast into Hell, and (e) the Qur'an is Allah's final message to the world. **50.1a** Literally, *Qaf.* See Q 32.1, note. **50.1b-5** Three characteristics of Muhammad's ministry presented in this passage: (a) he is an Apostle of Allah, (b) he is a warner, and (c) those who reject his ministry will be

2   nay, they wonder that there has come to them a warner from amongst themselves; and the misbelievers say, "This is a wondrous thing!

3   What, when we are dead and have become dust?—that is a remote return!"

4   We well know what the earth consumes of them, for with us is a book that keeps (account).

5   Nay, they call the truth a lie when it comes to them, and they are in a confused affair.

Allah:
the source of all blessings

6   Do not they behold the heaven above them, how we have built it and adorned it, and how it has no flaws?

7   And the earth, we have stretched it out and thrown thereon firm mountains, and caused to grow thereon every beautiful kind.

8   An insight and a reminder to every servant who repents!

9   And we sent down from the heaven water as a blessing, and caused to grow therewith gardens and the harvest grain!

10   And the tall palm trees having piled up spathes,

11   for a provision to (our) servants; and we quickened thereby a dead land; thus shall the resurrection be!

Past illustrations of Allah's
judgments upon the wicked

12   Before them the people of Noah and the fellows of ar Rass and Thamûd

13   and 'Âd and Pharaoh called the apostles liars; and the brethren of Lot

14   and the fellows of the Grove and the people of Tubbâ'h all called the prophets liars, and the threat was cast into a state of confusion.

50.2 *This is a wondrous thing* — The response of the infidels in Mecca was sarcasm.

50.6-11 One of Muhammad's chief arguments against the Arabic Family Star religion was that Allah is the creator of the heavens and the earth. Harmony exists—not among the many gods that make up the Family Star pantheon—but in the way in which Allah holds the universe together and enables it to operate efficiently. Since this is true, Muhammad reasoned, Allah alone is to be feared and worshipped.

50.12a *ar-Rass* — This is a town of unknown location. Some scholars suggest that it is a town in the mid Arabian desert inhabited by the Thamudian people.

50.12b *Thamud* — a people who lived in the second century B.C. to the second century A.D. in the northern Arabian Desert (see Q 91 note).

50.13a *Ad* — This is a small tribe that lived in northwest Arabia in the first century, A.D. (see Q 54.17-21, note).

50.13b *Pharaoh* — the Egyptian opponent to Moses whose army was destroyed at the Red (Reed) Sea (see Ex 5-15).

50.13c *the brethren of Lot* — The people of Sodom who were destroyed by God. The term 'brethren" is used loosely, perhaps bet-

duly executed.

15   Were we then fatigued with the first creation? nay! but they are in obscurity concerning the new creation.

*The whispering soul
at the Last Judgment*

16   But we created man, and we know what his soul whispers; for we are nigher to him than his jugular vein!
17   When the two meeters meet, sitting the one on the right and the other on the left,
18   not a word does he utter, but a watcher is by him ready!
19   And the agony of death shall come in truth!— "that is what thou didst shun!"
20   And the trumpet shall be blown!— that is the threatened day!
21   And every soul shall come—with it a driver and a witness!
22   "Thou wert heedless of this, and we withdrew thy veil from thee,

and today is thine eyesight keen !"
23   And his mate shall say, "This is what is ready for me (to attest).
24   Throw into hell every stubborn misbeliever!
25   —who forbids good, a transgressor, a doubter!
26   who sets other gods with God— and throw him, ye twain, into fierce torment!"
27   His mate shall say, "Our Lord! I seduced him not, but he was in a remote error."
28   He shall say, "Wrangle not before me; for I sent the threat to you before.
29   The sentence is not changed with me, nor am I unjust to my servants."

Hell

30   On the day we will say to hell, "Art thou full?" and it will say, "Are there any more?"

---

ter phrased "compatriots."

50.14 *Tubba'h* — A civilization that dwelt in the whole of the southern Arabian Desert and which was finally overcome by the Abyssianians in the fourth century, A.D.

50.16 *we are nigher to him than his jugular vein* — In ancient Arabia, the jugular vein was oft mentioned in terms of death; to cut the jugular vein is to cause a quick and bloody death. This verse suggests that Allah is prepared to kill all His adversaries.

50.17 *when the two meeters meet* — That is, when the two sides of a person's conscience are awakened and begin to speak.

Verse 21 refers to these two sides as "a driver and a witness."

50.20 *the trumpet shall be blown* — This is the last trumpet that will initiate events, such as the general resurrection from the dead and the Last Judgment.

50.23 *and his mate shall say* — The spirit who accompanied each person throughout the days of his or her life is called a *mate*. This spirit will give an account of the person's life at the Last Judgment.

50.24-26 Grounds for being cast into Hell are: (a) ungratefulness, (b) rebellion, (c) forbidder of good, (d) exceeder of limits, and

Paradise

31 And Paradise shall be brought near to the pious,—not far off.

32 This is what ye are promised, to evry one who turns frequently (to God) and keeps His commandments:

33 who fears the Merciful in secret and brings a repentant heart.

34 "Enter into it in peace: this is the day of eternity!"

Allah

35 They shall have what they wish therein, and increase from us!

36 How many a generation have we destroyed before them, mightier than they in prowess! Pass through the land, is there any refuge?

37 Verily, in that is a reminder to whomsoever has a heart, or gives ear, and is a witness thereto.

38 We did create the heavens and the earth and what is between the two in six days, and no weariness touched us.

39 Be thou patient then of what they

say, and celebrate the praises of thy Lord before the rising of the sun and before the setting.

40 And through (some) of the night celebrate His praise and the additional adorations.

41 And listen for the day when the crier shall cry from a near place;

42 —the day when they shall hear the shout in truth—that is the day of coming forth!

43 Verily, we quicken and we kill, and unto us the journey is!

44 On the day when the earth shall be cleft asunder from them swiftly;— that is a gathering together which is easy to us!

Qur'an

45 We know what they say; nor art thou over them one to compel. Wherefore remind, by the Qur'ân, him who fears the threat.

Surah 45

In the name of the compassionate and merciful God.

(e) idolatry (cf. Gal 5:19-21).
50.30 The implied answer is that Hell is never full. Also see Prov 27:20 which states, "Death and Destruction are never satisfied, and neither are the eyes of man" (cf. Ps 55:23; Prov 15:11; Isa 5:14; Hab 2:5).
50.34 In contrast to the words spoken to the unrighteous (v. 24), the righteous will be told: "Enter into it in peace: this is the

day of eternity."
50.38 A reference to the Six Days of Creation found in the first chapter of Genesis.
50.40 In Islam, faithfulness requires prayers spoken at night (cf. Q 73.20).
50.41-43 The crier is Allah or an angel of Allah. The cry is that the appointed time of death has finally come.
50.45 *fears the threat* — One of the chief

1   H. M.

Signs from Allah

2   A revelation of the Book from God. the mighty, the wise.
3   Verily, in the heavens and the earth are signs to those who believe;
4   and in your creation and the beasts that are spread abroad are signs to a people who are sure;
5   and in the alternation of night and day, and the provision that God has sent down from heaven and quickened thereby the earth after its death, and in the veering of the winds are signs unto a people who have sense.
6   These are the signs of God which we recite to thee in truth; and in what new story after God and His signs will they believe?

Woe upon all
who ignore the signs

7   Woe to every sinful liar
8   who hears God's signs sent to him, then persists in being big with pride as though he heard them not—so give him the glad tidings of grievous woe
9   —and when he knows something of our signs takes them for a jest! These—for them is shameful woe,
10   behind them is hell, and what they have earned shall not avail them aught, nor what they have taken besides God for patrons; and for them is mighty woe.
11   This is a guidance, and those who misbelieve in the signs of their Lord, for them is torment of a grievous plague.

All creation is
subservient to Allah

12   God it is who subjects to you the sea that the ships may sail thereon at his bidding, and that ye may

aims of the Qur'an is to cause people to fear Allah's threat of Hell.
Surah 45. The title to this surah, *The Kneeling*, comes from verse 28. Its theme is the revelation of Allah to a disbelieving people. The primary revelation given to the people is the world itself. The subservience of all creation to the will of the Creator (Allah) is the sign. Since all of creation is surrendered to Allah, for people to live unsurrendered lives is a second sign: that of willful rebellion and a deserving eternal chastisement in Hell.
45.1 Literally *Ha Mim.* See Q 32.1, note.
45.2 *the Book* — According to Muhammad, this is the eternal Book that resides in Para-

dise which Allah revealed to his apostles. (see **The Perspicuous Book** on pp. 178-179).
45.3 *the heavens and the earth are signs to those who believe* — Muhammad believed that nature itself is a form of natural revelation that attests to the rightness of the eternal Book in Paradise that has been revealed to man (the Qur'an). The New Testament claims that natural revelation attests to the existence of God (see Rom 1:19-20).
45.9 According to this verse, those who laugh disrespectfully at the Qur'an will experience an "abasing chastisement" in Hell (see Q 45.35).
45.10 *besides God for patrons* — That is,

crave of His grace, and that haply ye may give thanks;

13   and He has subjected to you what is in the heavens and what is in the earth,—all from Him; verily, in that are signs unto a people who reflect.

*All people are
called to fear Allah*

14   Say to those who believe that they pardon those who hope not for God's days, that He may reward a people for that which they have earned.

15   Whosoever acts aright it is for his own soul, and whosoever does evil it is against it; then unto your Lord shall ye be returned.

Israel's failure

16   And we did bring the children of Israel the Book and judgment and prophecy, and we provided them with good things, and preferred them above the worlds.

17   And we brought them manifest proofs of the affair, and they disputed not until after knowledge had come to them, through mutual envy. Verily, thy Lord will decide between them on the resurrection day concerning that whereon they did dispute.

18   Then we did set thee over a law concerning the affair: follow it then, and follow not the lusts of those who do not know.

19   Verily, they shall not avail thee

the gods that the infidels worship instead of Allah.

45.11 *torment of a grievous plague* — This could include divine judgment on earth as well as in the afterlife.

45.14 Muhammad asserted that Muslims were to forgive infidels for their refusal to place their faith and trust in Allah. As such, they were not to engage in Jihad against the infidel. This verse was abrogated later in the Qur'an where Jihad was instituted against all infidels who were steadfast in their rejection of Allah (see **The Doctrine of Abrogation** on pp. 68-70, and **Jihad** on pp. 616-622).

45.15 According to the Qur'an, at the Last Judgment, each person will give an account for his or her own lives.

45.16 *the Book* — divine revelation. In this case, the eternal Book of God that re-

sides in Paradise and was revealed to the people of Israel in the form of the Old Testament (see **The Perspicuous Book** on pp. 178-179).

45.16-17 The point of this passage is that in spite of the favor that Allah granted the people of Israel, having provided for them much revelation and wisdom via an almost countless number of prophets, they turned against Allah. They will therefore be held accountable for this rejection at the Last Judgment.

The Bible makes a similar charge against the people of Israel (Isa 6:9-10; 29:13; Jer 6:10-11; Zech 7:11-12; Matt 13:10-16; 15:7-9; 23:1-39; Acts 7:51; and 2 Cor 3:14). Yet, an important difference exists between Islam and Christianity. The Bible also declares that God has not given up on the people of Israel. Eventually, they will return in humble

against God at all; and, verily, the wrong-doers are patrons of each other, but God is the patron of those who fear.

20 This is an insight for men and a guidance and a mercy to a people who are sure.

21 Do those who commit evil deeds count that we will make them like those who, believe and work righteous deeds, equal in their life and their death?—ill it is they judge.

The coming judgment

22 And God created the heavens and the earth in truth; and every soul shall be recompensed for that which it has earned, and they shall not be wronged.

23 Hast thou considered him who takes his lusts for his god, and God leads him astray wittingly, and has set a seal upon his hearing and his heart, and has placed upon his eye-

sight dimness? who then shall guide him after God? Will they not then mind?

24 They say, "It is only our life in this world, we die and we live, and naught destroys us but time!" But they have no knowledge of this; they do but suspect.

25 And when our signs are rehearsed to them with evidences their only argument is to say, "Bring our fathers, if ye speak the truth."

26 Say, "God quickens you, then He kills you, then He will gather you unto the resurrection day, there is no doubt therein; but most men do not know."

27 God's is the kingdom of the heavens and the earth, and on the day when the Hour shall arise on that day shall those who call it vain be losers!

28 And thou shalt see each nation kneeling, each nation summoned to its book, "Today are ye re-

---

repentance and embrace God in genuine salvation (Deut 30:1-3; Isa. 60:1-22; 66:18-23; Hos 3:4-5; Mic 4:1-2; 5:3; Zech 8:20-23; 14:9-21; and Rom 11:25-27).

45.18 The Muslim people were instructed to not follow the ways of those who rejected Allah.

45.23 *God leads him astray wittingly* — That is, Allah deliberately leads the infidel astray (see **Doctrine of al-Qadar** on pp. 264-266).

45.25 *Bring our fathers (back) if ye speak the truth* — According to the infidels of Mecca, their fathers (who were now dead) were not burning in Hell. If they could some-

how come back to life they could serve as witnesses and set the record straight.

45.26 Muslims were instructed to tell the infidels: "God quickens you, then He kills you, then He will gather you unto the resurrection day." The words were intended to strike fear into their hearts.

45.27 *the Hour* — This is the moment in time when all people will be summoned to appear at the Last Judgment (see Q 79.24, note).

45.28 *its book* — Muhammad believed that God sent apostles to every nation, warning them of the Last Judgment and the truths pertaining to God. What these apostles said

warded for that which ye have done."

29 This is our Book that speaketh to you with truth; verily, we have written down what ye have done.

30 But as to those who believe and do righteous deeds their Lord will make them enter into His mercy: that is the obvious bliss.

31 And as for those who misbelieve,— were not my signs recited to you and ye were too big with pride and ye were a sinful people?

32 And when it was said, "Verily, the promise of God is true, and the Hour there is no doubt therein;" ye said, "We know not what the Hour is, we only suspect, and we are not sure."

33 But there shall appear to them the evils of what they have done, and that shall encompass them at which they have been mocking.

34 And it shall be said, "Today will we forget you as ye forgat the meeting of this day of yours, and your resort shall be the fire, and ye shall have no helpers.

35 That is because ye took the signs of God for a jest and the life of this world deceived you; wherefore today ye shall not be brought forth therefrom, neither shall ye be taken back into favour."

36 God's then is the praise, the Lord of the heavens and the Lord of the earth, the Lord of the worlds!

37 His is the grandeur in the heavens and the earth, and He is the mighty and the wise!

---

was compiled in divine revelations (books) specific to each nation.

45.29 *our Book* — divine revelation. In this case, the eternal Book of God that resides in Paradise and was revealed to his apostles that have been sent to the peoples of the world and revealed in part to them (see *The Perspicuous Book* on pp. 178-179).

45.30 *believe and do right* — These words are repeated often in the Qur'an and serve as a brief summary of the Islamic gospel (see Q 103.3 note).

45.31 *my signs* — According to this verse, the communications (signs) recited to the people of Mecca were the surahs. Muhammad believed that the reason why they rejected the "signs" was because of their pride and sinfulness.

45.32 *the Hour* — This is the moment in time when all people will be summoned to

appear at the Last Judgment (see Q 79.24, note).

45.33 At the resurrection, the sins committed on earth will be revealed (see *The Last Judgment* on pp. 46-50).

45.34-35 Muhammad declared that throughout eternity, the damned will be forgotten. It is a form of poetic justice since these same people forgot Allah in this life.

45.35 One of the reasons for entering into Hell is whether or not one laughed disrespectfully of the Qur'an (see Q 45.9).

45.36 In this verse we see three titles given to Allah: *the Lord of the heavens, the Lord of the earth,* and *the Lord of the worlds.* Of the three, this third title, *the Lord of the worlds,* is the most often used in the Qur'an (see Q 1.2, note).

45.37 *He is the mighty and the wise* — This is one of Muhammad's favorite descrip-

Surah 44

In the name of Allah, the Benefi-cient, the Merciful.

1   H. M.

Qur'an

2   By the perspicuous Book!
3   verily, we have sent it down on a blessed night;
4   —verily, we had given warning
5   —wherein is decided every wise affair, as an order from us. Verily, we were sending (apostles)
6   —a mercy from thy Lord; verily, He both hears and knows:
7   from the Lord of the heavens and the earth and what is between the two, if ye were but sure.

No god but Allah

8   There is no god but He, He quickens and He kills—your Lord and the Lord of your fathers of yore!
9   Nay, they in doubt do play!
10   But expect thou the day when the heaven shall bring obvious smoke
11   to cover men—this is grievous torment!
12   Our Lord! remove from us the torment; verily, we are believers.
13   How can they have the reminder (now), when they have had a plain apostle,
14   and when they turned their backs away from him and said, "Taught! mad!"

---

tions of Allah (see Q 14.4; 16.60; 30.27; 35.2).

Surah 44. The title of this surah, *Smoke*, comes from verse 10. Following the theme of Last Judgment, this surah reminds the reader of two thoughts: (a) a divine judgment is coming, and (b) Muhammad is Allah's faithful herald of this coming judgment.

44.1 Literally, *Ha Mim*. See Q 32.1, note.

44.2-7 *a blessed night* — According to Islamic lore, the first night in which Muhammad received a revelation from God via the archangel Gabriel was called "the Blessed Night" (see Q 97.1-2). Four assurances are given by Allah to mankind: (a) the Qur'an was initially revealed to Muhammad on this "blessed night," (b) Allah is offering a warning to people, (c) Allah is the sender of apostles, and (d) Allah is the All-Hearing and the All-Knowing.

44.2 *perspicuous Book* — The perspicuous book is the divine revelation that eternally resides in Paradise and revealed in the various surahs that comprise the Qur'an (see *The Perspicuous Book* on pp. 178-179).

44.5 *we were sending (apostles)* — A recurring theme in the Qur'an is that Allah has send numerous apostles to the various peoples of the world to serve as warners of divine judgment to come and the need to live righteous lives so as to survive this judgment (see *The Apostles* on pp. 396-398).

44.8 *There is no god but He* — Again, Muhammad drew attention to the Doctrine of Tauhid—absolute monotheism.

44.10 According to this verse, the skies will bring forth a pall of smoke—an indicator of the coming general resurrection from the dead and the Last Judgment.

44.14 The Meccan people accused Muham-

15   Verily, we will remove the torment a little, (but) ye will surely return!

16   On the day when we will assault with the great assault, verily, we will take vengeance.

Judgment came upon the Egyptians who rejected Moses

17   And we already tried the people of Pharaoh when there came to them a noble apostle:

18   "Send back to me God's servants; verily, I am to you a faithful apostle;"

19   and, "Exalt not yourselves above God; verily, I come to you with obvious authority.

20   And, verily, I seek refuge in my Lord and your Lord, that ye stone me not.

21   And if ye believe not in me then let me alone!"

22   Then he called upon his Lord, "Verily, these are a sinful people.

23   So journey with my servants by night—verily, ye will be pursued.

24   But leave the sea in quiet—verily, they are a host to be drowned!"

25   How many gardens and springs have they left,

26   and corn lands and a noble place,

27   and comfort wherein they did enjoy themselves!

28   Thus—and we gave them for an inheritance to another people.

29   And the heaven wept not for them, nor the erth, nor were they respited.

30   But we saved the children of Israel from shameful woe!

31   —from Pharaoh; verily, he was

mad of being crazy (see Q 68.2, note).

44.16 *we will take vengeance* — A consistent theme in the Qur'an is that Allah will exact vengeance on all infidels with relish. In the New Testament, we see a different understanding of God. God yearns for all people to repent. "The Lord is not slow in keeping his promise, as some understand slowness. He is patient with you, not wanting anyone to perish, but everyone to come to repentance" (2 Pet 3:9).

44.17 *a noble apostle* — Moses.

44.18 *Deliver to me the servants of Allah, surely I am a faithful apostle to you* — This statement is a loose paraphrase from the Book of Exodus: "Afterward Moses and Aaron went to Pharaoh and said, 'This is what the Lord, the God of Israel, says: "Let my people go, so that they may hold a festival to me in the desert"'" (Ex 5:1).

44.19 *Exalt not yourselves above god; verily I come to you with obvious authority* — This statement is another loose paraphrase from the Book of Exodus: "The God of the Hebrews has met with us. Now let us take a three-day journey into the desert to offer sacrifices to the Lord our God, or he may strike us with plagues or with the sword" (Ex 5:3).

44.20-21 These two statements are nowhere found in the Book of Exodus. Muhammad perhaps invented them to fill out the narrative.

44.22-24 Nowhere in the Book of Exodus were these words spoken. According to the Book of Exodus, when Moses and the people of Israel left Egypt and traveled toward the Red (Reed) Sea, Moses had no divine fore-

haughty, one of the extravagant!

32   And we did choose them, wittingly, above the worlds;

33   and we gave them signs wherein was an obvious trial!

*Judgment came upon
the people of Tubba'h*

34   Verily, these say,

35   "It is but our first death,

36   so bring our fathers, if ye do speak the truth!"

37   Are they better than the people of Tubbâ'h, and those before them? We destroyed them—verily, they were sinners!

Hell

38   Nor did we create the heavens and the earth, and what is between the two in sport:

39   we did but create them in truth, though most of them know it not!

40   Verily, the day of separation is their appointed term;

41   the day when master shall not avail client at all, nor shall they be helped;

42   save whomsoever God shall have mercy on; verily, He is the mighty, the merciful!

43   Verily, the Zaqqûm tree

44   (shall be) the food of the sinful:

45   as it were melting, shall it boil in their bellies

46   like the boiling of hot water!

47   — "Take him and hale him into the midst of hell!

48   then pour over his head the torment of hot water!

49   —Taste! verily, thou art the mighty, the honourable!

50   Verily, this is that whereon ye did dispute!"

Paradise

51   Verily, the pious shall be in a safe

---

knowledge of the impending drowning of the Egyptian army, as this passage from the Qur'an claims he had.

44.32 *we did choose them* — Muhammad acknowledged that the Jewish people are the chosen people of God. Yet, later in the Qur'an Muhammad noted that the Jewish people failed to live righteous lives, fell into the sin of idolatry, and thereby became the cursed (unchosen) people of God (see Q 2.88-103, 159-161; 4.52-53, 155-157; 5.12-19, 78; 7.138-169).

The New Testament asserts that though most of the Jewish people have rejected the Christian gospel, they will one day turn back to God in a massive revival (see Rom 11:25-27). Like a branch that has been broken off the tree, they will eventually be regrafted and restored (see Rom 11:13-24).

44.34-37 The Tubba'h civilization dwelt in the whole of the southern Arabian Desert and which was finally overcome by the Abyssinians in the fourth century, A.D.

44.43 *The Zaqqum tree* — This is a mythical tree that exists in Hell. Its fruit is the food of sinners. It is poisonous and likened to the taste of boiling oil (see Q 17.60 and 37.62, 56.52, and **Hell** on pp. 80-82).

44.51-59 Five characteristics of Paradise: (a) a secure place, (b) full of gardens and

place!
52 in gardens and springs,
53 they shall be clad in satin and stout silk face to face.
54 Thus!—and we will wed them to bright and large-eyed maids!
55 They shall call therein for every fruit in safety.
56 They shall not taste therein of death save their first death, and we will keep them from the torment of hell!
57 Grace from thy Lord, that is the grand bliss!
58 And we have only made it easy for

thy tongue, that haply they may be mindful.
59 "Then watch thou; verily, they are watching too!"

Surah 37

In the name of the merciful and compassionate God.

War in the lower heavens

1 By the (angels) ranged in ranks,
2 and the drivers driving,

springs, (c) people wear fine and thick silk, (d) sitting face to face in a state of love, (e) wed with the Houris (virgins), and (f) full of fruit (see **Paradise** on pp. 76-77).

Heaven is also a major theme and a great comfort within the Judeo-Christian tradition. John R. W. Stott comments: "Christians are confident about the future, and our Christian 'hope' (which is a sure expectation) is both individual and cosmic. Individually, apart from Christ, the fear of personal death and dissolution is almost universal. For us in the West Woody Allen typifies this terror. It has become an obsession with him. True, he can still joke about it. 'It's not that I'm afraid to die,' he quips, 'I just don't want to be there when it happens.' But mostly he is filled with dread. In a 1977 article in *Esquire* he said: 'The fundamental thing behind all motivation and all activity in the constant struggle against annihilation and against death. It's absolutely stupefying in its terror, and it renders anyone's accomplishments meaningless.' Jesus Christ, however, rescues his disciples from this horror. We will not only survive death, but be raised from it. We are to be

given new bodies like his resurrection body, with new and undreamed-of powers...Our hope of the future, however, is also cosmic. We believe that Jesus Christ is going to return in spectacular magnificence, in order to bring history to its fulfillment in eternity. He will not only raise the dead, but regenerate the universe; he will make all things new" (*The Contemporary Christian*, p. 83).

Surah 37. The title of this surah, *Those Arranged in Ranks*, comes from verse one. The purpose of this surah is to clarify the relationship between life in this world and the life to come. Allah is presented as Lord of the heavens and, as such, stands opposed to the occult sciences that dominated Arabia in the seventh century. Allah has provided guidance for the Meccan people with Muhammad.

Muhammad also reminded the reader that guidance has been provided for peoples of earlier epochs with other apostles. Several are mentioned, with the most notable example being Abraham. In his discussion of Abraham, Muhammad referenced the offering of his son on the altar.

3   and the reciters of the reminder,

4   "Verily, your God is one,

5   the Lord of the heavens and the
     earth and what is between the two,
     and the Lord of the sunrises!"

6   Verily, we have adrned the lower
     heaven with the adornment of the
     stars,

7   and to preserve it from every re-
     bellious devil,

8   that they may not listen to the ex-
     alted chiefs; for they are hurled at
     from every side,

9   driven off, and for them is lasting
     woe;

10   save such as snatches off a word,
     and there follows him a darting
     flame!

The scoffers

11   Ask them whether they are stron-

ger by nature or (the angels) whom
we have created? We have created
them of sticky clay.

12   Nay, thou dost wonder and they
     jest!

13   and when they are reminded they
     will not remember;

14   and when they see a sign they make
     a jest thereof,

15   and say, "This is naught but obvi-
     ous sorcery.

16   What! when we are dead, and have
     become earth and bones, shall we
     then be raised?

17   what! and our fathers of yore?"

Answering the scoffers

18   Say, "Yes, and ye shall shrink up,

19   and it shall only be one scare, and,
     behold, they shall look on,

20   and they shall say, 'O, woe is us!

37.1-3 The oath that serves as the introduction to this surah addresses angels who
follow with order and discipline the messages
in the Qur'an, who use the Qur'an to re-
prove the evil ones, and who recite its messages faithfully.

37.4 Muhammad begins the surah with a
reminder of the Doctrine of Tauhid—God is
one (see Q 112).

37.5-7 According to Muhammad, the lower
heaven is the realm of the stars, of which is
protected against the menacing work of the
devils. This is a subtle rebuke to the polytheists who understood the stars to be the
gods that they worshipped (see **Polytheism in Seventh Century Arabia** on pp.
92-97).

37.8 *exalted chiefs* — devils. The stars are

kept from listening to the demons, who are
hurled at from every side. In seventh century Arabia, the stars were thought to be
animate beings who could listen and respond
to words spoken to them. Muhammad embraced this animate understanding of the
stellar realm.

37.10 The exception to that which is mentioned in verses 8-9 are the few demons
that are embraced (snatched) by the sooth-
sayers on the earth to do their bidding.

37.11 The Muslim people were encouraged
to ask the polytheists if Allah is powerful
enough to resurrect those made of "sticky
clay"—that is, human beings.

37.15 According to Muhammad, infidels
called his surahs the work of sorcery. This is
due to the Arabic poetic and rhythmic liter-

this is the day of judgment,
21 this is the day of decision, which
    ye did call a lie!'
22 Gather ye together, ye who were
    unjust, with their mates and what
    they used to serve
23 beside God, and guide them to the
    way of hell,
24 and stop them; verily, they shall be
    questioned.
25 'Why do ye not help each other?'
26 nay, on that day they shall resign
    themselves,
27 and some shall draw near to oth-
    ers to question each other,
28 and they shall say, 'Verily, ye came
    to us from the right.'
29 They shall say, 'Nay, ye were not
    believers,
30 nor had we any authority over you;
    nay, ye were an outrageous
    people.
31 And the sentence of our Lord shall
    be due for us; verily we shall surely
    taste thereof;
32 we did seduce you—verily, we
    were erring too!'
33 therefore, verily, on that day they

shall share the torment:
34 thus it is that we will do with the
    sinners.
35 Verily, when it is said to them,
    'There is no god but God,' they
    get too big with pride,
36 and say, 'What! shall we leave our
    gods for an infatuated poet?'
37 Nay, he came with the truth, and
    verified the apostles;
38 verily, ye are going to taste of griev-
    ous woe,
39 nor shall ye be rewarded save for
    that which ye have done!'"

Paradise

40 Except God's sincere servants,
41 these shall have a stated provision
42 of fruits, and they shall be
    honoured
43 in the gardens of pleasure,
44 upon couches facing each other;
45 they shall be served all round with
    a cup from a spring,
46 white and delicious to those who
    drink,
47 wherein is no insidious spirit, nor

ary structure. No human being, it was alleged, could write poetry at this level of so-
phistication.
37.18-23 The resurrection that infidels scoff
will come upon them suddenly. They will
then respond with cries of dread as they are
led to Hell.
37.25-39 Regrets of the scoffers: (a) they
were not believers, (b) they were inordinate,
(c) the sentence of the Lord has come to
pass, and (d) they will share the chastisement together.

37.35 *There is no god but God* — Again,
Muhammad addressed the Doctrine of Tauhid—absolute monotheism.
37.40-50 Characteristics of Paradise: (a)
an abundance of fruit, (b) people will be
highly honored, (c) gardens of pleasure, (d)
thrones facing one another, (e) a shared
bowl, and (f) a private harem. The term
"gardens of pleasure" refers to a place of
erotic pleasures (see Q 10.9; 22.56; 31.8;
56.12-26; and 68.34, and *Paradise* on pp.
76-77, and *The Virgins* on pp. 107-109).

shall they be drunk therewith;

48   and with them damsels, restrain-
     ing their looks, large eyed;

49   as though they were a sheltered
     egg;

50   and some shall come forward to
     ask others;

A conversation in Paradise

51   and a speaker amongst them shall
     say, "Verily, I had a mate,

52   who used to say, 'Art thou verily
     of those who credit?

53   What! when we are dead, and have
     become earth and bones, shall we
     be surely judged?'"

54   He will say, "Are ye looking
     down?"

55   and he shall look down and see him
     in the midst of hell.

56   He shall say, "By God, thou didst
     nearly ruin me!

57   And had it not been for the favour
     of my Lord, I should have been
     among the arraigned."

58   — "What! shall we not die

59   save our first death? and shall we
     not be tormented?

60   —Verily, this is mighty bliss!

61   for the like of this then let the work-
     ers work."

62   Is that better as an entertainment,
     or the tree of Ez Zaqqûm?

63   Verily, we have made it a trial to
     the unjust.

64   Verily, it is a tree that comes forth
     from the bottom of hell;

65   its spathe is as it were the heads of
     devils;

66   verily, they shall eat therefrom, and
     fill their bellies therefrom.

67   Then shall they have upon it a mix-
     ture of boiling water;

68   then, verily, their return shall be to
     hell.

69   Verily, they found their fathers err-
     ing,

70   and they hurried on in their tracks;

71   but there had erred before them
     most of those of yore,

72   and we had sent warners amongst
     them.

73   Behold, then, what was the end of
     those who were warned,

74   save God's sincere servants!

Noah

75   Noah did call upon us, and a gra-

37.51-74 While in Paradise, a believer will comment that he had an acquaintance on earth who was not a believer and who scoffed about the resurrection. He will then look down and notice that this person is now in Hell. Finally, he will say to him: "By God, thou didst nearly ruined me! (v. 56).

Speaking across the gulf from Paradise to Hell is reminiscent of the biblical story of the rich man and Lazarus (see Lk 16:19-31).
37.62 *The Tree of Ez Zaqqum* — This is a mythic tree in Hell. Its fruit is poisonous and has the appearance of the heads of serpents (also see Q 17.60, 44.43 and 56.52).
37.72 *we had sent warners amongst them* — That is, we had sent apostles to them, warning of the coming Last Judgment and to take heed by living a righteous life and

cious answer did we give;

76   and we saved him and his people
      from a mighty trouble;

77   and we made his seed to be the
      survivors;

78   and we left for him amongst pos-
      terity

79   "peace upon Noah in the worlds;

80   verily; thus do we reward those
      who do well;

81   verily, he was of our believing ser-
      vants."

82   Then we drowned the others.

Abraham

83   And, verily, of his sect was
      Abraham;

84   when he came to his Lord with a
      sound heart;

85   when he said to his father and his
      people, "What is it that ye serve?

86   with a lie do ye desire gods beside
      God?

87   What then is your thought respect-
      ing the Lord of the worlds?"

88   And he looked a look at the stars

89   and said, "Verily, I am sick!"

90   and they turned their backs upon
      him fleeing.

91   And he went aside unto their gods
      and said, "Will ye not eat?

92   What ails you that ye will not
      speak?"

93   And he went aside to them smiting
      with the right hand.

94   And they rushed towards him.

95   Said he, "Do ye serve what ye hew
      out,

96   when God has created you, and
      what ye make?"

97   Said they, "Build for him a pyre,
      and throw him into the flaming
      hell!"

98   They desired to plot against him,
      but we made them inferior.

embracing the one true God (see **The Apostles** on pp. 396-398).

37.75-82 Praise was given to Noah and his offspring for their obedience to God. They were spared the catastrophe of the Great Deluge, known as Noah's Flood, that impacted the world (see Gen 6-9).

37.83-99 Praise was also given to Abraham. These verses are an imaginative description of the time when Abraham dwelt in the city of Ur of the Chaldeans and Haran and turned his heart away from idolatry to the one true God (cf. Gen. 11:28-12:5).

37.91-93 This critique on idolatry is reminiscent of Ps 115:4-8.

37.97-98 This episode of the threat to throw Abraham into a furnace (burning pyre) is not found in the Book of Genesis. According to the *Midrash Rabbah*, Abraham and Nimrod were contemporaries. This passage states that Abraham "'Behold, I [Nimrod] will cast you into it and let your God whom you adore come and save you from it.'...When Abram descended into the fiery furnace and was saved, he [Nimrod] asked him [Haran], 'Of whose belief are you?' 'Of Abram's,' he replied. Thereupon he seized and cast him [Haran] in the fire; his inwards were scorched and he died in his father's presence" (*Mid. Gen.* 38.13; also see *Sahih Bukhari* 6.60.86-87). Islamic scholar al-Tabari believed that Abraham was sixteen years old at the time (*The History of al-Tabari*, p. 2:68). Also see Q 21.51-73; 29.24; 85.4-10.

Abraham's sacrifice

99   Said he, "Verily, I am going to my Lord, He will guide me.

100   My Lord! grant me (a son), one of the righteous;"

101   and we gave him glad tidings of a clement boy.

102   And when he reached the age to work with him, he said, "O my boy! verily, I have seen in a dream that I should sacrifice thee, look then what thou seest right." Said he, "O my sire! do what thou art bidden; thou wilt find me, if it please God, one of the patient!"

103   And when they were resigned, and Abraham had thrown him down upon his forehead,

104   we called to him, "O Abraham!

105   thou hast verified the vision; verily, thus do we reward those who do well.

106   This is surely an obvious trial."

107   And we ransomed him with a mighty victim;

108   and we left for him amongst posterity,

109   "Peace upon Abraham;

110   thus do we reward those who do well;

111   verily, he was of our servants who believe!"

112   And we gave him glad tidings of Isaac, a prophet among the righteous;

113   and we blessed him and Isaac;— of their seed is one who does well, and one who obviously wrongs himself.

The *Midrash Rabbah* is dated to the second century, A.D. It therefore predates Muhammad and the Qur'an by five centuries. Muhammad acquired knowledge of this narrative and then chose to include it in this surah.

37.99-113 This is the story of Abraham sacrificing his son as a sacrifice to God. According to the Book of Genesis, Abraham offered his son Isaac on a pyre on Mount Moriah, yet saved from death at the last moment (see Gen 22:1-19).

According to mainstream Islamic scholarship, the son sacrificed in this story was Ishmael and the location of the sacrifice was Mount Mina—a few miles from Mecca. The celebration of the Festival of Sacrifice each year during the observance of the Hajj is testimony to its dominance in mainstream Islamic tradition (see the **Festival of Sacri-** *fice* on p. 226). Accordingly, Islamic scholars typically discount the Old Testament account on the grounds that Old Testament scribes corrupted the original Genesis 22 passage by replacing *Ishmael* with *Isaac* in their copies of the book of Genesis.

Yet, curiously, two problems present themselves in this passage: (a) nowhere is Ishmael mentioned, and (b) Isaac is mentioned (vv. 112-113). If Muhammad intended to correct an inaccuracy in the Old Testament narrative and note that it was Ishmael, and not Isaac offered on the pyre, why did he not clearly and forthrightly state this? Why did he fail to mention Ishmael's name?

Not all Islamic scholars are in agreement with this mainstream interpretation. The famous Islamic scholar al-Tabari (tenth century), for example, claimed that it was Isaac that

Moses and Aaron

114 And we were gracious unto Moses and Aaron.

115 We saved them and their people from mighty trouble,

116 and we helped them and they had the upper hand;

117 and we gave them both the perspicuous Book;

118 and we guided them to the right way;

119 and we left for them amongst posterity,

120 "Peace upon Moses and Aaron;

121 verily, thus do we reward those who do well;

122 verily, they were both of our servants who believe!"

Elijah

123 And verily Elyâs was of the apostles;

124 when he said to his people, "Will

ye not fear?

125 do ye call upon Baal and leave the best of Creators,

126 God your Lord and the Lord of your fathers of yore?"

127 But they called him liar; verily, they shall surely be arraigned,

128 save God's sincere servants.

129 And we left for him amongst posterity,

130 "Peace upon Elyâsîn;

131 verily, thus do we reward those who do well;

132 verily, he was of our servants who believe!"

Lot

133 And, verily, Lot was surely among the apostles;

134 when we saved him and his people altogether,

135 except an old woman amongst those who lingered;

136 then we destroyed the others;

Abraham attempted to sacrifice (see *The History of al-Tabari,* vol 2, pp. 82-89). Moreover, Thomas Patrick Hughes added, "The two commentators al-Kamalan quote a number of traditions on the subject. They say Ibn 'Umar, Ibn 'Abbas, Hassan, and 'Abdullah ibn Ahmad relate that it was Isaac; whilst Ibn Mas'ud, Mujahid, 'Ikrimah, Qatadah, and Ibn Ishaq say it was Ishmael. But whatever may be the real facts of the case, it is certain that popular tradition amongst both Sunnis and Shi'iahs assigns the honour to Ishmael, and believe the great Festival of Sacrifice, the 'Idu 'l-Azha, to have been established to commemorate the event" (*Dictionary of Islam,* p. 219).

37.113 *we blessed him and Isaac* — That is, Allah blessed Abraham and Isaac. The seed that does well is Jacob. The seed that obviously wrongs himself is Esau.

37.117 *the perspicuous Book* — See **The Perspicuous Book** on pp. 178-179.

37.123 *Elyas* — Elijah.

37.123-132 This account draws from the story of Elijah before the prophets of Baal at Mount Carmel (see 1 Kings 18:16-46).

37.133-138 This account draws from the story of Lot and the destruction of Sodom and Gomorrah (Gen 19:1-29). The "old woman...who lingered" mentioned in this epi-

137   verily, ye pass by them in the morn-
       ing
138   and at night; have ye then no sense?

Jonah

139   And, verily, Jonah was amongst the
       apostles;
140   when he ran away into the laden
       ship;
141   and he cast lots and was of those
       who lost;
142   and a fish swallowed him, for he
       was to be blamed;
143   and had it not been that he was of
       those who celebrated God's
       praises
144   he would surely have tarried in the
       belly thereof to the day when men
       shall be raised.
145   But we cast him on to the barren
       shore; and he was sick;
146   and we made to grow over him a
       gourd tree;
147   and we sent him to a hundred thou-
       sand or more,
148   and they believed; and we gave
       them enjoyment for a season.

Absolute monotheism

149   Ask them, "Has thy Lord daugh-
       ters while they have sons?
150   or have we created the angels fe-
       males while they were witnesses?"
151   is it not of their lie that they say,
152   "God has begotten?" verily, they
       are liars.
153   Has he preferred daughters to sons?
154   what ails you? how ye judge!
155   will ye not be mindful,
156   or have ye obvious authority?
157   then bring your Book if ye do speak
       the truth.
158   And they made him to be related to
       the ginns, while the ginns know
       that they shall be arraigned;
159   celebrated be God's praises from
       what they attribute!
160   —save God's sincere servants.
161   "Verily, ye and what ye worship
162   shall not try any one concerning
       him,
163   save him who shall broil in hell;
164   there is none amongst us but has
       his appointed place,
165   and, verily, we are ranged,

sode was Lot's wife who looked back at the city of Sodom and was turned into a pillar of salt (Gen 19:26).

37.139-148 This account draws upon the four chapters of the Book of Jonah. In the Qur'an, the story of Jonah carries the distinction of being the only account where the people heeded the warning of an apostle sent from Allah and repented.

37.149-166 A dominant theme throughout the Qur'an is the Doctrine of Tauhid—a strict monotheism: Allah is one. Such think-

ing was an assault on the Arabic Family Star religious system that characterized Arabia in the seventh century (see **Polytheism in Seventh Century Arabia** on pp. 92-97).

37.163 According to the Qur'an, to affirm anything less than a strict monotheism is to be an infidel and subject to eternal torment.

37.164 *appointed place* — People are either predestined to Paradise or Hell (see **The Doctrine al-Qadar** on pp. 264-266).

37.167-170 According to Muhammad, the people's complaint against him was that if

166 and, verily, we celebrate His praises."

Turn away from all unbelief

167 And yet they say,
168 "Had we a reminder from those of yore
169 we should surely have been of God's sincere servants."
170 But they misbelieved in it; but soon shall they know.
171 But our word has been passed to our servants
172 who were sent that they should be helped;
173 that, verily, our hosts should gain mastery for them.
174 Then turn thou thy back upon them for a time,
175 and look upon them, for soon they too shall look.
176 Would they hasten on our torment?

177 but when it descends in their court, ill will the morning be of those who have been warned!
178 But turn thy back upon them for a time;
179 and look, for soon they too shall look.

Final Words of Praise

180 Celebrated be the praises of thy Lord, the Lord of glory, above what they attribute!
181 and peace be upon the apostles
182 and praise be to God, the Lord of the worlds!

Surah 30

In the name of merciful and compassionate God.

---

only they had a divine writ from which to know the truth about God, then they would believe. Yet, this surah insisted that they indeed have such a divine writ (the Qur'an) and yet they still disbelieved.

37.171 *our word* — divine revelation.

37.175 Eventually, all infidels will see the truth, but it will too late for them (cf. Heb 9:27).

Surah 30. The title to this surah, *The Greeks*, comes from verse 2. The occasion of this surah is the defeat of the armies of the Byzantine (Roman) Empire along the frontier with Persia—an empire who principal language was Greek. Emperor Phocus, the Roman emperor, suffered military defeats from Khusrau II (Parvez), the Sassanid king

of Persia (A.D. 615). Following these defeats, Phocus was deposed by Heraclius, who ascended to the emperorship of the Byzantine Empire. This transition of emperors took place in A.D. 610, the year that Muhammad's ministry in Mecca commenced.

Khusrau Parviz continued his war against the Byzantine Empire. He conquered Antioch and Damascus in A.D. 613 and then Jerusalem in A.D. 614. Thousands of Christians were slaughtered by the Persians in Palestine at this time. Also at this time, the alleged original cross from which Jesus was crucified was seized and carried off to Hegra (al-Hijr). Furthermore, all the churches in Palestine were destroyed. The following year, Jordan and the Sinai Peninsula were

Festival of Sacrifice

On the tenth and final day of the Hajj, the Muslim pilgrims sacrifice a lamb, goat or camel on Mount Mina. The blood shed has nothing to do with the atonement for sin (a belief central to both Judaism and Christianity). "Their meat will never reach to God, nor yet their blood, but the piety from you will reach Him" (Q 22.37). The sacrifice is a symbol of the willingness of Muslims to make whatever sacrifices that falls within the will of God as a way of striving after the Right Direction that leads to eternal life (see Q 72.1). The slaughtered meat is then divided into thirds. One third is eaten by the immediate family and relatives. One third is given away to friends. One third is donated to the poor.

On a certain occasion when this illustrious father (Abraham) was performing the rites of the pilgrimage at Mecca, Abraham said to his beloved child, "I dreamed that I must sacrifice you; now consider what is to be done with reference to such an admonition." Ishmael replied, "Do as you shall be commanded of God. Verify your dream. You will find me endure patiently." But when Abraham was about to sacrifice Ishmael, the Most High God made a black and white sheep his substitute, a sheep which had been pasturing forty years in Paradise, and was created by the direct power of God for this event. Now every sheep offered on Mount Mina, until the Day of Judgment is a substitute, or a commemoration of the substitute for Ishmael.

—Muhammad Baqir Al-Majlisi, *Hayat Al-Qulub*

The slaughter is not considered expiation for sin. Muslims do not believe that a blood sacrifice is necessary to eradicate the effects of sin...[It is] a commemorative rite meant to instill in worshipers a sense of honor and respect for parents and a willingness to sacrifice to God that which is most dear.

— Margot Patterson, *Islam Considered*, p. 21

1   A.L.M.

Battle of Nineveh

2   The Greeks are overcome
3   in the highest parts of the land; but
     after being overcome
4   they shall overcome in a few years;
     to God belongs the order before
     and after; and on that day the be-
     lievers shall rejoice in the help of
     God;
5   —God helps whom He will, and
     He is mighty, merciful.

Ignorance of the hereafter

6   —God's promise!—God breaks
     not His promise, but most men do
     not know!
7   They know the outside of this
     world's life, but of the hereafter
     they are heedless.
8   Have they not reflected in them-
     selves, that God created not the
     heavens and the earth, and what is
     between the two except in truth,
     and for a stated and appointed
     time? but, verily, many men in the
     meeting of their Lord do disbelieve.
9   Have they not journeyed on in the
     land and seen how was the end of
     those before them who were
     stronger than they, and who turned
     up the ground, and cultivated it
     more than they do cultivate it? and
     there came to them their apostles
     with manifest signs; for God would
     never wrong them: it was them-
     selves they wronged!
10   Then evil was the end of those who
     did evil, in that they said the signs
     of God were lies and mocked
     thereat.

conquered, extending the Sassanid Empire to the frontiers of Egypt. By A.D. 619, the whole of Egypt had fallen to the Sassanid Empire. In A.D. 623, Heraclius waged a counterattack against Khusrau Parviz and took back much of the land.

Reflecting on this military campaign, Muhammad wrote this surah with the intent of demonstrating a parallel future event: the time when Allah would conquer all the peoples of the earth at the Last Judgment. **30.1** Literally, *Alif Lam Mim*. See Q 32.1, note.

30.2-5 The Greeks mentioned in this passage were the soldiers of the Byzantine Empire. This passage, according to Islamic scholars, is a prophecy. Written at the time when the Byzantines had been defeated by the Persians, it prophesied that the Byzantines would regroup and successfully counterattack, which they did at the Battle of Nineveh (627). Yet, the qur'anic surahs were collected (many from people's memories, scraps of paper, pieces of wood or bones) and formed into a book in the latter decades of the seventh century, long after the Byzantine counterattack. The possibility therefore exists that the passage was redacted into the Qur'an, reflecting what had already transpired in this battle (see **The Qur'an** on pp. 150-153).

30.6-10 This passage puts forth the Doctrine of Tauhid: Allah is sovereign over all the earth. Those who fail to recognize Allah will suffer eternally for their faithlessness and disobedience. In Muhammad's day, most

Last Judgment

11   God, produces a creation, then He makes it go back again, then unto Him shall ye return.

12   And on the day when the Hour shall rise, the sinners shall be confused;

13   and they shall not have amongst their partners intercessors; and their partners shall they deny.

14   And on the day when the Hour shall rise, on that day shall they be scattered apart;

Paradise

15   and as for those who believe and do right, they in the garden shall be joyful;

Hell

16   and as for those who misbelieved and said our signs and the meeting of the hereafter were lies, they shall be in the torment arraigned.

Praise belongs to Allah

17   Celebrated be the praises of God, when ye are in the evening and when ye are in the morning!

18   for to Him belongs praise in the heavens and the earth! and at the evening, and when ye are at noon.

19   He brings forth the living from the dead, and brings forth the dead from the living; and He quickens the earth after its death, and thus shall ye too be brought forth.

Six signs from Allah

20   And of His signs is this, that He hath created you from dust; then, behold, ye are mortals who are spread abroad.

21   And of His signs is this, that He hath created for you of yourselves wives with whom ye may cohabit; He has made between you affection and pity. Verily, in that are signs unto a people who reflect.

22   And of His signs is the creation of the heavens and the earth, and the diversity of your tongues and colours; verily, in that are signs

---

people were unconcerned about the realities of the hereafter. This lack of interest, he explained, is tantamount to dealing unjustly with their own souls.

30.11-14 Those who were so unconcerned about the hereafter will have a marked change of attitude at the Last Judgment when their fate is revealed to them.

30.15 *believe and do right* — These words are repeated often in the Qur'an and serve as a brief summary of the Islamic gospel (see

Q 103.3 note).

30.18-19 This is a reference to the Resurrection from the Dead.

30.20-27 In this passage, six signs are presented that demonstrate the sovereignty of Allah over the earth. They are reminders that a resurrection of the dead and a Last Judgment are indeed coming. The signs are: (1) our creation from the dust of the earth, (2) the blessing of marriage, (3) the heaven and earth and plurality of languages, (4) light-

unto the worlds.

23 And of His signs is your sleep by night and by day and your craving after His grace. Verily, in that are signs unto a people who do hear.

24 And of His signs is this, that He shows you lightning for fear and hope; and sends down from the sky water, and quickens therewith the earth after its death; verily, in that are signs unto a people who have sense.

25 And of His signs is this, that the heavens and the earth stand by His order; then when He calls you from the earth, lo! ye shall come forth.

26 His are those who are in the heavens and the earth, and all to Him are devoted.

27 And He it is who produces a creation and then makes it to go back again; for it is very easy to Him; and His are the loftiest similitudes in the heavens and the earth; and He is the mighty, wise!

Parable of Religions

28 He has struck out for you a parable from yourselves; have ye of

what your right hand possess partners in what we have bestowed upon you, so that ye share alike therein? do ye fear them as ye fear each other?—Thus do we detail the signs unto a people who have sense.

Interpretation of the parable

29 Nay, when those who are unjust follow their lusts without knowledge,—and who shall guide him whom God has led astray? and they shall have none to help.

30 Set thy face steadfast towards the religion as an 'Hanîf, according to the constitution whereon God has constituted men; there is no altering the creation of God, that is the standard religion, though most men do not know.

31 Turn repentant towards Him; and fear Him, and be steadfast in prayer; and be not of the idolaters.

32 Of those who have divided their religion and become sects, every party in what they have, rejoice.

33 And when distress touches men they call upon their Lord, repen-

ning and rain, (5) the blessings of sleep, and (6) the moment when each person will die and face Allah in the afterlife.

30.27 *He is the mighty, wise* — This is one of Muhammad's favorite descriptions of Allah (see Q 14.4; 16.60; 35.2; 45.37).

30.28 The story of the parable is that of a people holding hands with others in a partnership. Both sides benefit from the part-

nership. Yet they fear their partners just as they fear those within their own communities.

30.29-37 The interpretation of the parable addresses right and wrong religions. According to Muhammad, most of the peoples of the earth are polytheistic (worshippers of many gods—idolaters). Only a few were monotheists. For those, however, who were

tant towards Him; then when He has made them taste mercy from Himself, behold! a party of them associate others with their Lord,

34   that they may disbelieve in what we have brought them;—but enjoy yourselves; for hereafter ye shall know!

35   Or have we sentdown to them authority which speaks of what they do associate with Him?

36   And when we have made men taste of mercy, they rejoice therein; and if there befall them evil for what their hands have sent before, behold! they are in despair.

37   Have they not seen that God extends provision to whom He pleases, or doles it out? verily, in tat are signs unto a people who believe.

That which pleases Allah

38   Then give to the kinsman his due, and to the poor and to the wayfarer; that is better for those who desire the face of God, and these it is who are prosperous.

39   And what ye put out to usury that it may increase with the wealth of men, it shall not increase with God; but what ye put out in alms, desiring the face of God—these it is who shall gain double.

40   It is God who created you and then provided for you; and then will make you die, and then will quicken you again; is there any of your partners who can do aught of that? Celebrated be His praises, and exalted be He above what they associate with Him!

41   Trouble hath appeared in the land and the sea, for what men's hands have gained! to make them taste a part of that which they have

monotheistic and remained pure and faithful to Allah, "He had made them taste mercy from Himself" (v. 33) and were therefore people characterized by joy.

30.30 *Hanif* — This is an Arabic term that references pre-Islamic worshippers who embraced monotheism (see Q 3.67, 95; 4.125; 6.79; 10.105; 16.120; 22.31; and 98.5).

30.32-36 *divided their religion and become sects* — In pagan Arabia, a minority of Arabs worshipped only one of the many gods within the Arabian pantheon. Yet, when the true God—Allah—reached out and blessed them, they attributed the blessings to some other deity. Accordingly, they demonstrated themselves to be two-faced infidels and would be judged accordingly in the

afterlife.

30.38-45 According to Muhammad, people are to (a) give to the poor apart from usury, (b) take note of the sad fate of the polytheists, and (c) remain committed to the right religion (that is, the religion that worships Allah—and only Allah).

30.39 Usury, the charging of interest for loans, is forbidden in the Qur'an. Consequently, banks in the Muslim world today typically charge large fees for their services in the place of interest (also see Q 2.275-281; 3.130-132; 4.160-161).

30.41 Muhammad believed that trouble in this life is unavoidable, yet this fact should motivate people to turn back to Allah. The Bible makes a similar claim (Gen 3:16-19; 5:29;

done,—haply they may return!

42 Say, "Journey on in the land, and behold what was the end of those before you,—most of them were idolaters!"

43 Set thy face steadfast to the standard religion, before there come a day from God which there is no averting; on that day shall they be parted into two bands.

44 He who misbelieves, upon him is his misbelief; but whoso does right, for themselves they are spreading couches:

45 That He may reward those who believe and do right of His grace; verily, He loves not the misbelievers!

Signs of Allah's mercy

46 And of His signs is this, that He sends forth the winds with glad tidings, to make you taste of His mercy, and to make the ships go on at His bidding, and that ye may crave of His grace, and haply ye may give thanks.

47 We have sent before thee apostles unto their people, and they came to them with manifest signs: and we took vengeance upon those who sinned, but due from us it was to help the believers.

48 God it is who sends forth the winds to stir up clouds; then He spreads them forth over the sky as he pleases; and He breaks them up and ye see the rain come forth from amongst them; and when He causes it to fall upon whom He pleases of His servants, behold they hail it with joy,

49 although before it was sent down upon them they were before then confused!

Double predestination

50 Look then to the vestiges of God's mercy, how He quickens the earth after its death; verily, that is the

Ps 22:2; 34:17; 55:17; 72:12; 88:1; 127:2; Eccl 1:2-3, 13-14; 2:11, 17; Isa 24:5-6; Lam 2:18; Rom 8:20-22).

30.44 *spreading couches* — This is a reference to the harems in Paradise and the couches, upon which, they will be reclining (see Q 15.20; 52.20; 56.15; 76.13).

30.45a *believe and do right* — These words are repeated often in the Qur'an and serve as a brief summary of the Islamic gospel (see Q 103.3 note).

30.45b *He loves not the misbelievers* — Muhammad understood Allah to love the righteous and hate the infidel. In the Bible, how- ever, God is understood to love both the righteous and the unrighteous (see Ex 23:4-5; Prov 25:21-22; Matt 5:43-48; Lk 6:27-28, 34-35; Rom 12:20-21).

30.46-49 Signs of Allah's mercy: (a) He sends winds so that ships may sail and cause people to seek His grace and be grateful, (b) He sends apostles so that people will know the truth, (c) He punishes the wicked and rewards the righteous, (d) He sends forth rain, and (e) He will resurrect the dead.

30.50-57 This passage is an in-depth presentation of the Doctrine al-Qadar—double predestination. The Qur'an affirms the no-

quickener of the dead, and He is mighty over all!

51 But if we should send a wind and they should see it yellow, they would after that become misbelievers.

52 But, verily, thou canst not make the dead to hear, nor canst thou make the deaf to hear the call, when they turn their backs and flee;

53 nor hast thou to guide the blind out of their error; thou canst only make those to hear who believe in our signs and who are resigned.

54 God it is who created you of weakness, then made for you after weakness strength; then made for you after strength, weakness and grey hairs: He creates what He pleases, for He is the knowing, the powerful!

55 And on the day when the Hour shall rise, the sinners shall swear that they have not tarried save an hour; thus were they wont to lie!

56 But those who are given knowledge and faith will say, "We have tarried according to the Book of God,

until the day of resurrection;" and this is the day of resurrection, but ye—ye do not know.

57 And on that day their excuse shall profit not those who did wrong; nor shall they be asked to please God again.

Allah's stamp

58 We have struck out to men in this Qur'ân every kind of parable; but if thou shouldst bring them a sign then those who misbelieve will surely say, "Ye are but followers of vanity;

59 thus does God set a stamp upon the hearts of those who do not know."

60 Be thou patient then; verily, God's promise is true! and let them not flurry thee who are not sure.

Surah 26

In the name of the merciful and compassionate God.

---

tion of divine predestination. Only those who are "given knowledge and faith" will be justified before Allah (v 56). He grants them spiritual strength (v. 54). The rest are spiritually deaf and blind and cannot hear or see spiritual truth (see **Doctrine of al-Qadar** on pp. 264-266).

30.56 *the Book of God* — divine revelation. In this case, the divine revelation refers to that which was given to the numerous apostles and then passed on to the

peoples of the world. This divine revelation is the eternal Book of God in Paradise (see **The Perspicuous Book** on pp. 178-179).

30.58-60 *thus does God set a stamp upon the hearts* — Allah sets a seal on the hearts of those who do not know the truth. This explains why the proclamation of Islamic truth is often rejected by infidels (see Q 4.155; 7.100-101; 9.87, 93; 10.74; 16.108; 40.35; 47.16; 63.3).

Surah 26. The title of this surah, *The Po-*

1   T. S. M.

Hardheartedness

2   Those are the signs of the perspicu-
     ous Book;

3   haply thou art vexing thyself to
     death that they will not be believ-
     ers!

4   If we please we will send down
     upon them from the heaven a sign,
     and their necks shall be humbled
     thereto.

5   But there comes not to them any
     recent Reminder from the Merci-
     ful One that they do not turn away
     from.

6   They have called (thee) liar! but
     there shall come to them a mes-
     sage of that at which they mocked.

7   Have they not looked to the earth,
     how we caused to grow therein

     of every noble kind?

8   verily, in that is a sign; but most of
     them will never be believers!

9   but, verily, thy Lord He is mighty
     and merciful.

First Example:
the hardheartedness of Pharaoh

10   And when thy Lord called Moses
     (saying), "Come to the unjust
     people,

11   to the people of Pharaoh, will they
     not fear?"

12   Said he, "My Lord! verily, I fear
     that they will call me liar;

13   and my breast is straitened, and my
     tongue is not fluent; send then unto
     Aaron,

14   for they have a crime against me,
     and I fear that they may kill me."

15   Said He, Not so; but go with our

ets, comes from verse 224. The background to this surah is that the people of Mecca persistently rejected the message of Muhammad. Muhammad viewed this as a sign of hardheartedness and wrote the surah as a condemnation of their unbelief.

Moreover, seven other apostles are referenced in the surah: Moses, Abraham, Noah, Hud, Zali'h, Lot, and Sho'haib (Jethro). Muhammad commented upon the resistance they experienced from the recipients of their prophecies. The point was that just as the messages of previous apostles were rejected, it should be not surprising that Muhammad's message would be rejected by most of the people of Mecca. It is, as Q 26.5b-6 states, "...they turn aside from it. So they have indeed rejected (the

truth), therefore the news of that which they mock shall soon come to them."
26.1 Literally, *Ta Sin Mim.* See Q 32.1, note.
26.2 *the perspicuous Book* — The perspicuous (clear) book refers to divine revelation; in this case, the Qur'an (see **The Perspicuous Book** on pp. 178-179).
26.8-9 *Verily, in that is a sign; but most of them will never be believers! but, verily, thy Lord He is mighty and merciful* — This phrase is repeated eight times in this surah (Q 26.8-9, 67-68, 111-112, 121-122, 139-140, 170-171, 174-175 and 190-191).
26.10-68 The story begins with the incident at the burning bush and ends at the Crossing of the Red (Reed) Sea (see Ex 3-15). The point of this story is that Pharaoh

signs, verily, we are with you listening.

16   "And go to Pharaoh and say, 'Verily, we are the apostles of the Lord
of the worlds

17   (to tell thee to) send with us the
children of Israel.'"

18   And he [Pharaoh] said, "Did we not
bring thee up amongst us as a
child? and thou didst dwell
amongst us for years of thy life;

19   and thou didst do thy deed which
thou hast done, and thou art of the
ungrateful!"

20   Said he [Moses], "I did commit
this, and I was of those who erred.

21   And I fled from you when I feared
you, and my Lord granted me judgment, and made me one of His
messengers;

22   and this is the favour thou hast
obliged me with, that thou hast
enslaved the children of Israel!"

23   Said Pharaoh, "Who is the Lord of
the worlds?"

24   Said he [Moses], "The Lord of the
heavens and the earth and what is
between the two, if ye are but
sure."

25   Said he [Pharaoh] to those about
him, "Do ye not listen?"

26   Said he [Moses], "Your Lord and
the Lord of your fathers of yore!"

27   Said he [Pharaoh], "Verily, your

apostle who is sent to you is surely
mad!"

28   Said he [Moses], "The Lord of the
east and of the west, and of what
is between the two, if ye had but
sense!"

29   Said he [Pharaoh], "If thou dost
take a god besides Me I will surely
make thee one of the imprisoned!"

30   Said he [Moses], "What, if I come
to thee with something obvious?"

31   Said he [Pharaoh], "Bring it, if thou
art of those who tell the truth!"

32   And he threw down his rod, and,
behold, it was an obvious serpent!

33   and he plucked out his hand, and,
behold, it was white to the spectators!

34   He [Pharaoh] said to the chiefs
around him, "Verily, this is a knowing sorcerer,

35   he desires to turn you out of your
land! what is it then ye bid?"

36   They said, "Give him and his
brother some hope, and send into
the cities to collect

37   and bring to thee every knowing
sorcerer."

38   And the sorcerers assembled at the
appointed time on a stated day,

39   and it was said to the people, "Are
ye assembled?

40   Imply we may follow the sorcerers if we gain the upper hand."

repeatedly and unrelentingly resisted Moses.
The net result was the destruction of Egypt
and the Egyptian army.
26.23 *the Lord of the worlds* — This term
is one of Muhammad's favorite depictions of

Allah (see Q 1.2, note). The phrase is never
mentioned in the Bible.
26.27 Pharaoh accused Moses of being
crazy. The implication is that this corresponded to words spoken by the Meccan

41 And when the sorcerers came they said to Pharaoh, "Shall we, verily, have a hire if we gain the upper hand?"

42 Said he [Pharaoh], "Yes; and, verily, ye shall then be of those who are nigh (my throne)."

43 And Moses said to them, "Throw down what ye have to throw down."

44 So they threw down their ropes and their rods and said, "By Pharaoh's ight, verily, we it is who shall gain the upper hand!"

45 And Moses threw down his rod, and, lo, it swallowed up what they falsely devised!

46 And the sorcerers threw themselves down, adoring.

47 Said they, "We believe in the Lord of the worlds,

48 the Lord of Moses and Aaron!"

49 Said he [Pharaoh], "Do ye believe in Him ere I give you leave? Verily, he is your chief who has taught you sorcery, but soon ye shall know. I will surely cut off your hands and your feet from opposite sides, and I will crucify you all together!"

50 They said, "No harm; verily, unto our Lord do we return!

51 verily, we hope that our Lord will forgive us our sins, for we are the

52 first of believers!"

52 And we inspired Moses, "Journey by night with my servants; verily, ye are pursued."

53 And Pharaoh sent into the cities to collect;

54 Verily, these are a small company.

55 And, verily, they are enraged with us;

56 but we are a multitude, wary!

57 "Turn them out of gardens and springs,

58 and treasuries, and a noble station!"

59 —thus,—and we made the children of Israel to inherit them.

60 And they followed them at dawn;

61 and when the two hosts saw each other, Moses' companions said, "Verily, we are overtaken!"

62 Said he [Moses], "Not so; verily, with me is my Lord, He will guide me."

63 And we inspired Moses, "Strike with thy rod the sea;" and it was cleft asunder, and each part was like a mighty mountain.

64 And then we brought the others.

65 And we saved Moses and those with him all together;

66 then we drowned the others;

67 and that is a sign: but most of them will never be believers!

68 And, verily, thy Lord He is mighty, merciful.

people against Muhammad (see Q 68.2, note).

26.47-51 These verses are not found in the Exodus account. According to the Exodus account, the sorcerers in Pharaoh's court

neither repented nor turned to Moses.

26.53-63 In this passage, two significant episodes leading to the exodus of the Israelites from Egypt were not included: (a) the Passover Meal, and (b) the death of the

Second Example:
the hardheartedness of
Abraham's father

69   And recite to them the story of
      Abraham;
70   when he said to his father and his
      people, "What do ye serve?"
71   They said, "We serve idols, and we
      are still devoted to them."
72   He said, "Can they hear you when
      ye call,
73   or profit you, or harm?"
74   They said, "No; but we found our
      fathers doing thus,"
75   He said, "Have ye considered what
      ye have been serving,
76   ye and your fathers before you?
77   Verily, they are foes to me, save
      only the Lord of the worlds,
78   who created me and guides me,
79   and who gives me food and drink.
80   And when I am sick He heals me;
81   He who will kill me, and then bring
      me to life;
82   and who I hope will forgive me my
      sins on the day of judgment!
83   Lord, grant me judgment, and let
      me reach the righteous;
84   and give me a tongue of good re-
      port amongst posterity;
85   and make me of the heirs of the
      paradise of pleasure;

86   and pardon my father, verily, he is
      of those who err;
87   and disgrace me not on the day
      when they are raised up again;
88   the day when wealth shall profit
      not, nor sons,
89   but only he who comes to God with
      a sound heart.
90   And paradise shall be brought near
      to the pious;
91   and hell shall be brought forth to
      those who go astray,
92   and it shall be said to them, "Where
      is what ye used to worship
93   beside God? can they help you, or
      get help themselves?"
94   And they shall fall headlong into it,
      they and those who have gone
      astray,
95   and the hosts of Iblîs all together!"
96   They shall say, while they quarrel
      therein,
97   "By God! we were surely in an
      obvious error,
98   when we made you equal to the
      Lord of the worlds!
99   but it was only sinners who led us
      astray.
100   But we have no intercessors
101   and no warm friend;
102   but had we a turn we would be of
      the believers."
103   —Verily, in that is a sign, but most

first born by the death angel of God.
26.69-104 This passage is loosely based upon Gen. 11-28-31. The point of this passage is that idolatry is evil and that God admonished Abraham to repent and become a monotheist.

26.90 According to this verse, salvation is the reward for the pious. Piety, according to the Qur'an, is a meritorious activity that weighs heavily in the celestial balance at the Last Judgment. Such thinking, however, stands opposed to the Christian doctrine of

104 of them will never be believers; and, verily, thy Lord He is mighty and merciful.

Third Example:
the hardheartedness of
the people of Noah's day

105 The people of Noah said the apostles were liars,
106 when their brother Noah said to them, "Will ye not fear?
107 verily, I am a faithful apostle to you;
108 then fear God and obey me.
109 I do not ask you for it any hire; my hire is only with the Lord of the worlds.
110 So fear God and obey me."
111 They said, "Shall we believe in thee, when the reprobates follow thee?"
112 He said, "I did not know what they were doing;
113 their account is only with my Lord, if ye but perceive.
114 And I am not one to drive away the believers,
115 I am only a plain warner."
116 They said, "Verily, if thou desist not, O Noah! thou shalt surely be of those who are stoned!"
117 Said he, "My Lord! verily, my people call me liar;
118 open between me and between

them an opening, and save me and those of the believers who are with me!"
119 So we saved him and those with him in the laden ark,
120 then we drowned the rest;
121 verily, in that is a sign, but most of them will never be believers;
122 and, verily, thy Lord He is mighty and merciful.

Fourth Example:
the hardheartedness of
the people of Hud's day

123 And 'Âd called the apostles liars;
124 when their brother Hûd said to them, "Will ye not fear?
125 Verily, I am to you a faithful apostle;
126 then fear God and obey me.
127 I do not ask you for it any hire; my hire is only with the Lord of the worlds.
128 Do ye build on every height a landmark in sport,
129 and take to works that haply ye may be immortal?
130 "And when ye assault ye assault like tyrants;
131 but fear God and obey me;
132 and fear Him
133 who hath given you an extent of

salvation by grace. In the Bible, salvation is a question of *forgiveness*, not of *merit* (see **The Last Judgment** on pp. 46-50).
26.105-122 This passage is based upon the story in the Book of Genesis, chapters six through eight.

26.123-140 Hud was the legendary prophet of the people of Ad (see Q 54.17-21, note). According to Muhammad, Hud was born five generations after Noah. The people of Ad had forgotten the spiritual teachings of Noah and resorted to idolatry.

cattle and sons,

134   and gardens and springs.

135   Verily, I fear for you the torment of a mighty day!"

136   They said, "It is the same to us if thou admonish

137   or art not of those who do admonish; this is nothing but old folks' fictions,

138   for we shall not be tormented!"

139   And they called him liar! but we destroyed them. Verily, in that is a sign, but most of them will never be believers.

140   And, verily, thy Lord is mighty, merciful.

Fifth Example:
the hardheartedness of the Thamud
people of Zali'h's day

141   Thamûd called the apostles liars;

142   when their brother Zâli'h said to them, "Do ye not fear?

143   verily, I am to you a faithful apostle;

144   so fear God and obey me.

145   I do not ask you for it any hire; my hire is only with the Lord of the worlds.

146   Shall ye be left here in safety

147   with gardens and springs,

148   and cornfields and palms, the spathes whereof are fine?

149   and ye hew out of the mountains

houses skilfully.

150   But fear God and obey me;

151   and obey not the bidding of the extravagant,

152   who do evil in the earth and do not act aright!"

153   They said, "Thou art only of the infatuated;

154   thou art but mortal like ourselves; so bring us a sign, if thou be of those who speak the truth!"

155   He said, "This she-camel shall have her drink and you your drink on a certain day;

156   but touch her not with evil, or there will seize you the torment of a mighty day!"

157   But they hamstrung her,

158   and on the morrow they repented; and the torment seized them; verily, in that is a sign; but most of them will never be believers:

159   but verily, thy Lord He is mighty, merciful.

Sixth Example:
the hardheartedness
of the people in Lot's day

160   The people of Lot called the apostles liars;

161   when their brother Lot said to them, "Do ye not fear?

162   verily, I am to you a faithful apostle;

Hud's admonitions were twofold (a) repent from idolatry, and (b) stop oppressing people like tyrants. The people refused to repent and suffered divine judgment. In contrast, the Bible does not include any reference to either the people of Ad or Hud.

26.141-159 See Q 91, note.

26.160-175 This story is based upon Gen-

163 then fear God and obey me.

164 I do not ask you for it any hire; my hire is only with the Lord of the worlds.

165 Do ye approach males of all the world

166 and leave what God your Lord has created for you of your wives a nay, but ye are people who transgress!"

167 They said, "Surely, if thou dost not desist, O Lot! thou shalt be of those who are expelled!"

168 Said he, "Verily, I am of those who hate your deed;

169 my Lord! save me and my people from what they do."

170 And we saved him and his people all together,

171 except an old woman amongst those who lingered.

172 Then we destroyed the others;

173 and we rained down upon them a

rain; and evil was the rain of those who were warned.

174 Verily, in that is a sign; but most of them will never be believers.

175 And, verily, thy Lord He is mighty, merciful, compassionate.

Seventh Example:
the hardheartedness of the people
of Petra in Sho'haib's day

176 The fellows of the Grove called the apostles liars;

177 Sho'hâib said to them, "Will ye not fear?

178 verily, I am to you a faithful apostle,

179 then fear God and obey me.

180 I do not ask you for it any hire; my hire is only with the Lord of the worlds.

181 Give good measure, and be not of those who diminish;

---

esis 19. The sin that Lot preached against to the people of Sodom was the sin of homosexuality (see Q 26.165-166).

26.164 *the Lord of the worlds* — This is one of Muhammad's favorite depictions of Allah (see Q 1.2, note). The phrase, however, is never mentioned in the Bible.

26.165-166 *do ye approach males* — This is a depiction of the sin of homosexuality. Muhammad called it a transgression.

26.170-171 In this passage, the biblical account differs from the qur'anic account. In the biblical account, Lot did not preach to the people of Sodom of their sinfulness and was reluctant to leave the city, since he had become a man of prominence (he sat at the gates). two angels came to Lot and

beseeched him to flee the city before it was destroyed. Lot reluctantly left the city with his family. In the qur'anic account, Lot behaved righteously and was a preacher of righteousness.

26.171 The "old woman" in this verse is identified in Genesis 19:26 as Lot's wife. Yet, here again the Qur'an differs from the biblical account. In this account, no mention is given of her becoming a pillar of salt (Gen 19:16).

26.176 *fellows of the Grove* — Literally, the people of Madyan (Midian). They lived in the region southeast of Mount Sinai.

26.176-191 According to Islamic lore, Sho'haib was a descendent of Abraham and the father-in-law to Moses. The Old Testa-

182	and weigh with a fair balance,
183	and do not cheat men of their goods; and waste not the land, despoiling it;
184	and fear Him who created you and the races of yore!"
185	Said they, "Thou art only of the infatuated;
186	and thou art only a mortal like ourselves; and, verily, we think that thou art surely of the liars;
187	so make a portion of the heaven to fall down upon us, if thou art of those who tell the truth!"
188	Said he, "My Lord knows best what ye do!"
189	but they called him liar, and the torment of the day of the shadow seized them; for it was the torment of a mighty day:
190	verily, in that is a sign; but most of them will never be believers;
191	but, verily, thy Lord He is mighty, merciful!

Allah has warned people throughout history

192	And, verily, it is a revelation from the Lord of the worlds;
193	the Faithful Spirit came down with it
194	upon thy heart, that thou shouldst be of those who warn;
195	—in plain Arabic language,
196	and, verily, it is (foretold) in the scriptures of yore!
197	Have they not a sign, that the learned men of the children of Israel recognise it?
198	Had we sent it down to any barbarian,
199	and he had read it to them, they would not have believed therein.
200	Thus have we made for it a way into the hearts of the sinners;
201	they will not believe therein until they see the grievous woe!
202	and it shall come to them suddenly

ment identifies him with two names: Jethro (Ex 3:1) and Hobab (Num 10:29). The Qur'an added a third name: Sho'haib.

The Midianite people existed throughout the Old Testament era and into the Christian era. They were nomads—tent dwellers—not sedentary (that is, not living in caves in mountainous terrain, as Muhammad asserted). Jethro, father-in-law to Moses, was a Midianite. In the Book of Judges, Gideon fought against the Midianites.

Apart from Muhammad's account in the Qur'an, a person by the name of Sho'haib is not known to have existed. Nevertheless, in accord with Islamic tradition, a well preserved tomb of Sho'haib is located in Jordan, two kilometers west of the town of Mahis. Another site for the tomb of Sho'haib is located in the lower Galilee region of Israel in the town of Hattin, recognized by the Druze people as the official site.

26.192-200 Muhammad understood his ministry as that of a warner. He was to speak the truth of Allah in "plain Arabic language." His words were just as divinely authoritative as "the scriptures of the ancients" and were a sign to them in ways similar to the signs given to the learned Israelite people.

26.195 *in plain Arabic language* — some Islamic scholars believe that the Qur'an must

while they do not perceive!

203   They will say, "Shall we be re-
       spited?

204   —What! do they wish to hasten on
       our torment?"

205   What thinkest thou? if we let them
       enjoy themselves for years,

206   and then there come to them what
       they are threatened,

207   that will not avail them which they
       had to enjoy!

208   But we do not destroy any city
       without its having warners

209   as a reminder, for we are never
       unjust.

210   The devils did not descend there-
       with:

211   it is not a work for them; nor are
       they able to do it.

212   Verily, they are deposed from lis-
       tening;

Admonitions

213   call not then with God upon other
       gods, or thou wilt be of the tor-
       mented;

214   but warn thy clansmen who are
       near of kin.

215   And lower thy wing to those of the

be read in Arabic (see Q 12.2; 13.37; 20.113; 26.195; 39.28; 42.7; and 43.3). This statement de-legitimizes all translations of the Qur'an (see **The Qur'an** on pp. 150-153).

In contrast, the Judeo-Christian tradition makes no such requirement in regards to its sacred Scriptures. It encourages translations, evident in the Septuagint (Greek translation of the Old Testament), verses from which are repeatedly found in the New Testament. In the current age, thousands of translations of the Bible exist in the many languages of the world.

26.201-212 According to this passage, Allah had always sent "warners" prior to the onset of judgment upon a people. Their hard-heartedness justified the judgment that befell them. Muhammad was convinced that the people of Mecca were treating his ministry no differently than that which the warners of previous eras experienced.

26.210-212 The point here is that devils did not come down to earth to reveal the Qur'an. Moreover, they do not wish to hear it. This passage may be a subtle rebuke to the ginn worshippers of Mecca.

26.213 People are admonished not to worship Allah as one among many gods. Such syncretism is a version of polytheism and worthy of divine punishment.

The Judeo-Christian tradition carries similar sentiments. John R. W. Stott has rightly commented: "It is written that Yahweh, 'whose name is Jealous, is a jealous God' (Ex 34:14). Now jealousy is the resentment of rivals, and whether it is good or evil depends on whether the rival has any business to be there. To be jealous of someone who threatens to outshine us in beauty, brains or sport is sinful, because we cannot claim a monopoly of talent in those areas. If, on the other hand, a third party enters a marriage, the jealousy of the injured person, who is being displaced, is righteous, because the intruder has no right to be there. It is the same with God, who says, 'I am the Lord, that is my name! I will not give my glory to another or my praise to idols' (Isa. 42:8). Our Creator and Redeemer has a right to our exclusive allegiance, and is 'jealous' if we transfer it to anyone or anything else" (*The Spirit, the*

believers who follow thee;

216   but if they rebel against thee, say, "Verily, I am clear of what ye do,"

217   and rely thou upon the mighty, merciful One,

218   who sees thee when thou dost stand up,

219   and thy posturing amongst those who adore.

220   Verily, He both hears and knows!

Demonic deception

221   Shall I inform you upon whom the devils descend?

222   they descend upon every sinful liar,

223   and impart what they have heard; but most of them are liars.

224   And the poets do those follow who go astray!

225   Dost thou not see that they wander distraught in every vale?

226   and that they say that which they do not do?

227   save those who believe, and do right, and remember God much,

and defend themselves after they are wronged; but those who do wrong shall know with what a turn they shall be turned.

Surah 15

In the name of merciful and compassionate God.

1   A. L. R.

The remorse of the infidels

Those are the signs of the Book and of a perspicuous Qur'ân.

2   Many a time will those who disbelieve fain they had been resigned.

3   Leave them to eat and enjoy themselves and let hope beguile them, but they at length shall know!

4   We never destroyed a city without it had its noted doom.

5   No nation can hasten on its appointed time, nor put it off.

Church and the World, p. 278).

26.214-216 People were admonished to warn the infidels. If the infidels rejected the warning, those who warned them were to consider themselves as having fulfilled their responsibility and now free to move on with their lives (cf. Matt 10:14 and Lk 9:5 where Jesus made a similar comment, and Acts 13:51 where Paul and Barnabas acted in a similar fashion).

26.221 According to Muhammad, infidels were affected by demons who kept them bewildered and bound in lies (cf. 2 Cor 4:4; 11:3, 13-15 where the Bible makes similar

statements).

Surah 15. Because of the unending rejection of the people of Mecca to Muhammad's ministry, discouragement began to set in among the small Muslim community in Mecca. The purpose of this surah was to reaffirm the rightness of Muhammad's ministry, acknowledge once again his divine calling, and explain the fate of all infidels.

15.1a Literally, *Alif Lam Ra.* See Q 32.1, note.

15.1b *the Book* — divine revelation. In this case, the eternal divine revelation that resides in Paradise and which directly corre-

6   But they say, "O thou to whom the Reminder has been sent down! verily, thou art possessed.

7   Why dost thou not bring us the angels if thou dost tell the truth?"

8   We sent not down the angels save by right; nor even then would these be respited.

9   Verily, we have sent down the Reminder, and, verily, we will guard it.

10   And we sent before thee among the sects of those of yore.

11   But there never came an apostle to them but they mocked at him.

The spirit of delusion

12   Such conduct also will we put into the hearts of the sinners.

13   They will not believe therein, but the course of those of yore is run.

14   But had we opened to them a door of the sky and they had mounted

sponds to the Qur'an.

15.5 Muhammad believed that the sovereignty of Allah is so complete that the moment a nation's demise is established by Allah, it cannot be changed.

15.6 *the Reminder* — That is, the Qur'an. Muhammad believed that the Qur'an is the repository of eternal truths. Maulana Muhammad Ali describes it as "the perfect expression of the Divine will" (*The Religion of Islam*, p. 5).

15.6-7 *thou art possessed* — The Meccan people ridiculed Muhammad, calling him demon-possessed (insane). They chided him, demanding that he bring down angels from Paradise that they could see as a means of validating his ministry. In short, they demanded miracles. Curiously, the miracle where Muhammad allegedly divided the moon in half (see Q 54.1-5) was not cited by Muhammad as an answer to their demands.

Though Muhammad criticized the Meccan people for making such a demand, according to the Bible, the presence of miracles was a necessary credential of an Old Testament prophet (Deut 13:1-5) or a New Testament apostle (Acts 2:43; 5:12; 14:3; Rom 15:17-19; Heb 2:1-4). Even Jesus Christ

pointed to his miracles as a means of establishing His credentials (Jn 5:36; 6:14; 7:31). The Meccan people, then, were following in a long-standing tradition to expect a self-proclaimed apostle to perform miracles as a way of establishing credentials and validating his prophetic office. Throughout Muhammad's life, the absence of miracles was a continuing problem. Even after his death, the criticism continued. This was one of the complaints of John of Damascus (A.D. 676-749) in his assessment of Islam (see **John of Damascus** on pp. 247-248).

15.9 *the Reminder* — the Qur'an. According to Muhammad, the Qur'an is of divine inspiration ("we sent down the Reminder") and it will remain uncorrupted ("we will guard it"). Yet, elsewhere in the Qur'an Muhammad claimed that Allah sent down other divine inspirations, such as the Old and New Testaments, but did not guard them from corruption (see Q 4.46, 157-158, 172-173; 5.13, 73).

Christians note an inconsistency in this verse. If Allah is indeed almighty and sovereign and capable of guarding His divine revelation that He sent to the earth, why did He not guard all His divinely inspired scriptures? It impugns His power and sovereignty

up into it all the while;

15   then also had they said, "Our eyesight is only intoxicated; nay, we
are an enchanted people!"

16   And we have placed in the sky the
signs of the zodiac, and have made
them seemly to the beholders;

17   and we have guarded them from
every pelted devil;

18   save from such as steal a hearing,
and there follows him an obvious
shooting-star.

*The sovereignty of Allah
over all the earth*

19   And the earth we have stretched
out and have thrown on it firm
mountains, and have caused to
grow upon it of everything a measured quantity.

20   And we have made for you means
of livelihood therein, and for those
for whom ye have not to provide.

21   Nor is there aught but the treasuries of it are with us, and we do not
send it down save in a noted quantity.

22   And we send forth the impregnat-
ing winds, and we send down
water from the sky, and we give it

to you to drink, nor is it ye who
store it up.

23   And we, verily, we quicken and kill;
and we are of (all things) heirs.

24   And we already know the foremost
of you, and we know the laggards
too!

25   And, verily, it is your Lord who will
gather you; verily, He is wise and
knowing.

The fall of Satan

26   And we did create man from
crackling clay of black mud
wrought in form.

27   And the ginns had we created before of smokeless fire.

28   And when thy Lord said to the angels, Verily, I am creating a mortal
from crackling clay of black mud
wrought into shape;

29   "And when I have fashioned it,
and breathed into it of my spirit,
then fall ye down before it adoring."

30   And the angels adored all of them
together,

31   save Iblîs, who refused to be
among those who adored.

32   He said, "O Iblîs! what ails thee

to allow some of His divinely inspired Scriptures to suffer corruption, and not others
(see **The Qur'an** on pp. 150-153).
15.12-15 According to Islam, all infidels have
been given a spirit of delusion so that they
may not believe the truth of Islam (see **Doctrine of al-Qadar** on pp. 264-266).
15.26 *crackling clay of black mud* — This is

another description from the Qur'an of the
origin of the human being (see Q 96.2, note).
15.27 *ginns* — genies (see **Occultism in
Seventh Century Arabia** on pp. 123-125).
15.31 *Iblis* —Satan. Important differences,
however, exist between the biblical and
qur'anic understanding of Satan. In Islam,
Iblis was cast out of Paradise because he

that thou art not among those who adore?"

33 Said he, "I would not adore a mortal whom Thou hast created from crackling clay of black mud wrought into form."

34 He said, "Then get thee forth therefrom, and, verily, thou art to be pelted!

35 And, verily, the curse is upon thee until the day of judgment."

36 Said he, "O my Lord! respite me until the day when they shall be raised."

37 He said, "Then, verily, thou art of the respited

38 until the day of the noted time."

39 He said, "O my Lord! for that Thou hast seduced me I will surely make it seem seemly for them on earth, and I will surely seduce them all together;

40 save such of Thy servants amongst them as are sincere."

Paradise and Hell

41 Said He, "This is a right way

against me.

42 Verily, my servants thou hast no authority over, save over those who follow thee of such as are seduced:

43 and, verily, hell is promised to them all together.

44 It has seven doors; at every door is there a separate party of them."

45 Verily, those who fear God shall dwell amidst gardens and springs:

46 "Enter ye therein with peace in safety!"

47 And we will strip off whatever ill-feeling is in their breasts; as brethren on couches face to face.

48 No toil shall touch them therein, nor shall they be brought forth therefrom.

49 Inform my servants that I am the pardoning, the merciful;

50 and that my woe is the grievous woe.

The destruction of Sodom

51 And inform them concerning Abraham's guests

refused to bow down and give obeisance to Adam. His chief ministry is to deceive people, causing them to disbelieve Islamic dogma (see Q 2.34-35; 7.10-12; 15.31-35; 17.61-64; 38.71-85).

In the Bible, Satan was cast out of Heaven because he refused to bow down in worship to God. Instead, he sought to become like the Most High (Isa. 14:12 15; Ezek 28:12-19).

15.41-50 Description of Hell: (a) it has seven

gates, (b) a place of a painful punishment. Description of Paradise: (a) likened to an oasis, a place of gardens and fountains, (b) whatever rancor still exists in their hearts will be rooted out, (c) a place of no toil, and (d) a place of eternal security.

15.44 The Qur'an has seven different doors for Hell. They correspond to the seven levels in Hell: (1) Hell, (2) flaming fire, (3) crushing disaster, (4) burning fire, (5) scorching fire, (6) fierce fire, and (7) abyss (see *Hell*

52   when they entered in unto him and said, "Peace!" he said, "Verily, we are afraid of you."

53   They said, "Be not afraid! verily, we give thee glad tidings of a knowing boy."

54   He said, "Do ye give me this glad tidings although old age has touched me? give me the glad tidings then!"

55   They said, "We give the glad tidings of the truth, then be not of those who despair!"

56   He said, "Who would despair of the mercy of his Lord save those who err?"

57   He said, "What is your business, O ye messengers?"

58   They said, "Verily, we are sent unto a sinful people;

59   save only Lot's family, them will we save all together,

60   except his wife; we have decreed, verily, she shall be of those who linger."

61   And when the messengers came unto Lot's family,

62   he said, "Verily, ye are a people whom I recognise not."

63   They said, "Nay, but we have come

to thee with that whereof they did doubt.

64   And we have brought thee the truth, and, verily, we speak the truth!

65   Travel then with thy family in the deep darkness of the night, and follow thou their rear; and let not any one of you turn round to look; but go on to where ye are bidden."

66   And we decided for him this affair because the uttermost one of these people should be cut off on the morrow.

67   Then the people of the city came, glad at the tidings.

68   Said he, "Verily, these are my guests, therefore disgrace me not;

69   but fear God, and put me not to shame."

70   They said, "Have we not forbidden thee everybody in the world?"

71   He said, "Here are my daughters, if do it ye must."

72   —By thy life! verily, they were surely in their intoxication blindly wandering on!

73   And the noise caught them at the dawn.

74   And we made the higher parts (of the cities) their lower parts, and

on pp. 80-82).

15.51-77 The story of the destruction of Sodom is based upon the Genesis account (Gen. 17-19).

15.53 The prophesied birth a boy in this passage is not named. Yet, the Genesis account does name him: Isaac (Gen 17:19).

15.60 According to this passage, it was the will of Allah that Lot's wife be left be-

hind and die in the judgment. In the Genesis account, Lot's wife fled Sodom yet died because she disobeyed the word of the angels and turned and looked at the city while it was destroyed (Gen 19:26).

15.73 *the noise* — This is the mysterious noise that is often mentioned in the Qur'an that is said to bring destruction upon cities and civilizations (see Q 54.22-31, note).

John of Damascus

Mansour bin Sarjun (676-749) is looked upon by many Christian historians as the greatest Christian theologian of the eighth century. Eastern Orthodox churches consider him to be the last of the great teachers of the early church, the so-called Fathers of the Church.

Mansour was born and raised in Damascus. At the time of the first Muslim expansion and the conquering of the territory that included Damascus, Damascus contained many civil servants who happened to be Christians—Mansour's grandfather among them. Rather than eradicating the Christians and replacing them with Muslims, the Muslim leaders made use of their considerable expertise in the running of their newly expanding empire. Mansour's grandfather served as a high government official in the supervision of the acquisition of taxes throughout the Muslim empire. When Mansour reached adulthood, he served as a chief administrator to the Muslim caliph in Damascus.

When ordained to the priesthood, Mansour left Damascus. He adopted the monastic name of John and served at the monastery at Mar Saba (near Jerusalem)—one of the oldest monasteries in the world. He distinguished himself as a scholar in the fields of music, astronomy, theology, and mathematics. His mathematical acumen was such that he rivaled Pythagoras in arithmetic and Euclid in geometry.

Yet, it is in his work in theology that John is best remembered. During the iconoclastic controversy in the eighth century, where icons were routinely destroyed across the Christian world on the grounds that they were a violation of the Second Commandment (Ex 20:4-6), John was a leading and quieting voice arguing in favor of icons. He noted that they offered the illiterate a way in which to know biblical stories and related Christian truths.

In his book *The Fount of Knowledge*, John wrote extensively on all the theological heresies of his day. Because of his intimate knowledge of Islam, he wrote much on this religion, comparing and contrasting it with mainstream Christian thought. According to John, anyone could write documents and claim that they were divinely inspired. That which set apart genuine revelation from false was (a) the accompaniment of miracles in the author's life, and (b) the testimony of other prophets who wrote similarly and pointed to the coming of a new prophet.

Yet, John explained, Muhammad failed these two requisites. First, conspicuously absent in his life were miracles. Indeed, in a number of surahs he acknowledged this deficiency, noting that the Meccan people repeatedly criticized him for the lack of miracles (see Q 6.35; 10.19-20; 11.12; 13.6-7; 15.6-7; 17.90-95; 20.133-135; 25.7, 20-29; 29.50). One miracle is mentioned in the Qur'an, where Muhammad allegedly split the moon in half (see Q 54.1-5), yet this episode is only briefly mentioned once and curiously never repeated by Muhammad in subsequent surahs, in spite of the continued criticisms from his opponents that his ministry lacked miracles. Second, conspicuously absent in non-Islamic sacred literature (e.g., the Bible) are prophetic words that foreshadowed the coming of Muhammad and his new theological insights.

The one exception to the second point mentioned above is the word *periklutos* that Muhammad believed was included in Jn 14:26. This word, said Muhammad, was a foreshadowing of his coming ministry (see Q 61.6, note). Nevertheless, the word nowhere appears in any New Testament manuscripts. The word in Jn 14:26 is *parakletos* (not *periklutos*) and is a reference to the future ministry of the Holy Spirit.

His [John of Damascus'] theology was definitely Byzantine but a great part of his life was lived in direct personal encounter with people outside this tradition, namely with Muslims.

—Daniel J. Sahas, *John of Damascus on Islam*, p. 127

The fact that John treats Islam as a Christian heresy is significant. He regards it simply from an intellectual dogmatic point of view, and recognizes a near kinship between it and Christianity, but fails to appreciate the power and originality of Muhammad as a prophet. Muhammad's claim to be a prophet is judged by its lack of miraculous sanction, and of any prediction of his appearance...The pressure of this Christian argument may have strengthened the tendency to ascribe miracles to Muhammad. Moslems accuse Christians of being polytheists; Christians retort that Moslems mutilate God, making Him ἄλογος, without reason. John displays considerable knowledge of the Qur'an, pointing out many absurdities in it.

—Richard Bell, *Transactions*, p. 37

rained down on them stones of baked clay.

75 Verily, in that is a sign to those who mark.

76 And, verily, the (cities) are on a path that still remains.

77 Verily, in that is a sign to the believers.

The City of Hegra

78 And the fellows of the Grove too were unjust;

79 and we took vengeance on them, and, verily, they both are for an obvious example.

80 And the fellows of El 'Hagr called the messengers liars,

81 and we brought them our signs, but they therefrom did turn away.

82 And they did hew them in the mountain houses to dwell in in safety.

83 But the noise caught them in the morn;

84 and that which they had earned availed them naught.

Reaffirmation of Muhammad's calling as an apostle to the people of Mecca

85 We did not create the heavens and the earth and all that is between them both, save in truth. And, verily, the Hour is surely coming; then do thou pardon with a fair pardon.

86 Verily, thy Lord He is the creator, the knowing!

87 We have already brought thee Seven of the Repetition, and the mighty Qur'ân.

88 Let not thine eyes strain after what we have allowed a few pairs of them to enjoy, nor grieve for them; but lower thy wing to the believers,

89 and say, "Verily, I am an obvious warner."

90 As we sent down (punishment) on the separatists

91 who dismember the Qur'ân.

92 But, by thy Lord! we will question them, one and all,

93 about what they have done.

94 Therefore, publish what thou art bidden, and turn aside from the idolaters.

95 Verily, we are enough for thee against the scoffers.

96 Who place with God other gods; but they at length shall know!

15.74 *stones of baked clay* — In this passage, the divine judgment that destroyed Sodom and Gomorrah was "stones of baked clay" (cf. Q 11.82; 51.33). Yet, according to Q 54.34, that which destroyed Sodom and Gomorrah was "a heavy sand storm." The Bible, however, states that the two cities were destroyed by a burning sulphur raining down from the sky (Gen 19:23).

15.78 *fellows of the Grove* — That is, the people of Midian (see Q 26.176, note).

15.80 *El Hagr* — That is, the City of Hegra.

15.80-83 The two phrases, "dwellers of the Rock" and they who "hewed houses in the mountains in security" refer to the people who inhabited the City of Hegra (see **Hegra** on p. 28).

15.85-99 The reaffirmation of Muhammad's

97   And we knew that thy breast was straitened at what they say.

98   Then celebrate the praises of thy Lord, and be thou of those who adore.

99   And serve thy Lord until the certainty shall come to thee.

Surah 51

In the name of merciful and compassionate God.

Curses and Blessings

1   By the scatterers who scatter!

2   and by those pregnant with their burden!

3   and by those running on easily!

4   and by the distributors of affairs!

5   —verily, what ye are threatened with is surely true!

6   And, verily, the judgment will surely take place!

7   By the heaven possessed of paths;

8   verily, ye are at variance in what ye say!

9   He is turned from it who is turned.

10   Slain be the liars,

11   who are heedless in a flood (of ignorance).

12   They will ask, "When is the day of judgment?"

13   The day when at the fire they shall be tried.

14   — "Taste your trial! this is what ye wished to hasten on!"

15   Verily, the pious are in gardens and springs,

16   taking what their Lord brings them. Verily, they before that did well.

17   But little of the night they slept;

18   and at the dawn they asked for-

---

calling can be divided into the three phrases. Each begins with the word "verily." (1) "Verily, thy Lord He is the creator, the knowing," (2) "And say: "Verily, I am an obvious warner," and (3) "Verily, we are enough for thee against the scoffers."

15.91 *who dismember the Qur'an* — That is, those who severely criticize the qur'anic surahs. The "separatists" were those who, figuratively speaking, tore the Qur'an apart. It is possible that they tore into pieces one of the scraps of paper where a surah had been originally recorded. This verse is used as justification to punish any and all people who mistreat written copies of the Qur'an (e.g., soil, burn, tear apart, flush down toilets).

Surah 51. The title of this surah, *The Scat-terers*, comes from verse 1. This surah completes the Fourth Period. It is an encouragement that the teachings of Islam cannot be stopped and that judgment is certain upon the infidels. Several historical figures—Abraham, Sarah, Lot, Moses, the people of Ad, Thamud, and Noah—are featured. Their ministry is presented as a reminder to believe and do good as a way of avoiding divine judgment.

51.10-14 Muhammad cursed the liars of Mecca. He stated that they were engulfed in ignorance and discount the coming Day of Judgment which will be followed by "the fire."

51.15-23 This passage is an encouragement to believers. They shall be in gardens and fountains and will receive blessings from

giveness.

19 And in their wealth was what was due to him who asked, and him who was kept back from asking.

20 And in the earth are signs to those who are sure,

21 and in yourselves,—what! do ye not then see?

22 And in the heaven is your provision and that which ye are promised.

23 But by the Lord of the heaven and the earth! verily, it is the truth,—like that which ye do utter!

Abraham and Sarah

24 Has the tale of Abraham's honoured guests reached thee?

25 When they entered in unto him and said, "Peace!" he said, "Peace!—a people unrecognised."

26 And he went aside unto his people and fetched a fat calf,

27 and brought it nigh unto them; said

he, "Will ye then not eat?"

28 And he felt a secret fear of them: said they, "Fear not." And they gave him glad tidings of a knowing boy.

29 And his wife approached with a noise, and smote her face, and said, "An old woman, barren!"

30 Said they, "Thus says thy Lord, He is knowing, wise."

Lot

31 Said he, "And about what is your errand, O ye messengers?"

32 They said, "Verily, we are sent unto a sinful people,

33 to send upon them stones of clay,

34 marked from thy Lord for the extravagant."

35 And we sent out therefrom such as were in it of the believers;

36 but we only found therein one house of Muslims.

37 And we left therein a sign to those

the Lord. They will be characterized as "doers of good," and will enjoy their sleep. For them it will not be as it was on the earth: sleeping little, asking forgiveness each morning, striving with thieves.

51.24-30 In this passage, Allah is shown to be gracious and the bestower of good gifts. The reader is reminded of the blessing offered to Abraham and Sarah: the miracle birth of a child, promised them in spite of Sarah's advanced years (after her childbearing years have been completed).

51.31-37 Allah rescued the family of Lot from the coming judgment of Sodom.

51.33 The destruction of Sodom and Go-

morrah was the result of Allah sending "stones of clay" upon them (see Q 15.74 where a similar statement is made). Yet Q 54.34 states that Sodom and Gomorrah were destroyed in a violent sand storm. The Bible, however, states that the two cities were destroyed by a burning sulphur raining down from the sky (Gen 19:23).

51.36 *one house of Muslims* — That is, one house of people who were submissive to Allah.

51.38-40 Because Pharaoh rejected the message from Moses, accusing him of being a magician and a madman, the Egyptian army perished in the Red (Reed) Sea. Again, this

who fear the grievous woe.

Moses and Pharaoh

38 And in Moses; when we sent him to Pharaoh with obvious authority.
39 But he turned his back towards his column, and said, "A sorcerer or mad!"
40 And we seized him and his hosts and hurled them into the sea; for he was to be blamed.

The people of Ad

41 And in 'Âd, when we sent against them a desolating wind,
42 that left naught on which it came without making it ashes!

The people of Thamud

43 And in Thamûd, when it was said to them, "Enjoy yourselves for a season."
44 But they revolted against the bid-

ding of their Lord; and the noise caught them as they looked on.
45 And they could not stand upright, and they were not helped!

The people of Noah's day

46 And the people of Noah of yore; verily, they were an abominable people.
47 And the heaven—we have built it with might, and, verily, we do surely give it ample space!
48 And the earth—we have spread it out; and how well we lay it out!
49 And of everything have we created pairs, haply ye may be mindful.

Seek refuge in Allah

50 Flee then to God; verily, I am a plain warner from Him to you!
51 And do not set with God another god; verily, I am a plain warner from Him to you!
52 Thus there came no apostle to those before them, but they said, "A sor-

is a thinly veiled comparison between Muhammad and Moses. Since the people of Mecca had repeatedly accused Muhammad of being a sorcerer and mad (Q 37.15; 51.52; 68.2, 51; 81.22), Muhammad noted that Moses too was similarly criticized by Pharaoh.

51.41-42 Divine judgment fell upon the legendary people of Ad in the form of a tornado (see Q 26.123-140; 46.21-26; 54.17-21; 69.6-8; and 89.6-8).

51.43-45 Like the people of Ad, the people of Thamud suffered divine punishment when they "revolted against the commandment

of their Lord" that came to them via the prophet Zali'h (see Q 91, note).

51.46-49 The people of Noah's day rejected the ministry of Noah and suffered the consequences of a horrific divine retribution (see **The Apostles** on pp. 396-398).

51.50-55 Seeking refuge in Allah involves three activities: (1) refrain from polytheism—worship only Allah, (2) recognize Muhammad as anointed from Allah—a plain warner, and (3) turn one's back upon the scoffers of the one true religion—Islam.

51.52 The people of Mecca accused Mu-

cerer, mad!"
53 Do they bequeath it to each other? Yea, they are an outrageous people!
54 So turn thy back upon them, so thou wilt not be to blame.
55 And remind; for, verily, the reminder shall profit the believers.

Woe to the infidels

56 And I have not created the ginn and mankind save that they may worship me.

57 I do not desire any provision from them, and I do not wish them to feed me.
58 Verily, God, He is the provider, endowed with steady might.
59 Verily, for those who injure (the Apostle) shall be a portion like the portion of their fellows, but let them not hurry Me!
60 Then woe to those who misbelieve from their day which they are threatened.

hammad of being mad—out of his mind (see Q 68.2, 51, 81.22).
51.57 The pagan Arabs left food at the Ka'ba altars throughout Arabia as an act of devotion to their gods. Muhammad repudiated this custom.

INTRODUCTION

The Fifth Period

When the two year boycott of the Bani Hashim clan failed, the chieftains of Mecca searched for a new strategy in dealing with the Muslim problem. As it turned out, a new strategy fell into their laps.

Two unexpected events took place. Abu Talib, the leader of the Bani Hashim clan and one of the chieftains of Mecca, died. Following the death of his own parents when just a small child, Abu Talib had raised Muhammad from childhood and was, in many respects, the only father he ever knew. And hardly a month later, Muhammad's wife Khadijah died. During the previous ten years, these two individuals had been Muhammad's principal protectors. They had stood up to the leaders of Mecca, demanding that Muhammad be allowed to preach the message of his new Islamic religion. And since they were successful and re-spected business people who had brought much revenue into the city, the leaders of Mecca were reluctant to be too rigorous in their opposition to them. Now that they were dead, a more direct approach in eradicating this Muslim problem was possible.

Almost immediately, the persecution of the Muslim people intensified. Several of Muhammad's close associates were bound hand and foot, roped together, and left lying on the public highway. Pieces of putrefying offal was thrown into Muhammad's cooking pot by passersby. A sheep's uterus filthy with blood and excrement was thrown at him while he was praying. People walked up to him and threw handfuls of dirt into his face. And so it went. Muhammad suffered "from humiliation, derision and from being treated either like a madman or an outcast. Some people would even fling pebbles at him while he was praying and others kicked stones at him so that he had to run away with bleeding feet."[1] Still, the Meccan chieftains, however, were reluctant to physically harm or kill Muhammad since such an act could have resulted in a citywide war.

With few options and not knowing whether or not the chieftains were planning his assassination, Muhammad traveled to Ta'if by camel, a city to the east of Mecca, seeking refuge and armed support. This was a desperate move, and he knew it. The people of Ta'if were just as idolatrous as those in Mecca and would likely be disinclined to receive him favorably. And, indeed, that is what happened. He was told that he was not welcome and that he needed to return to Mecca. On his return trip, he later explained in two of his surahs, someone remarkable took place. He encountered a company of ginns who listened and responded favorably to his Islamic message. They converted and became Muslim devotees. Afterwards, Muhammad took refuge in the cave of Mount Hira (the cave where he allegedly first encountered the archangel Gabriel). He sent a message by means of a runner to Mecca, requesting permission to re-enter the city. Permission was granted.

Back in Mecca, Muhammad continued to write and preach. On several occasions, he included Jewish and Christian apocryphal literature in his surahs, with the apparent intent to make the case that his Islamic religion was compatible with Judaism and Christianity—two established religions that were accepted in Mecca. He also endorsed the longstanding practice of pilgrimages to the Ka'ba altar in Mecca, albeit in a fashion that corresponded to Islamic theology. And finally, he briefly commented on his alleged miraculous Night Journey to Jerusalem and the Seventh Heaven, an event that he called the Isra and Mi'raj. This was intended to offer the miraculous credentials that the chieftains of Mecca demanded.

Still, Muhammad felt threatened and feared for his life. In the early months of 622, he sent some of his Muslim converts as emigrants to the city of Yathrib (Medinah). This was done in preparation of his own migration, which took place a few months later.

---

[1] Marco Schöller, "Opposition to Muhammad," *Encyclopedia of the Qur'an*, vol. 3, p. 577.

Surah 46

In the name of the merciful and compassionate God.

1   H. M.

Qur'an

2   The revelation of the Book from God the mighty, the wise.

First appeal to infidels

3   We have only created the heavens and the earth and what is between the two in truth and for an appointed time; but those who misbelieve from being warned do turn aside.

4   Say, "Have ye considered what ye call on beside God? Show me what they have created of the earth? or have they share in the heavens? Bring me a book before this or a vestige of knowledge, if ye do tell the truth!

5   But who is more in error than he who calls beside God on what will never answer him until the resurrection day and who are heedless of their calling,

6   and when men are gathered together are enemies of theirs and do deny their service?"

Second appeal to infidels

7   And when our evident signs are recited to them, those who misbelieve say of the truth when it comes to them, "This is obvious magic."

8   Or do they say, "He has forged it?" Say, "If I have forged ye cannot obtain for me aught from God; He knows best what ye utter concerning it; He is witness enough between me and you, and He is the forgiving, the merciful."

Surah 46. The title of this surah, *The Sand Dunes*, comes from verse 21. The surah initiates the Fifth Period of the Qur'an, the final period prior to Muhammad's migration (*Hijrah*) to Medinah. In it, he described his brief visit to the City of Ta'if. It was his hope that the people of Ta'if would come to his aid against the people of Mecca. They did not. The surah begins with a catechism, explaining how to argue effectively with infidels. It then addresses Muhammad's encounter with a party of ginns (genies) during his return trip from Ta'if to Mecca. The surah concludes with two themes. The first is a warning of divine judgment to the Quraysh tribe in Mecca. The second is Allah telling Muhammad to have patience with the Quraysh tribe and other infidels in Mecca.

46.1 Literally, *Ha Mim*. See Q 32.1, note.

46.3-6 The people of Mecca were asked to reconsider their commitment to polytheistic worship.

46.7-8 The people of Mecca claimed that the Qur'an was the product of magic. Muhammad responded by denouncing the assertion as absurd.

46.9 *nor do I know what will be done with me* — In this verse, Muhammad acknowledged that he did not know his personal fate in the afterlife. All he knew was that

Third appeal to infidels

9   Say, "I am not an innovator among
    the apostles; nor do I know what
    will be done with me or with you
    if I follow aught but what I am
    inspired with; nor am I aught but
    a plain warner."

Fourth appeal to infidels

10 Say, "Have ye considered, if it is
    from God and ye have disbelieved
    therein, and a witness from the
    children of Israel testifies to the
    conformity of it, and he believes
    while ye are too big with pride?
    Verily, God guides not the unjust
    people."

11 And those who misbelieve say of
    those who believe, "If it had been
    good, they would not have been
    beforehand with us therein;" and
    when they are not guided thereby,
    then will they say, "This is an old-
    fashioned lie."

12 But before it was the Book of

Moses, a model and a mercy; and
this is a book confirming it in Arabic language, to warn those who
do wrong and as glad tidings to
those who do well.

Characteristics of believers

13 Verily, those who say, "Our Lord
    is God," and then keep straight,
    there is no fear for them, and they
    shall not be grieved.
14 These are the fellows of Paradise
    to dwell therein for aye, a recom-
    pense for that which they have
    done.

Parental relationships

15 We have prescribed for man kind-
    ness towards his parents. His
    mother bore him with trouble and
    brought him forth with trouble;
    and the bearing of him and the
    weaning of him is thirty months;
    until, when he reaches puberty,
    and reaches forty years, he says,

he had been commissioned by Allah (see Q 6.15) and that he strived to be obedient. This is a curious statement since elsewhere in the Qur'an he believed that Allah had forgiven all his sins—past, present, and future (see Q 48.1-2).

46.10 *Have ye considered* — Muhammad wanted the people of Mecca to think of the way in which the Jewish people rejected Moses, and then to compare that response with the way in which they were rejecting him. The Jewish people rejected the Book of Moses (the Pentateuch), and they were rejecting the Qur'an (a book confirming it in the Arabic language).

46.14 *These are the fellows of Paradise* — These are those who are destined for Paradise (see Q 10.26; 11.23; 25.24; 36.55; 46.16).

46.15-16 Believers who treat their parents with respect and pass on to their own offspring the Islamic faith are promised a special mercy in the afterlife.

46.16 *pass over their offenses* — Accord-

"Lord! stir me up that I may be thankful for thy favours wherewith thou hast favoured me and my parents; and that I may do right to please Thee; and make it right for me in my offspring; verily, I turn repentant unto Thee, and, verily, I am of those resigned."

16   There are those from whom we accept the best of what they have done, and we pass over their offenses—amongst the fellows of Paradise; the promise of truth which they have been promised.

17   But he who says to his parents, "Fie upon you! Do ye promise me that I shall be brought forth when generations have passed away before me?"—then shall they both cry to God for help. Woe to thee! Believe! Verily, the promise of God is true. Then says he, "This is but old folks' tales."

18   There are those against whom the

sentence was due amongst the nations who have passed away before them of ginns and men; verily, they have been the losers;

19   and for all are degrees of what they have done, so that He may repay them their works, and they shall not be wronged.

20   And the day when those who misbelieve shall be exposed to the fire: "Ye made away with your good things in your worldly life, and ye enjoyed them; wherefore today shall ye be rewarded with the torment of disgrace, for that ye were big with pride in the earth without the right, and for that ye did abomination."

The example of Ad

21   Remember too the brother of 'Âd when he warned his people at El A'hqâf,—though warners have

ing to the Qur'an, sins are qualitatively assessed. Lesser sins are subject to being passed over at the Last Judgment, provided that, on balance, the person lived a life of integrity and faithfulness in most other areas (see Q 103.3, note). In Islam, the two great sins are the sin of *shirk* (idolatry) and a refusal to recognize Muhammad as a prophet of Allah. Anyone found guilty of either would not successfully pass through the Last Judgment and enter Paradise (see Q 3.32; cf. Q 3.32; 4.69, 79-80, 136; 5.80-81; 8.13, 20-23; 24.47, 48, 50-52, 54; 33.33, 71; 48.9-10; 57.19; 59.4; 72.22-23, 81.19-21 and 46.16, note).

46.16 *fellows of Paradise* — Dwellers of Heaven (see Q 10.26; 11.23; 25.24; 36.55; 46.14).

46.17a *Fie upon you!* — That is, "Curses on you!" (cf. Q 17.23; 21.67).

46-17b *old folks' tales* — Non-Muslims claimed that Muhammad's surahs were little more than old folks' tales: based upon well-known writings of the ancient world (see Q 6.25; 16.24; 23.83; 25.5; 26.137; 27.68; 68.15; 83.13).

46.21 *El A'Ahqaf* — That is, Sand Dunes. Some Islamic scholars believe that two cities of Ad existed. The one described in this verse was situated in sand dunes. The other

passed away before him and after him,—"Serve not other than God; verily, I fear for you the torment of a mighty day!"

22 They said, "Hast thou come to us to turn us from our gods? then bring us what thou dost threaten us with, if thou art of those who speak the truth!"

23 Said he, "Knowledge is only with God: but I will preach to you that which I am sent with, though I see you are a people who are ignorant."

24 And when they saw a traversing cloud approaching their valleys they said, "This is a cloud to give us rain." "Nay, but it is what ye sought to hasten on—a wind in which is grievous torment;

25 it will destroy everything at the order of its Lord!" And in the morning naught was seen save their dwellings. Thus do we reward the sinful people!

26 We had established them in what we have established you, and we made for them hearing and eye-sight and hearts; but neither their hearing nor their eyesight nor their hearts availed them aught, since they did gainsay the signs of God, and that encompassed them whereat they had mocked.

Towns near Mecca

27 And we destroyed the cities that are around you:—and we turned about the signs that haply they might return.

28 Why did not those help them, whom beside God they took for gods that could draw nigh to Him? Nay! they strayed away from them; for that was their lie and what they had forged.

The ginns

29 And when we turned towards thee some of the ginn listening to the Qur'ân, and when they were present at (the reading of) it, they said, "Be silent!" and when it was

---

Ad was described as dwelling in "castles on its plains and hewed out mountains into houses" (Q 7.73)—that is, Hegra in north-west Arabia (see **Hegra** on p. 28).

Nevertheless, current archeological research points to a single tribe by the name of Ad. This tribe existed in the second century, A.D. north of Medinah. No evidence exists of an earlier tribe by the same name dated to the postdiluvian period associated with Noah.

46.27-28 Similar to the destruction that the people of Ad experienced, a number of towns near Mecca had experienced similar destructions and were brought to ruin. According to Muhammad, the reason for their demise was the people's involvement in idolatry.

46.29-33 This event allegedly took place while Muhammad was returning to Mecca from the City of Ta'if and parallels the story mentioned in the subsequent surah (Q 72.1-19).

Two interpretations of this episode

over they turned back to their people, warning them.

30 Said they, "O our people! verily, we have heard a book sent down after Moses, verifying what came before it, guiding to the truth, and unto the right way.

31 O our people! respond to God's crier and believe in Him, and He will pardon you your sins and will deliver you from grievous woe."

32 And whoso responds not to God's crier shall not frustrate Him in the earth, and shall not have any patrons beside Him:—these are in obvious error!

33 Did they not see that God who created the heavens and the earth, and was not wearied with creating them, is able to quicken the dead?—nay, verily, He is mighty over all!

*An encouragement to
remain steadfast*

34 And the day when those who

dominate Islamic scholarship. First, Muhammad's ministry was not limited to the human race. He encountered a group of *ginns* (genies) who were poised to accept his message of repentance and submission to Allah and were committed to live on the Narrow Path that leads to eternal life. Ibn Ishaq and two Hadiths are representative of this interpretation (see *The Life of Muhammad*, pp. 193-194; *Sahih Muslim* 4.30.0902 and *Sahih Mwatta* 54.12.33).

Second, Muhammad made contact with evil people, whom he figuratively characterized as ginns (genies). In his book *The Religion of Islam*, Maulana Muhammad Ali maintains that these individuals were "evidently foreign Christians" or "a party of the Jews" (p. 146). Since they had previously been opposed to Muhammad's message, they were characterized in the Qur'an as devilish in nature.

Christian scholarship is open to the first interpretation. The Bible affirms the existence of Satan and demons and, therefore, affirms the possibility that Muhammad indeed made contact with evil spirits (ginns). Their embrace of Muhammad's message, however,

does not imply the rightness of Muhammad's message and their repentance and conversion. Rather, it is a tacit admission that Muhammad had been deceived by demons. According to the Bible, demons are known to acquiesce some of our beliefs as a form of deception. In spite of their tacit beliefs, their overall strategy remains to deceive and control us (see 2 Cor 2:11; 11:3, 14; Gal 1:8; Rev 12:9).

C. S. Lewis said it well: "Like a good chess player, he [Satan] is always trying to manoeuvre you into a position where you can save your castle only by losing your bishop" (*The Weight of Glory*, p. 118). John R. W. Stott adds: "The devil disturbs the church as much by error as by evil. When he cannot entice Christian people into sin, he deceives them with false doctrine" (*The Message of Galatians*, p. 24).

Christian scholarship is also open to the second interpretation since metaphorical statements are found elsewhere in the Qur'an. Yet, the fact that canonical Hadiths affirm the first interpretation makes the case that the seventh century Muslim community did not understand this episode metaphori-

misbelieve shall be exposed to the fire,—"Is not this the truth?" they shall say, "Yea, by our Lord!" He shall say, "Then taste the torment for that ye did misbelieve!"

35 Then do thou be patient, as the apostles endowed with a purpose were patient, and hasten not on (their punishment). It shall be to them, on the day they see what they are threatened with, as though they had tarried but an hour of the day. A preaching this! Shall any perish but the people who work abomination?

Surah 72

In the name of merciful and compassionate God

1 Say, "I have been inspired that there listened a company of the ginn, and they said, 'We have heard a marvellous Qur'ân

2 that guides to the right direction; and we believe therein, and we join no one with our Lord,

3 for, verily, He—may the majesty of our Lord be exalted!—has taken to Himself neither consort nor son.

cally. This testimony mitigates against such an interpretation.

Moreover, Christian scholarship is open to a third interpretation: Muhammad fabricated the entire episode as a way of increasing his stature among the people of Mecca. Since this appears to be what happened with the story of the splitting of the moon (see Q 54.1-5), it is possible that Muhammad used this technique once again.

46.34-35 When placed in front of the fires of Hell, Muhammad believed that his opponents will regret their rejection of his message. He was therefore admonished to "be patient" and not to hasten their doom.

This response stands in contrast to attitudes exemplified by godly Christians. Ray Stedman wrote of a congregation that dismissed its pastor. When asked why the congregation did so, one parishioner said: "The pastor kept telling us we were going to hell." When asked what the new pastor says, the parishioner added: "He keeps saying we're going to hell, too." When asked the difference between the two, the man explained:

"When our first pastor said we were going to hell, he sounded like he was glad. But when our new pastor says it, he sounds like it is breaking his heart" (*From Guilt to Glory*, vol 2, p. 10).

Surah 72. The title of this surah, *The Ginn*, comes from verse 1. This surah develops in greater detail the story of Muhammad's encounter with a party of *ginns* during his return trip from Ta'if (see Q 46.29-33).

72.1 *a company of the ginn* — the word "company" (*nafar*) indicates that the number of ginns (genies) that Muhammad allegedly encountered to be between three and ten. Ibn Ishaq claimed that the number was seven (see *The Life of Muhammad*, p. 194).

72.2 *right direction* — These two words are repeated in the Qur'an. It refers to the way to eternal life. In the Qur'an, it is also called "the right path," "the level path," "the road," "the right way," "the path of God," "the way of the Lord," "the way of God," "our way," "the path of rectitude," "the way of peace," "God's way," "the level way" and "the straightest path" (see Q 1.6; 2.142, 256,

4   And, verily, a fool among us spake
     against God wide of the mark!

5   And we thought that men and ginn
     would never speak a lie against
     God.

6   And there are persons amongst men
     who seek for refuge with persons
     amongst the ginn; but they in-
     crease them in their perverseness.

7   And they thought, as ye thought,
     that God would not raise up any
     one from the dead.

8   But we touched the heavens and
     found them filled with a mighty

9   guard and shooting-stars;
     and we did sit in certain seats
     thereof to listen; but whoso of us
     listens now finds a shooting-star
     for him on guard.

10   And, verily, we know not whether
     evil be meant for those who are in
     the earth, or if their Lord means
     right by them.

11   And of us are some who are pi-
     ous, and of us are some who are
     otherwise: we are in separate
     bands.

12   And we thought that we could not

261-262; 3.51, 101; 4.68, 160, 168, 175; 5.12, 16; 6.39, 126, 153; 7.16, 86, 146; 10.25; 14.3; 16.76, 88, 125; 17.9; 21.51; 22.25; 24.46; 29.69; 40.29, 38; 60.1; 72.29; 98.7).

72.3 *God has taken to Himself neither consort nor son* — This was a criticism of the Arabic Star Family religious system. It operated on the assumption that the gods were part of a vast family, mating and giving birth to new gods (see **Polytheism in Seventh Century Arabia** on pp. 92-97). Muhammad believed that only one God existed— Allah. He neither mated nor gave birth to daughter or son gods.

72.8-9 According to this passage, a band of ginns (genies) often situated themselves in the ceiling of heaven and listened to the angels as they spoke to one another and to Allah. Such eavesdropping was evil and some were struck with meteorites (shooting stars) as a form of punishment. This idea of ginns situating themselves in the heavens and eavesdropping on angels has a Zoroastrian origin.

The passage also suggests that the band

of ginns that Muhammad encountered on his return trip from Ta'if (if indeed the story was not a pure fabrication) were not Christians or Jews (see Q 46.29-33, note). In this passage, the evil spirits are clearly supernatural beings. If the "ginns" of the previous passage were human beings, some form of clarification would have been necessary to distinguish a metaphorical description of evil spirits in one surah and a non-metaphorical description in the surah that immediately followed. Since no such clarification is offered, it stands to reason that a consistent interpretation is the correct one. Hence, in both passages a non-metaphorical interpretation is the preferred interpretation.

72.11-15 Muhammad claimed that some of the ginns were pious, while others were evil. Consequently, the pious ones turned to Muhammad and embraced the Islamic religion, thereby becoming Muslims. They are described as those who "strive after the right direction." The rest, said Muhammad, were "fuel for the fire" (see Q 46.29-33, note).

72.18 *the mosques* — The Ka'ba altar is sometimes called a mosque. This verse may

frustrate God in the earth, and could not frustrate Him by flight.

13   But, verily, when we heard the guidance we believed therein, and he who believes in his Lord shall fear neither diminution nor loss.

14   And, verily, of us are some who are Muslims, and of us some are trespassers; but those of us who are Muslims they strive after right direction;

15   and as for the trespassers they are fuel for hell.

16   And if they will go right upon the way, we will irrigate them with copious water

17   to try them thereby; and whoso turns from the remembrance of his Lord He will drive him to severe torment.

18   And (say) that the mosques are God's, and that ye should not call on any one with God,

19   and that when God's servant stood up to pray they called out to him and well-nigh crowded upon him."

Four statements

20   Say, "I only call upon my Lord, and I join no one with Him."

21   Say, "Verily, I cannot control for you either harm, or right direction."

22   Say, "Verily, as for me none can protect me against God, nor do I find any refuge beside Him,

23   —except delivering the message from God and His errands: and whoso rebels against God and His Apostle, verily, for him is the fire of hell for them to dwell therein for ever and for aye!"

24   Until when they see what they are threatened with, then shall they surely know who is most weak at helping and fewest in numbers!

be a reference to a time when Muhammad called out to Allah while standing in the precinct of the Ka'ba altar.

72.20-28 The surah concludes with a short catechism. Muslims were instructed to memorize four statements that are useful when debating their infidel opponents.

72.20 The first statement is a reaffirmation in monotheism and belief in Allah—the Doctrine of Tauhid (see Q 112).

72.21a The second statement is a release of spiritual responsibility to whom one speaks. Since one's eternal destiny had already been assigned by Allah, a corresponding resignation inevitably emerges. Only those who were predestined to accept the Islamic gospel would listen. Those who were

predestined to reject the message would not listen (see **The Doctrine of al-Qadar** on pp. 264-266).

72.21b *right direction* — This is a reference to the path to eternal life (see Q 72.2, note).

72.22-23 The third statement is a declarative testimony that spiritual refuge is found in Allah alone. Those who disobey Allah and "His Messenger" (Muhammad) will suffer the fire of Hell. Only when seen in this light are the true weak ones (the infidels) made manifest (see Q 3.32).

72.24-28 The fourth statement is an affirmation that Allah does not reveal his secrets—except to Muhammad. Muhammad knows the secrets of Allah and has revealed

The Doctrine of al-Qadar

Double Predestination

Among the many doctrines within Islam, perhaps none has generated as much discussion as the Doctrine al-Qadar. It makes the case that Allah is absolutely sovereign in all He says and does—to the extent that He predestinates, to the minutest details, all activities on the earth. In terms of salvation, Allah chooses whether a person goes to Paradise or Hell—the doctrine is commonly known as *double predestination*.

The Doctrine al-Qadar is grounded upon four beliefs in the nature of Allah. The first is His knowledge (*al-alam*). Due to His eternal knowledge (omniscience), Allah knows everything within His creation, which includes the choices that they will make. The second is His writing (*kitabat*). Prior to the creation of the universe, Allah wrote down everything pertaining to His creation, including the destiny of all His creatures. The third is His will (*mashii'at*). Nothing occurs within creation apart from the will of Allah. The fourth is creation (*al-Khalaq*). Not only did Allah create all that is, He also created the actions of all that is. Kenneth Cragg writes, "So God is the One Who leads astray, as well as the One Who guides."[1]

Still, the Qur'an also insists that people are responsible for their own behavior and will therefore be held accountable for their lives at the Last Judgment. Hence, the Doctrine of al-Qadar cannot be understood to be a pure determinism. With this in mind, the Doctrine of al-Qadar is similar to what is found in the Christian faith. Hans Küng explains that the general tenor of this Islamic doctrine

> runs roughly along the same lines as that of such great Christian theologians as Augustine, Luther, and Calvin. All three men repeatedly and forcefully emphasized the influence of God's grace (with Calvin's double predestination being the extreme instance), without, however, fully excluding responsibility—and consequently, freedom—from the picture of human weal and woe.[2]

Divine sovereignty and human responsibility, then, remain an unresolved paradox within Islam, just as it does within the Christian faith.

The Doctrine al-Qadar is found in a number of surahs in the Qur'an, such as:

- All things have been created after a fixed decree (Q 54.49)

- No one can die except by the permission of God (Q 3.139)

- God has fixed the destinies of all peoples (Q 6.39)

- Nothing can befall people outside that which God has predestined (Q 9.51)

It is also found in two articles in the *Second Great Creed of Islam:*

- *Article Six.* Allah created the creatures free from unbelief and belief. Then He addressed and gave them commandments and prohibitions. Thereupon some turned to unbelief. And their denial and disavowal of the truth was caused by Allah's abandoning them. And some of them believed— as appeared in their acting, consenting and declaring—through the guidance and help of Allah...

- *Article Twenty-two.* Allah guideth whomsoever He pleaseth, by grace, and He leadeth astray whomsoever He pleaseth, by justice. His leading astray means His abandoning, and the explanation of "abandoning" is that He does not help a man by guiding him towards deeds that please Him. This is justice on His part, and so is His punishment of those who are abandoned on account of sin...

Some within the Islamic world, the Mutazilites, attempted to overcome the paradox (divine predestination versus human self determination) by favoring human responsibility at the expense of divine sovereignty. They argued that people have free wills and can either choose belief or unbelief. Otherwise, they asked, what then is the difference between praising Allah or sinning against Him, faith and infidelity, and good and evil? In all such cases, everyone is doing the will of God. The notion of Allah setting seals or stamps upon hearts, rendering it impossible for them to believe (Q 2.7; 7.100-101; 9.87, 93; 10.74; 16.108; 30.58-60; 40.35; 47.16; 63.3) is interpreted metaphorically—that is, infidels are so opposed to the teachings of the Qur'an that it is *as if* Allah had set a stamp on their hearts, preventing them from attaining to a life of faith and obedience. Nevertheless, the Doctrine of the Mutazilites has been roundly condemned as heresy by mainstream Islamic scholarship.

In spite of the delicate balance in the Qur'an between the doctrine of divine sovereignty and human responsibility, a view of pure determinism (fatalism) has taken root in the Muslim world. It exists in the popular mind as well as in the writings of many Islamic theologians. Maulana Muhammad Ali is representative of this perspective, writing: "The doctrine of predestination...thus finds no support from the Qur'an which gives to man the choice to follow one way or the other."[3] This is perhaps due to the extreme doctrine of double predestination (Allah predestines certain people to Hell) that is often mentioned in the surahs.

The Christian faith. Many Christians are uncomfortable with the doctrine of predestination, and most find the doctrine of double predestination to be repugnant. The problem for these Christians is that both concepts result in the collapse of the notion of human free will—and with it, morality and accountability. Morality and accountability cannot exist in a world of pure determinism. Pure determinism treats people as if they are little more than Marionette puppets, tied to strings and wholly controlled by the Marionette puppeteer.

In response, many Christians believe that Scripture presents the notion of paradox (opposing views held in tension). God is sovereign over His creation and therefore elects people to salvation (predestination), yet also enables people to make their own spiritual choices (self-determination). God is responsible, but so too is the human being. C. S. Lewis put it this way: "I think we must take a leaf out of the scientists' book. They are quite familiar with the fact that, for example, Light has to be regarded *both* as a wave and as a stream of particles. No one can make these two views consistent. Of course reality must be self-consistent; but till (if ever) we can *see* the consistency it is better to hold two inconsistent views than to ignore one side of the evidence" (*Letters of C. S. Lewis*, Aug 3, 1953).

---

[1] Kenneth Cragg, *The Call of the Minaret*, p. 41.
[2] Hans Küng, *Christianity and World Religions*, p. 89; also see Küng, *Islam: Past Present & Future*, pp. 222-226.
[3] Maulana Muhammad Ali, *The Religion of Islam*, p. 242.

Today, many of Calvin's admirers, myself included, have abandoned the doctrine of double predestination.

—William Stacy Johnson, *John Calvin: Reformer for the 21st Century*, p. 48

Although many Muslim scholars argue that the Qur'an puts great emphasis on the free choice and moral conduct of individuals and communities, popular Islamic thinking and practice are often very fatalistic. Fatalism as a doctrine espouses that all events are subject to fate or inevitable predeterminism. Similar to the concept of fatalism, predestination (Arabic *taqdir*) is the belief that an omniscient and omnipotent God has determined all events. It means that a person cannot do anything that will change the course of history because events are outside of that person's realm of control. Fatalism may also be used as a rationale for not caring about what happens since efforts are futile in the end.

Mark Kerry, *Tigers of the Tigris*, p. 70

The belief in predestination practically always had an ascetic effect among the simple warriors of the early Islamic faith, which in the realm of ethics exerted largely external and ritual demands, but the ascetic effects of the Islamic belief in predestination were not rational, and for this reason they were repressed in everyday life. The Islamic belief in predestination easily assumed fatalistic characteristics in the beliefs of the masses.

—Max Weber, Guenther Roth, and Claus Wittich, *Economy and Society*, p. 575

In Islam the controversy is complicated by the clearly expressed koranic doctrine of predestination. This doctrine has a double aspect: God's universal, eternal decree (*qada*), and the application of the decree in time and place and to a particular individual (*qadar*). This makes God the direct cause of whatever happens to man. The Koran is explicit on this point and its commentators are wholeheartedly committed to it.

—Philip Khuri Hitti, *Islam: A Way of Life*, p. 128

This tension between predestination and freedom, which has never been resolved, also exists in Christianity. A kind of predestination that abolishes human freedom (in the sense of so-called double predestination to salvation or hell) is to be rejected...God does not predestine anyone to evil or to destruction.

—Richard Schenk, *Progress, Apocalypse, and Completion of History and Life after Death of the Human Person in the World Religion*, p. 121

When his Muslim guide took him across a steep scree slope in Macedonia, Cyrus Hamlin was horrified. If God wanted them to get across, they would, was the reply. When it came to cholera, Hamlin noted, "the Moslems and the Jews were the greatest sufferers; the latter for their filth, the former for their fatalism." He told of a "pleasant old Turkish neighbor," dining on a cucumber. Didn't he know the dangers of raw vegetables, especially cucumbers, during cholera? "'What do I care,' he replied. 'What is written is written...My appetite demands these and I shall eat them.' He died...during the night."

—Christopher Hamlin, *Cholera: the Biography*, p. 76

25   Say, "I know not if what ye are threatened with be nigh, or if my Lord will set for it a term.

26   He knows the unseen, and He lets no one know His unseen,

27   save such apostle as He is well pleased with: for, verily, He sends marching before him and behind him a guard!"

28   That He may know that they have delivered the errands of their Lord, for He compasses what they have, and reckons everything by number.

Surah 35

In the name of the merciful and compassionate God.

The one true God

1   Praise belongs to God, the originator of the heavens and the earth; who makes the angels His messengers, endued with wings in pairs, or threes or fours; He adds to creation what He pleases; verily, God is mighty over all!

2   What God opens to men of His mercy there is none to withhold; and what He withholds, there is none can send it forth after Him; for He is the mighty, the wise.

Appeal to turn to Allah

3   O ye folk! remember the favours of God towards you; is there a creator beside God, who provides you from the heavens and from the earth? There is no god but He; how then can ye lie?

4   And if they call thee liar, apostles

---

them via his many surahs.

Surah 35. The title to this surah, *The Originator*, comes from verse 1. The overall theme of the surah is the Doctrine of Tauhid—absolute monotheism, Allah is the only God. With this in mind, the surah follows two familiar themes: (a) a call to the infidel to reconsider his or her rejection of Allah and give Him his rightful due, and (b) a reaffirmation of Muhammad's calling as a prophet sent from Allah to warn people of the divine punishment awaiting them if they fail to return to Allah and worship Him alone.

35.1 Muhammad believed that angels had wings: some with two, four, six, or eight wings. Similarly, the Old Testament described seraphim as having six wings (see Isa 6:2).

35.2 As the surah unfolds, Allah is understood to possess seven titles: "the Originator of the heavens and the earth" (v. 1), "the Mighty, the Wise" (v. 2), "Mighty, Forgiving" (v. 28), and "Forgiving, Multiplier of Rewards" (v. 30, 34), "the Knower" (v. 38), "Forbearing and Forgiving" (v. 41), and "Knowing and Powerful" (v. 44).

35.3 *O ye folk!* — This phrase is repeated three times in this surah (vv. 3, 5, 15). In each case, the addressees are infidels since the phrase "when are you turned away?" implies that the people being addressed are infidels. Muhammad's use of the phrase is an appeal for people to turn away from false gods and to Allah.

35.5 *the beguiler* — The devil is the beguiler (v. 6). Muhammad encouraged people to see through the deception and submit

were called liars before thee, and unto God affairs return.

5   O ye folk! verily, God's promise is true; then let not the life of this world beguile you, and let not the beguiler beguile you concerning God.

6   Verily, the devil is to you a foe, so take him as a foe; he only calls his crew to be the fellows of the blaze.

7   Those who misbelieve, for them is keen torment. But those who believe and do right, for them is forgiveness and a great hire.

8   What! is he whose evil act is made seemly for him, so that he looks upon it as good,—? Verily, God leads astray whom He pleases and guides whom He pleases; let not thy soul then be wasted in sighing for them; verily, God knows what they do!

9   It is God who sends the winds, and they stir up a cloud, and we irrigate therewith a dead country, and we quicken therewith the earth

after its death; so shall the resurrection be!

10   Whosoever desires honour — honour belongs wholly to God; to Him good words ascend, and a righteous deed He takes up; and those who plot evil deeds, for them is keen torment, and their plotting is in vain.

Three illustrations

11   God created you from earth, then from a clot; then He made you pairs; and no female bears or is delivered, except by His knowledge; nor does he who is aged reach old age, or is aught diminished from his life, without it is in the Book; verily, that is easy unto God.

12   The two seas are not equal: one is sweet and fresh and pleasant to drink, and the other is salt and pungent; but from each do ye eat fresh flesh, and bring forth ornaments

themselves to Allah. Otherwise, he warned, they will become "fellows of the blaze" (v. 6).

35.7 *believe and do right* — These words are repeated often in the Qur'an and serve as a brief summary of the Islamic gospel (see Q 103.3, note).

35.8 The Qur'an presents Allah as fully sovereign; so much so, in fact, that those who believe do so because "Allah makes err whom he pleases and guides aright whom He pleases." This is the doctrine of double predestination (see **The Doctrine of al-Qadar** on pp. 264-266).

35.11 *the Book* — This is a reference to God's Book in Paradise which details all the activities on earth.

35.11-13 Muhammad used three illustrations to make the case that Allah is wholly sovereign in all that He says and does: (a) the intricacies of conception and birth, (b) the balancing presence of fresh and salt water, and (c) the balancing of night with day. His point was that nobody and nothing can resist the will of Allah.

35.13 *not a straw* — In contrast to Allah, the gods that the people of Mecca worship "possess not a straw"—they have no value

which ye wear; and thou mayest see the ships cleave through it, that ye may search after His grace, and haply ye may give thanks.

13 He turns the night into day, and He turns the day into night; and He subjects the sun and the moon, each of them runs on to an appointed goal; that is God, your Lord! His is the kingdom; but those ye call on beside Him possess not a straw.

14 If you call upon them they cannot hear your call, and if they hear they cannot answer you; and on the resurrection day they will deny your associating them with God; but none can inform thee like the One who is aware.

Warning

15 O ye folk! ye are in need of God but God, He is independent, praiseworthy.

16 If He please He will take you off,

and will bring a fresh creation;

17 for that is no hard matter unto God.

18 And no burdened soul shall bear the burden of another; and if a heavily laden one shall call for its load (to be carried) it shall not be carried for it at all, even though it be a kinsman!—thou canst only warn those who fear their Lord in the unseen and who are steadfast in prayer; and he who is pure is only pure for himself; and unto God the journey is.

19 The blind is not equal with him who sees,

20 nor the darkness with the night,

21 nor the shade with the hot blast;

22 nor are the living equal with the dead; verily, God causes whom He pleases to hear, and thou canst not make those who are in their graves hear;

Muhammad's calling reaffirmed

whatsoever.

35.15-23 Muhammad's warning is addressed to the infidels in Allah of the coming judgment. The warning is that Allah will replace the polytheists in Mecca with true believers in Allah.

35.18 *no burdened soul shall bear the burden of another* — That is, each person will face his or her own sins at the Last Judgment (see **The Last Judgment** on pp. 46-50).

The Bible makes a similar claim, yet with an important difference. Those who have

placed their faith in Jesus Christ will still give an account of their lives lived on the earth. Yet this accounting is not to determine their eternal destiny. This is because the question of our salvation has been secured by Jesus Christ. He bore the sins of the world when He died on the cross. "He himself bore our sins in his body on the tree..." (1 Pet 2:24).

The judgment that Christians will face in the afterlife has a different purpose. It is to determine the rewards they will or will not receive in Heaven. The Apostle Paul

23 thou art but a warner!

24 Verily, we have sent thee in truth a herald of glad tidings and a warner; and there is no nation but its warner has passed away with it.

25 And if they called thee liar, those before thee called their apostles liars too, who came to them with manifest signs, and the Scriptures, and the illuminating Book.

26 Then I seized those who misbelieved, and what a change it was!

Qur'an

27 Dost thou not see that God has sent down from the heaven water, and has brought forth therewith fruits varied in hue, and on the mountains dykes, white and red, various in hue, and some intensely black,

28 and men and beasts and cattle, vari-

ous in hue? thus! none fear God but the wise among His servants; but, verily, God is mighty, forgiving.

29 Verily, those who recite the Book of God, and are steadfast in prayer, and give alms of what we have bestowed in secret and in public, hope for the merchandise that shall not come to naught;

30 that He may pay them their hire, and give them increase of His grace; verily, He is forgiving, grateful.

31 What we have inspired thee with of the Book is true, verifying what was before it; verily, God of His servants is well aware and sees.

32 Then we gave the Book for an inheritance to those whom we chose of our servants, and of them are some who wrong themselves, and of them are some who take a

wrote: "For we must all appear before the judgment seat of Christ, that each one may receive what is due him for the things done while in the body, whether good or bad" (2 Cor 5:10). The word "bad" in this verse means *useless* or *worthless*. Some lives will be deemed to have been less purposeful than others (also see 1 Cor 3:10-15).

Those who have not placed their faith in Jesus Christ will also give an account of their lives. Yet, because they did not embrace the gospel (that is, were not pardoned for their sins) they will face the full force of divine punishment and be cast into Hell. A just and holy God can do no less.

35.23-26 Muhammad is described as a warner in line with the many other warners

that God has sent to the earth to warn people of judgment to come.

35.25a *if they call thee liar* — In the Qur'an, unbelief is often equated with calling Muhammad a liar.

35.25b *the Scriptures* — Old and New Testaments.

35.25c *the illuminating Book* — The previous scriptures inspired of God, such as the Old Testament, is described here as an illuminating book.

35.29 *the Book of God* — the Qur'an. The faithful are called upon to recite the Qur'an in the form of prayers. The Qur'an is affirmed to be "the truth." It is given as an inheritance to those whom Allah has chosen to receive it.

middle course, and of them are some who vie in good works by the permission of their Lord; that is great grace.

Paradise

33 Gardens of Eden shall they enter, adorned therein with bracelets of gold and pearls; and their garments therein shall be silk;

34 and they shall say, "Praise belongs to God, who has removed from us our grief; verily, our Lord is forgiving, grateful!

35 who has made us alight in an enduring abode of His grace, wherein no toil shall touch us, and there shall touch us no fatigue."

Hell

36 But those who misbelieve, for them is the fire of hell; it shall not be decreed for them to die, nor shall aught of the torment be lightened from them; thus do we reward every misbeliever;

37 and they shall shriek therein, "O our Lord! bring us forth, and we will do right, not what we used to do!"—"Did we not let you grow old enough for every one who would be mindful to be mindful? and there came to you a warner!— So taste it, for the unjust shall have none to help!"

38 verily, God knows the unseen things of the heavens and of the earth; verily, He knows the nature of men's breasts,

39 He it is who made you vicegerents in the earth, and he who misbelieves, his misbelief is against himself; but their misbelief shall only increase the misbelievers in hatred with their Lord; and their misbelief shall only increase the

35.33 *Gardens of Eden* — That is, the gardens in Paradise (also see Q 9.72; 16.31; 18.31; 19.61; 20.76; 38.50; 40.8; 61.12; 98.8). The gardens of Paradise await all who observe all that is written in the Qur'an. As such, the *Gardens of Eden* is not to be confused with the biblical Garden of Eden mentioned in the Gen. 2:8, 10, 15, 23, 24; and 4:16 where Adam and Eve lived prior to their Fall into Sin.

35.33-35 Description of Paradise: it is a place of lush gardens. People will wear bracelets of gold and pearls and their dress shall be silk. It is also place of perpetual rest—toil shall not touch those there, nor fatigue afflict them.

35.39-42 Description of Hell: it is a place of unending torment. The condemned are described as the ungrateful ones. People will regret their past lives and yearn for an opportunity to repent. Yet no such opportunity will be granted. They will also be reminded that they rejected "the warner" (Muhammad, *et al.*).

35.39 *vicegerents* — In the Arabic, the word is *khalifah*, or *caliphs*. In the Qur'an, the term is used to describe man's rightful supremacy on the earth (see Q 2.30; 6.165; 7.69, 74, 142; 38.39). In Q 2.30, for example, it is said that Allah was about to establish a *caliph* on the earth to possess it.

35.40 Muhammad challenged the polythe-

misbelievers in loss.

Final appeal

40   Say, "Have ye considered your associates whom ye call on beside God?" show me what they created of the earth; have they a share in the heavens, or have we given them a book that they rest on a manifest sign? nay, the unjust promise each other naught but guile.

41   Verily, God holds back the heavens and the earth lest they should decline; and if they should decline there is none to hold them back after Him; verily, He is clement, forgiving.

42   They swore by God with their most strenuous oath, verily, if there come to them a warner they would be more guided than any one of the nations; but when a warner comes to them, it only increases them in aversion,

43   and in being big with pride in the earth, and in plotting evil; but the

plotting of evil only entangles those who practise it; can they then expect aught but the course of those of yore? but thou shalt not find any alteration in the course of God; and they shall not find any change in the course of God.

44   Have they not journeyed on in the land and seen what was the end of those before them who were stronger than they? but God, nothing can ever make Him helpless in the heavens or in the earth; verily, He is knowing, powerful.

45   Were God to catch men up for what they earn, He would not leave upon the back of it a beast; but He respites them until an appointed time. When their appointed time comes, verily, God looks upon His servants.

Surah 36

In the name of the merciful and compassionate God.

ists to demonstrate the prowess of their gods (cf. Ps 115:1-8).

35.43 According to this verse, Allah is immutable; that is, He never changes. Not only does Allah not change, neither does He alter that which was established and planned in eternity past. Everything will come to pass without variation. It is here where the Doctrine of al-Qadar (double predestination) is rooted. Whether people believe or disbelieve, even this choice was established previously by Allah (see **The Doctrine of al-**

Qadar on pp. 264-266).

35.44 Allah is all-knowing and all-powerful (cf. Ps 147:4-5 and Matt 19:26).

35.45 The surah ends on a sour note, warning of the coming doom upon all who reject Allah.

Surah 36. The title of this surah, *Ya Seen*, comes from verse one. In the Muslim world, one of the titles of Muhammad is *Ya Seen* (Oh Human). This surah is regarded as one of the principal surahs in the Qur'an since it addresses issues related to the hereafter. It

1   Y. S.

*Reaffirmation of
Muhammad's call*

2   By the wise Qur'ân,
3   verily, thou art of the apostles
4   upon a right way.
5   The revelation of the mighty, the
     merciful!
6   That thou mayest warn a people
     whose fathers were not warned,
     and who themselves are heedless.

Double predestination

7   Now is the sentence due against
     most of them, for they will not
     believe.
8   Verily, we will place upon their
     necks fetters, and they shall reach
     up to their chins, and they shall
     have their heads forced back;
9   and we will place before them a
     barrier, and behind them a barrier;
     and we will cover them and they
     shall not see;
10   and it is all the same to them if thou
     dost warn them or dost warn them
     not, they will not believe.

Blessings on the elect

11   Thou canst only warn him who
     follows the reminder, and fears the
     Merciful in the unseen; but give
     him glad tidings of forgiveness and
     a noble hire.
12   Verily, we quicken the dead, and
     write down what they have done

is often recited as funerals.

Feeling threatened and challenged by those who had been resisting his message, Muhammad wrote this surah as an answer to his opponents. Included in the surah is an adaptation of the story of Paul and Barnabas while they were ministering in the city of Antioch of Pisidia (Acts 13). The purpose of the story is the drive home the point that all who oppose the message of divinely sent apostles will be judged—in this life as well as the afterlife.

36.1 Literally, *Ya Seen*. See Q 32.1 note.
36.3-6 The surah begins with a declaration that Muhammad is God's appointed messenger exemplifying the "right way." This being stated, Islamic scholarship generally looks upon Muhammad as perfect and infallible. Some believe Muhammad was only perfect and infallible in terms of his authorship of the Qur'an. Other add that Muhammad was also perfect and infallible in his personal life: a Christ-like figure for those within the Islamic faith (the Doctrine of Isma—see Q 94.1-3, note).
36.7-10 One of Muhammad's perplexing questions was the resistance of the Meccan people to his message. Since his belief in monotheism was so eminently logical to him, he struggled to understand why it was not logical to most of the people of Mecca. His answer was his conviction that only those that Allah chooses to believe will believe. Those who Allah chooses not to be believe will remain in unbelief. Whether warned or not warned, "they will not believe" (see *The Doctrine of al-Qadar* on pp. 264-266).
36.11-12 Blessings on the elect: (a) forgiveness, (b) honorable reward, and (c) life to the dead.

before, and what vestiges they
leave behind; and everything have
we counted in a plain model.

Paul and Barnabas

13 Strike out for them a parable: the
fellows of the city when there
came to it the apostles;
14 when we sent those two and they
called them both liars, and we
strengthened them with a third;
and they said, "Verily, we are sent
to you."
15 They said, "Ye are only mortals like
ourselves, nor has the Merciful
sent down aught; ye are naught but
liars."
16 They said, "Our Lord knows that
we are sent to you,
17 and we have only our plain message to preach."
18 They said, "Verily, we have au-
gured concerning you, and if ye
do not desist we will surely stone

you, and there shall touch you from
us a grievous woe."
19 Said they, "Your augury is with
you; what! if ye are reminded—?
Nay, ye are an extravagant
people!"

The runner

20 And there came from the remote
part of the city a man hastening
up. Said he, "O my people! follow
the apostles;
21 follow those who do not ask you a
hire, and who are guided.
22 What ails me that I should not
worship Him who originated me,
and unto whom I must return?
23 Shall I take gods beside Him? If
the Merciful One desires harm for
me, their intercession cannot avail
me at all, nor can they rescue me.
24 Verily, I should then be in obvious
error;
25 verily, I believe in your Lord, then

36.13-19 The city mentioned in this passage was Antioch of Pisidia. The story is
that of Paul and Barnabas when they first
entered the city with the intent of preaching the gospel and establishing a church (see
Acts 13:14-52).

The people of Antioch, said Muhammad,
possessed magical powers (auguries) from
which they could determine whether the
gospel preached by Paul and Barnabas was
true or false. They determined that Paul
and Barnabas were false teachers and threatened to stone them if they did not leave
forthwith.

36.20-27 At that moment, a person came

forward and admonished the people of Antioch to listen and receive the message of
Paul and Barnabas.

The New Testament account differs
from Muhammad's rendition on several points.
Nowhere in the story did the people of
Antioch make use of auguries to determine
the veracity of the message of Paul and
Barnabas. Rather, they listened to the sermon preached by Paul in the local synagogue.
After listening and considering the message,
a few devout Jews embraced the gospel.

The next Sabbath Day, however, a large
number of Jews sought to drive Paul and
Barnabas from their city. It was then that

listen ye to me!"

26 It was said, "Enter thou into Paradise!" said he, "O, would that my people did but know!

27 for that my Lord has forgiven me, and has made me of the honoured."

*The sudden destruction
of Antioch of Pisidia*

28 And we did send down upon his people no hosts from heaven, nor yet what we were wont to send down;

29 it was but a single noise, and lo! they were extinct.

30 Alas for the servants! there comes to them no apostle but they mock at him!

31 Have they not seen how many generations we have destroyed before them? verily, they shall not return to them;

32 but all of them shall surely altogether be arraigned.

33 And a sign for them is the dead earth which we have quickened and brought forth therefrom seed, and from it do they eat;

Paul and Barnabas boldly said: "We had to speak the word of God to you first. Since you reject it and do not consider yourselves worthy of eternal life, we now turn to the Gentiles. For this is what the Lord has commanded us: 'I have made you a light for the Gentiles, that you may bring salvation to the ends of the earth'" (Acts 13:46-47).

When the Gentiles heard this, they "were glad and honored the word of the Lord; and all who were appointed for eternal life believed" (Acts 13:48-49).

36.29 *a single noise* — Muhammad declared that after rejecting the message and ministry of Paul and Barnabas, Allah sent down "a single noise" that instantly and completely brought destruction upon the city of Antioch (see Q 54.22-31, note).

Not only does the biblical account make no mention of a sudden destruction of Antioch of Pisidia, historical and archeological evidence states that Antioch enjoyed a long and rich existence since the first century. Retired Roman legionaries settled in the city, causing it to become a Roman colony

of unusual strength and prestige. Following Emperor Constantine's liberalization of Christianity in A.D. 311, the city played an important role in church councils and the formation of early Christian theology. Moreover, this region gave rise to a number of important theologians of the Patristic era of the Church. Unfortunately, in the eighth century the city found itself in the midst of an ongoing struggle between Muslim and Byzantine/Crusader armies, situated in the direct path of both sides. In the midst of the many of the battles that were waged, the city changed hands a number of times. Following this extended military campaign—a campaign that lasted decades—Antioch never fully recovered. Nevertheless, it continued as a city and attracted newcomers. According to a 1950 census, forty villages with 50,000 people lived in the area.

36.31 Muhammad's point was that when a people reject the message of divinely sent apostles, they will suffer in this life and the afterlife (see Q 26.192-212 and 45.28).

36.32 A reference to the Last Judgment.

34   and we made therein gardens and palms and grapes, and we have caused fountains to gush forth therein,

35   that they may eat from the fruit thereof, and of what their hands have made; will they not then give thanks?

Doxology to Allah

36   Celebrated be the praises of Him who created all kinds, of what the earth brings forth, and of themselves, and what they know not of!

37   And a sign to them is the night, from which we strip off the day, and lo! they are in the dark;

38   and the sun runs on to a place of rest for it; that is the ordinance of the mighty, the wise.

The sovereignty of Allah over nature

39   And the moon, we have ordered for it stations, until it comes again to be like an old dry palm branch.

40   Neither is it proper for it to catch up the moon, nor for the night to outstrip the day, but each one floats on in its sky.

41   And a sign for them is that we bear their seed in a laden ship,

42   and we have created for them the like thereof whereon to ride;

43   and if we please, we drown them,

36.33 In the Islamic faith, ingratitude is one of the major sins that carries much weight at the Last Judgment.

36.36-38 Muhammad is the author of this doxology; that is, they are his words of praise offered to Allah. This doxology poses a problem for Islam. Due to its strict adherence to monotheism, only the words of Allah are understood to be divinely inspired. The words authored by Muhammad that are found in the Qur'an are not divinely inspired, since that would result in Muhammad taking on divine attributes—a version of idolatry that is strictly prohibited. Other passages (e.g., Q 19.64-65) include the alleged words of angels, which exasperate the problem. A number of non-Islamic scholars have pointed out the internal contradiction within the Qur'an due to passages such as these (also see Q 3.8-9; **The Qur'an** on pp. 150-153).

Some Islamic scholars have attempted to resolve this problem by including the word *say* in front of the words spoken by Muhammad, which causes the original author of the words to be Allah. Yet this too is problematic since the addition of the word *say* results in a tampering with the Qur'an.

The Judeo-Christian tradition has no such problem with its sacred Scripture. It maintains that sacred Scripture is a product of holy people being "carried along by the Holy Spirit" (2 Pet 1:21) as they spoke or wrote divine writ. Hence, in the Judeo-Christian tradition, sacred Scripture is a paradox: it is both wholly the words of men and wholly the words of God (cf. 2 Sam 23:2). Divine inspiration cannot be divided and thereby applies to Scripture, regardless of who the speaker happens to be (see Q 53.4, note).

36.39 *the moon* — This is a subtle denunciation of the Arabic Star Family religious system which placed much importance on the

and there is none for them to appeal to; nor are they rescued,

44   save by mercy from us, as a provision for a season.

45   And when it is said to them, "Fear what is before you and what is behind you, haply ye may obtain mercy;"

46   and thou bringest them not any one of the signs of their Lord, but they turn away therefrom;

47   and when it is said to them, "Expend in alms of what God has bestowed upon you," those who misbelieve say to those who believe, "Shall we feed him whom, if God pleased, He would feed? ye are only in an obvious error."

48   They say, "When shall this promise come to pass, if ye do tell the truth?"

49   They await but a single noise, that shall seize them as they are contending.

50   And they shall not be able to make a bequest; nor to their people shall they return;

Last Judgment

51   but the trumpet shall be blown, and, behold, from their graves unto their Lord shall they slip out!

52   They shall say, "O, woe is us! who has raised us up from our sleeping-place? this is what the Merciful promised, and the apostles told the truth!"

53   It shall be but a single noise, and lo! they are all arraigned before us.

54   And on that day no soul shall be wronged at all, nor shall ye be rewarded for aught but that which ye have done.

Paradise

55   Verily, the fellows of Paradise upon that day shall be employed in enjoyment;

56   they and their wives, in shade upon thrones, reclining;

57   therein shall they have fruits, and they shall have what they may call for.

---

worship of the moon.

36.48 Infidels mocked Muhammad's threats.

36.51 Muhammad believed that the resurrection of the dead will occur at the blasting of a final trumpet (cf. 1 Cor 15:52; 1 Thess 4:16).

36.52a *who has raised us up from our sleeping-place?* — That is, who raised us up from the grave?

36.52b *the apostles told the truth* — see *The Apostles* on pp. 398-400.

36.54 At the Last Judgment, people will be judged out of the works that they did

(cf. Matt 16:27; Rom 2:6; 2 Cor 5:10; and Rev. 20:11-15).

36.55-58 Five characteristics of Paradise: (a) places of shade, (b) reclining on raised couches, (c) fruit, (d) people will have whatever they desire, and (e) a place of peace.

36.56 *their wives* — These women are the *houri*— that is, the maidens in the harems (see *The Virgins* on pp. 107-109).

36.59-62 *children of Adam* — Human beings, a reference from the Book of Genesis (Gen 1:27-28; 2:20). The purpose of Satan is to lead people astray (cf. 2 Chron 18:20-

58 "Peace!"—a speech from the merciful Lord!

Allah rebukes the infidels

59 "Separate yourselves to-day, O ye sinners!

60 Did I not covenant with you, O children of Adam! that ye should not serve Satan? verily, he is to you an open foe;

61 but serve ye me, this is the right way.

62 But he led astray a numerous race of you; what! had ye then no sense?

Hell

63 This is hell, which ye were threatened;

64 broil therein today, for that ye misbelieved!"

65 On that day we will seal their mouths, and their hands shall speak to us, and their feet shall bear witness of what they earned.

66 And if we please we could put out their eyes, and they would race along the road; and then how could they see?

67 And if we pleased we would transform them in their places, and they should not be able to go on, nor yet to return.

68 And him to whom we grant old age, we bow him down in his form; have they then no sense?

Qur'an

69 We have not taught him poetry, nor was it proper for him; it is but a reminder and a plain Qur'ân,

70 to warn him who is living; but the sentence is due against the misbelievers.

Final appeal

22; Jn 8:44; Acts 5:3; 13:10; 2 Cor 11:3; 2 Thess 2:9-11; Rev 12:9).

36.64 *broil* — This is a favorite term in the Qur'an to describe the horrors of Hell (see Q 82.15, note).

36.65 Two characteristics of Hell: (a) those imprisoned will have their mouths sealed and will speak by means of sign language with their hands and feet, and (b) their eyes will be put out.

36.66-67 Muhammad believed that since Allah is sovereign over all creation, He could have transformed human beings into monsters or animals akin to dogs or horses. No such statement is found in the Bible since man was made in the image of God (see Gen 1:26-27; 9:6; James 3:9). For God to transform people into monsters or animals would require Him to debase the image of God.

36.68 The opponents of Muhammad called him mad. In reply, he said that his opponents had "no sense."

36.69-70 This passage offers a glimpse into the debate raging in Mecca. The infidels regarded Muhammad's surahs as mere poetry. Muhammad's retort was that it was "a plain Qur'an"—a word of truth that shows the way to eternal life.

36.71-83 Muhammad's final appeal has four

71   Have they not seen that we have created for them of what our hands have made for them, cattle, and they are owners thereof?

72   and we have tamed them for them, and of them are some to ride, and of them are what they eat,

73   and therein have they advantages and beverages; will they not then give thanks?

74   But they take, beside God, gods that haply they may be helped.

75   They cannot help them; yet are they a host ready for them.

76   But let not their speech grieve thee: verily, we know what they conceal and what they display.

77   Has not man seen that we have created him from a clot? and lo! he is an open opponent;

78   and he strikes out for us a likeness; and forgets his creation; and says, "Who shall quicken bones when they are rotten?"

79   Say, "He shall quicken them who produced them at first; for every creation does He know;

80   who has made for you fire out of a green tree, and lo! ye kindle therewith."

Final doxology

81   Is not He who created the heavens and the earth able to create the like thereof? yea! He is the knowing Creator;

82   His bidding is only, when He desires anything to say to it, "BE," and it is.

83   Then celebrated be the praises of Him in whose hands is the kingdom of everything! and unto Him shall ye return.

Surah 19

In the name of the merciful and compassionate God.

---

points: (a) people need to be grateful to Allah who has provided all the blessings they enjoy, (b) people need to admit that the gods that they worship cannot help them, (c) people need to recognize that it is Allah who created them, and (d) people did to take note of Hell awaiting them.

36.81-83 Again, we see Muhammad speaking words of praise to Allah (see note Q 36.36-38 and **The Qur'an** on pp. 150-153).

36.82 *"BE"*— Allah's sovereignty over all creation is illustrated in the fact that all He needs to do is say one word—*be*—and whatever it is He wishes comes into existence (see Q 3.47, 59; 16.40; 19.35; 40.68).

Surah 19. The title of this surah is *Mary*, and takes its name from verse 16. Its overarching theme is how the patriarchs of the Old Testament and major figures in the New Testament were genuine apostles who served as warners to the people of whom they ministered. Muhammad saw himself as an apostle within this same tradition. The word "Book" is mentioned seven times in the surah, suggesting that the Qur'an was of a divine origin. A peculiar feature in this surah is Muhammad's use of apocryphal literature pertaining to the infancy and childhood of Jesus which circulated widely in Arabia.

Many scholars have wondered where

1   K. H. Y. 'H. Z.

Zechariah

2   The mention of thy Lord's mercy to His servant Zachariah,

3   when he called on his Lord with a secret calling.

4   Said he, "My Lord! verily, my bones are weak, and my head flares with hoariness;—and I never was unfortunate in my prayers to Thee, my Lord!

5   But I fear my heirs after me, and my wife is barren; then grant me from Thee a successor,

6   to be my heir and the heir of the family of Jacob, and make him, my Lord! acceptable."

7   "O Zachariah! verily, we give thee glad tidings of a son, whose name shall be John. We never made a namesake of his before."

8   Said he, "My Lord! how can I have a son, when my wife is barren, and I have reached through old age to decrepitude?"

9   He said, "Thus says thy Lord, It is easy for Me, for I created thee at first when yet thou wast nothing."

10   Said he, "O my Lord! make for me a sign." He said, "Thy sign is that thou shalt not speak to men for three nights (though) sound."

11   Then he went forth unto his people from the chamber, and he made signs to them: "Celebrate (God's) praises morning and evening!"

John the Baptist

12   "O John! take the Book with strength;" and we gave him judgment when a boy,

13   and grace from us, and purity;

14   and he was pious and righteous to his parents, and was not a rebellious tyrant.

15   So peace upon him the day he was born, and the day he died, and the

---

Muhammad acquired his knowledge of the Bible. According to Ibn Ishaq, Muhammad acquired much of his knowledge of the Bible from a Christian slave in Mecca. He explained that Muhammad used to spend time al-Marwa (a small hill on the outskirts of Mecca) with a young Christian called Jabr, a slave who served the Banu al-Hadrami, a tribe of whom Muhammad was a member (*The Life of Muhammad*, p. 180). In addition to Jabr, some scholars believe that Muhammad also received some of his knowledge of the Judeo-Christian tradition from Waraqa bin Naufal, Khadijah's cousin (Khadijah was Muhammad's first wife).

Waraqa was a Jew who had converted to Christianity, and then converted to Islam (see Q 16.103, note, and Spencer, *The Truth About Muhammad*, pp. 38, 53).

19.1 Literally, *Kaf Ha Ya Ain Suad.* See Q 32.1, note.

19.2-11 Based upon Lk 1:5-25, this story addresses Zechariah's vision with the angel Gabriel. It was said that his offspring (John) would be a prophet sent from God.

19.12 *the Book* — Allah's revelation given to the Jewish people: the Old Testament.

19.16a *the Book* — The New Testament, specifically, the Gospels according to Matthew

day he shall be raised up alive.

Mary

16   And mention, in the Book, Mary;
      when she retired from her family
      into an eastern place;
17   and she took a veil (to screen her-
      self) from them; and we sent unto
      her our spirit; and he took for her
      the semblance of a well-made man.
18   Said she, "Verily, I take refuge in
      the Merciful One from thee, if thou
      art pious."
19   Said he, "I am only a messenger
      of thy Lord to bestow on thee a
      pure boy."
20   Said she, "How can I have a boy
      when no man has touched me, and
      when I am no harlot?"
21   He said, "Thus says thy Lord, It is
      easy for Me! and we will make him
      a sign unto man, and a mercy from
      us; for it is a decided matter."
22   So she conceived him, and she re-
      tired with him into a remote place.
23   And the labour pains came upon
      her at the trunk of a palm tree, and
      she said, "O that I had died before
      this, and been forgotten out of
      mind!"

24   and he called to her from beneath
      her, "Grieve not, for thy Lord has
      placed a stream beneath thy feet;
25   and shake towards thee the trunk
      of the palm tree, it will drop upon
      thee fresh dates fit to gather;
26   so eat, and drink, and cheer thine
      eye; and if thou shouldst see any
      mortal say, 'Verily, I have vowed
      to the Merciful One a fast, and I
      will not speak today with a human
      being.'"
27   Then she brought it to her people,
      carrying it; said they, "O Mary!
      thou hast done an extraordinary
      thing!
28   O sister of Aaron! thy father was
      not a bad man, nor was thy mother
      a harlot!"

Jesus

29   And she pointed to him, and they
      said, "How are we to speak with
      one who is in the cradle a child?"
30   He said, "Verily, I am a servant of
      God; He has brought me the Book,
      and He has made me a prophet,
31   and He has made me blessed wher-
      ever I be; and He has required of
      me prayer and almsgiving so long

and Luke.

19.16-28 Based upon Luke 1:26-38 and
2:2-7, this story presents the vision of Gabriel to Mary. In this vision, the virgin birth of
Jesus was prophesied.

19.23-28 This aspect of the story of Jesus
is nowhere found in the New Testament.
Its source is the twentieth chapter from the

Infancy Gospel of Pseudo-Matthew—an apocryphal and non-canonical book (see **The
Child Jesus** on p. 284). In it, Mary allegedly said that during childbirth labors, she
wished she had died prior to onset of the
pains (v. 23).

19.28 *Aaron* — Nowhere in the New Testament is the brother of Mary named. The

as I live,

32   and piety towards my mother, and
      has not made me a miserable ty-
      rant;

33   and peace upon me the day I was
      born, and the day I die, and the
      day I shall be raised up alive."

34   That is, Jesus the son of Mary,—
      by the word of truth whereon ye
      do dispute!

35   God could not take to himself any
      son! celebrated be His praise! when
      He decrees a matter He only says
      to it, "BE," and it is;

36   and, verily, God is my Lord and
      your Lord, so worship Him; this
      is the right way.

37   And the parties have disagreed
      amongst themselves, but woe to
      those who disbelieve, from the wit-

38   nessing of the mighty day!
      they can hear and they can see,
      on the day when they shall come
      to us; but the evildoers are today
      in obvious error!

39   And warn them of the day of sigh-
      ing, when the matter is decreed
      while they are heedless, and while
      they do not believe.

40   Verily, we will inherit the earth and
      all who are upon it, and unto us
      shall they return!

Abraham

41   And mention, in the Book,
      Abraham; verily, he was a confes-
      sor,—a prophet.

42   When he said to his father, "O my
      sire! why dost thou worship what

likelihood is high that Muhammad confused *Mary*, the mother of Jesus, with *Miriam*, the sister of Moses and Aaron.

19.29-33 The source of this passage is the *Arabic Infancy Gospel of the Savior*, verse one. It is also a non-canonical apocryphal account of the birth of Jesus. This story describes the infant Jesus, while still in the cradle declaring that he is the Son of God, the Logos, and the Savior of the world. In this surah, Muhammad altered the story by editing out the phrase that Jesus is the Son of God, since it mitigates against his claim that Allah can have no son (see **Jesus in the Cradle** on pp. 285-287; and Q 5.110).

19.30 *the Book* — It is unclear what book is meant.

19.34 Nowhere in this account is it mentioned that Jesus would be resurrected from the dead in a fashion that corresponded to the New Testament teachings (that is, raised from dead on the third day following his crucifixion). Here, the phrase "I am raised to life" (v. 33) is a reference to the resurrection at the Last Day.

19.33 This is one of two verses in the Qur'an that described the death of Jesus. The other verse is Q 4.157.

19.35 *BE"* — Allah's sovereignty over all creation is illustrated in the fact that all He needs to do is say one word—*be*—and whatever it is He wishes comes into existence (see Q 3.47, 59; 16.40; 36.82; 40.68).

19.41 *the Book* — The Book of Genesis.

19.41-50 This passage is based upon a story of Abraham included in the book of Genesis. The emphasis is on his conversion from polytheism to monotheism and his admonition to his father to turn away from the worship of multiple gods. The dialogue between

The Child Jesus

And it came to pass on the third day of their journey, while they were walking, that the blessed Mary was fatigued by the excessive heat of the sun in the desert; and seeing a palm tree, she said to Joseph: "Let me rest a little under the shade of this tree." Joseph therefore made haste, and led her to the palm, and made her come down from her beast.

And as the blessed Mary was sitting there, she looked up to the foliage of the palm, and saw it full of fruit, and said to Joseph: "I wish it were possible to get some of the fruit of this palm." And Joseph said to her: "I wonder that thou sayest this, when thou seest how high the palm tree is; and that thou thinkest of eating of its fruit. I am thinking more of the want of water, because the skins are now empty, and we have none wherewith to refresh ourselves and our cattle."

Then the child Jesus, with a joyful countenance, reposing in the bosom of His mother, said to the palm: "O tree, bend thy branches, and refresh my mother with thy fruit." And immediately at these words the palm bent its top down to the very feet of the blessed Mary; and they gathered from it fruit, with which they were all refreshed. And after they had gathered all its fruit, it remained bent down, waiting the order to rise from Him who bad commanded it to stoop.

Then Jesus said to it: "Raise thyself, O palm tree, and be strong, and be the companion of my trees, which are in the paradise of my Father; and open from thy roots a vein of water which has been hid in the earth, and let the waters flow, so that we may be satisfied from thee." And it rose up immediately, and at its root there began to come forth a spring of water exceedingly clear and cool and sparkling.

And when they saw the spring of water, they rejoiced with great joy, and were satisfied, themselves and all their cattle and their beasts. Wherefore they gave thanks to God.

—*Infancy Gospel of Pseudo Matthew*, ch. 20

Jesus in the Cradle

Surah 19:29-33	Arabic Infancy Gospel of the Savior
29 And she pointed to him, and they said, "How are we to speak with one who is in the cradle a child?"	1 We find what follows in the book of Joseph the high priest, who lived in the time of Christ.
30 He said, "Verily, I am a servant of God; He has brought me the Book, and He has made me a prophet,	Some say that he is Caiaphas. He has said that Jesus spoke, and, indeed, when He was lying in His cradle said to
31 and He has made me blessed wherever I be; and He has required of me prayer and almsgiving so long as I live,	Mary His mother: I am Jesus, the Son of God, the Logos, whom thou hast brought forth, as the Angel Gabriel an-
32 and piety towards my mother, and has not made me a miserable tyrant;	nounced to thee; and my Father has sent me for the salvation of the world.
33 and peace upon me the day I was born, and the day I die, and the day I shall be raised up alive."	

Muhammad had access to a number of apocryphal and canonical texts pertaining to the Jewish and Christian religions. In the writing of his surahs, he drew from these sources to develop and support his arguments, paraphrasing the sources to suit his purposes. If the source material contained information that spoke contrary to his peculiar theological stances, his paraphrases included modifications that violated the integrity of the source material.

We see this paraphrasing technique in the passage of Jesus in the Cradle, an account that is found in apocryphal literature but not found in the canonical New Testament. Muhammad's paraphrase was both an embellishment of the source material and an elimination of troubling material. Specifically, the *The Arabic Infancy Gospel of the Savior* presented Jesus as the Son of God, Muhammad edited this statement out of his version found in Q 19.29-33.

Copies of the *Arabic Infancy Gospel of the Savior* are only available to us in the Arabic language. It was first mentioned in a commentary on the Gospel of Matthew by Isho'dad of Merv and was widely read in the Arabian Peninsula. It is clearly historical fiction.

———•◆•◄———

In the four Gospels, there is no mention that the baby Jesus spoke. The only recorded words from his childhood were at age twelve when His parents found Him in the temple in Jerusalem (see Lk 2:41-50). The Qur'an finds the baby Isa [Jesus] proclaiming from the cradle that he is the prophet for Allah...Why would Islam have Jesus speaking from the cradle? There does seem to be an agenda here, for the first words amount to a direct renunciation of the Christian doctrine of His deity.

—Emir Fethi Caner and Ergun Mehmet Caner,
More than a Prophet: An Insider's Response to Muslim Beliefs, pp. 52, 53

The most common title used for Jesus in the Qur'an is "Jesus, son of Mary." This emphasizes his virgin birth and is in contrast to any suggestion that he should be thought of as the son of God.

—C. T. R. Hewer, *Understanding Islam*, p. 183

The Qur'an presents a Jesus (Isa) who declares his humanity in the cradle (Surah 5) denies His divinity (Surah 19), and prophesies the coming of Muhammad (Surah 61). All cults attempt to either correct Christianity or replace Christianity, and all cults view themselves as the sole voice for God on the Earth. Islam does this as well.

—Ed Hindson and Ergun Caner,
The Popular Encyclopedia of Apologetics, p. 280

can neither hear nor see nor avail thee aught?

43 O my sire! verily, to me has come knowledge which has not come to thee; then follow me, and I will guide thee to a level way.

44 O my sire! serve not Satan; verily, Satan is ever a rebel against the Merciful.

45 O my sire! verily, I fear that there may touch thee torment from the Merciful, and that thou mayest be a client of Satan."

46 Said he, "What! art thou averse from my gods, O Abraham? verily, if thou dost not desist I will certainly stone thee; but get thee gone from me for a time!"

47 Said he, "Peace be upon thee! I will ask forgiveness for thee from my Lord; verily, He is very gracious to me:

48 but I will part from you and what ye call on beside God, and will pray my Lord that I be not unfortunate in my prayer to my Lord."

49 And when he had parted from them and what they served beside God, we granted him Isaac and Jacob, and each of them we made a prophet;

50 and we granted them of our mercy, and we made the tongue of truth lofty for them.

Moses

51 And mention, in the Book, Moses; verily, he was sincere, and was an apostle,—a prophet.

52 We called him from the right side of the mountain; and we made him draw nigh unto us to commune with him,

53 and we granted him, of our mercy, his brother Aaron as a prophet.

Ishmael

54 And mention, in the Book, Ishmael; verily, he was true to his promise, and was an apostle,—a prophet;

55 and he used to bid his people prayers and almsgiving, and was acceptable in the sight of his Lord.

Enoch

56 And mention, in the Book, Idrîs; verily, he was a confessor,—a prophet;

57 and we raised him to a lofty place.

Abraham and his father Terah is fictitious. In it, Abraham compared polytheistic worship to the worship of demons. According to this passage, Allah blessed Abraham's commitment to monotheism with the birth of his son Isaac and his grandson, Jacob.

19.51 *the Book* — The Pentateuch (Genesis through Deuteronomy)

19.54 *the Book* — It is unclear which book is meant (if any), since no ancient Scriptures prior to the Qur'an exist that described Ishmael as an apostle or prophet.

19.56 *Idris* — Enoch.

19.56 *the Book* — Enoch is mentioned in Gen 5:18-24, Heb 11:5-6, and Jude 14-16.

19.57 *we raised him* — Enoch was raised

The call for repentance

58   These are those to whom God has
      been gracious, of the prophets of
      the seed of Adam, and of those
      whom we bore with Noah, and of
      the seed of Abraham and Israel, and
      of those we guided and elected;
      when the signs of the Merciful are
      read to them, they fall down ador-
      ing and weeping.
59   And successors succeeded them,
      who lost sight of prayer and fol-
      lowed lusts, but they shall at length
      find themselves going wrong,
60   except such as repent and believe
      and act aright; for these shall en-
      ter Paradise, and shall not be
      wronged at all,

Paradise

61   —gardens of Eden, which the
      Merciful has promised to His ser-
      vants in the unseen; verily, His
      promise ever comes to pass!
62   They shall hear no empty talk

therein, but only "peace;" and they
shall have their provision therein,
morning and evening;
63   that is Paradise which we will give
      for an inheritance to those of our
      servants who are pious!

Admonition from the angels

64   We do not descend save at the bid-
      ding of thy Lord; His is what is
      before us, and what is behind us,
      and what is between those; for thy
      Lord is never forgetful,
65   —the Lord of the heavens and the
      earth, and of what is between the
      two; then serve Him and persevere
      in His service. Dost thou know a
      namesake of His?

Last Judgment

66   Man will say, "What! when I have
      died shall I then come forth alive?
67   Does not man then remember that
      we created him before when he
      was naught?"

(raptured) to Heaven without first dying (see Gen 5:24). Elijah was the only other individual to be raised (raptured) to Heaven without first dying (see 2 Kings 2:1-12).

19.58-59 Following the biblical characters mentioned in these two verses, evil generations emerged who had forgotten the divine message, neglected prayers, and followed sensual desires.

19.60 *believe and act aright* — These words are repeated often in the Qur'an and serve as a brief summary of the Islamic gospel (see Q 103.3, note).

19.61 *gardens of Eden* — The gardens in Paradise (also see Q 16.31; 18.31; 20.76; 35.33; 38.50; 40.8, and Q 35.33, note).

19.61-63 Characteristics of Paradise: gardens of perpetuity, peace, an unending provision of sustenance.

19.64-65 Islamic scholarship struggles with passages such as this. Since in this case the speakers are angels, and not Allah, are the words divine or angelic? (see 36.36-38, note; *The Qur'an* on pp. 150-153).

19.66-74 At the Last Judgment, the unrighteous will regret their rejection of Allah

68   And by thy Lord! we will surely gather them together, and the devils too; then we will surely bring them forward around hell, on their knees!

69   Then we will drag off from every sect whichever of them has been most bold against the Merciful.

70   Then we know best which of them deserves most to be broiled therein.

71   There is not one of you who will not go down to it,—that is settled and decided by thy Lord.

72   Then we will save those who fear us; but we will leave the evildoers therein on their knees.

73   And when our signs are recited to them manifest, those who misbelieve say to those who believe, "Which of the two parties is best placed and in the best company?"

74   And how many generations before them have we destroyed who were better off in property and appearance?

The mercy of Allah

75   Say, "Whosoever is in error, let the Merciful extend to him length of days!—until they see what they are threatened with, whether it be the torment or whether it be the Hour, then they shall know who is worse placed and weakest in forces!"

76   And those who are guided God will increase in guidance. And enduring good works are best with thy Lord for a reward, and best for restoration.

Coming judgment

77   Hast thou seen him who disbelieves in our signs, and says, "I shall surely be given wealth and children?"

78   Has he become acquainted with the unseen, or has he taken a compact with the Merciful?

79   Not so! We will write down what he says, and we will extend to him

and be cast into Hell.

19.75 *the Hour* — The hour of the resurrection from the dead (see Q 79.42, note).

19.75-76 Muhammad believed that Allah extends mercy to the those chosen for salvation. Eventually their eyes are opened causing them to know and follow the straight path of good works that leads to an eternal reward. Paradise, then, is the awarded to those predestined to believe.

19.76 According to Muhammad, salvation is a question of leading a life full of good works (merit). In the Christian faith, salvation is a gift given to all who receive it (for-

giveness).

John R. W. Stott explains: "The gospel offers blessings; what must we do to receive them? The proper answer is 'nothing.' We do not have to *do* anything. We have only to *believe*. Our response is not 'the works of the law' but 'hearing with faith', that is, not obeying the law, but believing the gospel. For obeying is to attempt to do the work of salvation ourselves, whereas believing is to let Christ be our Saviour and to rest in his finished work" (*The Message of Galatians*, p. 75). Stott adds: "When God justifies sinners, he is not declaring bad people

a length of torment,

80   and we will make him inherit what he says, and he shall come to us alone.

81   They take other gods besides God to be their glory.

82   Not so! They shall deny their worship and shall be opponents of theirs!

Double predestination

83   Dost thou not see that we have sent the devils against the misbelievers, to drive them on to sin? but,

84   be not thou hasty with them. Verily, we will number them a number (of days),

85   —the day when we will gather the pious to the Merciful as ambassadors,

86   and we will drive the sinners to hell like (herds) to water!

87   They shall not possess intercession, save he who has taken a compact with the Merciful.

The nature of God

88   They say, "The Merciful has taken to Himself a son:"

89   —ye have brought a monstrous thing!

90   The heavens well-nigh burst asunder thereat, and the earth is riven, and the mountains fall down broken,

91   that they attribute to the Merciful a son!

92   but it becomes not the Merciful to take to Himself a son!

93   there is none in the heavens or the earth but comes to the Merciful as a servant;

94   He counts them and numbers them by number,

95   and they are all coming to Him on the resurrection day singly.

96   Verily, those who believe and act aright, to them the Merciful will give love.

97   We have only made it easy for thy tongue that thou mayest thereby give glad tidings to the pious, and warn thereby a contentious people.

98   How many a generation before them have we destroyed? Canst thou

to be good, or saying that they are not sinners after all, he is pronouncing them legally righteous, free from any liability to the broken law, because he himself in his Son borne the penalty of their lawbreaking" (*The Cross of Christ*, p. 190).

19.81 This is a description of the sin of *shirk*. According to Muhammad, all who worship gods other than the one true God (Allah) will suffer in Hell.

19.83-87 Allah has sent demons upon the

infidels to encourage them in their sinfulness (see *The Doctrine of al-Qadar* on pp. 264-266).

19.88-92 Again, Muhammad condemned the Arabic Star Family religious system which insisted upon the doctrine that gods procreated and gave birth to other gods (see *Polytheism in Seventh Century Arabia* on pp. 92-97).

19.96 *believe and act aright* — These words are a brief summary of the Islamic gospel (see

find any one of them, or hear a whisper of them?

Surah 18

In the name of the merciful and compassionate God.

Absolute monotheism

1 Praise belongs to God, who sent down to His servant the Book and put no crookedness therein,
2 —straight, to give warning of keen violence from Him; and to give the glad tidings to the believers,
3 who do what is right, that for them is a goodly reward wherein they shall abide for ever and for aye;
4 and to give warning to those who say, "God hath taken to Himself a son."

5 They have no knowledge thereof, nor their fathers; a serious word it is that comes forth from their mouths! verily, they only speak a lie!
6 Haply thou wilt grieve thyself to death for sorrow after them, if they believe not in this new revelation.

Allah: Creator of the earth

7 Verily, we have made what is on the earth an ornament thereof, to try them, which of them is best in works;
8 but, verily, we are going to make what is thereon bare soil.

Sleepers of the Cave

9 Hast thou reckoned that the Fellows of the Cave and Er-raqîm were a wonder amongst our signs?

Q 103.3, note).
Surah 18. The title of this surah, *The Cave*, comes verse 9. It contains four long narratives: (a) the story of the Sleepers of the Cave, (b) the parable of two men, (c) the story of Moses and the Wiseman, and (d) the story of Alexander the Great.
18.1 *the Book* — The surah begins with an affirmation of the divine inspiration of the Qur'an.
18.4-6 Muhammad addressed and condemned the Arabic Star Family religious system, which argued for the birthing of gods from other gods (see **Polytheism in Seventh Century Arabia** on pp. 92-97). He claimed that those who believed this doctrine had obtained it from their fathers with-

out engaging in necessary critical analysis. Moreover, his "new revelation" showed this doctrine to be a lie.
18.9a *the Fellows of the Cave* — According to Ibn Ishaq, the leaders of Mecca attempted to discredit Muhammad with a test that involved the legend of the Sleepers of the Cave.

In previous surahs, Muhammad had included information about questionable legends, claiming his recounting of the legends to be historically accurate. Yet the leaders of Mecca knew otherwise, that the legends were fiction: unsubstantiated myths without historical foundation.

In his biography of Muhammad, Ibn Ishaq explained that when Muhammad held a meet-

10	When the youths resorted to the cave and said, "O our Lord! bring us mercy from Thee, and dispose for us our affair aright!"	12	Then we raised them up again, that we might know which of the two crews could best calculate the time of their tarrying.
11	And we struck their ears (with deafness) in the cave for a number of years.	13	We will narrate to thee their story in truth. Verily, they were youths who believed in their Lord, and we

ing in which he spoke to them about Allah and warned about a coming judgment upon all who failed to worship Allah. One of his opponents—a man by the name of al Nadr—spoke up, declaring that he could tell better stories than Muhammad. He then recounted stories about Persia, Rustum, and Isbandiyar, which he claimed were better stories than those that Muhammad had been sharing (*The Life of Muhammad*, p. 136).

Convinced that Muhammad was a charlatan who was deceiving the people of Mecca, they sought a way in which to publicly expose and discredit him. They sent two men to Yathrib (Medinah) to speak with several Jewish rabbis, seeking help. After explaining to the rabbis the nature of Muhammad's surahs, and how he made use of ancient scriptures and legends which impressed some of the people of Mecca, they asked them for their counsel. The rabbis counseled that they should confront Muhammad with a test. They were to ask him three questions, the answers to which were not widely known in the Middle East: (a) what happened to the Sleepers of the Cave? (b) what happened to the mighty traveler who reached the confines of the eastern and western edges of the earth? and (c) what is the nature of the spirit? If he could correctly answer each of the questions, they reasoned, he was likely an authentic prophet. If he could not, he was to be regarded as a rogue prophet, a charlatan who peddled in

lies for his own personal gain, and publicly expose him.

The Quraysh leaders of Mecca then posed these three questions to Muhammad. He said to them that he would give them the answer the following day (*Ibid.*, pp. 136, 137). Muhammad, however, delayed his response for fifteen days. This prompted the people of Mecca to spread reports: "Muhammad promised us an answer on the morrow, and today is the fifteenth day we have remained without an answer" (*Ibid.*, 137). On the fifteenth day, Muhammad responded to the challenge with a newly composed surah. In it, he offered an answer to the first two questions—that of the Sleepers of the Cave (Q 18.9-26) and the mighty traveler (Q 18.83-98). He, however, made no attempt to answer the third question.

18.9b *Er-raqim* — Islamic scholars differ on the meaning of this word. Some claim that it refers to the place where the event of the Sleepers of the Cave took place. Others believe it means "inscription"—a plaque set up in the cave as a memorial.

18.9-26 The story of the Sleepers of the Cave is a legend that has many pre-Christian pagan versions, the most ancient being one mentioned by Aristotle regarding sleepers in the city of Sardis. Other versions exist. A monophysite priest, Jacob of Saruq of Edessa, also wrote a version of the legend, giving the story a Christian context. It was then that Gregory of Tours learned of the legend

added to their guidance,

14   and we braced up their hearts, when they stood up and said, "Our Lord is the Lord of the heavens and the earth, we will not call upon any god beside Him, for then we should have said an extravagant thing.

15   These people of ours have taken to other gods beside Him. Though they do not bring any manifest authority for them. And who is more unjust than he who forges against God a lie?"

16   "So when ye have gone apart from them and what they serve other than God, then resort ye to the cave. Our Lord will unfold His mercy to you, and will dispose for you your affair advantageously."

17   And thou mightst have seen the sun when it rose decline from their cave towards the right hand, and when it set leave them on the left hand, while they were in the spacious part thereof. That is one of the signs of God. Whom God guides he is guided indeed, and whom He leads astray thou shalt surely find for him no patron to

---

and included it in his book *Glory of the Martyrs*. At that time that the legend became known on a much wider popular level. Still, its mythic and non-historical quality is seen in Gregory's retelling since the Roman Emperor Theodosius the Great or Theodosius the Younger (one or the other is mentioned in Gregory's retelling) made no reference to the story in their own official Roman records.

According to the legend (as told by Gregory of Tours), during the reign of the Roman Emperor Decius (third century), seven young men refused to recant of their belief in the gospel of Jesus Christ. Instead, they entered a cave near the city of Ephesus and went to sleep (approximately in A.D. 250). When Decius discovered their location, he had the cave sealed. They awoke in A.D. 435 when a landowner opened the cave, thinking to use it as a cattle pen. They left the cave and returned to Ephesus. They were astonished that the Christian persecution had ceased and that Ephesus was now adorned with many Christian symbols. They then died.

The story had since inspired many other legends, one of the more famous being Washington Irving's *Rip van Winkle* (see ***The Seven Sleepers of Ephesus*** on pp. 297-299).

18.15 *who is more unjust than he who forges against God a lie?* — These words, allegedly spoken by the protagonists in the story, were also a subtle rebuke to the people of Mecca who had made the same charge against Muhammad.

18.17a Muhammad claimed that the rays of the sun did not bother the sleepers while inside the cave. His account, however, contradicted the account presented by Gregory since the cave, according to Gregory had been sealed by Emperor Decius, disallowing any rays from the sun to enter.

18.17b *Whom God guides he is guided indeed, and whom He leads astray though shalt surely find for him no patron to guide aright* — In this verse, Muhammad also inserted a brief statement of double predestination (see ***The Doctrine of al-Qadar*** on pp. 264-266).

18.18 The inclusion of the dog guarding the threshold to the cave is nowhere men-

18 Thou mightst have reckoned them waking though they were sleeping, as we turned them towards the right and towards the left; and their dog spreading out his fore-paws on the threshold. Hadst thou come suddenly upon them thou wouldst surely have turned and fled away from them, and wouldst surely have been filled by them with dread.

19 Thus did we raise them up that they might question each other. Spake a speaker amongst them, "How long have ye tarried?" They said, "We have tarried a day or part of a day." They said, "Your Lord knows best your tarrying; so send one of you with this coin of yours to the city, and let him look which of them has purest food, and let him bring you provision thereof; and let him be subtle and not let any one perceive you.

20 Verily, they—should they perceive you—would stone you, or would force you back again unto their faith, and ye would never prosper then."

21 Thus did we make their people acquainted with their story, that they might know that God's promise is true; and that the Hour, there is no doubt concerning it. When they disputed amongst themselves concerning their affair, and said, "Build a building over them, their Lord knows best about them;" and those who prevailed in their affair said, "We will surely make a mosque over them."

22 They will say, "Three, and the fourth of them was their dog:" and they will say, "Five, and the sixth of them was their dog:" guessing at the unseen: and they will say, "Seven, and the eighth of them was their dog." Say, "My Lord knows best the number of them; none knows them but a few." Dispute not therefore concerning them

tioned in the story, as presented by Gregory of Tours. Again, Muhammad's account makes no mention to the role of Emperor Decius, who sealed them inside the cave.

18.19 Since, according to Muhammad's account, the cave had not been sealed, nothing prevented them from leaving the cave after their long sleep.

18.21 Muhammad believed that the people of Ephesus, when learning of the sleepers, condemned them to death by sealing the cave with a mosque erected over its opening. The historical record demonstrates an opposite response. A church was indeed built, but not to seal the sleepers inside the cave. Rather, it was to commemorate the alleged miraculous event. In addition, the church was built years later, long after the alleged event took place.

18.22 Muhammad did not know the exact number of the sleepers. He suggested three, five or seven sleepers, along with their dog. He then added that only Allah and a few people knew that exact number of the sleepers. Yet, if Muhammad was indeed a prophet, as he claimed to be, why was he

save with a plain disputation, and ask not any one of them concerning them.

23 And never say of anything, "Verily, I am going to do that tomorrow,"

24 except "if God please;" and remember thy Lord when thou hast forgotten, and say, "It may be that my Lord will guide me to what is nearer to the right than this."

25 They tarried in their cave three hundred years and nine more.

26 Say, "God knows best of their tarrying. His are the unseen things of the heavens and the earth—He can see! and hear!" They have no patron beside Him, nor does He let any one share in His judgment.

Declaration of condemnation

27 So, recite what thou art inspired with of the Book of thy Lord; there is no changing His words; nor shalt thou ever find a refuge beside Him;

28 and keep thyself patient, with those who call upon their Lord morning and evening, desiring His face; nor let thine eyes be turned from them, desiring the adornment of the life of this world; and obey not him whose heart we have made heedless of remembrance of us, and who follows his lusts, for his affair is ever in advance (of the truth).

29 But say, "The truth is from your Lord, so let him who will, believe;

---

not included in the number of "the few" who knew the exact number of sleepers?

18.24 *"If God please"*— A custom throughout the Muslim world is to say, "if Allah pleases," when commenting about some future event.

The New Testament says something similar: "Now listen, you who say, 'Today or tomorrow we will go to this or that city, spend a year there, carry on business and make money.' Why, you do not even know what will happen tomorrow. What is your life? You are a mist that appears for a little while and then vanishes. Instead, you ought to say, 'If it is the Lord's will, we will live and do this or that'" (James 4:13-16).

18.25 Muhammad claimed that they slept in the cave 309 years. Yet, Gregory's account placed the duration of their sleep to be approximately 140 years. This is because Decius was emperor from 249-251. Schol-

ars are not sure which of the two Theodosiuses was intended (either Theodosius I who served as emperor between 379-395 or Theodosius II who served as emperor between 408-450). In either case, the duration of slumber of the Seven Sleepers was substantially less than 309 years.

18.26 *God's knows best* — Clearly, Muhammad did not know the details of the story of the Sleepers in the Cave. His account was full of errors. He also attempted to explain away his lack of accuracy by noting that the details are "the unseen things of the heavens and the earth." Only Allah rightly knows the details, he explained.

18.27 *the Book* — The Qur'an, once again, is noted to be the absolute truth—none can alter His Words, the truth is from your Lord.

18.29 Again, Muhammad reminds the reader of the doctrine of double predestination. Those who are destined to believe will

and let him who will, disbelieve."
Verily, we have prepared for the
evildoers a fire, sheets of which
shall encompass them; and if they
cry for help, they shall be helped
with water like molten brass,
which shall roast their faces:—an
ill drink and an evil couch!

Paradise

30   Verily, those who believe and act
      aright,—verily, we will not waste
      the hire of him who does good
      works.

31   These, for them are gardens of
      Eden; beneath them rivers flow;
      they shall be adorned therein with
      bracelets of gold, and shall wear
      green robes of silk, and of brocade;
      reclining therein on thrones;—
      pleasant is the reward, and goodly
      the couch!

Parable of Two Men

32   Strike out for them a parable: Two
      men, for one of whom we made
      two gardens of grapes, and sur-
      rounded them with palms, and put
      corn between the two.

33   Each of the two gardens brought
      forth its food and did not fail in
      aught. And we caused a river to
      gush forth amidst them;

34   and he had fruit, and said unto his
      fellow, who was his next door
      neighbour, "I am more wealthy
      than thee, and mightier of house-
      hold."

35   And he went in unto his garden,
      having wronged himself: said he,
      "I do not think that this will ever
      disappear;

36   and I do not think that the hour is
      imminent; and if even I be sent
      back unto my Lord, I shall find a

believe, and those who are destined to unbelief, will not believe. This eliminates the
need for rational debate and discussion (see
The Doctrine of al-Qadar on pp. 264-266).
18.30 *believe and act aright* — these words
are repeated often in the Qur'an and serve
as a brief summary of the Islamic gospel (see
Q 103.3, note).
18.30-31 Characteristics of Heaven: (a)
gardens of perpetuity, (b) flowing rivers, (c)
people will bear bracelets of gold and wear
green robes of fine silk interwoven with gold,
and (d) people will recline on raised couches.
18.31 *gardens of Eden* — That is, the gardens in Paradise (also see Q 16.31; 19.61;
20.76; 35.33; 38.50; 40.8). Paradise is also
described as that of an oasis with well sup-

plied aquifers, an underground river system
sufficiently close to the surface to keep the
surface of the oasis fertile and green (see Q
16.31; 20.76; 25.10; 39.20; 85.11).
18.32-43 In this parable, the first man was
given by Allah two gardens of grape vines,
surrounded with palms and in the midst of
cornfields. The gardens always produced
large crops. The first man boasted of his
wealth and assumed that it would never
cease. The second man, who had a smaller
garden and possessed less wealth, was thankful to Allah for what he possessed. He then
disputed with the first man, pointing out his
arrogance and need for humility before Allah. One day, the first man's garden ceased
to bear fruit and he came to regret his arro-

The Seven Sleepers of Ephesus

by Gregory of Tours

*Gregory of Tours (538-594) became bishop of Tours in southern Gaul in
573. His ten volume work,* The History of the Franks, *is the most known
of all his writings to the modern reader. It is an account of the
Christianization of Gaul. He also wrote* The Life of the Fathers *and* Glory
of the Martyrs. *It is a record of the spirituality and godliness of notable
Christian individuals.*

Here is an account of seven brothers who are buried at Ephesus. During
the reign of the emperor Decius when there was a persecution against
the Christians, seven men were captured and brought before the emperor. These seven men were named Maximianus, Malchus, Martinianus,
Constantinus, Dionysius, Johannes and Serapion. Although they were
tempted by various suggestions to yield, they never acquiesced. Because of his regard for them the emperor granted time to think, so that

they would not die im-
mediately. But the
seven men shut them-
selves up in one cave,
and there they lived for
many days. One of them
would leave, purchase
supplies, and bring back
necessities.

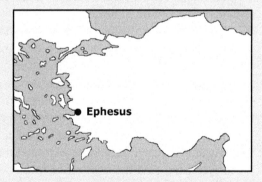

Ephesus

When the emperor
returned to Ephesus,
the seven men requested of the Lord that he design to rescue them
from this danger. They prayed, and while bowed to the ground they fell
asleep. When the emperor learned that they were staying in this cave,
by the will of God he ordered that the mouth of the cave be blocked off
with huge stones. He said: "Let those who refuse to sacrifice to our
gods die there." While this was being done, a Christian wrote the names

of the martyrs on a lead tablet and secretly put it in the entrance to the cave before it was blocked off.

After many years had gone by and peace had been granted to the churches, Theodosius, a Christian, became emperor. The impure heresy of the Sadducees, who denied that there would be a resurrection, was spreading. Then a citizen of Ephesus who decided to use this mountain as a sheepfold for his flocks overturned stones for the construction of walls for his pens. Not knowing what had happened within, he opened the entrance to the cave; but he did not find the inner chamber that was further inside.

The Lord sent the breath of life to the seven men and they awoke. Thinking that they had been asleep for only one night, they sent a young man from their number to purchase food. When the young man came to the gate of the city, he was surprised upon seeing an image of the glorious cross and hearing the people take oaths in the name of Christ. As soon as he presented the coins that he had from the reign of Decius, a merchant seized him and said: "You have found a hoard that was buried years ago." The young man denied [the accusation] and was brought to the bishop and the judge of the city, who denounced him. Compelled by force the young man revealed the hidden mystery and brought them to the cave where the other men were. As the bishop entered, he found the lead tablet on which everything the men had endured was recorded in writing.

The bishop spoke with the men; then the bishop and the judge quickly announced this news to the emperor Theododius. The emperor came and honored them by kneeling on the ground. The seven men spoke to the same emperor with these words: "A heresy has spread, glorious Augustus, that attempts to mislead the Christian people from the promises of God by saying that there is no resurrection of the dead. Therefore, because, as you know, we will all be held responsible before the tribunal of Christ in accordance with what the apostle Paul wrote [cf. 2 Cor. 5:10], the Lord has ordered us to be awakened and to say the kingdom of God." The emperor Theodosius listened and glorified the Lord who did not allow his people to perish. But the men again lay down on the ground and fell asleep.

When the emperor Theodosius wished to construct tombs of gold for them, he was warned in a vision not to do so. Even today the men lie asleep in that spot, covered by cloaks made of silk or linen. The record of their suffering, which with the assistance of a Syrian I translated into Latin, gives a fuller account.

—Gregory of Tours, *Glory of the Martyrs*, §94
first published *c.* 588

The Companions of the Cave (*Ashab el Kahf*) are the legendary "Seven Sleepers of Ephesus." Muhammad borrowed the story from Christian traditions and introduced it as a revelation into the Koran.

—Harold Alfred Macmichael, *A History of the Arabs in the Sudan*, p. 352

This story of "The Seven Sleepers of Ephesus" is told by Christian and Muslim alike in that part of the world. That little dog is one of the few animals allowed into Mohammedan heaven.

—Amy E. Spaulding, *The Wisdom of Storytelling in an Information Age*, p. 140

Mohammed seems to have entertained a sympathy for these mythic beings, whose adventures are told in the eighteenth chapter of the Koran. The name of their dog, somewhat variously known as Kitmir or Al Rakim, used to be written on the outside of letters in order to ensure their safe passage across the sea, and this happy animal is one of the few to whom paradise is specifically promised.

—Harrison Griswold Dwight, *Constantinople, Old and New*, p. 127

But here is proof of the greatness of the writer. It is a story not uncommon; but Irving tells it in such a way that everybody knows about Rip Van Winkle, though few have heard of Frederick Barbarossa, the Sleepers of Ephesus, or Peter Klaus. It is the genius of the writer which enables him to take stories which might be told by any one, and by his way of telling make them his own. This is what Shakespeare did in so many of his plays (for he rarely invented his plots), and this is what Irving has done in "Rip Van Winkle."

—Edward Everett Hale, *Knickerbocker Stories from the Old Dutch Days of New York*, p. 19

better one than it in exchange."

37   Said unto him his fellow, who was his next door neighbour, "Thou hast disbelieved in Him who created thee from earth, and then from a clot, then fashioned thee a man;

38   but God, He is my Lord; nor will I associate any one with my Lord.

39   Why couldst thou not have said, when thou didst go into thy garden, 'What God pleases! there is no power save in God,'—to look at, I am less than thee in wealth and children;

40   but haply my Lord will give me something better than thy garden, and will send upon it thunder-claps from the sky, and it shall be on the morrow bare slippery soil;

41   or on the morrow its water may be deeply sunk, so that thou canst not get thereat!"

42   And his fruits were encompassed, and on the morrow he turned down the palms of his hands for what he had spent thereon, for it was fallen down upon its trellises. And he said, "Would that I had never associated any one with my Lord!"

43   And he had not any party to help him beside God, nor was he helped.

Interpretation of the parable

44   In such a case the patronage is God's, the true; He is best at rewarding and best at bringing to an issue.

45   Strike out for them, too, a parable of the life of this world; like water which we send down from the sky, and the vegetation of the earth is mingled therewith;—and on the

---

gance.

Jesus spoke a parable that presented a similar theme. "The ground of a certain rich man produced a good crop. He thought to himself, 'What shall I do? I have no place to store my crops.' Then he said, 'This is what I'll do. I will tear down my barns and build bigger ones, and there I will store all my grain and my goods. And I'll say to myself, "You have plenty of good things laid up for many years. Take life easy; eat, drink and be merry."' But God said to him, 'You fool! This very night your life will be demanded from you. Then who will get what you have prepared for yourself?' This is how it will be with anyone who stores up things for himself but is not rich toward God" (Lk 12:16-21).

18.37 *from a clot* — In this passage, Muhammad believed that man originated from a clot (see Q 96.2, note).

18.44-58 A number of principles emerge from this parable: (a) it is Allah who gives and withholds rain, (b) it is Allah who gives and withholds wealth, (c) it is Allah who has appointed a time for all people to stand before Him, (d) the gods of the polytheists will offer no help to people at the Last Judgment, and (e) Allah has sent messengers to people to warn them of the Last Judgment, including the messenger who has given people the Qur'an.

In short, Muhammad's parable made the case of the certainty of divine judgment. Divine judgment comes in this life as well as the afterlife for those who fail to be thank-

morrow it is dried up, and the winds scatter it; for God is powerful over all.

46 Wealth and children are an adornment of the life of this world; but enduring good works are better with thy Lord, as a recompense, and better as a hope.

47 And the day when we will move the mountains, and thou shalt see the (whole) earth stalking forth; and we will gather them, and will not leave one of them behind.

48 Then shall they be presented to thy Lord in ranks.—Now have ye come to us as we created you at first! nay, but ye thought that we would never make our promise good!

49 And the Book shall be placed, and thou shalt see the sinners in fear of what is in it; and they will say, "Alas, for us! what ails this Book, it leaves neither small nor great

things alone, without numbering them?" and they shall find present what they have done; and thy Lord will not wrong any one.

50 And when we said to the angels, "Adore Adam," they adored him, save only Iblîs, who was of the ginn, who revolted from the bidding of his Lord. "What! will ye then take him and his seed as patrons, rather than me, when they are foes of yours? bad for the wrong-doers is the exchange!"

51 I did not make them witnesses of the creation of the heavens and the earth, nor of the creation of themselves, nor did I take those who lead astray for my supporters.

52 On the day when He shall say, "Call ye my partners whom ye pretend" and they shall call on them, but they shall not answer them; and we will set the vale of perdition between them;

---

ful to Allah and follow the ways of Allah.

18.46 Muhammad believed that a life of good works has more value than wealth and children since salvation is predicated upon a life of good works. Much wealth and many children have no bearing on one's eternal destiny.

Jesus also prioritized eternal life to anything else one might seek to acquire in this life. He asked: "What good will it be for a man if he gains the whole world, yet forfeits his soul? Or what can a man give in exchange for his soul?" (Matt 16:26). And, said Jesus, a person must not even allow his or her own family to stand between him or her from God and the Gospel of Jesus Christ

(see Matt 10:34-39; Lk 14:25-27; Jn 21:15; Phil 3:7-9).

18.49 *the Book* — the Book that will be opened at the Last Judgment.

18.50 *Iblis* — Satan. This passage repeats what he said earlier about Satan in Q 15.26-40. Here Muhammad described Satan as one of the ginns. He added that those committed to the Arabic Star Family worship are worshippers of Satan and the ginns (see *Occultism in Seventh Century Arabia* on pp. 123-125).

18.51 *I did not make them witnesses of the creation of the heavens and the earth* — that is, Allah did not make the gods witnesses of the sun, moon, and stars. These

53   and the sinners shall see the fire, and shall think that they are going to fall therein, and shall find no escape therefrom.

54   We have turned about in this Qur'ân for men every parable; but man is ever at most things a caviller.

55   Naught prevented men from believing when the guidance came to them, or from asking pardon of their Lord, except the coming on them of the course of those of yore, or the coming of the torment before their eyes.

56   We sent not prophets save as heralds of glad tidings and as warners; but those who misbelieve wrangle with vain speech to make void the truth therewith; and they take my signs and the warnings given them as a jest.

57   Who is more unjust than he who, being reminded of the signs of his Lord, turns away therefrom, and forgets what his hands have done before? verily, we will place veils upon their hearts lest they should understand, and dulness in their ears! And if thou shouldst call them to the guidance, they will not be guided then for ever.

58   But thy Lord is forgiving, endowed with mercy; were He to punish them for what they have earned He would have hastened for them the torment. Nay rather, they have their appointed time, and shall never find a refuge beside Him.

Sodom and Gomorrah

59   These cities, we destroyed them when they were unjust; and for their destruction we set an appointed time.

Moses and the wiseman

60   And when Moses said to his servant, "I will not cease until I reach the confluence of the two seas, or else I will go on for years."

61   But when they reached the

---

alleged gods are mere pretenders. Again, these two verses are a rebuke to all who were committed to Arabic Star Family worship.

18.54 *caviller* — cavalier. In this case, it means a haughty disregard for the Qur'an. In v. 56, Muhammad explained what he meant: "those who misbelieve wrangle with vain speech to make void the truth therewith."

18.57 *we will place veils upon their hearts* — Again, Muhammad referenced the doctrine of double predestination. In addition, Muhammad said that he was told by Allah to possess a cavalier (haughty disregard) attitude toward his opponents (see ***The Doctrine al-Qadar*** on pp. 264-266).

18.60-82 This particular story of Moses is not found in the Old Testament.

The setting of the story is the junction of the two rivers. It is not known which two rivers are intended. Some Islamic scholars assume it to be the junction of the Red Sea and the Indian Ocean. Others have thought

confluence of the two they forgot their fish, and it took its way in the sea with a free course.

62 And when they had passed by, he said to his servant, "Bring us our dinners, for we have met with toil from this journey of ours."

63 Said he, "What thinkest thou? when we resorted to the rock, then, verily, I forgot the fish, but it was only Satan who made me forget it, lest I should remember it; and it took its way in the sea wondrously!"

64 Said he, "This is what we were searching for: So they turned back upon their footsteps, following them up.

65 Then they found a servant of our servants [Wiseman], to whom we had given mercy from ourselves, and had taught him knowledge from before us.

66 Said Moses to him, "Shall I follow thee, so that thou mayest teach me, from what thou hast been taught, the right way?"

67 Said he [Wiseman], "Verily, thou canst never have patience with me.

68 How canst thou be patient in what thou compre-hendest no knowledge of?"

69 He [Moses] said, "Thou wilt find me, if God will, patient; nor will I rebel against thy bidding."

70 He [Wiseman] said, "Then, if thou followest me, ask me not about anything until I begin for them the mention of it."

71 So they set out until when they rode in the bark, he scuttled it. Said he [Wiseman], "Hast thou scuttled it to drown its crew? Thou hast produced a strange thing."

72 Said he [Wiseman], "Did I not tell thee, verily, thou canst never have patience with me?"

73 Said he [Moses], "Rebuke me not for forgetting, and impose not on me a difficult command."

74 So they set out until they met a boy, and he killed him. And he (Moses) said, "Hast thou killed a pure person without (his killing) a person? thou hast produced an unheard-of thing."

75 Said he [Wiseman], "Did I not tell thee, verily, thou canst not have patience with me?"

it to be the junction of the Mediterranean Sea with the Pacific Ocean. Still others look upon it allegorically—the junction of the streams of knowledge.

As the story unfolds, three episodes take place that puzzle Moses. The first was the drilling of a hole in a boat, rendering it unusable. The second was the killing of a boy. The third was the stabilizing of a teetering wall.

Towards the end of the story, the wise man (some scholars believe the wiseman to be Jethro/Sho'haib) explained the hidden wisdom of the three events. First, the boat was damaged so that a wealthy man who would soon be coming would not seize it by force. Second, the boy was killed because he lacked purity and would draw his parents away from Allah. Third, the wall was straightened because under it was a treasure that

76   Said he [Moses], "If I ask thee about anything after it, then do not accompany me. Now hast thou arrived at my excuse."

77   So they set out until when they came to the people of a city; and they asked the people thereof for food; but they refused to entertain them. And they found therein a wall which wanted to fall to pieces, and he set it upright. Said (Moses), "Hadst thou pleased thou mightst certainly have had a hire for this."

78   Said he [Wiseman], "This is the parting between me and thee. I will give thee the interpretation of that with which thou couldst not have patience.

79   As for the bark it belonged to poor people, who toiled on the sea, and I wished to damage it, for behind it was a king who seized on every bark by force.

80   And as for the youth, his parents were believers, and we feared lest he should impose upon them rebellion and misbelief.

81   So we desired that their Lord would give them in exchange a better one than him in purity, and nearer in filial affection.

82   And as for the wall, it belonged to two orphan youths in the city, and beneath it was a treasure belonging to them both, and their father was a righteous man, and their Lord desired that they should reach puberty, and then take out their treasure as a mercy from thy Lord; and I did it not on my own bidding. That is the interpretation of what thou couldst not have patience with."

Alexander the Great

83   And they will ask thee about DHu 'Qarnâin, say, "I will recite to you a mention of him;

84   verily, we stablished for him in the

Allah wished the people to discover later in life.

In each case, Moses was anxious in his desire to understand the morals of each of the stories. And this was precisely the underlying message that the wise man wished to share with him. The most valuable and deepest truths can only be ascertained by those who possess a quiet and patient spirit. Impatience always leaves one frustrated and foolish.

18.83 *DHu 'Qarnain* — The two horned one. Ancient literature identifies Alexander the Great as DHu 'Qarnain. The name DHu 'Qarnain was used of Alexander in the book *The Romance of Alexander the Great,* an Aramaic book which was disseminated among Nastoric Christians in pre-Islamic Arabia. Moreover, some copies of the book carried the title: *DHu 'Qarnain.*

It is odd that Muhammad identified Alexander the Great as one of Allah's chosen apostles. Alexander was a zealot pagan and a committed polytheist. He consulted the priests of the Greek gods before going to war. He also claimed that he was the son of the Greek god Zeus (also known as Ammon among the Egyptians). He therefore not only believed that God has sons, but that he was one of them.

earth, and we gave him a way to everything;

85 and he followed a way

86 until when he reached the setting of the sun, he found it setting in a black muddy spring, and he found thereat a people." We said, "O DHu 'Qarnâin! thou mayest either torment these people, or treat them well."

87 Said he, "As for him who does wrong, I will torment him, then shall he be sent back to his Lord, and He will torment him with an unheard-of torment;

88 but as for him who believes and acts aright, for him is an excellent reward, and we will tell him our easy bidding."

89 Then he followed a way

90 until when he reached the rising of the sun, he found it rise upon a people to whom we had given no shelter therefrom.

91 So! And we comprehended the knowledge of what (forces) he

had with him.

92 Then he followed a way

93 until when he reached the point between the two mountains, he found below them both a people who could scarcely understand speech.

94 They said, "O DHu 'Qarnâin! verily, Yâgûg and Mâgûg are doing evil in the land. Shall we then pay thee tribute, on condition that thou set between us and them a rampart?"

95 He said, "What my Lord hath established me in is better; so help me with strength, and I will set between you and them a barrier.

96 "Bring me pigs of iron until they fill up the space between the two mountain sides." Said he, "Blow until it makes it a fire." Said he, "Bring me, that I may pour over it, molten brass."

97 So they could not scale it, and they could not tunnel it.

98 Said he, "This is a mercy from my Lord; but when the promise of my

---

18.86 The Ptolemaic understanding of the universe (a system that included the notion of a flat earth) was commonly believed in the ancient world. In this scheme, the sun set in the west, where it died, and, the following morning, returned to life in the east. In accordance to this understanding of the universe, Muhammad believed that Alexander the Great reached the western edge of the earth: the place of the setting of the sun. He described it as "a black muddy spring."

This explanation was Muhammad's answer to the second question posed by his opponents in Mecca earlier in this surah (see

Q 18.9a note).

18.94 *Yagug and Magug* — Gog and Magog. In this passage, Gog and Magog merely meant those who "are doing evil in the land." People complained to Alexander about the evil that they had done in the world. Alexander responded by building a dam between two mountains made of pig iron and molten brass to keep them detained. They could neither scale the dam nor tunnel underneath. One wonders, however, why Gog and Magog could not have merely maneuvered to either side of the dam as a way of overcoming their confinement.

Lord comes to pass, He will make it as dust, for the promise of my Lord is true."

Hell

99   And we left some of them to surge on that day over others, and the trumpet will be blown, and we will gather them together.

100   And we will set forth hell on that day before the misbelievers,

101   whose eyes were veiled from my Reminder, and who were unable to hear.

102   What! did those who misbelieve reckon that they could take my servants for patrons beside me? Verily, we have prepared hell for the misbelievers to alight in!

103   Say, "Shall we inform you of those who lose most by their works?

104   those who erred in their endeavours after the life of this world, and who think they are doing good deeds."

105   Those who misbelieve in the signs of their Lord and in meeting Him, vain are their works; and we will not give them right weight on the resurrection day.

106   That is their reward,—hell! for that they misbelieved and took my signs and my apostles as a mockery.

Paradise

107   Verily, those who believe and act aright, for them are gardens of Paradise to alight in,

108   to dwell therein for aye, and they shall crave no change therefrom.

Final plea

In the Bible, Gog and Magog are prophetic words that pertain to end time prophecies. Gog represents an evil leader who ruled the land of Magog. Gog and the people of Magog will invade Israel from the north and be destroyed by God (see Ezekiel 38 and 39).

18.99-106 This surah describes Hell as "the entertainment of the unbelievers" (Q 18.102). Those in Hell are "the great losers." They are in Hell because they rejected the communications of Allah (i.e., the Qur'an) and mocked His messengers (i.e., Muhammad).

18.101 *whose eyes were veiled from my Reminder* — That is, the eyes of the infidels were veiled so that they could neither see nor understand the message of the Reminder

(the Qur'an). Once again, Muhammad referenced the doctrine of double predestination (see **The Doctrine of al-Qadar** on pp. 264-266).

18.105 Those who had fallen into the sin of idolatry will receive no benefit from their good works at the Last Judgment. All their alleged good works will have been declared to be vain (see **The Last Judgment** on pp. 46-50).

18.107a *believe and act aright* — These words are repeated often in the Qur'an and serve as a brief summary of the Islamic gospel (see Q 103.3, note).

18.107b *gardens of Paradise* — The oases awaiting the righteous in Paradise (see **Paradise** on pp. 76-77).

18.109 *Were the sea ink for the words of*

109   Say, "Were the sea ink for the words of my Lord, the sea would surely fail before the words of my Lord fail; aye, though we brought as much ink again!"

110   Say, "I am only a mortal like yourselves; I am inspired that your God is only one God. Then let him who hopes to meet his Lord act righteous acts, and join none in the service of his Lord."

Surah 27

In the name of the merciful and compassionate God.

1   T. S.

Qur'an

Those are the signs of the Qur'ân

and the perspicuous Book;

2   a guidance and glad tidings to the believers,

3   who are steadfast at prayer, and give alms, and of the hereafter are sure;

4   verily, those who believe not in the hereafter we have made seemly for them their works, and they shall wander blindly on!

5   These are they who shall have an evil torment, and they in the hereafter shall be those who most lose!

6   Verily, thou dost meet with this Qur'ân from the wise, the knowing One!

The calling of Moses

7   When Moses said to his people, "Verily, I perceive a fire, I will bring you therefrom news; or I will bring you a burning brand; haply ye may

---

my Lord — See Q 31.27 where a similar sentiment was expressed by Muhammad. Also see Jn 20:25 where the Apostle John wrote similar words in regards to Jesus Christ.

18.110 *act righteous acts* — This is because one's eternal destiny is dependent upon the amassing of righteous acts (see **Last Judgment** on pp. 46-49).

Surah 27. The title of this surah, *The Ants*, comes from verse 18. A feature unique to this surah and which has generated a great deal of discussion in scholarship is the section where Muhammad recounted the story of Solomon and the Queen of Sheba (vv. 15-44). It is a fanciful account mentioned in non-canonical Jewish ancient literature and therefore not in either the Jewish or Christian canons. The overall theme of the surah is Muhammad's understanding of apostles—divinely commissioned individuals throughout history who served as warners to those who were in rebellion to Allah.

27.1a Literally, *Ta Sin*. See Q 32.1, note.

27.1b *the perspicuous Book* — The eternal book in heaven that was revealed to Muhammad (see **The Perspicuous Book** on pp. 178-179).

27.1b-6 According to Muhammad, the Qur'an has two effects: (a) it is a guidance to those who keep up prayer and offer alms to the poor, and (b) it is a witness against those who are blind and destined for Hell.

27.7-14 This passage is rooted in Exodus 3-4 where Moses stood before the Lord at

be warmed."

8   But when he came to it he was
called to, "Blessed be He who is in
the fire, and he who is about it!
and celebrated be the praises of
God, the Lord of the worlds!

9   O Moses! verily, I am God, the
mighty, wise;

10   throw down thy staff!" and when
he saw it quivering, as though it
were a snake, he turned back fleeing, and did not return. "O Moses!
fear not; verily, as for me—
apostles fear not with me;

11   save only those who have done
wrong and then substitute good for
evil; for, verily, I am forgiving, merciful!

12   but put thy hand in thy bosom, it
shall come forth white without

hurt;—one of nine signs to Pharaoh and his people; verily, they are
a people who act abominably."

13   And when our signs came to them
visibly, they said, "This is obvious
sorcery!"

14   and they gainsaid them—though
their souls made sure of them—
unjustly, haughtily; but, behold
what was the end of the evildoers!

Solomon:
the ants and birds

15   And we gave David and Solomon
knowledge; and they both said,
"Praise belongs to God, who hath
preferred us over many of His servants who believe!"

---

the burning bush.

27.12 *nine signs* — Muhammad believed
that Allah visited the land of Egypt with nine
plagues. The Book of Exodus mentioned
ten divine judgments that visited the land
of Egypt during the confrontation between
Moses and Pharaoh—not "nine signs," as
mentioned in this verse (also see Q17.101
where the same error is repeated, and **How
Many Plagues Were There?** on p. 565).

27.14 *they gainsaid them* — That is, they
rejected their words.

27.15-44 With few variations, this passage
corresponds to the apocryphal account of
the visit of the Queen of Sheba mentioned
in the first chapter of the *Second Targum of
Esther* (also known as the *Targum Sheni*).
Its inclusion in the Qur'an has generated a
much discussion within qur'anic scholarship,
with the question being: who copied who?

Is the qur'anic account based upon the *Second Targum of Esther*, or is the account in
the *Second Targum of Esther* based upon
the Qur'an?

The question is important since it
touches upon the claim that the Qur'an is
an eternal document existing in Paradise and
guarded by Allah. If Muhammad indeed copied this story from the *Second Targum of
Esther*, then this surah is an example of the
Qur'an being a historical document that borrowed from earlier writings—and not an eternal document, as alleged.

The *Second Targum of Esther*, along
with the other targums, is an Aramaic translation of the Hebrew Bible. Targums tend
to contain embellishments and legends not
included in the Hebrew Bible and were never
regarded by ancient or contemporary Jewish scholars to be part of divine revelation.

16   And Solomon was David's heir; and said, "O ye folk! we have been taught the speech of birds, and we have been given everything; verily, this is an obvious grace!"

17   And assembled for Solomon were his hosts of the ginns, and men, and birds, and they were marshalled;

18   until they came upon the valley of the ants. Said an ant, "O ye ants! go into your dwellings, that Solomon and his hosts crush you not while they do not perceive."

19   And he smiled, laughing at her speech, and said, "O Lord! excite me to be thankful for Thy favour, wherewith Thou hast favoured me and my parents, and to do righteousness which may please Thee; and make me enter into Thy mercy amongst Thy righteous servants!"

Since the *Second Targum of Esther* is mentioned in the *Jerusalem Talmud* and cited in the *Tractrate Sopherim* (XIII:6), knowledge of its existence dates back to at least the fourth century, A.D. This points to the fact that the *Second Targum of Esther* existed prior to that century. Furthermore, a number of scholars link the legend of the Queen of Sheba to Josephus (first century, A.D.) who claimed that the legend originated in Arabia or Greece. This places the origin of the legend prior to the birth of Christ.

Islamic scholarship has rejected these claims by stressing that the earliest surviving manuscript of the *Second Targum of Esther* to be the eighth century. And since Muhammad lived in the early seventh century, this points to the fact that the Qur'an predates the Targum.

A second observation made by Islamic scholars is that the description of Solomon's throne corresponds to that which is found in Arabic culture and therefore reflects the qur'anic influence upon the *Second Targum of Esther*.

These two responses from Islamic scholarship, however, have three problems. (a) Islamic scholars are selective in the application of their criterion. The earliest surviving manuscript of the Qur'an is also eighth century. The eighth century dating of the *Second Targum of Esther,* therefore, proves nothing since both documents are dated to the same period of time. (b) Islamic scholarship has failed to adequately address the much earlier citations in ancient literature of the existence of the *Second Targum of Esther* prior to the fourth century, A.D. (c) The description of Solomon's throne in the *Second Targum of Esther* may indeed reflect the influence of Arabic culture, yet Arabic culture predated the Qur'an by multiple centuries (see Rafat Amari, *Islam: In Light of History*, pp. 39-43).

27.16 In both the *Second Targum of Esther* and this passage in the Qur'an, Solomon talked to animals. This is a highly fanciful dialogue. The *Second Targum of Esther* was never regarded as divinely inspired in either the Jewish or Christian faiths and was therefore not included in their canons. In contrast, the Qur'an is the Islamic canon, believed to be divinely inspired, and the account is included in its pages.

27.17 *ginns* — In the *Second Targum of Esther*, Solomon was described as having included in his assembled host demons. In this passage, they are called ginns.

27.18-19 This fanciful passage of Solomon coming close to walking upon and destroy-

20 And he reviewed the birds, and said, "How is it I see not the hoopoe? is he then amongst the absent?

21 I will surely torment him with a severe torment; or I will surely slaughter him; or he shall bring me obvious authority."

22 And he tarried not long, and said, "I have compassed what ye compassed not; for I bring you from Sebâ a sure information:

23 verily, I found a woman ruling over them, and she was given all things, and she had a mighty throne;

24 and I found her and her people adoring the sun instead of God, for Satan had made seemly to them their works, and turned them from the path, so that they are not guided.

25 Will they not adore God who brings forth the secrets in the heavens, and knows what they hide and what they manifest?

26 —God, there is no god but He, the Lord of the mighty throne!"

A letter

27 Said he [Solomon], "We will see whether thou hast told the truth, or whether thou art of those who lie.

28 Go with this my letter and throw it before them, then turn back away from them, and see what they return."

29 Said she [the queen], "O ye chiefs! verily, a noble letter has been thrown before me.

30 It is from Solomon, and, verily, it

---

ing a colony of ants, and then talking with them, is not mentioned in the *Second Targum of Esther*.

27.20 The bird described in the *Second Targum of Esther* is a wild rooster. In this passage, it is a hoopoe (see the illustration on this page). The hoopoe is a small elegant bird, related to the hornbill. It gets its name from its small shrill call—a hoop—which rings clear and repeated two or three times.

27.24 In the *Second Targum of Esther*, the Queen of Sheba was described as a worshipper of the ocean. In this passage, she is described as a worshipper of the sun.

27.27-28 Having heard this report from the birds, Solomon decided to check out its accuracy by sending a letter via the birds to the queen. In the version of the *Second Targum of Esther*, no such test was per-

formed. Solomon took the report of the wild rooster as factual and sent a letter of ultimatum to the Queen of Sheba, demanding complete subservience from her.

The Hoopoe

is, "In the name of the merciful and compassionate God.

31   Do not rise up against me, but come to me resigned!'"

32   She [the queen] said, "O ye chiefs! pronounce sentence for me in my affair. I never decide an affair until ye testify for me."

33   They [the advisors] said, "We are endowed with strength, and endowed with keen violence; but the bidding is thine, see then what it is that thou wilt bid."

34   She [the queen] said, "Verily, kings when they enter a city despoil it, and make the mighty ones of its people the meanest; thus it is they do!

35   So, verily, I am going to send to them a gift, and will wait to see with what the messengers return."

The response from
the Queen of Sheba

36   And when he [the messenger] came to Solomon, he said, "Do ye proffer me wealth, when what God has given me is better than what He has given you? nay, ye in your gifts rejoice!

37   return to them, for we will surely come to them with hosts which they cannot confront; and we will surely drive them out therefrom mean and made small!"

A ginn beguiles
the Queen of Sheba

38   Said he [Solomon], "O ye chiefs! which of you will bring me her throne before they come to me re-

27.31 *come to me resigned* — That is, come to me in full submission (that is, as a Muslim). According to the *Second Targum of Esther*, Solomon's letter was an ultimatum. Either she come to him in full submission, or he would marshal an army of animals, birds, and ginns to attack and destroy her kingdom.

27.34 In this passage, the Queen of Sheba assumed that Solomon would attack her if she did not submit to his demands. In contrast, the *Second Targum of Esther* states that the threat of war was stated outright by Solomon.

27.36 In the letter of response, the Queen of Sheba first commented that the gifts offered by Solomon could not compare with the wealth that her nation already possesses. In the *Second Targum of Esther*, the queen

made no comment about the comparison of wealth between the two nations. She merely said that she would arrive in three years.

27.37 The Queen of Sheba then commented that the gifts that she would offer are of such higher quality that the other gifts would be despised.

27.38 When Solomon learned that the Queen of Sheba was coming to him in a state of submissive obedience, he sought counsel from the ginns (demons), seeking a way in which to seize her throne.

27.39-40 A contest was devised between "a demon of the ginns" and another ginn who "had a knowledge of the Book" (that is, divine revelation) to see who could fulfill Solomon's wishes. The demon of the ginn is characterized as "ungrateful" whereas the

39   signed?"
      Said a demon of the ginns, "I will
      bring thee it before thou canst rise
      up from thy place, for I therein am
      strong and faithful."
40   He who had the knowledge of the
      Book said, "I will bring it to thee
      before thy glance can turn." And
      when he saw it settled down be-
      side him, he said, "This is of my
      Lord's grace, that He may try me
      whether I am grateful or ungrate-
      ful, and he who is grateful is only
      grateful for his own soul, and he
      who is ungrateful,—verily, my
      Lord is rich and generous."
41   Said he [Solomon], "Disguise for

      her her throne; let us see whether
      she is guided, or whether she is of
      those who are not guided."
42   And when she came it was said,
      "Was thy throne like this?" She
      said [the queen], "It might be it;"
      and we were given knowledge be-
      fore her, but we were resigned.
43   But that which she served beside
      God turned her away; verily, she
      was of the unbelieving people.
44   And it was said to her, "Enter the
      court;" and when she saw it, she
      reckoned it to be an abyss of wa-
      ter, and she uncovered her legs.
      Said he, "Verily, it is a court paved
      with glass!" Said she [the queen],

ginn of the Book is characterized as "grateful." The idea that this contest would beguile the queen and take her throne is nowhere mentioned in the *Second Targum of
Esther.*

27.40a *the Book* — That is, revelation from
Allah. It is unclear which book is meant since
no ancient Scripture referenced this incident.
It is possible that it is part of Muhammad's
fictional story and therefore should be regarded similarly, as a fictional book of revelation.

27.40b *This is of my Lord's grace, that He
may try me whether I am grateful or ungrateful* — That is, whether I recognize that
my spiritual powers come from God or come
from my own self.

27.40c *he who is grateful is only grateful
for his own soul* — That is, a thankful heart
will redound to one's own benefit at the
Last Judgment (see Q 17.15).

27.41-42 The grateful ginn cast a spell on
the Queen of Sheba so that she could not

distinguish her throne from common chairs
in Solomon's palace.

27.43 Muhammad commented that the
false god that the queen worshipped beguiled her so that she did not discover the
truth about the changing of the thrones.
The reason why the treachery succeeded
was because "she was of the unbelieving
people"—that is, she was not a follower of
Allah.

27.44 The Queen of Sheba, still enchanted,
entered the courts of Solomon, thinking the
court was an "abyss of water." She then
uncovered her legs to walk into the mirage.
When Solomon said that the court was
"paved with glass" she awoke from her en-
chantment, repented, and turned to the one
true God—the Lord of the worlds, Allah (see
Q 1.2, note).

      In the *Second Targum of Esther,* the
queen entered into Solomon's bathhouse
(swimming pool, sauna, changing room).
Seeing the water, she raised her dress to

"My Lord! verily, I have wronged myself, but I am resigned with Solomon to God the Lord of the worlds!"

The plot against Zali'h

45 And we sent unto Thamûd their brother Zâli'h, "Serve God;" but behold, they were two parties who contended!

46 Said he, "O my people! why do ye hasten on evil acts before good deeds? why do ye not ask forgiveness of God? Imply ye may obtain mercy."

47 They said, "We have taken an augury concerning thee and those who are with thee." Said he, "Your augury is in God's hands; nay, but ye are a people who are tried!"

48 And there were in the city nine persons who despoiled the land and did not right.

49 Said they, "Swear to each other by God, we will surely fall on him by night and on his people; then we will surely say unto his next of kin, 'We witnessed not the destruction of his people, and we do surely tell the truth!'"

50 And they plotted a plot, and we plotted a plot, but they did not perceive.

51 Behold, how was the end of their plot, that we destroyed them and their people all together!

52 Thus are their houses overturned, for that they were unjust; verily, in that is a sign to people who do know!

53 But we saved those who believed and who did fear.

Lot

54 And Lot when he said to his people, "Do ye approach an abomi-

wade across. Seeing the hair on her legs, Solomon commented, "Your beauty is the beauty of women, but your hair is the hair of men. Now hair is beautiful for a man but shameful for a woman." The queen responded by testing Solomon with three riddles. When he answered each one correctly, she praised him for his wisdom and gave him the gifts.

27.45-53 Once again, Muhammad repeated the story of the Thamud people (see Q 91, note). According to this passage, two parties contended with the prophet Zali'h. The first party preached repentance and submission to God. The second party resisted the message, and plotted the murder of Zali'h

and his family.

27.50-53 In spite of the fact that the people plotted to kill Zali'h, they were not aware that Allah was also plotting against the plotters. In the end, the evil people were destroyed by Allah. The only survivors were "those who believed and who did fear."

This account, then, is a reiteration of a major theme found in the Qur'an: those who judge the apostles will themselves be judged (see Q 26.192-212 and 45.28).

27.54-58 This passage is a summary of Gen 19:1-26—the destruction of Sodom and Gomorrah. Lot was driven out of the city because he is one "who would keep pure" (v 56). Lot and his entire family were saved,

nable sin while ye can see?

55   do ye indeed approach men lustfully rather than women? nay! ye
are a people who are ignorant."

56   But the answer of his people was
only to say, "Drive out Lot's family from your city! verily, they are
a folk who would keep pure."

57   But we saved him and his family
except his wife, her we destined
to be of those who lingered;

58   and we rained down upon them rain,
and evil was the rain of those who
were warned.

No god but Allah

59   Say, "Praise belongs to God; and
peace be upon His servants whom
He has chosen! Is God best, or
what they associate with Him?"

60   He who created the heavens and
the earth; and sends down upon
you from the heaven water; and
we cause to grow therewith gardens fraught with beauty; ye could

not cause the trees thereof to
grow! Is there a god with God?
nay, but they are a people who
make peers with Him!

61   He who made the earth, settled,
and placed amongst it rivers; and
placed upon it firm mountains; and
placed between the two seas a barrier; is there a god with God? nay,
but most of them know not!

62   He who answers the distressed
when he calls upon Him and removes the evil; and makes you
successors in the earth; is there a
god with God? little is it that ye
are mindful.

63   He who guides you in the darkness,
of the land and of the sea; and who
sends winds as glad tidings before
His mercy; is there a god with God?
exalted be God above what they
associate with Him!

64   He who began the creation and
then will make it return again; and
who provides you from the heaven
and the earth; is there a god with

except his wife (cf. Gen 19:26).

27.55 *do ye indeed approach men lustfully rather than women?* — a description of homosexuality (cf. Q 52.24; 76.19).

27.58 *rained down upon them rain* — In this passage, the destruction of Sodom and Gomorrah is described as a rain with evil (destruction) in the rain. Elsewhere in the Qur'an, the destruction of the two cities was a result of a sandstorm (Q 29.40; 54.34), or stones of baked clay (Q 11.82; 15.74; 51.33). The Bible, however, states that the two cities were destroyed by burning sulphur raining down from the sky (Gen 19:28).

27.59-64 Five times in this passage, a question is asked: *is there a god with God?* The presumed answer is no. The true God is presented as majestic, the creator of the heavens and the earth, the one who holds all things together. Muhammad offered five rejoinders: (a) the Meccan people claimed that Allah has peers, (b) most of the Meccan people were ignorant of the truth, (c) most of the Meccan people were not mindful to know the truth, (d) the true God was exalted above the false beliefs of the Meccan people, and (e) Muhammad challenged the Meccan people to bring their proofs to him

Second Targum of Esther
1:36-37

The Second Targum of Esther is an Aramaic translation of the Book of Esther. It embellishes the biblical account with apocryphal material, some of which not germane to the story of Esther. Scholars place the composition of this document anywhere between the fourth and seventh centuries, A.D.

In the third year of King Nebukhadnezzar the House of Israel wept, sighed and exclaimed: "Woe to us, the enemy has prevailed over us, he has plundered our land, he has destroyed our provinces, he has banished us into exile and has treated us improperly. Our elderly (he placed) in chains, and our princes he banished into exile, our youths he slew by sword and our children he hauled into captivity; he took away the crown of our glory from us. Now when the kings of David's dynasty rose (to power) they reigned over the entire world. David was succeeded by Solomon, whom the Holy One, Blessed be He, appointed to rule over wild beasts and (over) the fowl of the skies, and over all the earth, as well as (over) demons (and over) spirits (and) over the screeching owls. He spoke the language of each of them, and they understood his speech, for thus it is written, "and he spoke of trees" (1 Kings 5:13).

Once when King Solomon's heart became cheerful through wine, he summoned all the kings of the East and the West who were near him, (near) the Lord of Israel, he hosted them in the royal palace of his kingdom. Another time when King Solomon's heart became cheerful through wine, he ordered that wild beasts, birds of the sky and reptiles of the earth be brought. (Also) that lyres, cymbals, timbrels and lutes be brought to him, those upon which his father David played. Another time, when King Solomon's heart became cheerful through wine, he ordered that wild beasts, birds of the sky, reptiles of the earth, as well as demons, spirits and screeching owls, be brought to dance before him, so as to show his greatness to all the kings who were hosted in his presence. Now the royal scribes would call them by their names, and all of them would assemble and come to him without being bound or forced or anyone leading them.

At that time the wild rooster was missing from among the fowl and could not be found. So the king ordered that it should be brought and in anger sought to destroy it. Then the wild rooster replied before King Solomon, saying to him,

> Hear my words, my lord, O king, incline your ear and listen (to) my utterances. Have not three months (passed) that I have given advice and counsel, my words are truth; I did not eat food, nor did I drink water before I flew throughout the whole world inspecting it, saying: Is there a country whose ruler is not subservient to my lord, O king? Whereupon I noticed a certain country in the land of the East, its name was the city of Qitor, whose dust is so precious and whose gold and silver exists like dung in the streets. Trees stand there since the time of creation, and they drink water from the Garden of Eden. Great crowds of people are there (with) crowns upon their heads, standing there since (the time of) the Garden of Eden. They do not know anything about waging war; they are unable to draw the bow. However, truly I have seen a single woman rule over all of them, and her name is Queen of Sheba. Now if it pleases my lord, I will gird my loins like a warrior and proceed to go to the city of Qitor, to the land of Sheba. I will bind their kings in chains and its rulers in fetters of iron and bring them to my lord, the king.

Then the scribes of the king were summoned, and they wrote a letter and tied the letter to the wing of the wild rooster, which proceeded to ascend heavenward and soared soaringly. It then flew among the birds, which proceeded to follow it in flight; they went on to the city of Qitor to the land of Sheba.

Toward morning the Queen of Sheba went out to worship the sea, when (suddenly) the birds obscured the sunlight, which caused her to take hold of her clothes and tear them. Whereupon she was very stunned. As she was in her very stunned state, the wild rooster descended toward her, and she observed a letter tied to its wing. So she untied (it) and read it; and what was written in it—

> From me, the kingdom of Solomon: Peace to you, peace to your princes. As you know, the Holy One, Blessed be He, appointed me to reign over the wild beasts, over the fowl of the heavens and over demons and spirits. Now all the kings of the East, the West, the South and the North come to greet me. Now if you wish to come and greet me, I will show you greater honor than all those whom I have hosted before me. But if you do not wish to come and greet me, I will send kings and legions against you (which belong) to King Solomon. The wild beasts are the kings, the fowl of the heavens are the riders, the armies

are the spirits, and the demons and the Liliths are the legions (who will) strangle you in your beds inside your houses; the wild beasts will kill you in the field; the fowl of the heavens (will) eat your flesh from you.

When the Queen of Sheba heard the words of the letter, she took hold of her clothes and tore them. She then summoned her elders and princes and said to them: "Do you not know what King Solomon sent to me?" They replied, saying, "We do not know King Solomon, nor do we recognize his kingdom." But she did not trust (them) and did not heed their words.

She then summoned all the ships of the sea and had them loaded with bracelets, pearls, and precious gems. She sent him six thousand boys and girls, all of whom were (born) the same time, all of whom were of the same stature, all of whom were of the same proportion, and all of whom were dressed in purple. She then wrote a letter and sent it to King Solomon through them from the city of Qitor to the Land of Israel, a seven-year journey: "And now, with prayer and supplication which I will plead before you, I will come to you at the end of three years."

Now it came about at the end of three years that the Queen of Sheba came to King Solomon. When it was told to King Solomon that the Queen of Sheba had arrived, he had Benayahu son of Yehoyada go out to meet her. His beauty was comparable to Venus that emerges at morning time, it was comparable to the lustrous star that continues to sparkle among the (other) stars, it was comparable to the lily that stands by the brooks of water.

When the Queen of Sheba saw Benayahu son of Yehoyada, she descended from her carriage. Whereupon Benayahu responded by saying to the Queen of Sheba: "Why have you descended from your carriage?" She replied by saying: "Are you King Solomon?" To which he responded by saying: "I am not King Solomon, but only one of his servants who attend him." Immediately she responded by uttering proverbs to her princes: "If you do not see the lion, you see his lair; though you do not see King Solomon, you do see a handsome man who stands before him."

Then Benayahu son of Yehoyada brought her before King Solomon. Now when King Solomon heard that she was coming to him, King Solomon arose and went to sit down in a bathhouse. When the Queen saw that the king was sitting in a bathhouse, she thought to herself the king must be sitting in water. So she raised her dress in order to wade across. Whereupon he noticed the hair on her leg, to which King Solomon responded by saying: "Your beauty is the beauty of women, but your hair is the hair of men. Now hair is beautiful for a man but shameful for a woman."

Whereupon the Queen of Sheba answered, saying to him: "O lord, king. I will cite you three riddles; if you will solve them for me I will acknowledge that you are a wise man, but if not, (you are) like the rest of mankind." Thereupon she asked: "What is a wooden well, an iron pale which draws up stones and brings forth worth?" He replied saying: "(It is) a makeup box." She continued asking: "What is the thing that emerges as dust from the earth, its food is dust from the earth, it pours out as water and sticks to the house?" He responded: "(It is) naphtha." She asked again, saying: "What is it that as an oracle goes ahead of all, cries out loudly and bitterly, its head is like a bulrush; it is a cause of praise to the free, of shame to the unfortunate; a cause of praise to the dead, of shame to the living, of joy to the birds, of agitation to the fish." He replied: (It is) flax." Whereupon she commented, saying to him: "I would not have believed it. Praiseworthy are your people, praiseworthy are these your servants."

Whereupon he brought her into the royal palace. Now when the Queen of Sheba saw the greatness and glory of King Solomon, she offered praise to the One Who created him, saying: "Blessed be the Lord, your God who has chosen you to place you on the throne of His kingdom to do righteousness and justice." She then gave the king a great deal of fine gold, while the king gave her what she desired. Now when the kings of the East and the West and the North and the South heard of his reputation, all of them together trembling came from their lands, with great honor and much dignity, as well as with gold and precious stones and pearls.

Note: In ancient Israel, bathhouses were elaborate facilities, designed for bathing, swimming, relaxing, and discussing politics. The largest bathhouse discovered by archeologists was near Sderot (along the border of the Gaza Strip). Its size was approximately twenty meters by twenty meters, contained at least six rooms, which included a changing room, separate rooms where cold and hot water tubs were available, and a sauna.

God? so bring your proofs if ye do speak the truth!

Catechism

65 Say, "None in the heavens or the earth know the unseen save only God; but they perceive not when they shall be raised!"
66 —nay, but their knowledge attains to somewhat of the hereafter; nay, but they are in doubt concerning it! nay, but they are blind!
67 And those who disbelieved said, "What! when we have become dust and our fathers too, shall we indeed be brought forth?
68 We were promised this, we and our fathers before us, this is nothing but old folks' tales!"
69 Say, "Journey on through the land and see how was the end of the sinners!
70 and grieve not for them, and be not straitened at what they plot."
71 They say, "When shall this threat be if ye do tell the truth?"
72 Say, "It may be that there is press-

ing close behind you a part of what ye would hasten on!"
73 But, verily, thy Lord is full of grace to men, but most of them will not be thankful;
74 and, verily, thy Lord knows what their breasts conceal and what they manifest;
75 and there is no secret thing in the heaven or the earth, save that it is in the perspicuous Book!

Qur'an

76 Verily, this Qur'ân relates to the people of Israel most of that whereon they do dispute;
77 and, verily, it is a guidance and a mercy to the believers.

*Two characteristics
of the infidels*

78 Verily, thy Lord decides between them by His judgment, for He is mighty, knowing.
79 Rely thou then upon God, verily, thou art standing on obvious truth.

and make their case.

27.65-75 The Muslim people were instructed to respond to the polytheists with three catechized arguments: (a) only Allah knows the invisible truths of the spirit world, including the resurrection from the dead, (b) look at the lives of sinful people to determine if their lives have lasting value, and (c) most sinners are unaware of the grace bestowed upon them from Allah and are therefore ungrateful.

27.75 *the perspicuous Book!* — Allah's Book

in Paradise that has every deed recorded—past, present, and future (see **The Perspicuous Book** on pp. 178-179).

27.78-81 Two characteristics of infidels: (a) they are spiritually dead and hence cannot hear or see spiritual truth, and (b) they will be marshaled before Allah and rebuked for their rejection of the Qur'an. In this respect, the Qur'an and the New Testament are in agreement. In reference to spiritual blindness, see Matt 15:14; 23:17-26 and Rev 3:17. In reference to the Day of Judgment,

80   Verily, thou canst not make the dead to hear, and thou canst not make the deaf to hear the call when they turn their backs on thee;

81   nor art thou a guide to the blind, out of their error: thou canst only make to hear such as believe in our signs, and such as are resigned.

Last Judgment

82   And when the sentence falls upon them we will bring forth a beast out of the earth that shall speak to them, (and say) that, "Men of our signs would not be sure."

83   And the day when we will gather from every nation a troop of those who said our signs were lies; and they shall be marshalled;

84   until they come, and He will say, "Did ye say my signs were lies, when ye had compassed no knowledge thereof? or what is it that ye were doing?"

85   and the sentence shall fall upon them for that they did wrong, and they shall not have speech.

86   Did they not see that we have made the night for them to rest in, and the day to see by? verily, in that are signs to people who believe.

87   And the day when the trumpet shall be blown and all who are in the heavens and the earth shall be startled, save whom God pleases! and all shall come abjectly to Him.

88   And thou shalt see the mountains, which thou dost deem solid, pass away like the passing of the clouds;—the work of God who orders all things; verily, He is well aware of what ye do!

89   He who brings a good deed shall have better than it; and from the alarm of that day they shall be safe:

90   but those who bring an evil deed shall be thrown down upon their faces in the fire. Shall ye be rewarded save for what ye have done?

Calling of Muhammad

91   I am bidden to serve the Lord of this country who has made it sacred, and whose are all things; and I am bidden to be of those who

see Matt 25:31-46; Acts 17:31; Rom 2:5; 2 Tim 4:1; Jude 15 and Rev 20:11.

27.87-88 The Last Judgment will commence with the blowing of a trumpet (cf. Matt 24:31; 1 Cor 15:52; 1 Thess 4:16; and Rev 8-10). Following the blowing of the trumpet, cataclysmic events will transpire on the earth, such as the passing away of the mountains.

27.89 Those who are rich in good deeds will enter into the blessedness of Paradise. Again, we see here a brief reference to the doctrine of meritocracy (see **The Last Judgment** on pp. 46-50).

27.90 *the fire —* This verse rightly parallels that which is taught in the New Testament in its depiction of the Last Judgment (see Matt 25:41; Mark 9:43-48; and Rev 20:14-15; see **Hell** on pp. 80-82).

27.91-93 *I am bidden to be of those who*

are resigned,

92 and to recite the Qur'ân; and he who is guided he is only guided for himself; and he who errs,— say, "I am only of those who warn!"

93 And say, "Praise be to God, He will show you His signs, and ye shall recognise them; for thy Lord is not heedless of what ye do!"

Surah 42

In the name of the merciful and compassionate God.

1 'H. M.

2 'H. S. Q.

Doxology

3 Thus does God, the mighty, the wise, inspire thee and those before thee.

4 His is what is in the heavens and what is in the earth, and He is the high, the mighty!

5 The heavens well-nigh cleave asunder from above them; and the angels celebrate the praises of their Lord, and ask forgiveness for those who are on the earth. Ay, verily,

---

are resigned — That is, Muhammad has been chosen to be one of the submissive ones to Allah.

27.92a *to recite the Qur'an* — Muhammad saw himself as the spokesperson for Allah, the reciter of the Qur'an.

27.92b *I am one of those who warn!* — That is, Muhammad saw himself as a warner, a divinely appointed apostle of Allah. It is one of Muhammad's favorite descriptions of himself: that of a warner and a reciter of the Qur'an.

Surah 42. The title of this surah, *The Counsel*, comes from verse 38. In this surah, Muhammad was faced with a theological problem. On the one hand, he insisted that Allah was Almighty God, the creator and sustainer of all that is. Nothing can thwart His will. On the other hand, most people were polytheists and idolaters—which means, in so many words, that they were thwarting His will. The purpose of this surah was to address this question pertaining to the sovereignty of Allah and the free will of man.

His answer was an appeal to the doctrine of double predestination. Those who turn to Allah were predestined to do so. Equally, those who rejected Allah were predestined to do so (see **The Doctrine of al-Qadar** on pp. 264-266).

This surah also begins and ends with an affirmation of Muhammad as Allah's divinely inspired messenger.

42.1-2 Literally, *Ha Mim. Ain Sin Qaf.* See 32.1 note.

42.3 This verse makes the case that Muhammad is not only inspired of God, he is included in a long line of other apostles that have been inspired and used of God. Later in the surah, a sample of these other apostles are mentioned: Noah, Abraham, Moses, and Jesus (v 13). He also characterized himself, once again, as a warner (v. 7).

42.7a Many Islamic scholars insist that the Qur'an must be read in the Arabic language to be rightly understood (see Q 12.2; 13.37; 20.113; 26.195; and 39.28).

In contrast, the Judeo-Christian tradition

God, He is the forgiving and merciful!

6   but those who take beside Him patrons, God watches over them, and thou hast not charge over them.

Arabic Qur'an

7   Thus have we revealed an Arabic Qur'ân, that thou mayest warn the Mother of cities and all around it; and warn them of a day of gathering, there is no doubt therein;—a part in Paradise and a part in the blaze.

The call for repentance

8   But had God pleased He would have made them one nation; but He makes whom He will enter into His mercy; and the unjust have neither patron nor help.

9   Do they take other patrons besides Him, when God He is the patron, and He quickens the dead and He is mighty over all?

10   But whatsoever ye dispute about, the judgment of it is God's. There is God for you!—my Lord! upon Him do I rely, and unto Him I turn repentant.

Allah's supreme sovereign authority

11   The originator of the heavens and the earth, He has made for you from yourselves wives; and of the cattle mates; producing you thereby. There is naught like Him, for He both hears and sees.

12   His are the keys of, the heavens and the earth, He extends provision to whom He will, or doles it out; verily, He knows everything.

Divine election

13   He has enjoined upon you for reli-

permits and encourages translations of both Old and New Testaments in the languages of the world. Though a degree of precision is lost in translations, it is not enough to outweigh the benefits of reading Scripture in one's mother tongue. Moreover, the New Testament apostles set the example by making use of the Septuagint (a widely recognized Greek translation of the OT) in their citations of the Old Testament in the New Testament documents.

42.7b *the Mother of cities* — Mecca, since in its center is the Ka'ba altar (see Q 6.92).

42.8-10 Repentance is necessary since God will one day quicken the dead. The implica-tion is that if people do not repent, they will face a merciless God at the Last Judgment (see **Last Judgment** on pp. 46-49).

42.11-12 Allah's sovereign authority is demonstrated in that He is: (a) the creator of the heavens and the earth, (b) the creator of wives for men, (c) the one who provides mates for the cattle, (d) the possessor of the keys of heaven and earth, and (e) is omniscient—knows everything. This summary parallels that which we find in the Bible pertaining to God (see Gen 1-2, Matt 16:19 and Rev. 1:18).

42.13-14 The fact that people turned away from the correct religion and into idolatry is

gion what He prescribed to Noah and what we inspired thee with, and what we inspired Abraham and Moses and Jesus,—to be steadfast in religion, and not to part into sects therein —a great thing to the idolaters is that which ye call them to! God elects for Himself whom He pleases and guides unto Himself him who turns repentant.

14 But they did not part into sects until after the knowledge had come to them, through mutual envy; and had it not been for thy Lord's word already passed for an appointed time, it would surely have been decided between them; but, verily, those who have been given the Book as an inheritance after them, are in hesitating doubt concerning it.

*The fundamentals of
Muhammad's ministry*

15 Wherefore call thou, and go straight on as thou art bidden, and follow not their lusts; and say, "I believe in the Book which God has sent down; and I am bidden to judge justly between you. God is our Lord and your Lord; we have our works and ye have your works; there is no argument between us and you. God will assemble us together and unto Him the journey is."

Divine wrath

16 But those who argue about God after it has been assented to, their arguments shall be rebutted before their Lord; and upon them shall be wrath, and for them shall be keen torment.

17 God it is who has sent down the Book with truth, and the balance; and what shall make thee know

because Allah called them into it. Hence, Allah predestines people to faithfulness and faithlessness (see **The Doctrine of al-Qadar** on pp. 264-266).

42.14, 15, 17 *the Book* — The eternal Book of Allah that exists in Paradise (see **The Perspicuous Book** on pp. 178-179).

42.15a The fundamentals of Muhammad's ministry are the following: (a) a declaration of loyalty to the Qur'an, (b) the discernment of the spirituality of people, and (c) a confidence that all disputes and debates will be settled at the Last Judgment.

42.15b *there is no argument between us and you* — Muhammad's behavior was wholly sanctioned and affirmed by Allah. This points

to an infallibility and purity to Muhammad's words and works, a belief widely held in the Muslim world today—the Doctrine of Isma (see Q 94.1-3, note).

42.17a *the Book* — This refers to any divine revelation that accompanied apostles sent from Allah (see Q 42.14, note).

42.17b *the balance* — This refers to the celestial balance that weighs a person's good and bad works. The direction of the tipping of this balance will determine one's eternal fate, whether one enters Paradise or Hell (see **The Last Judgment** on pp. 46-50).

42.17-18 *the Hour* — This refers to the moment in time when people will be summoned to the Last Judgment. At this Hour

whether haply the Hour be nigh?
18   Those who believe not would hurry it on; and those who believe shrink with terror at it and know that it is true. Ay, verily, those who dispute concerning the Hour are in remote error!

Divine blessings

19   God is kind to His servants; He provides whom He will, and He is the mighty, the glorious.
20   He who wishes for the tilth of the next world, we will increase for him the tilth; and he who desires the tilth of this world, we will give him thereof: but in the next he shall have no portion.
21   Have they associates who have enjoined any religion on them which God permits not?—but were it not for the word of decision it would have been decreed to them. Verily, the unjust,—for them is grievous woe.
22   Thou shalt see the unjust shrink with terror from what they have gained as it falls upon them; and those who believe and do right, in meads of Paradise, they shall have what they please with their Lord;—that is great grace!
23   That is what God gives glad tidings of to His servants who believe and do righteous acts. Say, "I do not ask for it a hire —only the love of my kinsfolk." And he who gains a good action we will increase good for him thereby; verily, God is forgiving and grateful!
24   Or will they say he has forged against God a lie? But if God pleased He could set a seal upon thy heart; but God will blot out falsehood and verify truth by His word; verily, He knows the nature of men's breasts!
25   He it is who accepts repentance from His servants and pardons their offences and knows that which ye do.
26   And He answers the prayer of those who believe and do right, and gives

during the Last Judgment.

42.20 According to Muhammad, those who seek the blessings in the afterlife will live accordingly and be granted such blessings. Those who have no interest in the afterlife will live accordingly on earth and forfeit the blessings of the afterlife.

42.20 *tilth* — This refers to a plot of land useful for planting crops

42.21 *the word of decision* — It is Allah who decides whether a person is elected to Paradise or to Hell.

42.22 *great grace* — This refers to the blessings of Paradise.

42.22-23 *believe and do right* — These words are repeated often in the Qur'an and serve as a brief summary of the Islamic gospel (see Q 103.3 note).

42.23 The point here is that righteous acts should not be performed for personal gain (cf. Matt 6:16-18).

42.24-26 *He knows the nature of men's breasts* — Only God knows all things, including whether or not our repentance is genuine or tainted with hypocrisy.

42.26 *believe and do right* — These words

them increase of His grace; but the misbelievers,—for them is keen torment.

Various ways in which God communicates with people

27 And if God were to extend provision to His servants they would be wanton in the earth. But He sends down by measure what He pleases; verily, of His servants He is well aware and sees.

28 He it is who sends down the rain after they have despaired; and disperses His mercy, for He is the praiseworthy patron.

29 And of His signs is the creation of the heavens and the earth, and what He hath spread abroad therein of beasts; and He is able to collect them when He will.

30 And what misfortunes befall you it is for what your hands have earned; but He pardons much;

31 yet ye cannot make Him helpless in the earth, nor have ye, besides God, either a patron or a helper.

32 And of His signs are the ships that sail like mountains in the sea.

33 If He will, He calms the wind, and they become motionless on the back thereof: verily, in that are signs to every patient, grateful person:

34 —or He makes them founder for what they have earned; but He pardons much.

35 But let those who wrangle about our signs know that they shall have no escape!

Characteristics of godliness

36 And whatever ye are given it is but a provision of the life of this world; but what is with God is better and more lasting for those who believe and who upon their Lord rely,

37 and those who avoid great sins and abominations, and who when they are wroth forgive,

38 and who assent to their Lord, and are steadfast in prayer, and whose affairs go by counsel amongst themselves, and who of what we have bestowed on them give alms,

39 and who, when wrong befalls them, help themselves.

40 For the recompence of evil is evil like unto it; but he who pardons

---

are repeated often in the Qur'an and serve as a brief summary of the Islamic gospel (see Q 103.3 note).

42.27-35 Allah's signs (ways in which He communicates with people) are: (a) rain, (b) the animals of the earth, (c) the existence of the heavens and the earth, (d) divine pardon, and (e) wind which enables ships to sail.

42.37 Summary of the righteous life: (a) avoid the great sins and abominations, (b) forgive those who sin against them, (c) strive after God, (d) be steadfast in prayer, (e) follow good counsel, (f) be generous in the giving of alms, and (g) seek social justice. All who follow this path will be rewarded with eternal life.

42.40 According to Muhammad, for the

and does well, then his reward is with God; verily, He loves not the unjust.

41 And he who helps himself after he has been wronged, for these—there is no way against them.

42 The way is only against those who wrong men and are wanton in the earth without right; these—for them is grievous woe.

43 But surely he who is patient and forgives,—verily, that is a determined affair.

Characteristics of ungodliness

44 But whomsoever God leads astray he has no patron after Him; and thou mayest see the unjust when they see the torment say, "Is there no way to avert this?"

45 and thou mayest see them exposed to it, humbled with abasement, looking with a stealthy glance. And those who believe shall say, "Verily, the losers are they who have lost themselves and their families too upon the resurrection day!" Ay, verily, the unjust are in lasting torment!

46 And they shall have no patrons to help them beside God, and whomsoever God leads astray, there is no way for him.

47 Assent to your Lord before the day comes of which there is no averting from God; there is no refuge for you on that day; and for you there is no denial.

48 But if they turn aside, we have not sent thee to them as a guardian, thou hast only thy message to preach. And, verily, when we have made man taste of mercy from us he rejoices therein; but if there befall them an evil for what their hands have done before—then, verily, man is ungrateful!

The sovereignty of God

49 God's is the kingdom of the heavens and the earth, He creates what He pleases, He grants to whom He pleases females, and He grants to whom He pleases males, or

50 He gives them in pairs, males and females and He makes whom He pleases barren; verily, He is knowing, powerful!

one who has been wronged, he is to address the wrong and work towards a just resolution. Yet, a higher good can be achieved by forgiving the wrongdoer and demanding no retribution for the wrong committed. This is because the possibilities of a genuine peace is greater. In addition, one receives a special reward from Allah.

42.44-48 Characteristics of ungodliness: (a) they will eventually regret their rejection of true godliness, (b) are losers, (c) are led astray by God, and (d) ungrateful.

42.46 *whomsoever God leads astray* — This is a reference to the doctrine of double predestination (see **The Doctrine of al-Qadar** on pp. 264-266).

42.51 It is not for any mortal that Allah should speak to him or her, except: (a) via

Muhammad:
a divinely inspired guide

51   It is not for any mortal that God should speak to him, except by inspiration, or from behind a veil, or by sending an apostle and inspiring, by His permission, what He pleases; verily, He is high and wise!

52   And thus have we inspired thee by a spirit at our bidding; thou didst not know what the Book was, nor the faith: but we made it a light whereby we guide whom we will of our servants. And, verily, thou shalt surely be guided into the right way,

53   —the way of God, whose is what is in the heavens and what is in the earth. Ay, to God affairs do tend!

Surah 40

In the name of the merciful and compassionate God.

1   'H. M.

Qur'an

2   The sending down of the Book from God, the mighty, the knowing,

3   the forgiver of sin and accepter of repentance, keen at punishment, long-suffering! there is no god but He! to whom the journey is!

People who wrangle
with God's revelation

4   None wrangle concerning the signs

inspiration, (b) from behind the veil, and/or (c) via an apostle. The first approach points to a divinely inspired document. The second approach points to the enlightenment from within one's own mind. The third approach points to the declarative statements from a prophet.

42.52 According to this verse, Allah sovereignly chose Muhammad to be His prophet.

42.52 *the Book* — This is the eternal Book of Allah guarded in Paradise (see **The Perspicuous Book** on pp. 178-179).

42.53 *the way of God* — The right direction, the path to eternal life (see Q 72.2, note).

Surah 40. The title of this surah, *The Believer*, comes from verse 28. This surah is a call to the Muslim believers to remain steadfast in their faith to Allah and the Qur'an. With this in mind, a major theme is the con-

trast of the fate of the believers (Paradise) with that of the infidels (Hell). The phrase "O my people" is repeated six times, which illustrates the surah's sermonic tone.

40.1 Literally, *Ha Mim*. See Q 32.1, note.

40.2 The Qur'an is described as being sent down from heaven (see **The Qur'an** on pp. 150-153).

40.3 *there is no god but He* — The Doctrine of Tauhid (see Q 112, note).

40.4-6 According to Muhammad, the way in which the people of Mecca rejected the ministry and message of Muhammad was no different than the way in which people always rejected Allah's appointed spokesperson: with contempt and derision. This pattern reaches as far back as far as the antediluvian Noahic Age. And, in each case, the infidels were judged by Allah and cast into "the Fire" (Hell).

of God but those who misbelieve; then let not their going to and fro in the cities deceive thee.

5   The people of Noah before them called the prophets liars; and the confederates after them; and every nation schemed against their Apostle to catch him. And they wrangled with falsehood that they might refute the truth thereby, but I seized them, and how was my punishment!

6   Thus was the sentence of thy Lord due against those who misbelieved, that they are the fellows of the Fire!

*People who accept
God's revelation*

7   Those who bear the throne and those around it celebrate the praise of their Lord, and. believe in Him, and ask pardon for those who believe: "Our Lord! thou dost embrace all things in mercy and knowledge, then pardon those who turn repentant and follow thy way,

and guard them from the torment of hell!

8   Our Lord! make them enter into gardens of Eden which thou hast promised to them, and to those who do well of their fathers, and their wives, and their seed; verily, thou art the mighty, the wise!

9   and guard them from evil deeds, for he whom thou shalt guard from evil deeds on that day, thou wilt have had mercy on, and that is mighty bliss!"

Future regrets

10   Verily, those who misbelieve shall be cried out to, "Surely, God's hatred is greater than your hatred of each other when ye were called unto the faith and misbelieved?"

11   They shall say, "Our Lord! Thou hast killed us twice, and Thou hast quickened us twice; and we do confess our sins: is there then a way for getting out?"

12   That is because when God alone

In the New Testament, we see similar observations (see Matt 23:30-39; Acts 7:51-52; 1 Thess 2:15).

40.7 *those who bear the throne and those around it* — This is a reference to the angels of Paradise. The angels offer prayers to God, beseeching Him to pardon those who repent of their sins and turn to God.

40.8 *Garden of Eden* — That is, the gardens in Paradise (also see Q 16.31; 18.31; 19.61; 20.76; 35.33; 38.50).

40.11a *thou hast killed us twice* — The first death occurs at the close of their life on

earth; the second death occurs when cast into Hell.

40.11b *thou hast quickened us twice* — The first quickening occurs at the moment of birth (or conception). The second quickening occurs at the moment of resurrection when they stand before God at the Last Judgment.

40.11-12 Those who will be cast into Hell will repent of their sins, yet to no avail because it has come too late (cf Phil 2:11; Heb 9:27).

40.12 *God, the high, the great* — This

was proclaimed ye did disbelieve; but when partners were joined to Him ye did believe; but judgment belongs to God, the high, the great!

Call for repentance

13 He it is who shows you His signs, and sends down to you from heaven provision; but none is mindful except him who turns repentant;

14 then call on God, being sincere in your religion to Him, averse although the misbelievers be!

The ministry of the warner

15 Exalted of degrees! The Lord of the throne! He throws the spirit by His bidding upon whom He will of His servants, to give warning of the day of meeting.

16 The day when they shall be issuing forth, naught concerning them shall be hidden from God. Whose is the kingdom on that day?— God's, the one, the dominant!

17 today shall every soul be recompensed for that which it has earned. There is no wrong today; verily, God is quick at reckoning up!

18 And warn them of the day that approaches, when hearts are choking in the gullets; those who do wrong shall have no warm friend, and no intercessor who shall be obeyed.

19 He knows the deceitful of eye and what men's breasts conceal,

20 and God decides with truth; but those they call on beside Him do not decide at all: verily, God, He both hears and looks.

phrase, in the Muslim world, is called Takbir (*Allahu akbar*). See Q 34.23 note.

40.13 *him who turns repentant* — Repentance is a major theme in the Qur'an. It is turn from unbelief to belief and from evil works to works of righteousness—specifically, fulfilling the Five Pillars that serve as the foundation of Islamic theology. In the Islamic faith, then, entrance into Paradise is based upon a system of merit (see **The Last Judgment** on pp. 46-50).

In the Christian faith, salvation is based upon faith—apart from the works of the law (Gal 2:16; Eph 2:8-10; 2 Tim 1:9 and Titus 3:3-8). This disagreement of salvation by the works of the law (Islam) versus salvation by faith apart from the works of the law (Christianity) is one of the major dividing lines between the two religions.

40.15a *Exalted of degrees* — That is, the Lord of the throne is exalted above every created thing.

40.15b Allah sovereignly chooses the ones whom will be his warners—that is, prophets or apostles. It is not an office that one vaingloriously aspires to. The Meccan people believed that Muhammad had chosen himself to such an office.

The Christian religion agrees with this assessment. A person is divinely chosen to such a high office. Yet the Christian religion would also agree that the Meccan people had rightly identified Muhammad as a false prophet (see Gal 1:6-9).

40.20 *those they call on beside Him* — That is, their false gods.

The fate of
previous infidels

21   Have they not journeyed on in the
      earth and seen how was the end
      of those who journeyed on before
      them? They were stronger than
      them in might, and their vestiges
      are in the land; but God caught
      them up in their sins, and they had
      none to guard them against God.

22   That is for that their apostles did
      come to them with manifest signs,
      and they misbe-lieved, and God
      caught them up; verily, He is
      mighty, keen to punish!

The example of Pharaoh,
Haman, and Korah

23   And we did send Moses with our
      signs, and with obvious authority,

24   unto Pharaoh and Hâmân and
      Qarûn. They said, "A lying sor-
      cerer!"

25   and when they came to them with
      truth from us, they said, "Kill the
      sons of those who believe with
      him, and let their women live!" but
      the stratagem of the misbelievers
      is only in error!

26   And Pharaoh said, "Let me kill
      Moses; and then let him call upon
      his Lord! verily, I fear that he will
      change your religion, or that he will
      cause evil doing to appear in the
      land."

27   And Moses said, "Verily, I take ref-
      uge in my Lord and your Lord from

40.22 *He is mighty, keen to punish* — Muhammad encouraged the people of Mecca
to consider the fate of people of times past
who resisted God.

40.23-38 Muhammad drew on three historical people who resisted Allah and suffered
accordingly: Pharaoh, Qarun, and Haman.
Qarun (Korah) was a Hebrew who resisted
Moses. Haman, according to this passage,
was an Egyptian advisor and builder, who
sided with Pharaoh against Moses. Scholars,
however, have not been able to verify this
person in Egyptian history. He is neither mentioned in the Egyptian annals nor in the Old
Testament.

It has been suggested by scholars that
Muhammad conflated three stories into one:
the story of Esther where Haman is mentioned (Esther 3-9), the story of Moses (Ex
5-13), and the story of the building of the
Tower of Babel (Gen 11:1-8). Marraccio, con-

fessor to Pope Innocent XI in 1698 noted in
his Latin translation of the Qur'an: "Mahumet
[Muhammad] has mixed up Sacred stories.
He took Haman as the advisor of Pharaoh
whereas in reality he was an advisor of
Ahasuerus, King of Persia. He also thought
that Pharaoh ordered construction for him
of a lofty tower from the story of the Tower
of Babel. It is certain that in the Sacred
Scriptures there is no such story of the Pharaoh. Be that as it may, he has related a
most incredible story" (also see Q 28.4-13,
36-38 where Haman is again mentioned).
Moreover, the dialogues in this section are
imaginative inventions by Muhammad. They
are not found in any other documents (biblical or otherwise).

40.28 In this story, the unidentified man is
best understood to be Muhammad's alter-
ego. This is because he echoed Muhammad's
own words that he had previously spoken

every one who is big with pride and believes not on the day of reckoning."

28 And a believing man of Pharaoh's people, who concealed his faith, said, "Will ye kill a man for saying, 'My Lord is God, when he has come to you with manifest signs from your Lord? and if he be a liar, against him is his lie; and if he be truthful, there will befall you somewhat of that which he threatens you; verily, God guides not him who is an extravagant liar.'

29 O my people! yours is the kingdom today, ye are eminent in the land, but who will help us against the violence of God, if it comes upon us?" Said Pharaoh, "I will only show you what I see, and I will only guide you into the way of right direction."

30 And he who believed said, "O my people! verily, I fear for you the like of the day of the confederates,

31 the like of the wont of the people of Noah and 'Âd and Hâmân, and

of those after them; for God desires not injustice for His servants.

32 O my people! verily, I fear for you the day of crying out,

33 —the day when ye shall turn your backs, fleeing, with no defender for you against God; for he whom God leads astray, for him there is no guide!

34 And Joseph came to you before with manifest signs, but ye ceased not to doubt concerning what he brought you, until, when he perished, ye said, 'God will not send after him an apostle;' thus does God lead astray him who is extravagant, a doubter.

35 Those who wrangle concerning the signs of God without authority having come to them are greatly hated by God and by those who believe; thus does God set a stamp upon the heart of every tyrant too big with pride!"

36 And Pharaoh said, "O Hâmân! build for me a tower, haply I may reach the tracts,

---

to the people of Mecca in other surahs. The point of the believing man is threefold: (a) speaking lies about Allah is no justification for putting a man to death, (b) Allah will deal directly with the one who lies on Allah's behalf, and (c) if the man is speaking the truth and another person should kill him, he will face a divine retribution.

40.29-35 Again, the unidentified man (Muhammad's alter-ego) continued in his criticism of Pharaoh (and, by extension, the leaders of Mecca). This man commented that: (a) the kingdom of Allah is before the people,

(b) if believers are not courageous in their struggle against unbelievers, they will all suffer the same fate, and (c) Allah leads astray the proud and extravagant—that is, the infidels.

40.35 *does God set a stamp upon the heart* — Allah sets a seal on the hearts of those who do not know the truth. The stamp prevents them from attaining to a life of belief and obedience (see Q 4.155; 7.100-101; 9.87, 93; 10.74; 16.108; 30.59; 47.16; 63.3; *The Doctrine of al-Qadar* on pp. 264-266).

40.36-38 This passage is a conflation of

37   —the tracts of heaven, and may mount up to the God of Moses, for, verily, I think him a liar." And thus was his evil deed made seemly to Pharaoh, and he was turned from the way; but Pharaoh's stratagem ended only in ruin,

38   and he who believed said, O my people! follow me, I will guide you to the way of the right direction.

A plea

39   O my people! verily, the life of this world is but a provision, but, verily, the hereafter, that is the abode of stability!

40   Whoso does evil, he shall only be recompensed with the like thereof; and whoso does right, be it male or female and a believer, these shall enter into Paradise; they shall be provided therein without count.

41   O my people! why should I call you to salvation, and you call me to the fire?

42   Ye call on me to disbelieve in God, and to join with Him what I have no knowledge of; but I call you to

the mighty forgiving One!

43   no doubt that what ye call me to, ought not to be called on in this world or in the hereafter, and that we shall be sent back to God, and that the extravagant, they are the fellows of the Fire!

The fire

44   But ye shall remember what I say to you; and I entrust my affair to God, verily, God looks upon His servants!"

45   And God guarded him from the evils of what they plotted, and there closed in upon Pharaoh evil woe.

46   The fire—they shall be exposed to it morning and evening; and "on the day the Hour shall arise," enter, O people of Pharaoh! into the keenest torment.

47   And when they argue together in the fire, and the weak say to those who were big with pride, "Verily, we were followers of yours, can ye then avail us against a portion of the fire?"

48   Those who were big with pride shall say, "Verily, we are all in it;

the stories of the Tower of Babel (Gen 11:1-8), the story of the exodus (Ex 5-13), and the Book of Esther. Etymologically speaking, the name *Haman* is rooted in Persia, not Egypt, which offers further evidence that Muhammad conflated the two stories (see Q 28.4-13, 36-38).

40.39-43 Muhammad pleaded with his listeners to give priority to the afterlife. His

argument echoed the argument of "the believing man"—Muhammad's alter-ego (vv 28-38).

40.44-50 Three characteristics of Hell: (a) unending torments of fire, (b) people in Hell will plead for leniency, and (c) their calls for mercy will be unheeded.

40.46 *the Hour* — This refers to the hour when people will be resurrected from the

verily, God has judged between His servants."

49 And those who are in the fire shall say unto the keepers of hell, "Call upon your Lord to lighten from us one day of the torment."

50 They shall say, "Did not your apostles come to you with manifest signs?" They shall say, "Yea!" They shall say, "Then, call!"—but the call of the misbelievers is only in error.

A plea for patience

51 Verily, we will help our apostles, and those who believe, in the life of this world and on the day when the witnesses shall stand up:

52 the day when their excuse shall not avail the unjust; but for them is the curse, and for them is an evil abode.

53 And we did give Moses the guidance; and we made the children of Israel to inherit the Book,

54 as a guidance and a reminder to those endowed with minds.

55 Be thou patient, then; verily, God's promise is true: and ask thou forgiveness for thy sins, and celebrate the praise of thy Lord in the evening and in the morn.

56 Verily, those who wrangle concerning the signs of God without authority having come to them, there is naught in their breasts but pride; but they shall not attain it: do thou then seek refuge in God; verily, He both hears and looks!

57 Surely the creation of the heavens and the earth is greater than the creation of man: but most men know it not.

58 The blind and the seeing shall not be deemed alike, nor those who believe and do right and the evildoer; little is it that they remember.

59 Verily, the Hour will surely come; there is no doubt therein; but most men do not believe!

A call to monotheism

---

dead and placed before Allah at the Last Judgment (see Q 79.42, note).

40.51-59 The plea: since Allah will help people in this life and the afterlife, believers are called upon to remain patient, seek Allah's forgiveness for past sins, and worship God every morning and evening. They will avoid the fate of Hell that will befall all infidels (see **Divine Forgiveness in Islam** on pp. 158-161).

40.53 *the Book* — This initially meant the Pentateuch and eventually the entire Old Testament. Muhammad acknowledged that it was a reliable guidance (that is, accurate words) for those who read it (see Q 15.9, note).

40.58a *the blind* — In the Bible, the unbeliever is characterized as being blind (cf. Isa 56:10-11; 23:16-26; Jn 9:39-41).

40.58b *believe and do right* — These words are repeated often in the Qur'an and serve as a brief summary of the Islamic gospel (see Q 103.3 note).

40.59 *the Hour* — This refers to the hour

60   And your Lord said, "Call upon me, I will answer you; verily, those who are too big with pride to worship shall enter into hell, shrinking up."

61   God it is who has made for you the night to repose therein, and the day to see by; verily, God is Lord of grace to men, but most men give no thanks!

62   There is God for you! your Lord! the creator of everything! there is no god but He, how then can ye lie?

63   Thus did those lie who gainsaid the signs of God.

64   God it is who has made for you the earth as a resting-place, and a heaven as building, and has formed you and made excellent your forms; and has provided you with good things! there is God for you!—your Lord! then blessed be God, the Lord of the worlds!

65   He is the living One, there is no god but He! then call on Him, being sin-cere in your religion to Him; praise be to God, the Lord of the worlds!

66   Say, "Verily, I am forbidden to serve those whom ye call on beside God, since there have come to me manifest signs from my Lord, and I am bidden to be resigned unto the Lord of the worlds."

67   He it is who created you from the earth, then from a clot, then from congealed blood, then He brings you forth a child; then ye reach to puberty; then do ye become old men,—though of you there are some who are taken away before,—that ye may reach an appointed time, and haply ye may have some sense.

68   He it is who quickens and kills, and when He decrees a matter, then He only says to it, "BE," and it is.

A call for
commitment to God

69   Hast thou not seen those who

when all people are resurrected from the dead and summoned to the Last Judgment (see Q 79.42, note).
40.62 *there is no god but He* — Once again, Muhammad drew the listener to the Doctrine of Tauhid, an absolute monotheism (see Q 112, note).
40.65 *the Lord of the worlds* — This is a common term for Allah (see Q 1.2, note).
40.66 This recitation closely parallels the First Pillar of Islam. The one feature missing is an affirmation that Muhammad is the prophet of Allah. Yet an allusion to this sec-ond feature is found in vv. 78-85.
40.67 According to Muhammad, the human being was created from the earth, a clot and then congealed blood (see Q 96.2). No scientific evidence supports this claim.
40.68a *He it is who quickens and kills* — cf. Job 1:21; Eccl. 12:7.
40.68b *BE"* — Allah's sovereignty over all creation is illustrated in the fact that all He needs to do is say one word—be—and whatever it is He wishes comes into existence (see Q 3.47, 59; 16.40; 19.35; 36.82).
40.70 *the Book* —This refers to the eternal

wrangle concerning the signs of God how they are turned away?

70 Those who call the Book, and what we have sent our apostles with, a lie, soon shall they know

71 —when the fetters are on their necks and the chains,

72 as they are dragged into hell!—then in the fire shall they be baked.

73 Then it shall be said to them, "Where is what ye did associate

74 beside God?" They shall say, "They have strayed away from us; nay, we did not call before upon anything!"—thus does God lead the misbelievers astray.

75 There! for that ye did rejoice in the land without right; and for that ye did exult;

76 enter ye the gates of hell, to dwell therein for aye; for evil is the resort of those who are too big with pride!

77 But be thou patient; verily, the promise of God is true; and whether we show thee a part of what we promised them, or whether we surely take thee to ourself, unto us shall they be returned.

*A call for commitment
to God's revelation*

78 And we did send apostles before thee: of them are some whose stories we have related to thee, and of them are some whose stories we have not related to thee; and no apostle might ever bring a sign except by the permission of God; but when God's bidding came it was decided with truth, and there were those lost who deemed it vain!

79 God it is who has made for you cattle, that ye may ride on some of them;—and of them ye eat,

80 and ye have in them advantages;—and that ye may attain thereon a want which is in your breasts; upon them and upon ships are ye borne.

81 He shows you His signs; which sign then of your Lord do ye deny?

82 Have they not journeyed on in the

Book in Paradise, guarded by Allah, sent to the apostles on earth (see **The Perspicuous Book** on pp. 178-179).

40.70-75 A number of people in Mecca described Muhammad's surahs as lies. Muhammad prophesied that at the Last Judgment they will be cast into Hell because of their unbelief in the surahs (the Qur'an).

40.74 Because of Muhammad's belief in Allah's absolute sovereign rule, those who rejected his ministry did so because they were predestined to reject his ministry (see **The Doctrine of al-Qadar** on pp. 264-266).

40.78 Throughout the Qur'an, a number of apostles have been mentioned, including Adam, Noah, Abraham, Lot, Moses, David, Solomon, Jesus, Hud, Zali'h, and Loqman. The apostle most often mentioned in the Qur'an, of course, is Muhammad (see **The Apostles** on pp. 398-400).

40.81 *signs* — supernatural acts, such as miracles or divinely inspired words.

land and seen how was the end of those before them, who were more numerous than they and stronger in might, and in their vestiges which are still in the land? but of no avail to them was that which they had earned.

83 And when there came to them their apostles with manifest signs they rejoiced in what knowledge they had; but there closed in upon them that whereat they had mocked.

84 And when they saw our violence they said, "We believe in God alone, and we disbelieve in what we once associated with Him."

85 But their faith was of no avail to them when they saw our violence—the course of God with His servants in time past, and there the misbelievers lose!

Surah 38

In the name of the merciful and compassionate God.

1   S.

Characteristics of infidels

By the Qur'ân with its reminder!

2   nay, but those who misbe-lieve are in pride, schism!

3   How many a generation have we destroyed before them, and they cried out, but it was no time to escape!

4   And they wonder that a warner has come from amongst themselves, and the misbelievers say, "This is a magician, a liar!"

5   What! does he make the gods to

Surah 38. The title of this surah, *Suad*, comes from verse one. This surah is a reminder for Muslims to stay committed to Allah and the ministry of Muhammad. All who do not will be subject to a severe divine judgment. Muhammad drew upon several Old Testament patriarchs to make his case. He also drew upon the ministry of Satan (Iblis) whose role is to deceive as many people as he can to make his case. Once again, this surah is a return to the familiar themes of Paradise and Hell as a motivators to live righteously.

38.1a Literally, *Suad.* See Q 32.1 note.

38.1b-20 Infidels are characterized by: (a) pride, (b) schisms, (c) deep regrets, (d) rejections of the warners—apostles—who have spoken to them, (e) commitments to their false gods, and (f) rejection of divine revela-

tion.

38.4a *a warner has come from amongst themselves* — This is one of Muhammad's favorite titles for himself.

38.4b A constant complaint directed to Muhammad by the Meccan people was that he was a liar (see Q 26.6, 12; 35.4; 52.11; 67.9; and 68.8).

38.4-7 The Meccan people ridiculed Muhammad, accusing him of attempting to take all the gods in the Arabic Star Family pantheon and merging them into a single God—Allah. The chiefs of the people called Muhammad's message "a fiction" and advised the people to persevere with the worship of their gods.

38.10 *let them climb up the ropes thereof* — Let them climb up the ropes to Paradise, if they can. This verse is best understood as

be one God? verily, this is a wondrous thing.

6   And the chiefs of them went away:
     "Go on and persevere in your gods;
     this is a thing designed;

7   we never heard this in any other
     sect; this is nothing but a fiction!

8   Has a reminder come down upon
     him from amongst us?" nay, they
     are in doubt concerning my re-
     minder; nay, they have not yet
     tasted of my torment!

9   Have they the treasures of the
     mercy of thy mighty Lord, the
     giver?

10   or have they the kingdom of the
     heavens and of the earth, and what
     is between the two?—then let them
     climb up the ropes thereof.

11   Any host whatever of the confed-
     erates shall there be routed.

Examples from the past

12   Before them did Noah's people,
     and 'Âd, and Pharaoh of the stakes
     call the apostles liars;

13   and Thamûd and the people of Lot,
     and the fellows of the Grove, they
     were the confederates too.

14   They all did naught but call the
     apostles liars, and just was the pun-
     ishment!

15   Do these await aught else but one
     noise for which there shall be no
     pause?

16   But they say, "O our Lord, hasten
     for us our share before the day of
     reckoning!"

Example of David

17   Be patient of what they say, and
     remember our servant David en-
     dowed with might;

18   verily, he turned frequently to us.
     Verily, we subjected the mountains
     to celebrate with him our praises
     at the evening and the dawn;

19   and the birds too gathered together,
     each one would oft return to him;

20   and we strengthened his kingdom,
     and we gave him wisdom and de-
     cisive address.

---

a fanciful hyperbole (exaggerated speech)
directed back to the Meccan people.

38.12a *Noah's people* — the antediluvian
people who perished in the Great Flood (see
Gen 6:11-12).

38.12b *Ad* — This is a legendary city in the
Syrian desert (see Q 89.6 note).

38.12c *Pharaoh* — the Pharaoh of the Hebrew exodus from Egypt (see Gen 5-13).

38.13a *Thamud* — This is a people who
lived in the seventh century B.C. to the second century A.D. in the northern Arabian
Desert. See Q 91 note.

38.13b *the people of Lot* — That is, the
people of Sodom (see Gen 19:1-29).

38.13c *fellows of the Grove* — Literally, the
people of Madyan (Midian). See Q 26.176
note.

38.15 *one noise* — This is the mysterious
noise that brings divine judgment upon a rebellious people (see Q 54.22-31, note).

38.19 Muhammad believed that the kings
of ancient Israel made use of birds as scouts
in their armies. These kings were enabled
to communicate with birds and thereby
gained valuable intelligence about the en-

21   Has there come to thee the story of the antagonists when they scaled the chamber wall?

22   when they entered in unto David, and he was startled at them, they said, "Fear not, we are two antagonists; one of us has injured the other; judge then between us with the truth and be not partial, but guide us to a level way.

23   Verily, this is my brother: he had ninety-nine ewes and I had one ewe; and he said, 'Give her over to my charge;' and he overcame me in the discourse."

24   Said he [David], "He wronged thee in asking for thy ewe in addition to his own ewes. Verily, many associates do injure one another, except those who believe and do what is right, and very few are they!" And he thought that we were trying him; and he asked pardon of his Lord and fell down bowing, and did turn;

25   and we pardoned him; for, verily, he has a near approach to us and an excellent resort.

26   O David! verily, we have made thee a vicegerent, judge then between men with truth and follow not lust, for it will lead thee astray from the path of God. Verily, those who go astray from the path of God, for them is keen torment, for that they did forget the day of reckoning!

*The sovereignity
of Allah*

27   And we have not created the heavens and the earth, and what is between the two, in vain. That is what those who misbelieved did think, but woe from the fire to those who misbelieve!

28   Shall we make those who believe and do right like those who do evil in the earth? or shall we make the pious like the sinners?

29   A blessed Book which we have sent down to thee that they may con-

emy.

38.21-26 This passage addressed King David's act of adultery with Bathsheba. According to the story, as presented in 2 Samuel 11-12, David saw Bathsheba disrobed and bathing one day, lusted after her, and soon afterwards committed adultery with her. When he learned that she was pregnant, he had her husband Uriah the Hittite killed. He then married her. It was then that Nathan the Prophet confronted David of his sin, using the story of sheep to make his point.

The story, as presented in the Qur'an, roughly parallels the biblical account. The principal difference is that Muhammad had two "antagonists" scaling a wall and confronting David, rather than Nathan the Prophet, who confronted David without scaling a wall.

38.24 *believe and do what is right* — These words are repeated often in the Qur'an and serve as a brief summary of the Islamic gospel (see Q 103.3, note).

38.26 *vicegerent* — Literally, a *caliph* (see Q 35.39, note).

38.28 *believe and do right* — These words are repeated often in the Qur'an and serve as a brief summary of the Islamic gospel (see Q 103.3, note).

sider its verses, and that those endowed with minds may be mindful.

Example of Solomon

30 And we gave to David, Solomon, an excellent servant; verily, he turned frequently to us.

31 When there were set before him in the evening the steeds that paw the ground,

32 and he said, "Verily, I have loved the love of good things better than the remembrance of my Lord, until (the sun) was hidden behind the veil;

33 bring them back to me;" and he be-

34 gan to sever their legs and necks. And we did try Solomon, and we threw upon his throne a form; then he turned repentant.

35 Said he, "My Lord, pardon me and grant me a kingdom that is not seemly for any one after me; verily, thou art He who grants!"

36 And we subjected to him the wind to run on at his bidding gently wherever he directed it;

37 and the devils—every builder and diver,

38 and others bound in fetters

39 —"this is our gift, so be thou lavish or withhold without account!"

40 And, verily, he had with us a near approach, and a good resort.

38.29 *A blessed Book* — The Qur'an is described as being "sent down" to Muhammad (see **The Perspicuous Book** on pp. 178-179).

38.30-33 This passage presents the time when Solomon turned away from the Lord and became enamored with the things of this world. The Bible makes a similar observation: "He [Solomon] followed Ashtoreth the goddess of the Sidonians, and Molech the detestable god of the Ammonites. So Solomon did evil in the eyes of the Lord; he did not follow the Lord completely, as David his father had done" (1 Kings 11:5-6).

38.34 A number of Islamic scholars have attempted to explain the meaning of this verse. One commentator claimed that Solomon gave his magical signet ring to one of his wives who, in turn, gave it to Satan who then sat down on the throne. After forty days, Satan flew away and cast the ring into the sea. It was then swallowed by a fish. A

fisherman unknowingly caught the fish and gave it to Solomon for food. When Solomon cut open the fish, he saw the ring and gave praise to the Lord (see *The History of al-Tabari*, vol. 3, pp. 170-172).

A second commentator claimed that when a son was born to Solomon, the demons who had been made subservient to Solomon, plotted to kill the son. When Solomon learned of their plot, he caused his son to rise up into the clouds so that he could hide him. He, however, was surprised when Allah set a dead body on the throne in his place. This prompted Solomon to turn in repentance to Allah (see the account by al-Zamukhshari in *The Qur'an and its Exegesis*, pp. 107-109).

A third commentator claimed that Solomon once said: "Tonight I shall visit seventy wives and each shall bear a knight who will fight for God." Yet he failed to add the words: "If God wills." Only one became preg-

Example of Job

41   And remember our servant Job
      when he called upon his Lord that
      "the devil has touched me with toil
      and torment!"
42   "Stamp with thy foot, this is a cool
      washing-place and a drink."
43   And we granted him his family, and
      the like of them with them, as a
      mercy from us and a reminder to
      those endowed with minds,
44   —"and take in thy hand a bundle,
      and strike therewith, and break not
      thy oath!" Verily, we found him pa-
      tient, an excellent servant; verily,
      he turned frequently to us.
45   And remember our servants
      Abraham and Isaac and Jacob, en-
      dowed with might and sight;
46   verily, we made them sincere by a
      sincere quality—the remembrance
      of the abode;
47   and, verily, they were with us of
      the elect, the best.

Examples of Ishmael,
Elisha, and Ezekiel

48   And remember Ishmael and Elisha
      and DHu-l-kifl, for each was of the
      righteous.

A reminder
of Paradise and Hell

49   This is a reminder! verily, for the
      pious is there an excellent resort,
50   —gardens of Eden with the doors
      open to them;
51   —reclining therein; calling therein
      for much fruit and drink;
52   and beside them maids of modest
      glance, of their own age,
53   —"This is what ye were promised
      for the day of reckoning!"
54   —"This is surely our provision, it
      is never spent!"
55   This!—and, verily, for the rebel-
      lious is there an evil resort,
56   —hell; they shall broil therein, and

nant and the child she bore became a mon-
ster. The reason for the monster-child was
because Solomon had failed to say: "If God
wills." Later, this monster-child sat on his
throne (see the account by al Zamukhshari
in (see Gätje, *The Qur'an and its Exegesis*,
pp. 107-109).

38.41-47 This is a brief summary of the
Book of Job.

38.48 DHu-l-kifl, which literally means the
possessor of a *kifl* (double portion), is believed by some scholars to be a reference of
the prophet Ezekiel.

38.49 *for the pious* — That is, for those
who observe the Five Pillars that serve as

the foundation of Islamic theology, Paradise
is opened up to them (see **The Last Judg-**
ment on pp. 46-50).

38.50 *gardens of Eden* — The gardens in
Paradise (also see Q 16.31; 18.31; 19.61;
20.76; 35.33; 40.8). It is a place of an endless supply of food, sex, and relaxation.

38.52 *maidens of modest glance, of their*
own age — When the righteous enter Paradise, they will be assigned their own harems
(see **The Virgins** on pp. 107-109).

38.54 *it is never spent* — This provision of
a celestial harem will last forever.

38.55-64 Horrific description of Hell: (a)
people broiled on couches, (b) people sub-

an ill couch shall it be!

57   This,—so let them taste it!—hot water, and pus,

58   and other kinds of the same sort!

59   "This is an army plunged in with you! there is no welcome for them! verily, they are going to broil in the fire!"

60   They shall say, "Nay, for you too is there no welcome! it was ye who prepared it beforehand for us, and an ill resting-place it is!"

61   They shall say, "Our Lord! whoso prepared this beforehand for us, give him double torment in the fire!"

62   And they shall say, "What ails us that we do not see men whom we used to think amongst the wicked?

63   whom we used to take for mockery? have our eyes escaped them?"

64   Verily, that is the truth; the contention of the people of the fire.

A reminder of
absolute monotheism

65   Say, "I am only a warner; and there is no god but God, the one, the victorious,

66   the Lord of the heavens and the earth, and what is between the two, the mighty, the forgiving!"

67   Say, "It is a grand story,

68   and yet ye turn from it!"

69   I had no knowledge of the exalted chiefs when they contended.

70   I am only inspired that I am a plain warner.

Satan's fall into sin

71   When thy Lord said to the angels, "Verily, I am about to create a mortal out of clay;

72   and when I have fashioned him, and breathed into him of my spirit, then fall ye down before him adoring."

73   And the angels adored all of them,

74   save Iblîs, who was too big with pride, and was of the misbelievers.

75   Said He, "O Iblîs! what prevents

merged in boiling water and pus, and (c) people will argue back and forth, wishing greater torments for others than for themselves.

38.56, 59 *broil* — This is one of Muhammad's favorite descriptions of Hell.

38.57 *so let them taste it* — Allah will respond to the infidels condemned to Hell with contempt, a raw insensitivity, and a stunningly cold indifference.

38.65, 70 *a warner* — This is one of Muhammad's favorite descriptions of himself.

38.65 *there is no god but God* — The Doctrine of Tauhid (see Q 112).

38.65, 70 *warner* — This is one of Muhammad's favorite descriptions of himself.

38.71 *out of clay* — In this verse, Muhammad described the creation of man as being "out of clay" (see Q 96.2, note).

38.71-85 According to this passage, the original sin of Satan (Iblis) was his refusal to bow down and give obeisance to Adam. The stated reason was that Adam was made of clay (substance of little value) whereas Satan was made from fire (substance of high value). Rather than cast into Hell, Allah granted to Satan the ministry of deception, deceiving people into believing lies about

thee from adoring what I have created with my two hands? art thou
too big with pride? or art thou
amongst the exalted?"

76   Said he, "I am better than he, Thou
hast created me from fire, and him
Thou hast created from clay."

77   Said He, "Then go forth therefrom,
for, verily, thou art pelted, and, verily, upon thee is my curse unto the
day of judgment."

80   Said he, "My Lord! then respite me

81   until the day when they are raised."

82   Said He, "Then thou art amongst
the respited until the day of the
stated time." Said he, "Then, by
Thy might! I will surely seduce
them all together,

83   except Thy servants amongst them
who are sincere!"

84   Said He, "It is the truth, and the
truth I speak;

85   I will surely fill hell with thee and
with those who follow thee
amongst them all together."

Conclusion

86   Say, "I do not ask thee for it any
hire, nor am I of those who take
too much upon myself.

87   It is but a reminder to the servants,

88   and ye shall surely know its story
after a time."

Surah 25

*In the name of the merciful and compas-
sionate God.*

Doxology

1   Blessed be He who sent down the
Discrimination to His servant that
he might be unto the world a
warner;

2   whose is the kingdom of the heavens and the earth, and who has not
taken to Himself a son, and who
has no partner in His kingdom, and

Allah so that their condemnation would be sure (see Q 7.16-18; 15.26-40; 17.61-64).
38.86-88 Muhammad was instructed by Allah to say that his ministry was not moti-vated by money. With time, Muhammad was reminded, people will know the rightness of his ministry.
Surah 25. The title of this surah, *The Dis-crimination*, is taken from verse one. This surah is a defense of Muhammad's ministry. He offered answers to his critics, revealed their future fate in Hell, defended the legiti-macy of the Qur'an, and explained why an-gels did not revealed themselves as a way of validating his message.

25.1a *the Discrimination* — Literally, that which distinguishes true from false. It is one of several synonyms of the Qur'an mentioned in the Qur'an. The most common synonym is simply: the Book (e.g., v. 35).
25.1b *unto the world* — The Qur'an is in-tended to be a revelation given to the en-tire world.
25.1c *a warner*— This is one of Muhammad's favorite descriptions of himself. It is men-tioned repeatedly in the Qur'an.
25.2 *who has not taken to Himself a son* — Again, Muhammad returned to the topic of the Arabian Star Family religious system that typified the culture of Arabia (see **Polythe-**

created everything, and then decreed it determinately!

Catechism

3   And they take beside Him gods who create not aught, but are themselves created, and cannot control for themselves harm or profit, and cannot control death, or life, or resurrection.

4   And those who misbelieve say, "This is nothing but a lie which he has forged, and another people hath helped him at it;" but they have wrought an injustice and a falsehood.

5   And they say, "Old folks' tales, which he has got written down while they are dictated to him morning and evening."

6   Say, "He sent it down who knows the secret in the heavens. and the

earth; verily, He is ever forgiving, merciful!"

7   And they say, "What ails this prophet that he eats food and walks in the markets?—unless there be sent down to him an angel and be a warner with him...

8   Or there be thrown to him a treasury or he have a garden to eat therefrom...!" and the unjust say, "Ye only follow an infatuated man."

9   See how they strike out for thee parables, and err, and cannot find a way.

10 Blessed be He who, if He please, can make for thee better than that, gardens beneath which rivers flow, and can make for thee castles!

11 Nay, but they call the Hour a lie; but we have prepared for those who call the Hour a lie a blaze:

12 when it seizes them from a far-off place they shall hear its raging and

ism in Seventh Century Arabia on pp. 92-97). His criticism of the polytheism also served as a criticism of the Doctrine of the Trinity, a centerpiece of Christian theology (see **The Doctrine of the Trinity** on pp. 735-736).

25.3-16 In the form of a catechism, Muhammad responded to the following accusations made by his critics: (a) he forged a lie and has been assisted by other people, (b) his surahs are old folks' tales, (c) he is a mere mortal like everyone else who "eats food and walks in the markets," (d) his followers are merely following an infatuated man. Muhammad's answer is the following: (a) his critics are liars, (b) the Qur'an is truly from God, and (c) they will know the truth

at the time of the Hour at the Last Judgment when they are cast into Hell.

25.7 Muhammad's critics insisted that unless his ministry was accompanied by supernatural phenomena, such as angels, it lacked an adequate validation (see Q 11.12 and **John of Damascus** on pp. 247-248).

25.10 *gardens* — This is an oft-repeated theme in the Qur'an is that of Paradise being described as a garden (see Q 55.46-51 note) beneath which rivers flow, well supplied aquifers sufficiently close to the surface to keep the oasis fertile and green (see Q 16.31; 18.31; 20.76; 25.10; 39.20; 85.11).

25.11 *the Hour* — This is the hour of decision when people are either cast into Hell or

roaring;

13   and when they are thrown into a narrow place thereof, fastened together, they shall call there for destruction.

14   Call not today for one destruction, but call, for many destructions!

15   Say, "Is that better or the garden of eternity which was promised to those who fear—which is ever for them a recompense and a retreat?"

16   They shall have therein what they please, to dwell therein for aye: that is of thy Lord a promise to be demanded.

The Lord's rebuke
of the infidels

17   And the day He shall gather them and what they served beside God, and He shall say, "Was it ye who led my servants here astray, or did they err from the way?"

18   They shall say, "Celebrated be Thy praise, it was not befitting for us to take any patrons but Thee; but Thou didst give them and their fa-

thers enjoyment until they forgot the Reminder and were a lost people!"

19   And now have they proved you liars for what ye say, and they cannot ward off or help. And he of you who does wrong we will make him taste great torment.

The question of angels

20   We have not sent before thee any messengers but that they ate food and walked in the markets; but we have made some of you a trial to others: will ye be patient? thy Lord doth ever look.

21   And those who do not hope to meet us say, "Unless the angels be sent down to us, or we see our Lord...!" They are too big with pride in their souls and they have exceeded with a great excess!

22   The day they shall see the angels,— no glad tidings on that day for the sinners, and they shall say, "It is rigorously forbidden!"

23   And we will go on to the works

---

enter into Paradise (see Q 79.42, note).

25.18a *it was not befitting for us to take any patrons but Thee* — That is, it was not fitting for them to serve false gods (see **Polytheism in Seventh Century Arabia** on pp. 92-97).

25.18b *the Reminder* — A common synonym for the Qur'an.

25.19a *now have they proved you liars for what you say* — That is, now the false gods have proven those who worshipped them

to be liars.

25.19b *we will make them taste great torment* — This is a cold and detached attitude towards the infidels at the time of their condemnation to Hell.

25.20-29 Muhammad's critics insisted that unless angels came down and accompanied him, or if the Lord revealed himself to them, they would not believe Muhammad's message. Muhammad responded by noting that they would see angels at the Last Judgment,

which they have done, and make them like motes in a sunbeam scattered!

24 The fellows of Paradise on that day shall be in a better abiding-place and a better noonday rest.

25 The day the heavens shall be cleft asunder with the clouds, and the angels shall be sent down descending.

26 The true kingdom on that day shall belong to the Merciful, and it shall be a hard day for the misbelievers.

27 And the day when the unjust shall bite his hands and say, "O, would that I had taken a way with the Apostle!

28 O, woe is me! would that I had not taken such a one for a friend now,

29 for he did lead me astray from the Reminder after it had come to me, for Satan leaves man in the lurch!"

The Lord's affirmation
of the Qur'an

30 The Apostle said, "O my Lord! verily, my people have taken this Qur'ân to be obsolete!"

31 Thus have we made for every prophet an enemy from among the sinners; but thy Lord is good guide and helper enough.

32 Those who misbelieve said, "Unless the Qur'ân be sent down to him all at once...!" —thus—that we may stablish thy heart therewith, did we reveal it piecemeal.

33 Nor shall they come to thee with a parable without our bringing thee the truth and the best interpretation.

34 They who shall be gathered upon their faces to hell,—these are in the worst place, and err most from the path.

The fate of past infidels

35 And we did give to Moses the Book, and place with him his brother Aaron as a minister;

yet then it would be too late to repent and believe the message of the Qur'an (see **John of Damascus** on pp. 247-248).

25.27 *the Apostle* — This is another of Muhammad's favorite titles of himself.

25.32 *did we reveal it piecemeal* — According to this passage, the Qur'an was revealed to Muhammad verbatim, word by word, and one surah at a time. Accordingly, Muhammad was merely a passive listener in this process, offering none of his own thoughts or creativity. Scholarship, particularly non-Islamic scholarship, disagrees with this understanding of the Qur'an. Rather than passive in the process, Muhammad was fully actively involved in the composition of the surahs (see **The Perspicuous Book** on pp. 178-179; and **The Qur'an** on pp. 150-153).

25.35-45 In the past, infidels resisted the message of the Lord's warners and suffered enormously for their unbelief. This included the people of Egypt in the days of Moses and Aaron, the people of Noah's day who were drowned in the Great Flood, and the people of Ad, Thamud, and the people of ar-Rass. In each case, said Muhammad, the people rejected the divine message and messenger.

36   and we said, "Go ye to the people who say our signs are lies, for we will destroy them with utter destruction."

37   And the people of Noah, when they said the apostles were liars, we drowned them, and we made them a sign for men; and we prepared for the unjust a grievous woe.

38   And 'Âd and Thamûd and the people of ar-Rass, and many generations between them.

39   For each one have we struck out parables, and each one have we ruined with utter ruin.

40   Why, they have come past the cities which were rained on with an evil rain; have they not seen them?—nay, they do not hope to be raised up again.

41   And when they saw thee they only took thee for a jest, "Is this he whom God has sent as an apostle?

42   he well-nigh leads us astray from our gods, had we not been patient about them." But they shall know, when they see the torment, who errs most from the path.

43   Dost thou consider him who takes his lusts for his god? wilt thou then be in charge over him?

44   or dost thou reckon that most of them will hear or understand? they are only like the cattle, nay, they err more from the way.

*The Lord is sovereign
over His creation*

45   Hast thou not looked to thy Lord how He prolongs the shadow? but had He willed He would have made it stationary; then we make the sun a guide thereto,

46   then we contract it towards us with an easy contraction.

47   And He it is who made the night for a garment; and sleep for repose, and made the day for men to rise up again.

48   And He it is who sent the winds with glad tidings before His mercy; and we send down from the heavens pure water,

49   to quicken therewith the dead country, and to give it for drink to what we have created,—the cattle and many folk.

25.35 *the Book* — the Pentateuch (see **The Perspicuous Book** on pp. 178-179).

25.36 *say our signs are lies* — that is, all who reject the Qur'an are condemned to Hell.

25.38a *Ad* — Ad is an ancient tribe that inhabited the region of northwest Arabia (see Q 54.17-21, note).

25.38b *Thamud* — This is a people who lived in the seventh century B.C. to the second century A.D. in the northern Arabian Desert. See Q 91 note.

25.38c *ar-Rass* — This is a mythic town of unknown location, some scholars suggest that it was a town in the central Arabian desert.

25.44 Muhammad described the infidels as brute cattle. His point was that they lack fundamental sensibilities and rational thought.

25.45-50 This line of reasoning is reminiscent of the questions posed by God to Job (see Job 38-41).

50 We have turned it in various ways amongst them that they may remember; though most men refuse aught but to misbelieve.

51 But, had we pleased, we would have sent in every city a warner.

52 So obey not the unbelievers and fight strenuously with them in many a strenuous fight.

The divine mandate

53 He it is who has let loose the two seas, this one sweet and fresh, that one bitter and pungent, and has made between them a rigorous prohibition.

54 And He it is who has created man from water, and has made for him blood relationship and marriage relationship; for thy Lord is mighty.

55 Yet they worship beside God what can neither profit them nor harm them; but he who misbelieves in his Lord backs up (the devil).

56 We have only sent thee to give glad tidings and to warn.

57 Say, "I ask you not for it a hire unless one please to take unto his Lord a way."

58 And rely thou upon the Living One who dies not; and celebrate His praise, for He knows well enough about the thoughts of His servants.

59 He who created the heavens and the earth, and what is between them, in six days, and then made for the throne; the Merciful One, ask concerning Him of One who is aware.

60 And when it is said, "Adore ye the Merciful!" they say, "What is the Merciful? shall we adore what thou dost order us?" and it only increases their aversion.

The zodiac

61 Blessed be He who placed in the heavens zodiacal signs, and placed therein the lamp and an illuminating moon!

25.52 *fight strenuously with them in many a strenuous fight* — Literally, "jihad against the infidels with a great jihad" (also see Q 4.95; 5.35; 8.72, 74-75; 9.16, 41, 44, 73, 81; 16.110; 22.78; 29.6, 69; 47.31; 60.1; 66.9).

25.54 *blood relationship and marriage relationship* — That is, family relationships and in-law relationships.

25.55 False gods can neither profit nor harm people. Yet, unbeknown to most people, false gods give room to the devil to hold people in their unbelief and assure their eventual condemnation.

25.56 According to this passage, Muhammad is reminded that he is not responsible in how people respond to his message. His responsibility is merely to be faithful in warning people. The Bible makes a similar claim (see Isa 6:1-13).

25.59 *in six days* — See Gen 1:1-31 where the heavens and earth is described as occurring in six days. Yet, this verse contradicts Q 41.9-12 where the heavens and earth are said to have been created in eight days.

25.61 *zodiacal signs* — Though Muhammad embraced Allah as the one true God, he also

62   And He it is who made the night and the day alternating for him who desires to remember or who wishes to be thankful.

Characteristics of
Muslim piety

63   And the servants of the Merciful are those who walk upon the earth lowly, and when the ignorant address them, say, "Peace!"

64   And those who pass the night adoring their Lord and standing

65   and those who say, "O our Lord! turn from us the torment of hell; verily, its torments are persistent;

66   verily, they are evil as an abode and a station."

67   And those who when they spend are neither extravagant nor miserly, but who ever take their stand between the two;

68   and who call not upon another god with God; and kill not the soul which God has prohibited save deservedly; and do not commit for-

nication: for he who does that shall meet with a penalty;

69   doubled for him shall be the torment on the resurrection day, and he shall be therein for aye despised.

70   Save he who turns again and believes and does a righteous work; for, as to those, God will change their evil deeds to good, for God is ever forgiving, merciful.

71   And he who turns again and does right, verily, he turns again to God repentant.

72   And those who do not testify falsely; and when they pass by frivolous discourse, pass by it honourably;

73   and those who when they are reminded of the signs of their Lord do not fall down thereat deaf and blind;

74   and those who say, "Our Lord! grant us from our wives and seed that which may cheer our eyes, and make us models to the pious!"

75   These shall be rewarded with a high place for that they were patient: and

---

studied and affirmed the constellations that make up the zodiac (see Q 86.1 note; **Polytheism in Seventh Century Arabia** on pp. 92-97).

25.63-68 Characteristics of the Muslim believers: (a) they walk upon the earth lowly, (b) offer greetings of peace, (c) are persistent in their desire to avoid Hell, (d) are neither extravagant nor miserly, (e) committed monotheists, and (f) avoid the sins of murder and fornication.

25.64 *pass the night adoring their Lord and standing* — A common practice among Mus-

lims is to spend part of each night in prayer, while standing (see Q 73.3-6, note, and **al-Salat** on pp. 169-170).

25.70 *change their evil deeds to good* — With an abundance of good works, the impact of bad works is neutralized and even reversed. This is due to God's mercy and forgiveness (see **Divine Forgiveness in Islam** on pp. 158-161).

25.71-76 A list of good works: (a) repentance, (b) righteous testimony, (c) avoidance of frivolous conversations, (d) attentiveness to divine revelation, and (e) honor-

they shall meet therein with salutation and peace,

76   —to dwell therein for aye; a good
abode and station shall it be!

Final warning

77   Say, "My Lord cares not for you
though you should not call (on
Him); and ye have called (the
Apostle) a liar, but it shall be (a punishment) which ye cannot shake
off."

Surah 20

*In the name of the merciful and compas-
sionate God.*

1   T. H.

Qur'an

2   We have not sent down this Qur'ân
to thee that thou shouldst be
wretched;

3   only as a reminder to him who fears

---

able parents.

25.75 *rewarded with a high place* — A
person's station in Paradise is dependent
upon the degree of good works amassed in
his or her life. Those with more good works
are located closer to Allah in the seventh
heaven. Those with less good works, are
located on a lower level (see **Paradise** on
pp. 76-77).

25.77 *My Lord cares not for you* — This
statement is associated with Muhammad's
belief in double predestination (see **The Doctrine of al-Qadar** on pp. 264-266). Since
Allah predestined certain people to Hell, it
stands to reason that He also possesses a
cavalier disinterest in the needs and wishes
of the infidel. It is a formula where the first
clause naturally gives rise to the second.

Many Christians are uneasy with the doctrine of double predestination. One of their
reasons is the formula mentioned above: we
tend to conform to that which we worship.
If God predestines certain people to Hell, a
troubling corollary emerges where we tend
to harden our hearts towards those who are
steadfastly opposed to the Christian faith.
Our understanding of theology (whatever
our theology happens to be) gives shape to

our ethical behavior.

With this in mind, William Stacy Johnson
has written: "Any vision of how God works
in the world has potential social consequences. The vision that double predestination paints in which some are included and
others excluded by an arbitrary divine order
tempts us to view some as 'insiders' and others as 'outsiders'—some as loved by God and
others not. When we do this, we need to
remember that Calvin himself called double
predestination a 'horrible decree.'" Johnson
then recounted the story of King Philip's War
in seventeenth century colonial Massachu-
setts where the Puritans justified the massacre of thousands of Indians on the grounds
that they were not of the elect. Johnson
concluded, "To dehumanize others is to dehumanize ourselves. It is all the more revolting when we are helped in our dehumaniza-
tion by invoking particular understandings of
Christian doctrine" (*John Calvin*, pp. 48-49).

Surah 20. The title of this surah, *Ta Ha*,
comes from verse one. The overall theme
of the surah is, as verse 99 states, a reminder
of the story of Moses. It makes the case
that (a) God has sent apostles and warners
to peoples of times past (in this case, Moses),

4   —descending from Him who cre-
     ated the earth and the high heav-
     ens,
5   the Merciful settled on the throne!
6   His are what is in the heavens, and
     what is in the earth, and what is
     between the two, and what is be-
     neath the ground!
7   And if thou art public in thy
     speech—yet, verily, he knows the
     secret, and more hidden still.
8   God, there is no god but He! His
     are the excellent names.

The burning bush

9   Has the story of Moses come to
     thee? When he saw the fire and
     said to his family, "Tarry ye; ver-
     ily, I perceive a fire!
10   Haply I may bring you therefrom a
     brand, or may find guidance by the

fire."
11   And when he came to it he was
     called to, "O Moses!
12   verily, I am thy Lord, so take off
     thy sandals; verily, thou art in the
     holy valley Tuvâ,
13   and I have chosen thee. So listen
     to what is inspired thee;
14   verily, I am God, there is no god
     but Me! then serve Me, and be
     steadfast in prayer to remember
     Me."
15   Verily, the hour is coming, I almost
     make it appear, that every soul may
     be recompensed for its efforts.
16   "Let not then him who believes not
     therein and follows his lusts ever
     turn thee away therefrom, and thou
     be ruined."
17   "What is that in thy right hand, O
     Moses?"
18   Said he, "It is my staff on which I

and (b) they rejected their message in a manner that parallels the way in which the Meccan
people were currently rejecting Muhammad's
message. The surah also includes four notable parentheses (vv. 73-76, 98-101, 102-
111 and 112-114). In each, a theological
effort is made to explain notable Islamic beliefs regarding the doctrines of salvation, Allah, the Last Judgment, and the divine revelation. The surah also includes a brief description of Adam's fall into sin. A parallel is
presented showing how the Meccan people
had fallen into sin similar to that of Adam.

20.1 Literally, *Ta Ha*. See 32.1, note.

20.2 *Qur'an* — The word *Qur'an* means to
recite and to remind.

20.8 The Doctrine of Tauhid: an absolute
monotheism (see Q 112, note).

20.9 *the fire* — The burning bush. Accord-
ing to some Islamic scholars, the fire that
Moses saw was actually the heavenly light of
Allah surrounding the bush.

20.9-37 This account is based upon the
story found in the book of Exodus (see Ex
3:1-4:17).

20.12 *the holy valley Tuva* — This is the
valley where Moses encountered the burning bush. The word *Tuva* in the Arabic language means "twice." Scholars typically understand this to mean a valley that is twice
hallowed—meaning an intensely holy valley.
In contrast, the Book of Exodus states that
Moses encountered the burning bush on the
side of a mountain (see Q 79.16; Ex 3:1-2).

20.14 This verse presents the Doctrine of
Tauhid: an absolute monotheism (see Q 112,

lean, and wherewith I beat down leaves for my flocks, and for which I have other uses."

19 Said He, "Throw it down, O Moses!"

20 and he threw it down, and behold! it was a snake that moved about.

21 Said He, "Take hold of it and fear not; we will restore it to its first state."

22 But press thy hand to thy side, it shall come forth white without harm,

23 —another sign! to show thee of our great signs!

24 "Go unto Pharaoh, verily, he is outrageous!"

25 Said he, "My Lord! expand for me my breast;

26 and make what I am bidden easy to me;

27 and loose the knot from my tongue,

28 that they may understand my speech;

29 and make for me a minister from my people,

30 —Aaron my brother;

31 gird up my loins through him,

32 and join him with me in the affair;

33 that we may celebrate Thy praises much

34 and remember Thee much."

35 "Verily, Thou dost ever behold us!"

36 He said, "Thou art granted thy request, O Moses!

37 and we have already shown favours

unto thee at another time.

Baby Moses

38 When we inspired thy mother with what we inspired her,

39 'Hurl him into the ark, and hurl him into the sea; and the sea shall cast him on the shore, and an enemy of mine and of his shall take him;'—for on thee have I cast my love, that thou mayest be formed under my eye.

40 When thy sister walked on and said, 'Shall I guide you to one who will take charge of him?' And we restored thee to thy mother, that her eye might be cheered and that she should not grieve.

Story of Moses committing murder

And thou didst slay a person and we saved thee from the trouble, and we tried thee with various trials. And thou didst tarry for years amongst the people of Midian; then thou didst come (hither) at (our) decree, O Moses!

The commissioning of Moses

41 And I have chosen thee for myself.

note).

20.38-40a This account is a faithful depiction of the story found in the book of Exodus (see Ex 2:1-10).

20.40b This account is a faithful depiction of the story found in the book of Exodus

42 Go, thou and thy brother, with my signs, and be not remiss in remembering me.

43 Go ye both to Pharaoh; verily, he is outrageous!

44 and speak to him a gentle speech, haply he may be mindful or may fear."

45 They two said, "Our Lord! verily, we fear that he may trespass against us, or that he may be outrageous."

46 He said, "Fear not; verily, I am with you twain. I hear and see!

47 So come ye to him and say, 'Verily, we are the apostles of thy Lord; send then the children of Israel with us; and do not torment them. We have brought thee a sign from thy Lord, and peace be upon him who follows the guidance!

48 Verily, we are inspired that the torment will surely come upon him who calls us liars and turns his back.'"

Moses confronts Pharaoh

49 Said he, "And who is your Lord, O Moses?"

50 He said, "Our Lord is He who gave everything its creation, then guided it."

51 Said he, "And what of the former generations?"

52 He said, "The knowledge of them is with my Lord in a book; my Lord misleads not, nor forgets!

53 Who made for you the earth a bed; and has traced for you paths therein; and has sent down from the sky water,—and we have brought forth thereby divers sorts of different vegetables.

54 Eat and pasture your cattle therefrom; verily, in that are signs to those endued with intelligence.

55 From it have we created you and into it will we send you back, and from it will we bring you forth another time."

56 We did show him our signs, all of them, but he called them lies and did refuse.

57 Said. he, "Hast thou come to us, to turn us out of our land with thy magic, O Moses?

58 Then we will bring you magic like it; and we will make between us and thee an appointment; we will not break it, nor do thou either;— a fair place."

59 Said he, "Let your appointment be for the day of adornment, and let

(see Ex 2:11-15).

20.41-48 This account is a faith account of the story in the book of Exodus (see Ex 4:19-23).

20.49-61 This account is based upon the story in the book of Exodus (see Ex 5:1-23). The dialogue, however, is imagined— not found in either biblical or apocryphal literature.

20.52 *a book* — divine revelation.

20.62-72 This account is based upon the story in the book of Exodus (see Ex 7:8-14). Again, the dialogue is imagined, not found in either biblical or apocryphal litera-

the people assemble in the fore-noon."

60 But Pharaoh turned his back, and collected his tricks, and then he came.

61 Said Moses to them, "Woe to you! do not forge against God a lie; lest He destroy you by torment; for disappointed has ever been he who has forged."

The snakes
in Pharaoh's court

62 And they argued their matter among themselves; and secretly talked it over.

63 Said they, "These twain are certainly two magicians, who wish to turn you out of your land by their magic, and to remove your most exemplary doctrine.

64 Collect therefore your tricks, and then form a row; for he is prosperous today who has the upper hand."

65 Said they, "O Moses! either thou must throw, or we must be the first to throw."

66 He said, "Nay, throw ye!" and lo! their ropes and their staves appeared to move along.

67 And Moses felt a secret fear within his soul.

68 Said we, "Fear not! thou shalt have the upper hand.

69 Throw down what is in thy right hand; and it shall devour what they have made. Verily, what they have made is but a magician's trick; and no magician shall prosper wherever he comes."

70 And the magicians were cast down in adoration; said they, "We believe in the Lord of Aaron and of Moses!"

71 Said he, "Do ye believe in Him before I give you leave? Verily, he is your master who taught you magic! Therefore will I surely cut off your hands and feet on alternate sides, and I will surely crucify you on the trunks of palm trees; and ye shall surely know which of us is keenest at torment and more lasting."

72 Said they, "We will never prefer thee to what has come to us of manifest signs, and to Him who originated us. Decide then what thou canst decide; thou canst only decide in the life of this world! Verily, we believe in our Lord, that He may pardon us our sins, and the

---

ture.

20.71 *surely crucify you* — The speaker in this verse is Pharaoh. He threatened to cut the hands, feet, and crucify his magicians for bowing before Moses and Aaron. The problem with this passage, of course, is that crucifixion was not practiced in the ancient world prior to the sixth century, B.C. The story of the Exodus occurred in the fourteenth century, B.C. Hence, Muhammad inserted events known in his culture to an earlier culture where such events were not known (see Q 7.124-126). Moreover, in the biblical account, Pharaoh did not threaten

magic thou hast forced us to use; and God is better and more lasting!"

First Parenthesis:
Doctrine of Salvation

73   Verily, he who comes to his Lord a sinner,—verily, for him is hell; he shall not die therein, and shall not live.

74   But he who comes to Him a believer who has done aright

75   —these, for them are the highest ranks,

76   —gardens of Eden beneath which rivers flow, to dwell therein for aye; for that is the reward of him who keeps pure.

The Red Sea

77   And we inspired Moses, "Journey by night with my servants, and strike out for them a dry road in the sea. Fear not pursuit, nor be afraid!"

78   Then Pharaoh followed them with his armies, and there overwhelmed them of the sea that which overwhelmed them.

79   And Pharaoh and his people went astray and were not guided.

The manna and quail

80   O children of Israel! We have saved you from your enemy; and we made an appointment with you on

to cut off the hands and feet of his magicians.

20.73-76 This passage presents a stark contrast between the Christian and Islamic faiths. Islam teaches that entrance into Paradise is based upon a meritorious lifestyle—the amassing for oneself more good than bad works (Q 20.74, 112; 90.11; 93.6-11; 81.15-29 and 84.20-25). Forgiveness has a limited role, insufficient to overturn the role of personal merit (see **Divine Forgiveness in Islam** on pp. 158-161). If one approaches the Lord at the Last Judgment as a sinner, this is indicative of a life that lacked merit. Accordingly, such a person will be cast into Hell.

In contrast, the Christian faith insists that the only way in which to enter Heaven is to approach the Lord as a sinner and seek divine forgiveness. This is because all people are steeped in sin and incapable of overcoming their sinfulness, other than to acknowledge it and embrace God's forgiveness. Divine forgiveness is grounded in divine atonement (spiritual cleansing) by means of the blood of Jesus Christ (see Lk 18:13; Rom 4:7; Titus 3:3-8; 1 Jn 1:8-9).

20.76 *gardens of Eden* — That is, the gardens in Paradise (also see Q 16.31; 18.31; 19.61; 35.33; 38.50; 40.8). Also in the Qur'an is the imagery of Paradise being an oasis with well supplied aquifers sufficiently close to the surface to keep the oasis fertile and green (see Q 16.31; 18.31; 20.76; 25.10; 39.20; 85.11).

20.77-79 This account is based upon the story in the book of Exodus (see Ex 14:1-31). The dialogue is imagined.

20.80 According to Muhammad, Moses ascended Mt. Sinai, yet did not receive the Ten Commandments—an important omission. The original Exodus account, of course, in-

the right side of the mount; and we sent down upon you the manna and the quails.

81 Eat of the good things we have provided you with, and do not exceed therein, lest my wrath light upon you; for whomsoever my wrath lights upon he falls!

82 Yet am I forgiving unto him who repents and believes and does right, and then is guided.

The golden calf

83 But what has hastened thee on away from thy people, O Moses?

84 He said, "They were here upon my track and I hastened on to Thee, my Lord! that thou mightest be pleased."

85 Said He, "Verily, we have tried thy people, since thou didst leave, and es Sâmarîy has led them astray."

86 And Moses returned to his people, wrathful, grieving! Said he, "O my people! did not your Lord promise you a good promise? Has the time seemed too long for you, or do you

desire that wrath should light on you from your Lord, that ye have broken your promise to me?"

87 They said, "We have not broken our promise to thee of our own accord. But we were made to carry loads of the ornaments of the people, and we hurled them down, and so did es Sâmarîy cast;

88 and he brought forth for the people a corporeal calf which lowed." And they said, "This is your god and the god of Moses, but he has forgotten!"

89 What! do they not see that it does not return them any speech, and cannot control for them harm or profit?

90 Aaron too told them before, "O my people! ye are only being tried thereby; and, verily, your Lord is the Merciful, so follow me and obey my bidding."

91 They said, "We will not cease to pay devotion to it until Moses come back to us."

92 Said he, "O Aaron! what prevented thee, when thou didst see them go

---

cluded the story of the Ten Commandments at Mt. Sinai (see Ex 19:1-20:26).

20.80-82 This account is based upon a story in the book of Exodus (see Ex 15:22-16:36). The dialogue is imagined.

20.83-97 This account is based upon the story in the book of Exodus (see Ex 32:1-35). The dialogue is imagined.

20.88 *a corporeal calf which lowed* — Muhammad believed that the golden calf miraculously came to life and made sounds

(lowed). The Bible makes no such claim (see Q 7.148).

20.85, 95 *es Samariy* — That is, the Samaritan. The terms *Samaritan* and *Samaria*, however, did not appear in the ancient record until the eighth century, B.C., following the Assyrian occupation of Israel. Once again, Muhammad conflated two biblical stories into one by introducing into his story of the golden calf (fourteenth century, B.C.) with the name of a person who did not exist prior to the

astray,

93   from following me? Hast thou then
      rebelled against my bidding?"

94   Said he, "O son of my mother! seize
      me not by my beard, or my head!
      Verily, I feared lest thou shouldst
      say, 'Thou hast made a division
      amongst the children of Israel, and
      hast not observed my word.'"

95   Said he, "What was thy design, O
      Sâmarîy?"

96   Said he, "I beheld what they be-
      held not, and I grasped a handful
      from the footprint of the messen-
      ger and cast it; for thus my soul
      induced me."

97   Said he, "Then get thee gone; ver-
      ily, it shall be thine in life to say,
      'Touch me not!' and, verily, for
      thee there is a threat which thou
      shalt surely never alter. But look at
      thy god to which thou wert just
      now devout; we will surely burn
      it, and then we will scatter it in
      scattered pieces in the sea.

Second Parenthesis:
Pledge to monotheism

98   "Your God is only God who,—
      there is no god but He,—He
      embraceth everything in His
      knowledge."

99   Thus do we narrate to thee the his-
      tory of what has gone before, and
      we have brought thee a reminder
      from us.

100   Whoso turns therefrom, verily, he
      shall bear on the resurrection day
      a burden:

101   —for them to bear for aye, and evil
      for them on the resurrection day
      will it be to bear.

Third Parenthesis:
the Last Judgment

102   On the day when the trumpet shall
      be blown, and we will gather the
      sinners in that day blue-eyed.

103   They shall whisper to each other,
      "Ye have only tarried ten days."

104   We know best what they say,
      when the most exemplary of them
      in his way shall say, "Ye have only
      tarried a day."

105   They will ask thee about the moun-

eighth century, B.C.

20.96 According to the saying of Samariy
(the Samaritan), Aaron took a handful of dirt
from the footprint of "the messenger" and
shaped it into the golden calf. Islamic scholars believe the dirt refers to the horse print
of the horse of the archangel Gabriel. This
explanation is at wide variance with the biblical account, which states that the people
donated their own gold ornaments which
were cast into a golden calf.

20.98-101 The fundamental doctrine of
Islam—the Doctrine of Tauhid—is again articulated. It served as the critical fault line
between the infidels of Mecca and the Muslim people. According to Muhammad, all who
fail to embrace the Doctrine of Tauhid, says
this passage, will discover that the resurrection day is a burden, since they will be cast
into the fires of Hell.

20.102-111 Two events surrounding the
Last Judgment will include: (a) leveling of

tains; say, "My Lord will scatter them in scattered pieces,

106 and He will leave them a level plain,

107 thou wilt see therein no crookedness or inequality."

108 On that day they shall follow the caller in whom is no crookedness; and the voices shall be hushed before the Merciful, and thou shalt hear naught but a shuffling.

109 On that day shall no intercession be of any avail, save from such as the Merciful permits, and who is acceptable to Him in speech.

110 He knows what is before them and what is behind them, but they do not comprehend knowledge of Him.

111 Faces shall be humbled before the Living, the Self-subsistent; and he who bears injustice is ever lost.

Fourth Parenthesis:
the Arabic Qur'an

112 But he who does righteous acts and is a believer, he shall fear neither wrong nor diminution.

113 Thus have we sent it down an Arabic Qur'ân; and we have turned about in it the threat,—haply they may fear, or it may cause them to remember.

114 Exalted then be God, the king, the truth! Hasten not the Qur'ân before its inspiration is decided for thee; but say, "O Lord! increase me in knowledge."

Adam's fall into sin

115 We did make a covenant with Adam of yore, but he forgot it, and

the mountains, and (b) no intercessors to plead mercy on behalf of infidels.

20.112-114 According to this passage, the Qur'an provides a sure revelation of the Last Judgment, enabling one to know the truth and avoid the threat of hellfire.

20.113 *an Arabic Qur'an* — Muhammad insisted that the Qur'an, in its original form, was wholly Arabic. Many Islamic scholars have therefore concluded that the Qur'an should not be translated. Other scholars, however, have identified a number of non-Arabic words in the Qur'an (see Q 12.2; 13.37; 26.195; 42.7; 43.3 and Q 39.28 note; **The Qur'an** on pp. 150-153).

20.115-123 This account is based upon the story in the book of Genesis (see Gen 2:20-3:13). In important details, this account differs from the original Genesis ac-

count. This differences are the following. (a) In the qur'anic account, Adam and Eve were neither hungry nor naked. In the Genesis account, they both ate food, were naked, and were not ashamed of their nakedness (Gen 2:25). (b) In the qur'anic account, Satan beguiled Adam; in the Genesis account, Satan beguiled Eve (Gen 3:1-6). (c) In the qur'anic account, the lie spoken by Satan was the following: Adam would be guided to the tree of immortality and acquire a kingdom without end.

In the Genesis account, Satan's lie was that the woman would not die and know the difference between good and evil (in other words, lose her innocence). (d) In the qur'anic account, following Adam's fall into sin, he was promised the arrival of one who would guide him and lead him into the

we found no firm purpose in him.

116 And when we said to the angels, "Adore Adam," they adored, save Iblîs, who refused.

117 And we said, "O Adam! verily, this is a foe to thee and to thy wife; never then let him drive you twain forth from the garden or thou wilt be wretched.

118 Verily, thou hast not to be hungry there, nor naked! and, verily,

119 thou shalt not thirst therein, nor feel the noonday heat!"

120 But the devil whispered to him. Said he, "O Adam! shall I guide thee to the tree of immortality, and a kingdom that shall not wane?

121 And they eat therefrom, and their shame became apparent to them; and they began to stitch upon themselves some leaves of the garden; and Adam rebelled against his Lord, and went astray.

122 Then his Lord chose him, and relented towards him, and guided him.

123 Said he, "Go down, ye twain, therefrom altogether, some of you foes to the other. And if there should come to you from me a guidance; then whoso follows my guidance

shall neither err nor be wretched.

Fate of all infidels

124 But he who turns away from my reminder, verily, for him shall be a straitened livelihood; and we will gather him on the resurrection day blind!"

125 He shall say, "My Lord! wherefore hast Thou gathered me blind when I used to see?"

126 He shall say, "Our signs came to thee, and thou didst forget them; thus today art thou forgotten!"

127 Thus do we recompense him who is extravagant and believes not in the signs of his Lord; and the torment of the hereafter is keener and more lasting!

128 Does it not occur to them how many generations we have destroyed before them?—they walk in their very dwelling-places; verily, in that are signs to those endued with intelligence.

129 And had it not been for thy Lord's word already passed (the punishment) would have been inevitable and (at) an appointed time.

truth. In the Genesis account, no such guide was promised, other than a future messianic figure who would crush Satan's head (Gen 3:15).

20.116 *Iblis* — Satan.

20.120 *the tree of immortality* — Muhammad claimed that Satan tempted Adam to eat from the *Tree of Immortality*. According

to the third chapter of Genesis, the tree is identified as the *Tree of the Knowledge of Good and Evil* (see Gen 2:9; 3:1-6).

20.124-129 According to Muhammad, at the Last Judgment the infidels will be blinded. They will then be rebuked for rejecting the divine revelation that had been made available to them while on the earth.

Admonition to faithfulness

130   Bear patiently then what they say, and celebrate the praises of thy Lord before the rising of the sun, and before its setting, and at times in the night celebrate them; and at the ends of the day; haply thou mayest please (Him).

131   And do not strain after what we have provided a few of them with—the flourish of the life of this world, to try them by; but the provision of thy Lord is better and more lasting.

132   Bid thy people prayer, and persevere in it; we do not ask thee to provide. We will provide, and the issue shall be to piety.

Final warnings

133   They say, "Unless he bring us a sign from his Lord—What! has there not come to them the manifest sign of what was in the pages of yore?"

134   But had we destroyed them with torment before it, they would have said, "Unless Thou hadst sent to us an apostle, that we might follow Thy signs before we were abased and put to shame."

135   Say, "Each one has to wait, so wait ye! but in the end ye shall know who are the fellows of the level way, and who are guided!"

Surah 43

In the name of the merciful and compassionate God.

1   'H. M.

20.130-132 Admonitions to faithfulness: (a) bear patiently what the warners say, (b) worship Allah each day, (c) pray incessantly, and (d) be content with what one has. These admonitions parallel what is found in the Bible (see Gal 6:9; 1 Thess 5:16-25).

20.133-135 The people of Mecca rejected Muhammad's message, saying that they would only believe him provided that he presented a genuine miracle (a sign) to validate his message (see **John of Damascus** on pp. 247-248).

Muhammad's response was that such a miracle had indeed been provided: the Qur'an itself. It possessed a heightened level of literary achievement that reached beyond that which a mortal could have written. He then condemned the people of Mecca for refusing to accept him as Allah's apostle (see Q 10.38, note).

Surah 43. The title of this surah, *Gold*, comes from verse 35. The surah is a reassurance to Muhammad and his followers that his message and ministry was of Allah, and that the religion of the polytheists (Star Family worshippers) was human origin and thereby false. In this surah, Muhammad vacillated between two arguments in making his case: (a) he drew on a number of biblical leaders: Abraham, Moses, and Jesus whose ministry paralleled his own, and (b) he reaffirmed the divine origin of the Qur'an.

43.1 Literally, *Ha Mim*. See Q 32.1, note.

43.2 *the perspicuous Book* — the Qur'an

	Arabic Qur'an		*Polytheism*
2	By the perspicuous Book,	9	And if thou shouldst ask them who
3	verily, we have made it an Arabic		created the heavens and the earth,
	Qur'ân; haply ye will have some		they will surely say, "The mighty,
	sense.		the knowing One created them,"
4	And it is in the Mother of the Book	10	who made for you the earth a couch
	with us,—high and wise.		and placed for you therein roads,
5	Shall we then push aside from you		haply ye may be guided:
	the Reminder, because ye are a	11	and who sent down from the
	people who are extravagant?		heaven water in due measure; and
6	How many prophets have we sent		we raised up thereby a dead coun-
	amongst those of yore?		try; thus shall ye too be brought
7	and there never came to them a		forth;
	prophet but they did mock at him;	12	and who has created all species;
8	then we destroyed them—more		and has made for you the ships and
	valiant than these; and the example		the cattle whereon to ride
	of those of yore passed away.	13	that ye may settle yourselves on

(see **The Perspicuous Book** on pp 178-179).

43.3 *we have made it an Arabic Qur'an —* Muhammad insisted that the Qur'an, in its original form, was wholly Arabic. Other scholars, however, have identified a number of non-Arabic words in the Qur'an (see Q 12.2; 13.37; 20.113; 26.195; 42.7 and Q 39.28 note; **The Qur'an** on pp. 150-153).

In reply, non-Muslims ask: if the Qur'an was indeed divinely inspired, and was restricted to the Arabic language, are we to conclude that God intends only Arabic speaking people to know His Word? Christians encourage translations of the Bible. Indeed, a major feature in Christian missions has been the translation of the Bible into as many languages in the world as possible. As of 2005, the Summer Institute of Linguistics reported that at least one book of the Bible has been translated into 2,400 of the 6,900 languages in the world.

43.4 *the Mother of the Book* — the Qur'an. Its title suggests that the Qur'an is not a divine revelation, it is superior to all other divine revelations (see **The Qur'an** on pp. 150-153).

43.5 *the Reminder* — the Qur'an.

43.6-8 Muhammad claimed that differing peoples of the world were destroyed because they consistently resisted the prophets (apostles) sent from Allah who sought to show them the way of righteousness and salvation. The implication is that the same would happen to the people of Mecca (see **The Apostles** on pp. 398-400).

43.9-25 In this passage, Muhammad laid out a monotheistic foundation to the Arabic Star Family religious system. He noted that the polytheists admitted that the Arabic Star Family religious system required a primordial God to set into motion the initial creation of the heavens and the earth. Yet, said the polytheists, this primordial God then brought

their backs; then remember the favour of your Lord when ye settled thereon, and say, "Celebrated be the praises of Him who hath subjected this to us! We could not have got this ourselves;

14 and, verily, unto our Lord shall we return!"

15 Yet they make for Him of His servants offspring; verily, man is surely obviously ungrateful.

16 Has He taken of what He creates daughters, and chosen sons for you?

17 Yet when the tidings are given any one of that which he strikes out as a similitude for the Merciful One, his face grows black and he is choked.

18 What! one brought up amongst ornaments, and who is always in contention without obvious cause?

19 And have they made the angels, who are the servants of the Merciful One, females? Were they wit-

nesses of their creation? their witness shall be written down, and they shall be questioned;

20 and they say, "Had the Merciful pleased we should never have worshipped them." They have no knowledge of that, they only conjecture.

21 Have we given them a book before it to which they might hold?

22 Nay; they say, "We found our fathers (agreed) upon a religion, and, verily, we are guided by their traces."

23 Thus, too, did we never send before thee to a city any warner, but the affluent ones thereof said, "Verily, we found our fathers (agreed) upon a religion, and, verily, we are led by their traces."

24 Say, "What! if I come to you with what is a better guide than what ye found your fathers agreed upon?" and they will say, "Verily, we in what ye are sent with disbe-

into existence offsprings—lesser gods who are His sons and daughters. Muhammad agreed with the initial aspect of the Arabic Star Family religious system, yet rejected the second aspect.

43.12-14 This passage is read today on Muslim airlines prior to the commencement of its flight. This is the case, in spite of the fact that the passage merely mentions travel by animal—and not by airline. The idea is that the passage applies indirectly to all forms of travel.

43.17 *his face grows black* — That is, Muhammad believed that when news (tidings) is brought to a polytheist of the birth of one

of their gods (a god in the likeness of the Merciful One), his face darkens and he is choked with inward grief (see Q 10.26-27; 39.60).

43.21 *a book* — Divine revelation. According to this verse, no legitimate divine revelation exists that affirms the notion of God bringing into exists infant gods (see vv. 15, 16).

43.23-24 Muhammad's point was that prophets were sent from Allah to reveal divine truth to an otherwise ignorant people. Once the truth was known, they were obligated to respond in obedience and convert to the Islamic faith.

lieve!"

25 Then we took vengeance on them, and see how was the end of those who called the (apostles) liars.

Abraham

26 When Abraham said to his father and his people, "Verily, I am clear of all that ye serve,

27 except Him who created me; for, verily, He will guide me:"

28 and he made it a word remaining among his posterity, that haply they might return.

Ingratitude and self-delusion of the infidels

29 Nay; but I let these (Meccans) and their fathers have enjoyment until the truth came to them, and an apostle.

30 And when the truth came to them they said, "This is magic, and we therein do disbelieve!"

31 And they say, "Unless this Qur'ân

were sent down to a man great in the two cities..."

32 Is it they who distribute the mercy of thy Lord? We distribute amongst them their livelihood in the life of this world, and we exalt some of them above others in degrees, that some may take others into subjection; but the mercy of thy Lord is better than that which they amass.

33 And but that men would then have been one nation, we would have made for those who misbelieve in the Merciful One roofs of silver for their houses, and steps up thereto which they might mount;

34 and to their houses doors, and bedsteads on which they might recline;

35 and gilding,—for, verily, all that is a provision of the life of this world, but the hereafter is better with thy Lord for those who fear!

36 And whosoever turns from the reminder of the Merciful One, we will chain to him a devil, who shall be his mate;

43.26-28 Abraham was an example of a faithful witness. He confronted his neighbors, friends, and associates in his native city of Ur because of their polytheistic beliefs.

43.29-31 According to Muhammad, the Meccan people were self-deluded in two ways: (a) they claimed that Muhammad was a magician, and (b) they claimed that unless Muhammad was great in two cities, they would not believe in him.

43.32 *some may be take others into subjection* — That is, some may take others into slavery (see Q 2.222b, note).

43.32-42 Muhammad's reply to his opponents in Mecca who resisted his ministry was fourfold: (a) divine mercy is better than the wealth of the Meccan people, (b) they will eventually be chained to the devil, (c) they will eventually regret their rejection of Muhammad's message and ministry, and (d) they will eventually be punished by God.

43.35 *gilding* — That is, gold plating on the furniture and other objects in Heaven.

43.36-38 According to Muhammad, all who reject the Qur'an will experience a peculiar curse in this life. They will be chained to a

37   and, verily, these shall turn them from the path while they reckon that they are guided;

38   until when he comes to us he shall say, "O, would that between me and thee there were the distance of the two orients, for an evil mate (art thou)!"

39   But it shall not avail you on that day, since ye were unjust; verily, in the torment shall ye share!

40   What! canst thou make the deaf to hear, or guide the blind, or him who is in obvious error?

41   Whether then we take thee off we will surely take vengeance on them;

42   or whether we show thee that which we have promised them; for, verily, we have power over them.

Qur'an

43   Say, "Dost thou hold to what is inspired thee?" verily, thou art in the right way,

44   and, verily, it is a reminder to thee and to thy people, but in the end they shall be asked.

45   And ask those whom we have sent before thee amongst the prophets, "Did we make gods beside the Merciful One for them to serve?"

Moses

46   We did send Moses with our signs to Pharaoh and his chiefs, and he said, "Verily, I am the apostle of the Lord of the worlds; but when he came to them with our signs, lo, they laughed at them!"

47   And we did not show them a sign,

48   but it was greater than its fellow; and we seized them with the torment, haply they might turn.

49   And they said, "O thou magician! pray for us to thy Lord, as He has engaged with thee: verily, we are guided."

50   And when we removed from them the torment, behold they broke their word.

51   And Pharaoh proclaimed amongst his people; said he, "O my people! is not the kingdom of Egypt mine? and these rivers that flow beneath me? What! can ye then not see?

52   Am I better than this fellow, who is contemptible, who can hardly

demon who will become his or her mate and keep him or her committed to the path that leads to eternal damnation.

43.44 *a reminder* — Once again, Muhammad reminded his listeners that the Qur'an is divinely inspired. Most notably, it is a reminder that Allah is one (the Doctrine of Tauhid—an absolute monotheism).

43.46-50 Muhammad emphasized the fu-tility of resisting an apostle sent from Allah. The people of Egypt only affirmed Moses as an apostle sent from God after divine judgment fell upon them. Yet when the judgment was removed, they returned to their previous idolatrous ways. They were, as is often said today, "foxhole conversions."

43.51 Pharaoh assumed for himself privileges reserved for Almighty God.

explain himself?

53   Unless then bracelets of gold be cast upon him, or there come with him angels as his mates...!"

54   And he taught his people levity; and they obeyed him: verily, they were an abominable people.

55   And when they had annoyed us we took vengeance on them, and we drowned them all together,

56   and we made them a precedent and an example to those after them.

Jesus

57   And when the son of Mary was set forth as a parable, behold thy people turned away from him

58   and said, "Are our gods better, or is he?" They did not set it forth to thee save for wrangling. Nay, but

they are a contentious people.

59   He is but a servant whom we have been gracious to, and we have made him an example for the children of Israel.

60   And if we please we can make of you angels in the earth to succeed you.

61   And, verily, he is a sign of the Hour. Doubt not then concerning it, but follow this right way;

62   and let not the devil turn you away; verily, he is to you an open foe!

63   And when Jesus came with manifest signs he said, "I am come to you with wisdom, and I will explain to you something of that whereon ye did dispute, then fear God, obey me;

64   verily, God, He is my Lord and your Lord, serve Him then, this is

43.55 This is a reference to the drowning of the Egyptian army at the Red (Reed) Sea.

43.57-65 Muhammad turned to Jesus as another example of an apostle sent from God, yet rejected by the people to whom he ministered.

43.58 Muhammad assumed that the people of Israel in the days of Jesus were polytheistic, as were the people of Mecca.

This, however, is historically inaccurate. Earlier in their history, Israel had fallen into polytheism. Yet, following the First Diaspora, they returned to monotheism. According to the New Testament, in the days of Jesus their sin was not idolatry but the rejection of Jesus as Messiah.

43.58-59 According to the Qur'an, Jesus was a servant and an example for the children of Israel. Nothing is said, however, of

Jesus being God the Son. The reason, of course, is that a strict monotheism makes no allowance for this.

Christians reply that they too affirm monotheism—but a complex monotheism. God is one yet existing in three Persons: God the Father, God the Son, and God the Holy Spirit (see **The Doctrine of the Trinity** on pp. 735-736, and the **Nicene-Constantinopolitan Creed** on p. 740).

43.60 That is, if God pleased He could have made angels walk behind Jesus as a way of demonstrating his credentials as being truly sent from God.

43.61 *the Hour* — The moment when people will be summoned to the Last Judgment (see Q 79.42, note).

43.64-65 One of the chief complaints of the leaders of Israel was Jesus' claim to de-

the right way."

65 But the confederates disputed amongst themselves; and woe to those who are unjust from the torment of a grievous day!

The delights of Paradise

66 Do they expect aught but that the Hour will come upon them suddenly while they do not perceive?

67 Friends on that day shall be foes to each other, save those who fear.

68 O my servants! there is no fear for you on that day; nor shall ye be grieved

69 who believe in our signs and who are resigned.

70 Enter ye into Paradise, ye and your wives, happy!

71 Dishes of gold and pitchers shall be sent round to them; therein is what souls desire, and eyes shall be delighted, and ye therein shall dwell for aye;

72 for that is Paradise which ye are given as an inheritance for that

which ye have done.

73 Therein shall ye have much fruit whereof to eat.

The torments of Hell

74 Verily, the sinners are in the torment of hell to dwell for aye.

75 It shall not be intermitted for them, and they therein shall be confused.

76 We have not wronged them, but it was themselves they wronged.

77 And they shall cry out, "O Mâlik! let thy lord make an end of us;" he shall say, "Verily, ye are to tarry here."

The plans of Allah

78 We have brought you the truth, but most of you are averse from the truth.

79 Have they arranged the affair? then will we arrange it too!

80 Or do they reckon that we did not hear their secrets and their whispering? Nay, but our messengers

---

ity (see Lk 5:21-26; Jn 8:58 and 10:25-33). This dispute, however, is wholly absent from Muhammad's description of the controversy that the leaders of Israel had with Jesus.

43.66-73 Characteristics of Paradise: (a) dishes of gold and pitchers will be provided, and (b) an abundance of fruit to eat.

43.74-77 Characteristics of Hell: (a) a place of confusion, and (b) a yearning to cease to exist.

43.76 *We have not wrong them, but it was themselves they wronged* — That is,

people are culpable for their own sin; they therefore have no cause to blame God (see Q 16.33-34 note and 16.35 note).

43.77 *Malik* — This is an Arabic word meaning *king*. It is one of the names for Allah.

43.78 According to this verse, Islam is the truth. Infidels are opposed to the truth.

43.80 Muhammad insisted that Allah is omniscient. The Bible makes a similar (Ps 33:13-15, 139:11-12; 147:5; Prov 15:3; Isa 40:14; 46:10; Heb 4:13; and 1 Jn 3:20).

43.81 This is a mere hypothetical state-

are with them writing down.

81   Say, "If the Merciful One has a son then am I the first to worship him.

82   Celebrated be the praise of the Lord of the heavens and the earth! the Lord of the throne, above all they attribute to Him!

83   But leave them to ponder and to play until they meet that day of theirs which they are promised.

84   He it is who is in the heaven a God and in the earth a God! and He is the wise, the knowing.

85   And blessed be he whose is the kingdom of the heavens and the earth, and what is between both, and His is the knowledge of the Hour, and unto Him shall ye be brought back!

86   And those they call on beside Him shall not possess intercession except those only who bear witness for the truth and who do know.

87   And if thou shouldst ask them who

created them they shall surely say, "God!" How then can they lie?

Shunning infidels

88   And what he says, "O Lord, verily, these are a people who do not believe;

89   shun them then and say, 'Peace!' for they at length shall know!"

Surah 12

In the name of the merciful and compassionate God.

1   A. L. R.

Arabic Qur'an

Those are the signs of the perspicuous Book.

2   Verily, we have revealed it, an Ara-

---

ment. According to Muhammad, it is theologically impossible for more than one God to exist.

43.85 *the Hour* — This is the moment in time when people will be judged by Allah at the Last Judgment (see Q 79.42, note).

43.88-89 According to this passage, Muhammad is called by Allah to shun infidels.

Surah 12. The title of this surah, *Joseph*, comes from verse 4. Its purpose is to draw a parallel with the Old Testament patriarch Joseph with the trials that Muhammad was facing in his final year in Mecca. Similar to Joseph, people from Muhammad's own family (*e.g.*, Abu Lahab) had become some of his most fierce opponents. This surah, then,

makes the case that apostles sent from Allah have a long history of being rejected and persecuted from their own families and extended families. Nevertheless, they are ultimately cared for by Allah who eventually vindicates them and puts down their opponents. Interspersed in this surah are several summaries designed to give a divine perspective of the story as it unfolds (Q 12.6, 15, 21-22, 34, 42, 56-57, 68, 76).

12.1a Literally, *Aif Lam Ra*. See Q 32.1, note.

12.1b *the perspicuous Book* — the Qur'an (see **The Perspicuous Book** on pp. 178-179).

12.2 *an Arabic Qur'an* — Muhammad in-

bic Qur'ân; haply ye may understand.

3   We tell thee the best of stories, in
inspiring thee with this Qur'ân,
though thou Wert before it among
the heedless.

Joseph's dream

4   When Joseph said to his father, "O
my sire! verily, I saw eleven stars,
and the sun, and the moon,—I saw
them adoring me!"

5   He said, "O my boy! tell not thy
vision to thy brethren, for they will
plot a plot against thee; verily, the
devil is to man an open foe."

6   Thus does thy Lord choose thee,

and teach thee the interpretation of
sayings, and fulfil His favour upon
thee, and upon Jacob's people, as
He fulfilled it upon thy two forefathers before thee, Abraham and
Isaac,—verily, thy Lord is knowing, wise!

The brothers' plot

7   In Joseph and his brethren were
signs to those who enquire!

8   When they said, "Surely, Joseph
and his brother are dearer to our
father than we, a band although we
be; verily, our father is in obvious
error.

9   Slay Joseph, or cast him in some

sisted that the Qur'an, in its original form, was wholly Arabic. Other scholars, however, have identified a number of non-Arabic words in the Qur'an (see Q 13.37; 20.113; 26.195; 42.7; 43.3 and Q 39.28 note; **The Qur'an** on pp. 150-153).

12.4-6 This passage is based upon Gen 37:2-11. Yet, Muhammad's account has several variances. Muhammad claimed that Joseph first shared his dream with his father, rather than his brothers, and that his father cautioned him not to share the dream with his brothers.

In contrast, the biblical account claims that Joseph first revealed the two dreams to his brothers in a field (each dream reinforcing the other) and then repeated the dreams in the presence of his father. Everyone—Jacob and the brothers—were indignant with Joseph. As a result of these provocative dreams, the brothers cultivated a deep jealousy against Joseph: "When he

told his father as well as his brothers, his father rebuked him and said, 'What is this dream you had? Will your mother and I and your brothers actually come and bow down to the ground before you?' His brothers were jealous of him, but his father kept the matter in mind" (Gen 37:10-11).

In a Hadith, Muhammad affirmed the supernatural origin of dreams. He explained that "a good dream is from Allah, and a bad or evil dream is from Satan; so if anyone of you has a bad dream of which he gets afraid, he should spit on his left side and should seek Refuge with Allah from its evil, and then it will not harm him" (*Sahih Bukhari* 4.54.513). Spitting on one's left side suggests that Satan approaches a person from the left and Allah approaches a person from the right.

12.7-15 This account is an imaginative dialogue between the brothers as they plotted to eliminate Joseph. At first, they considered killing Joseph. They then revised their

land; that your father's face may be free for you, and ye may be, after he is gone, a people who do right."

10 A speaker from amongst them spake, "Slay not Joseph, but throw him into the bottom of the pit; some of the travellers may pick him up, if so ye do."

11 Said they, "O our father! what ails thee that thou wilt not trust us with Joseph while we are unto him sincere?

12 Send him with us tomorrow to revel and to play, and, verily, we over him will keep good guard."

13 Said he, "Verily, it grieves me that ye should go off with him, for I fear lest the wolf devour him while ye of him do take no heed."

14 Said they, "Why, if the wolf should devour him while we are (such) a band, verily. we then should deserve to lose!"

15 And when they had gone off with him and agreed to put him in the

depths of the pit, and we inspired him, "Thou shalt surely inform them of this affair of theirs and they shall not perceive."

The brothers' lie

16 And they came to their father at eve and weeping

17 said, "O our father! verily, we went forth to race and left Joseph by our goods, and the wolf devoured him,—but thou wilt not believe us, truth tellers though, we be."

18 And they brought his shirt with lying blood upon it. Said he, "Nay, but your souls have induced you to do this; but patience is fair! and God is He whom I ask for aid against that which ye describe."

The selling of Joseph

19 And travellers came and sent their water-drawer; and he let down his bucket. Said he, "O glad tidings!

plan by placing in a deep pit and give him to travelers who happened to pass by.

Again, the Genesis account differs from the qur'anic account. When one of the brothers, Reuben, heard of their plan to kill Joseph, "he tried rescue him from their hands. 'Let's not take his life,' he said. 'Don't shed any blood. Throw him into this cistern here in the desert, but don't lay a hand on him.' Reuben said this to rescue him from them and take him back to his father" (Gen 37:21-22).

12.16-18 This passage is based upon Gen 37:31-35. Again, it differs from the biblical

account. It presents Jacob as suspicious of his sons' explanation (v. 18). In the biblical account, Jacob was not suspicious: "Then Jacob tore his clothes, put on sackcloth and mourned for his son many days. All his sons and daughters came to comfort him, but he refused to be comforted. 'No,' he said, 'in mourning will I go down to the grave to my son.' So his father wept for him" (Gen 37:34-35).

12.19-22 This passage is based upon Gen 37:25-28. According to Muhammad, travelers discovered Joseph in the pit, rescued him, and made him chattel. This occurred when

this is a youth." And they kept him secret, as a chattel; but God knew what they were doing.

20 And they sold him for a mean price,—drachmæ counted out,—and they parted with him cheaply.

21 And the man from Egypt who had bought him said to his wife, "Honour his abiding here; it may be he will be of use to us, or we may adopt him as a son." Thus did we stablish Joseph in the land; and we did surely teach him the interpretation of sayings; for God can overcome His affairs, though most men do not know.

22 And when he had reached his strength we brought him judgment and knowledge, for thus do we reward those who do good.

Potiphar's wife

23 And she in whose house he was desired him for his person; and she locked the doors and said, "Come along with thee!" Said he, "Refuge in God! verily, my Lord has made good my abiding here; verily, the wrong-doers shall not prosper."

24 And she was anxious for him, and he would have been anxious for her, had it not been that he saw

---

the sons were back with their father.

Again, the Bible offers a different narrative. It states that the travelers came when the brothers were present and the brothers sold Joseph to them: "As they sat down to eat their meal, they looked up and saw a caravan of Ishmaelites coming from Gilead. Their camels were loaded with spices, balm and myrrh, and they were on their way to take them down to Egypt." Judah schemed with his brothers (with only Reuben being absent), asking, "What will we gain if we kill our brother and cover up his blood? Come, let's sell him to the Ishmaelites and not lay our hands on him; after all, he is our brother, our own flesh and blood." The brothers agreed to the plan, pulled Joseph out of the cistern, and sold him for twenty shekels to the Ishmaelites, who took him to Egypt (Gen 37:25-28).

12.21 The man of Egypt is not identified. The Genesis account, however, identifies him as Potiphar (Gen 37:36).

12.23-29 According to Muhammad, Potiphar's wife enticed Joseph to commit adultery. Joseph refused, pleading God's help. As he ran from her, she tore his shirt. Afterwards, however, she accused Joseph of attempted rape and she fought him off, tearing his shirt in the process. Potiphar discerned the truth of the matter in his examination of the side of the shirt that was torn. Since it was torn in the back, it was evidence that Joseph had indeed attempted to flee, rather than commit rape. Potiphar then rebuked his wife.

Once again, this account differs from the biblical account. In the biblical account, Joseph's clothing was not torn. Instead, Potiphar's wife grabbed Joseph's cloak as he fled. In addition, Potiphar took the side of his wife and placed Joseph in prison: "When his master heard the story his wife told him, saying, 'This is how your slave treated me,' he burned with anger. Joseph's master took him and put him in prison, the place where

the demonstration of his Lord; thus did we turn evil and fornication from him; verily, he was of our sincere servants.

25 And they raced to the door and she rent his shirt from behind; and they met her master at the door. Said she, "What is the recompense of him who wishes evil for thy family, but that imprisonment or a grievous torment?"

26 Said he, "She desired me for my person." And a witness from among her family bore witness: "If his shirt be rent from in front, then she speaks the truth and he is of the liars;

27 but if his shirt be rent from behind, then she lies and he is of the truth tellers."

28 And when he saw his shirt rent from behind he said, "This is one of your tricks; verily, your tricks are mighty!

29 Joseph! turn aside from this. And

do thou, woman, ask pardon for thy fault; verily, thou wert of the sinners."

The banquet

30 And women in the city said, "The wife of the prince desires her young man for his person; he has infatuated her with love: verily, we see her in obvious error."

31 And when she heard of their craftiness, she sent to them and prepared for them a banquet, and gave each of them a knife; and she said, "Come forth to them!" And when they saw him they said, "Great God!" and cut their hands and said, "God forbid! This is no mortal, this is nothing but an honourable angel."

32 Said she, "This is he concerning whom ye blamed me. I did desire him for his person, but he was too continent. But if he do not what I

the king's prisoners were confined" (Gen 39:19-20).

12.30 According to Muhammad, having been disgraced by her husband, the wife of Potiphar suffered an additional disgrace from the scorns of the women in the city.

12.31a According to Muhammad, Potiphar's wife responded to the scorn she suffered from the women of the city by inviting them to a banquet where Joseph would be present. When they saw him, they too were overcome with sexual passion. Due to their passionate exhilaration, they mistakenly cut their own hands. In his commentary, Ibn Kathir explained, "They thought highly of him

and were astonished at what they saw. They started cutting their hands in amazement at his beauty, while thinking that they were cutting the citron with their knives."

12.31b *Great God!* — This phrase, in the Muslim world, is called Takbir (*Allahu akbar*). See Q 34.23 note.

12.32 According to Muhammad, Potiphar's wife reprimanded them, saying, "This is he concerning whom ye blamed me." She then described Joseph as "continent"—in this context, sexually frigid. Sensing a rise in sexual desire within his soul, Joseph beckoned Potiphar to send him to prison as a way of escaping temptation. Potiphar acquiesced,

bid him he shall surely be imprisoned and shall surely be among the small!"

33 Said he, "My Lord! Prison is dearer to me than what they call on me to do; and unless Thou turn from me their craftiness I shall feel a passion for them and shall be among the ignorant!"

34 And his Lord answered him and turned from him their craftiness; verily, He both hears and knows!

Prison

35 Then it appeared good to them, even after they had seen the signs, to imprison him until a time.

36 And there entered the prison with him two young men. Said one of them, "Verily, I see myself pressing wine." And the other said, "Verily, I see myself bearing on my

head loaves from which the birds do eat; inform us of the interpretation thereof; verily, we see that thou art of those who do good."

37 He said, "There shall not come to you any food with which ye are provided, but I will inform you both of its interpretation before it comes to you. That is (some) of what my Lord has taught me; verily, I have left the faith of a people who do not believe in God, while in the future too they disbelieve.

38 And I have followed the faith of my fathers, Abraham and Isaac and Jacob; we could not associate aught with God; that is from God's grace upon us and upon men: but most men give not thanks.

39 O ye twain fellow-prisoners! Are manifold lords better, or God, the one, the dominant?

40 What ye worship beside Him are

---

placing him in prison. This story of the banquet does not appear in the biblical account. **12.35-42** While in prison, Joseph befriended two inmates, both of whom had dreams. One dreamt that he was pressing wine. The other dreamed that loaves of bread were on his head whereupon birds were perched and eating. Joseph interpreted the dreams: (a) the first inmate will be restored to his post and pour out wine for his lord, and (b) the second inmate will be crucified and the birds shall eat his head.

This account roughly parallels the biblical account (Gen 40:1-23). An important difference, however, exists in regards to the form of execution that the first inmate would undergo. Crucifixion (v. 41) was a

form of execution not known in that era. Muhammad conflated historical realities of a later period and incorrectly inserted them in this earlier era (see Q 20.71, note).

12.37 *I have left the faith of a people who do not believe in God, while in the future too they disbelieve* — These condemning words allegedly spoken by Joseph were meant to parallel Muhammad's own words of condemnation directed towards the people of Mecca.

12.38 These words by Joseph are curiously similar to the arguments that Muhammad had been having with his Meccan opponents.

12.40 Here Muhammad presented the Doctrine of Tauhid (an absolute monotheism) in the story of Joseph.

naught but names which ye have named, ye and your fathers, for which God has sent down no authority. Judgment is only God's; He bids you worship only Him. That is the standard of religion,— but most men do not know.

41 O ye twain fellow-prisoners! as for one of you, he shall pour out wine for his lord: and as for the other, he shall be crucified, and the birds shall eat of his head. The matter is decreed whereon ye asked me for a decision!"

42 And he said to him whom he thought would escape of those two, "Remember me with thy lord!" But Satan made him forget the remembrance of his lord, so he tarried in prison a few years.

Pharaoh's dream

43 Then said the king, "Verily, I see seven fat kine which seven lean kine devoured; and seven green ears of corn and others dry. O ye chiefs! Explain to me my vision, if a vision ye can expound!"

44 Said they, "Confused dreams, and naught of the exposition of such dreams know we!"

45 Then he who had escaped of those twain said,—remembering after a while,—"Verily, I will inform you of the interpretation thereof, so send me."

Joseph's interpretation
of the dream

46 "Joseph! O thou truth teller! explain to us the seven fat kine which seven lean devoured; and the seven green ears of corn and others dry. Haply I may go back to the men, haply they then may know!"

47 He said, "Ye shall sow for seven years, as is your wont; but what ye reap, let it remain in the ear, except a little whereof ye shall eat.

48 Then there shall come after that seven severe (years) which shall devour what ye have put by before for them, save a little of what ye shall preserve.

49 Then there will come after that a year in which men shall have rain

---

12.43-45 Pharaoh (the king) had a dream of seven fat kine (cows) devoured by seven lean kine (cows), and seven green ears of corn and seven dry ears. None of his counselors could offer an interpretation of the dream, except the bearer of wine who remembered that Joseph could indeed interpret dreams. This qur'anic account is based upon Gen 41:1-14.

Here the Palmer translation of the Qur'an

is faulty. A better translation of term would have been *grain*.

12.46-49 According to Muhammad, Joseph interpreted the dream as the following: seven abundant years of harvest would be followed by seven years of drought. He therefore counseled the Pharaoh to conserve food during the seven abundant years so as to have enough to survive the seven severe years. This account accurately corresponds

and in which they shall press."

Joseph's innocence
established

50   Then said the king, "Bring him to me." And when the messenger came to him, he said, Go back to thy lord, and ask him, 'What meant the women who cut their hands? Verily, my lord knows their craftiness!'"

51   He said, "What was your design when ye desired Joseph for his person?" They said, "God forbid! we know no bad of him." Said the wife of the prince, "Now does the truth appear! I desired him for his person and, verily, he is of those who tell the truth."

52   "That" (said Joseph) "was that he might know that I did not betray him in his absence, and that God guides not the craft of those who do betray!

53   Yet I do not clear myself, for the soul is very urgent to evil, save what my Lord has had mercy on;

verily, my Lord is forgiving and merciful!"

Blessings afforded to Joseph

54   And the king said, "Bring him to me. I will take him specially for myself." And when he had spoken with him he said, "Verily, to-day thou art with us in a permanent place of trust."

55   He said, "Place me over the treasures of the land; verily, I will be a knowing keeper."

56   Thus did we stablish Joseph in the land that he might settle in what part thereof he pleased—we overtake with our mercy whom we will, nor do we waste the hire of those who do good;

57   and surely the hire of the future life is better for those who believe and who have feared.

The brothers come to Egypt

58   And his brethren came to Joseph, and they entered in unto him and

---

to the biblical story found in Gen 41:15-36. **12.50-53** According to Muhammad, the Pharaoh (the king) asked for a clarification for the reason for Joseph's imprisonment. He learned from Potiphar and Potiphar's wife that Joseph was indeed innocent of any crime. This account, however, is just as fanciful and unconvincing as the story of the banquet (vv. 30-34).
12.54-57 According to Muhammad, Pharaoh (the king) was convinced of Joseph's interpretation and elevated him to "a per-

manent place of trust" in his kingdom. He placed him in charge of the king-dom's agriculture.

Again, a difference exists in Muhammad's and the biblical account. In the biblical account, it was Pharaoh's idea to elevate Joseph to the position of governor of all agriculture (see Gen 41:39-45)—not Joseph who suggested that he become governor to Pharaoh (v. 55).
12.58-62 This passage is a summary of the biblical passage of Gen 42:6-28. It differs

he knew them, but they recognised not him.

59 And when he had equipped them with their equipment he said, "Bring me a brother that ye have from your father; do ye not see that I give good measure, and that I am the best of entertainers?

60 But if ye bring him not to me, no measure shall ye have with me, nor shall ye come nigh me."

61 They said, "We will desire him of our father and we will surely do it."

62 Then he said to his young men, "Put their chattels in their packs, haply they may know it when they are come back to their family; haply they may return."

The brothers return to Jacob

63 And when they returned to their father, they said, "O our father! Measure is withheld from us; so send with us our brother that we may get measure, and, verily, him we will keep!"

64 He said, "Shall I entrust you with him, save as I entrusted you with his brother before? but God is the

best of keepers, and He is the most merciful of the merciful."

65 And when they opened their goods they found their chattels restored to them. Said they, "O our father! What more can we crave? Here are our chattels restored to us, and we shall guard our brother, and shall have an additional measure beside that—a small measure."

66 He said, "I will by no means send him with you until you give me a compact from God that ye will surely bring him to me, unless ye be encompassed." So when they had given him their compact he said, "God over what ye say has charge."

67 And he said, "O my sons! enter not by one gate, but enter by several gates; but I cannot avail you aught against God. Judgment is only God's; upon Him do I rely, and on Him do the reliant rely."

The brothers' return to Egypt

68 And when they had entered as their father bade them, it availed them nothing against God, save for a want in Jacob's soul which it ful-

from the biblical passage, however, in that in this surah a "measure" was withheld as collateral. What is meant by "measure," however, is not explained. Moreover, in the biblical passage, the brother who was sequestered is identified: Simeon.

12.62 *chattels* — property; in this case, silver coins (see Gen 42:28).

12.63-67 This passage is a summary of the biblical passage of Gen 42:29-43:14. Again, the difference between this passage and that of the Bible is the question of "measure" (Q 12.58-62, note).

12.68-69 This passage is based upon the biblical passage of Gen 43:15-45:15. Again, important details differ from the biblical ac-

filled; for, verily, he was possessed of knowledge, for that we had taught him;—but most men do not know.

69 And when they entered in unto Joseph, he took his brother to stay with him, and said, "Verily, I am thy brother—then take not ill that which they have been doing."

*The stolen goblet and
the sequestering of Benjamin*

70 And when he had equipped them with their equipment he placed the drinking cup in his brother's pack; then a crier cried out, "O ye caravan! verily, ye are thieves!"

71 They said, approaching them, "What is it that ye miss?"

72 Said they, "We miss the goblet of the king, and whoso brings it shall have a camel-load, and I am guarantee thereof,"

73 They said, "By God! Ye knew we came not to do evil in the land, and that we were not thieves."

74 They said, "And what shall be the recompense thereof if ye be liars?"

75 They said, "The recompense thereof is he in whose pack it is found—he shall be the recompense thereof; thus do we recompense

the unjust."

76 And he began with their sacks before the sacks of his brother; then he drew it forth from his brother's sack. Thus did we devise a stratagem for Joseph. He could not take his brother by the king's religion except God pleased; —we raise the degrees of whomsoever we please, and over every possessor of knowledge is one who knows.

77 They said, "If he has stolen, a brother of his has stolen before him." But Joseph kept it secret in his soul and disclosed it not to them. Said he, "Ye are in a bad case, and God knows best about what ye describe."

78 They said, "O prince! Verily, he has a father, a very old man; take then one of us instead of him; verily, we can see that thou art of those who do good."

79 Said he, "(I seek) refuge in God from taking any save him with whom we found our property; verily, we should then be certainly unjust."

80 And when they despaired of him they retired to consult privately. Said the eldest of them, "Do ye not know that your father has taken a compact from God against you?

count. In this passage, Joseph revealed himself to Benjamin, the younger brother (v 69) without revealing himself to the other ten brothers. When the brothers returned to their father, Benjamin refused to share with the others what he had learned from Joseph. In the biblical passage, no such revelation of Joseph to Benjamin took place at this time.

12.70-82 This passage of the stolen goblet is based upon the biblical passage of Gen 44:1-34. It roughly agrees with the biblical

Aforetime ye exceeded in the matter of Joseph—I will surely not quit the land until my father give me leave, or God judge for me, for He is the best of judges.

81 "Return ye to your father and say, 'O our father! verily, thy son has committed theft, and we bore testimony to naught but what we knew; for of the unforeseen we were not keepers!'

82 Ask then in the city where we were, and of the caravan in which we approached it, for, verily, we tell the truth."

The brothers return
to their father

83 Said he [Jacob], "Nay, your souls have induced you to do this thing. But patience is fair. It may be that God will give me them all together;—verily, He is knowing, wise."

84 And he turned away from them and said, "O my lament for Joseph!" and his eyes grew white with grief, for he repressed (his woe).

85 They said, "By God! thou wilt not cease to remember Joseph till thou art at the point of death, or art of those who perish!"

86 Said he, "I only complain of my emotion and my grief to God, for I know that from God which ye know nothing of.

87 O my sons! go and enquire concerning Joseph and his brother, and despair not of God's comfort; for, verily, none need despair of God's comfort save a misbelieving people!"

The brothers return to Egypt

88 And when they entered in unto him they said, "O prince! distress has touched both us and our families, and we have brought trifling chattels. So give us full measure and bestow upon us in charity; verily, God rewards the charitable."

Joseph reveals his identity
to his brothers

89 He said, "Do ye know what ye did

account.
12.83-87 This part of the story of Joseph is not mentioned in the biblical account. According to the biblical account, when Joseph decided to sequester Benjamin, the brothers fell into deep anguish, commenting that if they returned without Benjamin, their father would die of grief (Gen 44:30-34). It was then that Joseph, who also was troubled with deep anguish, revealed himself to his

brothers. The return trip to Jacob, as per this passage, then, never took place.
12.88 According to the biblical story, the story described in this verse never took place since the brothers never returned to their father to report the sequestering of Benjamin (see Q 12.83-87, note).
12.89-93 This passage is based upon the biblical passage of Gen 45:1-15. Two details, however, differ. First, the brothers did

with Joseph and his brother, while ye were ignorant?"

90 They said, "Art thou then indeed Joseph?" He said, "I am Joseph, and this is my brother; God has been gracious towards us. Verily, whoso fears God and is patient,—verily, God wastes not the hire of those who do good!"

91 They said, "By God! God has chosen thee over us; and we indeed were sinners."

92 He said, "No reproach against you today! God will pardon you, for He is the most merciful of the merciful.

93 Take this my shirt, and throw it over the face of my father, he will become able to see; and bring me your families all together."

*The restoration of
the family in Egypt*

94 And when the caravan departed, their father said, "Verily, I find the smell of Joseph, unless ye think I dote!"

95 They said, "By God! thou art in thy old error."

96 And when the herald of glad tid-

ings came he threw it on his face, and he was restored to sight. Said he, "Did I not tell you that I know from God that of which ye know not?"

97 They said, "O our father! ask pardon for us of our sins;—verily, we were sinners!"

98 He said, "I will ask pardon for you from my Lord; verily, He is the pardoning and merciful."

99 And when they entered in unto Joseph, he took his father to stay with him, and said, "Enter ye into Egypt, if it please God, safe."

100 And he raised his father upon the throne, and they fell down before him adoring. And he said, "O my sire! This is the interpretation of my vision aforetime; my Lord has made it come true, and He has been good to me, in bringing me forth out of prison, and bringing you from the desert, after Satan had made a breach between me and my brethren;—verily, my Lord is kind to whomsoever He will;—verily, He is the knowing, the wise!

101 O my Lord! thou hast given me dominion, and hast taught me the interpretation of sayings; O origina-

not discover Joseph's true identity, as per v. 90. Rather, Joseph revealed himself to the brothers (Gen 45:1-3). Second, Joseph did not instruct his brothers to take back his shirt to his father as evidence that he was still alive, as per v. 93.

12.94-101 This passage is based upon the biblical passage of Gen 45:21-28; 46:29-34.

It differs, however, from the biblical account. In this account, Jacob was raised upon a throne and then Joseph reminded the family of the dream which stated that his family would one day bow down to him (Q 12.4-6). In the biblical account, nothing was said of Jacob being placed upon a throne, nor of Joseph reminding his family of the dream.

tor of the heavens and the earth! Thou art my patron in this world and the next; take me to Thyself resigned, and let me reach the righteous!"

Muhammad's application
of the story of Joseph

102   That is one of the stories of the unseen which we inspire thee with, though thou wert not with them when they agreed in their affair, when they were so crafty.

103   —And yet most men, though thou shouldst be urgent, will not believe.

104   Thou dost not ask them for it a hire; it is naught but a reminder to the world.

105   How many a sign in the heavens and the earth do they pass by and turn away therefrom!

106   Nor do most of them believe in God without associating (other gods) with Him.

107   Are they safe, then, from overwhelming vengeance coming on them from the torment of God? or from the Hour coming upon them suddenly while they do not perceive?

108   Say, "This is my way; I call now unto God on clear proof, I and those who follow me; and celebrated be God's praises, for I am not of the idolaters."

109   Nor did we ever send before thee any save men whom we inspired, of the people of the cities. Have they not journeyed on in the earth, and beheld how was the end of those before them? But the abode of the future is surely better for those who believe;—what! have they then no sense?

110   Until when the apostles despaired and they thought that they were proved liars, our help came to them, and—whosoever we pleased was saved; but our violence is not averted from the sinful people.

Conclusion

111   Their stories were a lesson to those endowed with minds. It was not a tale forged, but a verification of what was before it, and a detailing of everything, and a guide and a

---

12.102-111 Muhammad presented three applications of the story of Joseph, each of which reflected his own situation in Mecca. *First,* he noted that Joseph remained committed to a belief in Allah "without associating (other gods) with Him" (v. 106)—in other words, he was a monotheist, committed to the Doctrine of Tauhid. *Second,* he noted that apostles sent from God to speak the

truth are often persecuted and placed in dire circumstances, so much so that some despaired of being thought liars. In this respect, Muhammad understood his own ministry to be remarkably similar to that of Joseph. *Third,* he noted that a day of vindication will eventually come to all apostles that had been sent by Allah. Muhammad was confident that it would also take place for

mercy to a people who believe.

Surah 11

In the name of the merciful and compassionate God.

1   A. L. R.

The herald

A book whose signs are confirmed and then detailed, from the wise one, the aware:

2   that ye worship not other than God,—verily, I am to you from Him a warner and a herald of glad tidings;

3   and that ye seek pardon from your Lord, then turn again to Him! He will cause you to enjoy a good provision to a named and appointed time, and will give His grace to every one deserving grace; but if ye turn your backs, I fear for you the torment of a great day.

4   Unto God is your return, and He is mighty over all.

The delusion of infidels

5   Do they not, verily, fold up their breasts, that they may hide from Him? But when they cover themselves with their garments, does He not know what they conceal and what they display? verily, He

---

him, as well, in regards to his struggles against the people of Mecca. He too would someday be vindicated by Allah.

Surah 11. The title of this surah, *Hud*, comes from verse 50. The overall theme of the surah is an encouragement for the Meccan people to reconsider their rejection of Allah. The phrase "O my people" occurs sixteen times in this surah, which sets its tone. Muhammad drew on a number of past apostles and the response of the peoples of their day as examples and encouragements for the Meccan people to not follow in their unbelief. He also saw himself as an apostle in the same tradition (Noah, Hud, Zali'h, Abraham, Lot, Jethro, and Moses) and yearned for the Meccan people to recognize him as such.

11.1a Literally, *Alif Lam Ra.* See Q 32.1, note.

11.1b *A book* — the Qur'an.

11.2 One of Muhammad's favorite descrip-

tions of himself is that of a warner. In this verse he also described himself as "a herald of glad tidings."

11.3 Muhammad's point is that people who seek pardon from Allah will receive it and be given grace to avoid "the torment of a great day." These two terms *(pardon and grace)* are also major themes in the Bible. In the Bible, *pardon* and *grace* are connected to the notion of substitutionary atonement (see **Divine Forgiveness in Islam** on pp. 158-161).

11.5-11 This passage presents the Doctrine of Divine Omniscience. Muhammad's point is that the infidel cannot effectively hide his or her sins from Allah. Allah knows all and will judge each person accurately and thoroughly.

The New Testament makes a similar claim about God: "Oh, the depth of the riches of the wisdom and knowledge of God! How

knows the nature of men's breasts!

6   There is no beast that walks upon the earth but its provision is from God. He knows its settlement and its resting-place; all is in the perspicuous Book.

7   He it is who created the heavens and the earth in six days, and His throne was upon the water that He might try you, which of you did best. But shouldst thou say, "Ye will be raised up after death," those who misbelieve will surely say, "This is naught but obvious sorcery;"

8   and if we keep back from them the torment to a stated generation, they will surely say, "What hinders it?"—Aye! on the day it comes to them there is no turning it away from them, but that shall close in on them at which they mocked.

9   And if we make man taste of mercy from us and then strip it off from him, verily, he is despairing, ungrateful;

10   and if we make him taste of comfort after distress has touched him, he will surely say, "The evils have gone away from me;" verily, then he is joyful and boasting.

11   Save those who are patient and do right; these—for them is pardon and a mighty hire!

The destiny of infidels

12   Haply thou art leaving part of what is revealed to thee and thy breast is straitened thereby, lest they should say, "Why is not a treasure sent down to him? or why did not an angel come with him?—thou art only a warner, and God is guardian over all."

13   Or they will say, "He hath devised it;" say, "Bring ten sûrahs like it devised; and call upon whom ye can beside God, if ye do tell the truth!"

14   And if they do not answer, then know that it is revealed by the

unsearchable his judgments, and his paths beyond tracing out! Who has known the mind of the Lord? Or who has been his counselor? Who has ever given to God, that God should repay him? For from him and through him and to him are all things. To him be the glory forever! Amen" (Rom 11:33-36).

11.6 *the perspicuous book* — Allah's book in Paradise which records all that existed, exists, and will exist (see **The Perspicuous Book** on pp. 178-179).

11.7 The Six Days of Creation. This premise is based upon the first chapter of Genesis.

11.8 This is further evidence that the

people of Mecca mocked Muhammad's message of a coming divine judgment due to their idolatrous/polytheistic beliefs and practices.

11.12 Again, Muhammad observed that one of arguments of his opponents was that if his message was indeed sent from Allah, it would have been accompanied by angels (see Q 25.7; 43.60, and **John of Damascus** on pp. 247-248).

11.13-14 *"Bring ten surahs like it devised"* — The opponents of Muhammad claimed that he devised (authored) the Qur'an. Muhammad countered by challenging his oppo-

knowledge of God, and that there is no god but He—are ye then resigned?

15 Whosoever shall wish for the life of this world and its ornaments, we will pay them their works therein, and they shall not be cheated.

16 These are those for whom there is nothing in the hereafter save the Fire; and void is what they made therein, and vain what they were doing!

17 Is he (like them) who stands upon a manifest sign from his Lord, which is a witness from Him, and recites it, with the book of Moses

before him for a model and a mercy? These believe in it; and whosoever of the crews disbelieves in him, the Fire is his promise. Be not thou in doubt about it; verily, it is truth from thy Lord, though most men do not believe.

18 Who is more unjust than he who forges against God a lie? they shall be set before their Lord, and the witnesses shall say, "These it is who lied against their Lord." Aye! God's curse is on the unjust

19 who turn men away from the path, and crave to make it crooked, and in the hereafter disbelieve!

20 They cannot make Him helpless in

---

nents to devise ten surahs of their own. Then the two sets of surahs could be set side by side, compared, and contrasted.

Though the remarks of John R. W. Stott were not directed specifically to Islam, his words are applicable to this religion. He wrote, "Jesus warned his disciples of false prophets. So did Paul and Peter. Still today there are many voices clamoring for our attention, and many cults gaining widespread popular support. Some of them claim a special revelation or inspiration to authenticate their particular doctrine. There is need for Christian discernment. For many are too gullible, and exhibit a naive readiness to credit messages and teachings which purport to come from the spirit-world. There is such a thing, however, as a misguided tolerance of false doctrine. Unbelief (*do not believe every spirit*, 1 Jn 4:1) can be as much a mark of spiritual maturity as belief. We should avoid both extremes, the superstition which believes everything and suspicion which believes

nothing" (*The Letters of John*, p. 156).

11.15a *ornaments* — That is, the amenities of life.

11.15b *they shall not be cheated* — If their concerns are only rewards for this world, they will not be cheated. But they will receive no rewards in the afterlife (at the Last Judgment).

Jesus made a similar observation: "And when you pray, do not be like the hypocrites, for they love to pray standing in the synagogues and on the street corners to be seen by men. I tell you the truth, they have received their reward in full" (Matt 6:5).

11.17 *the book of Moses* — That is, the first five books in the Bible, the Pentateuch. In this verse, Muhammad affirms the divine inspiration of the Pentateuch, calling it "a manifest sign for his Lord," "a witness from Him," and "truth from thy Lord."

11.18-22 Again, Muhammad addressed the question of lies. The Meccan people, he insisted, were speaking lies about his mes-

the earth, nor have they other than God for patrons. Doubled for them is the torment. They could not hear, nor did they see!

21   Those it is who lose themselves; and that which they did devise has strayed away from them.

22   No doubt but that in the hereafter these are those who lose!

The destiny of believers

23   Verily, those who believe and do what is right, and humble themselves to their Lord, they are the fellows of Paradise; they shall dwell therein for aye.

24   The two parties' likeness is as the blind and the deaf, and the seeing and the hearing shall they two be equal in likeness? will ye not mind?

Noah

25   We did send Noah unto his people, "Verily, I am to you an obvious

warner;

26   that ye should not worship any save God. Verily, I fear for you the torment of the grievous day."

27   But the chiefs of those who misbelieved amongst his people said, "We only see in thee a mortal like ourselves; nor do we see that any follow thee except the reprobates amongst us by a rash judgment; nor do we see that you have any preference over us; nay more, we think you liars!"

28   He said, "O my people! let us see! if I stand upon a manifest sign from my Lord, and there come to me mercy from him, and ye are blinded to it; shall we force you to it while ye are averse therefrom?

29   O my people! I do not ask you for wealth in return for it; my hire is only from God; nor do I repulse those who believe; verily, they shall meet their Lord. But I see you, a people who are ignorant.

30   O my people! who will help me

sages. Typical to what we see in the Qur'an, his response was to curse them. "These are those," he said, "who lose" in the hereafter.

11.23 *believe and do what is right* — These words are repeated often in the Qur'an and serve as a brief summary of the Islamic gospel (see Q 103.3 note).

11.24 Muhammad describes the "two parties," that is, the believers and infidels, at the Last Judgment, as hearing and seeing (the believers) and blind and deaf (the infidels).

11.25-48 In this section of the surah, Muhammad returned to a familiar theme: comparing past patriarchs and the opposition they endured with his own situation at Mecca. Here he drew upon the story of Noah to make this point (see **The Apostles** on pp. 398-400).

11.27 *We only see in thee a mortal like ourselves* — This is a similar complaint that the people of Mecca had made against Muhammad.

11.31 Noah was criticized for being a mere mortal (and not an angel), and yet allegedly

against God, were I to repulse you? do ye not then mind?

31 I do not say that I have the treasures of God; nor do I know the unseen; nor do I say, 'Verily, I am an angel;' nor do I say of those whom your eyes despise, 'God will never give them any good!' —God knows best what is in their souls— verily, then should I be of the unjust."

32 They said, "O Noah! thou hast wrangled with us, and hast multiplied wranglings with us; bring us then what thou hast threatened us with, if thou art of those who tell the truth."

33 Said he, "God will only bring it on you if He pleases, nor can ye make Him helpless; nor will my advice profit you,

34 should I wish to advise you, if God wish to lead you into error. He is your Lord, and unto Him shall ye be returned."

35 Do they say, "He has devised it?" Say, "If I have devised it, then on

me be my sin. But I am clear of that wherein ye sin."

36 And Noah was inspired, "None shall surely believe amongst thy people but those who have believed already; take not then ill that which they do.

37 And make the ark under our eyes, and at our inspiration; and plead not with me for those who have done wrong; verily, they shall be drowned."

38 So he made the ark, and every time the chiefs of his people passed by him they jested at him. Said he, "If ye jest at us, verily, we shall jest at you even as ye are jesting, and ye shall surely know.

39 He to whom a torment comes, it shall shame him, and there shall light upon him lasting torment."

40 Until at length when our order came, and the oven boiled, we said, "Load therein of every kind two, and likewise thy family,—save those on whom the sentence has already been passed—likewise

delivered divine revelations. This same complaint had been directed to Muhammad (see Q 11.12; 25.7; and 43.60).

11.35 *He has devised it* — That is, the Meccans believed that he wrote the surah on his own; it is not a divine revelation. This same complaint had been directed against Muhammad by the Meccan leaders (see Q 11.13).

11.36-44 This passage is based upon Gen 6:9-8:22.

11.38 Muhammad claimed that Noah ridiculed the people who ridiculed him.

11.40 *the oven boiled* — That is, when the water gushes forth in torrents. The Sumerian Flood myth stated that the primary cause of the Flood was the subterranean sea boiling over which then reached the surface of the earth (see Q 11.40, note). Muhammad believed that Noah was ordered to load the ark with animals at the onset of the storm. In contrast, the Bible claims that the ark was loaded seven days prior to the onset of the storm (see Gen 7:1-4).

11.41-43 Muhammad asserted that one of the sons of Noah refused to enter the

those who believe;" but there believed not with him save a few.

41 And he said, "Ride ye therein; in the name of God is its course, and its mooring. Verily, my Lord is forgiving and merciful."

42 And it floated on with them mid waves like mountains; and Noah cried to his son who had gone aside, "O my boy! ride with us and be not with the misbelievers."

43 Said he, "I will betake me to a mountain that shall save me from the water." Said he, "There is none to save today from the command of God, except for him on whom He may have mercy." And the wave came between them, and he was amongst the drowned.

44 And it was said, "O earth! swallow down thy water!" and, "O heaven! hold!" and the water abated; and the affair was decided, and it settled on Gûdî, and it was said, "Away with the people who are evildoers!"

45 And Noah went unto his Lord and said, "My Lord, verily, my son is

of my people, and, verily, Thy promise is true, and Thou art the justest of judges."

46 He said, "O Noah! he is not of thy people; verily, it is a work that is not right. Then, ask me not for that of which thou knowest naught. Verily, I admonish thee that thou shouldst not be of the ignorant."

47 He said, "My Lord, verily, I seek refuge in Thee from asking Thee for aught of which I know nothing; and, unless Thou dost forgive me and have mercy on me, I shall be of those who lose."

48 It was said, "O Noah! descend in safety from us, and blessings upon thee and upon (some) nations of those who are with thee; but (some) nations we will allow to enjoy prosperity and then there shall touch them from us grievous woe."

*Introduction
to the following stories*

49 These are stories of the unseen

ark, declaring that he would travel to one of the mountain peaks to be saved from the rising waters. The waters continued to rise and he finally drowned.

The biblical account states otherwise. Everyone in his family entered the ark and was saved. "Noah and his sons and his wife and his sons' wives entered the ark to escape the waters of the flood" (Gen 7:7).

11.44 *settled on Gudi* — A disagreement exists between the book of Genesis and the

Qur'an as to where Noah's ark finally rested following the Great Flood. Genesis 8:4 states that it settled on the mountains of Ararat, located in eastern Turkey near the Georgian border. The Qur'an states that it settled on Mt. Gudi (also known as Mt. Judi), located in southeast Turkey near the Iraqi border (see **Noah's Ark...Where Is It?** on p. 388). **11.49** Muhammad claimed that the story of Noah and the Great Flood was unknown to the Meccan people and himself prior to

which we reveal to thee; thou didst not know them, thou nor thy people before this. Be patient, then; verily, the issue is for those who fear.

Hud

50 And unto 'Âd (we sent) their brother Hûd; he said, "O my people! serve God; ye have no god but Him. Ye do but devise a lie.

51 O my people! I do not ask you for hire in return; my hire created me: have ye then no sense?

52 "O my people! ask pardon of your Lord; then turn to Him; He will send the skies down on you in torrents; and He will add strength to your strength: do not then turn back sinners."

53 They said, "O Hûd! thou hast not come to us with a manifest sign; nor will we leave our gods at thy word; nor will we believe in thee.

54 We can only say that some of our gods have attacked thee with evil." Said he, "Verily, I call God to witness, and do ye bear witness too, that I am free from that which ye associate beside Him.

55 Plot then against me altogether, and give me no delay.

56 Verily, I rely upon God, my Lord and your Lord. There is no beast that walks, but He taketh it by its forelock. Verily, my Lord is on the right way!

57 But if ye turn your backs,—then I have conveyed to you what I was sent to you with; and my Lord will make another people your successors. Ye cannot harm Him at all; verily, my Lord is guardian over all!"

58 And when our order came we saved Hûd, and those who believed with him, by mercy from us; and we saved them from harsh torment.

---

the initial presentation of this surah.

11.50a According to Muhammad, the sin of the people of Ad was their polytheistic worship—a sin which happened to be the same as the Meccan people. Hud's message was repentance from the sin of polytheism and to the one true God, the Doctrine of Tauhid—an absolute monotheism (see Q 54.17-21, note).

11.50b *serve God; ye have no god but Him* — See Q 11.84 where the same words were spoken to the people of Midian. To the people of Ad were spoken similar words: "worship God; ye have no god but Him" (Q 11.61).

11.52 *ask pardon of your Lord; then turn*

to Him — This phrase is repeated three times in this surah (Q 11.52, 61, 90). It is addressed to the people of Ad, Thamud, and Midian.

11.54 Because Hud's warnings were unheeded by the people of Ad, he declared that he was "free from that which ye associate beside Him." This too paralleled Muhammad's own response to the people of Mecca (see Q 43.91-92).

11.58 *and those who believed with him, by mercy from us* — This phrase is repeated three times in this surah (Q 11.58, 66, 94) to Hud, Zali'h, and Sho'haib.

11.59 The infidels of Ad, said Muhammad, were cursed and will undergo a severe chas-

59   That (tribe of) 'Âd denied the signs of their Lord, and rebelled against His apostles, and followed the bidding of every headstrong tyrant.

60   They were followed in this world by a curse, and on the resurrection day—"Did not 'Âd disbelieve their Lord? Aye! away with 'Âd the people of Hûd!"

Zali'h

61   And unto Thamûd (we sent) their brother Zâli'h; said he, "O my people! worship God; ye have no god but Him. He it is that produced you from the earth, and made you live therein! Then ask pardon of Him; then turn again to Him: verily, my Lord is nigh and answers!"

62   They said, "O Zâli'h! thou wert amongst us one we hoped in before this: dost thou forbid us to worship what our fathers worshipped? verily, we are in hesitat-

ing doubt as to that to which thou callest us."

63   He said, "O my people! let us see; if I stand upon a manifest sign from my Lord, and there come from Him mercy, who will help me against God if I rebel against Him? Ye will add only to my loss.

64   O my people! this she-camel of God is a sign for you; leave her, then, to feed in God's earth, and touch her not with evil, or there will catch you torment that is nigh."

65   But they did hamstring her, and he said, "Enjoy yourselves in your houses for three days;—that is the promise that shall not be belied."

66   And when our order came we saved Zâli'h, and those who believed with him, by our mercy, from disgrace upon that day. Verily, thy Lord He is powerful and mighty.

67   And the noise caught those who had done wrong; and on the mor-

---

tisement at the Last Judgment. Once again, this corresponds to the words of judgment that Muhammad had spoken to the people of Mecca.

11.61a *worship God; ye have no god but Him* — Zali'h admonished the Thamudian people to repent and turn to Allah (see Q 11.50, 84 where almost the same words were spoken to the people of Ad and Midian).

11.61b *ask pardon of Him; then turn again to Him* — This phrase is repeated three times in this surah (Q 11.52, 61, 90). It is addressed to the people of Ad, Thamud, and Midian.

11.61-68 The legend of Thamud is repeated multiple times in the Qur'an (Q 91, note, cf. Q 26.141-159; 54.22-31; 69.4-8; 89.9).

11.62 Again, a parallel thought was presented by Muhammad regarding the people of Thamud with the people of Mecca. The people of Thamud criticized Zali'h for forbidding them of worshipping the gods of their fathers. The people of Mecca made a similar criticism of Muhammad.

11.66 *and those who believed with him, by our mercy* — This phrase is repeated three times in this surah (Q 11.58, 66, 94) to Hud, Zali'h, and Sho'haib (Jethro).

row they were lying corpses in their houses,

68 as though they had never dwelt therein. Did not Thamûd indeed disbelieve in their Lord? Aye! away with Thamûd!

Abraham

69 Our messengers did come to Abraham with glad tidings; they said, "Peace!" He said, "Peace be it!" nor did he delay to bring the roasted calf.

70 But when he saw that their hands reached not thereto, he could not understand them, and harboured fear of them. They said, "Fear not. Verily, we are sent unto the people of Lot."

71 And his wife was standing by, laughing; and we gave her the glad tidings of Isaac, and of Jacob after Isaac.

72 Said she, "Alas for me! shall I bear a son when I am an old woman, and this husband of mine an old man? Verily, this is a wonderful thing!"

73 They said, "Dost thou wonder at the bidding of God? God's mercy and blessings upon you, ye people of the house! Verily, He is to be praised and glorified."

74 And when his terror left Abraham, and the glad tidings came to him, he wrangled with us about the people of Lot;

75 verily, Abraham was clement, pitiful, relenting.

76 "O Abraham! avoid this; verily, the bidding of thy Lord has come; verily, there is coming to them torment that cannot be put off."

Lot

77 And when our messengers came to Lot, he was grieved for them; but his arm was straitened for them, and he said, "This is a troublesome day!"

78 And his people came to him, rushing at him, for before that they used to work evil. He said, "O my people! here are my daughters,

11.69-76 This passage is based upon Gen 18:1-33.

11.70 *when he saw that their hands reached not thereto* — That is, when Abraham saw that the messengers did not reach to eat some of the meat.

11.71 According to Muhammad, Sarah laughed prior to hearing the news that she would give birth to Isaac. In contrast, the biblical account states that Sarah laughed after she heard of the news of her coming pregnancy with Isaac (see Gen 18:10-12).

11.74 *he wrangled with us about the people of Lot* — This is a summary of the intercessory prayer of Abraham on behalf of the people of Sodom. In the biblical account, he finally pleaded, "May the Lord not be angry, but let me speak just once more. What if only ten can be found there?" and the Lord answered, "For the sake of ten, I will not destroy it" (Gen 18:32).

11.77-83 Angels (messengers) came to Lot and admonished him and his family to flee the city of Sodom. This passage is based

Noah's Ark...Where Is It?

The Bible and the Qur'an differ in their understanding of the final resting place of Noah's Ark. On the one hand, Genesis 8:4 claims that "the ark came to rest on the mountains of Ararat" in the region of present day Armenia and eastern Turkey. On the other hand, Surah 11.44 claims that "it settled on Gudi." Mount Gudi (also known as Mount Judi) is situated approximately 200 miles (320 kilometers) to the southwest of the mountains of Ararat in Kurdistan (a politically contested area in southeast Turkey). Yet since some cartographers claim that Mount Gudi is part of the Ararat mountain range, the possibility exists that the contrast in the Bible and the Qur'an pertaining to the final resting place of Noah's Ark is a difference that lacks a distinction.

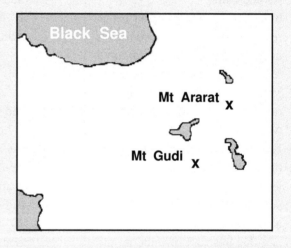

In the Qur'an, the ark comes to rest on Mount Judi in Turkey rather than Mt. Ararat as in the Bible. The Qur'an does not include the narrative about Noah's drunkenness, which has a prominent place in the Bible. The Qur'an also classifies Noah's wife as a nonbeliever.

—Diane Morgan, *The Essential Islam*, p. 40

they are purer for you; then, fear God, and do not disgrace me through my guests;—is there not among you one right-thinking man?"

79   They said, "Thou knowest that we have no claim on thy daughters; verily, thou knowest what we want!"

80   He said, "Had I but power over you; or could I but resort to some strong column...!"

81   (The angels) said, "O Lot! verily, we are the messengers of thy Lord, they shall certainly not reach thee; then travel with thy people in the darkness of the night, and let none of you look round except thy wife: verily, there shall befall her what befalls them. Verily, their appointment is for the morning! and is not the morning nigh?"

82   And when our bidding came, we

made their high parts their low parts. And we rained down upon them stones and baked clay one after another,

83   marked, from thy Lord, and these are not so far from the unjust!

Jethro (Sho'haib)

84   And unto Midian (we sent) their brother Sho'hâib. He said, "O my people! serve God; ye have no god but Him, and give not short measure and weight. Verily, I see you well off; but, verily, I fear for you the torments of an encompassing day.

85   O my people! give measure and weight fairly, and defraud not men of their things; and wreak not wrong in the earth, corrupting it.

86   God's residue is better for you if ye be believers. But I am not a

upon Gen 19:1-29.

11.81 According to Muhammad, the angels permitted Lot's wife to look back, knowing full well that judgment would await her as she did so. In the Genesis account, the angels instructed everyone who were fleeing— including Lot's wife—not to look back. In disobedience, she did so and was turned into a pillar of salt (Gen 19:26).

11.82 *rained down upon them stones of baked clay* — In the Qur'an, two versions are presented of the destruction of Sodom and Gomorrah. One is the destruction via baked clay, as we see here (see Q 15.74; 51.33), and the other is the destruction via an enormous sand storm (Q 29.40; 54.34). The Bible, however, speaks otherwise. Ac-

cording to Gen. 19:23, a burning sulphur rained down from heaven and destroyed the two cities.

11.84-95 *Sho'haib* — The Old Testament identifies him with two names: Jethro (Ex. 3:1) and Hobab (Num 10:29). The names *Hobab* and *Sho'haib* are phonetically similar, suggesting that it is the same person. According to Muhammad, Sho'haib (Jethro) served as an apostle to the Midianite people (see Q 26.176-191 note, for a fuller discussion of this individual).

11.84 *serve God; ye have no god but Him* — See Q 11.50 where the same words were spoken to the people of Ad. Almost the same words were spoken to the people of Thamud: "worship God; ye have no god

guardian over you."

87 They said, "O Sho'hâib! Do thy prayers bid thee that we should forsake what our fathers served, or that we should not do as we please with our wealth? Thou art, forsooth, the clement and straightforward one!"

88 He said, "O my people! Do ye see? If I stand upon a manifest sign from my Lord, and He provides me from Himself with a goodly provision, and I consent not with you to that which I forbid you, I only wish to better you so far as I can,—nor comes my grace through any one but God; on Him do I rely, and unto Him I turn.

89 O my people! let not a breach with me make you so sin that there befall you the like of that which befel the people of Noah, or the people of Hûd, or the people of Zâli'h—nor are the people of Lot so far from you!

90 Ask pardon, then, from your Lord, then turn to Him; verily, my Lord is merciful, loving!"

91 They said, "O Sho'hâib! we do not understand much of what thou sayest, and we see that thou art weak amongst us; and were it not for thy family we would stone thee, nor couldst thou be powerful over us."

92 He said, "O my people! are my family more esteemed by you than God? or have you taken Him as something to cast behind your backs? Verily, my Lord, whate'er ye do, doth comprehend.

93 O my people! act according to your power; verily, I too will act, and ye at length shall know! To whomsoever torment comes it shall disgrace him, and him who is a liar. Watch then; verily, I with you am watching too!"

94 And when our bidding came we saved Sho'hâib, and those who believed with him, by our mercy; and the noise caught those who had done wrong, and on the morrow they were in their houses prone,

95 as though they had not dwelt therein. Aye! "Away with Midian!"

---

but Him (Q 11.61).

11.87 Sho'haib (Jethro) was "the clement and straightforward one." The Bible understood Sho'haib similarly.

11.90 *ask pardon of your Lord; then turn to Him* — This phrase is repeated three times in this surah (Q 11.52, 61, 90). It is addressed to the people of Ad, Thamud, and Midian.

11.91 *were it not for thy family we would stone thee* — That is, because he was re-

lated to Moses, they would show deference to him.

11.94 *and those who believed with him, by our mercy* — This phrase is repeated three times in this surah (Q 11.58, 66, 94) to Hud, Zali'h, and Sho'haib (Jethro).

11.96-98 The point of this passage is that Moses was an apostle sent from Allah to Pharaoh. Pharaoh opposed his message and suffered judgment from Allah.

11.101 Again, Muhammad appealed to the

as it was, "Away with Thamûd!"

Moses

96 And we sent Moses with our signs and with obvious power

97 unto Pharaoh and his chiefs; but they followed Pharaoh's bidding, and Pharaoh's bidding was not straightforward.

98 He shall approach his people on the resurrection day, and take them down to water at the Fire,—an evil watering-place to water at!

Rewards and punishments

99 In this (world) were they followed by a curse; and on the resurrection day evil shall be the aid they are aided with!

100 That is one of the stories of the cities which we recite to thee— some of them are standing now and some mown down!

101 We did not wrong them, but they wronged themselves. Their gods availed them naught, on which they called instead of God, when once the bidding of thy Lord had come; nor did they add save to

their downfall!

102 Thus is thy Lord's overtaking when He overtakes the cities that have done wrong; verily, His over-taking is grievous, keen.

103 Verily, in that is a sign to him who fears the torment of the last day;— that is a day unto which men shall be gathered;—that is a witnessed day!

104 We will not delay it, save unto a numbered and appointed time.

105 The day when it shall come no soul shall speak save by His permission, and amongst them (shall be) the wretched and the glad.

106 And as for those who are wretched —why, in the Fire! there shall they groan and sob!

107 to dwell therein for aye, so long as the heavens and the earth endure; save what thy Lord will. Verily, thy Lord is one who works His will.

108 And as for those who are glad— why, in Paradise! to dwell therein for aye, so long as the heavens and the earth endure; save what thy Lord will,—a ceaseless boon!

Admonition to faith

Doctrine of Tauhid—absolute monotheism— as foundational to one's standing before Al- lah. Those who lived as polytheists would suffer eternal torments whereas those who remained faithful to the one true God would be rewarded with an entrance into Paradise.
11.105 At the Last Judgment, no soul shall speak except by permission from Allah.

11.107 According to this verse, one's abode in the Fire (Hell) is eternal—"as long as the heavens and the earth endure."
11.108 According to this verse, one's abode in Paradise is also eternal—"so long as the heavens and the earth endure."
11.109 In this surah, this is the third time that Muhammad repeated a problem that

109   Be not then in doubt concerning what these men do serve;—they only serve as their fathers served before; and we will give them their portion undiminished.

110   We gave Moses the Book before, and then they disagreed concerning it, and, had it not been for a word that had been passed by thy Lord, it would have been decided between them but, verily, they are (still) in hesitating doubt concerning it.

111   But, verily, every one thy Lord will surely repay for their works; verily, He of what they do is well aware!

112   Do thou then be upright, as thou art bidden, and whosoever turns repentantly with thee; and transgress ye not:—verily, He on what ye do doth look.

113   Lean not unto those who do wrong, lest the Fire touch you, for ye have no patrons but God; and, moreover, ye shall not be helped!

114   And be thou steadfast in prayer at the two ends of the day, and the (former and latter) parts of the night. Verily, good works remove evil works;—that is a reminder to the mindful!

115   And be thou patient, for God wastes not the hire of those who do good.

A final warning

116   And were there among the generations before you any endowed with a remnant (of piety) forbidding evildoing in the earth, save a few of those whom we saved; but the evildoers followed what they enjoyed, and were sinners.

117   Thy Lord would not have destroyed the cities unjustly while the people

---

typified infidels: they worshipped in a manner that corresponded to their fathers' paganism (see Q 11.62, 87).

11.110a *the Book* — The Pentateuch (Genesis through Deuteronomy).

11.110 Quite possibly, this passage is a criticism of the Jews who lived in Mecca. Muhammad was critical of them for not rightly believing their Jewish Scriptures (the Torah).

11.111-112 According to Muhammad, salvation was a combination of being repaid for one's works, along with an attitude of repentance (see Q 11.3, note).

11.113 People should be careful with the friends they keep. Infidels can influence a person to unbelief. The future is catastrophic since all infidels are cast in the Fire.

11.114 Muhammad admonished Muslims to begin and end each day with prayer (see Q 73.3-6, note, and **al-Salat** on pp. 169-170). In the Islamic tradition, prayers are prescribed and obligatory throughout the day. The first prayer is called *fajr*, and offered before sunrise. The last is called *'isha* and is to be offered after night has set in. The other prayers are laid out in a regimented schedule throughout the day.

The abundance of good works (such as prayer) can have the effect of removing, or replacing, bad works. In the hadithic literature, Muhammad said: "Fear Allah wherever you are, and follow up a bad deed with a good one and it will wipe it out, and behave well towards people" (*Imam An-Nawawi's 40*

of them were welldoers.

118 Had thy Lord pleased, He would have made men one nation; but they will not cease to differ,

119 save those thy Lord has had mercy on. For this has He created them, and the word of thy Lord is fulfilled, "I will surely fill hell with ginns and mankind altogether."

120 And all that we relate to thee of the stories of the apostles is what will stablish thy heart: and herein has the truth come to thee, and an admonition and a reminder to the believers.

121 Say to those who believe not, "Act according to your power, verily, we are acting too!

122 And wait ye, verily, we are waiting too!"

A final admonition
to serve God

123 God's are the unseen things of the heavens and of the earth; and unto Him the affair doth all return. Then serve Him and rely on Him; for thy Lord is not heedless of that which ye do.

Surah 10

In the name of the merciful and compassionate God.

1 A. L. R.

Warnings

Hadiths, no. 18; also see Q 11.3; 25.70-76; 39.73; 40.13; 41.36 and 72.14).

11.119 *ginns* — genies (see **Occultism in Seventh Century Arabia** on pp. 123-125).

11.118 *one nation* — The world, said Muhammad, has divided into a multitude of nations due to their stubborn differences. The only nations that has held together are the ones which yielded to Allah and were the recipients of His mercy. The passage, then, is a subtle affirmation of the notion of the islamification of the world. It speaks to the "one Muslim nation" concept presented here and elsewhere in the Qur'an (see Q 10.19; 42.8 and 43.33; **Islamification** on pp. 851-852).

11.120 Muhammad saw himself as "a reminder to the believers" (see Q 18.101; 20.3, 99, 124; 25.18, 29; 36.11, 69; 38.1, 8, 43, 49, 87; 40.54 and 43.5).

Surah 10. The title of this surah, *Jonah,* comes from verse 98. It is a lengthy discussion on the topic of repentance, a frequent theme in the Qur'an. The reasons for repentance are enumerated, consequences are foretold for those who fail to repent, and examples are presented of previous messengers sent from God who called their contemporaries to repent. Muhammad saw himself as part of this long line of divinely chosen messengers.

10.1a Literally, *Alif Lam Ra.* See Q 32.1, note.

10.1b *the wise Book* — Muhammad described the Qur'an as a wise book and inspired of God.

10.3, 5-6 According to this passage, the first reason to worship Allah is that Allah is the Creator of the heavens and the earth. "That is God for you—your Lord," Muham-

Those are the signs of the wise Book!

2 was it a wonder to the folk that we inspired a man from amongst themselves, "Warn thou the folk; and give glad tidings, to those who believe, that for them there is an advance of sincerity gone before them with their Lord?" The misbelievers say, "Verily, this is an obvious sorcerer!"

Two reasons
to worship Allah

3 Verily, your Lord is God, who created the heavens and the earth in six days; then He made for the throne, to govern the affair; there is no intercessor, except after His permission. That is God for you—your Lord! Then worship Him—do ye not mind?

4 To Him is your return all of you—God's promise in truth; verily, He produces the creature, then He makes it return again, that He may recompense those who believe and do what is right with justice; but those who misbelieve, for them is a drink of boiling water, and grievous woe, for that they did misbelieve.

5 He it is who made the sun for a brightness, and the moon for a light, and decreed for it mansions, that ye may know the number of the years and the reckoning.—God only created that in truth. He details the signs unto a people who do know.

6 Verily, in the alternation of night and day, and in what God has created of the heavens and the earth, are signs unto a people who do fear.

Paradise and Hell

7 Verily, those who hope not for our meeting, and are content with the life of this world, and are comforted thereby, and those who are

mad said. Therefore, "worship Him." The Bible makes a similar argument (see Ps 33:6-9; 119:90; 139:13; Rom 1:19-20).
10.4a *believe and do what is right* — These words are repeated often in the Qur'an and serve as a brief summary of the Islamic gospel (see Q 103.3 note).
10.4b According to this verse, the second reason to worship Allah was that all people will one day be summoned to Allah and receive their recompense from Him (see **The Last Judgment** on pp. 46-50).
10.7-9 Muhammad divided people in two broad categories: (a) those who are not

concerned about a Last Judgment, neglect divine revelation, and therefore emphasize life in this world, and (b) those who believe and do what is right.
10.8 *their resort is the fire* — The eternal destiny of infidels is the fire. In Hadith, Muhammad reportedly said that "people will be thrown into Hell (Fire) and it will keep on saying, 'Is there any more?' till the Lord of the worlds puts His Foot over it, whereupon its different sides will come close to each other, and it will say, 'Qad! Qad! (enough! enough!) by Your Izzat (honor and power)" (*Sahih Bukhari* 9.93.481).

8 neglectful of our signs,
—these, their resort is fire for that which they have earned!

9 Verily, those who believe and do what is right, their Lord guides them by their faith; beneath them shall rivers flow in the gardens of pleasure.

10 Their cry therein shall be, "Celebrated be Thy praises, O God!" and their salutation therein shall be, "Peace!" and the end of their cry shall be, "Praise (belongs) to God, the Lord of the worlds!"

11 And if God should hasten on the bad to men as they would hasten on the good, their appointed time would surely be fulfilled. But we will let those who hope not for our meeting go on in their rebellion, blindly wandering on.

Smugness

12 When distress touches man, he calls us to his side, whether sitting or standing; but when we have removed from him his distress, he passes on as though he had not called on us in a distress that

---

10.9a *believe and do what is right* — These words are repeated often in the Qur'an and serve as a brief summary of the Islamic gospel (see Q 103.3 note).

10.9b *beneath them rivers shall flow* — An oft repeated imagery of Paradise is that of gardens of sensual pleasure with underground rivers (aquifers) sufficiently close to the surface to keep the oases fertile and green (see Q 16.31; 18.31; 20.76; 25.10; 39.20; 85.11).

10.9-10 The eternal destiny of the righteous is Paradise. Paradise is described as: (a) rivers that flow in the gardens of pleasure, (b) a place of worship, and (c) a place of peace. In an earlier surah, Muhammad used the phrase "gardens of pleasure" in relationship to the harems of maidens in Paradise that will be assigned to the righteous (see Q 56.12-26). The word "pleasure" refers to sensual and erotic pleasure (also see Q 22.56; 31.8; 37.40-50; 68.34, and *The Virgins* on pp. 107-109).

10.10 *the Lord of the worlds!* — This is a common name for Allah in the Qur'an (see Q 1.2, note).

10.11 In this life, the unrighteous are described as rebellious to God and spiritually blind. The Bible characterizes the unrighteous in similar terms (see Matt 15:14; 23:16-26; Jn 9:39-41 and Titus 1:10).

10.12 Muhammad's point is that material comfort and the absence of trials tend to cause a person to depend less upon Allah. The inverse is equally true: trials tend to drive a person to Allah.

The Bible makes a similar claim. An indefinable fragrance exists within the spirits of those who have suffered on account of their submission and obedience to Christ. They possess a peculiar meekness and a gentleness foreign to all other people. In his first epistle, the Apostle Peter made a remarkable statement where he spoke of such people. He said that 'he who has suffered in his body is done with sin' (1 Pet 4:1). The Apostle was not speaking of a form of sinless perfection attainable in this life, but of a quality of life especially characterized by holiness.

The Apostles

A major theme in the Qur'an is the role of apostles in presenting divine revelation to people on earth. Muhammad believed that Allah commissioned various individuals throughout history as apostles. He said that "every nation has its apostle" (Q 10.47) and "every nation has its appointed time" (Q 10.49). Maulana Muhammad Ali has written, "The Qur'an...not only establishes the theory that prophets have appeared in all nations; it goes further and renders it necessary that a Muslim should believe in all those prophets."[1] If a nation failed to heed the message of its apostle, it would be destroyed in a horrific judgment (see Q 26.191-212; 43.6-8; 45.28).

Undergirding the message of the apostles was the notion of *the judgment of history*. They maintained that since there is no god but Allah, all who fail to worship the one true God would suffer accordingly. As history unfolded, they would be judged—severely. Moreover, they would then suffer the greater and more permanent judgment at the Last Judgment where they would be cast into the flames of Hell forever. The Qur'an states: "We have already destroyed generations before you when they did wrong, and there came to them their apostles with manifest signs, but they would not believe. Thus do we reward the sinful people" (Q 10.13).

A corollary to this doctrine was the belief that Muhammad was not only an apostle, he was the last apostle. The divine revelations he presented to the people of Mecca and Medinah—the 114 surahs that constitute the Qur'an—were the final revelations offered to the world. They are most complete and therefore most authoritative. Muslims were commissioned by Allah to take the message of the Qur'an to the world. The vision was the earth being comprised of "one nation" living in obedience and subjection to Allah (see Q 23.52). Their purpose, then, were to "expand and extend Islam until the whole world is under Muslim rule."[2]

This notion of *the judgment of history* underwent a change at the midpoint of the Qur'an. The Meccan surahs (Periods 1 through 5) defined this judgment as divine retribution independent of human participation (such as Noah's flood and the plagues of Egypt). The Medinan surahs (Period 6), however, defined this judgment as divine retribution that invited—indeed, required—human participation. It is here, in the Medinan surahs, then, that we see the Doctrine of Jihad (Holy War) emerge and take shape.

The various apostles mentioned in the Qur'an are: Adam, Enoch, Noah, Abraham, Lot, Moses, Aaron, David, Solomon, Elijah, Ezekiel, Jonah, John the Baptist, Jesus, Zali'h, Hud, Jethro, Loqman, and DHu 'Qarnain (Alexander the Great). Curiously, neither Ishmael nor Isaac are mentioned as apostles. Another curiosity is that the hadithic record notes that Muhammad believed "Allah created Adam, making him sixty cubits [ninety feet] tall" (*Sahih Bukhari* 4.55.543). This listing of apostles, however, is only a sampling of the multitudes of apostles that Allah had commissioned. A. J. Wensinck writes that the full number of Apostles "do not exceed the number of 315, whereas that of the Prophets varies between 1000 and 224,000."[3] Other scholars put forth differing numbers.

The catastrophes most often mentioned in the Qur'an as examples of *the judgment of history* are: Noah's Flood, the destruction of Sodom and Gomorrah, and the destruction of Pharaoh's army at the Red Sea. Muhammad also believed that the people of Mecca would someday be destroyed by Allah for rejecting his message and ministry. This occurred when Muhammad declared jihad on Mecca and conquered the city in A.D. 630.

The Christian faith. The New Testament also speaks of apostles, but in a manner that differs considerably from that which is mentioned in the Qur'an. Following a night of prayer, Jesus chose his apostles whom He mentored during His three year ministry prior to His death and resurrection. One defected and committed suicide—Judas Iscariot—and replaced by Matthias. Saul of Tarsus was later added to the band of twelve, known as the Apostle to the Gentiles. Jesus then commissioned them to take the gospel to all the world, baptizing them and making disciples (see Matt 28:19-20; Acts 1:8).

The apostles were given the commission of evangelizing the world (Matt 28:18-20; Mk 16:15-16; Lk 24:47-18; Acts 1:8), but to do so peacefully and gently, independent of jihads or any other form of coercion. "Go!" Jesus said, "I am sending you out like lambs among wolves" (Lk 10:3). The fact that in the history of the Church, especially during the Middle Ages, jihadic activities occurred in the name of Christ (the most notable ones being the Crusades, the Inquisition, and the pogroms directed against the Jews), they do not change the original mandate given by Jesus. As one Christian missionary wrote, "We should have been glad to go on peacefully prosecuting our labors of love, and peacefully announcing the Gospel truths to every sinner within our reach."[4]

---

[1] Maulana Muhammad Ali, *The Religion of Islam*, p. 167.
[2] Paul Fregosi, *Jihad in the West*, p. 20.
[3] A. J. Wensinck, *The Muslim Creed*, p. 204.
[4] N. De Pressense, *The Christian World*, p. 111.

Besides the Last Judgment, the Qur'an developed the doctrine of the Judgment of History. While the Last Judgment will be concerned with the performance of individuals, the Judgment of History is visited upon nations, peoples, and communities on the basis of their collective performance. Because the Qur'an was immediately concerned with changing the attitudes of the Arabs—particularly Meccans—as a society, from the start it cited stories of earlier peoples and communities that met their doom because of their persistence in evil ways and their rejection of the call of their prophets...This attitude strongly imbues the Qur'anic teaching with the idea of the eventual vindication and success of the truth; Muhammad and his message must, therefore, be successful, despite heavy odds, since this is God's design.

—Marjorie Kelly, *Islam: the Religious and Political Life of a World Community*, p. 46

For some observers, the triumph of Islam in the East in the seventh century was regarded as the judgment of history upon a degenerate Christianity. In the Letters to the Seven Churches in Revelation 1-3, the Apostle John warned the churches of these problems. The degeneration had already begun...It helps explain the readiness of Christian Arabs to accept Islam. Similarly today, the Church is in a state of degeneration...In many Western countries, Islam is on the rise as Christians are accepting it as an acceptable alternative to Christianity.

—David J. Jonsson, *The Clash of Ideologies*, p. 21

When, in 1096, the Crusades were launched, the Jihad had already been in action against Christendom for nearly five hundred years. It was the Jihad's recent successes in Spain that inspired, so to speak, the pope to create the Crusades and to order the Crusaders to march to the Holy Land.

—Paul Fregosi, *Jihad in the West*, p. 17

touched him. Thus unto the extravagant is made seemly that which they have done.

Examples from history

13 We have already destroyed generations before you when they did wrong, and there came to them their apostles with manifest signs, but they would not believe. Thus do we reward the sinful people.

*Example of
the Meccan people*

14 Then we made you their successors in the earth after them, that we may see how ye will act.

15 But when our evident signs are recited to them, those who hope not for our meeting say, "Bring a Qur'ân other than this; or change it." Say, "It is not for me to change it of my own accord; I do not follow aught but what I am inspired with; verily, I fear, if I rebel against my Lord, the torment of a mighty day!"

*The question of
divine revelation*

16 Say, "Had God pleased, I should not have recited it to you, nor taught you therewith. I have tarried a lifetime amongst you before it;—have ye not then any sense?"

10.13 This is a major theme in the Qur'an: just as Allah judged peoples in times past, He will judge the people of Mecca in the current time. To make his case, Muhammad drew from biblical as well as non-biblical sources (e.g., Noah, Abraham, Lot, Moses, John the Baptist, Jesus, Hud, Sho'haib, and Zali'h). Jesus made a similar argument regarding the unbelievers of His day (see Matt 23:33-39).

10.15 *if I rebel against my Lord* — Even Muhammad had no absolute confidence that he would avoid Hell in the afterlife. Like everyone else, he believed that he could fail the test of righteousness, lapse into sin, and live as an apostate. Therefore, he declared openly that all people—including himself—needed to live circumspectly, lest they find themselves condemned to Hell (see Q 13.37; 17.73; **The Last Judgment** on pp. 46-50).

In contrast, the Bible offers salvation as a free gift—not of works. This provides a person a sense of confidence that Heaven awaits him or her, provided that he or she has received the gift of eternal life in Jesus Christ. That is, once given, the gift of salvation cannot be taken away. James Montgomery Boice wrote, "Christianity does not have a shaky foundation. It is not a gospel of percentages and possibilities. It is a certain gospel. It is the message of our complete ruin in sin but of God's perfect and certain remedy in Christ" (*Foundations of the Christian Faith*, p. 526). John R. W. Stott adds: "Justification is a gift of God's sheer grace, not a reward for any merit or works of ours. For God's 'grace' is his spontaneous generosity, his free and unmerited favour, his gracious kindness to the undeserving. Grace is God loving, God stooping, God coming, God giving" (*Believing and Obeying Jesus Christ*, p. 69).

17   Who is more unjust than he who forges against God a lie, or says His signs are lies? verily, the sinners shall not prosper.

18   They worship beside God what can neither harm them nor profit them, and they say, "These are our intercessors with God!" Say, "Will ye inform God of aught in the heavens or the earth, that He knows not of?" Celebrated be His praise! and exalted be He, above what they associate with Him!

The question of
Muhammad's credentials

19   People were but one nation once, then they disagreed; and had it not been for thy Lord's word already passed, there would have been decided between them that concerning which they disagreed.

20   They say, "Why is not a sign sent down upon him from his Lord?"

Muhammad's response

Say, "The unseen is only God's; but wait ye for a while, verily, I with you am one of those who wait!"

10.17 Muhammad wondered out loud which fate is worse: (a) he who writes a document and falsely ascribes it to God as divinely inspired, or (b) he who calls false that which is truly a divine revelation. He offered no answer to this question other than to say that "sinners shall not prosper."

10.18 The gods of the Meccan people, Muhammad insisted, "can neither harm them nor profit them." That is to say, they have no power whatsoever, other than to deceive. The Bible makes similar statements of idols (see Ps 115:4-8; 135:15-18; Isa 40:19-20; 1 Cor 8:4-6).

10.19-20 Muhammad's critics were relentless in their insistence that his surahs be accompanied with a miraculous sign (see Q 6.4-8; 10.19-20; 13.27; 29.50). Muhammad responded by noting that at the beginnings of human civilization, people divided into separate communities due to disagreements. Muhammad believed that the remedy of the divisions in Mecca was the divine word, not the manifestation of miraculous signs.

Christians, of course, disagree with this argument. Discerning the divine word from rogue or charlatan prophets required the presence of miraculous signs as a way of confirming (that is, credentialing) that which is truly from God. Muhammad's appeal to an ancient civilization, then, was a *non sequitur.* It offered no help in answering the pressing question that the people of Mecca were asking: was Muhammad a prophet sent from God, or was he not? (see **John of Damascus** on pp. 247-248).

"Authentic Christianity," writes John R. W. Stott, "the Christianity of Christ as his apostles, is supernatural Christianity. It is not a tame and harmless ethic, consisting of a few moral platitudes, spiced with a dash of religion. It is rather a resurrection religion, a life lived by the power of God" (*Christ the Controversialist,* p. 63). It is grounded, first and foremost, in the resurrection of Jesus Christ from the dead. Surrounding this signature event are multitudes of miracles (Jn 20:30-31; 21:25).

Strategem of the infidels

21 When we have let men taste of mercy after distress which has touched them, lo! they use a stratagem against our signs! Say, "God is quicker at stratagem." Verily, our messengers write down what stratagem ye use.

22 He it is who makes you travel in the land and sea, until when ye are in the ships—and these carry them afloat with a favouring wind, and they rejoice therein, there comes to them a violent wind, and there comes to them the wave from every place, and they think that they are encompassed about then they call on God, sincere in religion towards Him, "If thou dost save from this we will surely be of those who thank."

23 But when He has saved them, lo! they are wilful in the earth unjustly;—O ye folk! your wilfulness against yourselves is but a provision of this world's life; then unto us is your return, and we will inform you of that which ye have done!

24 Verily, the likeness of this world's life is like water which we send down from the sky, and the plants of the earth, from which men and cattle eat, are mingled therewith; until when the earth puts on its gilding and is adorned, the people thereof think that they have power over it. Our order comes to it by night or. day, and we make it as it were mown down—as though it had not yesterday been rich!—Thus do we detail the signs unto a people who reflect.

25 God calls unto the abode of peace, and guides whom He will into the right path.

Black and white skin

26 To those who do what is good, goodness and increase! nor shall blackness or abasement cover their faces! these are the fellows of

10.21-25 Infidels, said Muhammad, turn to Allah in times of trial—yet turn away when the trial is removed. It is a stratagem that they believe works to their advantage. Yet it is, Muhammad added, nothing more than an approach destined to fail—for Allah knows that such a stratagem is not "the right path" (see Q 72.2, note).

10.26-27 Muhammad described the appearance of those at the Last Judgment as either possessing white skin (the righteous) or black skin (the unrighteous). Those with black skin are "the Fellows of the Fire."

Some have wondered if a racial overtone is present in this passage—that is, people with Negroid features are condemned to the fires of Hell. Since nothing exists in mainstream Islamic scholarship to support this view, such an interpretation should be discarded. The references to dark and light skin are of symbolic importance—nothing more (see Q 39.60; 43.17). The Bible makes use of a similar scheme of colors (See Ps 51:7; Isa. 1:18; 50:10; Eph 6:12; 2 Pet 1:19; Rev

Paradise, they shall dwell therein for aye.

27 But, as for those who have earned ill, the reward of evil is the like thereof; abasement shall cover them! they shall have none to defend them against God;—as though their faces were veiled with the deep darkness of the night; these are the fellows of the Fire, and they shall dwell therein for aye.

Absolute monotheism

28 And on the day we gather them all together then we will say to those who associated other gods (with us), "To your places, ye and your associates!" and we will part them; and their associates will say, "It was not us ye worshipped.

29 —But God is witness enough between us and you, that we were heedless of your worshipping us."

30 There shall every soul prove what it has sent on before; and they shall be returned unto God, their God, their true sovereign, and that which they devised shall stray away from them.

Catechism

31 Say, "Who provides you from the heaven and the earth? who has dominion over hearing and sight? and who brings forth the living from the dead, and brings forth the dead from the living? and who governs the affair?" And they will say, "God." Say, "Do ye not then fear?"

32 That is God, your true Lord! and what is there after the truth but error? how then can ye turn away?

33 Thus is the word of thy Lord verified against those who commit abomination; verily, they will not believe.

34 Say, "Is there any of your associates who can produce a creature and then turn it back again?" Say, "God produces a creature, then turns it back again; how then can ye lie?"

35 Say, "Is there any of your associates who guides unto the truth?" Say, "God guides unto the truth." Is then He who guides unto the truth more worthy to be followed, or he that guides not except he be himself guided? What ails you then, how ye judge?

36 But most of them follow only suspicion; verily, suspicion does not avail against the truth at all; verily,

7:14).

10.28-30 Muhammad condemned Arabic Star Family religious beliefs with his reiteration of the Doctrine of Tauhid—absolute monotheism. All who fail to embrace this doctrine, said Muhammad, will be gathered "on the day" (the Last Judgment) and suf-

fer accordingly.

10.31-36 Polytheists were encouraged to reconsider their rejection of monotheism with seven key questions. Each of the questions was intended to draw the person back to a monotheistic orientation and worship of Allah.

God knows what they do.

Qur'an

37 This Qur'ân could not have been devised by any beside God; but it verifies that which was before it, and details the Book—there is no doubt therein—from the Lord of the worlds.

38 Do they say, "He hath devised it?" say then, "Bring a sûrah like it,—and call, if ye can, on other, than God, if ye do tell the truth!"

39 Yet they call that a lie, the knowledge of which they cannot compass, while its interpretation has not yet come to them; so did those before them charge with lying, and see what was the end of the un-

10.37 *This Qur'an* — The divine Book in Paradise (see **The Perspicuous Book** on pp. 178-179). The phrase "this Qur'an could not have been devised by any beside God" is the bedrock credential of faith for Muslims. It is commonly believed in the Muslim world that Muhammad was illiterate and therefore could not have been its author. This notion is based upon Q 2.78 which uses the Arabic word *ummiyyun* which means *unlettered* or *illiterate*. Muslims also believe that the literary style and contents far exceeds the abilities of any human being.

Christians are of a different opinion. First, the use of the word *ummiyyun* in Q 2.78 could also be defined as a people without a written Scripture, as was the case of the Muslim people prior to the completion of the Qur'an (see Q 3.20). Second, in his early adulthood Muhammad ran a commercial business in Mecca. It would have been impractical for him to have done so if he were illiterate. Third, the Qur'an is replete with historical and archeological errors. Moreover, it is dependent upon apocryphal writings that are spurious, clearly fictional, and full of error. Hence, rather than receive the surahs directly from the archangel Gabriel in the form of dictation, Christians maintain that Muhammad researched numerous documents, seeking to make a case for his new theology (the

best that he could) about Allah.

10.38 Muhammad challenged those who insisted that the Qur'an was of his own composition and not of a divine origin. He posited that his opponents should produce their own surahs and then allow others to compare the two. He was confident that his was of a vastly superior quality which demonstrated its divine authorship (see Q 17.88, note).

In his commentary of this surah, Ibn Kathir explained: "The Qur'an has a miraculous nature that cannot be imitated. No one can produce anything similar to the Qur'an, nor ten Surahs or even one Surah like it. The eloquence, clarity, precision and grace of the Qur'an cannot be but from Allah. The great and abundant principles and meanings within the Qur'an—which are of great benefit in this world and for the Hereafter—cannot be but from Allah. There is nothing like His High Self and Attributes or like His sayings and actions. Therefore His Words are not like the words of His creatures."

10.39 Muhammad argued that the charge that he was a liar was an old ploy, used by peoples throughout history who rejected the apostles sent from God (see **The Apostles** on pp. 398-400).

10.40 *Lord knows best who are corrupters* — Muhammad claimed that the Qur'an is the

just!

40 Of them are some who believe therein; and of them are some who do not believe therein but thy Lord knows best who are corrupters.

41 But if they call thee liar, say, "I have my work, and ye have your work; ye are clear of what I work, and I am clear of what ye work."

The fate of the
spiritually deaf and blind

42 There are some of them who listen to thee—canst thou make the deaf to hear, although they have no sense?

43 And of them are some who look at thee—canst thou guide the blind, although they cannot see?

44 Verily, God wrongs not man at all, but men do wrong themselves.

45 And on the day when we will gather them together it will be as though they had not tarried save an hour of the day, they shall know each other. Lost are those who called the meeting with God a lie, and were not guided!

46 Either we will show thee something of that with which we threatened them, or we will take thee to ourself, for unto us is their return; then is God a witness to what they do.

47 Every nation has its apostle; and when their apostle comes to them, it is decided between them with justice, and they are not wronged.

48 But they say, "When is this threat (to come), if ye tell the truth?"

last revelation in a series of revelations from God. It comprises the unaltered and direct words of God. The document is therefore unique in that it is the only revealed book that exists today in the precise form and content in which it was originally revealed.

All other revelations (e.g., the Old and New Testaments) have been corrupted due to scribal errors—intended and unintended. Hence all these sacred literatures contain false doctrine, such as the Doctrines of the Trinity and the Incarnation (see notes on Q 10.68-70; 37.149-166; 39.4; 41.47 and 10.68-70). In his commentary, Ibn Kathir claimed that the earlier revelations show "the changes, perversions, and corruption that have taken place within these Books." Christian scholars reject this claim, countering that the Qur'an is a document replete with error.
10.42 Muhammad characterized the infidel

as spiritually deaf and blind. His point was that it was impossible to communicate spiritual truths to such people. Their fate is settled and at the Last Judgment they will be held accountable for their refusal to follow the path that leads to eternal life.

According to the Bible, unbelievers are also characterized as spiritually deaf and blind (Isa 43:8; Matt 23:16; Jn 9:39; Rev 3:17). Yet, the Bible also states that God opens their spiritual eyes and ears so that they can know and understand spiritual truth (Eph 1:18-22; cf Ps 119:18; Lk 24:45; Acts 16:14; 26:18; 1 Cor 2:9-16; 2 Cor 4:4-6; Eph 5:8).
10.44 Sin is ultimately a violation of one's self and brings injury to one's self (see Ps 38:3, 18; Rom 6:12).
10.47 *Every nation has its apostle* — Muhammad believed that every nation had a divine messenger, like himself, sent to draw

49　Say, "I have no power over my-self for harm or for profit, save what God will. Every nation has its appointed time; when their ap-pointed time comes to them they cannot delay it for an hour or bring it on."

Short catechism

50　Say, "Let us see now when the tor-ment comes to you, by night or day, what will the sinners fain bring on there-of?

51　And when it has fallen—will ye be-lieve in it now!—And yet ye wish to bring it on!

52　Then shall it be said to those who have done wrong, Taste ye the tor-ment of eternity! shall ye be rec-ompensed except for that which ye have earned?"

53　They will ask thee to inform them whether it be true. Say, "Aye, by my Lord! verily, it is the truth, nor can ye weaken him."

54　And if every soul that hath done wrong had whatever is in the earth, it would give it as a ransom. They will utter their repentance when they see the torment; and it shall be decided between them with jus-tice, nor shall they be wronged.

55　Is not indeed what is in the heav-ens and what is in the earth God's? is not indeed the promise of God true? Though most of them know not.

56　He quickens and He kills, and unto Him are ye returned!

57　O ye folk! there has come to you a warning from your Lord, and a balm for what is in your breasts, and a guidance and a mercy to be-lievers.

58　Say, "By the grace of God and by His mercy,—and in that let them rejoice! It is better than that which they collect!"

59　Let us see now what God has sent

people back to God. Most people, however, rejected their message (see **The Apostles** on pp. 398-400).

10.49 *Every nation has its appointed time* — Muhammad also believed that every na-tion will experience divine judgment in this life (prior to the hereafter) if it rejects the message of its divine messenger. Through-out the Qur'an, Muhammad illustrated such appointed times (e.g., Noah's Flood, the de-struction of Sodom and Gomorrah, the de-struction of the Thamudian people, and the destruction of Ad).

10.50-54 Throughout the Qur'an, the fun-damental reason to repent and return to Allah is the threat of eternal condemnation. One is to repent now during this life rather than weight for the moment when one is stand-ing before God at the Last Judgment. People will repent at that time, Muhammad explained, yet to no avail.

10.55-70 This passage is a series of addi-tional appeals designed to draw the infidel to repentance. The general thrust of the argument is that Allah is the sovereign Lord of all creation. He is all-knowing and all-pow-erful. To call Allah a liar and resist Him is futile. It is much better to receive His grace

down to you of provision! and yet ye have made. of it unlawful and lawful. Say, "Does God permit you, or against God do ye forge lies?"

60 What will those who forge lies against God think on the resurrection day? Verily, God is Lord of grace towards men, but most of them do not give thanks!

61 Nor shalt thou be in any affair, nor shalt thou recite concerning it a Qur'ân—nor shall ye do a work, without our being witness against you, when ye are engaged therein: nor does the weight of an atom escape thy Lord in earth or in heaven; nor is there less than that or greater, but it is in the perspicuous Book.

62 Are not, verily, the friends of God those on whom there is no fear, neither shall they be grieved?

63 —They who believed and who did fear

64 —for them are good tidings in the life of this world, and in the future too; there is no changing the words

of God! That is the mighty happiness!

65 Let not their speech grieve thee; verily, power is wholly God's! He both hears and knows.

66 Is not, verily, whoever is in the heavens and whoever is in the earth God's? What then do they follow who call on associates other than God? Verily, they follow nothing but suspicion, and verily, they are telling naught but lies.

67 He it is who made for you the night, that ye might rest therein, and the day to see therein; verily, in that are. signs unto a people who can hear.

68 They say, "God has taken to Himself a son." Celebrated be His praises! He is the rich one! His is whatever is in the heavens, and whatever is in the earth. Ye have no authority for this! will ye say against God, that which ye do not know?

69 Say, "Verily, those who forge against God a lie shall not prosper!"

---

rather than face His stern judgment.

10.61 *the perspicuous Book* — The divine Book in Paradise (see ***The Perspicuous Book*** on pp. 178-179).

10.64 *there is no changing the words of God!* — Muhammad believed in the immutability (unchangeableness) of the Qur'an.

Christians ask: why, then, are there abrogated verses in the Qur'an? Why did God not guard other words of God from corruption? Why did Muhammad claim that the

Bible had been corrupted and is no longer trustworthy? (see Q 4.46, 157-158, 172-173; 5.13, 73; also see Q 15.9, note, and ***The Doctrine of Abrogation*** on pp. 68-70).

10.68-70 *God has taken to Himself a son* — previously in the Qur'an, the word *ibn* (son) was used. Here Muhammad used the word *walid* (physical son). It is an apparent reference to the Christian claim that Jesus Christ is God the Son (see ***The Doctrine of***

70 A provision in this world—then unto us is their return! then we will make them taste keen torment for that they misbelieved.

Noah

71 Recite to them the story of Noah, when he said to his people, "O my people! if my stay with you be grievous to you, and my reminding you of the signs of God, yet upon God do I rely! Collect then your affairs and your associates; nor let your affair (be ordered) for you in the dark; then decide respecting me, and do not wait;

72 and if ye turn your backs, I ask you not for hire; my hire is only due from God, and I am bidden to be of those resigned."

73 But they called him a liar; and we saved him, and those with him, in the ark; and we made these successors, and drowned those who had said our signs were lies; see then how was the end of those who had been warned!

74 Then we raised up after him apostles unto their people, and they came to them with manifest signs; but they would not believe in what they had called a lie before. Thus do we set a stamp upon the hearts of the transgressors.

Moses and Aaron

75 Then we raised up after them Moses and Aaron, unto Pharaoh and his chiefs with our signs; but they were too big with pride, and

the **Trinity** on pp. 735-736; the **Nicene-Constantinopolitan Creed** on p. 740). This passage is a condemnation of this foundational Christian doctrine.

In response, without apology Christians declare that Jesus Christ is indeed God the Son. A failure to recognize Him as He reveals Himself is a sign of disbelief (see Jn 8:24).
10.71-74a According to 2 Peter 2:5, Noah was "a preacher of righteousness." In this passage, Muhammad imagined what a typical sermon from Noah would have been like, and what would have been the response of his detractors. Not surprisingly, the give and take during this antediluvian era sounded remarkably similar to the give and take between Muhammad and his detractors in Mecca.
10.74b *Thus do we set a stamp upon the hearts of the transgressors* — Allah sets a

seal on the hearts of those who do not know the truth. This explains why the proclamation of Islamic truth is often rejected by infidels (see Q 4.155; 7.100-101; 9.87, 93; 16.108; 30.59; 40.35; 47.16; 63.3; **The Doctrine of al-Qadar** on pp. 264-266).
10.75-93 Similar to Muhammad's depiction of the Noahic story (vv. 71-74), his presentation of the story of Moses and Aaron and their conflict with Pharaoh (see Ex 7-14), is similar with his own struggle with the Meccan people. Consider the following:

First, Pharaoh accused Moses with sorcery (the story of the snake—Gen. 7:8-10; cf. Q 27.13). Muhammad had also been accused with sorcery by the people of Mecca (Q 11.7).

Second, the Egyptians rejected Moses' message of monotheism. The reason for

were a sinful people;

76 and when the truth came to them from us they said, verily, "This is obvious sorcery."

77 Moses said, "Will ye say of the truth when it comes to you, Is this sorcery? But sorcerers shall not prosper."

78 They said, "Hast thou come to turn us away from what we found our fathers at, that there may be for you twain grandeur in the earth? but we will not believe you."

79 And Pharaoh said, "Bring me every knowing sorcerer;"

80 and when the sorcerers came, Moses said to them, "Throw down what ye have, to throw!"

81 and when they threw down, Moses said, "What ye have brought is sorcery! verily, God will make it vain; verily, God rights not the work of evil-doers!"

82 But God verifies the truth by His words, although the sinners are averse therefrom.

83 But none believed in Moses, save a

race of his own people, through fear of Pharaoh and his chiefs; lest he should afflict them, for verily, Pharaoh was lofty in the earth, and verily, he was extravagant.

84 And Moses said, "O my people! if ye did believe in God, then on Him rely, if ye be resigned."

85 They said, "Upon God do we rely. O our Lord! make us not a cause of trial for a people who do wrong,

86 but save, us by Thy mercy from the people who misbelieve!"

87 And we inspired Moses and his brother thus, "Establish, ye twain, houses for your people in Egypt; and make ye your houses a qiblah; and be ye steadfast in prayer, and give glad tidings to those who believe."

88 Moses said, "O our Lord! verily, Thou hast brought to Pharaoh and his chiefs ornaments and wealth in the life of this world; O our Lord! that they may err from Thy way! O our Lord! confound their wealth and harden their hearts that

their unbelief, said Muhammad, was due to their commitment to the religion of their fathers (v. 78). A parallel response existed between Muhammad and the people of Mecca (see Q 11.109; 12.40; 27.67-68; 31.21; 34.43; 43.22-24; 45.25 and 53.23).

Third, Moses noted in his prayer that the Egyptians were people of wealth. Likewise, elsewhere in the Qur'an, Muhammad noted that the infidels of Mecca were people of wealth (Q 18.34-46; 19.77).

Fourth, following the miraculous crossing of the Red (Reed) Sea, Moses reaffirmed

his belief in monotheism (v. 90). This too happened to be Muhammad's principal message in the Qur'an—the Doctrine of Tauhid (see Q 112, note).

10.87 *make ye your houses a qiblah* — In the Islamic tradition, a *qiblah* refers to the direction that one faces during *Salah* (formalized prayer). Most mosques contain a niche in a wall that indicates the direction of *qiblah*. In the context of this verse, the word means that the Hebrew people were to treat their homes as an especially sacred sanctuary.

they may not believe until they see grievous woe!"

89 He said, "Your prayer is answered; be upright then, ye two, and follow not the path of those who do not know!"

90 And we brought the children of Israel across the sea; and Pharaoh and his hosts followed them eager and hostile, until when drowning overtook him, he said, "I believe that there is no god but He in whom the children of Israel believe, and I am of those who are resigned!"

91 —"Now! but thou didst rebel aforetime, and wert of those who do evil;

92 but today we will save thee in thy body, that thou mayest be to those who come after thee a sign, for verily, many men are careless of our signs!"

93 And we established the people of Israel with a sure establishment, and we provided them with good

things; nor did they disagree until there came to them the knowledge. Verily, thy Lord shall decide between them on the resurrection day concerning that whereon they did dispute.

Overcoming doubt

94 And if thou art in doubt of that which we have sent down unto thee, ask those who read the Book before thee verily, the truth is come to thee from thy Lord, be not then of those who are in doubt.

95 And be not of those who say the signs of God are lies, or thou wilt be of those who lose!

96 Verily, those against whom God's word is pronounced will not believe,

97 even though there come to them every sign, until they see the grievous woe.

98 Were it not so, a city would have

10.90 *I am of those who are resigned* — that is, "I am a Muslim." According to Muhammad, when Pharaoh was drowning in the Red (Reed) Sea, he confessed that there is no god other than the God of the Israelites, and then added that he was a Muslim. The Old Testament makes no such claim regarding Pharaoh. Curiously, elsewhere in the Qur'an it states that Pharaoh died as an infidel (see Q 17.101-103; **The Doctrine of Abrogation** on pp. 68-70).

10.94 *the Book* — Here the *Book* refers to the Scriptures—the Old and New Testaments. Curiously, Allah allegedly told Muhammad that if he had doubts regarding the di-

vine inspiration of the Qur'an, he was to ask the opinion of Jews and Christians. Their counsel was regarded by Allah as trustworthy. The assumption is that both Jews and Christians would endorse the Qur'an as a divinely inspired document. Yet, elsewhere in the Qur'an Muhammad was told that both the Old and New Testaments are full of error (see Q 10.40 note).

10.95-98 Those who overcome doubt, said Muhammad, avoid divine judgment and receive divine blessings. The people of Ninevah, under the ministry of Jonah, were cited as an example of a city repenting of its sins and turning to the one true God.

believed and its faith would have, profited it. But (none did) except the people of Jonas; when they believed we removed from them the torment of disgrace in this world, and we gave them provision for a while.

Double predestination

99   But had thy Lord pleased, all who are in the earth would have believed altogether; as for thee, wilt thou force men to become believers?

100   It is not for any person to believe save by the permission of God; He puts horror on those who have no sense.

Final catechism

101   Say, "Behold what is in the heavens and in the earth! but signs and warners avail not a people who do not believe.

102   Do they await aught but the like of the days of those who passed away before them?" Say, "Wait ye then! verily, I am with you one of those who wait."

103   Then we will save our apostles and those who believe; thus is it due from us to save believers.

104   Say, "O ye folk! if ye are in doubt concerning my religion, I will not worship those ye worship other than God; but I worship God, who takes you to Himself, and I am bidden to be of the believers!"

105   And, "Make steadfast thy face to the religion as a 'Hanîf; and be not of the idolaters;

106   and call not besides God on what can neither profit thee nor harm thee; for if thou dost, verily, thou art then of the unjust!"

107   And should God touch thee with harm, there is none to remove it save He; and if He wish thee well, there is none to repel His grace; He makes it fall on whom He will of His servants; for He is pardoning and merciful!

108   Say, "O ye people! there has come to you the truth from your Lord, and he who is guided, his guidance is only for his soul; and he who errs, errs only against it; and I am not a guardian over you."

109   Follow what is revealed to thee, and be patient until God judges, for He is the best of judges.

10.99-100 In the final analysis, Muhammad explained, only those who are predestined by Allah to eternal life will repent of their sins. His appeals for repentance and a turning towards Allah and "the right path," then, are predicated upon predestination (see **The Doctrine of al-Qadar** on pp. 264-266).

10.101-108 Muhammad concluded the surah with the claim that he was instructed of Allah to avoid the infidels and remain steadfast in his worship of Allah.

10.105 *Hanif*—A pre-Islamic Arabian monotheist (see Q 30.30, note).

10.107 *there is none to repel His grace* — This is another reference to double predes-

Surah 14

In the name of the merciful and compassionate God.

1   A. L. M.

Qur'an

A book which we have sent down to thee, to bring men forth from darkness into light, by permission of their Lord, unto the way of the mighty and praiseworthy one.

The fate of the infidels

2   God is He whose is whatsoever is in the heavens and whatsoever is in the earth. Alas for the misbelievers, for their torment is keen!

3   Who love this world's life better than the next, and turn folks from the path of God, and crave to make it crooked; these are in remote error.

4   We have not sent any apostle save with the language of his people, that he might explain to them. But God leads whom He will astray, and guides whom He will; and He is the mighty, the wise.

Moses

5   We did send Moses with our signs,

---

tination (see **The Doctrine of al-Qadar** on pp. 264-264).

Surah 14. The title of this surah, *Abraham*, comes from verse 35. Oddly, the surah mentions Abraham by name only once. The surah is a plea for people to turn to God in repentance and embrace his divinely inspired surahs. The word *woe* in mentioned three times in the surah: evil woe (v. 6), rigorous woe (v. 17), and grievous woe (v. 22). The final verse of the surah summarizes its overall message of the oneness of God: "This is a message to be delivered to men that they may be warned thereby, and know that only he is God,—one,—and that those who have minds might remember" (v. 52).

14.1a Literally, *Alif Lam Ra.* See Q 32.1, note.

14.1b *a book* — The Qur'an, that which is eternal in Paradise guarded by God and "sent down" to Muhammad by way of dictation via the archangel Gabriel (see **The Perspicu-** ous **Book** on pp. 178-179).

14.3 *the path of God* — This is a synonym for "the right direction," "the right path" and "the right way" (see Q 72.2, note). It describes the way to eternal life.

14.4 *God leads whom He will astray, and guides whom He will* — Allah sent apostles to the various peoples of the world to share truths from Allah's perspicuous book in a language common to the receivers of the message. Yet, even with the ministry of the apostles, the doctrine of double predestination holds sway (see **The Doctrine of al-Qadar** on pp. 264-266).

14.4b *He is the mighty, the wise!* — This is one of Muhammad's favorite descriptions of Allah (see Q 16.60; 30.27; 35.2; 45.37).

14.5-8 This passage from the life of Moses comes from the period following the miraculous crossing of the Red (Reed) Sea and during the period of testing in the wilderness. The comment from Moses (v. 8) is a sum-

"Bring forth thy people from the darkness into the light, and remind them of the days of God!" verily, in that are signs to every patient, grateful one.

6   When Moses said to his people, "Remember the favours of God towards you, when He saved you from Pharaoh's people, who sought to wreak you evil woe, slaughtering your sons and letting your women live;" in that was a great trial for you from your Lord.

7   When your Lord proclaimed, "If ye give thanks I will surely give you increase; but if ye misbelieve, verily, my torment is severe!"

8   And Moses said, "If ye misbelieve, ye and those who are on the earth altogether—then, verily, God is rich, and to be praised!"

Allah's many apostles

9   Has not the story come to you of those who were before you, of the people of Noah, and 'Âd, and Thamûd, and those who came after them? none knows them save God. Apostles came unto them with manifest signs; but they thrust their hands into their mouths and said, "Verily, we disbelieve in that which ye are sent with, and we are in hesitating doubt concerning that to which ye call us!"

10   Their apostles said, "Is there doubt about God, the originator of the heavens and the earth? He calls you to pardon you for your sins, and to respite you until an appointed time." They said, "Ye are but mortals like ourselves; ye wish to turn us from what our fathers used to serve. Bring us, then, obvious authority!"

11   Their apostles said unto them, "We are only mortals like yourselves; but God is gracious unto whomsoever He will of His servants, and it is not for us to bring you an authority, save by His permission; but upon God do the believers rely!"

12   What ails us that we should not rely on God when He has guided us in our paths? we will be surely patient in your hurting us; for upon God rely those who do rely.

mary of many comments mentioned in Exodus, Numbers, and Deuteronomy that address Moses' admonitions to the people of Israel (e.g., Deut. 9:7-29; 32:1-52).
14.9-15 According to this passage, Allah has sent apostles to the peoples of the world to speak the truth about God to them so that they could avoid the torments of Hell and enter the bliss of Paradise. Noah, Hud (the apostle sent to the people of Ad), and Zali'h (the apostle sent to the people of Thamud) are merely three examples of this numerous host of apostles. Yet in most all cases, the people rejected the message of the apostles. Their typical response to the apostles was that they would either "drive you forth from our land," or "ye shall return to our faith."
14.11 *save by His permission* — Once again, Muhammad referenced double predestination. People can only believe and be saved by the permission of Allah (see ***The Doc-***

13 And those who misbelieved said to their apostles, "We will drive you forth from our land; or else ye shall return to our faith!" And their Lord inspired them, "We will surely destroy the unjust;

14 and we will make you to dwell in the land after them. That is for him who fears my, place and fears my threat!"

15 Then they asked for an issue; and disappointed was every rebel tyrant!

Hell

16 Behind such a one is hell, and he shall be given to drink liquid puss!

17 He shall try to swallow it, but cannot gulp it down; and death shall come upon him from every place, and yet he shall not die; and behind him shall be rigorous woe!

18 The likeness of those who disbelieve on their Lord,—their works are as ashes whereon the wind blows fiercely on a stormy day. They have no power at all over that which they have earned.—That is the remote error!

Allah's sovereign control

19 Dost not thou see that God created the heavens and the earth in truth? If He please He can take you off and bring a new creation;

20 nor is that hard for God!

21 They all come out to God; and the weak say to those who were big with pride, "We were followers of yours, can ye now avail us aught against God's torment?" They say, "If God had guided us we would have guided you. It is the same to us if we are agonized or if we are penitent, we have no escape."

22 And Satan says, when the affair is decided, "Verily, God promised you a promise of truth; but I promised you and failed you; for I had no authority over you. I only called you, and ye did answer me; then blame me not, but blame yourselves; I cannot help you, nor can you help me. I disbelieved in your

trine of al-Qadar on pp. 264-266).

14.13-15 The destruction presented in this passage addresses the destruction that takes place in our current world (see Q 21.11).

14.16-18 Characteristics of Hell: (a) the unrighteous will gag on liquid puss that they are forced to swallow, (b) eternal torment, (c) a rigorous woe, (d) works will be turned to ashes and blown away, and (e) a complete powerlessness to stop the suffering.

14.21 According to this verse, Muhammad believed that eventually the followers of the leaders of Mecca would recognize the error of the doctrines that they had been taught and would seek refuge from the coming terror of the Fire in the afterlife. Yet it would be too late. With much regret, the leaders would tell the people of Mecca: "If God had guided us we would have guided you...we have no escape."

14.22 Satan will also voice words of regret to the infidels. Not only did Satan lie to them, resulting in their damnation, Satan himself will be cast into the Fire.

associating me (with God) before; verily, the wrong-doers, for them is grievous woe!"

23   But I will cause those who believe and do aright to enter gardens beneath which rivers flow, to dwell therein for aye by the permission of their Lord; their salutation therein is "Peace!"

Parable of the Tree

24   Dost thou not see how God strikes out a parable? A good word is like a good tree whose root is firm; and whose branches are in the sky

25   it gives its fruit at every season by

the permission of its Lord—but God strikes out parables for men that haply they may be mindful.

26   And the likeness of a bad word is as a bad tree, which is felled from above the earth, and has no staying place.

Hell

27   God answers those who believe with the sure word in this world's life and in the next; but God leads the wrong-doers astray; for God does what He will.

28   Dost not thou see those who have changed God's favours for mis-

14.23a *believe and do aright* — These words are repeated often in the Qur'an and serve as a brief summary of the Islamic gospel (see Q 103.3 note).

14.23b *beneath which rivers flow* — In the Qur'an is the imagery of Paradise being an oasis with well supplied aquifers sufficiently close to the surface to keep the oasis fertile and green (see Q 16.31; 18.31; 20.76; 25.10; 39.20; 85.11).

14.23c Three characteristics of Paradise: (a) a place of gardens and rivers, (b) a place of peace, and (c) a place that is granted to those whom God gives permission to enter. Once again, we see Paradise described in terms that a person raised in a searing hot and dry desert with few oases would understand and appreciate.

14.24-26 According to this parable, a good word is likened to a good tree. It is reminiscent of the parabolic images found in the First Psalm. Yet it differs in one important aspect. Whereas the imagery in the Psalm

places the responsibility upon the individual to avoid evil people and meditate upon the law of the Lord, in this parable the responsibility is placed upon Allah who speaks good and bad words. The good words result in good people who are blessed of God. The bad words result in bad people who are cursed of God. As such, this parable illustrates the doctrine of double predestination (see **The Doctrine of al-Qadar** on pp. 264-266).

14.27 *God leads the wrongdoers astray* — That is, Allah deliberately causes the infidel to think wrong thoughts about spirituality and the afterlife. This is the oft-mentioned doctrine of double predestination. Allah predestines some to eternal life and others to eternal damnation (see **The Doctrine of al-Qadar** on pp. 264-266).

Though some Christians affirm the doctrine of double predestination, many do not. John R. W. Stott, for example, is representative of those who do not. "Just as it is

belief, and have made their people to alight at the abode of perdition?

29 —in hell they shall broil, and an ill resting-place shall it be!

30 And they made peers for God, to lead men astray from His path. Say, "Enjoy yourselves, for, verily, your journey is to the Fire."

*Admonition to prayer
and the givings of alms*

31 Say to my servants who believe, that they be steadfast in prayer and expend in alms of what we have bestowed upon them in secret and in public, before there comes the day when there shall be no buying and no friendship.

32 God it is who created the heavens and the earth; and sent down from the sky water, and brought forth therewith fruits as a provision for you; and subjected to you the ships, to float therein upon the sea at His bidding; and subjected for you the rivers;

33 and subjected for you the sun and the moon, constant both; and subjected for you, the night and the day;

34 and brought you of everything ye asked Him: but if ye try to number God's favours, ye cannot count them;—verily, man is very unjust and ungrateful.

Abraham's prayer

35 And when Abraham said, "My

---

the nature of light to shine, so it is the nature of God to reveal himself. True, he hides himself from the wise and clever, but only because they are proud and do not want to know him; he reveals himself to 'babies,' that is, to those humble enough to receive his self-disclosure...The chief reason why people do not know God is not because he hides from them, but because they hide from him" (*Between Two Worlds*, p. 93).

14.28-30 Muhammad beckoned people to look with amazement at the actions of the infidels. Not only did they exchange the favors of Allah for misbelief, they encouraged their followers to do the same thing, thus assuring both their perdition in the Fire in the afterlife.

The passage is reminiscent of the words of Jesus who was critical of the scribes and Pharisees of his day who were blind guides leading blind people. He said: "Woe to you, teachers of the law and Pharisees, you hypocrites! You shut the kingdom of heaven in men's faces. You yourselves do not enter, nor will you let those enter who are trying to" (Matt 23:13).

14.31 People are admonished to be people of prayer and generous with their giving of alms in this life. All such activities will benefit them in the afterlife when their works are weighed to determine whether they were good or bad (see **The Last Judgment** on pp. 46-50).

14.34 *man is very unjust and ungrateful* — Such is a summary of man in his natural state. Entering Paradise requires that people turn away from such a life-style and adopt a life-style characterized by justice and gratitude.

14.35-41 In this passage, Abraham prayed. The prayer is neither found in the Bible nor

Lord, make this land safe, and turn me and my sons away from serving idols.

36 My Lord, verily, they have led many men astray; but he who follows me, verily, he is of me; but he who rebels against me,—verily, thou art pardoning, merciful!

37 "O our Lord! verily, I have made some of my seed dwell in a valley without corn, by thy Sacred House. O our Lord! let them be steadfast in prayer and make the hearts of men yearn towards them, and provide them with fruits, haply they may give thanks.

38 O our Lord! verily, Thou knowest what we hide and what we publish; for naught is hid from God in the earth or in the sky."

39 "Praise to God who hath bestowed on me, notwithstanding my old age, Ishmael and Isaac!—verily, my Lord surely hears prayer.

40 O my Lord! make me steadfast in prayer, and of my seed likewise! O our Lord! and accept my prayer!

41 O our Lord! pardon me and my parents and the believers on the reckoning day!"

Last Judgment

42 So think not God careless of what the unjust do; He only respites them until the day on which all eyes shall stare!

43 Hurrying on, raising up their heads, with their looks not turned back to them, and their hearts void; and warn men of the day when the torment shall come!

44 And those who have done wrong shall say, "O our Lord! respite us until an appointed time nigh at hand, and we will respond to Thy call, and follow the apostles!"—"What! did ye not swear before, ye should have no decline?"

45 And ye dwelt in the dwellings of

---

apocryphal literature. It is therefore a likely fabricated by Muhammad. The prayer contains a number of themes. Abraham petitioned the Lord to rid his land of idolatry. He then petitioned the Lord to fulfill the same in his day in regards to the people of Mecca. After that, he prayed for his two sons, Ishmael and Isaac, to become steadfast in prayer and resolute against idolatry. He noted that he had hid nothing that Allah had willed that he publish for the peoples of Mecca. In conclusion of his prayer, Abraham asked for forgiveness for his sins, the sins of his parents, and all the believers under his care. His concern was that they would be able to pass through "the reckoning day" and enter Paradise (see **Divine Forgiveness in Islam** on pp. 158-161).

14.36 *thou art pardoning, merciful* — See **Divine Forgiveness in Islam** on pp. 158-161.

14.37 *thy Sacred House* — The Ka'ba altar.

14.42-51 Characteristics of the Last Judgment: (a) it will be day when "all eyes shall stare," (b) people will not look at the unjust in the eyes, (c) the unjust will have hearts that are void, (d) the unjust will plead for more time and another opportunity to live righteously, (e) the heavens and earth will be changed for a new earth and a new

those who had wronged themselves; and it was made plain to
you how we did with them; and
we struck out parables for you:

46 but they plotted their stratagems,
but with God is a stratagem for
them, although at their stratagem
the mountains should give way.

47 Think then not indeed that God fails
in his promise to his apostles;—
verily, God is mighty, the Lord of
vengeance;

48 on the day when the earth shall be
changed for another earth, and the
heavens too; and (all) shall go forth
unto God, the one, the dominant.

49 Thou shalt see the sinners on that
day bound together in fetters;

50 with shirts of pitch, and fire covering their faces;

51 —that God may reward each soul
according to what it has earned;

verily, God is swift at reckoning
up!

Conclusion

52 This is a message to be delivered
to men that they may be warned
thereby, and know that only He is
God, —one,—and that those who
have minds may remember.

Surah 6

*In the name of the merciful and compas-
sionate God.*

A rebuke to polytheism

1 Praise belongs to God who created
the heavens and the earth, and
brought into being the darkness

---

heaven, (f) the sinners will be bound together in fetters with shirts of pitch and fire
on their faces, and (g) sinners will receive
the reward that they have earned—eternal
torment (see **The Last Judgment** on pp.
46-50).

Surah 6. The title of this surah, *The Cattle*,
comes from verse 136. According to the
tradition of Ibn Abbas, this surah was revealed to Muhammad while in Mecca. Asma—
a daughter of Yazid and a first cousin of Hadrat
Muaz-bin Jabl, said: "During the revelation
of this surah, the Holy Prophet was riding on
a she-camel and I was holding her nose-
string. The she-camel began to feel the
weight so heavily that it seemed as if her
bones would break under it" (see *Syed
Maududi's Commentary*). The implication is

that the divine revelation possessed its own
physical weight and burdened the camel.

This surah is a review of themes already
discussed in previous surahs. In it, Muhammad rebuked the practice of polytheism, he
spoke of the horrors of the Last Judgment,
the necessity of faith, the example of Allah's
many apostles in world history, Allah's sovereign control over the universe, his concerns
about the Jews and Christians, and the problem of pagan superstitions.

6.1-9 Muhammad claimed that even if Allah
were to have provided him with miraculous
signs, the people of Mecca would still have
rejected him. They would have claimed that
he was a magician or a sorcerer. This, said
Muhammad, was regrettable since Allah had
judged the polytheists who had lived before

and the light. Yet do those who misbelieve hold Him to have peers.

2   He it is who created you from clay; then He decreed a term,—a term ordained with Him. And yet ye doubt thereof.

3   He is God in the heavens and the earth. He knows your secret conduct and your plain, and He knows what ye earn.

4   There came not to them any sign of, the signs of their Lord, but they turned away;

5   and they have called the truth a lie now that it has come to them, but there shall come to them the message of that at which they mocked.

6   Do not they see how many a generation we have destroyed before them, whom we had settled in the earth as we have not settled for you, and sent the rain of heaven upon them in copious showers,

and made the waters flow beneath them? Then we destroyed them in their sins, and raised up other generations after them.

7   Had we sent down to thee a book on paper, and they had touched it with their hands, still those who misbelieve would have said, "This is naught but obvious magic."

8   They say, "Why has not an angel been sent down to him?" but if we had sent down an angel, the affair would have been decided, and then they would have had no respite.

9   And had we made him an angel, we should have made him as a man too; and we would have made perplexing for them that which they deem perplexing now.

First catechism

10   There have been prophets before

them and was about to judge them in a similar fashion.

6:1 *Hold Him to have peers* —That is, the infidels, because of their belief in polytheism, believed that Allah was one of many gods.

6.2 In this verse, Muhammad argued that people were created "from clay" (see Q 96.2, note).

6.3 *He is God in the heavens and the earth* — This description of Allah corresponds with the biblical understanding of God (see Gen 1:1; 2:4; Deut 10:14; Neh 9:6; Ps 50:4; 89:11; 135:6; Isa 42:5; Heb 1:10 and Rev 10:6).

6.4 *they have called the truth a lie* — Muhammad declared that the natural incli-

nation of people was to turn Allah's truth into falsehood. Again, this notion corresponds with the biblical understanding of sin (see Ps 144:8 and Rom 1:23).

6.8-9 Part of the Meccan people's rejection of Muhammad was the lack of the supernatural events to validate his ministry, such as the manifestation of an angel sent from God (see Q 10.19-20a, note). Muhammad dismissed this request, claiming that if an angel had indeed appeared, "the affair would have been decided, and then there would have had no respite"—that is, faith would no longer have been required (see **John of Damascus** on pp. 247-248; 1 Cor 1:22-23; Heb 11:1-2).

6.10-30 The purpose of this catechism was

thee mocked at, but that encompassed them which the scoffers among them mocked at.

11   Say, "Go about in the earth, then wilt thou see how has been the end of those who called them liars."

12   Say, "Whose is what is in the heavens and the earth?" Say, "God's, who has imposed mercy on himself." He will surely gather you together for the resurrection day. There is no doubt in that, but those who waste their souls will not believe.

13   His is whatsoever dwells in the night or in the day, He both hears and knows.

14   Say, "Other than God shall I take, for a patron, the Originator of the heavens and the earth? He feedeth men, but is not fed." Say, "I am bidden to be the first of those resigned;" and it was said to me, "Be not thou of the idolaters."

15   Say, "I fear, if I rebel against my Lord, the torment of the mighty day."

16   Whomsoever it is averted from on that day, God will have had mercy on; and that is obvious happiness.

to provide the listener with a set questions and answers that could serve as arguments against the infidels of Mecca.

6.11 Muhammad encouraged his detractors to examine the consequences of other cultures and communities in history where the sin of *shirk* (idolatry) was practiced. In each case, he maintained, the cultures and civilizations were destroyed.

6.12 *those who waste their souls will not believe* — That is, those who indulge in wickedness will not believe. This is a telling description of sinful people. The Bible speaks similarly of the wicked: "You will keep your turbans on your heads and your sandals on your feet. You will not mourn or weep but will waste away because of your sins and groan among yourselves" (Ezek 24:23).

6.12 *God's, who has imposed mercy upon himself* — That is, Allah restrained Himself from exacting judgment on the infidels. Yet, this is only a temporary restraint since the Day of Judgment will come some day in the future when vengeance will be realized.

6.13 *He both hears and knows* — This is the Doctrine of Omniscience. Allah is all-know-

ing. The Bible makes a similar claim about God (see Ps 33:13-15; 139:11-12; 147:5; Prov 15:3; Isa 40:14; 46:10; 1 Jn 3:20 and Heb 4:13).

6.14 Muhammad was critical of the Meccan people's commitment to *shirk*—idolatry. His point in this verse was to question why would people place their faith in a patron of Allah (i.e., a god or a goddess) when they could go directly to Allah, the creator of the heavens and the earth, and place their faith in Him? It made no sense. The Bible makes a similar argument against idolatry (see Deut 4:28; Ps 135:15-18; Jer 10:5, 14; 1 Cor 12:2).

6.15 *I fear, if I rebel against my Lord* — As part of the first catechism, Muhammad wanted to make the point that Muslims should not adopt a wrongful assurance that they would unquestionably enter Paradise, simply because they were Muslims. They too, he said, had to remind themselves that if they rebelled they would face the "torment of the mighty day." In contrast, the Bible offers a quiet assurance of salvation to all who place their faith in Christ. The Apostle

17 And if God touch thee with harm, there is none to take it off but He; and if He touch thee with good, He is mighty over all.

18 He is sovereign over His servants, He is the wise, the aware!

19 Say, "What is the greatest witness?" Say, "God is witness between you and me." This Qur'ân was inspired to me to warn you and those it reaches. Do ye really bear witness that with God are other gods? Say, "I bear not witness thereto" say, "He is but one God, and I am clear of your associating (gods with him)."

20 Those to whom we have brought the Book know him as they know their sons;—those who lose their souls do not believe.

Paul, for example said, "I know whom I have believed, and am convinced that he is able to guard what I have entrusted to him for that day" (2 Tim 1:12; cf. Ps 31:5; Acts 7:59; Eph 1:8; 1 Jn 5:13). See **Last Judgment** on pp. 46-50.

6.17 *He is mighty over all* — This is the Doctrine of Divine Sovereignty. If Allah should choose to bless, none can stop Him. If Allah should choose to do harm, none can stop Him. The Bible speaks similarly of God (see Ex 33:19; Isa 27:11; Rom 9:15-18).

6.18 *He is the wise, the aware* — This is the Doctrine of Omniscience. Allah is all-knowing. The Bible speaks similarly (see Ps 33:13-15; 139:11-12; 147:5; Prov 15:3; Isa 40:14; 46:10; 1 Jn 3:20 and Heb 4:13). John R. W. Stott adds: "You can never take God by surprise. You can never anticipate him. He always makes the first move. He is always there 'in the beginning.' Before man existed, God acted. Before man stirs himself to seek God, God has sought man. In the Bible we do not see man groping after God; we see God reaching after man" (*Basic Christianity*, p. 11).

6.19 *the greatest witness* — According to Muhammad, the greatest witness given to man is Allah Himself via the words of the Qur'an. According to Christians, the greatest witness given to man is God Himself via the Old and New Testaments.

This, then, is one of the fundamental differences between Islam and Christianity. Each religious tradition turns to a different sacred literature as its *scientia Dei* (knowledge of God). And each religious tradition makes use of faith as its starting point in its affirmation of its sacred literature. Yet the Islamic faith tends to be characterized by fideism (faith in faith)—an untested faith. The typical Muslim is less interested in rigorous theological reflection than he or she is in submission and obedience to whatever the Qur'an says. The Christian, on the other hand, is forever testing his or her faith against archeology, historical findings, the question of consistencies within the sacred text—indeed, the veracity of the Bible itself. Doubt is not the enemy of faith; rather, it is useful in propelling the Christian forward towards a deepening of faith. It is, said Anselm of Canterbury, a question of "faith seeking knowledge." We can perhaps modify Anselm's famous statement by saying it is a question of "faith seeking knowledge seeking faith, seeking knowledge, etc.," with neither faith nor knowledge serving as the starting point.

6.20 *the Book* — Literally, the Scriptures. It is a reference to the Bible. We know this since it is phrased as an action already completed. According to Muhammad, Christians

*Lamentations
at the Last Judgment*

21 Who is more unjust than he who forges against God a lie, or says His signs are lies? verily, the unjust shall not prosper.

22 On the day when we shall gather them all together, then shall we say to those who have associated others with ourself, "Where are your associates whom ye did pretend?"

23 Then they will have no excuse but to say, "By God our Lord, we did not associate (others with thee)!"

24 See how they lie against themselves, and how what they did forge deserts them!

25 And they are some who listen unto thee, but we have placed a veil upon their hearts lest they should understand it, and in their ears is dullness of hearing; and though they saw each sign they would not believe therein; until when they come to thee to wrangle with thee, the unbelievers say, "These are but old folks' tales."

26 They forbid it and they avoid it;— but they destroy none but themselves; yet they do not perceive.

27 But couldst thou see when they are set over the fire and say, "Would that we were sent back! we would not call our Lord's signs lies, but we would be of the believers?"

28 Nay! now is shown to them what they did hide before; and could they be sent back, they would return to that they were forbidden, for they are very liars.

29 They say there is naught but this life of ours in the world and we shall not be raised.

30 But couldst thou see when they are set before their Lord; he says, "Is not this the truth?" They say, "Yea, by our Lord!" He says, "Then taste the torment, for that ye did misbelieve!"

*The cavalier attitude
of infidels*

---

know the rightness of Muhammad's surahs just as they "know their sons." In his commentary, Ibn Kathir explained, "They received good news from the previous Messengers and Prophets about the coming of Muhammad, his attributes, homeland, his migration, and the description of his Ummah." Their rejection of his surahs, then, is not due to honest analysis but rather because of spiritual duplicity: "see how they lie against themselves" (v. 24).

6.25 *we have placed a veil upon their hearts* — Again, Muhammad presented the doctrine of double predestination. Though people heard Muhammad, they did not understand or believe because Allah had "placed a veil upon their hearts lest they should understand." In addition, Allah caused a "dullness of hearing" and in inability to see and comprehend the divine signs (see **The Doctrine of al-Qadar** on pp. 264-266).

6.27-30 According to Muhammad, when placed before the Fire the infidels will speak of their deep regret that they called the Qur'an and the other signs (revelations) given by God lies.

31   Losers are they who disbelieved in
      meeting God, until when the hour
      comes suddenly upon them they
      say, "Woe is us for our neglect
      thereof!" for the shall bear their
      burdens on their backs, evil is what
      they bear.
32   The life of this world is nothing but
      a game and a sport, and surely the
      next abode were better for those
      who fear. What! do they not un-
      derstand?
33   Full well we know that verily that
      which they say grieves thee; but
      they do not call thee only a liar, for
      the unjust gainsay the signs of God.
34   Called liars too were apostles be-

fore thee; but they were patient of
being called liars and of being hurt
until our help came to them; for
there is none to change the words
of God—now has there come to
thee the story of those He sent.

The necessity of faith

35   And if their turning from thee be
      hard for thee, and if thou canst
      seek for a shaft down into the
      earth, or a ladder up into the sky,
      to bring them a sign—but if God
      pleased He would bring them all to
      guidance, be thou not then of the
      ignorant.

6.31-34 The cavalier attitude of the infidels is noted: (a) only at the Last Judgment will they understand the eternal woe that is upon them, (b) in this world, life is "nothing but a game and a sport," (c) in this world, they call Allah a liar and gainsay (declare false) his signs (revelation), and (d) they had called the apostles prior to Muhammad in similar fashion.

6.34 *there is none to change the words of God* — Muhammad asserted the immutability of the Qur'an, which he believed to be the unadulterated word of God.

Yet, Christians then ask: why, then, are there abrogated verses in the Qur'an? And, why did Allah not guard other words of Allah from corruption? Muhammad declared that both Old and New Testaments had been corrupted and are no longer trustworthy (see Q 4.46, 157-158, 172-173; 5.13, 73; also see Q 15.9, note; **The Doctrine of Abrogation** on pp. 68-70).

6.35 In the popular parlance of seventh

century, Hell was believed to exist deep in the earth and Paradise was believed to exist high above the earth. The comments about a "shaft down into the earth" reflected a way to go down and verify the existence of Hell. Similarly, the comments about a "ladder up into the sky" reflected a way to go up into the sky and verify the existence of Paradise.

Some Muslim mystics believe that access to the depths of the earth and the heights of Paradise is still possible. It can happen either (a) in the physical body, or (b) in an astral (disembodied) projection.

6.35-39 According to Muhammad, the people of Mecca were demanding miracles from Muhammad to validate his prophetic credentials. Yet, Muhammad's answer was that such a display of miracles would mitigate against the more important need of faith on the part of the Meccan people. They have *the Book*—the Qur'an— and, according to Muhammad, that is sufficient (see **John of**

36   He only answers the prayer of those who listen but the dead will God raise up, then unto Him shall they return.

37   They say, "Unless there be sent down some sign from his Lord"— say, "Verily, God is able to send down a sign, but most of them do not know.

38   There is not a beast upon the earth nor a bird that flies with both its wings, but is a nation like to you; we have omitted nothing from the Book; then to their Lord shall they be gathered.

39   Those who say our signs are lies— deafness, dumbness, in the dark! whom He pleases does God lead astray, and whom He pleases He places on the right way.

Second catechism

40   Say, "Look you now! if there should come God's torment, or there should come to you the hour, on other than God would ye call, if ye do tell the truth?"

41   Nay, it is on Him that ye would call, and He will avert that which ye call upon Him for if He but please; and ye shall forget that which ye did associate with Him.

42   Ere this we sent unto nations before thee, and we caught them in distress and trouble that haply they might humble themselves.

43   And do they not, when our violence falls upon them, humble themselves?—but their hearts were hard, and Satan made seemly to

Damascus on pp. 247-248).

6.38 *we have omitted nothing from the Book* — That is, the Qur'an is the complete revelation of Allah.

6.39a *whom He pleases does God lead astray, and whom He pleases He places on the right way* — Muhammad once again reminded the reader of the doctrine of double predestination (see **The Doctrine of al-Qadar** on pp. 264-266).

6.39b *the right way* — a synonym for "the right direction." It stands alongside the phrase "believe and do right" as shorthand for the Islamic definition of salvation (see Q 72.2, note).

6.40-73 This is a second series of catechismal instruction in this surah designed to show the folly of unbelief in Allah. It contains seven couplets characterized by a question, an answer, and sometimes a follow-up explana-

tion.

6.40-45 The first question-and-answer couplet addresses the issue of fundamental belief. Muhammad believed that when calamities enter a person's life, whether they be calamities related to this life or the afterlife, people are predisposed to call upon Allah, the true God, and forsake the gods that they had previously worshipped.

6.41 *ye shall forget that which ye did associate with Him* — That is, you forget your gods and goddesses that you worshipped alongside the true God.

6.42-44 Muhammad maintained that, in contrast to believers, infidels harden their hearts against Allah when calamities strike. This hardness of heart is the result of Satan's enticements to resist Allah (also see 2 Cor 11:3, 14; Eph 6:11-12; 2 Tim 2:25-26; 1 Pet 5:8).

them that which they had done.

44 And when they forgot what they were reminded of, we opened for them the gates of everything, until when they rejoiced at what they had, we caught them up suddenly, and lo! they were in despair.

45 And the uttermost part of the people who did wrong were cut off; praise be to God, Lord of the worlds!

46 Say, "Look you now! if God should catch your hearing and your sight, and should set a seal upon your hearts—who is god but God to bring you it again?"

47 Say, "Look you now! if God's torment should come upon you suddenly or openly, would any perish save the people who do wrong?"

48 We do not send our messengers save as heralds of glad tidings and of warning, and whoso believes and acts aright, there is no fear for them, and they shall not be grieved,

49 but those who say our signs are lies, torment shall touch them, for that they have done so wrong.

50 Say, "I do not say to you, mine are the treasuries of God, nor that I know the unseen; I do not say to you, I am an angel—if I follow aught but what I am inspired with"—say, "Is the blind equal to him who sees—?" what! do ye not reflect?

51 Admonish therewith those who fear that they shall be gathered unto their Lord; there is no patron for them but Him, and no intercessor; haply they may fear.

52 Repulse not those who call upon their Lord in the morning and in the evening, desiring His face; they have no reckoning against thee at all, and thou hast no reckoning against them at all;—repulse them and thou wilt be of the unjust.

53 So have we tried some of them by others, that they may say, "Are

6.46 The purpose of the second question-and-answer couplet was to address the issue of calamities in the lives of the believers. The answer was that they should fear no such calamities sent from God. It is only for those who "say our signs [revelations] are lies" should fear the prospects of eternal torment (Hell).

6.50 The third question-and-answer couplet was more pastoral in nature. From the perspective of Allah, believers (those who see) are not equal with infidels (those who are spiritually blind). Those who feared Allah were to be encouraged. They would be gathered unto their Lord, encouraged as they

perform their prayers, blessed for their thankful hearts towards God, and would be the recipients of the peace of Allah.

6.53 *Does not God know those who give thanks?* — The question of thankfulness is a central theme in the Islamic world. Allah watches it carefully and links it directly with genuine faith. The Judeo-Christian faith makes the same association between thankfulness and faith (see Job 1:21; Eph 5:20; Phil 4:6; Col 3:17; 1 Thess 5:18; Heb 13:15).

C. S. Lewis wrote: "We ought to give thanks for all fortune: if it is 'good,' because it is good, if 'bad' because it works in us patience, humility and the contempt of this

these those unto whom God has been gracious amongst ourselves?" Does not God know those who give thanks?

54 And when those who believe in our signs come to thee, say, "Peace be on you! God hath prescribed for Himself mercy; verily, he of you who does evil in ignorance, and then turns again and does right,—verily, He is forgiving and merciful."

55 Thus do we detail our signs, that the way of the sinners may be made plain.

56 Say, "I am forbidden to worship those ye call upon beside God;" say, "I will not follow your lusts, for

then should I err and not be of the guided."

57 Say, "I stand on a manifestation, from my Lord, which ye call a lie, I have not with me what ye fain would hasten on,

58 that the matter might be settled between me and you; but God knows best who are the unjust."

59 With Him are the keys of the unseen. None knows them save He; He knows what is in the land and in the sea; and there falls not a leaf save that He knows it; nor a grain in the darkness of the earth, nor aught that is moist, nor aught that is dry, save that is in His perspicuous Book.

---

world and the hope of our eternal country" (*Letters of C. S. Lewis*, Aug 10, 1948).

John R. W. Stott adds: "We are to be 'always and for everything giving thanks' (Eph 5:20). Most of us give thanks for some things. There is no time at which, and no circumstances for which, they do not give thanks. They do so 'in the name of our Lord Jesus Christ', that is because they are one with Christ and 'to God the Father', because the Holy Spirit witnesses with their spirit that they are God's children and that their Father is wholly good and wise. Grumbling, one of Israel's besetting sins, is serious because it is a symptom of unbelief. Whenever we are moaning and groaning, it is proof positive that we are not filled with the Spirit. Whenever the Holy Spirit fills believers, they thank their heavenly Father at all times for all things" (*Baptism and Fullness*, p. 58).

6.54 *He is forgiving and merciful* — Allah will pardon their sins (see **Divine Forgive-**

ness in Islam on pp. 158-161; and Q 11.3, note).

6.55 *the way of sinners* — The central characteristic of "the way of the sinners" is the embrace of polytheism.

6.56 Muhammad declared in the fourth question-and-answer couplet: "I am forbidden to worship those ye call upon beside God" (v. 56). Only God, said Muhammad, (a) holds the "keys of the unseen," (b) is omniscient, (c) controls every aspect of people's lives—from dawn to dusk, (d) provides people with guardian angels, and (e) and appoints the day of each person's death.

6.59a *keys of the unseen* — This refers to power and authority to predestine every act that takes place in the world, including each leaf that falls to the ground.

6.59b *His perspicuous Book* — This is the book in Paradise that details and predestines each and every action and event that occurs on earth (see **The Perspicuous Book**

60   He it is who takes you to Himself at night, and knows what ye have gained in the day; then He raises you up again, that your appointed time may be fulfilled; then unto Him is your return, and then will He inform you of what ye have done.

61   He triumphs over His servants; He sends to them guardian angels, until, when death comes to Any one of you, our messengers take him away; they pass not over any one,

62   and then are they returned to God, their true sovereign. Is not His the rule? but He is very quick at reckoning up.

63   Say, "Who rescues you from the darkness of the land and of the sea?" ye call upon Him in humility and in secret, "Indeed, if He would rescue us from this, we will surely be of those who give Him thanks."

64   Say, "God rescues from the darkness thereof, and from every trouble, yet ye associate others with Him."

65   Say, "He is able to send torment on you from above you and from beneath your feet, and to confuse you in sects, and to make some of you taste the violence of others." See how we turn about the signs, that haply they may discriminate.

66   Thy people called it a lie, and yet it is the truth. Say, "I have not charge over you;

on pp. 178-179).

6.63-64 The fifth question-and-answer couplet addressed the Doctrine of Divine Providence. Muhammad presented the illustration of a person rescued from darkness, whether it be on land or sea, to make his case. All such rescues, he maintained, were because Allah moved providentially to bring about the desired outcome.

When it comes to divine providence, Christians are in agreement with the Qur'an. Without suspending the laws of nature, God gives shape to events to that they result in His desired outcome. Most answers to prayer involve the outworking of divine providence. Oswald Chambers added: "The attitude of a Christian towards the providential order in which he is placed is to recognize that God is behind it for purposes of His own" (*Biblical Ethics*, p. 35), and "The circumstances of a saint's [that is, a Christian's] life are ordered by God, and not by happy-go-lucky chance. There is no such thing as chance in the life of a saint [that is, a Christian], and we shall find that God by His providence brings our bodies into circumstances that we cannot understand a bit, but the Spirit of God understands; He is bringing us into places and among people and under conditions in order that the intercession of the Holy Spirit in us may take a particular line" (*If Ye Shall Ask*, p. 107).

6.65-70 The sixth question-and-answer couplet addressed Muhammad's responsibility over those who rejected his message. He maintained that those individuals misunderstood and twisted the meanings of the Qur'an to such an extent that they were plunge into deep confusion. Muhammad believed that he was admonished by Allah to leave them alone. "Leave those who have taken their religion for a play and a sport" (v.

67 to every prophecy is a set time, and in the end ye shall know."

68 When thou dost see those who plunge deeply into the discussion of our signs, turn from them until they plunge deeply into some other discourse; for it may be that Satan may make thee forget; but sit not after thou hast remembered, with the unjust people.

69 Those who fear are not bound to take account of them at all, but mind!—haply they may fear.

70 Leave those who have taken their religion for a play and a sport, whom this world's life hath deceived, and remind them thereby that a soul shall be given up for what it has earned; nor has it, beside God, patron or intercessor; and though it should compensate with the fullest compensation, it would not be accepted. Those who are given up for what they

have gained, for them is a drink of boiling water, and grievous woe for that they. have misbelieved.

71 Say, "Shall we call on what neither profits us nor harms us, and be thrown back upon our heels after God has guided us, like him whom Satan hath led away bewildered in the earth, who has companions who call him to guidance, 'Come to us?'" Say, "Verily, God's guidance is the guidance, and we are bidden to resign ourselves unto the Lord of the worlds,

72 and be ye steadfast in prayer and fear Him, for He it is to whom we shall be gathered."

73 He it is who has created the heavens and the earth in truth; and on the day when He says, "BE," then it is. His word is truth; to Him is the kingdom on the day when the trumpets shall be blown; the knower of the unseen and of the

70). At the Last Judgment they would get their due: "drink of boiling water" in Hell.

6.68 *Satan may make thee forget* — Muhammad admitted that when disputing with infidels, he may had been subject to the influence of Satan who caused him to forget certain divine teachings. This admission may be a subtle reference to the Satanic Verses Controversy where Muhammad allegedly experienced a forgetfulness brought on by Satan (see **The Satanic Verses Controversy** on pp. 135-138).

6.71-73 The seventh and final question-and-answer couplet addressed the issue of a surrendered lifestyle to the Lord. According to Muhammad, it was Allah who should

guide every aspect of the believer's life.

These sentiments correspond to the Christian faith. The way James Montgomery Boice put it: "If Madison Avenue executives were trying to attract people to the Christian life, they would stress its positive and fulfilling aspects. They would speak of Christianity as a way of wholeness of life and all happiness. Unfortunately, we who live in the West are so conditioned to this way of thinking (and to precisely this type of Christian evangelism or salesmanship) that we are almost shocked when we learn that the first great principle of Christianity is negative. It is not, as some say, 'Come to Christ, and all your troubles will melt away.' It is as the

evident; He is wise and well aware.

Abraham

74 When Abraham said to his father Âzar, "Dost thou take idols for gods? verily, I see thee and thy people in obvious error."

75 Thus did we show Abraham the kingdom of heaven and of the earth, that he should be of those who are sure.

76 And when the night overshadowed him he saw a star and said, "This is my Lord;" but when it set he said, "I love not those that set."

77 And when he saw the moon be-

ginning to rise he said, "This is my Lord;" but when it set he said, "If God my Lord guides me not I shall surely be of the people who err."

78 And when he saw the sun beginning to rise he said, "This is my Lord, this is greatest of all;" but when it set he said, "O my people! verily, I am clear of what ye associate with God;

79 verily, I have turned my face to him who originated the heaven and the earth, as a 'Hanîf, and I am not of the idolaters."

80 And his people disputed with him;—he said, "Do ye dispute with me concerning God, when He has

Lord himself declared, 'If any man would come after me, let him deny himself and take up his cross and follow me. For whoever would save his life will lose it, and whoever loses his life for my sake will find it. For what will it profit a man, if he gains the whole world and forfeits his life?'" (*Foundations of the Christian Faith*, p. 459).

6.74a *Azar* — Muhammad called Abraham's father Azar. According to the Bible, however, his name was Terah (see Gen 11:27). This discrepancy is not a contradiction. In his book *Church History,* Eusebius of Caesarea called Abraham's father *Athar* which is phonetically close to *Thara* (Terah). The Greek *Athar* is easily converted into the Arabic *Azar*. Hence, the variances in his name could easily be explained as a question of phonetic dissonance that exists when any two languages interface with one another (see *A Comprehensive Commentary on the Qur'an*, p. 177, n. 75).

6.74b Abraham was critical of his father's

commitment to the worship of idols (see Josh 24:2; Jubilees 12:1-8).

6.74-82 This passage is a fanciful story about Abraham and his belief in astrology.

6.76 According to this verse, Abraham saw a star and worshipped it. Yet, he rejected this adoration when the star set beneath the horizon.

6.77 According to this verse, Abraham saw the moon rise above the horizon and worshipped it. Yet, he then rejected this adoration when the moon set beneath the horizon.

6.78 According to this verse, Abraham saw the sun rise and worshipped it, Yet he then rejected this adoration when he saw the sun set beneath the horizon.

6.79 Finally, Abraham worshipped the one true God, the creator of the heavens and the earth and became a *Hanif*—that is, a monotheist (see Q 30.30, note).

6.80-82 The gods worshipped by the people of Ur were Sin (the Akkadian moon

guided me? but I fear not what ye associate with Him unless my Lord should wish for anything. My Lord doth comprehend all things in His knowledge, will ye not then remember?

81 How should I fear what ye associate with Him, when ye yourselves fear not to associate with God what He has sent down to you no power to do? Which then of the two sects is worthier of belief, if indeed ye know?"

82 Those who believe and do not obscure their faith with wrong, they are those who, shall have security, and they are guided.

*The example of God's
many apostles*

83 These are our arguments which we gave to Abraham against his people;—we raise the rank of whom we will; verily, thy Lord is wise and knowing.

84 And we gave to him Isaac and Jacob, each did we guide. And Noah we guided before and all his seed,—David and Solomon and Job and Joseph and Moses and Aaron,—for thus do we reward those who do good.

85 And Zachariah and John and Jesus and Elias, all righteous ones;

86 and Ishmael and Elisha and Jonas and Lot, each one have we preferred above the worlds;

87 and of their fathers and their seed and brethren; we have chosen them and guided them into a right way.

88 That is God's guidance; He guides those whom He will of His servants; and if they associate aught with Him,—vain is that which they have worked.

89 It is to these we give the Book and judgment and prophecy; and if these disbelieve therein we have given them in charge to a people

god), Shamash, and Ishtar. Nevertheless, Abraham disputed with the people of Ur and defended his belief in monotheism. These words parallel the dispute that Muhammad had been having with the Meccan people as he defended his belief in monotheism and condemned their belief in polytheism.

6.81 *Which then of the two sects* — That is, which then of the two systems of belief is correct—monotheism or polytheism?

6.82 *believe and do not obscure their faith with wrong* — This phrase is a variation of "believe and do right," a phrase repeated often in the Qur'an and serve as a brief summary of the Islamic gospel (see Q 103.3

note).

6.83-89 According to Muhammad, Allah sent many apostles into the world who were righteous ("we have chosen them and guided them into a right way"), and who were given divine revelation ("the Book and judgment and prophecy"). Those apostles mentioned in this passage are: Abraham, Isaac, Jacob, Noah, David, Solomon, Job, Joseph, Moses, Aaron, Zechariah, John the Baptist, Jesus, Elias (Elijah), Ishmael, Elisha, Jonas (Jonah), and Lot. Each one is mentioned in the Bible.

6.89 *the Book* — The eternal Book in Paradise that reveals Allah, man, sin, and salvation (see **The Perspicuous Book** on pp.

who shall not disbelieve.

Third catechism

90   It is these that God hath guided,
and by their guidance be thou led.
Say, "I will not ask you for it a
hire: it is naught save a reminder
to the worlds."

91   They do not prize God at His true
worth when they say, "God has
never revealed to mortal anything."
Say, "Who revealed the Book
wherewith Moses came, a light and
a guidance unto men? Ye put it on
papers which ye show, though ye
hide much; and ye are taught what
ye knew not, neither you nor your
fathers." Say, "God," then leave
them in their discussion to play.

92   This is the Book which we have
revealed, a blessing and a confirmation to those which were before it, and that the mother of cit-

ies may be warned, with those who
are round about her. Those who
believe in the last day believe
therein, and they unto their prayers
will keep.

The example of false apostles

93   Who is more unjust than he who
devises against God a lie, or says,
"I am inspired," when he was not
inspired at all? and who says, "I
will bring down the like of what
God has sent down;" but didst thou
see when the unjust are in the
floods of death, and the angels
stretch forth their hands, "Give ye
forth your souls; today shall ye be
recompensed with the torment of
disgrace, for that ye did say against
God what was not true, and were
too proud to hear His signs.

94   And ye come now single-handed
as we created you at first, and ye

178-179).

6.90-92 The purpose of this third catechism is to affirm the Old Testament as a divinely inspired document. Muhammad asserted that its truths are eternal and therefore should be read and revered by the people of Mecca. Still, according to Muhammad, the Old Testament was to be interpreted in a way that paralleled his own surahs.

6.91 Muhammad claimed that the Jews of Mecca were not interpreting their own Scriptures accurately.

6.92 *the mother of cities* — Mecca. Mecca was believed to be the mother of cities because in its center is the Ka'ba altar (see Q 42.7). See **The City of Mecca** on pp. 32-

34.

6.93 Muhammad regarded the most unjust to be those who falsely claimed to be inspired of God. The Christian cannot help but see an irony in this verse. Though Muhammad condemned false prophets, Christians look upon Muhammad as a false prophet. The New Testament states: "But even if we or an angel from heaven should preach a gospel other than the one we preached to you, let him be eternally condemned! As we have already said, so now I say again: If anybody is preaching to you a gospel other than what you accepted, let him be eternally condemned!" (Gal 1:8-9).

6.94 *we see not with you your interces-*

have left behind your backs that which, we granted you; and we see not with you your intercessors whom ye pretended were partners amongst you; betwixt you have the ties been cut asunder; and strayed away from you is what ye did pretend."

Allah's sovereign control over the world

95 Verily, God it is who cleaves out the grain and the date-stone; He brings forth the living from the dead, and it is He who brings the dead from the living. There is God! how then can ye be beguiled?

96 He it is who cleaves out the morning, and makes night a repose, and the sun and the moon two reckonings—that is the decree of the mighty, the wise!

97 He it is who made for you stars that ye might be guided thereby in the darkness of the land and of the sea. Now have we detailed the signs unto a people who do know.

98 He it is who made you spring from one soul, and gave you a settlement and a depository. Now have we detailed the signs unto a people who discern.

99 He it is who sends down from the heavens water; and we bring forth therewith growths of everything;

sors — That is, at the Last Judgment Allah will not see the gods of the infidels protecting them from their impending doom. The words are full of sarcasm and mockery, belittling the infidels previous involvement in the sin of *shirk*—idolatry.

6.95 According to Muhammad, life and death are in the hands of Allah. He is the source of life and the One who determines the moment of one's death. He also has the power to effect the resurrection from the dead. The Bible makes a similar claim about God (see Deut 32:39; 2 Kings 5:7; Jn 5:21; Acts 26:8; Rom 4:17-19).

6.96 Muhammad claimed that it was Allah—and not the gods that the polytheists worshipped—who created day and night. The Bible makes a similar claim about God (Gen 1:3-31; 8:22; Ps 74:16; 104:20; Isa 45:7).

6.97 *we detailed the signs* — Foundational to navigation across the desert or the sea was the positioning of the stars against the horizon and the sun, moon, and stars. Muhammad's argument was that of Natural Revelation. It is Allah who made the sun, moon, and stars and thereby made navigation possible. They are indicators not only of Allah's benevolent and providential care but of Allah's existence and sovereign control over all things.

6.98 *made you spring from one soul* — Muhammad argued that people should be able to deduce that all humankind originated from one couple (Adam and Eve). It is Allah who created the first couple who served as the progenitors of the human race. This too, Muhammad concluded, is evidence of Natural Revelation ("signs unto a people who discern").

6.99 *in that ye have a sign* — The food that exists on the earth is an indicator not only of Allah's benevolent and providential care, but of Allah's existence and sovereign control over all things. Again, this is evidence

and we bring forth therefrom green things, wherefrom we bring forth grain in full ear; and the palm, from its spathe come clusters within reach; and gardens of grapes and olives and pomegranates, alike and unlike;—behold its fruit when it fruits and ripens! verily, in that ye have a sign for the people who believe.

False beliefs

100   Yet they made the ginn partners with God, though He created them! and they ascribed to Him sons and daughters, though they have no knowledge; celebrated be His praise!" and exalted be He above what they attribute to Him!

101   The inventor of the heavens and the earth! how can He have a son, when He has no female companion, and when He has created everything, and everything He knows?

An insight from Allah

102   There is God for you,—your Lord! There is no god but He, the Creator of everything; then worship Him, for He o'er everything keeps guard!

103   Sight perceives Him not, but He perceives men's sights; for He is the subtle, the aware.

104   Now has an insight from your Lord come unto you, and he who looks therewith it is for himself; but he Who is blind thereto, it is against his soul; and I am not your keeper.

105   Thus do we turn about the signs, that they may say, "Thou hast stud-

---

of Natural Revelation ("a sign for the people who discern").

6.100a *ginn* — genie. Instead of understanding the implications of Natural Revelation, people turned to ginns (genies) and worshipped them (see **Occultism in Seventh Century Arabia** on pp. 123-125).

6.100 *they ascribed to Him sons and daughters* — the Arabic Star Family religious system that dominated the ancient Middle East, including Arabia, asserted that the gods whom they worshipped procreated and brought into existence new gods. Muhammad condemned religion, insisting in the rightness of monotheism. Allah was the only God.

6.102 *There is no god but He* —Muhammad's rebuttal to those who, from his point of view, fell into the sin of *shirk* (vv 100-

101), was a reaffirmation of the Doctrine of Tauhid—an absolute monotheism (see Q 112; see also 6.106; 10.90; 11.14; 20.8, 98; 27.26; 35.3; 39.6; 40.3, 62, 65; 44.8; 73.9).

6.104 *an insight from your Lord* — This insight is sevenfold. The first part of this insight (v. 104) is that whoever chooses to see the right path to Allah, does so for his own good; and whoever chooses to remain blind, does so for his own hurt.

The second part of the insight (v. 105) is that divine revelation has many facets, all requiring rigorous study. Those who take the time to study will know the truth.

The third part of the insight (v. 106) is that one must follow (embrace) the Doctrine of Tauhid (absolute monotheism) and shun the sin of *shirk* (idolatry).

ied," and that we may explain to those who know.

106   Follow what is revealed to thee from thy Lord; there is no god but He, and shun the idolaters.

107   But had God pleased, they would not have associated aught with Him; but we have not made thee a keeper over them, nor art thou for them a warder.

108   Do not abuse those who call on other than God, for then they may abuse God openly in their ignorance. So do we make seemly to every nation their work, then unto their Lord is their return, and He will inform them of what they have done.

109   They swore by God with their most strenuous oath, that if there come to them a sign they will indeed believe therein. Say, "Signs are only in God's hands;—but what will make you understand that even when one has come, they will not believe?"

110   We will overturn their hearts and their eyesights, even as they believed not at first; and we will leave them, in their rebellion, blindly wandering on.

111   And had we sent down unto them the angels, or the dead had spoken to them, or we had gathered everything unto them in hosts, they would not have believed unless that God pleased—but most of them are ignorant.

The enemies of the prophets

112   So have we made for every prophet an enemy,—devils of men and ginns; some of them inspire others with specious speech to lead astray; but had thy Lord pleased they would not have done it; so leave them with what they do devise.

113   And let the hearts of those who be-

The fourth part of the insight (v. 107) is the doctrine of double predestination. If Allah had so willed, those who have fallen into the sin of *shirk* would not have done so (see **The Doctrine of al-Qadar** on pp. 264-266).

The fifth part of the insight (v. 108) is that Muhammad was not to plead for the repentance of those who refuse to believe.

The sixth part of the insight (vv. 109, 111) is that miracles (signs) would only generate faith, provided that Allah so willed that the miracles (signs) generated faith. The same is true of the manifestation of angels, the voice from the dead, and so on.

The seventh part of the insight (v. 110) is that Allah chose to leave the unrighteous "in their rebellion, blindly wandering on."

6.112 *devils of men and ginns* — That is, evil ones from among men and ginns. Some of them inspire the unrighteous with "specious speech to lead astray." The work of evil men and ginns, however, are still under the overarching control of Allah. This is because Allah ordained their ministry of deception upon the earth (see **The Doctrine of al-Qadar** on pp. 264-266; Q 16.63; 17.61-64; 36.59-62; 38.71-85).

6.113 Muhammad encouraged the infidels to continue in their unbelief. This stands in

lieve not in the hereafter listen to it; and let them be well pleased with it; and let them gain what they may gain!

Jews and Christians

114 Of other than God shall I crave a decree, when it is He who has sent down to you the Book in detail, and those to whom we gave the Book know that it is sent down from thy Lord, in truth? be thou not then of those who doubt.

115 The words of thy Lord are fulfilled in truth and justice; there is none to change His words, for He both hears and knows.

116 But if thou followest most of those who are in the land, they will lead thee astray from the path of God, they only follow suspicion and they only (rest on) conjecture.

117 Thy Lord, He knows best who errs from His path, and He knows best the guided.

Blessed and unblessed food

118 Eat then of what God's name has been pronounced over, if ye believe in His signs.

119 What ails you that ye do not eat from what God's name is pronounced over, when He has detailed to you what is unlawful for you? Save what ye are forced to; but, verily, many will lead you astray by their fancies, without

contrast to the sentiments found in the Bible (see Rom 9:1-5; 2 Pet 3:9).

6.114 *the Book* — The eternal Book that accurately describes the nature of God, man, sin, salvation, and so on (see **The Perspicuous Book** on pp. 178-179). In this case, the Book is the Old and New Testaments since He had already given it to people on the earth; "those who doubt" were the Jews and Christians.

6.114 *the Book* — That is, the Qur'an. Muhammad claimed that he was admonished by Allah to remain devoted to the Qur'an, which he believed contained truth and justice. Others (e.g., Jews and Christians) who had received their version of the Book (the Old and New Testaments) had become doubters and suspicious of its true content and had entered into falsehood. Their doubts were grounded in their skepticism

and rejection of Muhammad's interpretation of the Old and New Testaments.

6.115 *there is none to change His words* — Muhammad asserted the immutability of the Qur'an, which he believed to be the word of God. Christians ask: why, then, are there abrogated verses in the Qur'an? And, why did Allah not guard other words of Allah from corruption, such as the Old and New Testaments? Muhammad had alleged that both Old and New Testaments had been corrupted and are no longer trustworthy (see Q 4.46, 157-158, 172-173; 5.13, 73; also see Q 15.9, note, **The Doctrine of Abrogation** on pp. 68-70).

6.118-121 Muhammad believed that Allah instructed to eat whatever had been blessed and to avoid what had been identified as unlawful. This passage is the foundation of the *Halal Tradition* in Islam. It requires that

knowledge. Verily, thy Lord knows best the transgressors.

120   Leave alone the outside of sin and the inside thereof; verily, those who earn sin shall be recompensed for what they have gained.

121   But eat not of what the name of God has not been pronounced over, for, verily, it is an abomination. Verily, the devils inspire their friends that they may wrangle with you; but if ye obey them, verily, ye are idolaters.

The two ways

122   Is he who was dead and we have quickened him, and made for him a light, that he might walk therein amongst men, like him whose likeness is in the darkness whence he cannot come forth? Thus is made seemly to the misbelievers what

they have done.

123   And thus have we placed in every town the great sinners thereof, that they may use craft therein; but they use not craft except against themselves, although they do not understand.

124   And when there comes to them a sign, they say, "We will not believe until we are brought like what the apostles were brought;" God knows best where to put His message. There shall befall those who sin, meanness in God's eyes, and grievous torment for the craft they used.

125   Whomsoever God wishes to guide, He expands his breast to Islam; but whomsoever He wishes to lead astray, He makes his breast tight and straight, as though he would mount up into heaven; thus does God set His horror on those who

---

the jugular vein, windpipe and food pipe of the animal be severed after the butcher recites: "In the name of Allah." Ian MacLachlan writes: "Halal may be performed by any adult Muslim, provided that just prior to slaughter, a prayer is recited: *'Bismillah-e-Allah-o-Akbar'* ('with the name of Allah who is great') (*Kill and Chill*, p. 252). Whatever food that has not been blessed must be avoided since whoever eats unblessed food has become an idolater (has committed the sin of *shirk*).

6.122a *we have quickened him* — Islamic commentators agree that this phrase is to be taken metaphorically; that is, it refers to people who were spiritually dead and then quickened to spiritual life (see Eph 2:1-5

where a similar metaphor is used).

6.122b *made for him a light* — Divine revelation (the Book).

6.123 *that they may use craft therein* — That they may scheme to achieve their own unrighteous ends.

6.124 The excuse of unrighteous people is that they will not believe unless they receive a direct revelation from Allah "like what the apostles were brought." This excuse will not impress Allah, however, who will respond with meanness in His eyes and a grievous torment.

6.125 *Islam* — The word literally means *submission*. Once again, the doctrine of double predestination is brought to bear in this par-

do not believe.

126   This is the way of thy Lord—
       straight. We have detailed the signs
       unto a mindful people;

127   for them is an abode of peace; and
       their Lord, He is their patron for
       what they have done.

Last Judgment

128   And on the day when He shall
       gather them all together, "O assem-
       bly of the ginns! ye have got much
       out of mankind." And their clients
       from among mankind shall say, "O
       our Lord! much advantage had we
       one from another;" but we reached
       our appointed time which thou
       hadst appointed for us. Says He,
       "The fire is your resort, to dwell
       therein for aye! save what God
       pleases; verily, thy Lord is wise and
       knowing."

129   Thus do we make some of the un-
       just patrons of the others, for that
       which they have earned.

130   O assembly of ginns and men! did
       there not come to you apostles
       from among yourselves, relating to
       you our signs, and warning you
       of the meeting of this very day of
       yours? They say, "We bear wit-
       ness against ourselves." The life
       of this world deceived them, and
       they bear witness against them-
       selves that they were unbelievers.

Judgment on towns

131   That is because thy Lord would
       never destroy towns unjustly while
       their people are careless;

132   but for every one are degrees of
       what they have done; and thy Lord
       is not careless of that which they
       do.

ticular argument: (a) those whom Allah wishes to guide, He expands his breast, and (b) those whom Allah wishes to lead astray, He tightens the breast (see **The Doctrine of al-Qadar** on pp. 264-266).

6.126 Muhammad described the way of the Lord as *straight*, meaning that it is clear and predictable (see Q 72.2, note; also see Matt 3:3; Mk 1:3; Lk 3:4-5; Jn 1:23; 2 Pet 2:15 where a similar metaphor is used in the New Testament).

6.127 *an abode of peace* — Paradise.

6.128 *ginns* — genies. The men with whom the ginns spent their time are called *clients* and *unjust patrons*, suggesting a formalized working relationship with ginn priests and prognosticators where commitments and

monies were exchanged (see **Occultism in Seventh Century Arabia** on pp. 123-125).

6.130a *ginns* — genies.

6.130b At the Last Judgment, the unrigh-teous ginns and men will be questioned about the apostles that Allah had sent to them. These apostles will bear witness that the unrighteous were indeed infidels.

6.131-134 In this passage, the words "thy," "you," and "ye" refer to the unrigh-teous people. Divine judgment comes in two ways: in this life and in the afterlife (see **The Apostles** on pp. 398-400). To the de-gree that people live unrighteously, their towns will be destroyed. Allah will then cause other righteous people to succeed them— living where unrighteous people previously

133 Thy Lord is rich, merciful; if He pleases He will take you off, and will cause what He pleases to succeed you; even as He raised you up from the seed of other people.

134 Verily, what ye are promised will surely come, nor can ye frustrate it.

135 Say, "O my people! act according to your power, verily, I am acting too; and soon shall ye know whose is the future of the abode!" verily, the unjust shall not prosper.

Reasons for judgment

136 They set apart for God, from what He raises of tilth and of cattle, a portion, and they say, "This is God's;"—as they pretend—"and this is for our associates;" but that which is for their associates reaches not to God, and that which was for God does reach to their associates;—evil is it what they judge.

137 Thus too have their associates made seemly to many of the idolaters the killing of their children, to destroy them, and to obscure for them their religion; but had God pleased they would not have done it, leave them alone and that which they have forged.

138 And they say, "These cattle and tilth are inviolable; none shall taste thereof, save such as we please as they pretend—and there are cattle

lived—just as surely as they were born from the seed of their own parents. Nothing can frustrate this judgment.

6.135 Muhammad then spoke out to the Muslim people ("O my people"), telling them to act according to their power in reference to their future abode. When taken in context with vv. 131-134, this *abode* refers to the towns that will be destroyed and then given to them. Hence, the Muslim people are to participate in the divine judgment on the unrighteous.

This passage (Q 6.131-135), then, is a foreshadowing of the Doctrine of Jihad that will be developed in later surahs. It is also a foreshadowing of the notion of islamification (see Q 21.10-15; **Jihad** on pp. 616-622 and **Islamification** on pp. 851-852).

6.136-140 The reasons for divine judgment on the infidels: (a) hypocrisy in the setting aside of a portion of the wealth for Allah—verse 136, (b) infanticide—verses 137, 140, (c) hypocrisy in the offering of certain cattle as an offering to Allah, and (d) shifting standards in regards to the birth of calves—verse 139.

In the pre-Islamic Arabic world, infanticide was a common occurrence, typically involving unwanted female babies (see Q 16.57-59; 81.8). Infanticide was also a part of the occult in Arabia where the sacrificing of one's own children to the ginns was a way of demonstrating religious devotion. Muhammad's own grandfather was a worshipper of the ginns and considered sacrificing Muhammad's father (while a child) to the ginns (see Ibn Ishaq, *The Life of Muhammad*, pp. 66-68). Though the practice of elective abortions is not specifically mentioned in this verse, according to mainstream Islam, it is implied. Accordingly, elective abortions too are forbidden (see Q 81.8).

whose backs are prohibited, and cattle over whom God's name is not pronounced,—forging a lie against Him! He shall reward them for what they have forged."

139 And they say, "What is in the wombs of these cattle is unlawful for our wives, but if it be (born) dead, then are they partners therein." He will reward them for their attribution; verily, He is wise and knowing.

140 Losers are they who kill their children foolishly, without knowledge, and who prohibit what God has bestowed upon them, forging a lie against God; they have erred and are not guided.

Pagan superstitions

141 He it is who brought forth gardens with trailed and untrailed vines, and the palms and corn land, with various food, and olives, and pomegranates, alike and unlike. Eat

from the fruit thereof whene'er it fruits, and bring the dues thereof on the day of harvest, and be not extravagant; verily, He loves not the extravagant.

142 Of cattle are there some to ride on and to spread. Eat of what God has bestowed upon you, and follow not the footsteps of Satan; verily, he is to you an open foe.

143 Eight pairs,—of sheep two, and of goats two; say, "Are the two males unlawful, or the two females, or what the wombs of the two females contain? inform me with knowledge if ye tell the truth."

144 And of camels two, and cows two; say, "Are the two males unlawful, or the two females, or what the wombs of the two females contain? Were ye witnesses when God ordained for you these?—Then who is more unjust than he who devises a lie against God, to lead men astray without knowledge? verily, God guides not the unjust

6.141 The righteous are told to grow gardens and bring forth a harvest for Allah.

6.142a *cattle are there some to ride on and to spread* — That is, some cattle are to be rode and some are to be slaughtered.

6.142b *Satan* — Muhammad claimed that Satan is the foe of all believers. The Bible makes a similar claim (see Zech 3:1; Jn 8:44; 2 Cor 11:14).

6.142-143 This passage is a description of a practice in seventh century Arabia that addressed the dedication of animals to the gods. Muhammad criticized the practice of

setting aside pairs of animals based upon sex, number, and the sequence of their offspring, and then dedicating them to one of their gods (that is, dedicated animals were regarded as a good luck charm to guarantee the well-being of the rest of the herds). The animals were free to pasture and never slaughtered for meat. Muhammad described such activity as "a lie against God, to lead men astray without knowledge." Eight pairs of animals are mentioned in his passage: (a) two sheep, (b) two goats, (c) two camels, and (d) two cows. Also see Q 5.103 where

people."

145 Say, "I cannot find in what I am inspired with anything unlawful for the taster to taste; unless it be dead (of itself), or blood that has been shed, or the flesh of swine,—for that is a horror—or an abomination that is consecrated to other than God. But he who is forced, not wilfully nor transgressing,—then, verily, thy Lord is forgiving and merciful."

146 To those who were Jews did we prohibit everything that hath a solid hoof; and of oxen and sheep did we prohibit to them the fat, save what the backs of both do bear, or the inwards, or what is mixed with bone; with that did we recompense them for their rebellion, for, verily, we are true.

147 And if they give thee the lie, say, "Your Lord is of ample mercy, nor shall His violence be turned back from the sinful people."

Fourth catechism

148 Those who associate others with God will say, "Had God pleased, we had not so associated, nor our fathers; nor should we have forbidden aught." Thus did they give the lie to those who came before them, until they tasted of our violence! Say, "Have ye any knowledge? if so, bring it forth to us: ye only follow suspicion, and ye do but conjecture."

149 Say, "God's is the searching argument; and had He pleased He would have guided you all."

150 Say, "Come on then with your witnesses, who bear witness that God has prohibited these!" but if they do bear witness, bear thou not witness with them; nor follow the lust of those who say our signs are lies, and those who do not believe in the last day, or those who for their Lord make peers.

this form of paganism is mentioned.

6.145 As a rebuttal, Muhammad insisted that there was nothing unlawful about slaughtering and eating whatever animal is in one's herd. The exceptions were: (a) those animals who died apart from an intended slaughter, (b) blood, and (c) pork.

6.146 Muhammad reminded his listeners of Jewish dietary law. Jews were not permitted to eat: (a) animals with a solid hoof, (b) the fat from oxen or sheep, apart from the back or the entrails, and (c) that which is mixed with bone.

6.148-153 Muhammad once again turned to catechismal instruction. This time, its pur-

pose was to provide Muslim followers with rebuttals to those "who associate others with God" (idolatry).

6.148-150 Muhammad began the catechism by addressing the doctrine double predestination. At the Last Judgment, the polytheists will say: "Had God pleased, we had not so associated [with idolatry], nor our fathers; nor should we have forbidden naught." The comments, in other words, were both a lament and an accusation against Allah (see **The Doctrine of al-Qadar** on pp. 264-266).

6.151-152 Muhammad listed a number of sins of which they would be judged at the

151   Say, "Come! I will recite what your Lord has forbidden you, that ye may not associate aught with Him, and (may show) kindness to your parents, and not kill your children through poverty;—we will provide for you and them;—and draw not nigh to flagrant sins, either apparent or concealed, and kill not the soul, which God hath forbidden save by right; that is what God ordains you, haply ye may understand."

152   And draw not nigh unto the wealth of the orphan, save so as to better it, until he reaches full age; and give weight and measure with justice. We do not compel the soul save what it can compass; and when ye pronounce, then be just, though it be in the case of a relative. And God's compact fulfill ye; that is what He ordained you, haply ye may be mindful.

153   Verily, this is my right way; follow it then, and follow not various paths, to separate yourselves from His way; that is what He has ordained you, haply ye may fear!

Jews and Christians

154   Then we gave Moses the Book, complete for him who acts aright, and a decision and a guidance and a mercy; haply in the meeting of their Lord they will believe.

155   This is the Book which we have sent down; it is a blessing; follow it then and fear; haply ye may obtain mercy.

156   Lest ye say, "The Book was only sent down to two sects before us; verily, we, for what they read, care naught."

157   Or, lest ye should say, "Had we had

Last Judgment: (a) idolatry—associating aught with Allah, (b) failure to show kindness to one's parents, (c) infanticide, (d) flagrant sins, (e) murder, (f) taking money from orphans—except to improve their monies until they reach adulthood, and (g) make dishonest transactions—that is, inaccurate weights and measure.

6.152b *God's compact* — That is, the law of Allah. Muhammad believed that it was a person's moral obligation to use his or her natural talents (physical as well as mental) to the glory of Allah.

6.153 *my right way* — The way of righteousness (see Q 72.2, note).

6.154, 155 *the Book* — That is, the Pentateuch (see **The Perspicuous Book** on pp. 178-179). It is described here as an expression of righteousness ("for him who acts aright"). Muhammad then admonished his listeners to "follow it and fear." Those who did so, he said, would "obtain mercy." This is a curious statement since elsewhere in the Qur'an Muhammad said that the Old Testament has been corrupted and no longer trustworthy (see Q 10.40 note).

6.156 *two sects before us* — That is, the Jews and the Christians. The Jews and the Christians were the only sects known to the Arabians to be recipients of sacred Scripture. Muhammad's problem was that he believed that the Jews and Christians did not follow ("care naught") that which they read in their own sacred Scriptures ("the Book").

a book revealed to us we should surely have been more guided than they;" but there is come to them a manifest sign from their Lord, and a guidance and a mercy; who then is more unjust than he who calls God's signs lies, and turns from them? we will reward those who turn from our signs with an evil punishment for that they turned away.

158   What do they expect but that the angels should come for them, or that thy Lord should come, or that some signs of thy Lord should come? On the day when some signs do come, its faith shall profit no soul which did not believe before, unless it has earned some good by its faith. Say, "Wait ye expectant, then we wait expectant too."

159   Verily, those who divided their religion and became sects, thou hast

not to do with them, their matter is in God's hands, He will yet inform them of that which they have done.

Fifth catechism

160   He who brings a good work shall have ten like it; but he who brings a bad work shall be recompensed only with the like thereof, for they shall not be wronged.

161   Say, "As for me, my Lord has guided me to the right way, a right religion,—the faith of Abraham the 'Hanîf, for he was not of the idolaters."

162   Say, "Verily, my prayers and my devotion and my life and my death belong to God, the Lord of the worlds.

163   He has no partner; that is what I am bidden; for I am first of those who are resigned."

6.157 Muhammad maintained that if the Jews and Christians had rightly read their own sacred Scriptures they would have recognized that the surahs he had been presenting to the people of Mecca were of the same origin. That is, the revelations of the Jews, Christians, and Muslims had originated from the same eternal Book in Heaven. Therefore, since they called Muhammad's surahs falsehoods ("he who calls God's signs lies"), they condemned themselves and would suffer an "evil punishment"—be cast into the fires of Hell.

6.158 Jews and Christians, said Muhammad, were deluded into thinking that angels, the Lord, or new revelations would come and

defend their decision in rejecting his qur'anic surahs.

6.159 Muhammad was critical of the Jews and Christians who had divided themselves into sects, rather than remain interconnected with other religions of *the Book*, such as his small Muslim community in Mecca. Muhammad added that God "will yet inform them" about the wrongness of what they have done.

6.160-165 The final catechism is a reaffirmation that the Islamic faith is the "right religion" (v. 161).

6.165 *vicegerents* — The Arabic term is *khalifah*, or *caliph*. It is a divine office of man's rightful supremacy on the earth under Allah's

164   Say, "Other than God shall I crave
       for a Lord when He is Lord of all?"
       but no soul shall earn aught save
       against itself; nor shall one bear-
       ing a burden bear the burden of
       another; and then unto your Lord
       is your return, and He will inform
       you concerning that whereon ye
       do dispute.

165   He it is who made you vicegerents,
       and raised some of you above oth-
       ers in degree, to try you by that
       which he has brought you;—ver-
       ily, thy Lord is swift to punish, but,
       verily, He is forgiving and merci-
       ful.

Surah 64

*In the name of the merciful and compas-
sionate God.*

Doxology

1   What is in the heavens and what is
       in the earth celebrates God's
       praises; His is the kingdom, and
       His is the praise, and He is mighty
       over all!

The sovereignty of Allah

2   He it is who created you, and of
       you is (one) a misbeliever and
       (one) a believer; and God on what
       ye do does look.

3   He created the heavens and the
       earth in truth; and has formed you
       and made excellent your forms; and
       unto Him the journey is!

4   He knows what is in the heavens
       and the earth, and knows what ye
       conceal and what ye display; for
       God knows the nature of men's

watchful eyes (see Q 35.39, note).
Surah 64. The title of this surah, *The Day
of Cheating*, comes from verse 9. The dual
theme of this short surah is faith and obedience. The sequence begins with faith which
then leads to obedience., and which finally
leads to altruistic living—seen in a repudiation of covetousness and the practice of the
giving of alms.

  This surah has traditionally been difficult
to place chronologically. It could easily fit in
either the Meccan or Medinan period. This
is due to its simple message that spans the
entire chronological breadth of the Qur'an.
64.1 The surah begins with a doxology to
Allah. It is reminiscent of what is found repeatedly in the Bible (see Ps 146:1-2; 147:1;
148:1; 149:1; 150:1-6). Since it is a doxol-

ogy to Allah, it could therefore not be words
spoken by Allah. In Islam, only words specifically spoken by Allah were understood to
be divinely inspired (see Q 36.36-38, note;
and **The Qur'an** on pp. 150-153).
64:2-4 Muhammad drew attention to the
omniscient (all-knowing) and omnipotent (all-
powerful) attributes of Allah. Most notably,
Allah knows what people conceal and that
which resides deep in their hearts. They
are answerable to Allah, particularly in regards
to His sovereign control over the entire universe.
64.5-10 According to this passage, foundational to unbelief and unrighteousness is a
rejection of the apostles who proclaimed
Allah's Word. They are the "fellows of the
Fire" (v. 10). See **The Apostles** on pp. 398-

breasts!

Two ways

5   Has there not come to you the story
of those who misbelieved before,
and tasted the evil result of their
affair, and for them was grievous
woe?

6   That is because their apostles came
to them with manifest signs, and
they said, "Shall mortals guide us?"
and they misbelieved and turned
their backs. But God was independent of them; for God is rich and
to be praised!

7   Those who misbelieve pretend that
they shall surely not be raised: say,

"Yea! by my Lord! ye shall surely
be raised: then ye shall be informed
of that which ye have done;" for
that is easy unto God.

8   So believe in God and His Apostle
and the light which we have sent
down; for God of what ye do is
well aware!

9   On the day when he shall gather
you to the day of gathering, that is
the day of cheating! but whoso believes in God and acts aright, He
will cover for him his offences,
and will bring him into gardens beneath which rivers flow, to dwell
therein for aye! that is the mighty
bliss!

10   But those who misbelieve and say

400.
64.6 The central problem with the infidels
is that they understand that the apostles
were ordained by Allah and sent to them to
encourage repentance and a return to Allah. As has been noted in previous surahs,
this was the problem that the Meccan people
had with Muhammad.
64.7 According to this verse, a second characteristic of infidels is a rejection of the belief that all people will one day be resurrected
from the dead and stand before Allah at the
Last Judgment. Muhammad countered by
speaking prophetically: they shall surely be
raised and shall be informed of that which
they have done.
64.8 Muhammad appealed to his listeners
to: (a) believe in Allah, and (b) believe in His
Apostle (Muhammad). Muhammad believed
that his surahs were "the light" which Allah
had sent down. In contrast, Jesus said: "I
am the light of the world" (Jn 8:12; cf. Matt

5:15; Jn 1:4-5; 3:19-21; 9:5; 2 Cor 4:6; 1 Jn
1:5).
64.9a *that is the day of cheating!* — That
is, that is a day of loss and gain. The infidels
will lose and the believers will gain.
64.9b *whoso believes in God and acts aright*
— These words are repeated often in the
Qur'an and serve as a brief summary of the
Islamic gospel (see Q 103.3 note).
64.9c *He will cover for him his offences* —
Provided that on balance a person believes
and acts aright, Allah will cover the sins that
he or she committed in life (see ***Divine Forgiveness in Islam*** on pp. 158-161).
64.9d *gardens beneath which rivers flow*
— In the Qur'an is the imagery of Paradise
being an oasis with well supplied underground
aquifers sufficiently close to the surface to
keep the oasis fertile and green (see ***Paradise*** on pp. 76-77).
64.10 *fellows of the Fire* — People who
inhabit Hell. Muhammad's point is that all

our signs are lies, they are the fellows of the Fire, to dwell therein for aye! and evil shall the journey be!

Call to
outward obedience

11   No calamity befalls but by the permission of God: and whoso believes in God, He will guide his heart; for God all things doth know!

12   So obey God and obey the Apostle: but if ye turn your backs—our Apostle has only his plain message to preach!

13   God, there is no god but He; and upon Him let the believers rely!

Call to
inward obedience

14   O ye who believe! verily, among your wives and children are foes of yours: so beware of them! But if ye pardon, and overlook it, and forgive,—verily, God is forgiving, compassionate!

15   Your property and your children are but a trial; and God, with Him is mighty hire!

16   Then fear God as much as ye can! and hear, and obey, and expend in alms: it is better for yourselves. But whosoever is saved from his own covetousness—these are the prosperous!

17   If ye lend to God a goodly loan, He

who reject the Qur'an will be condemned to Hell.

64.11-13 In spite of the calamities of life, people are admonished in this passage to obey Allah and Muhammad. This is because: (a) no calamity can befall someone apart from the will of Allah, and (b) Allah will guide the heart through the calamity.

In the Bible, the Book of Job makes a similar case regarding the watchful eye and care of God during times of calamity (also see Ps 3:1-8; Heb 12:1-3; 1 Pet 4:1-3). The primary difference in the Bible, of course, is that the reader is admonished to reject false prophets (Gal 1:6-9). In this context, Muhammad should be rejected due to the voluminous differences in his surahs with biblical teachings.

64.13 Muhammad brought into the discussion the Doctrine of Tauhid (absolute monotheism) as the final reason for one to main-

tain steadfast obedience to Allah.

64.14-15 Muhammad observed that some of the Muslims had wives and children who were infidels. They were admonished to beware of them, yet also to be gentle—quick to pardon, overlook, and forgive.

The New Testament makes a similar point. Christians are to love those in their families, even if they are unbelievers (see Matt 5:43-48; Lk 6:27-36). With love, God may draw them to a saving knowledge of Christ.

64.16 *fear God* — Central to Islamic spirituality is to fear, hear, and obey God. And a central part of obedience is to give alms to the poor and avoid covetousness. Such people, said Muhammad, "are the prosperous."

64.17 *double it for you* — Muhammad's point was that a person cannot out-give Allah. Whatever is given to Allah will be re-

will double it for you, and will for-give you; for God is grateful, clem-ent!

18 He knows the unseen and the vis-ible; the mighty, the wise!

Surah 28

In the name of the merciful and compas-sionate God.

1 T. S. M.

The perspicuous Book

2 Those are the signs of the perspicu-ous Book;

The story of baby Moses

3 we recite to thee from the history of Moses and Pharaoh in truth unto a people who believe.

4 Verily, Pharaoh was lofty in the land and made the people thereof sects; one party of them he weakened, slaughtering their sons and letting their women live. Verily, he was of the despoilers.

5 And we wished to be gracious to

turned to the individual by Allah double the value. Allah will also grant forgiveness for sins based upon offerings given to Him.

Historically, various sects within the Church have embraced a similar understanding of gifts and offerings. The most notable example was the practice of Indulgences by the Roman Catholic Church in medieval Europe. People were given the opportunity to reduce their time in Purgatory based upon the quantity of offerings given to the Church. This practice sparked the Protestant Reformation which was wholly opposed to this concept. Martin Luther's Ninety-Five Theses nailed to the door in Wittenberg, Germany, was a critique against the practice of Indulgences.

Also, the theological position known as the Prosperity Gospel has emerged within the modern-day Protestant Church. It operates on the premise that whatever sum of money is given to God, a larger yield of money will somehow be returned to him or her. The Prosperity Gospel, however, is not part of mainstream Christian thought. Scrip-

ture neither supports nor warrants the practice.

Surah 28. The title of this surah, *The Narrative*, comes from verse 25. In this surah, Muhammad returned to a familiar theme: throughout the ages, Allah has sent apostles to the peoples of the world, showing them the truth about Himself, the coming judgment, and salvation from Hell. To make his case, Muhammad showcased two stories from the lives of Moses and Korah. He also reminded the listener that he too is an apostle, part of the line of apostles chosen by Allah.

28.1 Literally, *Ta Sin Mim*. See Q 32.1, note.

28.2 *the perspicuous Book* — In this case, the perspicuous Book refers to the divine revelations given to Moses. The version of these revelations given to Muhammad were believed to recite "in truth unto a people who believe" (see **The Perspicuous Book** on pp. 178-179).

28.3-13 This passage is based upon Exodus 1:6-2:10. Though the dialogue is Mu-

those who were weakened in the earth, and to make them models, and to make them the heirs;

6   and to establish for them in the earth; and to show Pharaoh and Hâmân and their hosts what they had to beware of from them.

7   And we inspired the mother of Moses, "Suckle him; and when thou art afraid for him then throw him into the river, and fear not and grieve not; verily, we are going to restore him to thee, and to make him of the apostles!"

8   And Pharaoh's family picked him up that he might be for them a foe and a grief; verily, Pharaoh and Hâmân and their hosts were sinners.

9   And Pharaoh's wife said, "He is a cheering of the eye to me, and to thee. Kill him not; it may be that he will profit us, or that we may take him for a son;" for they did not perceive.

10   And the heart of Moses' mother was void on the morrow; she well-

nigh disclosed him, had it not been that we bound up her heart that she might be of the believers.

11   And she said to his sister, "Follow him up." And she looked after him from afar, and they did not perceive.

12   And we made unlawful for him the wet-nurses. And she said, "Shall I guide you to the people of a house who will take care of him for you, and who will be sincere respecting him?"

13   So we restored him to his mother that her eye might be cheered, and that she might not grieve, and that she might know that the promise of God is true, though most of them know not.

Moses as a
young adult in Egypt

14   And when he reached puberty, and was settled, we gave him judgment and knowledge; for thus do we reward those who do well.

---

hammad's own invention, the storyline closely follows that of the Exodus account, with the one exception being the presence of Haman (vv 6, 8).

28.8 *Haman* — Two errors are present in this verse. The first error addresses the presence of Haman in the Exodus story. He correctly belongs to the story found in the Book of Esther (see Q 40.23-38, note). The second error addresses chronology. In this surah, Haman was alive and served as advisor to the Pharaoh during the period of

Moses' infancy. In the narrative of Surah 40, however, Haman was alive and served as an advisor to the next Pharaoh, when Moses returned eighty years later and led the Israelites out of Egypt in the exodus. Hence, Muhammad's inclusion of Haman in this and the fortieth surah demonstrates a chronological impossibility.

28.14-21 This passage is based upon Exodus 2:11-15a. Though the dialogue is Muhammad's own fabrication, it faithfully follows the storyline found in the book of Exo-

15 And he entered into the city at the time the people thereof were heedless, and he found therein two men fighting; the one of his sect and the other of his foes. And he who was of his sect asked his aid against him who was of his foes; and Moses smote him with his fist and finished him. Said he, "This is of the work of Satan, verily, he is a misleading obvious foe."

16 Said he, "My Lord! verily, I have wronged my soul, but forgive me." So He forgave him; for He is forgiving and merciful.

17 Said he, "My Lord! for that Thou hast been gracious to me, I will surely not back up the sinners."

18 And on the morrow he was afraid in the city, expectant. And behold, he whom he had helped the day before cried (again) to him for aid. Said Moses to him, "Verily, thou art obviously quarrelsome."

19 And when he wished to assault him who was the enemy to them both, he said, "O Moses! dost thou desire to kill me as thou didst kill a person yesterday? thou dost only desire to be a tyrant in the earth; and thou dost not desire to be of those who do right!"

20 And a man came from the remote parts of the city running, said he, "O Moses! verily, the chiefs are deliberating concerning thee to kill thee; go then forth; verily, I am to you a sincere adviser!"

21 So he went forth therefrom, afraid and expectant. Said he, "Lord, save me from the unjust people!"

Moses in Midian

22 And when he turned his face in the direction of Midian, he said, "It may be that my Lord will guide me to a level path!"

23 And when he went down to the water of Midian he found thereat a

---

dus.

28.15a *the one of his sect* — That is, a Hebrew.

28.15b *the other of his foes* — That is, an Egyptian.

28.16 *forgive me* — Muhammad believed that Allah forgave him since God is "forgiving and merciful" (see **Divine Forgiveness in Islam** on pp. 158-161).

28.22-28 This passage is based upon Ex 2:15b-25. Once again, though the dialogue is Muhammad's own fabrication, it faithfully follows the storyline found in the book of Exodus—with two exceptions. The first exception is the episode at the well. According to the Exodus narrative, Moses "came to their [the women's] rescue" when the men drove them away. In this passage, the impression is left that Moses watered the women's animals after the men had finished watering their animals.

The second exception is the episode of the marital contract between Moses and Jethro, the young women's father. According to this passage, a contract of eight years of labor was required of Moses for the privilege of marrying one of his daughters. In the book of Exodus, no such contract ne-

nation of people watering their flocks. And he found beside them two women keeping back their flocks. Said he, "What is your design?" They said, "We cannot water our flocks until the herdsmen have finished; for our father is a very old man."

24 So he watered for them; then he turned back towards the shade and said, "My Lord! verily, I stand in need of what Thou sendest down to me of good."

25 And one of the two came to him walking modestly; said she, "Verily; my father calls thee, to reward thee with hire for having watered our flocks for us." And when he came to him and related to him the story, said he, "Fear not, thou art safe from the unjust people."

26 Said one of them, "O my sire! hire him; verily, the best of those whom thou canst hire is the strong and faithful."

27 Said he, "Verily, I desire to marry thee to one of these daughters of mine, on condition that thou dost serve me for hire eight years; and if thou shalt fulfil ten it is of thyself; for I do not wish to make it wretched for thee; thou wilt find me, if it please God, of the righteous!"

28 Said he, "That is between you and me; whichever of the two terms I fulfil, let there be no enmity against me, for God over what we say keeps guard."

The burning bush

29 And when Moses had fulfilled the appointed time, and was journeying with his people, he perceived from the side of the mountain a

---

gotiation is mentioned.

28.25 *And one of the two came to him walking modestly* — Modesty is an important attribute in Islam. In the hadithic literature, Muhammad once said that "the character of Islam is modesty" (*Sahih Mwatta* 47.2.9). Again, in another Hadith, Muham-mad explained that the Islamic faith is "self respect, modesty, bashfulness, and scruples" (*Sahih Bukhari* 1.2.8). In a third, Muhammad said that "whoever among you can marry, should marry, because it helps him lower his gaze and guard his modesty" (*Sahih Bukhari* 7.62.4).

28.27-28 *eight years...ten* — The two terms of the contract were either eight years or ten years. The eight years was what Jethro expected. The additional two years was understood as an act of grace that was not required but desired. At the time of the contract, Moses refused to decide which of the two spans of time he would honor.

Yet, this contract—regardless of the years required—is not found in the biblical account. It is an apparent conflation of the story of the marriage of Moses and Zipporah (Ex 2:21-22) with the story of the marriage of Jacob and Rachel (Gen 29:18).

28.29-35 This passage is based upon Ex 3:1-4:17. The story presented in this passage is a simplified presentation of the narrative found in the book of Exodus. Three noteworthy differences exist, as mentioned below.

fire; said he to his people, "Tarry ye here; verily, I have perceived a fire, haply I may bring you good news therefrom, or a brand of fire that haply ye may be warmed."

30   And when he came to it he was called to, from the right side of the wady, in the blessed valley, out of the tree, "O Moses! verily, I am God the Lord of the worlds;

31   so throw down thy rod"; and when he saw it quivering as though it were a snake, he turned away and fled and did not return. "O Moses! approach and fear not, verily, thou art amongst the safe.

32   Thrust thy hand into thy bosom, it shall come out white, without hurt; and then fold again thy wing, that

thou dost now stretch out through dread; for those are two signs from thy Lord to Pharaoh and his chiefs; verily, they are a people who work abomination!"

33   Said he, "My Lord! verily, I have killed a person amongst them, and I fear that they will kill me:

34   and my brother Aaron, he is more eloquent of tongue than I; send him then with me as a support, to verify me; verily, I fear that they will call me liar!"

35   Said He, "We will strengthen thine arm with thy brother; and we will make for you both authority, and they shall not reach you in our signs; ye two and those who follow you shall gain the upper hand."

28.30a *wady* — a valley. According to this verse, the burning bush was located in a wady (or valley). This description stands opposed to the Exodus account, which states that the burning bush was located on a mountainside (see Ex 3:1-3).

28.30b An important alteration between the two accounts is centered on the way in which God identified himself to Moses. The account found in the book of Exodus reads: "Moses said to God, 'Suppose I go to the Israelites and say to them, "The God of your fathers has sent me to you," and they ask me, "What is his name?" Then what shall I tell them?' God said to Moses, 'I AM WHO I AM. This is what you are to say to the Israelites: "I AM has sent me to you"' (Ex 3:13-14). In the Hebrew, the name God spoke was YHWH (or Yahweh). It is the common name for God found in the Old Testament, mentioned over 6800 times.

In contrast, in this surah the account reads: "O Moses! verily, I am God the Lord of the worlds." This name—*God the Lord of the worlds*—is a typical identification of God throughout the qur'anic surahs (see Q 1.2, note). Hence, Muhammad replaced YHWH (Yahweh) with "the Lord of the worlds." What is more, nowhere in the Qur'an is the name YHWH (Yahweh) mentioned. This omission appears to be deliberate. Yahweh was the name for God used exclusively of the Jewish people and which predicated their covenant relationship with Him. Moreover, in the New Testament, Jesus identified himself as Yahweh (see Jn 8:58).

28.33 According to this verse, one of Moses' reasons for rejecting the Lord's commission was his previous sin of murder. Nowhere in the Exodus account did Moses comment on that episode to the Lord.

28.36-38 This passage is based upon Ex

*The return of
Moses to Egypt*

36   And when Moses came to them
       with our manifest signs, they said,
       "This is only sorcery devised; and
       we have not heard of this amongst
       our fathers of yore."
37   Moses said, "My Lord knows best
       who comes with guidance from
       Him, and whose shall be the issue
       of the abode. Verily, the unjust shall
       not prosper!"
38   And Pharaoh said, "O ye chiefs! I
       do not know any god for you ex-
       cept me; then set fire, O Hâmân!
       to some clay and make for me a
       tower, haply I may mount up to
       the God of Moses; for, verily, I
       think he is of those who lie!"

The Red Sea

39   And he grew big with pride, he and
       his armies in the land, without right;
       and they thought that they to us
       should not return.

40   And we overtook him and his army,
       and we flung them into the sea;
       behold, then, how was the end of
       the unjust!

*Muhammad: a member
of the apostolic line*

41   But we made them models calling
       to the fire; and on the resurrection
       day they shall not be helped;
42   and we followed them up in this
       world with a curse; and on the res-
       urrection day they shall be ab-
       horred!
43   And we gave Moses the Book, af-
       ter that we had destroyed the
       former generations, as an insight
       to men and a guidance and a
       mercy; haply they may be mind-
       ful!
44   Thou wast not upon the western
       side when we decided for Moses,
       but afar off; nor wast thou of the
       witnesses.
45   But we raised up (other) genera-
       tions, and life was prolonged for

5:1-13:22. Haman once again appears in this passage (see Q 28.4-13, note, and Q 40.23-38, note).

28.38 *set fire...to some clay and make for me a tower* — Nowhere in the Exodus account is this episode mentioned. It is possibly a conflation of the stories of the Tower of Babel (Gen 11:1-9) with the conflict between Pharaoh and Moses in the Book of Exodus.

28.39-40 This passage is based upon Exodus 14:1-31.

28.41-43 According to Muhammad, Pharaoh and his army were models (examples) of those who were destined to the fire.

28.44 *Thou wast not upon the western side* — That is, the western side of Mount Sinai. The point is that Muhammad was not on the western side of Mt. Sinai when Moses received divine revelation. Rather, he was "afar off" (of a different era) and not "of the witnesses" of this event.

28.45 *was not staying amidst the people of Midian* — Muhammad was not among the

them; and thou wast not staying amidst the people of Midian, reciting to them our signs; but we were sending our apostles.

46 Nor wast thou by the side of the mountain when we called; but it is a mercy from thy Lord, that thou mayest warn a people to whom no warner has come before thee; haply they may be mindful!

47 And lest there should befall them a mishap for what their hands have sent before, and they should say, "Our Lord! why didst thou not send to us an apostle? for we would have followed thy signs and been of the believers."

48 And when the truth comes to them from us they say, "We are given the like of what Moses was given." Did they not disbelieve in what Moses was given before?—they say, "Two works of sorcery back up each other;" and they say, "Verily, we do disbelieve in all."

49 Say, "Bring, then, a book from God which shall be a better guide than both, and I will follow it, if ye do tell the truth!"

50 And if they cannot answer thee, then know that they follow their own lusts; and who is more in error than he who follows his own lust without guidance from God? verily, God guides not an unjust people!

51 And we caused the word to reach them, haply they may be mindful!

people of Midian reciting to the Midianite people divinely inspired surahs. Rather, Allah sent other apostles to do this work.

28.46a *Nor wast thou by the side of the mountain* — According to some Islamic scholars, this second reference to the mountain is also Mt. Sinai and refers to the calling of Moses to the ministry at the burning bush.

28.46b Even though Muhammad was not among the people of Midian when other apostles spoke divine words to them (v. 45), and was not with Moses when he was called at the burning bush (vv. 44, 46), Muhammad was nevertheless called to serve as a warner to "a people to whom no warner has come before thee."

28.47 Muhammad's ministry as an apostle eliminates the excuse that at the Last Judgment no apostle had been sent to them to warn of judgment to come.

28.48 The people of Mecca rejected Mu-

hammad just as they would have rejected Moses had he been sent to them.

28.49-50 Muhammad's challenge to the Meccan people was for them to bring forth a divine revelation that was "a better guide" than the Mosaic revelations (the Pentateuch) and the revelation given to them (the Qur'an). Muhammad then chided them: "I will follow it, if ye do tell the truth!" Their inability to do, said Muhammad, demonstrated that they were indeed followers of their own lusts.

In response, a Christian answer to Muhammad's challenge is that the Bible—both Old and New Testaments—is such a divinely inspired Book. And it was available in Mecca in the early seventh century, evidenced by Muhammad's constant references to it. Christians (then and now) look upon the Bible as "a better guide" than both miracles (that which Muhammad described as "works of sor-

The straight path

52   Those to whom we gave the Book
      before it, they believe therein;
53   and when it is recited to them they
      say, "We believe in it as truth from
      our Lord; verily, we were resigned
      before it came!"
54   These shall be given their hire twice
      over, for that they were patient, and
      repelled evil with good, and of what
      we have bestowed upon them give
      alms.
55   And when they hear vain talk, they
      turn away from it and say, "We
      have our works, and ye have your
      works. Peace be upon you! we do
      not seek the ignorant!"
56   Verily, thou canst not guide whom
      thou dost like, but God guides
      whom He pleases; for He knows
      best who are to be guided.
57   And they say, "If we follow the
      guidance we shall be snatched

away from the land." Have we not
established for them a safe sanctuary, to which are imported the
fruits of everything as a provision
from us? but most of them do not
know.

*Allah's response
to the infidels*

58   How many a city have we destroyed
      that exulted in its means of sub-
      sistence? These are their dwellings,
      never dwelt in after them, except
      a little; for we were the heirs.
59   But thy Lord would never destroy
      cities until He sent to the metropo-
      lis thereof an apostle, to recite to
      them our signs; nor would we de-
      stroy cities unless their people
      were unjust.
60   Whatever thing ye may be given, it
      is a provision for this world's life
      and the adornment thereof; but

cery") and the qur'anic surahs.

28.52-57 Muhammad then returned to his theme of apostles having been sent to differing peoples and cultures. He recited the actions of those who responded correctly to these apostles: (a) they believed in the divine revelations of the Book presented by these apostles, (b) they were patient and repelled evil with good, (c) they gave alms to the poor, (d) they rejected the vain talk of the ignorant, believing that if they follow such guidance they would be "snatched away from the land."

28.54-57 According to Muhammad, Allah's response to upright people was: (a) a double reward for their good works, and (b) the

provision of a safe sanctuary.

28.56 *God guides whom He pleases* — Once again, Muhammad drew attention to the doctrine of double predestination (see **The Doctrine of al-Qadar** on pp. 264-266).

28.58-60 According to Muhammad, no city has ever been destroyed by Allah without Allah first sending an apostle to its people, warning them of judgment to come if they did not repent. This destruction typically occurred in two ways: (a) natural disasters, and (b) due to the ravages of war. This passage, then, is a hint or a foretelling of the Doctrine of Jihad that will be presented in greater clarity later in the Medinan surahs (the Sixth Period). See **The Apostles** on

what is with God is better and more enduring; have ye then no sense?

61   Is He to whom we have promised a goodly promise, which he shall meet with, like him to whom we have given the enjoyment of the life of this world, and who upon the resurrection day shall be of the arraigned?

62   And on the day when He will call them and will say, Where are those associates which ye did pretend?"

63   And those against whom the sentence is due shall say, "Our Lord! these are those whom we have seduced; we seduced them as we were seduced ourselves: but we clear ourselves to thee; —they did not worship us!"

64   And it will be said, "Call upon your partners;" and they will call upon them, but they will not answer them, and they shall see the torment; would that they had been guided.

65   And the day when He shall call them and shall say, "What was it

66   and the history shall be blindly confusing to them on that day, and they shall not ask each other.

67   But, as for him who turns again and believes and does right, it may be that he will be among the prosperous.

68   For thy Lord creates what He pleases and chooses; they have not the choice! Celebrated be the praise of God! and exalted be He above what they associate with Him!

69   Thy Lord knows what they conceal in their breasts and what they manifest.

Absolute monotheism

70   He is God, there is no god but He; to Him belongs praise, in the first and the last; and His is the judgment; and unto Him shall ye return!

Night and day

71   Have ye considered, if God were

---

ye answered the apostles?"

pp. 398-400; *Jihad* on pp. 616-622).

28.61-69 This passage is a description of Allah mocking the infidels at the Last Judgment. In his mockery, Allah will ask them to bring forth their gods to protect them from their impending doom. He will also chide them for rejecting the message of the apostles that He had sent to them.

28.68 *thy Lord creates what He pleases and chooses* — It is Allah who creates believe and unbelief. He does so, based upon His own pleasures. This, once again, is a

reference to the doctrine of double predestination (see *The Doctrine of al-Qadar* on pp. 264-266).

28.70 Muhammad returned, once again, to the fundamental creed of Islam: the Doctrine of Tauhid — absolute monotheism (see Q 112, note).

28.71-74 According to Muhammad, Allah is sovereign over all creation, including the phenomena of night and day. In contrast, the gods worshipped by the Meccan people have no power.

to make for you the night endless until the resurrection day, who is the god, but God, to bring you light? can ye not then hear?

72   Say, "Have ye considered, if God were to make for you the day endless until the day of judgment, who is the god, except God, to bring you the night to rest therein? can ye not then see?"

73   But of His mercy He has made for you the night and the day, that ye may rest therein, and crave of His grace, haply ye may give thanks.

74   And the day when He shall call them and shall say, "Where are my partners whom ye did pretend?"

75   And we will pluck from every nation a witness; and we will say,

"Bring your proof and know that the truth is God's;" and that which they had devised shall stray away from them.

The example of Korah

76   Verily, Korah was of the people of Moses, and he was outrageous against them; and we gave him treasuries of which the keys would bear down a band of men endowed with strength. When his people said to him, "Exult not; verily, God loves not those who exult!

77   but crave, through what God has given thee, the future abode; and forget not thy portion in this world, and do good, as God has done good

28.74 *Where are my partners whom ye did pretend? —* That is, where are the gods worshipped by the infidels?

28.75 *witness from every nation —* According to Muhammad, Allah has sent a witness (apostle) to every nation, warning of judgment to come.

28.76 *God loves not those who exult! —* Muhammad claimed that Allah does not love those who exult (are joyous). The Bible speaks otherwise of God, noting repeatedly that God joyous and encourages others to also be joyous (see Ps 19:8; 21:1; 42:4; 47:1; 66:1; 98:4; Lk 10:21; Jn 15:11; Rom 15:13; 3 Jn 4).

28.76-82 The example of Korah mentioned in this passage is based upon Num 16:1-50. In this story, Korah and 250 men challenged the leadership (apostleship) of Moses. Yahweh responded by opening up the earth and swallowing Korah and his followers (Num

26:10). In this qur'anic passage, an imaginative dialogue between Korah and the followers of Moses is presented. Also presented is the account of the earth swallowing Korah and his house (v. 81; also see Q 7.155).

The moral to the story is stated in v. 78: "he did not know that God had destroyed before him many generations of those who were stronger than he, and had amassed more." The story of Korah, then, was meant by Muhammad to serve as a warning to all who oppose Allah's chosen apostles. Judgment will come, not only in the afterlife but in the current life, as well. The story ends with ominous words: "Ah, ah! the unbelievers shall not prosper!"

28.77a *do good, as God has done good to thee —* One of Korah's many sins was his unwillingness to show charity (be generous with his possessions) to others. In the hadithic literature, Muhammad reportedly said,

to thee; and seek not evil doing in the earth; verily, God loves not the evildoers!"

78   Said he, "I have only been given it for knowledge which I have!" did he not know that God had destroyed before him many generations of those who were stronger than he, and had amassed more? But the sinners. need not to be asked concerning their crimes.

79   And he went out amongst the people in his ornaments; those who desired the life of this world said, "O would that we had the like of what Korah has been given! verily, he is endowed with mighty fortune!"

80   But those who had been given knowledge said, "Woe to you! the reward of God is better for him who believes and does right; but none shall meet with it except the patient.

81   And we clave the earth with him and with his house; and he had no troop to help him against God, nor was he of those who were helped!"

82   And on the morrow those who had yearned for his place the day before said, "Ah, ah! God extends provision to whom He pleases of His servants, or He doles it out; had not God been gracious to us, the earth would have cleft open with us! Ah, ah! the unbelievers

"If I had gold equal to the mountain of Uhud, I would love that, before three days had passed, not a single Dinar thereof remained with me if I found somebody to accept it excluding some amount that I would keep for the payment of my debts" (*Sahih Bukhari,* 9.90.334; also see Al-Ghazali, *Inner Dimensions of Islamic Worship,* pp. 53-73).

28.77b *God loves not the evildoers!* — According to Muhammad, Allah does not love evildoers. Rather, His love is restricted to the righteous.

In the Bible, God's relationship with evildoers is more complex. In one sense, God hates evil and strives against evildoers (Gen 6:13; Ps 7:11; Ezek 7:2-6). Yet, in another sense, God loves the sinner (Prov 25:21-22; Matt 5:43-48; Rom 12:14, 20-21; 1 Cor 4:12-13; 1 Pet 3:9). The point of contact between these two perspectives is the cross of Jesus Christ. The Apostle Paul wrote: "But God demonstrates his own love for us

in this: While we were still sinners, Christ died for us" (Rom 5:8).

John R. W. Stott explains: "Man is, in fact, the object of God's love and wrath concurrently. The God who condemns man for his disobedience has already planned how to justify him...God's wrath is seen in the corruption of man and of society, his remedy for sin is seen in the gospel. There are thus two revelations of God. His righteousness (or way of salvation) is revealed in the gospel, because his wrath is revealed from heaven against all unrighteousness. So the God of the Bible is a God of love and wrath, of mercy and judgment. And all the restlessness, pleasure-seeking, and escapism that mark the life of man in every age, and all the world over, are symptomatic of his judicial estrangement from God" (*Our Guilty Silence,* p. 42).

28.83-88 Muhammad concluded this surah with a final plea. It was his hope that people

shall not prosper!"

Final plea

83   That is the future abode; we make it for those who do not wish to be haughty in the earth, nor to do evil, and the end is for the pious.

84   He who brings a good deed shall have better than it; and he who brings an evil deed-those who do evil deeds shall only be rewarded for that which they have done.

85   Verily, He who hath ordained the Qur'ân for thee will restore thee to thy returning place. Say, "My Lord knows. best who brings guidance, and who is in obvious error;

86   nor couldst thou hope that the Book would be thrown to thee, save as a mercy from thy Lord! be not then a backer up of those who misbelieve;

87   and let them not turn thee from the signs of God, after they have been sent down to thee; but call unto thy Lord and be not of the idolaters;

88   and call not with God upon any other god; there is no god but He! everything is perishable, except His face; His is the judgment, and unto Him shall ye return!"

Surah 23

In the name of the merciful and compassionate God.

Righteous behaviors

1   Prosperous are the believers

2   who in their prayers are humble,

3   and who from vain talk turn aside,

4   and who in almsgiving are active.

5   And who guard their private parts

would listen and obey the apostles Allah had sent to all the peoples of the earth. Since he saw himself as part of this long line of apostles and the Qur'an as the divine revelation given to the people of Mecca, he was convinced that those who heeded its message would be restored to Allah.

Surah 23. The title of this surah, *The Believers,* comes from verse one. In it, Muhammad returned to the familiar theme of divinely commissioned apostles. Throughout time, he explained, Allah has anointed certain people to be His spokespeople to the cultures and civilizations on earth. Typically, their words were rejected, called lies, and they themselves were abused. In the end,

however, divine retribution befell those who rejected their ministries in the form of national catastrophes. The apostles highlighted in this surah are Noah, Moses, Aaron, Jesus, Mary, and several additional unnamed apostles.

23.1-11 This is a listing of six specific righteous behaviors that Muhammad believed would cause one to be "prosperous" in their personal lives and in the afterlife "inherit Paradise" (v 11). They are: (a) humility in prayer, (b) the rejection of vain talk, (c) being active in the giving of alms, (d) sexually chastity, except for their relationships with their wives, (e) integrity in their trusts and covenants, and (f) the disciplined maintenance

6   —except for their wives or what their right hands possess for then, verily, they are not to be blamed;

7   —but whoso craves aught beyond that, they are the transgressors

8   —and who observe their trusts and covenants,

9   and who guard well their prayers:

10   these are the heirs

11   who shall inherit Paradise; they shall dwell therein for aye!

The natural world

12   We have created man from an extract of clay;

13   then we made him a clot in a sure depository;

14   then we created the clot congealed blood, and we created the congealed blood a morsel; then we created the morsel bone, and we

clothed the bone with flesh; then we produced it another creation; and blessed be God, the best of creators!

15   Then shall ye after that surely die;

16   then shall ye on the day of resurrection be raised.

17   And we have created above you seven roads; nor are we heedless of the creation.

18   And we send down from the heaven water by measure, and we make it rest in the earth; but, verily, we are able to take it away;

19   and we produce for you thereby gardens of palms and grapes wherein ye have many fruits, and whence ye eat.

20   And a tree growing out of Mount Sinai which produces oil, and a condiment for those who eat.

21   And, verily, ye have a lesson in the

of their prayer life.

23.5 *who guard their private parts* — That is, who keep themselves sexually pure.

23.6 *what their right hands possess* — Men were permitted to have sexual relationships with their slaves (concubines).

23.12-22 Muhammad made a case from natural theology to demonstrate the omnipotent power of Allah. By inference, this argument marginalized and ultimately rendered unnecessary and useless the gods worshipped by the polytheists at Mecca. Not only is Allah the creator of the human being, he also created the Seven Heavens, the rain, all the vegetation on the earth, cattle, and milk. Since the polytheists believed that their gods were responsible for various items (various foods, animals, inanimate objects, etc.),

Muhammad's declaration that Allah has power over all of creation was intended to invalidate and render useless these alleged gods.

23.12-14 Muhammad believed that the formation of the first man began with an extract of clay that was configured into a clot, which then became congealed blood, which then took the shape of a morsel, bone, and flesh (see Q 96.2, note).

23.17 *seven roads* —That is, the paths to the seven levels of Paradise.

23.20 *a tree growing out of Mount Sinai which produces oil* — The olive tree, native to the lands surrounding the eastern Mediterranean Sea.

23.21 *drink of what is in their bellies* — That is, they drink milk.

cattle; we give you to drink of what is in their bellies; and ye have therein many advantages, and of them ye eat,

22   and on them and on ships ye are borne!

Noah

23   We sent Noah unto his people, and he said, "O my people! worship God, ye have no god but Him; do ye then not fear?"

24   Said the chiefs of those who misbelieved among his people, "This is nothing but a mortal like

yourselves who wishes to have preference over you, and had God pleased He would have sent angels; we have not heard of this amongst our fathers of yore:

25   he is nothing but a man possessed; let him bide then for a season."

26   Said he, "Help me, for they call me liar!"

27   And we inspired him, "Make the ark under our eyes and inspiration; and when the oven boils over, conduct into it of every kind two, with thy family, except him of them against whom the word has passed; and do not address me for

---

23.21b *of them ye eat* — That is, they eat beef.

23.23-30 Muhammad then returned to the familiar theme of previous apostles that had ministered to an obstinate people who were subsequently judged by Allah. In this passage, he addressed the ministry of Noah. The dialogue that Muhammad invented paralleled the dialogue that had been occurring between himself and his opponents in Mecca. The moral of the story was that the people of Mecca would be utterly destroyed via divine retribution, just as had the antediluvian people of Noah's day who rejected Noah's message and ministry.

23.23 In his presentation of the ministry of Noah, Muhammad began with a recitation of the Doctrine of Tauhid, absolute monotheism, the central creed of Islam (see Q 112). This doctrine was also a major bone of contention between Muhammad and the people of Mecca.

23.24a *This is nothing but a mortal like yourselves* — Muhammad had also been ac-

cused by the Meccan people of being just a mortal with no extraordinary powers. Hence, his claim to being a channel of divine revelation was false (see Q 36.15).

23.24b *He would have sent angels* — Muhammad had also been chided by the Meccan people since no angels visibly accompanied him, with the purpose of validating his alleged divine inspiration (see Q 25.20-29).

23.25 *a man possessed* — That is, a man who has lost his mind, someone who has gone crazy, possessed by evil spirits.

23.26 *they call me liar!* — Muhammad also noted that the people of Mecca had called him a liar (Q 35.4, 25).

23.27a *when the oven boils over* — That is, when the water gushes forth in torrents. The Sumerian Flood myth stated that the primary cause of the Flood was the subterranean sea boiling over which then reached the surface of the earth (see Q 11.40, note).

23.27b *except him of them against whom the word has passed* — Muhammad believed that certain animals were prohibited from en-

those who do wrong, verily, they are to be drowned!

28 But when thou art settled, thou and those with thee in the ark, say, 'Praise belongs to God, who saved us from the unjust people!'

29 And say, 'My Lord! make me to alight in a blessed alighting-place, for Thou art the best of those who cause men to alight!'"

30 Verily, in that is a sign, and, verily, we were trying them.

An unnamed prophet

31 Then we raised up after them another generation;

32 and we sent amongst them a prophet of themselves (saying), "Serve God, ye have no god but He; will ye then not fear?"

33 Said the chiefs of his people who misbelieved, and called the meeting of the last day a lie, and to whom we gave enjoyment in the life of this world. This is only a

mortal like yourselves, who eats of what ye eat, and drinks of what ye drink;

34 and if ye obey a mortal like yourselves, verily, ye will then be surely losers!

35 Does he promise you that when ye are dead, and have become dust and bones, that then ye will be brought forth?

36 "Away, away with what ye are threatened,

37 —there is only our life in the world! We die and we live, and we shall not be raised!

38 He is only a man who forges against God a lie. And we believe not in him!"

39 Said he, "My Lord! help me, for they call me liar!"

40 He said, "Within a little they will surely awake repenting!"

41 And the noise seized them deservedly; and we made them as rubbish borne by a torrent; so, away with the unjust people!

---

tering the ark. According to the Genesis account (Gen 7:1-16), no animals were prohibited.

23.29 Noah wished to "alight in a blessed alighting-place" for God (see Q 18.107 and 35.35 where this phrase is similarly used).

23.31-41 In this passage, Muhammad described an unnamed prophet ministering as Allah's apostle to an unnamed group of people. The prophet's ministry experienced the same forms of opposition as did Noah previously (vv 23-30). First, the prophet proclaimed the Doctrine of Tauhid—absolute monotheism—to a people who were com-

mitted polytheists (see Q 112). The people responded by calling the prophet a liar and that he was not imbued with the gift of divine revelation. Third, they mocked his teaching regarding a general revelation from the dead.

The prophet responded to these accusations with the precise words spoken by Noah ("My Lord, help me, for they call me liar!"— see v. 26). Following this plea to Allah, total destruction came to the people (v. 41).

23.40 *they will surely awake repenting —* That is, when destruction comes, they will

Other unnamed prophets

42   Then we raised up after them other generations.
43   No nation can anticipate its appointed time, nor keep it back.
44   Then we sent our apostles one after another. Whenever its apostle came to any nation they called him a liar; and we made some to follow others; and we made them legends; away then with a people who do not believe!

Moses and Aaron

45   Then we sent Moses and his brother Aaron with our signs, and with plain authority
46   to Pharaoh and his chiefs, but they

were too big with pride, and were a haughty people.

47   And they said, "Shall we believe two mortals like ourselves, when their people are servants of ours?"
48   So they called them liars, and were of those who perished.
49   And we gave Moses the Book, that haply they might be guided.

Jesus and Mary

50   And we made the son of Mary and his mother a sign; and we lodged them both on a high place, furnished with security and a spring.

One nation

51   O ye apostles! eat of the good

repent...but it will be too late to rescue them from divine judgment.

23.42-44 In this passage, Muhammad noted that the pattern has always been the same in reference to the ministry of apostles. The people called them liars. Allah responded by visiting them with divine judgment.

23.45-49 The ministry of Moses and Aaron followed the pattern outlined in vv 42-44.

23.45 *plain authority* — Muhammad insisted that divine revelation constitutes a "plain" or "obvious" authority to anyone who reads or listens objectively; that is, without prejudice or bias (see Q 27.21; 37.156; 40.23; 44.19; 51.38; 52.38).

23.47 Patterned after the previous stories in this surah, Pharaoh accused Moses and Aaron as being mere mortals—that is, not imbued with the gift of divine revelation (see Q 23.24a, note).

23.48 Muhammad believed that whenever a people called the apostles liars, they would be visited upon by Allah with destruction. It was a coupling of events that could not be avoided.

23.49 *the Book* — The eternal Book in Paradise that explains the nature of God, man, salvation, Paradise, Hell, and so on. According to Muhammad, parts of *the Book* have been "sent down" (Q 15.6, 9; 46.30) to the earth to divinely appointed apostles, Moses being one such individual (see **The Perspicuous Book** on pp. 178-179).

23.50a Muhammad believed that Jesus and Mary were also examples (signs) of the abuse heaved upon divinely ordained apostles.

23.50b *we have lodged them both on a high place, furnished with security and a spring* — That is, Jesus and Mary are now in Paradise.

things and do right; verily, what
ye do I know!

52 And, verily, this nation of yours is
one nation, and I am your Lord;
so fear me.

Sects and divisions

53 And they have become divided as
to their affair amongst themselves
into sects, each party rejoicing in
what they have themselves.

54 So leave them in their flood (of error) for a time.

55 Do they reckon that of which we
grant them such an extent, of
wealth and children,

56 we hasten to them as good
things—nay, but they do not per-

ceive!

Characteristics
of godliness

57 Verily, those who shrink with terror at their Lord,

58 and those who in the signs of their
Lord believe,

59 and those who with their Lord join
none,

60 and those who give what they do
give while their hearts are afraid
that they unto their Lord will return,

61 —these hasten to good things and
are first to gain the same.

62 But we will not oblige a soul beyond its capacity; for with us is a

---

23.51-52 Muhammad envisioned a world
that comprised of only one nation—led by
the divinely appointed apostles, all of whom
preach the same message in regards to this
life and the afterlife. And since he saw himself as the final or ultimate apostle, this one
nation would necessarily recognize and embrace his apostleship as that of the Supreme
and Final Prophet (see **The Shahadah** on
pp. 58-61). All nations that oppose the
apostles, then, will experience divine retribution and national catastrophes (see **The
Apostles** on pp. 398-400). This passage,
then, lays the groundwork for the notion of
islamification; that is, only one nation has a
divinely ordained right of existence—that
being a singular Muslim nation (see
Islamification on pp. 851-852). It also lays
the groundwork for the Doctrine of Jihad,
which would emerge in later surahs (see
Jihad on pp. 616-622).

23.53-55 In contrast to the above passage (vv 51-52), infidels oppose this notion
of "one nation." They are characterized by
sects and divisions, each division rejoicing in
that which it possesses (v 53) and living in a
flood of error—for a time (v 54).

23.56 *do not perceive* — As noted earlier
in this surah, that which these people "do
not perceive" (v 56) is that the "appointed
time" (v 43) of their utter destruction will
indeed come. Such destruction comes in
two phases: (a) *in this life*—e.g., the Great
Flood, the destruction of Pharaoh's army at
the Red Sea, the destruction of Sodom and
Gomorrah in the times of Abraham and Lot,
and (b) *in the afterlife* when people are cast
into Hell.

23.57-62 Characteristics of godly people:
(a) they possess a fear of the Lord, (b) they
believe in divine revelation, (c) they eschew
idolatry, (d) they practice the giving of alms,

book that utters the truth, and they shall not be wronged.

Characteristics
of ungodliness

63   Nay, their hearts are in a flood (of error) at this, and they have works beside this which they do.

64   Until we catch the affluent ones amongst them with the torment; then lo! they cry for aid.

65   Cry not for aid today! verily, against us ye will not be helped.

66   My signs were recited to you, but upon your heels did ye turn back,

67   big with pride at it, in vain discourse by night.

68   Is it that they did not ponder over the words, whether that has come to them which came not to their fathers of yore?

69   Or did they not know their apostle, that they thus deny him?

70   Or do they say, "He is possessed by a ginn?" Nay, he came to them with the truth, and most of them

are averse from the truth.

71   But if the truth were to follow their lusts, the heavens and the earth would be corrupted with all who in them are!—Nay, we brought them their reminder, but they from their reminder turn aside.

72   Or dost thou ask them for a tribute? but the tribute of thy Lord is better, for He is the best of those who provide.

73   And, verily, thou dost call them to a right way;

74   but, verily, those who believe not in the hereafter from the way do veer.

75   But if we had mercy on them, and removed the distress they have, they would persist in their rebellion, blindly wandering on!

76   And we caught them with the torment but they did not abase themselves before their Lord, nor did they humble themselves;

77   until we opened for them a door with grievous torment, then lo! they are in despair.

and (e) they are committed to good works.
23.63-65 The ungodly are gripped by error and only turn in repentance when divine judgment befalls them.
23.66-71 Infidels are gripped by pride and therefore reject divine revelation when it is presented to them. They refuse to ponder the words. They also look upon the apostles as possessed by a *ginns*—that is, they believe that they are either demon possessed or crazy (see Q 17.47 and 23.25).
23.70 *ginn* — genie (see **Occultism in Seventh Century Arabia** on pp. 123-125).

23.71 *their reminder* — The divinely appointed apostle that had been sent to them.
23.72-74 Infidels reject the events foretold regarded the hereafter.
23.75-77 Infidels refuse to humble themselves before the Lord, persisting in their rebellion. Muhammad described them as people "blindly wandering on" (see Q 6.50, 104; 10.11, 42; 17.96-97; 27.4, 81; 40.58). The Bible makes a similar characterization of unbelievers (see Isa 56:10-11; Matt 15:14; 23:16-19, 24-26; and Jn 9:39-41).
23.78 Infidels are not thankful to Allah.

78 He it is who produced for you hearing, and sight, and minds,—little is it that ye thank.

79 And He it is who created you in the earth, and unto Him shall ye be gathered.

80 And He it is who gives you life and death and His is the alternation of the night and the day; have ye then no sense?

81 Nay, but they said like that which those of yore did say.

82 They said, "What! when we have become earth and bones, are we then going to be raised?

83 We have been promised this, and our fathers too, before;—this is naught but old folks' tales!"

Catechism

84 Say, "Whose is the earth and those who are therein, if ye but know?"

85 They will say, "God's." Say, "Do ye not then mind?"

86 Say, "Who is Lord of the seven heavens, and Lord of the mighty throne?"

87 They will say, "God." Say, "Do ye not then fear?"

88 Say, "In whose hand is the dominion of everything; He succours but is not succoured, if ye did but know?"

Unthankfulness to Allah is one of the fundamental sins in the Islamic worldview.

23.79-83 According to Muhammad, infidels do not believe in the resurrection of the dead.

23.84-89 Muhammad insisted that a complete and unreserved surrender to Allah—an attitude known as *islam*—is the only natural and rational position a person can maintain to the Creator. With this in mind, in his catechismal instruction, the Muslim follower was given a series of three questions and answers on the theme of sovereign lordship. The point was to use argumentation as a tool in showing the inconsistencies and irrationality of the infidel's unbelief. It also, by inference, reinforced the believer's submission to the sovereign lordship of Allah.

23.84-85 The first question-and-answer couplet in this catechism dealt with natural theology. Its point was this: since Allah created the earth and everything on the earth, people are obligated to yield and submit to Him (see Rom 1:18-20 where a similar argument is used in the New Testament).

23.86 *seven heavens* — The idea that heaven is divided into seven layers has a long tradition (see **Paradise** on pp. 76-77; Q 13.17; 23.86; 41.12; 65.12; 78.12).

Zoroastrianism (founded in the sixth century, B.C.), is the ancient religion of Iran. It claimed that Paradise was divided into seven layers. It is widely believed in modern scholarship that Muhammad knew of many of the beliefs that comprise Zoroastrianism.

The Jewish Talmud also claims that heaven is divided into seven layers: *Vilon, Raki'a, Shehaqim, Teh, Zebul, Ma'on, Machon,* and *Araboth*. David N. Livingstone adds, "There is no evidence of the notion of an ascent through seven heavens prior to the end of the first century, A.D. when it was probably invented, perhaps by Rabbi Akiva, the principal figure of early Merkabah mysticism" (*The Dying God: the Hidden History of Western Civilization*, p. 191).

89   They will say, "God's." Say, "Then
      how can ye be so infatuated?"

      Falsehoods of the ungodly

90   Nay, we have brought them the
      truth, but, verily, they are liars!
91   God never took a son, nor was
      there ever any god with Him;—then
      each god would have gone off with
      what he had created, and some
      would have exalted themselves
      over others,—celebrated be His
      praises above what they attribute
      (to Him)!

      Hell

92   He who knows the unseen and the
      visible, exalted be He above what
      they join with Him!
93   Say, "My Lord! if Thou shouldst
      show me what they are threat-
      ened,
94   —my Lord! then place me not

      amongst the unjust people."
95   Repel evil by what is better.
96   We know best what they attribute
      (to thee).
97   And say, "My Lord! I seek refuge
      in Thee from the incitings of the
      devils;
98   and I seek refuge in Thee from their
      presence!"
99   Until when death comes to any one
      of them he says, "My Lord! send
      ye me back,
100   haply I may do right in that which
      I have left!"   Not so! —a mere
      word he speaks! —but behind
      them is a bar until the day they shall
      be raised.
101   And when the trumpet shall be
      blown, and there shall be no rela-
      tion between them on that day, nor
      shall they beg of each other then!
102   And he whose scales are heavy,—
      they are the prosperous.
103   But he whose scales are light,—
      these are they who lose themselves,

The New Testament mentions three layers of Heaven (see 2 Cor 12:1-2). Most Christian scholars believe them to be: (a) the
lower atmosphere where the birds fly, (b)
the sphere of the celestial bodies—sun,
moon, and stars, (c) and the abode of God.
23.86-87 The second question-and-answer
dealt with special revelation. Since Allah created the Seven Heavens (information that
could only be known via divine revelation),
people are obligated to submit to Him.
23.92-110 In this passage, the contrast is
between the sovereign Lord (the word *Lord*
is mentioned seven times) and the ungodly.

The ungodly will plead with the Lord, but to
no avail. According to Muhammad, all who
committed the sin of *shirk* and rejected the
Doctrine of Tauhid will be cast into Hell.
23.101 *the trumpet shall be blown* — This
is the trumpet that will initiate all the events
pertaining to the Last Judgment. The New
Testament also stated that the blowing of a
trumpet was associated with end time
events (see 1 Cor 15:52; 1 Thess 4:16).
23.102 *And he whose scales are heavy—
they are prosperous* — That is, he whose
scales (balances) are heavy with good works.
According to the Qur'an, salvation is predi-

in hell to dwell for aye!

104 The fire shall scorch their faces, and they shall curl their lips therein!

105 "Were not my signs recited to you? and ye said that they were lies!"

106 They say, "Our Lord! our misery overcame us, and we were a people who did err!

107 Our Lord! take us out therefrom, and if we return, then shall we be unjust."

108 He will say, "Go ye away into it and speak not to me!"

109 Verily, there was a sect of my servants who said, "Our Lord! we believe, so pardon us, and have mercy upon us, for Thou art the best of the merciful ones."

110 And ye took them for a jest until ye forgat my reminder and did laugh thereat.

Paradise

111 Verily, I have recompensed them this day for their patience; verily, they are happy now.

112 He will say, "How long a number of years did ye tarry on earth?"

113 They will say, "We tarried a day or part of a day, but ask the Numberers."

114 He will say, "Ye have only tarried a little, were ye but to know it.

115 Did ye then reckon that we created you for sport, and that to us ye would not return?"

Conclusion

116 But exalted be God, the true; there is no god but He, the Lord of the noble throne!

117 and whoso calls upon another god with God has no proof of it, but, verily, his account is with his Lord; verily, the misbelievers shall not prosper.

118 And say, "Lord, pardon and be merciful, for Thou art the best of the merciful ones!"

Surah 22

cated upon one having more good works than bad (see **The Last Judgment** on pp. 46-50).

23.105 At the Last Judgment, the ungodly will be reminded of the divine revelations that had been given to them (e.g., the Qur'an) of which they called lies.

23.107-108 The ungodly will plead for another opportunity to live their lives on the earth whereupon they would respond attentively to the Qur'an. The request will be denied.

23.111-118 In contrast to the ungodly, in the afterlife the godly will be happy. As they reflect back on the years of their lives on earth, they will faintly remember the number of years they lived prior to death.

23.116-118 The surah ends with a reiteration of the Doctrine of Tauhid—absolute monotheism. Those who misbelieve (that is, reject absolute monotheism and have fallen into the sin of *shirk*) "shall not prosper." Their fate is Hell.

Surah 22. The title of the surah, *The Pil-*

In the name of the merciful and compassionate God.

The coming hour

1　O ye folk! fear your Lord. Verily, the earthquake of the Hour is a mighty thing.

2　On the day ye shall see it, every suckling woman shall be scared away from that to which she gave suck; and every pregnant woman shall lay down her load; and thou shalt see men drunken, though they be not drunken: but the torment of God is severe.

3　And amongst men is one who wrangles about God without knowledge, and follows every rebellious devil;

4　against whom it is written down that whoso takes him for a patron, verily, he will lead him astray, and will guide him towards the torment of the blaze!

The course of human life

5　O ye folk! if ye are in doubt about the raising (of the dead),—verily, we created you from earth, then from a clot, then from congealed blood, then from a morsel, shaped or shapeless, that we may explain to you. And we make what we please rest in the womb until an appointed time; then we bring you forth babes; then let you reach your full age; and of you are some who die; and of you are some who are kept back till the most decrepit age, till he knows no longer aught of knowledge. And ye see the earth parched, and when we send down water on it, it stirs and swells, and brings forth herbs of every beauteous kind.

6　That is because God, He is the truth, and because He quickens the dead, and because He is mighty over all;

7　and because the Hour is coming, there is no doubt therein, and because God raises up those who are in the tombs.

---

grimage, comes from verse 27. A major theme in this surah is the rite of Pilgrimage to the Ka'ba altar in Mecca. This pilgrimage, known as the *Hajj* in Arabic, is one of the centerpieces in Islamic worship. It is also one of the Five Pillars that serve as the foundation of Islamic theology, in both the Sunni and Shi'ite traditions. Another theme included in the surah is the theme of fighting on behalf of Allah. And finally, the theme of righteousness versus unrighteousness is reiterated for Muslims, with encouragements to remain steadfast in their faith and obedient to Allah.

22.1-4 Muhammad began this surah with an appeal to the infidels to reconsider their unbelief. He described them as those who wrangle about Allah without knowledge (v 3; cf v. 8).

22.1, 7 *the Hour* — The Hour refers to the moment when people are raised from the dead and summoned before Allah at the Last Judgment (see Q 79.42, note).

22.5 Muhammad again addressed the na-

Two kinds of fools

8 And amongst men is one who wrangles about God without knowledge or guidance or an illuminating book;

9 twisting his neck from the way of God; for him is disgrace in this world, and we will make him taste, upon the resurrection day, the torment of burning.

10 That is for what thy hands have done before, and for that God is not unjust unto His servants.

11 And amongst men is one who serves God (wavering) on a brink; and if there befall him good, he is comforted; but if there befall him a trial, he turns round again, and loses this world and the next—that is an obvious loss.

12 He calls, besides God, on what can neither harm him nor profit him;— that is a wide error.

13 He calls on him whose harm is nigher than his profit,—a bad lord and a bad comrade.

The divine challenge

14 Verily, God makes those who believe and do aright enter into gardens beneath which rivers flow; verily, God does what He will.

15 He who thinks that God will never help him in this world or the next— let him stretch a cord to the roof and put an end to himself; and let him cut it and see if his stratagem will remove what he is enraged at.

16 Thus have we sent down manifest signs; for, verily, God guides

ture of man's creation (see Q 96.2, note), describing man's origin as coming from "a clot." **22.8-10** The first kind of fool is the one, said Muhammad, who "wrangles about God without knowledge." Such a person is a disgrace, discussing theology independently of divine *guidance* (words from apostles) or an *illuminating book* (divine revelation). Upon the day of resurrection (the Hour), he or she will enter into the fires of Hell. **22.11-13** A second kind of fool is the one whose dedication and surrender to Allah wavers—tempted to fall into the sin of apostasy. In times of trial, he or she calls upon the gods for help, rather than upon Allah. As a result, such a person suffers loss in "this world and the next." **22.14a** *believe and do aright* — These words are repeated often in the Qur'an and

serve as a brief summary of the Islamic gospel (see Q 103.3 note). **22.14b** *beneath which rivers flow* — In the Qur'an is the oft repeated imagery of Paradise being an oasis, underneath which are aquifers sufficiently close to the ground to provide fertility and greenery (see Q 16.31; 20.76; 25.10; 39.20; 85.11; also see **Paradise** on pp. 76-77). **22.15** Those who disagree with this premise (v. 14) are invited to find success in life independent of Allah and see for themselves how they manage. The word *roof* may also be translated *sky*, and *sky* is perhaps a better choice here. The discussion of "stretch a cord," then, is probably best understood to be a metaphor. Muhammad challenged a person to find a way to Paradise independently of Allah—by one's own efforts (such

whom He will.

Jews, Sabaeans,
Christians and Magians

17   Verily, those who believe, and those
      who are Jews, and the Sabæans,
      and the Christians, and the
      Magians, and those who join other
      gods with God, verily, God will de-
      cide between them on the resur-
      rection day; verily, God is witness
      over all.

Two classes of people

18   Do they not see that God, whoso-
      ever is in the heavens adores Him,
      and whosoever is in the earth, and
      the sun, and the moon, and the
      stars, and the mountains, and the
      beasts, and many among men,
      though many a one deserves the
      torments? Whomsoever God
      abases there is none to honour him;
      verily, God does what He pleases.
19   These are two disputants who dis-

---

as climbing a rope).

22.16 The correct answer, Muhammad explained, is to rely upon "manifest signs"—that
is, divine revelation.

22.17 Four groups are identified in this
verse: Jews, Sabaeans, Christians, and
Magians. The *Jews* were those who embrace Old Testament revelation and corresponding oral tradition—the Talmud and
Mishna. The *Sabaeans* were an ancient culture that worshipped the sun, moon, and
Venus and lived in the southern tip of the
Arabian peninsula (present-day Yemen); today residual groups exist in Iraq. The *Christians* were closely associated with Judaism.
The essential difference between themselves
and the Jews turned on the doctrine of the
Messiah. The Jews rejected Jesus Christ as
Messiah whereas the Christians believed Him
to be the Promised Messiah prophesied in
the Old Testament. The *Magians* were of
the Zoroastrian faith centered in Persia (modern-day Iran). All four religions mentioned in
this verse were present in the Middle East,
with devotees likely traveling along the caravan routes that in the Arabian Peninsula.
They were therefore likely known to the
Meccan people in the seventh century, A.D.

Muhammad's point was that people
should be permitted to discuss religion
openly. Moreover, they should leave it with
Allah to clarify the correct answers pertaining to religious beliefs on Resurrection Day.
This perspective would undergo a change
later in the Qur'an where Muslims were called
upon to become the instruments of Allah in
exacting divine retribution on the infidels (see
Jihad on pp. 616-622; the **Doctrine of Abrogation** on pp. 68-70).

22.18 Muhammad identified two disputants
(religious opponents). The first adored the
true God: Allah. The second worshipped
the sun, moon, stars, mountains, or beasts
(characteristics of Arabian Star Family religion).
Leaning on his belief in double predestination, Muhammad was confident that the religious choices that people made were predetermined and their eternal destinies also
predetermined. As he put it, "God does what
he pleases" (cf. vv. 14, 16, 23, and 54).

22.19-22 Those who have fallen into the
sin of *shirk* (idolatry) will suffer accordingly at
the Last Judgment by experiencing the torments of Hell.

22.23 *believe and do right* — These words
are repeated often in the Qur'an and serve

pute about their Lord, but those who misbelieve, for them are cut out garments of fire, there shall be poured over their heads boiling water,

20 wherewith what is in their bellies shall be dissolved and their skins too,

21 and for them are maces of iron.

22 Whenever they desire to come forth therefrom through pain, they are sent back into it: "And taste ye the torment of the burning!"

23 Verily, God will make those who believe and do right enter into gardens beneath which rivers flow; they shall be bedecked therein with bracelets of gold and with pearls, and their garments therein shall be of silk,

24 and they shall be guided to the goodly speech, and they shall be guided to the laudable way.

The Hajj

25 Verily, those who misbelieve and who turn men away from God's path and the Sacred Mosque, which we have made for all men alike, the dweller therein, and the stranger, and he who desires therein profanation with injustice, we will make him taste grievous woe.

26 And when we established for Abraham the place of the House, (saying), "Associate naught with me, but cleanse my House for those who make the circuits, for those

---

as a brief summary of the Islamic gospel. In contrast to the first class of people, those "who believe and do right" will enter into the gardens of Paradise with all its related blessings (see Q 103.3 note).

22.25 *God's path* — This is the way that leads to eternal life (see Q 72.2, note). In this verse, the term "God's path" may have a double meaning. It may also refer to the sacred pilgrimage to Mecca (the Hajj) that all faithful Muslims are required to perform.

22.25, 26 *Sacred Mosque...the House* — the Ka'ba altar (see Q 106.3, note).

22.26 *Abraham* — Hagar and Ishmael were forced to leave the household of Sarah and Isaac. According to some hadithic literature, Abraham accompanied them as they traveled southward into the Arabian desert. They traveled as far as the present site of Mecca. Abraham then left them and returned

to Canaan to be with Sarah and Isaac. While in the desert, Hagar and Ishmael encountered the archangel Gabriel who directed them to an oasis (the story is based upon Gen 21:15-18). Years later, Abraham returned to Mecca. It was at this time that he and his son Ishmael constructed the Ka'ba altar (see *Bukhari* 4.55.583-584). Later, Abraham established the annual pilgrimage to the altar that was observed throughout the Arabian world.

This claim, however, is challenged by the evidence in ancient literature which states that Mecca was founded in the fourth century, A.D. Prior to this time, the area where Mecca now stands was open desert (see ***The City of Mecca*** on pp. 32-34).

In pre-Islamic times (fourth through early seventh century, A.D.), the Hajj in Mecca included visitations to locations outside the

who stand to pray, for those who bow, and for those too who adore.

27 And proclaim amongst men the Pilgrimage; let them come to you on foot and on every slim camel, from every deep pass,

28 that they may witness advantages for them, and may mention the name of God for the stated days over what God has provided them with of brute beasts, then eat thereof and feed the badly off, the poor."

29 Then let them finish the neglect of

their person, and let them pay their vows and make the circuit round the old House.

30 That do. And whoso magnifies the sacred things of God it is better for him with his Lord. Cattle are lawful for you, except what is recited to you; and avoid the abomination of idols, and avoid speaking falsely,

31 being 'Hanîfs to God, not associating aught with Him; for he who associates aught with God, it is as though he had fallen from heaven,

city, at Mina, Muzdalifah, and Arafat, under the auspices of the occultic ginn priests. The primary purposes of the pilgrimages were to plead for rain and other personal concerns. Rituals lasted several days. Notable events included the worship of the two idols in front of the Ka'ba altar, circumambulations, praying at Mina, the cutting of one's hair, and the throwing of stones at two stone altars (see **Polytheism in Seventh Century Arabia** on pp. 92-97).

Rather than disconnecting wholly from this ancient practice, Muhammad incorporated many of the rituals of this pagan pilgrimage into his Islamic version of the Hajj. Most notably, he transformed its focus from pagan worship to the sole worship of Allah. He also linked the Hajj with the biblical Abraham. This too was a common practice in the ancient Middle East. Attaching a biblical patriarch to a pilgrimage enhanced its spiritual importance.

The pilgrimage that Muhammad envisioned was to be characterized by the following: (a) monotheism, (b) while at the altar, people were to worship in a fashion

called *circumambulation*—that is, they were to make circuits around the altar in a counterclockwise direction as a way of paying homage to Allah, (c) devotees utilized two differing worshipful postures—standing and bowing, (d) devotees were to proclaim the importance of the Hajj in their prayers, and (e) all who made the pilgrimage believed that they would witness spiritual advantages for themselves (see **The Hajj** on pp. 480-482).

22.27 According to this passage, Abraham was ordered by Allah to a minaret—that is, a tower—from which he called people to commence the rites of the pilgrimage. This too was a borrowed rite, whose origin was the occultic ginn worship. Ginn priests and priestesses called out to the people to commence seasons of prayer from a tower.

22.30-31 All forms of idolatry were forbidden at the altar. It is this final requirement—the prohibition of polytheism—that was offensive to the people of Mecca. This constituted the essence of the quarrel between Muhammad and the Quraysh tribe of Mecca.

22.31 *Hanifs* — A *Hanif* was a pre-Islamic monotheist (see Q 30.30, note).

and the birds snatch him up, or the wind blows him away into a far distant place.

32 That—and he who makes grand the symbols of God, they come from piety of heart.

33 Therein have ye advantages for an appointed time, then the place for sacrificing them is at the old House.

Consecration

34 To every nation have we appointed rites, to mention the name of God over what He has provided them with of brute beasts; and your God is one God, to Him then be re-signed, and give glad tidings to the lowly,

35 whose hearts when God is men-tioned are afraid, and to those who are patient of what befalls them, and to those who are steadfast in prayer and of what we have given them expend in alms.

36 The bulky (camels) we have made for you one of the symbols of God, therein have ye good; so mention the name of God over them as they stand in a row, and when they fall down (dead) eat of them, and feed the easily contented and him who begs. Thus have we subjected them to you; haply, ye may give thanks!

37 Their meat will never reach to God, nor yet their blood, but the piety from you will reach to Him. Thus hath He subjected them to you that ye may magnify God for guiding you: and give thou glad tidings to those who do good.

Apostasy

38 Verily, God will defend those who believe; verily, God loves not any misbelieving traitor.

Jihad

39 Permission is given to those who fight because they have been

22.34-37 Five characteristics of Islamic pi-ety: (a) hearts that fear when God's name is mentioned, (b) patient in times of trial, (c) steadfast in prayer, (d) generous in the giving of alms and food for the poor, and (e) give thanks for livestock and food.

22.38 *misbelieving traitor* — That is, an apostate, a person who embraced and then turned away from the Muslim faith.

22.39-48 In this passage, Muhammad in-troduced the idea of Just War Theory (the Doctrine of Jihad). Here Allah gave permis-sion to the Muslim believers who have been wronged to fight (v. 39). The reason for Jihad is also given: "who have been driven forth from their homes undeservedly" (v. 40). This explains one of the longstanding dis-putes in our present era between the na-tion of Israel and the Palestinian people. Since all of Palestine was historically once un-der Muslim control and ownership, it should be restored. This claim, therefore, makes no allowance for Israel to continue to exist as a nation (see Q 2.191).

wronged,—and, verily, God to help them has the might,

40 —who have been driven forth from their homes undeservedly, only for that they said, "Our Lord is God;" and were it not for God's repelling some men with others, cloisters and churches and synagogues and mosques, wherein God's name is mentioned much, would be destroyed. But God will surely help him who helps Him; verily, God is powerful, mighty.

41 Who, if we stablish them in the earth, are steadfast in prayer, and give alms, and bid what is right, and forbid what is wrong; and God's is the future of affairs.

42 But if they call thee liar, the people of Noah called him liar before them, as did 'Âd and Thamûd,

43 and the people of Abraham, and the people of Lot,

44 and the fellows of Midian; and Moses was called a liar too: but I let the misbelievers range at large,

45 and then I seized on them, and how great was the change!

45 And how many a city have we destroyed while it yet did wrong, and it was turned over on its roofs, and (how many) a deserted well and lofty palace!

46 Have they not travelled on through the land? and have they not hearts to understand with, or ears to hear with? for it is not their eyes which are blind, but blind are the hearts which are within their breasts.

47 They will bid thee hasten on the torment, but God will never fail in his promise; for, verily, a day with thy Lord is as a thousand years of what ye number.

48 And to how many a city have I given full range while it yet did wrong! then I seized on it, and unto me was the return.

Allah versus Satan

49 Say, "O ye folk! I am naught but a

22.40 As the Muslim fights, Allah too "will surely help him." His assistance is due to the fact that the Muslims and Allah have the same objectives in the war, which is the islamification of newly acquired territory. This is the essence of the Doctrine of Jihad.

22.41 *if we establish them in the earth* — The purpose of Jihad is to establish the Muslims in the earth; that is, islamification (see **Islamification** on pp. 851-852).

22.42-45 Those who call Muhammad a liar will be destroyed, just as the people in Noah's day were destroyed, the people of Ad and Thamud were destroyed, the people in

Abraham and Lot's day were destroyed, and the people of Midian were destroyed.

22.47 *God will never fail in his promise* — Muslims were called upon to wait patiently for the impending destruction upon these people, remembering that Allah's sense of time often differs from that of human beings. The way Muhammad put it, "a day with thy Lord is as a thousand years of what ye number" (cf. Ps 90:4; 2 Pet 3:8).

22.48 *how many a city have I given full range* — That is, how many a city did Allah allow to grow until the day when He seized and destroyed it.

plain warner to you,

50 but those who believe and do right, for them is forgiveness and a generous provision;

51 but those who strive to discredit our signs, they are the fellows of hell!"

52 We have not sent before thee any apostle or prophet, but that when he wished, Satan threw not something into his wish; but God annuls what Satan throws; then does God confirm his signs, and God is knowing, wise

53 —to make what Satan throws a trial unto those in whose hearts is sickness; and those whose hearts are hard; and, verily, the wrong-doers are in a wide schism

54 —and that those who have been given "the knowledge" may know that it is the truth from thy Lord, and may believe therein, and that their hearts may be lowly; for, verily, God surely will guide those who believe into a right way.

The fate of the infidel

55 But those who misbelieve will not cease to be in doubt thereof until the Hour comes on them suddenly, or there comes on them the torment of the barren day.

56 The kingdom on that day shall be God's, He shall judge between them; and those who believe and do aright shall be in gardens of

22.49-54 Though Satan is powerful in encouraging people to misbelieve, Allah is more powerful. Allah is capable of (a) annulling what Satan throws into the hearts of people, and (b) confirming His revelation to people's hearts.

Sheikh Mohammed al Ghazali has written, "Satan's insinuations are efforts made to obliterate and pervert the truth, keeping people ignorant of it. In every community there are hordes of people who will say and do the most outrageous and disgraceful things in order to distort the truth and confuse the masses about it. But the surah reassures us that God watches over His revelation and will protect it against such harmful and destructive activities. Satan's efforts will also appear in the form of distortions, misinterpretations, and fabrications which are introduced over time into God's messages, causing people to reject, destroy, mistrust,

and ridicule them. Be that as it may, the truth as advocated by God's prophets and messengers will be protected and its followers will ultimately prevail" (*A Thematic Commentary on the Qur'an*, vol 2, p. 146).

22.50 *believe and do right* — These words are repeated often in the Qur'an and serve as a brief summary of the Islamic gospel (see Q 103.3 note).

22.52 *God annuls what Satan throws* — Muhammad noted that Satan sought to draw away from Allah previous prophets. Yet, Satan was unsuccessful due to the stronger power and authority of Allah.

22.55-57 The future of infidels is the following: (a) they will continue to doubt divine revelation until the Hour when they are summoned to the Last Judgment, and (b) they shall be cast into Hell (see Q 79.42, note; *Hell* on pp. 80-82).

22.56a *believe and do aright* — These

pleasure,

57 but those who misbelieve and say our signs are lies, these—for them is shameful woe.

The fate of the believer

58 And those who flee in God's way, and then are slain or die, God will provide them with a goodly provision; for, verily, God is the best of providers.

59 He shall surely make them enter by an entrance that they like; for, verily, God is knowing, element.

60 That (is so). Whoever punishes with the like of what he has been injured with, and shall then be outraged again, God shall surely help him; verily, God pardons, forgives.

The sovereign control of Allah

61 That for that God joins on the night to the day, and joins on the day to the night, and that God is hearing, seeing;

62 that is for that God is the truth, and for that what ye call on beside Him is falsehood, and that God is the high, the great.

63 Hast thou not seen that God sends down from the sky water, and on the morrow the earth is green? verily, God is kind and well aware.

64 His is what is in the heavens and what is in the earth; and, verily, God is rich and to be praised.

65 Hast thou not seen that God has subjected for you what is in the earth, and the ship that runs on in

words are a brief summary of the Islamic gospel (see Q 103.3 note).

22.56b *gardens of pleasure* — In an earlier surah, Muhammad used this phrase in relationship to the harems of maidens in Paradise that will be bequeathed to the righteous (see Q 56.12-26; also see Q 10.9; 31.8; 37.40-50; 68.34).

22.58 *those who flee in God's way* — That is, those who run in the direction of Allah. This is a way of describing those who believe and do aright. At the time of their death, they will receive a "goodly provision."

22.60 If the believer is attacked and retaliates in a manner commensurate with the injury that he has received, and then is attacked again, Allah will surely help him (see *Jihad* on pp. 616-622).

22.61-66 This passage is a summary of the absolute sovereignty of Allah. It is Allah who

causes the days to grow shorter and nights longer (and vice versa). Allah is the perfection of truth. No lies, deception, or falsehood can survive His scrutiny. It is also Allah who brings the rain and causes vegetation to grow. In addition, it is Allah who enables ships to sail, who holds the stars in the sky, and who causes death and the subsequent resurrection.

22.62 *God is the high, the great* — This phrase, in the Muslim world, is called Takbir (*Allahu akbar*). See Q 34.23 note.

22.66 *man is indeed ungrateful* — The sin of unthankfulness is one of the most serious sins in the Islamic hierarchy of sins. Ungratefulness is manifested by the refusal to surrender absolutely and fully to the will of Allah. In the Judeo-Christian tradition, ungratefulness is an equally serious sin, and for the same fundamental reasons.

the sea at His bidding, and He holds back the sky from falling on the earth save at His bidding? verily, God to men is gracious, merciful.

66 He it is who quickens you, then makes you die, then will He quicken you again—verily, man is indeed ungrateful.

Religious pluralism

67 For every nation have we made rites which they observe; let them not then dispute about the matter, but call upon thy Lord; verily, thou art surely in a right guidance!

68 But if they wrangle with thee, say, "God best knows what ye do."

69 God shall judge between them on the resurrection day concerning that whereon they disagreed.

70 Didst thou not know that God knows what is in the heavens and the earth? verily, that is in a book; verily, that for God is easy.

71 And they serve beside God what He has sent down no power for, and what they have no knowledge of; but the wrong-doers shall have none to help them.

72 When our signs are read to them manifest, thou mayest recognise in the faces of those who misbelieve disdain; they well-nigh rush at those who recite to them our signs. Say, "Shall I inform you of something worse than that for you, the Fire which God has promised to those

22.67 Muhammad recognized that differing cultures possess differing religions and religious rites with which to worship God. The religions of Adam, Noah, Abraham, Moses, Zali'h, and Hud, for example, affirmed religious rites that differed from those of the Islamic religion—yet they were accepted by Allah. This is because, said Muhammad, the theologies of these religions possessed the same essential qualities—that is, they all corresponded to the same primordial religion that honored Allah as the one true God. Still, said Muhammad, Islam is the greatest of these religions since its sacred literature (the Qur'an) is based upon the most complete divine revelation.

Nevertheless, Islam's embrace of other religions has limits. It offers no quarter to any theological system that denies cardinal Islamic doctrines, such as absolute monotheism—the Doctrine of Tauhid—and a salvation

based one's personal merit. Accordingly, Christiainty was rejected. This is due to a series of doctrines that were foundaetional to Christianity: the Doctrines of the Trinity, the Hypostatic Union and the Incarnation of Christ, for example, fall outside the sphere of right doctrine and were therefore repudiated and condemned by Muhammad (see *The Apostles Creed* on p. 87; the *Doctrine of the Trinity* on pp. 735-736; the *Nicene Constantinopolitan Creed* on p. 740; and the *Definition of Chalcedon* on pp. 785-786).

22.68-72 According to this passage, Muhammad was content to wait until the Resurrection Day and the Last Judgment for the differences between the many religions to be sorted out. At the Last Judgment some will enter eternal life and others will enter the flames of Hell. Yet, as stated in a previous note (Q 22. 67, note), this idea is ac-

who misbelieve? an evil journey shall it be!"

The Parable of the Fly

73 O ye folk! a parable is struck out for you, so listen to it. Verily, those on whom ye call beside God could never create a fly if they all united together to do it, and if the fly should despoil them of aught they could not snatch it away from it— weak is both the seeker and the sought.

74 They do not value God at His true value; verily, God is powerful, mighty.

75 God chooses apostles of the angels and of men; verily, God hears and sees.

76 He knows what is before them and what is behind them; and unto God affairs return.

The threefold calling

77 O ye who believe! bow down and adore, and serve your Lord, and do well, haply ye may prosper;

78 and fight strenuously for God, as is His due.

Preparations for the calling

He has elected you, and has not put upon you any hindrance by your religion,—the faith of your father Abraham. He has named you Muslims before and in this (book), that the Apostle may be a witness against you, and that ye may be witnesses against men. Be ye then steadfast in prayer, and give alms, and hold fast by God; He is your sovereign, and an excellent sovereign, and an excellent help!

companied by the belief that Allah also executes judgment on the infidels in this life, and that sometimes Allah utilizes people as His instruments in the exacting of this judgment (see Q 6.131-135; 14.13-15; 22.38-48; 23.51-52; 25.52 and 28.58-60; **The Apostles** on pp. 398-400; **Jihad** on pp. 616-622).

22.73-76 In this parable, Muhammad's point was that among all the creatures of the earth, a fly is regarded as one of the smallest and weakest. Yet, the gods that the polytheists worshipped could not create even a fly. In contrast, Allah not only created the fly, He is powerful and mighty, the creator of the heavens and the earth. He has also chosen "apostles of the angels and of men" (v. 75).

22.78 *fight strenuously for God, as is His due* — That is, "jihad a great jihad for Allah, as is His due" (see Q 4.95; 5.35; 8.72, 74-75; 9.16, 41, 44, 73, 81; 16.110; 22.78; 25.52; 29.6, 69; 47.31; 60.1; 66.9).

Surah 21. The title of this surah, *The Prophets*, and comes from verse 41. This surah presents the foolishness of the infidel. Muhammad believed that divine judgment would surely fall upon all infidels. It was just a question of time. A noteworthy feature of this surah is the presentation of a number of previous historic "apostles." These apostles are Noah, Abraham, Lot, Moses, Aaron, David, Solomon, Job, Jonah, Zechariah, Mary, and Jesus. In each case,

Surah 21

In the name of the merciful and compassionate God.

The foolishness of the infidel

1   Their reckoning draws nigh to men, yet in heedlessness they turn aside.

2   No reminder comes to them from their Lord of late, but they listen while they mock,

3   and their hearts make sport thereof! And those who do wrong discourse secretly (saying), "Is this man aught but a mortal like yourselves? will ye acceed to magic, while ye can see?"

4   Say, "My Lord knows what is said in the heavens and the earth, He hears and knows!"

5   "Nay!" they say, "—a jumble of dreams; nay! he has forged it; nay! he is a poet; but let him bring us a sign as those of yore were sent."

6   No city before them which we de-stroyed believed—how will they believe?

7   Nor did we send before them any but men whom we inspired? Ask ye the people of the Scriptures if ye do not know.

8   Nor did we make them bodies not to eat food, nor were they immortal.

9   Yet we made our promise to them good, and we saved them and whom we pleased; but we destroyed those who committed excesses.

The destruction of cities

10   We have sent down to you a book in which is a reminder for you; have ye then no sense?

11   How many a city which had done wrong have we broken up, and raised up after it another people!

12   And when they perceived our violence they ran away from it.

13   "Run not away, but return to what ye delighted in, and to your dwell-

the peoples to whom they ministered rejected their message and suffered divine judgment.

21.1-5 Muhammad commented that though the infidels of Mecca rejected the divine revelation that he presented, they had not received divine revelations from any of the gods that they worshipped.

21.6 Muhammad reverted to an old argument: people who lived in prior eras also rejected the message of divinely appointed apostles and suffered accordingly (the de-struction of their cities, see Q 14.13-15; 22.45-48; 28.58-60). The implication is that it would be no different for the infidels who lived in Mecca.

21.10-15 Not only will the cities of the infidels be destroyed by Allah, Allah will then raise up another people to live in and rebuild the cities (see Q 6.131-135; *Jihad* on pp. 616-622; and *Islamification* on pp. 851-852).

21.11-12 The judgment that Allah would bring to bear on the cities of the infidels would

ings! haply ye will be questioned."

14 Said they, "O woe is us! verily, we were wrong-doers."

15 And that ceased not to be their cry until we made them mown down,—smouldering out!

Polytheism

16 We did not create the heaven and the earth and what is between the two in play.

17 Had we wished to take to a sport, we would have taken to one from before ourselves; had we been bent on doing so.

18 Nay, we hurl the truth against falsehood and it crashes into it, and lo! it vanishes, but woe to you for what ye attribute (to God)!

19 His are whosoever are in the heavens and the earth, and those who are with Him are not too big with pride for His service, nor do they weary.

20 They celebrate His praises by night and day without intermission.

21 Or have they taken gods from the earth who can raise up (the dead)?

22 Were there in both (heaven and earth) gods beside God, both would surely have been corrupted. Celebrated then be the praise of God, the Lord of the throne, above what they ascribe!

23 He shall not be questioned concerning what He does, but they shall be questioned.

24 Have they taken gods beside Him? Say, "Bring your proofs. This is the reminder of those who are with me, and of those who were before me." Nay, most of them know not the truth, and they do turn aside.

25 We have not sent any prophet before thee, but we inspired him that, "There is no god but Me, so serve ye Me."

26 And they say, "The Merciful has taken a son; celebrated be His praise!"—Nay, honoured servants;

be characterized by "violence." In the end, they would be "broken up"—that is, utterly destroyed.

21.18 When the truth of Allah confronts falsehood, falsehood is crushed and vanishes. The Christian tradition agrees with this insight, yet with two noteworthy caveats: (a) truth is that which corresponds to the Bible (Ps 5:6; Prov 6:16-19; Isa 1:28; Rev 21:8), and (b) falsehood will linger in the world until it is finally and thoroughly put down by God when the Messiah establishes his messianic kingdom on the earth (Isa 11:1-5; 59:17). According to Jesus, this messianic

kingdom remains an unfulfilled prophecy, an event that is still future (see Acts 1:6-7; cf. Isa 9:6-7; Dan 7:27).

21.19-21 Those described in these verses are the ones who offer praise of Allah, whether on earth or Paradise. This would include angels, genies, men, and women.

21.24 *Bring your proofs* — At the Last Judgment, infidels will be told to bring forth proofs that the gods they worshipped were indeed gods. None will pass the test.

21.25 Muhammad once again mentioned the Doctrine of Tauhid—absolute monotheism (see Q 112, note).

27 they do not speak until He speaks; but at His bidding do they act.

28 He knows what is before them, and what is behind them, and they shall not intercede except for him whom He is pleased with; and they shrink through fear.

29 And whoso of them should say, "Verily, I am god instead of Him," such a one we recompense with hell; thus do we recompense the wrong-doers.

The one true God

30 Do not those who misbelieve see that the heavens and the earth were both solid, and we burst them asunder; and we made from water every living thing—will they then not believe?

31 And we placed on the earth firm mountains lest it should move with them, and He made therein open roads for paths, haply they may be guided!

32 and we made the heaven a guarded roof; yet from our signs they turn aside!

33 He it is who created the night and the day, and the sun and the moon, each floating in a sky.

The folly of fools

34 We never made for any mortal before thee immortality; what, if thou shouldst die, will they live on for aye?

35 Every soul shall taste of death! we will test them with evil and with good, as a trial; and unto us shall they return!

36 And when those who misbelieve see thee, they only take thee for a jest, "Is this he who mentions your gods?" Yet they at the mention of the Merciful do disbelieve.

37 Man is created out of haste. I will show you my signs; but do not hurry Me.

38 And they say, "When will this threat (come to pass), if ye tell the truth?"

39 Did those who misbelieve but know when the fire shall not be warded off from their faces nor from their

---

21.26-29 Muhammad then condemned the Arabic Star Family religious system that dominated Arabia (see **Polytheism in Seventh Century Arabia** on pp. 92-97.

21.30-33 The one true God is the creator of the heavens and the earth. He is therefore sovereign over His entire dominion, ruling out the possibility of competing gods.

21.34-44 Muhammad believed that infidels consistently twist and misunderstand truths pertaining to Allah and the Last Judgment.

They also fail to understand that their eternal destiny is Hell.

21.36 In response, infidels ridiculed Muhammad, refusing to take his surahs seriously (see Q 18.56; 23.110; 25.41; 31.6; 37.12-14; 39.56; 45.9, 35).

21.38-41 Muhammad's detractors were also curious about the timing of the General Resurrection and Last Judgment. His answer was that it would come upon them unexpectedly and suddenly.

The Hajj

The Hajj is the authorized religious pilgrimage to Mecca. It is a requirement incumbent upon every Muslim male, provided that he is free, sane,
in good health, and has sufficient money to make the journey. If a
woman makes the journey, she must do so in the accompaniment of her
husband or a near male relative. The pilgrimage is required at least once
in one's lifetime.

In addition, the Hajj is to be made in the appointed seasons, which
are: *Shawwal* (the tenth month of the lunar Islamic calendar), *Zu l-
Qa'dah* (the eleventh month of the lunar Islamic calendar), and the first
ten days of *Zu l-Hijjah* (the twelfth month of the lunar Islamic calendar).
Since the lunar Islamic calendar is eleven to twelve days shorter than the
solar year, Islamic lunar months migrate through the four seasons.

The specifics of the tradition. The Hajj begins with the journey
itself. People are to make the journey wearing the same kind of clothing
(white shrouds for men and simple white dresses for women) so that
there would be no distinction between rich and poor.

Just prior to entering Mecca, the Muslim pilgrim bathes, recites two
prayers, and removes his or her clothing, replacing them with the sacred
robe. Sandals may be worn, but no shoes or boots. As the final stage of
the journey is then completed, the pilgrim sings the *Talbiyah* (the lyrics
of which indicate that the pilgrim is awaiting orders from the Master).

Upon arrival at Mecca, the pilgrim commences the rituals associated
with the Ka'ba altar:

- The pilgrim performs legal ablutions and then kisses the Ka'ba altar.

- The pilgrim worships in a circumambulation movement (a counter-clock-
  wise movement) around the altar. At first, he or she completes seven
  rotations around the altar (three times in a quick or running pace and four
  times at a slow pace). Each time as he or she passes by the altar, the
  corner of the altar is kissed.

- The pilgrim proceeds to the *Maqamu Ibrahim* (Abraham's station) where he or she recites the 119th verse of the Second Surah and then recites two prayers (see Q 3.97, note).

- The pilgrim returns to the Ka'ba altar and kisses it once again.

- The pilgrim goes to the gate of the temple leading to Mount al-Safa, ascends the hill, reciting the 153rd verse of the Second Surah. Once upon the summit, he or she turns towards the Ka'ba altar and repeats three times the following: "There is no deity but God! God is great! There is no deity but God alone! He has performed His promise, and has aided His servant and has put to flight the hosts of infidels by Himself alone!"

- The pilgrim runs to the summit of Mount al-Marwah and descends seven times, reciting prayers.

The above routine is repeated six consecutive days.

- On the seventh day, the pilgrim listens to a sermon at the Great Mosque.

- On the eighth day, the pilgrim travels to Mount Mina and spends the night there, performing various prayers.

- On the ninth day, the pilgrim travels to the Plain of Arafat where a second sermon is heard. The pilgrim then leaves for al-Muzdalifah.

- On the tenth day, the pilgrim celebrates the Festival of Sacrifice at Mount Mina. Early in the morning he or she recites prayers and then proceeds to Three Pillars, called "the Great Devil." The pilgrim casts seven stones at each of the pillars. He or she then returns to Mina where an animal is

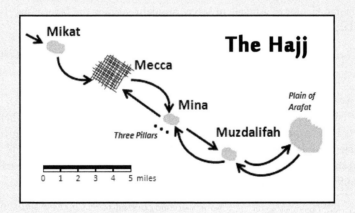

> sacrificed—either a sheep, goat, cow, or camel. The pilgrim plunges a
> knife into the throat of the animal, saying: "God is great! O God, accept
> this sacrifice from me!" The pilgrim then returns to Mecca and recites a
> final prayer.
>
> This concludes the Hajj.

———— ◆•◆•◆ ————

Modernist Islamic thinkers see the hajj as a treasure-house of fluid symbols carrying infinite meanings everyone is free to interpret and reinterpret as they choose. Inviting Muslims to think of the hajj creatively is part of modernists' wider commitment to democratizing religious knowledge. In their view, "reading" the hajj's inner meaning is similar to reading any sacred text, including the Qur'an—every mortal mind can grasp a fraction of God's message, but no human authority, no matter how learned and esteemed, can monopolize the discussion or claim the final word.

—Robert R. Bianchi, *Guests of God*, p. 23

Ever since I was old enough to understand the meaning of the pilgrimage, I have dreamed of the day when I would go to Mecca to perform the hajj. It was my dream to be able to go while I was young enough and physically able to undertake, on my own power, the physical rigors of this fifth pillar of Islam.

—Jihan Sadat, *My Hope for Peace*, p. 57

The Mohammedan Hajj or pilgrimage to Mecca annually spreads the fanaticism. No missionary or Christian dare enter the city, save in disguise.

—George Smith, *Short History of Christian Missions*, p. 222

The bond between Moslem and Moslem is today much stronger than that between Christian and Christian. Of course, Moslems fight bitterly among themselves, but these conflicts never quite lose the aspect of family quarrels and tend to be adjourned in presence of infidel aggression...Islam's solidarity is powerfully buttressed by two of its fundamental institutions: the "Hajj," or pilgrimage to Mecca, and the caliphate...It is the Hajj rather than the caliphate which has exerted the more consistently unifying influence.

—Lothrop Stoddard, *The New World of Islam*, p. 46

backs, and they shall not be helped!

40   Nay, it shall come on them suddenly, and shall dumb-founder them, and they shall not be able to repel it, nor shall they be respited.

41   Prophets before thee have been mocked at, but that whereat they jested encompassed those who mocked.

Last Judgment

42   Say, "Who shall guard you by night and by day from the Merciful?" Nay, but they from the mention of their Lord do turn aside.

43   Have they gods to defend them against us? These cannot help themselves, nor shall they be abetted against us.

44   Nay, but we have granted enjoyment to these men and to their fathers whilst life was prolonged. Do they not see that we come to the land and shorten its borders? Shall they then prevail?

45   Say, "I only warn you by inspiration;" but the deaf hear not the call

when they are warned.

46   But if a blast of the torment of thy Lord touches them, they will surely say, "O, woe is us! verily, we were wrong-doers!"

47   We will place just balances upon the resurrection day, and no soul shall be wronged at all, even though it be the weight of a grain of mustard seed, we will bring it; for we are good enough at reckoning up.

Moses and Aaron

48   We did give to Moses and Aaron the Discrimination, and a light and a reminder to those who fear;

49   who are afraid of their Lord in secret; and who at the Hour do shrink.

50   This is a blessed reminder which we have sent down, will ye then deny it?

Abraham

51   And we gave Abraham a right direction before; for about him we

---

21.39 Description of Hell: fire will cling to people's faces and backs. It is also a place of hopelessness, where the tormented ones "shall not be helped."

21.42-43 According to these verses, the Last Judgment is an event that is inevitable. No person or spirit can forestall or sidestep it.

21.45 This verse is a reminder that Muhammad's surahs were divinely inspired (see Q 53.4, note).

21.47 At the Last Judgment, the eternal destiny of people will be weighed in "just balances" that will determine the quantities and qualities of their works (see **The Last Judgment** on pp. 46-50).

21.48-50 This passage states that God gave to Moses and Aaron "the Discrimination"— that is, divine revelation that distinguishes right from wrong. It was "a light and a reminder for those who fear." As such, Muhammad affirmed the divine inspiration of the

knew.

52 When he said to his father and to his people, "What are these images to which ye pay devotion?"

53 Said they, "We found our fathers serving them."

54 Said he, "Both you and your fathers have been in obvious error."

55 They said, "Dost thou come to us with the truth, or art thou but of those who play?"

56 He said, "Nay, but your Lord is Lord of the heavens and the earth, which He originated; and I am of those who testify to this;

57 and, by God! I will plot against your idols after ye have turned and shown me your backs!"

58 So he brake them all in pieces, except a large one they had; that haply they might refer it to that.

59 Said they, "Who has done this with our gods? verily, he is of the wrong-doers!"

60 They said, "We heard a youth mention them who is called Abraham."

61 Said they, "Then bring him before the eyes of men; haply they will

bear witness."

62 Said they, "Was it thou who did this to our gods, O Abraham?"

63 Said he, "Nay, it was this largest of them; but ask them, if they can speak."

64 Then they came to themselves and said, "Verily, ye are the wrong-doers."

65 Then they turned upside down again: "Thou knewest that these cannot speak."

66 Said he, "Will ye then serve, beside God, what cannot profit you at all, nor harm you?

67 fie upon you, and what ye serve beside God! have ye then no sense?"

68 Said they, "Burn him, and help your gods, if ye are going to do so!"

69 We said, "O fire! be thou cool and a safety for Abraham!"

70 They desired to plot against him, but we made them the losers.

71 And we brought him and Lot safely to the land which we have blessed for the world,

72 and we bestowed upon him Isaac

Pentateuch (Genesis, Exodus, Leviticus, Numbers, and Deuteronomy).

21.51 *a right direction* — That is, a knowledge of the way to eternal life (see Q 72.2, note).

21.51-73 This narrative of Abraham's idolatrous father is based upon Josh 24:2. In this biblical passage, it states: "Joshua said to all the people, 'This is what the Lord, the God of Israel, says: "Long ago your forefathers, including Terah the father of Abraham

and Nahor, lived beyond the River and worshiped other gods.'" The dialogue of this narrative comes from Muhammad's own imagination.

21.67 *fie upon you* — That is, curses upon you (see Q 17.23; 46.17).

21.68-69 Nowhere in the Bible is it stated that Abraham was thrown into a fire and then protected by God. The origin of this story is found in the Jewish *Midrash Rabbah* (c. A.D. 200) in its commentary on Genesis

and Jacob as a fresh gift,

73   and each of them we made righ-
       teous persons; and we made them
       high priests to guide (men) by our
       bidding, and we inspired them to
       do good works, and to be stead-
       fast in prayer, and to give alms;
       and they did serve us.

Lot

74   And Lot, to him we gave judgment
       and knowledge, and we brought
       him safely out of the city which
       had done vile acts; verily, they were
       a people who wrought abomina-
       tions!
75   And we made him enter into our
       mercy; verily, he was of the righ-
       teous!

Noah

76   And Noah, when he cried
       aforetime, and we answered him
       and saved him and his people from
       the mighty trouble,
77   and we helped him against the
       people who said our signs were
       lies; verily, they were a bad people,
       so we drowned them all together.

David and Solomon

78   And David and Solomon, when
       they gave judgment concerning the
       field, when some people's sheep
       had strayed therein at night; and
       we testified to their judgment;
79   and this we gave Solomon to un-
       derstand. To each of them we gave

(see Q 29.24; 37.97-98 note; 85.4-10).

21.73 *righteous persons* — Literally, *imams.* Allah turned Isaac and Jacob into imams. Five characteristics of imams: they (a) provide guidance to men, (b) characterized by good works, (c) are steadfast in prayer, (d) give alms, and (e) serve God.

21.74-75 This description is based upon Gen 19:1-29. Lot was given "judgment and knowledge" from two angels who brought him safely out of Sodom "which had done vile acts." As he and his family were leaving the city, it was destroyed by Allah.

21.76-77 This description is based upon Gen 7:1-24. Noah served as a warner to the people of his age. He and his family were saved from the Great Flood by means of an ark that God had instructed him to build.

21.76-77 This story, that of the sheep straying into someone else's field and de-stroyed a crop, is not mentioned in the Bible, nor anywhere else in ancient literature. Some scholars presume that the story belongs to Arabian lore.

According to legend, David awarded the entire flock of sheep to an owner whose crop was destroyed by a straying sheep. So-lomon, thinking the judgment too severe, appealed to his father to adjudicate his deci-sion. He stated that the awarding of sheep should only be temporary—until after one season of shearing and birth of newborn lambs occurred. David agreed and adjusted his decision.

21.79 *and to David we subjected the moun-tains to celebrate our praises, and the birds too* — Muhammad believed that when David sang, the birds and mountains listened and were inspired to sing songs in response.

judgment and knowledge; and to David we subjected the mountains to celebrate our praises, and the birds too,—it was we who did it.

80   And we taught him the art of making coats of mail for you, to shield you from each other's violence; are ye then grateful?

81   And to Solomon (we subjected) the wind blowing stormily, to run on at his bidding to the land which we have blessed,—for all things did we know,

82   —and some devils to dive for him, and to do other works beside that; and we kept guard over them.

Job

83   And Job, when he cried to his Lord, "As for me, harm has touched me, but Thou art the most merciful of the merciful ones."

84   And we answered him, and removed from him the distress that was upon him; and we gave his family, and the like of them with them, as a mercy from us, and a remembrance to those who serve us.

Ishmael, Enoch and Ezekiel

85   And Ishmael, and Idrîs, and DHu 'l Kifl, all of these were of the patient:

86   and we made them enter into our mercy; verily, they were among the righteous.

Jonah

87   And DHu'nnûn, when he went away in wrath and thought that we

---

21.80 Arabian lore also claimed that David was the first to invent coats of mail used in combat. Archeologists, however, date the invention of coats of mail to the fourth century, B.C., six centuries after David.

21.81 Some Islamic scholars believe that Solomon mounted the wind to make a pilgrimage to "the land which we have blessed," Harran, a city known for ancient pilgrimages.

21.82 Muhammad believed that demons worked on behalf of Solomon by diving into the depths of the sea to acquire various treasures. In contrast, the godly people mentioned in the Bible (including Solomon) recognized the evil associated with demons and refused any cooperation with them.

21.83-84 This account is based upon the book of Job in the Old Testament. He was assaulted with a series of trials and afflictions, yet when he prayed God answered and restored his family (see Job 42).

21.85-86 DHu-l-kifl, which literally means the possessor of a *kifl* (double portion), is believed by some scholars to be the prophet Ezekiel. Muhammad identified Ishmael, Enoch, and Ezekiel as righteous patriarchs. Idris is Arabic for Enoch, the eighth generation from Adam (Gen 4:17-18).

21.87 *There is no god but Thou* — This is another reference to the Doctrine of Tauhid (see Q 112, note).

21.87-88 DHu'nnun is believed by some scholars to refer to the prophet Jonah. His prayer in the darkness is a reference to the episode when he prayed while in the belly of the large fish (Jonah 2).

had no power over him; and he cried out in the darkness, "There is no god but Thou, celebrated be Thy praise! Verily, I was of the evil-doers!"

88   And we answered him, and saved him from the trouble. Thus do we save believers!

Zechariah

89   And Zechariah, when he cried unto his Lord, "O Lord! leave me not alone; for thou art the best of heirs."

90   And we answered him, and bestowed upon him John; and we made his wife right for him; verily, these vied in good works, and called on us with longing and dread, and were humble before us.

Mary and Jesus

91   And she who guarded her private parts [chastity], and we breathed into her of our Spirit, and we made her and her son a sign unto the worlds.

One nation

92   Verily, this your nation is one nation; and I am your Lord, so serve me.

93   But they cut up their affair amongst themselves; they all shall return to us;

94   and he who acts aright, and he who is a believer, there is no denial of his efforts, for, verily, we will write them down for him.

21.89-90 This is a description of Zechariah's prayer when he encountered an angel of the Lord while in the Temple (Lk 1:5-22). Following this prayer, his wife Elizabeth became pregnant and gave birth to their child: John the Baptist.

21.91 This episode in this verse refers to the time when the angel Gabriel visited Mary and announced that the Holy Spirit would impregnate her with seed that would be Jesus Christ. According to the Bible, "The angel answered, 'The Holy Spirit will come upon you, and the power of the Most High will overshadow you. So the holy one to be born will be called the Son of God'" (Lk 1:35-36).

21.92 *this your nation is one nation* — In Islam, one of its principal doctrines is the Doctrine of One Nation; that is, islamification.

It teaches the submission of the entire world to Allah and is grounded in the notion that Allah is the only God. The submission of the entire world to Allah, then, is not only logical, it is inevitable. Currently, the world is divided into many diverse and sinful nations. Yet this, said Muhammad, was because of their sinfulness. Some time in the future, these nations "shall return to us" (v. 93). See **Islamification** on pp. 851-852.

21.94 *he who acts aright, and he who is a believer, there is not denial of his efforts* — That is, he who is a believer and strives to restore this unity will be rewarded.

21.95-96 *Yagug and Magug* — That is, Gog and Magog (see Q 18.94). At the end of times, Gog and Magog will emerge "from every hummock" (every corner of the earth) and resist the effort to achieve the

Gog and Magog

95   There is a ban upon a city which we have destroyed that they shall not return,

96   until Yâgûg and Mâgûg are let out, and they from every hummock shall glide forth.

97   And the true promise draws nigh, and lo! they are staring—the eyes of those who misbelieve! O, woe is us! we were heedless of this, nay, we were wrong-doers!

98   Verily, ye, and what ye serve beside God, shall be the pebbles of hell, to it shall ye go down!

99   Had these been gods they would not have gone down thereto: but all shall dwell therein for aye;

100   for them therein is groaning, but they therein shall not be heard.

101   Verily, those for whom the good (reward) from us was fore-ordained, they from it shall be kept far away;

102   they shall not hear the slightest sound thereof, and they in what their souls desire shall dwell for aye.

103   The greatest terror shall not grieve them; and the angels shall meet them, (saying), "This is your day

islamification of the world. Allah will respond to their challenge and conquer them.

In his book *A Thematic Commentary on the Qur'an,* Sheikh Mohammed al Ghazali has written that when Muhammad emerged as a prophet, the Jews and Christians rejected him. Moreover, this division would continue onward until some future date when the "hordes from the eastern part of the globe, who had never received divine revelation, would sweep across the civilized world, plundering and pillaging everything in their way." Though some scholars identify the Mongols and Tatars who, in the thirteenth century, invaded Baghdad and conquered much of the Muslim world, this interpretation is incorrect. Al Ghazali explains that this passage clearly states that the emergence of Gog and Magog would usher in the Hour, the Day of Resurrection, and the Day of Judgment. This clearly did not take place in the thirteenth century. Hence, al Ghazali concludes, the fulfillment of this prophecy is still future (vol 2, pp. 135, 136).

The Bible presents Gog and Magog differently. According to chapters 38 and 39 of the Book of Ezekiel, Gog and Magog will emerge in end-time prophecy and seek to draw the world away from the one true God. They will be utterly defeated. Then, the Messiah will come and establish His kingdom upon the earth. According to the Book of the Revelation, this kingdom will be headed by Jesus Christ, the Messiah. Since Muhammad is not recognized as a genuine apostle or prophet of God, he will have no role or presence in this kingdom. This is one of the fundamental points where Christianity and Islam differ.

21.97 *the true promise draws nigh* — That is, the promise of Muslim domination throughout the world. The infidels will exclaim, "O woe is us! we were heedless of this, nay, we were wrongdoers!"

21.103 *This is your day which ye were promised* — That is, this is your day of judgment.

21.104a *The day when we roll up the heav-*

which ye were promised!"

104 The day when we will roll up the heavens as es-Sigill rolls up the books; as we produced it at its first creation will we bring it back again—a promise binding upon us; verily, we are going to do it.

A final appeal

105 And already have we written in the Psalms after the reminder that "the earth shall my righteous servants inherit,"

106 Verily, in this is preaching for a people who serve me!

107 We have only sent thee as a mercy to the worlds.

108 Say, "I am only inspired that your God is one God; are ye then re-

signed?"

109 But if they turn their backs say, "I have proclaimed (war) against all alike, but I know not if what ye are threatened with be near or far!"

110 Verily, He knows what is spoken openly, and He knows what ye hide.

111 I know not, haply it is a trial for you and a provision for a season.

112 Say, "My Lord! judge thou with truth! and our Lord is the Merciful whom we ask for aid against what they ascribe!"

Surah 17

In the name of the merciful and compassionate God.

---

ens — an apocalyptic event that will affect the skies. This is a possible reference to Rev. 6:14, which states: "The sky receded like a scroll, rolling up, and every mountain and island was removed from its place."

21.104b *es-Sigill* — A form of magic.

21.105 This is a possible reference to Psalm 37:29, which states: "the righteous will inherit the land and dwell in it forever."

21.105-112 Muhammad reminded his readers once again of the Doctrine of Tauhid (absolute monotheism). The word "war" in verse 109 is implied (bracketed) and therefore not in the original Arabic.

21.110 Allah is omniscient—he knows public as well as secret knowledge.

Surah 17. The title of this surah, *The Night Journey*, comes from verse one. The surah begins with a brief description of the Night Journey by Muhammad to the Temple Mount

in Jerusalem. One night, while in Mecca, he was allegedly transported by an angelic Buraq (half mule, half donkey, with wings) at supersonic speeds to Jerusalem (the Isra) whereupon he ascended to the seventh heaven and met Allah (the Mi'raj). Afterwards, he descended to Temple Mount and then returned to Mecca. The entire journey took place in one night.

Most of what is known of the Night Journey comes from hadithic literature—and not this surah—which is odd since the Night Journey occupies a prominent place in Islamic theology, worldview, and lore. It would seem that this episode would have satisfied the Quraysh' demands for a *bone fide* miracle to validate Muhammad's ministry. It is because of this that Christians rightly wonder why it was not given greater prominence with a sufficient breadth of detail in this surah (see

The Night Journey	the Remote Mosque, the precinct of which we have blessed, to show him of our signs! verily, He both hears and looks.
1 Celebrated be the praises of Him who took His servant a journey by night from the Sacred Mosque to	2 And we gave Moses the Book and

The Night Journey on pp. 502-504; also see *Sahih Muslim* 1.75.0309).

Following the Night Journey, Muhammad moved on to other topics in this surah pertinent to the Islamic faith.

17.1 This verse is a summary of the Night Journey. Muhammad claimed that he was taken from the Ka'ba altar (the Sacred Mosque) to Temple Mount in Jerusalem (the Remote Mosque, "the precinct of which we have blessed"). Not mentioned in the verse, but later explained in the hadithic literature, was the ascension from Jerusalem (that is, the *Mi'raj)* to the Seventh Heaven. While in Paradise, Muhammad was reportedly shown divine revelations ("our signs").

This verse has generated considerable debate within Islamic scholarship. First, the phrase, "from the Sacred Mosque" is understood differently within the hadithic literature. One Hadith asserts that Muhammad was at the Ka'ba altar when the journey began. It states: "While I was between being asleep and awake in the apartments near the Ka'ba at the holy mosque, Gabriel came to me with the (angelic steed) Buraq." Yet, an opposing Hadith states: "After the evening prayer Muhammad slept in the dwelling of Umm Hani, when he was taken on the night journey (to Jerusalem) and returned in the same night." Umm Hani was his cousin, the daughter of Abu Talib. If this second Hadith is correct, it would mean that the phrase "from the Sacred Mosque" meant "from *the precincts of* the Sacred Mosque."

Second, not all Islamic scholars are in agreement as to the timing of the journey. Though the prevailing opinion is that it occurred within the last year of Muhammad's stay in Mecca (just prior to his emigration to Medinah), some scholars maintain that it occurred prior to the Blessed Night (that is, prior to the night when he allegedly received the first surah from the archangel Gabriel).

Third, the hadithic literature is not in agreement as to the nature of the journey. Though a number of Hadiths claim that he journeyed with his body, two Hadiths argue otherwise. In one, A'isha states: "By God, the body of the Messenger of God was not missed (during the night journey); rather, the ascension to heaven took place only with the spirit." In another, Mu'awiya claims that the journey "took place only with the spirit"— essentially, an event where the spirit temporarily left his body (see Brook Olson Vuckovic, *Heavenly Journeys, Earthly Concerns*, pp. 79-80).

17.2a When placed in the context of verse one, Muhammad compared the revelation that he received on this event with the divine revelations given to Moses when he composed the Pentateuch (Genesis, Exodus, Leviticus, Numbers and Deuteronomy).

17.2b *the Book* — This refers to the Pentateuch (the first five books of the Bible).

17.2c *Take ye to no guardian but me* — It is unclear which verse from the Pentateuch Muhammad had in mind here. Perhaps the intended verse is the following: "Fear the Lord your God, serve him only and take your oaths in his name" (Deut 6:13; cf. Ex 20:3;

made it a guidance to the children of Israel: "Take ye to no guardian but me."

3   Seed of those we bore with Noah (in the ark)! verily, he was a thankful servant!

Two diasporas

4   And we decreed to the children of Israel in the Book, "Ye shall verily do evil in the earth twice, and ye shall rise to a great height (of pride)."
5   And when the threat for the first

(sin) of the two came, we sent over them servants of ours, endued with violence, and they searched inside your houses; and it was an accomplished threat.

6   Then we rallied you once more against them, and aided you with wealth and sons, and made you a numerous band.

7   "If ye do well, ye will do well to your own souls; and if ye do ill, it is against them!" And when the threat for the last came to harm your faces and to enter the mosque as they entered it the first time, and

---

Deut 10:20; 13:4).

17.3 Muhammad compared his Night Journey with the journey of Noah and his family. The point is this: just as Noah was a thankful servant for what Allah did on his behalf, Muhammad is equally thankful for what Allah did for him.

17.4a *the Book* — That is, the Scriptures, the Old Testament.

17.4b The Old Testament does not contain this verse, or even a paraphrase of this verse.

17.5 This is a reference to Phase One of the First Diaspora (the exile of the northern kingdom—eighth century, B.C.). Shalmaneser V of the Assyrians overran the northern kingdom of Israel and sent the Jewish people into exile. Though the Jewish people were guilty of many sins, the fundamental sin that caused God to send judgment upon the northern kingdom was the widespread practice of idolatry (see 2 Kings 16:3; 17:8-13).

17.6 This is a reference to Phase Two of the First Diaspora. The Babylonians overran

the southern kingdom of Judah and sent the Jewish people into exile (sixth century, B.C.). The fundamental sin that caused God to send judgment upon the southern kingdom was also idolatry (see 1 Kings 14:22-24; 2 Chron 28:25-26; Isa 1:1-31).

17.7 This is a reference to the Second Diaspora. This event took place in the first century, A.D. when the Jewish people were once again sent into exile. The word *mosque* is a general term for temple; in this case, it likely referred to Herod's Temple that was destroyed by the Roman general Titus in A.D. 70. With its destruction, the Second Diaspora commenced. Jews were scattered across the Mediterranean world, the Arabian peninsula, and as far east as India. Eventually, the extent of the Second Diaspora reached to the four corners of the earth.

According to Jesus, the reason for the Second Diaspora was unbelief—not idolatry. The Jewish people, by in large, failed to recognize and embrace Him as their Messiah. As Jesus approached Jerusalem, he wept over it and said, "If you, even you, had only

to destroy what they had got the upperhand over with utter destruction.

8 It may be that thy Lord will have mercy on you;—but if ye return we will return, and we have made hell a prison for the misbelievers.

A mighty woe

9 Verily, this Qur'ân guides to the straightest path, and gives the glad tidings to the believers who do aright that for them is a great hire;

10 and that for those who believe not in the hereafter, we have prepared

a mighty woe.

11 Man prays for evil as he prays for good; and man was ever hasty.

12 We made the night and the day two signs; and we blot out the sign of the night and make the sign of the day visible, that ye may seek after plenty from your Lord, and that ye may number the years and the reckoning; and we have detailed everything in detail.

13 And every man's augury have we fastened on his neck; and we will bring forth for him on the resurrection day a book offered to him wide open.

---

known on this day what would bring you peace—but now it is hidden from your eyes. The days will come upon you when your enemies will build an embankment against you and encircle you and hem you in on every side. They will dash you to the ground, you and the children within your walls. They will not leave one stone on another, because you did not recognize the time of God's coming to you" (Lk 19:42-44).

17.8 *but if ye return we will return* — That is, if the Jewish people returned to their idolatry, Allah would return with additional judgment. Once again, the Jewish people were minded that Hell is "a prison for the misbelievers (infidels)."

17.9 *the straightest path* — That is, the path to eternal life (see Q 72.2, note). Muhammad believed that the Qur'an was the most straight path, an accurate and reliable revelation available to mankind. In contrast, the New Testament refers to all the sacred literatures that present different gospels as the wrong path, a path cursed of God (see

Gal 1:8-9; 2 Cor 11:13-15; 2 Jn 10-11).

17.10 For those who believe not in the hereafter (that is, general resurrection, Last Judgment, Paradise and Hell), will suffer "a mighty woe"—the wrath of Allah.

17.13 *every man's augury* — That is, every man's omen. The Arab word translated augury is *ta'ir*, which literally means *bird*. Seventh century Arabs were fond of identifying and establishing good and bad omens for purposes of prognostication. One common omen was determined by the direction of birds in flight. Hence, the phrase "a bird tied around one's neck" meant "an omen that could result in one's death."

The particular omen of which Muhammad had in mind addressed events that would transpire at the Last Judgment. The omen focused on their rejection of his message his message. People will be handed a book which contains an accounting of all the works committed during their lives. As they read they will discover that they have become witnesses against themselves.

14   "Read thy book, thou art accoun-
      tant enough against thyself today!"

15   He who accepts guidance, accepts
      it only for his own soul: and he
      who errs, errs only against it; nor
      shall one burdened soul bear the
      burden of another. Nor would we
      punish until we had sent an apostle.

16   And when we desired to destroy a
      city we bade the opulent ones
      thereof; and they wrought abomi-
      nation therein; and its due sentence
      was pronounced; and we de-
      stroyed it with utter destruction.

17   How many generations have we
      destroyed after Noah! but thy Lord
      of the sins of his servant is well
      aware, and sees enough.

18   Whoso is desirous of this life that
      hastens away, we will hasten on
      for him therein what we please,—
      for whom we please. Then we will
      make hell for him to broil in—de-
      spised and outcast.

A mighty blessing

17.15a *He who accepts guidance, accepts it only for his own soul* — Each person is accountable for activities done in his or her own life. If he or she did good works during their lives, it will redound to their benefit. If he or she did bad works during their lives, it will redound to their own hurt (also see Q 27.40). This, then, is a reference to the concept of salvation by individual merit. The Bible opposes this doctrine, insisting upon the Doctrine of Salvation by Faith—apart from works (see Eph 2:8-9; Titus 3:3-7).

17.15b *Nor would we punish until we had sent an apostle* — A familiar theme in the Qur'an is the notion that Allah first sends apostles to a given community of people (whether the community be small, such as a city, or large, such as a nation) to serve as warners of judgment to come. If the people refuse to heed the warning, a fierce and violent judgment inevitably comes (see Q 10.13, 74; 12.110; 14.13, 47; 20.47, 134; 25.37, 41-42, 77; 26.105-191; 28.59; 30.9-10, 47; 36.32-34, 52-54; 37.37-39, 139-148; 38.12-16; 39.70 71; 40.5-6, 22, 51-52; 70, 78, 83-85; 41-14-18, 43; 43.25; 72.23; 44.13-33; 50.13-14; 51.59; 52.11-16; 54.9-16; 69.10; 77.11-15; 91.11-15; also see **The Apostles** on pp. 398-400; and **Jihad** on pp. 616-622).

According to Muhammad, divine judgment comes in two phases: (a) in the current life, and (b) in the hereafter. A classic example of judgment that came in the current life is the Great Flood during the ministry of Noah (see Q 10.71-74; 11.25-48; 21.76-77; 23.23-30; 25.25-48; 26.105-122; 37.75-82; 40.5-6; 53.52-54; 54.9-15; 71.1-28). A second example is the two Diasporas that befell the Israelite people (see Q 17.4-8, and **The Apostles** on pp. 398-400).

17.16 *we bade the opulent ones thereof* — According to Muhammad, Allah brought utter destruction to the people of numerous cities that failed to heed His warnings and repent and turn to Him. Moreover, Allah forced the people of these cities to engage in abominations (see **The Doctrine of al-Qadar** on pp. 264-266).

17.18 Following the destruction wrought by Allah in this life, He will cast infidels into Hell. Such individuals, Muhammad said, are the "despised and outcast."

17.19-20 Those who are faithful to Allah and strive to live so that they will receive a favorable outcome at the Last Judgment will

19   But whoso desires the next life, and strives for it and is a believer—these, their striving shall be gratefully received.

20   To all—these and those—will we extend the gifts of thy Lord; for the gifts of thy Lord are not restricted.

21   See how we have preferred some of them over others, but in the next life are greater degrees and greater preference.

The straight path

22   Put not with God other gods, or thou wilt sit despised and forsaken.

23   Thy Lord has decreed that ye shall not serve other than Him; and kindness to one's parents, whether one or both of them reach old age with thee; and say not to them, "Fie!" and do not grumble at them, but speak to them a generous speech.

24   And lower to them the wing of humility out of compassion, and say, "O Lord! have compassion on them as they brought me up when I was little!"

25   Your Lord knows best what is in your souls if ye be righteous, and, verily, He is forgiving unto those who come back penitent.

26   And give thy kinsman his due and the poor and the son of the road; and waste not wastefully,

27   for the wasteful were ever the devil's brothers; and the devil is ever ungrateful to his Lord.

28   But if thou dost turn away from them to seek after mercy from thy Lord, which thou hopest for, then speak to them an easy speech.

29   Make not thy hand fettered to thy neck, nor yet spread it out quite open, lest thou shouldst have to sit down blamed and straitened in means.

---

be "gratefully received." They are the ones who will receive "the gifts of thy Lord" (see **The Last Judgment** on pp. 46-50).

17.22-38 Muhammad presented a listing of eleven meritorious activities that typify the straight path that leads to eternal life.

17.22-23a The first meritorious activity was *an affirmation of monotheism*—the Doctrine of Tauhid (cf. Ex 20:3; Deut 5:7; 6:14; Josh 24:18-24; Ps 73:25; 81:9; Isa 43:10; 44:8; 45:21-22; 46:9; Jer 25:6; 35:15; Col 2:18).

17.23b-24 The second meritorious activity was *the honoring of one's parents*. The word "fie" means "curse" (see Q 21.67; 46.17; also see Ex 20:12; 21:15-17; Lev 19:3, 32; Prov 1:8-9; 15:5; 20:20; 23:22-

25; 28:24; 30:11, 17; Matt 15:4-6; Eph 6:1-3; Col 3:20).

17.25 The third meritorious activity was *a humble and penitent heart* (cf. Job 42:6; Isa 1:27; 44:22; 59:20; Jer 15:19; Ezek 14:6; 18:32; Matt 4:17; Acts 2:38).

17.26-30 The fourth meritorious activity was *a generous spirit*. Such generosity should manifest itself in the giving of alms, helping those who are traveling, and a thrifty and non-materialistic life-style. The phrase "thy hand fettered to thy neck" is a figure of speech signifying miserliness (cf. Deut 15:11; Ps 112:9; Prov 11:25-26; 19:17; Ecc 11:1-2; Isa 58:7, 10; Lk 11:41; 12:33; Acts 4:35; 20:35; Rom 12:13; 1 Tim 6:18; Heb

30   Verily, thy Lord spreads out provision to whomsoever He will or He doles it out. Verily, He is ever well aware of and sees His servants.

31   And slay not your children for fear of poverty; we will provide for them; beware! for to slay them is ever a great sin!

32   And draw not near to fornication; verily, it is ever an abomination, and evil is the way thereof.

33   And slay not the soul that God has forbidden you, except for just cause; for he who is slain unjustly we have given his next of kin authority; yet let him not exceed in

slaying; verily, he is ever helped.

34   And draw not near to the wealth of the orphan, save to improve it, until he reaches the age of puberty, and fulfil your compacts; verily, a compact is ever enquired of.

35   And give full measure when ye measure out, and weigh with a right balance; that is better and a fairer determination.

36   And do not pursue that of which thou hast no knowledge; verily, the hearing, the sight, and the heart, all of these shall be enquired of.

37   And walk not on the earth proudly; verily, thou canst not cleave the

---

13:16; James 2:15-16; 1 Jn 3:16-18).

17.31 The fifth meritorious activity was *the caring of all one's children*. This statement challenged a practice in seventh century Arabia of burying alive unwanted female babies "for fear of poverty." Such deplorable activity, said Muhammad, is "a great sin" (cf. 2 Kings 8:12; 15:16; Ps 137:8-9; Hos 13:16; Amos 1:13; Nah 3:10).

17.32 The sixth meritorious activity was *sexual purity*; that is, the avoidance of the sin of fornication. Such activity, said Muhammad, is "an abomination" (cf. Ex 20:14; Lev 18:20; 20:10; Prov 2:15-18; 6:24-35; 7:18-27; Jer 5:8-9; 29:22-23; Mal 3:5; Matt 5:27-28; Mk 10:11-12; Eph 5:3-5; Heb 13:4).

17.33 The seventh meritorious activity was *the refusal to commit murder* "except for just cause." One such just cause is kinsman vengeance (provided that it is based upon a legal death sentence). Another form of legitimate killing, though not mentioned in this verse, is the participation in Jihad (see Q

5.32; 22.38-48; *Jihad* on pp. 616-622; and *Saving One Life* on pp. 725-726). The Bible also prohibits murder (see Gen 9:5-6; Ex 20:13; 21:14, 20; 21:29; Lev 24:21; Num 35:16-34; Deut 5:17; 19:11-13; Prov 1:11-18; Jer 26:15; 1 Jn 3:12-15).

17.34 The eighth meritorious activity was *the care for the needs of orphans* (cf. Job 29:12-13; Ps 68:5; Isa 1:16-18; 1 Jn 3:17-19).

17.35 The ninth meritorious activity was *honesty in commercial transactions*. In other words, the avoidance of false balances (cf. Lev 19:35-36; Deut 25:13-15; Prov 11:1; 16:11; 20:10, 23; Ezek 45:10; Hos 12:7; Amos 8:5; Mic 6:11).

17.36 The tenth meritorious activity is *the avoidance of slander, gossip, and the giving of false testimony* (cf. Gen 20:16; Lev 19:16; Ps 15:3; 101:5-7; Prov 10:18; James 4:11).

17.37 The eleventh meritorious activity was to *walk humbly upon the earth* (cf. Isa 57:15; 66:2; Mic 6:8; Matt 5:3; Lk 18:13-17; James 4:6-10; 1 Pet 5:5-6).

earth, and thou shalt not reach the mountains in height.

38   All this is ever evil in the sight of your Lord and abhorred.

Polytheism

39   That is something of what thy Lord has inspired thee with of wisdom; do not then put with God other gods, or thou wilt be thrown into hell reproached and outcast.

40   What! has your Lord chosen to give you sons, and shall He take for Himself females from among the angels? verily, ye are speaking a mighty speech.

41   Now have we turned it in various ways in this Qur'ân, so let them bear in mind; but it will only increase them in aversion.

42   Say, "Were there with Him other gods, as ye say, then would they seek a way against the Lord of the throne."

43   Celebrated be His praises, and exalted be He above what they say with a great exaltation!

44   The seven heavens and the earth celebrate His praises, and all who therein are; nor is there aught but what celebrates His praise: but ye cannot understand their celebration;—verily, He is clement and forgiving.

The veil over hearts

45   And when thou readest the Qur'ân we place between thee and those who believe not in the hereafter a covering veil.

46   And we place covers upon their hearts, lest they should understand, and dulness in their ears. And when thou dost mention in the Qur'ân thy Lord by Himself they turn their backs in aversion.

47   We know best for what they listen when they listen to thee; and when

17.38 This is a summary statement that encompasses the previous sixteen verses (vv. 22-37), the road that leads to eternal life. It would later be codified and become part of Shari'a Law: mandatory requirements of Muslim life. The Judeo-Christian worldview also has its defining characteristics of that which characterizes holiness. The Ten Commandments (Ex 20:1-17) reduced them to ten, the Book of Malachi (Mal 6:8) reduced them to three, and Jesus reduced them to two (Matt 22:37-40). Yet, unlike Islam, within the Judeo-Christian worldview salvation is not earned through meritorious activity (see **The Last Judgment** on pp. 46-

50).

17.39-44 Again, Muhammad addressed the Arabic Star Family religious system, claiming that all who embrace this religion will "be thrown into hell" (see **Polytheism in Seventh Century Arabia** on pp. 92-97).

17.45-46 The reason infidels reject the message of the Qur'an is because Allah has placed a veil upon their hearts and a dullness in their ears (see **The Doctrine of al-Qadar** on pp. 264-266).

17.47 Muhammad asserted that the Meccan people accused him of being "a man enchanted"—that is, crazy (also see Q 7.184; 26.27; 44.14; 51.52; 52.29; 68.2, 51).

they whisper apart—when the wrongdoers say, "Ye only follow a man enchanted."

48 Behold, how they strike out for you parables, and err, and cannot find the way!

49 They say, "What! when we have become bones and rubbish are we to be raised up a new creature?"

50 Say, "Be ye stones, or iron,

51 or a creature, the greatest your breasts can conceive—!" Then they shall say, "Who is to restore us?" Say, "He who originated you at first;" and they will wag their heads and say, "When will that be?" Say, "It may, perhaps, be nigh."

52 The day when He shall call on you and ye shall answer with praise to Him, and they will think that they have tarried but a little.

Double predestination

53 And say to my servants that they speak in a kind way; verily, Satan makes ill-will between them; verily, Satan was ever unto man an open foe.

54 Your Lord knows you best; if He please He will have mercy upon you, or if He please He will torment you: but we have not sent thee to take charge of them.

55 And thy Lord best knows who is in the heavens and the earth; we did prefer some of the prophets over the others, and to David did we give the Psalms.

Idolatry

56 Say, "Call on those whom ye pretend other than God;" but they shall not have the power to remove distress from you, nor to turn it off.

57 Those on whom they call, seek themselves for a means of ap-

17.48 According to Muhammad, an inability to rightly interpret Allah's parables is evidence of the veil that Allah has placed over one's eyes.

17.51 Muhammad admitted that he did not know the date of the general resurrection of the dead, commenting: "It may, perhaps, be nigh (near)."

17.54 *If He please...* — According to Muhammad, salvation was always dependent upon the prior sovereign choosing of Allah. Those whom He chose to show mercy would be saved. Those whom He chose to torment would be cast into Hell (see **The Doctrine of al-Qadar** on pp. 264-266).

17.55 *and to David did we give the Psalms*

— Muhammad recognized the Old Testament psalms to be divinely inspired. Curiously, the psalms speak prophetically of Jesus Christ as the Savior, the Son, and the King. He was crucified and rose from the dead (see Ps 2:7; 16:8-10; 22:1-21; 45:6-7; 68:18; 96:13; 110:1-4).

17.56-57 Muhammad chided his opponents to call upon their gods to remove distress from their lives. He also chided them to compare their gods with Allah. He was convinced that the pagan gods had no power to save from the distress or eternal condemnation.

17.58-59 Muhammad claimed that the eternal Book in Paradise states that Allah will bring judgment upon each and every city ("be-

proaching their Lord, (to see) which of them is nearest: and they hope for His mercy and they fear His torment; verily, the torment of thy Lord is a thing to beware of.

The Lord's judgment
on idolators

58 There is no city but we will destroy it before the day of judgment, or torment it with keen torment;— that is in the Book inscribed.

59 Naught hindered us from sending thee with signs, save that those of yore said they were lies; so we gave Thamûd the visible she-camel, but they treated her unjustly! for we do not send (any one) with signs save to make men fear.

60 And when we said to thee, "Verily, thy Lord encompasses men!" and we made the vision which we showed thee only a cause of sedition unto men, and the cursed tree as well; for we will frighten them, but it will only increase them in great rebellion.

Satan's fall into sin

61 And when we said to the angels "Adore Adam;" and they adored, save Iblîs, who said, "Am I to adore one whom Thou hast created out of clay?"

62 Said he, "Dost thou see now? this one whom Thou hast honoured above me, verily, if Thou shouldst respite me until the resurrection day, I will of a surety utterly de-

fore the day of judgment") that has fallen into the sin of idolatry. The divine judgment that befell Thamud is a case in point (see Q 91, note).

17.60a *thy Lord encompasses men!* — That is, Allah surrounds people with the intent of destroying them.

17.60b *only a cause of sedition* — That is, divine revelation causes people to rebel further against Allah.

17.60c *the cursed tree* — That is, the cursed tree of Zaqqum. This is a mythical tree that exists in Hell. Its fruit is the food of sinners. It is poisonous and likened to the taste of boiling oil (see Q 37.62, 44.43 and 56.52).

17.61-64 According to this passage, Allah commanded the angels in Paradise to adore Adam. All did so, except Satan (Iblis), who

had contempt for a creature made from clay. Allah responded by banishing Satan from his sight, along with his followers (the fallen angels). Allah then empowered Satan to deceive people with false promises that would drive them to unbelief (see Q 7.16-18; 15.26-40; 38.71-85).

The Bible presents a different understanding of the fall of Satan into sin. Rather than disobeying God by refusing to adore Adam, Lucifer sought to become "like the Most High" (Isa 14:14). Some Christian theologians believe that it was at this time that a third of the angels in Heaven sided with Lucifer in this revolt against God (see Rev 12:4). God was victorious over the rebellion and banished Satan and his followers from the ranks of angels. Henceforth, Lucifer was called Satan and his followers were called

63 Said He, "Begone! and whoso of them follows thee—verily, hell is your recompense, an ample recompense.

64 Entice away whomsoever of them thou canst with thy voice; and bear down upon them with thy horse and with thy foot; and share with them in their wealth and their children; and promise them, but Satan promises them naught but deceit.

65 Verily, my servants, thou hast no authority over them; thy Lord is guardian enough over them!"

The sin of ungratefulness

66 It is your Lord who drives the ships for you in the sea that ye may seek after plenty from Him; verily, He is ever merciful to you.

67 And when distress touches you in the sea, those whom ye call on, except Him, stray away from you; but when He has brought you safe to shore, ye turn away; for man is ever ungrateful.

68 Are ye sure that He will not cleave with you the side of the shore, or send against you a heavy sandstorm? then ye will find no guardian for yourselves.

69 Or are ye sure that He will not send you back therein another time, and send against you a violent wind, and drown you for your misbelief? then ye will find for yourselves no protector against us.

Last Judgment

70 But we have been gracious to the children of Adam, and we have borne them by land and sea, and have provided them with good things, and have preferred them over many that we have created.

71 The day when we will call all men by their high priest; and he whose book is given in his right hand— these shall read their book, nor shall they be wronged a straw.

72 But he who in this life is blind shall be blind in the next too, and err

---

fallen angels—or demons. This event took place prior to the creation of Adam (see Isa 14:12-17 and Ezek 28:12-19).

17.66-69 In this passage, Muhammad argued against the sin of ungratefulness. He drew on an illustration of a storm at sea. In such an event, the gods commonly worshipped by the pagans are set aside. The people intuitively turn to the one true God, Allah, for help. Yet, once on shore, the people turn away, "ever ungrateful." Allah would respond to such ungratefulness by not assisting such individuals when a new problem entered their lives. Muhammad's point was that ungratefulness has consequences. Because of the infidels penchant for worshipping gods rather than the one true God, they will experience no protection from Allah in times of need (see Q 16.54-56).

17.73-77 The point of this passage is that Allah does not extend favoritism to his prophets. Had Muhammad come close to straying

farther from the way.

*God's attitude
towards prophets*

73   They had well-nigh beguiled thee
      from what we inspired thee with,
      that thou shouldst forge against us
      something else, and then they
      would have taken thee for a friend;
74   and had it not been that we
      stablished thee, thou wouldst have
      well-nigh leant towards them a
      little:
75   then would we have made thee taste
      of torment both of life and death,
      then thou wouldst not have found
      against us any helper.
76   And they well-nigh enticed thee

away from the land, to turn thee
out therefrom; but then—they
should not have tarried after thee
except a little.

77   (This is) the course of those of our
      prophets whom we have sent be-
      fore thee; and thou shalt find no
      change in our course.

A call to prayer

78   Be thou steadfast in prayer from
      the declining of the sun until the
      dusk of the night, and the reading
      of the dawn; verily, the reading of
      the dawn is ever testified to.
79   And for the night, watch thou
      therein as an extra service. It may
      be that thy Lord will raise thee to a

away from Allah and wrote/spoke something false about Allah, Allah would have responded by condemning him to "taste of torment both of life and death" (v. 75).

17.73 *well-nigh beguiled thee* — Muhammad noted an event that well-nigh beguiled him into apostasy. He did not specify, however, the event in question. One possibility is the event of the Satanic Verses that some scholars believed took place earlier in his ministry while still in Mecca (see Q 53.19-22 note; also see Q 10.15; 13.37). In his commentary, *The Message of the Qur'an*, Islamic scholar Muhammad Asad alluded to this same episode, yet in a fashion that showed Muhammad faithfully resisting the temptation to yield to Satan. Asad explained that the Meccan leaders demanded that Muhammad give recognition to their deities. If he did so, they promised to recognize him as a prophet and make him their spiritual leader.

Yet, said Asad, Muhammad rejected their offer (p. 479). For a fuller examination of this issue, see **The Satanic Verses Controversy** on pp. 135-137.

17.78a Muhammad believed that he was called to spiritual steadfastness. He was to pray from noon (from the declining of the sun) until midnight (the dusk of the night). Most Islamic scholars do not believe that Muhammad was in a continuous state of prayer during this time. Rather, this was the period of time when the five prescribed prayers took place.

17.78b *the reading of the dawn is ever testified to* — Many Islamic scholars claim that this meant the witness of the angels; others claim that it meant the witness within Muhammad's own soul.

17.79 *watch thou therein as an extra service* — In the early hours of the morning (while still night), Muhammad prayed an ad-

laudable station.

80   And say, "O my Lord! make me enter with a just entry; and make me come forth with a just coming forth; and grant me from Thee authority to aid."

81   And say, "Truth has come, and falsehood has vanished! verily, falsehood is transient."

82   And we will send down of the Qur'ân that which is a healing and a mercy to the believers, but it will only increase the wrong-doers in loss.

83   And when we favour man he turns away and retires aside, but when evil touches him he is ever in despair.

84   Say, "Every one acts after his own manner, but your Lord knows best who is most guided in the way."

The nature of divine revelation

85   They will ask thee of the spirit. Say, "The spirit comes at the bidding of my Lord, and ye are given but a little knowledge thereof."

86   If we had wished we would have taken away that with which we have inspired thee; then thou wouldst have found no guardian against us,

87   unless by a mercy from thy Lord; verily, His grace towards thee is great!

88   Say, "If mankind and ginns united together to bring the like of this Qur'ân, they could not bring the like, though they should back each other up!"

89   We have turned about for men in

ditional sixth prayer. During his sixth prayer, Muhammad recited the words mentioned in these two verses.

17.82 According to this passage, a knowledge of the Qur'an will cause those who are destined to righteousness to be righteous and those destined to unrighteousness to continue in their unrighteousness (see **The Doctrine of al-Qadar** on pp. 264-266).

17.85-100 Muhammad carried a supposed conversation with the infidels regarding the nature of divine revelation. His point was that no matter how compelling the words and no matter what miracles accompanied them, infidels would always have their reasons to remain in unbelief (see Isa 6:9-13).

17.85 *they will ask thee of the spirit* — That is, they will ask you of divine revelation (the *spirit*, according to Islam, is the *spirit* of

revelation). The concept of a divine spirit is not to be confused with the Christian concept of the Holy Spirit—the Third Person of the Trinity.

17.86-87 Whether or not a person is a recipient of divine revelation is a question of the sovereign choosing of Allah. Allah owes no man anything.

17.88 According to this verse, the Qur'an itself is a miracle document and attests to its own divine origin. This is based on the notion that no person or genie (ginn) could have written such a document. In this respect, the Qur'an is self-authenticated. It needs no additional credentials. Decades later, in the late seventh century, this argument of self-authentication would be used to counter John of Damascus' critique of the Qur'an—that it lacked divine credentials or

The Night Journey

The Night Journey is briefly mentioned in the Qur'an in the beginning of the seventeenth surah (Q 17.1-2). Among Muslims, it is defined by two words:

- the *Isra* (the trip from Mecca to Temple Mount)
- the *Mi'raj* (the ascent from Temple Mount into Paradise)

Muhammad allegedly took a journey from the Sacred Mosque (the Ka'ba altar) to the Remote Mosque (the Jerusalem Temple). Implied in the account is the notion that Muhammad returned the Mecca the same night. The filling of the details of this event occurred in the hadithic and biographic literature, specifically that of the Muslim historian Ibn Ishaq (*c.* 704-767) in his book *The Life of Muhammad*. Several oral traditions had taken root in the Muslim world that described this alleged supernatural journey.

'Abdullah bin Mas'ud. According to the tradition relayed by 'Abdullah bin Mas'ud, the archangel Gabriel came to Muhammad one night accompanied by a *buraq* (half mule, half donkey, with wings). Muhammad mounted the animal and was miraculously transported to the temple in Jerusalem. When he arrived, he found "Abraham, the friend of God, Moses, and Jesus assembled with a company of the prophets." After a season of prayer, Muhammad was confronted with a test. Three vessels were placed before him: one containing milk, the second wine, and the third water. Muhammad said:

> I heard a voice saying when these were offered to me: If he takes the water he will be drowned and his people also; if he takes the wine he will go astray and his people also; and if he takes the milk he will be rightly guided and his people also. So I took the vessel containing milk and drank it.

Gabriel then said to him: "You have been rightly guided and so will your people be, Muhammad" (*The Life of Muhammad*, p. 182).

Al Hasan. According to the tradition relayed by al Hasan, while sleeping near the Ka-ba altar in Mecca, the archangel Gabriel came to Muhammad and awoke him. Muhammad reportedly said:

> Gabriel came and stirred me with his foot. I sat up but saw nothing and lay down again. He came a second time and stirred me with his foot. I sat up and saw nothing and lay down again. He came to me the third time and stirred me with his foot. I sat up and he took hold of my arm and I stood beside him and he brought me out to the door of the mosque and there was a white animal, half mule, half donkey, with wings on its sides with which it propelled its feet.

The *buraq* transported Muhammad to Jerusalem. There he found Abraham, Moses, Jesus and a company of prophets. Muhammad then took the lead, serving as their imam, and led in prayer. He was then brought two vessels, one with milk and the other with wine. Muhammad drank the wine, whereby Gabriel praised him, saying, "You have been rightly guided to the way of nature...Wine is forbidden you."

Then Muhammad returned to Mecca. The following morning, he told the people of Mecca what had happened the night before. Nobody believed him. Even many of his Muslim followers thought him mad and gave up their faith in him. Seeing a crisis in the making, Abu Bakr—one of Muhammad's close associates—settled the matter with words of faith:

> If he says so then it is true. And what is so surprising in that? He tells me that communications from God from heaven to earth come to him in an hour of a day or night and I believe him, and that is more extraordinary than that at which you boggle!

He then asked Muhammad to describe Jerusalem to him. Hearing Muhammad's words, Bakr concluded that it was an accurate depiction of Jerusalem. He could only have known this information if he had indeed visited Jerusalem the night before. He said: "I testify that you are the apostle of God" (*The Life of Muhammad*, pp. 182-183).

The Hadithic literature. According to the *Sahih Bukhari*, Muhammad settled the dispute in Mecca regarding his alleged Night Journey by standing up in the Al-Hijr (the unroofed portion of the Ka'ba altar) whereupon he described Jerusalem to them in a vision: "When the people of Quraish did not believe me (i.e., the story of the Night Journey), I stood up in the Al-Hijr and Allah displayed Jerusalem in front of me and I began describing it to them while I was looking at it."

Also included in the hadithic literature is a further description of the Night Journey. In the first heaven, he greeted Adam. In the second heaven, he greeted John the Baptist and Jesus. In the third heaven, he greeted Joseph. In the fourth heaven, he greeted Enoch. In the fifth heaven, he greeted Aaron. In the sixth heaven, he greeted Moses. In the seventh heaven, he greeted Abraham. In each case, they returned the greeting, praising Muhammad with the words: "Oh pious son and pious Prophet." Moreover, during his visit in the sixth heaven, Moses wept. "I weep," Moses said, "because after me there has been sent (as Prophet) a young man whose followers will enter Paradise in greater numbers than my followers."

After his greeting of Abraham in the seventh heaven, Muhammad was taken to the Lote Tree, which is the utmost boundary, beyond which was the Sacred House where Allah resided. At the Lote Three he was given three vessels: the first filled with wine, the second filled with milk, and the third filled with honey. He chose the milk. He was then ordered by Allah to tell his Muslim followers to offer fifty prayers a day as a form of worship to Him. When Muhammad told Moses of this command, Moses advised him to appeal the order, asking that it be reduced. Muhammad returned to Allah, first appealing that it be reduced to ten prayers, and then to five. Allah agreed to the reduction. Moses explained to Muhammad that each of the five prayers would be credited as ten, yielding the sum of fifty prayers each day. Moses also explained to Muhammad the way in which good and bad deeds were credited to Muslim followers:

> He who intends to do a good deed and does not do it will have a good deed recorded for him; and if he does it, it will be recorded for him as ten; whereas he who intends to do an evil deed and does not do, it will not be recorded for him; and if he does it, only one evil deed will be recorded.

Following his visit to the seven heavens, Muhammad was then transported back to Mecca (*Sahih Bukhari* 5.58.227 and *Sahih Muslim* 1.309).

It was possibly at his lowest ebb that Muhammad experienced what was arguably the most intense spiritual experience of his life, in which it is said he left his physical body and ascended "into the heavens," where he underwent a series of visionary, psycho-spiritual experiences described in the Koran as an "ascension" (*mi'raj*) or "night journey" (*isra*).

—Colin Turner, *Islam: the Basics*, p. 23

This event is recorded as *Al-Miraj*, in Surah 17.1. It is very important to note that this one verse in the Koran, on which they base Mohammed's heavenly journey, doesn't actually specify whether this journey was literal or visionary. Interpreters are on opposite sides of what this night journey actually meant. Not the least of their challenges is that Mohammed's wife said he was by her side the whole night and never left her physically. Also of consternation to Muslim scholars is that a very similar episode exists in Zoroaster's legend of a heavenly journey, which predates Islam. Textual critics continue to battle over whether this story was borrowed by Islam.

—Ravi Zacharias, *Jesus Among Other Gods*, p. 190

This large mosque on the southwest end of the Temple Mount is by tradition built on the site where Gabriel brought Muhammad to pray on the night he rose to heaven. The original wooden mosque, built by Omar, the general who conquered Jerusalem, was replaced in the early eighth century by Caliph el-Walid. It has been often rebuilt, enlarged, and embellished by succeeding rulers, including a major refurbishing from 1938 to 1943. The ornate wooden pulpit (*minbar*) was a donation of Saladin. The mosque can accommodate four thousand men for prayer.

—Linda Kay Davidson and David Martin Gitlitz, *Pilgrimage*, p. 284

I placed it [the location of Solomon's Temple], not in the center of the original Temple Mount, but over the rock mass lying beneath the Dome of the Rock, generally referred to as es-Sakhra, "the Rock" in Arabic...In the end, the conclusion that this unique depression [on the rock mass] marked the emplacement of the Ark of the Covenant inside the Holy of Holies is inescapable.

—Leen and Kathleen Ritmeyer, *Secrets of Jerusalem's Temple Mount*, pp. 100, 117

Today the Foundation Stone is enshrined in the Dome of the Rock. Known to Muslims as es-Sakhra—"the Rock"—it is revered for its association with the Temple. (On a wall of the Dome is the inscription "The Rock of the Temple—from the Garden of Eden.") It is also revered for its connection with Muhammad and his Night Journey. For it was from this outcropping of bedrock that Muhammad ascended into the heavens. The guide will point out an indentation in the Rock. This is Muhammad's footprint, he avows, left behind as the Prophet—accompanied by the angel Gabriel—leap onto a stairway of light and ascended to Paradise. The guide points out, too, the imprint of Gabriel's fingers. The angel had to restrain the Rock, he explains, which wanted to follow them upwards. And the rock has another indentation, which has caused a stir in archeological circles. For it may be tangible evidence that the Rock served as a pedestal for the Ark of the Covenant.

—*The Book of King Solomon*, p. 241

Dome of the Rock

The Dome of the Rock is located on Temple Mount in Jerusalem and is its most prominent building on that site. Palestine was conquered in 638 by Omar (second caliph). The Dome of the Rock was completed in 691 under the caliphate of Abd al-Malik (the fifth caliph). It constitutes the oldest continuously used building in the world. The dome is technically not a mosque, but a shrine, commemorating the alleged ascent of Muhammad into Paradise. Al-Aqsa Mosque, located several hundred yards south of the Dome of the Rock, is the only mosque situated on Temple Mount.

The Dome of the Rock also possesses a triumphalistic intent, built on the precise location of Solomon's Temple (the First Temple), Herod's Temple (the Second Temple), and the place where Jewish tradition believes that Abraham offered Isaac as a sacrifice. Moreover, inscriptions inside the dome mention Jesus, not as the Son of God—but as Allah's faithful servant.

this Qur'ân every parable; but most men refuse to accept it, save ungratefully.

90 And they say, "We will by no means believe in thee, until there gush forth for thee a fountain from the earth;

91 or there be made for thee a garden of palms and grapes, and rivers come gushing out amidst them;

92 or thou make the sky to fall down upon us in pieces; or thou bring us God and the angels before us;

93 or there be made for thee a house of gold; or thou climb up into the heaven; and even then we will not believe in thy climbing there, until thou send down on us a book that we may read!" Say, "Celebrated be the praises of my Lord! was 1 aught but a mortal apostle?"

94 Naught prohibited men from be-

lieving when the guidance came to them, save their saying, "God has sent a mortal for an apostle."

95 Say, "Were there angels on the earth walking in quiet, we had surely sent them an angel as an apostle."

96 Say, "God is witness enough between me and you; verily, He is ever of His servants well aware, and sees."

97 He whom God guides, he is guided indeed; and he whom God leads astray, thou shalt never find patrons for them beside Him; and we will gather them upon the resurrection day upon their faces, blind, and dumb, and deaf; their resort is hell; whenever it grows dull we will give them another blaze!

98 That is their reward for that they disbelieved in our signs, and said, "What! when we are bones and

the anticipation from previous prophets (see Q 10.38, note; **John of Damascus** on pp. 247-248).

In contrast, Christian scholars make the case that the Bible is both self-authenticating and outwardly authenticated. Its self-authentication comes via the Holy Spirit who speaks to the heart of the individual and makes the case that it is indeed the Word of God (1 Cor 2:9-16). Its outward authentication comes via four forms of evidence: (a) miracles that accompanied the it during the time of its writing, (b) archeological evidence that has supported its claims, (c) the historical accuracy of the content of the Bible, and (d) the changed lives of its devotees that manifest grace and love (see Q 6.19 note).

17.89 *every parable* — That is, every spiritual lesson.

17.90-95 Muhammad's point is that even if miracles accompanied the surahs that he had been reciting to the infidels at the Ka'ba altar, they would remain steadfast in their unbelief (see Q 6.35-39; 10.19-20a, 15.6-7; 21.1-5, and **John of Damascus** on pp. 247-248).

17.96-97 Again, Muhammad presented the sovereignty of Allah (the doctrine double predestination) in connection to illumination of divine revelation. Infidels, he explained, are spiritually blind, dumb, and deaf because Allah willed that they be so (see **The Doctrine of al-Qadar** on pp. 264-266).

17.98-99 Again, Muhammad noted that the infidels of Mecca disbelieved in the res-

rubbish, shall we then be raised up a new creation?"

99   Could they not see that God who created the heavens and the earth is able to create the like of them, and to set for them an appointed time; there is no doubt therein, yet the wrong-doers refuse to accept it, save ungratefully!

100   Say, "Did ye control the treasuries of the mercy of my Lord, then ye would hold them through fear of expending; for man is ever niggardly!"

Moses and Pharaoh

101   And we did bring Moses nine manifest signs; then ask the children of Israel (about) when he came to them, and Pharaoh said to him, "Verily, I think thee, O Moses! enchanted."

102   He said, "Well didst thou know that none sent down these save the Lord of the heavens and the earth as visible signs; and, verily, I think thee, O Pharaoh! ruined."

103   And he desired to drive them out of the land; but we drowned him and those with him, one and all.

104   And after him we said to the children of Israel, "Dwell ye in the land; and when the promise of the hereafter comes to pass, we will bring you in a mixed crowd (to judgment)."

Conclusion

105   In truth have we sent it down, and in truth has it come down; and we have not sent thee as aught but a herald of glad tidings and a warner.

106   And a Qur'ân which we have divided, that thou mayst read it to

---

urrection from the dead.

17.100 Muhammad's point is that man, by his nature, is materialistic—dependent upon wealth and possessions. As he put it, "man is ever niggardly." This attitude is in contrast to Allah, who is self-sufficient and generous with all that He has.

17.101-104 In this passage, Muhammad returned to a familiar story: the confrontation between Moses and Pharaoh. Yet this passage contains two variances from the biblical record. First, Book of Exodus comments on ten "mighty acts of judgment" (Ex 7:4), not "nine manifest signs" as it is presented in this surah (see Q 27.12-13 where the same variance is repeated). Second, in the book of Exodus comments that Pharaoh's army

was drowned in the Red (Reed) Sea (Ex 15:19)—Pharaoh, however, survived. Yet, Muhammad noted that both Pharaoh and his army drowned (v. 103). See **How Many Plagues Were There?** on p. 565.

17.105-111 Muhammad ended the surah with a reiteration of four fundamental insights: (a) the Qur'an is a divinely inspired document that Allah sent down to the earth as a warning to all peoples, (b) the sovereign will of Allah will determine who will believe and who will not believe in this message, (c) Muslims are to offer their prayers with humility—in a manner that is neither overly public nor overly private, and (d) Allah has not taken to himself a Son. These four points condemned the Star Family religious system that domi-

mankind leisurely, and we sent it down, sending it down."

107 Say, "Believe ye therein, or believe not; verily, those who were given the knowledge before it, when it is read to them fall down upon their beards adoring!

108 and they say, 'Celebrated be the praises of our Lord! verily, the promise of our Lord is ever fulfilled'

109 —they fall down upon their beards weeping, and it increases their humility."

110 Say, "Call on God, or call on the Merciful One, whichever ye may call on Him by for His are the best of names." And do not say thy prayers openly, nor yet murmur them, but seek a way between these.

111 And say, "Praise belongs to God, who has not taken to Himself a son, and has not had a partner in His kingdom, nor had a patron against (such) abasement." And magnify Him greatly!

Surah 16

In the name of the merciful and compassionate God.

Sovereign power of God

1 God's bidding will come; seek not then to hasten it on. Celebrated be His praises from what they join with Him!

2 He sends down the angels with the Spirit at His bidding upon whom He will of His servants (to say), "Give warning that there is no god but Me; Me therefore do ye fear."

3 He created the heavens and the earth in truth! Exalted be He above that which they join with Him

---

nated the Arabian Peninsula in the seventh century (see **Polytheism in Seventh Century Arabia** on pp. 92-97).

Surah 16. The title of this surah, *The Bee*, comes from verse 68. Discouragement had begun to develop within the nascent Muslim community, evidenced by some turning away from the Islamic faith and back to their previously held beliefs. Muhammad attempted to combat this discouragement by strengthening the faith of his followers with two familiar themes: (a) righteousness versus unrighteousness, and (b) a vivid reminder of the Last Judgment and events that will transpire at that judgment. Muhammad said, "God's bidding will come" (v. 1). Since he believed this to be true, the only rational response was submission to Allah and a patient awaiting for His blessings.

16.1 *God's bidding will come* — That is, the will of Allah cannot be stopped.

16.2 *with the Spirit* — That is, Allah endows the angels (specifically, Gabriel) with divine inspiration (see Q 17.85, note). Hence, the term "Spirit" is not to be confused with the term "Holy Spirit," the Second Person of the Trinity, as understood in Christian theology (see Q 16.102, note).

16.3 Allah is exalted above all the gods that the Meccan people worshipped (see **Polytheism in Seventh Century Arabia** on pp. 92-97).

4   He created man from a clot; and yet, behold, he is an open opponent!

5   The cattle too have we created for you; in them is warmth and profit, and from them do ye eat.

6   In them is there beauty for you when ye drive them home to rest, and when ye drive them forth to graze.

7   And they bear your heavy burdens to towns which ye could not otherwise reach, except with great wretchedness of soul;—verily, your Lord is kind and merciful.

8   And horses too, and mules, and asses, for you to ride upon and for an ornament.—He creates also what ye know not of.

9   God's it is to show the path; from it some turn aside: but had He pleased He would have guided you one and all.

10   He it is who sends down water from the sky, whence ye have drink, and whence the trees grow whereby ye feed your flocks.

11   He makes the corn to grow, and the olives, and the palms, and the grapes, and some of every fruit;— verily, in that is a sign unto a people who reflect.

12   And He subjected to you the night and the day, and the sun, and the moon, and the stars are subjected to His bidding. Verily, in that are signs to a people who have sense.

13   And what He has produced for you in the earth varying in hue, verily, in that is a sign for a people who are mindful.

14   He it is who has subjected the sea, that ye may eat fresh flesh therefrom; and ye bring forth from it ornaments which ye wear,—and thou mayest see the ships cleaving through it,—and that ye may search after His grace,—and haply

16.4a *He created man from a clot* — See Q 96.2, note.

16.4b *behold, he is an open opponent* — That is, in spite of the rich blessings of Allah in having created man, the infidel is now an open opponent—evidence of ingratitude.

16.5-7 Cows were used in seventh century Arabian culture as beasts of burden, leather for clothing, meat for food, and overall financial profit.

16.8 *and for an ornament* — That is, for public display and as a recognition of personal wealth. The more horses, mules and asses a person owned, the more ornate and attractive he appeared in the eyes of his fellow man.

16.9 *God's it is to show the path* — It is ultimately Allah who enables a person to become a person of faith. This is a reference, once again, to the doctrine of double predestination (see **Doctrine of al-Qadar** on pp. 264-266).

16.10-16 Muhammad believed that the entire universe operates in harmony with the will of Allah. In this passage, His will includes the activity of (a) rain, (b) corn, (c) olives, (d) palms, (e) grapes, (f) night and day, (g) sea, (h) mountains, (i) rivers, (j) roads, and (k) stars. As mentioned earlier (v. 9), faith in Allah is foreordained.

16.14 *search after His grace* — That is, search after the many blessings of Allah.

ye may give thanks.

15   And He has cast firm mountains on the earth lest it move with you; and rivers and roads; haply ye may be guided.

16   And landmarks; and by the stars too are they guided.

17   Is He who creates like him who creates not?—are they then unmindful?

18   But if ye would number the favours of God, ye cannot count them. Verily, God is forgiving; merciful.

Polytheism

19   God knows what ye keep secret, and what ye disclose.

20   And those on whom ye call beside God cannot create anything, for they are themselves created.

21   Dead, not living, nor can they perceive! When shall they be raised?

22   Your God is one God, and those who believe not in the hereafter their hearts are given to denial, and they are big with pride!

23   Without a doubt God knows what ye keep secret and what ye, disclose! Verily, He does not love those big with pride!

24   And when it is said to them, "What is it that your Lord has sent down?" they say, "Old folks' tales!"

25   Let them bear the burden of their sins entirely on the resurrection day, and some of the burdens of those whom they led astray without knowledge.—Aye! an ill burden shall they bear.

26   Those who were before them devised a stratagem, but God brought their building off its foundations, and the roof fell over them, and the torment came to them, from

16.19-21 Since Allah is omniscient, He knows all who have fallen into idolatry—the worship of false gods. These gods are, said Muhammad, "dead, not living, nor can their perceive" (cf. Deut 4:28; Ps 135:15-18; Jer 10:5, 14; 1 Cor 8:4; 12:2).

16.22-24 The remedy to the sin of *shirk* (idolatry) is a belief in monotheism. Because of this, Muhammad presented, once again, the Doctrine of Tauhid (see Q 112). Yet, the polytheists of Mecca insisted that this doctrine was nothing more than "old folks' tales" handed down by their forefathers (see Q 6.25; 23.83; 25.5; 26.137; 27.68; 46.17; 68.15; 83.13).

16.25 According to this verse, teachers of

false theology will face a stiffer judgment at the Last Day than will those of the students. They will bear their own burdens entirely plus "some of the burdens of those whom they led astray." The New Testament makes a similar observation: "Not many of you should presume to be teachers, my brothers, because you know that we who teach will be judged more strictly" (James 3:1; cf. Matt 23.13-14).

16.26 *brought the building off its foundation* — To make his point, Muhammad spoke of the judgment Allah brought upon the Philistines during the ministry of Samson (Jud 16:25-30). Similarly, just as the Philistines were committed to idolatry, so too were the

whence they could not perceive.

27   Then on the resurrection day He will put them to shame, and say, "Where are your associates whom ye divided into parties about?" Those to whom knowledge is brought will say, "Verily, disgrace today, and evil are upon the misbelievers!"

28   Those whom the angels took away were wronging themselves; then they offered peace: "We have done no evil."—"Yea! verily, God knows what ye did.

29   Wherefore enter ye the doors of hell, to dwell therein for aye; for ill is the resort of the proud."

Paradise

30   And it will be said to those who

fear God, "What is it that your Lord has sent down?" They will say, "The best," for those who do good, good in this world; but certainly the abode of the next is best, and surely pleasant is the abode of those who fear.

31   Gardens of Eden which they shall enter, beneath them rivers flow; therein shall they have what they please;—thus does God reward those who fear Him.

32   To those whom the angels take off in a goodly state they shall say, "Peace be upon you! enter ye into Paradise for that which ye have done."

Double predestination

33   Do they expect other than that the

Meccan people. They used the Ka'ba altar as a centerpiece of their idolatrous worship. In addition, the altar generated the side benefit of an economic boom for the city since pilgrims came to Mecca in religious pilgrimages. Just as Samson knocked down the Philistine altar, Muhammad believed that Allah would eventually knock the Ka'ba altar off its foundation and cause the roof to fall down on at the time that "they could not perceive."

Accordingly, this verse was an anticipation of the time when Muhammad would leave Mecca, initiate a Holy War (Jihad) against Mecca, and conquer it. Muhammad conquered Mecca in 630. At that time, he decapitated many of the Meccan leaders as divine retribution for their pagan beliefs. He did not, however, destroy the Ka'ba altar.

16.27 In addition to the judgment that will befall people in this life, in the afterlife—at the Last Judgment—an additional judgment will take place. After being mocked for the sins that they committed while on earth, they will enter into "the doors of hell" (v. 29).

16.31 *Garden of Eden* — That is, the gardens in Paradise (also see Q 18.31; 19.61; 20.76; 35.33; 38.50; 40.8).

16.32 According to Muhammad, these words of blessing are pronounced by angels to those who successfully pass through the Last Judgment. The New Testament has a similar rejoinder spoken by God Himself to those who enter Heaven: "Come and share your master's happiness!" (Matt 25:21, 23). See **Paradise** on pp. 76-77 for a further description and contrasts between the Islamic and Christian visions of Heaven.

angels should come to take them off, or that thy Lord's bidding should come?—thus did those before them; God did not wrong them; but it was themselves they wronged.

34 And the evil which they had done befell them, and that environed them at which they used to mock!

35 And those who associated (others with God) said, "Had God pleased we had not served aught beside Him, neither we nor our fathers; nor had we prohibited aught without Him;"—thus did those before them: but have messengers aught to do but to deliver their message plainly?

36 We have sent in every nation an apostle (to say), "Serve ye God, and avoid Tâghût!" and amongst them are some whom God has guided, and amongst them are

some for whom error is due;—go ye about then on the earth, and behold how was the end of those who called (the apostles) liars!

37 If thou art ever so eager for their guidance, verily, God guides not those who go astray, nor have they any helpers.

*General resurrection
from the dead*

38 They swear by their most strenuous oath, "God will not raise up him who dies."—Yea! a promise binding on him true!—but most men do not know.

39 To explain to them that which they disputed about, and that those who misbelieved may know that they are liars.

40 We only say unto a thing we wish, "BE," and it is.

16.33 *God did not wrong them; but it was themselves they wronged* — That is, people are culpable for their own sin. This is a phrase that occurs repeatedly in the Qur'an (cf. Q 10.44; 11.101; 16.118; 30.9 and 43.76).

16.35 *And those who associated (others with God)* — That is, the idolaters. The polytheists used the doctrine of double predestination against Muhammad. They placed the blame directly upon Allah for their unwillingness to embrace Muhammad's message. They said: "Had God pleased we had not served aught [other gods] beside Him, neither we nor our fathers; nor had we prohibited aught without Him" (see **The Doctrine of al-Qadar** on pp. 264-266).

16.36a *Taghut* — This is an Arabic word that means *idolatry* and *religious impurity*. Anyone who claims to be holy outside of Islam's definition of holiness is *Taghut* (see Q 39.17).

16.36b-37 Muhammad again attempted an answer to those who resisted his message on the grounds of double predestination (the Doctrine of al-Qadar). He explained that the apostles were sent to all the peoples of the world proclaiming the right beliefs about Allah and eternal life. Hence, they all were given opportunity to believe (see **The Apostles** on pp. 398-400).

16.38-40 Muhammad insisted that polytheists did not believe in a general resurrection. It is a categorical denial of Allah's ulti-

The blessings of God

41   But those who fled for God's sake, after they were wronged, we will surely establish them in this world with good things; but the hire of the future life is greater, if ye did but know.

42   Those who are patient, and upon their Lord rely!

God's apostles

43   And we have not sent before thee any but men whom we inspire,— ask ye those who have the Reminder, if ye know not yourselves,—with manifest signs and with scriptures;

44   and we have sent down the Re-minder to thee too, that thou mayest explain to men what has been sent down to them, and haply they may reflect.

45   Are those who were so crafty in evil sure that God will not cleave open the earth with them, or bring them torment from whence they cannot perceive,

46   or seize them in their going to and fro? for they cannot make Him helpless.

47   Or that He should seize them with a gradual destruction? for, verily, your Lord is kind, merciful.

Nature of holiness

48   Do they not regard whatever thing God has created; its shadow falls

---

mate judgment of good and evil.

16.40 *"BE"* — Allah's sovereignty over all creation is illustrated in the fact that all He needs to do is say one word—*be*—and whatever it is He wishes comes into existence (see Q 3.47, 59; 19.35; 36.82; 40.68).

16.41-42 The blessings of Allah are promised for the faithful in both this life and the afterlife, though the blessings of the afterlife are far greater.

16.43 Muhammad believed that every apostle ordained by Allah to serve as a warner has been endowed with both "manifest signs" and "scriptures." Manifest signs meant *miracles* (see Q 40.34 where "manifest signs" meant the ability to accurately prophecy the future, and Q 20.72 where "manifest signs" meant the ability to perform magic). The term "scriptures" meant *divinely inspired writings:* either portions of divine writ or the entire eternal book.

This observation poses two problems for Islam. First, both the Old and New Testaments are part of these "manifest signs" and "scriptures" (see Q 10.94); yet, they contain numerous teachings that contradict teachings found in the Qur'an. Second, repeatedly the Qur'an notes that Muhammad did not perform miracles (see **John of Damascus** on pp. 247-248).

16.44 According to this verse, Muhammad is described as having received the Reminder (scripture) but not the manifest signs (miracles).

16.45-47 The crafty and evil people were convinced that divine judgment would never befall them.

16.48-53 In this passage, Muhammad defined the nature of holiness: (a) the genuine worship of Allah, (b) spiritual humility, (c)

on the right or the left, adoring God and shrinking up?

49 Whatever is in the heavens and in the earth, beast or angel. adores God; nor are they big with pride!

50 They fear their Lord above them, and they do what they are bidden.

51 And God says, "Take not to two gods; God is only one; me then do ye fear!"

52 His is what is in the heavens and in the earth; to Him is obedience due unceasingly; other than God then will ye fear?

53 And whatever favours ye have, they are from God; then, whenever distress touches you, unto Him ye turn for succour.

Sin of apostasy

54 Yet, when He removes the distress from you, lo! a party of you join

partners with their Lord.

55 That they may disbelieve in what we have brought them and may enjoy,—but at length they shall know!

56 And they set aside for what they know not a portion of what we have bestowed upon them.—By God! ye shall be questioned concerning that which ye have devised.

Sin of infanticide

57 They make for God daughters;—celebrated be His praise!—and for themselves they like them not.

58 When any one of them has tidings of a female child, his face is overclouded and black, and he has to keep back his wrath.

59 He skulks away from the people, for the evil tidings he has heard;—

obedience to the will of Allah, (d) a rejection of the sin of Shirk—polytheism, (e) thankfulness for the blessings of Allah, and (f) a propensity to turn to Allah for succor when distress touches them.

16.54-56 Muhammad observed that some Muslims turned to Allah in times of distress, yet turned away from Allah and to one of the gods worshipped by the polytheists when the times of distress were removed (see Q 17.66-69). Muhammad warned them: "At length they shall know!" At the time of the Last Judgment, they "shall be questioned" concerning that which they had devised.

Later in the Qur'an, Muhammad added that faithful Muslims were called upon to exact divine judgment upon apostates by killing

them (see Q 9.73; 66.9; **The Doctrine of Abrogation** on pp. 68-70).

The Christian faith also addresses the sin of apostasy. The New Testament makes the point, however, that those who apostasize (turn away) from the faith were never genuine believers in the first place. "They went out from us, but they did not really belong to us. For if they had belonged to us, they would have remained with us; but their going showed that none of them belonged to us" (1 Jn 2:19). Unlike Islam, Christians were never admonished to exact divine retribution on apostates by killing them, as was the case with those who apostasized from the Muslim faith.

16.59 *bury it in the dust* — A custom of

is he to keep it with its disgrace, or to bury it in the dust?—aye! evil is it that they judge!

Nature of evil

60   For those who disbelieve in the future life is a similitude of evil: but for God is the loftiest similitude; for He is the mighty, the wise!

61   If God were to punish men for their wrong-doing He would not leave upon the earth a single beast; but He respites them until a stated time; and when their time comes they cannot put it off an hour, nor can they bring it on.

62   They set down to God what they abhor themselves; and their tongues describe the lie that "good is to be theirs." Without a doubt theirs is the Fire, for, verily, they shall be sent on there!

63   By God! we sent (messengers) to nations before thee, but Satan made their works seemly to them, for he is their patron today, and for them is grievous woe!

---

seventh century Arabia was the infanticide of newly born baby girls. In a culture where older people relied upon the provisions of their grown offspring to care for their material needs, boys were more prized than girls. This is because boys, when married, remained part of the immediate family clan and contributed to the material wealth.

Muhammad spoke against this custom. He explained that men struggled with anger and sulked at the knowledge that their newborn child was a girl. They considered such news as "evil tidings" (v. 59a). Consequently, that which some of these fathers had done was to bury their newborn girls "in the dust" (v 59b). Also see Q 6.137, 140; and 81.8 where the sin of infanticide is again mentioned. Muhammad condemned this practice: "aye! evil is it that they judge!"

Though the practice of elective abortions is not mentioned in this verse, according to mainstream Islam, it is implied. Hence, elective abortions too are forbidden.

16.60 *He is the mighty, the wise!* — This is one of Muhammad's favorite descriptions of Allah (see Q 14.4; 30.27; 35.2; 45.37). Ac-

cording to Muhammad, fundamental to the nature of evil is a disbelief that a Last Judgment is coming where all the accounts of all the good and evil in the world will be settled.

16.62 *They set down to God what they abhor themselves* — That is, they are blasphemers. They claim that it is because of Allah that a wide host of activities that they abhor has entered their lives. They also believe that they will be blessed by cursing Allah. Without a doubt, said Muhammad, their eternal destiny is the Fire.

16.63 Muhammad maintained that Satan is the great deceiver. He has made the infidel's own works appear "seemly to them." That is, Satan has confused their minds causing them to think their bad works were good works.

The New Testament makes a similar observation about Satan. He is called "the father of lies" (Jn 8:44), "the enemy of everything that is right" (Acts 13:10), "cunning" (2 Cor 11:3), one who "masquerades as an angel of light" (2 Cor 11:14), and the one "who leads the whole world astray" (Rev 12:9), and the one "who is now at work in

Allah's manifold blessings

64 We have only sent down to thee the Book that thou mayest explain to them that which they did dispute about, and as a guidance and a mercy to a people who believe.

65 And God sends down water from the sky, and quickens therewith the earth after its death; verily, in that is a sign to a people who can hear.

66 Verily, ye have in cattle a lesson; we give you to drink from that which is in their bellies, betwixt chyme and blood, pure milk,— easy to swallow for those who drink.

67 And of the fruit of the palms and the grapes ye take therefrom an intoxicant and a goodly provision; verily, in that is a sign to a people who have sense!

68 And thy Lord inspired the bee, "Take to houses in the mountains, and in the trees, and in the hives they build.

69 Then eat from every fruit, and walk in the beaten paths of thy Lord;" there cometh forth from her body a draught varying in hue, in which is a cure for men; verily, in that are signs unto a people who re-

those who are disobedient" (Eph 2:2).

16.64-69 According to Muhammad, within the eternal Book is a presentation of the blessings that Allah has given to people on earth: (a) rain, (b) milk from cows, (c) fruit from palms—dates, (d) wine, and (e) honey.

16.67 *the grapes ye take therefrom an intoxicant and a goodly provision* — The Muslim culture's prohibition against intoxicants is well known. Yet, the Qur'an is ambiguous about wine, with statements in different surahs that both encourage and discourage its consumption. Chronologically, Q 16.67 was written first. It was written while in Mecca and presents a most liberal position on wine, noting that it is one of the gifts that Allah has given to mankind (cf. Q 47.15). Much later, while in Medinah, Muhammad described intoxication as a sin (Q 2.219) and "an abomination of Satan's work" (Q 5.90). He made this statement after observing that people were intoxicated during daily prayers, he added: "O ye who believe! approach not prayer while ye are drunk" (Q 4.43).

This variance in the Qur'an speaks of the presence of progressive revelation in the Qur'an. It also points to the Doctrine of Abrogation (see **The Doctrine of Abrogation** on pp. 68-70). "Al-Qaffal said that the wisdom of issuing the prohibition in these stages lies in the following: God knew that the people had been accustomed to drinking wine and drawing from it its many uses. Thus he (also) knew that it would be unbearable for them if he had prohibited them all at once (from the use of wine) and thus unquestionably (for this reason) he made use of these stages and kindness in the prohibition" (cited in Gätje, *The Qur'an and Its Exegesis*, p. 201).

16.68 *the bee* — Muhammad saw the activities of the bee as a sign (divine revelation) of the presence of a vast intelligence working behind the scenes (Allah). How else, he reasoned, can one explain the nature of bee hives and the production of honey?

16.70-74 According to Muhammad, Allah sovereignly predetermined the details of a

flect.

Allah's discriminations

70   God created you; then He will take you to Himself; but amongst you are some whom He will thrust into the most decrepit age; so that he may not know aught that once he knew. Verily, God is knowing, powerful.

71   And God has preferred some of you over others in providing for you; but those who have been preferred will not restore their provision to those whom their right hands possess that they may share equally therein:—is it God's favours they gainsay?

72   And God has made for you from amongst yourselves wives, and has made for you from your wives sons and grandchildren; and has provided you with good things;— is it in vanity that they believe, while for God's favour they are ungrateful?

73   And they serve beside God what cannot control for them any provision from the heavens or the earth, and have no power at all.

74   Do not then strike out parables for God! Verily, God knows, but ye do not know.

Parable of Two Slaves

75   God has struck out a parable; an owned slave, able to do nothing; and one whom we have provided with a good provision, and who expends therefrom in alms secretly and openly:—shall they be held equal?—Praise be to God, most of them do not know!

Parable of Two Men

76   And God has struck out a parable: two men, one of them dumb, able to do nothing, a burden to his lord; wherever he directs him he comes not with success; is he to be held equal with him who bids what is

---

person's life: how long a person will live, a person's stature in society, a person's wealth or lack thereof, the person's sex, and progeny. Yet, most people are ungrateful for these divinely ordained decisions. They (a) gainsay (deny) Allah's favors, remain ungrateful, and (c) serve false gods that "have no power at all."

16.75 In this parable, two slaves are presented. The first slave is unable to do anything. The second slave accomplishes much and gives alms to the poor secretly and openly. Muhammad rhetorically asked: "Shall

they be held equal?" The implied answer is no. And so it is with people. Infidels are identified with the first slave. The faithful believers—those who follow the straight path of Islam (see Q 72.2)—are identified with the second slave.

16.76 In this parable, two people are presented. The first man is dumb and unable to do anything, likened to infidels. The second man is righteous and on "the right way" to eternal life, likened to Muslims.

16.77-88 In Muhammad's application of the two parables, he expected people to strive

just and who is on the right way?

*Application of
the two parables*

77 God's are the unseen things of the heavens and the earth; nor is the matter of the Hour aught but as the twinkling of an eye, or nigher still! Verily, God is mighty over all!

78 God brings you forth out of the wombs of your mothers knowing naught; and He makes for you hearing, and sight, and hearts,— haply ye may give thanks!

79 Do they not see the birds subjected in the vault of the sky?—none holds them in but God: verily, in that is a sign unto a people who believe.

80 God made for you in your houses a repose; and made for you, of the skins of cattle, houses, that ye may find them light, on the day ye move your quarters and the day when ye abide; and from their wool, and from their fur, and from their hair come furniture and chattels for a season.

81 And God has made for you, of what He has created, shades; and has made for you shelters in the mountains; and He has made for you shirts to keep you from the heat, and shirts to keep you from each other's violence:—thus does He fulfil His favours towards you,— haply ye yet may be resigned.

82 But if they turn their backs, —thine is only to preach thy plain message.

83 They recognise the favours of God, and yet they deny them, for most men are ungrateful.

84 And on the day when we shall send from every nation a witness; then shall those who misbelieve not be allowed (to excuse themselves), and they shall not be taken back into favour.

85 And when those who join their partners with God say, "Our Lord! these be our partners on whom we used to call beside Thee."

86 And they shall proffer them the speech, "Verily, ye are liars!" And they shall proffer on that day peace unto God;

87 and that which they had devised shall stray away from them.

to be like the second slave and the second man. The many blessings given by Allah to each person (birth, the ability to hear, see and feel, homes, clothing, food, money, and shade) should bring about a sense of thanksgiving to Allah and a commitment to strive to live a life pleasing to Him.

Yet those who turn their backs on Allah ("they recognize the favours of God, and yet they deny them") will suffer divine judgment. Allah will send them a witness (prophet or apostle) to preach the right way to eternal life. If these people persist in their polytheism ("join their partners with God"), Allah will add "torment to their torment" (see **The Apostles** on pp. 398-400).

16.85-87 *these be our partners* — That is, these are the gods whom we worship.

88 Those who misbelieve and turn folks off God's path, we will add torment to their torment, for that they were evildoers.

89 And on the day when we will raise up in every nation a witness against them from among themselves, and we will bring thee as a witness against these; for we have sent down to thee a book explaining clearly everything, and a guidance, and a mercy, and glad tidings to the believers.

God's path

90 Verily, God bids you do justice and good, and give to kindred (their due), and He forbids you to sin, and do wrong, and oppress; He admonishes you, haply ye may be mindful!

91 Fulfil God's covenant when ye have covenanted, and break not your oaths after asseverating them, for ye thereby make God your surety; verily, God knows what ye do.

92 And be not like her who unravels her yarn, fraying it out after she hath spun it close, by taking your oaths for mutual intrigue, because one nation is more numerous than another; God only tries you therewith, but He will make manifest to you on the resurrection day that whereon ye did dispute.

93 But had God pleased He would have made you one nation; but He leads astray whom He will, and guides whom He will;—but ye shall be questioned as to that which ye have done.

94 Take not therefore your oaths for mutual intrigue, lest a foot slip after being planted firmly, and ye taste of evil for that ye turned folks off the path of God, and for you

16.88 *God's path* — That is, the path to eternal life (see Q 72.2, note).

16.89 *we have sent down to thee a book* — That is, Allah has sent down to Muhammad the eternal book (see **The Perspicuous Book** on pp. 178-179).

16.90-97 In this passage, Muhammad clarified the path that leads to eternal life. Generally speaking, it is a life of integrity: (a) doing justice and goodness to all people, (b) caring for one's family, (c) avoiding oppressive behavior towards other people, (d) fulfilling God's covenant, and (e) not breaking oaths for mutual intrigue. At the day of resurrection (v. 92), Allah will examine the activities of a person's life and determine his or her eternal fate (see **The Last Judgment** on pp. 46-50).

16.92 *be not like her who unravels her yarn* — This is a proverb, meaning that a person should not throw aside and ruin that which he or she had previously taken care in organizing and pulling together.

16.93 The reason for the multiplicity of nations in the world is due to (a) the predetermined will of Allah, and (b) the sinfulness of people who have been led astray by Allah.

16.95 *sell not God's covenant* — That is, do not fail to fulfill completely the covenants of Allah. The Bible makes a similar admonition (see Num 30:2; Deut 23:21-23; Ps

there be mighty woe!

95 And sell not God's covenant for a little price; with God only is what is better for you, if ye did but know.

96 What ye have is spent, but what God has endures; and we will recompense the patient with their hire for the best deeds they have done.

97 Whoso acts aright, male or female, and is a believer, we will quicken with a goodly life; and we will recompense them with their hire for the best deeds they have done.

Reading the Qur'an

98 When thou dost read the Qur'ân, ask refuge with God from Satan the pelted one.

99 Verily, he has no power over those who believe and who upon their Lord rely.

100 His power is only over those who take him for a patron, and over the idolaters.

101 And whenever we change one verse for another,—God knows best what He sends down. They say, "Thou art but a forger!"— Nay, most of them do not know.

102 Say, "The Holy Spirit brought it down from thy Lord in truth, to stablish those who believe, and for a guidance and glad tidings to those who are resigned."

103 We knew that they said, "It is only some mortal who teaches him."— The tongue of him they lean towards is barbarous, and this is plain Arabic.

50:14; 76:11; 119:106; Eccl 5:4; Matt 5:33).

16.97 *whoso acts aright...and is a believer* — these words are repeated often in the Qur'an and serve as a brief summary of the Islamic gospel (see Q 103.3, note).

16.98a When reading the Qur'an, said Muhammad, the faithful Muslim was admonished to seek refuge with Allah so that the beguiling misinterpretations Satan would be thwarted.

16.98b-100 According to Muhammad, Satan has power over those who are involved in the occult ("take him for a patron") and those who are committed to Arabic Star Family religion ("idolaters").

16.101 *and whenever we change one verse for another* — See the **Doctrine of Abrogation** on pp. 68-70).

16.102 *the Holy Spirit brought it down* — That is, Allah brought it down. The point is

that the Qur'an is the product of divine inspiration. It is intended to establish those who believe, to serve as guidance and glad tidings for those who are resigned (surrendered) to Allah. Hence, the term "Holy Spirit" is not to be confused with the Second Person of the Trinity, as understood in Christian theology (see Q 16.2).

16.103 Muhammad's opponents believed that "some mortal" (i.e., some individual) served as the true source of much that was included in Muhammad's surahs. Ibn Ishaq, Muhammad's most authoritative biographer, acknowledged this possibility. As mentioned in an earlier surah (see Q 19, note), Muhammad used to spend time with a Christian slave by the name of Jabr at a hill on the outskirts of Mecca, al-Marwa, who taught him much of the Judeo-Christian tradition. The people of Mecca had observed Muhammad spend-

104 Verily, those who believe not in God's signs, God will not guide them, and for them is grievous woe.

105 Only they are the forgers of a lie who believe not in God's signs; and these, they are the liars.

Sin of apostasy

106 Whoso disbelieves in God after having believed, unless it be one who is forced and whose heart is quiet in the faith,—but whoso expands his breast to misbelieve,—on them is wrath from God, and for them is mighty woe!

107 That is because they preferred the love of this world's life to the

next;—but, verily, God guides not the unbelieving people.

108 These are they on whose hearts, and hearing, and eyesight, God has set a stamp, and these, they are the careless.

109 Without a doubt that in the next life they will be the losers.

*Blessings for those
who persevere*

110 Then, verily, thy Lord, to those who fled after they had been tried, and then fought strenuously and were patient,—verily, thy Lord after that will be forgiving and merciful.

111 On the day every soul will come to

ing much time with Jabr and concluded that his understanding of these two religions (Judaism and Christianity) came from a mortal, and not from Gabriel the archangel, as Muhammad alleged (*The Life of Muhammad*, p. 180).

Some scholars add to Ishaq's commentary, noting that Muhammad received much of his knowledge of the Judeo-Christian tradition from Waraqa bin Naufal, Khadijah's cousin (Khadijah was Muhammad's first wife) and a Christian slave called Jabr (see Q 19, note).

16.106 *whoso disbelieves in God after having believed* — This is the classic definition of apostasy. Muhammad asserted that for each apostate awaits the wrath of God and a mighty woe. Later in the Qur'an, Muhammad added that faithful Muslims were called upon to exact divine judgment upon apostates by killing them (see Q 9.73; 66.9; **The**

Doctrine of Abrogation on pp. 68-70).
16.108 *God has set a stamp* — That is, due to the doctrine of double predestination a stamp from God is placed upon the hearts of infidels, making it impossible for them to respond positively to the Islamic faith (see Q 4.155; 7.100-101; 9.87, 93; 10.74; 30.59; 40.35; 47.16; 63.3; **The Doctrine of al-Qadar** on pp. 264-266).
16.110 *fought strenuously* — Literally, engaged in a great jihad (see Q 4.95; 5.35; 8.72, 74-75; 9.16, 41, 44, 73, 81; 22.78; 25.52; 29.6, 69; 47.31; 60.1; 66.9). According to this passage, fighting strenuously in the Cause of Jihad will be rewarded with a relationship with Allah who is forgiving and merciful.
16.111 *every soul shall be paid what it has earned* — This is the Islamic gospel, a gospel of meritorious behavior (see **The Last Judgment** on pp. 46-50).

wrangle for itself, and every soul shall be paid what it has earned, and they shall not be wronged.

Parable of the city

112 God has struck out a parable: a city which was safe and quiet, its provision came to it in plenty from every place, and then it denied God's favours, and God made it feel the clothing of hunger and fear, for that which they had wrought.

113 And there came to them an apostle from amongst themselves, but they called him a liar, and the torment seized them, while yet they were unjust.

Muslim dietary law

114 Eat, then, from what God has provided you with, things lawful and good, and give thanks for the favours of God, if it be Him ye serve.

115 He has only forbidden you that which dies of itself, and blood, and the flesh of swine, and that which is devoted to other than God; but he who is forced, neither revolting nor transgressing, it is no sin for him: verily, God is forgiving and merciful.

116 And say not of the lie your tongues pronounce, "This is lawful, and this is unlawful," forging against God a lie; verily, those who forge against God a lie shall not prosper.

117 A little enjoyment—then for them is grievous woe!

Jewish dietary law

118 For those who are Jews we have forbidden what we have narrated to thee before; we did not wrong them, but it was themselves they wronged.

119 Then, verily, thy Lord to those who have done evil in ignorance and then repented after that and done aright,—verily, thy Lord after-

16.112-113 This parable depicts a city characterized by safety and quietness, with an abundance of provisions from Allah and faithful to His ways. Then the inhabitants of the city turned away from Allah (apostasized). Allah responded by bringing hunger and fear into their lives. When an apostle came to warn them of the judgment to come, they continued in their apostasy by rejecting his message, calling him a liar. Allah then responded by seizing them with torment (see *The Apostles* on pp. 398-400).

16.114-115 Islamic dietary law requires one

to give thanks to Allah before eating. That which is forbidden includes: (a) carrion, (b) blood, (c) pork, and (d) food devoted to other gods. Caveat: the partaking of such food is not a sin if one is forced to eat it.

16.118-119 According to Muhammad, none of the truly wholesome foods are forbidden to the Muslim. They are only forbidden to the Jews because of their persistent sinning against Allah.

16.120-124 Abraham, said Muhammad, was an example of one who remain committed to monotheism. He was, hence, a *Hanif*

wards is forgiving and merciful.

Example of Abraham

120   Verily, Abraham was a high priest, a 'Hanîf, and was not of the idolaters:,

121   thankful for His favours; He chose him and He guided him unto the right way

122   And we gave him in this world good things; and, verily, in the next he will be among the righteous.

123   Then we inspired thee, "Follow the faith of Abraham, a 'Hanîf, for he was not of the idolaters."

124   The Sabbath was only made for those who dispute thereon; but, verily, thy Lord will judge between them on the resurrection day concerning that whereon they do dispute.

Contending for
the Islamic faith

125   Call unto the way of thy Lord with wisdom and goodly warning; and wrangle with them in the kindest way; verily, thy Lord He knows best who has erred from His way, for He knows best the guided ones.

(see Q 30.30, note).

16.121 *the right way* — The way of works that leads to eternal life (see Q 72.2, note).

16.124 According to Muhammad, Sabbath Day observance was ordained for only those who hold divergent views about Abraham; that is, the Jewish people. Jews had wandered from a correct understanding of Abraham and "the right way" that he espoused. They believe that they are the chosen people due to their genealogical relationship with Abraham.

On this issue, Christians agree with Muhammad—but only to a point. Jesus also criticized the Jewish people of His day who relied upon their genealogical relationship with Abraham to validate their salvation and status as being the chosen people. He said: "And do not think you can say to yourselves, 'We have Abraham as our father.' I tell you that out of these stones God can raise up children for Abraham. The ax is already at the root of the trees, and every tree that does not produce good fruit will be cut down and thrown into the fire" (Matt 3:8-10).

Yet the "good fruit" to which Jesus referred was not meritorious living. Rather, it was the trusting in divine forgiveness and the provision made via blood atonement. The Jewish people had lost sight of this spiritual truth. The way in which the Apostle Paul put it: "What then shall we say? That the Gentiles, who did not pursue righteousness, have obtained it, a righteousness that is by faith; but Israel, who pursued a law of righteousness, has not attained it. Why not? Because they pursued it not by faith but as if it were by works" (Rom 9:32-34).

Accordingly, though the Christian faith is critical of the Jewish people's reliance upon their genealogical relationship with Abraham and "a law of righteousness" is attain favor with God, the Christian faith is also critical of Islam's teaching that they way to salvation is also via a law of righteousness. In both cases, the answer is Jesus Christ who provided the way of divine forgiveness via His death on the cross (Rom 5:1-11).

16.125a *the way of thy Lord* — This is a synonym for "the right way" of works that

126 But if ye punish, punish (only) as ye were punished; but if ye are patient, it is best for those who are patient.
127 Be thou patient then; but thy patience is only in God's hands. Do not grieve about them; and be not in a strait at their craftiness;—
128 verily, God is with those who fear Him, and with those who do well.

Surah 13

In the name of the merciful and compassionate God

1 A. L. M. R.

Qur'an

Those are, the signs of the Book, and that which is sent down to thee from thy Lord is the truth; but most people will not believe.

*The sovereignty of God
over all creaton*

2 God it is who has raised the heavens without columns that ye can see; then He made for the throne, and subjected the sun and the moon; each one runs on to a stated and appointed time; He governs the affair, details the signs;—haply of the meeting with your Lord ye will be sure.
3 And He it is who has stretched out the earth and placed therein firm mountains and rivers, and of ev-

leads to eternal life (see Q 72.2, note).
16.125b-128 Muslims were called upon to wrangle with the infidels "in the kindest way." This approach was to be characterized by: (a) punishment in a manner proportionate to the way in which they have punished you, (b) patience in one's dealings with the infidel, (c) not grieving the fate of an infidel, and (d) not distressed over the false arguments that infidels advance.
16.127 *a strait at their craftiness* — That is, distressed (in a strait) due to their disingenuous argumentations (craftiness).
16.128 Allah is with those who (a) fear Him, and (b) do well.
Surah 13. The title of this surah, *The Thunder*, comes from verse 13. Its theme is found in its final verse: "Those who misbelieve say, 'Thou art not sent!' Say, 'God is witness enough between me and you, and so is he

who has the knowledge of the Book!" Its purpose, then, was to defend Muhammad's ministry against the constant criticism from his opponents who had been calling his ministry a fraud.
13.1a Literally, *Alif Lam Mim Ra*. See Q 32.1, note.
13.1b *the Book...sent down to thee* — that is, the Perspicuous Book. This is the alleged eternal book guarded in Paradise by Allah that was sent down to Muhammad (see **The Perspicuous Book** on pp. 178-179).
13.2 According to Muhammad, Allah controls all the celestial bodies, including the sun and the moon. This assertion stands opposed to the Arabian Star Family Religion, which assigned differing celestial bodies to differing gods.
13.3 According to Muhammad, Allah also controls the earth, mountains, rivers, and

ery fruit has He placed therein two kinds. He makes the night cover the day;—verily, in that are signs unto a people who reflect.

4   And on the earth are neighbouring portions, and gardens of grapes and corn and palm's growing together (from one root) and not growing together; they are watered with one water, yet we distinguish one over the other as food;—verily, in that are signs unto a people who have sense.

Coming resurrection

5   And if thou shouldst wonder, wondrous is their speech: "What! when we have become dust, shall we really then be created anew?" These are they who disbelieve in their Lord, and these are they with fetters round their necks, and these are the fellows of the Fire; they shall dwell therein for aye!

6   They will wish thee to hasten on the evil rather than the good; examples have passed away before them:

The challenge to Muhammad's prophetic credentials

but thy Lord is possessor of forgiveness unto men, notwithstanding their injustice; but, verily, thy Lord is keen to punish.

7   Those who misbelieve say, "Unless a sign be sent down upon him from his Lord..." —Thou art only a warner, and every people has its guide.

---

fruit. This is another denial of the Arabic Star Family Religion, which ascribed gods to earthly objects, as well, including the earth, mountains, rivers, and fruit.

13.4a *grapes and corn and palm* — This is a third denial of the Arabic Star Family Religion, which ascribed gods to grapes, corn, and palm trees.

13.4b *signs unto a people who have sense* — That is, since Allah is sovereign over all creation, this leaves nothing left for the gods of the Arabic Star Family Religion (cf. Rom 1:18-20 where a similar argument is made by the Apostle Paul).

13.5-6a Those in the Arabic Star Family Religion believed that once a person died, his or her spirit entered the subterranean netherworld where it remained, dwelling with the gods. It was a religion where people were not judged for their sins. Muhammad's assertion of a resurrection of the body and the Last Judgment, then, contradicted this religious scheme. Understandably, it became a bone of contention between Muhammad and the polytheists (see **Polytheism in Seventh Century Arabia** on pp. 92-97).

13.6b-7 Another source of contention between the people of Mecca and Muhammad was his lack of prophetic credentials. All divinely appointed prophets, they reasoned, were endowed with miraculous powers that demonstrated that they were indeed divinely ordained. Muhammad had no such powers. This, they said, invalidated his alleged prophetic ministry (see v. 27 and **John of Damascus** on pp. 247-248).

13.7-11a Muhammad's answer to his critics: he was called by Allah to only be a warner

8 God knows what each female bears, and what the wombs fall short of or add; for dimensions of everything are with Him.

9 He who knows the unseen and the visible,—the great, the lofty one.

10 Alike among you is he who keeps secret his speech and he who displays it; and he who hides by night and he who stalks abroad by day.

11 Each of them has pursuers before him and behind him, to keep guard over him at the command of God; verily, God changes not what a people has until they change it for themselves. And when God wishes evil to a people there is no averting it, nor have they a protector beside Him.

12 He it is who shows you the light-ning for fear and hope; and He brings up the heavy clouds.

13 And the thunder celebrates His praise, and the angels too for fear of Him; and He sends the thunder-clap and overtakes therewith whom He will;—yet they wrangle about God! But He is strong in might.

14 On Him is the call of truth, and those who call on others than Him shall not be answered at all, save as one who stretches out his hand to the water that it may reach his mouth, but it reaches it not! The call of the misbelievers is only in error.

15 And God do those who are in the heavens and the earth adore, whether they will or no! as do their shadows also morn and eve.

and a guide—nothing more. He also appealed to the omniscience of Allah. He knows (a) the sex of each unborn child, (b) those who will suffer miscarriages, (c) the length of the gestation of each pregnancy, (d) that which is beyond the reach of the human mind, and (e) that which is knowable to the human mind. He sees and knows everything. Hence, since only Allah is all-knowing, the Meccan people were out of order to criticize Allah for not sending a sign (a miracle) to validate Muhammad's ministry.

13.11b *God changes not what a people has until they change it for themselves —* In the eighteenth century, Benjamin Franklin was to say something similar: God helps those who help themselves.

13.11c According to Muhammad, when Allah decides that evil comes to a particular people, nothing can avert it.

13.12-13 According to Muhammad, Allah is all-powerful. He sends lightning, thunder, and heavy rain. The implied question is: who are we, then, to wrangle with His decisions about how he chooses to endow his apostles? If He should choose to not supply them with miraculous powers, that is His pre-rogative.

13.14 Muhammad also noted that if his opponents should seek knowledge from the gods that they worship, they will receive no answers. It is as if they attempted to gather water into their outstretched hands and then attempted to drink. The water would slip between the fingers, with nothing left.

13.15 *whether they will or no —* Further-more, Muhammad explained, all creation is subject to the will of Allah. Those who sub-mit willingly, of course, are surrendered to His will. Yet those who reject Allah are also

Parable of the Scum

16   Say, "Who is Lord of the heavens and the earth?" say, "God;" say, "Do ye take beside God patrons who cannot control profit or harm for themselves?" say, "Shall the blind and the seeing be held equal? or shall the darkness and the light be held, equal? or have they made associates with God who can create as He creates, so that the creation seem familiar to them?" say, "God is the creator of everything, and He is the one, the dominant."

17   He sends down from the sky water, and the water-courses flow according to their bulk, and the torrent bears along the floating scum: and from what they set fire to, craving ornaments or utensils, comes a scum like that;—thus does God hit the truth and the falsehood;—and as for the scum it is thrown off, and as for what profits man it stays on the earth. Thus does God strike out parables!

Interpretation of the parable

18   For those who respond to their Lord is good; but those who respond not to Him, had they all that is in the earth and the like thereof as well, they would give it for a ransom; these shall have an evil reckoning up! and their resort is hell,—an evil couch shall it be!

The straight path

19   Is he who knows that naught but the truth is sent down upon thee from thy Lord like him who is blind? Only those possessed of minds will remember!

in submission to Him since Allah has willed that they remain in unbelief (see **The Doctrine of al-Qadar** on pp. 264-266).

13.17a *water-courses flow according to their bulk* — That is, riverbeds enable water to flow according to their volume. The term *wadi* (riverbed) is normally dry and only experiences water runoff after particularly strong rainstorms.

13.17b *floating scum* — Since wadis are dry most of the year, when they are transformed into rivers due to heavy rain falls, large amounts of scum (debris: sticks, leaves, human utensils, garbage, etc.) are carried along on its surface. The water is therefore contaminated and needs to be strained before being useful. In the same way, truth and falsehood tend to flow together. Falsehood needs to be strained so that one can rightly distinguish right from wrong.

13.18 Muhammad compared the infidels with scum. They remain unsubmissive to Allah and will, at the Last Judgment, receive "an evil reckoning."

13.19-22 Muhammad reminded his listeners the characteristics of "the straight path." Those on the straight path that leads to eternal life will: (a) fulfill Allah's covenant, (b) are fearful of an evil reckoning at the Last Judgment are therefore sufficiently motivated to avoid it, (c) are patient in craving a look at their Lord's face, (d) steadfast in prayer, and (e) generous in the giving of alms (see Q 72.2, note).

20 Those who fulfil God's covenant and break not the compact,

21 and those who attain what God has bidden to be attained, and dread their Lord and fear the evil reckoning up;

22 and those who are patient, craving their Lord's face, and are steadfast in prayer, and expend in alms of what we have bestowed upon them secretly and openly, and ward off evil with good,—these shall have the recompense of the abode,

23 gardens of Eden, into which they shall enter with the righteous amongst their fathers and their wives and their seed; and the angels shall enter in unto them from every gate:—

24 "Peace be upon you! for that ye were patient; and goodly is the recompense of the abode."

The fate of apostates

25 And those who break God's cov-

enant after compacting for it, and who cut asunder what God hath bidden to be joined, and who do evil in the earth, these—upon them is the curse of God, and for them is an evil abode.

Double predestination

26 God extends his bounty freely to whomsoever He will, or He metes it out; and they rejoice in the life of this world, but the life of this world is naught but a (temporary) provision compared with the next.

27 Those who misbelieve say, "Unless a sign is sent down upon him from his Lord..." Say, "God leads whom He will astray, but guides unto Him those who turn again.

28 Those who believe and whose hearts are comforted by the mention of God,—aye! by the mention of God shall their hearts be comforted,

29 who believe and do what is right.

13.23 Those who are successful in living according to "the straight path" will enter into the "gardens of Eden" (that is, their heavenly abodes). Their wives will be with them (see **The Virgins** on pp. 107-109).

13.24 The angels will tell them: "Peace be upon you! for that ye were patient, and goodly is the recompense of the abode."

13.25 *those who break God's covenant after compacting for it* — That is, apostates (see Q 16.106; 22.38).

13.27 *God leads whom He will astray, but guides unto Him those who turn again* — this is a classic definition of double predesti-

nation. Allah intentionally leads astray those predestined to Hell. Those who turn to Him do so because He has chosen to reveal the truth to them. Accordingly, all who require a miraculous signs in Muhammad's ministry to validate the rightness of his words have been predestined to Hell (see v. 7). See **Doctrine of al-Qadar** on pp. 264-266.

13.28 Muhammad believed that the mention of the name of Allah brings calm to the heart to faithful Muslims.

13.29 *believe and do what is right* — This is a summary of the Islamic gospel (see Q 103.3, note).

Good cheer for them and an excellent resort."

The nature of Muhammad's ministry

30 Thus have we sent thee to a nation before which other nations have passed away, to recite to them that which we have inspired thee with; yet they misbelieve in the merciful! Say, "He is my Lord; there is no god but He; upon Him do I rely, and unto Him is my repentance."

31 And though it were a Qur'ân by which the mountains were moved, or by which the earth were cut up, or the dead made to speak—nay, God's is the command altogether! Did not those who believed know that if God had pleased He would have guided men altogether? And

a striking calamity shall not cease to overtake those who misbelieve for what they have wrought, or to alight close by their dwellings; until God's promise comes—verily, God fails not in His promise.

32 Before thee have apostles been mocked at; and those who misbelieved have I allowed to range at large; and then it caught them up! How then was my punishment?

Foolishness of the infidel

33 Shall He who is standing over every soul (to note) what it has earned—? And they join partners with God! Say, "Name them; can ye inform Him of what He does not know in the earth? or is it for name's sake only (that ye call upon

13.30 Muhammad believed that he was called to recite divine revelation. The centerpiece of his message was the Doctrine of Tauhid—absolute monotheism. Moreover, Allah is sovereign over the entire earth.

13.31a Muhammad believed that the Qur'an is a supernatural book that, when read, can cause supernatural events, such as the moving of mountains, earthquakes, and the resurrection of the dead.

13.31b *a striking calamity shall not cease to overtake those who misbelieve* — That is, infidels will suffer calamitous misfortune in this life for their persistent unbelief.

13.32 *it caught them up* — That is, Allah will bring destruction upon those who reject the ministry of the apostles at a moment that takes them by surprise.

13.33a Muhammad contrasted Allah (who stands over every soul and will remit each one that which it has earned) with the infidel who insisted on continuing in his or her polygamous beliefs.

13.33b Muhammad believed that Allah encouraged the infidels to name their gods with whatever name they wished. Their behavior was idolatrous and they would suffer eternal torment in the afterlife.

13.33c *whomsoever God doth lead astray, no guide has he* — Once again, Muhammad pointed out the doctrine of double predestination that prompted people to follow error. They will be tormented in this life and experience a greater torment in the afterlife (see ***The Doctrine of al-Qadar*** on pp. 264-266).

them)? "Nay, then, stratagem. is made seemly to those who misbelieve, and they turn folks from the path of God! But whomsoever God doth lead astray, no guide has he."

34 For them is torment in this world's life; but surely the torment of the next is more wretched still—nor have they against God a keeper.

Paradise and Hell

35 The likeness of the Paradise which those who fear God are promised, beneath it rivers flow, its food is enduring, and likewise its shade! That is the recompense of those who fear; but the recompense of misbelievers is the Fire!

36 And those to whom we brought the Book rejoice in that which we have

sent down to thee; but of the confederates are some who deny a part thereof. Say, "I am only bidden to serve God and not to associate any with Him; on Him I call and to Him is my recourse."

37 Thus have we sent it down, an Arabic judgment, but hadst thou followed their lusts, after the knowledge that has come to thee, thou hadst not had against God a patron or a keeper.

The abrogation of holy writ

38 And we sent apostles before thee, and we made for them wives and seed; and no apostle could bring a sign save by God's permission;— for every period there is a book.

39 God blots out what He will, or He confirms; and with Him is the

---

13.35 *the likeness of the Paradise* — The description of heaven in the Qur'an is only an approximation (a likeness). Moderate Muslim scholars point to this verse to mitigate against the literalness of the seventy-two virgins in Paradise, and other usual features of Paradise mentioned in the Qur'an (see **Paradise** on pp. 76-77).

13.36 *the Book...which we have sent down* — That is, the eternal Book in Paradise has been sent down via the archangel Gabriel to Muhammad (see **The Perspicuous Book** on pp. 178-179 and **The Qur'an** on pp. 150-153).

13.37a *an Arabic judgment* — That is, the Qur'an was written in Arabic (see Q 12.2; 20.113; 26.195; 39.28; 42.7; 43.3; also see **The Qur'an** on pp. 150-153).

13.37b Muhammad commented that it was possible for him to turn away from Islam, in spite of the fact that he was a chosen apostle, and thereby discover Allah to be against him. Even he was susceptible to the sin of apostasy (see Q 10.15 and 17.73).

13.38 *for every period there is a book* — That is, every age has its own holy writ. Muhammad believed that Allah sent an apostle to the earth in each and every period of time with a corresponding holy writ to serve as a warner and a guide.

13.39a *God blots out what He will, or He confirms* — That is, Allah abrogates whatever He wishes in His divine revelation. When read in context of the previous verse, Muhammad's point was that holy scripture in previous ages has undergone a process of

Mother of the Book.

Muhammad's duty

40   Either we will let thee see a part of what we threaten them with, or we will take thee to Ourself; but thy duty is only to deliver thy message, and ours to reckon up.

41   Did they not see that we come to the land and diminish the borders thereof? God judges, and there is none to reverse His judgment, and He is swift at reckoning up!

42   And those who were before them were crafty too; but God's is the craft altogether! He knows what every soul earns; and the misbelievers shall know whose is the recompense of the abode.

43   And those who misbelieve say, "Thou art not sent!" Say, "God is witness enough between me and you; and so is he who has the knowledge of the Book!"

Surah 29

In the name of the merciful and compassionate God

1   A. L. M.

editing by Allah. Yet, in all cases, that which Allah sent down to earth for his apostles to present to people was the perspicuous book (the eternal book guarded by Allah in the heavens). See Q 2.106; 87.6-7; **The Perspicuous Book** on pp. 178-179, **The Qur'an** on pp. 150-153, and **The Doctrine of Abrogation** on pp. 68-70.

Many Christians see an inconsistency here. Why would God, who is perfect in all His doings and all-knowing, give to His apostles a revelation that was less than perfect and required editing? One would think that a revelation, existing eternally in the heavens, would by definition be perfect and require no alterations.

13.39b *the Mother of the Book* — That is, the eternal book that exists in Paradise (see **The Perspicuous Book** on pp. 178-179).

13.40-43 As the surah draws to a close, Muhammad summarized that which he had been saying in the surah: (a) His calling and message were ordained from Allah, (a) Allah

brings judgment to whomsoever He wishes, (c) Allah will weigh the works of every person in a balance at the Last Judgment and give to each person whatever he or she has earned, and (d) the infidels will be cast into an abode of everlasting torment.

Surah 29. The title to this surah, *The Spider,* comes from verse 41. The theme of this surah is that one is to strive hard after Allah. A central insight is that divine judgment has fallen and will fall on all who remain steadfast in their resistance to Allah. They will be crushed as if they were living in a small and frail spider's house. Towards the end of the surah, Muhammad instructed his believers how to respond to the challenges presented by Jews and Christians to the Islamic faith.

29.1 Literally, *Alif Lam Mim.* See Q 32.1, note.

29.2 *"We believe," and not be tried* — Muhammad rejected the notion of salvation by faith apart from a meritorious lifestyle. He

The fate of the infidel	*Striving after God*
2 Do men then reckon that they will be left alone to say, "We believe," and not be tried?	5 He who hopes for the meeting of God,—verily, God's appointed time will come; and He both hears and knows!
3 we did try those who were before them, and God will surely know those who are truthful, and He will surely know the liars.	6 And he who fights strenuously, fights strenuously only for his own soul; verily, God is independent of the worlds.
4 Do those who do evil reckon that they can outstrip us? evil is it that they judge.	7 Those who believe and do right, we will surely cover for them their

insisted that faith must be tried in the crucible of life where works are given opportunity to manifest themselves. Only those who are successful in amassing a life of good works will be allowed into Paradise (see **The Last Judgment** on pp. 46-50).

Christians takes the opposite position: salvation is a free gift based upon the sacrifice of Jesus Christ on the cross. Theologians call it the Doctrine of Substitutionary Atonement. His death on the cross served as a substitute punishment for the sins of the world.

John R. W. Stott explains: "What is there about the cross of Christ which angers the world and stirs them up to persecute those who preach it? Just this: Christ died on the cross for us sinners, becoming a curse for us (Gal 3:13). So the cross tells us some very unpalatable truths about ourselves, namely that we are sinners under the righteous curse of God's law and we cannot save ourselves. Christ bore our sin and curse precisely because we could gain release from them in no other way. If we could have been forgiven by our own good works, by being circumcised and keeping the law, we may be quite sure that there would have been no cross. Every time we look at the

cross Christ seems to say to us, 'I am here because of you. It is your sin I am bearing, your curse I am suffering, your debt I am paying, your death I am dying.' Nothing in history or in the universe cuts us down to size like the cross. All of us have inflated views of ourselves, especially in self-righteousness, until we have visited a place called Calvary. It is there, at the foot of the cross, that we shrink to our true size. And of course men do not like it. They resent the humiliation of seeing themselves as God sees them and as they really are. They prefer the comfortable illusions" (*The Message of Galatians*, p. 179).

29.6 *he who fights strenuously, fights strenuously only for his own soul* — Literally, he who jihads a great jihad, jihads on behalf of his own soul (see Q 8.72, 74-75; 16.110; 22.78; 25.52; 29.69; 47.31). That is, the one who fights a great jihad will be benefitted at the Last Judgment (see Q 6.131-135; 16.26; 21.10-15; 22.39-48; **Jihad** on pp. 616-622).

29.7 *believe and do right* — This is a summation of the Islamic gospel (see Q 103.3, note). According to Islam, divine forgiveness is offered to those who lives were, on balance, righteousness (see **Divine Forgive-**

offences; and we will surely reward them with better than that
which they have done.

8   And we have enjoined on man kindness to his parents; and if they
strive with thee that thou mayest
join with me, what thou hast no
knowledge of, then obey them not;
to me is your return, and I will inform you of that which ye have
done.

9   But those who believe and do right,
we will make them enter amongst
the righteous.

10 And there are those among men
who say, "We believe in God!" but
when they are hurt in God's cause,
they deem the trials of men like the
torment of God; but if help come
from thy Lord they will say, "Verily, we were with you!" does not
God know best what is in the
breasts of the worlds?

11 God will surely know those who
believe, and will surely know the
hypocrites.

12 And those who misbelieved said to
those who believed, "Follow our
path, we will bear your sins;" but
they could not bear their sins at
all; verily, they are liars!

13 But they shall surely bear their own
burdens, and burdens with their
burdens; and they shall surely be
asked upon the resurrection day
concerning what they did devise:

Noah

14 And we sent Noah to his people,
and he dwelt among them for a
thousand years save fifty years;
and the deluge overtook them while
they were unjust:

15 but we saved him and the fellows
of the ark, and we made it a sign

---

ness in Islam on pp. 158-161; and **The Last Judgment** on pp. 46-50).

29.8 Muhammad enjoined people to show kindness to their parents (see Q 31.14-15). Yet, if parents insisted that their children be polytheists ("join with me what thou hast no knowledge of"), the children were instructed by Muhammad to disobey them.

29.9 *believe and do right* — This is a summation of the Islamic gospel (see Q 103.3, note).

29.10 Muhammad expected his followers to be sufficiently strong in the faith to be able to withstand the trials that the infidels bring upon them. Those who do turn away from Allah and follow the beliefs of the infidels were reminded that Allah is all-knowing and sees their lack of dedication and hypocrisy.

29.13 *they shall surely bear their own burdens* — at the Last Judgment they will be held accountable for the evils done in life.

29.14 Muhammad stated that Noah had been an apostle sent from Allah to an unbelieving people. According to the Bible, the statement that Noah "dwelt among them" for 950 years is incorrect since, according to Gen 9:28-29, Noah's entire life-span was 950 years. He was 600 years old when the Flood came, he dwelt with his people 600 years, not 950 years.

29.16 Muhammad then spoke of Abraham, noting how he stood opposed to idolatry and admonished the people of the City of

unto the worlds.

Abraham

16   And Abraham when he said to his
people, "Serve God and fear Him,
that is better for you if ye did but
know.

17   Ye only serve beside God idols and
do create a lie; verily, those whom
ye serve beside God cannot control for themselves provision; then
crave provision with God, and
serve Him, and give thanks to Him;
unto Him shall ye return!

18   And if ye say it is a lie, nations before you called (the apostles) liars
too; but an apostle has only his plain
message to preach!"

19   Have they not seen how God produces the creation, and then turns
it back? verily, that to God is easy.

20   Say, "Journey ye on in the land,
and behold how the creation appeared; then God produces another production: verily, God is
mighty over all!"

21   He torments whom He will, and has
mercy on whom He will; and unto

Him shall ye be returned.

22   Nor can ye make Him helpless in
the earth, nor in the heavens; nor
have ye beside God a patron or a
helper.

23   And those who disbelieve in God's
signs and in meeting with Him,
these shall despair of my mercy;
and these, for them is grievous
woe.

24   But the answer of his people was
only to say, "Kill him or burn him!"
But God saved him from the fire;
verily, in that are signs unto a
people who believe.

25   He said, "Verily, ye take beside God
idols, through mutual friendship in
the life of this world; then on the
day of judgment ye shall deny each
other, and shall curse each other,
and your resort shall he the fire,
and ye shall have none to help."

26   And Lot believed him. And (Abraham) said, "Verily, I flee unto my
Lord! Verily, He is mighty, wise!

27   and we granted him Isaac and Jacob; and we placed in his seed
prophecy and the Book; and we
gave him his hire in this world;

Ur to repent from the sin of idolatry and embrace monotheism. Abraham's message was
presented plainly, yet the people of Ur none-
theless accused him of speaking lies. This
exchange between the people of Ur and
Abraham paralleled the exchange in Mecca
between Muhammad and the Quraysh
people.
29.21 Muhammad inserted the doctrine of
double predestination into Abraham's minis-

try (see **The Doctrine of al-Qadar** on pp.
264-266).
29.22 *beside God a patron or a helper* —
That is, multiple gods: Allah and other gods.
29.24 Muhammad believed that the infidels attempted to place Abraham in a fire as
a way of silencing his ministry (see Q 37.97-
98, note, and Q 21.51-73; 85.4-10).
29.27 *the Book* — That is, the eternal Book
of God (see **The Perspicuous Book** on pp.

and, verily, he in the next shall be among the righteous."

Lot

28 And Lot when he said to his people, "Verily, ye approach an abomination which no one in all the world ever anticipated you in!

29 What! do ye approach men? and stop folks on the highway? and approach in your assembly sin?" but the answer of his people was only to say, "Bring us God's torment, if thou art of those who speak the truth!"

30 Said he, "My Lord! help me against a people who do evil!"

31 And when our messengers came to Abraham with the glad tidings, they said, "We are about to destroy

the people of this city. Verily, the people thereof are wrong-doers."

32 Said he, "Verily, in it is Lot;" they said, "We know best who is therein; we shall of a surety save him and his people, except his wife, who is of those who linger."

33 And when our messengers came to Lot, he was vexed for them, and his arm was straitened for them; and they said, "Fear not, neither grieve; we are about to save thee and, thy people, except thy wife, who is of those who linger.

34 Verily, we are about to send down upon the people of this city a horror from heaven, for that they have sinned;

35 and we have left therefrom a manifest sign unto a people who have sense."

178-179).

29.28-35 Muhammad turned his attention to Lot, presenting him as an apostle sent to the people of Sodom and Gomorrah.

29.29 *Bring us God's torment* — These words were presented as mockery. Muhammad believed that he too had been mocked by the people of Mecca (see Q 6.5; 16.34; 18.106; 21.2; 36.48).

29.34 *a horror from heaven* — In other passages in the Qur'an, the judgment upon Sodom and Gomorrah were described as a horrific sandstorm (Q 54.34; 29.40), or the raining down from the sky of stones of baked clay (Q 11.82; 15.74; 51.33).

29.35 Muhammad believed that Muslims were endowed with "sense" (rational understanding) with which to rightly understand divine revelation. The inverse is also true:

people who failed to recognize divine revelation and respond in humble obedience to it lacked "sense" (see Q 10.16, 42, 100; 11.51; 12.109; 13.4; 16.12, 67; 21.10, 67; 23.80; 26.28; 28.60; 29.63; 36.62, 68; 37.138; 39.43; 40.67; 43.3; 45.5; 67.10; 89.5).

The Christian Scriptures, however, offer a competing claim: it is only those blessed by the illuminating work of the Holy Spirit who can rightly read and understand divine revelation. It is therefore not a question of possessing "sense," as it is being enlightened and guided by the Spirit (see Jn 16:13-15; 1 Cor 2:10-16; 1 Jn 2:20, 27). Anselm of Canterbury said that the acquisition of spiritual truth was a question of "faith seeking understanding." This is not to disparage the role of rational analysis. The point is that

Jethro (Sho'haib)

36 And unto Midian we sent their brother Sho'hâib, and he said, "My people, serve God, and hope for the last day; and waste not the land, despoiling it."

37 But they called him liar; and the convulsion seized them, and on the morrow they lay in their dwellings prone.

Ad and Thamud

38 And 'Âd and Thamûd—but it is plain to you from their habitations; for Satan made seemly to them their works, and turned them from the way, sagacious though they were!

Korah, Pharaoh, and Haman

39 And Korah and Pharaoh and Hâmân—Moses did come to them with manifest signs, but they were too big with pride in the earth, al-

---

rigorous rational analysis and an enlightened faith go hand in hand.

Oswald Chambers explained: "Everything He [Jesus] taught was contrary to common sense. Not one thing in the Sermon on the Mount is common sense. The basis of Christianity is neither common sense nor rationalism, it springs from another centre, viz., a personal relationship to God in Christ Jesus in which everything is ventured on from a basis that is not seen" (*Shade of His Hand*, pp. 146-147).

Chambers also wrote: "The danger with us is that we want to water down the things that Jesus says and make them mean something in accordance with common sense; if it were only common sense, it was not worthwhile for Him to say it. The things Jesus says about prayer are supernatural revelations" (*My Utmost for His Highest*, May 26th).

29.36-37 Muhammad turned to the story of Sho'haib (Jethro), the father-in-law to Moses (see Q 11.84-95; and 26.176-191, note). Muhammad believed that the divine retribution that the Midianite people experienced was a major earthquake that destroyed their dwelling places in the Sinai

Desert. Yet, according to archeological evidence, the Midianites lived throughout the Old Testament era and into the Christian era—far beyond the ancient period when Moses and Jethro lived. They were nomads—tent dwellers—not sedentary (living in caves in mountainous terrain).

29.38 According to Muhammad, the people of Ad and Thamud lived in consecutive periods of time in the city of Hegra (Hijr)—a city located in northwestern Arabia and south of the City of Petra. They took for themselves "castles on its plains and hewed out mountains into houses" (Q 7.73; also see **Hegra** on p. 28). The Ad people were also understood to be unusually tall people (see Q 54.16-21 note, Q 7:69). Muhammad believed that these two civilizations were destroyed by Allah due to their rejection of the apostles that had been sent to them.

29.39 According to Muhammad, others that were judged by Allah were Korah, Pharaoh and Haman (see Q 28.8, 36-38, 76-82, note, and Q 40.23-38, note).

29.40a Muhammad explained that in each of the cases mentioned above (vv. 14-39), those judged by Allah had been seized in their sin.

though they could not outstrip us!

Summary of the judgments

40 And each of them we seized in his sin; and of them were some against whom we sent a sandstorm; and of them were some whom the noise seized; and of them were some with whom we cleaved the earth open; and of them were some we drowned: God would not have wronged them, but it was themselves they wronged.

Parable of the Spider

41 The likeness of those who take, beside God, patrons is as the likeness of a spider, that takes to himself a house; and, verily, the weakest of houses is a spider's house,

if they did but know!

42 Verily, God knows whatever thing they call upon beside Him; for He is the mighty, wise.

43 These are parables which we have struck out for men; but none will understand them, save those who know.

44 God created the heavens and the earth in truth; verily, in this is a sign unto believers.

Responses to Jews and Christians

45 Recite what has been, revealed to thee of the Book; and be steadfast in prayer; verily, prayer forbids sin and wrong; and surely the mention of God is greater; for God knows what ye do.

46 And do not wrangle with the people

29.40b The forms of judgment were: (a) sandstorms, (b) the mysterious noise [see Q 54.22-31, note], (c) an opening of the earth, and (d) the Flood.

29.41 Muhammad equated those who reject the message of divinely appointed apostles and formulate their own religious systems with spiders. Spiders construct their own houses in which they live. Their houses are small and frail and easily destroyed. In like manner, the houses of the infidels were also frail and easily destroyed.

29.42 Allah knows the nature of whatever it is that infidels worship—whether they be the gods of the Arabic Star Family religion, deified people, or forces of nature.

29.44 Only those who understand Allah as the creator of the heavens and the earth

have taken the first step towards true religion. Similarly, the Bible begins with the statement: "In the beginning, God created the heavens and the earth" (Gen 1:1).

29.45-55 Muhammad admonished his followers to remain committed to the straight path that leads to eternal life. With this in mind, they were to be wary of the Jews and Christians (that is, people of the Book) who would contend with them and attempt to draw they away from the Islamic faith. In this passage, he offered them a three responses to such challenges.

29.45 The Muslim believers *first response* was to cultivate personal piety: (a) remain steadfast in prayer, and (b) recite the qur'anic surahs.

29.46a The *second response* of Muslim be-

of the Book, except for what is better; save with those who have been unjust amongst them and who say, "We believe in what is sent down to us, and what has been sent down to you; our God and your God is one, and. we are unto Him resigned."

47 Thus did we send down to thee the

Book; and every one to whom we have given the Book believes therein. But these will not believe therein though none gainsay our signs except the misbelievers.

48 Thou couldst not recite before this any book, nor write it with thy right hand, for in that case those who deem it vain would have

lievers was to avoid wranglings (that is, discussions and debates) with "the people of the Book." In this case, "the people of the Book" were Jews and Christians, since they were people known to be committed to a sacred literature (the Jews were devoted to the Old Testament and Christians were devoted to the Old and New Testaments for the Christians).

29.46b *except for what is better* — That is, do not wrangle other than in a polite and kind manner.

29.46c *save among those who have been unjust amongst them* — That is, the one exception to polite and kind discourse with Jews and Christians were those who had been unjust with them. With such people, a more aggressive wrangling was permitted.

29.46d Muslims were admonished to tell the Jews and Christians that the Old and New Testaments teach the same fundamental doctrine as that which was being presented in the qur'anic surahs. They were to teach the doctrine of monotheism (the Doctrine of Tauhid) and the requirement that all people live in submission to God.

29.47a *Thus did we send down to thee the Book* — Muhammad believed that he received this doctrine via divine revelation. It corresponded to previous sacred scriptures (that is, the Old and New Testaments). Many Jews and Christians affirmed this doctrine.

29.47b *But these will not believe therein* — Yet there were some Jews and Christians who resisted and continued in their unbelief. More than likely, Muhammad had in mind the Christians who insisted upon the Doctrine of the Trinity, which he claimed was a form of polytheism: the belief in multiple gods (see **The Doctrine of the Trinity** on pp. 735-736).

29.48 *Thou couldst not recite before this any book* — Prior to his ministry, Muhammad claimed that he had not recited or written sacred literature. Islamic scholars take this verse, along with Q 7.157-158, to make the case that Muhammad was illiterate, unable to read or write. Moreover, they add that since such a large volume of surahs emerged from his ministry, it could only mean that the surahs had a supernatural origin (also see Q 2.78; 7.157; and 10.48).

Non-Islamic scholars have consistently rejected this claim of Muhammad's illiteracy. They have noted that prior to his alleged call to the ministry as a prophet he had been involved in the business of caravans. The caravan business—by its very nature of buying, selling, and inventorying goods—required businessmen to be literate. In addition, most of the people of Mecca were literate due to the fact that it had become a major intersection of several caravan routes and therefore deeply involved in the caravan negotia-

doubted.

49 Nay, but it is evident signs in the breasts of those who are endued with knowledge, and none but the unjust would gainsay our signs!

50 They say, "Unless there be sent down upon him signs from his Lord—;" say, "Verily, signs are with God, and, verily, I am an obvious warner!"

51 Is it not enough for them that we have sent down to thee the Book which thou dost recite to them? verily, in that is a mercy and a reminder to a people who believe.

52 Say, "God is witness enough between me and you; He knows what is in the heavens and what is in the earth; and those who believe in falsehood and misbelieve in God, they shall be the losers."

53 They will wish thee to hasten on the torment; but were it not for a stated and appointed time, the torment would have come upon them suddenly, while yet they did not perceive.

54 They will wish thee to hurry on the torment, but, verily, hell encompasses the misbelievers!

55 On the day when the torment shall cover them from above them and from beneath their feet, and He shall say, "Taste that which ye have done!"

Future blessings

56 O my servants who believe! verily, my land is spacious enough; me therefore do ye worship.

57 Every soul must taste of death, then unto us shall ye return;

58 and those who believe and act

tions. These same scholars also disregard Muhammad's claims that the surahs came to him via supernatural angelic visitations. Rather, they say, the surahs were the result of his own study and creative thought.

29.49 Muhammad believed that the divine origin of his surahs were self-evident—clear to the hearts of any person endowed with simple intuitive perception. Only those who are morally unjust would reject this claim.

29.50 According to Muhammad, the Jews and Christians who insisted that miraculous signs accompany Muhammad's ministry to validate his prophetic calling were morally unjust—making demands upon Allah that they had no right to make (see **John of Damascus** on pp. 247-248).

29.51 The *third response* of Muslim believ-

ers was to affirm the notion that the Qur'an is sufficient in itself, therefore not requiring miracles to provide an external validation. sign. That is, the Qur'an was self-authenticating, its own miraculous sign.

29.52-55 Muhammad was convinced that one's attitude toward the Qur'an served as a litmus test, distinguishing true believers from those who embraced falsehood. What is more, all who reject the Qur'an will suffer in Hell.

29.56 *my land is spacious enough* — That is, the entire earth belongs to Allah. Allah will grant to his faithful followers (those who worship Him) the blessings of land.

29.58a *believe and act aright* — A summary of the Islamic gospel (see Q 103.3, note).

aright, we will surely inform them of upper chambers in Paradise, beneath which rivers flow; to dwell therein for aye—pleasant is the hire of those who work!

59 those who are patient and rely upon their Lord!

60 How many a beast cannot carry its own provision! God provides for it and for you; He both hears and knows!

Two questions

61 And if thou shouldst ask them, "Who created the heavens and the earth, and subjected the sun and the moon?" they will surely say, "God!" how then can they lie?

62 God extends provision to whomsoever He will of His servants, or doles it out to him; verily, God all things doth know.

63 And if thou shouldst ask them, "Who sends down from the heavens water and quickens therewith the earth in its death?" they will

29.58b *upper chambers in Paradise* — That is, the higher levels in Paradise (see **Paradise** on pp. 76-77).

29.58c *pleasant is the hire for those who work* — That is, pleasant is the reward for those who strived faithfully after God.

29.59-60 Those who rely on the Lord will be blessed with godly provision.

29.61-63a Muhammad suggested that Muslims ask the Jew and Christian two questions: (a) who created the heavens and the earth? and (b) Who sends down from the heavens water and quickens therewith the earth in its death" In both cases, Jews and Christians would answer: God. How, then, Muhammad mused, could they not see that the qur'anic surahs and Bible parallel one another, possessing doctrines that are fundamentally the same?

The answer, Jews and Christians would say, is a *non sequitur*. The problem between Islam and Judeo-Christianity is not centered on the doctrine of creation but rather the doctrine of redemption (salvation).

In the Old Testament, Jews relied on the blood of two goats dedicated to God as a substitutionary atonement for their sins at the ceremony of *Yom Kippur* (the Day of

Atonement—see Leviticus 16). That is, the animals were put to death in their place so that the blessing of salvation could be offered to them.

Christians believe that the Jewish sacrifice at Yom Kippur was a prefiguring of the blood of Jesus Christ that was shed on the cross. His death served as a substitutionary atonement for the sins of the entire world. Speaking of Jesus, the Apostle Paul said: "God presented him as a sacrifice of atonement, through faith in his blood. He did this to demonstrate his justice" (Rom 3:25), and "Since we have now been justified by his blood, how much more shall we be saved from God's wrath through him!" (Rom 5:9). Christians also believe that Jesus Christ is God incarnate, the Second Person of the Trinity.

Since Muhammad denied the doctrine of blood atonement and its relationship to divine salvation, Muhammad was determined to be a false teacher and the Qur'an to be rejected as a false sacred literature.

29.63b-66 The nature of religious hypocrisy is: (a) a cavalier attitude towards life, (b) devotedness to God when in peril but then ascribing the blessings offered by God to the gods, and (c) a rejection of divine

surely say, "God!" say, "And praise
be to God!"

Hypocritical religion

Nay, most of them have no sense.
64   This life of the world is nothing but
     a sport and a play; but, verily, the
     abode of the next world, that is
     life,—if they did but know!
65   And when they ride in the ship they
     call upon God, making their reli-
     gion seem sincere to Him; but
     when He saves them to the shore,
     behold, they associate others with
     Him;
66   that they may disbelieve in our
     signs; and that they may have some
     enjoyment: but soon they shall
     know.
67   Have they not seen that we have

made a safe sanctuary whilst
people are being snatched away
around them? is it then in falsehood that they will believe, and for
the favours of God be ungrateful?
68   But who is more unjust than he
     who devises against God a lie, or
     calls the truth a lie when it comes
     to him? Is there not in hell a resort
     for the misbelievers?
69   but those who fight strenuously for
     us we will surely guide them into
     our way, for, verily, God is with
     those who do well.

Surah 7

*In the name of the merciful and compas-
sionate God*

revelation.
29.67 *a safe sanctuary* — That is, an inner
peace where people are free from fear of
despair. In contrast, Muhammad believed
that the infidel was "snatched away" (presumably by Satan) in falsehood and ungratefulness.

The Christian faith also speaks of a safe
sanctuary (an inner peace) offered to the
believer. Yet it is offered as a free gift due
to the nature of salvation, which is also a
free gift (Ps 4:8; Jn 14:27; Rom 5:1; 8:6;
15:13; Gal 5:22; Phil 4:7; Col 1:20; 3:15; 1
Thess 5:23 and Heb 12:11).

John R. W. Stott comments, "Although
'grace' and 'peace' are common monosyl-
lables, they are pregnant with theological
substance. In fact, they summarize Paul's
gospel of salvation. The nature of salvation

is peace, or reconciliation—peace with God,
peace with men, peace within. The source
of salvation is grace, God's free favour, irrespective of any human merit or works, his
loving-kindness to the undeserving. And this
grace and peace flow from the Father and
the Son together" (*The Message of Galatians*, p. 16).
29.69a *those who fight strenuously for us*
— Literally, those who jihad a great jihad for
us (see Q 8.72, 74-75; 16.110; 22.78;
25.52; 29.6; 47.31).
29.69b *our way* — This is a synonym for
the straight path that leads to eternal life
(see Q 72.2, note).
Surah 7. The title of this surah, *The Faculty of Discernment*, comes from verse 46.
The phrase, "the Lord of the worlds" occurs
five times in the surah. The surah has as its

1   A. L. M. S.

Muhammad's calling

2   A book revealed to thee,—so let
there be no straitness in thy breast,
that thou mayest warn thereby,—
and a reminder to the believers.

3   Follow what has been revealed to
you from your Lord, and follow
not beside Him patrons; little is it
that ye mind.

Muhammad's warning

4   Yet how many a town have we destroyed, and our violence came
upon it by night, or while they slept
at noon;

5   and their cry, when our violence
came upon them, was only to say,
"Verily, we were unjust!"

6   But we will of a surety question
those to whom the prophets were
sent,

overall theme the divine retribution of Allah upon the civilizations who rejected the message of his duly called apostles. It begins with a discussion of the fall of Satan and subsequent fall of Adam, with a warning to the children of Adam (that is, all humanity) to be repent and turn to Allah—and Allah alone. Muhammad then moved to a brief review of the ministries of five apostles mentioned in other surahs. In each case, those who were the recipients of their ministries rejected their message of repentance and were then duly destroyed by Allah (Great Flood, earthquakes, and rain). Then, at the midpoint of the surah (verse 103), Muhammad turned his attention to the people of Israel, and stayed with this concern for the remainder of the surah. His point was that the Israelite people also rejected the message of their duly called apostle—Moses—and were judged accordingly. The surah ended with an appeal for Muslims to remain faithful to Allah.

7.1 Literally, *Alif Lam Mim Sad*. See Q 32.1, note.

7.2a *A book revealed to thee* — Muhammad insisted that the surahs that he presented to the people of Mecca were not of his own invention. Rather, they were revealed to him from the archangel Gabriel.

Islamic scholars refer to this revelation as having been dictated to Muhammad who then memorized what he heard. The surahs were later transcribed by a number of Muhammad's followers.

7.2b *let there be no straitness in thy breast* — That is, let there be no doubts in your heart about the truthfulness of the qur'anic surahs.

7.2c Muhammad believed that the nature of his ministry was to be that of a *warner* to the infidels and a *reminder* to the believers.

7.3 Muhammad also believed that his responsibility was to follow the path that leads to eternal life and not to fall into the sin of polygamy ("follow not beside Him patrons").

7.4-5 According to this passage, Allah destroyed numerous towns with violence, all at unexpected moments, due to their refusal to heed the message of the apostles that had been sent to them (see **The Apostles** on pp. 398-400).

7.6-7 At the Last Judgment, Allah will repeat to the infidels the message of the apostles that had been sent to them. The message will serve as a validation of the sentence of condemnation that will be spoken to them.

7.7-8 At the Last Judgment, the celestial

7   and we will narrate to them with knowledge, for we were not absent.

8   The balance on that day is true, and whosesoever scales are heavy, they are prosperous;

9   but whosesoever scales are light, they it is who lose themselves, for that they did act unjustly by our signs.

Satan's fall into sin

10   We have established you in the earth, and we have made for you therein livelihoods; little is it that ye thank;

11   and we created you, then we fashioned you, then we said unto the angels, "Adore Adam," and they adored, save Iblîs [Satan], who

was not of those who did adore.

12   Said He, "What hinders thee from adoring when I order thee?" he said, "I am better than he; Thou hast created me from fire, and him Thou hast created out of clay."

13   Said He, "Then go down therefrom; what ails thee that thou shouldst be big with pride therein? go forth! verily, thou art of the little ones."

14   He [Satan] said, "Respite me until the day when they shall be raised."

15   He said, "Verily, thou art of the respited;"

16   said he, "For that Thou hast led me into error, I will lie in wait for them in Thy straight path;

17   then I will surely come to them, from before them and from behind them; and most of them Thou

balance will either be heavy (with many good works) or light (with few good works). One's eternal destiny will be determined by whether the balance is heavy or light (see **The Last Judgment** on pp. 46-50).

7.10-12 Muhammad believed that the original sin of Satan (Iblis) was his failure to bow down and show obeisance to Adam. Satan's reason for not showing obeisance to Adam was that he was better than Adam since he was created from the fire and Adam from clay.

The Bible presents a different account of Satan's fall into sin. According to Isa 14:13-15, the archangel Lucifer desired to raise his throne above the stars of God and make himself "like the Most High." It was an act of profound insubordination and a desire to be worshipped. This was the original sin.

The consequences of this action was condemnation and a change of names: from Lucifer to Satan. The book of the Revelation suggests that a third of the angels in heaven followed Lucifer and were part of the failed insurrection (see Rev 12:4).

In the biblical account, not only do the details of Satan's fall into sin differ from the Qur'an, the chronology differs. In the Qur'an, Satan fell into sin after the creation of Adam. In the biblical account, it occurred prior to the creation of Adam.

7.13-14 Allah condemned Satan, casting him out of Paradise. Satan requested a respite (a temporary relief) from judgment, until the Day of Resurrection.

7.16 *Thy straight path* — This is a summary of the Islamic gospel (see Q 72.2, note).

7.16-18 Since Satan believed that Allah

shalt not find thankful."

18 He said, "Go forth therefrom, despised, expelled; whoso follows thee, I will surely fill hell with you altogether."

Adam's fall into sin

19 "But, O Adam, dwell thou and thy wife in Paradise and eat from whence ye will, but draw not nigh unto this tree or ye will be of the unjust."

20 But Satan whispered to them to display to them what was kept back from them of their shame, and he said, "Your Lord has only forbidden you this tree lest ye should be twain angels, or should become of the immortals;"

21 and he swore to them both, "Verily, I am unto you a sincere adviser;"

22 and he beguiled them by deceit, and when they twain tasted of the tree, their shame was shown them, and they began to stitch upon themselves the leaves of the garden. And their Lord called unto them, "Did I not forbid you from that tree there, and say to you, Verily, Satan is to you an open foe?"

23 They said, "O our Lord! we have wronged ourselves—and if Thou dost not forgive us and have mercy on us, we shall surely be of those who are lost!"

24 He said, "Go ye down, one of you to the other a foe; but for you in the earth there is an abode, and a

was responsible for leading him into error, he requested that he be sent to the earth where he would lead others into error (sin). Allah granted Satan this request (see Q 15.26-40; 17.61-64; 38.86-88).

The Bible presents a similar account of Satan. Rather than being cast into the Lake of Fire, God permitted Satan to remain on the earth and beguile people to sin. The angels that had followed Lucifer in his original sin were also cast down to the earth and became fallen angels (or demons). Satan and his demons will continue in this activity until the time in which God summons all the wicked to the Great White Throne. Just prior to this event, Satan and the demonic horde wicked will finally be cast into the Lake of Fire (Rev 20:10).

7.19 *Paradise* — In this case, Paradise refers to the original Garden of Eden that exists on the earth, the original home of Adam and Eve (see Gen 2:8). Typically in the Qur'an, however, Paradise refers to a realm in the afterlife (see **Paradise** on pp. 76-77). **7.19-25** This passage is based upon Gen. 3:1-20. It varies slightly from the biblical account. The qur'anic account claims that Satan spoke to both Adam and Eve (v. 20). In the biblical account, Satan spoke only to the woman (Gen 3:1). The qur'anic account claims that the content of Satan's lie was: if Adam and Eve ate of the fruit of the tree, they would be like angels and achieve immortality. In the biblical account, the woman was told that she would become like God, know the difference between good and evil, and not be punished with death (Gen 3:4-5). The statement in the Qur'an ("ye should be twain angels"—v. 20) corresponds to the qur'anic insistence that no-

25 provision for a season." He said, "Therein shall ye live and therein shall ye die, from it shall ye be brought forth."

Admonition to the sons of Adam

26 O sons of Adam! we have sent down to you garments wherewith to cover your shame, and plumage; but the garment of piety, that is better. That is one of the signs of God, haply ye may remember.

27 O sons of Adam! let not Satan infatuate you as he drove your parents out of Paradise, stripping from them their garments, and showing them their shame; verily, he sees you—he and his tribe, from whence ye cannot see them. Verily, we have made the devils patrons of those who do not believe,

28 and when they commit an abomi-

---

body can be likened unto Allah. Rather than being tempted to be like God, Adam and Eve were tempted to be like angels.

The qur'anic account claims that after they ate of the fruit they begged forgiveness from God for their sin (v. 23). In the biblical account, neither begged for forgiveness. Rather, when confronted by God, Adam cast the blame on the woman for the sin, and the woman cast the blame on the serpent for beguiling her (Gen 3:12-13).

The qur'anic account claims that Adam and Eve were punished by being cast out of the garden ("go ye down"), and by losing their status of immortality (vv. 25-26). In the biblical account, the woman was judged with pain in childbirth, having her husband as her head, and experiencing the loss of immortality; the man was judged by working by the sweat of his brow and experiencing the loss of immortality. Both were then cast from the Garden (Gen 3:24).

7.26a *sons of Adam* — That is, all the descendents of Adam, the entire human race. The daughters of Adam are also included since the word "sons" could also be rightly translated "children."

7.26b *cover your shame* — That is, cover your nakedness.

7.26c *plumage* — birds' feathers. The word is used metaphorically to describe the beauty of one's clothing.

7.26d Muhammad's point was that not only did Allah provide clothing for people, as He did for Adam and Eve (Gen 3:21), He also provided a more important clothing, that of personal piety. People were admonished to pursue lives of piety as a way of overcoming the shame of sin.

7.27a Muhammad believed that it was Satan who drove Adam and Eve from Paradise (the Garden of Eden), and then stripped them of their garments. According to the Book of Genesis, it was God Himself who drove Adam and Eve from the Garden of Eden (Gen 3:23). Moreover, they were not stripped of the garments—by Satan or anyone else.

7.27b Muhammad asserted that Satan and his demonic horde ("he and his tribe") see people, though people cannot see them. Moreover, Satan and his horde are attached and control the lives of those who do not believe. The Bible makes a similar claim (see Matt 12:43-45; Jn 8:44; 2 Cor 4:4; Eph 2:1-3; 1 Jn 5:19; Rev 12:9).

nation they say, "We found our
fathers at this, and God bade us
do it." Say, "God bids you not to
do abomination; do ye say against
God that which ye do not know?"

29 Say, "My Lord bids only justice:—
set steadfastly your faces at every
mosque and pray to Him, being sincere in your religion. As He
brought you forth in the beginning,
shall ye return.

30 A sect He guides, and for a sect of
them was error due; verily, they
did take the devils for their patrons
instead of God, and they did count
that they were guided."

31 O sons of Adam! take your ornaments to every mosque; and eat
and drink, but do not be extravagant, for He loves not the extravagant.

32 Say, "Who has prohibited the ornaments of God which He brought
forth for His servants, and the good

things of His providing?" say, "On
the day of judgment they shall only
be for those who believed when in
the life of this world." Thus do
we detail the signs unto a people
that do know.

33 Say, "My Lord has only prohibited
abominable deeds, the apparent
thereof and the concealed thereof,
and sin, and greed for that which
is not right, and associating with
God what He has sent down no
power for, and saying against God
that which ye do not know."

34 Every nation has its appointed time,
and when their appointed time
comes they cannot keep it back an
hour, nor can they bring it on.

35 O sons of Adam! verily, there will
come to you apostles from
amongst you, narrating unto you
my signs; then whoso fears God
and does what is right, there is no
fear for them, nor shall they grieve.

7.28-29 People are told not to make excuses for sin, such as was the custom of
their fathers or the culture in which they
live, (see James 1:13-14).

7.29 *at every mosque* — That is, at every
temple where Allah is rightly worshipped.

7.30a *a sect He guides* — That is, Muhammad believed that Allah guided the small sect
of Muslim believers.

7.30b *they did make devils for their patrons instead of God* — That is, Muhammad
believed that people who worshipped anyone other than Allah were, in fact, worshippers of demons (see **Polytheism in Seventh Century Arabia** on pp. 92-97). The
Bible makes a similar claim (see Deut 32:16-

17; Ps 106:37-39; 1 Cor 10:19-20; Rev 9:20).

7.31 *take your ornaments to every mosque*
— That is, take your adornment (beautiful
clothing) to your temples, but do not do so
in an extravagant fashion.

7.32 *the ornaments of God which He
brought forth* — That is, the beautiful things
of life. Muhammad's point is that while everyone benefits from the good things of life,
in the afterlife only the righteous will enter
heaven enjoy them.

7.34 *Every nation has its appointed time* —
That is, every nation has its appointed time
from which divine judgment will come, bringing destruction. This can only be averted if
the nation listens to its apostle and repents

FIFTH PERIOD

36 But those who say my signs are lies, and who are too big with pride for them, these are the fellows of the Fire, they shall dwell therein for aye!

Last Judgment

37 Who is more unjust than he who devises against God a lie, or says His signs are lies? These, their portion of the Book shall reach them, until when our messengers come to take their souls away, and say, "Where is what ye used to call upon instead of God?" they say, "They have strayed away from us;" and they shall bear witness against themselves that they have been misbelievers.

Hell

38 He will say, "Enter ye—amongst the nations who have passed away before you, both of ginns and men—into the fire;" whenever a nation enters therein, it curses its mate; until, when they have all reached it, the last of them will say unto the first, "O our Lord! these it was who led us astray, give them double torment of the fire!" He will say, "To each of you double! but ye do not know."

39 And the first of them will say unto the last, "Ye have no preference over us, so taste ye the torment for that which ye have earned!"

40 Verily, those who say our signs are lies and are too big with pride for them; for these the doors of heaven shall not be opened, and they shall not enter into Paradise until a camel shall pass into a needle's eye.

41 It is thus that we reward the sinners; for them is a couch of hell-fire, with an awning above them! thus do we reward the unjust!

Paradise

42 But those who believe and do what is right—we will not oblige a soul

prior to this time (see **The Apostles** on pp. 398-400).

7.37 According to Muhammad, all who were part of the Arabic Star Family religion and called the Islamic teaching of monotheism a lie will be condemned to Hell at the Last Judgment (see **Polytheism in Seventh Century Arabia** on pp. 92-97).

7.38-39 According to Muhammad, anyone who happened to be a leader and led others astray by resisting the Islamic faith will receive a double portion of torment in Hell.

7.40 *they shall not enter into Paradise until a camel shall pass into a needle's eye* — That is, they shall never enter into Paradise since it is impossible for a camel to pass through a needle's eye (see Matt 19:24; Mk 10:25; Lk 18:25 where this same figure of speech is used, yet in a different context).

7.41 *a couch of hell-fire* — The couch of hell-fire is a stark contrast to the couches awaiting the righteous with their harems in Paradise (see Q 13.18; 38.56).

7.42 *believe and do what is right* — This is

more than its capacity—they are the fellows of Paradise, they shall dwell therein for aye.

43 We will strip away what ill feeling is in their breasts—there shall flow beneath them rivers, and they shall say, "Praise belongs to God who guided us to this! for we should not have been guided had not God guided us!—the apostles of our Lord did come to us with truth!" And it shall be cried out to them, "This is Paradise which ye have as an inheritance for that which ye have done!"

The veil

44 And the fellows of Paradise will call out to the fellows of the Fire, "We have now found that what our Lord promised us is true; have ye found that what your Lord promised you is true?" They will say, "Yea!" And a crier from amongst them will cry out, "The curse of God is on the unjust

45 who turn from the way of God and crave to make it crooked, while in the hereafter they do disbelieve!"

46 And betwixt the two there is a veil, and on al Aarâf are men who know each by marks; and they shall cry out to the fellows of Paradise, "Peace be upon you!" they cannot enter it although they so desire.

47 But when their sight is turned towards the fellows of the Fire, they

---

a summary of the Islamic gospel (see Q 103.3, note).

7.43a According to Muhammad, in Paradise all ill feelings will be stripped away and replaced with feelings that are wholesome and joyous. The Bible says something similar where in heaven God "will wipe every tear from their eyes. There will be no more death or mourning or crying or pain, for the old order of things has passed away" (Rev 21:4).

7.43b *for that which ye have done!* — According to Islam, salvation is understood in terms of living a meritorious life combined with worshipping the one true God: Allah.

This definition of salvation stands in contrast to salvation to that which is presented in the New Testament. In the New Testament, salvation is achieved by Jesus Christ who cleansed people of their sins. C. S. Lewis wrote: "We are told that Christ was killed for us, that His death has washed out our sins, and that by dying He disabled death itself. That is the formula. That is Christianity. That is what has to be believed" (*Mere Christianity*, p. 58).

7.44-53 Muhammad believed that in the afterlife Paradise will be divided from Hell by a veil (v. 46). On either side of the veil, people will be able to communicate with one another. Those in Paradise will mock those in the Fire by reminding them of the truths that had been presented to them in the previous life and yet rejected. In reply, those in Hell will cry out to those in Paradise, pleading for water to alleviate the torment that they are experiencing.

Situated between these two realms is a region where a third group of people dwell: the people of *al Aaraf* (those who possess the faculty of discernment). In their previous lives, they possessed a lukewarm attitude towards questions pertaining to spiri-

say, "O our Lord! place us not with the unjust people."

48 And the fellows on al Aarâf will cry out to the men whom they know by their marks, and say, "Of no avail to you were your collections, and what ye were so big with pride about;

49 are these those ye swore that God would not extend mercy to? Enter ye Paradise; there is no fear for you, nor shall ye be grieved."

50 But the fellows of the Fire shall cry out to the fellows of Paradise, "Pour out upon us water, or something of what God has provided you with." They will say, "God has prohibited them both to those who misbelieve;

51 who took their religion for a sport and a play; whom the life of the world beguiled."—Today do we forget them as they forgot the

52 meeting of this day, and for that they did deny our signs!

52 Now we have brought them a book explaining it in knowledge, a guidance and a mercy to a people who believe.

53 Do they wait now for aught but its interpretation?—on the day when its interpretation shall come, those who forgot it before will say, "There did come to us the apostles of our Lord in truth, have we intercessors to intercede for us? or, could we return, we would do otherwise than we did." They have lost themselves, and that which they devised has strayed away from them.

The God of nature

54 Verily, your Lord is God who created the heavens and the earth in

tuality. They neither did much good nor much bad. They now look into Paradise, longing to enter but prevented from doing so. They also look into Hell and exclaim: "O our Lord! place us not with the unjust people."

In contrast, according to the Bible, only two categories of people exist in the afterlife: those in Heaven and those in Hell. A third group situated between the two is nowhere mentioned. A sphere called Limbo has been advanced by certain Roman Catholic scholars. It is a place assigned to those who did not partake of the Catholic sacraments yet lived fundamentally good lives. Limbo, however, has never been part of official Roman Catholic dogma.

7.48 *men whom they know by their marks* — That is, the people of *al Aaraf* will know the sinners from the righteous by distinguishing marks on their bodies.

7.51 *we forget them* — Those in the Fire are the forgotten ones. Yet, prior to this moment, they will be given a copy of the eternal book (that is, the Perspicuous Book) and be reminded that during their life on earth they had been reminded of its truths from the apostles, but they rejected this message (see **The Perspicuous Book** on pp. 178-179).

7.54-56 With this vision of Paradise, Hell, and the place situated between the two thus explained, Muhammad reminded his listeners to follow the straight path that leads

six days; then He made for the Throne. He covers night with the day—it pursues it incessantly—and the sun and the moon and the stars are subject to His bidding. Aye!—His is the creation and the bidding,—blessed be God the Lord of the worlds

55 Call on your Lord humbly and secretly, verily, He loves not the transgressors.

56 And do not evil in the earth after it has been righted; and call upon Him with fear and earnestness; verily, the mercy of God is nigh unto those who do well.

57 He it is who sends forth the winds as heralds before His mercy; until when they lift the heavy cloud which we drive to a dead land, and send down thereon water, and bring forth therewith every kind of fruit;—thus do we bring forth the dead; haply ye may remember.

58 And the good land brings forth its vegetation by the permission of its Lord; and that which is vile brings forth naught but scarcity. Thus do we turn about our signs for a people who are grateful.

Noah

59 We did send Noah unto his people,

---

to eternal life. Allah is described as having made the heavens and earth in six days (cf. Gen 1:1-31) and sitting on His throne with absolute authority over all of creation. It is in this respect that Allah is "the Lord of the worlds" (see Q 1.2, note). With Allah so described, people are admonished to yield to His sovereign authority by praying in secret with fear, humility, and in earnestness. They are also admonished, by implication, to turn away from all other gods, which are nothing but false gods.

The Bible makes a similar claim (see Ps 8:1-9; 19:1-14; 29:1-11; 89:1-13; 135:1-7; 139:1-24; Isa 40:21-24; Acts 17:22-34). In his sermon at the Areopagus in Athens, the Apostle Paul proclaimed as the Creator and Sustainer of the universe. He spoke of God's greatness, the one who brought all things into existence, who holds all things together, and to whom all people owe their existence. It was an argument from natural revelation. His purpose in sharing these thoughts was to make the point that the Athenians' commitment to idolatry was inexcusable. God was offended by their false worship and expected them to repent. It was then, when he began speaking of Jesus Christ as the one who had risen from the dead to secure their salvation, that the Athenians stopped the sermon and walked away (see Acts 17:22-31).

7.57 *thus to we bring forth the dead* — That is, thus does God bring forth life from dead land by means of rain and seeds germinating, growing to plants, and then bearing fruit.

7.59-64 Muhammad returned to a familiar theme—the ministry of Noah (see Gen 6-8). The focus of his ministry was to proclaim the doctrine of monotheism to a people beholden to a polytheistic understanding of deity. If they failed to repent they would experience "the torment of the mighty day" (v. 59). The people, in response, said that he was "in obvious error" (v. 60). Because

and he said, "O my people! serve God, ye have no god but Him; verily, I fear for you the torment of the mighty day."

60 Said the chiefs of his people, "Verily, we do surely see you in obvious error."

61 Said he, "O my people! there is no error in me; but I am an apostle from the Lord of the worlds.

62 I preach to you the messages of my Lord, and I give you sincere advice; and I know from God what ye know not.

63 What! do ye wonder that there came to you a reminder from your Lord by a man from amongst yourselves, to warn you, and that ye may fear? but haply ye may receive mercy."

64 But they called him a liar, and we rescued him and those who were with him in the ark; and we drowned those who said our signs were lies, verily, they were a blind

people.

Hud

65 And unto 'Âd (we sent) their brother Hûd, who said, "O my people! serve God, ye have no god save Him; what! will ye not then fear?"

66 Said the chiefs of those who misbelieved amongst his people, "Verily, we see thee in folly, and, verily, we certainly think thou art of the liars."

67 He said, "O my people! there is no folly in me; but I am an apostle from the Lord of the worlds;

68 I preach to you the messages of your Lord; and, verily, I am to you a faithful adviser.

69 What! do ye then wonder that there comes to you a reminder from your Lord by a man from amongst yourselves, to warn you? remember when He made you vicegerents af-

---

the people rejected his message, they suffered a cataclysm that brought an end to their civilization: the Great Flood.

7.61 *I am an apostle from the Lord of the worlds* — see Q 1.2, note; also see Q 7.67.

7.65-72 Muhammad then returned to another of his favorite apostles: Hud, the legendary apostle who lived among the Ad people. The people of Ad lived in the City of Hegra (Hijr), approximately five hundred miles northwest of Mecca, along the caravan route that leads northward to Jerusalem (see **Hegra** on p. 28).

According to Muhammad, the primary message of Hud was the rightness of mono-

theism and the need for the people of Ad to repent of their polytheism. Since the people of Ad rejected his message, calling Hud a liar, they experienced a "horror and wrath" (v. 71).

7.67 *I am an apostle from the Lord of the worlds* — see Q 1.2, note; also see Q 7.61.

7.69a *He made you vicegerents after Noah's people* — In the Arabic, the word vicegerents is *khalifah*, or *caliphs*. Muhammad believed that the people of Ad became the *caliphs* (rulers of the land) following the death of Noah's family (see Q 35.39, note).

Yet, the archeological record asserts that the Ad people are dated to the second cen-

ter Noah's people and increased you in length of stature; remember, then, the benefits of God, haply ye may prosper!"

70 They said, "Hast thou come to us that we may worship God alone, and leave what our fathers used to worship? then bring us what thou dost threaten us with, if thou art of those who tell the truth!"

71 He said, "There shall fall upon you from your Lord horror and wrath; do ye wrangle with me about names, which ye and your fathers have named yourselves, for which God sent down no power; wait then expectant, and I with you will wait expectant too!

72 But we rescued him and those with him, by mercy from ourselves, and we cut off the hindermost parts of those who said our signs were lies and who were not believers."

Zali'h

73 Unto Thamûd (we sent) their brother Zâli'h, who said, "O my

people! worship God; ye have no god but Him: there has come to you a manifest sign from your Lord. This she-camel of God's is a sign for you; leave her then to eat in the land of God, and touch her not with evil, or there will overtake you grievous woe.

74 And remember how he made you vicegerents after 'Âd and stablished you in the earth, so that ye took for yourselves castles on its plains and hewed out mountains into houses; and remember the benefits of God, and waste not the land, despoiling it."

75 Said the chiefs of those who were big with pride from amongst his people to those who were weak,—to those amongst them who believed, "Do ye know that Zâli'h is sent from his Lord?" They said, "We do believe in that with which he is sent."

76 Said those who were big with pride, "Verily, in what ye do believe we disbelieve."

77 Then they did hamstring the camel,

tury, A.D.—not to an antediluvian age. Aware of this problem, some Islamic scholars have asserted that two Ad civilizations existed—one in the ancient period associated with Noah and the other of the second century, A.D. Still, no archeological evidence exists of two Ad civilizations nor are two such civilizations mentioned in the Qur'an (see Q 54.17-21, note). The Qur'an consistently assumes a singular civilization by this name. The ruins of Hegra (Hijr) are dated to the second century, A.D. (see **Hegra** on p. 28).

7.69b *increased you in length of stature* — According to Muhammad, the Ad people were an unusually tall people (see Q 54.16-21 note).

7.73-79 Muhammad then reminded his audience of Zali'h, the legendary apostle who lived among the Thamudian people. These people, Muhammad explained, moved into the City of Hegra following the demise of the people of Ad (v. 74). This means that they too were a civilization that existed in the years immediately following the Great

and rebelled against the bidding of their Lord and said, "O Zâli'h! bring us what thou didst threaten us with, if thou art of those who are sent."

78 Then the earthquake took them, and in the morning they lay prone in their dwellings;

79 and he turned away from them and said, "O my people! I did preach to you the message of my Lord, and I gave you good advice! but ye love not sincere advisers."

Lot

80 And Lot, when he said to his people, "Do ye approach an abomination which no one in all the world ever

anticipated you in?

81 verily, ye approach men with lust rather than women—nay, ye are a people who exceed."

82 But his people's answer only was to say, "Turn them out of your village, verily, they are a people who pretend to purity."

83 But we saved him and his people, except his wife, who was of those who lingered;

84 and we rained down upon them a rain;—see then how was the end of the sinners!

Jethro (Sho'haib)

85 And unto Midian did we send their brother Sho'hâib, who said, "O my

---

Flood—a postdiluvian age (see v. 69). Yet, the archeological record disputes this claim, dating the people of Thamud to the 8th century, B.C. and that they continued into the 5th century, A.D. (see Q 91, note).

According to Muhammad, central to his message was monotheism (the Doctrine of Tauhid) and a corresponding call for the people of Thamud to turn away from their polytheistic beliefs.

The people of Thamud rejected the ministry of Zali'h by eating the she-camel that Allah supernaturally provided as a sign (miraculously created out of a rock).

Due to their insolence (being "big with pride"), Muhammad explained that Allah sent a "grievous woe" (v. 73) upon the Thamudian people. He sent an earthquake to Hegra in the middle of the night. By morning all the Thamudian polytheists were dead. It is not clear whether the few Thamudian be-

lievers in Zali'h's message survived the earthquake. Zali'h then walked away from the devastation, saying, "O my people! I did preach to you the message of my Lord, and I gave you good advice! but ye love not sincere advisers" (v. 79).

7.74 *vicegerents*— In the Arabic, the word vicegerents is *khalifah*, or *caliphs*. Muhammad believed that the people of Ad became the *caliphs* (rulers of the land) following the death of Noah's family (see Q 35.39, note).

7.80-84 Muhammad reminded his audience, once again, of the ministry of Lot. In this passage, he addressed the sin of homosexuality: a major sin of the inhabitants of Sodom and Gomorrah (see Gen 19:1-26). Because the people rejected his message, Allah sent to them a torrential rain that destroyed their cities. Elsewhere in the Qur'an, the destruction was described as a sandstorm (Q 29.40; 54.34) or the raining down of baked clay

people! serve God, ye have no god save Him. There has come to you a manifest sign from your Lord; then give good weight and measure, and be not niggardly of your gifts to men, and do not evil in the earth after it has been righted. That is better for you if ye are believers;

86 and sit not down in every path, threatening and turning from the path of God those who believe in Him, and craving to make it crooked. Remember when ye were few and He multiplied you; and see what was the end of the evildoers!

87 And if there be a party of you who believe in what I am sent with, and a party who believe not, then wait patiently until God judges between us, for He is the best of judges."

88 Said the crowd of those who were big with pride amongst His people, "We will of a surety turn thee out, O Sho'hâib! and those who be-

lieve with thee, from our village; or else thou shalt return unto our faith." Said he, "What even if we be averse therefrom?

89 We shall have devised a lie against God if we return unto your faith, after God has saved us from it; and what should ail us that we should return thereto, unless that God our Lord should please? our Lord embraces everything in His knowledge;—on God do we rely. O our Lord! open between us and between our people in truth, for Thou art the best of those who open."

90 And the chiefs of those who disbelieved amongst his people said, "If ye follow Sho'hâib, verily, ye shall be the losers;"

91 then there took them the earthquake, and in the morning they lay in their dwellings prone.

92 Those who called Sho'hâib a liar, (were) as though they had not dwelt therein!—Those who called Sho'hâib a liar, they were the los-

(see Q 11.83' 15.74; 51.33; **The Doctrine of Abrogation** on pp. 68-70).

7.85-96 Muhammad brought to the attention of his audience a person by the name of Sho'haib (Jethro), the father-in-law to Moses (see Q 11.84-95, note). According to Muhammad, Sho'haib (Jethro) served as Allah's apostle to the Midianite people. Because the Midianite people rejected his ministry, Allah brought destruction upon this people—an enormous earthquake that resulted in widespread death. Sho'haib (Jethro) survived the earthquake and walked

away, saying: "O my people! I preached to you the messages of my Lord, and I gave you good advice; how should I be vexed for a people who do misbelieve?" (v. 93).

The archeological record, however, disagrees with this alleged destruction of the Midianite people. Rather than being destroyed in the days of Moses (c. 1500 B.C.), they continued as tent dwellers well into the Christian era (see Q 11.84-95, note).

7.86 *the path of God* — This is a summary of the Islamic gospel (see Q 72.2, note). It stands in contrast to the crooked path (see

ers then!

93 And he turned away from them and said, "O my people! I preached to you the messages of my Lord, and I gave you good advice; how should I be vexed for a people who do misbelieve?"

94 We have not sent unto a city any prophet except we overtook the people thereof with trouble and distress, that haply they might humble themselves;

95 and then did we give them, in exchange for evil, good, until they increased and said, "Distress and joy both touched our fathers;" then we overtook them suddenly ere they could perceive.

96 —Had the people of the town but believed and feared, we would have opened up for them blessings from the heavens and from the earth; but they said it was a lie, so we overtook them for that which they had

earned.

Four questions

97 Were the people of these cities then secure that our violence would not come on them by night, while they slept?

98 were the people of these cities secure that our violence would not come on them in the morning whilst they played?

99 were they secure from the craft of God? none feel secure from the craft of God except a people that shall lose.

100 Is it not shown to those who inherit the earth after its (former) people, that, did we please, we would smite them in their sins, and would set a stamp upon their hearts, and then they should not hear?

101 These cities, we do relate to thee

Q 7.175-185).

7.93 *how should I be vexed for a people who do misbelieve?* — Sho'haib (Jethro) is characterized as possessing a coldhearted disinterest when divine judgment befell infidels. It corresponds to the coldhearted disinterest of Allah toward infidels (see Q 25.19; 31.24; 38.57; 39.41).

7.97-102 In review of the examples mentioned previously in this surah—Noah, Hud, Zali'h, Lot, and Jethro—Muhammad asked four questions: (a) Were the people of these cities secure that divine judgment could be averted in the evening? (b) Were the people of these cities secure that divine judgment could be averted in the morning? (c) Were

the peoples of these cities secure from the craftiness of Allah? (d) Were the peoples who replaced those who had been destroyed secure in their lives, or should they take care to remain committed to Allah?

The point of the four questions was to bring to light the truth that nobody should feel secure within themselves in regards to avoiding divine judgment. Moreover, those who occupy the lands and cities of those who had been destroyed need to take care that they remain committed to the path of Allah and do not apostasize from the faith, otherwise they too will be destroyed (see **The Apostles** on pp. 398-400; **Islamification** on pp. 851-852).

their stories. There came to them our apostles with manifest signs; but they did not at all believe in what they called a lie before.—Thus doth God set a stamp upon the hearts of those who misbelieve.

102 Nor did we find in most of them a covenant; but we did find most of them workers of abomination.

The story of Israel (Part One):
Moses and the contest of snakes

103 Then we raised up after them Moses with our signs to Pharaoh and his chiefs; but they dealt unjustly therewith, and see what was the end of the evildoers!

104 Moses said, "O Pharaoh! verily, I am an apostle from the Lord of the worlds;

105 it is not right for me to speak against God aught but the truth. I have come to you with a manifest

sign from my Lord; send then the children of Israel with me."

106 Said he, "If thou hast come with a sign, then bring it, if thou art of those who speak the truth."

107 Then he threw his rod down, and lo! it was an obvious snake;

108 and he drew out his hand, and lo! it was white to the beholders.

109 Said the chiefs of Pharaoh's people, "Verily, this is surely a knowing magician;

110 he desires to turn you out of your land;—what is it then ye bid?"

111 They said, "Give him and his brother some hope; and send into the cities to collect

112 and bring you every knowing magician."

113 And the magician came to Pharaoh and said, "Is there indeed a reward for us if we are conquerors?"

114 He said, "Yea! and ye shall be of those who draw nigh unto me."

7.101 *stamp upon their hearts* — This is the mysterious stamp that Allah places on the hearts of infidels that makes it impossible for them to hear and respond to the message of the apostles and repent of their evil ways (see Q 16.108, note, and Q 4.155; 9.87, 93; 10.74; 30.59; 40.35; 47.16; 63.3; **The Doctrine of al-Qadar** on pp. 264-266). **7.103-168** The next section of this surah addresses the story of Israel, beginning with the confrontation between Moses and Pharaoh and ending with the Israelite people in exile—cursed of God. Muhammad's point was to clarify how and why the Israelite people fell into the sin of idolatry and became cursed of Allah.

7.103-126 The story of Israel begins with the story of the rod of Moses being miraculously transformed into a snake before Pharaoh in his court (see Ex 7:6-13). The narrative in this passage is more extensive than the Exodus account, adding imaginative details and dialogue. It follows the biblical account with the one main exception being the response of the Egyptian sorcerers who, said Muhammad, bowed before Moses and acknowledged his superiority when the snake of Moses ate their snakes (vv. 120-126). Their response enraged Pharaoh who decided to cut off their hands and feet and then crucify them.

The practice of crucifixion was unknown

115   They said, "O Moses! wilt thou cast down (thy rod) or shall we be (first) to throw?"

116   Said he, "Throw down;" and when they threw down, they did enchant the people's eyes, and made them dread, and brought a mighty magic.

117   But we inspired Moses (saying), "Throw down thy rod, and it will gulp down that which they devise;"

118   and the truth stood fast, and vain was that which they had done;

119   and they were conquered there, and turned back feeling small!

120   and the magicians threw themselves down adoring.

121   Said they, "We believe in the Lord of the worlds,

122   the Lord of Moses and Aaron!"

123   Said Pharaoh, "Do ye believe in him ere I give you leave? This is craft which ye have devised in the land, to turn its people out therefrom,

but soon shall ye know!

124   I will cut off your hands and your feet from opposite sides, then I will crucify you altogether!"

125   They said, "Verily, we unto our Lord return!

126   nor dost thou take vengeance on us, save for that we believe in the signs of our Lord, when they come to us. "O our Lord! pour out upon us patience, and take us to Thyself resigned."

The story of Israel (Part Two): the plagues and exodus

127   And the chiefs of Pharaoh's people said, "Will ye leave Moses and his people to do evil in the land, and to leave thee and thy gods?" Said he, "We will have their sons slain and their women we will let live, for, verily, we are triumphant over them."

in the ancient world, not to have been invented until the sixth century, B.C. The story of the Exodus, however, occurred in the fourteenth century, B.C. Muhammad's insertion of crucifixion in the story demonstrates his lack of historical understanding (see Q 20.71).

7.127-137 This passage is roughly based upon the Exodus account (Ex 7:14-14:31). It is the story of the plagues that impacted Egypt through the ministry of Moses and the subsequent exodus of the Israelite people from Egypt, concluding with their successful passage through the Red (Reed) Sea.

Nevertheless, three variations from the biblical account exist in this presentation.

First, in the qur'anic presentation, Pharaoh threatened to kill the Israelite sons, following the episode of the rods turning into snakes (v. 127). The biblical account makes no reference of such a threat. Second, the qur'anic account claims that one of the plagues being a great flood that overcame Egypt (v. 133). The biblical account makes no reference to a Great Flood impacting Egypt. Third, the qur'anic account identifies five plagues (v. 133). The biblical account identifies ten plagues. A noteworthy omission was the plague of the death of the firstborn and the corresponding Passover Meal that functioned as a protection from the plague (see ***How Many Plagues Were***

128 Said Moses unto his people, "Ask for aid from God and be patient; verily, the earth is God's! He gives it for an inheritance to whom He pleases of His servants, and the future is for those who fear."

129 They said, "We have been hurt before thou didst come to us, and since thou hast come to us." Said he, "It may be that your Lord will destroy your foe, and will make you succeed him in the earth; and He will see how ye act."

130 We had overtaken Pharaoh's people with the years (of dearth) and scarcity of fruits, that haply they might remember;

131 but when there came to them a good thing they said, "This is ours;" and if there befell them an evil, they took the augury from Moses and those with him;—is not their augury only in God's hands? —but most of them know not.

132 And they said, "Whatever thou dost bring us as a sign to enchant us therewith, yet will we not believe in thee."

133 Then we sent upon them the flood and the locusts and the lice and the frogs and the blood,—signs detailed; but they were big with pride and were a people who did sin.

134 And when there fell upon them the plague, they said, "O Moses! call upon thy Lord for us, as He has covenanted with thee; verily, if thou dost remove the plague from us, we will believe in thee; and we will assuredly send with thee the children of Israel."

135 But when we removed from them the plague until the appointed time which they should reach, lo! then they broke their promise.

136 But we took vengeance on them, and we drowned them in the sea, for that they said our signs were lies and were careless thereof.

137 And we gave as an inheritance unto the people who had been weak, the eastern quarters of the earth and the western quarters thereof, which we had blest; and the good word of thy Lord was fulfilled on the children of Israel, for that they were patient; and we destroyed that which Pharaoh and his people had made and that which they had piled.

The story of Israel (Part Three): Moses and the golden calf

138 And with the children of Israel we passed across the sea; and they

There? on p. 565).

7.130 The years of dearth refers to the seven years of drought that Joseph correctly prognosticated and which caused him to be elevated in high office in Egypt (Gen 41:25-27).

7.133 Muhammad claimed that among the plagues that God sent to Egypt were the plagues of the flood and lice. Neither is mentioned in the biblical account.

7.138 This passage is centered on the event of the golden calf first mentioned in

came unto a people devoted to their idols, and said, "O Moses! make for us a god as they have gods." Said he, "Verily, ye are ignorant people."

139   Verily, these—destroyed shall be that which they are given to; and vain is that which they have done.

140   He said, "Other than God then do ye crave for a god, when He has preferred you above the worlds?"

141   And when we saved you from Pharaoh's people who wrought you evil woe, killing your sons, and letting your women live; and in that was a mighty trial from your Lord.

142   And we appointed for Moses thirty nights, and completed them with ten (more), so that the time appointed by his Lord was completed to forty nights. And Moses said unto his brother Aaron, "Be thou my vicegerent amongst my people, and do what is right, and follow not the path of the evildoers."

143   And when Moses came to our appointment, and his Lord spake unto him, he said, "O my Lord! show me,—that I may look on thee!" He said, "Thou canst not see me; but look upon the mountain, and if it remain steady in its place, thou shalt see me;" but when his Lord appeared unto the mountain He made it dust, and Moses fell down in a swoon! And when he came to himself, he said, "Celebrated be thy praise! I turn repentant unto Thee, and I am the first of those who are resigned."

144   He said, "O Moses! verily, I have chosen thee over the people with my messages and my words, take then what I have brought thee, and be of those who thank."

145   And we wrote for him upon tablets an admonition concerning ev-

---

Ex 32:1-35. Generally speaking, Muhammad's presentation accurately followed the biblical account.

7.142a *thirty nights...with ten more* — After the Israelite people traveled to the base of Mount Sinai, God summoned Moses to the summit of Mount Sinai. In his absence, he appointed Aaron as vicegerent in his stead (cf. Ex. 24:18).

7.142b *vicegerent* — In the Arabic, the word vicegerents is *khalifah*, or *caliphs*. Muhammad believed that the people of Ad became the *caliphs* (rulers of the land) following the death of Noah's family (see Q 35.39, note).

7.143a *He made it dust* — Muhammad believed when Allah appeared before Moses, a mountain was reduced to dust. This feature of the narrative is neither included in the biblical account nor in any of the apocryphal literature. Most likely, it was original with Muhammad.

7.143b *I am the first of those who are resigned* — that is, "I am the first of those who have submitted to Allah." Muhammad claimed that he himself was the first Muslim. Yet, this is an inconsistency within the Qur'an since earlier in the Qur'an, Muhammad mentioned Adam, Noah, Zali'h, Hud, Abraham, and Lot as worshippers of Allah.

7.145 *tablets* — That is, the tablets of the Ten Commandments.

erything, and a detailing of every-thing: "Take them then with firm-ness, and bid thy people take them for what is best thereof. I will show you the abode of those who work abominations;

146   I will turn from my signs those who are big with pride in the earth without right; and if they see ev-ery sign they shall not believe therein, and if they see the path of rectitude they shall not take it for a path; but if they see the path of error they shall take it for a path;— that is because they have said our signs are lies and have been care-less of them."

147   But those who say our signs and the meeting of the last day are lies,—vain are their works: shall they be rewarded save for that which they have done?

148   And Moses' people after him took to themselves of their ornaments a corporeal calf that lowed; did they not see that it could not speak with them, nor could it guide them in the path? They took it and they were unjust;

149   but when they bit their hands with fruitless rage and saw that they had gone astray, they said, "Verily, if our Lord have not compassion on us and forgive us we shall surely be of those who lose!"

150   And when Moses returned unto his

7.146 This verse makes an astounding claim. Because of their sins of idolatry (e.g., the sin of the golden calf—v. 148), Allah cursed the people of Israel with spiritual blindness. Be-cause of this blindness, henceforth (a) they would not take the *path of rectitude*—the path that leads to eternal life, and (b) they would take the *path of error*—the path that leads to eternal condemnation. The episode of the golden calf, then, is a major turning point in the history of the Jewish people. It was the first of several divine judgments that befell them.

The biblical account speaks otherwise. Though the Lord considered abandoning the people of Israel and beginning afresh by form-ing a new chosen people through the de-scendents of Moses (see Ex 33:1), He re-lented and continued to bless the people of Israel (Ex 33:4-17).

Fifth century Christian scholar Cassiodorus wrote: "What a holy man, most worthy of all praise! When he came down from Mt. Sinai to the camp and saw the people exult-antly and sacrilegiously posturing before the idol, he was roused to anger, broke the tab-lets in front of them and ordered one or other of them to be slain by the sword. But when comprehensive disaster loomed, he prayed that he himself should be destroyed rather than that the entire nation should per-ish. Both attitudes were devoted and splen-did. Moses was right to converse with the divine clemency since he loved to carry out its decrees. At the same time that power is revealed by which we often escape the pun-ishment of deserved death through the prayers of the saints" (*Exposition of the Psalms 105:23*).

7.148 *a corporeal calf that lowed* — Mu-hammad believed that the golden calf had come to life and made a lowing sound. In contrast, the biblical account makes no such claim (see Q 20.88).

people angry and grieved, he said, "Evil is it that ye have done after me! Would ye hasten on the bidding of your Lord?" and he threw down the tablets and took his brother by the head to drag him towards him, but he said, "O son of my mother! verily, the people weakened me and well-nigh killed me; make not then mine enemies glad about me, and put me not with the unjust people."

151   He said, "O Lord! pardon me and my brother, and let us enter into Thy mercy; for Thou art the most merciful of the merciful.

152   Verily, these have taken to themselves a calf; there shall reach them wrath from their Lord, and abasement in the life of this world; for thus do we reward those who forge a lie.

153   But those who have done bad works, and then turn again after them and believe—verily, thy Lord,

after that, is forgiving and merciful."

154   And when Moses' wrath calmed down he took the tables, in the inscription of which was guidance and mercy for those who dread their Lord.

155   And Moses chose from his people seventy men for our appointment; and when the earthquake took them he said, "O my Lord! hadst Thou willed, Thou hadst destroyed them before and me. Wilt Thou destroy us for what the fools amongst us have done? This is naught but Thy trial, wherewith Thou dost lead astray whom Thou pleasest and guidest whom Thou pleasest; Thou art our patron! forgive us and have mercy on us, for Thou art the best of those who do forgive!

156   And write down for us in this world good, and in the future too; verily, we are guided unto Thee." He [Allah] said, "My punishment—

7.151-155 According to this verse, Moses pleaded with Allah to pardon himself and his brother for the events related to the sin of the golden calf. He also pleaded on behalf of all the Israelite people. "Wilt Thou destroy us for what the fools amongst us have done?" (v. 155). He reminded Allah of the Doctrine al-Qadar ("Thou dost lead astray whom Thou pleasest and guidest whom Thou pleasest"), the implication being that Allah knew all along which Jews would fall into the sin of idolatry and which Jews would not. Since this was the case, judging the entire nation of Israel would not reflect divine justice (see **The Doctrine of al-Qadar**

on pp. 264-266).

7.155 *seventy men* — According to this passage, the earth opened its mouth and swallowed seventy men. The biblical record, however, speaks otherwise. Only once did the earth open its mouth and swallow a number of men, and this occurred much later, during the rebellion of Korah (Num 26:10), and the number of men who died was 250 (see Q 28.76-82).

7.156 According to this passage, Allah responded to Moses by reiterating the doctrine of double predestination. Allah would continue to bless those whom He had chosen to guide into "the path of rectitude" (v.

with it I fall on whom I will; and my mercy embraceth everything; and I will write it down for those who fear, and who give alms, and those who in our signs believe,

157 —who follow the Apostle —the illiterate prophet, whom they find written down with them in the law and the gospel, bidding them what is reasonable and forbidding them what is wrong, and making lawful for them what is good, and making unlawful evil things; and setting down for them their burdens and the yokes which were upon them;—to those who believe in him and aid him and help him and follow the law which has been sent down with him—they shall be the prosperous.

158 Say, 'O ye folk! verily, I am the Apostle of God unto you all,—of Him whose is the kingdom of the heavens and the earth, there is no god but He! He quickens and He kills! believe then in God and His Apostle, the illiterate prophet,— who believes in God and in His words—then follow him that haply ye may be guided.'"

The story of Israel (Part Four):
the drift into apostasy

159 Amongst Moses' people is a nation guided in truth, and thereby act they justly.

160 And we cut them up into twelve tribes, each a nation; and we revealed unto Moses, when his people asked him for drink, "Strike with thy staff the rock!" and there

146)—a path also known as the path of God, our way, the straight path, the right way, the way of the Lord, and the right direction (see Q 72.2, note).

Included in this path was a commitment by the people to submit to the authority and follow "the Apostle"—Moses. They were to "believe in him and aid him and help him and follow the law which has been sent down with him" (v. 157). If they followed Moses, they would be guided by Allah (see **The Doctrine of al-Qadar** on pp. 264-266).

7.157a *the illiterate prophet* — Muhammad characterized himself as illiterate (see Q 2.78 note).

7.157b *whom they find written down with them in the law and the gospel* — Muhammad believed that he is mentioned in the law and the gospel; that is, in both Old and New Testaments. Later in the Qur'an (Q 61.6), Muhammad made the case that the term *parakletos* (Jn 14:16) is a misspelling of the term *periklutos* (which means the much praised one) and is a subtle reference to Muhammad. No textual evidence, however, exists among NT manuscripts to support this claim (see Q 61.6, note).

7.159-166 According to this passage, following the incident of the golden calf, the Israelite people again drifted into apostasy. Early episodes of this apostasy took place while in the wilderness, times when Allah sent water from the rock to quench their thirst, clouds to provide shade, and manna and quail to provide sustenance.

Citing Allah, Muhammad added, "Yet they did not wrong us, but it was themselves they wronged." His point, of course, was that sin

gushed forth from it twelve springs, each folk knew their drinking place. And we overshadowed them with the cloud; and sent down upon them the manna and the quails, "Eat of the good things we have provided you with!"—Yet they did not wrong us, but it was themselves they wronged.

161   And when it was said unto them, "Dwell in this city and eat therefrom as ye will, and say 'hittatun and enter the gate adoring; so will we pardon you your sins;—we will increase those who do well.'"

162   But those amongst them who did wrong changed it for another word than which was said to them; and we sent upon them a plague from heaven for that they were unjust.

163   Ask them too about the city which

stood by the sea, when they transgressed upon the Sabbath; when their fish came to them on the Sabbath day sailing straight up to them; but on the days when they kept not the Sabbath, they came not to them, thus did we try them for the abominations that they wrought.

164   And when a nation from amongst them said, "Why do ye warn a people whom God would destroy, or punish with severe torment?" they said, "As an excuse to your Lord, that haply they may fear."

165   But when they forgot what they had been reminded of, we saved those who forbade evil, but we overtook those who did wrong with punishment;—evil was the abomination that they did,

166   but when they rebelled against what

---

always results in suffering and the one who suffers the most is the instigator of the sin. The converse is equally true. The one who benefits the most from well doing is the person himself or herself "who do well" (v. 161).

7.161a *Dwell in this city* — That is, dwell in the land of Palestine. In his commentary, Muhammad Asad noted that the word *qaryah* usually refers to a *village* or *town*, but it can also be understood to mean *land*. In this verse, he says, it means *land* (*The Message of the Qur'an*, p. 20).

7.161b *hittatun* — This is an Arabic word meaning *repentance*. The point of this verse is that Allah wished for the Israelite people to act humbly and obediently, now that they were in their own land (see Q 2.58).

7.162 According to Muhammad, many Is-

raelites changed the word *hittatun* (repentance) "for another word"—presumably, a word that reflected arrogance and an unwillingness to repent for their sins. Accordingly, Allah "sent upon them a plague from heaven for that they were unjust."

7.163 The Qur'an fails to mention which Jewish city transgressed the Sabbath and suffered loss. Most likely it refers to a number of cities that engaged in this practice.

7.164 According to this passage, some people who were dwelling among them asked others in Palestine why warn a people of their sinfulness when Allah has determined to destroy them. Muhammad's answer was: "As an excuse (to be free from blame) from before Allah."

7.166 *Become ye apes* — According to this passage, Allah judged a number of the Jew-

How Many Plagues Were There?

According to the book of Exodus, the people of Egypt were visited by ten plagues. God sent the plagues to motivate Pharaoh to listen to Moses and allow the Hebrew people leave Egypt. The plagues were:

1.	Plague of Blood	Exod 7:14-25
2.	Plague of Frogs	Exod 7:25-8:11
3.	Plague of Lice	Exod 8:16-19
4.	Plague of Flies	Exod 8:20-32
5.	Plague of Death to Livestock	Exod 9:1-7
6.	Plague of Boils	Exod 9:8-9
7.	Plague of Hail	Exod 9:13-35
8.	Plague of Locusts	Exod 10:1-20
9.	Plague of Darkness	Exod 10:21-29
10.	Plague of Death to Firstborn	Exod 11:1-12:36

In contrast, according to the Qur'an the people of Egypt were visited by nine plagues: "But put thy in thy bosom, it shall come forth white without hurt;—one of the nine signs to Pharaoh and his people, verily, they are a people who act abominably'" (Q 27.12; also see Q 17.101). These "nine manifest signs," however, are *not* enumerated in the Qur'an, as they are in the Bible. Neither does the Qur'an explain which one of the ten plagues mentioned in the biblical account should not be included.

| they were forbidden, we said to them, "Become ye apes, despised and spurned!" | 167 | And then thy Lord proclaimed that He would surely send against them till the resurrection day, those who should wreak them evil torment; verily, thy Lord is quick at following up, but, verily, He is forgiving, |

The story of Israel (Part Five): Israel cursed of God

---

ish people for their arrogance and refusal to submit to Allah by transforming them into apes (see Q 2.63-66; 5.60). According to Q 2.65, the sin that these Jews committed that resulted in this unusual judgment was the breaking of the Sabbath. In addition, according to Q 5.60, they were transformed into "apes and swine."

Due to a tendency among many Muslims to interpret the Qur'an literally, a common interpretation of this passage is that the Jews were physiologically transformed into apes and pigs. In the hadithic literature, Muhammad asked, "What about those apes and swine which suffered metamorphosis?" He then added, "The deniers of truth were tormented and suffered metamorphosis" (*Sahih Muslim* 33.7.6440).

More contemporaneously, Al-Azhar Sheikh Muhammad Sayyid Tantawi, a high ranking cleric in the Sunni Muslim world, called Jews "the enemies of Allah, descendents of apes and pigs" (Asra Nomani, *Standing Alone*, p. 261). In addition, Hezbollah Secretary General Hassan Nasrallah described Jews as "the grandsons of apes and pigs" (Andrew Bostom, *The Legacy of Islamic Antisemitism*, p. 145). In another Hadith, Muhammad added Christians to this condemnation. He said that some Christians and Jews "had entered into the hole of the lizard," implying that they had been transformed into lizards (*Sahih Muslim* 34.3.6448).

Still, not all Islamic scholars are in agreement with such a literal interpretation of this

passage. Mujahid comments: "[Only] their hearts were transformed, that is, they were not [really] transformed into apes; this is but a metaphor *(mathal)* coined by God with regard to them" (62:5). Muhammad Asad adds that the expression "like an ape" is often used in classical Arabic literature "to describe a person who is unable to restrain his gross appetites or passions" (*The Message of the Qur'an*, p. 260).

Ibrahim Al-ʽAli offers a similar observation: that the souls of Jews had merely become like that of apes and pigs. He explains that this punishment of Jews is not limited to a few Jews in the distant past. Rather, the punishment "left its impression in the souls of the Jews who came after them: their spirit, their opinions, their feelings, and their ways of thought—which are reflected in face and external appearance—became like their nature and like the appearance of apes and pigs, and this profoundly affected their ways of behavior" (*Filastin al-Muslimah*, London, Sept 1996, pp. 55-56).

Whether taken literally or figuratively, this association of Jews with apes and pigs is widespread in the Muslim world. It is found in the past as well as the present in both religious writings, sermons, speeches, prose and fiction.

7.167 Because of the sinfulness of the majority of the Israelite people, Muhammad believed that Allah "would surely send against them till the resurrection day, those who should wreak them evil torment" (v. 167).

merciful.

168 We cut them up in the earth into nations. Of them are the righteous, and of them are the reverse of that; we have tried them with good things and with bad things haply they may return.

169 But there succeeded them successors who inherited the Book! They take the goods of this lower world and say, "It will be forgiven us." But if the like goods came to them they would take them too! Was

there not taken from them a covenant by the Book, that they should not say against God aught but the truth? Yet they study therein! But the abode of the future life is better for those who fear—do ye not then understand?

The straight path

170 But those who hold fast by the Book and are steadfast in prayer—verily, we will not waste the hire of

---

The evil torment upon the Jewish people, then, would come via a people doing Allah's work in exacting divine judgment. In addition, this "evil torment" would continue until the Resurrection Day—that is, until the end of time. Many Muslim people in our current age see themselves as Allah's soldiers, that is, as Allah's executioners against the Jewish people (see **Jihad** on pp. 616-622).
7.168 The Israelite people, Muhammad explained, had fallen into such debauchery that by the first century, A.D., they were driven from the land of Palestine and dispersed among the nations of the world ("cut them up in the earth into nations"). Historians refer to this event as the Second Diaspora that took place in A.D. 70.
7.169 *successors who inherited the Book* — According to Muhammad, following the onset of the Second Diaspora, the spiritual inheritance that had been bequeathed to the Jewish people was transferred to the Christians. They became the "successors who inherited the Book." In this case, "the Book" referred to both the Old and New Testaments. Still, Muhammad added, the Jewish people continue to see themselves as God's chosen people and that, no matter

what they do, are still the recipients of divine favor. This is based upon a belief in an unconditional covenant of grace in the Old Testament given to them from God (see Gen 12:1-3; 15:1-19).

Within the Christian faith, scholars are divided as to the spiritual status and future of the Jewish people. On one side are those who believe that the Jewish people have indeed been set aside and have forever forfeited their spiritual status as the chosen people of God. They therefore have no spiritual inheritance. This occurred at the time when the Jewish people, as a nation, rejected Jesus as Messiah (see Matt 27:25; Jn 19:15). This event was followed, soon afterward, by the Second Diaspora.

On the other side are those who believe that the Jewish people have been temporarily set aside, yet will one day experience a massive revival and be restored to God (see Rom 11:1-32). Nevertheless, in the interim period, some Jews are embracing Jesus Christ as their Messiah and becoming part of the Church. They refer to themselves as Messianic Jews.
7.170 Individual repentance, said Muhammad, is still possible—no matter who that per-

those who do right.

171 And when we shook the mountain over them, as though it were a shadow, and they thought it would fall upon them (saying), "Take ye what we have given you with firmness, and remember what is therein; haply ye may fear."

172 And when thy Lord took from the children of Adam out of their loins their seed, and made them bear witness against themselves, "Am I not your Lord?" They said, "Yea! we do bear witness"

173 —lest ye should say on the day of resurrection, "Verily, for this we did not care;" or say, "Verily, our fathers associated others with God before us, and we were but their seed after them: wilt Thou then destroy us for what vaindoers did?"

174 —Thus do we detail the signs; haply they may return.

The crooked path

175 Read to them the declaration of him to whom we brought our signs, and who stepped away therefrom, and Satan followed him, and he was of those who were beguiled.

176 Had we pleased we would have exalted him thereby, but he crouched upon the earth and followed his lust, and his likeness was as the likeness of a dog, whom if thou shouldst attack he hangs out his tongue, or if thou should leave him,

---

son happens to be.

7.171a *And when we shook the mountain over them* — This is a reference to the shaking of Mt. Sinai at the time of the giving of the Ten Commandments (see Ex 19:18-19). The way in which Muhammad described this event, Mt. Sinai was supernaturally elevated over them, forming a shadow where they dwelt, and causing fear that it would soon fall down upon them. The biblical account makes no such claim of the mountain being lifted from the earth.

7.171b The quotation in the second half of the verse is a paraphrase, most likely associated with Deut 4:2; 12:32; and Josh 1:7. Muhammad's point was that the Jewish people should have remained committed to the ways of the Lord, just as it was clearly stated at the base of Mt. Sinai at the time when they received the Ten Commandments.

7.172 In addition to the illustration of the mountain shaking in the previous verse, Muhammad also offered an illustration from the words spoken to the children of Adam. He believed that they were admonished to say that they were devoted to God. If they should fail to follow through with that vow, then the vow itself would bear witness against them at the Last Judgment. No such words spoken by "the children of Adam" are mentioned in the Bible.

7.175 Those who step away from "the straight path," said Muhammad, will find themselves beguiled by Satan (see Q 7.16-18; 15.26-40; 17.61-64; 38.86-88).

7.176 Those who reject "the straight path" and its corresponding divine revelation (signs) are likened to dogs who crouch upon the earth, follow their lusts, and hang out their tongues. To be called a dog in the Middle East is a particularly offensive comment.

hangs out his tongue too. That is the likeness of the people who say our signs are lies. Tell them then these tales—haply they may reflect.

177 Evil is the likeness of a people who say our signs are lies; themselves it is they wrong!

178 Whom God doth guide,—he is on the right path: whom He rejects from his guidance,—such are the persons who perish.

179 We have created for hell many of the ginn and of mankind; they have hearts and they discern not therewith; they have eyes and they see not therewith; they have ears and they hear not therewith; they are like cattle, nay, they go more astray! these it is who care not.

180 But God's are the good names; call on Him then thereby, and leave those who pervert His names; they shall be rewarded for that which they have done.

181 And of those, whom we have created is a nation who are guided in truth and thereby act with equity;

182 but they who say our signs are lies, we will bring them down by degrees from whence they know not.

183 I will let them range;—verily, my stratagem is efficacious!

184 Do they not then reflect that their companion is not possessed? he is but an obvious warner!

185 Do they not behold the kingdoms of the heavens and of the earth, and what things God has created, and (see that), it may be, their time is already drawing nigh? in what

7.177-179 All who reject Muhammad's claim to being a divinely appointed prophet are described as spiritually deaf and blind—likened to cattle who have no spiritual sense. Along with the ginns (genies), they are condemned to Hell.

The New Testament also describes the unbeliever as spiritual blind (see 1 Cor 2:6-16; 2 Cor 4:4). Yet, through the power of the Holy Spirit and the Word of God, the spiritual eyes of the unbeliever are being opened. In other words, rather than maintaining a belief in the doctrine of double predestination, the believer is encouraged to reach out and evangelize the lost, assuming that all who hear the gospel are able to respond in faith believing.

7.180-181 All faithful Muslims were looked upon by Muhammad as citizens of their own peculiar nation—a Muslim nation (see *Islamification* on pp. 851-852).

7.182 *bring them down by degrees* — Muhammad believed that infidel nations would be brought down incrementally. In the end, the divine stratagem would be effective and a complete judgment upon the infidel nations would be exacted.

7.184 *their companion is not possessed* — That is, Muhammad countered the claims of his opponents by insisting that he was neither crazy nor demon-possessed. This was an oft-repeated criticism of Muhammad by his opponents (see Q 17.47; 23.25; 26.27; 44.4; 51.52; 52.29; 68.2, 51).

7.186-188 Having presented the characteristics of the straight and crook paths (the two paths that lead to either Paradise or Hell), Muhammad turned his attention to a

relation then will they believe?

Double predestination

186 He whom God leads astray there is no guide for him! He leaves them in their rebellion, blindly wandering on.
187 They will ask you about the Hour, for what time it is fixed?—say, "The knowledge thereof is only with my Lord; none shall manifest it at its time but He; it is heavy in the heavens and the earth, it will not come to you save on a sudden." They will ask as though thou wert privy to it, say, "The knowledge thereof is only with God,"—but most folk do not know.
188 Say, "I cannot control profit or harm for myself, save what God will. If I knew the unseen I should surely have much that is good, nor would evil touch me; I am but a

warner and a herald of good tidings unto a people who believe."

Folly of polytheism

189 He it is who created you from one soul, and made therefrom its mate to dwell therewith; and when he covered her she bore a light burden and went about therewith; but when it grew heavy they called on God, Lord of them both, "Surely if thou givest us a rightly-shaped child we shall of a surety be of those who thank."
190 And when He gave them both a rightly-shaped child they joined partners with Him for that which He had given them, but exalted be God above that which they associate with Him.
191 Will they associate with Him those who cannot create aught, but are themselves created,

more fundamental question: that of double predestination (see **The Doctrine of al-Qadar** on pp. 264-266). It is this doctrine that determined which spiritual path each person was traveling. For the faithful Muslim, it also gave rise to a lack of empathy or compassion for those on the crooked path. Since Allah lacked a concern for such people, a similar attitude existed among His devotees.

7.189a *He who created you from one soul* — That is, every person is genealogically linked to one individual: Adam.

7.189b *and made therefrom its mate to dwell therewith* — That is, a man might draw towards a woman as a mate.

7.189c *and when he covered her she bore a light burden and went about therewith* — That is, when a man made love to a woman she would become pregnant with child.

7.189d *but when it grew heavy they called on God* — That is, towards the end of the pregnancy when the child "grew heavy," they called on Allah for assistance and vowed to give thanks to Allah if they should receive "a rightly-shaped child."

7.190-198 Yet after the birth of the child, they ascribed to gods other than Allah ("partners with Him") for the blessings on the newborn. They therefore associate with gods "who cannot create aught, but are themselves created, which have no power to help

192   which have no power to help them,
        and cannot even help themselves?

193   But if ye call them unto guidance
        they will not follow you. It is the
        same to them if Thou dost call
        them or if Thou dost hold thy
        tongue.

194   Those whom ye call on other than
        God are servants like yourselves.
        Call on them then, and let them
        answer you, if so be ye tell the
        truth!

195   Have they feet to walk with? or
        have they hands to hold with? or
        have they eyes to see with? or have
        they ears to hear with? Call upon
        your partners; then plot against
        me, and do not wait.

196   Verily, my patron is God, who hath
        sent down the Book, and He is the
        patron of the righteous.

197   But those whom ye call on beside
        Him cannot help you, nor can they
        even help themselves.

198   But if ye call them unto the guid-
        ance they will not hear, thou
        mayest see them looking towards
        thee, yet they do not see.

Final thoughts

199   Take to pardon, and order what is
        kind, and shun the ignorant;

200   and if an incitement from the devil
        incites you, then seek refuge in
        God: verily, He both hears and
        knows.

201   Verily, those who fear God, if a
        wraith from the devil touch, men-
        tion Him, and lo! they see.

202   And their brethren he shall increase
        in error, then they shall not desist.

203   Shouldst Thou not bring them a sign
        they say, "Hast Thou not yet made
        choice of one?" Say, "I only fol-
        low what is inspired to me by my
        Lord. These are perceptions from
        my Lord, and a guidance and a
        mercy to a people who believe."

204   And when the Qur'ân is read, then
        listen thereto and keep silence;
        haply ye may obtain mercy.

205   And remember thy Lord within thy-
        self humbly and with fear, not
        openly in words, in the morning
        and in the evening; and be not of
        those who do not care.

them, and cannot even help themselves."

7.199-201 Muhammad concluded this surah with a scattering of thoughts. He first addressed Muslim believers. They were to: (a) seek the pardon of Allah for sins, (b) order one's life in a way that pleases Allah, (c) shun the ignorant—that is, the infidel, and (d) turn to Allah when the demonic temptation comes.

7.202 Muhammad then spoke of the infidel. He said that the infidel would "increase in error" and "shall not desist."

7.203 Muhammad addressed the lingering criticism that he could not quell: the lack of divine miracles to validate his ministry. If he were a genuine prophet sent from God, why were there no miracles accompanying his ministry? His answer was that he did not know. He merely followed the dictates of Allah (see *John of Damascus* on pp. 247-248).

7.204-206 Muhammad admonished the Muslim believer to treat the qur'anic surahs

206   Verily, they who are with my Lord   5   and from the evil of the envious
       are not too big with pride for His   when he envies."
       service, but they do celebrate His
       praise, and Him they do adore.

Surah 114

In the name of the merciful and compas-
sionate God

Surah 113

In the name of the merciful and compas-
sionate God

1   Say, "I seek refuge in the Lord of   1   Say, "I seek refuge in the Lord of
     the daybreak,   men,
2   from the evil of what He has cre-   2   the King of men,
     ated;   3   the God of men,
3   and from the evil of the night when   4   from the evil of the whisperer, who
     it cometh on;   slinks off,
4   and from the evil of the blowers   5   who whispers into the hearts of
     upon knots;   men!
                                                   6   —from ginns and men!"

---

as divine revelation and cultivate a life of true piety before Allah.

Surah 113. In this surah, Muhammad was encouraged to resist the Meccan leadership and take to refuge in Allah. According to a Hadith, Aisha (Muhammad's favorite wife) said that whenever Muhammad "became ill, he used to recite *al-Muawidhatan* (i.e. the last two surahs of the Qur'an—surahs 113 and 114) and then blow his breath and passed his hand over himself. When he had his fatal illness, I started reciting *al-Muawidhatan* and blowing my breath over him as he used to do, and then I rubbed the hand of the Prophet over his body" (*Sahih Bukhari* 5.59.714).

113.4 *blowers upon knots* — To blow upon knots was a technique used in sorcery. The sorcerer tied knots on a string and blew on them as a way of conjuring a curse on someone, prognosticating the future, or bringing about a healing. The blowing upon knots was commonly practiced by polytheists throughout Arabia, including the customs practiced at the Ka'ba altar in Mecca.

Surah 114. The title of this surah, *The Men*, comes from verse one. Similar to Surah 113, the theme of this surah is seeking refuge in Allah. He is called: the Lord of men, the King of men, and the God of men. He also sought protection from (a) Satan who subtly whispers into the hearts of men, tempting them to sin, and (b) from ginns and men (see ***Polytheism in Seventh Century Arabia*** on pp. 92-97).

INTRODUCTION

The Sixth Period

B y 622, the situation in Mecca had deteriorated to the point that Muhammad decided to leave. The untimely deaths of his two protectors—his uncle Abu Talib, and his wife Khadijah—left him vulnerable to his many enemies. He therefore migrated to Yathrib (Medinah) to begin life anew. The day was September, 9, 622, a truly historic day. It denotes the first day of the first year on the Islamic calendar, just as the birth of Jesus Christ *(Anno Domini)* denotes the first year on the Julian and Gregorian calendars.

The City. Yathrib was a collection of small villages and forts (known as a district) situated near a large oasis, approximately 200 miles north of Mecca. The people of the city were divided into Jewish and Arabic sectors. The Jewish tribes occupied the place of economic superiority in Yathrib which generated resentment among the Arabic tribes. This was because the Jews were a people given to farming, whereas the Arabs were given to a less productive desert way of life, a life limited to bare necessities. It was, as the great medieval Islamic scholar Ibn Khaldun explained, the interplay between the desert and the sown.[1] Through the years, the strained relationships between the Jews and Arabs had resulted in brief episodes of violence, including, on one occasion, a citywide war.

The Plan. Prior to leaving Mecca, Muhammad met with several Arab representatives of Yathrib. They invited him to their city to help them work out their longstanding political differences. The Arabs had often raided the Jews in the region of Yathrib (known as The District), and the Jews used to say in response, "A prophet will be sent soon. His day is at hand. We shall follow him and kill you by his aid."[2] So, when Muhammad arrived in Yathrib, most of the Arabs thought that he was the one foretold by the Jews. They said to one another: "This is the very prophet of whom the Jews warned us. Don't let them get to him before us!"[3] With this in mind, they quickly embraced Muhammad as their Prophet—and Muhammad was more than willing to accommodate their interests against the Jews.

The Conquest. The Sixth Period of the Qur'an opens with Muhammad in Yathrib. Within a few short years (less than a decade) the Jews in Yathrib would either be annihilated or banished. In both cases, their possessions—which included their vast farmland holdings—

would be confiscated and redistributed among the Muslim people. A military jihad would be launched against the people of Mecca, at first raiding the caravans that passed through Mecca, and then with battles and sieges. When Muhammad finally captured Mecca the jihad turned northward, against the Byzantine Empire.

The Islamic State. Now in Yathrib (also called Medinah—which means the City of the Prophet) the Islamic community had transformed itself into a theocracy (a Muslim state) with Muhammad serving as its resident Prophet. Among the many themes presented in this period are the following:

(a) *The House of Islam.* We see the development of a new theme in the Qur'an: the building of the Islamic state. It was organized as both a religion and a state—a theocracy. And since the central teaching of the Qur'an is that "there is no god but Allah," the purview of this Islamic theocracy was global in scope. Muslim scholars would later bring clarity to this doctrine, describing it as the House of Islam and the House of War: the Dar al-Islam and the Dar al-harb. The House of Islam referred to all those lands controlled by the Islamic theocratic state. All other lands belonged to the House of War. Because Allah was the only one true God, the creator of the heavens and the earth, the House of Islam was destined to increase its boundaries and eventually occupy the entire earth. Much attention is given in this final section of the Qur'an as to the laws of this Islamic theocracy. Again, Muslim scholars would later bring clarity to these laws, codifying them into that which would be called Shari'a Law.

(b) *The Doctrine of Jihad.* A second theme in these surahs is the development of the Doctrine of Jihad. In the previous surahs, Muhammad presented the argument that Allah had sent numerous apostles to the peoples of the world to draw them to Himself and became faithful reposers (people who believed and acted aright, travelers on the straight path that leads to eternal life). Those who steadfastly refused this message suffered horrific retributions from the hand of Allah. In this final sixth period of the Qur'an, Muhammad declared that Allah wished to use the Muslim community as His instruments in exacting divine retribution on the infidels.

(c) *The Mecca-Medinah military campaign.* The sixth period witnessed the Mecca-Medinah military campaign. It began with Muhammad sending out raiders to attack and sack caravans traveling to and from Mecca. Their first successful raid was the Battle of Badr in 624. The elation of Muhammad's band of men was short-lived, however, since they were soundly defeated at the Battle of Uhud the following year. The Battle of the Trench took place three years later. The battle was a siege that Muhammad and his Muslim warriors successfully withstood. After the confederate army withdrew, Muhammad exacted retribution on a major Jewish tribe of Medinah, slaughtering them in the town center. Finally, with the help of Bedouin Arabs, Muhammad's small army attacked and defeated Mecca in 630.

(d) *The Jews and Christians.* A fourth theme of the sixth period addressed the Jews and Christians. Muhammad declared that both groups to be idolatrous and therefore worthy of divine judgment. This was due to their steadfast rejection of the Doctrine of Tauhid (the Islamic version of monotheism) and their unwillingness to embrace him as Allah's final prophet.

(e) *Shari'a Law.* With the clarification of a sacred theology and a sacred government, the third necessary component to the Muslim community were sacred laws, laws that addressed questions of faith as well as civil and criminal questions. And since Shari'a Law was

codified within several of the qur'anic surahs, it was regarded as divinely inspired. Its authority was such that no other legal document or system of laws could supersede it or exist side
by side. It was the final word of authority. When the Muslims conquered Mecca, for
example, the previously held laws of the city were annulled and replaced by Shari'a Law.

(f) Muhammad. We also see in this period Muhammad's self-promotion to an exalted
status. Eternal salvation required one to not only worship Allah, but to show due deference
to Muhammad, recognizing him to be Allah's final prophet sent into the world. People were
to ask permission prior to entering his presence, and when in his presence to speak in a
reverentially subdued voice.

Moreover, since Allah was understood to be the one and only God, the God of the
heavens and the earth, Muhammad's vision was for the Islamic state to eventually reach
across the entire earth. All peoples everywhere were to be either Muslims or under Muslim
rule.

---

[1] See Ibn Khaldun, *The Muqaddimah: An Introduction to History.* vol 1, pp. 308-310.
[2] Ibn Ishaq, *The Life of Muhammad*, p. 198.
[3] Ibid.

Surah 98

In the name of the merciful and compassionate God

1   Those of the people of the Book and the idolaters who misbelieve did not fall off until there came to them the manifest sign,

2   —an apostle from God reading pure pages

3   wherein are right scriptures:

4   Nor did those who were given the Book divide into sects until after there came to them the manifest sign.

5   But they were not bidden aught but to worship God, being sincere in religion unto Him as 'Hanîfs, and to be steadfast in prayer, and to give alms: for that is the standard religion.

6   Verily, those who disbelieve amongst the people of the Book and the idolaters shall be in the fire of hell, to dwell therein for aye; they are wretched creatures!

7   Verily, those who believe and act aright, they are the best of creatures;

8   their reward with their Lord is gardens of Eden, beneath which rivers flow, to dwell therein for aye; God shall be well pleased with them, and they with Him! that is for him who fears his Lord!

Surah 2

In the name of the merciful and compassionate God

Surah 98. The title of this surah, *The Manifest Sign*, comes from verse one. It contains heated rhetoric directed towards two groups of people: (a) the people of the Book—the Jews and Christians, and (b) the idolaters—those committed to the Arabic Star Family religious worship. Both groups are described as "wretched creatures," condemned to the fires of Hell for eternity. The reason for these harsh words is centered on their rejection of Muhammad's alleged apostleship and his alleged divinely inspired surahs. This initial surah, then, sets the theme of much of what is to follow in the Sixth Period.

98.4-5 It was Muhammad's belief that the division of the Jews and Christians into sects was a result of their rebellion against divine revelation (the manifest signs). If they would have remained committed to God's Word, he added, they would have maintained their essential unity. The implication is that their multiple sects was *de facto* evidence of rebellion against Allah and a variance to "the standard religion" (cf. Jn 17:20-21).

98.5 *Hanifs* — Pre-Islamic monotheists (see Q 30.30, note).

98.7 *those who believe and act aright* — This is a summary of the Islamic gospel (see Q 72.2, note).

98.8 *gardens of Eden* — This is a reference to the gardens in Paradise (see Q 35.33, note).

Surah 2. The title of this surah, *The Cow*, comes from verse 67. With his recent migration to Yathrib (Medinah), Muhammad was no longer under the pressures and threats from the leaders of Mecca. Moreover, he

1   A. L. M.

Qur'an

2   That is the book! there is no doubt
     therein; a guide to the pious,
3   who believe in the unseen, and are
     steadfast in prayer, and of what
     we have given them expend in
     alms;
4   who believe in what is revealed to
     thee, and what was revealed be-
     fore thee, and of the hereafter they
     are sure.
5   These are in guidance from their
     Lord, and these are the prosper-
     ous.

The crooked path

6   Verily, those who misbelieve, it is
     the same to them if ye warn them
     or if ye warn them not, they will
     not believe.
7   God has set a seal upon their hearts
     and on their hearing; and on their
     eyes is dimness, and for them is
     grievous woe.
8   And there are those among men
     who say, "We believe in God and

was now free to codify what he expected from his Muslim followers. This, then, is the first surah that laid out the specifics of Shari'a Law (see **Shari'a Law** on pp. 610-612).

Soon after moving into Yathrib (Medinah), Muhammad attempted to bring the entire city under the authority of Allah and his prophetic authority. This surah reflects these historical settings and societal opportunities. Among his many maneuverings in Yathrib, Muhammad took aim and challenged the legitimacy of the Jewish and Christian religions. He also challenged the polytheism also present in Yathrib, yet less so. At the midpoint of the surah, he turned his attention to his Muslim converts, explaining the specifics of a number of issues pertaining to civil law. The second half of the surah, then, is a codified version of "the way" (shari'a) that leads to eternal life. In this surah, then, the Doctrine of Islamification is clarified and sharpened (see **Islamification** on pp. 851-852).

In this surah, Muhammad also laid out the basics of the Doctrine of Jihad—holy war.

This doctrine presented the theological groundwork and justification for a just and holy war that he would soon initiate against his enemies in Mecca and Medinah.

2.1 Literally, *Alif, Lam, Mim.* See Q 32.1, note.

2.2-5 Muhammad began the surah with a reaffirmation of the Qur'an being an inspired document. He noted that it was (a) wholly true, (b) a guide to the pious who believe in the unseen, (c) an encouragement to prayer and the giving of alms, (d) divine revelation, (e) a guidance from the Lord, and (f) the way of prosperity.

2.6 *if ye warn them or if ye warn them not, they will not believe* — Muhammad believed that the obstinacy of the infidels was such that whether or not warned, their response would be the same: total rejection of Qur'an. Yet, said Muhammad, this attitude was due to the fact that "God has set a stamp upon their hearts and on their hearing, and on their eyes" (v. 7; cf. Q 7.100-101; 9.87, 93; 10.74; 16.108; 30.58-60; 40.35; 47.16; 63.3). Spiritual understanding is thereby ren-

in the last day;" but they do not believe.

9 They would deceive God and those who do believe; but they deceive only themselves and they do not perceive.

10 In their hearts is a sickness, and God has made them still more sick, and for them is grievous woe because they lied.

11 And when it is said to them, "Do not evil in the earth," they say, "We do but what is right."

12 Are not they the evildoers? and yet they do not perceive.

13 And when it is said to them, "Believe as other men believe," they say, "Shall we believe as fools believe?" Are not they themselves the fools? and yet they do not know.

14 And when they meet those who believe, they say, "We do believe;" but when they go aside with their devils, they say, "We are with you; we were but mocking!"

15 God shall mock at them and let them go on in their rebellion, blindly wandering on.

16 Those who buy error for guidance, their traffic profits not, and they are not guided.

Parable of the Fire

dered impossible (see **The Doctrine of al-Qadar** on pp. 264-266).

2.8-15 Muhammad was aware of the problem of hypocrisy within the Muslim faith. Hypocrites maintained a pretense of faith yet were either (a) superficial in their faith and failed to follow through with its rigid requirements, or (b) were two-faced in that which they professed to believe.

The Christian religion also struggles with the problem of hypocrisy. Jesus Christ spoke of such people, saying, "Everything they do is done for men to see" (Matt 23:5; cf. Matt 6:1-16; Lk 20:46-47; Jn 5:44; 12:43; Phil 2:3). And this is especially true of Christian leaders. Oswald Chambers aptly wrote: "Beware of hypocrisy with God, especially if you are in no danger of hypocrisy among men... Impressive preaching is rarely Gospel-preaching: Gospel-preaching is based on the great mystery of belief in the Atonement, which belief is created in others, not by my impressiveness, but by the insistent conviction of the Holy Spirit" (*Disciples Indeed*, p. 45).

2.16 *those who buy error for guidance* — That is, those who have taken error for exchange for guidance. Common in the seventh century Arabia were occultists (followers of the ginns) who charged money for their prognostications (see vv. 14-16). Muhammad's point was that all who sought wisdom from such people had wasted their money and were not rightly guided (see **Occultism in Seventh Century Arabia** on pp. 123-125).

The Bible also warns people to avoid all forms of occultism. Those who do so run the risk of becoming influenced or controlled by demons. "Do not turn to mediums or seek out spiritists, for you will be defiled by them. I am the LORD your God" (Lev 19:31) and "I will set my face against the person who turns to mediums and spiritists to prostitute himself by following them, and I will cut him off from his people" (Lev 20:6; Deut 18:10-14; Isa 8:19).

17 Their likeness is as the likeness of one who kindles a fire; and when it lights up all around, God goes off with their light, and leaves them in darkness that they cannot see.

18 Deafness, dumbness, blindness, and they shall not return!

*Parable of
the Storm Cloud*

19 Or like a storm cloud from the sky, wherein is darkness and thunder and lightning; they put their fingers in their ears at the thunderclap, for fear of death, for God encompasses the misbelievers.

20 The lightning well-nigh snatches off their sight, whenever it shines for them they walk therein; but when it is dark for them they halt; and if God willed He would go off with their hearing and their sight; verily, God is mighty over all.

The straight path

21 O ye folk! serve your Lord who created you and those before you; haply ye may fear!

2.17-18 In this parable, the light from the fire is a metaphor for spiritual truth. Muhammad's point is that all who sought spiritual light apart from Allah would quickly discover that Allah takes away whatever light they did possess, leaving them in spiritual darkness (see v. 171).

2.19-20 In this parable, the thunder and lightning represent spiritual truth that can be both heard and seen. Muhammad's point was that spiritual truth is so bright that it almost blinds infidels, leaving them in utter darkness once the truth is taken away. The sound of spiritual truth is also terrifying, causing them to cover their ears in fear.

2.21 In contrast to the crooked path that leads to eternal condemnation is the straight path that leads to eternal life (see Q 72.2, note). It is grounded, said Muhammad, with the attitude of fearing the Lord and a commitment to serve Him.

The Bible makes a similar observation about the acquisition of spiritual wisdom. "The fear of the Lord is the beginning of wisdom; all who follow his precepts have good understanding. To him belongs eternal praise" (Ps 111:10). This fear, however, is not a worrisome terror of the possibility of being thrown into the fires of Hell, as is the case with Islam. That concern has been settled at the cross of Jesus. Rather, it is an abiding desire to surrender our hearts to the lordship of Jesus Christ.

John R. W. Stott explains, "There is no more integrating Christian principle than the affirmation 'Jesus Christ is Lord.' It is of the essence of integrated discipleship that we both confess his lordship with our lips and enthrone him as Lord in our hearts. We assume the easy yoke of his teaching authority. We seek to 'take captive every thought to make it obedient to Christ' (2 Cor 10:5). And when Jesus is Lord of our beliefs, opinions, ambitions, standards, values and lifestyle, then we are integrated Christians, since then 'integrity' marks our life. Only when he is Lord do we become whole" (*The Contemporary Christian*, p. 177).

2.22 *earth...a bed and the heaven a dome* — As was typical of his age, Muhammad un-

22   who made the earth for you a bed
      and the heaven a dome; and sent
      down from heaven water, and
      brought forth therewith fruits as a
      sustenance for you; so make no
      peers for God, the while ye know!

23   And if ye are in doubt of what we
      have revealed unto our servant,
      then bring a chapter like it, and call
      your witnesses other than God if
      ye tell truth.

24   But if ye do it not, and ye shall
      surely do it not, then fear the fire
      whose fuel is men and stones, pre-
      pared for misbelievers.

25   But bear the glad tidings to those
      who believe and work righteous-
      ness, that for them are gardens
      beneath which rivers flow; when-
      ever they are provided with fruit
      therefrom they say, "This is what

we were provided with before,"
and they shall be provided with the
like; and there are pure wives for
them therein, and they shall dwell
therein for aye.

Parable of the Gnat

26   Why, God is not ashamed to set
      forth a parable of a gnat, or any-
      thing beyond; and as for those who
      believe, they know that it is truth
      from the Lord; but as for those
      who disbelieve, they say, "What is
      it that God means by this as a par-
      able? He leads astray many and He
      guides many;"—but He leads
      astray only the evildoers;

27   who break God's covenant after the
      fixing thereof, and cut asunder
      what God has ordered to be joined,

derstood the cosmos in terms of Ptolemaic astronomy. The earth was flat with the sun, moon, stars, and planets moving overhead in an arc across the sky.

2.24 *fear the fire whose fuel is men and stones, prepared for misbelievers* — The straight path, said Muhammad, requires the believer to remain fearful of the possibility of being cast into Hell (see **The Last Judgment** on pp. 46-50).

Those within the Christian faith, however, stand firmly opposed to such thinking. For those who have received Christ as Savior, the fear of Hell has forever been replaced with the attitude of thankfulness and a settled anticipation of Heaven. "And this is the testimony: God has given us eternal life, and this life is in his Son. He who has the Son has life; he who does not have the

Son of God does not have life" (1 Jn 5:11-12).

2.25a *those who believe and work righteousness* — This is a summary of the Islamic gospel, the way to eternal life. It is a variation of the phrase "believe and do right" oft repeated in the Qur'an (see Q 103.3, note).

2.25b *pure wives for them* — According to Muhammad, one of the blessings of those who enter Paradise is to be bequeathed with their own harems (see **The Virgins** on pp. 107-109).

2.26 In this parable, the gnat is a metaphor for the human being—small and insignificant. Muhammad's point is that Allah is able to lead astray or guide as many as He wishes since, from His perspective, man is nothing more than a gnat (see **The Doc-**

and do evil in the earth;—these it is who lose.

28 How can ye disbelieve in God, when ye were dead and He made you alive, and then He will kill you and then make you alive again, and then to Him will ye return?

29 It is He who created for you all that is in the earth, then he made for the heavens and fashioned them seven heavens; and He knows all things.

The fall of Adam

30 And when thy Lord said unto the angels, "I am about to place a vicegerent in the earth," they said, "Wilt Thou place therein one who will do evil therein and shed blood? we celebrate Thy praise and hallow Thee." Said (the Lord), "I know what ye know not."

31 And He taught Adam the names, all of them; then He propounded them to the angels and said, "Declare to me the names of these, if ye are truthful:

32 They said, "Glory be to Thee! no knowledge is ours but what Thou thyself hast taught us, verily, Thou art the knowing, the wise."

33 Said the Lord, "O Adam declare to them their names;" and when he had declared to them their names He said, "Did I not say to you, I know the secrets of the heavens and of the earth, and I know what ye show and what ye were hiding?"

34 And when we said to the angels, "Adore Adam," they adored him save only Iblîs, who refused and was too proud and became one of the misbelievers.

35 And we said, "O Adam dwell, thou

trine of al-Qadar** on pp. 264-266).

2.28 Muhammad was incredulous of the way in which the infidel reasons. He could not understand how a person could refuse to submit to Allah, seeing that he or she was first lifeless, then given life, then will die, and finally will be resurrected and stand before Allah at the Last Judgment.

2.29 *He knows all things* — That is, Allah is omniscient. The Bible makes a similar claim about God (see Ps 33:13-15; 139:11-12; 147:5; Prov 15:3; Isa 40:14; 46:10; 1 Jn 3:20; Heb 4:13).

2.30 In this case, the vicegerent (or *caliph*) was Adam. As *caliph*, Adam was given authority over the entire earth (see Q 35.39, note).

2.31-34 According to some Islamic scholars, since Allah taught Adam the name of all the animals, Adam also knew all things (the secrets) that pertained to the animals, causing him to be extremely wise. Allah then challenged the angels if they knew the names of the animals. When they acknowledged that they did not, they were ordered to give obeisance to Adam—since he was their intellectual superior. All the angels gave obeisance to Adam, except Iblis (Satan). Because of his rebellion, Satan became the first infidel (see Q 7.10-12; 15.31-35; 17.61-64; 38.71-85).

2.35 Adam and Eve were instructed by Allah to not "draw near a particular tree" in Paradise (that is, the Garden of Eden). This

and thy wife, in Paradise, and eat therefrom amply as you wish; but do not draw near this tree or ye will be of the transgressors."

36 And Satan made them backslide therefrom and drove them out from what they were in, and we said, "Go down, one of you the enemy of the other, and in the earth there is an abode and a provision for a time."

37 And Adam caught certain words from his Lord, and He turned towards him, for He is the compassionate one easily turned.

38 We said, "Go down therefrom altogether and haply there may come from me a guidance, and whoso follows my guidance, no fear is theirs, nor shall they grieve.

39 But those who misbelieve, and call our signs lies, they are the fellows of the Fire, they shall dwell therein for aye."

Appeal to the Jews

40 O ye children of Israel! remember my favours which I have favoured you with; fulfil my covenant and I will fulfil your covenant; me therefore dread.

41 Believe in what I have revealed, verifying what ye have got, and be not the first to disbelieve in it, and do not barter my signs for a little price, and me do ye fear.

42 Clothe not truth with vanity, nor hide the truth the while ye know.

43 Be steadfast in prayer, give the alms, and bow down with those who bow.

44 Will ye order men to do piety and forget yourselves? ye read the

corresponds to the story of the Tree of the Knowledge of Good and Evil mentioned in Gen 2:17. In the biblical account, however, they received no instructions in reference to drawing near the tree. They were merely ordered to not eat from its fruit.

2.36 *Satan made them backslide* — That is, Satan successfully enticed Adam and Eve to draw near the tree.

2.37-38 When Adam turned to Allah in repentance, Allah forgave him. It is here where the Islamic gospel is stated: "whoso follows my guidance, no fear is theirs, nor shall they grieve. But those who misbelieve, and call our signs lies, they are the fellows of the Fire, they shall dwell therein for aye" (v. 38). It is a salvation based upon "belief and doing right" (see Q 103.3, note; also see

The Last Judgment on pp. 46-50, and **Divine Forgiveness in Islam** on pp. 158-161).

2.43 *bow down with those who bow* — Muhammad was convinced that the Jewish people had fallen into sin, as had Adam and Eve (v. 36). Yet, unlike Adam and Eve, they had turned away from the guidance of Allah and were therefore on the crooked path that leads to eternal damnation. Muhammad's appeal, then, was for the Jews to turn back to the straight path—to listen and submit to the teachings in his surahs.

2.44 Muhammad chided the Jewish people, noting that they read the Old Testament (the Book), yet did not follow in what the Old Testament teaches. The implication is that the Old Testament and the qur'anic

45	Book, do ye not then understand? Seek aid with patience and prayer, though it is a hard thing save for the humble,	47	O ye children of Israel! remember my favours which I have favoured you with, and that I have preferred you above the worlds.
46	who think that they will meet their Lord, and that to Him will they return.	48	Fear the day wherein no soul shall pay any recompense for another soul, nor shall intercession be ac-

surahs present the same teachings.

2.48a *fear the day wherein no soul shall pay any recompense for another soul* — That is, people should fear the Last Judgment since it is a day when each person will stand on the merits of what he or she did in life—and will not benefit from the merits of anyone else.

As such, Muhammad firmly rejected the Doctrine of Substitutionary Atonement, which happens to be one of the cornerstone doctrines in the Bible—both Old and New Testaments. In the Old Testament, God established the rite of blood atonement. On *Yom Kippur* (the Day of Atonement) one goat was slain for the sins that the people of Israel had committed in the previous twelve months. Their sins were transferred to the goat who was killed in their place. A second goat was set free to live the remainder of its life in the wilderness. The two goats were known as the *scapegoats* (see Lev. 16:1-34). These two goats provided an atonement for sin for the Jewish people.

According to the New Testament, this Old Testament rite anticipated the day when Jesus Christ would be the true sacrifice for the sins of the world. "The law is only a shadow of the good things that are coming—not the realities themselves. For this reason it can never, by the same sacrifices repeated endlessly year after year, make perfect those who draw near to worship" (Heb 10:1). The "realities" are centered in

the death of Jesus Christ on the cross: "But when this priest (Jesus Christ) had offered for all time one sacrifice for sins, he sat down at the right hand of God" (Heb 10:12).

Therefore, say Christians, we are admonished "to enter the Most Holy Place by the blood of Jesus, by a new and living way opened for us through the curtain, that is, his body, and since we have a great priest over the house of God, let us draw near to God with a sincere heart in full assurance of faith, having our hearts sprinkled to cleanse us from a guilty conscience and having our bodies washed with pure water. Let us hold unswervingly to the hope we profess, for he who promised is faithful. And let us consider how we may spur one another on toward love and good deeds" (Heb 10:19-24).

John R. W. Stott explains, "If the uniqueness of Christianity is the uniqueness of Christ, wherein does his uniqueness lie? Historically speaking, it is found in his birth, death and resurrection. As for his birth, he was 'conceived by the Holy Spirit, born of the Virgin Mary,' and therefore is both God and man. As for his death, he died for our sins, in our place, to secure our salvation. As for his resurrection, he thereby conquered death and possesses universal authority. Or, to express these historical events theologically, the uniqueness of Jesus lies in the incarnation, the atonement and the exaltation. Each is unparalleled" (*The Authentic Jesus*, p. 73).

2.48b *nor shall intercession be accepted*

cepted for it, nor shall compensa- tion be taken from it, nor shall they	be helped. 49 When we saved you from

for it — Since in previously written surahs, Muhammad spoke otherwise, that intercession shall accepted for an individual (e.g., Q 20.109; 21.28; 34.23), the benefits of intercession are limited to only those whose lives achieved a certain degree of merit in this life: Muslim believers. The infidel who rejected Allah and Muhammad in this life shall not benefit whatsoever by intercessory prayer at the Last Judgment (see Q 39.44 note).

Another possible interpretation, though not widely held in the Muslim world, is that this passage abrogated all previous passages pertaining to the teaching of intercession. The founder of the Islamic sect Wahhabism, Muhammad ibn Abd al-Wahhab, insisted that "there can be no intercessory prayer" (Stephen Schwartz, *The Two Faces of Islam*, p. 69; also see **The Doctrine of Abrogation** on pp. 68-70).

The strict Wahhabistic view is not widely held since Muslims typically look to family members who have achieved a high degree of merit to intercede on their behalf in the afterlife, such as those who have died as martyrs in the cause of Jihad. Still, in spite of such intercessions, Muslims press forward, seeking to achieve their own lives of merit. Accordingly, a degree of uncertainty and tension exists among many Muslims when it comes to this question of intercession (see **Divine Forgiveness in Islam** on pp. 158-161).

In contrast, the New Testament claims that intercession takes place on behalf of Christian believers. In the Epistles to the Hebrews, we are told: "Therefore he (Jesus Christ) is able to save completely those who come to God through him, because he always lives to intercede for them" (Heb 7:25). And, "My dear children, I write this to you so that you will not sin. But if anybody does sin, we have one who speaks to the Father in our defense—Jesus Christ, the Righteous One" (1 Jn 2:1). And, "In the same way, the Spirit helps us in our weakness. We do not know what we ought to pray for, but the Spirit himself intercedes for us with groans that words cannot express. And he who searches our hearts knows the mind of the Spirit, because the Spirit intercedes for the saints in accordance with God's will" (Rom 8:26-27).

James Montgomery Boice comments: "A wonderful word is used for [the] mediatorial function of the Lord Jesus Christ, doubly wonderful because it is also used of the earthly ministry of the Holy Spirit on our behalf. In the Greek language the word is *parakletos* ...The picture, then, is of something we might call a heavenly law firm with us as clients. It has a heavenly branch presided over by the Lord Jesus Christ and an earthly branch directed by the Holy Spirit. Each of them pleads for us. It is the Spirit's role to move us to pray and to intensify that prayer to a point of which we ourselves are not capable...Similarly, it is the ministry of the Lord in heaven to interpret our prayers aright and plead the efficacy of his sacrifice as the basis of our coming to God. The consequence of this is that we can have great boldness in prayer. How could we ever have boldness if the answering of our prayers depended either upon the strength with which we pray or upon the correctness of the petitions themselves? Our prayers are weak, as Paul

Pharaoh's people who sought to wreak you evil and woe, slaughtering your sons and letting your women live; in that was a great trial for you from your Lord.

50   When we divided for you the sea and saved you and drowned Pharaoh's people while ye looked on.

51   When we treated with Moses forty nights, then ye took the calf after he had gone and ye did wrong.

52   Yet then we forgave you after that; perhaps ye may be grateful.

53   And when we gave Moses the Scriptures and the Discrimination; perhaps ye will be guided.

54   When Moses said to his people, "O my people! Ye have wronged yourselves in taking this calf; repent unto your Creator and kill each other, that will be better for you in your Creator's eyes; and He turned unto you, for He is the compassionate one easily turned."

55   And when ye said to Moses, "O Moses! we will not believe in thee until we see God manifestly," and the thunderbolt caught you while ye yet looked on.

56   Then we raised you up after your death; perhaps ye may be grateful.

57   And we overshadowed you with the cloud, and sent down the manna and the quails; "Eat of the

---

confesses, and we often pray wrongly. But we are bold, nevertheless, for we have the Holy Spirit to strengthen the requests, and the Lord Jesus Christ to interpret them rightly" (*Foundations of the Christian Faith*, pp. 303-304).

2.48c *nor shall compensation be taken from it, nor shall they be helped* — Allah will neither listen nor respond to anyone offering to pay a recompense for another person at the Last Judgment.

Yet again, the New Testament speaks otherwise. Jesus Christ is our recompense. He paid the penalty of our sins at the cross. The Apostle Paul admonished the leaders of the church: "Be shepherds of the church of God, which he bought with his own blood" (Acts 20:28; cf 1 Cor 6:20; 7:23; 2 Pet 2:1).

2.49-63 Muhammad then pressed his case against the Jews, bringing to their attention repeated illustrations from the Old Testament of how the Lord had come to their aid and cared for their needs. Interspersed with these illustrations are the phrases: "perhaps ye may be grateful" (v. 52), "perhaps ye will be guided" (v. 53), "perhaps ye may be grateful" (v. 56), and "haply yet ye may fear" (v. 63). According to Muhammad, in each case they were not grateful, guided, or restored to a fear of the Lord. His point was that the Israelite people refused to follow the straight path that leads to eternal life. In its place, they remained committed to the crooked path that leads to eternal damnation.

2.50 This is the episode the passing of the Israelite people through the Red (Reed) Sea (see Ex. 14:1-31).

2.51-54 This is the episode the sin of the golden calf and the giving of the Ten Commandments (see Ex 32-33).

2.55-56 Neither of these two episodes is mentioned in the Old Testament.

2.57 This is the episode of the feeding of the Israelite people with manna and quail

good things we have given you."
They did not wrong us, but it was
themselves they were wronging.

58   And when we said, "Enter this city
and eat therefrom as plentifully as
ye wish; and enter the gate worshipping and say 'hittatun.' So will
we pardon you your sins and give
increase unto those who do well."

59   But those who did wrong changed
it for another word than that which
was said to them: and we sent
down upon those who did wrong,
wrath from heaven for that they
had so sinned.

60   When Moses, too, asked drink for
his people and we said, "Strike with
thy staff the rock," and from it
burst forth twelve springs; each
man among them knew his drinking place. "Eat and drink of what
God has provided, and transgress
not on the earth as evildoers."

61   And when they said, "O Moses, we
cannot always bear one kind of
food; pray then thy Lord to bring
forth for us of what the earth
grows, its green herbs, its cucum-

bers, its garlic, its lentils, and its
onions." Said he, "Do ye ask what
is meaner instead of what is best?
Go down to Egypt,—there is what
ye ask." Then were they smitten
with abasement and poverty, and
met with wrath from God. That
was because they had misbelieved
in God's signs and killed the prophets undeservedly; that was for that
they were rebellious and had transgressed.

Appeal to Jews,
Christians and Sabaeans

62   Verily, whether it be of those who
believe, or those who are Jews or
Christians or Sabæans, whosoever
believe in God and the last day and
act aright, they have their reward
at their Lord's hand, and there is
no fear for them, nor shall they
grieve.

Jews transformed into apes

63   And when we took a covenant with

(see Ex 16:1-36).

2.58-59 According to some Islamic scholars, the word *city* could be perhaps best
translated *country*. The episode described
in this verse, then, is that of the Israelite
people entering Palestine. The word *hittatun* means repentance (see Q 7.161, note).

2.60 This is the episode of the striking of
the rock (see Ex 17:5-7).

2.61 This is the episode when the Israelite
people yearned for the foods of Egypt (Num

11:4-9).

2.62a *Sabaeans* — The *Sabaeans* were an
ancient culture that worshipped the Sun,
Moon, and Venus and centered in the southern tip of the Arabian Peninsula (present-
day Yemen); today residual groups exist in
Iraq (see Q 22.17, note).

2.62b *believe in God...and act aright* —
This is a summary of the Islamic gospel (see
Q 103.3, note).

2.63 *when we took covenant with you* —

you and held the mountain over you; "Accept what we have brought you with strong will, and bear in mind what is therein, haply ye yet may fear."

64 Then did ye turn aside after this, and were it not for God's grace towards you and His mercy, ye would have been of those who lose.

65 Ye know too of those among you who transgressed upon the Sabbath, and we said, "Become ye apes, despised and spurned."

66 Thus we made them an example unto those who stood before them, and those who should come after them, and a warning unto those who fear.

Example of the cow

67 And when Moses said to his people, "God bids you slaughter a cow," they said, "Art thou making a jest of us?" Said he, "I seek refuge with God from being one of the unwise."

68 They said, "Then pray thy Lord for us to show us what she is to be." He answered, "He saith it is a cow, nor old, nor young, of middle age between the two; so do as ye are bid."

69 They said, "Pray now thy Lord to show us what her colour is to be." He answered, "He saith it is a dun cow, intensely dun, her colour delighting those who look upon her."

70 Again they said, "Pray thy Lord to show us what she is to be; for cows appear the same to us; then we, if God will, shall be guided."

71 He answered, "It is a cow, not broken in to plough the earth or irrigate the tilth, a sound one with no blemish on her." They said, "Now hast thou brought the truth." And they slaughtered her, though they came near leaving it undone.

72 When too ye slew a soul and disputed thereupon, and God brought forth that which ye had hidden,

73 then we said, "Strike him with part of her." Thus God brings the dead

---

That is, when God established the Mosaic Covenant with the Israelite people at Mount Sinai (see Ex 19-20).

2.65 *Become ye apes* — As judgment against those Jews who transgressed the Sabbath, Muhammad claimed that Allah transformed them into apes (see Q 7.165-166, note). Moreover, Q 5.60 notes that Allah transformed them into "apes and swine."

2.67-74 This passage is based upon the Mosaic ordinance located in Deut 21-1-9 which explains that which is to be done when a person has been slain and the assailant is

not known (see Q 2.72). Those in a town closest to the incident were to take a heifer that has never been worked and sacrifice it before the Lord. The dialogue in this passage is imaginary, a dramatization by Muhammad to explain this event.

2.69 *it is a dun cow* — it is a yellow cow.

2.71 This verse corresponds to Deut 21:3, which states the that heifer chosen for sacrifice must be one that "has never been worked and has never worn a yoke."

2.73 *Strike him with part of her* — Some Islamic scholars interpret this verse as follows:

to life and shows you His signs, that haply ye may understand.

74   Yet were your hearts hardened even after that, till they were as stones or harder still, for verily of stones are some from which streams burst forth, and of them there are some that burst asunder and the water issues out, and of them there are some that fall down for fear of God; but God is never careless of

what ye do.

*The condemnation of
the Jewish people*

75   Do ye crave that they should believe you when already a sect of them have heard the word of God and then perverted it after they had understood it, though they knew?

76   And when they meet those who be-

Allah instructed the people to strike the dead man with part of the heifer that had been slain, after which the dead man would come back to life and point our his murderer. This was meant as a "sign," a divine miracle to demonstrate Allah's power and presence. The biblical account, however, does not include this command to strike the dead corpse with the intent of bringing the man back to life.

Other Islamic scholars claim that this verse should be interpreted metaphorically. Muhammad Asad said, "God brings the dead to life" is best understood figuratively. Rather than a literal resurrection from the dead, in this verse the phrase means "the prevention of bloodshed and the killing of innocent persons...be it through individual acts of revenge, or in result of an erroneous judicial process" (*The Message of the Qur'an*, p. 24).

2.74a With this verse, the moral to the story of the sacrificed cow is presented. In spite of Allah's miraculous sign (v. 73), the hearts of the Jewish people were "hardened even after that, till they were as stones or harder still."

2.74b *some that burst asunder and the water issues out* — That is, in the midst of the Jewish people's spiritual hardness, their stony hearts will break apart. The flow of

water from the rocks (hearts) illustrates the exodus of moisture, leaving them utterly dry, completely lacking any spiritual vitality whatsoever.

2.75 *Do ye crave that they should believe you* — That is, "Muhammad, can you hope that the Jewish people will believe in what you are preaching?" This is a rhetorical question, with its answer being no, since the Jewish people were beyond hope. The reason for this was because the Jewish people knowingly perverted the word of Allah "after they had understood it." This is perhaps a reference to a passage in Jeremiah, which states: "A cry is heard on the barren heights, the weeping and pleading of the people of Israel, because they have perverted their ways and have forgotten the Lord their God" (Jer 3:21).

It could also be a reference to one of the Jewish groups in Yathrib (Medinah) who rejected Muhammad's teachings soon after he arrived. The Jews in Yathrib were divided into three *banus* (tribes) that lived together in their own neighborhoods (rather than being a consolidated city, Yathrib (Medinah) was a loosely arranged amalgam of neighborhoods). In the ensuing years, the Jews would prove to be some of Muhammad's most ardent opponents in Yathrib

lieve they say, "We believe," but when one goes aside with another they say, "Will ye talk to them of what God has opened up to you, that they may argue with you upon it before your Lord? Do ye not therefore understand?"

77 Do they not then know that God knoweth what they keep secret and what they make known abroad?

78 And some of them there are, illiterate folk, that know not the Book, but only idle tales; for they do but fancy.

79 But woe to those who write out the Book with their hands and say "this is from God;" to buy therewith a little price! and woe to them for what their hands have written,

and woe to them for what they gain!

80 And then they say, "Hell fire shall not touch us save for a number of days." Say, "Have ye taken a covenant with God?" but God breaks not His covenant. Or do ye say of God that which ye do not know?

81 Yea! whoso gains an evil gain, and is encompassed by his sins, those are the fellows of the Fire, and they shall dwell therein for aye!

82 But such as act aright, those are the fellows of Paradise, and they shall dwell therein for aye!

83 And when we took from the children of Israel a covenant, saying, "Serve ye none but God, and to your two parents show kindness, and to your kindred and the or-

(Medinah).

The New Testament notes that most of the Jewish people turned away from Jesus as Messiah in the first half of the first century, A.D. Yet, hope was presented that the hardening of the Jewish people was only "in part" (Rom 11:25), and that some day in the future a vast revival would take place, in which "all Israel will be saved" (Rom 11:26).

2.76 Muhammad accused the Jews of taking aside recent converts of Islam, confiding with them that they too had been believers, with the intent of subtly drawing them away from Muhammad's teachings.

2.78 *idle tales* — Muhammad also accused some of the Jews as being illiterate and therefore not knowledgeable of the Old Testament. As such, they were beholden to "idle tales"—that is, myths and fables.

2.79 Muhammad accused some of the Jews

of writing their own scriptures and then fraudulently claiming them to be part of the Old Testament.

2.80 *shall not touch us save for a number of days* — Muhammad claimed that some of the Jewish people believed in a realm in the afterlife similar to the Roman Catholic doctrine of Purgatory. Muhammad rejected this notion. He insisted that they "shall dwell therein for aye"—that is, their stay in Hell would be for all eternity.

2.83-84 Muhammad believed that the essence of the Mosaic Covenant was a list of ethical commands that enabled the Jewish people to "act aright" (v. 82). Curiously, Muhammad failed to mention the rites of blood sacrifice that served as the foundation of the Old Testament Doctrine of Substitutionary Atonement (see Lev. 16:1-34), without which the list of ethical commands were

phans and the poor, and speak to men kindly, and be steadfast in prayer, and give alms;" and then ye turned back, save a few of you, and swerved aside.

84   And when we took a covenant from you, "shed ye not your kinsman's blood, nor turn your kinsmen out of their homes;" then did ye confirm it and were witnesses thereto.

85   Yet ye were those who slay your kinsmen and turn a party out of their homes, and back each other up against them with sin and enmity. But if they come to you as captives ye ransom them!—and yet it is as unlawful for you to turn them out. Do ye then believe in part of the Book and disbelieve in part? But the reward of such among

you as do that shall be nought else but disgrace in this worldly life, and on the day of the resurrection shall they be driven to the most grievous torment, for God is not unmindful of what ye do.

86   Those who have bought this worldly life with the Future, the torment shall not be lightened from them nor shall they be helped.

87   We gave Moses the Book and we followed him up with other apostles, and we gave Jesus the son of Mary manifest signs and aided him with the Holy Spirit. Do ye then, every time an apostle comes to you with what your souls love not, proudly scorn him, and charge a part with lying and slay a part?

---

meaningless (see Q 2.48a, note; **The Last Judgment** on pp. 46-50).

2.85-86 Muhammad accused the Jewish people of wanton sinfulness against their own people: (a) murder, (b) abandonment, and (c) the selling of captives for profit. As such, they were only partially committed to the Old Testament. The reward for such behavior, Muhammad concluded, was a severe torture from Allah in the afterlife.

2.87 Muhammad noted that following the ministry of Moses, Allah sent many other apostles, culminating with the ministry of Jesus. In each case, the apostles presented the way of Allah, yet the Jewish people remained obstinate and rebellious. "Do ye then, every time an apostle comes to you with what your souls love not, proudly scorn him, and charge a part with lying and slay a part?" (v. 87).

Jesus spoke similarly of the Jews: "Woe to you, teachers of the law and Pharisees, you hypocrites! You build tombs for the prophets and decorate the graves of the righteous. And you say, 'If we had lived in the days of our forefathers, we would not have taken part with them in shedding the blood of the prophets.' So you testify against yourselves that you are the descendants of those who murdered the prophets. Fill up, then, the measure of the sin of your forefathers!...Jerusalem, Jerusalem, you who kill the prophets and stone those sent to you, how often I have longed to gather your children together, as a hen gathers her chicks under her wings, but you were not willing. Look, your house is left to you desolate. For I tell you, you will not see me again until you say, 'Blessed is he who comes in the name of the Lord'" (Matt 23:29-39). Neverthe-

88 They say, "Our hearts are uncircumcised;" nay, God has cursed them in their unbelief, and few it is who do believe.

89 And when a book came down from God confirming what they had with them, though they had before prayed for victory over those who misbelieve, yet when that came to them which they knew, then they disbelieved it,—God's curse be on the misbelievers.

90 For a bad bargain have they sold their souls, not to believe in what God has revealed, grudging because God sends down of His grace on whomsoever of His servants He will; and they have brought on themselves wrath after wrath and for the misbelievers is there shameful woe.

*Reasons for the curse
upon the Jewish people*

91 And when they are told to believe in what God has revealed, they say, "We believe in what has been revealed to us;" but they disbelieve in all beside, although it is the truth confirming what they have. Say, "Wherefore did ye kill God's

less, the New Testament maintains a confident expectation that the Jewish people will be restored some day in the future when "all Israel will be saved" (Rom 11:26).

2.88 *God has cursed them in their unbelief* — As a result, Muhammad concluded that Allah has cursed the Jewish people. He also wrote: "For a bad bargain they have sold their souls" (v. 90). In addition, "they have brought on themselves wrath after wrath... and a shameful woe" (v. 90). It is only a few that would be believers.

2.91-103 Once again, Muhammad laid out the reason for the Jewish people having become a cursed people. They (a) rejected their own divine Scriptures, (b) killed the prophets that God had sent to them, (c) committed idolatry with the golden calf, (d) were full of greed, (e) were enemies of the archangels Gabriel and Michael, (f) were the enemies of Allah and his apostles, (g) were followers of the devil, and (h) were practitioners of sorcery.

In regards to the Jewish people, many Christians differ. They note that the Jewish people possess a mixed record. On some occasions, they acted admirably. On other occasions, they did not. On balance, they fell short. It was for this reason that Jesus bemoaned their overall record (see Matt 23:1-39). The Apostle Paul, himself a Jew, wrote: "I speak the truth in Christ—I am not lying, my conscience confirms it in the Holy Spirit— I have great sorrow and unceasing anguish in my heart. For I could wish that I myself were cursed and cut off from Christ for the sake of my brothers, those of my own race, the people of Israel. Theirs is the adoption as sons; theirs the divine glory, the covenants, the receiving of the law, the temple worship and the promises. Theirs are the patriarchs, and from them is traced the human ancestry of Christ, who is God over all, forever praised! Amen" (Rom 9:1-5).

An important difference between the Christian and Islamic attitudes toward the Jewish people, however, is centered on the

prophets of yore if ye were true believers?"

92   Moses came to you with manifest signs, then ye took up with the calf when he had gone and did so wrong.

93   And when we took a covenant with you and raised the mountain over you, "Take what we have given you with resolution and hear;" they said, "We hear but disobey;" and they were made to drink the calf down into their hearts for their unbelief. Say, "An evil thing is it which your belief bids you do, if ye be true believers."

94   Say, "If the abode of the future with God is yours alone and not mankind's: long for death then if ye speak the truth:

95   But they will never long for it because of what their hands have sent on before; but God is knowing as to the wrong doers.

96   Why, thou wilt find them the greediest of men for life; and of those who associate others with God one would fain live for a thousand years,—but he will not be reprieved from punishment by being let live, for God seeth what they do.

---

questions of *attitude* and *hope*. The Qur'an labels them a cursed people, sees them as the enemies of God, and treats them as such. In contrast, many Christians love them and anticipate their future redemption when they will embrace Jesus Christ as their Messiah.

This attitude and sense of hope within the Church, unfortunately, has not always been the case. During the Middle Ages, a dominant attitude within the Church was similar to that of Islam, an attitude which gave rise to pogroms and other forms of harsh treatment. Fortunately, modern-day Christianity has bemoaned what had previously been done in the name of Christ and turned from it with the deepest of regrets.

John R. W. Stott well articulates a correct attitude regarding the church's previous persecution of the Jews. "The blaming of the Jewish people for the crucifixion of Jesus is extremely unfashionable today. Indeed, if it is used as a justification for slandering and persecuting the Jews (as it has been in the past), or for anti-Semitism, it is absolutely indefensible. The way to avoid anti-Semitic prejudice, however, is not to pretend that the Jews were innocent, but, having admitted their guilt, to add that others shared in it. This was how the apostles saw it. Herod and Pilate, Gentiles and Jews, they said, had together 'conspired' against Jesus (Acts 4:27). More important still, we ourselves are also guilty. If we were in their place, we would have done what they did. Indeed, we *have* done it. For whenever we turn away from Christ, we 'are crucifying the Son of God all over again and subjecting him to public disgrace' (Heb 6:6). We too sacrifice Jesus to our greed like Judas, to our envy like the priests, to our ambition like Pilate. 'Were you there when they crucified my Lord?' the old negro spiritual asks. And we must answer, 'Yes,' we were there. Not as spectators only but as participants, guilty participants, plotting, scheming, betraying, bargaining, and handing him over to be crucified. We may try to wash our hands of responsibility like Pilate. But our attempt

97 Say, "Who is an enemy to Gabriel?" for he hath revealed to thy heart, with God's permission, confirmation of what had been before, and a guidance and glad tidings to believers.

98 Who is an enemy to God and His angels and His apostles and Gabriel and Michael?—Verily, God is an enemy to the unbelievers.

99 We have sent down to thee conspicuous signs, and none will disbelieve therein except the evildoers.

100 Or every time they make a covenant, will a part of them repudiate it? Nay, most of them do not believe.

101 And when there comes to them an apostle confirming what they have, a part of those who have received the Book repudiate God's book, casting it behind their backs as though they did not know.

102 And they follow that which the devils recited against Solomon's kingdom;—it was not Solomon who

misbelieved, but the devils who misbelieved, teaching men sorcery,—and what has been revealed to the two angels at Babylon, Hârût and Mârût yet these taught no one until they said, "We are but a temptation, so do not misbelieve." Men learn from them only that by which they may part man and wife; but they can harm no one therewith, unless with the permission of God, and they learn what hurts them and profits them not. And yet they knew that he who purchased it would have no portion in the future; but sad is the price at which they have sold their souls, had they but known.

103 But had they believed and feared, a reward from God were better, had they but known.

The straight path

104 O ye who believe! say not *râ'hinâ*, but say *unthurnâ*, and hearken; for unto misbelievers shall be grievous

will be as futile as his. For there is blood on our hands. Before we can begin to see the cross as something done *for* us (leading us to faith and worship), we have to see it as something done *by* us (leading us to repentance)" (*The Cross of Christ*, p. 59).
2.97 *Who is an enemy to Gabriel?* Muhammad believed that the Jewish people understood the archangel Gabriel to be their enemy.
2.100 Muhammad reminded his audience that most of the Jews "do not believe" in

the revelation that Allah sent down to them.
2.102 *Harut and Marut* — According to Muhammad, these are the two angels that were sent to the earth and earned the art of sorcery. Since then, they taught others the same occultic art.
2.104a *O ye who believe* — Muhammad was addressing fellow Muslims (also see vv. 178, 183, 208, 254, 264, 267, 278, 282).
2.104b *ra'hina* — listen.
2.104c *unthurna* — have patience.
2.105 The straight path is predicated upon

woe.

105   They who misbelieve, whether of those who have the Book or of the idolaters, would fain that no good were sent down to you from your Lord; but God specially favours with His mercy whom He will, for God is Lord of mighty grace.

106   Whatever verse we may annul or cause thee to forget, we will bring a better one than it, or one like it; dost thou not know that God is mighty over all?

107   Dost thou not know that God's is the kingdom of the heavens and the earth? nor have ye besides God a patron or a help.

108   Do ye wish to question your apostle as Moses was questioned aforetime? but whoso takes misbelief in exchange for faith has

erred from the level road.

109   Many of those who have the Book would fain turn you back into misbelievers after ye have once believed, through envy from themselves, after the truth has been made manifest to them; but pardon and shun them till God brings His command; verily, God is mighty over all.

110   Be ye steadfast in prayer, and give alms; and whatsoever good ye send before for your own souls, ye shall find it with God, for God in all ye do doth see.

*The question of
religious exclusivism*

111   They say, "None shall enter Paradise save such as be Jews or

---

the notion of double predestination (see **The Doctrine of al-Qadar** on pp. 264-266). It is, therefore, not a question of correct reasoning. Rather, it is a question of the bestowal of divine favor that enables a person to know the way to eternal life. If Allah does not guide a person's mind, that person will neither know nor understand the straight path that leads to eternal life.

2.106 *Whatever verse we may annul —* Two interpretations of this verse are the following: (a) It had been pointed out to Muhammad that what he had said in earlier surahs was contradicted in later ones. His answer was the Doctrine of Abrogation. (b) Muhammad anticipated important changes to come in his future surahs and intended to prepare his audience for the new teachings (see **The Doctrine of Abrogation** on

pp. 69-71, and Q 87.6-7, note, and Q 13.39, note).

2.107-108 In this passage, Muhammad directed his attention to infidels and asked two questions. The first question challenged the doctrine of polytheism and insisted that Allah is one—the Doctrine of Tauhid. The second question challenged the Jew's proclivity to question Muhammad's authority.

2.109-110 Muhammad then turned his attention to the newly converted Muslim believers. They were admonished to "pardon and shun" those who "have the Book"—that is, Jews and Christians. They were also admonished to remain steadfast in prayer (see **al-Salat** on pp. 169-170), give alms (see **al-Zakat** on pp. 115-116), and doing good (see **Last Judgment** on pp. 46-49).

2.111 The theological issue being examined in this verse is *universalism versus particularism.* Muhammad noted that both Judaism and Christianity were not universalist religions. Both made the claim that salvation from sin was limited to their own particular understanding and practice of spiritual truth.

Muhammad was correct in this observation. Christians believed that the Jews were not saved from the penalty of sin since they failed to acknowledge Jesus as Messiah. The Jews, on the other hand, believed that the Christians were not saved from the penalty of sin since they were not "the chosen people" and did not practice efficacious Jewish rituals. Moreover, both Jews and Christians believed that the polytheistic Arabs and the Muslim Arabs were not saved from the penalty of sin.

Speaking to Jews and Christians, Muhammad challenged these exclusivist claims, saying: "bring your proofs, if ye be speaking truth."

The following is an answer. According to the Christian faith, the fundamental difference between Judaism and Christianity is centered on the question of substitutionary atonement. In Judaism, the sins of the people were ritually placed upon two goats, one was then slaughtered and the other set free. This ritual was performed annually, on *Yom Kippur*—the Day of Atonement (see Lev. 16:1-34. In Christianity, the sins of the people were placed upon Jesus Christ who died on the cross. The Christian faith sees Jesus as the realization of the Old Testament ritual at *Yom Kippur* (Heb 10:1-12; cf. Mk 16:15-16; Jn 3:16, 36; 14:6; 1 Tim 2:5). Orthodox Judaism, of course, does not.

Since the destruction of the Temple in Jerusalem in A.D. 70, the Jewish people have not been able to perform the *Yom Kippur* ritual as prescribed in the OT due to the absence of a Temple. Christians generally understand this to be the providential act of God that de-legitimized the ritual. *Yom Kippur* was replaced with that which had been accomplished at the cross of Jesus Christ.

Notwithstanding, each year at *Yom Kippur,* orthodox (practicing) Jews perform all the rituals related to the event with the exception of the sacrifice of the one goat and the release of the second. They believe that God, in His mercy, understands their quandary of having no Temple and has therefore made providential allowances on their behalf. Still, they look forward to a future day when the Temple will be rebuilt and the sacrifice of the goat reestablished as an enduring annual event. It is with this in mind that orthodox Jews long for the day when the Jewish Temple will be rebuilt in Jerusalem on Temple Mount.

A key question asked in our current culture is this: is it not the height of *chutzpah* to insist that there is only one way that leads to Heaven, as Jews and Christians are prone to say? Many people believe that it is *chutzpah.* They have no problem with people embracing either Judaism or Christianity and journeying on that spiritual path—provided that they are agreeable to other spiritual paths. This approach is demonstrative of tolerance, an attitude that is prized in our current culture.

Conservative Christians, however, see it otherwise. Christian scholar Erwin Lutzer frames the question this way: "Does Christ belong on the same shelf with Buddha, Krishna, Bahá ú lláh, and Zoroaster?" His answer is a *resounding no.* As he explains in his book *Christ Among Other gods:* (1) Jesus had an extraordinary birth, (2) Jesus had an extraordinary life, (3) Jesus possessed an extraordinary authority, (4) Jesus had an extraordinary death, (5) Jesus had an extraor-

Christians;" that is their faith. Say thou, "Bring your proofs, if ye be speaking truth."

112   Aye, he who resigns his face to God, and who is kind, he shall have his reward from his Lord, and no fear shall be on them, and they shall not grieve.

113   The Jews say, "The Christians rest on nought;" and the Christians say, "The Jews rest on nought;" and yet they read the Book. So, too, say those who know not, like to what these say; but God shall judge between them on the resurrection day concerning that whereon they

---

dinary resurrection, (6) Jesus underwent an extraordinary ascension into Heaven, and (7) Jesus has promised an extraordinary return to the earth.

In short, Jesus Christ is unique among the founders of all the world religions. He is the God of Gods and the Lord of Lords, the Second Person of the Trinity, and the Savior of the world. Whereas all other religions are attempts to reach out and understand the realm of the spirit, in Christianity the direction is reversed. God reached down and revealed Himself to people. He initially did this through His prophets. He ultimately did so via Jesus Christ who was God in the flesh. "I and the Father are one," Jesus said. He added: "He who has seen me has seen the Father." It is in this respect that Jesus has become an extraordinary stumbling block in our world.

As noted earlier, to think of Jesus as the God the Son and the Savior of the world is an assault on human reason—an unwarranted act of *chutzpah*. Religious multi-culturalism demands that each culture be permitted to fashion religion via its own cultural norms.

Yet, this argument collapses the moment the God of the universe genuinely enters our world and speaks. At that moment, all legitimate religious truth finds itself instantly grounded to this singular God. And, all religious truth that remains opposed to this God is patently false. This God, says the Chris-

tian, has entered the world and has spoken throughout the pages of the Bible—and most completely when Jesus Christ entered the world as a baby (see 1 Cor 1:20-25).

2.112 Muhammad insisted that true religion can be reduced to the following: (a) a full surrender to God, and (b) kindness. At the Last Judgment, the works of each person will be weighed in the balance to see if he or she has succeeded in accomplishing these two requirements (see **The Last Judgment** on pp. 46-50). Elsewhere in the Qur'an, he added other requirements, such as performing a Hajj, acknowledging Muhammad as the Prophet of Allah, and the giving of alms as part and parcel of the straight way that leads to eternal life.

2.113 *rest on naught* — Muhammad understood the Jews and Christians as thinking in terms of mutual exclusivity; that is, each accused the other of possessing a faith that is baseless. And yet, he added, they read the same Scriptures. His implication is that both Jews and Christians lack sound reasoning.

A Christian response is that the fundamental difference between Jews and Christians turns on the identification of the Messiah. Jews believe that Jesus is not the Messiah. Christians believe that He is.

2.114 *mosques* — This is an Arabic word meaning any houses of worship, no matter the religion. Muhammad's point was that all

do dispute.

114   But who is more unjust than he who prohibits God's mosques, that His name should not be mentioned there, and who strives to ruin them? 'Tis not for such to enter into them except in fear, for them is disgrace in this world, and in the future mighty woe.

115   God's is the east and the west, and wherever ye turn there is God's face; verily, God comprehends and knows.

116   They say, "God takes unto Himself a son. Celebrated be His praise!" Nay, His is what is in the heavens and the earth, and Him all things obey.

117   The Originator of the heavens and the earth, when He decrees a matter He doth but say unto it, "BE," and it is.

118   And those who do not know (the Scriptures) say, "Unless God speak to us, or there comes a sign." So spake those before them like unto their speech. Their hearts are all alike. We have made manifest the signs unto a people that are sure.

119   We have sent thee with the truth, a

---

houses of worship should be honored and protected—provided that the religion be monotheistic in orientation. This is true, writes Muhammad Asad, "whether it be a mosque or a church or a synagogue." Moreover, any attempt to impede people from worshipping in their houses of worship is also condemned (*The Message of the Qur'an*, p. 33).

A Christian response to this verse is to question its qur'anic consistency in light of other verses in the Qur'an. These opposing verses condemn the Christian faith (see Q2.48; 7.114-117, 154-159; 22.17; 29.45-55), characterize Jews as apes and swine (see Q 2.65, and Q 7.165-166, note), and make the point that people are to be sent against the Jewish people who will "wreak them evil torment" (that is, engage in a military Jihad) until the resurrection day (Q 7.167).

2.115 According to Muhammad, Allah is omnipresent ("the east and the west") and omniscient ("comprehends and knows").

2.116 Whereas in previous surahs Muham-

mad's rejection of the notion that "God takes unto Himself a son" was directed against the worshippers of the Arabic Star Family religion, in this verse the immediate context indicates that his criticism was directed against the Christian religion (see v. 113). He opposed the notion that Jesus Christ is God the Son. As such, his criticism was directed at the heart of mainstream Christian thought: the doctrine of the Trinity (see *The Doctrine of the Trinity* on pp. 735-736; *The Nicene-Constantinopolitan Creed* on p. 740).

2.118 Muhammad accused the Jews and Christians of not knowing their own Scriptures since, he maintained, Allah does not demand miraculous signs to validate one's ministry. In contrast, Jews and Christians maintain that miraculous signs were common to the Bible. Moreover, false prophets could be discerned by means of a careful examination of their teachings and credentials (see Prov 2:1-5; Acts 17:11; Gal 1:6-9; *John of Damascus* on pp. 247-248).

2.119 *We have sent thee with the truth,*

bearer of good tidings and of warning, and thou shalt not be questioned as to the fellows of hell.

120 The Jews will not be satisfied with thee, nor yet the Christians, until thou followest their creed. Say, "God's guidance is the guidance" and if thou followest their lusts after the knowledge that has come to thee, thou hast not then from God a patron or a help.

121 They to whom we have brought the Book and who read it as it should be read, believe therein; and whoso disbelieve therein, 'tis they who lose thereby.

122 O children of Israel! remember my favours with which I favoured you, and that I have preferred you over the worlds.

123 And fear the day when no soul shall pay a recompense for a soul, nor shall an equivalent be received therefrom, nor any intercession avail; and they shall not be helped.

124 And when his Lord tried Abraham with words, and he fulfilled them, He said, "Verily, I will set thee as a high priest for men." Said he, "And of my seed?" God said, "My covenant touches not the evildoers."

---

a bearer of good tidings and of warning — That is, we have sent to thee (Muhammad) divine revelation. You will not be held accountable for those who are destined for Hell.

2.120 *The Jews will not be satisfied with thee, nor yet the Christians* — Muhammad finally accepted the inevitable: neither the Jews nor the Christians would ever accept the teachings found in the Qur'an. Accordingly, said Muhammad, if he were ever to accept the Jewish or Christian faith (which he described as a religion of lusts), Allah would abandon him.

2.121 Muhammad insisted that if the Old and New Testaments were rightly read, their interpretations would parallel the Qur'an.

2.122-123 Muhammad beckoned the Jewish people to abandon their belief in the Doctrine of Substitutionary Atonement. At the Last Judgment, he told them that they would receive no benefit from any such "recompense for a soul" (see Q 2.83-84, note).

2.124 Muhammad also beckoned the Jewish people to abandon their belief in the Abrahamic Covenant, a covenant that serves as a cornerstone of Orthodox Judaism. This covenant establishes the descendents of Abraham, through the seed of Isaac and then Jacob, to be the chosen people of God (see Gen 12:1-3; 15:1-6; 17:1-16; 21:12). According to Muhammad, righteous living ("believe and do right") is more foundational than reliance upon a covenant.

The New Testament offers an interpretation of the Abrahamic Covenant that stands apart from both the Jewish and Islamic interpretations. Jesus said: "And do not think you can say to yourselves, 'We have Abraham as our father.' I tell you that out of these stones God can raise up children for Abraham. The ax is already at the root of the trees, and every tree that does not produce good fruit will be cut down and thrown into the fire" (Matt 3:8-10).

The "good fruit" to which Jesus referred was repentance that leads to faith in Jesus Christ as the Messiah sent from God. And

Abraham's prayer

125 And when we made the House a place of resort unto men, and a sanctuary, and (said) take the station of Abraham for a place of prayer; and covenanted with Abraham and Ishmael, saying, "Do ye two cleanse my house for those who make the circuit, for those who pay devotions there, for those who bow down, and for those too who adore."

126 When Abraham said, "Lord, make this a town of safety, and provide the dwellers there with fruits, such as believe in God and the last day!" (God) said, "And he who misbelieves, I will give him but little to enjoy, then will I drive him to the torment of the fire, an evil journey will it be."

127 And when Abraham raised up the foundations of the House with

---

since a central facet of the messiahship of Jesus was His death, burial, and resurrection as understood in terms of the Doctrine of Substitutionary Atonement, the "good fruit" required Jews to place their faith in the message of the cross of Jesus Christ. Regrettably, though, "the message of the cross is foolishness to those who are perishing, but to us who are being saved it is the power of God" (1 Cor 1:18). See Q 3.65-69, note.

2.125a *covenanted with Abraham and Ishmael* — Muhammad claimed that the worship of the Ka'ba altar in Mecca is historically rooted with Abraham who consecrated the altar with his own special prayer. This assertion dates the Ka'ba altar at Mecca to the third millennium, B.C.

The historical record, however, speaks otherwise. Neither the city of Mecca nor the Ka'ba altar located in that city existed prior to the fourth century, A.D. (see **The City of Mecca** on pp. 32-34). What is more, prior to Muhammad's ministry and writings, the Ka'ba altar in Mecca had no tradition associating it with Abraham. Rather, as was the case with all the Ka'ba altars in the Arabian Peninsula, it was associated with Arabian paganism (see **Polytheism in Seventh Century Arabia** on pp. 92-97).

2.125b *the station of Abraham* — Three Islamic traditions are associated with this term. (a) It is a stone located in Mecca with Abraham's footprint. This was the place where Abraham allegedly stood when building the Ka'ba altar; it became soft and left an imprint. (b) It is the entire sacred area surrounding the Ka'ba altar. (c) Each of the stations associated with the Hajj is known as the station of Abraham (see **The Hajj** on pp. 480-482; Q 3.97).

2.125c *for those who make the circuit* — That is, for those who worship in the form of a circumambulation. It was the custom of the ancient Arab world for worshippers of Arabian paganism to "make a circuit" around their respective Ka'ba altars. Muhammad claimed that this ancient custom had its origin with Abraham at the Ka'ba altar in Mecca (see Q 22.26, note; **The Hajj** on pp. 480-482).

2.126 *make this a town of safety* — This verse makes the case that the city of Mecca existed in the days of Abraham. The historical record, however, speaks otherwise, that its founding occurred in the 4th century, A.D. (see **The City of Mecca** on pp. 32-34).

2.127-128 *a nation resigned unto Thee* — According to Muhammad, all true worship-

Ishmael, "Lord! receive it from us, verily, thou art hearing and dost know.

128 Lord! and make us too resigned unto Thee, and of our seed also a nation resigned unto Thee, and show us our rites, and turn towards us, verily, Thou art easy to be turned and merciful.

129 Lord! and send them an apostle from amongst themselves, to read to them Thy signs and teach them the Book and wisdom, and to purify them; verily, Thou art the mighty and the wise."

130 Who is averse from the faith of Abraham save one who is foolish of soul? for we have chosen him in this world, and in the future he is surely of the righteous.

131 When his Lord said to him, "Be resigned," he said, "I am resigned unto the Lord of the worlds."

132 And Abraham instructed his sons therein, and Jacob (saying), "O my sons! verily, God has chosen for you a religion, do not therefore die unless ye be resigned."

133 Were ye then witnesses when Jacob was facing death, when he said to his sons, "What will ye serve when I am gone?" They said, "We will serve thy God, the God of thy fathers Abraham, and

---

pers of Allah constitute their own peculiar nation, a nation that emerged from the offspring of Abraham through the line of Ishmael. As such, loyalty to the Muslim faith is deemed more fundamental than the loyalty to any nation to which a Muslim happened to be a legal citizen (see Q 23.51-52, note). Writing autobiographically, Ayaan Hirsi Ali has written: "We were first and foremost Muslim and only then Somali...Shari'a, or Islamic law, comes before any law or rule instituted by people. And it is every Muslim's duty to follow the Shari'a as strictly as possible" (*The Caged Virgin*, pp. ix, x, 29; also see **Shari'a Law** on pp. 610-612).

2.129a *send them an apostle from amongst them* — According to this verse, Abraham prayed that the Lord would send "an apostle" to read to them divine revelation (the Book). Islamic tradition believes that this prayer was fulfilled in Muhammad and his apostleship.

2.129b *teach them the Book* — That is, teach them the eternal book in Paradise (see

The Qur'an on pp. 150-153; and *The Perspicuous Book* on pp. 178-179).

2.130 *the faith of Abraham* — Muhammad asserted that the Islamic faith was one and the same with the faith of Abraham. Moreover, the faith of Abraham rightly corresponded with the previous apostles, tracing back to Adam. It is the one true primordial religion.

2.131a *I am resigned* — That is, "I am a Muslim." Muhammad believed that Abraham embraced the Islamic faith along with its doctrine of meritocracy. Christians adamantly disagree, insisting that "Abraham's faith was credited to him as righteousness" (Rom 4:9). Also see Q 3.65-69, note.

2.131b *the Lord of the worlds* — This is one of Muhammad's favorite titles for Allah (see Q 1.2, note).

2.132-133 Muhammad believed that Abraham admonished both his sons (Ishmael and Isaac) and Jacob to embrace the true faith—which, according to Muhammad, was the Is-

Ishmael, and Isaac, one God; and we are unto Him resigned."

134 That is a nation that has passed away, theirs is what they gained; and yours shall be what ye have gained; ye shall not be questioned as to that which they have done.

Further admonitions to
the Jews and Christians

135 They say, "Be ye Jews or Christians so shall ye be guided." Say, "Not so! but the faith of Abraham the 'Hanîf, he was not of the idolaters."

136 Say ye, "We believe in God, and what has been revealed to us, and what has been revealed to Abraham, and Ishmael, and Isaac, and Jacob, and the Tribes, and what was brought to Moses and Jesus, and what was brought unto the Prophets from their Lord; we will not distinguish between any one of them, and unto Him are we resigned."

137 If they believe in that in which ye believe, then are they guided; but if they turn back, then are they only in a schism, and God will suffice thee against them, for He both hears and knows.

138 The dye of God! and who is better than God at dyeing? and we are worshippers of Him.

139 Say [to the Jews and Christians], "Do ye dispute with us concerning God, and He is our Lord and your Lord? Ye have your works and we have ours, and unto Him are we sincere."

140 Do ye say that Abraham, and Ishmael, and Isaac, and Jacob, and the Tribes were Jews or Christians? Say, "Are ye more knowing than God? Who is more unjust than one who conceals a testimony that he has from God?" But God is not careless of what ye do.

141 That is a nation that has passed away; theirs is what they gained, and yours shall be what ye have gained; ye shall not be questioned

---

lamic faith (the Doctrine of Tauhid).

2.135 The rebuttal of the Jews and Christians to Muhammad's understanding of "the faith of Abraham" was to say to the Muslim community needed to become either Jews or Christians if they wished to be guided in the right spiritual path.

2.136-137 Muhammad believed that his teachings corresponded to the inspired Scriptures that had revealed to Abraham, Ishmael, Isaac, Jacob, the Twelve Tribes of Israel, Moses, Jesus, and the other prophets.

2.138 *the dye of God!* — This is a figure of speech. Muhammad believed that the Islamic religion correctly reflected God's colors (or teachings).

2.139 When comparing the works of the Muslims with those of the Jews and Christians, he believed that Muslims works were sincere before God.

2.141 *that is a nation that has passed away* — That is, the Jewish nation has passed away. The current nation of Israel in the Middle East is therefore an offense to Muslim sensibilities and a contradiction to this verse.

The direction of prayer

142 The fools among men will say, "What has turned them from their *qiblah*, on which they were agreed?" Say, "God's is the east and the west, He guides whom He will unto the right path."

143 Thus have we made you a middle nation, to be witnesses against men, and that the Apostle may be a witness against you. We have not appointed the *qiblah* on which thou wert agreed, save that we might know who follows the Apostle from him who turns upon his heels; although it is a great thing save to those whom God doth guide. But God will not waste your faith, for verily, God with men is kind and merciful.

144 We see thee often turn about thy

as to that which they have done.

face in the heavens, but we will surely turn thee to a *qiblah* thou shalt like. Turn then thy face towards the Sacred Mosque; wherever ye be, turn your faces towards it; for verily, those who have the Book know that it is the truth from their Lord;—God is not careless of that which ye do.

145 And if thou shouldst bring to those who have been given the Book every sign, they would not follow your *qiblah*; and thou art not to follow their *qiblah*; nor do some of them follow the *qiblah* of the others: and if thou followest their lusts after the knowledge that has come to thee then art thou of the evildoers.

146 Those whom we have given the Book know him as they know their sons, although a sect of them do surely hide the truth, the while they know.

2.142a *qiblah* — The direction of prayer. Prior to Muhammad's alleged call to the prophethood and throughout the early period of his ministry when he lived in Mecca, he prayed before the southern wall of the Ka'ba altar in a northern direction: towards Jerusalem. After his migration to Medinah, "he continued to pray northwards, with only Jerusalem as his qiblah (direction of prayer)" (*The Message of the Qur'an*, p. 39).

2.142b *the right path* — a summary of the Islamic gospel (see Q 72.2, note).

2.143a *a middle nation* — The Muslim community was to be a conduit between the teachings of Muhammad and the needs of the world. Muslims were, in so many words,

to be a witness, as they understood it, of the true faith to the world.

2.143b *we have not appointed the qiblah on which thou wert agreed* — That is, Allah had not appointed the direction northward towards Jerusalem, which had been the previous custom of Muhammad.

2.144-145 *turn then thy face toward the Sacred Mosque* — That is, the *qiblah* changed. Muhammad was to pray towards the Ka'ba altar in Mecca. This has been the custom within Islam ever since this time.

2.146 *know him as they know their sons* — Muhammad asserted that Jews and Christians (the people of the Book) deliberately hide the truth about true spirituality.

147 The truth (is) from thy Lord; be not therefore one of those who doubt thereof.

148 Every sect has some one side to which they turn (in prayer); but do ye hasten onwards to good works; wherever ye are God will bring you all together; verily, God is mighty over all.

149 From whencesoever thou comest forth, there turn thy face towards the Sacred Mosque, for it is surely truth from thy Lord; God is not careless about what ye do.

150 And from whencesoever thou comest forth, there turn thy face towards the Sacred Mosque, and wheresoever ye are, turn your faces towards it, that men may have no argument against you, save only those of them who are unjust; and fear them not, but fear me and I will fulfil my favours to you, perchance ye may be guided yet.

151 Thus have we sent amongst you an apostle of yourselves, to recite to you our signs, to purify you and teach you the Book and wisdom, and to teach you what ye did not know;

152 remember me, then, and I will remember you; thank me, and do not misbelieve.

Martyrdom

153 O ye who do believe! seek aid from patience and from prayer, verily, God is with the patient.

154 And say not of those who are slain in God's way (that they are) dead, but rather living; but ye do not perceive.

155 We will try you with something of fear, and hunger and loss of wealth, and souls and fruit; but give good tidings to the patient,

156 who when there falls on them a calamity say, "Verily, we are God's and, verily, to Him do we return."

157 These, on them are blessings from

2.148 Muhammad also questioned whether Jews and Christians were people "who hasten onwards to good works."

2.149-150 Muhammad was convinced that those who pray towards the Ka'ba altar in Mecca are those committed to the truth—"wheresoever ye are, turn your faces towards it." They were also instructed not to fear the infidel nor give account to their arguments that oppose Islamic doctrine.

2.151a Muhammad maintained that he was the divinely chosen apostle, called to recite divine revelation and teach spiritual wisdom.

2.151b *the Book* — That is, the eternal book in Paradise (see **The Perspicuous Book** on pp. 178-179).

2.154 *slain in God's way* — That is, those who experienced martyrdom for the sake of Allah. Muhammad commented that they were not dead but alive—that is, in Paradise. His point is that those who die as martyrs in the Cause of Jihad sidestep the Last Judgment and are admitted directly into Paradise (see Q 3.169-173, note).

2.156 According to this verse, Muslims who die in cause of Islam will be blessed of Allah

their Lord and mercy, and they it is who are guided.

158 Verily, Zafâ and Merwah are of the beacons of God, and he who makes the pilgrimage unto the House, or visits it, it is no crime for him to compass them both about; and he who obeys his own impulse to a good work,—God is grateful and doth know.

Jews and Christians cursed

159 Verily, those who hide what we have revealed of manifest signs and of guidance after we have manifested it to men in the Book, them God shall curse, and those who curse shall curse them too.

160 Save those who turn and do right and make (the signs) manifest; these will I turn to again, for I am easy to be turned and merciful.

161 Verily, those who misbelieve and die while still in misbelief, on them is the curse of God, and of the angels, and of mankind altogether;

162 to dwell therein for aye; the torment shall not be lightened for them, no shall they be looked upon.

Monotheism vs. polytheism

163 Your God is one God; there is no God but He, the merciful, the compassionate.

164 Verily, in the creation of the heavens and the earth, and the alterna-

in the afterlife.

2.158 *Zafia and Merwah* — These are two outcrops of rocks situated in Mecca, near the Ka'ba altar. According to Islamic legend, it is the scene where Hagar was distraught with thirst and fear and encountered the angel of God (see Gen. 21:15-19; also see Q 106.3, note and **The Banishment of Hagar and Ishmael** on pp. 38, 39 and **The Hajj** on pp. 480-482).

2.159a *men of the Book* — According to Ibn 'Abbas and a number of other Islamic scholars, the Book mentioned here is the Bible. Consequently, the men of the Book refer to Jews and Christians.

2.159b *God shall curse* — Because the Jews and Christians hid (rejected) the teachings of the qur'anic surahs, Muhammad said that they were cursed of Allah.

2.159c *those who curse shall curse them too* — That is, all righteous people who are

able to correctly assess moral issues (i.e., Muslims) shall curse the Jews and Christians.

2.160 *save those who turn and do right* — The only Jews and Christians who will be spared from being cursed are those who repent and become Muslims.

2.161 *on them is the curse* — The Jews and Christians who remain infidels (reject the qur'anic surahs) will be cursed of Allah, the angels, and mankind (a teaching that laid the groundwork for the Doctrine of Jihad).

2.162 — *the torment shall not be lightened for them* — That is, they will receive the most intense torture.

2.163 Foundational to the Islamic faith is an absolute monotheism (the Doctrine of Tauhid). Christianity failed this Islamic test due to the Doctrine of the Trinity that is foundational to its theology (see Q 2.136-137, note). The Jewish people also failed this test due to their repeated excursions

tion of night and day, and in the ship that runneth in the sea with that which profits man, and in what water God sends down from heaven and quickens therewith the earth after its death, and spreads abroad therein all kinds of cattle, and in the shifting of the winds, and in the clouds that are pressed into service betwixt heaven and earth, are signs to people who can understand.

165 Yet are there some amongst mankind who take to themselves peers other than God; they love them as they should love God; while those who believe love God more. O that those, who are unjust could only see, when they see the torment, that power is altogether God's! Verily, God is keen to torment.

166 When those who are followed clear themselves of those who followed them, and see the torment, and the cords are cut asunder,

167 those who followed shall say, "Had we but another turn, then would we clear ourselves of them as they have cleared themselves of us." So will God show them their works; for them are sighs, and they shall not come forth from out the fire.

Dietary law

168 O ye folk! eat of what is in the earth, things lawful and things good, and follow not the footsteps of Satan, verily, to you he is an open foe.

169 He does but bid you evil and sin, and that ye should speak against God what ye do not know.

170 When it is said to them, "Follow what God has revealed," they say, "Nay, we will follow what we found our fathers agreed upon." What! and though their fathers had no sense at all or guidance?

into the sin of idolatry (see Q 2.51-54, note).
2.164 Muhammad believed Allah to be the supreme sovereign ruler of the universe, controlling the minutest of details transpiring on the earth.
2.165a *they love them as they should love God* — Muhammad believed that the love Christians had for Jesus was idolatrous, since it was coupled with worship that should have been limited to God (see Jn 14:15, 21-24; 15:9-10; 17:26; 21:15-17; 1 Cor 16:22-24; Eph 6:24).
2.165b *God is keen to torment* — That is, Allah is eager to inflict torture on infidels.
2.166-167 In the context of this passage,

Muhammad believed that at the Last Judgment Jesus will disown those who falsely worshipped him as the Son of God. They will then regret their false beliefs and wish for a second opportunity to worship Allah aright and avoid their impending torture.
2.168-173 In this passage, Muhammad addressed Shari'a Dietary Law. Prohibitions were minimal, in contrast with Jewish dietary laws, which were extensive. The only dietary restrictions codified by Muhammad were: (a) no carrion, (b) no blood, (c) no pork, and (d) no foods consecrated to idols (also see Q 2.173 and Q 6.118-121, note, where the Halal Tradition is mentioned, and

171 The likeness of those who misbelieve is as the likeness of him who
shouts to that which hears him not,
save only a call and a cry; deafness, dumbness, blindness, and
they shall not understand.

172 O ye who do believe! eat of the
good things wherewith we have
provided you, and give thanks unto
God if it be Him ye serve.

173 He has only forbidden for you what
is dead, and blood, and flesh of
swine, and whatsoever has been
consecrated to other than God; but
he who is forced, neither revolting nor transgressing, it is in no
sin for him; verily, God is forgiving and merciful.

*The straight
and crooked paths*

174 Verily, those who hide what God
has revealed of the Book, and sell
it for a little price, they shall eat
nothing in their bellies save fire and
God will not speak to them on the
day of resurrection, nor will He purify them, but for them is grievous woe.

175 They who sell guidance for error,
and pardon for torment, how patient must they be of fire!

176 That (is), because God has revealed
the Book with truth, and verily
those who disagree about the Book
are in a wide schism.

Q 16.114-117).

2.171 Muhammad likened infidels to those who suffered from deafness, dumbness, and blindness (see Q 2.18, note).

2.173 Though unanimous agreement exists among Islamic scholars that swine are not to be eaten, a lack of agreement exists in regards to water swine (hippopotamus). Some scholars claim that it can be eaten while others argue that the animal falls under the category of swine and therefore should not be eaten.

2.174a *those who hide what God has revealed* — That is, those who suppress divine revelation.

2.174b *the Book* — That is, the eternal book in Paradise that has been revealed, in part or in whole, to the duly appointed apostles (see **The Perspicuous Book** on pp. 178-179).

2.174c *sell it for a little price* — That is, barter it away for minimal gains one finds in

life. Muhammad claimed that Jews and Christians taught spiritual truths to others for a price, thereby corrupting their integrity.

2.175a *They who sell guidance for error* — In seventh century Arabia, pagan prognosticators were common, offering advice that they claimed came from the ginns for a fee (see **Occultism in Seventh Century Arabia** on pp. 123-125). Muhammad believed that all such guidance was spiritual error.

2.175b *They who sell...pardon* — This verse could possibly be a reference to the Council of Epaon (A.D. 517) which bestowed canonical penances for the sinner for a fixed sum of money or other acts of righteousness. Canonical penances were acts of contrition that demonstrated to the Church that the sinner was truly sorrowful and repentant. This practice later gave rise to the practice of Indulgences in the thirteenth century. By the sixteenth century, the practice was in widespread use and gave rise to se-

177   Righteousness is not that ye turn your faces towards the east or the west, but righteousness is, one who believes in God, and the last day, and the angels, and the Book, and the prophets, and who gives wealth for His love to kindred, and orphans, and the poor, and the son of the road, and beggars, and those in captivity; and who is steadfast in prayer, and gives alms; and those who are sure of their covenant when they make a covenant; and the patient in poverty, and distress, and in time of violence; these are they who are true, and these are those who fear.

Laws pertaining to homicide

178   O ye who believe! Retaliation is prescribed for you for the slain: the free for the free, the slave for the slave, the female for the female; yet he who is pardoned at all by his brother, must be prosecuted in reason, and made to pay with kindness. That is an alleviation from your Lord, and a mercy; and he who transgresses after that for him is grievous woe.

179   For you in retaliation is there life, O ye possessors of minds! it may be ye will fear.

*Laws pertaining to
wills and inheritances*

180   It is prescribed for you that when

vere criticism by Martin Luther and other clerics within the Church who rebelled and eventually broke free from the Roman Catholic Church. The result was a new branch of the Church: Protestantism.

2.177 *Righteousness is not that ye turn your faces towards the east or the west* — That is, righteousness is not a question of faithfully fulfilling the *qiblah,* the direction of prayer (see Q 2.142-152, note). According to Muhammad, if all that one possesses are outward forms of righteousness, a person is not righteous. True piety also requires righteous actions. These include: (a) belief in Allah, (b) belief in the Last Judgment, (c) a dedication to divine revelation, (d) a dedication to the teachings of the prophets, (e) the giving of alms, (f) and the care of the poor, the orphans, the travelers, and those held in captivity, (g) remaining steadfast in prayer, and (h) patient in poverty, times of

distress and violence. In Islam, then, inward and outward piety are intertwined, giving rise to Shari'a Law (see **Shari'a Law** on pp. 610-612).

2.178a *O ye who believe* — Muhammad was addressing fellow Muslims (also see vv. 104, 183, 208, 254, 264, 267, 278, 282).

2.178b *retaliation is prescribed for you for the slain* — A freeman may not be killed as retribution for a slave who had been killed and a man may not be killed in retribution for a woman who had been killed. Yet, some Islamic scholars believe that this verse had been abrogated by Q 5.45 which states that retribution for murder shall be "a life for a life" without mention of social or sexual status.

2.178b *yet he who is pardoned at all by his brother, must be prosecuted with reason* — the term "brother" refers to a fellow citizen examining the case. Mitigating circumstances

one of you is face to face with death, if he leave (any) goods, the legacy is to his parents, and to his kinsmen, in reason. A duty this upon all those that fear.

181 But he who alters it after that he has heard it,—the sin thereof is only upon those who alter it; verily, God doth hear and know.

182 And he who fears from the testator a wrong intention, or a crime, and doth make up the matter between the parties, it is no sin to him; verily, God is forgiving and merciful.

Siyam (the law of fasting)

183 O ye who believe! There is prescribed for you the fast as it was prescribed for those before you; haply ye may fear.

184 A certain number of days, but he

amongst you who is ill or on a journey, then (let him fast) another number of days. And those who are fit to fast may redeem it by feeding a poor man; but he who follows an impulse to a good work it is better for him; and if ye fast it is better for you, if ye did but know.

185 The month of Ramadhân, wherein was revealed the Qur'ân, for a guidance to men, and for manifestations of guidance, and for a Discrimination. And he amongst you who beholds this month then let him fast it; but he who is sick or on a journey, then another number of days;—God desires for you what is easy, and desires not for you what is difficult,—that ye may complete the number, and say, "Great is God," for that He has guided you; haply ye may give thanks.

can be introduced in the trial, with the result being a reduction of the penalty.

2.180-182 The dispersal of one's inheritance is to be divided to "his kinsman, in reason." The division of wealth is explained in greater detail in Q 4.11-12.

2.182 If a person has reason to believe that a mistake has been committed by the testator—intentional or unintentional—an adjustment to the settlement is permitted.

2.183 *O ye who believe* — Muhammad was addressing fellow Muslims (also see vv. 104, 178, 208, 254, 264, 267, 278, 282).

2.184 *a certain number of days* — A Muslim is to fast during the month of Ramadan. It is an abstention from food, drink, and sexual intercourse from dawn to sunset (whenever

the sun is in the sky). If a person is unable to fulfill the fast as prescribed, he or she may redeem the days not fulfilled by feeding a poor man (see **Siyam** on p. 817).

2.185a *the month of Ramadhan* — The ninth month on the Islamic year. The months on the Islamic year are based upon a lunar calendar of thirty days and hence migrates throughout the four seasons (winter, spring, summer, fall) over the course of years. The month of Ramadan is sacred among Muslims since it is believed to be the month whereupon Muhammad first received divine revelations from the archangel Gabriel—the Night of Power (see Q 97).

2.185b *Great is God* — This is the Islamic phrase known as the *Takbir* (*Allahu akbar*).

Law of prayer

186 When my servants ask thee concerning me, then, verily, I am near; I answer the prayer's prayer whene'er he prays to me. So let them ask me for an answer, and let them believe in me; haply they may be directed aright.

The prohibition of sex during the month of fasting

187 Lawful for you on the night of the fast is commerce with your wives; they are a garment unto you, and ye a garment unto them. God knows that ye did defraud yourselves, wherefore He has turned towards you and forgiven you; so now go in unto them and crave what God has prescribed for you, and eat and drink until a white thread can be distinguished by you from a black one at the dawn. Then fulfill the fast until the night, and go not in unto them, and ye at your devotions in the mosques the while. These are the bounds that God has set, so draw not near thereto. Thus does God make manifest His signs to men, that haply they may fear.

Law of wealth

188 Devour not your wealth among yourselves vainly, nor present it to the judges that ye may devour a part of the wealth of men sinfully, the while ye know.

See Q 34.23 note.

2.186 *I answer the prayer's prayer* — In the Islamic world, prayer is a complicated matter since Islamic theology also presents a version of divine sovereignty which implies that the will of Allah is already determined in eternity past and cannot be swayed (see **Divine Forgiveness in Islam** on pp. 158-161 for a further discussion of this question).

2.187a *commerce with your wives* — That is, have sexual intercourse with your wives. According to this verse, men were permitted to have sexual intercourse with their wives on the night preceding the month of Ramadan. The implication is that sexual intercourse is to be abstained throughout the month of Ramadan. Only eating and drinking is permitted during the night hours.

2.187b *God knows that ye did defraud yourselves* — That is, Allah knows that you unnecessarily restricted yourself in regards to sex.

2.187c *what God has prescribed for you* — sex is an Allah-ordained activity.

2.187d *Then fulfill the fast until the night, and go not in unto them* — Muslims were mandated to fulfill the sexual fast until night. At nightfall they were still prohibited from going "in unto them" (that is, from having sexual relations).

2.188a *Devour not your wealth among yourselves vainly* — That is, do not devour your possessions wrongfully. Rather, spend your money responsibly and righteously.

2.188b Those who were wealthy were prohibited from displaying their wealth in such a way of influencing outcomes of criminal or civil trials.

Shari'a Law

Since Islam is both a theology (sacred beliefs) and a theocracy (sacred government), it is inevitable that a theo-jurisprudence (sacred law) would emerge. This version of jurisprudence is technically called: Shari'a Law— an Arabic word meaning *the way*, the way that leads to eternal life.

Shari'a Law emerged in the eighth century during the Abbasid dynasty (the second dynasty of Islamic caliphs). Legal scholars sifted through the thousands of hadithic sayings attributed to Muhammad and the Qur'an. The intent was to establish a thoroughly structured law that addressed cultic, private and criminal questions.

Yet, Shari'a Law was not officially codified in the eighth century— nor has it ever been. Instead, it remained an unsystematized collection of rules and regulations that has spawned on-going debates and discussions among Islamic legal scholars. Shari'a Law, writes Abou El Fadl, contains "a wide range of ethical and moral principles, legal methodologies, and many conflicting and competing judgments."[1] He adds,

> To help visualize the phenomenon that I am describing, perhaps I should mention my own personal library on Islamic law. It contains fifty thousand titles...As I repeatedly remind my students, the fifty thousand titles do not simply present the same ideas and doctrines over and over again. Rather, each book is unique, and special in terms of the ideas and doctrines presented.[2]

Still, in spite of the variances of interpretation, a broad consensus exists in the Muslim world on three themes within Shari'a Law. In each, the notion of *subordination* serves as the main idea. They are:

- the subordination of the entire world to Allah and His Prophet Muhammad—that is, worldwide islamification

- the subordination of non-Muslims to Muslims

- the subordination of women to men

Woven into this threefold definition, Shari'a Law contains material that addresses behavior that is (a) obligatory, (b) meritorious, (c) neutral or indifferent, (d) reprehensible yet not forbidden, and (e) forbidden and subject to punishment.[3]

Fundamentalist Islam. Fundamentalist Muslims have taken Shari'a Law one step further. They insist that Shari'a Law, rightly understood, offers a singular interpretation—a seamless ideology that contains no conflicting or competing judgments. Most importantly, it brings clarity to the nature of the ideal Islamic state. In this state, writes D. P. Sharma, "sovereignty would belong to God alone and would be exercised on his behalf by an ideological state, it would be administered for God solely by Muslims who adhered to its ideology...Non-Muslims, who could not share its ideology, and women, who by nature could not devote their entire lives to it, would have no place in high politics. Everything would come under the purview of this Islamic state."[4]

Syed Abu-al Maududi (1903-1979), founder of the terrorist organization Jamaat-e-Islami that has inserted itself into the Pakistani-Indian conflict, readily admitted that Shari'a Law stands opposed to the principles of democracy that typify many nations in the West. Speaking of the Islamic state that embraces Shari'a Law, he commented: "In such a state no one can regard any field of his affairs as personal and private. Considered from this aspect the Islamic State bears a resemblance to the Fascist and Communist states." He added: "The state in Islam is based on an ideology and its objective is to establish that ideology."[5]

Maududi's writings have left a legacy for fundamentalist Islam that has carried forward to the present day. Typical to this fundamentalist ideology are the following:

- the death sentence on Muslim apostates

- clitoridectomy for Muslim women

- the permission for Muslim girls to be married at the age of nine

- death to Jews and all who give support to Jews

In short, fundamentalist Muslims are committed to a literal and stark reading of the Qur'an. Shari'a Law is its natural outgrowth, an inflexible system of laws that encompasses the entirety of one's life (politics, religion, and social mores). It is also geo-political in scope. Because of this, it is deemed a threat to most non-Muslim nations and cultures.

1 Abou El Fadel, *The Great Theft*, p. 33
2 Ibid, pp. 33-34
3 See *The Columbia Encyclopedia*, p. 2584.
4 D. P. Sharma, *The New Terrorism*, p. 80.
5 Maududi, *Islamic Law and Constitution*, p. 146.

Democracy and freedom are an affront to Allah. All constitutions are an offense to Allah and must be destroyed and replaced with Sharia Law. For Muslims, Sharia Law is the Rule of Law...Sharia is the legal code ordained by Allah for all mankind. To violate Sharia or not to accept its authority is to commit rebellion against Allah, which Allah's faithful are required to combat...It is the long term goal of Islam to replace the US Constitution with the Sharia, since it contradicts Islam. For that matter, democracy violates Sharia law. Democracy assumes equality of all peoples. Islam teaches that a Muslim is a better person than kafirs [infidels] and that the kafirs should submit to Islam. But in voting, a Muslim's vote is equal to a kafir's vote. This violates Islamic law, since a Muslim and a kafir are never equal.

—Jake Neuman, *God of Moral Perfection*, p. 23

Sharia has been connected to the idea of "spiritual law" and a "system of divine law." Social, economic and political issues as well as religious rituals are covered by Sharia. Some laws with Sharia are treated as divinely ordained and can never be altered. Other laws within Sharia are created by lawyers and judges. Lawmakers are seen as establishing what is a human approximation of that which is seen as divine. The Islamic lawmakers are endeavoring to interpret divine principles. Whilst the specific opinions and laws created by lawyers and judges are not considered divine, Sharia law in general is considered to be divine.

—Larry Mead and David Sagar, *Fundamentals of Ethics*, pp. 33, 34

The genius of Islam is finally law and not theology. In the last analysis the sense of God is a sense of Divine command. In the will of God there is none of the mystery that surrounds His being. His demands are known and the believer's task is not so much exploratory, still less fellowship, but rather obedience and allegiance.

—Kenneth Cragg, *The Call of the Minaret*, p. 57

No formal legal code was created at this time, or subsequently, the sharia being more a discussion of how Muslims ought to behave. In the process, human actions were classified on a five point scale: obligatory, meritorious, indifferent, reprehensible, forbidden.

—Francis Robinson, *The Cambridge Illustrated History of the Islamic World*, p. 212

Phases of the moon

189 They will ask thee about the phases of the moon; say, "They are indications of time for men and for the pilgrimage." And it is not righteousness that ye should enter into your houses from behind them, but righteousness is he who fears; so enter into your houses by the doors thereof and fear God; haply ye may prosper yet.

Law of Jihad

190 Fight in God's way with those who fight with you, but transgress not; verily, God loves not those who do transgress.

191 Kill them wherever ye find them, and drive them out from whence they drive you out; for sedition is worse than slaughter; but fight them not by the Sacred Mosque until they fight you there; then kill

---

2.189 The religious observances within Islam is based upon the lunar calendar. It indicates the arrival of the month of Ramadan and all the religious rituals associated with it—including the pilgrimage to Mecca (see **The Hajj** on pp. 480-482).

2.190 *Fight in God's way with those who fight with you* — Literally, wage jihad with those who wage jihad with you. Islamic scholars understand jihad to be meritorious when it is done in terms of self-defense. The phrase "but transgress not" is understood by Islamic scholars to mean that they were not to be the aggressors. According to other surahs, by rejecting the messages and ministry of divinely appointed apostles, the infidel has become the aggressor since he has offended Allah. Just as Allah is now fighting against the infidel, the Muslim is summoned to fight alongside Allah "in God's way"—that is, in Allah's righteous cause (see Q 10.13, 49; 22.39-40; 26.192-212; 43.6-8; **Jihad** on pp. 616-622).

2.191a *kill them wherever ye find them* — when waging Jihad, Muslims were admonished to bring death to all infidels opposing them (also see Q 9.5, known as *The Verse of the Sword*).

2.191b *drive them out from whence they drive you out* — A motivation for Jihad is to restore lands that had once been in Muslim hands yet since taken over by the infidel. The fact that the infidel had taken possession of previously owned Islamic land is, in the eyes of Allah, an act of aggression against Allah (see Q 22.40).

This verse has given justification for the current struggle between Israel and the surrounding Arab nations in the Middle East. Since, at one time, Palestine had been occupied and ruled by Muslims, any non-Muslims who now occupy and rule the region are aggressors. They must be driven out of the land any way possible, including Jihad. Islam has the same attitude towards Spain (the Iberian Peninsula) since it too was once under Muslim rule.

2.191c *for sedition is worse than slaughter* — That is, oppression is worse than slaughter. According to this verse, for a land to be occupied and ruled by non-Muslims is, by definition, a form of oppression and "worse than slaughter." Therefore, under such conditions, to slaughter (to wantonly kill) the unjust occupiers is less atrocious than living in an occupied territory. In our current world, this

them, for such is the recompense of those that misbelieve.

192 But if they desist, then, verily, God is forgiving and merciful.

193 But fight them that there be no sedition and that the religion may be God's; but, if they desist, then let there be no hostility save against the unjust.

194 The sacred month for the sacred month; for all sacred things demand retaliation; and whoso transgresses against you, transgress against him like as he transgressed against you; but fear ye God, and know that God is with those who fear.

195 Expend in alms in God's way and be not cast by your own hands into perdition; but do good, for God loves those who do good.

Laws pertaining to the Hajj

196 And fulfil the pilgrimage and the visitation to God; but if ye be besieged, then what is easiest for you by way of gift. But shave not your heads until your gift shall reach its destination; and he amongst you who is sick or has a hurt upon his head, then the redemption is by fasting or by alms or by an offering. But when ye are safe again,

verse has given justification for some Muslims to slaughter non-Muslims in Palestine.

2.191d *fight them not by the Sacred Mosque until they fight you there* — At the time of the writing of the second surah, Mecca was still occupied by Arab tribes that had resolutely rejected Muhammad's ministry. He therefore prohibited any warfare to be waged in the proximity of the Ka'ba altar (the Sacred Mosque) unless the infidel initiated warfare in that same proximity.

2.191e *such is the recompense of those who misbelieve* — That is, the waging of Jihad was a just recompense for those who refused to submit to Allah.

2.192 *But if they desist* — That is, infidels who surrender are to be shown mercy. The implication is that all who refuse to surrender are to be fought until they are either killed or accept Muslim terms of surrender.

2.193 *fight them until there be no sedition and that the religion may be God's* — That is, Jihad is to be waged until all unjust occu-

pation of Muslim lands is quenched and the Islamic faith is restored in the land as the one true religion. In reference to the current Israeli-Arab conflict in Middle East, this verse validates the notion that jihad is to be waged against the Jew until all Jews are pushed out of Palestine and the Islamic faith is established as the one true faith.

2.194a *the sacred month for the sacred month* — Most Islamic scholars interpret this phrase to mean: "fight during the sacred months if you are attacked."

2.194b *God is with those who fear* — That is, Allah will ultimately bless those who fight in His cause.

2.195 *expend in alms* — In this context, alms were understood as charitable gifts given to advance the Cause of Allah (Jihad). Accordingly, this verse has offered justification for Islamic charities to give financial support of jihadistic causes.

2.196 *fulfill the pilgrimage and the visitation to God* — That is, fulfill the obligation of

then let him who would enjoy the visitation until the pilgrimage (bring) what is easiest as a gift. And he who cannot find (anything to bring), then let him fast three days on the pilgrimage and seven when ye return; these make ten days complete. That is, for him whose family are not present in the Sacred Mosque; and fear God and know that God is keen to punish.

197 The pilgrimage is (in) well-known months: whosoever then makes it incumbent on himself (let him have neither) commerce with women, nor fornication, nor a quarrel on the pilgrimage; and whatsoever of good ye do, God knoweth it; then provide yourself for your journey; but the best provision is piety. Fear ye me ye who possess minds.

198 It is no crime to you that ye seek good from your Lord; but when ye pour forth from 'Arafât, remember God by the sacred beacon. Remember Him how He guided you, although ye were surely before of those who err.

199 Then pour ye forth from whence men do pour forth and ask pardon of God; verily, God is forgiving and merciful.

---

the Hajj (see **The Hajj** on pp. 480-482). Yet, if someone is held back by unexpected difficulties, then a Muslim is to give whatever gift one can easily afford.

2.196c *shave not your heads until you gift shall reach its destination* — That is, do not shave your head until your gift is sacrificed at the Festival of Sacrifice on the tenth day of the Hajj (see **The Festival of Sacrifice** on p. 226 and **The Hajj** on pp. 480-482).

2.196d *he amongst you who is sick or has a hurt upon his head* — That is, those who are sick are exempted from the Hajj, yet are required to redeem themselves with fasting or by giving alms or by an offering.

2.196e *when ye are safe again* — That is, when you are in a position to be able to perform the Hajj, bring a gift that is affordable.

2.196f *he who cannot find (anything to bring), let him fast three days on the pilgrimage and seven when ye return* — Those who are not able to bring a gift are required to fast three days while on the pilgrimage and seven days after returning home.

2.197a *the pilgrimage is (in) well-known months* — Since the Hajj always occurs in the month of Ramadan, its plural form in this verse refers to its annual observance.

2.197b *let him neither have commerce with women* — That is, while on pilgrimage, men are not permitted to have sexual relations with women.

2.197c *fear ye me ye who possess minds* — That is, fear Allah all those who possess righteous minds.

2.198a *when ye pour forth from Arafat* — when the pilgrims finish their time at the Plains of Arafat on the ninth day of the Hajj (see **The Hajj** on pp. 480-482).

2.198b *remember God by the sacred beacon* — That is, remember how you met Allah at the sacred place at the Plains of Arafat. Pilgrims are to remain until sunset at Arafat and then proceed to Mount Mina to celebrate the Festival of Sacrifice.

2.199 *ask pardon of God* — Muslims are to ask Allah to forgive their past sins. This,

Jihad

Jihad—Holy War, Guerra Santa, Guerre Sacrée, Heiliger Krieg—has entered the vernacular in many nations in the West. It is now so common that this Arabic word and its cognates are often left untranslated. It has typically been associated with terrorism, violence and war. Moderate Muslims, however, disagree, insisting that the word literally means "strenuous striving," specifically a striving in reference to one's personal devotion to Allah. As such, they think of *jihad* in terms of a quiet and peaceful activity, something akin to Yoga. Both definitions have found a home within the Islamic world and both have long traditions.

The Qur'an. To acquire an accurate understanding of what the concept of *jihad*, we should begin with an examination in how the word was used in classic Muslim literature—specifically, the Qur'an. The Qur'an is the most dominant document within Islam since it is its sacred scripture, believed to be divinely inspired and without error.

In the latter surahs of the Qur'an, the word *jihad* emerged and its definition given. With an even uniformity, its message was this:

- Allah is sovereign over all creation.

- Infidels have offended him for having rejected His sovereign rule.

- If infidels refuse to repent and humbly bow before Allah, his Prophet, and the Qur'an, they will endure His wrath—in this life as well as the life to come.

- All Muslims are called upon to participate with Allah in bringing judgment to unrepentant infidels.

- All Muslims who refuse to participate in bringing judgment upon infidels are also worthy of the wrath of Allah. This is because their unwillingness to participate is a sign that they are not living in true submission to Allah.

- This overall scheme has been in force since the earliest of Allah's apostles sent to the earth and will stay in force until the final Resurrection of the Dead.

In addition, the Qur'an makes the case that all legitimate warfare be defensive in nature. Accordingly, jihadists must never be the aggressors against the infidel; aggression must first come from the infidel (Q 2.190-191). Aggression against Islam is defined by the following:

- Offending Allah by steadfastly refusing to listen and heed the message of repentance by his chosen prophets.

- Occupying and governing land previously occupied and governed by Muslim rulers.[1]

In short, by standing in the way of the islamification of the world, the infidel was deemed the aggressor.

Jihad in the early seventh century. Following Muhammad's migration to Yathrib (Medina), he initiated a military Jihad. In a Hadith, Muhammad said: "I love to fight in the way of Allah and be killed, to fight and again be killed, and to fight again and be killed."[2] Jihad took place on two fronts. The first front was waged against the infidels in Mecca who had had ample opportunity to accept his message and ministry. The second front was waged against the infidels in Yathrib itself. Muhammad's second front was slower in developing since he wished to give the citizens of Yathrib ample opportunity to accept his message. After a few years, however, his patience wore thin and he concluded that the Jews of Yathrib were wholly unrepentant. He therefore initiated a jihad against them.

Jihad through the centuries. Muhammad's writings, sayings and biography has become a seminal inspiration for jihadism in both the past and the present. After his death, jihadism drove the Muslim warriors across the Arabian Peninsula, vanquishing Muslim apostates and the remaining pagan infidels. Jihad then moved north into modern-day Iraq, Iran, and Palestine and east into modern-day India where it swept across that Asian subcontinent. Moving west, jihad swept across the Sahara Desert and then north into the Iberian peninsula. Jihad went west again across modern-day Turkey, the Balkans and up as far as Vienna, Austria, where the tide finally turned and the Islamic quest for world conquest stalled.

Ibn Khaldun, a fourteenth century Islamic scholar, explained the ideology of jihadism:

> In the Muslim community, the holy war is a religious duty, because of the universalism of the [Muslim] mission and [the obligation to] convert everybody to Islam either by persuasion or by force...The other religious groups did not have a universal mission, and the holy war was not a religious duty for them, save only for purposes of defense...Islam is under obligation to gain power over other nations.[3]

Ibn Hudayl, another a fourteenth century scholar, offered a defense for the jihadic conquest of the Iberian Peninsula and other parts of Europe:

> It is permissible to set fire to the lands of the enemy, his stores of grain, his beasts of burden—if it is not possible for the Muslims to take possession of them—as well as to cut down his trees, to raze his cities, in a word, to do everything that might ruin and discourage him...[being] suited to hastening the Islamization of that enemy or to weakening him. Indeed, all this contributes to a military triumph over him or to forcing him to capitulate.[4]

Muhammad Taqi Usmani, a respected Muslim scholar who sat for twenty years as a Shari'a judge in Pakistan's Supreme Court, asserted that jihads were waged "because it was truly commendable for establishing the grandeur of the religion of Allah."[5] This notion of the grandeur of the religion of Allah pointed to the Doctrine of the Two Houses. According to an early Islamic scholar, Ibn Taymiyyah, the world was divided into two houses: the *Dar al-Islam* (the House of Peace) and the *Dar al-harb* (the House of War). The *Dar al-Islam* constituted that region of the world where Muslim rule and law prevailed. The *Dar al-harb* constituted the rest of the world. Thomas Asbridge writes: "The express purpose of the *jihad* was to wage a relentless holy war in the *Dar al-harb*, until such time as all mankind had accepted Islam, or submitted to Muslim rule. No permanent peace treaties with non-Muslim enemies were permissible, and any temporary truces could last no more than ten years."[6] The logic behind this teaching was that Allah was sovereign over all creation. Faithfulness to Allah, then, required Muslims to actively participate in the conversion of the *Dar al-harb* into the *Dar al-Islam*.

Yusuf al-Qaradawi, a widely regarded Muslim cleric and scholar, defined jihadism as the following:

> It has been determined by Islamic law that the blood and property of people

of Dar Al-Harb [the House of the Infidel] are not protected...In modern war, all of society, with all its classes and ethnic groups, is mobilized to participate in the war, to aid its continuation, and to provide it with the material and human fuel required for it to assure the victory of the state fighting its enemies. Every citizen in society must take upon himself a role in the effort to provide for the battle. The entire domestic front, including professional, laborers, and industrialists, stands behind the fighting army, even if it does not bear arms.[7]

In short, the Qur'an, canonical Hadiths, and respected Islamic scholars present Islam as a religion that is committed to the islamification of the entire world. Seen in this context, the Muslim wars of the first several centuries were not understood as a form of imperialistic aggrandizement as they were a form of spiritual liberation. Muslim warriors were, in so many words, freedom-fighters. Moreover, they understood themselves as warriors who fought defensively. In his book, *Future Jihad,* Walid Phares explains,

For centuries, the jihad machine presented and consolidated the arguments for *fatah* as "defensive." Under this logic, launching a military offensive across the Strait of Gibraltar into another continent was a move to protect the Maghreb [north Africa] from the infidels—just as invading the Maghreb had been to defend Egypt. Invading Egypt had been necessary to shield Syria, and to start with, conquering the whole Fertile Crescent was to deter Byzantinium from marching into Arabia. When the soldiers of the caliphate were chasing after Hindu villagers thousands of miles to the east of the peninsula and raiding cities in the middle of France thousands of miles to the west, the argument never wavered. It was always because of an aggressor to be retaliated against.[8]

The Greater Jihad. In the mid-ninth century, a new form of jihad emerged in the Muslim world: the greater jihad. It contrasted the previous definition, the lesser jihad, which was associated with Holy War. With this new definition, the enemy of Islam was defined as all that was inside one's soul that stood opposed to Allah. Accordingly, it was a rigorous moral self-examination, a jihad that was waged against one's own self. The great Islamic theologian al-Ghazali (d. 1111) championed this dual understanding of Jihad. Two forms of jihad existed, he said, "the greater jihad" and "the lesser jihad." Both had a role and the truly dedicated Muslim was required to be a jihadist in both senses. Still, he added, "the greater jihad" was more meritorious. 'Abdul-Qadir Gilani (d. 1166) explained:

[There are] two types of jihads: the outer and the inner. The inner is the jihad of the soul, the passion, the nature, and Satan. It involves repentance from rebelliousness and errors, being steadfast about it, and abandoning the forbidden passions. The outer is the jihad of the infidels who resist Him and His Messenger [Muhammad] and to be pitiless with their swords, their spears, and their arrows—killing and being killed. The inner jihad is more difficult than the outer jihad because it involves cutting the forbidden customs of the soul, and exiling them, so as to have as one's example the Divine commands and to cease from what it forbids. Whoever takes God's commands as his example with regard to two types of jihad will gain a reward in this world and the next. Bodily wounds on the martyr are just like someone cutting their hand—there is no real pain in it—and death with regard to the soul of the *mujahid* who repents from his sins is like a thirsty man drinking cold water.[9]

With this dual definition of jihad, a new form of Islam emerged: Sufism. Sufi warriors quickly gained a reputation as being the elite fighting forces in the Muslim armies of the ninth through twelfth centuries. Similar to the samurai warriors of medieval Japan, they were disciplined in the inner world of their own minds as well as skilled warriors who effectively waged war against the infidel.[10] This paradigm persisted until the early thirteenth century when Sufism abandoned its warlike tendencies and transformed itself into a version of monkish mysticism, not unlike Buddhism and other mystical traditions.[11] Its Islamic distinctives, however, remained inasmuch as it persisted in the "repetition, contemplation, and internalization of the divine word of the Qur'an, and the imitation of Muhammad as exemplar and Perfect Man."[12]

Moderate Islam. At the outset of the twentieth century, most of the Muslim world was ruled by Europeans—either by European nations who directly imposed their laws on Muslim societies, or through proxies, carpetbaggers, or local elites who did the bidding of European leaders. The net result was an influx of western values into the Muslim world. And the effect of these values was intensified via radio, television, the worldwide web, and travel to western nations.

The Muslim world responded to this influx of western values in two ways. Resistance movements emerged that returned to the writings of the classic Islamic literature (the Qur'an and the canonical Hadiths) and became radicalized. Many other Muslims, however, rediscovered the literature of "the greater jihad" (spiritual warfare, moral renewal, introspection, meditation) of the ninth through eleventh centuries and defined jihad in these categories. Yet, rather than understand jihad as having two faces (the greater and the lesser), these Muslims were committed to only "the greater jihad." It is here, with these Muslims, that Moderate Islam was born.

Moderate Muslims claim that at its essence jihad has nothing to do with warfare. The word literally means *intense struggle.* They admit that in the Qur'an the word is often associated with military activities, yet this is due to the lawlessness that typified the Middle East in the seventh century. Muhammad is understood as a man shaped by the times in which he lived, an era where meaningful peace treaties were non-existent and warfare and bloodshed ubiquitous. Placed in that context, the violence that he promoted was to be considered a special case—not part of the essence of the qur'anic message and certainly not to be replicated in our current age. Accordingly, jihad is best understood as something akin to the meditative state of yoga practiced by devotees of Eastern religions and the strivings after godliness that characterize most all religions. Abou El Fadl explains:

> Jihad is a core principle in Islamic theology; it means to strive, to apply oneself, to struggle, and persevere. In many ways, jihad connotes a strong spiritual and material work ethic in Islam. Piety, knowledge, health, beauty, truth, and justice are not possible without jihad—without sustained and diligent hard work. Therefore, cleansing oneself from vanity and pettiness, pursuing knowledge, curing the ill, feeding the poor, and standing up for truth and justice even at great personal risk are all forms of jihad.[13]

Summary. In the Islamic world, the Doctrine of Jihad possesses a range of understandings. Broadly speaking, it is defined by the following: (a) Holy War directed against infidels and apostate Muslims, (b) a combination of Holy War and inner discipline where one wages war against one's own inclinations to sinfulness, and (c) inner discipline. In Islamic history, all three are represented. In the Qur'an and other early Islamic documents, the term *jihad* was always associated with the notion of Holy War. Several centuries later, the doctrine was split into "greater" and "lesser"—where the "greater jihad" addressed the inner discipline of the soul and the "lesser jihad" addressed Holy War. In this period, the faithful Muslim was called upon to engage in both the "greater" and the "lesser" since both were understood to be essential and therefore indivisible from one another. In more recent centuries, and typically in those

regions of the Islamic world influenced by Western values, jihad has
evolved into a definition limited to the "greater jihad."

[1] See Q 10.13; 22.39-40; 26.192-212; and 43.6-8.
[2] *Sahih Muslim* 20.28.4626.
[3] Ibn Khaldun, *The Muqudimmah: An Introduction to History,* p. 473.
[4] Ibn Hudayl, *L'Ornement des Ames,* p. 195.
[5] *London Times,* Sept. 8, 2007.
[6] Thomas Asbridge, *The Crusades,* p. 25.
[7] Quoted in the London based Arabic language daily newspaper: *Asharq al-Awast* (July 19, 2003).
[8] Walid Phares, *Future Jihad,* p. 36.
[9] Abdul-Qadir Gilani, *The Sublime Revelation,* p. 83.
[10] See David Cook, *Understanding Jihad,* pp. 44-48, and Hans Küng, *Islam: Past, Present & Future,* p. 325.
[11] See Daisaku Ikeda, Majid Tehranian, *Global Civilization: A Buddhistic-Islamic Dialogue,* p. 28; Philip K. Hitti, *The Origins of the Druze People and Religion,* p. 51.
[12] Carl W. Ernst, *Words of Ecstasy in Sufism,* p. 2.
[13] Abou El Fadl, "Peaceful Jihad," in *Taking Back Islam,* p. 37.

Many contemporary Muslim writers, recognizing the negative connotations that *jihad* has acquired in European languages, maintain that the word means nothing more than "striving." Yet this position, predominant among Muslims apologists writing in non-Muslim (primarily Western) languages, is disingenuous. To gain a sense of the word's true meaning, one must begin by looking at its usage in classical Muslim literature, primarily in Arabic, but also in other Muslim languages, as well as its function in Muslim history and historiography.

—David Cook, *Understanding Jihad,* p. 1

It is only among the jurists that the word *jihad* lost its original wider significance and began to be used in the narrower sense of *qital* (fighting)…Together with this narrowing of the significance of *jihad,* the further idea was developed that the Muslims were to carry on a war against unbelieving nations and countries, whether they were attacked or not, an idea quite foreign to the Qur'an.

—Maulana Muhammad Ali, *The Religion of Islam,* p. 409

Muhammad himself waged a series of proto-jihad campaigns to subdue the Jews, Christians, and pagans of Arabia. As numerous modern-day pronouncements by leading Muslim theologians confirm…Muhammad has been the major inspiration for jihadism, past and present Jihad was pursued century after century because jihad embodied an ideology and a jurisdiction. Both were formally conceived by Muslim juriconsults and theologians from the eighth to ninth centuries onward, based on their interpretation of Koranic verses and long chapters in the "hadith," or acts and sayings of the Muslim prophet Muhammad, especially those recorded by al-Bukhari (d. 869) and Muslim (d. 874).

—Andrew G. Bostom, *The Legacy of Jihad*, p. iii

Time and again throughout Islamic history, pious men would follow the stages of the Prophet's life, withdrawing first from the world to develop their spirituality, then making the *hijra* with a devoted band of disciples to a distant place before launching the *jihad* that would reclaim the backsliding pagans for the true Islam.

—Malise Ruthven, *Islam in the World*, p. 77

Islam means "submission" to God. Jihad means "struggle" or "striving." It can be taken metaphorically or even mystically, but in raw physical terms it means a state of holy war, involving killing, and preparedness to die as a martyr, which is described as a painless trip to heaven to see the face of al-Llah, partly in the belief that Jesus did not die a painful death on the cross, but was "taken up" by God. Islam is unique for combining martyrdom with intentional violence. The fundamental tenet of Islamic faith *Shadadah*—"there is no God (reality) but al-Llah and Muhammad is his prophet" also means sacrifice, or martyrdom. In Muslim apocalyptic vision, the world is divided between Domain of Islam and the Domain of War—*Dar al-Harb*—invoking a utopian agenda of violent world conquest. Jihad in the Qur'an is striving, the "strivers" are mightily rewarded, death is mentioned in the same breath, and those dying in the cause of al-Llah have a special reward in paradise.

—Christine Fielder and Chris King, *Sexual Paradox*, p. 264

Jihadism is a movement based on a specific version of Islam, but it is only one way of looking at Allah's religion and certainly not the only one. There are many others that are much closer to political pluralism and tolerance, promoted by Islamic Reformists, who are in a minority position institutionally and culturally. The crisis of the Muslim world—the domination of Muslim religious institutions by fundamentalist religious authorities and heedless, erratic American policies in the Muslim world—have given Jihadism credibility in Muslims' eyes.

—Farhad Khosrokhavar, *Inside Jihadism*, p. 2

Radical Islamism, to which it has become customary to give the name Islamic fundamentalism, is not a single homogenous movement. There are many types of Islamic fundamentalism in different countries and even sometimes within a single country. Some are state-sponsored—promulgated, used, and promoted by one or other Muslim government for its own purposes; some are genuine popular movements from below.

—Bernard Lewis, *The Crisis of Islam*, p. 23

200 And when ye have performed your rites, remember God as ye remember your fathers, or with a keener memory still. There is among men such as says, "Our Lord! give us in this world;" but of the future life no portion shall he have.

201 And some there be who say, "Our Lord! give us in this world good and in the future good; and keep us from the torment of the fire!"

202 These,—they have their portion from what they have earned; for God is swift at reckoning up.

203 Remember God for a certain number of days; but whoso hastens off in two days, it is no sin to him, and he who lingers on it is no sin to him,—for him who fears. So

fear ye God and know that unto Him shall ye be gathered.

*The man of
the crooked path*

204 There is among men one whose speech about the life of this world pleases thee, and he calls on God to witness what is in his heart; yet is he most fierce in opposition unto thee.

205 And when he turns away, he strives upon the earth to do evil therein, and to destroy the tilth and the stock; verily, God loves not evil doing.

206 And when it is said to him, "Fear God," then pride takes hold upon

however, does not suggest a salvation by faith apart from works (see **Divine Forgiveness in Islam** on pp. 158-161).

2.200 *or with a keener memory still* — This passage suggests that the religious rites at the Plains of Arafat and Mina were performed by Arabs in pre-Islamic days, yet with less insight. They prayed that the Lord would give them this world, yet without a concern of the future life. The Muslim pilgrims, in contrast, have keener memories of the importance of this rite since they take in both a desire for this world and a future life in Paradise.

2.201 *keep us from the torment of the fire* — That is, keep us from the impending tortures of Hell.

2.203 *remember God for a certain number of days* — Following the Festival of Sacrifice (the tenth day) which concludes the Hajj, pilgrims are obliged to spend at least two

days in the valley between the Plains of Arafat and Mount Mina reflecting on Allah.

2.204-207 It has been supposed that Muhammad was speaking of two specific individuals that he personally knew, yet most Islamic scholars believe that this passage has a general meaning: it is a description of two people, one who follows the crooked path, the path that leads to the eternal torments of Hell, and the other who follows the straight path that leads to eternal bliss in Paradise.

2.204 The man of this verse possesses an eloquent tongue, speaking of this world and about life in general with pleasant words— and even calls upon Allah as a witness to what he says. He is also quite skillful in argumentation and debates.

2.205 This man is full of corruption. With conscious intention, he destroys the farms and livestock of other people.

him in sin; but hell is enough for him! surely an evil couch is that.

The man of
the straight path

207   And there is among men one who selleth his soul, craving those things that are pleasing unto God; and God is kind unto His servants.

The footsteps of Satan

208   O ye who believe! enter ye into the peace, one and all, and follow not the footsteps of Satan; verily, to you he is an open foe.

209   And if ye slip after that the manifest signs have come to you, then know that God is the mighty, the wise.

210   What can they expect but that God should come unto them in the shadow of a cloud, and the angels too? But the thing is decreed, and unto God do things return.

211   Ask the children of Israel how many a manifest sign we gave to them; and whoso alters God's favours after that they have come to him, then God is keen at following up.

212   Made fair to those who misbelieve is this world's life; they jest at those who do believe. But those who fear shall be above them on the resurrection day. God gives provision unto whom He will without account.

The sin of mankind

213   Men were one nation once, and God sent prophets with good tid-

---

2.207 *selleth his soul* — In contrast to the man described in vv. 204-206, the man who is so willing to please Allah that he would gladly sell his soul is the one blessed by Allah.

2.208 *O ye who believe* — Muhammad was addressing fellow Muslims (also see vv. 104, 178, 183, 254, 264, 267, 278, 282).

2.208-210 Muhammad beckons his audience to enter into the peace of Allah and not follow the footsteps of Satan. Those who slip after receiving divine revelation and enter into the path of Satan. They may anticipate Allah approaching them in the shadow of a cloud along with his angels (v. 210) with the intent of accepting their repentance. Still, they will discover that late repentance is not accepted with Allah.

2.210 *the thing is decreed* — That is, the Last Judgment is a firmly established event. Everyone will return to Allah and face Him at this judgment.

2.211 *the children of Israel* — According to this passage, the Israelite people are an example of those who received divine revelation, turned away, and followed in the footsteps of Satan. At the Last Judgment, they will discover it to be a grievous time.

2.213a *men were one nation once* — Initially, all mankind were one single community of people.

2.213b *God sent prophets with good tidings* — Once again, Muhammad noted the ministry of the apostles. They were sent to warn peoples of the consequences of the crooked path and the need for repentance (see **The Apostles** on pp. 396-398).

ings and with warnings, and sent down with them the Book in truth, to judge between men in that wherein they disagreed; but none did disagree therein save those who had been given it after that manifest signs had come to them, through greed amongst themselves; and God guided those who did believe to that truth concerning which they disagreed by His permission, for God guides whom He will unto the right path.

214   Did ye count to enter Paradise, while there had nothing come to you like those who passed away before you; there touched them violence and harm, and they were made to quake, until the Apostle and those who believed with him said, "When (comes) God's help? Is not God's help then surely

nigh?"

Law of almsgiving

215   They will ask thee what they are to expend in alms: say, "Whatsoever good ye expend it should be for parents and kinsmen, and the orphan and the poor, and the son of the road; and whatsoever good ye do, verily, of it God knows."

Law of Jihad (cont'd)

216   Prescribed for you is fighting, but it is hateful to you. Yet peradventure that ye hate a thing while it is good for you, and peradventure that ye love a thing while it is bad for you; God knows, and ye,—ye do not know!

217   They will ask thee of the sacred

2.213c *the Book in truth* — That is, the eternal book in heaven (see **The Perspicuous Book** on pp. 178-179).

2.213d *God guided those who did believe* — That is, Allah chooses those destined to believe (see **The Doctrine of al-Qadar** on pp. 264-266).

2.214 An intellectualized faith is not sufficient to enter into Paradise. A life of piety is also required, characterized by a willingness to suffer on behalf of Allah.

2.215 The recipients of alms include the following: (a) parents, (b) one's kinsmen, (c) orphans, (d) the poor, (e) and the traveler.

2.216 *Prescribed for you is fighting, but it is hateful to you* — The activity of Jihad is understandably an odious (unpleasant) thing,

yet is also necessary to those committed to faithfulness. Muslims were therefore required to overcome their emotional reservations about killing the infidel. Only then would they be truly obedient to the will of Allah.

2.217a Participating in Jihad during the sacred month (the month of Ramadan) was a great sin, yet turning people away from the way of God that leads to Paradise was a greater sin still. This jihad necessarily refers to warfare (and not the internal struggle of the soul, as moderate Muslims assert), since a jihad of the inner soul could not logically be prohibited during the sacred month.

2.217b *They will not cease fighting you* — That is, the aggressor is the one who motivates Muslims to turn away from their own religion (become apostates). It is because

month,—of fighting therein. Say, "Fighting therein is a great sin; but turning folks off God's way, and misbelief in Him and in the Sacred Mosque, and turning His people out therefrom, is a greater in God's sight; and sedition is a greater sin than slaughter." They will not cease from fighting you until they turn you from your religion if they can; but whosoever of you is turned from his religion and dies while still a misbeliever; these are those whose works are vain in this world and the next; they are the fellows of the Fire, and they shall dwell therein for aye.

218 Verily, those who believe, and those who flee, and those who wage war in God's way; these may hope for God's mercy, for God is forgiving and merciful.

Law of wine

219 They will ask thee about wine and *el mâisar*, say, "In them both is sin and profit to men; but the sin of both is greater than the profit of the same." They will ask thee what they shall expend in alms: say, "The surplus." Thus does God manifest to you His signs; haply ye may reflect

220 on this world and the next!

*Business transactions
with orphans*

They will ask thee about orphans: say, "To do good to them is best." But if ye interfere with them—they are your brethren, and God knows the evildoer from the well doer; and if God will He will surely trouble you. Verily, God is mighty, wise.

Law of marriage

221 Wed not with idolatrous women until they believe, for surely a be-

---

of this that Jihad is always defined in the Qur'an as a form of self-defense.

2.218 *those who flee* — That is, those who fled their homelands (Mecca) and migrated to Yathrib (Medinah) are blessed of Allah. After the conquest of Mecca by Muhammad in A.D. 630, this requirement was no longer applicable.

2.219a *wine* — In this passage, the drinking of wine is described as sin. It stands opposed to a previous surah in the Qur'an where the drinking of wine was described as "a goodly provision" (see Q 16.67, note). This, then, is an example of the Doctrine of

Abrogation. Earlier statements regarding wine in the Qur'an are abrogated (erased) and replaced with new ones (see Q 87.6-7, note, **The Doctrine of Abrogation** on pp. 68-70).

2.219b *el maisar* — These are games of chance intended for gambling. Such games, said Muhammad, are sinful.

2.220 *if ye interfere with them* — That is, if you involve yourselves in the lives of orphans. The point here is that a person is permitted to benefit through a business partnership with an orphan and gain monetarily from that partnership, provided that the interests of

lieving handmaid is better than an idolatrous woman, even though she please you. And wed not to idolatrous men until they believe, for a believing slave is better than an idolater, even though he please you. Those invite you to the fire, but God invites you to paradise and pardon by His permission, and makes clear His signs to men; haply they may remember.

Law of menstruation

222   They will ask thee about menstruation: say, "It is a hurt." So keep apart from women in their men-struation, and go not near them till they be cleansed; but when they are cleansed come in to them by where God has ordered you; verily, God loves those who turn to Him, and those who keep themselves clean.

Law of sex

223   Your women are your tilth, so come into your tillage how you choose; but do a previous good act for yourselves, and fear God, and know that ye are going to meet Him; and give good tidings unto those who do believe.

the orphan are not compromised or damaged. In this regard, "God knows the evil-doer from the well doer."

2.221a *idolatrous women* — Women who worship any god other than Allah. Muslims were instructed to not marry them. A handmaid (a slave-girl) who happens to be a Muslim believer is a better choice for marriage than an idolatrous woman (see Q 5.5).

2.221b This requirement applies equally to women interested in marrying an idolatrous man. The reason for this is that an unbelieving mate can easily influence a Muslim believer to apostasize from the Islamic faith and thereby invite them to the fire (Hell).

2.221c *paradise and pardon* — See **Divine Forgiveness in Islam** on pp. 158-161).

2.222a Sexual relationships are prohibited with women who are in the midst of their monthly menstruation cycle. The Old Testament makes a similar prohibition (see Lev 12:2; 15:19-30; 20:18; Ezek 18:5-6).

2.222b *God has ordered you* — The Qur'an looks upon sexual relationships as moral and upright, provided that they are limited to one's wives and slaves (see Q 70.29-30, note). The Bible comments that sexual relationships with one's spouse are honorable (see Gen 2:24; Prov 5:15-23; 1 Cor 7:3-4; 1 Tim 5:14; Heb 13:4).

2.223a *your women are your tilth* — That is, your women are your fertile ground. This is a figure of speech comparing the sexual relations with a woman with the sowing of seeds in a garden.

2.223b *so come into your tillage how you choose* — That is, engage in sexual relationships when or how you wish. This passage has been widely interpreted in the Muslim world to mean that a woman is to acquiesce to sex with her husband whenever he should make such requests. In one Hadith, Muhammad said, "If a husband calls his wife to his bed (i.e., to have sexual relation) and she refuses and causes him to sleep in anger, the angels will curse her till morning" (*Sahih*

Law of oaths

224 Make not God the butt of your oaths, that ye will keep clear and fear and make peace amongst men, for God both hears and knows.

225 He will not catch you up for a casual word in your oaths, but He will catch you up for what your hearts have earned; but God is forgiving and clement.

Law of divorce

226 Those who swear off from their women, they must wait four months; but if they break their vow God is forgiving and merciful.

227 And if they intend to divorce them, verily, God hears and knows.

228 Divorced women must wait for themselves three courses; and it is not lawful to them that they hide what God has created in their wombs, if they believe in God and in the last day. Their husbands will do better to take them back in that (case) if they wish for reconciliation; for, the same is due to them as from them; but the men should have precedence over them. God is mighty and wise.

Bakhari 4.54.460). In a second Hadith, Muhammad said, "When a man calls his wife to his bed, and she does not respond, the One Who is in the heaven is displeased with her until he (her husband) is pleased with her (*Sahih Muslim* 8.20.3367). Esteemed eleventh century Islamic scholar al-Ghazali added, "If the husband wants to enjoy her body, she should not refuse" (*Revival of Religious Learnings*, vol. 2, Section 3).

Not all within the Muslim world agree with this teaching. Irshad Manji, a Muslim feminist and heterodox in many of her beliefs, rejoins: "'Women are your fields,' it says...Are women partners or property?...What about the words 'when you please'? Doesn't that qualifier give men undue power? The question remains: Which paradigm does Allah advocate—Adam and Eve equals, or women as land to be plowed (excuse me, stroked) on a whim?" (*The Trouble with Islam Today*, p. 35).

2.224 *Make not God the butt of your oaths* — That is, do not allow your oaths to hold you to wrongful or foolish behavior. Accordingly, Allah would "not catch you up for a casual word in your oaths." A Hadith interprets this to mean that "he who took an oath, but he found something else better than that, should do that which is better and break his oath" (*Sahih Muslim* 15.4057; also see 15.3.4058).

2.226 *if they break their vow* — Divorce is a good example of what Muhammad meant in vv. 224-225).

2.228a *three courses* — That is, three menstrual cycles. A divorced woman must wait three menstrual cycles before remarrying some other man. The purpose of this is to determine if she is pregnant with the child of her former husband.

2.228b *the men should have precedence over them* — If it is determined that a woman is pregnant at the time of divorce, the baby in the womb is the property of the husband and must be surrendered to him following the birth (see Q 65.4).

2.229-230 A divorce may be pronounced

229   Divorce (may happen) twice; then keep them in reason, or let them go with kindness. It is not lawful for you to take from them anything of what you have given them, unless both fear that they cannot keep within God's bounds. So if ye fear that ye cannot keep within God's bounds there is no crime in you both about what she ransoms herself with. These are God's bounds, do not transgress them; and whoso transgresses God's bounds, they it is who are unjust.

230   But if he divorce her (a third time) she shall not be lawful to him after that, until she marry another husband; but, if he divorce her too, it is no crime in them both to come together again, if they think that they can keep within God's bounds. These are God's bounds which He explains to a people who know.

231   When ye divorce women, and they have reached the prescribed time,

then keep them kindly, or let them go in reason, but do not keep them by force to transgress for whoso does that, he is unjust to his own soul: and do not take God's signs in jest; and remember God's favours to you, and what He has sent down to you of the Book and wisdom, to admonish you thereby; and fear God, and know that God doth all things know.

232   When ye divorce women, and they have reached their prescribed term, do not prevent them from marrying their (fresh) husbands, when they have agreed with each other reasonably. That is what he is admonished with who amongst you believes in God and in the last day. That is more pure for you and cleaner. But God knows, and ye know not.

233   [Divorced] Mothers must suckle their children two whole years for one who wishes to complete the time of suckling; and on him to

twice by a husband and then revoked. But once pronounced a third time (an oral announcement), the divorce is final. He may not remarry her until she has been married to some other man and has had sexual relations with him. Then, following that divorce, she may be remarried to her former husband.
2.231a *when they have reached the prescribed time* — That is, when they have reached the end of their waiting time: three menstrual cycles (see v. 228a, note, Q 65.1-4).
2.231b *let them go in reason* — Husbands

are to make allowances for a kindly departure.
2.232a *When...they have reached their prescribed term* — See Q 228a, note.
2.232b *do not prevent them from marry their (fresh) husbands* — The former husbands are not to impede the remarriage of their former wives to some other man.
2.233 Divorced mothers are to nurse their babies who are now in the custody of the husbands. The former husbands are to not burden the former wives in performing this maternal function (see Q 65.6).

whom it is born its sustenance and clothing are incumbent; but in reason, for no soul shall be obliged beyond its capacity. A mother shall not be forced for her child; nor he to whom it is born for his child. And the same (is incumbent) on the heir (of the father). But if both parties wish to wean, by mutual consent and counsel. then it is no crime in them. And if ye wish to provide a wet-nurse for your children, it is no crime in you when you pay what you have promised her in reason. Fear God, and know that God on what ye do doth look.

*Laws pertaining
to widowhood*

234 Those of you who die and leave wives behind, let these wait by themselves for four months and ten days; and when they have reached their prescribed time, there is no crime in them for what they do with themselves in reason; for God of what ye do is well aware.

235 Nor is there any crime in you for that ye make them an offer of marriage, or that ye keep it secret, in your minds. God knows that ye will remember them; but do not propose to them in secret, unless ye speak a reasonable speech; and resolve not on the marriage tie until the Book shall reach its time; but know that God knows what is in your souls; so beware! and know that God is forgiving and clement.

*Laws pertaining to
divorce settlements*

236 It is no crime in you if ye divorce your women ere you have yet touched them, or settled for them a settlement. But provide maintenance for them; the wealthy according to his power, and the straitened in circumstances according to his power, must provide, in reason;—a duty this upon the kind.

237 And if ye divorce them before ye have touched them, but have already settled for them a settlement; the half of what ye have settled, unless they remit it, or he in whose hand is the marriage tie remits it; and that ye should remit is nearer to piety, and forget not liberality between you. Verily, God on what ye do doth look.

2.234-235 Widows are to wait four months and ten days prior to any possible remarriage. Following this time, they may remarry.

2.236 *a settlement* — Prior to marriage, a settlement (Arabic: *faridah*)—also known as a prenuptial agreement—is to be established between the bridegroom and bride. This is to occur as a protection in the case that the marriage should end in divorce.

2.237 If the marriage should be terminated prior to having had sexual relations, the wife is to receive half of the settlement (Arabic: *faridah*).

2.238 The posture for prayer during "the

The posture of prayer

238   Observe the prayers, and the middle prayer, and stand ye attent before God.

239   And if ye fear, then afoot or on
horseback; but when ye are in
safety remember God, how He
taught you while yet ye did not
know.

*Settlements for widows
and divorced women*

240   Those of you who die and leave
wives, should bequeath to their
wives maintenance for a year,
without expulsion (from their
home); but if they go out, there is
no crime in you for what they do
of themselves, in reason; but God

is mighty and wise.

241   And divorced women should have
a maintenance in reason,—a duty
this on those that fear.

242   Thus does God explain to you His
signs; haply ye may understand.

*Admonition to
participate in Jihad*

243   Dost thou not look at those who
left their homes by thousands, for
fear of death; and God said to them
"Die," and then He quickened them
again? Verily, God is Lord of grace
to men, but most men give no
thanks.

244   Fight then in God's way, and know
that God both hears and knows.

245   Who is there that will lend to God
a good loan? He will redouble it

middle prayer" (mid-afternoon prayer) is that
of standing. Some Islamic scholars believe
that the Arabic term is best translated "the
noblest prayer"—meaning that prayer is its
most noble when one stands at attention
before God (see Q 73.20, note, and **al-Salat**
on pp. 169-170).

2.240 *maintenance* — That is, a financial
settlement that provides for their welfare
for a year. In addition to the settlements,
widows were to be permitted to live in the
home of the deceased spouse for one year.
This law of living in the house for a year was
only enacted, provided that the deceased
husband did not bequeath the home to the
widow outright (see Q 4.12).

2.241-242 Divorced women were also to
receive a financial maintenance (see Q 2.236,
note).

2.243a Muslims were called upon to engage in Jihad and be prepared to die in the
struggle.

2.243b *He quickened them* — A phrase
used metaphorically to mean that God
helped these men to overcome their fear of
death.

2.244 *Fight then in God's way* — The way
of Allah is to punish the infidel for his determined resistance to the ministry and message of the divinely appointed apostles (see
The Apostles on pp. 396-398). In Muhammad's case, this meant that Muslims were
admonished to fight those who have steadfastly rejected Muhammad's call to repentance (see Q 2.190-195 and **Jihad** on pp.
616-622).

2.245 *lend to God a good loan* — Those
who participated in Jihad were likened to

many a double; God closes His hand and holds it out, and unto Him shall ye return.

The valor of David

246 Dost thou not look at the crowd of the children of Israel after Moses' time, when they said to a prophet of theirs, "Raise up for us a king, and we will fight in God's way?" He said, "Will ye perhaps, if it be written down for you to fight, refuse to fight?" They said, "And why should we not fight in God's way, now that we are dispossessed of our homes and sons?" But when it was written down for them to fight they turned back, save a few of them, and God knows who

are evildoers.

247 Then their prophet said to them, "Verily, God has raised up for you Tâlût as a king;" they said, "How can the kingdom be his over us; we have more right to the kingdom than he, for he has not an amplitude of wealth?" He said, "Verily, God has chosen him over you, and has provided him with an extent of knowledge and of form. God gives the kingdom unto whom He will; God comprehends and knows."

248 Then said to them their prophet, "The sign of his kingdom is that there shall come to you the ark with the *shechina* in it from your Lord, and the relics of what the family of Moses and the family of

those who lend to Allah. According to Muhammad, Allah always increases the loan "many a double"—that is, Allah multiplies the loan on behalf of the one making the loan. The implication is that if a person should die in the midst of waging Jihad (become a martyr), he would receive multiplied blessings from Allah in the afterlife.

2.246-251 This story comes from the book of First Samuel (chapters 8-17) which addresses the war between the Philistines and Israel in the days of King Saul. The story culminated with the battle of David and Goliath where David overcame and killed a much stronger enemy (1 Sam 17:41-51). Muhammad's point with this story is to encourage Muslims to have the same level of valor exemplified by David.

2.246a *a prophet of theirs* — That is, the Prophet Samuel.

2.246b Muhammad explained the acquisition of the first king of Israel in a way that matched the theme of Jihad that he was developing in this surah. He claimed that the reason Allah raised up Saul as their king was because of their cowardice. The biblical text makes no such claim. Rather, the reason why they received a king was because they demanded one, so that they could be like the other nations (see 1 Sam 8:4-5).

2.247 *Talut* — That is, King Saul.

2.248 *shechina* — the *shekinah* glory. The word *shekinah* is not found in the Hebrew Old Testament, but is often found throughout the Old Testament Targums (Aramaic paraphrases of the Old Testament). The word, then, is an invention of the post-exilic rabbis who attempted to explain the glory and power that accompanied God's presence

Aaron left; the angels shall bear it." In that is surely a sign to you if ye believe.

249   And when Tâlût set out with his soldiery, he said, "God will try you with a river, and he who drinks therefrom, he is not of mine; but whoso tastes it not, he is of mine, save he who laps it lapping with his hand." And they drank from it save a few of them, and when he crossed it, he and those who believed with him, they said, "We have no power this day against Gâlût and his soldiery," those who thought that they should meet their Lord said, "How many a small division of men have conquered a numerous division, by the permission of God, for God is with the patient."

250   And when they went out against Gâlût and his soldiery, they said, "Lord, pour out patience over us, and make firm our steps, and help us against the misbelieving people!"

251   And they put them to flight by the permission of God, and David killed Gâlût, and God gave him the kingdom and wisdom, and taught him of what He willed. And were it not for God's repelling men one with another the earth would become spoiled, but God is Lord of grace over the worlds.

Muhammad's apostleship

252   These are the signs of God, we recite them to thee in truth, for, verily, thou art of those who are sent.

(also see Q 48.4, 18, 26).

2.249a The episode of the soldiers who lapped with their hands water from a river and soldiers who did not is mentioned in the Book of Judges in connection with the story of Gideon (see Jud 7:4-8). Muhammad confused and blended this story with the story of Saul found in 1 Samuel.

2.249b *Galut* — Goliath.

2.251 *David killed Galut* — The valor of David killing the much more skilled and powerful Goliath served as an example for Muhammad in how he wanted his Muslim fighters to wage war.

In modern parlance, the imagery of David killing Goliath is used among Muslim jihadists as they wage war against larger and more powerful enemies. Reuven Paz writes: "Since this is an asymmetric war symbolized, in the jihadi's mind, as the struggle between David and Goliath, the key words in the terminology of the culture of global Jihad are 'heroism' against 'cowardice'; the search for the Hereafter against the search for peaceful life in this world; and 'self-sacrifice' or martyrdom in the face of powerful and well-organized armies...The Islamists seek only to deliver frequent and increasingly more sophisticated blows in order to best enable the Islamists to undermine the West's morale and sense of security" (*Global Jihad and WMD*).

2.252 Muhammad believed that he was called to be an apostle, a member of the apostolic line of apostles who had come before him.

2.253a *we have preferred one of them above another* — According to Muhammad, not all the divinely chosen apostles were of

The ranking of apostles

253   These apostles have we preferred one of them above another. Of them is one to whom God spake; and we have raised some of them degrees; and we have given Jesus the son of Mary manifest signs, and strengthened him by the Holy Spirit. And, did God please, those who came after them would not have fought after there came to them manifest signs. But they did disagree, and of them are some who believe, and of them some who misbelieve, but, did God please, they would not have fought, for God does what He will.

Admonition to give alms

254   O ye who believe! expend in alms

---

the same rank. Allah preferred some more than others.

Islamic scholars look to Muhammad as the most preferred apostle and therefore the prophet of highest rank. Muhammad Asad comments that Muhammad is unique among all of Allah's chosen apostles inasmuch as he is "the Last Prophet and the bearer of a universal message applicable to all people and to all times" (*The Message of the Qur'an*, p. 68).

Christians understand Muhammad to be a false apostle and a false prophet, since the message that he presented was a false gospel. He rejected a score of cardinal doctrines, all of which are linked to a correct understanding of the gospel (see **The Last Judgment** on pp. 46-50, **The Apostles Creed** on p. 87, the **Definition of Chalcedon** on pp. 785-786, and **The Nicene-Constantinopolitan Creed** on p. 740).

2.253b *we have given Jesus* — Muhammad understood Jesus to be an apostle of high rank. He is characterized as the son of Mary, the recipient of divine revelation (signs), and strengthened by the Holy Spirit. Jesus was, in short, a great human teacher who accurately taught eternal truths. Islamic scholars are in full agreement with this characterization of Jesus. He was a prophet sent from Allah and is to esteemed as such. He presented an understanding of morality to the Jewish people that encouraged almsgiving. He also taught the importance of prayer and was committed to a life of good works.

Though Christians agree with this characterization, they maintain that it falls short. The problem turns on the question of deity. Jesus claimed to be divine and acted as one who is divine. C. S. Lewis wrote: "You must make your choice. Either this man was, and is, the Son of God: or else a madman or something worse. You can shut him up for a fool; you can spit on him and kill him for a demon; or you can fall at his 'feet and call him Lord and God. But let us not come with any patronizing nonsense about him being a great human teacher. He has not left that open to us. He did not intend to" (*Mere Christianity*, p. 41).

2.253c *they did disagree* — The apostles who came after Jesus and other unnamed apostles were said to have disagreements with one another and fell into varying degrees of error. Yet even this, said Muhammad, was part of the sovereign will of Allah who predestined and foreordained these disagreements and errors.

2.254a *O ye who believe* — Muhammad

The Christian
Who Refused to Stay Buried

According to a canonical Hadith, while in Medinah a series of miracles took place that involved Muhammad's scribe. The scribe was previously a Christian who had converted to the Islamic faith. With time, however, he became disenchanted with the Islamic faith and re-converted to the Christian faith. Because of this betrayal, Allah killed him. When his Christian friends attempted to bury him, however, the earth refused to accept his body, spitting it out each time it was buried.

Christians reject the accuracy of this Hadith, asserting that it is fictional and fanciful.

There was a Christian who embraced Islam and read *Surat al-Baqara* [Surah 2] and *Al-Imran* [Surah 3], and he used to write (the revelations) for the Prophet. Later on he returned to Christianity again and he used to say, "Muhammad knows nothing but what I have written for him." Then Allah caused him to die, and the people buried him, but in the morning they saw that the earth had thrown his body out. They said, "This is the act of Muhammad and his companions. They dug the grave of our companion and took his body out of it because he had run away from them." They again dug the grave deeply for him, but in the morning they again saw that the earth had thrown his body out. They said, "This is an act of Muhammad and his companions. They dug the grave of our companion and threw his body outside it, for he had run away from them." They dug the grave for him, as deeply as they could, but in the morning they again saw that the earth had thrown his body out. So they believed that what had befallen him was not done by human beings and had to leave him thrown (on the ground).

— *Sahih Bukhari* 4.56.814

of what we have bestowed upon you, before the day comes in which is no barter, and no friendship, and no intercession; and the misbelievers, they are the unjust.

The greatness of God

255   God , there is no god but He, the living, the self-subsistent. Slumber takes Him not, nor sleep. His is what is in the heavens and what is in the earth. Who is it that intercedes with Him save by His permission? He knows what is be-

fore them and what behind them, and they comprehend not aught of His knowledge but of what He pleases. His throne extends over the heavens and the earth, and it tires Him not to guard them both, for He is high and grand.

The law of religious compulsion

256   There is no compulsion in religion; the right way has been distinguished from the wrong, and whoso disbelieves in Tâghût and believes in God, he has got hold of

---

was addressing fellow Muslims (also see vv. 104, 178, 183, 208, 264, 267, 278, 282).
2.254b According to Muhammad, the giving of alms is an essential part of true faith (see **al-Zakat** on pp. 115-116).
2.255a *there is not god but He* — This is the Doctrine of Tauhid (absolute monotheism) that serves as the cornerstone of the Islamic faith (see Q 112, note).
2.255b *Who is it that intercedes with Him save by His permission?* — Due to the Islamic Doctrine of Tauhid (absolute sovereignty of Allah), intercessory prayer is can only occur "save by His permission" (see **Divine Forgiveness in Islam** on pp. 158-161).
2.256a *There is no compulsion in religion* — Forcible conversions to the Islamic faith were prohibited. Conversions must occur from the heart since it is the heart that Allah sees and will judge and the Last Judgment. Hans Küng notes: "The much-quoted Qur'an verse 'No compulsion in religion' (2.256) still presupposes the pre-eminence of Islam and the rule of Muslims" (*Islam: Past, Present & Future*, p. 413).

For moderate Islam, this verse is oft-cited and serves as part of its core beliefs. S. A. Rahman commented: "This verse is one of the most important verses in the Qur'an, containing a charter of freedom of conscience unparalleled in the religious annals of mankind" (*Punishment of Apostasy in Islam*, p. 16). Abdelwahab Boase added: "It must be emphasized that *jihad* in the military sense does not have as its object the propagation of religion. The fallacy that Islam imposes on the non-Muslim the choice between 'conversion or the sword' is disproved by the Quranic injunction: 'There is no coercion in matters of faith'" ("Arabia" in *The Islamic World Review*, July 1986, p. 79).

Yet, fundamentalist Islam also embraces this verse, seeing within it no fundamental contradiction to its vision of world conquest (the islamification of all nations). Non-Muslims were allowed to worship in their own churches and maintain themselves as non-Muslims, provided that they refrained from idolatry. They did, however, have to pay *jizya* (poll taxes) and submit to Shari'a laws.

the firm handle in which is no breaking off; but God both hears and knows.

257　God is the patron of those who believe, He brings them forth from darkness into light. But those who misbelieve, their patrons are Tâghût, these bring them forth from light to darkness,—fellows of the Fire, they dwell therein for aye.

Parable of a
Resurrected Passerby

258　Do you not look at him who disputed with Abraham about his Lord, that God had given him the kingdom? When Abraham said, "My Lord is He who giveth life and death," he said, "I give life and death." Abraham said, "But verily, God brings the sun from the east, do thou then bring it from the west?" And he who misbelieved was dumb-founded, for God does not guide unjust folk.

259　"Or like him who passed by a village, when it was desolate and

Muhammad Siddiq Hasan Khan wrote: "One should not say of a person convened to Islam under the shadow of the sword, that he was compelled to the Faith for 'there is no compulsion in religion.' Another construction...confines the verse to the People of the Scriptures who submitted to the Muslims and agreed to pay *jizya* (poll-tax) but excludes the idolaters from its scope. In the case of the latter, only two alternatives are said to be open—Islam or the sword—on the authority of al Shabi, al Hasan, Qatadah and al-Dahhaq" (cited in Rahman, "Arabia" in *The Islamic World Review*, July 1986, p. 19).

Another Islamic jurist, Ibn Abi Zayd al-Qushayri (tenth century), wrote: "Jihad is a precept of Divine institution. Its performance by certain individuals may dispense others from it. We Malikis [one of four schools of Muslim jurisprudence] maintain that it is preferable not to begin hostilities with the enemy before having invited the latter to embrace the religion of Allah except where the enemy attacks first. They have the alterative of either converting to Islam or paying the poll tax (jizya), short of which war will be declared against them"

(*The Epistle on Sufism*, p. 165).

The interpretations of this verse within Islam, then, have a wide variance. They constitute a bone of contention within Islam itself; specifically, between the moderates and the fundamentalists (see Q 3.84, note, Q 3.85, note, and Q 109, note).

2.256b *the right way* — The way that leads to eternal life (see Q 72.2, note).

2.256c-257 *Taghut* — that is, idol. The sin of Shirk, Muhammad insisted, will lead people to the fires of Hell.

2.258 *he who misbelieved was dumb-founded* — Those who are not guided by Allah will remain dumbfounded when presented with spiritual truth.

2.258-259 Having stated once again the Doctrine of Tauhid (absolute monotheism) in v. 255, Muhammad then presented a parable that made the case that Allah has absolute power over life and death, a power that He reserves to Himself alone.

In this parable, Abraham described a scene where a passerby came to a desolate village and questioned the reality of the resurrection. Allah then caused the passerby to die and then raised him to life one hun-

turned over on its roofs, and said, 'How will God revive this after its death?' And God made him die for a hundred years, then He raised him, and said, 'How long hast thou tarried?' Said he, 'I have tarried a day, or some part of a day.' He said, 'Nay, thou hast tarried a hundred years; look at thy food and drink, they are not spoiled, and look at thine ass; for we will make thee a sign to men. And look at the bones how we scatter them and then clothe them with flesh.' And when it was made manifest to him, he said, 'I know that God is mighty over all.'"

Parable of the Four Birds

260 And when Abraham said, "Lord, show me how thou wilt revive the dead," He said, "What, dost thou not yet believe" Said he, "Yea, but that my heart may be quieted." He said, "Then take four birds, and take them close to thyself; then put a part of them on every mountain then call them, and they will come to thee in haste; and know that God is mighty, wise."

Parable of the Sower

261 The likeness of those who expend their wealth in God's way is as the likeness of a grain that grows to seven ears, in every ear a hundred grains, for God will double unto whom He pleases; for God both embraces and knows.

262 Those who expend their wealth in God's way, then do not follow up what they expend by taunting with it and by annoyance, these have their hire with their Lord, and no fear is on them, neither shall they grieve.

263 Kind speech and pardon are better than almsgiving followed by annoyance, and God is rich and clement.

dred years later. Yet, the passerby imagined that he had only slept for a few hours. When told that he had been asleep for one hundred years, observed that the food and drink in still good condition, and that his ass was still alive, he concluded that Allah was indeed mighty in power and able to bring life from death. According to Islamic lore, this passerby was Ezra, the Jewish High Priest (see Sabine Baring-Gould, *Legends of the Patriarchs*, pp. 178-179).

2.260 In a second parable, Abraham asked the Lord: "Lord, show me how thou wilt revive the dead?" The Lord told him to take four birds and hold them close to himself. Then he was to place the birds on different mountains and call the birds back. "They will come to thee in haste," the Lord said. The moral behind the parable is that when Allah calls to the dead, miracles take place.

2.261a In a third parable, Muhammad made the point that living a life that conforms to Allah's way, especially when it comes to money, reaps huge dividends—in this life and in the afterlife. The Bible presents a similar parable (see Matt 19:29; Lk 8:8).

2.261b *God's way* — That is, the way that leads to eternal life (see Q 72.2, note).

264   O ye who believe! make not your almsgiving vain by taunts and annoyance, like him who expends what he has for the sake of appearances before men, and believes not in God and the last day; for his likeness is as the likeness of a flint with soil upon it, and a heavy shower falls on it and leaves it bare rock; they can do nought with what they earn, for God guides not the misbelieving folk.

Parable of
the Garden on a Hill

265   But the likeness of those who expend their wealth craving the goodwill of God, and as an insurance for their souls, is as the likeness of a garden on a hill. A heavy shower falls on it, and it brings forth its eatables twofold; and if no heavy shower falls on it, the dew does; and God on what ye do doth look.

Parable of the
Garden of Palms and Vines

266   Would one of you fain have a garden of palms and vines, with rivers flowing beneath it, in which is every fruit; and when old age shall reach him, have weak seed, and there fall on it a storm wind with fire therein, and it gets burnt? Thus does God manifest to you His signs, mayhap ye will reflect.

Admonition to almsgiving

267   O ye who believe! expend in alms of the good things that ye have

2.263-264 According to Muhammad, not all good works are of the same value. Kind speech and pardon are more valuable than the giving of alms accompanied by attitudes of annoyance. Indeed, if one gives alms and then follows the act with attitudes of annoyance, that act has been voided, as far as Allah is concerned. The same is true if the gift was given with the intent of being seen by others. The Bible offers similar teachings (see Mt 6:2-5).

2.264 *O ye who believe* — Muhammad was addressing fellow Muslims (also see vv. 104, 178, 183, 208, 254, 267, 278, 282).

2.265 In a fourth parable, Muhammad believed that the giving of money for the cause of Allah (including the giving of alms) serves as an insurance at the time of the Last Judg-

ment. It is likened to a garden on a hill that either receives rain or dew and brings forth food (eatables) in its own season.

2.266 In a fifth parable, Muhammad envisioned a person with a garden of palms and vines with an aquifer flowing underneath to provide sustenance, and then is destroyed when the man reaches old age. The garden is a symbol of the blessings of life in the here and now, only to be destroyed by fire in the afterlife. This, Muhammad warned, is the fate of the infidel (the Bible presents a similar parable (see Mt 7:24-27).

2.267 *O ye who believe!* — Muhammad was addressing fellow Muslims (also see vv. 104, 178, 183, 208, 254, 264, 278, 282).

2.267-272 In the giving of alms, Muhammad offered a number of insights to assist

earned, and of what we have brought forth for you out of the earth, and do not take the vile thereof to spend in alms,—what you would not take yourselves save by connivance at it; but know that God is rich and to be praised.

268 The devil promises you poverty and bids you sin, but God promises you pardon from Him and grace, for God both embraces and knows.

269 He bringeth wisdom unto whom He will, and he who is brought wisdom is brought much good; but none will remember save those endowed with minds.

270 Whatever expense ye expend, or vow ye vow, God knows it; but the unjust have no helpers.

271 If ye display your almsgiving, then well is it; but if ye hide it and bring it to the poor, then is it better for you, and will expiate for you your evil deeds; for God of what ye do is well aware.

272 Thou art not bound to guide them; but God guides whom He will; and whatever good ye expend it is for yourselves, and do not expend save craving for God's face. And what ye expend of good, it shall be repaid you, and ye shall not be wronged,

273 —unto the poor who are straitened in God's way, and cannot knock about in the earth. The ignorant think them to be rich because of their modesty; you will know them by their mark, they do not beg from men importunately; but what ye spend of good God knows.

274 Those who expend their wealth by night and day, secretly and openly, they shall have their hire with their Lord. No fear shall come on them, nor shall they grieve.

Usury

275 Those who devour usury shall not rise again, save as he riseth whom Satan hath paralysed with a touch;

the almsgiver: (a) giving should come from one's own earnings, (b) do not give vile fruit or vegetables, (c) avoid the temptation of the devil to horde money, (d) look to Allah for wisdom in knowing what to give, (e) secret giving is better than public giving, (f) let the motivation for giving alms be the craving of the face of Allah, and (g) Allah will always repay the one who gives alms.

2.273 *you will know them by their mark —* That is, you will know them by their mark of piety. The mark is visible in their actions: (a) they are modest, and (b) they do not beg importunately (aggressively).

2.275 Muhammad condemned the practice of usury (*riba*)—the charging of interest on loans. This, he said, is Satanic. Moreover, he added that those who engage in usury are "the fellows of the Fire." Al-Tabari (tenth century Islamic scholar) is of the opinion that usury (*riba*) in this verse means a gift offered by someone to a person with the intention of receiving a greater gift in return. Other Islamic scholars (including Hasan Al-Basri and Ibn Al-Jawzi) disagree, noting that it means usury in its normative sense: the charging of interest on loans (see Q 4.161, note). It is because of this verse

and that is because they say "selling is only like usury," but God has made selling lawful and usury unlawful; and he to whom the admonition from his Lord has come, if he desists, what has gone before is his: his matter is in God's hands. But whosoever returns (to usury) these are the fellows of the Fire, and they shall dwell therein for aye.

276   God shall blot out usury, but shall make almsgiving profitable, for God loves not any sinful misbeliever.

277   Verily, those who believe, and act righteously, and are steadfast in prayer, and give alms, theirs is their hire with their Lord; there is no fear on them, nor shall they grieve.

278   O ye who believe! fear God, and remit the balance of usury, if ye be believers;

279   and if ye will not do it, then hearken to the proclamation of war from God and His Apostle; but if ye repent, your capital is yours. Ye shall not wrong, nor shall ye be wronged.

280   And if it be one in difficulties, then wait for easy circumstances; but that ye remit it as alms is better for you, if ye did but know.

281   Fear the day wherein ye shall return to God; then shall each soul be paid what it has earned, and they shall not be wronged.

The law concerning debts

282   O ye who believe! if ye engage to

that banks in the Muslim world typically charge large fees in the place of interest (also see Q 3.123-125; 4.160-161; 30.39).

2.276 In contrast to usury, Muhammad encouraged people to engage in almsgiving. It is profitable in that the giver will be repaid by Allah.

The biblical teaching on usury is the following: (a) The Old Testament encourages almsgiving and condemns the practice of usury (Lev 25:36-37; Deut 23:19-20; Ps 15:5; Jer 15:10 and Prov 28:8). (b) The New Testament encourages almsgiving yet does not condemn the practice of usury (Matt 25:27; Lk 19:23).

2.277 *believe, and act righteously* — This is a summary of the Islamic gospel (see Q 103.3, note). In this context, two of the Five Pillars are highlighted: almsgiving and

prayer (see *al-Zakat* on pp. 115-116 and *al-Salat* on pp. 169-170).

2.278 *O ye who believe!* — Muhammad was addressing fellow Muslims (also see vv. 104, 178, 183, 208, 254, 264, 267, 282).

2.279 *war from God and His Apostle* — That is, those who continue to practice usury were threatened by Muhammad with Jihad. In this Jihad, Muhammad threatened to take the capital (finances) of the practitioners of usury (*riba*).

2.280 For those people who are in difficulties, they are admonished to avoid the temptation of practicing usury (riba) and instead wait for "easy circumstances."

2.282a *O ye who believe!* — Muhammad was addressing fellow Muslims (also see vv. 104, 178, 183, 208, 254, 264, 267, 278).

2.282b This is the longest verse (ayah) in

one another in a debt for a stated time, then write it down, and let a scribe write it down between you faithfully; nor let a scribe refuse to write as God taught him, but let him write, and let him who owes dictate; but let him fear God his Lord, and not diminish therefrom aught; but if he who owes be a fool, or weak, or cannot dictate himself, then let his agent dictate faithfully, and let them call two witnesses out from amongst their men; or if there be not two men, then a man and two women, from those whom he chooses for witnesses, so that if one of the two should err, the second of the two may remind the other; and let not the witnesses refuse when they are summoned; and let them not tire of writing it, be it small or great, with its time of payment. That is more just in the sight of God, and more upright for testimony, and brings you nearer to not doubting.

Unless, indeed, it be a ready-money transaction between you,. which ye arrange between yourselves, then it is no crime against you that ye do not write it down; but bring witnesses to what ye. sell one to another, and let not either scribe or witness come to harm, for if ye do it will be abomination in you; but fear God, for God teaches you, and God knows all things.

283 But if ye be upon a journey, and ye cannot find a scribe, then let a pledge be taken. But if one of you trust another, then let him who is trusted surrender his trust, and let him fear God his Lord, and conceal not testimony, for he who conceals it, verily, sinful is his heart: God knows what ye do.

284 God's is what is in heaven and in the earth, and if ye show what is in your souls, or hide it, God will call you to account; and. He forgives whom He will, and punishes whom He will, for God is mighty

the Qur'an. It states that all contractual obligations related to the transfer of money in the form of loans and debts must be written down with witnesses attesting to its veracity and terms. The witnesses can be (a) two men, or (b) one man and two women. A combination of witnesses that was purely female (no men included in the group of witnesses) was prohibited. In contrast, the Bible—in either Old or New Testaments—make no distinction between male and female when it came to serving as witnesses.
2.282c *ready-money transaction* — An exception to the above clause in this verse is if

the transaction concerns ready merchandise which one transfers directly to the other.
2.282d *let not either scribe or witness come to harm* — Witnesses are not to be intimidated with harm or harmed due to their testimonies regarding the transactions of loans and debts.
2.283 *let a pledge be taken* — A second objection to the attestation by witnesses of loans and debts is if one is on a journey and witnesses cannot be found. Then an oral agreement may be enacted.
2.285a *what is sent down to him from his Lord* — Muhammad asserted that the surahs

over all.

Concluding prayer

285   The Apostle believes in what is sent down to him from his Lord, and the believers all believe on God, and His angels, and His Books, and His apostles,—we make no difference between any of His apostles,—they say, "We hear and obey, Thy pardon, O Lord! for to Thee our journey ends.

286   God will not require of the soul save its capacity. It shall have what it has earned, and it shall owe what has been earned from it. Lord,

catch us not up, if we forget or make mistake; Lord, load us not with a burden, as Thou hast loaded those who were before us. Lord, make us not to carry what we have not strength for, but forgive us, and pardon us, and have mercy on us. Thou art our Sovereign, then help us against the people who do not believe!"

Surah 3

In the name of the merciful and compassionate God.

---

were "sent down to him" from Allah, was dictated to him (see Q 76.23, note, and **The Qur'an** on pp. 150-153).

2.285b *His Books* — That is, the books sent down to the various apostles on the earth (see **The Perspicuous Book** on pp. 178-179).

2.286a *it shall have what it has earned* — That is, the destiny of each person is based upon that which he or she has done on the earth—salvation by individual merit.

2.286b *forgive us and pardon us* — According to Muhammad, provided that the balance of good works versus bad works in the afterlife tips favorably towards good works, Allah will forgive one's bad works (see **Divine Forgiveness in Islam** on pp. 158-161).

2.286c *help us against the people who do not believe!* — Muhammad saw the infidels as a threat. They were the aggressors against Allah and His people due to the fact that their rejection of Muhammad's message was steadfast. In some cases, they occu-

pied territory that had previously been under the control of the Muslim people. Muhammad believed that such was the case with the Ka'ba altar which was originally constructed by Abraham, Ishmael and the archangel Gabriel (all of whom were fully submitted to Allah). See Q 2.191b, note.

Surah 3. The title of this surah, *Imran's People*, comes from verse 33. This surah includes a series of accusations against Christians and Jews, addressing theological questions as well as practical behavior. The surah also addresses the Compact of Medinah. In this compact, the people of Medinah (Yathrib) embraced Muhammad as its Apostle. The surah addresses two battles waged against the people of Mecca: the Battle of Badr (A.D. 624) and the Battle of Uhud (A.D. 625). Muhammad's small army won the first and lost the second. He offered theological reasons for the victory and defeat. The surah ends with a prayer and a warning.

1   A. L. M.

Qur'an

2   God, there is no god but He, the
     living, the self-subsistent.
3   He has sent down to thee the Book
     in truth, confirming what was be-
     fore it, and has revealed the law,
4   and the gospel before for the guid-
     ance of men, and has revealed the
     Discrimination. Verily, those who
     disbelieve in the signs of God, for

     them is severe torment, for God is
     mighty and avenging.
5   Verily, God, there is nothing hid-
     den from Him in the earth, nor in
     the heaven;
6   He it is who fashions you in the
     womb as He pleases. There is no
     God but He, the mighty, the wise.
7   He it is who has revealed to thee
     the Book, of which there are some
     verses that are decisive, they are
     the mother of the Book; and oth-
     ers ambiguous; but as for those in

3.1 Literally, *Alif, Lam, Mim.* See Q 32.1, note.

3.2 *there is no god but He* — Muhammad began this surah with a reiteration of the Doctrine of Tauhid—absolute monotheism. This doctrine serves as the foundational teaching in the Qur'an (see Q 112, note). It stood opposed to the prevailing Arab paganism of his day as well as mainstream Christian theology.

3.3a *He has sent down to thee the Book in truth* — Muhammad asserted that the surahs were "sent down to him" from Allah, was dictated to him (see Q 76.23, note, and **The Qur'an** on pp. 150-153. The *Book* refers to the eternal book that Muhammad claimed exists in Paradise, guarded by Allah (see **The Perspicuous Book** on pp. 178-179).

3.3b-4a *confirming what was before it* — Muhammad believed that his surahs corresponded and complemented divine revelations from earlier apostles. Specifically, Muhe believed that the Qur'an clarified the teachings in the Jewish Torah (the first five books of the Old Testament) and the gospel (the Four Gospels in the New Testament).

The differences that do exist, such as the doctrine of substitutionary atonement, the teaching that Jesus is the Son of God, and teaching that Jesus died on the cross, are due to corruptions within the biblical text. All who disbelieve in the Qur'an are destined for a "severe torment" by an avenging God.

Jews and Christians, of course, disagree, claiming that Muhammad was a false prophet and that the Qur'an—which contains numerous differences with both Old and New Testaments—is what one would expect from a false prophet (see Deut 13:1-5; Jer 23:36; Gal 1:6-9; 2 Pet 2:1-3).

3.4b *the Discrimination* —That is, divine revelation that distinguishes right from wrong. (see Q 21.48-50, note). All infidels will be tortured by Allah, the one who is mighty and vengeful.

3.6 *There is no God but He* — Muhammad reminded the reader of the Doctrine of Tauhid—absolute monotheism, the doctrine that sets Islam apart from pagan Arabia and the Jews and Christians (see v. 18).

3.7a *the Book* — This is the eternal book in Paradise guarded by Allah and sent down to Muhammad, dictated to him by the archan-

whose hearts is perversity, they follow what is ambiguous, and do crave for sedition, craving for (their own) interpretation of it; but none know the interpretation of it except God. But those who are well grounded in knowledge say, "We believe in it; it is all from our Lord; but none will remember save those who possess minds.

Muhammad's prayer

8   O Lord! pervert not our hearts again when Thou hast guided them, and grant us mercy from Thee, for Thou art He who grants.

9   O Lord! Thou shalt gather together men unto the day wherein is no doubt. Verily, God will not depart from His promise."

The destiny of the infidel

10   Verily, those who misbelieve, their wealth shall not help them, nor their children, against God at all; and they it is who are the fuel of the fire.

11   As was the wont of Pharaoh's people, and those before them, they said our signs were lies, and God caught them up in their sins, for God is severe to punish.

12   Say to those who misbelieve, "Ye shall be overcome and driven together to hell, an ill couch will it be.

---

gel Gabriel (see **The Perspicuous Book** on pp. 178-179). Muhammad believed that the surahs he presented contained verses that were decisive, what he called "the mother of the Book." What he meant by "decisive" was that they were clear in and unambiguous, allowing only one legitimate interpretation. Other verses are ambiguous and open to a variety of interpretations. Muhammad believed that the infidels gravitated to the ambiguous verses and used them to plot sedition against him.

3.7b *those who possess minds* — That is, those who possess spiritual insight.

3.8-9 Muhammad responded by asking Allah for clarity of understanding of the Qur'an for his entire Muslim community.

Yet these verses presented, once again, an important question regarding the dictation theory of the Qur'an. If the Qur'an was indeed eternal and "sent down" to Mu-

hammad by the archangel Gabriel and then dictated to him, why then are there statements where Muhammad is offering a prayer to Allah? These words fail the test of eternality and dictation, since it was Muhammad dictating them to Allah in a real time situation located in a moment in history (see Q 36.39-42, and **The Qur'an** on pp. 150-153).

3.10 *fuel for the fire* — This is one of Muhammad's favorite descriptions of the infidel. At the Last Judgment, neither money nor the appeal of their children will be of any assistance in averting in fires of Hell.

3.11 *our signs were lies* — This is another of Muhammad's common descriptions of the infidel, that they characterize divine revelation as lies.

3.12 Muhammad's strategy in dealing with infidels is to proclaim the prospects of eternal condemnation that awaits them. Else-

13 Ye have had a sign in the two parties who met; one party fighting in the way of God, the other misbelieving; these saw twice the same number as themselves to the eyesight, for God aids with His help those whom He pleases." Verily, in that is a lesson for those who have perception.

*This life contrasted
with the afterlife*

14 Seemly unto men is a life of lusts, of women, and children, and hoarded talents of gold and silver, and of horses well-bred, and cattle, and tilth;—that is the provision for the life of this world; but God, with Him is the best resort.

15 Say, "But shall we tell you of a better thing than this?" For those who fear are gardens with their Lord, beneath which rivers flow; they shall dwell therein for aye, and pure wives and grace from God; the Lord looks on His servants,

16 who say, "Lord, we believe, pardon Thou our sins and keep us from the torment of the fire,"

where in the Qur'an, Muhammad presented the mercy of Allah on all who turn to Him.

The Bible makes a similar two-fold approach (the love and mercy of God and the justice of God with a corresponding condemnation) in motivating the unbeliever to turn to God and receive His salvation. Dependent upon the situation and the spiritual response of the unbeliever, the Christian is prompted by the Holy Spirit to either emphasize the mercy or justice of God. "Be merciful to those who doubt; snatch others from the fire and save them; to others show mercy, mixed with fear-hating even the clothing stained by corrupted flesh" (Jude 22-23; also see Matt 7:21-27; Eph 2:4-10; Titus 3:4-7).

3.13 *fighting in the way of God* — That is, engaging in jihad in the cause of Allah. The imagery here is that of two armies engaged in battle with one another: one army fighting in the way of Allah and the other army characterized by infidels. The first army saw the enemy of infidels as twice their size, nevertheless, "God aids with His help those whom He pleases."

Some Islamic scholars assume this verse to be a reference to the Battle of Badr where Muhammad's poorly equipped and outnumbered army of three hundred warriors routed a well-armed Mecca army of nearly one thousand soldiers. It was the first open battle between Muhammad's forces and the forces of Mecca. Yet, other Islamic scholars see this passage as a generalized description of battles where the forces of good defeated the forces of evil, in spite of the fact that they were severely outnumbered and should have been defeated, given the general nature of warfare.

3.14-17 Muhammad contrasted the priorities and focus of the infidel, which is on the wealth and provisions of this life with that of the faithful Muslim, which is on the wealth and provisions of the afterlife.

3.15 Description of Paradise: an oasis with well supplied aquifers flowing underneath the surface. Oases are also supplied with harems of "pure wives" (see **The Virgins** on pp. 107-109).

3.16 *pardon Thou our sins* — According to Muhammad, divine forgiveness is granted to

17   —upon the patient, the truthful, the devout, and those who ask for pardon at the dawn.

Islam

18   God bears witness that there is no god but He, and the angels, and those possessed of knowledge standing up for justice. There is no God but He, the mighty, the wise.

19   Verily, (the true) religion in God's sight is Islâm, and those to whom

the Book was given disagreed not until after that there was given to them knowledge, through mutual envy. But whoso disbelieves in God's signs, truly God is quick at reckoning up.

20   And if they would dispute with thee, then say, "I turn my face with resignation unto God, and whoso follows me." And say to those who have been given the Book, unto the Gentiles, "Are ye, too, resigned?" and if they are resigned, then are they guided. But if they

those who have earned it through a life of righteous deeds (see **Divine Forgiveness in Islam** on pp. 158-161). In this respect, divine pardon in Islamic theology is not to be confused with divine forgiveness as presented in both Old and New Testaments. In Christian theology, divine pardon is granted to those who have *not* earned it. Rather, it has been earned it on their behalf via the death and resurrection of Jesus Christ from the dead (see Jn 1:29, 36; Rom 5:1-11).

3.18 *There is no god but He* — Once again, Muhammad reminded the reader of the Doctrine of Tauhid—absolute monotheism, the doctrine that sets Islam apart from pagan Arabia and the Jews and Christians (see v. 6).

3.19 In this verse, Muhammad drew the lines of demarcation between Islam, on the one side, and Judaism and Christianity, on the other. According to most Islamic scholars, those to whom the Book (or Scriptures) was given were the Jews and Christians. The Jews were people of the Old Testament and the Christians were people of both Old and

New Testaments. Muhammad claimed that the reason the Jews and Christians rejected his ministry and message was due to envy—sectarian pride.

3.20 Muhammad decided that he was not to engage in interreligious dialogue with the Jews and Christians. Rather, he told Jews and Christians that he remained in submission to Allah and other Muslim believers. In other words, he would no longer dialogue with the infidel on the topic of religion (see Q 3.100). In its place, he was to merely preach to them about the rightness of Islam. This approach to inter-faith dialogue has carried forward, generally speaking, to the present day.

In contrast, the Christian faith encourages interreligious dialogue. It falls under the large umbrella of evangelism, serving as one of its three major components. The work of evangelism is understood as an effort to convince both the mind and the heart of unbelievers of the rightness of the Christian gospel, with a reliance upon the Holy Spirit to work quietly behind the scenes in people's hearts. Its three component parts

turn their backs, then thou hast only to preach, and God looks on his servants.

21 Verily, those who disbelieve in God's signs, and kill the prophets without right, and kill those from among men, who bid what is just,—to them give the glad tidings of grievous woe!

22 These are they whose works are void in this world and the next, and helpers have they none.

23 Did ye not see those who have been given a portion of the Book? They were called unto the Book of God to decide between them; and then a sect of them turned their backs and turned away;

---

are: (a) the preaching of the Word of God, (b) the testimony of a life of good works, and (c) the engagement of honest dialogue.

It is in the third part—honest dialogue—where people of differing religions are given a hearing to make their case and debate opposing points of view. Such dialogue takes place in formal and informal settings. Without this third component, the Christian faith comes across as overly authoritarian and insecure. It also promotes an aggressive approach to evangelism. The net result is the loss of credulity in the eyes of the non-Christian. David Hesselgrave rightly comments: "The mission fields are well populated with men and women who have been ushered into the heavenlies without knowing why they got on the elevator. Once back on earth they have no intention of being taken for another ride" (*Communicating Christ Cross-Culturally*, p. 152).

The importance of inter-religious dialogue is illustrated by C. S. Lewis. He turned from atheism to a belief in God, and finally to the Christian faith via long and lively discussions with other Christians. In a letter to a friend, he wrote: "I have just passed on from believing in God to definitely believing in Christ—in Christianity. I will try to explain this another time. My long night talk with Dyson and Tolkien had a good deal to do with it" (*Letters of C. S. Lewis to Arthur Greeves*,

Oct 1, 1931). In another letter, he added: "Dyson and Tolkien were the immediate human causes of my conversion. Is any pleasure on earth as great as a circle of Christian friends by a good fire?" (*Letters of C. S. Lewis*, Dec 21, 1941).

3.21 Muhammad noted that in the Old Testament, on numerous occasions, the Jewish people killed the prophets whom Allah had sent to them.

Jesus made a similar observation of the people of his day. He pronounced a series of woes upon the Jewish religious leaders, whom he called hypocrites, for honoring their Jewish heritage and decorating the graves of the prophets and other people distinguished in Jewish history, yet rejected His ministry. They, he explained were also the shedders of blood. He then added: "So you testify against yourselves that you are the descendants of those who murdered the prophets. Fill up, then, the measure of the sin of your forefathers! You snakes! You brood of vipers! How will you escape being condemned to hell? Therefore I am sending you prophets and wise men and teachers. Some of them you will kill and crucify; others you will flog in your synagogues and pursue from town to town. And so upon you will come all the righteous blood that has been shed on earth, from the blood of righteous Abel to the blood of Zechariah son

24   —that is because they say the fire shall not touch us save for a certain number of days. But that deceived them in their religion which they had invented.

25   How will it be when we have gathered them together for a day whereof there is no doubt, when each soul shall be paid what it has earned, and they shall not be wronged?

Allah sovereign
over the nations

26   Say, "O God, Lord of the kingdom! Thou givest the kingdom to whomsoever Thou pleasest, and strippest the kingdom from whomsoever Thou pleasest; Thou honourest whom Thou pleasest, and abasest whom Thou pleasest; in Thy hand is good. Verily, Thou art mighty over all.

27   Thou dost turn night to day, and dost turn day to night, and dost bring forth the living from the dead, and dost provide for whom Thou pleasest without taking count."

Permission to lie

28   Those who believe shall not take

---

of Berekiah, whom you murdered between the temple and the altar" (Matt 23:29-35).

Still, the Christian attitude toward Jewish unbelief differs from that which is presented in the Qur'an. The Christian attitude is to grieve for them (Rom 9:1-5) and await a time in the future when the Jewish people will return and acknowledge Jesus as Messiah (Zech 12:10; Rom 11:25-27).

3.24 *save for a certain number of days* — In this passage, Muhammad referenced the Doctrine of Purgatory, a teaching that asserted that an intermediate place existed between Paradise and Hell, a temporary punishment where the process of purification from sin continued. Once fully purged, the soul would then enter Paradise. In the Jewish apocryphal writings, it is briefly mentioned in 2 Macc 12:42-44. In the early centuries of the church, the doctrine was circulated and affirmed as part of the Apostolic Tradition. At the Second Council of Lyon (1274), the Council of Florence (1438-1445) and the Council of Trent (1545-1563) the doctrine was affirmed as part of official Roman Catholic dogma. The doctrine, however, has never been affirmed by Protestant Christianity.

Muhammad noted that the doctrine is a deception and part of their own theological inventions. Curiously, elsewhere in the Qur'an Muhammad affirmed a version of the Doctrine of Purgatory for Muslim believers (see Q 7.44-53, note).

3.25 *each soul shall be paid what it has earned* — That is, a salvation by works (meritocracy). Shadowed in this verse is the notion of a balance at the Last Judgment (see **The Last Judgment** on pp. 46-50).

3.26 Allah's authority and power reaches across the kingdoms or nations of the world. Allah raises up whom He pleases and deposes whom He pleases. The Bible makes a similar observation of God (Job 34:25-26; Dan 4:31-35; 5:5-6, 22-28; Jn 19:11; Rom 13:1).

3.28 *shall not take misbelievers for their patrons* — That is, let not believers take in-

misbelievers for their patrons, rather than believers, and he who does this has no part with God at all, unless, indeed, ye fear some danger from them. But God bids you beware of Himself, for unto Him your journey is.

29 Say, "If ye hide that which is in your breasts, or if ye show it, God knows it: He knows what is in the heavens and what is in the earth, for God is mighty over all."

The life of obedience

30 The day that every soul shall find what it has done of good present before it; and what it has done of evil, it would fain that there were between itself and that a wide interval. "God bids you beware of Himself, but God is gentle with His servants."

31 Say, "If ye would love God then follow me, and God will love you and forgive you your sins, for God is forgiving and merciful."

32 Say, "Obey God and the Apostle; but if ye turn your backs God loves

---

fidels as allies (also see Q 4.139). The one exception, however, is if the Muslim believer fears "some danger from them." Under such conditions, Muslims may enter alliances with infidels. Yet they must do so with duplicitous motivations. The overall strategy is to prevent the unbeliever from gaining the advantage.

Hence, Muslims were permitted to deceive infidels and forge insincere alliances with them when they perceived that it was to their advantage to do so. When in a position of weakness, they were permitted to make agreements. Yet, when in a position of strength, they were allowed to negate their agreements. With this in mind, in a Hadith Muhammad said, "By Allah, and Allah willing, if I take an oath and later find something else better than that. then I do what is better and expiate my oath" (*Sahih Bukhari*, 7.26.427).

3.29 This is a reiteration of that which is stated in the previous verse. Muslims were permitted to hide what was in their breasts and become allies with infidels when it was in their Islamic interests to do so.

3.30 This is a reference to the Last Judgment. It will be a time when what has been done of good will be presented alongside what has been done of evil (see ***The Last Judgment*** on pp. 46-50).

3.31 *God will love you and forgive you your sins* — Provided that the balance in the afterlife tilts towards good works, Allah will pardon the bad works committed in life (see ***Divine Forgiveness in Islam*** on pp. 158-161).

3.32 *Obey God and the Apostle* — Muhammad equated obedience to Allah with obedience to the Apostle (himself). This is because Muhammad believed his surahs to be divinely inspired. Stated otherwise, to disobey Muhammad was tantamount to disobeying Allah with the net result being eternal condemnation in Hell (see Q 4.69, 79-80, 136; 5.80-81; 8.13, 20-23; 24.47, 48, 50-52, 54; 33.33, 71; 48.9-10; 57.19; 59.4; 72.22-23, 81.19-21 and 46.16, note).

In the Christian faith, no individual is bequeathed such an exalted status. The one exception is Jesus Christ. Jesus said: "Anyone who has seen me has seen the Father"

not misbelievers."

The House of Amram

33   Verily, God has chosen Adam, and
      Noah, and Abraham's people, and
      Imrân's people above the world,
34   —a seed, of which one succeeds
      the other, but God both hears and
      knows.
35   When Imrân's wife said, "Lord! I

have vowed to Thee what is within
my womb, to be dedicated unto
Thee, receive it then from me. Verily, Thou dost hear and know."

36   And when she brought it forth she
      said, "Verily, I have brought it forth
      a female"—but God knew best
      what she brought forth; and a male
      is not like a female—"I have called
      her Mary, and I seek a refuge in
      Thee for her and for her seed from

(Jn 14:9), "I and the Father are one" (Jn 10:30), "Heaven and earth will pass away, but my words will never pass away" (Mk 13:31), "There is a judge for the one who rejects me and does not accept my words; that very word which I spoke will condemn him at the last day" (Jn 12:48), and "If you remain in me and my words remain in you, ask whatever you wish, and it will be given you" (Jn 15:7). What is more, since Muhammad is regarded as a false apostle, he is to be disregarded by all who seek after God.
3.33 *Imran's people* — That is, the House of Moses and Aaron. According to Num 26:59, the name of the father of Moses and Aaron was Amram, and the name of their mother was Jochebed. Moses and Aaron also had a sister: Miriam.
3.35 *Imran's wife* — That is, a woman from the House of Imran—not literally the wife of Imran (see **The House of Amram** on p. 654). This woman was to be the future mother of Mary and grandmother of Jesus. According to the *Infancy Gospel of James*, she was identified as Anna and her husband was Joachim. That placed Anna in the genealogical lineage that traced back to Aaron, Amram, and Levi. Elizabeth (Mary's cousin) was also of the House of Aaron (see Lk 1:5), which meant that her genealogical lineage

traced back to Aaron, Amram, and Levi. According to the *Infancy Gospel of James*, Anna prayed, "If I give birth, whether male or female, I will present it as a gift to the Lord my God, and it shall be a ministering servant to him all the days of its life" (4:1).

The New Testament claims that Jesus was of the House of Judah, not Levi. The only way in which the genealogy presented in this qur'anic passage can harmonize with the New Testament account is if Joachim was of the House of Judah. Mary is traditionally believed to also be of the House of Judah due to an interpretation of Luke 3:23-38 which claims that this particular genealogy was actually that of Mary—not Joseph (see Lk 3:33).

3.36a *I seek refuge in Thee for her* — When the baby proved to be a female, the mother decided to dedicate her to the Lord. This corresponds to the *Infancy Gospel of James* which states that following the birth of Mary, Anna said: "As the Lord my God lives, you shall not walk on this earth until I bring you into the Temple of the Lord" (6:1).
3.36b *and for her seed from Satan the pelted* — The woman also sought divine protection for her grandchild (Jesus) from Satan. Satan is described as "the pelted" or "the Pelted One." This is a reference to the

Satan the pelted."

37 And her Lord received her with a good reception, and made her grow up with a good growth, and Zachariah took care of her. Whenever Zachariah entered the chamber to her he found beside her a provision, and said, "O Mary, how hast thou this?" She said, "It is from God, for God provides for whom He pleases without count."

38 Therefore prayed Zachariah to his Lord, and said, "Lord, grant me from Thee a good seed. Verily, Thou hearest prayer."

39 And an angel cried out to him as he was standing praying in the chamber (and said) that "God gives thee the glad tidings of John, to confirm the Word from God,—of a chief and a chaste one, and a prophet from amongst the righteous."

40 He said, "My Lord, how can there be to me a boy when old age has reached me, and my wife is barren?" Said he, "Thus God does what He pleaseth."

41 He said, "My Lord, make for me a sign." He said, "Thy sign is that thou shalt not speak to men for three days, save by gesture; but remember thy Lord much, and celebrate His praises in the evening and the morning."

42 And when the angels said, "O Mary! verily, God has chosen thee, and has purified thee, and has chosen thee above the women of the world.

longstanding pre-Islamic tradition in Mecca to throw rocks at the Three Pillars called The Great Devil (see **The Hajj** on pp. 480-482).
3.37a Muhammad believed that Zechariah (Zachariah), Elizabeth's husband, became the guardian of Mary. The New Testament makes no such claim. To the contrary, Zechariah and Elizabeth lived "in the hill country of Judea" (Lk 1:39), whereas Mary lived in Nazareth of Galilee (Lk 1:26). It would have been impossible for Zechariah to serve as Mary's guardian from such a long distance.
3.37b *entered the chamber* — That is, entered one of the chambers in the Temple.
3.37c *he found beside her a provision* — That is, Zechariah found beside Mary a provision of food. This account is taken from the *Infancy Gospel of James*, which states: "Mary was in the Temple of the Lord like a dove being fed, and she received food from the hand of an angel" (8:1).
3.38-39 While in the Temple, Zechariah prayed that the Lord would give him a male child. An angel appeared to him and granted his request.
3.40-41 When asked for a sign, the angel said that he would remain mute for three days. This contradicts the New Testament account, which states that he was to remain mute until the birth of the child (see Lk 1:20).
3.42a *and when the angels said* — Muhammad believed that the announcement to Mary that she was chosen to be the mother of Jesus included more than one angel. This contradicts the New Testament which says that a singular angel made the announcement to her (Lk 1:35).
3.43-51 That which is missing in this lengthy announcement by the angels in this qur'anic

The House of Amram

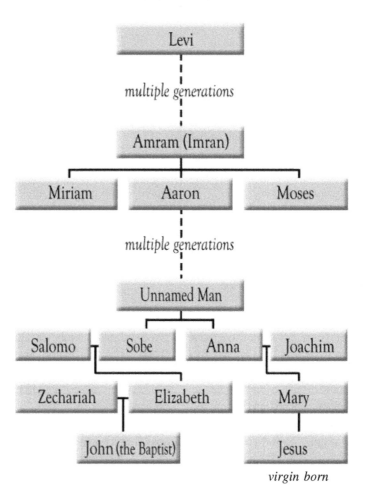

In the Qur'an, the genealogy of Jesus traces back to the Hebrew patriarch Levi. In contrast, the Bible traces the genealogy of Jesus traces back to the Hebrew patriarch Judah (see Matt 1:1-16 and Lk 3:23-38).

This chart is based upon Q 3.33-35 and the *Infancy Gospel of James* 4:1-7:10. The names Salomo (man) and Sobe (woman) come from Church Tradition.

43   O Mary! be devout unto thy Lord, and adore and bow down with those who bow.

44   That is (one) of the declarations of the unseen world which we reveal to thee, though thou wert not by them when they threw their lots which of them should take care of Mary, nor were ye by them when they did dispute."

45   When the angel said, "O Mary! verily, God gives thee the glad tidings of a Word from Him; his name shall be the Messiah Jesus the son of Mary, regarded in this world and the next and of those whose place is nigh to God.

46   And he shall speak to people in his cradle, and when grown up, and shall be among the righteous."

47   She said, "Lord! how can I have a son, when man has not yet touched me?" He said, "Thus God creates what He pleaseth. When He decrees a matter He only says BE and it is;

48   and He will teach him the Book, and wisdom, and the law, and the gospel,

49   and he shall be a prophet to the people of Israel (saying), that I have come to you, with a sign from God, namely, that I will create for you out of clay as though it

passage are the words: "So the holy one to be born will be called the Son of God" (Lk 1:35). Such an omission is what one would expect since Muhammad steadfastly rejected the possibility that a human could also be the Son of God. It violated the Doctrine of Tauhid—absolute monotheism. In its place, the Qur'an has the angels reporting that Jesus will be a prophet (v. 49).

3.46 *he shall speak to people in his cradle* — This is an reference to the apocryphal document, *The Arabic Gospel of the Infancy of Jesus* (see Q 19.29-33 and **Jesus in the Cradle** on pp. 285-286).

3.47a *when man has not yet touched me* — This verse affirms the virgin conception of Jesus (also see Matt 1:23; Lk 1:27, 34).

3.47b *He only says BE and it is* — Allah's sovereignty over all creation is illustrated in the fact that all He needs to do is say one word—*be*—and whatever it is He wishes comes into existence (see Q 3.59; 16.40; 19.35; 36.82; 40.68).

3.48 *The Book* refers to the eternal book in Paradise guarded by Allah (see **The Perspicuous Book** on pp 178-179). Wisdom perhaps refers to the Wisdom Books of the Old Testament (Job through the Song of Solomon). The *law* refers to the Old Testament Torah (Genesis through Deuteronomy). The *gospel* refers to the Four Gospels (Matthew through John).

3.49a *I will create for you out of clay as though it were the form of a bird* — The origin of this story is found in the apocryphal infancy gospel known as the *Gospel of Thomas* and then repeated in a later apocryphal document *The Arab Gospel of the Infancy of the Savior* (see **Jesus and the Clay Sparrows** on p. 658-659).

The *Gospel of Thomas* is one of the earliest of the Infancy Gospels, written about A.D. 150. It was popular in the early centuries of the Church and translated into many languages. The Gospel addresses the period of Jesus' life between his birth and the

were the form of a bird, and I will blow thereon and it shall become a bird by God's permission; and I will heal the blind from birth, and lepers; and I will bring the dead to life by God's permission; and I will tell you what you eat and what ye store up in your houses. Verily, in that is a sign for you if ye be believers.

50 And I will confirm what is before you of the law, and will surely make lawful for you some of that which was prohibited from you. I have come to you with a sign from your Lord,

51 so fear God and follow me, for God is my Lord, and your Lord,

so worship Him:—this is the right path."

52 And when Jesus perceived their unbelief, He said, "Who are my helpers for God?" Said the apostles, "We are God's helpers. We believe in God, so bear witness that we are resigned.

53 Lord, we have believed in what Thou hast revealed, and we have followed the Apostle, so write us down with those which bear witness."

The death of Jesus

54 But they (the Jews) were crafty, and God was crafty, for God is

---

event in the Temple mentioned in Luke 2:40 when he was twelve years of age. The family of Jesus is depicted as non-Jewish (Gentile) and Jesus is depicted as a child prodigy, sometimes as a child terror, performing a number of miracles. The *Gospel of Thomas* was never a candidate for inclusion in the New Testament canon.

The *Arabic Gospel of the Infancy of the Savior* is believed to be derived from the *Gospel of Thomas*. Since it was written in Arabic and widely disseminated throughout the Arab speaking world, it was readily accessible to Muhammad.

3.49b *I will heal the blind from birth, and lepers; and I will bring the dead to life* — the *Arabic Gospel of the Infancy of the Saviour* records people healed from the palsy, leprosy, fever, demon possession and even raised from the dead when placed next to the infant Jesus.

3.50 *I will make lawful for you some of that*

which was prohibited from you — That is, Jesus redefined kosher law for the Church (see Jn 16:12-15; Acts 10:9-16; 15:29; Rom 14:14-15, 20-21; 1 Cor 10:18-20; Gal 2:11-14; 1 Tim 4:4-5).

3.51 *the right path* — This is the path that leads to eternal life (see Q 72.2, note). In this verse, it is summarized as (a) fearing God, and (b) following Him.

3.52 *we are resigned* — That is, we are Muslims. After having been asked by Jesus, "Who are my helpers for God?" the apostles answered "We are God's helpers." They added that they bore witness that they were resigned (*islam*). This subtlety, lost in English translations, is clear in the Arabic. The apostles declared that they were Muslims (see Q 61.14).

3.54 *God is the best of crafty ones!* — That is, Allah is more adept in outmaneuvering His opponents (see vv. 28-29 where Muslims are encouraged to also be crafty).

the best of crafty ones!

55 When God said, "O Jesus! I will make Thee die and take Thee up again to me and will clear thee of those who misbelieve, and will make those who follow thee above those who misbelieve, at the day of judgment, then to me is your return. I will decide between you concerning that wherein ye disagree.

56 And as for those who misbelieve, I will punish them with grievous punishment in this world and the next, and they shall have none to help them."

57 But as for those who believe and do what is right, He will pay them their reward, for God loves not the unjust.

The nature of Jesus

58 That is what we recite to thee of the signs and of the wise reminder.

59 Verily, the likeness of Jesus with

3.55 *I will make Thee die and take Thee up again* — Elsewhere in the Qur'an (Q 4.157-158) it is stated that Jesus was not crucified. Rather, someone else was crucified in his place, unbeknown to the Jews who sought his crucifixion. According to this verse, then, Jesus died at a later date (following the episode of the mistaken identity crucifixion). Allah caused his death and then raised him to Paradise.

3.57 *believe and do what is right* — These words are repeated often in the Qur'an and serve as a brief summary of the Islamic gospel (see Q 103.3, note).

3.59a *the likeness of Jesus with God is as the likeness of Adam* — With this statement, Muhammad insisted that Jesus was a human being, as was Adam, and possessed a relationship with God, as did Adam. He was not the Son of God and had no rightful claims to deity. As such, Muhammad denied the Doctrine of the Hypostatic Union (that Jesus was fully God and fully man), and the Doctrine of the Trinity (that Jesus was the Second Person in the Godhead). This is because Muhammad insisted that Jesus could not have been the Son of God since it violated his understanding of monotheism—the Doctrine

of Tauhid.

For Christians, the Hypostatic Union of Christ is a foundational doctrine, standing alongside the Doctrine of the Trinity in importance. The Doctrine of Salvation is predicated upon it. The Arian Controversy that erupted in the third century, A.D. was centered on this theological question. It resulted in the formation of the Nicene-Constantinopolitan Creed (A.D. 381). This creed resulted in Arianism being declared a heresy. Anathema was pronounced upon all who embraced Arianism—that is, they were accursed, declared to be non-Christians, outside the saving faith found in Jesus Christ (see the **Definition of Chalcedon** on pp. 785-786, **The Doctrine of the Trinity** on pp. 735-736, and **The Nicene-Constantinopolitan Creed** on p. 740). The Athanasian Creed (*c.* A.D. 500), though never officially ratified, reaffirmed both the Definition of Chalcedon and the Nicene-Constantinopolitan Creed, In part, it states: "Furthermore it is necessary to everlasting salvation; that he also believe faithfully the Incarnation of our Lord Jesus Christ. For the right Faith is, that we believe and confess; that our Lord Jesus Christ, the Son of God, is God

Jesus and the Clay Sparrows

Surah 3.49

...and he shall be a prophet to the people of Israel (saying), that I have come to you, with a sign from God, namely, that I will create for you out of clay as though it were the form of a bird, and I will blow thereon and it shall become a bird by God's permission

The Arabic Gospel of the Infancy of the Savior 1:36

And He had made figures of birds and sparrows, which flew when He told them to fly, and stood still when He told them to stand, and ate and drank when He handed them food and drink. After the boys had gone away and told this to their parents, their fathers said to them: My sons, take care not to keep company with him again, for he is a wizard: flee from him, therefore, and avoid him, and do not play with him again after this.

The Gospel of Thomas 2

The child Jesus, when five years old, was playing in the ford of a mountain stream; and He collected the flowing waters into pools, and made them clear immediately, and by a word alone He made them obey Him. And having made some soft clay, He fashioned out of it twelve sparrows. And it was the Sabbath when He did these things. And there were also many other children playing with Him. And a certain Jew, seeing what Jesus was doing, playing on the Sabbath, went off immediately, and said to his father Joseph: Behold, your son is at the stream, and has taken clay, and made of it

> twelve birds, and has profaned the Sabbath. And Joseph, coming to the place and seeing, cried out to Him, saying, Why do you do on the Sabbath what is not lawful to do? And Jesus clapped His hands, and cried out to the sparrows, and said to them: Off you go! And the sparrows flew, and went off crying. And the Jews seeing this were amazed, and went away and reported to their chief men what they had seen Jesus doing.

Apocryphal gospels, judged spurious by the church, suggest what it might have looked like had Jesus succumbed to Satan's temptations. These fantastic accounts show the child Jesus making clay sparrows that he could bring to life with a puff of breath, and dropping dried fish into water to see them miraculously start swimming. He turned his playmates into goats to teach them a lesson, and made people go blind or deaf just for the thrill of healing them. The apocryphal gospels are the second-century counterparts to modern comic books about Superboy or Batgirl. Their value lies mainly in the contrast they form with the actual Gospels, which reveal a Messiah who did not use miraculous powers to benefit himself.

—Philip Yancey, *The Jesus I Never Knew*, p. 72

One of the most popular stories about Jesus from the Qur'an tells that Jesus turned clay figurines into actual birds (surah 5:110). It is possible to find uninformed Christians who assume that this is found in the Bible. However, the fact that Muhammad retells this story demonstrates what sources he is using to claim the life of Jesus as a prophet of Allah. The original story of this miracle is found in *The Infancy Gospel of Thomas*, which appeared in about 150. This was written long after the death of the Thomas for whom it is named and was never accepted as more than a literary fiction.

—Emir Fethi Caner and Ergun Mehmet Caner, *More Than a Prophet*, p. 112

While the Jesus of Islam performed many miracles, including the creation of a bird, Prophet Muhammad did no such thing...It is not a surprise that even Islamic scholars admit that Prophet Muhammad did not perform miracles. The Qur'an's account that Jesus created a bird from clay does not belong to the Gospel narratives in the New Testament. It was perhaps borrowed from the non-canonical *Gospel of Thomas* where Jesus supposedly "took clay and formed the images of twelve sparrows."

—Hussein Hajji Wario, *Cracks in the Crescent*, p. 220

God is as the likeness of Adam. He created him from earth, then He said to him BE, and he was;

60 —the truth from thy Lord, so be thou not of those who are in doubt.

61 And whoso disputeth with thee after what has come to thee of knowledge, say, "Come, let us call our sons and your sons, and our women and your women, and ourselves and yourselves: then we will imprecate and put God's curse on those who lie."

62 Verily, those are the true stories, and there is no god but God, and, verily, God He is the mighty, the wise;

63 but if they turn back, God knows the evildoers.

64 Say, "O ye people of the Book, come to a word laid down plainly between us and you, that we will not serve other than God, nor associate aught with him, nor take each other for lords rather than God." But if they turn back then say, "Bear witness that we are resigned."

Three accusations directed toward Jews and Christians

65 O people of the Book, why do ye dispute about Abraham, when the law and the gospel were not revealed until after him? What! do

and Man; God, of the Essence of the Father; begotten before the worlds...This is the catholic faith; which except a man believe truly and firmly, he cannot be saved." Also see Augustine, *On the Trinity* (first published in A.D. 415).

3.59b *then He said to him BE, and he was* — Allah's sovereignty over all creation is illustrated in the fact that all He needs to do is say one word—*be*—and whatever it is He wishes comes into existence (see Q 3.47; 16.40; 19.35; 36.82; 40.68).

3.61 *we will imprecate and put God's curse on those who lie* — That is, Muhammad believed that Allah would invoke a curse on all who lie (believe that Jesus is the Son of God).

3.62 *there is no god but God* — The reason Muhammad denied the deity of Christ is because of his steadfast insistence upon an absolute monotheism—The Doctrine of Tauhid.

3.64 Muhammad then appealed to the

people of the Book—that is, Christians—not to serve other than God or associate aught with him. That is to say, they were not to worship Jesus Christ. If they refused to repent and turn to Allah and worship Him alone, Muslims were instructed to turn away from them and cease from further interreligious dialogue. In the place of such dialogue, they were to merely proclaim the truths of Islam.

3.65 *why do ye dispute about Abraham* — Muhammad noted that Jews and Christians had differing views about Abraham and his role in their religions (see Q 2.124, note).

3.65-74 Muhammad then presented three accusations against Jews and Christians (people of the Book). In each, they were characterized as either willfully ignorant of spiritual truth or people of deceit.

3.65-69 *The first accusation addressed the Christian view of Abraham.* Muhammad maintained that the Law (the Old Testament) and the Gospel (the New Testament) were

ye not understand?

66 Here ye are, disputing about what ye have some knowledge of; why then do ye dispute about what ye have no knowledge of? God knows and ye know not.

67 Abraham was not a Jew, nor yet a Christian, but he was a 'Hanîf resigned, and not of the idolaters.

68 Verily, the people most worthy of Abraham are those who follow him and his prophets, and those who believe;—God is the patron of the believers.

69 A sect of the people of the Book would fain they could lead you astray, but they only lead themselves astray, and they do not per-

---

revealed after Abraham (v. 65). As such, he was neither a Jew nor a Christian—but a *Hanif,* a pre-Islamic monotheist (see Q 30.30, note). Hence, Abraham had more in common with Islam (which is also steadfastly monotheistic) than with either Judaism or Christianity.

A Christian response is that Abraham is inextricably associated with both Judaism and Christianity. This is due to the Abrahamic Covenant that has application to both religions.

Its initial application was Judaism. God declared, "I will make you into a great nation and I will bless you; I will make your name great, and you will be a blessing. I will bless those who bless you, and whoever curses you I will curse; and all peoples on earth will be blessed through you" (Gen 12:2-3; cf 17:1-8). The covenant was then confirmed by means of animal sacrifice (see Gen 15:1-21).

The Abrahamic Covenant went through a series of transmissions. At first, it was passed down to his son Isaac (Gen 17:21; 21:10-12; 26:2-5; 48:15; Ex 2:24; 3:6; Heb 11:9). After that, the covenant was passed down to Jacob who was also called Israel (Gen 27:25-33; 28:6; 46:2-4; Heb 8:8-12). After that, the covenant divided into twelve parts, to each of the twelve tribes of Israel (Gen 49:1-28; Num 23:21-24; Rom 11:26-27). In spite of their sinfulness when, for

example, the people of Israel indeed fell into various forms of idolatry, they remained the covenanted people of God (Ps 69:35-36; Jer 30:18-22; 31:3-7; 33:7-9; Amos 9:11-12; Acts 15:16-18).

Christians understand themselves to be within the Abrahamic Covenant. The link between Christians and the Abrahamic Covenant is found in Jesus Christ. He is a direct descendent of Abraham and the one from whom all the nations of the world are blessed (Matt 1:2-16). The Epistle to the Galatians makes the same point: "The promises were spoken to Abraham and to his seed. The Scripture does not say 'and to seeds,' meaning many people, but 'and to your seed,' meaning one person, who is Christ. What I mean is this: The law, introduced 430 years later, does not set aside the covenant previously established by God and thus do away with the promise. For if the inheritance depends on the law, then it no longer depends on a promise; but God in his grace gave it to Abraham through a promise" (Gal 3:16-18).

Hence, Jesus Christ is the fulfillment of the Abrahamic Covenant. In the Old Testament, animal sacrifices brought about a covering from sin. In the New Testament, the death of Jesus Christ brought about a cleansing from sin. In this respect, the Old Testament animal sacrifices pointed forward to (anticipated) the death of Jesus Christ on the

| ceive.
70   O people of the Book! why do ye | disbelieve in the signs of God, the
while ye witness them? |

cross (Heb 9:13-14). Everyone who places his or her faith in Jesus Christ, then, are part of the Abrahamic Covenant and blessed by God. They are cleansed from their sins.

Moreover, Abraham had no association with Mecca. Muhammad's claim that Hagar and Ishmael traveled to the present site of Mecca when banished by Abraham contradicts the biblical account (Gen 21:14-20) and other historical records in the Mediterranean world (see Q 106.3, note, and **The Banishment of Hagar and Ishmael** on pp. 38, 39; **The City of Mecca** on pp. 32-34).

The fundamental difference between the Islamic and the Judeo-Christian understanding of Abraham, then, turns on the question of covenant (promise). In Islam, no such covenant exists. Abraham serves as the example of obedience and faithfulness. In the Judeo-Christian tradition, salvation is predicated upon God's promises to people via substitutionary atonement. In the Old Testament, it occurred through animal sacrifice. In the New Testament, it occurred through the death, burial, and resurrection of Jesus. Islam has no such covenant. People are burdened with the prospect of facing a celestial balance from they face God, hoping that their good works outweigh their bad.

3.70 *The second accusation addressed the Christian understanding of divine revelation.* Muhammad's criticism is that Christians claim to be committed to divine revelation, yet disbelieve the most recent divine revelation given to them: the Qur'an. This demonstrates a hypocrisy, an inconsistency, and a willful ignorance on their part.

A Christian response is that Christians are indeed committed to divine revelation, yet believe that the Qur'an is not of divine origin. This is due to the following.

First, *the Qur'an contains internal contradictions.* It claims to have existed in eternity with Allah and "sent down" to the earth via the archangel Gabriel who then dictated it to Muhammad (see Q 2.285; 3.3; 10.94; 14.1; 15.6, 9; 16.30, 44, 64, 89; 18.1; 20.2; 21.10, 50; 22.16; 25.1, 32; 28.87; 34.6; 38.29; 39.41; 42.15, 17; 43.31; 46.30; 64.8; 76.23). Yet, the surahs contain numerous evidences of being tied to historical events. Repeatedly, Muhammad is found dialoguing with Allah or his audience in the surahs, which is further evidence of it not being a timeless document. Even some Islamic scholars have acknowledged this fact, with the added explanation that the surahs being "sent down" is not to be taken literally—but figuratively. Still, the surahs themselves speak otherwise. The Doctrine of Abrogation and Q 87.6-7, note) is further evidence of the Qur'an not being a timeless document in Paradise.

Second, *the Qur'an contains external contradictions.* Perhaps the most significant of the external contradictions is the lack of historical evidence for the existence of Mecca prior to the fourth century, A.D. In the ancient period, several accounts of the topography of the Arabian Peninsula were written—none of which noted a city at the present site of Mecca (see Q 106, note, and Q 106.3, note). Furthermore, the earliest accounts of Abrahamic pilgrimages to Mecca were the seventh century, A.D. Though pilgrimages to Mecca occurred prior to seventh century, Muhammad was the first to associate these pilgrimages with Abraham.

This calls into question one of the foundational pillars of Islam—that the Ka'ba altar is historically connected to Abraham and Ishmael, who lived approximately 1800 B.C. (see *The City of Mecca* on pp. 32-34).

Other external contradictions involve statements in the Qur'an pertaining to other "apostles," such as Zali'h, Hud, Sho'haib, and Alexander the Great (Dhu 'Qarnain), and the Story of the Seven Sleepers of Ephesus. In each case, historical and archeological evidence contradicts the qur'anic record (see Q 91; 26.176-191; 18.9-26; 18.83-98, and related notes).

Third, *the Qur'an lacks miraculous credentials*. This is the criticism first articulated by John of Damascus (see *John of Damascus* on pp. 247-248). A common characteristic found in both Old and New Testaments is the presence of miraculous phenomena with the one who made known divine revelation. This was especially true when the divine revelation presented truths previously not known. Moses is a good example of this, as was Jesus and the apostles. By claiming that the Qur'an was the final and most complete divine revelation, and that it cancelled truths previously mentioned in other divine revelations that stood opposed to it, indisputable miraculous phenomena would necessarily had to have accompanied it as a way of establishing divine credentials to a new divine revelation.

Fourth, *the Qur'an makes use of spurious apocryphal literature*. It draws on *The Arab Gospel of the Infancy of Jesus*, the *Gospel of Thomas*, the *Infancy Pseudo Matthew Gospel*, the *Infancy Gospel of James*, and the *Second Targum of Esther*, presenting them as canonical documents and historically accurate.

Fifth, *the Qur'an contradicts fundamental teachings found in the Bible*. One such teaching is the Doctrine of Substitutionary Atonement. This is found in both Old and New Testaments and serves as the foundation to the biblical understanding of salvation from sin. Salvation is presented in terms of substitution: in the OT the blood of an animal is sacrificed in lieu of the sinner, in the NT the blood of Jesus Christ is sacrificed in lieu of the sinner. It is therefore a free gift to those who genuinely turn to God and desire it. It is a system of faith and grace which generates an attitude of thanksgiving which, in turn, spawns a desire to live one's life dedicated to God. Fear is replaced by a settled peace and a lasting gratitude.

The Qur'an rejects this teaching, replacing it with the notion of a celestial balance where one's good and bad works are weighed and measured against one another in the afterlife. Whichever side is greater determines the eternal destiny of the soul. It is a doctrine of works which leaves the devotee preoccupied with his eternal destiny. In such a system, a person cannot know—until the moment when standing before God at the Last Judgment—which direction the celestial balance will ultimately tip.

Hence, Christians have no difficulty labeling the Qur'an as false. Throughout the Bible, the people of faith were warned of false prophets who would seek to lead them astray. This warning was not only for the emergence of false prophets in the biblical era. It also includes the following centuries—including the seventh century. In this respect, words from the Apostle Paul are applicable. He wrote: "But even if we or an angel from heaven should preach a gospel other than the one we preached to you, let him be eternally condemned! As we have already said, so now I say again: If anybody is preaching to you a gospel other than what you accepted, let him be eternally con-

71   O people of the Book! why do ye clothe the truth with falsehood and hide the truth the while ye know?

72   A sect of the people of the Book say, "Believe in what was revealed to those who believed at the first appearance of the day,

73   and disbelieve it at the end thereof,"—that (others) may perchance go back (from their faith)—"do not believe save one who followeth your religion." Say, "Verily, the (true) guidance is the guidance of God, that one should be given like what ye are given." Or would they dispute with you before your Lord, say, "Grace is in the hand of God, He gives it to whom he pleases, for God both comprehends and knows.

74   He specially favours with his mercy whom he pleases, for God is Lord of mighty grace."

The question of honesty

75   And of the people of the Book,

there are some of them who, if thou entrust them with a talent give it back to you; and some of them, if thou entrust them with a dînâr, he will not give it back to thee except so long as thou dost stand over him. That is because they say, "We owe no duty to the Gentiles;" but they tell a lie against God, the while they know.

76   Yea, whoso fulfils his covenant and fears,—verily, God loves those who fear.

77   Those who sell God's covenant and their oaths for a little price, these have no portion in the future life. God will not speak to them, and will not look upon them on the resurrection day, and will not purify them; but for them is grievous woe.

78   And, verily, amongst them is a sect who twist their tongues concerning the Book, that ye may reckon it to be from the Book, but it is not from the Book. They say, "It is from God," but it is not from God, and they tell a lie against God, the

demned!" (Gal 1:8-9).

3.71-74 *The third accusation addressed the question of consistency of the Christian message.* Muhammad's point was that Christians attempted to confuse Muslims by affirming truths found in the early surahs ("the first appearance of the day") yet denying truths found in the latter surahs ("at the end thereof").

A Christian response is that some of the teachings found in the early surahs are indeed useful—specifically, the teachings that opposed the Arab paganism that dominated

almost all of the Arabian Peninsula. Still, much of what is found in the Qur'an stands opposite Christian beliefs.

3.75-80 According to Islamic scholars, the "people of the Book" mentioned in this verse were the Jews. Muhammad accused the Jews of dishonesty. Though some paid back their debts, most did so provided that one stood over them. This was because, said Muhammad, they refused to pay "duty to Gentiles." That is, they claimed to be under no moral obligation to pay their debts to those who were non-Jews.

while they know.

79 It is not right for a man that God should give him a Book, and judgment, and prophecy, and that then he should say to men, "Be ye servants of mine rather than of God;" but be ye rather masters of teaching the Book and of what ye learn.

80 He does not bid you take the angels and the prophets for your lords; shall He bid you misbelieve again when you are once resigned?

The solemn compact

81 And when God took the compact from the prophets, "(This is) surely what we have given you of the Book and wisdom. Then shall come to you the Apostle confirming what is with you. Ye must believe in him and help him." He said, moreover, "Are ye resolved and have ye taken my compact on that (condition)?" They say, "We are resolved." He said, "Then bear witness, for I am witness with you;

82 but he who turns back after that, these are sinners."

83 What is it other than God's religion that they crave? when to Him is

Muhammad also noted that in their attempts to justify this deceit with their Scriptures, they twisted what the Old and New Testaments actually said, claiming that "It is from God" when it is not from God.

3.79 Muhammad accused the Jews of making the claims of being a privileged people with divine truths revealed only to them.

3.81a *And when God took the compact from the prophets* — That is, Allah accepted, through the prophets, a solemn pledge from the Jews and Christians in Yathrib. It was, in so many words, a pledge to remain loyal to Allah and Allah's Prophet—Muhammad.

It is believed that in the years prior to Muhammad's migration to Yathrib (Medinah), the city had been embroiled in its own inner struggles and violence as differing tribes (extended families) vied for power—specifically, the pagan Arabs were pitted against the Jews. Peace was finally achieved when the tribes agreed to the conditions of the solemn compact.

3.81b *Then shall come to you the Apostle confirming what is with you* — Muhammad

explained to the people of Yathrib (Medinah) that he was a divinely chosen apostle sent to them to help them maintain the peace and confirm the compact. The Arabs in Yathrib (Medinah) readily embraced Muhammad, seeing him as one who could provide political leverage in the city politics against the Jews.

3.81c *We are resolved* — According to Muhammad, the people of Yathrib accepted his apostleship. They then changed the name of the city to Medinah (meaning: the City of the Prophet). Yet this agreement did not have the full support of the people of Yathrib. Many remained suspicious of his intentions and many others remained steadfastly opposed to his alleged apostleship and sought help from the people of Mecca to eradicate Muhammad and his followers from Medinah (Yathrib).

3.82 Muhammad noted that all who rejected his apostleship were labeled *sinners.*

3.83 Muhammad rhetorically asked: who else, besides Allah, do people seek to worship, since everyone in Paradise and on the

Jesus

Jesus was one of the supreme apostles. He is less in stature than Muhammad, yet still a major prophet sent from Allah. So said Muhammad. Muhammad also believed that the canonical New Testament documents had been corrupted

Virgin birth. Muhammad agreed with mainstream Christian scholarship in that he affirmed that Jesus was born of a virgin (Q 3.47; 19.16-22). But apart from this one point of similarity, in most all other ways Muhammad's Jesus contradicted what is found elsewhere in the New Testament.

Infancy and early childhood. In the early years of the life of Jesus, Muhammad drew principally from apocryphal Christian sources—particularly the various *Infant Gospels* (see Q 3.49 and 19.23-28). In one apocryphal account, while still an infant lying in a crib, for example, Jesus spoke and proclaimed himself to be a prophet sent from God. Speaking to Joseph and Mary, the infant Jesus reportedly said:

> Verily, I am a servant of God; He has brought me the Book, and He has made me a prophet, and He has made me blessed wherever I be; and He has required of me prayer and almsgiving so long as I live, and piety towards my mother, and has not made me a miserable tyrant; and peace upon me the day I was born, and the day I die, and the day I shall be raised up alive.[1]

Predictably, and in accord with Islamic doctrine, Muhammad modified this apocryphal account by replacing the words "I am Jesus, the Son of God" with "He has made me a prophet sent from God."

In these apocryphal sources, Jesus is presented as a child prodigy, sometimes as a child terror, performing numerous miracles in childlike innocence, such as the fashioning a number of birds from clay figurines which then came to life and flew away. Clive Marsh and Steve Moyise write, "What is surprising about *The Infancy Gospel of Thomas* is that the child prodigy also has a dark side, wreaking vengeance on those who oppose him."[2]

As an adult, Muhammad explained, Jesus presented truths from the eternal book in Heaven: submission to Allah, the giving of alms, and the life of prayer—that which he called the gospel (according to Muhammad, the gospel was, not surprisingly, identical to his message of piety that he had been presenting in his surahs).

End time prophecy. Though not mentioned in the Qur'an, in the hadithic literature Jesus is presented as returning to the earth in the last days, prior to the general resurrection of the dead and related apocalyptic activities (*Sahih Muslim* 041.7015; 001.0293). His role is to serve the Mahdi (the Islamic Messiah) who is already upon the earth. He will also disavow the Christian faith and admonish all peoples everywhere to become a Muslim (*Sahih Bukhari* 3.43.656; *Sunan Abu Dawud* 37.4310). These two Hadiths state that Jesus will "break the cross" and "abolish the *jizya* tax." Being subject to the Jizya tax, which in times past was an alternative for those who refused to convert to Islam, will cease to be an option. This means that (a) Jesus will abolish the worship of the cross, and (b) offer only two options to people: conversion to the Islamic faith or death.[3] In short, when Jesus returns to the earth, he will abolish the Christian religion and order the death on all who refuse to convert to Islam.

The question of deity. Muhammad rejected out of hand the notion that Jesus Christ is the Second Person of the Trinity, an individual who is fully God and fully man (see Q 2.146, 159; 4.171; 5.17-18, 72, 116-118). He regarded this as a irresolvable contradiction. It is not only illogical, it swerved into idolatry—the sin of *shirk* (a sin which condemns one to eternal condemnation).

More recently, Islamic scholars have described the doctrine of Jesus being fully God and man as a form of doublethink. Muhammad Ata al-Rahim has written,

> Doublethink lies at the root of a Christian's basic assumption that Christ is God. It is around this assumption that the controversy of the two natures of Jesus has raged. One moment he is human. The next moment he is divine. First, he is Jesus, then he is Christ. It is only by the exercise of doublethink that a man can hold these two contradictory beliefs simultaneously. It is only by the exercise of doublethink that belief in the doctrine of the Trinity can be maintained.[4]

The term *doublethink* was coined by George Orwell in his book *Nineteen*

Eighty-four. It is, he explained, "to be conscious of complete truthful-ness while telling carefully constructed lies, to hold simultaneously two opinions which cancelled out, knowing them to be contradictory and believing in both of them, to use logic against logic...to forget, whatever it was necessary to forget, then draw it back into memory again at the moment it was needed."[5]

The question of the crucifixion. Muhammad also maintained that Jesus was not crucified (Q 4.157-158). Rather, without the Roman guards being aware, a substitute was slipped in and crucified in his place. This teaching, of course, negated one of the cardinal doctrines within the Church: that by means of his death on the cross, Jesus took upon himself the sins of the world (John 3:1-16; Rom 5;1-11; 2 Cor 5:21). After his death, which occurred sometime much later, Allah raised him back to life and caused him to ascend to heaven (Q 3.55; 4.158).

Without deity and without the cross, the Jesus of Islam is little more than a good example. He showed the way to eternal life by living a godly life.

CHRISTIAN RESPONSE

In contrast to Islam, the New Testament presents Jesus as the God-man—fully God and fully man. Christian scholarship maintains that the *Infant Gospels* that circulated in the Mediterranean world and the Middle East were fictional accounts, not to be taken seriously, written long after the first century. For the most part, the four Gospels addresses the ministry of Jesus as an adult. And, as an adult, it offers to us three fundamental truths regarding Him.

Jesus is the God-man. The New Testament presents Jesus as fully God and fully man, the Second Person of the Trinity.[6] Though Islamic scholars regard this as a form of *doublethink*, Christian scholars regard it as a *mystery* that the human mind can only lightly understand. Alister McGrath writes, "For the early fathers, Jesus had to be both God and man if salvation was to be a possibility. If Jesus was not God, he could not save; if Jesus was not man, man could not be saved." The relationship between the two, however, is a mystery. McGrath adds, "The early Christians were actually far more interested in *defending* this insight, rather than trying to *explain* it! We must never fall into the trap of suspecting that the fathers thought that they were explaining how

Jesus could be both God and man—it is clear that they were simply trying to find ways of making sense of a *mystery*, something which in the end defied explanation."[7]

Jesus is the Savior. The New Testament also presents Jesus as the Savior of the world. Salvation is explained as a legal transaction between God and man. Though guilty of sin, we are declared righteous because Jesus willingly came forward to be our substitute. He stood between us and God the Father and took to Himself the penalty of our sin. On the cross, He then experienced the complete wrath of God the Father. The Apostle Paul said: "God made him who had no sin to be sin for us, so that in him we might become the righteousness of God."[8] Describing Jesus as a sacrificial lamb, John the Baptist added: "Look, the Lamb of God who takes away the sin of the world."[9]

If Jesus merely served as a guide, as Muhammad claimed, He could point to holiness, but that is all. Oswald Chambers explained: "If Jesus is a teacher only, then all He can do is to tantalize us by erecting a standard we cannot come anywhere near." We need more than a teacher. We need someone who can provide a divine pardon for our sins whereupon we are given clemency and declared righteous. We also need someone who can energize us from within so that we can gradually be conformed to a life of righteousness. Guides cannot do this. A Savior can. Chambers added: "But if by being born again from above we know Him first as Savior, we know that He did not come to teach us only: *He came to make us what he teaches we should be*"[10]

End-time prophecy. Jesus is the long awaited Messiah prophesied in the Old Testament. According to many Christian scholars, in the last days He will return to the earth, subdue all the kings of the earth, and establish His millennial kingdom (Ps 72:11; Isa 11:1-16; Acts 1:6-7; 1 Tim 6:14-15; Rev 17:14; 19:11-16). It will be a kingdom that affirms the Christian faith.

---

[1]   Q 19.30-33. Here Muhammad made use of the *Arabic Gospel of the Infancy of the Savior* as his source.

[2]   Clive Marsh and Steve Moyise, *Jesus and the Gospels*, p. 66.

[3]   See al-Misri, *Reliance of the Traveller*, p. 603.

[4]   Muhammad Ata ur-Rahim, *Jesus, a Prophet of Islam*, p. 198.

[5]   Orwell, George, *Nineteen Eighty-Four*, p. 31.

[6]   In this respect, the Church creeds were accurate summations of New Testament doctrine (see the *Definition of Chalcedon* on pp. 787-788; the *Nicene-Con-*

stantinopolitan *Creed* on p. 744; and *The Doctrine of the Trinity* on pp. 739-740).
   7   Alister McGrath, *Understanding Jesus*, p. 98.
   8   2 Cor 5:21.
   9   Jn 1:29.
   10 Oswald Chambers, *Studies in the Sermon on the Mount*, p. 10.

There runs a great tenderness for Jesus, yet a sharp dissociation from his Christian dimension. Islam registers a profound attraction but condemns its Christian interpretation...Islam finds his nativity miraculous but his Incarnation impossible.

—Kenneth Cragg, *Jesus and the Muslim*, p. 278

The prophet Muhammad is linked closely with Jesus as carrying on the same message of God's unity and the unity of the human race. Jesus sought to free the Jews from their tribalism, and so did Muhammad with the Arabs, and indeed with the rest of humankind.

—Russell Stannard, *God for the 21st Century*, p. 73

Folk Islam turned to Jesus not only in his qualities as prophet and teacher but also as mediator, healer, and miracle worker with great power. The name of Jesus assumed personal and supernatural qualities. There were prayers in His name. There were shrines named after Him.

—George Braswell, *What You Need to Know About Islam and Muslims*, p. 115

According to Muslim interpretation, Jesus' teachings coincided exactly with Islam, but they were distorted by Paul the Apostle and assumed their present form as accepted by Christians. Other polemicists held Constantine the Great responsible for falsifying Jesus' teachings, incorrectly assuming he declared Jesus' teachings to be the state religion of the Holy Roman Empire. According to Muslim belief, Jesus will not be a judge at the Last Judgment, corresponding to Christian doctrine, but a witness for the true faith of his followers, who did go astray by following Paul.

—Heribert Busse, *Islam, Judaism, and Christianity*, p. 168

Islam insists that neither Jesus nor Muhammad brought a new religion. Both sought to call people back to what might be called "Abrahamic faith." This is precisely what we find emphasized in the book of James.

—James D. Tabor, *The Jesus Dynasty*, p. 315

resigned whosoever is in the heavens and the earth, will he or nill he, and to him shall they return!

84 Say, "We believe in God, and what has been revealed to thee, and what was revealed to Abraham, and Ishmael, and Isaac, and Jacob, and the tribes, and what was given to Moses, and Jesus, and the prophets from their Lord,—we will make no distinction between any of them,—and we are unto Him resigned.

85 Whosoever craves other than Islam for a religion, it shall surely not be accepted from him, and he shall, in the next world, he of those who lose."

86 How shall God guide people who have disbelieved after believing and bearing witness that the Apostle is true, and after there come to them manifest signs? God guides the unjust folk.

87 These, their reward is, that on them is the curse of God, and of the angels, and of men together;

88 they shall dwell therein for aye— the torment shall not be alleviated from them, nor shall they be respited;

89 save those who repent after that, and act aright, for verily, God is forgiving and merciful.

---

earth are surrendered to Him and everyone will someday return to Him?

3.84 Muhammad sought a religion in Yathrib (Medinah) that was ecumenical in nature. Allah was identified as the God of Abraham, Ishmael, Isaac, Jacob, the Twelve Tribes, Moses, Jesus, and the Prophets. "We will make no distinction between any of them," he said.

A genuine and workable ecumenism between religions, however, proved to be elusive. It required an agreement on the essentials with the freedom to disagree on the nonessentials. The essentials upon which Muhammad insisted were: (a) a resolute commitment to monotheism—the Doctrine of Tauhid, (b) a commitment to a works-based orientation towards salvation—and he defined that which constituted good versus bad works, and (c) a commitment to him as the divinely appointed Apostle or Prophet.

Hence, Muhammad articulated an ecumenism that required the capitulation of many cardinal beliefs held by the Jews and Christians.

3.85 *Whosoever craves other than Islam for a religion, it shall surely not be accepted from him* — After tipping his hat to ecumenism in the previous verse, Muhammad revealed his true beliefs. He believed Islam to be exclusively true. All other religions are false, are not accepted by Allah, and will ultimately cause one devoted to a different religion to be subject to eternal damnation (see Q 2.256a, note, and Q 109, note).

3.86-88 Muhammad warned that disloyalty to the conditions of the compact would result in "the curse of God, and of the angels, and of men together," along with being tortured throughout eternity. Being cursed by men was ominous, pointing to a possible future a Jihad.

3.89-90 The only ones saved from Jihad would be those who repented of their disloyalty. Yet, those whose disloyalty was severe, and then repented, would not be re-

90 Verily, those who misbelieve after believing, and then increase in misbelief, their repentance shall not be accepted; these are those who err.

91 Verily, those who misbelieve and die in misbelief, there shall not be accepted from any one of them the earth full of gold, though he should give it as a ransom. For them is grievous woe, and helpers have they none.

92 Ye cannot attain to righteousness until ye expend in alms of what ye love. But what ye expend in alms, that God knows.

The first temple

93 All food was lawful to the children of Israel save what Israel made unlawful to himself before that the law was revealed. Say, "Bring the law and recite it, if ye speak the truth."

94 But whoso forges against God a lie, after that, they are the unjust.

95 Say, "God speaks the truth, then follow the faith of Abraham, a 'hanîf, who was not of the idolaters."

96 Verily, the first House founded for men was surely that at Bekkah, for a blessing and a guidance to the worlds.

97 Therein are manifest signs,— Abraham's station, and whosoever enters in is safe. There is due to God from man a pilgrimage unto the House, for whosoever can find his way there. But whoso misbelieves—God is independent of the worlds.

Two accusations

98 Say, "O people of the Book! why

ceived back or spared.

3.91-92 Muhammad's point is that those who deny the truth and were persistent in their denial would not be saved from the wrath of Allah, no matter how much gold they offered in tribute. Rather than wait until the Last Judgment, they should spend that money now in alms for the poor and needy.

3.95 Muhammad believed that Abraham was a *Hanif,* that is, a pre-Islamic monotheist (see Q 30.30, note). Since (a) Abraham had left Ur of the Chaldeans due to overwhelming commitment to idolatry, (b) lived prior to the establishment of the Israelite nation, and (c) the Israelite people had historically often fallen into the sin of idolatry,

Muhammad's distinguished Abraham from the Arab pagans and the Israelite people.

3.96 *the first House* — That is, the first temple. Muhammad believed that the Ka'ba altar in Mecca (Bekkah) was the first temple ever constructed with the intent of worshipping the one true God. It was constructed, said Muhammad, by Hagar and Ishmael, with the help of the archangel Gabriel. This dated its construction to approximately 1800 B.C. Yet, as already noted, historians have no record of Mecca or a temple existing in that proximity prior to the fourth century, A.D. (see **The City of Mecca** on pp. 32-34).

3.97 *Abraham's station* — Three traditions are associated with the term *Abraham's sta-*

do ye misbelieve in God's signs, while God is witness of what ye do?"

99 Say, "O people of the Book! why do ye turn from the way of God him who believes, craving to make it crooked, while ye are witnesses? But God is not careless of what ye do."

Two warnings to the Muslims

100 O ye who believe! if ye obey the sect of those to whom the Book was brought, they will turn you, after your faith, to unbelievers again.

101 How can ye misbelieve while unto you are recited the signs of God, and among you is His Apostle? But whoso takes tight hold on God, he is guided into the right way.

102 O ye who believe! fear God with the fear that He deserves, and die not save ye be resigned.

The problem of disunity

103 Take tight hold of God's rope altogether, and do not part in sects; but remember the favours of God towards you, when ye were enemies and He made friendship between your hearts, and on the morrow ye were, by His favour, brothers. Ye were on the edge of a pit of fire, but he rescued you therefrom. Thus does God show to you His signs, perchance ye may be guided;

tion (see Q 2.125 note).

3.98 Muhammad accused the Jews and Christians of rejecting divine revelation; namely, the qur'anic surahs. Jews and Christians, of course, accused Muhammad of exactly the same thing.

3.99 Muhammad also accused the Jews and Christians in transforming the gospel (the straight path) into a false gospel (a crooked path). Jews and Christians, of course, accused Muhammad of exactly the same thing.

3.100a *O ye who believe* — That is, Muslims.

3.100b *the sect of those to whom the Book was brought* — This could refer to either Jews or Christians since both faiths are grounded in Scripture. Muhammad warned the Muslims not to listen to the Jews or Christians since they could possibly turn them away from the Islamic faith. Accordingly,

Muslims were not to engage in a genuine inter-faith dialogue (see Q 3.20 note).

3.101a Muhammad believed it to be incredulous that Muslims would apostasize from the Islamic faith, given that they were acquainted with the qur'anic surahs and had the Apostle (himself) among them.

3.101b *the right way* — This is the path that leads to eternal life (see Q 72.2, note).

3.102 Muhammad admonished the Muslim believers not to die without first being fully submitted to Allah.

3.103-109 Muhammad envisioned that his Muslim community would grow into a nation that would invite others to the good works that he preached. This required that the Muslims did not break apart into competing sects (v. 103). Such a breaking apart into competing sects, of course, took place in the decades following the death of Muham-

104   and that there may be of you a nation who shall invite to good, and bid what is reasonable, and forbid what is wrong; these are the prosperous.

105   Be not like those who parted in sects and disagreed after there came to them manifest signs; for them is mighty woe,

106   on the day when faces shall be whitened and faces shall be blackened. As for those whose faces are blackened,—"Did ye misbelieve after your faith, then taste the torment for your misbelief!"

107   But as for those whose faces are whitened, they are in God's mercy, and they shall dwell therein for aye.

108   These are the signs of God. We recite them to you in truth, for God desires not wrong unto the worlds.

109   God's is what is in the heavens and what is in the earth, and unto God affairs return.

The weakness of Jews and Christians

110   Ye were the best of nations brought forth unto man. Ye bid what is reasonable, and forbid what is wrong, believing in God. Had the people of the Book believed, it would have been better for them. There are believers among them, though most of them are sinners.

111   They shall surely not harm you save a hurt; and if they fight you, they shall show you their backs, then they shall not be helped.

112   They are smitten with abasement wherever they be found, save for the rope of God and the rope of man; and they draw on themselves wrath from God. They are smitten, too, with poverty; that is because they did disbelieve in God's signs, and kill the prophets undeservedly. That is because they did rebel and did transgress.

113   They are not all alike. Of the people of the Book, there is a nation upright, reciting God's signs throughout the night, as they adore the while.

---

mad (e.g., the Sunni-Shi'ite divide).
3.106a *faces shall be whitened and faces shall be blackened* — This is symbolic. It had no reference to racism. Whitened faces represent those whose lives are full of good works, blackened faces represent those whose lives are full of evil works.
3.106b *Did ye misbelieve after your faith* — Muhammad claimed that Muslims who fell back into unbelief would be tortured by Allah.
3.110 *the people of the Book* — That is,

Jews and Christians. Muhammad believed that when fighting against Jews or Christians, the Muslims would handily prevail. Jews and Christians will flee when faced in open battle.
3.112-114 Muhammad added that the Jews and Christians were cowardly and worthy of death by hanging. He added that because Jews and Christians rejected the Qur'an, they were smitten with poverty. Still, a few of them crossed over and became believers in Allah and devoted to "the straight path" that leads to eternal life.

114 They believe in God, and in the last day, and bid what is reasonable, and forbid what is wrong, and vie in charity; these are among the righteous.

115 What ye do of good surely God will not deny, for God knows those who fear.

116 Verily, those who misbelieve, their wealth is of no service to them, nor their children either, against God; they are the fellows of the Fire, and they shall dwell therein for aye.

Parable of the Wind

117 The likeness of what they expend in this life of the world, is as the likeness of wind wherein is a cold blast that falls upon a people's tilth who have wronged themselves and destroys it. It is not God who wrongs them, but it is themselves they wrong.

The requirement of separation

118 O ye who believe! take not to inti-

macy with others than yourselves; they will not fail to spoil you; they would fain ye came to trouble,—hatred is shown by their mouths; but what their breasts conceal is greater still. We have made manifest to you our signs, did ye but understand.

119 Ye it is who love them, but they love not you; and ye believe in the Book, all of it. But when they meet you they say, "We believe;" and when they go aside they bite their finger tips at you through rage. Say, "Die in your rage, for God doth know the nature of men's breasts."

120 If good luck touch you it is bad for them, but if bad luck befall you they rejoice therein; yet if ye are patient and fear, their tricks shall not harm you, for what they do God comprehends.

Battle of Badr

121 When thou didst set forth early from thy people to settle for the believers a camp to fight;—but

3.116 Muhammad maintained that Jews and Christians who remained steadfast in their resistance to the Islamic faith were "fellows of the Fire" and "shall dwell therein for aye."

3.117 Jews and Christians who refused to embrace Islam were likened to a cold blast of wind that destroyed their own garden (tilth). The Book of Psalms in the Old Testament makes use of a similar metaphor for evil people: "They [the wicked] are like chaff that the wind blows away. Therefore the

wicked will not stand in the judgment, nor sinners in the assembly of the righteous" (Ps 1:4-5).

3.121-129 In this passage, Muhammad described the Battle of Badr (March 17, 624, the seventeenth day of Ramadan). To this day, the seventeenth day of Ramadan is held in especially high regard. In this battle, Muhammad's warriors were outnumbered three-to-one. After a dual where three Meccan champions fought three Muslim champi-

God both hears and knows;

122 —when two companies of you were on the point of showing cowardice; but God was their guardian, for on God surely the believers do rely.

123 Why! God gave you victory at Bedr when ye were in a poor way; fear God, then, haply ye may give thanks.

124 When thou didst say unto the believers, "Is it not enough for you that your Lord assists you with three thousand of the angels sent down from on high?

125 Yea, if ye are patient and fear God, and they come upon you on a sudden, now, your Lord will assist you with five thousand of His angels, (angels) of mark.

126 God only made this as glad tidings for you to comfort your hearts withal,—for victory is but from God, the mighty, the wise;

127 —to cut off the flank of those who misbelieve, or make them downcast, that they may retire disappointed."

128 Thou hast nothing to do with the affair at all, whether He turn to-

ons (with all three Meccans slain and one of the Muslims slain) a general battle ensued. The fighting quickly became a free for all and at its conclusion, the Muslims routed the Meccan opponents. It was followed by widespread plundering by the Muslim soldiers (see **The Battle of Badr** on pp. 680-682).

According to a Hadith, the Meccan losses at the Battle of Badr were "seventy of whom were captured and seventy were killed" (*Sahih Bukhari* 4.52.276). Muslims losses were fourteen dead (Martin Lings, *Muhammad: His Life Based on the Earliest Sources*, p. 148).

In a Hadith, Muhammad guaranteed entrance into Paradise all Muslims who died in battle. "The example of a *Mujahid* in Allah's Cause—and Allah knows better who really strives in His Cause...Allah guarantees that He will admit the *Mujahid* in His Cause into Paradise if he is killed, otherwise He will return him to his home safely with rewards and war booty" (*Sahih Bukhari* 4.52.46).

In another Hadith, a woman whose son had died in the Battle of Badr came to Muhammad burdened and asked of the eternal destiny of her son. "O Allah's Prophet! Will

you tell me about Hartha?" Hartha died as a martyr in the Battle of Badr. She added, "If he is in Paradise, I will be patient; otherwise, I will weep bitterly for him." He said, "O mother of Hartha! There are Gardens in Paradise...and your son got...the best place in Paradise" (*Sahih Bukhari*, 4.52.64).

3.124 Muhammad claimed that Allah added "three thousand angels sent down from on high" to help his warriors win the battle. He also believed that Allah disheartened the enemy which resulted in their retreat and ultimate defeat. In a Hadith it is reported that Muhammad said during the battle that the archangel Gabriel was "holding the head of his horse and equipped with arms for the battle" (*Sahih Bukhari*, 5.59.330). It later became part of Islamic folklore that "the sign of the angels at Badr was white turbans flowing behind them" (Ibn Ishaq, *The Life of Muhammad*, p. 303).

3.125 Muhammad believed that victory in battle was determined by the degree of piety of the warriors.

3.128-129 Muslims were admonished not to enter into romantic or marital relationships

wards them again or punish them; for, verily, they are unjust.

129 God's is what is in the heavens and in the earth. He forgives whom He pleases, and punishes whom He pleases; for God is forgiving and merciful.

The straight path

130 O ye who believe! devour not usury

doubly doubled, but fear God, perchance ye may be prosperous;

131 fear the fire which is prepared for the unbelievers,

132 and obey God and His Apostle, perchance ye may get mercy.

133 And vie with one another for pardon from your Lord, and for Paradise, the breadth of which is as the heaven and the earth, prepared for those who fear;

with Jews or Christians. Muhammad characterized Jews and Christians as deceitful and disloyal when it came to romantic and marital love. To enter into such an emotionally committed relationship risked Muslims veering away from the Islamic faith.

Both the Old and New Testaments admonished believers similarly. "Do not be yoked together with unbelievers. For what do righteousness and wickedness have in common? Or what fellowship can light have with darkness? What harmony is there between Christ and Belial? What does a believer have in common with an unbeliever? What agreement is there between the temple of God and idols? For we are the temple of the living God. As God has said: 'I will live with them and walk among them, and I will be their God, and they will be my people. Therefore come out from them and be separate,' says the Lord. 'Touch no unclean thing, and I will receive you. I will be a Father to you, and you will be my sons and daughters, says the Lord Almighty'" (2 Cor 6:14-18; cf. Deut 7:2-3; Ezra 9:1-2, 11-12; Neh 13:23-26; Mal 2:11; James 4:4).

3.130a *O ye who believe* — that is, Muslim believers.

3.130b *devour not usury doubly doubled* — That is, do not gorge yourself on the mon-

ies gained through usury, doubling and redoubling it (also see Q 2.275-281; 4.160-161; 30.39).

3.131 *fear the fire* — Muhammad insisted that everyone, including Muslim believers, should fear the fires of Hell. This is because the Doctrine of Salvation by Works leaves nobody secure or confident when it comes to the Last Judgment. The one exception was the Muslim who died as a martyr in Allah's Cause (see Q 3.121-129, note).

3.132 *obey God and His Apostle* — Muhammad elevated his spiritual status to that of Allah. The Muslim believer was to obey both Allah and Muhammad. To disobey Muhammad was tantamount to disobeying Allah with the net result being an eternal condemnation in Hell (see Q 3.32; 4.69, 79-80, 136; 5.80-81; 8.13, 20-23; 24.47, 48, 50-52, 54; 33.33, 71; 48.9-10; 57.19; 59.4; 72.22-23, 81.19-21 and 46.16, note).

The Christian is called upon to worship God, who is understood to exist in Three Persons—Father, Son, and Holy Spirit. Accordingly, the Christian is to obey the Father, and His Son, and His Spirit (see **The Doctrine of the Trinity** on pp. 735-736 and the **Definition of Chalcedon** on pp. 785-786).

3.133 *pardon from your Lord* — see **Di-**

134   —for those who expend in alms, in prosperity and adversity, for those who repress their rage, and those who pardon men; God loves the kind.

135   Those who when they do a crime, or wrong themselves, remember God, and ask forgiveness for their sins,—and who forgives sins save God?—and do not persevere in what they did, the while they know;—

136   —these have their reward:—pardon from their Lord, and gardens beneath which rivers flow, dwelling therein for aye; for pleasant is the hire of those who act like this.

No sympathy for the infidel

137   Incidents have passed before your time, go on then in the earth, and see what was the end of those who called (the prophets) liars.

138   This is an explanation unto men, and a guidance and a warning unto those who fear.

139   Do not give way nor grieve, for ye shall have the upper hand if ye but be believers.

140   If a sore touch you, a sore like it has touched people: these are days which we make to alternate amongst mankind that God may know who it is that believe, and may take from you witnesses, for God loves not the unjust;

141   and that God may assay those who believe, and blot out the misbelievers.

142   Do ye think that ye can enter Paradise and God not know those of you who have fought well, or know the patient?

143   Why, ye longed for death before ye met it! Now ye have looked

vine Forgiveness in Islam on pp. 158-161.

3.134 the straight path that leads to eternal life is laid out in this verse: giving alms, repress rage, and forgive others. According to Muhammad, these three activities contributes to one earning salvation.

3.135 *ask for forgiveness for their sins —* see **Divine Forgiveness in Islam** on pp. 158-161.

3.136 The reward of the righteous: (a) pardon from their Lord, (b) living in an oasis

3.139-140 Muslim believers were not to show sympathy or grieve when infidels suffered and died.

The Battle of Badr offers a telling illustration of these two verses. Abu Jahl, one of Muhammad's uncles, was one of his most resolute foes. Since Muhammad began raiding Meccan caravans, Abu Jahl joined the Meccan army, hoping to defeat Muhammad. At the conclusion of the battle, Abu Jahl lay mortally wounded. Abdullah ibn Mas'ud, one of Muhammad's warriors, cut off his head. In a Hadith, it is reported that Muhammad rewarded Abdullah ibn Mas'ud by giving him Jahl's sword for his bravery in killing Jahl (*Abu Dawud*, 14.2716; also see 14.2703 and Ibn Ishaq, *The Life of Muhammad*, p. 304). Moreover, Muhammad ordered that all the corpses of the enemy be cast into a filthy well (latrine). He then stood before the well and harangued the dead for their folly in resisting him (*Sahih Bukhari* 5.59.314).

3.144a This passage was another refer-

upon it and ye halt!

No retreats from the infidel

144 Mohammed is but an apostle; apostles have passed away before his time; what if he die or is killed, will ye retreat upon your heels? He who retreats upon his heels does no harm to God at all; but God will recompense the thankful.

145 It is not for any soul to die, save by God's permission written down for an appointed time; but he who wishes for the reward of this world we will give him of it, and he who wishes for the reward of the future we will give him of it, and we will recompense the grateful.

146 How many prophets have myriads fought against! yet they did not give way at what befell them in God's way! Nor were they weak,

nor did they demean themselves:— God loves the patient.

147 And their word was only to say, "Lord, forgive us our sins and our extravagance in our affairs; and make firm our footing and help us against the misbelieving folk!"

148 and God gave them the reward of this world, and good reward for the future too, for God doth love the kind.

Submission to
infidels forbidden

149 O ye who believe! if ye obey those who misbelieve, they will turn you back upon your heels, and ye will retreat the losers.

150 Nay, God is your Lord, He is the best of helpers.

151 We will throw dread into the hearts of those who misbelieve, for that

ence to the Battle of Uhud. During the battle, it was rumored that Muhammad had been killed. This news demoralized his soldiers. It also contributed to their defeat and brought some of them close to apostasy— abandoning the Muslim faith.

3.144b *God will recompense the thankful* — That is, Allah will reward those who fight valiantly in battle. Similar phrases are used later in this passage: "we will recompense the grateful" (v. 145) and "God loves the patient" (v. 146) and "God doth love the kind" (v. 148). In each case, the words *thankful, grateful, patient,* and *kind* refer to the soldiers' dedication to Allah and their willingness to become martyrs for the Cause of Allah.

3.145 The reward of eternal life was given to those who are "grateful" to Allah. In this context, it meant striving hard and fighting to the uttermost on His behalf.

3.146 *God's way!* — That is, Allah's Cause. In this context, it means joining the Jihad that Allah has proclaimed against the infidel (see Q 2.190, note).

3.149 *O ye who believe!* — That is, Muslim believers. Muhammad was steadfast that the Muslim believers were not to place themselves under the power and control of the infidel. If they do so, he said, they would be the losers.

3.151 *We will throw dread into the hearts of those who misbelieve* — Terror (striking dread into the hearts of the infidel) is part

The Battle of Badr

March 17, 624

The turning point for Muhammad took place in 624 at the legendary Battle of Badr. Prior to the battle, his small army of raiders had attempted to ambush and plunder a number of caravans moving through the Arabian western desert. In each case, he failed. He either arrived too early or too late at the rendezvous points and thereby missed the opportunities to attack the caravans. Aware of Muhammad's intentions, the caravans had become protected with armed soldiers. Such was the case at Badr. When Muhammad's raiders approached the caravan, the protective soldiers of the caravan intervened.

The battle began with a dual. The Meccan army sent three soldiers to dual three of the best soldiers of the Muslims. Those chosen by Muhammad were from his own family: Ali, Al Humza, and Obeidah al Harith. At the conclusion of the dual, all three of the Meccan soldiers were dead. Obeidah was also dead. The heads of the three dead Meccan soldiers were then cut off.

Afterwards, the general offensive began. Muhammad's soldiers stormed the lines of Meccans, which resulted in a general melee. The demoralized Meccan soldiers quickly broke rank and fled. Muhammad would later say that the angel Gabriel came down and fought on behalf of the Muslims.[1]

The Muslim people saw their victory as confirmation that Allah had indeed anointed Muhammad as prophet. "God gave you victory at Badr when ye were in a poor way; fear God, then, haply ye may give thanks."[2] "O Prophet! urge the believers to war; if there are twenty patient ones of you they shall overcome two hundred, and if there are a hundred of you they shall overcome a thousand of those who disbelieve, because they are a people who do not understand."[3]

All the possessions of the caravan were taken as booty. This small Muslim raiding army had acquired a reputation. It was a force to be reckoned with. In addition, writes Robert Spencer, with this victory a specific set of assumptions were instilled in their minds:

- Allah will grant victory to his people against foes that are superior in numbers or firepower, so long as they remain faithful to His commands.

- Victories entitle the Muslims to appropriate the possessions of the vanquished as booty.

- Bloody vengeance against one's enemies belongs not solely to the Lord, but also to those who submit to him on the earth.

- Prisoners taken in battle against the Muslims may be put to death at the discretion of Muslim leaders.

- Those who reject Islam are "the vilest of creatures" (Qur'an 98.6) and thus deserve no mercy.

- Anyone who insults or even opposes Muhammad or his people deserves a humiliating death—by beheading if possible. (This is in accordance with Allah's command to "smite the necks" of the "unbelievers" (Qur'an 47.4)).[4]

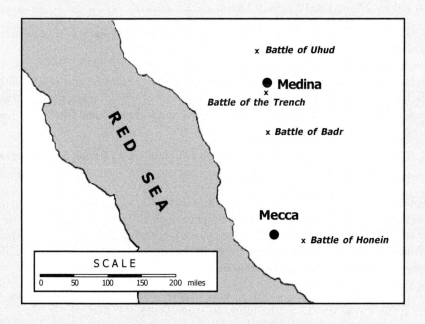

The Battle of Badr would later enter the canons of Muslim history as synonymous with the attitude of victory against all odds. In 1973, during the Yom Kippur War, Egypt's offensive against Israel was called "Operation Badr." The battle also inspired other Muslim warriors to engage in similar attacks of violence.

---

[1] Narrated by Ibn 'Abbas, *Sahih Bukhari*, 5.59.330.
[2] Q 3.123.
[3] Q 8.65.
[4] Robert Spencer, *The Politically Incorrect Guide to Islam and the Crusades* (Washington, D.C. Regnery Publishing, 2005), 10. Also see Q 47.4.

It was the noblest of battles and it was the day of criterion, on which Allah strengthened Islam and the Muslims, and on which He repelled polytheism and its adherents, in spite of the Muslims' smallness of numbers and the enemy's superiority of numbers, plus their abundance of steel, their complete preparedness, their powerful horses and their overweening pride and self-confidence. Allah strengthened His Messenger and made His Revelation manifest, honoured the Prophet and his followers and humiliated Satan and his cohorts.

—Sameh Strauch, *Biography of the Prophet*, p. 412

The presence of the Angels was felt by all, as a strength by the faithful and as a terror by the infidels, but that presence was only visible or audible to a few, and in varying degrees. Two men of a neighboring Arab tribe had gone to the top of a hill to see the issue and to take part—so they hoped—in the looting after the battle.

—Martin Lings, *Muhammad: His Life Based on the Earliest Sources*, pp. 151, 152

The home of the worldly nature is our bodily desires and passions (our *nafs*)...According to what has been reported, the Prophet, peace and blessings be upon him, after returning from the Battle of Badr said to his victorious friends: "You have now returned from the minor jihad to the major one." When he was asked, "What is the major jihad?" he replied: "It is jihad against the *nafs*." He is also reported to have said, "Real *mujahids* are those who fight against their *nafs*."

—Ergün Capan, *Terror and Suicide Attacks*, pp. 69, 70

they associate that with God. which He has sent down no power for; but their resort is fire, and evil is the resort of the unjust.

The Battle of Uhud

152 God has truly kept His promise, when ye knocked them senseless by His permission, until ye showed cowardice, and wrangled, and rebelled, after he had shown you what ye loved. Amongst you are those who love this world, and amongst you are those who love the next. Then He turned you away from them to try you; but He has pardoned you, for God is Lord of grace unto believers,—

153 when ye went up and looked not round upon any one, although the Apostle was calling you from your rear. Therefore did God reward you with trouble on trouble that ye should not grieve after what ye had missed, nor for what befell you, for God is well aware of what ye do.

---

of the Islamic *modis operandi.* In a Hadith, Muhammad acknowledged the value of terror, saying, "I have been made victorious with terror" (*Sahih Bukhari* 4.52.220; also see **Death of Abu Afak** on p. 686).

3.152-153 The Meccans depended upon trade with Syria for the city's survival. Due to Muhammad's continuing raids on caravans, the city had been placed in a crisis. The Meccans responded by altering the course of the caravans, having them travel across the open desert northward towards Persia. It was a lengthy and arduous journey. When Muhammad learned of one of these caravans, he sent a raiding party and encountered it at Nejd. The raid was successful and much booty was acquired.

Consequently, the Meccans decided to face Muhammad again in open battle. At the Battle of Uhud (March 19, 625), they assembled three thousand warriors and attacked Muhammad's army of one thousand. This time, Muhammad's army was routed. At the conclusion of the battle, Muhammad's face was bloodied and a tooth was knocked out. Vowing revenge, he said that the wrath of Allah would be fierce against the one who bloodied his face (Ibn Ishaq, *The Life of Muhammad,* p. 382).

The reason for the defeat, Muhammad later said, was because his warriors had not been fully obedient and faithful to Allah: "God has truly kept His promise, when ye knocked them senseless by His permission, until ye showed cowardice, and wrangled, and rebelled, after he had shown you what ye loved" (v. 152).

3.152a Muhammad reproached some of his soldiers, commenting that their love for this world was greater than was their love for the afterlife.

3.152b *He has pardoned you* — That is, Allah has given them a second chance. He forgave their sin, provided that they strive hard after him in the future.

3.153 *did God reward you with trouble on trouble* — That is, the realization of how shamefully they fought at Uhud was more grievous to them that what they missed: additional booty.

3.154 This verse is an illustration of the extreme form of predestination that Muham-

Allah's will cannot be averted

154   Then He sent down upon you after trouble safety,—drowsiness
creeping over one company of you,
and one company of you getting
anxious about themselves, suspecting about God other than the
truth, with the suspicion of the ignorant, and saying, "Have we any
chance in the affair?" Say, "Verily,
the affair is God's." They conceal
in themselves what they will not
show to thee, and say, "If we had
any chance in the affair we should

not be killed here." Say, "If ye were
in your houses, surely those
against whom slaughter was written down, would have gone forth
to fight even to where they are lying now; that God may try what is
in your breasts and assay what is
in your hearts, for God doth know
the nature of men's breasts."

155   Verily, those of you who turned
your backs on that day when the
two armies met, it was but Satan
who made them slip for something
they had earned. But God has now
pardoned them; verily, God is for-

mad taught. He believed that soldiers who
failed to leave Yathrib to fight in the battle
of Uhud, and thereby missed their appointment with death, would fall into a trance,
go to the now ended battlefield, lie down
and die (see **The Doctrine of al-Qadar** on
pp. 264-266).

3.154a *He sent down upon you after
trouble safety* — That is, Allah sent peace
after the battle.

3.154b *drowsiness creeping over one company of you* — That is, Allah caused one company of Muslims to become drowsy and not
think clearly.

3.154c *suspecting about God other than
the truth* — That is, they began to believe
lies, fearing that they were going to be killed
by the enemy.

3.154d *If ye were in your houses...* — That
is, if the soldiers remained in their houses in
Medinah and failed to join the battle.

3.154e *those against whom slaughter was
written down* — Their deaths were predestined, yet they averted their deaths by fail-
ing to enter the battle.

3.154f *would have gone forth to fight* —
Even though the battle was completed,
they would nevertheless go forth to the
battle and lie down and somehow die to fulfill
their predestined fate.

3.155 *it was but Satan who made them
slip for something they had earned* — Those
who fled from the face of the enemy were
tempted and controlled by Satan. When
placed in context with the other verses in
this passage, the reason for the defeat at
Uhud was a combination of cowardice and
the influence of Satan.

In the hadithic literature, a third possibility is presented: the warriors were drunk
(intoxicated with alcohol). One Muslim soldier explained the reason for the defeat:
"Some people drank alcoholic beverages in
the morning (of the day) of the Uhud battle
and on the same day they were killed as
martyrs, and that was before wine was prohibited" (*Sahih Bukhari*, 6.60.142).

A fourth possibility that explained the
Muslim defeat was that the Muslim army was
simply outnumbered. The Meccan army con-

giving and clement.

156 O ye who believe! be not like those who misbelieve, and say unto their brethren when they knock about in the earth, or are upon a raid, "Had they but been at home, they had not died and had not been killed." It was that God might make a sighing in their hearts, for God gives life and death; and God on what ye do doth look.

157 And if, indeed, ye be killed in God's way or die, surely forgiveness from God and mercy is better than what ye gather;

158 and if ye die or be killed it is to God ye shall be assembled.

159 It was by a sort of mercy from God thou didst deal gently with them, for hadst thou been rough and rude of heart they had dis-

persed from around thee. But pardon them, and ask forgiveness for them, and take counsel with them in the affair. As for what thou hast resolved, rely upon God; verily, God loves those who do rely.

160 If God help you, there is none can overcome you; but if He leave you in the lurch, who is there can help you after Him? Upon God then let believers rely.

Muhammad defends himself

161 It is not for the prophet to cheat; and he who cheats shall bring what he has cheated on the resurrection day. Then shall each soul be paid what it has earned, and they, shall not be wronged.

162 Is he who follows the pleasure of

---

sisted of three thousand soldiers. The Muslim army was one third the size: one thousand soldiers.

3.156-158 Apparently, a number of the Muslim people were gripped with deep regrets, believing that if only they would have remained at home and not attempted another caravan raid, many of their number would still be alive. Muhammad attempted to dissuade them of such thoughts. It was Allah who "gives life and death." If some should die, it was the will of Allah that they die.

3.159 According to this verse, following the defeat at Uhud, Muhammad did not reproach his followers due to the degree of their demoralization. If they had been reprimanded, the possibility existed that they would have permanently left him. Yet, curiously, a few

verses earlier Muhammad spoke otherwise, that he indeed reprimanded his soldiers (vv. 152-153).

3.160 Muhammad reminded his Muslim warriors that Allah is the one who grants victory. The implication is that devotion to Allah is fundamental to military victory.

3.161 *It is not for the prophet to cheat* — that is, Muhammad insisted that he did not deceive his followers by writing surahs and then falsely claiming them to be divine revelation. Apparently, following the defeat at Uhud, some of his followers questioned his prophetic credentials. It is also possible that the Jews in Yathrib (Medinah) who opposed his ministry began propagating the idea that he was a false prophet following his stunning defeat at Uhud.

3.162-163 Muhammad proclaimed that

The Death of Abu Afak

In addition to the raids on caravans, assassinations took place. Abu Afak, a Jewish man of one hundred and twenty years, wrote poetry critical of Muhammad, calling him a crazed man. To listen to Muhammad, he explained, required one to set aside one's rational intelligence. Muhammad ordered his assassination. In a Hadith, Ibn Sa'd wrote:

> then occurred the "sariyyah [raid] of Salim Ibn Umayr al-Amri against Abu Afak, the Jew, in [the month of] Shawwal in the beginning of the twentieth month from the hijrah [immigration from Mecca in 622] of the Apostle of Allah. Abu Afak, was from Banu Amr ibn Awf, and was an old man who had attained the age of one hundred and twenty years. He was a Jew, and used to instigate the people against the Apostle of Allah, and composed verses.
>
> Salim Ibn Umayr who was one of the great weepers and who had participated in [the Battle of] Badr, said, "I take a vow that I shall either kill Abu Afak or die before him." He waited for an opportunity until a hot night came, and Abu Afak slept in an open place. Salim ibn Umayr knew it, so he placed the sword on his liver and pressed it till it reached his bed. The enemy of Allah screamed and the people who were his followers, rushed to him, took to his house and interred him.[1]

Following his death, a Jewish woman with five small children was outraged and composed her own poetry, condemning Muhammad for what he had ordered. Muhammad then went to his pulpit and cried out: "Who will rid me of Marwan's daughter?" Another of Muhammad's followers took up the challenge and put her to death.[2]

---

[1] Ibn Sa'd, *Kitab Al-Tabaqat Al-Kabir*, vol.2, pp. 31-32; also see Ibn Ishaq, *The Life of Muhammad*, p. 675.

[2] See Ibn Ishaq, *The Life of Muhammad*, p. 676.

God, like him who has drawn on himself anger from God, whose resort is hell? An evil journey shall it be!

163 These are degrees with God, and God sees what ye do.

164 God was surely very gracious to the believers, when He sent amongst them an apostle from themselves, to recite to them His signs, and purify them, and teach them the Book and wisdom, although they surely were before his time in manifest error.

Hypocritical Muslims

165 Or when an accident befalls you, and ye have fallen on twice as much, ye say, "How is this?" Say, "It is from yourselves. Verily, God

is mighty over all."

166 And what befell you the day when the two armies met, it was by God's permission; that He might know the believers,

167 and might know those who behaved hypocritically; for it was said to them, "Come, fight in God's way," or "repel (the foe);" they said, "If we knew how to fight we would surely follow you." They were that day far nigher unto misbelief than they were to faith. They say with their mouths what is not in their hearts, but God doth know best what they hid.

168 Those who said of their brethren, whilst they themselves stayed at home, "Had they obeyed us they would not have been killed." Say, "Ward off from yourselves death,

false prophets were destined for Hell. Yet he was confident that Allah was able to distinguish one from the other, since He sees and knows everything.

3.164 Muhammad reiterated that he was a divinely chosen apostle who recited divine revelation to his followers and taught them divine wisdom.

3.165a *twice as much* — Muhammad sought to remind his followers that though they suffered a defeat, they had inflicted a defeat on their enemies twice its size at the Battle of Badr.

3.165b *It is from yourselves* — Muhammad added that the defeat at Uhud was because they were not sufficiently committed and dedicated to do the will of Allah. In other words, if they would have been wholly committed to Allah, no matter the size of the

enemy, they would have prevailed.

3.166-167a The purpose of the defeat, Muhammad added, was to reveal genuine believers from "those who behaved hypocritically." This is a reference to an event that took place prior to the Battle of Uhud. Three hundred of the Muslim soldiers turned back and returned to Medinah.

3.167b *They were that day far nigher unto misbelief than they were to faith* — That is, the hypocrites had come close to falling into the sin of apostasy.

3.168 Some of the Muslims were thankful that they stayed at home and did not join the fight at Uhud. With a tone of sarcasm, Muhammad exclaimed: "Ward off from yourselves death, if ye do speak the truth."

3.169-173 Muhammad believed that those who die in battle in Allah's Cause (that is,

if ye do speak the truth."

The martyr's reward

169   Count not those who are killed in
the way of God as dead, but living
with their Lord;—provided for, rejoicing in what God has brought
them of His grace,

170   and being glad for those who have
not reached them yet,—those left
behind them; there is no fear for
them, and they shall not be grieved;

171   glad at favour from God and grace,
and that God wasteth not the hire
of the believers.

172   Whoso answered to the call of God
and of His prophet after sorrow
had befallen them, for those, if
they do good and fear God, is a
mighty hire.

173   To whom when men said, "Verily,
men have gathered round you, fear
then them," it only increased their
faith, and they said, "God is
enough for us, a good guardian is
He."

174   Then they retired in favour from
God and grace; no evil touched
them; they followed the pleasure
of God, and God is Lord of mighty
grace.

---

those who die while participating in Jihads) are provided for in the afterlife. They have acquired "a mighty hire"—that is, their admission into Paradise is guaranteed (see Q 47.4-6 and Q 3.121-129 note).

Understanding the logic to this requires one to reflect on the nature of Islam itself. The word *islam* means surrender—specifically, it is surrender to the will of Allah. Since there is no act of surrender more complete than that of martyrdom in the Cause of Allah, those who die as martyrs fully embody the noblest virtues of *Islam.*

In contrast, Christians have a different understanding of martyrdom. Since Christianity affirms the Doctrine of Salvation by Faith *apart from works* (Eph 2:8-10; Titus 3:4-8), salvation is not predicated upon the degree or quality of one's surrender to the will of God. Rather, salvation is a question of faith in Jesus Christ, embracing Him as the Savior from sin. "God made him who had no sin to be sin for us, so that in him we might become the righteousness of God" (2 Cor 5:21; cf. Rom 5:1-11). Martyrdom, then, has no bearing on a person entering heaven. Rather, it is an expression of genuine faith—a demonstration of a thankful heart for all that Allah has done on behalf of the individual. It also serves as an example to others, of total commitment.

3.170a *and being glad for those who have not reached them yet* — Muslims were admonished to rejoice for their fallen brethren who died in the cause of Jihad.

3.170b *there is no fear for them* — That is, martyrs will experience no fear in the afterlife. Therefore, "they should not be grieved."

3.172 This is an allusion to those who died (suffered martyrdom) during the Battle of Uhud. They achieved "a mighty hire"—that is, they earned salvation and automatically entered Paradise.

3.173 When faced with imminent death, surrounded by enemy combatants, a committed Muslim possessed an increased faith with a steadfast confidence in Allah.

175   It is only that Satan who frightens his friends. Do not ye fear them, but fear me, if ye be believers.

176   Let them not grieve thee who vie with each other in misbelief. Verily, they cannot hurt God at all. God wills not to make for them a portion in the future life; but for them is mighty woe.

177   Verily, those who purchase misbelief for faith, they do not hurt God at all, and for them is grievous woe.

178   Let not those who misbelieve reckon that our letting them range is good for themselves. We only let them have their range that they may increase in sin. And for them is shameful woe.

179   God would not leave believers in the state which ye are in, until He discerns the vile from the good. And God would not inform you of the unseen, but God chooses of His apostles whom He pleases.

"Wherefore believe ye in God and His Apostle; and if ye believe and fear, for you is mighty hire."

Warning to the Jews

180   And let not those who are niggard of what God has given them of His grace, count that it is best for them;—nay, it is worse for them. What they have been niggard of shall be a collar round their necks upon the resurrection day. And God's is the heritage of the heavens and the earth, and God of what ye do is, well aware.

181   God heard the speech of those who said, "Verily, God is poor and we are rich." We will write down what they said, and how they killed the prophets undeservedly, and say, "Taste ye the torment of burning;"

182   this shall they suffer for what their hands have sent on before;—for, verily, God is no unjust one to His

---

3.175 *It is only Satan who frightens his friends* — Muhammad believed that it was possible that Satan would cause one's friends to become fearful if a Muslim should contemplate becoming a martyr on behalf of the Cause of Allah. The Muslim should not allow their fear dissuade him or her from the path that Allah has determined for him or her.

3.177-179 According to Muhammad, a rejection of the call to martyrdom was a sign of unbelief and possible spiritual apostasy.

3.180-186 According to most Islamic scholars, this passage is an indictment of the materialism that characterized the Jews in

Yathrib (Medinah). They would suffer, Muhammad said, in the afterlife when they "taste the torment of burning" (v. 181).

3.180 *a collar round their necks* — Collars were used to keep slaves confined. The point was that wealth serves to enslave, in this life as well as the afterlife.

3.181 *God is poor and we are rich* — That is, we are richer than Allah. The Jews satirized Allah, insisting that He was a god without wealth. Their words, however, will be used against them when they are condemned to the tortures of Hell.

3.183-184 The Jews demanded a sign from

servants,

183 —who say, "Verily, God has covenanted with us that we should not believe in an apostle until he gives us a sacrifice which fire devours." Say, "There have come to you apostles before me with manifest signs, and with what ye talk about; why then did ye kill them, if ye speak the truth?"

184 And if they did call thee a liar, apostles before thee have been called liars too, who came with manifest signs, and with scriptures, and with the illuminating Book.

185 Every soul must taste of death; and ye shall only be paid your hire upon the resurrection day. But he who is forced away from the fire and brought into Paradise is indeed happy; but the life of this world is but a possession of deceit.

186 Ye shall surely be tried in your wealth, and in your persons, and ye shall surely hear from those who have had the Book brought them before you, and from those who associate others with God, much harm. But if ye be patient and fear,—verily, that is one of the determined affairs.

187 When God took the compact from those who have had the Book brought them that "Ye shall of a surety manifest it unto men, and not hide it," they cast it behind their backs, and bought therewith a little price,—but evil is what they buy.

188 Count not that those who rejoice in what they have produced, and love to be praised for what they have not done,—think not that they are in safety from woe,—for them is grievous woe!

Final prayer

189 God's is the kingdom of the heavens and the earth, and God is mighty over all!

190 Verily, in the creation of the heavens and the earth, and in the succession of night and day, are, signs to those possessed of minds;

191 who remember God standing and

Muhammad, similar to the sign that was given to the prophet Elijah at Mount Carmel (see 1 Kings 18:20-46). Muhammad's response was that even when miraculous signs had been given to the Jews, they still killed the prophets and remained idolatrous (see Jer 2:30; Matt 5:12; 23:37; Acts 7:51-52).

3.186-188 This passage was a warning that harm was soon to come upon the Jews in Yathrib (Medinah) for having offended Allah. They would be tried in their wealth (that is, it will be taken from them) and in their persons (that is, they will suffer personal harm). The destruction that the Jews of previous eras experienced would serve as a testimony of the suffering that would soon be brought to bear on them. For them, Muhammad said, "is grievous woe."

3.189 Muhammad drew the attention of his listeners to the greatness of Allah and encouraged them to remain committed and surrendered to do His will.

sitting or lying on their sides, and reflect on the creation of the heavens and the earth. "O Lord! thou hast not created this in vain. We celebrate Thy praise; then keep us from the torment of the fire!

192 Lord! verily, whomsoever Thou hast made to enter the fire, Thou hast disgraced him; and the unjust shall have none to help them.

193 Lord! verily, we heard a crier calling to the faith, 'Believe in your Lord,' and we did believe. Lord! forgive us our sins and cover our offences, and let us die with the righteous.

194 Lord! and bring us what Thou hast promised us by Thy apostles, and disgrace us not upon the resurrection day; for, verily, Thou dost not break Thy promises!"

195 And the Lord shall answer them, "I waste not the works of a worker amongst you, be it male or female,—one of you is from the other. "Those who fled, and were turned out of their houses, and were harmed in my way, and who fought and were killed, I will cover their offences, and I will make them enter into gardens beneath which rivers flow." A reward from God; for God, with Him are the best of rewards.

Final admonition

196 Let it not deceive you that those who misbelieve go to and fro in the earth.

197 It is a slight possession, and then their resort is Hell; an evil couch shall it be.

198 But those who fear their Lord, for them are gardens beneath which rivers flow, and they shall dwell therein for aye,—an entertainment from God; and that which is with God is best for the righteous.

199 Verily, of the people of the Book are some who do believe in God, and in what has been revealed to you, and what was revealed to them, humbling themselves before God, and selling not the signs of God for a little price. These shall

3.191 In Islamic theology, one does not know his or her eternal destiny until at the Last Judgment when a decision is rendered. Hence, the preoccupation and fear of Hell, as illustrated in this verse.

3.192 *whomsoever Thou has made to enter the fire* — This is a reference to double predestination (see **The Doctrine of al-Qadar** on pp. 264-266).

3.193 *forgive us our sins* — According to Muhammad, divine forgiveness is only extended to those whose lives merit forgiveness (see **Divine Forgiveness in Islam** on pp. 158-161).

3.195 Muhammad envisioned Allah answering his prayer with a reminder of the reward awaiting all who had become martyrs in his Cause. They will enter the gardens of Paradise (see vv. 169-179).

3.196-200 The Muslim believers were reminded to not be deceived by the infidels who would draw them away from Islam and cause them to become apostates (see Q 3.20, 100).

have their reward with their Lord; verily, God is quick at reckoning up.

200   O ye who believe! be patient and vie in being patient, and be on the alert, and fear God, that haply ye may prosper.

Surah 8

In the name of the merciful and compassionate God.

The spoils of war

1   They will ask thee about the spoils.

Say, "The spoils are God's and the Apostle's; fear God and settle it amongst yourselves; obey God and the Apostle if ye do believe."

2   Verily, the believers are those who, when God's name is mentioned, their hearts sink with fear; and when His signs are rehearsed to them they increase them in faith; and on their Lord do they rely;

3   who are steadfast in prayer, and of what we have bestowed, upon them give in alms;

4   these are in truth believers; to them are degrees with their Lord, and forgiveness, and a generous provision.

Surah 8. The title of this surah, *The Spoils*, comes from v. 1. It addresses various concerns related to the Doctrine of Jihad, including the dividing of spoils, the treatment of prisoners, the entering into treaties with non-Muslims, suing of peace, and the effects of personal piety in the outcome of battles. **8.1** *the spoils are God's and the Apostle's* — That is, the spoils of war (war booty) were not the property of the soldiers. Rather, they were to be distributed under the authority of Muhammad, guided by the will of Allah.

The occasion for this statement was an event that occurred in the aftermath of the Battle of Badr. According to Ibn Ishaq, those who had fought and remained at the battlefield claimed the booty for themselves. Yet, those who fought and pursued the enemy by leaving the battlefield also insisted that if it were not for their efforts in routing the enemy the battle would not have been won. Hence, they too made a claim on the booty.

Moreover, those who had guarded Muhammad and had not engaged directly in the battle made an additional claim on the booty. In response, on a sand hill called Sayar, Muhammad gathered his warriors together and divided the booty evenly among them, irrespective of their role in the battle (see *The Life of Muhammad*, pp. 307-308).

8.2-4 Apparently, a number of the warriors grumbled over the amount of booty that they received. In response, Muhammad explained that true Muslim believers were content to fear Allah, remain steadfast in prayer, give alms, and accepted the amount of the war booty that he deemed appropriate.

8.4 *degrees with their Lord* — That is, the level of Paradise that they will inhabit. The higher levels are closer to the dwelling of Allah and therefore more elegant. The lower levels are still elegant, but less so. The "generous provision" refers to the provisions in Paradise.

Battle of Badr

5   As thy Lord caused thee to go forth from thy house with the truth, although a sect of the believers were averse therefrom.
6   They wrangled with thee about the truth after it was made plain, as though they were being driven on to death and looked thereon;
7   and when God promised you that one of the two troops should be yours, and ye would fain have had those who had no arms God wished to prove the truth true by His words, and to cut off the hin-

dermost parts of those who misbelieve
8   —to prove the truth true, and to make vain the vain, although the sinners are averse.
9   When ye asked for succour from your Lord, and He answered you, "I will assist you with a thousand angels, with others in reserve."
10   God made it only glad tidings to quiet your hearts therewith; for victory is only from God! verily, God is mighty and wise.
11   When drowsiness covered you as a security from Him,—and He sent down upon you from the heavens

8.5a *as the Lord caused thee to go forth from thy house with the truth* — That is, as Allah caused you to go forth from your house in the cause of truth. Muhammad equated the Cause of Jihad with the Cause of Truth. In his eyes, they were the same.

8.5b-6 *although a sect of the believers were averse therefrom* — Some of the Muslim soldiers were reluctant to attack the Meccan caravan in the Valley of Badr, believing that they would die in the ensuing battle.

8.7a Muhammad claimed that prior to the battle Allah told him that half of the enemy would be destroyed.

8.7b *cut off the hindermost parts* — Muhammad claimed that Allah promised him victory over all of western Arabia—to the hindermost parts. The Battle of Badr, then, was reckoned as the first of many Islamic victories.

8.8 Muhammad believed that the victory of Badr validated his assertion that the way of Islam was the way of truth. The purpose of the victory was to establish truth in western

Arabia and to clearly show the vanity (emptiness, worthlessness) of the way of the unbelievers. With this in mind, Muhammad renamed the region of northwestern Arabia the *Hejaz*, meaning the area of ignorance, barbarism or vanity.

This is illustrated by a comment made by Muhammad following the battle. As the dead Meccan soldiers were cast into a pit near the site of the battle, he said: "O people of the pit, have you found that what God threatened is true? For I have found that what my Lord promised me is true." When those nearby asked why he was speaking to dead people, he replied that they heard him (Ibn Ishaq, *The Life of Muhammad*, p. 305).

8.9 Muhammad believed that he was assisted by a thousand angels (with others in reserve) in the victory at the Battle of Badr (see Q 3.124, note). The implication is that the Muslim jihadists were not entitled to the spoils since the victory of the battle rightly belonged to the angels.

8.11 *when drowsiness covered you as a*

water to purify you withal, and to take away from you the plague of Satan, and to tie up your hearts and to make firm your footsteps.

12   When your Lord inspired the angels—"Verily, I am with you; make ye firm then those who believe; I will cast dread into the hearts of those who misbelieve,—strike off their necks then, and strike off from them every finger tip."

13   That is, because they went into opposition against God and His Apostle; for he who goes into opposition against God and His Apostle—verily, God is keen to punish.

14   There, taste it! since for the misbelievers is the torment of the Fire.

Five characteristics
of the heroic soldier

15   O ye who believe! when ye meet those who misbelieve in swarms, turn not to them your hinder parts;

16   for he who turns to them that day his hinder parts save turning to fight or rallying to a troop, brings down upon himself wrath from God, and his resort is hell, and an ill journey shall it be!

17   Ye did not slay them, but it was God who slew them; nor didst thou shoot when thou didst shoot, but God did shoot, to try the believers from Himself with a goodly trial; verily, God both hears and knows.

18   There I verily, God weakens the

security from Him — That is, when a profound sense of calm entered your heart. Muhammad believed that Allah sent down to him water from Paradise to purify his heart from the plague of Satan (the terror of Satan) and thereby establish his feet so that he could make war.

8.12a   As the battle ensued, the Meccan forces, which outnumbered the Muslim forces by three-to-one, were disheartened and the routed. Muhammad believed that this was due to the hidden unseen work of angels who struck fear in the hearts of the enemy.

8.12b   In the aftermath of the battle, Muhammad ordered his soldiers to cut off the heads and finger tips of the slain Meccan soldiers.

8.13   According to Muhammad, all who opposed Allah and Muhammad would be tortured in Hell forever (see Q 3.32, and 46.16,

note). Muhammad was subtly elevated himself to the status normally reserved for Allah.

8.15   The phrase "O ye who believe" is mentioned five times in this passage (vv. 15, 20, 24, 27, 29). In each case, it addresses a different aspect of commendable attitudes related to Islamic spirituality while in combat.

8.15-19   The first characteristic of the heroic soldier addressed the question of *the temptation to retreat while in battle*. Muslim soldiers were not to retreat in the face of a larger enemy force. The only exception was for the purposes of regrouping and counterattacking. Those who fled the battle as cowards would bring upon themselves the wrath of Allah.

8.17   *it was God who slew them* — That is, all glory belongs to Allah for the victory in battle. It was Allah who directed the ar-

stratagem of the misbelievers.

19   If ye wish the matter to be decided, a decision has now come to you; but if ye desist, it is better for you; and if ye turn back we will turn too, and your troop shall avail nothing, great in number though it be, since God is with the believers!

20   O ye who believe! obey God and His Apostle, and turn not from Him while ye hear,

21   and be not like those who say, "We hear," and yet they hear not.

22   Verily, the worst of beasts in God's sight are the deaf, the dumb who do not understand.

23   Had God known any good in them, He would have made them hear; but had He made them hear, they would have turned back and have swerved aside.

24   O ye who believe! answer God and His Apostle when He calls you to that which quickens you; and know that God steps in between man and his heart; and that to Him ye shall be gathered.

25   And fear temptation, which will not light especially on those of you who have done wrong; but know that God is keen to punish.

26   Remember when ye were few in number and weak in the land, fearing lest people should snatch you away; then He sheltered you and aided you with victory, and provided you with good things; haply ye may give thanks.

27   O ye who believe! be not treacherous to God and His Apostle; nor

---

rows so that they reached their targets and defeated the enemy.

8.19a *If ye wish the matter to be decided* — That is, if you prayed for victory, you will receive victory.

8.19b *if ye desist, it is better for you* — That is, if you refrain from sinning and maintain a life of piety, victory would come your way.

8.19c *if ye turn back we will turn too* — That is, if you turn back on Allah and live a life of sin, Allah will deny the Muslims victory in the field of battle.

8.20-23 The second characteristic of the heroic soldier addressed the question of *obedience to the voice of both Allah and Muhammad.* Those who did not were likened to the spiritually deaf and dumb, characteristics of the infidel (see Q 2.18, 171). Again, Muhammad elevated his status to a level commensurate with Allah. That is, to disobey Muhammad in tantamount to disobeying Allah with the net result being an eternal condemnation in Hell (see Q 3.32; 4.69, 79-80, 136; 5.80-81; 8.13, 24.47, 48, 50-52, 54; 33.33, 71; 48.9-10; 57.19; 59.4; 72.22-23 and 46.16, note).

8.24-26 The third characteristic of the heroic soldier addressed the question of *the call to battle.* In the Battle of Uhud, some of the Muslims refused to leave their homes in Medinah and join in the battle (see Q 3.156-158). Muhammad claimed that those who refused to fight would one day face Allah who was "keen to punish." Those who did fight, on the other hand, would be sheltered by Allah who would aid them in being victorious in battle.

8.27-28 The fourth characteristic of the heroic soldier addressed the question of

be treacherous to your engagement while ye know!

28   Know that your wealth and your
children are but a temptation, and
that God—with Him is mighty
hire!

29   O ye who believe! if ye fear God
He will make for you a discrimination, and will cover for you your
offences, and will forgive you; for
God is Lord of mighty grace.

The craftiness of the infidel

30   And when those who, misbelieve
were crafty with thee to detain thee
a prisoner, or kill thee, or drive thee
forth; they were crafty, but God
was crafty too, for God is best of

crafty ones!

31   But when our verses were rehearsed to them they said, "We
have already heard.—If we
pleased we could speak like this;
verily, this is nothing but tales of
those of yore."

32   When they said, "O God! if this be
truth, and from Thee, then rain
upon us stones from heaven or
bring us grievous woe!"

33   But God would not torment them
while thou art amongst them; nor
was God going to torment them
while they asked Him to forgive.

34   But what ails them that God should
not torment them while they turn
folk away from the Holy Mosque,
though they are not the guardians

treachery to Allah and Muhammad. Heroic
soldiers were not treacherous. Treachery
would occur if a soldier was to commit to
fight and then turn away from that commitment due to concerns of his family, if he were
to die in battle.

8.28-29 The fifth characteristic of the heroic solider addressed the question of *the
rewards of Allah*. Allah's rewards are: (a)
the soldier would become a discriminator—a
keen awareness of the knowledge of right
and wrong, which is indispensable for the
one seeking eternal life, and (b) cover your
offences and forgive you—another provision
for the one seeking eternal life.

8.30 At times, infidels would have their
moments of victory. They would either cap-
ture, kill, or drive Muslims from lands that are
rightfully theirs. And this they would accomplish due to their cunning and craftiness. Yet,
Muhammad explained, Allah is all the more

cunning and crafty. Accordingly, the victory
of infidels is only momentary. In the end,
the victory will belong to Allah.

8.31 A common attitude of the infidel was
to regard the Qur'an as the composition of
man and not of God (see Q 3.70, note).

8.32-33 This statement was a taunt believed by some Islamic scholars to reference
the destruction of Sodom and Gomorrah, spoken by the Meccan people while Muhammad
still lived in Mecca. Since Muhammad often
referenced the destruction of these cities
as the judgment of Allah upon infidels, they
taunted him asking that such a destruction
befall their city.

8.34-35 When this surah was first presented, Mecca was under the control of Muhammad's enemies. He therefore noted that
the infidels also falsely saw themselves as the
guardians of the Ka'ba altar in Mecca. Because they disrespected the altar, they would

thereof—its guardians are only the pious?—but most of them know not.

35 Their prayer at the House was naught but whistling and clapping hands!—taste then the torment for that ye misbelieved!

36 Verily, those who misbelieve expend their wealth to turn folk from the path of God; but they shall spend it, and then it shall be for them sighing, and then they shall be overcome! Those who misbelieve, into hell shall they be gathered!

37 —that God may distinguish the vile from the good, and may put the vile, some on the top of the other, and heap all up together, and put it into hell!—These are those who lose!

38 Say to those who misbelieve, if they

desist they will be forgiven what is past; but if they return,—the course of those of former days has passed away.

39 Fight them then that there should be no sedition, and that the religion may be wholly God's; but if they desist, then God on what they do doth look.

40 But if they turn their backs, then know that God is your Lord; a good Lord is He, and a good help;

Battle of Badr

41 and know that whenever ye seize anything as a spoil, to God belongs a fifth thereof, and to His Apostle, and to kindred and orphans, and the poor and the wayfarer; if ye believe in God and what we have revealed unto our servants on the

---

be tortured by Allah for their sacrilege.

8.36 Muhammad noted that the infidels spend their wealth turning people away from the genuine worship of Allah.

8.37 The imagery is that of clearing a battlefield of the dead by piling them on top of one another. Muhammad's point was that Allah would act similarly towards the wicked at the Day of Judgment.

8.38-39a Muhammad noted that in spite of their momentary victories, the craftiness of the infidels would eventually prove to be inadequate, since they would be fighting against Allah himself. They were therefore invited to repent before divine judgment fell upon them. But if they would not repent, Muhammad said that a Jihad should be waged against them.

8.39b According to Muhammad, the goal of Jihad is bring about a world where there is "no sedition, and that the religion may be wholly God's"—that is, a world where the religion of Islam reigned supreme.

8.41a *to God belongs a fifth thereof, and to His Apostle* — Most Islamic scholars believe that this verse teaches that four-fifths of the booty was to be distributed among those who took part in the war effort, and one-fifth was to be left for the Islamic government, headed by Muhammad.

8.41b *and to the kindred and orphans* — In regards to the one-fifth of the booty, the family members of those who died in battle were to be provided, as well as the poor and the wayfarer.

8.42a *When ye were on the near side of*

day of the discrimination,—the day when the two parties met; and God is mighty over all.

42   When ye were on the near side of the valley, and they were on the far side, and the camels were below you; had ye made an appointment then ye would have failed to keep your appointment—but it was that God might accomplish a thing that was as good as done! that he who was to perish might perish with a manifest sign; and that he who was to live might live with a manifest sign; for, verily, God hears and knows!

43   When God showed thee them in thy dream as though they were but few; but had He shown thee them as though they were many, ye would have been timid, and ye would have quarrelled about the matter;—but God preserved you; verily, He knows the nature of men's breasts!

44   And when He showed them to you, as ye encountered them, as few in your eyes; and made you seem few in their eyes; that God might accomplish a thing that was as good as done; for unto God do things return!

45   O ye who believe! when ye encounter a troop, then stand firm and remember God; and haply ye may prosper!

46   and fear God and His Apostle, and do not quarrel or be timid, so that your turn of luck go from you; but be ye patient, verily, God is with the patient.

47   And be not like those who went forth from their homes with insolence, and for appearance sake before men, and to turn folks off God's way; for all they do God comprehends.

48   And when Satan made their works

the valley — That is, when the Muslim army was near the valley of Badr. Prior to the battle, the Muslims were encamped on the northern side of the valley and the caravan was approaching the valley from the southern side.

8.42b he was to perish might perish with a manifest sign — Muhammad claimed that all who lived and died at the Battle of Badr were predestined by Allah to either live or die.

8.43 Prior to the battle, Muhammad claimed Allah revealed to him in a dream that those within the caravan were few in number. He then shared this information with the Muslim soldiers, encouraging them to press forward and attack. Now, in the aftermath of the battle, it was clear to him that the enemy had indeed been large—three times the size of Muhammad's Muslim soldiers. The purpose of this verse was to explain why the dream proved to be false. Allah deliberately deceived Muhammad with this dream as a way of motivating the army to attack.

8.45-47 Muhammad was disturbed that some of the Muslims refused to leave their lives of comfort in Yathrib (Medinah) and participate in the raiding of caravans. (A possible explanation for their reluctance was that up until the Battle of Badr, only one of the caravan raids had been successful.)

8.48 Muhammad believed that Satan encouraged the Meccan forces to attack the

appear seemly to them, and said, "There is none amongst mankind to conquer you today, for, verily, I am your neighbour!" and when the two troops came in sight of each other, he turned upon his heels and said, "Verily, I am clear of you! verily, I see what you see not! verily, I fear God, for God is keen to punish!"

49 And when the hypocrites and those in whose hearts was sickness said, "Their religion hath beguiled these men, but he who relies upon God, verily, God is mighty and wise."

The consequences of unbelief

50 Couldst thou see when the angels take away the souls of those who misbelieve; they smite them on their faces and hinder parts— "Taste ye the torment of burning!
51 that is for what your hands have sent on before; and for that God is not unjust one towards his ser-

vants."

52 As was the wont of Pharaoh's people and those before them! they disbelieved in the signs of God, and God overtook them in their sins; verily, God is strong and keen to punish.

53 That is because God is not one to change a favour He has favoured a people with, until they change what they have in themselves, and for that God both hears and knows.

54 As was the wont of Pharaoh's people and those before them! they said our signs were lies, and we destroyed them in their sins, and drowned Pharaoh's people; and all of them were evil-doers.

The treachery of the infidel

55 Verily, the worst of beasts in God's eyes are those who misbelieve and will not believe;
56 with whom if thou dost make a

Muslim army, claiming that he would guarantee victory for them. Yet when Satan saw that Allah was fighting on the side of the Muslim soldiers, he turned and fled, leaving the Meccan soldiers to their own fate.
8.49 Muhammad explained that the Meccan soldiers believed that the Muslims were beguiled into thinking that their Islamic religion would grant them the victory. Yet, they were the ones who had been beguiled.
8.50-51 In the afterlife, angels will smite the faces and hinder parts (backs) of the infidels as they are cast into Hell.
8.52 Fundamental to all unbelief is a refusal

to believe in divine revelation. Muhammad believed that the Qur'an was divinely inspired. Jews and Christians, of course, disagreed.
8.54 According to Muhammad, people who reject divine revelation are punished in this life as well as the afterlife. An illustration of punishment in this life was the drowning of Pharaoh's army in the Red (Reed) Sea (see Ex. 14:1-31; also see **The Apostles** on pp. 396-398).
8.55-56 Muhammad believed that the infidels cannot be trusted to keep their word in regard to treaties. "They break their league each time, for they fear not God."

league, they break their league each time, for they fear not God;

57 but shouldst thou ever catch them in war, then make those who come after them run by their example, haply they may remember then.

58 And shouldst thou ever fear from any people treachery, then throw it back to them in like manner; verily, God loves not the treacherous.

59 Deem not that those who misbelieve can win; verily, they cannot make (God) Powerless!

Peace treaties

60 Prepare ye against them what force and companies of horse ye can, to make the enemies of God; and your enemies, and others beside them, in dread thereof. Ye do not know them, but God knows them! and whatever ye expend in God's way

He will repay you; and ye shall not be wronged.

61 But if they incline to peace, incline thou to it too, and rely upon God; verily, He both hears and knows.

62 But if they wish to betray thee, then God is enough for thee! He it is who supports thee with His help and with the believers;

63 and reconciles their hearts! Didst thou expend all that is in the earth thou couldst not reconcile their hearts, but God reconciled them, verily, He is mighty and wise!

Guaranteed victory

64 O thou prophet! God is sufficient for thee, with those of the believers who follow thee!

65 O thou prophet! urge on the believers to fight. If there be of you twenty patient men, they shall conquer two hundred; if there be of

8.57 *make those who come after them run by their example* — That is, bring destruction on the enemy and on those who follow after them.

8.58 Muslims were under no compulsion to keep a treaty with the infidel, provided that they feared that the infidel would break the treaty. Yet, Muhammad Asad comments, "The 'reason to fear treachery' must not, of course, be based on mere surmise but on clear, objective evidence" (*The Message of the Qur'an*, p. 282).

8.59 *deem not that those who misbelieve can win* — That is, never imagine that the infidel will ever win a war against Allah.

Muhammad maintained that they are destined to defeat.

8.60-65 When engaged in war, the Muslim is instructed to be fully committed to defeat the infidel, knowing that Allah is on his side. Each jihadist soldier was to quote the verse Q 8.60-65 in preparation for battle.

8.61-63 If the infidel should sue for peace, the Muslim should be inclined to grant peace. If the Muslim suspicioned that the request for peace was insincere, the Muslim should still pursue peace, unless clear evidence spoke otherwise.

8.64-65 These are two appeals from Allah: (a) Allah has guaranteed victory to Muham-

you a hundred, they shall conquer a thousand of those who misbelieve, because they are a people who did not discern.

66   —Now has God made it light for you; He knows that there is a weakness amongst you: but if there be amongst you but a patient hundred, they will conquer two hundred; and if there be of you a thousand, they will conquer two thousand, by the permission of God,— for God is with the patient!

Prisoners of war

67   It has not been for any prophet to take captives until he hath slaugh-

tered in the land! Ye wish to have the goods of this world, but God wishes for the next, for God is mighty, wise!

68   Were it not for a book from God that had gone before, there would have touched you, for that which ye took, a mighty punishment.

69   Eat of what spoils ye have taken, what is lawful and good; and fear God, verily, God is forgiving and merciful.

70   O thou prophet! say to such of the captives as are in your hands, "If God knows of any good in your hearts, he will give you better than that which is taken from you, and will forgive you; for God is for-

mad and his followers, (b) Muslim followers are urged to carry on the fight against the infidel. Even when greatly outnumbered, Muhammad believed that they will still be victorious: twenty Muslims will conquer two hundred infidels, one hundred Muslims will conquer one thousand infidels.

Historically, however, Muslim armies were not always victorious, even when facing smaller infidel armies (e.g., the Battle of Tours in 732, the two battles for Vienna that occurred in 1529 and 1683). Islamic scholars have therefore concluded that this passage teaches that Muslim victories are guaranteed only to Muslim soldiers and armies that are characterized by an unreserved and wholly committed faith in Allah.

8.66 Due to the lack of courage among the Muslim people, Allah adjusted the arithmetic of battle to accommodate their spiritual insecurities: one hundred Muslims would conquer two hundred infidels, and one thou-

sand Muslims will conquer two thousand infidels.

8.67 According to this verse, infidel captives could be taken only in war, provided that a slaughter of the enemy first took place (see *Jihad* on pp. 616-622).

8.68 This verse is a reference to the Battle of Badr where a large number of captives were taken. The term "a book from God" is a reference to a divine decree. If it were not for this decree, divine punishment would have befallen the Muslim people for the captives that they took.

8.69 Muslims were permitted to take possession of and consume the spoils of war; that is, they were permitted to take possession of the property of the vanquished.

8.70 The prisoners of war were encouraged to convert to Islam. If they did so, they would receive more than that which had been taken from them—that is, Allah will forgive and show mercy in the form of

giving and merciful."

71   But if they desire to betray thee,—
they have betrayed God before! but
He hath given you power over
them; for God is knowing, wise!

*Blessings
accorded to jihadists*

72   Verily, those who believe and have
fled and fought strenuously with
their wealth and persons in God's
way, and those who have given refuge and help, these shall be next
of kin to each other. But those who
believe, but have not fled, ye have
naught to do with their claims of
kindred, until they flee as well. But
if they ask you for aid for religion's
sake, then help is due from you,

except against a people between
whom and you there is an alliance;
for God on what ye do doth look.

73   And those who misbelieve, some
of them are next of kin to others—
unless ye act the same there will
be sedition in the land, and great
corruption.

74   Those who believe and have fled
and fought strenuously in God's
cause, and those who have given
a refuge and a help, those it is who
believe; to them is forgiveness and
generous provision due.

75   And those who have believed afterwards and have fled and fought
strenuously with you; these too are
of you, but blood relations are
nearer in kin by the Book of God.
Verily, God all things doth know.

eternal life.

8.71 Prisoners of war who refused to convert were to remain under the power and
authority of Muhammad.

8.72a *those who believe and have fled —*
That is, those who believe in Islam and left
Mecca and emigrated to Medinah.

8.72b *fought strenuously with their wealth
and persons in God's way —* Literally, jihad
against them a great jihad with their wealth
and personal well-being in the Cause of Allah
(see Q 4.95; 5.35; 8.74-75; 9.16, 41, 44,
73, 81; 16.110; 22.78; 25.52; 29.6, 69;
47.31; 60.1; 66.9).

8.72c *those who have given refuge and
help —* That is, have cared for the needs of
other Muslims.

8.72d *these shall be next of kin to each
other —* They were to understand and treat
one another as if they were of the same

family.

8.72e *those who believe, but have not
fled —* Muslims that have not left Mecca
were to be shunned until they fled as well.

8.72f *except against a people between
whom and you there is an alliance —* When
Muslims live in a non-Muslim nation or city-
state, an Islamic state was not permitted to
make demands in how the non-Muslim nation treats its Muslim inhabitants.

8.73 *those who misbelieve —* Non-Muslims
have more in common with one another than
they do with Muslim nations. Hence, relations between Muslim and non-Muslim nations or city-states will always be tenuous
and subject to suspicion.

8.74 *fought strenuously in God's cause —*
Literally, jihad against them a great jihad in
the Cause of Allah (see Q 4.95; 5.35; 8.72;
9.16, 41, 44, 73, 81; 16.110; 22.78; 25.52;

Surah 47

In the name of the merciful and compassionate God.

Two paths

1 Those who misbelieve and turn folk from God's way, He will make their works go wrong.

2 But those who believe and do right and believe in what is revealed to Muhammad, —and it is the truth from their Lord,—He will cover for them their offences and set right their mind.

3 That is because those who misbelieve follow falsehood, and those who believe follow the truth from their Lord. Thus does God set forth for men their parables.

Rules of warfare

4 And when ye meet those who misbelieve—then striking off heads until ye have massacred them, and bind fast the bonds! Then either a free grant (of liberty) or a ransom until the war shall have laid down its burdens. That!—but if God please He would conquer them— but (it is) that He may try some of you by the others. And those who are slain in God's cause, their works shall not go wrong;

5 He will guide them and set right their mind;

6 and will make them enter into Paradise which He has told them of.

29.6, 69; 47.31; 60.1; 66.9).
Surah 47. The title of this surah, *Muhammad*, comes from verse 2. The focus of this surah is the Doctrine of Jihad, with a particular focus on the need to be fully committed and willing to sacrifice all for the Cause of Allah—with the end being the utter defeat of the infidel. Those who were fainthearted and unwilling to participate in Jihad were condemned as hypocrites and destined for the fires of Hell.
47.1-3 That which is presented in this passage are the straight and crooked paths. Those of the *crooked path* are characterized by the following: (a) they encourage people to turn away from the Islamic faith, (b) they are followers of falsehood, and (c) they are destined to have their works go wrong. Those of the *straight path* are characterized by the following: (a) Allah will cover their offenses at the Last Judgment, (b) they are followers of truth, and (c) Allah will set right their minds.
47.2 *those who believe and do right* — A summary of eternal life, according to Islam (see Q 103.3, note).
47.4a *striking off heads* — Jihad is to be waged ruthlessly, no sympathy offered to the enemy. The preferred method of combat was decapitation. Those who survived the battle were to be put in bonds. Captives were either to be granted their freedom or ransomed for money.
47.4b *those who are slain in God's cause* — Those who suffer martyrdom as jihadists in the Cause of Allah would be blessed by Allah. Allah would enable them to enter Paradise (see Q 3.121-129, note and Q 3.169-173, note).
47.7 *if ye help God* — That is, if you en-

7	O ye who believe! if ye help God, He will help you, and will make firm your footsteps.
8	But as for those who misbelieve—confound them! and He will make their works go wrong.
9	That is because they were averse from what God has revealed; but their works shall be void!
10	Have they not journeyed through the land and seen how was the end of those before them? God destroyed them; and for the misbelievers is the like thereof.
11	That is because God is the patron of those who believe, and because the misbelievers have no patron.
12	Verily, God causes those who believe and do right to enter into gar-

dens beneath which rivers flow; but those who misbelieve enjoy themselves and eat as the cattle eat; but the fire is the resort for them!

13 How many a city, stronger than thy city which has driven thee out, have we destroyed, and there was none to help them!

Paradise and Hell

14 Is he who rests upon a manifest sign from his Lord like him, the evil of whose works is made seemly to him, and who follow their lusts?

15 The similitude of Paradise which is promised to the pious,—in it are rivers of water without corruption,

---

gage in the Cause of Allah by becoming jihadists. Allah does not need help in vanquishing His enemies since He is sovereign over all the universe. Nevertheless, as a test to the faithfulness of Muslims, they were called upon to participate in the Cause of Allah by their readiness to kill (see Q 2.190).

47.8-9a Jihadists were instructed to confound (confuse) infidels as part of their overall strategy in defeating them. This means that lying, deception and duplicity were acceptable tactics as Muslims engage in Jihad.

47.9b *their works shall be void* — Muhammad encouraged Muslims to consider the fate of previous infidel nations, such as Pharaoh's Egypt, the people of Noah's day, the people of Ad, the Midianites, etc. Without exception "God destroyed them" (v. 10). Such would also be the case with infidel nations in the current age.

47.12a *those who believe and do right —*

This is a summary of the Islamic gospel (see Q 103.3, note). Such individuals were the promised gardens of Paradise (see **Paradise** on pp. 76-77).

47.12b *those who misbelieve* — They were promised the fires of Hell.

47.13 According to Muhammad, Allah destroyed cities much stronger than Mecca ("thy city which has driven thee out"). The implication was that Allah would also bring judgment upon the people of Mecca.

47.14 The question presented in this verse can be paraphrased as follows: how is one to compare the faithful Muslim with those "who follow their lusts"? The answer is given in v. 15.

47.15 According to Muhammad, the faithful Muslim would enter Paradise whereas those who follow their lusts would enter the Fire for all eternity. Paradise was described as a place of four delightful rivers: the river

and rivers of milk, the taste whereof changes not, and rivers of wine delicious to those who drink; and rivers of honey clarified; and there shall they have all kinds of fruit and forgiveness from their Lord! (Is that) like him who dwells in the fire for aye? and who are given to drink boiling water that shall rend their bowels asunder?

16 Some of them there are who listen to thee, until when they go forth from thee they say to those who have been given the knowledge, "What is this which he says now?" These are those on whose hearts God has set a stamp and who follow their lusts.

17 But those who are guided, He guides them the more, and gives them the due of their piety.

18 Do they wait for aught but the Hour, that it should come to them suddenly? The conditions thereof have come already; how, when it has come on them, can they have their reminder?

19 Know thou that there is no god but God; and ask pardon for thy sin and for the believers, men and women; for God knows your return and your resort!

Words for the fainthearted

20 Those who misbelieve say, "Why has not a sûrah been revealed?" but when a decisive sûrah is re-

---

of water, the river of milk, the river of wine, and the river of honey. In contrast, Hell is described as a place where the inhabitants drink boiling water which rend their bowels asunder.

The use of the word *similitude* at the beginning of this verse suggests that this description of Paradise is not to be taken literally. It is rather a metaphoric depiction.

The use of the term *rivers of wine* in the description of Paradise is curious since wine is both blessed and condemned in the Qur'an (Q 16.67, note). In this verse, the context presents wine as a desirable and blessed beverage.

47.16 *these are those on whose hearts God has set a stamp* — According to Muhammad, Allah sets a seal on the hearts of those who do not know the truth. The stamp prevents them from attaining to a life of belief and obedience. This explains why the proc-

lamation of Islamic truth is often rejected by infidels (see Q 7.100-101; 9.87, 93; 10.74; 16.108; 30.59; 40.35; 63.3; **The Doctrine of al-Qadar** on pp. 264-266).

47.18 *the Hour* — That is, the hour of the Last Judgment.

47.19 *there is no god but God* — That is, there is no god but Allah (the Doctrine of Tauhid). This is the central creed of Islam. The final destiny of each person is predicated upon how one responds to this creed in terms of faith and works.

47.20-21 According to this passage, Jihad is indeed stressful and required enormous personal sacrifice. Yet, some Muslims were fainthearted when it came to Jihad and looked for excuses to avoid direct participation. They claimed that no divine revelation had been revealed that authorized Jihad, in spite of many surahs that have done so. Muhammad coerced them to fight by present-

vealed and fighting is mentioned therein, thou mayest see those in whose heart is sickness looking towards thee with the look of one fainting in death.

21 Preferable for them were obedience and a reasonable speech! But when the matter is determined on, then if they believed God it were better for them.

22 Would ye perhaps, if ye had turned back, have done evil in the land and severed the bonds of kinship?

23 It is these whom God has cursed, and has made them deaf, and has blinded their eyesight!

24 Do they not peruse the Qur'ân? or are there locks upon their hearts?

25 Verily, those who turn their backs after the guidance that has been manifested to them—Satan induces them, but (God) lets them go on for a time!

26 That is for that they say to those who are averse from what God has revealed, "We will obey you in part of the affair!" but God knows their secrets!

27 How will it be when the angels take their souls, smiting their faces and their backs?

28 This is because they follow what angers God and are averse from His goodwill; and their works are void.

29 Do those in whose hearts is sickness reckon that God will not bring their malice forth?

30 But did we please we would show thee them, and thou shouldst know them by their cognizances. But thou shalt know them by their distorting their speech, and God knows their works!

31 But we will try you until we know those among you who fight strenu-

---

ing new surahs that he claimed were divinely inspired that required their participation. If they did not participate, it would reflect that they were infidels.

47.22 The rhetorical question was intended to make the point that the alternative to Jihad is to live in a land where evil was rampant. When seen in this light, Jihad is always the correct choice.

47.23-25 Those who failed to see the value and necessity of Jihad were cursed by Allah. They were made spiritually deaf and blind. Again, a rhetorical question suggests that they either had not read the Qur'an or had locks upon their hearts, making it impossible to rightly understand the Qur'an. Moreover, they were induced by Satan to turn away

from fighting in the Cause of Allah.

47.26 *We will obey you in part of the affair* — According to Muhammad, Allah was not impressed with Muslims who were only partially committed to Jihad. In the afterlife, they would be smitten on their faces and backs by angels and all their righteous deeds would be nullified.

47.30 Muhammad claimed that fainthearted Muslims (those unwilling to participate in Jihad) could be identified by their outward appearances, specifically: distortions in their speech. That is, their hypocrisy was evident by means of a careful analysis of the words they choose and their tone of voice.

47.31 *those among you who fight strenuously* — Literally, those among you who ji-

ously and the patient; and we will try the reports concerning you.

32 Verily, those who misbelieve and turn folks off God's path, and break with the Apostle after the guidance that has been manifested to them, cannot harm God at all, and their works shall be void!

33 O ye who believe! obey God, and obey the Apostle; and make not your works vain.

34 Verily, those who misbelieve and turn folks off God's path, and then die misbelievers, God will not pardon them.

Final admonition

35 Then faint not, nor cry for peace while ye have the upper hand; for God is with you and will not cheat you of your works!

36 The life of this world is but a play

and a sport; but if ye believe and fear God, He will give you your hire. He does not ask you for (all) your property;

37 if He were to ask you for it and to press you, ye would be niggardly, and he would bring your malice out.

38 Here are ye called upon to expend in God's cause, and among you are some who are niggardly; and he who is niggardly is but niggardly against his own soul: but God is rich and ye are poor, and if ye turn your backs He will substitute another people in your stead, then they will not be like you.

Surah 62

In the name of the merciful and compassionate God.

had a great jihad (also see Q 8.72, 74-75; 16.110; 22.78; 25.52; 29.6, 69). The point here is that Allah will try the Muslim people to determine those who are committed to Jihad and those who are not.

47.32 Those Muslims who are not committed to Jihad and break with Muhammad after guidance "has been manifested to them" will not enter Paradise in the afterlife. Instead, "their works shall be void."

47.35 Muhammad demanded that the Muslim people neither be fainthearted nor cry for peace on behalf of the infidel when they "have the upper hand."

47.36 *The life of this world is but a play and a sport* — That is, in contrast to the afterlife, this life is of little importance.

47.38 *among you are some who are niggardly* — That is, some Muslims were unwilling to sacrifice any of their possessions for the Cause of Allah. Those so characterized were niggardly against their own souls. This is a serious indictment against fainthearted Muslims—those unwilling to participate in Jihad. Muhammad described them as bringing disaster upon themselves ("against his own soul"), suggesting disaster in the afterlife. Not only that, the work of Jihad will continue forward, but with other people filling their roles and gaining the rewards of eternal life.

Surah 62. The title of this surah, *The Congregation Day*, comes from v. 9. This surah juxtaposes three groups of people against

Muhammad	*Jews*
1 What is in the heavens and what is in the earth celebrates the praises of God the King, the holy, the mighty, the wise!	5 The likeness of those who were charged with the law and then bore it not as in the likeness of an ass bearing books: sorry is the likeness of the people who say God's signs are lies! but God guides not an unjust people.
2 He it is who sent unto the Gentiles a prophet amongst themselves to recite to them His signs and to purify them, and to teach them the Book and the wisdom, although they were before in obvious error.	6 Say, "O ye who are Jews! if ye pretend that ye are the clients of God, beyond other people; then wish for death if ye do speak the truth!"
3 And others of them have not yet overtaken them; but He is the mighty, the wise!	7 But they never wish for it, through what their hands have sent before! but God knows the unjust.
4 That is God's grace, He gives it to whomsoever He will; for God is Lord of mighty grace.	8 Say, "Verily, the death from which

one another: Muhammad, the Muslim community, and the Jewish people. *Muhammad* is presented as Allah's prophet sent to unlettered peoples (the Gentiles) to turn them from error and to the truth. The *Muslim people* are presented as people not committed to prayer. They prefer to continue in their merchandising activities than to set aside time for congregational prayers. The *Jewish people* are presented as people who have rejected divine revelation (God's signs), wrongly see themselves as the chosen people of God (clients of God). They are cowardly people who flee death. Nevertheless, they will face death and then face Allah who sees all things and will reward them accordingly with the fires of Hell.

62.2a *the Gentiles* — That is, unlettered (illiterate) people. In this context, it could also mean: all non-Jews.

62.2b *the Book* — That is, the eternal book that exists in Paradise (see **The Perspicu-**

ous Book on pp. 178-179).

62.4 *He gives it to whomsoever He will* — That is, the grace of Allah is limited to His foreordination (see **The Doctrine of al-Qadar** on pp. 264-266).

62.5 Muhammad claimed that the Jews with the Torah (the law) are likened to an ass carrying a load of books, but cannot benefit from them.

62.6a *ye pretend that ye are the clients of God* — That is, Jews pretend that they are the chosen people of God.

62.6b *then wish for death if ye do speak the truth!* — That is, if the Jewish people were indeed the chosen people of God, then they should wish for death in order to be with God in Heaven (also see Q 2.94-95).

62.8 *the death from which ye flee will surely meet you* — That is, eventually the Jews will die and face God at the Last Judgment.

62.9 *the Congregation Day* — That is, con-

ye flee will surely meet you; then shall ye be sent back to Him who knows the unseen and the visible, and He will inform you of that which ye have done."

Muslims

9   O ye who believe! when the call to prayer is made upon the Congregation Day, then hasten to the remembrance of God, and leave off traffic; that is better for you, if ye did but know!

10   And when prayer is performed, then disperse abroad in the land, and crave of God's grace; and remember God much; haply ye may prosper!

11   But when they see merchandise or sport they flock to it and leave thee

standing! Say, "What is with God is better than sport and than merchandise, for God is the best of providers!"

Surah 5

In the name of the merciful and compassionate God.

The sacred month

1   O ye who believe! fulfil your compacts.—Lawful for you are brute beasts, save what is here recited to you, not allowing you the chase while ye are on pilgrimage; verily, God ordaineth what He will.

2   O ye who believe! do not deem the monuments of God to be lawful,

gregational prayers at noon on Fridays. Muslims were encouraged to set aside the normal work of the day to attend prayer.

62.10-11 Muhammad was critical of the Muslim people who were more interested in commercial activities or sports than with prayer.

Surah 5. The title of this surah, *Table from Heaven*, comes from v. 112. The surah begins with a reminder of one's social and spiritual obligations and concludes with a reminder of one's utter dependence upon Allah. In the middle of the surah is a long section where Muslims were reminded not to form spiritual alliances with either Jews or Christians, nor imitate their way of life. This is because their divine revelations—the Old and New Testaments—have been irreparably corrupted by their scribes and sages. In

particular, Christians were taken to task for corrupting the New Testament with its claim that Jesus—and Mary—are to be worshipped. In contrast, the Qur'an, said Muhammad, is not only without corruption, it has "perfected for you your religion" (v. 3). The phrase "O ye who believe" is repeated sixteen times, giving the surah a sermonic quality.

5.1a *O ye who believe!* — Muhammad's target audience in this surah are the Muslim believers (also see vv. 2, 6, 8, 11, 35, 51, 54, 57, 87, 90, 94, 95, 101, 105, and 106).

5.1b Muhammad noted that it is lawful to hunt and eat brute beasts—specifically, cattle and all animals like cattle. The one exception is when on a pilgrimage (the Hajj) to worship at the Ka'ba altar in Mecca.

5.2a *do not deem the monuments of God to be lawful* — That is, do not deem the

nor the sacred month, nor the offering, nor its neck garlands, nor those who sojourn at the sacred house, craving grace from their Lord and His pleasure. But when ye are in lawful state again, then chase; and let not ill-will against the people who turned you from the Sacred Mosque make you transgress; but help one another in righteousness and piety, and do not help one another to sin and enmity; but fear God,—verily, God is keen to punish.

Dietary law

3   Forbidden to you is that which dies of itself, and blood, and the flesh of swine, and that which is devoted to other than God, and the strangled and the knocked down, and that which falls down, and the gored, and what wild beasts have eaten—except what ye slaughter in time—and what is sacrificed to idols, and dividing carcases by arrows. Today shall those who disbelieve in your religion despair; do

monuments of Allah, or the sacred month, or the offerings, or neck garlands, or those who sojourn to the Ka'ba altar as lawful for normal activity and behavior. Rather, these items and periods of time are sacred and stand outside of normal lawful activity. Moreover, the sacredness of these items and periods of time date to pre-Islamic times and extended throughout the Arabian Peninsula. The word *monuments* in this verse means symbols and applies to anything set aside for the worship of Allah.

5.2b *the sacred month* — Ramadan, a month where bloodshed was prohibited throughout the Arabian Peninsula. The *offering* referred to animals that were brought to Mecca for sacrifice. The *neck garlands* referred to garlands hung around the necks of the animals designated for sacrifice.

5.2c *when ye are in lawful state again* — That is, when the sacred period of time (Ramadan) is passed and conventional laws came to apply once again.

5.2d *the Sacred Mosque* — That is, the Ka'ba altar in Mecca. Muhammad longed for the day when the Ka'ba altar would be used

for the worship of Allah, rather than that of the Arabian Star Family religious system. The polytheists also made use of all sacred items and events mentioned earlier in this verse, yet from within the context of polytheistic worship.

5.3a Certain meats were forbidden: (a) carrion, (b) pork, (c) animals that had been strangled, (d) animals that had been beaten to death, (e) animals that had been killed by a fall, (f) animals that had gored, and (g) animals that had been killed by beasts of prey. In addition, meat that had been blessed by any god other than Allah was forbidden. The one exception is for those "forced by hunger" (that is, extreme hunger) to eat such meat. In such cases Allah is forgiving and compassionate (also see Q 2.173 and Q 6.128-130, note, regarding the Muslim tradition of Halal meat).

5.3b *dividing carcases by arrows* — This is a reference to the use of divining arrows cast at meat with the purpose of prognosticating the future. The organs of dead carcasses were inspected, which people believed offered clues pertaining to the future. This

ye not then fear them, but fear me—Today is perfected for you your religion, and fulfilled upon you is my favour, and I am pleased for you to have Islâm for a religion. But he who is forced by hunger, not inclined willfully to sin, verily, God is forgiving, compassionate.

4 They will ask thee what is lawful for them? say, "Lawful for you are good things and what ye have taught beasts of prey (to catch), training them like dogs;—ye teach them as God taught you;—so eat of what they catch for you, and mention the name of God over it, and fear God, for verily, God is swift in reckoning up."

5 Lawful for you today are good things, and the food of those to whom the Book has been given is lawful for you, and your food is lawful for them;

Marital laws

and chaste women of those who believe, and chaste women of those to whom the Book has been given before you,—when you have given them their hire, living chastely and not fornicating, and not taking paramours. But whoso disbelieves in the faith, of a truth his work is vain, and he shall be in the next life of those who lose.

Prayer purification laws

6 O ye who believe! when ye rise up to prayer wash your faces, and your hands as far as the elbows, and wipe your heads, and your feet down to the ankles. And if ye are polluted, then purify yourselves. But if ye are sick, or on a journey, or if one of you comes from the

---

was a practice common among the pagans of the Middle East (see Ezek 21:21).

5.5a Muslims were permitted to eat foods approved in the Bible (*the Book*). The non-kosher foods mentioned in the Old Testament roughly corresponds to what is mentioned in verse 3 (see Lev 11:1-47). The New Testament, however, is much less restrictive than the Old Testament in regards to food (see Acts 10:9-16; Rom 14:14-21; 1 Cor 10:25; 1 Tim 4:3-5).

5.5b Muslim men were permitted to marry non-Muslim women, provided that they were "women of those to whom the Book (the Bible) has been given before you." Conditions include the following: (a) women were to be given "their hire"—that is, a dowry,

and (b) there was to be no premarital sex. Curiously, the Qur'an made no provision for Muslim women to marry non-Muslim men. Elsewhere, however, Muslim men were instructed not to marry idolatrous women (see Q 2.221).

5.6 In preparation for prayer, a man was required to do the following: (a) wash his face, (b) wash his hands as far as the elbows, (c) wipe his head, and (d) wipe his feet to the ankles. Additional laws required the Muslim to wash himself with water or fine sand. This requirement was necessary if he: (a) was sick, (b) was on a journey, (c) had just relieved himself, that is, bathroom duties, or (d) had recently had sex with his wife, he was to either wash himself with

privy, or if ye have touched women and cannot find water, then take fine surface sand and wipe your faces and your hands therewith. God does not wish to make any hindrance for you; but he wishes to purify you and to fulfil his favour upon you; haply ye may give thanks.

7   Remember the favour of God to you and His covenant which He covenanted with you, when ye said, "We hear and we obey;" and fear God, verily, God knows the nature of men's breasts.

General jurisprudence

8   O ye who believe! stand steadfast to God as witnesses with justice; and let not ill-will towards people make you sin by not acting with equity.   Act with equity, that is

nearer to piety, and fear God; for God is aware of what ye do.

9   God has promised to those who believe and work righteousness, that for them is pardon and a mighty hire.

10   But those who disbelieve and call our signs lies, these are the fellows of hell.

11   O ye who believe! remember God's favour towards you, when a people intended to stretch their hands against you, but He withheld their hands from you; and upon God let believers rely.

The failure of
the Jews and Christians

12   God did take a compact from the children of Israel, and raised up of them twelve wardens; and God said, "Verily, I am with you, if ye

water or fine sand (see Q. 4.43b). Moreover, if he was polluted (if he imbibed alcoholic beverages—Q 4.43a), he was to wait until the effects of the alcohol wore off.

5.8 Muslims were admonished to "act with equity" in regards to all matters pertaining to Muslim justice. They were never to permit hatred cause them to deviate from objective analysis and honest and equitable resolutions.

5.9 Pardons were to be forthcoming to those who maintained a public testimony of religious faithfulness and righteous behavior.

5.10 In contrast, those who rejected the Islamic faith were to be treated harshly, since they were "the fellows of hell." They were to remember that such individuals were pre-

viously their enemies ("stretched their hands against you"). See **Dhimmitude** on pp. 716-717.

5.12a Muhammad believed that the salvatory relationship between Allah and Israel was predicated upon Jews following the *straight path* that leads to eternal life. This included them remaining steadfast in prayer, giving of alms, believing in divinely ordained apostles, and giving monetarily to Allah's causes (see Q 72.2, note).

    In contrast, the Bible speaks otherwise. Central to God's relationship with the children of Israel was the doctrine of substitutionary atonement: the blood of a sacrificial animal shed to cover the sins of the people (see Lev. 16:1-34).

be steadfast in prayer, and give alms, and believe in my apostles, and assist them, and lend to God a goodly loan; then will I cover your offences and make you enter gardens beneath which rivers flow: and whoso disbelieves after that, he hath erred from the level way."

13 And for that they broke their compact, we cursed them, and placed in their hearts hardness, so that they perverted the words from their places, and forgot a portion of what they were reminded of. But thou wilt not cease to light upon treachery amongst them, save a few of them; but pardon them and shun them; verily, God loves the kind.

14 And of those who say, "Verily, we are Christians," we have taken a compact; but they have forgotten a portion of what they were re-minded of; wherefore have we excited amongst them enmity and hatred till the resurrection day; but God will tell them of what they have done.

15 O ye people of the Book! our Apostle has come to you to explain to you much of what ye had hidden of the Book, and to pardon much. There has come to you from God a light, and a perspicuous Book;

16 God guides thereby those who follow His pleasure to the way of peace, and brings them into a right way.

17 They misbelieve who say, "Verily, God is the Messiah the son of Mary;" say, "Who has any hold on God, if he wished to destroy the Messiah the son of Mary, and his mother, and those who are on earth altogether?" God's is the kingdom

---

5.12b *a compact* — That is, a covenant.
5.12c *twelve wardens* — That is, twelve tribes.
5.12d *the level way* — The level way is that which leads to eternal life. It is also called *the straight path* (see Q 72.2, note).
5.13 According to Muhammad, the Jewish people broke their own covenant, perverted the words of Scripture, and forgot others. Allah therefore cursed them and caused their hearts to become hard (see **The Doctrine of al-Qadar** on pp. 264-266).
5.14a *we have taken a compact* — That is, Christians have their own covenant with God.
5.14b *they have forgotten a portion of what they were reminded of* — According to Muhammad, Christians routinely ignore certain passages in the New Testament.
5.15 Muhammad believed that in his surahs, he reminded both the Jews and the Christians ("people of the Book"), that which they had set aside in the Bible. The surahs, he said, are a light from Allah that reveal the eternal book that exists in Paradise (see **The Perspicuous Book** on pp. 178-179).
5.16 *the way of peace* — This is another way of saying *the straight path* or *the right way* that leads to eternal life (see Q 72.2, note).
5.17 Muhammad's chief complaint against the Christians was their claim that Jesus Christ was divine (see **The Apostles Creed** on p. 87, **The Definition of Chalcedon** on pp. 785-786, **The Nicene-Constantinopolitan**

of the heavens and the earth and what is between the two; He createth what He will, for God is mighty over all!

18   But the Jews and the Christians say, "We are the sons of God and His beloved." Say, "Why then does He punish you for your sins? nay, ye are mortals of those whom He has created! He pardons whom He pleases, and punishes whom He pleases; for God's is the kingdom of the heavens and the earth, and what is between the two, and unto Him the journey is."

19   O people of the Book! our Apostle has come to you, explaining to you the interval of apostles; lest ye say, "There came not to us a herald of glad tidings nor a warner." But there has come to you now a herald of glad tidings and a warner, and God is mighty over all!

Kadesh Barnea

20   When Moses said to his people, "O my people! remember the favour

Creed on p. 740, and Q 2.111, note).

5.18a *the Jews and the Christians say, "We are the sons of God and His beloved"* — This is a curious statement. Muhammad was mistaken inasmuch as the Jewish people in the Old Testament never referred to themselves as "the sons of God" or even as "the children of God." On two occasions, they did refer to themselves as "the people of God" (Jud 20:2; 2 Sam 14:13). Their preferred nomenclature was: "the servants of the Lord" and "the children of Israel." Also, on only two occasions did the Jewish people refer to themselves as the beloved of the Lord (Deut 33:12; Jer 11:15). Muhammad was correct, however, in his characterization of Christians calling themselves "sons of God" (Matt 5:9; Rom 8:14, 19; Gal 3:26). They were also often called: "children of God" (Jn 1:12; Rom 8:21; Phil 2;15; 1 Jn 3:1-2, 10; 5:2, 19). Since both Jews and Christians understood their relationship with God to be centered on love, for them to think of themselves as "His beloved" was an accurate characterization.

5.18b *He pardons whom He pleases, and punishes whom He pleases* — In contrast to the love and familial relationship with God that Jews and Christians cherished, Muhammad emphasized the sovereign power of Allah (see *The Doctrine of al-Qadar* on pp. 264-266).

5.18c *between the two, and unto Him, the journey is* — This is the journey that leads to eternal life. Muhammad also characterized this journey as an arduous journey. It stood in contrast to the Jewish and Christian understanding where eternal life was better defined as a promise and a covenant (see Ps 105:42; 119:41, 76; Rom 4:16; 9:8; Gal 3:17-19, 29; 4:28; Eph 2:12; 3:6; 2 Tim 1:1; Heb 4:1; 2 Pet 3:13).

5.19 *the interval of the apostles* — That is, the line of apostles, which includes Muhammad's alleged apostleship. Muhammad believed that both the Jews and Christians were ignorant of the role of the apostles throughout history in revealing the eternal book of God (see *The Perspicuous Book* on pp. 178-179). Their purpose was to (a) warn people of eternal damnation to all who fail to follow the straight path, and (b) herald glad tidings to all who successfully followed the straight path.

of God towards you when He made amongst you prophets, and made for you kings, and brought you what never was brought to anybody in the worlds.

21 O my people! enter the Holy Land which God has prescribed for you; and be ye not thrust back upon your hinder parts and retreat losers:"

22 They said, "O Moses! verily, therein is a people, giants; and we will surely not enter therein until they go out from thence; but if they go out then we will enter in."

23 Then said two men of those who fear,—God had been gracious to them both—"Enter ye upon them by the door, and when ye have entered it, verily, ye shall be victorious; and upon God do ye rely if ye

be believers."

24 They said, "O Moses! we shall never enter it so long as they are therein; so, go thou and thy Lord and fight ye twain; verily, we will sit down here."

25 Said he, "My Lord, verily, I can control only myself and my brother; therefore part us from these sinful people."

26 He said, "Then, verily, it is forbidden them; for forty years shall they wander about in the earth; so vex not thyself for the sinful people."

Cain and Abel

27 Recite to them the story of the two sons of Adam; truly when they offered an offering and it was accepted from one of them, and was

5.20-24 Muhammad illustrated his point regarding the disobedience and faithlessness of the Jewish people with the story of Kadesh-Barnea in the Old Testament (Num 13:1-14:45). As the people of Israel were camped at Kadesh-Barnea, spies were sent into the Holy Land to determine the nature of the enemy. The report that came back was dismal and discouraging. The enemy was determined to be too powerful, some of whom were giants. Only two of the spies, Caleb and Joshua, believed that God would give them the victory. The majority report prevailed and the people refused to enter the land.

5.25-26 According to Muhammad, Moses asked the Lord to separate himself from the Israelite people. The biblical story speaks otherwise, that the Lord was angered by

the people's response and was prepared to destroy them. He said: "How long will these people treat me with contempt? How long will they refuse to believe in me, in spite of all the miraculous signs I have performed among them? I will strike them down with a plague and destroy them, but I will make you into a nation greater and stronger than they" (Num 14:11-12). Moses then interceded for the people and the Lord relented. Instead, the people were sentenced to wander in the wilderness for forty years.

5.27-34 This passage addresses the story of Cain and Abel (see Gen. 4:1-16). Both presented to the Lord offerings, yet the Lord accepted Abel's offering of a sheep and rejected Cain's grain offering. Infuriated by the Lord's rejection, Cain took out his anger on his brother, whom he killed.

Dhimmitude

The ideal Muslim state is where all its inhabitants are Muslim believers. Throughout history, however, this has seldom been the case. To accommodate the presence of Muslims and non-Muslims living side by side in Muslim states, the tradition of *dhimmitude* (which euphemistically means *protection*) came into being. It is based upon Q 5.9-11, which states:

> God has promised to those who believe and work righteousness, that for them is pardon and a mighty hire. But those who disbelieve and call our signs lies, these are the fellows of hell. O ye who believe! remember God's favour towards you, when a people intended to stretch their hands against you, but He withheld their hands from you; and upon God let believers rely.

Infidels who lived in Islamic lands were offered three options:

- *convert to Islam.* If they did so, their status would be upgraded from that of infidel to believer, with corresponding social and economic privileges.

- *refuse to convert to Islam.* In that case, they would remain in the status of infidel and be subject to corresponding social and economic disadvantages.

- *refuse to convert to Islam and refuse to accept social and economic disadvantages.* In that case, the military solution would be applied and they would be slaughtered as a form of ethnic cleansing.

In Islamic lands, two sets of laws existed; one for Muslims, and another for non-Muslims. The laws designated for Muslims were decisively advantageous over the laws for non-Muslims. Moreover, all one had to do to move from one set of laws to the other was to convert to Islam. And, indeed, this was its fundamental motivation. *Dhimmitude* included the following:

- the prohibition of arms for vanquished non-Muslims

- the prohibition of church bells

- restrictions concerning the renovation and restoration of homes, churches, synagogues, and temples

- inequality between Muslims and non-Muslims in regards to taxes and penal law

- requirement to wear special clothing

The poll tax was demanded from children, widows, orphans, and the dead. An-Nawawi explained: "Our religion compels the poll tax to be paid by dying people, the old, even in a state of incapacity, the blind, monks, workers, and the poor, incapable of practicing a trade. As for people who seem to be insolvent at the end of the year, the sum of the poll tax remains a debt to their account until they should become solvent."[1] Andrew Bostom adds, "Onerous taxation, combined with indebtedness to Muslim creditors, forced Christian and Jewish peasants to abandon their mortgaged lands to their Muslim overlords, and go into exile or become slaves."[2]

An important question debated by scholars is whether the practice of *dhimmitude* resides in the distant past or is a problem in our current times. In her two books, *Islam and Dhimmitude: Where Civilizations Collide* (2002) and *Eurabia: the Euro-Arab Axis* (2005), Bat Ye'or has noted that since the idea of *dhimmitude* is rooted in the Qur'an and codified in Shar'ia law, it should be of no surprise to see it re-emerge on the current world stage.[3] Moderate Islamic scholars disagree, arguing for an understanding of Islam that defines *dhimmitude* as a relic of the ancient past.

---

[1] Bat Ye'or, *Islam and Dhimmitude*, p. 70.
[2] Andrew Bostom, *The Legacy of Jihad*, p. 30.

The basic element of dhimmitude is a land expropriation through a pact of "land for peace." The vanquished populations of territories taken during a millennium of *jihad* were "protected," providing they recognized the Islamic ownership of their lands, which had now become *dar al-Islam*, and that they submitted to Islamic authority.

—David J. Jonsson, *The Clash of Ideologies*, p. 523

Not only does such dhimmitude protect Islam from truths about itself, it also protects Islam from the "offensive"—that is, non-Islamic—aspects of the world outside Islam. Norwegian authorities prohibit Jewish symbols—stars of David, Israeli flags—at an Oslo anniversary commemoration of Kristallnacht to prevent "trouble" (this in a city that regularly hosts pro-Palestinian events). France's chief rabbi warns French Jews against wearing yarmulkes in public to prevent violence...The University of the Incarnate Word in Texas exchanges its crusader mascot for a cardinal (the bird, not the prelate), also for fear of giving offense...It's easy to see why dhimmi populations in Islamic lands would collude in "protecting" Islam from such "offense" or criticism; they fear the sharia consequences. But why do Westerners, in the media, the White House, the United Nations, or the tourist board collude in these same "protections"? Why the refusal to acknowledge patent differences between Islam and the West?

—Diana West, *The Death of the Grown-Up*, p. 184

More problematic, though, is Bat Ye'or's concept of dhimmitude as the primary, legitimate means by which to describe the state of non-Muslims living under Islamic jurisdiction throughout Islamic history. She describes this way of life under *jihad* as a civilization, a polity, an identity that has permeated, delineated, and defined all of *dhimmi* experience since the beginning of Islam. With regard to the medieval context, her portrayal of dhimmitude conjures up visions of rapidly shrinking and profoundly impotent Christian and Jewish minorities, cowering in a proverbial corner of the Islamic world.

—Kurt J. Werthmuller, *Coptic Identity and Ayyubid Politics in Egypt*, p. 20

This relationship between conqueror and conquered was institutionalized as part of the Sharia and still serves as a blueprint today for the treatment of non-Muslims under Islamic rule...The spirit of dhimmitude is pervasive in the Muslim world, regardless of how religious a country is. Even the more secular Muslim countries, such as Egypt and Jordan, discriminate against non-Muslims. There are exceptions, Turkey being one of them, but even in those places Islamic fundamentalism is gaining support. Dhimmitude is institutionalized apartheid in its most blatant form, part of the official law in the *dar al-Islam.*

—Tal Ben-Shahar, *A Clash of Values*, p. 15

The history of dhimmitude has yet to be accepted by the Muslim intelligentsia...Dhimmitude should be recognized, not only on a human and moral level, but also as a grave modern political problem. As long as the prejudices and ideologies that have justified dhimmitude for Jews, Christians and other religious groups are not clearly denounced in the Muslim world, they will continue to influence Muslim politics and perceptions of these peoples. The reactions will be more detrimental to the Muslims themselves, especially those living in Western countries. It is therefore important that Muslim religious and political leaders denounce the sources of intolerance in their own culture, in order to build the bridges of a universal reconciliation.

—Malka Hillel Shulewitz, *The Forgotten Millions*, p. 49

not accepted from the other, that one said, "I will surely kill thee." He said, "God only accepts from those who fear.

28 If thou dost stretch forth to me thine hand to kill me, I will not stretch forth mine hand to kill thee; verily, I fear God the Lord of the worlds;

29 verily, I wish that thou mayest draw upon thee my sin and thy sin, and be of the fellows of the Fire, for that is the reward of the unjust."

30 But his soul allowed him to slay his brother, and he slew him, and in the morning he was of those who lose.

31 And God sent a crow to scratch in the earth and show him how he might hide his brother's shame, he said, "Alas, for me! Am I too helpless to become like this crow and hide my brother's shame?" and in the morning he was of those who did repent.

32 For this cause have we prescribed to the children of Israel that whoso kills a soul, unless it be for another soul or for violence in the land, it is as though he had killed men altogether; but whoso saves one, it is as though he saved men altogether. Our apostles came to them

---

5.28 *I fear God the Lord of the worlds* — The title, "God the Lord of the worlds" is nowhere found in the Bible. Muhammad used it as a substitute for the word Yahweh (see Gen 4:1-13). Yahweh (YHWH) is oft-mentioned in the Old Testament, yet never mentioned in the Qur'an. This dialogue between Cain and Abel, however, is not mentioned in the Genesis account.

5.31 According to this passage, Cain had no idea what to do with a dead corpse, since this was the first of all human deaths. When he saw a crow bury one of its fellow crows by scratching at the earth, he got the idea to bury his dead brother Abel.

This story of the crow, however, is not mentioned in the Bible. It was taken from the *Midrash Tanhuma*, a commentary on the Book of Genesis that includes Hebrew legends, written in the fifth century, A.D. (see **Saving One Life** on pp. 725-726).

5.32-33 Having mentioned the murder of Abel in the previous verse, Muhammad clarified the ethics of killing. He explained that the killing of another human being is sin, with only two exceptions. The first exception is "for another soul" (v. 32)—that is, capital punishment is justified upon the one who commits the crime of murder. The second exception is "for violence in the land" (v. 32)—that is, when one is engaged in the work of Jihad. This is clarified in v. 33 where it is stated that death is "the reward of those who make war against God and His Apostle, and strive after violence in the earth." The kind of death one could expect during Jihad, he added, is being "slaughtered or crucified, or their hands cut off and their feet on alternate sides." Another possibility is that they should be "banished from the land."

The phrase: "whoso kills a soul, unless it be for another soul or for violence in the land, it is as though he had killed men altogether; but whoso saves one, it is as though he saved men altogether" (v. 32) was not original with Muhammad. He acquired it from

with manifest signs; then, verily, many of them did after that commit excesses in the earth.

33   The reward of those who make war against God and His Apostle, and strive after violence in the earth, is only that they shall be slaughtered or crucified, or their hands cut off and their feet on alternate sides, or that they shall be banished from the land;—that is a disgrace for them in this world, and for them in the next is mighty woe;

34   save for those who repent before ye have them in your power, for know ye that God is forgiving, merciful.

The two ways

35   O ye who believe! fear God and crave the means to approach Him, and be strenuous in His way, haply ye will prosper then.

36   Verily, those who disbelieve, even though they had what is in the earth, all of it, and the like thereof with it, to offer as a ransom from the punishment of the resurrection day, it would not be accepted from them; but for them is grievous woe.

37   They may wish to go forth from the Fire, but they shall not go forth therefrom, for them is lasting woe.

Penalty for thievery

38   The man thief and the woman thief, cut off the hands of both as a punishment, for that they have erred;—an example from God, for God is mighty, wise.

39   But whoso turns again after his injustice and acts aright, verily, God will turn to him, for, verily, God is forgiving, merciful.

---

the *Mishnah Sanhedrin*, written four hundred years earlier (see Q 7.33; **Saving One Life** on pp. 725-726).

5.35 *be strenuous in His way* — That is, be jihadistic in the Cause of Allah (see Q 4.95; 8.72, 74-75; 9.16, 41, 44, 73, 81; 16.110; 22.78; 25.52; 29.6, 69; 47.31; 60.1; 66.9). When taken in context of the previous two verses, the implication is that Muhammad desired Muslims to be actively engaged in the work of Jihad. Believing in Allah, fearing Him, craving a relationship with Him, and the work of Jihad are presented as interconnected. Those who engage in all four activities will prosper.

5.36-37 In contrast are those who disbelieve and acquire money and possessions.

They will discover at the Last Judgment that all their wealth will have no value in gaining them entrance into Paradise. They may wish to avoid the fires of Hell, but to no avail.

5.38 The penalty for thievery, whether it be a man or a woman, is to have a hand cut off. The severity of the punishment serves as a warning and example for others. In a Hadith, Muhammad added that "the hand should be cut off for stealing something that is worth a quarter of a Dinar or more" (*Sahih Bukhari* 8.81.780). In another Hadith, Muhammad added that "Allah curses the thief who steals an egg." The penalty for this crime, he added, was that "his hand is to be cut off" (*Sahih Bukhari* 8.81.791).

5.39-40 Exemptions from this severe pun-

40 Do ye not know that God, His is the kingdom of the heavens and the earth; He punishes whom He pleases, and forgives whom He pleases, for God is mighty over all?

General jurisprudence

41 O thou Apostle! let not those grieve thee who vie in misbelief; or those who say with their mouths "We believe," but their hearts do not believe; or of those who are Jews, listeners to a lie,—listeners to other people, but who come not to thee. They pervert the words from their places and say, "If this is what ye are given, take it; but if ye are not given it, then beware!" but he whom God wishes to mislead, thou canst do nothing with God for him;

these are those whose hearts God wishes not to purify, for them in this world is disgrace, and for them in the next is mighty woe,

42 —listeners to a lie, eaters of unlawful things! But if they come to thee, then judge between them or turn aside from them; but if thou turnest aside from them they shall not harm thee at all, but if thou judgest, then judge between them with justice, verily, God loves the just.

43 But how should they make thee their judge, when they have the law wherein is God's judgment? Yet they turn back after that, for they do not believe.

44 Verily, we have revealed the law in which is guidance and light; the prophets who were resigned did

ishment were granted to those who, following the crime, repent immediately. According to Islamic scholars, this exemption was typically limited to Muslim thieves. Non-Muslims found guilty of thievery were seldom granted this exemption (see Q 5.10, note, and **Dhimmitude** on pp. 716-717).

5.41a Muhammad felt compelled to comment about the Muslim hypocrites (apostates) and Jews. He believed that they were only willing to accept rulings that corresponded to their own understandings of jurisprudence.

5.41b *they pervert the words from their places* — That is, they distort their own Scriptures to make them say what they want to hear.

5.41c *he whom God wishes to mislead, thou canst do nothing with God for him* —

That is, because of Muhammad's high view of the sovereignty of Allah, those who distort Scripture were predestined by Allah to do so (see **The Doctrine of al-Qadar** on pp. 264-266).

5.42 *But if they come to thee* — Most Islamic scholars believe that this phrase referred to a historic event where the Jews in Medinah were considering to bring a case to Muhammad.

5.43 Muhammad believed that in spite of their beliefs in the Torah (Old Testament Law), the Jews turned a deaf ear to the Torah when involved in legal disputes.

5.44a Muhammad was admonished to not accept bribes.

5.44b *whoso will not judge by what God has revealed, these be the misbelievers* — This phrase is repeated three times in this

judge thereby those who were Jews, as did the masters and doctors by what they remembered of the Book of God and by what they were witnesses of. Fear not men, but fear me, and sell not my signs for a little price; for whoso will not judge by what God has revealed, these be the misbelievers.

45 We have prescribed for thee therein "a life for a life, and an eye for an eye, and a nose for a nose, and an ear for an ear, and a tooth for a tooth, and for wounds retaliation;" but whoso remits it, it is an expiation for him, but he whoso will not judge by what God has revealed, these be the unjust.

46 And we followed up the footsteps of these (prophets) with Jesus the son of Mary, confirming that which was before him and the law, and we brought him the gospel, wherein is guidance and light, verifying what was before it of the law, and a guidance and an admonition unto those who fear.

47 Then let the people of the gospel judge by that which is revealed therein, for whoso will not judge by what God has revealed, these

be the evildoers.

48 We have revealed to thee the Book in truth verifying what was before it, and preserving it; judge then between them by what God has revealed, and follow not their lusts, turning away from what is given to thee of the truth. For each one of you have we made a law and a pathway; and had God pleased He would have made you one nation, but He will surely try you concerning that which He has brought you. Be ye therefore emulous in good deeds; to God is your return altogether, and He will let you know concerning that wherein ye do dispute.

49 Wherefore judge thou between them by what God has revealed, and follow not their lusts; but beware lest they mislead thee from part of what God has revealed to thee; yet if they turn back, then know that God wishes to fall on them for some sins of theirs,—verily, many men are evildoers.

50 Is it the judgment of the Ignorance they crave? but who is better than God to judge for people who are sure?

passage, with slight variations (see vv. 45 and 47 where the word "misbelievers" is replaced with "unjust" and "evildoers").

5.45 Muhammad drew attention to the passage from the Old Testament, Exodus 21:23-36, which established an equitable jurisprudence.

5.46 Muhammad recognized Jesus as an

example of a righteous judge.

5.48 *be ye therefore emulous in good deeds* — Muslims were encouraged to be eager to surpass one another with lives of good deeds.

5.50 *the judgment of the Ignorance* — That is, pagan jurisprudence.

5.51a Muhammad insisted that the Muslims

Alliances with infidels

51 O ye who believe! take not the Jews and Christians for your patrons: they are patrons of each other; but whoso amongst you takes them for patrons, verily, he is of them, and, verily, God guides not an unjust people.

52 Thou wilt see those in whose hearts is a sickness vieing with them; they say, "We fear lest there befall us a reverse." It may be God will give the victory, or an order from Himself, and they may awake repenting of what they thought in secret to themselves.

53 Those who believe say, "Are these they who swore by God with their most strenuous path that they were surely with you?"—their works are

in vain and they shall wake the losers.

54 O ye who believe! whoso is turned away from his religion—God will bring (instead) a people whom He loves and who love Him, lowly to believers, lofty to unbelievers, strenuous in the way of God, fearing not the blame of him who blames. That is God's grace! He gives it unto whom He pleases, for God both comprehends and knows.

55 God only is your patron, and His Apostle and those who believe, who are steadfast in prayer and give alms, bowing down.

56 Whoso taketh as patrons God and His apostles and those who believe;—verily, God's crew, they are victorious!

---

make no alliances with Jews or Christians, since they were, he explained, an "unjust people."

5.51b *they are patrons of each other* — That is, Jews form alliances with Jews, and Christians form alliances with Christians.

5.52-53 Muhammad warned that if Muslims make alliances with either Jews or Christians, they will eventually apostasize from the Islamic faith and become one of them. Though at one time these Muslims were "most strenuous" (jihadistic in dedication), eventually their works would become vain.

The Bible makes similar observations about alliances with nonbelievers. Christians were cautioned to avoid such alliances, especially marriages with nonbelievers (see Deut 7:2-3; Ezra 9:1-2; Neh 13:1-3; Ps 106:35; 1 Cor 15:33; 2 Cor 6:14-18; James 4:4)

5.54 Those Muslims who made alliances with non-Muslims and turned away from the Islamic religion (that is, became apostates) would discover that Allah will replace them with people more dedicated and strenuous in the way of Allah (that is, more jihadistic in the Cause of Allah).

5.55-56 Muhammad reminded the apostates that Allah is the only true God and Muhammad is the only true Apostle. They are the victorious ones. Accordingly, to disobey Muhammad was tantamount to disobeying Allah. The net result was eternal condemnation in Hell (see Q 3.32; 4.69, 79-80, 136; 5.80-81; 8.13, 20-23; 24.47, 48, 50-52, 54; 33.33, 71; 48.9-10; 57.19; 59.4; 72.22-23; 81.19-21 and 46.16, note).

Christians, on the other hand, remind the Muslim apostates that Islam is a false religion

57 O ye who believe! take not for patrons those who take your religion for a jest or a sport, from amongst those who have been given the Book before and the misbelievers; but fear God if ye be believers.

58 Nor those who, when ye call to prayer, take it for a jest and a sport; that is because they are a people who do not understand.

59 Say, "O people of the Book! do ye disavow us, for aught but that we believe in God, and what was revealed to us before, and for that most of you are evildoers?"

60 Say, "Can I declare unto you some-

thing worse than retribution from God?" Whomsoever God has cursed and been wroth with—and he has made of them apes and swine—and who worship Tâghût, they are in a worse plight and are more erring from the level path.

61 When they come to you they say, "We believe;" but they entered in with unbelief, and they went out therewith, and God knows best what they did hide.

62 Thou wilt see many of them vieing in sin and enmity, and in eating unlawful things,—evil is it that they have done.

and Muhammad a false prophet. By turning to Jesus Christ as Savior they will find true grace and freedom, an assured confidence of Heaven, and a freedom from guilt. George Braswell writes, "An appropriate and decisive evangelism to Muslims is based on the following: (a) the message and life of Jesus Christ, (b) a clear knowledge of Islam, (c) an appreciation of the challenges and struggles of Muslim peoples, (d) a love for individual Muslims and their families, (e) a presentation of biblical truths, and (f) a sharing of one's own Christian faith." He adds: "Methods and styles of evangelism to Muslims may differ to needs, circumstances, and personalities. Especially with much history of uncongenial relations between Christianity and Islam, it is wise to tread carefully but deliberately and intentionally" (*What You Need to Know about Islam and Muslims*, pp. 148, 149).

5.57 Muhammad called Muslims to separate themselves from all who ridicule their religion, which, he said, includes Jews and Christians

("those who have been given the Book").
5.58 Muhammad also called Muslims to separate themselves from all insincere Muslims—most clearly evidenced by their lack of a prayer regimen (see *al-Salat* on pp. 169-170).
5.59 *O people of the Book!* — That is, Jews.
5.60 *apes and swine* — Muhammad believed that Jews were cursed of God. Some of them were transformed into "apes and swine" (see Q 2.65; 7.165-166 note).

Whether this verse and the others cited above are taken literally or figuratively, they have affected Muslim attitudes of Jews. Ayaan Hirsi Ali explains: "Many madrassas [schools] imbue their pupils with an irrational hatred of Jews and an aversion to nonbelievers, a message that is also frequently repeated in the mosques. Jews are consistently portrayed as the instigators of evil in books, on cassette tapes, and by the media. I myself experienced how insidious the effects of years of this indoctrination can be: the first time I saw a Jew with my own eyes,

Saving One Life

In recent years, one of the most oft-cited verses in the Qur'an is the thirty-second verse of the fifth surah. It states:

> ...whoso kills a soul, unless it be for another soul or for violence in the land, it is as though he had killed men altogether; but who saves one, it is as though he saved men altogether.

The verse is repeatedly used to defend moderate Islam and to condemn the wanton killings that is often associated with Jihad. President George W. Bush cited this verse days after the 9/11 Terrorist Attack, making the point that Islamic jihadists neither represent mainstream Islam nor the Qur'an.

When placed in proper context, however, this verse speaks otherwise. Its immediate context is an act of murder unrelated to Jihad (Q 5.27-31; also see Gen 4:1-16). It states that killing is only permitted providing that one of two conditions are met: (a) *provided that it be for another soul*—that is, capital punishment for the crime of murder, or (b) *provided that it be done due to violence in the land*. The following verse (Q 5.33) clarifies what is meant by *violence in the land:*

> The reward of those who make war against God and His Apostle, and strive after violence in the earth, is only that they shall be slaughtered or crucified, or their hands cut off and their feet on alternate sides, or that they shall be banished from the land;—that is a disgrace for them in this world, and for them in the next is mighty woe (Q 5.33).

This second proviso justifies the killing of a human being if that person makes war against (which includes the notion of resisting) Allah and Muhammad (see Q 2.190-191; 10.13; 22.39-40; 26.192-212; 43.6-8).

It is worth nothing that this and the previous verse are borrowed from ancient Jewish writings. The story of the crow scratching the dirt and burying a fellow crow (Q 5.31) comes from Jewish folklore included in the *Midrash Tanhuma* (fifth century, A.D.). It states:

> After Cain slew Abel, the body lay outstretched upon the earth, since Cain did
> not know how to dispose of it. Thereupon, the Holy One, blessed be He,
> selected two clean birds and caused one of them to kill the other. The surviv-
> ing bird dug the earth with its talons and buried its victim. Cain learned from
> this what to do. He dug a grave and buried Abel.[1]

The ethics related to the killing (Q 5.32) comes from another Jewish
writing, *Mishnah Sanhedrin*, (fifth century, B.C.). It states:

> For we find concerning Cain who killed his brother, it is written, "the bloods of
> your brother cry"; it does not say, "your brother's blood" but "bloods"—his
> blood and the blood of his offspring. Another interpretation of "brother's
> blood"—his blood was dashed on the trees and on the stones. Therefore man
> was created singly, to teach you that whoever destroys a single soul of Israel,
> Scripture accounts it as if he had destroyed a full world; and whoever saves
> one soul of Israel, Scripture accounts it as if he has saved a full world (Mish.
> San. 4:5)

---

[1] *Midrash Tanhuma*, pp. 31-32. Some scholars have incorrectly sourced this
legend to the *Targum of Pseudo-Jonathan*. None of the Hebrew Targums mention
this legend.

This passage is not really a prohibition against murder, for two reasons. First, the passage (Sura
5:32) begins with the address to the "Children of Israel." This represents a particular historical
context. It is not addressed to Muslims. Rather, it is a warning to the Jews not to engage in warfare
against Muhammad. Second, it has an important proviso: if there is "corruption in the earth." This
is sometimes translated as "making mischief in the land." While this would certainly include
making war against the Muslims, it could also include resisting the Muslim advance into the land.

—Kerby Anderson, *Islam*, p.71

The greatest danger to Christians and Jews has come when they have been subdued and forced
to submit within an Islamic society. In such a setting, there is no concept of religious pluralism or
liberty. The Qur'anic mandate is that anyone found guilty of "spreading mischief in the land"
(surah 5:32)...is subject to one of four punishments...Muslim countries widely differ, however, in
regard to the definition of "treason" against Allah and the Islamic state. In the perfect example of
Muhammad, the criteria extend beyond violent uprising to verbal insurrection. Missionaries are

criminals guilty of treason under this interpretation.

—Ergun Mehmet Caner, Emir Fethi Caner, *Unveiling Islam*, p. 55

Enough already...Qur'an 5:32 actually says Noble Qur'an 5:32 "...We ordained for the Children of Israel that if anyone killed a person not in retaliation of murder, or (and) to spread mischief in the land—it would be as if he killed all mankind, and if anyone saved a life, it would be as if he saved the life of all mankind..." So, not only did you remove the exception for killing, you stop short of reciting the very next verse. You and your Islamic apologist brethren are warping a passage that epitomizes the motivations of Muslims to kill and torture Israelis and all of mankind to "prove" how peaceful Islam is.

—Craig Winn, *Open Letter to President Bush*

The Koran's commands to Muslims to wage war against non-Muslims in the name of Allah are unmistakable. Such commands are authoritative because they were revealed late in the Prophet's career and abrogate earlier instructions to coexist peacefully with infidels. Without knowledge of the principles of abrogation, Westerners will continue to misread the Koran. Some, however, manage to misread the Koran in a way that even knowledge of abrogation would not remedy. President George W. Bush, for example, has cited Surah 5:32 on at least two occasions to emphasize Islam's peacefulness...One expects that the president's point would have come across somewhat differently had he not neglected to keep reading [Surah 5:33].

—Gregory M. Davis, *Religion of Peace?* pp. 39-40

There are three distinct interpretations of the events of September 11. The first view is that the terrorist acts do not represent Islam. President George W. Bush best expressed this notion when he said that "Islam is a religion of peace." One of the leading Muslims to echo this is Yusuf Islam (the former rock musician Cat Stevens, who now helps promote Muslim education in England). "Today, I am aghast at the horror of recent events and feel it a duty to speak out," he said in a London newspaper. "Not only did terrorists hijack planes and destroy life; they also hijacked the beautiful religion of Islam." During an interfaith ceremony at Yankee Stadium on September 23, Imam Izak-El M. Pasha pleaded, "Do not allow the ignorance of people to have you attack your good neighbors. We are Muslims, but we are Americans. We Muslims, Americans, stand today with a heavy weight on our shoulders that those who would dare do such dastardly acts claim our faith. They are no believers in God at all."

—James A. Beverley, "Islam A Religion of Peace," *Christianity Today*, Jan 7, 2002.

Wishing that Islam is "a religion of peace," however earnestly, does not make it so, and naively lulls the wisher into a false sense of security.

—David Goldmann, *Resurgent Islam and America*, p. 112

63   The masters and their doctors pro-
     hibit them from speaking sin and
     eating unlawful things,—evil is
     what they have performed.
64   The Jews say, "God's hand is fet-
     tered;" their hands are fettered and
     they are cursed for what they said;
     nay! His hands are outspread, He
     expends how He pleases! and that
     which has been sent down to thee
     from thy Lord will surely increase
     many of them in their rebellion and
     misbelief, for we have cast
     amongst them enmity and hatred
     till the resurrection day. Whenever
     they light a fire for war, God puts
     it out; they strive for corruption in
     the earth, but God loves not the
     corrupt.
65   But did the people of the Book be-
     lieve and fear, we would cover their
     offences, and we would make
     them enter into gardens of plea-
     sure;
66   and were they steadfast in the law

and the gospel, and what has been
sent down to them from their
Lord, they should eat from above
them and below them. Amongst
them are a nation who are moderate, but many of them—bad is what
they do.

The straight path

67   O thou Apostle! preach what has
     been revealed to thee from thy
     Lord; if thou do it not thou hast
     not preached His message, and
     God will not hold thee free from
     men; for God guides not people
     who misbelieve.
68   Say, "O people of the Book! ye rest
     on naught until ye stand fast by
     the law and the gospel, and what
     is revealed to you from your Lord."
     But what has been revealed to thee
     from thy Lord will of a surety in-
     crease many of them in rebellion
     and misbelief, vex not thyself then

I was surprised to find a human being of flesh
and blood" (*The Caged Virgin*, p. 30).
5.64a *God's hand is fettered* — That is,
Allah is unwilling to open His hand and bless
anyone who is not a Jew.
5.64b *rebellion and misbelief* — That is, refusal to submit to Allah and acknowledge
Muhammad as His Prophet.
5.65a *we would cover their offences* —
That is, Allah would forgive their transgressions. The notion of covering offenses did
not discount the Islamic requirement of one
earning his or her salvation by means of an
accumulation of righteous acts (see **Divine
Forgiveness in Islam** on pp. 158-161).

5.65b *gardens of pleasure* — That is, Paradise (see **Paradise** on pp. 76-77).
5.67 *preach what has been revealed to
thee* — Muhammad believed that he was
under divine compulsion to preach the Islamic message to all people. If he did not,
Allah would not protect him from infidels.
5.68 Muhammad believed that the Jews
and Christians had no valid ground for their
faith unless they held fast to the Torah and
the Gospel. Yet, the teachings of the
Qur'an, he maintained, correspond to the
Torah and the Bible, rightly understood.
Hence, their rejection of the Qur'an is evidence that they were also rejecting their

for a people who misbelieve.

69 Verily, those who believe and those who are Jews, and the Sabæans, and the Christians, whosoever believes in God and the last day, and does what is right, there is no fear for them, nor shall they grieve.

Jewish and Christian rebelliousness

70 We took a compact of the children of Israel, and we sent to them apostles; every time there came to them an apostle with what their souls loved not, a part of them they

did call liars and a part of them they slew.

71 And they reckoned that there would be no disturbance; but they were blind and deaf! and then God turned again towards them: and then many amongst them were blind and deaf! but God saw what they did.

72 They misbelieve who say, "Verily, God is the Messiah the son of Mary;" but the Messiah said, "O children of Israel! worship God, my Lord and your Lord," verily, he who associates aught with God, God hath forbidden him Paradise,

own Scriptures.

5.69a *those who believe* — That is, Muslims.

5.69b *the Sabaeans* — The *Sabaeans* were an ancient culture that worshipped the Sun, Moon, and Venus and centered in the southern tip of the Arabian Peninsula (present-day Yemen); today residual groups exist in Iraq (see Q 22.17).

5.69c *there is no fear for them* — Muhammad believed that peoples other than Muslims could earn salvation, provided that their lives were characterized by an abundance of righteous deeds. Yet, elsewhere in the Qur'an he maintained that a believer must also believe and obey Muhammad in order to be saved (see Q 4.69, 79-80, 136).

5.70a *we took a compact of the children of Israel* — That is, we made a covenant with the children of Israel. The covenant that Muhammad imagined was neither the Abrahamic Covenant, the Davidic Covenant, the Palestinian Covenant, nor the Mosaic Covenant, all four of which are mentioned in

the Old Testament. Rather, it was a commitment to send apostles to the children of Israel, revealing to them the eternal book (see **The Perspicuous Book** on pp. 178-179 and **The Apostles** on pp. 396-398).

5.70b *every time there came to them an apostle* — Muhammad identified the many prophets that God sent to the children of Israel as *apostles*. His point was that the Israelite people chaffed against the prophets (apostles) and often killed them. Jesus made a similar point where He called the Jewish leaders as "whitewashed tombs" (see Matt 23:27-39).

5.71 *many amongst them were blind and deaf* — That is, many were spiritually blind and deaf.

5.72 Muhammad believed that Jesus never identified himself as God and rejected all attempts to worship him as such. All who worship Jesus as God will enter the fires of Hell. Yet, the New Testament speaks otherwise on this point (see Matt 1:23; Jn 1:1; 10:30-33; 20:28; Rom 9:5; Phil 2:6; Titus 2:13;

and his resort is the Fire, and the unjust shall have none to help them.

73 They misbelieve who say, "Verily, God is the third of three;" for there is no God but one, and if they do not desist from what they say, there shall touch those who misbelieve amongst them grievous woe.

74 Will they not turn again towards God and ask pardon of Him? for God is forgiving and merciful.

75 The Messiah, the son of Mary, is only a prophet: prophets before him have passed away; and his mother was a confessor; they used

both to eat food.—See how we explain to them the signs, yet see how they turn aside!

76 Say, "Will ye serve, other than God, what can neither hurt you nor profit you?" but God, He both hears and knows.

77 Say, "O people of the Book! exceed not the truth in your religion, and follow not the lusts of a people who have erred before, and who lead many astray, and who go away from the level path."

Enemies and friends

78 Those of the children of Israel who

Heb 1:8-13; 2 Peter 1:1; 1 Jn 5:20; also see **The Apostles Creed** on p. 87; the **Definition of Chalcedon** on pp. 785-786, **The Nicene-Constantinopolitan Creed** on p. 740, **The Doctrine of the Trinity** on pp. 735-736; and Q 2.111, note).

5.73 *there is no God but one* — In this verse, Muhammad took aim at the Doctrine of the Trinity saying, "There is no God but one." Yet, according to mainstream Christian thought, the Doctrine of the Trinity does not reject the doctrine of monotheism. It is a complex monotheism: God is one who exists in Three Persons—God the Father, God the Son, and God the Holy Spirit (see **The Doctrine of the Trinity** on pp. 735-736).

C. S. Lewis explained: "Flatlanders, attempting to imagine a cube, would either imagine the six squares coinciding, and thus destroy their distinctiveness, or else imagine them set out side by side, and thus destroy the unity. Our difficulties about the Trinity are of much the same kind" (*Christian Re-*

flections, p. 80).

Millard Erickson added: "We do not hold the Doctrine of the Trinity because it is self-evident or logically cogent. We hold it because God has revealed that this is what he is like" (*Christian Theology*, p. 342).

5.75 Muhammad insisted that Jesus Christ was not divine. In this verse, he made his case by noting that Jesus ate bread. His point was that God is transcendent from His creation and therefore does not engage in such activities as eating bread. From a Christian perspective, this comment merely draws attention to his inability to grasp the notion that Jesus Christ is fully God and fully man (see the **Definition of Chalcedon** on pp. 785-786).

5.77 *the level path* — That is, the way that leads to eternal life (see Q 72.2, note). Muhammad believed that all who believe in the Doctrine of the Trinity are on the crooked path that leads to eternal damnation.

5.78a *cursed by the tongue of David* —

disbelieved were cursed by the tongue of David and Jesus the son of Mary; that is because they rebelled and did transgress;

79 they would not desist from the wrong they did; evil is that which they did.

80 Thou wilt see many of them taking those who disbelieve for their patrons; evil is that which their

souls have sent before them, for God's wrath is on them, and in the torment shall they dwell for aye.

81 But had they believed in God and the prophet, and what was revealed to him, they had not taken these for their patrons; but many of them are evildoers.

82 Thou wilt surely find that the strongest in enmity against those who

---

Muhammad believed that David cursed the people of Israel. In contrast, the Bible states otherwise, that David never cursed the Israelite people. His cursings were directed to the enemies of the people of Israel, not to the Israelites themselves. This was true even of Israelites who sought to kill him, such as King Saul (see 1 Sam 24:5-15).

5.78b *cursed by the tongue of...Jesus the son of Mary* — Jesus cursed the leaders of the Israel (see Matt 23:1-39; Lk 13:34-35).

According to the New Testament, the cursing by Jesus was not meant as a complete condemnation by God of the Israelite people. Rather, the Jewish people are still regarded as God's chosen people, in spite of their rebellion, and will eventually be restored (see Isa 45:17; 54:6-10; Jer 31:31-37; Ezek 37:21-28; 39:25-29; Hos 3:5; Amos 9:14-15; Zech 10:6-12; Rom 11:25-27).

The pogroms initiated by Christians against the Jews during the last two thousand years, then, were wrongheaded and based upon a faulty theology. Pope John Paul II recognized this error, stating, "There are no words strong enough to deplore the terrible tragedy of the *Shoah*" (Address at the Yad Vashem Museum, Jerusalem, March 23, 2000). The word *Shoah* is the Hebrew word for the Holocaust. He added: "My own personal memories are of all that hap-

pened when the Nazis occupied Poland during the war. I remember Jewish friends and neighbors, some of whom perished, while others survived."

Speaking to the Jewish people, Beatrice S. Neall added: "If you are a Jew, chances are you have never encountered the real Jesus. You have glimpsed him through accounts of pogroms, persecutions, inquisitions, and the denunciations of Catholic popes and Protestant Reformers. Your ancestors have fled from country to country, seeking a safe haven from his followers. The cross makes you shudder, along with the taunt that you killed Jesus. We Christians deeply regret the abuses perpetrated against the Jewish people in the name of Jesus. But we feel that if only these historic barriers could be broken down, and you could understand the real Jesus, you would admire him too" (*Outreach to Judaism*).

5.80-81 Muhammad believed that the wrath of God is upon the Jewish people. The reason is that they have not rightly believed in Allah nor His Prophet (Muhammad). They will therefore suffer the tortures of Allah throughout eternity (see Q 3.32, and 46.16, note).

5.82 Muhammad rated the opponents to Islam as the following: the Jews and pagan idolaters are "the strongest in enmity," and

believe are the Jews and the idolaters; and thou wilt find the nearest
in love to those who believe to be
those who say, "We are Christians;" that is because there are
amongst them priests and monks,
and because they are not proud.

83 And when they hear what has been
revealed to the prophet, you will
see their eyes gush with tears at
what they recognise as truth therein; and they will say, "O our Lord!
we believe, so write us down
amongst the witnesses.

84 Why should we not believe in God
and the truth that is given to us,
nor desire that our Lord should
make us enter with the upright
people?"

85 Therefore has God rewarded them,
for what they said, with gardens
beneath which rivers flow, to dwell
therein for aye; that is the reward

of those who do good;

86 but those who disbelieve and say
our signs are lies they are the fellows of hell.

Dietary law

87 O ye who believe! forbid not the
good things which God has made
lawful for you, nor transgress;
verily, God loves not the transgressors.

88 But eat of what God has provided
you lawfully of good things; and
fear God, in whom ye believe.

Law of oaths

89 God will not catch you up for a
casual word in your oaths, but He
will catch you up for having what
ye make deliberate oaths about;
and the expiation thereof is to feed

the Christians to be "the nearest in love."
The reason for the favorable assessment of
the Christians is that "they are not proud."
In this context, it is questionable if Muhammad included those Christians who affirm the
deity of Christ in this favorable assessment
(see Q 5.72-73). More than likely, he meant
Arian Christians (those who rejected the
deity of Christ and the Doctrine of the Trinity). In the seventh century, Christians who
affirmed Arian theology were known to have
lived in the Middle East, including the Arabian Peninsula.

5.83-84 Muhammad believed that the humility of the Christians was illustrated in the
way in which the priests and monks responded to the surahs: their eyes gushed

with tears at what they recognize as truth
therein. As suggested in the previous note,
these priests and monks were religious clergy
committed to Arian theology. Both Arian
Christians and Muslims affirmed an absolute
monotheism and rejected the Doctrine of
the Trinity.

5.85 Muhammad commented that such
Christians (more than likely, Arian in theological orientation) were on the straight path
that leads to eternal life. This is because
they too rejected the doctrine of the deity
of Jesus Christ.

5.89 Muhammad claimed that Allah would
not hold a Muslim accountable for oaths spoken casually. Yet, Allah would hold a Muslim
accountable for oaths spoken deliberately.

ten poor men with the middling food ye feed your families withal, or to clothe them, or to free a neck; but he who has not the means, then let him fast three days. That is the expiation of your oaths, when ye have sworn to keep your oaths; thus does God explain to you His signs,—haply ye may be grateful.

Wine, gambling, idolatry,
and witchcraft

90   O ye who believe! verily, wine, and el mâisar, and statues, and divining (arrows) are only an abomina-

tion of Satan's work; avoid them then that haply ye may prosper.

91   Satan only desires to place enmity and hatred between you by wine and mâisar, and to turn you from the remembrance of God and from prayer; but will ye not desist,

92   and obey God, and obey the apostles, and beware, for if ye turn back then know that our Apostle has only his message to preach?

93   There is no crime in those who believe and do right, for having tasted food, when they fear God, and believe, and do what is right, and then fear Him, and believe, and then

---

Oaths spoken deliberately, yet not fulfilled, could only be expiated if the person (a) fed ten poor men with a middling (moderate and average size) meal, (b) clothed ten poor men, or (c) freed a neck (free a human being from bondage). For those who had no means with which to do the above option, then a person was to fast for three days.

5.90 Muhammad prohibited the imbibing of wine, the involvement in gambling (*maisar*), the worship of statutes, and the practice of witchcraft. He described them as "an abomination of Satan's work." His prohibition of wine is a retraction of a previous surah, where it was described as "a goodly provision" (see Q 16.67; the **Doctrine of Abrogation** on pp. 68-70).

In regards to the divining of arrows, Thomas Harwell Home writes, "The manner of divining by arrows was thus: they wrote on several arrows the names of the cities against which they intended to make war, and then putting them promiscuously all together into a quiver, they caused them to

be drawn out in the manner of lots; and that city whose name was on the arrow first drawn out was the first they assaulted. This method of divination was practiced by the idolatrous Arabs, and prohibited by Muhammad, and was likewise used by the ancient Greeks, and other nations" (*An Introduction to the Critical Study and Knowledge of the Holy Scriptures*, vol. 3, pp. 388-389).

5.91 Muhammad understood wine and gambling (*maisar*) as activities that increased hatred between Muslim believers and discouraged people from true Islamic piety, such as public prayer, the giving of alms, obedience to Allah and obedience to the apostles (namely, Muhammad).

5.91-92 Muhammad reminded the Muslims of the dietary law presented in vv. 3-5; also see Q 2.168, and Q 6.118-121 where the tradition of Halal is mentioned).

5.93 *believe and do right* — This is a summary of the Islamic gospel (see Q 103.3, note). For emphasis, this phrase (in various forms) is repeated three times in one verse.

fear, and do good, for God loves those who do good.

Laws pertaining to the Hajj

94   O ye who believe! God will try you with something of the game that your hands and your lances take, that God may know who fears Him in secret; and whoso transgresses after that, for him is grievous woe.

95   O ye who believe! kill not game while ye are on pilgrimage. But he amongst you who kills it purposely, his compensation is the like of that which he has killed, in sheep—of which two equitable persons amongst you shall be judge—an offering brought to the Kaabah; or as an expiation, the food of poor persons, or an equivalent thereof in fasting, that he may taste the evil result of his deed. God pardons bygones; but whoso returns, God will take vengeance on him, for God is mighty and the avenger.

96   Lawful for you is the game of the sea, and to eat thereof; a provision for you and for travellers; but forbidden you is the game of the land while ye are on pilgrimage; so fear God to whom ye shall be gathered.

97   God has made the Kaabah, the sacred House, to be a station for men, and the sacred month, and the offering and its neck garland; this is that ye may know that God knows what is in the heavens and what is in the earth, and that God knows all things.

98   Know that God is keen to punish, but that God is forgiving, merciful.

99   The Apostle has only to preach his message, but God knows what ye show and what ye hide.

100 Say, "The vile shall not be deemed equal with the good, although the abundance of the vile please thee." Fear God then, O ye who have minds! haply ye may prosper.

*Prohibition against
additional laws*

101 O ye who believe! ask not about

5.94 During one's pilgrimage on the Hajj, a pilgrim was not permitted to kill wild game. If he should violate this law, he was to either (a) bring a sheep to the Festival of Sacrifice for sacrifice, (b) bring an offering to the Ka'ba altar which will then be distributed among the poor, or (c) perform a religious fast. If the option of a sheep was chosen, two equitable men were to determine the size of the sheep so that its flesh value approximated that which was wrongfully killed. The final two options—providing food for the poor or fasting—were only offered to the pilgrims who were too poor to purchase a sheep.

5.96 While on the Hajj, pilgrims may eat seafood.

5.97 *neck garland* — All animal offerings were to have garlands draped around their necks.

The Doctrine of the Trinity

The famous Christian theologian, Augustine of Hippo, once said: "Deny the Trinity and lose your salvation, try to understand the Trinity and lose your mind." This is because the Doctrine of the Trinity is fundamentally a paradox: God is one, yet exists in Three Persons.

The oneness of God is stated throughout the Bible, the most oft-cited verse perhaps being Deut. 6:4, which states: "Hear, O Israel: the LORD our God, the LORD is one." Yet this one God existed in Three Persons: God the Father, God the Son, and God the Holy Spirit. Each Person is distinct from the other two, yet of the same essence. Early church creeds further defined this doctrine: the Nicene Creed (325) and the Constantinopolitan Creed (381). These two creeds are typically understood as one creed: the Nicene-Constantinopolitan Creed.

Our problems with the doctrine is that the finite mind has difficulties and limits in understanding infinitude. C. S. Lewis explained: "Flatlanders, attempting to imagine a cube, would either imagine the six squares coinciding, and thus destroy their distinctiveness, or else imagine them set out side by side, and thus destroy the unity. Our difficulties about the Trinity are of much the same kind."[1] Millard Erickson added: "We do not hold the doctrine of the Trinity because it is self-evident or logically cogent. We hold it because God has revealed that this is what he is like."[2]

Briefly stated, the Scriptures that teach the Trinity are the following:

- **God is one** (Deut 6:4; Isa 44:8; 45:5-6; Mk 12:29; 1 Cor 8:4)
- **the Father is God** (Matt 18:14; Lk 10:21; Jn 4:23; 6:27; 20:17; Rom 1:7; 15:6; Gal 1:1; Eph 1:17; 4:6; 5:20; Phil 1:2; 2:11; 4:20; Col 1:2-3; 3:17; 1 Thess 1:1; 3:11; 2 Thess 1:1-2; 2:16; 1 Tim 1:2; Titus 1:4; Phile 3; James 1:27; 1 Pet 1:2-3; Jude 1)
- **the Son is God** (Isa 9:6; Jn 1:1; 10:30-33; 20:28; Rom 9:5;

Phil 2:6; Titus 2:13; Heb 1:8-9; 2 Pet 1:1; 1 Jn 5:20; Rev 1:17
with Isa 44:6)

- **the Holy Spirit is God** (Acts 5:1-4)

Liturgical formulas: Matt 28:19; 2 Cor 13:14; and Jude 20; cf. Matt
3:16-17; Luke 1: 35; Heb 9:14; 1 Pet 1:2; 3:18.

---

[1] C. S. Lewis, *Christian Reflections*, p. 80.
[2] Millard Erickson, *Christian Theology*, p. 342.

Islamic critics of Christianity regularly criticize Christians for apparently deviating from the emphasis upon the unity of God (often referred to by the Arabic word *tawhid*) through the doctrine of the Trinity. This doctrine is argued to be a late invention, which distorts the idea of the unity of God, and ends up teaching that there are three gods. The witness of the Qur'an to what Mohammed thought that Christians believe is not quite as clear as might be hoped for, and had led some interpreters of Islam to suggest that it believes that Christians worship a trinity consisting of God, Jesus and Mary.

—Alister E. McGrath, *Christian Theology: An Introduction*, p. 247

Trinitarianism is flatly condemned in Islam on the grounds that it denies the sole worship of God...The Qur'an makes a fundamental distinction between God and all else, including human beings who are finite creatures. God alone is infinite as well as absolute. To point to an individual such as Jesus, with delimitations of birthplace and birthdate, and then to say simply that he is God, or the second person in the godhead, is, according to the Qur'an, impossible and unpardonable. The Qur'anic judgment against those who uphold the doctrine of Trinity is similar to its judgment against idolaters.

—Solomon Alexander Nigosian, *Islam: Its History, Teaching, and Practices*, p. 75

The Bible does not teach the doctrine of the Trinity. Neither the word "trinity" itself nor such language as "one-in-three," one "essence (or "substance"), and three "persons" is biblical language. The language of the doctrine is the language of the ancient church taken from classical Greek philosophy. But the church did not simply invent this doctrine. It used the language and concepts available to it to interpret what the Bible itself says about who God is and how God is present and at work in the world. Although scripture does not teach the doctrine itself, it says some things about God that made the doctrine necessary.

—Shirley C. Guthrie, *Christian Doctrine*, p. 77

things which if they be shown to you will pain you; but if ye ask about them when the (whole) Qur'ân is revealed, they shall be shown to you. God pardons that, for God is forgiving and clement.

102 People before you have asked about that, yet on the morrow did they disbelieve therein.

Pagan superstitions prohibited

103 And God has not ordained any Ba'hîrah or Sâïbah, nor Wazîlah nor 'Hâmî, but those who misbelieve invent a lie against God, for most of them do not understand.

104 And when it is said to them, "Come round to what God has revealed unto His Apostle," they say, "Enough for us is what we found our fathers agreed upon." What!

though their fathers knew nothing and were not guided.

105 O ye who believe! mind yourselves; he who errs can do you no hurt when ye are guided: unto God is your return altogether, and He will declare to you that which ye do not know.

Last Will and Testaments

106 O ye who believe! let there be a testimony between you when any one of you is on the point of death—at the time he makes his will—two equitable persons from amongst you; or two others from some other folk, if ye be knocking about in the land, and the calamity of death befall you; ye shall shut them both up after prayer, and they shall both swear by God, if ye doubt them, (saying), "We will not

5.101 Muslims were admonished not to ask additional questions about the Islamic faith on the grounds that too much divine revelation could be too painful. In his commentary, Muhammad Asad notes that by leaving certain issues unspoken, the Muslim was allowed a degree of latitude so that he could "act in accordance with his conscience" as he sought the well-being of the Islamic community (*The Message of the Qur'an*, p. 190).

5.103 *God has not ordained Ba'hirah or Saibah, nor Wazilah nor Hami* — These four terms were used by pagan Arabs for cattle set aside for religious devotion. Based upon size, sex, and order in the birthing process, certain cows were set aside and allowed to pasture and never slaughtered for meat (see

Q 6.152-153 where this practice is also mentioned). These animals served, in so many words, as good luck charms. Muhammad asserted that this practice was not ordained of Allah and should not be practiced by Muslims.

5.106-108 According to the Qur'an, laws concerning Last Will and Testaments included the following: at the point of death, a person was to speak to two reliable witnesses of his intentions regarding the dispositions of all personal property. The two witnesses were warned not to take bribes and alter the testimony at the time of disbursement. Yet, if heirs of the deceased should challenge the testimony of the two witnesses, a hearing was to be held where a final deci-

sell (our testimony) for a price, though it were to a relative, nor will we hide God's testimony, verily, then, we should be among sinners."

107 But if it shall be lit upon that they too have deserved the imputation of sin, then let two others stand up in their place with those who think them deserving of the imputation, the nearest two in kin, and they shall both swear by God, "Indeed, our testimony is truer than the testimony of those two, and we have not transgressed, for then we should surely be of the unjust:"

108 thus is it easier for men to bear testimony according to the purport thereof, else must they fear lest an oath be given to rebut their own oath; but let them fear God and listen, for God guides not the people who do ill.

*Review of the
ministry of Jesus*

109 On the day when God shall assemble the apostles and shall say, "How were ye answered?" they will say, "We have no knowledge; verily, thou art He who knoweth the unseen."

110 When God said, "O Jesus, son of Mary! remember my favours towards thee and towards thy mother, when I aided thee with the Holy Ghost, till thou didst speak to men in the cradle and when grown up. And when I taught thee the Book and wisdom and the law and the gospel; when thou didst create of clay, as it were, the likeness of a bird, by my power, and didst blow thereon, it became a bird; and thou didst heal the blind from birth, and the leprous by my permission; and when thou didst bring forth the dead by my permission; and when I did ward off the children of Israel from thee, when thou didst come to them with manifest signs, and those who

sion would be rendered.

5.109 Muhammad believed that following the General Resurrection from the Dead, Allah will gather together all the apostles and review the particular ministries that they had while on the earth.

5.110 Muhammad summarized a number of events that he believed were associated with Jesus: (a) the Holy Ghost enabled Jesus to speak forth the Word of God while in the cradle and while an adult, (b) God taught Jesus of the Law and the Gospel, (c) the Holy Ghost aided Jesus in forming clay birds and then breathing life into them, (d) while

an infant Jesus healed blind and the lepers, and raised the dead, and (e) Jesus warned the people of Israel of spiritual truths, of which they readily rejected.

The source of Muhammad's information was apocryphal Christian literature; specifically, of *The Arab Gospel of the Infancy of the Savior* and *The Gospel of Thomas*, both of which were in circulation in the Middle East in the seventh century (see **Jesus in the Cradle** on pp. 285-286; **Jesus and the Clay Sparrows** on p. 658-659; and Q 19.29-33).

5.111 Muhammad believed that the twelve

misbelieved amongst them said, 'This is naught but obvious magic.'

The table of food

111 And when I inspired the apostles that they should believe in him and in my Apostle, they said, 'We believe; do thou bear witness that we are resigned.'"

112 When the apostles said, "O Jesus, son of Mary! is thy Lord able to send down to us a table from heaven?" He said, "Fear God, if ye be believers;"

113 and they said, "We desire to eat therefrom that our hearts may be at rest, and that we may know that what thou hast told us is the truth, and that we may be thereby amongst the witnesses."

114 Said Jesus the son of Mary, "O God, our Lord! send down to us a table from heaven to be to us as a

festival,—to the first of us and to the last, and a sign from Thee,—and grant us provision, for Thou art the best of providers."

115 God said, "Verily, I am about to send it down to you; but whoso disbelieves amongst you after that, verily, I will torment him with the torment which I have not tormented any one with in all the worlds."

Denial of the Trinity

116 And when God said, "O Jesus, son of Mary! is it thou who didst say to men, take me and my mother for two gods, beside God?" He said, "celebrate Thy praise! what ails me that I should say what I have no right to? If I had said it, Thou wouldst have known it; Thou knowest what is in my soul, but I know not what is in Thy soul; verily, Thou art one who knoweth

apostles of Jesus believed in both Jesus and Muhammad. Since Muhammad had not yet been born, the inference is that the future birth and ministry of Muhammad was implied or subtly presented in the teachings of Jesus (see Q 61.6 note, where the controversy of *parakletos* and *periklutos* is discussed).

5.112-115a Muhammad was mistaken in his recounting of the story of a table of food being sent down from heaven. The story applies to Peter, not Jesus. It also occurred in a private moment when Peter was in prayer on a rooftop, not in the presence of the other apostles. And finally, it took place after the resurrection of Jesus and His as-

cension to heaven (see Acts 10:9-16).

5.115b Within a few years, said Muhammad, Allah would torture all infidels with an intensity unknown in all previous eras. This is an allusion to the era of Islam and the increase of tortures to all who resisted Muhammad's message (see **Jihad** on pp. 616-622).

5.116 *take me and my mother for two Gods* — Muhammad claimed that Christians wrongly ascribed divinity to both Jesus and Mary. This has caused many to conclude that Muhammad wrongly defined the doctrine of the Trinity as: God the Father, God the Son, and the Virgin Mary. Islamic scholar

Nicene-Constantinopolitan Creed

A.D. 381

In the early church, a controversy emerged regarding the nature of the Godhood. In A.D. 325, the first ecumenical council was convened in Nicaea (present-day northwest Turkey) where the Doctrine of the Trinity was affirmed. In A.D. 381, a second ecumenical council was convened in Constantinople to add a few words to the Nicene Creed that further explained the nature of the Holy Spirit.

THE CREED

We believe in one God, the Father All Governing, creator of heaven and earth, of all things visible and invisible;

And [we believe] in one Lord Jesus Christ, the only-begotten Son of God, begotten from the Father before all time, Light from Light, true God from true God, begotten not created, of the same essence as the Father, through whom all things came into being, who for us men and because of our salvation came down from heaven, and was incarnate by the Holy Spirit and the Virgin Mary and became human. He was crucified for us under Pontius Pilate, and suffered and was buried, and rose on the third day, according to the Scriptures, and ascended to heaven, and sits on the right hand of the Father, and will come again with glory to judge the living and dead. His Kingdom shall have no end.

And [we believe] in the Holy Spirit, the Lord and life-giver, who proceeds from the Father, who is worshiped and glorified together with the Father and Son, who spoke through the prophets; and in one, holy, catholic, and apostolic church. We confess one baptism for the remission of sins. We look forward to the resurrection of the dead and the life of the world to come. Amen.

the unseen.

117 I never told them save what Thou didst bid me,—'Worship God, my Lord and your Lord,' and I was a witness against them so long as I was amongst them; but when Thou didst take me away to thyself Thou wert the watcher over them, for Thou art witness over all.

118 If Thou shouldst, punish them, verily, they are Thy servants; if Thou shouldst forgive them, verily, Thou art the mighty and the wise."

Benediction

119 God said, "This is the day when their confession shall profit the confessors, for them are gardens beneath which rivers flow, to dwell therein for ever and for aye." God is well pleased with them, and they well pleased with Him; that is the mighty happiness.

120 God's is the kingdom of the heavens, and the earth, and all that is therein, and He is mighty over all.

Surah 59

In the name of the merciful and compassionate God.

Banu 'n-Nadir

1 What is in the heavens and in the earth celebrates God's praises; He

---

Abdullah Yusuf Ali, for example, wrote: "The worship of Mary, though repudiated by the Protestants, was widely spread in the earlier Churches, both in the East and the West" (*The Meaning of the Qur'an*).

Indeed, within the official Church of the seventh century, Mary began acquiring an increasingly prominent place in Christian dogma. Roles that the New Testament restricted to the Holy Spirit (e.g., the Divine Comforter, the Interceder of people's prayers, and the One responsible for the execution of miracles) were gradually handed over to Mary. As such, in the eyes of many, Mary was in the process of becoming a surrogate Holy Spirit.

In recent years, this observation has been acknowledged by some theologians within Roman Catholicism, including the esteemed Roman Catholic theologian Yves Congar. Congar pointed out "that certain pre-Vatican II styles of devotion to Mary, the Mother of the Lord, were actually a displacement of what should have been a liturgical and theological focus on the Holy Spirit. He concedes, therefore, a basis for the Protestant criticism that Catholics have attributed to Mary what really belongs to the Holy Spirit" (*Yves Congar: Theologian of the Church*, p. 308).

5.119a *this is the day when their confession shall profit the confessors* — This is a day of blessing, a reference to the Last Judgment.

5.119b *gardens beneath which rivers flow* — Repeatedly in the Qur'an is the imagery of Paradise is presented as an oasis with well supplied aquifers (see **Paradise** on pp. 76-77).

Surah 59. The title of this surah, *The Ban-*

is the mighty, the wise!

2 He it was who drove those of the people of the Book who misbelieved forth from their houses, at the first emigration; ye did not think that they would go forth, and they thought that their fortresses would defend them against God; but God came upon them from whence they did not reckon, and cast dread into their hearts! They ruined their houses with their own hands and the hands of the believers; wherefore take example, O ye who are

endowed with sight!

3 Had it not been that God had prescribed for them banishment, He would have tormented them in this world; but for them in the next shall be the torment of the Fire!

4 that is because they opposed God and His Apostle: and whoso opposes God, verily, God is keen to punish!

5 What palm trees ye did cut down or what ye left standing upon their roots was by God's permission, and to disgrace the workers of

ishment, is based on v. 3. The occasion of this surah is the conflict between Muhammad and the Banu 'n-Nadir, a Jewish tribe in Medinah, and its banishment from the city.

Shortly after Muhammad's emigration to the Medinah (Yathrib), the Compact of Medinah was confirmed (see Q 3.81-92), a covenant which recognized him as the city's official prophet and apostle. Following the military success at the Battle Badr in 624, it seemed to most people of Medinah that Muhammad was indeed blessed of Allah.

Yet following his defeat at Uhud in A.D. 625, perceptions changed. The Banu 'n-Nadir entered into a secret alliance with the people of Mecca, with the hope of expelling Muhammad and his followers from Medinah. When Muhammad learned of this alliance, he offered this Jewish tribe two options: either (a) they face him and his Muslim army in open combat, or (b) leave the city. If they chose the second option, they could return each year to harvest their crops.

The Jewish tribe chose the second option, yet requested a ten day respite to gather their possessions. During this time, they secretly conspired with other Arabs in

Medinah to attack Muhammad and his small Muslim army. They then remained in their fortified settlements and declared war against Muhammad. After a twenty-one day siege of their settlements, which resulted in no loss of life, the promised support of the Arabs did not materialize and the Jewish tribe surrendered. They left Medinah. Most emigrating to Syria. Their farm lands were forfeited and divided among a number of the Muslims in Medinah.

59.1-2 The surah begins with words of celebration of Muhammad's victory over the Banu 'n-Nadir, a Jewish tribe in Medinah. They were driven from the houses in the first emigration from the city. Others were therefore warned not to follow in their example.

59.3 *God had prescribed for them banishment* — Rather than torturing them, Allah chose banishment.

59.4 Muhammad believed that all who opposed Allah and Muhammad will be punished (also see Q 3.32, and 46.16, note).

59.5 *palm trees* — Certain palm trees were cut down in preparation of the siege against the fortresses of the Jewish settlement.

59.6a *the spoils* — The spoils included the

abomination;

6 and as for the spoils that God gave to His Apostle from these (people) ye did not press forward after them with horse or riding camel; but God gives His Apostle authority over whom He pleases, for God is mighty over all!

7 What God gave as spoils to His Apostle of the people of the cities is God's, and the Apostle's, and for kinsfolk, orphans, and the poor, and the wayfarer, so that it should not be circulated amongst the rich men of you. And what the Apostle gives you, take; and what he forbids you, desist from; and fear God, verily, God is keen to punish!

8 And (it is) for the poor who fled, who were driven forth from their houses and their wealth, who crave grace from God and His goodwill, and help God and the Apostle; they are the truthful.

9 And those who were settled in the abode and the faith before them, love those who fled to them; and they do not find in their breasts a need of what has been given to them; preferring them to themselves, even though there be poverty amongst them; and whoso is preserved from his own covetousness, these are the prosperous!

10 And those who came after them say, "Our Lord, forgive us and our brethren who were beforehand with us in the faith, and place not in our hearts ill-will towards those who believe—our Lord! verily, thou art kind, compassionate!"

The Arab hypocrites

11 Dost thou not look on those who were hypocritical, saying to their brethren who misbelieved amongst the people of the Book, "If ye be driven forth we will go forth with you; and we will never obey any one concerning you; and if ye be

homes of the Jewish tribe and their farmlands.

59.6b *ye did not press forward after them with horse or riding camel* — That is, a military battle was not initiated.

59.7 *God gave as spoils to His Apostle* — The spoils were given to Muhammad and his kin, orphans, the poor, and the sojourner. Allah chose Muhammad to disperse the spoils to those in need.

59.9a *settled in the abode* — That is, content in their life on this earth

59.9b *love those who fled to them* — That is, love all who come to them seeking ref-

uge and protection from the infidels who wish them harm.

59.10 With a forward look into the future, Muhammad anticipated people embracing the Islamic faith with a sense of true submission to the Lord, not like that of the Banu 'n-Nadir (the Jewish tribe) that had been banished.

59.11-12 Muhammad then turned his attention to the Arabs in Medinah who had originally agreed to help the Jews in their fight against the Muslim presence in Medinah. These Arabs had agreed to go into exile with the Banu 'n-Nadir. They also

fought against we will help you."
But God bears witness that they
are surely liars!

12   If they be driven forth, these will
not go forth with them; and if they
be fought against, these will not
help them; or if they do help them,
they will turn their backs in flight;
—then shall they not be helped!

13   Ye indeed are a keener source of
fear in their hearts than God; that
is because they are a people who
do not understand!

14   They will not fight against you in a
body save in fortified cities, or
from behind walls; their valour is
great amongst themselves;—thou
dost reckon them as one body, but
their hearts are separated. This is
because they are a people who
have no sense!

15   Like unto those before them, recently; they tasted the evil result
of their affair, and for them is
grievous woe.

16   Like unto the devil when he said to
man, "Disbelieve." But when he

disbelieved, he said, "Verily, I am
clear of thee! Verily, I fear God the
Lord of the worlds!"

17   And the end of them both shall be
that they shall both be in the Fire,
to dwell therein for aye! for that is
the reward of the unjust!

Muslims

18   O ye who believe! fear God; and
let each soul look to what it sends
on for the morrow; and fear God;
verily, God is well aware of what
ye do!

19   And be ye not like those who forget God, and He makes them forget themselves; they are the workers of abomination!

20   Not deemed alike shall be the fellows of the Fire and the fellows of
Paradise: the fellows of Paradise
they are the blissful!

Qur'an

21   Had we sent down this Qur'ân

agreed to fight alongside the Jews, if war
ensued. Yet, said Muhammad, they were
liars and therefore could not be trusted in
whatever they said.

59.14 The Jews and the Arab hypocrites
(apostates), said Muhammad, were cowards.
They had valor "from behind walls," yet were
truly a people "who have no sense."

59.15 *Like unto those before them* — Like
the vanquished Meccans at the Battle of
Badr.

59.16 *Like unto the devil* — Muhammad
also likened his opponents in Medinah as unto

the devil himself.

59.17 Muhammad condemned to Hell both
the Jews of the Banu 'n-Nadir and the Arabs
who had originally pledged to help them resist the Muslim people (see vv. 11-12).

59.18-20 The Muslim people were encouraged to remain steady and faithful to Allah
and not follow in the example of those "who
forget God"—that is the Banu 'n-Nadir (the
Jewish tribe) who had turned against Muhammad.

59.21 Muhammad contrasted an inert
mountain with the hard-heartedness of the

upon a mountain, thou wouldst have seen it humbling itself, splitting asunder from the fear of God! These parables do we strike out for men; haply they may reflect!

Allah

22 He is God than whom there is no god; who knows the unseen and the visible; He is the merciful, the compassionate!
23 He is God than whom there is no god; the King, the Holy, the Peace-Giver, the Faithful, the Protector, the Mighty, the Repairer, the Great!—celebrated be the praises of God above what they join with Him.
24 He is God, the Creator, the Maker, the Fashioner; His are the excellent names! His praises, whatever are in the heavens and the earth do celebrate; for God is the mighty, the wise!

Surah 4

In the name of the merciful and compassionate God.

Civil laws

1 O ye folk! fear your Lord, who created you from one soul, and created therefrom its mate, and diffused from them twain many men and women. And fear God, in whose name ye beg of one another, and the wombs; verily, God over you doth watch.
2 And give unto the orphans their property, and give them not the vile in exchange for the good, and devour not their property to your own property; verily, that were a great sin.

---

infidels. If the Qur'an were sent down and placed upon a mountain it would humble itself. Yet when the Qur'an is recited to infidels, they remain proud and resistant.

59.22 *He is God than whom there is no god* — Muhammad concluded this surah by repeating the Doctrine of Tauhid twice (vv. 22-23; also see Q 112, note). Muhammad then added a number of titles of Allah: the King, Holy, the Peace-Giver, the Faithful, the Protector, the Mighty, the Repairer, the Great, the Creator, the Maker, and the Fashioner.

Surah 4. The title of this surah, *The Women*, comes from v. 1. A major theme is the rights and obligations of the Muslim wo-man. The surah also addresses questions related to war and peace, laws of inheritance, and the relationship between Muslims, non-Muslims, and apostates. Moreover, the Jewish and Christian religions were compared and contrasted with Islam, with special attention given to questions related to the crucifixion of Jesus.

4.1a *who created you from one soul* — That is, who created you from Adam (see Gen. 1:27-28; 2:20; 3:20).

4.1b *and created therefrom its mate* — That is, who created you from Eve.

4.2 Muhammad admonished the Muslim people to not abuse orphans. Rather, they were to properly care for their needs.

3   But if ye fear that ye cannot do justice between orphans, then marry
what seems good to you of
women, by twos, or threes, or
fours; and if ye fear that ye cannot be equitable, then only one, or
what your right hands possess.
That keeps you nearer to not being partial.

4   And give women their dowries
freely; and if they are good enough
to remit any of it of themselves,
then devour it with good digestion
and appetite.

5   But do not give up to fools their
property which God has made you
to stand by; but maintain them
from it, and clothe them, and speak
to them with a reasonable speech.

6   Prove orphans until they reach a
marriageable age, and if ye perceive in them right management,

then hand over to them their property, and do not devour it extrava-
gantly in anticipation of their growing up. And he who is rich, let him
abstain; but he who is poor, let him
devour in reason, and when ye
hand over to them their property,
then take witnesses against them;
but God sufficeth for taking account.

Inheritances

7   Men should have a portion of what
their parents and kindred leave, and
women should have a portion of
what their parents and kindred
leave, whether it be little or much,
a determined portion.

8   And when the next of kin and the
orphans and the poor are present
at the division, then maintain them

4.3a *if ye fear that ye cannot do justice between orphans* — In pre-Islamic Arabia, guardian men were permitted to marry orphan girls under their care. Muhammad taught that if men could not properly care for orphan girls under their care (do justice between orphans), they were encouraged to marry other women.

4.3b *by twos, or threes, or fours* — Muslim men were permitted to be married to a maximum of four wives simultaneously (the law of polygamy). They were to strive to not be partial with any one of their wives. In his own life, Muhammad violated this ordinance, being married to numerous wives simultaneously (see Q 33.50, note; **Muhammad's Many Wives** on p. 823).

4.3c *or what your right hands possess* —

Men were permitted to have sex with their female slaves (concubines). See Q 4.25-26; 23.5-6; 33.50; 70.29-30.

4.5 *But do not give up to fools their property* — That is, manage the property and possessions of the feebleminded and the orphans.

4.6 *Prove orphans* — That is, test orphans to see if they are able to manage their own possessions and property.

4.7 Direct descendents, whether men or women, are to be given the shares of the inheritances.

4.8-10 Next of kin and orphans have no legal claim on the distribution of inheritances, yet should be reasonably considered. Otherwise family squabbles could result in serious familial problems.

out of it, and speak to them a reasonable speech.

9 And let these fear lest they leave behind them a weak seed, for whom they would be afraid; and let them fear God, and speak a straightforward speech.

10 Verily, those who devour the property of orphans unjustly, only devour into their bellies fire, and they shall broil in flames.

Legal shares

11 God instructs you concerning your children; for a male the like of the portion of two females, and if there be women above two, then let them have two-thirds of what (the deceased) leaves; and if there be but one, then let her have a half; and as to the parents, to each of them a sixth of what he leaves, if he has a son; but if he have no son, and his parents inherit, then let his mother have a third, and if he have brethren, let his mother have a

sixth after payment of the bequest he bequeaths and of his debt. Your parents or your children, ye know not which of them is nearest to you in usefulness:—an ordinance this from God; verily, God is knowing and wise!

12 And ye shall have half of what your wives leave, if they have no son; but if they have a son, then ye shall have a fourth of what they leave, after payment of the bequests they bequeath or of their debts. And they shall have a fourth of what ye leave, if ye have no son; but if ye have a son, then let them have an eighth of what ye leave, after payment of the bequest ye bequeath and of your debts. And if the man's or the woman's (property) be inherited by a kinsman who is neither parent nor child, and he have a brother or sister, then let each of these two have a sixth; but if they are more than that, let them share in a third after payment of the bequest he bequeaths and of

4.11-12 The legal shares of inheritances are to be given as follows: (a) the share of a male heir shall be the equal of the shares of two female heirs, (b) if the deceased leaves two or more daughters and no sons, their shares are two thirds of the inheritance, (c) if the deceased leaves only one daughter, she is to receive half of the inheritance, (d) if the deceased leaves a son, his parents is to receive a sixth of the shares, (e) if the deceased does not have a son, the father receives two-thirds and the mother one third of the shares, (f) if the deceased has brethren, his mother is to receive one sixth after the payment of all debts and the remainder divided among the brethren, (g) a man is to receive half of the inheritances of his wives, if they have no sons, (h) a man is to receive a fourth of what his wives leave, if they have sons, (i) the wives shall receive a fourth of what a man leaves, if he had no son, (j) the wives shall receive an eighth of what a man leaves, if he had a son, and (k) if a man assigns a kinsman who is neither parent nor child, yet have a brother or sister, each one is to receive one sixth of

his debts, without prejudice,—an ordinance this from God, and God is knowing and clement!

13   These be God's bounds, and whoso obeys God and the Apostle He will make him enter into gardens beneath which rivers flow, and they shall dwell therein for aye;—that is the mighty happiness.

14   But whoso rebels against God and His Apostle, and transgresses His bounds, He will make him enter into fire, and dwell therein for aye; and for him is shameful woe.

Adultery

15   Against those of your women who commit adultery, call witnesses four in number from among yourselves; and if these bear witness, then keep the women in houses until death release them, or God shall make for them a way.

16   And if two of you commit it, then hurt them both; but if they turn again and amend, leave them alone, verily, God is easily turned, compassionate.

17   God is only bound to turn again towards those who do evil through ignorance and then turn again, Surely, these will God turn again to, for God is knowing, wise.

18   His turning again is not for those who do evil, until, when death comes before one of them, he says, "Now turn again;" nor yet for those who die in misbelief. For such as these have we prepared a grievous woe.

Inheritance laws

19   O ye who believe! it is not lawful for you to inherit women's estates the inheritance.

4.15a *call witnesses four in number* — Wives convicted of adultery (confirmed through the witness of four people) were to be confined in their homes for the remainder of their lives (see Q 24.2 where it is stated that the penalty for adultery is twenty-four lashes). Sanaz Alasti has noted that "in Islam, there are no clear instructions about stoning in the Qur'an" (*Comparative Study of Stoning Punishment in the Religions of Islam and Judaism*) See **Honor Killing** on pp. 799-800.

4.15b *or God shall make for them a way* — Forgiveness and the release of punishment is possible through repentance.

4.16a *if two of you commit it* — That is, if a man and woman are found guilty of adultery, then both are to be punished. Most Islamic scholars believe that homosexual liaisons are also subject to the same penalty.

4.16b *but if they turn again and amend* — A release of the penalty is possible if the guilty parties repent of their sin. This verse was abrogated by Q 24.2 which legislated one hundred stripes for the crime of adultery (see Q 87.6-7, note).

4.17 Repentance was available to only those who committed adultery "through ignorance"—that is, without knowledge that the paramour was already married.

4.18 If a person waited until the moment of death, and then repented, that repentance would not be regarded as genuine.

4.19a *it is not lawful for you to inherit*

against their will; nor to hinder them, that ye may go off with part of what ye brought them, unless they commit fornication manifestly; but associate with them in reason, for if ye are averse from them, it may be that ye are averse from something wherein God has put much good for you.

20 But if ye wish to exchange one wife for another, and have given one of them a talent, then take not from it anything. What! would you take it for a calumny and a manifest crime?

21 How can ye take it when one of you has gone in unto the other, and they have taken from you a rigid compact?

*Forbidden
marital relationships*

22 And do not marry women your fathers married,—except bygones,—for it is abominable and hateful, and an evil way;

23 unlawful for you are your mothers, and your daughters, and your sisters, and your paternal aunts and maternal aunts, and your brother's daughters, and your sister's daughters, and your foster mothers, and your foster sisters, and your wives' mothers, and your step daughters who are your wards, born of your wives to whom ye have gone in; but if ye have not gone in unto them, then it is no crime in you; and the lawful spouses of your sons from your own loins, and that ye form a connexion between two sisters,—except bygones,—verily, God is forgiving, merciful;

women's estates against their will — That is, a man was not permitted to forcibly keep an unloved wife with the purpose of acquiring her inheritance (dower) following her death.
4.19b *unless they commit fornication* — If a woman has been determined to have committed adultery (with four witnesses attesting to this fact), upon divorce the man was entitled to have his dower returned to him.
4.20-21 If a man wished to divorce a wife and replace her with a new wife, the divorced wife was entitled to the dower that had been given to her at the time of the first marriage.
4.22 A man was not permitted to marry one of his father's wives who had been divorced. If such a marriage took place, forgiveness was accepted, provided that the

sin had been committed prior to the time of the presentation of this surah (in a bye-gone era).
4.23a A man was not permitted to have sexual relations with his (a) mother, (b) daughters, (c) sisters, (d) paternal and maternal aunts, (e) nieces, (f) foster mothers, (g) foster sisters, (h) mothers-in-law, and (i) stepdaughters.
4.23b If a marriage had not yet been consummated, a man could lawfully marry the woman's daughters.
4.23c A man could not marry the wives of his sons who were now divorced from them.
4.23d A man may not marry two sisters at the same time, unless the marriages occurred prior to the presentation of this surah (in a bye-gone era)

24   and married women, save such as your right hands possess,—God's Book against you!—but lawful for you is all besides this, for you to seek them with your wealth, marrying them and not fornicating; but such of them as ye have enjoyed, give them their hire as a lawful due; for there is no crime in you about what ye agree between you after such lawful due, verily, God is knowing and wise.

25   But whosoever of you cannot go the length of marrying marriageable women who believe, then take of what your right hands possess, of your maidens who believe;—though God knows best about your faith. Ye come one from the other; then marry them with the permission of their people, and give them their hire in reason, they being chaste and not fornicating, and not receivers of paramours. But when they are married, if they commit fornication, then inflict upon them half the penalty for married women; that is for whomso-

ever of you fears wrong; but that ye should have patience is better for you, and God is forgiving and merciful.

26   God wishes to explain to you and to guide you into the ordinances of those who were before you, and to turn towards you, for God is knowing, wise.

27   God wishes to turn towards you, but those who follow their lusts wish that ye should swerve with a mighty swerving!

28   God wishes to make it light for you, for man was created weak.

Commerical enterprise

29   O ye who believe! devour not your property amongst yourselves vainly, unless it be a merchandise by mutual consent. And do not kill yourselves; verily, God is compassionate unto you.

30   But whoso does that maliciously and unjustly, we will broil him with fire; for that is easy with God.

31   If ye avoid great sins from which

4.24 A man was permitted to marry other women, provided that he gave her an appropriate dower (that which is lawfully due). It was also lawful for him to have sexual relations with his slaves (what "your right hands possesses").

4.25a If a man was not inclined to marry a free woman, he could maintain a concubine relationship with any of his female slaves, provided that they embrace the Islamic faith.

4.25b *give them their hire* — That is, give

them a dower.

4.25c If a concubine committed fornication, she was to receive half the penalty of a wife who committed fornication.

4.29a *devour not your property amongst yourselves vainly* — Do not engage in profit through trade and commerce, unless through mutual consent of both parties.

4.29b *do not kill yourselves* — That is, do not destroy one another through unethical commercial activities.

ye are forbidden, we will cover your offences and make you enter with a noble entrance.

32 And do not covet that by which God has preferred one of you over another. The men shall have a portion of what they earn, and the women a portion of what they earn; ask God for His grace, verily, God knows all.

33 To every one have we appointed kinsfolk as heirs of what parents and relatives and those with whom ye have joined right hands leave;

so give them their portion, for, verily, God is over all a witness.

Male and female status

34 Men stand superior to women in that God hath preferred some of them over others, and in that they expend of their wealth: and the virtuous women, devoted, careful in their husbands' absence, as God has cared for them. But those whose perverseness ye fear, admonish them and remove them

4.31 Some Islamic scholars identify seven great sins: (a) idolatry, (b) murder, (c) slandering a blameless woman, (d) consuming the wealth of orphans, (e) usury, (f) abandoning the Cause of Allah, and (g) obstinacy towards one's parents. The greatest sin is the sin of *shirk* (idolatry) and the least severe is the harboring of a sinful thought in one's mind.

4.34a *Men stand superior to women* — Muhammad insisted that men stand superior to women. Male superiority and dominance exists within the overall sphere of jurisprudence, including inheritances and issues pertaining to child custody. This included the following: male heirs are to receive twice the size of inheritances than female heirs (Q 4.11), in court cases, a male witness has twice the testimonial weight as a female witness (Q 2.282), and polygamy was established as a right for Muslim men (Q 4.3).

Moreover, in the cases of divorce, children were placed in the custody of the fathers since fathers functioned as the natural guardian of their children's persons and property. Mothers were granted no guardianship whatsoever. According to Shari'a Law,

after the father, guardianship was transferred to a child's paternal grandfather. "Under the laws of countries such as Kuwait, guardianship passes to the next relative on the father's side if the father and paternal grandfather are unable to act as guardian" (Kristine Uhlman, *Overview of Shari'a and Prevalent Customs in Islamic Societies—Divorce and Child Custody*, §8.0; also see Q 2.233; 65.6).

The esteemed medieval Islamic scholar al-Ghazali defined the woman's role: "If she goes out of his house without his permission, the angels curse him till she returns to his house or till she repents. The Prophet said: When a woman stays within her house, she becomes more near to God. Her prayer in the courtyard of her house is more meritorious than her prayer in mosque. Her prayer in a room is better than her prayer in her courtyard. The Prophet said: A woman is like a private part. When she comes out, the devil holds her high. He said: There are ten private parts of a woman. When she gets married, the husband keeps one private part covered; and when she dies, the grave covers the other parts. The duties of a wife towards her husband are many, two

into bed-chambers and beat them; but if they submit to you, then do not seek a way against them; verily, God is high and great.

35   And if ye fear a breach between the two, then send a judge from his people and a judge from her people. If they wish for reconcili-

ation, God will arrange between them; verily, God is knowing and aware.

Kindness and generosity

36   And serve God, and do not associate aught with Him; and to your

---

out of them are essentially necessary. The first one is to preserve chastity and to keep secret the words of her husband and the second thing is not to demand unnecessary things and to refrain from unlawful wealth which her husband earns" *(The Revival of Religious Learnings*, vol. 2, pp. 42-43).

4.34b *and beat them* — This phrase has received enormous attention by scholars studying Islamic culture since it implies that the Qur'an legitimizes domestic violence.

Within Islam, the interpretation of the phrase "and beat them" has resulted in a divide within moderate and fundamentalist Islamic scholars. Moderate Islamic scholars minimize its *prima facie* interpretation with a number of alternate interpretations: (a) the adjective *lightly* is implied and should therefore read: *and lightly beat them*, (b) the form of beating is verbal, not physical, and is therefore best understood to mean: *and beat them with rigorous argumentations*, or (c) the word *beating* is a euphemism for *making love* and therefore means to resolve conflicts between married couples with sex (see Yvonne Yzzbeck Haddad and John Esposito, *Islam, Gender and Social Change*).

In contrast, fundamentalist Islamic scholars insist upon its *prima facie* interpretation. They maintain that the phrase legitimizes domestic violence as a way of motivating submission to Allah by those who persist in rebellion. Mohammed Idriss writes, "There is

evidence that some *Ulama* [Islamic scholars] believe that a husband is permitted to use force, referring to the Qur'an in relation to passages on the social interaction between husbands and wives. One of the most often cited verses in this context is verse 4:34 entitled *Surah An-Nisa"* (*Honor, Violence, Women and Islam*, p. 97). Azis Azmah adds, "The Islamic family is seen as a hotbed of authoritarianism, patriarchy, misogyny and domestic violence" (*Islam in Europe*, p. 77). Ayaan Hirsi Ali adds, "Every society that is still in the rigid grip of Islam oppresses women" (*Infidel*, p. 296). In many passages in the Qur'an, Allah is seen using violence and the threat of violence to encourage submission. It is therefore understandable to assume that a similar approach would be advocated in domestic relationships.

4.34c *if they submit to you, then do not seek a way against them* — That is, if they submit, then do not impose additional beatings.

4.34d *God is high and great* — In the Muslim world, this phrase is called Takbir (*Allahu akbar*). See Q 34.23 note.

4.35 *if ye fear a breach between the two* — That is, if you fear that the marital relationship is being irreconcilably damaged, seek two arbiters to help bring about a reconciliation.

4.36a *serve God, and do not associate aught with Him* — A Muslim is to be wholly

parents show kindness, and to kindred, and orphans, and the poor, and the neighbour who is akin, and the neighbour who is a stranger, and the companion who is strange, and the son of the road, and what your right hands possess, verily, God loves not him who is proud and boastful;

37 who are miserly and bid men be miserly too, and who hide what God has given them of His grace;—but we have prepared for the misbelievers shameful woe.

38 And those who expend their wealth in alms for appearance sake before men, and who believe not in God nor in the last day;—but whosoever has Satan for his mate, an evil mate has he.

39 What harm would it do them if they believed in God and in the last day, and expended in alms of what God has provided them with? but God

knows about them.

40 Verily, God would not wrong by the weight of an atom; and if it's a good work, He will double it and bring from Himself a mighty hire.

41 How then when we bring from every nation a witness, and bring thee as a witness against these

42 on the day when those who misbelieve and rebel against the Apostle would fain that the earth were levelled with them? but they cannot hide the news from God.

Prayer purification laws

43 O ye who believe! approach not prayer while ye are drunk, until ye well know what ye say; nor yet while polluted,—unless ye be passing by the way,—until ye have washed yourselves. But if ye are sick, or on a journey, or one of you come from the privy, or if ye

committed to Allah, careful to avoid all forms of idolatry.

4.36b A Muslim is to be characterized by kindness and generosity. These two virtues are to be extended to all peoples, from those within one's family to the complete stranger. One is also to show kindness and generosity to one's slaves.

4.38 Those who give alms for appearance sake will gain no benefit for the deed at the Last Judgment.

In the Sermon on the Mount, Jesus said something similar: "So when you give to the needy, do not announce it with trumpets, as the hypocrites do in the synagogues and on the streets, to be honored by men.

I tell you the truth, they have received their reward in full. But when you give to the needy, do not let your left hand know what your right hand is doing, so that your giving may be in secret. Then your Father, who sees what is done in secret, will reward you" (Matt 6:2-4).

4.40 *He will double it* — Muhammad believed that alms given in the right spirit will receive a double benefit at the Last Judgment (see **The Last Judgment** on pp. 46-50).

4.43 Muslims were not to attend public prayers while intoxicated or physically unclean (polluted) (see **al-Salat** on pp. 169-170 and Q 5.6, note).

have touched a woman, and ye cannot find water, then use good surface sand and wipe your faces and your hands therewith; verily, God pardons and forgives.

Jews

44   Do ye not see those who have been given a portion of the Book? they buy error, and they wish that ye may err from the way!
45   But God knows best who your enemies are, and God suffices as a patron, and sufficient is God as a help.
46   And those who are Jews, and those who pervert the words from their places, and say, "We hear but we rebel, and do thou listen without hearing," and (who say) "râ'hinâ," distorting it with their tongues and taunting about religion. But had they said, "We hear and we obey, so listen and look upon us," it would have been better for them

and more upright—but may God curse them in their misbelief, for they will not believe except a few.
47   O ye who have been given the Book! believe in what we have revealed, confirming what ye had before; ere we deface your faces and turn them into hinder parts, or curse you as we cursed the fellows of the Sabbath when God's command was done.
48   Verily, God pardons not associating aught with Him, but He pardons anything short of that to whomsoever He pleases; but he who associates aught with God, he hath devised, a mighty sin.
49   Do ye not see those who purify themselves? nay, God purifies whom He will, and they shall not be wronged a straw.
50   Behold, how they devise against God a lie, and that is manifest sin enough.
51   Do ye not see those to whom a portion of the Book has been given?

4.44 *those who have been given a portion of the Book* — that is, the Jews.
4.45 *God knows best who your enemies are* — The implication is that the Jews were the enemies of all Muslims.
4.46a *pervert the words from their places* — Muhammad accused Jews of perverting the words of their own Scriptures (the Old Testament).
4.46b *ra'hina* — listen.
4.46c Muhammad summoned Allah to curse the Jews for their persistent unbelief.
4.47a *O ye who have been given the Book!* — That is, you who have been given the

Old Testament. Muhammad harkened Jews to believe the Qur'an.
4.47b *ere we deface your faces and turn them into hinder parts* — That is, ban certain people by driving them into exile. They would be cursed just as God cursed those who desecrated the Sabbath.
4.48 *God pardons not associating aught with Him* — Muhammad believed that Allah will not pardon those who practice idolatry.
4.49 *do you not see those who purify themselves?* — That is, do you not see those who think that they are spiritually pure? The implication is that they are not pure.

They believe in Gibt and Tâghût, and they say of those who misbelieve. "These are better guided in the way than those who believe."

52 These are those whom God has cursed, and whom God has cursed no helper shall he find.

53 Shall they have a portion of the kingdom? Why even then they would not give to men a jot.

54 Do they envy man for what God has given of His grace? We have given to Abraham's people the Book and wisdom, and we have given them a mighty kingdom:

55 And of them are some who believe therein, and of them are some who turn from it, but Hell is flaming enough for them.

56 Verily, those who disbelieve in our signs, we will broil them with fire; whenever their skins are well done, then we will change them for other skins, that they may taste the torment. Verily, God is glorious and wise.

57 But those who believe and do aright, we will make them enter gardens beneath which rivers flow, and they shall dwell therein for ever and aye, for them therein are pure wives, and we will make them enter into a shady shade.

Honesty

58 Verily, God bids you pay your trusts to their owners, and when ye judge between men to judge with justice. Verily, God, excellent is what He admonishes you with; verily, God both hears and sees.

59 O ye who believe! obey God, and obey the Apostle and those in au-

---

4.51 *Gibt and Taghut* — two pagan gods. Two Jews from Medinah, Huyayy ibn Ahtab and Ka'b ibn al-Ashraf, traveled to Mecca with a number of other Jews to sign a covenant with the Quraysh tribe. The intent was to attack and defeat Muhammad. Yet, by entering into a covenant with the Quraysh people, these Jews aligned themselves with pagan Arabs who worshipped pagan gods: Gibt and Taghut. According to Muhammad, this was another illustration of Jewish complicity with idolatry.

4.52 *those whom God has cursed* — That is, the Jews are cursed of Allah.

4.54 *do they envy man* — Muhammad claimed that the Jewish people believed that they alone were the beneficiaries of Abraham's faith. They therefore were envious

of those who made the same claim—that is, the Muslims.

4.55-56 Muhammad claimed that those who disbelieved in the Qur'an ("our signs") have turned away from the faith of Abraham. They will therefore enter into the fires of Hell and be tortured throughout eternity.

4.57 *believe and do aright* — This is a summary of the Islamic gospel (see Q 103.3, note). They are the ones who will enter the gardens of Paradise (see **Paradise** on pp. 76-77). In Paradise, they will enjoy their "pure wives...in shady shade" (see **The Virgins** on pp. 107-109).

4.58-59 Muhammad summoned the Muslim people to be characterized by honesty in all their doings, whether in financial transactions, judicial decisions, or spiritual issues.

thority amongst you; and if ye quarrel about anything, refer to God and the Apostle, if ye believe in God and the last day; that is better and fairer as a settlement.

Hypocrisy

60   Do ye not see those who pretend that they believe in what has been revealed to them, and what was revealed before thee; they wish to refer their judgment to Tâghût, but they are bidden to disbelieve therein, and Satan wishes to lead them into a remote error.

61   And when it is said to them, "Come round to what God has sent down and unto the Apostle," thou seest the hypocrites turning from thee, turning away.

62   How then when there befalls them a mischance through what their hands have sent on before? then will they come to you, and swear by God, "We meant naught but good and concord."

63   These, God knows what is in their hearts. Turn thou away from them and admonish them, and speak to them into their souls with a searching word.

64   We have never sent an apostle save that he should be obeyed by the permission of God; and if they, when they have wronged themselves, come to thee and ask pardon of God, and the Apostle asks pardon for them, then they will find God easy to be turned, compassionate.

65   But no! by thy Lord! they will not believe, until they have made thee judge of what they differ on; then they will not find in themselves aught to hinder what thou hast decreed, and they will submit with submission.

66   But had we prescribed for them, "Kill yourselves, or go ye forth out of your houses," they would not have done it, save only a few of them but had they done what they are admonished, then it would have been better for them, and a more firm assurance.

67   And then we would surely have brought them from ourselves a mighty hire,

68   and would have guided them into a

4.60-61 *Taghut* — idolatry. The hypocrites (Muslim apostates), said Muhammad, listened to the Qur'an, yet gave greater weight to the teachings found in the pagan idolatry of Arabia.

5.64-65 Muhammad insisted that nobody can believe and obey him apart from "the permission of God" (see **The Doctrine of al-Qadar** on pp. 264-266).

4.66 *Kill yourselves, or go ye forth out of your houses* — That is, if Allah had ordered most Muslims to kill themselves (commit suicide for the Cause of Allah) or go forth and leave their houses for the Cause of Allah) they "would not have done it" due to their lack of devotion. Yet, it would have been better if they would have sacrificed whatever Allah ordered them to do.

right path.

69 Whoso obeys God and the Apostle, these are with those God has been pleased with, of prophets and confessors and martyrs and the righteous;—a fair company are they.

70 That is grace from God, and God knows well enough.

Herald

71 O ye who believe! take your precautions and sally in detachments or altogether.

72 Verily, there is of you who tarries behind, and, if a mischance befalls you, says, "God has been gracious to me, since I am not with them a martyr."

73 But if there befalls you grace from

God, he would say—as though there were no friendship between you and him—"O would that I had been with thee to attain this mighty happiness!"

74 Let those then fight in God's way who sell this life of the world for the next; and whoso fights in God's way, then, be he killed or be he victorious, we will give him a mighty hire.

75 What ails you that ye do not fight in God's way, and for the weak men and women and children, who say, "Lord, bring us out of this town of oppressive folk, and make for us from Thee a patron, and make for us from Thee a help?"

76 Those who believe fight in the way

4.68 *right path* — This is a summary of the Islamic gospel (see Q 72.2, note).

4.69 A parallel relationship exists between Allah and Muhammad: believers are called upon to obey them both. Whosoever obeys both Allah and Muhammad will find pleasure with Allah (see Q 3.32; 4.69, 136; 5.80-81; 8.13, 20-23; 24.47, 48, 50-52, 54; 33.33, 71; 48.9-10; 57.19; 59.4; 72.22-23, 81.19-21 and 46.16, note).

4.70 *that is grace from God* — That is, obedience to Allah and Muhammad was only possible to those whom Allah has chosen to obey (see **The Doctrine of al-Qadar** on pp. 264-266).

4.71 Muhammad cautioned Muslims to be careful, whether they go forth to war in small detachments or in a much larger group.

4.72-73 During war, some Muslims tarried behind and were spared bloodshed and gave

thanks to Allah. Yet, those who died in battle as martyrs have attained to a "mighty happiness"—Paradise. Hence, said Muhammad, it matters not whether one lives or dies in Jihad—both are blessed.

4.74a *Let those then fight in God's way who sell this life of the world for the next* — Muhammad encouraged Muslims to be wholly devoted to Jihad. Their focus should be on the afterlife, not this life.

4.74b *whoso fights in God's way, then, be he killed or be he victorious, we will give him a mighty hire* — All active participants in Jihad (whether they die in battle or not) will be given a mighty hire (Paradise).

4.75 Muhammad bewailed the Muslims who were fainthearted and refused to participate in Jihad.

4.76 Muhammad divided the Muslims into two camps: those who believed and those

of God; and those who disbelieve fight in the way of Tâghût; fight ye then against the friends of Satan, verily, Satan's tricks are weak.

The problem of cowardice

77 Do ye not see those to whom it is said, "Restrain your hands, and be steadfast in prayer and give alms;" and when it is prescribed for them to fight then a band of them fear men, as though it were the fear of God or a still stronger fear, and they say, "O our Lord! why hast thou prescribed for us to fight, couldst thou not let us abide till our near appointed time?" Say, "The enjoyment of this world is but slight, and the next is better for him who fears;"—but they shall not be wronged a straw.

78 Wheresoe'er ye be death will over-take you, though ye were in lofty towers. And if a good thing befall them, they say, "This is from God," but if a bad thing, they say, "This is from thee." Say, "It is all from God." What ails these people? they can hardly understand a tale.

79 What befalls thee of good it is from God; and what befalls thee of bad it is from thyself.

Obedience to Muhammad

We have sent thee to mankind as an apostle, and God sufficeth for a witness.

80 Whoso obeys the prophet he has obeyed God; and he who turns back—we have not sent thee to watch over them.

81 They say, "Obedience!" but when they sally forth from you, a com-

who disbelieved. Believers were characterized as those who fought in the Way of God—that is, Jihad. Those who refused to fight were committed to the Way of *Taghut*—that is, the way of idolatry. With this statement, Muhammad made no allowance for a third way—a way that allowed Muslims to remain neutral from the requirement of Jihad. Moreover,

4.77a *Restrain your hands, and be steadfast in prayer and give alms* — Muhammad was describing people who refused to fight (curbed their hands) and devoted themselves to prayer and the giving of alms.

4.77b *The enjoyment of this world is but slight* — Muhammad reminded such individuals that the enjoyment of this world is slight when compared to Paradise in the afterlife. It is therefore much more reasonable to experience the hardships of this life, if by so doing one entered the bliss of Paradise.

4.76-77a When engaged in Jihad, whether one lives or dies, all participants are promised entrance into Paradise.

4.79b-80 Muhammad is elevated to a status that parallels Allah. He stated that obedience to himself is tantamount to obedience to Allah. The reverse is equally true: disobedience to himself is tantamount to disobedience to Allah (see Q 3.32; 4.69, 136; 5.80-81; 8.13, 20-23; 24.47, 48, 50-52, 54; 33.33, 71; 48.9-10; 57.19; 59.4; 72.22-23, 81.19-21 and 46.16, note).

4.81 Jihadistic soldiers were not to ques-

pany of them brood by night over something else than that which thou hast said but God writes down that over which they brood. Turn then from them and rely on God, for God sufficeth for a guardian.

82 Do they not meditate on the Qur'ân? if it were from other than God they would find in it many a discrepancy.

Dealing with hypocrites

83 And when there comes to them a matter of security or fear they publish it; but if they were to report it to the Apostle and to those in authority amongst them, then those of them who would elicit it from them would know it; but were it not for God's grace upon you and His mercy ye had followed Satan,

save a few.

84 Fight, then, in the way of God; impose not aught on any but thyself, and urge on the believers; it may be that God will restrain the violence of those who misbelieve, for God is more violent and more severe to punish.

85 Whoso intercedes with a good intercession shall have a portion therefrom; but he who intercedes with a bad intercession shall have the like thereof, for God keeps watch over all things.

86 And when ye are saluted with a salutation, salute with a better than it, or return it;—verily, God of all things takes account.

87 God, there is no God but He! He will surely assemble you on the resurrection day, there is no doubt therein; who is truer than God in his discourse?

tion the authority of Muhammad or his directives in battle. Throughout history, Islamic scholars have understood this authority to have been passed down to the *caliphs* (successors to Muhammad), also known as *vicegerents*, and the imams.

4.82 *many a discrepancy* — Muhammad believed that all sacred literatures, other than the Qur'an, contain many errors. In contrast, Christian scholars have noted many discrepancies in the Qur'an (see Q 3.70 note, **The Doctrine of Abrogation** on pp. 68-70).

4.83-91 In Muhammad's day, not all who claimed to be Muslims were dedicated to the cause of advancing Islam, fighting in Jihad, and maintaining strict loyalty to Muhammad.

Muhammad categorized them as hypocrites. He believed that they will face a horrific afterlife when their true works are made known at the Last Judgment.

4.83 Some of the Muslims were traitors (apostates), sharing sensitive military or political information with the enemies of Muhammad.

4.84 All Muslims were urged to engage in the work of Jihad.

4.85 Communication and intercession with the enemy were permitted, provided that their overall purpose was the advancement of the Cause of Allah.

4.87 Muhammad reminded his listeners that the only God was Allah—the Doctrine of Tauhid (see Q 112). It is this doctrine that dis-

88 Why are ye two parties about the hypocrites, when God hath overturned them for what they earned? Do ye wish to guide those whom God hath led astray? Whoso God hath led astray ye shall not surely find for him a path.

89 They would fain that ye misbelieve as they misbelieve, that ye might be alike; take ye not patrons from among them until they too flee in God's way; but if they turn their backs, then seize them and kill them wheresoever ye find them, and take from them neither patron nor help,

90 —save those who reach a people betwixt whom and you is an alliance—or who come to you while their bosoms prevent them from fighting you or fighting their own people. But had God pleased He would have given you dominion over them, and they would surely have fought you. But if they retire from you and do not fight you, and offer you peace—then God hath given you no way against them.

91 Ye will find others who seek for quarter from you, and quarter from their own people; whenever they return to sedition they shall be overturned therein: but if they retire not from you, nor offer you peace, nor restrain their hands, then seize them and kill them wheresoever ye find them;—over these we have made for you manifest power.

When a Muslim kills
another Muslim

92 It is not for a believer to kill a be-

tinguished the Muslim people from all their enemies.

4.88 According to Muhammad, Allah had already overturned the work of the hypocrites (apostates). At the Last Judgment, they will have nothing to show on the positive side of the balance. Hence, they will all be condemned to Hell. Moreover, in this life they will never find the right path that leads to eternal life.

4.89 *seize them and kill them wheresoever ye find them* — Within Islam was a struggle between sincere and hypocritical Muslims. Muhammad believed that he was ordered by Allah to make war against the hypocrites.

Following his death, the Ridda Wars were waged across the Arabian Peninsula, cleansing Islam of the hypocrites who resisted Muslim leadership in Medinah/Mecca (see *The Ridda Wars* on p. 771). In recent centuries, this verse has motivated the Wahhabis to engage in an internal cleansing of the Muslim world. This verse has also motivated the Sunnis and Shi'ites to wage war against one another.

4.90 *save those who reach a people betwixt whom and you is an alliance* — The one exception to warring against hypocrites are those who dwell among and have ties with a people with whom you are bound by a peace treaty.

4.91 Muhammad believed that hypocrites will look for places to live that are outside the sphere of war. Still, if they continued in their sedition, then "seize them and kill them."

liever save by mistake; and whosoever kills a believer by mistake then let him free a believing neck; and the blood-money must be paid to his people save what they shall remit as alms. But if he be from a tribe hostile to you and yet a believer, then let him free a believing neck. And if it be a tribe betwixt whom and you there is an alliance, then let the blood-money be paid to his friends, and let him free a believing neck; but he who cannot find the means, then let him fast for two consecutive months—a penance this from God, for God is knowing, wise.

93   And whoso kills a believer purposely, his reward is hell, to dwell therein for aye; and God will be wrath with him, and curse him, and prepare for him a mighty woe.

94   O ye who believe! when ye are knocking about in the way of God be discerning, and do not say to him who offers you a salutation, "Thou art no believer," craving after the chances of this world's life, for with God are many spoils! So were ye aforetime, but God was gracious to you, be ye then discerning; verily, God of what ye do is well aware.

Commitment and discernment during Jihad

95   Not alike are those of the believers who sit at home without harm, and those who are strenuous in God's way with their wealth and their persons. God hath preferred those

4.92a *free a believing neck* — The penalty for accidentally killing another Muslim in war was the granting of the freedom of a slave who happened to be a Muslim believer. The money was to be paid to the deceased man's relatives.

4.92b *but if he be from a tribe hostile to you and yet a believer* — If a Muslim kills another Muslim (who happens to be a member of an enemy tribe), he was to free a slave who was a Muslim believer.

4.92c If it be a tribe whom and you there was an alliance, and a Muslim is killed, a slave who happened to be a believer was still to be to freed and money given to the deceased man's friends.

4.92d *he who cannot find the means* — Those who cannot pay the fine were required to fast for two consecutive months

as a penance.

4.93 Whoever intentionally killed a Muslim was cursed and condemned to Hell.

4.94 *when ye are knocking about in the way of God* — Muhammad was concerned that his Muslim warriors, covetous for the spoils of war, would attack people without first determining whether or not they were Muslims. Some simply assumed that they were not Muslims and would venture forth in their raid. This, he said, was wrong.

4.95 *strenuous in God's way with their wealth and their persons* — That is, jihadistic in the Cause of Allah with both their wealth and personal safety. Muhammad believed that Allah is much more favorable for the Muslim who is active in Jihad than the Muslim who is not (see Q 5.35; 8.72, 74-75; 9.16, 41, 44, 73, 81; 16.110; 22.78; 25.52; 29.6,

who are strenuous with their wealth and their persons to those who sit still, by many degrees, and to each hath God promised good, but God hath preferred the strenuous for a mighty hire over those who sit still,

96   —degrees from him, and pardon and mercy, for God is forgiving and merciful.

97   Verily, the angels when they took the souls of those who had wronged themselves, said, "What state were ye in?" they say, "We were but weak in the earth;" they said, "Was not God's earth wide enough for you to flee away therein?" These are those whose resort is hell, and a bad journey shall it be!

98   Save for the weak men, and women, and children, who could not compass any stratagem, and were not guided to a way;

99   these it may be God will pardon, for God both pardons and forgives.

100   Whosoever flees in the way of God

shall find in the earth many a spacious refuge, and he who goes forth from his house, fleeing unto God and His prophet, and then death catches him up,—his hire devolves on God, and God is forgiving and merciful.

The importance of
prayer during Jihad

101   And when ye knock about in the earth, it is no crime to you that ye come short in prayer, if ye fear that those who disbelieve will set upon you; verily, the misbelievers are your obvious foes.

102   When thou art amongst them, and standest up to pray with them, then let a party of them stand up with thee, and let them take their arms; and when they adore, let them go behind you, and let another party who have not yet prayed come forward and pray with thee; and let them take their precautions and their arms. Fain would those who misbelieve that ye were careless of

69; 47.31; 60.1; 66.9).

4.96 *degrees for him* — That is, a higher level of Paradise awaits him.

4.97a *the angels when they took the souls of those who had wronged themselves* — That is, at the moment of death, the angels took the souls of the deceased and asked them of the quality of their lives. Those who say that they were weak in the earth would be rebuked.

4.97b-99 *Was not God's earth wide enough for you?* — That is, was not Allah's earth

large enough to allow you to emigrate to the place of Muslim strongholds?

4.100 Muhammad believed that all immigrants would be blessed.

4.101-102 *when ye knocked about in the earth* — That is, when you look for opportunities to fight the enemy. During Jihad, Muslims were to be wary of ambushes during their times of prayer. The solution was for other Muslims to stand guard with their weapons at the ready when another Muslim was performing his daily prayers.

your arms and your baggage, that they might turn upon you with a single turning. And it is no crime to you if ye be annoyed with rain or be sick, that ye lay down your arms; but take your precautions— verily, God has prepared for those who misbelieve a shameful woe.

103 But when ye have fulfilled your prayer, remember God standing and sitting and lying on your sides; and when ye are in safety then be steadfast in prayer; verily, prayer is for the believers prescribed and timed!

The importance of
endurance during Jihad

104 And do not give way in pursuit of the people; if ye suffer they shall surely suffer too, even as ye suffer; and ye hope from God, but they hope not! and God is knowing, wise.

Separation from the hypocrites
and the fainthearted

105 Verily, we have revealed to thee the Book in truth that thou mayest judge between men of what God has shown thee; so be not with the treacherous a disputant;

106 but ask God's pardon: verily, God is forgiving, merciful.

107 And wrangle not for those who defraud themselves; for God loves not him who is a fraudulent sinner.

108 They hide themselves from men; but they cannot hide themselves from God, for He is with them while they brood at night over speeches that please Him not;—but God doth compass what they do!

109 Here are ye, wrangling for them about this world's life;—but who shall wrangle with God for them on the day of judgment, or who shall be a guardian over them?

4.103a When in warlike situations, jihadists were not required to keep to the prescribed times for prayer. On such occasions, they were to keep in mind that Allah was always with them, whether they should be standing, sitting, or lying down.

4.103b In times of safety, when battle is neither imminent nor upon them, jihadists were to remember the prescribed times for prayer (see **al-Salat** on pp. 169-170).

4.104 The jihadists were not to relent from pursuing the enemy. If the jihadist was weary, he should remember that the enemy was also weary.

4.105-107 Muhammad, and all Muslims by implication, have been given the Qur'an (the Book). Muhammad believed that it is *the Book in truth*, enabling all Muslims to discern truth from error. He therefore admonished all faithful Muslims not to engage in lengthy debates with "the treacherous"—that is, the Muslim hypocrites and fainthearted believers.

4.108 *they brood at night over speeches that please Him not* — That is, a chief characteristic of the hypocrites and fainthearted believers was that were impressed ("they brood at night") with the speeches from of non-Muslims.

4.110 The only activity that Muhammad was willing to countenance of the hypocrites

The Sunnis and Shi'ites

Following the death of Muhammad in 632, the leadership of the nascent Muslim nation passed to the caliphs (successors). The second caliph, Umar (also known as Omar), found himself at an important crossroads.

The Muslim empire, such as it was, was pushing against the borders of the Byzantine Empire to the northwest and Sasanian Empire to the northeast. Would he seek a peaceful coexistence or would he push against these two empires and take a portion of their land? He led the Muslim people to a decisive victory against the Byzantine Empire at the Battle of Yarmuk Valley (east of the Sea of Galilee) in 636. With this victory the Muslims gained control of Egypt and the entire Palestinian region. He also led them to a decisive victory against the Sasanian Empire (Persia) at the Battle of Qadisiya (along the Euphrates River) in 637. With this victory, the Muslims gained control of present day Iraq and Iran.

Now in control of the entire Middle East, the Muslims became major players on the world scene. Property and wealth throughout the Middle East were redistributed on a massive scale. Old ruling classes were replaced with a new one. And, most importantly, the Muslims were in a position to significantly alter the culture of the Middle East by pressing people throughout the empire to accept the Islamic faith.

The First Civil War. The third caliph was Uthman. Because he ruled unfairly—giving lucrative appointments to his own family and spending money for his own self-aggrandizement—unrest developed among those with power in the Muslim world. Uthman was assassinated. Then Ali ibn Abi Talib—the cousin and son-in-law to Muhammad—claimed the title as fourth caliph. Lesley Hazleton writes, "If there was a single person who seemed destined to be Muhammad's successor, it was Ali, his first cousin and the man whose name the Shia were to take as their own. They were, and are, the followers of Ali, or in Arabic, *Shiat Ali*—Shia for short."[1] But Muawiyah of the Umayyad clan also claimed the title as fourth caliph. A civil war erupted (656-661) with Ali and his Shi'ite army on one side and Muawiyah and his Sunni army on the other. The war came to an abrupt end when Ali was assassinated in 661.

The Second Civil War. Upon Muawiyah's death in 680, the Shi'ite army sought revenge for Ali assassination and attempted to make Ali's son al-Husayn the fifth caliph. A second civil war broke out which continued for twelve years (680-692). It ended with the death of al-Husayn and, once again, the defeat of the Shi'ite army.[2]

The Following Centuries. Following the Second Civil War, two dynasties emerged in Islam. The Umayyad dynasty was the first and ruled the Islamic empire for eighty years. During this era, the empire expanded from Spain (the western frontier) to India (the eastern frontier). High leadership was limited to descendents of the Quraysh tribe of Mecca. The dynasty was characterized by self-aggrandizement and wanton corruption. Because of its widespread corruption, the Umayyad dynasty collapsed and replaced by the Abbasidians. The Abbasid dynasty opened important leadership in the empire to all ethnic groups. Moreover, its liberal policies made possible the Golden Age of Islam.[3] The Abbasid dynasty continued until the mid-tenth century.

The Lasting Legacy. These two civil wars and early dynasties established the Sunnis as the dominant sect within Islam and pushed the Shi'ites to the margins of Islam. Still, the Shi'ites refused to remain defeated. They understood themselves to be the rightful heirs of the caliphate, a caliphate rooted to the geneaology of Ali. Accordingly, skirmishes between the two sects have persisted throughout the centuries. Currently, the majority of the Islamic world is Sunni. In the early twenty-first century, Sunni Muslims number approximately one billion three hundred million. In contrast, Shia Muslims number approximately 180 million. Shia Muslims constitute the majorities in Iran, Iraq, Yemen, with large followings in India, Pakistan, East Africa, Lebanon, and Syria.

---

[1] Lesley Hazleton, *After the Prophet: the Epic Story of the Shia-Sunni Split in Islam*, p. 32.

[2] For an insightful summary of the first and second civil wars in Islam, see Hans Küng, *Islam: Past, Present & Future*, pp. 189-201.

[3] Ibid., pp. 201-304.

In recent years, the public has started to hear more about Sunni and Shia Islam. People hear buzzwords and news highlights and sometimes get confused. Put simply, Sunni and Shia are two denominations in Islam, similar to Catholic and Protestant in Christianity. There are distinctions and differences in interpretations, traditions, and beliefs, but they are still under the same umbrella of Islam. All Sunnis do not hate all Shias, and all Shias do not hate all Sunnis.

—Nawar Shora, *The Arab-American Handbook*, p. 33

Shia-Sunni conflicts are wide spread in countries where there are democratic governments like, in India and Pakistan...In India and Pakistan clashes between Shias and Sunnis take place even for minor issues. It may be over burial sites of Tazias or routes to be followed for Tazia processions. Authorities in these countries step up security arrangements throughout the district or province to prevent any outbreak of sectarian violence during Muharram. Preparations are made months in advance to ensure no untoward incident takes place during the months of Muharram. The most dangerous hours for sectarian violence are when Shia Muslims take out processions through localities dominated by Sunni Muslims. There is always the danger of attack by militant Sunni Muslims in such areas. At other times Shia and Sunni mosques are protected from attacks by either sect. Heavy contingent of police remain present around mosques during Muharram.

—D. P. Sharma, *The New Terrorism: Islamist International*, p. 320

Shia friends complained to me that foreign journalists such as myself always exaggerated the extent of Sunni-Shia divisions in Iraq. They would say they had Sunni friends and relatives married to Sunni, but then they would add all-important exclusion clauses to this supposed amity, such as saying that all former Baathists should be arrested. Sunni friends would likewise claim that sectarian strife was less than I supposed, but would then go on to dismiss Sistani, Muqtada, and the Shia religious parties as all pawns of Iran.

—Patrick Cockburn, *Muqtada al-Sadr and the Battle for the Future of Iraq*, p. 166

Two days after the publication of the Saudi statement, Shaykh al-Barrak, the first cleric to sign the Saudi statement, issued a separate and a more extreme and vicious *fatwa* against the Shia. He accused the Shia of duplicity, conniving, and deception and said that "because of their false religion, they are more dangerous to Muslims than Jews and Christians." He concluded by saying that "the Sunni and Shia *mathhabs* (beliefs) are completely contradictory and cannot be reconciled; the talk of Sunni-Shia rapprochment is utterly false."

—Emile A. Nakhleh, *A Necessary Engagement*, p. 29

On one day alone, 14 September 2005, Shia-Sunni tit-for-tat street fights resulted in 11 bomb blasts, the death of 180 people and the wounding of another 560 (Vincent 2005). The insurgency has escalated in 2006 with the destruction of 23 February of the Golden Mosque in Samarra, one of the holiest Shia sites. Fifty Sunni mosques were destroyed in retaliation, and according to one report as many as 1300 people died in the sectarian conflicts that broke out. Talk of a new "religious war" in Iraq has now taken on a serious tone.

—Marika Vicziany, *Controlling Arms and Terror in the Asia Pacific*, p. 9

110 Yet whoso does evil and wrongs himself, and then asks pardon of God, shall find God forgiving and merciful;

111 and whoso commits a crime, he only commits it against himself, for God is knowing, wise.

112 And whoso commits a fault or a sin and throws it on the innocent, he hath to bear a calumny and a manifest sin.

113 Were it not for God's grace upon thee, and His mercy, a party of them would have tried to lead thee astray; but they only lead themselves astray; they shall not hurt you in aught: for God hath sent down upon thee the Book and the wisdom, and taught thee what thou didst not know, for God's grace was mighty on thee.

114 There is no good in most of what they talk in private save in him who bids almsgiving, or kindness, or reconciliation between men; and whoso does this, craving the good pleasure of God, we will give to him a mighty hire.

115 But he who severs himself from the prophet after that we have made manifest to him the guidance, and follows other than the way of the believers, we will turn our backs on him as he hath turned his back; and we will make him reach hell, and a bad journey shall it be.

Idolatry

116 Verily, God forgives not associating aught with Him, but He pardons anything short of that, to whomsoever He will; but whoso associates aught with God, he hath erred a wide error.

117 Verily, they call not beside Him on aught save females; and they do not call on aught save a rebellious

and fainthearted was a sincere repentance.

4.113 A second characteristic of hypocritical and fainthearted Muslims was to seek to lead astray other Muslims who are steadfast and committed to their faith.

4.114-115 According to Muhammad, most of what hypocritical and fainthearted Muslims said in private conversations was of no value. The only good works that they performed was: (a) the giving of alms, (b) showing kindness, and (c) seeking reconciliation between people. Still, if they distanced themselves from Muhammad after having been enlightened in the teachings of the Qur'an, they would suffer the fires of Hell.

4.116a *God forgives not associated aught with Him* — That is, Allah does not forgive those who participate in idolatry.

4.116b *a wide error* — Muhammad believed that the sin of idolatry (that is, the sin of Shirk) was so grievous that all idolaters would be condemned to Hell, no matter the quality and quantity of good works he or she otherwise possesses.

4.117 Once again, Muhammad referenced the pagan Arabic Star Family religious system of seventh century Arabia. In this pantheon of gods, many were believed to be female. Muhammad condemned the entire system, describing this as a form of devil worship.

4.118-121 Muhammad believed that Allah would curse the idolater by leading him or

devil.

118 God curse him! for he said, "I will take from thy servants a portion due to me;

119 and I will lead them astray; and I will stir up vain desires within them; and I will order them and they shall surely crop the ears of cattle; and I will order them and they shall surely alter God's creation;" but he who takes the devil for his patron instead of God, he loses with a manifest loss.

120 He promises them, and stirs up vain desires within them; but the devil promises only to deceive.

121 These, their resort is hell; they shall not find an escape therefrom!

122 But those who believe, and do what is right, we will make them enter into gardens beneath which rivers flow, to dwell therein for aye,—

God's promise in truth; and who is truer than God in speech?

123 Not for your vain desires, nor the vain desires of the people of the Book. He who doeth evil shall be recompensed therewith, and shall not find for him beside God a patron, or a help.

124 But he who doeth good works,— be it male or female,—and believes, they shall enter into Paradise, and they shall not be wronged a jot.

125 Who has a better religion than he who resigns his face to God, and does good, and follows the faith of Abraham, as a 'Hanîf?—for God took Abraham as a friend.

126 And God's is what is in the heavens and in the earth, and God encompasses all things!

The concerns of women

her further into the sin of idolatry. One of the practices of the pagan Arabs was to dedicate some of their cattle to their gods by slitting their ears. Muhammad believed that Allah encouraged this practice, resulting in an increase of sin and a deepening of their punishment in Hell.

4.124 *But he who doeth good works —* This is a summary of the Islamic gospel (see Q 103.3, note). Muhammad believed that those who earned salvation by believing and doing what is right will enter Paradise (see **The Last Judgment** on pp. 46-50). In contrast, those who did evil would be cast in the fires of Hell.

Herein, in bold relief, we see the Islamic gospel. It is a salvation earned through good works. Those who failed in this endeavor

with lives characterized by evil would be cast into Hell. The gospel of Jesus Christ differs from the Islamic gospel inasmuch it is predicated upon the work of Jesus Christ who earned salvation for us via his death and resurrection. Our part is to believe and embrace that which He did on our behalf (see Rom 5:1-11; Eph 2:8-9 and Titus 3:3-8).

4.125a *resigns his face to God, and does good —* This is a summary of the Islamic gospel (a variation of what is presented in vv. 122, 124). In this verse, resigning oneself to Allah—that is, submitting to Allah—is regarded as the same as believing in Allah.

4.125b *Abraham, as a Hanif —* Muhammad believed that Abraham was a pre-Islamic monotheist, also known as a *Hanif* (see Q 30.30, note). This fact, said Muhammad,

127   They will ask thee a decision about women; say, "God decides for you about them, and that which is rehearsed to you in the Book; about orphan women to whom ye do not give what is prescribed for them, and whom ye are averse from marrying; and about weak children; and that ye stand fairly by orphans—and what ye do of good, verily, that God knows."

128   And if a woman fears from her husband perverseness or aversion, it is no crime in them both that they should be reconciled to each other, for reconciliation is best. For souls are prone to avarice; but if ye act kindly and fear God, of what ye do He is aware.

129   Ye are not able, it may be, to act equitably to your wives, even though ye covet it; do not however be quite partial, and leave one as it were in suspense; but if ye be reconciled and fear, then God is forgiving and merciful;

130   but if they separate, God can make both independent out of His abundance; for God is abundant, wise.

131   God's is what is in the heavens and what is in the earth!

The judgment of God
upon unbelieving peoples

We have ordained to those who have been given the Book before you, and to you too that ye fear God—but if ye misbelieve, verily, God's is what is in the heavens and what is in the earth, and God is rich and to be praised!

132   God's is what is in the heavens and what is in the earth! and God sufficeth for a guardian!

133   If He will He can make ye pass away, O men! and can bring others—God is able to do all that.

134   He who wishes for a reward in this world—with God is the reward of this world and of the next, and God both hears and sees.

---

linked the faith of Abraham with the Islamic faith.

4.127 Men are required to treat equitably and with charity all who under their charge, whether they be orphan women, feeble-minded children, or orphans.

4.128 If discord should exist between husband and wife, they should make every effort to seek reconciliation.

4.129-131a In the cases of polygamy, some wives may sense that they were being neglected due to the attention given to the other wives. In such cases, reconciliation was to be pursued. If reconciliation was un-successful, divorce was a suitable solution.

4.131b *those who have been given the Book before you* — That is, the Perspicuous Book. A continuing theme in the Qur'an is that throughout history Allah has sent numerous apostles to civilizations, seeking to bring them into conformity with the eternal book that exists in Paradise. Yet most civilizations rejected the messages of their duly appointed apostles and were thereby destroyed by Allah (see **The Perspicuous Book** on pp. 178-179 and **The Apostles** on pp. 396-398).

4.135a *O ye who believe* — That is, Mus-

The call for full devotion

135   O ye who believe! be ye steadfast
in justice, witnessing before God
though it be against yourselves, or
your parents, or your kindred, be
it rich or poor, for God is nearer
akin than either. Follow not, then,
lusts, so as to act partially; but if
ye swerve or turn aside, God of
what ye do is well aware.

136   O ye who believe! believe in God
and His apostles, and the Book
which He hath revealed to His
Apostle, and the Book which He
sent down before; for whoso disbelieves in God, and His angels,
and His Apostle, and the last day,
has erred a wide error.

137   Verily, those who believe and then
misbelieve, and then believe and
then misbelieve, and then increase

in misbelief, God will never pardon them, nor will He guide them
in the path.

138   Give to the hypocrites the glad tidings that for them is grievous woe!

139   Those who take the misbelievers
for their patrons rather than believers—do they crave honour from
them? Verily, honour is altogether
God's!

140   He hath revealed this to you in the
Book, that when ye hear the signs
of God disbelieved in and mocked
at, then sit ye not down with them
until they plunge into another discourse, for verily, then ye would
be like them. Verily, God will gather
the hypocrites and misbelievers into
hell together.

141   Those who lie in wait for you, and
if the victory be yours from God,
say, "Were we not with you?" and

lims.

4.135b *be ye steadfast in justice* — Muslims were called to a life of absolute justice,
even if it required them to bear witness
against their own activities, the activities of
their parents or relatives. Their financial status had no bearing on this demand. The
deciding question was whether he himself
or his family members have become hypocrites ("act partially") or apostates ("swerve
or turn aside").

4.136a Muslims were told to devote themselves to Muhammad and the Qur'an. They
were also to acknowledge that Allah sent
down other revelations prior to the Qur'an,
such as the Old and New Testaments.

4.136b *a wide error* — Those who failed
to believe in Allah, the angels, and Muham-

mad as "His Apostle," and the Last Judgment
have committed a wide error. This meant
that the destiny of all who committed such
an error was Hell. Stated otherwise, to disobey Muhammad was tantamount to disobeying Allah, with the net result being an
eternal condemnation in Hell (see Q 3.32;
4.69, 79-80; 5.80-81; 8.13, 20-23; 24.47,
48, 50-52, 54; 33.33, 71; 48.9-10; 57.19;
59.4; 72.22-23 and 46.16, note).

4.137-138 Muhammad believed that Muslims who experienced recurring episodes of
apostasy would not be forgiven by Allah at
the Last Judgment.

4.135-137 Muhammad accused Muslim
apostates (hypocrites) of insincere motives.
Because of this, Muslim believers were instructed to not take them into their confi-

The Ridda Wars

A.D. 632-633

Following Muhammad's death in 632, the Muslim people found themselves at an important crossroad. Would they maintain a centralized government or would they allow themselves to splinter into a series of separate communities, each headed by its own political leader? Muhammad's close associates pressed for centralization—one Muslim nation—arguing that this was a key feature in Muhammad's vision for the Muslim people (see Q 23.51-52; *cf.* 10.19; 11.118-119; 42.8; 43.33). Yet a number of Muslim communities disagreed and pressed for decentralization. In addition, the leaders in some of these break away communities claimed to be prophets themselves.

In Medinah, Abu Bakr was selected caliph (successor) of the Muslim people. One of his first orders was to stop the splintering within Islam. Wars were waged—known as the Ridda (Apostasy) Wars. Abu Bakr's army swept across the Arabian Peninsula and attacked the wayward Muslim communities and tribes. The decisive battle took place in Yamama in eastern Arabia. At the end of the two year military campaign, Abu Bakr and his Muslims in Mecca-Medinah were in control of most of the Arabian Peninsula.

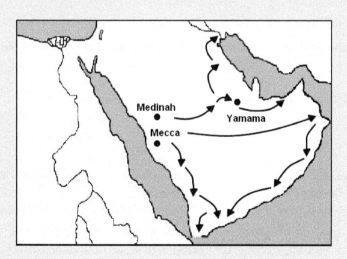

After the death of Mohammed, there took place the *hurub al ridda*, or wars of reinstating Islam among tribes that decided to quit it. These military campaigns were very bloody. The *dawla*, or state of Islam, was at stake: A domino effect might erode the demography of the new *umma*. In later times, and especially in the twentieth century, the ideology of jihadism would refer to these wars as a reason to attack any Muslim who would divert from religion or change faith. Cases of jihadist execution of former Muslims or of converts to other religions are widespread at the hands of the modern-day radicals.

—Walid Phares, *Future Jihad*, p. 28

Once the apostasy had been suppressed, closer unity followed with greater zeal to sacrifice all in a larger struggle. The end of the Ridda wars left the Arabs poised for Holy War for the sake of Islam, ready to challenge even Byzantium and Iran.

—Abd al-Husain Zarrinkub, *The Cambridge History of Iran*, p. 1

Battles following Muhammad's death in 632 were fought against groups that broke away from the nascent Muslim community. Called the Ridda wars, the wars of apostasy, they probably had little to do with apostasy in the sense of a rejection of faith or dogma—since the content of Muslim faith and dogma had yet to be fully defined, and since many members of these recalcitrant tribes had never even put aside their own religions. They had joined the Muslims in the traditional fashion of forging a temporary alliance. The Ridda wars were aimed at countering this traditional perfidy at enforcing a new unity of the Arabs under the leadership of Muhammad's community in Medina.

—Sarah Chayes, *The Punishment of Virtue*, p. 204

Immediately after Muhammad's death it became necessary to fight a war to bring back to Islam the Arabian tribes that were starting to drift away from their religious obedience. These wars against apostasy, known as the wars of the *ridda*, were holy wars. In the later history of Islam other holy wars were fought against Muslims judged guilty of apostasy.

—Peter Partner, *God of Battles*, p. 118

In the early part of Abu Bakr's rule (632-634), there was severe repression of some Arab tribes who refused to pay the religious tax (*zakat*) or came to accept another prophet. They renounced Islam and tried to get away from the new state. Thus the war against them was called the "War of Apostasy."

—Ralph H. Salmi, *Islam and Conflict Resolution*, p. 26

if the misbelievers have a chance, they say, "Did we not get the mastery over you, and defend you from the believers?" But God shall judge between you on the resurrection day; for God will not give the misbelievers a way against believers.

142 Verily, the hypocrites seek to deceive God, but He deceives them; and when they rise up to pray, they rise up lazily to be seen of men, and do not remember God, except a few;

143 wavering between the two, neither to these nor yet to those! but whomsoever God doth lead astray thou shall not find for him a way.

144 O ye who believe! take not misbelievers for patrons rather than believers; do ye wish to make for God a power against you?

145 Verily, the hypocrites are in the lowest depths of hell-fire, and thou shalt not find for them a help.

146 Save those who turn again, and do right, and take tight hold on God, and are sincere in religion to God; these are with the believers, and God will give to the believers mighty hire.

The spiritual life

147 Why should God punish you, if ye are grateful and believe? for God is grateful and knowing.

148 God loves not publicity of evil speech, unless one has been wronged; for God both hears and knows.

149 If ye display good or hide it, or pardon evil, verily, God is pardoning and powerful!

The Jewish people

150 Verily, those who disbelieve in God and His apostles desire to make a distinction between God and His apostles, and say, "We believe in

dences and develop relationships.

4.145 According to Muhammad, the eternal destiny of Muslim apostates (hypocrites) is the "lowest depths of hellfire."

4.146a *turn again, and do right* — This is a variation on the phrase "believe and do right," which is a summary of the Islamic gospel (see Q 103.3, note).

4.146b *take tight hold on God, and are sincere in religion to God* — That is, those who are fully devoted to Allah.

4.147 *grateful and believe* — In terms of the spiritual life, these words represent two major themes in the Qur'an: thankfulness and faith.

4.148 *God loves not publicity of evil speech* — That is, Allah does not approve of evil being mentioned publicly, unless the one wronged is benefitted by the knowledge being made public. In all other situations, the evil that has taken place should be addressed and resolved privately. When the previous passage is taken into consideration, this would include the words spoken by Muslim apostates (hypocrites). Their words, said Muhammad, should not be given a public airing, unless a wider benefit to the Muslim people can be achieved.

4.150 Muhammad opposed those who embraced some of the past apostles, but not

part and disbelieve in part, and desire to take a midway course between the two:"

151 these are the misbelievers, and we have prepared for misbelievers shameful woe!

152 But those who believe in God and His apostles, and who do not make a distinction between any one of them,—to these we will give their hire, for God is forgiving and merciful!

153 The people of the Book will ask thee to bring down for them a book from heaven; but they asked Moses a greater thing than that, for they said, "Show us God openly;" but the thunderbolt caught them in their injustice. Then they took the calf, after what had come to them

of manifest signs; but we pardoned that, and gave Moses obvious authority.

154 And we held over them the mountain at their compact, and said to them, "Enter ye the door adoring;" and we said to them, "Transgress not on the Sabbath day," and we took from them a rigid compact.

155 But for that they broke their compact, and for their misbelief in God's signs, and for their killing the prophets undeservedly, and for their saying, "Our hearts are uncircumcised,"—nay, God hath stamped on them their misbelief, so that they cannot believe except a few,

156 —and for their misbelief, and for their saying about Mary a mighty

all of them. Both Jews and Christians were so characterized since they affirmed the ministries of Adam, Noah, Abraham, Moses, and so on, yet rejected others—especially the alleged apostleship of Muhammad. Moreover, they rejected the way in which Muhammad defined the ministries of these biblical patriarchs.

4.151 Muhammad believed that all who failed to fully embrace the apostles and their ministries, as defined by Muhammad, would face a shameful woe (the fires of Hell).

4.153a *Show us God openly* — Nowhere in the Old Testament did the Israelites request that Moses openly show them God. The New Testament records an event that may be the source of Muhammad's comment. Philip asked: "Lord, show us the Father and that will be enough for us" (Jn 14:8). The answer of Jesus is enlightening: "Any-

one who has seen me has seen the Father" (Jn 14:9).

4.153b *then they took the calf* — This is the story of the Golden Calf mentioned in Ex 32:1-35; also see Q 2.51-52, 92; 7.138-158 and 20.83-97). Muhammad's reason for addressing this story was to illustrate the Jewish people's fall into the sin of idolatry.

4.154a *the mountain at their compact* — Mt. Sinai where the Ten Commandments were given (see Ex 19:1-20:26).

4.154b *Enter ye the door adoring* —This statement is found in the Book of Psalm: "Enter into his gates with thanksgiving, and into his courts with praise: be thankful unto him, and bless his name" (Ps 100:4).

4.154c *transgress not on the Sabbath day* — This is the Fourth Commandment (Ex 20:8-11).

4.155-157a *God has stamped on them*

their misbelief — Muhammad believed that the Jewish people were a cursed people ("except a few"). This was due to six major transgressions that they committed: (a) they broke the Mosaic Covenant, (b) they refused to believe in divine revelation, (c) they killed their own prophets, (d) they declared that their hearts were uncircumcised, (e) they accused Mary of bearing an illegitimate child, and (f) they admitted that they killed their Messiah—Jesus.

These accusations are sweeping and warrant a response. The following is a Christian theological rejoinder:

First, the Jewish people broke the Mosaic Covenant. Yet, on several occasions nationwide repentances took place as the Jewish people grieved over their sins and sought divine restoration (Jud 20:26; 1 Sam 7:5-6; 2 Kings 10:1-28; 23:1-7; Neh 8:1-9:38). What is more, all people everywhere, said the Apostle Paul, have violated the ethical principles found in the Mosaic Law (Acts 13:39; Rom 3:9-20; 7:7-9; Gal 3:10-11). When seen in this light, the Jewish people are no different than the rest of humanity. It is just as the Apostle Paul said: "all have sinned and fall short of the glory of God" (Rom 3:23).

Second, the Jewish people experienced unbelief in divine revelation. Though this is true, on numerous occasions they demonstrated remarkable dedication to God's Word. The psalmist is representative of numerous Jews, who said: "Do not snatch the word of truth from my mouth, for I have put my hope in your laws" (Ps 119:43). Once again, they are no different from others who struggled to place their full trust in the Word of God. In the New Testament, a Jew said it well: "I do believe; help me overcome my unbelief!" (Mk 9:24).

Third, the Jewish people killed many of their own prophets. Throughout the history of the Old Testament, the Jewish people often resisted the prophets that God had sent to them. This is because the Jewish nation has always been a mixture of belief and unbelief. The Apostle Paul, who himself was a Jew, put it this way: "Not all who are descended from Israel are Israel" (Rom 9:6). Even in the present day, Jewish people are divided into the two broad categories of secular and religious Jews.

Fourth, the Jewish people have never declared their hearts to be uncircumcised. The closest a Jew has ever come to making such a statement comes from the pen of the Apostle Paul. He wrote: "Circumcision has value if you observe the law, but if you break the law, you have become as though you had not been circumcised" (Rom 2:25). Paul's point is that circumcision only has value if the Jew has placed his faith in God. For the Jew who has no faith, the outward rite of circumcision has no religious significance.

Fifth, some Jews declared Mary, the mother of Jesus, to have given birth to an illegitimate son. During the ministry of Jesus, it was said: "We are not illegitimate children" (Jn 8:41). Some scholars believe this to be a subtle vilification of Jesus due to the unusual circumstances surrounding her pregnancy (Lk 1:35). Rather than believing in a virginal insemination, they believed that he was conceived in a non-miraculous fashion outside of wedlock.

This charge of Jesus being an illegitimate son of Mary surfaces from time to time in history. Origen mentions it once in his *Against Celsus* (second century, A.D.) where he presented the Jewish accusation and his rebuttal to the charge (Ag. Cel. 1:28). In the apocryphal *The Gospel of Nicodemus* (fifth century, A.D.), the accusation surfaced once again: "Annas and Caiaphas said to Pilate:

calumny,

157 and for their saying, "Verily, we have killed the Messiah, Jesus the son of Mary, the apostle of God," .....but they did not kill him, and they did not crucify him, but a similitude was made for them. And verily, those who differ about him are in doubt concerning him; they have no knowledge concerning

'These twelve men who say that he was not born of fornication are believed. But we, the whole multitude, cry out that he was born of fornication and is a sorcerer'" (Nic 2).

Sixth, for the most part, Jews have not admitted that they killed their Messiah, Jesus Christ. The closest one can come to such a statement made by Muhammad is to reference the Jews who have turned to Jesus, believing him to be their Messiah. These Jewish Christians—Messianic Jews, as they prefer to be called—affirm that the Jewish leaders in Jerusalem were indeed complicit in the death of their Messiah.

Conclusion. Muhammad's attempt to discredit the Jewish people and then declare them worthy of Allah's stamp of unbelief, a stamp that condemns them to Hell, is unconvincing. Christians acknowledge that Jewish people, like all people, are sinful and in need of spiritual redemption. This redemption is found in Jesus Christ. Rather than discredit and demonize them, the general attitude of the New Testament is to hold the Jewish people in honor. The Apostle Paul wrote: "Theirs is the adoption as sons; theirs the divine glory, the covenants, the receiving of the law, the temple worship and the promises. Theirs are the patriarchs, and from them is traced the human ancestry of Christ, who is God over all, forever praised! Amen" (Rom 9:4-5). The Apostle Paul also wrote prophetically of the Jewish people: "And so all Israel will be saved, as it is written: 'The deliverer will come from Zion; he will turn godlessness away from Jacob. And this is my covenant with them when I take away their sins'" (Rom 11:26-27).

4.157b-158 they did not kill him, and they did not crucify him, but a similitude was made for them — Muhammad claimed that Jesus was not crucified. A substitute, possibly Judas Iscariot, was either intentionally or mistakingly placed on the cross by Roman soldiers. Hence, the Jews thought they had slain Jesus, but did not. This assertion is based upon a Docetic heresy in the early Church that maintained that either Judas Iscariot or Simon of Cyrene was crucified in the place of Jesus.

Mainstream Christians claim that this theory is not only wrong, it is preposterously wrong. The likelihood of an individual mistakenly crucified in the place of Jesus stretches the limits of credulity. Jesus had been a serious threat to the Jewish religious establishment. He was also a well-known public figure. The Jewish leaders knew who he was and were insistent that he be put to death. Because of this, any mistaken substitute would have been quickly identified.

It must be added, however, that the likelihood that Jesus died on the cross and then rose from the dead, according to the Scriptures, also stretches credulity to its limits. Yet, it is not implausible once a person embraces an "open system" worldview that allows God to enter our world, suspend the laws of nature, and perform miracles.

Along with the topics of the deity of

him, but only follow an opinion. They did not kill him, for sure!

158 nay, God raised him up unto Himself; for God is mighty and wise!

159 And there shall not be one of the people of the Book but shall believe in him before his death; and on the day of judgment he shall be a witness against them.

160 And for the injustice of those who are Jews have we forbidden them good things which we had made lawful for them, and for their obstructing so much the way of God,

161 and for their taking usury when we had forbidden it, and for their devouring the wealth of people in

vain—but we have prepared for those of them who misbelieve a grievous woe.

162 But those amongst them who are firm in knowledge, and the believers who believe in what is revealed to thee, let what is revealed before thee, and the steadfast in prayer, and the givers of alms, and the believers in God and the last day,—unto these we will give a mighty hire.

Muhammad

163 Verily, we have inspired thee as we inspired Noah and the prophets

Jesus Christ and the nature of salvation (by individual merit or as a gift), this topic of the crucifixion of Jesus Christ serves as a third major line of demarcation that divides Christianity from Islam. No theological middle ground between the two exists. Hence, when it comes to the prospects of the success of theological dialogue between representatives of these two religions, the only option is for one side to win the argument—not to achieve an agreeable compromise.

4.159 Muhammad claimed that all Christians will rightly believe, at the moment of their death, that Jesus was merely a prophet of Allah. Yet, this belief will come too late. At the Last Judgment, Jesus will be a witness to all who wrongly believed him to be the Son of God.

4.160 *the way of God* — Muhammad believed that the Jewish people had obstructed the true way of Allah. That true way is summarized in the Five Pillars of Islam.

4.161 *and for their taking usury* —

Muhammad condemned the Jews for their practice of usury. For them, he said, is a "grievous woe"—the flames of Hell.

Following the Second Diaspora of the first century and the emergence of the Church as the dominant religion in the West, Jewish people found themselves ostracized from most professions and the guilds. This cause them to be pushed into marginal occupations disdained by the Church, such as tax and rent collection and usury. Jews were therefore looked upon with an increasing sense of disdain since they were the ones who took other people's earnings (see Q 2.275-281; 3.123-125; 30.39).

4.162 *are firm in knowledge* — Muhammad acknowledged that some Jews are firm in knowledge by embracing the truths found in the qur'anic surahs. In other words, a few Jews converted to Islam. Provided that they remain steadfast in prayer, and the giving of alms, they will enter Paradise following the Last Judgment.

after him, and as we inspired Abraham, and Ishmael, and Jacob, and the tribes and Jesus, and Job, and Jonas, and Aaron, and Solomon; and to David did we give Psalms.

164 Of apostles we have already told thee of some before; and of apostles some we have not told thee of; but Moses did God speak to, speaking;

165 —apostles giving glad tidings and warning, that men should have no argument against God, after the apostles for God is mighty, wise!

166 But God bears witness to what He has revealed to thee: He revealed it in His knowledge, and the angels bear witness too; though God is witness enough.

167 Verily, those who misbelieve and obstruct the way of God, have

erred a wide error.

168 Verily, those who misbelieve and are unjust, God will not pardon them, nor will He guide them on the road

169 —save the road to hell, to dwell therein for aye;—that is easy enough to God!

170 O ye folk! the Apostle has come to you with truth from your Lord: believe then, for it is better for you. But if ye misbelieve, then God's is what is in the heavens and the earth, and God is knowing, wise.

Monotheism

171 O ye people of the Book! do not exceed in your religion, nor say against God aught save the truth. The Messiah, Jesus the son of Mary, is but the apostle of God and

4.163 Muhammad asserted, once again, that he was a divinely chosen apostle—in the same prophetic line as Noah, Abraham, Ishmael, Jacob (Israel), the patriarchs of the Twelve Tribes of Israel, Jesus, Job, Jonah, Aaron, Solomon, and David.

4.164 *some we have not told thee of* — Some Islamic scholars believe that Allah sent thousands of apostles to the various peoples of the world since the beginning of history (see **The Apostles** on pp 396-398). In the Qur'an, only a small number of these prophets were identified and discussed.

4.165 According to Muhammad, the purpose of the apostles was to give "glad tidings and warnings" to all people so that they will successfully pass through the testing at the Last Judgment.

4.171 *say not Three* — Christians were admonished to not affirm the Doctrine of the Trinity—one God existing in Three Persons (God the Father, God the Son, and God the Holy Spirit). He insisted that "God is only one God, celebrated by His praise that He should beget a Son!" (see the **Definition of Chalcedon** on pp. 785-786; **The Doctrine of the Trinity** on pp. 735-736; and **The Nicene-Constantinopolitan Creed** on p. 740).

In reply, Christians maintain that God is not three, as Muhammad asserted, but that God is Three-in-One (a Trinity). Nowhere in the Qur'an did Muhammad rightly articulate the Doctrine of the Trinity, as understood in mainline Christian scholarship. Instead, he caricaturized it as a form of polytheism, and

His Word, which He cast into Mary and a spirit from Him; believe then in God and His apostles, and say not "Three." Have done! it were better for you. God is only one God, celebrated be His praise that He should beget a Son! His is what is in the heavens and what is in the earth; and God sufficeth for a guardian.

172 The Messiah doth surely not disdain to be a servant of God, nor do the angels who are nigh to Him; and whosoever disdains His service and is too proud, He will gather them altogether to Himself.

173 But as for those who believe and do what is right, He will pay their hire and will give increase to them of His grace. But as for those who disdain and are too proud, He will punish them with a grievous woe,

and they shall not find for them other than God a patron or a help.

The straight path

174 O ye folk! proof has come to you from your Lord, and we have sent down to you manifest light.

175 As for those who believe in God, and take tight hold of Him, He will make them enter into mercy from Him and grace; and He will guide them to Himself by a right way.

*Laws pertaining
to inheritances*

176 They will ask thee for a decision; say, "God will give you a decision concerning remote kinship." If a man perish and have no child, but have a sister, let her have half of

then condemned it.

4.172-173 Muhammad acknowledged that the Messiah (Jesus Christ) was a servant of God. The New Testament makes a similar claim (Matt 12:18; 20:28; Lk 22:27; Jn 13:3-14; Rom 15:8; Phil 2:7). Yet Muhammad also stated that whoever rejects Jesus as a servant by ascribing to him a nature that is more than a servant (the teaching that Jesus is God) are "too proud" and will be punished in the fires of Hell.

4.173 *believe and do what is right* — This is a summary of the Islamic gospel (see Q 103.3, note).

4.174-175 Muhammad believed that the Qur'an is a "manifest light" which shows people the "right way" that leads to eternal life. The Qur'an is also described as a strong

rope that people are called upon to "to take tight hold of Him."

4.175 *believe in God, and take hold of Him* — This is a variation of the formula "believe and do right" mentioned throughout the Qur'an (see Q 103.3, note).

4.176 Before closing the surah, Muhammad revisited the laws of inheritance. He addressed the question of remote kinship. Muhammad decided that if a man should die and have no child, but had a sister, she should receive half of the shares. But if he should have two sisters, they were to receive two-thirds of the shares. If he should have brothers and sisters, then the brother would receive twice the portion of one of the sisters. If a woman should die and have no child yet have a brother, he would receive

what he leaves; and he shall be her heir, if she have no son. But if there be two sisters, let them both have two thirds of what he leaves; and if there be brethren, both men and women, let the male have like the portion of two females. God makes this manifest to you lest ye err; for God all things doth know.

Surah 58

In the name of the merciful and compassionate God.

The Oath of Zihar

1   God has heard the speech of her who wrangled with you about her husband, and complained to God; and God hears your gossip; verily, God both hears and sees.

2   Those among you who back out of their wives they are not their mothers: their mothers are only those who gave them birth; and, verily, they speak a wrong speech and a false. Verily, God both pardons and forgives.

3   But those who back out of their wives and then would recall their speech—then the, manumission of a captive before they touch each other; that is what ye are admonished, and God of what ye do is well aware!

4   But he who finds not (the means)—

the entire inheritance.

Surah 58. The title of this surah, *The Pleading Woman*, comes from v. 1. The surah contrasts the practice of divorce in pagan Arabia with Islamic law. It then addresses questions related to belief and unbelief. The surah ends with a brief discussion of the Muslim believer's attitude towards the infidel.

58.1 Islamic scholars claim that this surah begins with a complaint of a woman by the name of Khawlah bint Tha'labah. She had recently been divorced by her husband who then pronounced the *Oath of Zihar:* "Thou art henceforth unlawful to me as my mother's back" where the term *back* is a synonym for *body*. The point is that the husband would not have sexual relations with this woman any more than he would with his own mother. This was an oath widely used among the pagan polytheists in Arabia. A woman thus divorced was not permitted to remarry and had to remain forever in the custody of

her former husband.

58.2 *they speak a wrong speech and a false* — Muhammad responded to the complaint of the woman in the previous verse by abolishing the *Oath of Zihar*.

58.3a *the manumission of a captive before they touch each other* — That is, those who pronounce the *Oath of Zihar* to one of their wives, then wished to go back on what they have said, shall have to free a slave (provide manumission) to one of his slaves.

58.3b *God of what ye do is well aware* — That is, Allah is concerned of what is done in this world that either affirms to or rebels against His will. In the context of this verse, it means that Allah is aware of those who attempt to hold their wives in bondage to the *Oath of Zihar*.

58.4 *he who finds not (the means)* — That is, he who had not the wherewithal to free a slave must fast for two consecutive months before the couple were permitted to re-

then a fast for two months con-secutively, before they touch each other; and he who cannot endure that—then the feeding of sixty poor folk. That is that ye may believe in God and His Apostle; and these are the bounds of God; and for the mis-believers is grievous woe!

5 Verily, those who oppose God and His Apostle shall be upset, as those before them were upset. We have sent down manifest signs: for the misbelievers is shameful woe

6 on the day when God shall raise them all together, and shall inform them of what they have done. God has taken account of it, but they forget it; for God is witness over all!

Jewish conspiracies

7 Dost thou not see that God knows what is in the heavens and what is in the earth? and that there cannot be a privy discourse of three but He makes the fourth? nor of five but He makes the sixth? nor less than that nor more, but that He is with them wheresoe'er they be? then He will inform them of what they have done upon the resurrec-tion day; verily, God all things doth know!

8 Dost thou not look at those who were prohibited from privy talk, and then returned to that they were forbidden? and they too discourse together with sin and enmity and rebellion against the Apostle; and when they come to thee they greet thee with what God greets thee not; and they say in themselves, Why does not God torment us for what we say? Hell is enough for them! they shall broil therein, and an ill journey shall it be!

9 O ye who believe! when ye dis-course together, then discourse not in sin and enmity and rebellion

sume sexual relations with one another. If this was not possible, then the man was to feed sixty poor people.

58.5-6 Muhammad believed that all who failed to follow his instructions concerning the *Oath of Zihar* would suffer accordingly in the afterlife since Allah is a witness over all.

58.7 The historical setting of this passage was the struggles and intrigues that took place in Medinah. Muhammad and the Mus-lim community were on one side, and a Jewish tribe was on the other side. The Jews, said Muhammad, had been gathering together in secret devising plans to conquer Muham-mad and remove the Muslim presence from Medinah. Muhammad, having come to a knowledge of the meetings, noted that Al-lah was present in all such meetings. The implication was that Allah would confound their conspiracies.

58.8 *when they come to greet thee* — According to hadithic literature, the Jews of Medinah did not greet Muhammad or the other Muslims with the traditional *salaam* (peace). Rather, they spoke the Arabic word *sam* (death). For such disrespect, Muham-mad cursed them to the fires of Hell.

58.9 Muhammad warned the Muslim com-munity to remain separate from the Jewish people and their conspiracies. The problem

against the Apostle; but discourse together in righteousness and piety; and fear God, for unto Him ye shall be gathered!

10   Privy talk is only from the devil, and those who do believe may grieve: it cannot hurt them at all, except by the permission of God: and upon God let the believers rely.

Muslim assemblies

11   O ye who believe! when it is said to you, "Make room in your assemblies," then make room; God will make room for you; and when it is said to you, "Rise up," then rise up; God will raise all you who believe, as well as those who are given knowledge, in rank; for God of what ye do is well aware!

Almsgiving

12   O ye who believe! when ye address the Apostle, then give in charity before addressing him; that is better for you, and more pure. But if ye find not the means—then God is forgiving, compassionate.

13   What! do ye shrink from giving in charity before addressing him? then if ye do it not, and God relents towards you, then be steadfast in prayer, and. give alms, and fear God and His Apostle; for God is well aware of what ye do!

Religious separation

14   Dost thou not look at those who take for patrons a people God is wrath with? they are neither of you nor of them, and they swear to you a lie the while they know;

15   for them God has prepared severe torment; verily, evil is it they have done!

16   They take their faith for a cloak; and they turn men aside from the

was that not all the Muslims were wholly loyal to Muhammad in Medinah. Some had become disenchanted with him (perhaps due to the Muslim defeat at the Battle of Uhud and began conspiring with the Jews in Medinah.

58.10 All such conspiracies, said Muhammad, were devilish. True believers, he said, were to remain faithful to Allah.

58.11 Many Muslims, anxious to hear another divine revelation that had been given to Muhammad, thronged around him. In this passage, Muslims were reminded to remain dedicated to Muhammad and continue this practice.

58.12-13 Muhammad instructed the Muslim community to establish the tradition of giving something to charity prior to speaking to him. This was not mandated, since if one had no means with which to give to charity, Allah would forgive and show compassion. Such individuals, however, were instructed to show their dedication in other ways: steadfastness in prayer, the giving of alms, and remaining worshipful towards God and respectful of Muhammad.

58.14-21 Muslims were instructed to remain separate from all who rejected the qur'anic teachings. Since all such people were destined to eternal damnation, Muham-

path of God; and for them is shameful woe!

17 Their wealth shall not avail them, nor their children at all, against God; they are the fellows of the Fire, and they shall dwell therein for aye!

18 On the day when God raises them all together, then will they swear to Him as they swore to you; and they will think that they rest on somewhat—Ay, verily, they are liars!

19 Satan hath overridden them, and made them forget the remembrance of God: they are the crew of Satan; ay, the crew of Satan, they are the losers!

20 Verily, those who oppose God and His Apostle are amongst the most vile.

21 God has written, "I will surely prevail, I and my apostles;" verily, God is strong and mighty!

22 Thou shalt not find a people who believe in God and the last day loving him who opposes God and His Apostle, even though it be their fathers, or their sons, or their brethren, or their clansmen. He has written faith in their hearts, and He aids them with a spirit from Him; and will make them enter into gardens beneath which rivers flow, to dwell therein for aye! God is well pleased with them, and they well pleased with Him: they are God's crew; ay, God's crew, they shall prosper!

Surah 65

In the name of the merciful and compassionate God.

Divorce

1 O thou prophet! when ye divorce women, then divorce them at their

---

mad concluded that it was improper for those seeking eternal life in Paradise to befriend them. "Satan has overridden them," he explained. Not only were they "the losers" (v. 19), they were also "amongst the most vile" (v. 20)

58.22 The most important reason, said Muhammad, for Muslims to remain separate from those who rejected Islam is that at the Last Judgment one will not be able to find a person who truly loved Allah and Muhammad yet also loved those who contended against him. In other words, if a Muslim loved those who resisted Islam, Allah would not love him in the afterlife (i.e., he would go to Hell).

This is true even if those who contend against Islam are members of one's own family ("even though it be their fathers, or their sons, or their brethren, or their clansmen").

Surah 65. The title of this surah, *The Divorce*, comes from v. 1. Its primary theme is the waiting period that women must undergo before a marriage is finally dissolved, permitting them to remarry. At the end of the surah, Muhammad revisited the Doctrine of the Apostles.

65.1a *calculate the term* — That is, calculate the period of time between divorce and remarriage for women. According to Q 2.228 and 65.4, she must wait "three

term, and calculate the term and fear God your Lord. Do not drive them out of their houses unless they have committed manifest adultery. These are God's bounds, and whoso transgresses God's bounds has wronged himself. Thou knowest not whether haply God may cause something fresh to happen after that.

2   And when they have reached their appointed time, then retain them with kindness, or separate from them with kindness; and bring as witnesses men of equity from among you; and give upright testimony to God. That is what He admonishes him who believes in God and the last day; and whosoever fears God, He will make for him a (happy) issue, and will provide for him from whence he reckoned not.

3   And whosoever relies on God, He is sufficient for him: verily, God will attain His purpose—God has set for everything a period.

4   And such of your women as despair of menstruation—if ye doubt, then their term is three months; and such as have not menstruated too. And those who are heavy with child their appointed time is when they have laid down their burden; and whosoever fears God, He will make for him an easy affair.

5   That is God's command, He has sent it down to you; and whosoever fears God He will cover for him his offences and will make grand for him his hire.

6   Let them dwell where ye dwell, according to your means, and do not harm them, to reduce them to straits; and if they be heavy with child, then pay for them until they lay down their burdens; and if they suckle (the child) for you, then give them their hire, and consult among yourselves in reason; but if ye be in difficulties, and another

courses"—that is, three menstrual cycles (three months). The reason for this delay was to assure that any future pregnancy was not the child of the former husband. During the waiting time, divorced women were to remain in the homes of their former husbands—unless they had committed adultery.

65.1b *God may cause something fresh to happen* — That is, during this waiting period, a reconciliation between the two may transpire and the marriage restored.

65.2 At the completion of the three months, a kindly departure between the two divorced people was encouraged.

65.3 Divorce is always a trauma for both parties, yet those who rely upon Allah, Muhammad, said, will find that He is sufficient to carry them forward.

65.4 The waiting period for women, prior to remarriage, is three months (three menstrual cycles). This requirement holds for women who sill menstruate and those who are post-menopause. Women who are pregnant must wait until they give birth, and then the child is placed in the sole guardianship of the father (see Q 2.228).

65.6 Pregnant women were to remain in the homes of their former husbands and be paid for their services as wet nurses until the child was weaned (see Q 2.233).

Definition of Chalcedon

A.D. 451

In one of the first seven ecumenical councils of the early church, the early church convened its principal leaders and scholars in Chalcedon (present day northwest Turkey) to address a growing controversy regarding the nature of Jesus Christ. Some believed in Monophysitism (Jesus possessed only one nature) where his divine nature overcame his human nature. Others believed that Jesus was one Person with two natures (divine and human) that existed in full balance with one another. The Definition of Chalcedon declared as heresy the first view and affirmed the second.

THE DEFINITION

We, then, following the holy Fathers, all with one consent, teach people to confess one and the same Son, our Lord Jesus Christ, the same perfect in Godhead and also perfect in manhood;

truly God and truly man, of a reasonable [rational] soul and body;

consubstantial [co-essential] with the Father according to the Godhead, and consubstantial with us according to the Manhood;

in all things like unto us, without sin;

begotten before all ages of the Father according to the Godhead, and in these latter days, for us and for our salvation, born of the Virgin Mary, the Mother of God, according to the Manhood;

one and the same Christ, Son, Lord, only begotten, to be acknowledged in two natures, unconfusedly, unchangeably, indivisibly, inseparably;

the distinction of natures being by no means taken away by the union, but rather the property of each nature being preserved, and concurring in one Person and one Subsistence, not parted or divided into two persons, but one and the same Son, and only begotten, God the Word, the Lord Jesus Christ;

as the prophets from the beginning [have declared] concerning Him, and the Lord Jesus Christ Himself has taught us, and the Creed of the holy Fathers has handed down to us.

———————————•◆•◆•————————————

This Chalcedonian Definition represented a delicate balancing act...It took longer for the East to accept the Definition of Chalcedon than the West. In Egypt particularly, determined opposition arose to the formula. An Egyptian bishop, Proterius, said at Chalcedon that if he signed the statement he would be signing his death warrant. Six years later he was indeed killed by a mob because of that very act...In the West, by contrast, there was almost immediate satisfaction with Chalcedon. Soon, in fact, even most of the East came to agree that this was a good statement of the delicate mystery lying at the heart of Christianity itself.

—Mark A. Noll, *Turning Points*, p. 76

The Christological settlement at Chalcedon illustrates the catholicity of the theology of the ancient church. Three major schools of theology had been involved in the Christological controversies and were represented at Chalcedon: Alexandria, Antioch, and Western Christianity. The final result could have been produced by none of these schools of thought alone. Chalcedon was truly catholic in the very great degree in which it was the result of the shared theological wisdom of the Church.

—John H. Leith, *Creeds of the Churches*, p. 34

The Definition of Chalcedon set the standard of all subsequent Christological confessions in the majority of Christian churches, Eastern Orthodox, Roman Catholic, and Protestant.

—Daniel L. Migliore, *Faith Seeking Understanding*, p. 172

It was in the aftermath of Chalcedon that Islam was born, with its own unequivocal condemnation of even the possibility of an incarnation or trinity in God.

—Sandra Toenies Keating, Habib ibn Khidmah Takriti, *Defending the People of Truth*, p. 4

woman shall suckle the child for him, let him who has plenty expend of his plenty;

7   but he whose provision is doled out, let him expend of what God has given him; God will not compel any soul beyond what He has given it—God will make after difficulty ease!

The apostles

8   How many a city has turned away from the bidding of its Lord and His apostles; and we called them to a severe account, and we tormented them with an unheard-of torment!

9   And they tasted the evil results of their conduct; and the end of their conduct was loss!

10   God prepared for them severe torment—then fear God, ye who are endowed with minds! Ye who believe! God has sent down to you

a reminder;

11   —an apostle to recite to you God's manifest signs—to bring forth those who believe and act aright from darkness into light! and whoso believes in God and acts right He will bring him into gardens beneath which rivers flow, to dwell therein for ever and for aye! God has made goodly for him his provision!

12   God it is who created seven heavens, and of the earth the like thereof. The bidding descends between them, that ye may know that God is mighty over all, and that God has encompassed all things with His knowledge!

Surah 63

In the name of the merciful and compassionate God.

65.7 For those former husbands who were poor and without sufficient means to pay the expenses for the former wife, they were to pay what they were capable of paying.

65.8 *tormented them with an unheard-of torment* — Muhammad concluded this surah with a return to a familiar theme: divine torture. All who opposed the message of the apostles were tortured by Allah. In the afterlife, those who heeded their message and lived accordingly went to Paradise. Those who did not, went to Hell (see *The Apostles* on pp. 396-398; and *The Perspicuous Book* on pp. 178-179).

65.11 *believe and act aright* — This is a

summary of the Islamic gospel (see Q 103.3, note).

65.12 *seven heavens* — Muhammad believed that Paradise is divided into seven layers, with a ranking from bottom to top. The seventh heaven was the abode of Allah, the most pristine of all the heavens (see *Paradise* on pp. 76-77; Q 13.17; 41.12; 67.3; 71.15 and 78.12).

Surah 63. The title to this surah, *The Hypocrites*, comes from v. 1. Its theme is the problem Muhammad had with one of his opponents in Medinah, Abdullah bin Ubai bin Salul. Muhammad described him as a hypocrite (Muslim apostate) who threatened his

The hypocrites

1   When the hypocrites come to thee, they say, "We bear witness that thou art surely the Apostle of God;" but God knows that thou art His Apostle: and God bears witness that the hypocrites are liars!

2   They take their faith for a cloak, and then they turn folks from God's way—evil is that which they have done!

3   That is because they believed and then disbelieved, wherefore is a stamp set on their hearts so that they do not understand!

4   And when thou seest them, their persons please thee; but if they speak, thou listenest to their speech: they are like timber propped up: they reckon every noise against them! They are the foe, so beware of them!—God

fights against them, how they lie!

5   And when it is said to them, "Come, and the Apostle of God will ask forgiveness for you!" they turn away their heads, and thou mayest see them turning away since they are so big with pride!

6   It is the same to them whether thou dost ask forgiveness for them, or whether thou dost not ask forgiveness for them—God will not forgive them; verily, God guides not a people who work abomination!

7   They it is who say, "Expend not in alms upon those who are with the Apostle of God, in order that they may desert him!"—but God's are the treasures of the heavens and the earth; but the hypocrites have no sense!

8   They say, "If we return to el Medînah, the mightier will surely drive out the meaner therefrom;"

work in Medinah due to his disloyalty. The historical setting were events following Muhammad's defeat at the Battle of Uhud.

63.1-2 Shortly after the Battle of Uhud, a number of Muslims maintained an outward appearance of remaining Muslims, yet privately had become infidels.

63.3 *they believed that then disbelieved* — This is the classic definition of apostasy. Muhammad believed that Allah put His stamp on their hearts, an act that condemns them to Hell (see Q 4.155; 7.100-101; 9.87, 93; 10.74; 16.108; 30.59; 40.35; 47.16).

63.4 Muhammad looked upon apostate Muslims as his foes. By association, they are also the foes of all faithful Muslims. They are like "timber propped up," meaning that they are

as worthless as hollow pieces of wood unable to stand up on their own.

63.7 *Expend not in alms* — Much of Muhammad's political strength in Medinah depended upon the Muslims who had emigrated with him from Mecca. Yet these same Muslims were poor. Muhammad's opponents believed that if they refused to give alms to these people, many of them would leave and return to Mecca. If this were to happen, then Muhammad's political power would diminish, causing it to be easier to overcome him.

63.8a *el Medinah* — Medinah. This is a name which literally means: the City of the Prophet. The city's previous name was Yathrib, a name that it held for centuries.

but to God belongs the might, and to His Apostle and to the believers; but the hypocrites do not know!

The faithful

9   O ye who believe! let not your property nor your children divert you from the remembrance of God—for whosoever does that, they are those who lose!

10 But expend in alms of what we have bestowed upon you before death come on any one of you, and he says, "My Lord! wouldst thou but have respited me till an appointed time nigh at hand, then would I

surely give in charity and be among the righteous!" But God will never respite a soul when its appointed time has come: and God of what ye do is well aware!

Surah 24

In the name of the merciful and compassionate God.

Sexual sin

1   A chapter which we have sent down and determined, and have sent down therein manifest signs; haply

---

63.8b The hypocrites said that if they returned to Medinah, the more honorable Abdullah bin Ubai bin Salul (one of Muhammad's opponents) could expel Muhammad from the city and restore it to its pre-Islamic ways.

63.9-10 Muhammad believed that Muslim loyalty should be first to Allah, and second to property and children. This means that one's property and children should be sacrificed, if needed, for the Cause of Allah. The reason for this radicalized faith was a settled belief in the reality of the Last Judgment and one's subsequent eternal destiny.

Surah 24. The title of this surah, *The Light*, comes from v. 35. Its purpose was to face down the Muslims within Muhammad's ranks in Medinah who were secretly disloyal to him. Their profession of faith in Islam was superficial, a ploy to breed discord among the Muslim community. Repeatedly, Muhammad felt compelled to reiterate his authority as the Prophet of Allah, insisting that any disobedi-

ence to him was tantamount to disobedience to Allah.

The historical background to the surah are events following the Raid at the Wells of Muraysi in 626, a battle that took place after the Battle of the Trench. Muhammad had received news that a Jewish tribe (Banu al-Mustaliq) had taken their livestock to a watering place called al-Muraysi. He sent his Muslim raiders to the watering place where he defeated them (see **The Raid at the Wells of Muraysi** on pp. 796-797). On the return trip to Medinah, however, one of his wives was accused of adultery. This accusation generated a scandal in Medinah that Muhammad's opponents attempted to use to discredit him and drive him from their city.

24.1 *A chapter* — That is, a surah. Muhammad claimed that each of the surahs that he recited to people were not his creations. Rather, they were "sent down" from Paradise and were then dictated to Muhammad (see **The Perspicuous Book** on pp. 178-

ye may be mindful.

2   The whore and the whoremonger. Scourge each of them with a hundred stripes, and do not let pity for them take hold of you in God's religion, if ye believe in God and the last day; and let a party of the believers witness their torment.

3   And the whoremonger shall marry none but a whore or an idolatress; and the whore shall none marry but an adulterer or an idolater; God has prohibited this to the believers;

4   but those who cast (imputations) on chaste women and then do not bring four witnesses, scourge them with eighty stripes, and do not receive any testimony of theirs

179).

24.2 *whore and whoremonger* — The Arabic term is *zina*, which includes both the sins of fornication and adultery. The penalty for those found guilty of the sin was a flogging of one hundred stripes, for both man and woman. The hadithic literature, however, notes that Muhammad ordered death by stoning for those found guilty of adultery (see **Honor Killing** on pp. 799-800).

24.3 *shall marry none but a whore* — This verse has generated some debate among Islamic scholars. Some claim that it requires the adulterer and adulteress to marry one another (this is how the Palmer translation of the verse, seen above, presents it).

Muhammad Asad, however, claims that this interpretation is impossible since it would result in Muslims marrying idolatrous infidels. Muhammad could not have meant for such couples to marry this since it is prohibited elsewhere in the Qur'an (see Q 2.221; 5.5). Rather, Asad notes that since adultery is an illicit sexual union, the verb *yankihu*, which appears twice in this passage, should not be understood to be "he marries." A better interpretation would be "he couples with"— which includes unlawful sexual intercourse, namely fornication. Hence, both partners are equally guilty of a sexual crime and neither can use the defense that he or she was seduced by the other. Accordingly, Asad

concluded, both the adulterer and the adulteress should suffer the same penalty for their illicit sexual union (*The Message of the Qur'an*, p. 595).

Farooq Ibrahim offers a third interpretation, noting that the verse indeed states that an adulterer and adulteress were required to marry one another, yet this verse was abrogated by statements from the Sunnah and Hadithic literature where the penalty for adultery was death by stoning. He writes: "It is clear from the Qur'an, that either in the case of adultery or fornication the punishment is 100 lashes. Note that in the Surah 24:3, the people who commit this crime are still able to continue to live and marry, implying they are not to be put to death. But as we know from Shariah Law, the punishment for adultery is death by stoning. This ruling comes from the Sunnah... Hence we see here that existing Muslim Law is based on the Sunnah and not the Qur'an. Therefore, as some Muslim scholars correctly say, the Sunnah abrogates the Qur'an" (*The Problem of Abrogation in the Qur'an*). See **The Doctrine of Abrogation** on pp. 68-70; **Honor Killing** on pp. 799-800.

24.4-5 Those found guilty of false accusations against chaste women—that is, those who failed to produce four witnesses to back their accusation—were to be flogged with eighty stripes. A provision was made to elimi-

ever, for these are the workers of abomination.

5 Except such as repent after that and act aright, for, verily, God is forgiving and compassionate.

6 And those who cast (imputation) on their wives and have no witnesses except themselves, then the testimony of one of them shall be to testify four times that, by God, he is of those who speak the truth;

7 and the fifth testimony shall be that the curse of God shall be on him if he be of those who lie.

8 And it shall avert the punishment from her if she bears testimony four times that, by God, he is of those who lie;

9 and the fifth that the wrath of God shall be on her if he be of those who speak the truth.

The Hazrat Ayesha Scandal

10 And were it not for God's grace upon you and His mercy, and that God is relenting, wise...

11 Verily, those who bring forward the lie, a band of you—reckon it not as an evil for you, nay, it is good for you; every man of them shall have what he has earned of sin; and he of them who managed to aggravate it, for him is mighty

nate the penalty, provided that the one found guilty repented and pledged to act aright.

24.5 *repent after that and act aright —* This is a variation of "believe and act aright," a summary of the Islamic gospel (see Q 103.3, note).

24.6-7 If a husband should accuse one of his wives of adultery, he needed not bring any additional witnesses. He only needed to call on Allah as a witness four times. Such a calling on Allah, of course, was a mere formality. If he, however, should make a false accusation regarding one of his wives, he would bring upon himself a curse from Allah.

24.8-9 The accused wife could avert the testimony of her husband by calling upon Allah four times. If she was the one lying in her counter testimony, then she would bring upon herself a curse from Allah.

24.11 *a band of you —* That is, a group of people from Medinah who accused one of Muhammad's wives of unchastity.

Following the Raid at the Wells of Muraysi, one of Muhammad's wives, Hazrat Ayesha, had inadvertently been left behind one night. She slept alone on the ground, hoping that by morning the caravan would return, looking for her. Instead, another Muslim came across her the following morning, placed her on his camel, and caught up with the caravan. Nevertheless, one of Muhammad's chief opponents in Medinah—Abdullah bin Ubayy (a hypocritical Muslim)—slandered her. He said that she and the man who found her had spent the night together in adulterous activities. His hope was to generate a civil war among the Muslims in Medinah. In the following month, the news of the alleged adultery spread throughout Medinah, generating a serious scandal for Muhammad. With time, the scandal settled down as Muhammad instituted a series of laws that addressed questions related to the way in which the accusations of adultery were to be handled.

woe.

12   Why did not, when ye heard it, the believing men and believing women think good in themselves, and say, "This is an obvious lie?"

13   Why did they not bring four witnesses to it? but since they did not bring the witnesses, then they in God's eyes are the liars.

14   And but for God's grace upon you, and His mercy in this world and the next, there would have touched you, for that which ye spread abroad, mighty woe.

15   When ye reported it with your tongues, and spake with your mouths what ye had no knowledge of, and reckoned it a light thing, while in God's eyes it was grave.

16   And why did ye not say when ye heard it, "It is not for us to speak of this? Celebrated be His praises, this is a mighty calumny!"

17   God admonishes you that ye return not to the like of it ever, if ye be believers;

18   and God manifests to you the signs, for God is knowing, wise.

19   Verily, those who love that scandal should go abroad amongst those who believe, for them is grievous woe in this world and the next; for God knows, but ye do not know.

20   And but for God's grace upon you, and His mercy, and that God is kind and compassionate..!

Admonition to purity

21   O ye who believe! follow not the footsteps of Satan, for he who follows the footsteps of Satan, verily, he bids you sin and do wrong; and but for God's grace upon you and His mercy, not one of you would be ever pure; but God purifies whom He will, for God both hears and knows.

22   And let not those amongst you who have plenty and ample means swear that they will not give aught to their kinsman and the poor and those who have fled their homes in God's way, but let them pardon and pass it over. Do ye not like God to forgive you? and God is

24.13 If accusers are unable to bring forth four witnesses to corroborate their testimony of an alleged adultery, they were to be regarded as liars.

24.14-20 These words were addressed to the accusers of Muhammad's wife, Hadrat Ayesha. Muhammad condemned the accusers, since they lacked adequate corroborating testimony (four witnesses). All such people, he said, would experience a "grievous woe in this world and the next" (v. 19).

With this new law, the simmering civil war among the Muslims in Medinah was stopped.
24.21a *O ye who believe!* — That is, Muslims.
24.21b Both sins of sexual impropriety and the bearing of false testimony caused one to become impure, following in the footsteps of Satan.
24.22 Another sin was the refusal to give alms to the poor kinsmen who left their homes in Mecca and emigrated to Medinah.

forgiving, compassionate.

23 Verily, those who cast imputations on chaste women who are negligent but believing shall be cursed in this world and the next; and for them is mighty woe.

24 The day when their tongues and hands and feet shall bear witness against them of what they did,

25 on that day God will pay them their just due; and they shall know that God, He is the plain truth.

26 The vile women to the vile men, and the vile men to the vile women; and the good women to the good men, and the good men to the good women: these are clear of what they say to them—forgiveness and a noble provision!

27 O ye who believe! enter not into houses which are not your own houses, until ye have asked leave and saluted the people thereof, that

is better for you; haply ye may be mindful.

28 And if ye find no one therein, then do not enter them until permission is given you, and if it be said to you, "Go back!" then go back, it is purer for you; for God of what ye do doth know.

29 It is no crime against you that ye enter uninhabited houses —a convenience for you—and God knows what ye show and what ye hide.

Personal chastity

30 Say to the believers that they cast down their looks and guard their private parts; that is purer for them; verily, God is well aware of what they do.

31 And say to the believing women that they cast down their looks and guard their private parts, and dis-

---

Financial assistance from wealthy Muslims was to be given to these poor and needy Muslims.

24.23 *chaste women who are negligent but believing* — That is, chaste women who were unthinkingly careless in their activities which opened them up to slanderous accusations. Those who slander will be punished by Allah in this life as well as the afterlife.

24.24 *tongues and hands and feet* — At the Last Judgment, all the actions of the infidels (words and behaviors) will be examined and judged.

24.27-29 Muslims were instructed to not enter the homes of other people without proper salutations and permissions.

24.30a *cast down their looks* — Male Mus-

lims were instructed to look downward when in the presence of women, other than their own wives.

24.30b *guard their private parts* — That is, protect their chastity.

24.31a *cast down their looks* — Female Muslims were instructed to look downward when in the presence of men, other than their own husbands.

24.31b *guard their private parts* — That is, protect their chastity.

24.31c *display not their ornaments, except those which are outside* — That is, chastity for Muslim women required them to only display their faces, hands and feet in public.

24.31d *let them pull their kerchiefs over their bosoms* — That is, chastity for Muslim

play not their ornaments, except those which are outside;

Hijabs and burqas

and let them pull their kerchiefs over their bosoms and not display their ornaments save to their husbands and fathers, or the fathers of their husbands, or their sons, or the sons of their husbands, or their brothers, or their brothers' sons, or their sisters' sons, or their women, or what their right hands possess, or their male attendants who are incapable, or to children who do not note women's nakedness; and that they beat not with their feet that their hidden orna-

ments may be known—but turn ye all repentant to God, O ye believers! haply ye may prosper.

Marital opportunities

32   And marry the single amongst you, and the righteous among your servants and your hand-maidens. If they be poor, God will enrich them of His grace, for God both comprehends and knows.

33   And let those who cannot find a match, until God enriches them of His grace, keep chaste.

Slavery

And such of those whom your

women required them to drape their heads with headcoverings (Arabic: *hijabs*) that reached down over their bosoms. They could only remove the headcoverings in their homes in the presence of their husbands, fathers, sons, brothers, slaves ("what their right hands possess"), or children "who do not note women's nakedness" (also see *Sahih Bukhari* 1.8.368, 395; 6.60.10; 7.62.95, 166; 7.65.375). Burqas are the outer garments that cover the entire body.

Moderate Muslims interpret this legal ordinance of headcoverings figuratively. Muslim women were to maintain their personal modesty, privacy, and chastity. As such, they were not required to wear *burqas*—that is, they could reveal more than their faces, feet, and hands when in public.

24.31e *beat not with their feet that their hidden ornaments may be known* — Muslim women were to be careful with their hands

so that they did not inadvertently reveal anything other than their faces, hands, and feet. **24.31f** *turn ye all repentant to God* — That is, women who are properly clad encourages people to remain pious (repentant) before Allah.

24.32 Muslim men were encouraged to marry Muslim women, regardless of the financial status of the women.

24.33a All unmarried Muslim men were to remain sexually chaste. Nevertheless, according to Q 23.6, they were permitted to have sexual relations with their female slaves.

24.33b *your right hands possess* — That is, your slaves (including concubines).

24.33c *a writing* — That is, a legal document that grants a slave's manumission, known as *kitabah*. If a slave wished to purchase his or her freedom, a *kitabah* was to be drawn up. Slave owners were also required to give their slaves financial encour-

right hands possess as crave a writing, write it for them, if ye know any good in them, and give them of the wealth of God which He has given you. And do not compel your slave girls to prostitution, if they desire to keep continent, in order to crave the goods of the life of this world; but he who does compel them, then, verily, God after they are compelled is forgiving, compassionate.

Parable of the Star

34   Now have we sent down to you manifest signs, and the like of those who have passed away before you, and as an admonition to those who fear.

35   God is the light of the heavens and

the earth; His light is as a niche in which is a lamp, and the lamp is in a glass, the glass is as though it were a glittering star; it is lit from a blessed tree, an olive neither of the east nor of the west, the oil of which would well-nigh give light though no fire touched it—light upon light!—God guides to His light whom He pleases; and God strikes out parables for men, and God all things doth know.

Two ways

36   In the houses God has permitted to be reared and His name to be mentioned therein—His praises are celebrated therein mornings and evenings.

37   Men whom neither merchandize

agement to achieve their manumission by offering them a portion of their own wealth (some Islamic scholars believe that this gift should amount to one fourth of the price of manumission). Though encouraged to do so, slave owners were not required to offer manumission. Slaves could pay the price in installments, through work projects, or in lump sums of money.

24.33d *prostitution* — Muslim owners of slaves were not to compel their female slaves to engage in prostitution, as a way of acquiring additional revenues. The only exception was when the female slave was willing to become a prostitute. Nevertheless, if a slave owner compelled his female slave to enter into the practice of prostitution, Allah would forgive him of this deed.

24.35a *God is the light of the heavens and*

the earth — That is, Allah is the One who enlightens heaven and earth with Himself and His truths. Many Islamic scholars claim that this is parable of the light of Allah in the heart of the believer. The Bible makes a similar claim about God (see Isa 9:2; 42:6-7; 49:6; 60:1-3; Hos 6:3; Matt 4:14-16; Lk 1:76-77; 2:32; Jn 1:4-9; 3:19; 8:12; 9:5; 12:35; Acts 13:47; 26:23).

24.35b *God guides to His light whom He pleases* — Again, Muhammad believed that only those who were predestined would be guided to spiritual light (see **The Doctrine of al-Qadar** on pp. 264-266).

24.36-38 In this passage, Muhammad contrasted the way that leads to Paradise with the way that leads to the fires of Hell. Muhammad characterized the homes of devoted Muslims as: (a) those that bring much

Raid at the Wells of Muraysi

January 627

After a series of raids on caravans heading to and from Mecca, Muhammad suspicioned that the Jewish tribe of al-Mustaliq were secretly preparing to launch an attack on the Muslims. The al-Mustaliq tribe was immensely prosperous who lived in the environs of Medinah.

Therefore, Muhammad decided upon a preemptive strike. Describing the battle in one of the Hadiths, Ibn Aun explained:

> I wrote a letter to Nafi and Nafi wrote in reply to my letter that the Prophet had suddenly attacked Bani Mustaliq without warning while they were heedless and their cattle were being watered at the places of water. Their fighting men were killed and their women and children were taken as captives, the Prophet got Juwairiya on that day. Nafi said that Ibn 'Umar had told him the above narration and that Ibn 'Umar was in that army.[1]

Two hundred Jewish women were taken captive. The booty included two thousand camels, five hundred sheep and goats, along with a huge quantity of household goods. The Muslim soldiers were hungry for sex and Muhammad allowed them to rape the female Jewish captives. In another Hadith, Ibn Muhairiz explained:

> I entered the Mosque and saw Abu said al-Khudri and sat beside him and asked him about al-Azl (i.e., *coitus interruptus*). Abu said, "We went out with Allah's Apostle for the Ghazwa of Banu al-Mustaliq and we received captives from among the Arab captives and we desired women and celibacy became hard on us and we loved to do *coitus interruptus*. So when we intended to do *coitus interruptus* before asking Allah's Apostle who is present among us?" We asked him about it and he said, "It is better for you not to do so, for if any soul (till the Day of Resurrection) is predestined to exist, it will exist."[2]

Coitus interruptus was the termination of intercourse prior to ejaculation, which prevented pregnancies. Muhammad opposed the practice
of coitus interruptus since it interfered with Allah's sovereign control
over the question of pregnancies. He did, however, sanction the rape
of female captives (see Q 4.24; 23.5-6; 24.32; 33.50; 70.29-30).

Afterwards, when back in Medinah, many of the women who had
been raped were sold as slaves.

---

[1] Sahih Bukhari, 3.46.717; also see Sahih Muslim, 19.429.
[2] Sahih Bukhari, 5.59.459.

In January 627, after the introduction of the *hijah* for the Prophet's wives, a painful incident
showed how quickly any slur against his family could undermine Muhammad's position. He had
led an expedition against the Bani al-Mustaliq, a branch of Khuza'ah, which was preparing to raid
Medina. He took them by surprise at the Well of Muraysi on the Red Sea coast, north-west of
Medina, put them to flight and made off with 2,000 camels, 5,000 sheep and goats and 200 of their
women.

—Karen Armstrong, *Muhammad: A Biography of the Prophet*, p. 199

Muhammad allowed his men to rape the women captured in raids. However, after capturing the
women, Muslims faced a dilemma. They wanted to have sex with them but also wanted to return
them for ransom and therefore did not want to make them pregnant. Some of these women were
already married. Their husbands had managed to escape when taken by surprise and were still
alive. The raiders considered the possibility of *coitus interruptus* (withdrawing from intercourse
prior to ejaculation). Unsure of the best course of action, they went to Muhammad for
counsel...Muhammad [told] his men that *coitus interruptus* would be futile and ill-advised because it would be an attempt to thwart the irresistible will of Allah.

—Ali Sina, *Understanding Muhammad*, pp. 36, 37

It is obvious from these incidents that the goal of Muhammad in addition to preaching a new
religion of peace, was to negate the peacefulness of his religion by committing these horrendous
acts of murder, robbery, and rape of his victim's wives and daughters.

—John U. Hanna, *Cancer in America*, p. 107

nor selling divert from the remembrance of God and steadfastness in prayer and giving alms, who fear a day when hearts and eyes shall be upset;

38   —that God may recompense them for the best that they have done, and give them increase of His grace; for God provides whom He pleases without count.

Parable of the Mirage

39   But those who misbelieve, their works are like the mirage in a plain, the thirsty counts it water till when he comes to it he finds nothing, but he finds that God is with him; and He will pay him his account, for God is quick to take account.

Parable of the Deep Sea

40   Or like darkness on a deep sea, there covers it a wave above which is a wave, above which is a cloud—darknesses one above the other—when one puts out his hand he can scarcely see it; for he to whom God has given no light, he has no light.

The sovereign control of Allah

41   Hast thou not seen that God—all who are in the heavens and the earth celebrate His praises, and the birds too spreading out their wings; each one knows its prayer and its praise, and God knows what they do?

42   And unto Allah belongeth the Sovereignty of the heavens and the earth, and unto Allah is the journeying

43   Hast thou not seen that God drives the clouds, and then re-unites them, and then accumulates them, and thou mayest see the rain coming forth from their midst; and He sends down from the sky moun-

---

praise of Allah, (b) give a higher priority to devotion to Allah than to merchandising, (c) steadfast in prayer, (d) committed to the giving of alms, and (e) fearful of anything that would divert their attention from Allah.
24.38 *God may recompense them* — That is, eternal life is earned through good works (see **The Last Judgment** on pp. 46-50).
24.39 *their works are like the mirage in a plain* — The works of the infidels were likened by Muhammad to a mirage. They leave the impression of substance but are wholly inconsequential and unsatisfying.
24.40 *darkness on a deep sea* — Muham-

mad also likened the works of infidels to a dark night on the high seas with a thick cloud cover. If a sailor were in such a situation, he would be stranded and unable to navigate due to the lack of stars to offer guidance. Muhammad maintained that the lives of the infidels are likened to the darkness on a deep sea.
24.41-45 Muhammad returned to the familiar theme of Allah being in sovereign control of the universe. All activities on the earth are under His control and foreordination. This includes the forces of nature (clouds, rain, and lightning), the division between night

Honor Killing

The Islamic tradition of honoring killing is the practice where family honor is restored through the execution of a family member who sullied the family reputation through improper sexual activity. Typically, women are the ones subject to this discipline. Though members of other religions have also practiced honor killings, in Islam those who practice it look to their founder and principal prophet—Muhammad—for justification. The passage of scripture, Q 24.2, along with canonical hadithic literature, is where they look for justification.

There came to him (the Holy Prophet) a woman from Ghamid and said: Allah's Messenger, I have committed adultery, so purify me. He (the Holy Prophet) turned her away. On the following day she said: Allah Messenger, Why do you turn me away. Perhaps you turned me away as you turned away Ma'iz. By Allah, I have become pregnant, He said: Well, if you insist upon it, then go away until you give birth to (the child). When she was delivered she came with the child (wrapped) in a rag and said: Here is the child whom I have given birth to. He said: Go away and suckle him until you wean him. When she had weaned him, she came to him (the Holy Prophet) with the child who was holding a piece of bread in his hand. She said: Allah's Apostle, here is he as I have weaned him and he eats food. He (the Holy Prophet) entrusted the child to one of the Muslims and then pronounced punishment. And she was put in a ditch up to her chest and he commanded people and they stoned her. Khalid b. Walid came forward with a stone which he flung at her head and there spurted blood on the face of Khalid and so he abused her. Allah's Apostle (may peace be upon him) heard his (Khalid's) curse that he had hurled upon her. Thereupon he (the Holy Prophet) said: Khalid, be gentle. By Him in Whose Hand is my life, she has made such a repentance that even if a wrongful tax-collector were to repent, he would have been forgiven. Then giving command regarding her, he prayed over her and she was buried (*Sahih Muslim* 17.4206; also see *Sahih Bukhari* 7.63.195, 196).

———◆·●·◆———

Every year, hundreds of women and girls are murdered in the Middle East by male family members. The honor killing—the execution of a female family member for perceived misuse of her sexuality—is a thorny social and political issue...Given that honor killings often remain a private family affair, no official statistics are available on the practice or its frequency. According to a November 1977 report of the Women's Empowerment Project, published in *Al-Hayat Al-Jadida*, there were 20 honor killings in Gaza and the West Bank in 1996. One representative of the group added, "We know there are more, but no one publicizes it."

—Haideh Moghissi, *Women and Islam: Critical Concepts in Sociology*, p. 125

Muslim parents, those who are practicing honor killing, are directly motivated or influenced by the...scriptural and historical (Hadiths) support; hence they are able to commit heinous crimes called "honor killing" with (almost) impunity, exultantly and with ample satisfaction that they are following the strict Islamic ethical code to guard chastity, as the holy Prophet repeatedly cautioned Muslims so seriously to guard their women's chastity. Courts sanctioned that an adulteress should be buried up to her chest and stoned to death. Mullahs of Iran know the hadiths quite well.

—Jake Neuman, *God of Moral Perfection*, p. 165

"Honor killings" have sometimes been mistakenly attributed to Islamic teaching. Such killings, in which a woman's sexual activity is considered to have dishonored her family and provoked her murder, are rooted in cultural practices that are not synonymous with Islam and extend beyond the Islamic world Honor killings occur in many Middle Eastern societies, but not in Indonesia, the world's largest Muslim country...It should be noted that Islam originated in a patriarchal tribal society in which women had few rights, that much attributed to Islam is really due to the influence of local culture, and that there is a wide variance in how women are treated in Muslim societies.

—Margot Patterson, *Islam Considered*, p. 28

Honor killing is not an Islamic practice. Islam does not justify it. Honor killing is unknown, and would have been unheard of, in many Muslim societies. It has been practiced among Christians, Hindus, Buddhists, Confucians, and others, as documentary evidence shows.

—Unni Wikan, *In Honor of Fadime*, p. 248

tains with hail therein, and He makes it fall on whom He pleases, and He turns it from whom He pleases; the flashing of His lightning well-nigh goes off with their sight?

44 God interchanges the night and the day; verily, in that is a lesson to those endowed with sight.

45 And God created every beast from water, and of them is one that walks upon its belly, and of them one that walks upon two feet, and of them one that walks upon four. God creates what He pleases; verily, God is mighty over all!

The fate of the hypocrites

46 Now have we sent down manifest signs, and God guides whom He pleases unto the right way.

47 They will say, "We believe in God and in the Apostle, and we obey." Then a sect of them turned their backs after that, and they are not believers.

48 And when they are called to God and His Apostle to judge between them, lo! a sect of them do turn aside.

49 But had the right been on their side they would have come to him submissively enough.

50 Is there a sickness in their hearts, or do they doubt, or do they fear lest God and His Apostle should deal unfairly by them?—Nay, it is they who are unjust.

51 The speech of the believers, when they are called to God and His Apostle to judge between them, is

and day, and the activities of the animal kingdom.

24.46-57 Muhammad suspicioned that a number of people in Medinah who claimed to be Muslims were, in fact, insincere in their faith. They were seeking opportunities to conquer Muhammad and push the Muslims out of Medinah. In this passage, Muhammad openly declared that he was aware of their disloyalty. He attempted to turn the opinion of the middle-roaders (those Muslims who had been influenced by the hypocrites) back to himself by linking loyalty to Allah with himself and to clarify the eternal destiny of all hypocrites: the fires of Hell.

24.46 *the right way* — This is a summary of the Islamic gospel (see Q 72.2, note).

24.47 *We believe in God and in the Apostle* — Seven times in this passage Muhammad linked himself to Allah (vv 47, 48, 50, 51, 52, and 54). His intent was to make the case that loyalty to Allah requires loyalty to himself (see Q 3.32; 4.69, 79-80, 136; 5.80-81; 8.13, 20-23; 24, 48, 50-52, 54; 33.33, 71; 48.9-10; 57.19; 59.4; 72.22-23 and 46.16, note). Hence, Muslims were admonished to (a) believe in both, (b) not judge between them, (c) recognize that they were called to both, (d) obey both, and (e) be mindful that both will deal fairly with them. Towards the end of the passage, he added (without mentioning Allah) that they were to "be steadfast in prayer and give alms and obey the Apostle (v. 56).

24.48 *a sect of them do turn aside* — That is, Muhammad believed that a sect within the Muslim community had become traitors to the Islamic Cause due to their disloyalty.

only to say, "We hear and we obey;" and these it is who are the prosperous,

52 for whoso obeys God and His Apostle and dreads God and fears Him, these it is who are the happy.

53 They swear by God with their most strenuous oath that hadst Thou ordered them they would surely go forth. Say, "Do not swear reasonable obedience; verily, God knows what ye do."

54 Say, "Obey God and obey the Apostle; but if ye turn your backs he has only his burden to bear, and ye have only your burden to bear. But if ye obey him, ye are guided; but the Apostle has only his plain message to deliver."

55 God promises those of you who believe and do right that He will give them the succession in the earth as He gave the succession to those before them, and He will establish for them their religion which He has chosen for them, and to give them, after their fear, safety in exchange—they shall worship me, they shall not associate aught with me: but whoso disbelieves after that, those it is who are the sinners.

56 And be steadfast in prayer and give alms and obey the Apostle, haply ye may obtain mercy.

57 Do not reckon that those who misbelieve can frustrate (God) in the earth, for their resort is the Fire, and an ill journey shall it be.

*Chaste behavior
inside the home*

58 O ye who believe! let those whom your right hands possess, and those amongst you who have not reached puberty, ask leave of you three times: before the prayer of dawn, and when ye put off your clothes at noon, and after the evening prayer—three times of privacy for you: there is no crime on either you or them after these while ye are continually going one about the other. Thus does God explain to you His signs, for God is knowing, wise.

59 And when your children reach pu-

24.53 *they swear by god with their most strenuous oath* — That is, genuine Muslims swear with a jihadistic (fanatical) oath to Allah. In contrast, they were not to "swear reasonable obedience," for that did not exemplify a sufficient dedication. Accordingly, jihadistic dedication required a level of obedience that was beyond reason—a mixture of faith and fanaticism.

24.58a *O ye who believe!* — That is, Mus-

lims.

24.58b Homes in seventh century Arabia typically had only one room. Privacy while one dressed and undressed, then, required people to momentarily leave the home. Muhammad advised Muslims to dismiss children and slaves on three occasions during the day: "before the prayer of dawn, when ye put off your clothes at noon, and after the evening prayer."

berty let them ask leave as those before them asked leave. Thus does God explain to you His signs, for God is knowing, wise.

*Chaste behavior
for elderly women*

60   And those women who have stopped (child-bearing), who do not hope for a match, it is no crime on them that they put off their clothes so as not to display their ornaments; but that they abstain is better for them, for God both hears and knows.

Table customs

61   There is no hindrance to the blind, and no hindrance to the lame, and no hindrance to the sick, and none upon yourselves that you eat from your houses, or the houses of your fathers, or the houses of your mothers, or the houses of your brothers, or the houses of your sisters, or the houses of your paternal uncles, or the houses of your paternal aunts, or the houses of

your maternal uncles, or the houses of your maternal aunts, or what ye possess the keys of, or of your friend, there is no crime on you that ye eat all together or separately. And when ye enter houses then greet each other with a salutation from God, blessed and good. Thus does God explain to you His signs, haply ye may understand.

Respect for the Apostle

62   Only those are believers who believe in God and His Apostle, and when they are with Him upon public business go not away until they have asked his leave; verily, those who ask thy leave they it is who believe in God and His Apostle. But when they ask thy leave for any of their own concerns, then give leave to whomsoever thou wilt of them, and ask pardon for them of God; verily, God is forgiving and merciful.

63   Make not the calling of the Apostle amongst yourselves like your calling one to the other; God knows those of you who withdraw them-

24.60 *display their ornaments* — That is, display their feminine features. Older women advanced in age may discard their outer garments, provided that they did not reveal their feminine features.

24.61 Muhammad stated that Muslims were under no compulsion to eat his or her meals in the company of other family members.

24.62 Muhammad insisted that people who

entered his presence were not permitted to leave without requesting permission to do so.

24.63 Similarly, people were not to regard a summons from Muhammad to enter his presence as they did other people, with the option to either accept or reject the request. Since he saw himself as the Apostle, a summons from him was mandatory and must be

selves covertly. And let those who disobey his order beware lest there befall them some trial or there befall them grievous woe.

64   Ay, God's is what is in the heavens and the earth, He knows what ye are at; and the day ye shall be sent back to Him then He will inform you of what ye have done, for God all things doth know.

Surah 33

In the name of the merciful and compassionate God.

Initial admonition

1   O thou prophet! fear God and obey

not the misbelievers and hypocrites; verily, God is ever knowing, wise!

2   But follow what thou art inspired with from thy Lord; verily, God of what you do is ever well aware.

3   And rely upon God, for God is guardian enough.

General social laws

4   God has not made for any man two hearts in his inside; nor has He made your wives—whom you back away from—your real mothers; nor has He made your adopted sons your real sons. That is what ye speak with your mouths; but God speaks the truth and He guides to the path!

heeded.

Surah 33. The title of this surah, *The Allies*, comes from v. 9. It is closely related to the previous surah, Surah 24, and addressed similar concerns. The historical setting of the surah was the Battle of the Trench in A.D. 627 where a confederation of forces from a number of cities and towns, including a large force from Mecca, laid siege to Medinah. The Muslim forces, under the command of Muhammad, were nearly defeated. Yet after a month of siege, the Muslim forces successfully withstood the attack (see **The Battle of the Trench and its Aftermath** on pp. 813-815).

The second half of the surah addressed the scandal that emerged in Medinah regarding the marriage between Muhammad and Hazrat Zaynab. Another issue addressed the question of Muhammad's many wives, a num-

ber that far exceeded the limit of four wives that is stated previously in the Qur'an (see Q 4.3). These two issues called into question the sexual chastity of the Muslims in general and Muhammad in particular.

33.1 Muhammad began the surah with a firm rejection of the non-Muslims and hypocritical Muslims (apostates) in Medinah. The hypocrites were people who made an outward profession of faith in Islam, yet inwardly were working towards Muhammad's defeat and removal from Medinah.

33.2-3 Muhammad responded by reiterating the truths of the qur'anic surahs that he claimed were inspired from the Lord. He also rededicating himself to Allah.

33.4a *God has not made for any man two hearts in his inside* — This is a reference back to the previous passage (vv. 1-3) where Muhammad roundly criticized hypocritical Mus-

5   Call them by their fathers' names; that is more just in God's sight; but if ye know not their fathers, then they are your brothers in religion and your clients. There is no crime against you for what mistakes ye make therein; but what your hearts do purposely—but God is ever forgiving and merciful.

6   The prophet is nearer of kin to the believers than themselves, and his wives are their mothers. And blood relations are nearer in kin to each other by the Book of God than the believers and those who fled; only your doing kindness to your kindred, that is traced in the Book.

The prophetic lineage

7   And when we took of the prophets their compact, from thee and from Noah, and Abraham, and Moses, and Jesus the son of Mary, and took of them a rigid compact,

8   that He might ask the truth-tellers of their truth. But He has prepared for those who misbelieve a grievous woe.

The Battle of the Trench
(the cowards)

9   O ye who believe! remember God's favours towards you when hosts came to you and we sent against

lims.

33.4b *nor has He made your wives—whom you back away from—your real mothers —* This is a reference to the pre-Islamic pagan custom of the *Oath of Zihar* (see Q 58.1-6).

33.4c-5 *nor has He made your adopted sons your real sons —* This is a preview to Muhammad's discussion of his own scandal where he married his own daughter-in-law (see vv. 37-40). Muhammad's point was that the rights and social mores associated with a son is not the same as that of an adopted son. Hence, it was socially permissible for the wife of an adopted son to be married by the son's stepfather.

33.6a Muhammad claimed that since he was the chosen prophet of Allah, he was "nearer" (that is, more authoritative) than people in one's own family. In addition, Muhammad's many wives were nearer (that is, more authoritative) than one's own mother. Muslims were therefore compelled to offer him

their full loyalty, above that of loyalty to their own families.

33.6b Muhammad claimed that Muslim believers were "nearer" (that is, contained closer social ties) to other Muslims than they were to blood relations who were not Muslims. The way he put it, "your kindred...is traced in the Book (the Qur'an)." Muslims were compelled to offer a greater sense of loyalty to other Muslims than to non-Muslims, including non-Muslims in one's own family.

33.7 In line with the thoughts mentioned in the previous verse, Muslims were obligated to remain loyal to the prophets. This obligation reached back as far as Noah, Abraham, Moses, and Jesus and as far forward as Muhammad. As such, Muhammad saw himself as part of that prophetic lineage.

33.9-20 Muhammad then reminisced over the Battle of the Trench, a siege battle of which his small army was not defeated (see

them a wind and hosts that ye could not see—and God knew what ye were doing.

10 When they came upon you from above you and from below you, and when your eyesights were distracted and your hearts came up into your throats, and ye suspected God with certain suspicions.

11 There were the believers tried and were made to quake with a severe quaking.

12 And when the hypocrites and those in whose hearts was sickness said, "God and His Apostle have only promised us deceitfully."

13 And when a party of them said, "O people of Yathreb; there is no place for you (here), return then (to the city)." And a part of them asked leave of the prophet (to return), saying, "Verily, our houses are defenseless;" but they were not defenseless, they only wished for flight.

14 But had they been entered upon from its environs and then been asked to show treason they would have done so; but they would only have tarried there a little while.

15 They had covenanted with God before, that they would not turn their backs; and God's covenant shall be enquired of.

16 Say, "Flight shall avail you naught; if ye fly from death or slaughter, even then ye shall be granted enjoyment only for a little!"

17 Say, "Who is it that can save you from God, if He wish you evil, or wish you mercy?" but they will not find beside God a patron or a helper.

18 Say, "God knows the hinderers amongst you, and those who say to their brethren, 'Come along unto us,' and show but little valour;

19 —covetous towards you." When

The Battle of the Trench and its Aftermath on pp. 813-815).

33.9 *hosts that ye could not see* — Muhammad claimed that the reason for their victory in the Battle of the Trench was due to the presence of a host of invisible angels who fought on the side of the Muslims.

33.11 The threat of the enemy was such that Muhammad and his Muslim army feared defeat.

33.12a *hypocrites* — That is, apostate Muslims. These were Muslims whom Muhammad suspicioned to be on the side of the enemy.

33.12b *those in whose hearts was sickness* — Muslims who were deeply afraid.

33.13a *O people of Yathreb* — That is, O

people of Medinah. Yathrib (Yathreb) was its ancestral name. By using the name Yathrib, Muhammad's opponents were subtly saying that the city was no longer the City of the Prophet (which is what the name Medinah means).

33.13b *return then (to the city)* — A number of the Muslim soldiers were so fearful of death that they wished to abandon the trenches that surrounded the city and flee to their homes where they would mount a defense.

33.14-16 *treason* — Muhammad told the Muslim soldiers to remain in the trenches. All who retreated to their homes would be charged with treason.

fear comes thou wilt see them looking towards thee, their eyes rolling like one fainting with death; but when the fear has passed away they will assail you with sharp tongues, covetous of the best. These have never believed, and God will make vain their works, for that is easy with God.

20 They reckoned that the confederates would never go away; and if the confederates should come they would fain be in the desert with the Arabs, asking for news of you! and if they were amongst you they would fight but little.

The Battle of the Trench
(the brave)

21 Ye had in the Apostle of God a good example for him who hopes for God and the last day, and who remembers God much.

22 And when the believers saw the confederates they said, "This is what God and His Apostle promised us; God and His Apostle are true!" and it only increased them in faith and resignation.

23 Amongst the believers are men who have been true to their covenant with God, and there are some who have fulfilled their vow, and some who wait and have not changed with fickleness.

24 That God might reward the truthful for their truth, and punish the hypocrites if He please, or turn again towards them—verily, God is forgiving, merciful!

25 And God drove back the misbelievers in their rage; they gat no advantage—God was enough for the believers in the fight, for God is strong, mighty!

26 And He drove down those of the people of the Book who had helped

---

33.19 *sharp tongues*— Muhammad believed that some of his soldiers were fearful of the enemy yet spoke arrogantly against him.

33.20 After the enemy withdrew and returned to Mecca, many of the Muslim soldiers feared that the enemy would return and resume the siege. They therefore wished to be done with warfare, leave Medinah, and live as Bedouin Arabs.

33.21 Muhammad believed that he remained a good example of bravery for his Muslim soldiers throughout the battle.

33.22a *the confederates* — That is, the enemy. The people of Mecca amassed a large fighting force of neighboring cities to converge upon Medinah and defeat Muham-

mad.

33.22b *increased them in faith and resignation* — That is, increased their heroism and submission to Allah. Unlike the cowards mentioned in a previous passage (vv. 9-20), Muhammad believed that the challenge from the enemy forces merely increased the faith and heroic efforts of the brave Muslims.

33.23-24 Bravery, said Muhammad, was directly dependent upon one's devotion to Allah. Conversely, cowardice was directly dependent upon one's lack of devotion to Allah.

33.25 Muhammad believed that Allah was the one who provided the victory in the Battle of the Trench.

them from their fortresses and hurled dread into their hearts; a part ye slew and ye took captive a part:

27   and He gave you their land, and their dwellings, and their property for an inheritance, and a land ye had not trodden, for God is ever mighty over all.

Muhammad's wives

28   O thou prophet! say to thy wives, "If ye be desirous of the life of this world and its adornments, come, I will give you them to enjoy and I will let you range handsomely at large!

29   But if ye be desirous of God and His Apostle and of the abode of the hereafter, verily, God has prepared for those of you who do good a mighty hire!"

30   O ye women of the prophet! whosoever of you commits manifest fornication, doubled shall be her torment twice; and that is easy unto God!

31   But that one of you who is devoted to God and His Apostle and does right we will give her her hire twice

---

33.26a *hurled dread into their hearts* — According to Muhammad, the hurling of dread (or terror) into the hearts of the enemy is essential to military victory (see Q 8.12, 60).

In a widely studied text on Islamic warfare, Pakistani Brigadier General S. K. Malik emphasized that the instilling of terror is an essential feature in waging a successful jihad campaign: "Terror struck into the hearts of the enemies is not only a means, it is the end in itself. Once a condition of terror into the opponent's heart is obtained, hardly anything is left to be achieved. It is the point where the means and the end meet and merge. Terror is not a means of imposing decision upon the enemy; it is the decision we wish to impose upon him...The Book [Qur'an] does not visualize war being waged with 'kid gloves.' It gives us a distinctive concept of total war. It wants both, the nation and the individual, to be at war 'in toto,' that is, with all their spiritual, moral, and physical resources. The Holy Qur'an lays the highest emphasis on the preparation for war. It wants us to prepare ourselves for war to the utmost. The test of utmost preparation lies in our capability to instill terror into the hearts of the enemies" (*The Quranic Concept of War*, pp. 59, 152-153). See **Jihad** on pp. 616-622).

33.26b-27 Following the Battle of the Trench, Muhammad turned his attention to a Jewish tribe, the Banu Quraiza. The men of the tribe were accused of treason and put to death. Following their deaths, "their land, and their dwellings, and their property" were confiscated (see **The Battle of the Trench and its Aftermath** on pp. 813-815).

33.28 Muhammad offered divorce of any of his wives who were "desirous of the life of this world and its adornments."

33.29 Muhammad also offered to any of his wives the privilege to remaining married to him, provided that they remained devoted to his prophethood.

33.30 Muhammad warned his wives with the thought that any who committed fornication would endure a double torture in Hell.

33.31 Muhammad encouraged his wives with the thought that any whose lives were

over, and we have prepared for her a noble provision.

32 O ye women of the prophet! ye are not like any other women; if ye fear God then be not too complaisant in speech, or he in whose heart is sickness will lust after you; but speak a reasonable speech.

33 And stay still in your houses and show not yourselves with the ostentation of the ignorance of yore; and be steadfast in prayer, and give alms, and obey God and His Apostle—God only wishes to take away from you the horror as people of His House and to purify you thoroughly.

34 And remember what is recited in your houses of the signs of God and of wisdom; verily, God is subtle and aware!

Ten qualifications
for divine forgiveness

35 Verily, men resigned and women resigned, and believing men and believing women, and devout men and devout women, and truthful men and truthful women, and patient men and patient women, and humble men and humble women, and almsgiving men and almsgiving women, and fasting men and fasting women, and men who guard their private parts and women who guard their private parts, and men who remember God much, and women who remember Him—God has prepared for them forgiveness and a mighty hire.

Hazrat Zaynab Scandal

36 It is not for a believing man or for a believing woman, when God and His Apostle have decided an affair, to have the choice in that affair;

exemplary would be rewarded double in Paradise.

33.32 Muhammad warned his wives to not be overly soft in their speech with other men, since it could sexually arouse them and tempt them to lascivious behavior.

33.33a Muhammad admonished his wives to the following behaviors: (a) to quietly abide in their houses, (b) to avoid flirtatious activities (c) to be constant in prayer, (d) to be generous in the giving of alms, and (e) to obey Allah and His Prophet.

33.33b *people of His House* — That is, Muhammad's house. Muhammad identified his own house as Allah's house.

33.35 In the Islamic faith, forgiveness is a

blessing that is earned, not given as a gift earned. In this verse, Muhammad enumerated ten qualifications that would enable one to earn divine forgiveness: (1) a consistent submissiveness to Allah, (2) a belief in the Islamic faith, (3) a devotedness to the Islamic faith, (4) given to truthfulness, (5) patient, (6) humble, (7) generous in the giving of alms, (8) given to the practice of fasting, (9) chaste, and (10) given to remembering Allah often (see **Divine Forgiveness in Islam** on pp. 158-161).

33.36-40 In the fifth year since Muhammad's emigration to Medinah, a scandal erupted in Medinah that caused many to question Muhammad's prophetic calling.

and whoso rebels against God and His Apostle has erred with an obvious error.

37 And when thou didst say to him God had shown favour to and thou hadst shown favour to, "Keep thy wife to thyself and fear God;" and thou didst conceal in thy soul what God was about to display; and didst fear men, though God is more deserving that thou shouldst fear Him; and when Zâid had fulfilled his desire of her we did wed thee to her that there should be no hindrance to the believers in the matter of the wives of their adopted sons when they have fulfilled their desire of them: and so God's bidding to be done.

38 There is no hindrance to the prophet about what God has ordained for him—(such was) the course of God with those who have passed away before—and God's bidding is a decreed decree!

39 Those who preach God's messages and fear Him and fear not any one except God—but God is good enough at reckoning up.

40 Mohammed is not the father of any of your men, but the Apostle of God, and the Seal of the Prophets; for God all things doth know!

The three forms of spirituality

41 O ye who believe! remember God with frequent remembrance,

Muhammad found his daughter-in-law Zaynab to be sexually attractive and desired to marry her. Yet, she was currently married to his stepson, Zaid bin Harithah. "On the day the Prophet went out in search of him (Zaid), the door of his house was but a piece of fabric, therefore the wind blew it open and revealed Zaynab (with her sleeves up). And she fell into the Prophet's heart, and since then she hated the other (Zaid)" (*Tafsir al-Tabari* 22.13). Since Muhammad's marriage to Zaynab was looked upon as incest, a scandal erupted in Medinah. Muhammad attempted to settle the scandal and reassert his moral authority by including in one of his surahs a divinely inspired revelation that legitimized his actions (see *Sahih Bukhari* 9.93.516-517).

33.36 In this passage, Muhammad's first move was to reassert his calling as the Apostle of Allah and to thereby insist that

nobody had the right to question his decisions. Such questions, he noted, was a form of rebellion against Allah and his Apostle, and "an obvious error." All who rebelled in this fashion risked eternal damnation.

33.37 In his second move, Muhammad claimed that his wedding to Zaynab had been blessed of Allah. The former marriage with his stepson Zaid was described as a relationship where he had fulfilled his desire of her, implying that he was no longer attracted to her. Hence, for Muhammad to marry Zaynab did not constitute an offense to Zaid.

33.38 In his third move, Muhammad claimed that Allah had ordained his marriage to Zaynab.

33.39-40 In his fourth move, Muhammad claimed that Allah told him not to fear anyone except Allah, since he is "the Apostle of God with the Seal of the Prophets."

33.41-47 Muhammad clarified the essence

42 and celebrate His praises morning and evening.

43 He it is who prays for you and His angels too, to bring you forth out of the darkness into the light, for He is merciful to the believers.

44 Their salutation on the day they meet Him shall be "Peace!" and He has prepared for them a noble hire.

45 O thou prophet! verily, we have sent thee as a witness and a herald of glad tidings and a warner,

46 and to call (men) unto God by His permission, and as an illuminating lamp.

47 Give glad tidings then to the believers, that for them is great grace from God.

48 And follow not the unbelievers and the hypocrites; but let alone their ill-treatment, and rely upon God, for God is guardian enough.

Remarriages

49 O ye who believe! when ye wed believing women, and then divorce them before ye have touched them, ye have no term that ye need observe; so make them some provision, and let them go handsomely at large.

Muhammad's
special exception

50 O thou prophet! verily, we make lawful for thee thy wives to whom thou hast given their hire, and what thy right hand possesses out of the booty that God has granted thee, and the daughters of thy paternal uncle and the daughters of thy paternal aunts, and the daughters of thy maternal uncle and the daugh-

---

of spirituality by dividing it into a triad. The *first leg* is the devoted Muslim whose heart is drawn to Allah, celebrating His praises morning and evening. The *second leg* is Allah and His angels who pray on behalf of the Muslim believer, with the intend of bringing him or her out of darkness and into the light. In the afterlife, Allah will speak the word Peace to the Muslim and usher him or her into Paradise, which is described as "a noble hire" (something that the Muslim had earned through a life of good works). The *third leg* is Muhammad, who is described as "an illuminating lamp." He is both a warner of Hell and a herald of glad tidings of Paradise.

33.48 Left outside the triad of spirituality are the infidels and hypocrites (apostates).
33.49 Muslim women were required to wait three months after a divorce before entering into a new marriage (see Q 2.228, note, and 65.1-4). The one exception is the woman who was divorced prior to the sexual consummation of the marriage. For such women, no waiting period was required.
33.50 *a special privilege this for thee, above the other believers* — Muhammad claimed that Allah provided for him a special dispensation whereby he was permitted to have an unlimited number of wives at any one time. This stood in contrast to other Muslim men who were limited to four wives (see Q 4.3). They may divorce and then add another, provided that the total was never more than four women at the same time (see **Muhammad's Many Wives** on p. 823).

ters of thy maternal aunts, provided they have fled with thee, and any believing woman if she give herself to the prophet, if the prophet desire to marry her—a special privilege this for thee, above the other believers. We knew what we ordained for them concerning their wives and what their right hands possess, that there should be no hindrance to thee; and God is forgiving, merciful.

51 Put off whomsoever thou wilt of them and take to thyself whomsoever thou wilt, or whomsoever thou cravest of those whom thou hast deposed, and it shall be no crime against thee. That is nigher to cheering their eyes and that they should not grieve, and should be satisfied with what thou dost bring them all; but God knows best what is in their hearts; and God is knowing, clement.

52 It is not lawful to thee to take women after (this), nor to change them for (other) wives, even though their beauty please thee;

except what thy right hand possesses, for God is ever watchful over all.

Annoyances of Muhammad

53 O ye who believe! do not enter the houses of the prophet, unless leave be given you, for a meal—not watching till it is cooked! But when ye are invited, then enter; and when ye have fed, disperse, not engaging in familiar discourse. Verily, that would annoy the prophet and he would be ashamed for your sake, but God is not ashamed of the truth. And when ye ask them for an article, ask them from behind a curtain; that is purer for your hearts and for theirs. It is not right for you to annoy the prophet of God, nor to wed his wives after him ever; verily, that is with God a serious thing.

54 If ye display a thing or conceal it, verily, God all things doth know.

55 There is no crime against them (if they speak unveiled) to their fathers, or their sons, or their broth-

33.53-59 Muslims were cautioned not to annoy Muhammad since those who did so would be cursed "in this world and the next" (v. 57). In this passage, the word annoy (or cognates of the word) is mentioned four times (vv. 53, 57-59).

33.53a Muslims were not allowed to enter Muhammad's houses, except to partake of a meal. Yet even then they were not to watch the food's preparation. After completing the meal, they were to quickly leave,

not engaging in familiar discourse. Violators of this rule were an annoyance to Muhammad.

33.53b *when ye ask them for an article —* Muslims who requested anything of one of Muhammad's wives were required to make their request from behind a curtain.

33.53c *nor to wed his wives after him ever* — Muslim men were not permitted to marry any of Muhammad's wives, whether they be divorced from Muhammad or widowed (fol-

The Battle of the Trench
and its Aftermath

March-April, 627

In 627, the Jewish tribe Banu 'n-Nadir, banished from their ancestral grounds in Medinah, traveled to Mecca seeking help in vanquishing Muhammad. The leaders of Mecca were predisposed to their wishes. Muhammad's raiders had been successful in overcoming several caravans heading to and from Mecca, which disrupted the commercial lifeblood of their city. They decided to attack Medinah with the intent of putting an end to Muhammad and his nascent Islamic religion. A confederacy of forces were organized which then began its march upon Medinah.

Learning of the impending attack, Muhammad dug a trench around Medinah—ten yards wide and five feet deep. As the trench was dug, Muhammad praised his workers and promised them direct access into Paradise in the afterlife (Q 24.62) and rebuked those in Medinah who refused to help, claiming that Allah knew their thoughts and would reward them accordingly (Q 24.63-64). Muslim historians Tabari and Ibn Ishaq wrote of a legend that during the digging of the trench, the Muslims uncovered a white rock. Muhammad struck it with his pick ax and a flash of lightning spread across and illuminated the trench. This, said Muhammad, was an omen that they would eventually be victorious in the impending battle.

When the Meccan force arrived at Medinah, they were stunned at the sight of the trench, having never seen this kind of defensive military tactic in previous battles. A siege ensued that lasted one month. During this time, the supplies of the Meccan army dwindled, and camels and horses died due to a lack of food. Then, the siege extended into the month of Dzul Qaedah, the first of three consecutive months in the Arab tradition of no hostilities, a tradition strictly enforced throughout the

Arabian Peninsula. Moreover, since pilgrims would soon be arriving in Mecca to worship at the Ka'ba altar, the Meccans abandoned the fight and returned to Mecca.

During the siege, however, the Jewish tribe in Medinah—the Banu Qurayza—was suspicioned to have been in league with the Meccan army. Muhammad later claimed that the archangel Gabriel ordered him to attack this Jewish tribe.

> When the Prophet returned from the (battle) of Al-Khandaq (i.e., Trench) and laid down his arms and took a bath Gabriel came to him while he (i.e., Gabriel) was shaking the dust off his head, and said, "You have laid down the arms? By Allah, I have not laid them down. Go out to them (to attack them." The Prophet said, "Where?" Gabriel pointed towards Bani Quraiza. So Allah's Apostle went to them (i.e., Banu Quraiza) (i.e., besieged them).[1]

Gabriel also gave his judgment that "their warriors should be killed, their women and children should be taken as captives, and their properties distributed."[2]

The Banu Qurayza lived in their own community inside the Medinah district, within protective walls. A siege quickly ensued, which lasted twenty-five days. At its conclusion, the Jews surrendered unconditionally. A trial was then held and the verdict followed the directive of the archangel Gabriel. It was stated that the men should be killed, the property divided, and the women and children taken as captives. Muslim historian Ibn Ishaq explained:

> "Then they surrendered, and the apostle confined them in Medina in the quarter of d. al-Harith...Then the apostle went out to the market of Medina (which is still its market today) and dug trenches in it. Then he sent for them and struck off their heads in those trenches as they were brought out to him in batches...There were 600 or 700 in all, though some put the figure as high as 800 or 900...This went on until the apostle made an end of them.[3]

Sir William Muir added:

> Each company as it came up was made to sit down in a row on the brink of the trench destined for its grave, there beheaded, and the bodies cast therein...The butchery, begun in the morning, lasted all day, and continued by torchlight till the evening.[4]

Following the mass executions, Muhammad desired to take one of the Jewish women, Rihana, to be one of his wives. Yet, she refused. She then became his slave and concubine for the remainder of her life.

[1] *Sahih Bukhari* 5.59.448; also see 4.52.280; 8.74.278; *Sahih Dawud* 14.2665; 38.4390.
[2] Ibid.
[3] Ibn Ishaq, *The Life of Muhammad*, p. 464.
[4] William Muir, *The Life of Mohammad from Original Sources*, pp. 307, 308.

In the Battle of the Trench, he [Abu Sufyan] could not overcome the defenders who had fortified the city by erecting a large embankment from dirt they had unearthed in the creation of a large ditch. Abu Sufyan's troops were unprepared for the fortifications they were confronted with, and after an ineffectual siege, the coalition decided to go home.

—Ibn El-Neil, *The Truth about Islam*, p. 151

It was, therefore, not merely religious-ideological differences, but also and, primarily, material economic and political differences that resulted in the killing of between 600 and 900 men of the Jewish tribe, Banu-Qurayza, and the selling of the women and children into slavery. These men were systematically beheaded after they had surrendered, which appears to have been an unprecedented atrocity in the Hijaz. Muhammad then turned over the now-ownerless date plantations of the Jews to the Emigrants. A year before the massacre, Muhammad had sent into exile the Banu-al-Nadir, a second Jewish tribe of Medina, and confiscated their land as well.

—Irving M. Zeitlin, *The Historical Muhammad*, pp. 12, 13

Early in the twentieth century, a number of Orientalist scholars pointed to this episode [the Battle of the Trench] in Islamic history as proof that Islam was a violent and backward religion...In response to these accusations, some Muslim scholars have done considerable research to prove that the execution of the Banu Qurayza never happened, at least not in the way it has been recorded...In recent years, contemporary scholars of Islam, arguing that Muhammad's actions cannot be judged according to our modern ethical standards, have striven to place the execution of the Qurayza in its historical context. Karen Armstrong, in her beautiful biography of the Prophet, notes that the massacre, while revolting to a contemporary audience, was neither illegal nor immoral according to the tribal ethic of the time.

—Reza Aslan, *No god but God*, pp. 92, 93

ers, or their brothers' sons, or their sisters' sons, or their women, or what their right hands possess; but let them fear God—verily, God is witness over all.

56   Verily, God and His angels pray for the prophet. O ye who believe! pray for him and salute him with a salutation!

57   Verily, those who annoy God and His Apostle, God will curse them in this world and the next, and prepare for them shameful woe!

58   And those who annoy the believers for what they have not earned, such have to bear (the guilt of) calumny and obvious sin.

59   O thou prophet! tell thy wives and thy daughters, and the women of the believers, to let down over them their outer wrappers; that is nearer for them to be known and that they should not be annoyed; but God is forgiving, merciful.

Threat to Muhammad's
enemies in Medinah

60   Surely if the hypocrites and those

in whose hearts is a sickness and the insurrectionists in Medînah do not desist, we will surely incite thee against them. Then they shall not dwell near thee therein save for a little while.

61   Cursed wherever they are found—taken and slain with slaughter!

62   God's course with those who have passed away before: and thou shalt never find in God's course any alteration.

The Hour

63   The folk will ask thee about the Hour; say, "The knowledge thereof is only with God, and what is to make thee perceive that the Hour is haply nigh?"

64   Verily, God has cursed the misbelievers and has prepared for them a blaze!

65   To dwell therein for ever and for aye; they shall not find a patron or a helper!

66   On the day when their faces shall writhe in the fire they shall say, "O, would that we had obeyed God and

---

lowing Muhammad's death).

33.59 *let down over them their outer wrappers* — That is, while in public, women were to drape themselves with outer garments (*burqas*) to prevent men from being sexually aroused.

33.60 All the inhabitants in Medinah who were either insincere in the Islamic faith or secretly planning an insurrection were on notice by Muhammad that he would attack and

slaughter them. Such had already taken place following the Battle of the Trench (see **The Battle of the Trench and its Aftermath** on pp. 813-815).

33.63 *the Hour* — That is, the Hour when all people will be summoned to the Last Judgment. On that occasion, infidels will be cast into "a blaze" (Hell) to "dwell there forever." The chiefs and great men who led the masses astray into unbelief will suffer double

Siyam

One of the pillars of Islam is the practice of *siyam* (fasting). Faithful Muslims are called upon to fast as a way of demonstrating their dedication to Allah. Throughout the entire month of Ramadan (the ninth month of the Islamic calendar), Muslims are required to take neither food nor drink during the sunlight hours. Smoking and sexual intercourse is also prohibited. Its purpose is stated in Q 2.185: "for manifestations of guidance [from Allah], and for a Discrimination [the Qur'an]." Muhammad added: "God desires for you what is easy, and desires not for you what is difficult,—that ye may complete number, and say, 'Great is God,' for that He has guided you, haply ye may give thanks." Muslims typically spend much time in prayer and listen to recitations of the Qur'an.

At sunset of each of the days during Ramadan, the fast is broken and feasting begins. Arshad Khan writes, "There is no restriction on eating and drinking from sunset to the following dawn."[1] The feasting is often large, accompanied by joyous fellowship with Muslim friends and strangers.

Siyam is take place throughout the month of Ramadan since that is the month that Muhammad claimed that he first encountered the archangel Gabriel and was commissioned to be Allah's Prophet. Ramadan is not fixed to any corresponding month in the Gregorian (Western) calendar. This is because the number of days in each of the Islamic months is thirty; hence the Islamic year is 360 days. This creates a deficit of approximately five days each year. Accordingly, through the course of the centuries, Ramadan migrates through the four seasons—spring, summer, fall, and winter—and the twelve months of the Gregorian calendar.

---

[1] Arshad Khan, *Islam 101*, p. 54

Although physically rigorous, the month of fasting is also profoundly spiritual. It is a customary act of piety to read a portion of the Qur'an each night so as to have traversed the entire Qur'an during this holy month. Breaking of the fast in the evening can be a joyous affair and, indeed, in many Muslim communities the rigours of daylight abstentions are ameliorated by nights of compensatory enjoyment.

—Douglas Pratt, *The Challenge of Islam*, p. 86

Fasting is the means by which the Muslim voluntarily abandons certain legitimate frivolous enjoyments as a means of putting his soul to a test and promoting its capacity for perseverance, thus strengthening his will to keep away from sins, both obvious and obscure. The Muslim thereby samples enough of starvation to make him a warm-hearted, hospitable person, sympathetic with the poor who are in constant want.

—Mahmud Shaltout, *Islam, the Straight Path*, p. 116

In Islamic countries, life's rhythms adjust to this rigor, and people rest during the day and feast during the night. It is also common to recite the Qur'an, or listen to recitation, during this month, and the Qur'an has been separated into thirty sections for just this purpose. By denying themselves the basic food and water needed to survive, believers are reminded of their absolute dependence on God. Nightfall brings life to the cities once again, however. After the breaking of the fast at sunset, the streets fill with shoppers and shops re-open. Ramadan is also considered a time to remember God's mercy; shopkeepers set up tables on the street, inviting strangers to break the fast with them, and people make a special effort to see that no one goes hungry. Thus, night becomes day and day becomes night in Ramadan, an inversion of time which changes the believer's focus from the mundane to the divine.

—Jacob Neusner, Tamara Sonn, and Jonathan Brockopp,
Judaism and Islam in Practice, p. 30

Nevertheless, fasting has played a relatively subordinate role in Christianity compared to its importance in other traditions, particularly Islam. Fasting (sawm) during the ninth month of Ramadan is a central event in the Islamic year and one of the five pillars of islamic practice enjoined in the Qur'an itself. Over and above its place in the prescribed tradition, however, the practice of fasting is integral to many people's sense of what it means to be a Muslim. Some describe it as the most central of Islamic rituals.

—Catherine Bell, *Ritual: Perspectives and Dimensions*, p. 124

67 obeyed the Apostle!"
And they shall say, "Our Lord! verily, we obeyed our chiefs and our great men and they led us astray from the path!

68 Our Lord! give them double torment and curse them with a great curse!"

Final admonitions

69 O ye who believe! be not like those who annoyed Moses; but God cleared him of what they said, and he was regarded in the sight of God.

70 O ye who believe! fear God and speak a straightforward speech.

71 He will correct for you your works, and pardon you your sins; for he who obeys God and His Apostle has attained a mighty happiness.

72 Verily, we offered the trust to the heavens and the earth and the mountains, but they refused to bear it, and shrank from it; but man bore it: verily, he is ever unjust and ignorant.

73 That God may torment the hypocritical men and hypocritical women, and the idolaters and idolatresses; and that God may turn relenting towards the believing men and believing women; verily, God is ever forgiving, merciful.

for their sins (v. 68).

33.69 Muhammad compared the Muslims who were resisting his leadership with the Jews who resisted the leadership of Moses. The unspoken message was that Allah judged the Jews who resisted Moses with a variety of judgments, many of which resulted in numerous deaths (e.g., Ex 32:1-35; Num 14:1-19; 16:1-35; 21:1-9). Similarly, Allah would judge Muhammad's opponents.

33.71 *he who obeys God and His Apostle has attained a mighty happiness* — The Islamic gospel is predicated upon obedience to Allah and Muhammad (see **The Last Judgment** on pp. 46-50). To disobey Muhammad was tantamount to disobeying Allah with the net result being an eternal condemnation in Hell (see Q 3.32; 4.69, 79-80, 136; 5.80-81; 8.13, 20-23; 24.47, 48, 50-52, 54; 33.33; 48.9-10; 57.19; 59.4; 72.22-23; 81.19-21 and 46.16, note). Ayaan Hirsi Ali writes: "The relationship between Mu-

hammad and his god is vertical: God is almighty, He is one, and Muhammad obeys His commands. The relationship between Muhammad and his followers is simple and the same: Muhammad's will is the law" (*The Caged Virgin*, p. 41).

33.73 Muhammad concluded the surah with a final reproach and rebuke to the hypocrites (apostates) and idolaters—both men and women—who had been opposing his leadership in Medina. It was his belief that Allah would bring torment into their lives. He also trusted that Allah would become relenting (that is gracious) towards the believing Muslims. The impression of the surah is that Muhammad was indeed concerned about an insurrection forming in Medina to oust him from power.

Surah 57. The title of this surah, *Iron*, comes from v. 25. The theme of the surah is a series of spiritual reflections following the Conquest of Mecca in A.D. 630.

Surah 57

In the name of the merciful and compassionate God.

Allah

1 Whatever is in the heavens and the earth celebrates the praises of God, for He is the mighty, the wise!
2 His is the kingdom of the heavens and the earth: He quickens and He kills, and He is mighty over all!
3 He is the first and the last; and the outer and the inner; and He all things doth know!
4 He it is who created the heavens and the earth in six days, then He made for the throne; and He knows what goes into the earth and what goes forth therefrom, and what comes down from the sky and what goes up therein, and He is with you wheresoe'er ye be: for God on what ye do doth look!

5 His is the kingdom of the heavens and the earth, and unto God affairs return.
6 He makes the night succeed the day, and makes the day succeed the night; and He knows the nature of men's breasts.

Two questions

7 Believe in God and His Apostle, and give alms of what He has made you successors of. For those amongst you who believe and give alms—for them is mighty hire.
8 What ails you that ye do not believe in God and His Apostle? He calls on you to believe in your Lord; and He has taken a compact from you, if ye be believers.
9 He it is who sends down upon His servants manifest signs, to bring you forth from the darkness into the light; for, verily, God to you is kind, compassionate!

57.1-6 Muhammad began the surah with reflections on the grandeur and power of Allah. The kingdom of Allah, he explained, stretches across the heavens and the earth. He has the power to give and take life. He is the first and the last, the outer and the inner, all-knowing, the creator of the earth in six days, the one who causes night to follow day, and knows what is the hearts of all people. With this, Allah was characterized in ways that paralleled biblical themes.

57.7 Because Allah is the one true God, people are behooved to worship and obey Him, to live their lives in total surrender to His will, and to take careful note of His rev-

elations that have been given to them. This, he explained, entailed two things: (a) belief in Allah, and (b) a generosity in the giving of alms.

57.8 Muhammad asked two questions. The first question is found in this verse: "What ails you that ye do not believe in God and His Apostle?" His concern was a failure of many people in Medinah to understand that belief in Allah required a corresponding belief in Allah's Apostle: Muhammad. He maintained that a person could not believe in the one without also believing in the other (see Q 24.47, note; also see Q 3.32; 4.69, 79-80, 136; 5.80-81; 8.13, 20-23; 24.47, 48,

10   What ails you that ye give not alms in God's cause? for God's is the inheritance of the heavens and the earth. Not alike amongst you is he who gives alms before the victory and fights—they are grander in rank than those who give alms afterwards and fight. But to all does God promise good; and God of what ye do is well aware!

The fate of the hypocrites

11   Who is there who will lend a good loan to God? for He will double it for him, and for him is a generous reward.
12   On the day when thou shalt see believers, men and women, with their light running on before them and on their right hand —"Glad tidings for you today—Gardens beneath which rivers flow, to dwell therein for aye; that is the grand bliss!"
13   On the day when the hypocrites, men and women, shall say to those who believe, "Wait for us that we may kindle at your light." It will be said, "Get ye back, and beg a light." And there shall be struck out between them a wall with a door; within it shall be mercy, and outside before it torment.
14   They shall cry out to them, "We were not with you!" they shall say, "Yea, but ye did tempt yourselves, and did wait, and did doubt; and your vain hopes beguiled you; and the beguiler beguiled you about God.
15   "Wherefore today there shall not be taken from you a ransom, nor

---

50-52, 54; 33.33, 71; 48.9-10; 57.19; 59.4; 72.22-23, 81.19-21 and 46.16, note).

57.10a The second question is found in this verse: "What ails you that ye give not alms in God's cause?" Due to the context of this surah, the term "God's cause" is a reference to a military action (Jihad). Those who gave prior to battle, said Muhammad, were "grander in rank" (that is, given higher recognition) than the one who waited until after the victory.

Hence, the practice of almsgiving was not limited to charity for the poor. Almsgiving was also understood to be the giving of one's resources for the cause of Jihad (see *Jihad* on pp. 616-622).

57.10b *the victory* — Islamic scholars are in general agreement that the victory described in this verse was the victorious Conquest of Mecca (see *The Conquest of Mecca* on pp. 828-829).

57.11 *lend a good loan to God* — That is, give alms to the war effort. Allah will repay in the future life.

57.12 *light running on before them and on their right hand* — This is a metaphor. The word *light* is a metaphor for spiritual knowledge and purity. The words *right hand* are a metaphor for power and control.

57.13-15 At the Last Judgment, the hypocrites shall say to the true believers that they would like to borrow a little of their light (running before them and on their right hand), yet will be denied. Then a wall will come down between the believers and the hypocrites. The hypocrite will cry out for help but in vain. Their destiny will be the fires of Hell.

from those who misbelieved. Your resort is the fire; it is your sovereign, and an ill journey will it be!"

Admonition

16   Is the time come to those who believe, for their hearts to be humbled at the remembrance of God, and of what He has sent down in truth? and for them not to be like those who were given the Scriptures before, and over whom time was prolonged, but their hearts grew hard, and many of them were workers of abomination?

17   Know that God quickens the earth after its death!—we have manifested to you the signs; haply ye may have some sense!

18   Verily, those who give in charity, men and women, who have lent to God a goodly loan—it shall be doubled for them, and for them is a generous hire.

19   And those who believe in God and His Apostle, they are the confes-

sors and the martyrs with their Lord; for them is their hire and their light! But those who misbelieve and call our signs lies, they are the fellows of hell!

Call to commitment

20   Know that the life of this world is but a sport, and a play, and an adornment, and something to boast of amongst yourselves; and the multiplying of children is like a rain-growth, its vegetation pleases the misbelievers; then they wither away, and thou mayest see them become yellow; then they become but grit. But in the hereafter is a severe woe, and forgiveness from God and His goodwill; but the life of this world is but a chattels of guile.

21   Race towards forgiveness from your Lord and Paradise, whose breadth is as the breadth of the heavens and the earth, prepared for those who believe in God and

57.16a Muhammad called the Muslim believers to humility, to remembrance of Allah, and to remembrance of the Qur'an.

57.16b The Muslim believers were also admonished to not be like those who had been given the Scriptures previously (that is, Jews and Christians) and allowed their hearts to grow hard and become the workers of abominations.

57.17-19a Muslims were reminded that they had received divine revelation in the Qur'an, and were therefore admonished to be charitable to the poor and to remain com-

mitted to Allah and His Prophet, Muhammad.

57.19 True Muslim believers were divided into two categories: confessors and martyrs.

57.20 The infidels, said Muhammad, are given to sport, play, adornment, and large families. Their interests were nothing more than the "chattels of guile."

57.21 Committed Muslim believers, said Muhammad, should have their eyes focused elsewhere: on the prize of Paradise, available to all who rightly earn it. Central to such commitment is a belief in Allah and His

Muhammad's Many Wives

Not all Islamic scholars, nor the Hadiths, are in agreement with the number of wives that Muhammad acquired. The following list is based upon Islamic scholar Ali Dashti (*Twenty-three Years: A Study of the Prophetic Career of Muhammad*) who drew his research principally from the History of al-Tabari:

1.	Khadijah	16.	Mary the Copt
2.	Sauda bint Zam'a		(Christian)
3.	'Aisha	17.	Rayhanah bint Zayd
4.	Omm	18.	Omm Sharik
5.	Hafsah	19.	Maymuna
6.	Zaynab of Jahsh	20.	Zaynab the third
7.	Juwairya bint Harith	21.	Khawla
	(captive)	22.	Mulaytah bint Dawud
8.	Safiya bint Huyal	23.	al-Shanba' bint 'Amr
	(captive)	24.	al-'Aliyyah
9.	Maymuna of Hareth	25.	'Amrah bint Yazid
10.	Fatimah	26.	Qutaylah bint Qays
11.	Hend (widow)	27.	Sana bint Sufyan
12.	Asma of Saba	28.	Sharaf bint Khalifah
13.	Zaynab of Khozayma	29.	Women of Muhammad's
14.	Habla		right hand (captives)
15.	Asma of Noman		

A'isha remarked: "It seems to me that your Lord hastens to satisfy your desire" (*Sahih Muslim*, 8. 3453-3454)

———•▪◆▪•———

Several of Muhammad's marriages appear to have been principally intended as a further humiliation of vanquished enemies. After the Quraiza massacre [following the Battle of the Trench], he took Jewish Raihana as a concubine during his fifty-eighth year. That same year he married Juwairiya, the daughter of a tribal chief defeated by a raiding party that Muhammad led. Ishaq reports that her exceptional beauty "captivated every man who saw her." Safiya, the teenaged widow of the vanquished Jewish chief at Khaibar was subsequently selected as his tenth wife. Muhammad threw his mantle over that spoil of war after discerning that she did not appear to grieve as she was led past the corpses of her husband and father. He rejected the other woman who was brought with Safiya, calling her a she-devil because she shrieked on seeing the sight of her slain spouse.

—William E. Phipps, *Muhammad and Jesus*, p. 143

According to Umar, Hafsa, one of Muhammad's wives, had been angering the Prophet by talking back to him. So when Umar learned that Muhammad had divorced all his wives, he was not surprised; he exclaimed: "Hafsa is a ruined loser! I expected that would happen some day."

—Robert Spencer, *The Truth About Muhammad*, p. 22

Discrepancies occur in counting Muhammad's wives, because Muhammad's own "classification" system of wives and concubines creates confusion. Muhammad married at least nine women after the death of his first wife, Khadija. Muhammad divided these wives into classifications of intimate" (*Muqarribat*) and "remote" (*Ghair Muqarribat*). At the head of the list of intimates was Aishah, then Hafsah, Um Salma, and Zaynab.

—Ergun Mehmet Caner, Emir Fethi Caner, and Richard Land, *Unveiling Islam*, p. 135

Allah was not satisfied just giving Muhammad many wives, so he gave him a *carte blanche* to do as he wished. Allah did not even limit the number of women he could marry, as he had with all other Muslims. Rather, he gave him the right to grab any woman he desired, even married ones, forcing the husband to divorce his wife when the prophet desired to marry her.

—Mohammad al-Ghazoli, *Christ, Muhammad and I*, p. 31

As to polygamy, the Islamic rules of marriage or those of women's rights indicate how grave is the mistake of those who suppose that Muhammad legalized polygamy...Muhammad did not bring polygamy but corrected the practice. The social reform instituted by Muhammad found its practical effect on a vast and remarkable improvement in the status and the rights of women.

—Sayed Khatab and Gary D. Bouma, *Democracy in Islam*, p. 120

His apostles! and God's grace, He gives it to whom He pleases, for God is Lord of mighty grace!

Absolute control

22 No accident befalls in the earth, or in yourselves, but it was in the Book, before we created them; verily, that is easy unto God.

23 That ye may not vex yourselves for what ye miss, nor be overjoyed at what He gives you; for God loves no arrogant boaster,

24 who are niggardly and bid men be niggardly: but whoso turns his back, verily, God is rich, praise-worthy.

25 We did send our apostles with manifest signs; and we did send down among you the Book and the balance, that men might stand by justice; and we sent down iron in which is both keen violence and advantages to men; and that God might know who helps Him and His apostles in secret; verily, God is strong and mighty!

Lineage of apostles

26 And we sent Noah and Abraham; and placed in their seed prophecy and the Book; and some of them are guided, though many of them are workers of abomination!

27 Then we followed up their footsteps with our apostles; and we followed them up with Jesus the son of Mary; and we gave him the gos-

apostles. Forgiveness from the Lord is available to all who earn it (see **Divine Forgiveness in Islam** on pp. 158-161, and Q 33.35, note).

57.22 Muhammad believed that each and every activity that transpired on the earth was foreordained by Allah. In this respect, Allah is sovereign and in control of the universe.

The Bible makes a similar claim that God is sovereign over the universe (Ps 50:1; 66:7; 93:1; Isa 40:15,17; 1 Tim 6:15; Rev 11:17). Nowhere is it stated, however, that each and every action on the earth was written down beforehand in a Book. Rather, it is, as Christian theologians are prone to say, a balance between God's sovereign control and individual freedom. As such, the problem of a divine absolute determinism is avoided.

57.23 Muhammad cautioned believers to not be vexed over what they miss, or overjoyed for what they experience.

57.25a Muhammad believed that Allah sent down three things to help people understand His sovereignty over the universe: (a) the apostles with divine revelation, (b) the Qur'an and the celestial balance to weigh people's behaviors, and (c) iron. The purpose of iron was for violence (weaponry) and domestic uses (tools).

57.25b *who helps Him and His apostles in secret* — That is, whoever it is who assists the Cause of Allah with iron.

57.26-29 Muhammad concluded the surah with a reminder of the lineage of apostles. In this rendition, he began with Noah, then Abraham, and then Jesus, and finally with himself.

57.27 *monkery* — That is, monastic asceticism. Early Christianity approved of monas-

pel; and we placed in the hearts of those who followed him kindness and compassion—But monkery, they invented it; we only prescribed to them the craving after the goodwill of God, and they observed it not with due observance. But we gave to those who believe amongst them their hire; though many amongst them were workers of abomination!

28 O ye who believe! fear God, and believe in His Apostle: He will give you two portions of His mercy, and will make for you a light for you to walk in, and will forgive you; for God is forgiving, compassionate.

29 That the people of the Book may know that they cannot control aught of God's grace; and that grace is in God's hands, He gives it to whom He will; for God is Lord of mighty grace!

Surah 61

In the name of the merciful and compassionate God.

1 What is in the heavens and what is in the earth celebrates the praises of God, for He is the mighty, the wise!

Sincerity of faith

2 O ye who believe! say not what ye do not.

3 It is most hateful to God that ye say what ye do not.

---

tic asceticism (an extreme denial of the pleasures of this world). This practice still exists in the present day, though not to the extent that it was practiced and encouraged in the Early Church. Muhammad dismissed monastic asceticism as a mere invention of man.

57.28 Muhammad claimed that Muslim believers will receive a double blessing: spiritual guidance and forgiveness (see ***Divine Forgiveness in Islam*** on pp. 158-161, and 33.35 note).

57.29 Muhammad criticized the Jews and Christians for thinking that they can control Allah's grace by merely requesting it, thinking of it as a gift freely offered. Instead, Muhammad asserted, it is part of the sovereign will of God. "He gives it to whom He will" (see ***The Doctrine of al-Qadar*** on pp. 264-266).

Surah 61. The title of this surah, *The Ranks*, comes from v. 4. Its theme is consistency and commitment of belief. The concern was that some Muslim believers claimed to be committed to Allah and the teachings of Muhammad, yet their personal behavior demonstrated a lackluster half-heartedness. The solution, said Muhammad, was to rethink the Islamic faith and act accordingly.

61.2-3 Muhammad rebuked some of his Muslim followers. They talked the talk but did not walk the walk—their words did not match their behavior. This, Muhammad said, was "most hateful to God."

61.4 *God loves those who fight in His cause in ranks* — Muhammad was concerned that

4   Verily, God loves those who fight in His cause in ranks as though they were a compact building.

5   When Moses said to his people, "O my people! why do ye hurt me, when ye know that I am the apostle of God to you?" and when they swerved, God made their hearts to swerve; for God guides not the people who work abomination!

6   And when Jesus the son of Mary said, "O children of Israel! verily, I am the apostle of God to you, verifying the law that was before me and giving you glad tidings of an apostle who shall come after me, whose name shall be A'hmed"—but when he did come to them with manifest signs, they said, "This is manifest sorcery!"

7   And who is more unjust than he who forges against God a lie when called unto Islâm? but God guides

some of the Muslim men were unwilling to fight in the Cause of Jihad (see **Jihad** on pp. 616-622).

61.5 Muhammad turned to Moses as an example. He noted that those who hurt him with their lack of commitment were judged by God, causing them to serve into theological heresy.

61.6 *A'hmed* — Muhammad made the claim that Jesus spoke "of an apostle who shall come after me, whose name shall be A'hmed."

Islamic scholars interpret this to be a prophecy found in the New Testament of the future ministry of Muhammad. Jesus said: "And I will ask the Father, and he will give you another Counselor to be with you forever—the Spirit of truth" (Jn 14:16). In the Greek manuscript, the word *Counselor* is the term *parakletos*. Islamic scholars believe that this word was not in the original New Testament. The original manuscript, they maintain, used the word *periklutos*, which means "the much praised one." When translated into Arabic, *periklutos* becomes A'hmed.

Hence, when *parakletos* is correctly replaced by *periklutos*, Islamic scholars conclude, Jesus was prophesying the coming ministry of Muhammad. He, they say, is the

Spirit of Truth. "He it is who sent His Apostle with guidance and the religion of truth to set it above all religion; averse although the idolaters may be" (v. 9). For a further discussion of the alignment of Jn 14.16 with Q 61.6, see Kenneth Cragg *Jesus and the Muslim*, pp. 262-268.

Christian scholars, of course, disagree. In spite of the similarity in spelling, the substitution of *parakletos* with *periklutos* has no NT manuscript support. Sinaiticus and Vaticanus, the earliest New Testament manuscripts that include the complete Gospel of John, include the term *parakletos* in Jn 14:16. Even in manuscripts of later dates, the term *parakletos* is found. In no manuscript is the term *periklutos* found. All theologians are in agreement that the Holy Spirit is the One intended by Jesus. Later in the New Testament, the Holy Spirit came as a fulfillment of Jesus' words (see Acts 2:1-4).

In short, say Christian scholars, the attempt to substitute *parakletos* with *periklutos* is a blatant and unashamed effort to re-write history for the benefit of Islam. Jesus neither prophesied the future coming of Muhammad nor endorsed his ministry.

61.7-8 According to Muhammad, the most unjust people were those who called them-

The Conquest of Mecca

January 11, 630

In 628, one year after the Battle of the Trench, Muhammad organized a pilgrimage to Mecca. His intent was to return to the altar of Ka'ba to worship Allah. The Meccan people were stupefied by this move since Muhammad was their sworn enemy. They blocked his entry into the city at a place called al-Hudaybiyah. An agreement was reached which resulted in...

    (a)   a ten-year armistice between Medina and Mecca

    (b)   a decision that caravans would no longer be raided by Muhammad's men

    (c)   a Muslim pilgrimage to Mecca the following year

The treaty, however, gave Muhammad a free hand to attack one of Mecca's ally's to the north, the oasis of Khaybar, whose population (especially its Jewish population) was hostile to him. Then, in the spring of 629, Muhammad and his people completed their first religious pilgrimage to Mecca.

With Khaybar out of the way, Muhammad turned his attention on Mecca. In 630, he conquered it. Following the battle, the key leaders of Mecca were beheaded, the Ka'ba altar was purified from all vestiges of idolatry and polytheism, and all the inhabitants of Mecca were required to acknowledge Muhammad as Allah's Prophet. Muhammad made it compulsory for Muslims to wage *jihad* on non-Muslims whenever they were called to do so. "The Prophet said, on the day of the Conquest of Mecca, 'There is no migration (after the Conquest), but Jihad and good intentions remain; and if you are called for *Jihad*, you should immediately respond to the call.'"[1]

Two weeks later, the enemies of Muhammad counter-attacked. Twenty thousand men assembled a few miles to the east of Mecca advanced into the Hunayn Valley where they met Muhammad's army. Again, Muhammad was victorious.

Following this victory at Hunayn, Muhammad was the unchallenged political leader of the western Arabian Desert. He ruled the region from Medina. He fell ill two years later, in 632, and died in the city of Medinah. While on his deathbed, he gave his final command: "Expel the pagans from the Arabian Peninsula."[2]

During his life, Muhammad had taken part in twenty-seven raids against his enemies and had actually fought in nine of the engagements.[3] The Muslim people had become the dominant tribe in the Arabian Peninsula and were now poised to venture onward into new territories.

---

[1] *Sahih Bukhari* 4.52.311. Also see *Sahih Bukhari* 4.52.42 and *Sahih Muslim* 20.4597.

[2] *Sahih Bukhari* 4.52.288.

[3] Ibn Ishaq, *The Life of Muhammad*, pp. 659, 660.

Mahomet [Muhammad] had already resolved to make a grand attack upon his native city. But he kept his counsel secret even from his closest friends as long as it was possible. To divert attention, he dispatched a small body of men in another direction. Meanwhile he summoned his allies amongst the Bedouin tribes to join him at Medina, or to meet him a certain convenient points, which he indicated to them, on the road to Mecca. At the last moment he ordered his followers in the city to arm themselves, announced his intentions, and enjoined on all the urgent command that no hint regarding his hostile designs should in any way reach Mecca.

—Sir William Muir, *The Life of Muhammad from Original Sources*, pp. 388, 389

Muhammad then marched on Mecca with an army of, according to some reports, ten thousand Muslims. When the Meccans saw the size of their force, which Muhammad exaggerated by ordering his men to build many extra fires during the night as his men were assembled outside the city, they knew that all was lost. Many of the most notable Quraysh warriors now deserted and, converting to Islam, joined Muhammad's forces.

—Robert Spencer, *Muhammad: Founder of the World's Most Intolerant Religion*, p. 146

Muhammad had forbidden his men to loot the city so there was no booty with which to pay the army. To compensate his troops, especially the Bedouins, Muhammad took out large loans from the Meccan bankers and paid his men in cash.

—Richard A. Gabriel, *Muhammad: Islam's First Great General*, p. 176

not the unjust people.

8   They desire to put out the light of God with their mouths; but God will perfect His light, averse although the misbeliever be!

9   He it is who sent His Apostle with guidance and the religion of truth to set it above all religion; averse although the idolaters may be.

Call to fight strenuously

10 O ye who believe! shall I lead you to a merchandise which will save you from grievous woe?

11 To believe in God and His Apostle, and to fight strenuously in God's cause with your property and your

persons; that is better for you if ye did but know!

12 He will pardon you your sins, and bring you inter gardens beneath which rivers flow, and goodly dwellings in gardens of Eden—that is the mighty bliss!

13 And other things which ye love—help from God and victory nigh! so do thou give the glad tidings unto the believers!

Call to resist the Jews

14 O ye who believe! be ye the helpers of God! as Jesus son of Mary said to the apostles, "Who are my helpers for God?" Said the

---

selves Muslims yet spoke lies about Allah (apostates). The nature of these lies were either distortions of the Qur'an or disagreements with the Qur'an—Islam's sacred literature. And since the Qur'an presents theological truths (beliefs) and theocratic truths (governmental law), disagreements or distortions could apply to either.

This explains the Sunni-Shi'a divide that exists within Islam today. Each disagrees with the other on questions pertaining to theocracy. Accordingly, each declares the other to be the most unjust people who are attempting to put out the perfect light of Allah.

61.9 Muhammad believed that Islam was the religion of truth set above all other religions. Muslims who attempted to live at peace with those of idolatrous religions, then, were fundamentally at odds with the teachings in the Qur'an (see Q 2.190-191; **Islamification** on pp. 851-852).

61.10 *O ye who believe!* — That is, Muslims.

61.11-12a Muhammad prodded those who were stingy in their support of the war effort or in serving as jihadists. He noted that they risked losing their reward in Paradise. Only those who were generous in their contributions to Jihad would be pardoned and enter goodly dwellings.

61.12b *the gardens of Eden* — That is, Paradise (see Q 35.33, note).

61.13 A second blessing given to fully committed Muslims—those who fight jihadistically (strenuously) is help from Allah and victory in the Jihad.

61.14 In this dialogue between Jesus and his disciples, Muhammad's point was that being a helper of Allah required Muslims to aid believers and resist their enemies. Since the Jewish people had rejected the gospel as presented by Jesus, they were the enemies who were to be resisted (see Q 3.52 note).

apostles, "We are God's helpers!"
And a party of the children of Israel believed, and a party misbelieved. And we aided those who
believed against their enemies, and
they were on the morrow superior!

Surah 48

*In the name of the merciful and compas-
sionate God.*

Muhammad's victory

1   Verily, we have given thee an obvi-
    ous victory!
2   that God may pardon thee thy
    former and later sin, and may ful-

fil His favour upon thee, and guide
thee in a right way,

3   and that God may help thee with a
    mighty help.
4   It is He who sent down His
    shechina into the hearts of the be-
    lievers that they might have faith
    added to their faith—and God's are
    the hosts of the heavens and the
    earth, and God is knowing, wise—
5   to make the believers, men and
    women, enter into gardens be-
    neath which rivers flow, to dwell
    therein for aye; and to cover for
    them their offences; for that with
    God is a grand bliss:
6   and to torment the hypocrites, men
    and women, and the idolaters, men
    and women, who think evil
    thoughts of God—over them is a

Surah 48. The title of this surah, *The Victory*, comes from verse 27. Its setting is the
events surrounding the so-called "lesser pilgrimage" to the Ka'ba altar in Mecca in 629.
It was planned to take place in the month
of Dhu 'I-Qa'dah, one of the four months
when war hostilities were outlawed throughout the Arabian Peninsula (see Q 2.217
where Muhammad legitimized warfare against
the Meccan forces during the four months
of non-hostilities). An armed Meccan force
met Muhammad outside of Mecca at a place
called al-Hudaybiyah and denied him entrance. A peace treaty, however, was signed
during this encounter that was to last for
ten years. In exchange, Muhammad was
promised entrance to Mecca as a pilgrim to
visit the Ka'ba altar the following year.

Islamic scholars are in agreement that
the contents of this surah was presented to

the Muslim people on the trip back to
Medinah, following the signing of the peace
treaty (see **The Conquest of Mecca** on
pp. 828-829).

48.1-2 Muhammad claimed that Allah forgave all his sins: past, present, and future.
It stands in contradiction to previous verses
in the Qur'an (see Q 6.15; 46.9; and **The
Doctrine of Abrogation** on pp. 68-70).

48.3-4 The surah begins with a resolute
statement of victory. Muhammad saw the
Peace Treaty of al-Hudaybiyah as a victory
for his overall aims. He believed that Allah
assisted him and sent down His *shechina*
(shekinah glory) into the hearts of the Muslim people (see Q 2.248, note).

48.5-6 Muhammad also saw this victory as
prefiguring the victory in the afterlife when
the Muslim people would enter Paradise and
his opponents (hypocrites and idolaters)

turn of evil fortune, and God will be wrath with them and curse them, and has prepared for them hell, and an evil journey shall it be!

7   God's are the hosts of the heavens and the earth, and God is mighty, wise!

The special bond of allegiance

8   Verily, we have sent thee as a witness, and a herald of glad tidings, and a warner;

9   —that ye may believe in God and His Apostle, and may aid Him and revere Him and celebrate His praises morning and evening!

10   Verily, those who swear allegiance to thee do but swear allegiance to God—God's hand is above their

hands! and whoso perjures himself does but perjure himself against himself; but he who fulfils what he has covenanted with God, God shall bring him mighty hire.

11   The desert Arabs who were left behind shall say, "Our wealth and our people occupied us; ask pardon then for us!"—they speak with their tongues what is not in their hearts! Say, "Who can control for you aught from God, if He wish you harm or wish you advantage?" Nay, God of what ye do is well aware!

12   Nay, ye thought that the Apostle and the believers would not ever return again to their families; that was made seemly in your hearts! and ye thought evil thoughts, and

would be cast into the fires of Hell.

48.8 Muhammad understood his ministry to be that of a herald of glad tidings (explaining the straight path that leads to Paradise) and a warner (explaining the horrors of Hell to all who fail to follow the straight path).

48.9-10a Muhammad claimed that one needed to believe in both Allah and Allah's Apostle if one wished to enter Paradise. As he put it, "Those who swear allegiance to thee do but swear allegiance to God" (see Q 3.32; 4.69, 79-80, 136; 5.80-81; 8.13, 20-23; 24.47, 48, 50-52, 54; 33.33, 71; 48.9-10; 57.19; 59.4; 72.22-23, 81.19-21 and 46.16, note).

48.10b *God's hand is above their hands!* — The seal of allegiance in seventh century Arabia was a combined handclasp where all the participants formed a circle and clasped their hands together. Muhammad drew on

this tradition, saying that when a Muslim clasps the hand of Muhammad in a show of allegiance, the hand of Allah was also included in the clasping. It was therefore not only a covenant with Muhammad alone, it was also a covenant with Allah. Some Islamic scholars believe that this special handshake symbolized a *pledge of death*. All who made this handshake were pledging that they would fight unto death for the cause of Islam.

48.11-12 *the desert Arabs who were left behind* — Bedouin Arabs (the tribes of Ghifar, Muzaynah, Juhaynah, Ashja, Aslam and Dhayl) were allied with Muhammad and professed to be Muslims, yet refused to join Muhammad in his pilgrimage to Mecca. Their reason was a concern that the Meccan forces would ambush Muhammad and annihilate the pilgrims. Muhammad took their refusal to join him as

ye were a corrupt people.

13 Whoso believes not in God and His Apostle—we have prepared for the unbelievers a blaze!

14 God's is the kingdom of the heavens and of the earth. He pardons whom He pleases, and torments whom He pleases; and God is forgiving, merciful.

15 Those who were left behind shall say when ye have gone forth to spoils that ye may take, "Let us follow you;" they wish to change God's words. Say, "Ye shall by no means follow us; thus did God say before!" They will say, "Nay! but ye envy us!" Nay! they did not understand save a little.

16 Say to those desert Arabs who were left behind, "Ye shall be called out against a people endowed with vehement valour, and shall fight them or they shall become Muslims. And if ye obey, God will give you a good hire; but if ye turn your backs, as ye turned your backs before, He will torment you with grievous woe!"

17 There is no compulsion on the blind, and no compulsion on the lame, and no compulsion on the sick, but whoso obeys God and His Apostle, He will make him enter gardens beneath which rivers flow; but whoso turns his back He will torment with grievous woe.

Muhammad's gratitude

18 God was well pleased with the believers when they did swear allegiance to thee beneath the tree; and

a disgrace and a demonstration that they were not sincere in their Islamic faith and loyalty to him. As he put it, "Ye were a corrupt people" (v. 12).

48.13 Muhammad maintained that whosoever failed to believe in Allah and himself (Muhammad) are destined to Hell (see Q 3.32; 4.69, 79-80, 136; 5.80-81; 8.13, 20-23; 24.47, 48, 50-52, 54; 33.33, 71; 48.9-10; 57.19; 59.4; 72.22-23, 81.19-21 and 46.16, note).

48.15 In this verse, Muhammad entered into a hypothetical discussion. The next time the Bedouin tribesmen went forth into battle, he surmised, those who stayed behind would demand part of the booty. Yet, he insisted, those who refused to fight the enemies of Allah would not benefit from any shares of the booty.

48.16 Moreover, Muhammad insisted that the next time the Bedouin tribes enter into a battle, they would have to demonstrate vehement valor to redeem themselves from their previous cowardice and disobedience.

48.17 Muhammad then reminded the Bedouin tribesmen that obedience to Allah's Apostle is a prerequisite for entering into Paradise. Those who turned their backs on him would enter into the fires of Hell (see Q 3.32; 4.69, 79-80, 136; 5.80-81; 8.13, 20-23; 24.47, 48, 50-52, 54; 33.33, 71; 48.9-10; 57.19; 59.4; 72.22-23, 81.19-21 and 46.16 note).

4.18 Muhammad was pleased with the believers who accompanied him to al-Hudaybiyah. He believed that the *shechina* (shekinah glory) was present when the Peace Treaty was ratified (see Q 2.248, note).

He knew what was in their hearts, and He sent down His shechina upon them and rewarded them with a victory nigh at hand,

19 and many spoils for them to take; for God is mighty, wise!

20 God promised you many spoils and hastened this on for you, and restrained men's hands from you; and it may be a sign for the believers and guide you in a right way;

21 —and other (spoils) which ye could not gain; but God has encompassed them; for God is mighty over all.

22 And had those who misbelieved fought you, they would have turned their backs; then they would have found neither patron nor helper!

23 —God's course which has been followed before, and thou shalt find no change in the course of God!

24 He it was who restrained their hands from you, and your hands from them in the mid-valley of Mecca after He had given you the victory over them; for God on what ye do doth look!

25 Those who misbelieved and turned (you) away from the Sacred Mosque, and (turned away) the offering, kept from arriving at its destined place; and had it not been for believing men and believing women whom ye knew not, whom ye might have trampled on, and so a crime might have occurred to you on their account without your knowledge—that God may make whomsoever He pleases enter into His mercy. Had they been distinct from one another, we would have tormented those of them who misbelieved with grievous woe.

26 When those who misbelieved put in their hearts pique—the pique of ignorance—and God sent down

48.19 *spoils* — war booty. Clearly, no war booty was acquired at the Peace Treaty of al-Hudaybiyah. That which was meant was the hope of future war booty.

48.22 Muhammad believed that if the Meccan people would have ambushed Muhammad and his unarmed pilgrims at al-Hudaybiyah they would have been defeated since Allah would not have fought on behalf of the pilgrims.

48.23 *God's course* — In this context, *God's course* meant the Word of Allah. Accordingly, Muhammad believed that there is "no change" in the Word of Allah. Yet, the Doctrine of Abrogation speaks otherwise (see **The Doctrine of Abrogation** on pp. 68-70).

48.24a According to Muhammad, the reason why the Meccans did not attack Muhammad and his pilgrims was because Allah "restrained their hands."

48.24b *the mid-valley of Mecca* — That is, al-Hudaybiyah.

48.25a *the Sacred Mosque* — that is, the Ka'ba altar in Mecca.

48.25b Muhammad believed that Allah stopped Muhammad and his men from entering Mecca since, if they did so, they would have trampled to death the true believers worshipping at the Ka'b altar.

48.26 Muhammad believed that the Meccan leaders were embittered (piqued) at

His shechina upon His Apostle and upon the believers, and obliged them to keep to the word of piety, and they were most worthy of it and most suited for it; for God all things doth know.

27 God truly verified for His Apostle the vision that ye shall verily enter the Sacred Mosque, if God please, in safety with shaven heads or cut hair, ye shall not fear; for He knows what ye know not, and He has set for you, beside that, a victory nigh at hand.

28 He it is who sent His Apostle with guidance and the religion of truth to set it above all religion; for God is witness enough!

Muslim fanaticism

29 Mohammed is the Apostle of God, and those who are with Him are vehement against the misbelievers—compassionate amongst themselves; thou mayest see them bowing down, adoring, craving grace from God and His goodwill—their marks are in their faces from the effects of adoration—that is their similitude in the law and their similitude in the gospel; as a seedling puts forth its sprouts and strengthens it, and grows stout, and straightens itself upon its stem, delighting the sower!—that the misbelievers may be angry at

Muhammad. They prepared to attack Medinah, yet the shekinah glory settled down upon Muhammad and the Muslims, protecting them from harm (see Q 2.248 note).

48.27 According to the Peace Treaty at al-Hudaybiyah, the following year Muhammad was permitted to form a pilgrimage to the Ka'ba altar in Mecca. In preparation, they were required to shave their heads or cut their hair.

48.29a Muhammad characterized his Muslim followers as "vehement against the misbelievers." Other English translations, use the phrase: "hard against the disbelievers," "ruthless towards the disbelievers," "strong against the unbelievers," or "firm and unyielding towards all deniers of the truth." Set in the context of this surah, the peace treaty ratified at al-Hudaybiyah was only a means to an end. The end was the eventual conquest of Mecca.

48.29b Muhammad also characterized his

Muslim followers as compassionate amongst themselves. This is where their true loyalties lay. Ayaan Hirsi Ali writes that the Islamic worldview (view of mankind and the world) is based on groups, and its central concepts are honor and disgrace. "Within the community of the faithful, the fact that someone claims to be a Muslim is enough for other Muslims to regard that person as closer to them than any non-Muslim. Muslims feel an emotional bond with their oppressed brothers and sisters elsewhere in the world. When a group of Muslims—no matter where —is suffering or being oppressed (Kashmir, Palestine), the community of the faithful is commonly depicted as a bleeding body in pain" (*The Caged Virgin*, p. 39).

48.29c Muhammad finally characterized his Muslim followers as intensely dedicated to Allah. The marks on their faces were due to their many prostrations to the ground where their faces forcefully struck the floor or dirt.

them—God has promised those of them who believe and do right—forgiveness and a mighty hire.

Surah 60

In the name of the merciful and compassionate God.

1   O ye who believe! take not my en-emy and your enemy for patrons, encountering them with love for they misbelieve in the truth that is to come to you; they drive out the Apostle and you for that ye believe in God your Lord. If ye go forth fighting strenuously in my cause and craving my good pleasure, and secretly show love for them, yet do I know best what ye conceal and what ye display! and he of you

It was, said Muhammad, "the effects of adoration."

48.29d The Muslim fanatic is symbolized by the plant and Allah the sower of the seed. The similitude of this fanaticism is a seedling that puts forth its root and eventually becomes a sturdy plant that grows stout and brings delight to its sower.

48.29e *believe and do right* — This is a summary of the Islamic gospel (see Q 103.3, note).

Surah 60. The title of the surah, *The Examined One*, comes from v. 10. It has a singular theme: addressing problems associated with friendships between Muslims and non-Muslims. Its historical setting is the period after the Peace Treaty of Hudaybiyah and prior to the Conquest of Mecca.

60.1a *take not my enemy and your enemy for patrons* — That is, Muslims were instructed to not befriend non-Muslims who were actively hostile to the Islamic faith. This was due to the theocratic nature of Islam. The befriending of non-Muslim enemies threatened the Islamic government in Medinah.

In contrast, the Christian faith typically limits such separations from non-Christians to specific spheres—such as marriage, church memberships, professional partnerships, and the like (see 2 Cor 6:14-18). Otherwise, Christians are encouraged to build relationships with those who oppose the Christian faith. John R. W. Stott writes, "Close contact with people involves uncomfortable exposure of ourselves to them. It is much easier, in both fellowship and witness, to keep our distance. We are more likely to win the admiration of other people if we do. It is only at close quarters that idols are seen to have feet of clay. Are we willing to let people come close enough to us to find out what we are really like and to know us as we really are? True witness, born of friendship, requires a great degree of holiness in us as well as love" (*Motives and Methods in Evangelism*, p. 16).

60.1b *they drive out the Apostle and you for that ye believe in God your Lord* — This is a reference to Muhammad's forced emigration from Mecca to Medinah in 622.

60.1c *if ye go forth strenuously in my cause* — That is, if you go forth jihadistically in the Cause of Allah.

60.1d *secretly show love for them* — That is, quietly attempt to befriend them.

60.1e *the level path* — A summation of the Islamic gospel, the way to eternal life

who does so has erred from the level path.

2 If they find you they will be enemies to you, and they will stretch forth against you their hands and their tongues for evil, and would fain that ye should disbelieve;

3 neither your kindred nor your children shall profit you upon the resurrection day; it will separate you! but God on what ye do doth look!

4 Ye had a good example in Abraham and those with him, when they said to their people, "Verily, we are clear of you and of what ye serve beside God. We disbelieve in you: and between us and you is enmity and hatred begun for ever, until ye believe in God alone!" But not the speech of Abraham to his father, "Verily, I will ask forgiveness for thee, though I cannot control aught from God!" O our Lord! on thee do we rely! and unto thee we turn! and unto thee the journey is!

5 Our Lord! make us not a trial for

those who misbelieve; but forgive us! Our Lord! verily, thou art mighty, wise!

6 Ye had in them a good example for him who would hope in God and the last day. But whoso turns his back, verily, God, He is rich and to be praised.

7 Mayhap that God will place love between you and between those of them ye are hostile towards: for God is powerful, and. God is forgiving, compassionate.

8 God forbids you not respecting those who have not fought against you for religion's sake, and who have not driven you forth from your homes, that ye should act righteously and justly towards them; verily, God loves the just!

9 He only forbids you to make patrons of those who have fought against you for religion's sake, and driven you forth from your homes, or have aided in your expulsion; and whoever makes patrons of

(see Q 72.2, note).

60.2-3 Muhammad believed that all such friendships were built on false pretenses since the non-Muslim who actively opposed the Islamic faith would attempt to convert him or her away from Islam, if possible. Accordingly, the Muslim ran the risk of eternal damnation on the Resurrection Day.

60.4a Muhammad looked to Abraham as an example of religious and social separation. Abraham was from the prosperous and sophisticated City of Ur, yet separated from it due to its rampant idolatry. He then followed the word of the Lord who led him to

land of Canaan where he lived as a Bedouin tribesman (see Gen 12:1-4; Josh 24:2-4).

60.4b-5 *O our Lord...* — This is a prayer of dedication to live separated lives from non-Muslims.

60.7 Perhaps, said Muhammad, Allah would provide loving relationships and friendships from within the Muslim community to meet the needs of the believer.

60.8-9 Allah allows friends between Muslims and non-Muslims, provided that the non-Muslims are not hostile to the Islamic faith.

60.10 One of the stipulations mentioned in the Peace Treaty of al-Hudaybiyah was

them, they are the unjust!

The emigration of wives

10   O ye who believe! when there come believing women who have fled, then try them: God knows their faith. If ye know them to be believers do not send them back to the misbelievers—they are not lawful for them, nor are the men lawful for these—but give them what they have expended, and it shall be no crime against you that ye marry them, when ye have given them their hire. And do not ye retain a right over misbelieving women; but ask for what ye have spent, and let them ask for what they have spent. That is God's judgment: He judges between you, for God is knowing, wise!

11   And if any of your wives escape from you to the misbelievers, and your turn comes, then give to those whose wives have gone away the like of what they have spent; and fear God, in whom it is that ye believe.

12   O thou prophet! when believing women come to thee and engage with thee that they will not associate aught with God, and will not steal, and will not fornicate, and will not kill their children, and will not bring a calumny which they have forged between their hands and feet, and that they will not rebel against thee in what is reasonable, then engage with them and ask forgiveness for them of God—verily, God is forgiving, compassionate.

Conclusion

13   O ye who believe! take not for pa-

---

that children from Mecca who chose to emigrate to Medinah were to be returned to Mecca, if their guardians disapproved of the emigration. The truce, however, said nothing about wives who emigrated from one city to the other. Therefore, Muhammad formulated his own stipulations. If a woman wished to emigrate from Mecca to Medinah and was a believer in the Islamic faith, she was permitted to stay in Medinah. A Muslim man in Medinah could marry her, provided that he give her a *hire* (that is, a dower). If such a woman proved to not be a Muslim believer, the marriage was rendered null and void and dowers were to be returned.

60.11 If Muslim wives chose to emigrate to Mecca, Muhammad stipulated that they should be free to do so, with the dowers restored.

60.12 This verse is a reiteration of v. 10 with a clarification of the conditions upon which the examination of faith is to be determined. Muhammad claimed that he was a mediator between Allah and his wives, granting him the power to petition Allah to forgive their sins.

In contrast, no such mediation of husbands exist within the Christian faith. Jesus Christ is the sole mediator between God the Father and an individual (see Job 9:33; 1 Tim 2:5; Heb 4:14-16; 7:15; 8:6; 1 Jn 2:1).

60.13 Muhammad concluded the surah with a reiteration of the principle that served as the surah's major theme: Muslims were not

trons a people whom God is wroth against; they despair of the hereafter, as the misbelievers despair of the fellows of the tombs!

Surah 66

In the name of the merciful and compassionate God.

The secret oath

1   O thou prophet! wherefore dost thou prohibit what God has made lawful to thee, craving to please

thy wives? but God is forgiving, compassionate!

2   God has allowed you to expiate your oaths; for God is your sovereign, and He is the knowing, the wise!

*The scandal of
Mary the Coptic Christian*

3   And when the prophet told as a secret to one of his wives a recent event, and when she gave information thereof and exposed it, he acquainted her with some of it and avoided part of it. But when he in-

to befriend non-Muslims who were hostile to the Islamic faith.

Surah 66. The title of this surah, *The Prohibition*, comes from v. 1. This brief surah is one of the more controversial surahs in the Qur'an since it addresses another scandal in Muhammad's domestic life. This scandal involved his sexual activity with one of his concubines, Mary the Coptic Christian.

66.1-2 The surah begins with Allah rebuking Muhammad. In his attempt to please his wives, Muhammad had made oaths, where he would spend one night with each of his wives in rotation. To violate this rotation by spending a night with a wife out of order was therefore not allowed. Allah rebuked Muhammad, since this oath unnecessarily limited Muhammad from having sexual relations with whomever he wanted among his wives, whenever he wanted. Accordingly, in His mercy Allah allowed Muhammad to expiate (terminate) this oath.

66.3 The secret mentioned in this verse addressed Muhammad's relationship with one

of his concubines, Mary the Coptic Christian. It had been his custom to spend his time equally with his wives, spending one night with each in turn. Due to the problem of jealousies in his harem, the wives were mindful of whom he spent each night and the night when their turn would come.

On the night when it was Hafsa's turn to be with Muhammad, she was momentarily and unexpectedly out of the house. When she returned, she found Muhammad in her bed with Mary, the Coptic Christian. Infuriated, Hafsa reproached him and threatened to expose his behavior to the others in the harem. Muhammad pleaded with her to keep the tryst a secret.

At first she kept the incident secret, but then relented and went public with the story. Embittered, all the wives ostracized themselves from Muhammad. Muhammad responded by threatening to divorced all his wives with an oath. He then relented and maintained his marriages with them (see **The Day Muhammad Almost Divorced All His**

formed her of it, she said, "Who told thee this?" he said, "The wise one, the well-aware informed me.

4 If ye both turn repentant unto God—for your hearts have swerved!—but if ye back each other up against him—verily, God, He is the sovereign; and Gabriel and the righteous of the believers, and the angels after that, will back him up.

5 It may be that his Lord if he divorce you will give him in exchange wives better than you, Muslims, believers, devout, repentant, worshipping, given to fasting—such as have known men and virgins too."

The call for repentance

6 O ye who believe! save yourselves and your families from the fire, whose fuel is men and stones—over it are angels stout and stern;

they disobey not God in what He bids them, but they do what they are bidden!

7 O ye who disbelieve! excuse not yourselves today—ye shall only be rewarded for that which ye have done.

8 O ye who believe! turn repentant to God with sincere repentance; it may be that thy Lord will cover for you your offences and will bring you into gardens beneath which rivers flow!—the day God will not disgrace the Prophet nor those who believe with him; their light shall run on before them, and at their right hands! they shall say, "Our Lord! perfect for us our light and forgive us verily, Thou art mighty over all!"

9 O thou prophet! fight strenuously against the misbelievers and hypocrites and be stern towards them; for their resort is hell, and an evil journey shall it be!

Wives on pp. 844-847).

66.4-5 It was then that Muhammad received a new revelation from Allah via the archangel Gabriel. The wives were told that if they continued in their insolence and ostracization of Muhammad, he would divorce all of them and acquire new set of wives, better than those of the first harem.

66.6 Muhammad turned to the topic of repentance, reminding his listeners (including his wives) that all who disobey the revelations from Allah will be cast into Hell.

66.8 The believing Muslims (in this context, his wives) were admonished to turn in repentance so that the gardens of Paradise

would still be theirs in the afterlife.

66.9 *fight strenuously against the misbelievers and hypocrites* — That is, fight jihadistically against the non-Muslims and the apostate Muslims. Allah reminded Muhammad that he was to be resolute in his struggle against infidels and hypocrites (apostates). In the context of what came prior in this surah, the implication is that the hypocrites could possibly include some of his wives. If they did not repent, they would enter Hell.

66.10-12 Muhammad then turned his attention to four women in antiquity: Noah's wife, Lot's wife, Pharaoh's wife, and Mary the mother of Jesus.

The examples of four women

10 God strikes out a parable to those who misbelieve: the wife of Noah and the wife of Lot; they were under two of our righteous servants, but they betrayed them: and they availed them nothing against God; and it was said, "Enter the fire with those who enter."

11 And God strikes out a parable for those who believe: the wife of Pharaoh, when she said, "My Lord, build for me a house with Thee in Paradise, and save me from Pha-raoh and his works, and save me from the unjust people!"

12 And Mary, daughter of Imrân, who guarded her private parts, and we breathed therein of our spirit and she verified the words of her Lord and His books, and was of the devout.

Surah 9

Resumption of hostilities

1 An immunity from God and His

The first two women (v. 10) were the wives of two Old Testament patriarchs: Noah and Lot. According to Muhammad, they betrayed their husbands and entered the fires of Hell in the afterlife.

The third woman (v. 11) was the wife of Pharaoh. According to Muhammad, she prayed to the Lord asking to be saved from the works of Pharaoh and be given a place in Paradise. The impression is that the Lord answered her prayer.

The fourth woman was Mary (Miriam), also mentioned in v. 12. Muhammad claimed that she was the daughter of Imran, yet in Q 3.35 Imran was the father of the distant patriarch Aaron (see **The House of Amram** on p. 654). Because she was sexually chaste, she was mightily used of the Lord.

These illustrations are not sourced in any biblical or apocryphal documents, and are therefore to be regarded as imaginative inventions of Muhammad. His point was to underscore the message mentioned earlier in this surah to his own wives. If they wished to enter the pleasures of Paradise in the af-terlife, they could not rest of the laurels of being married to the Prophet. Instead, they needed to cultivate personal piety and submissiveness. Otherwise, they would be cast into the fires of Hell.

Christian scholarship has regarded this surah to be a useful insight look into the character of Muhammad. His surah was conveniently timed to help him out of a serious marital problem with his many wives. Not only did he place the blame on his wives for the problem, he also threatened them with divorce and eternal damnation if they did not submit to his authority.

Surah 9. The title of this surah, *Repentance*, comes from v. 104. This surah is the only one which does not begin with the conventional doxology. Some scholars have suggested that this surah and Surah 8 were originally one surah, which would explain the absence of a doxology. Yet, internal content strongly points to an interval of approximately seven years between the two surahs, which has caused most scholars to see Surah 9 as a separate surah.

Apostle to those idolaters with whom ye have made a league.

2   Roam ye at large in the land for four months, but know that ye cannot make God helpless, and that God disgraces the misbelievers.

3   A proclamation from God and His Apostle to the people on the day of the greater pilgrimage, that God is clear of the idolaters as is His Apostle! If then ye repent it is better for you; but if ye turn your backs, then know that ye cannot make God helpless. Give to those who misbelieve glad tidings of

grievous woe!

4   —Except to those of the idolaters with whom ye have made a league, and who then have not failed you at all, and have not backed up any one against you. Fulfil for them then your covenant until the time agreed upon with them; verily, God loves those who fear.

5   But when the sacred months are passed away, kill the idolaters wherever ye may find them; and take them, and besiege them, and lie in wait for them in every place

The historical setting of the surah was the situation in the Muslim community shortly after the Conquest of Mecca and prior to the military expedition to Tabuk in northwestern Saudi Arabia to attack a Byzantine army. Curiously, no Byzantine accounts of the military campaign exist. Since both Islamic and non-Islamic sources agree that the two armies never met, the general consensus is that an expedition may have taken place but a battle did not (see **The Expedition to Tabuk** on p. 862).

The fundamental premise of this surah is the islamification of the earth, with Jihad serving as a principal method in achieving this goal. Muhammad saw the Muslim nation as superior to all other civilizations, with the mandate to spread Islam to the entire earth and thereby bring all peoples everywhere in submission to Allah.

9.1 *an immunity from God and His Apostle* — That is, a repudiation of all idolaters by Allah and His Apostle to the idolaters. At this point in time, all peace treaties with the infidels in Arabia were cancelled.

9.2 *roam ye at large in the land for four months* — Muhammad provided a grace period of four months between the announcement of the cancellation of all peace treaties and the resumption of hostilities.

9.3 This proclamation was made on the Day of the Great Pilgrimage to Mecca in the month of Ramadan. The justification for the resumption of hostilities was due to the fact that the infidels were worshippers of idols.

9.4 The only infidels exempted from this impending war were the city-states that had faithfully maintained their peace treaties with Muhammad without infractions. They would be spared attack "until the time agreed upon with them" expired.

9.5 *The Verse of the Sword.* Once the conditions of *no hostilities* had passed, the idolaters were to be killed wherever Muslims found them. Two exceptions to this carnage were the following: (a) those who repented and became Muslims—showing forth a new faith with prayer and the giving of alms, and (b) those who willingly surrendered prior to the onset of hostilities. This second exception would eventually evolve into the *Tradition of Dhimmitude* and the institution of the poll tax known as *jizya* (see **Dhimmitude** on pp. 716-717).

In contrast, Jesus Christ admonished his followers to sheath the sword. At the time of his arrest, Jesus commanded Peter, "Put your sword away! Shall I not drink the cup the Father has given me?" (Jn 18:11). And then, before Pontius Pilate, Jesus said, "My kingdom is not of this world. If it were, my servants would fight to prevent my arrest by the Jews. But now my kingdom is from another place" (Jn 18:36). Jesus' point is that his followers were not to fight (make use of the sword) to prevent his coming crucifixion.

The words of Jesus were also a subtle renunciation of the notion of a Christian theocracy. And along with the renunciation of theocracy was the renunciation of Holy War. As Augustine once said, Christians are the citizens of two worlds. Although the two worlds impact one another, our heavenly citizenship is not to be confused with our earthly citizenship (see Augustine, *The City of God;* and Charles Colson, *Kingdoms in Conflict*). It is only when a religion sees itself as a theocracy that holy wars emerge with the resulting wave of violence enacted in the name of God.

The advancement of the Christian faith in the world, then, was to stand clear of theocracy and Holy War. This principle, of course, has not always been followed, evidenced by repeated theocracies and holy wars in Church history. Still, Jesus' words remain the touchstone—the canon, norm, yardstick—in determining authentic evangelism and missionary outreach.

In the place of the Doctrine of Holy War, Christian theologians have strived to develop an alternate concept: Just War Theory.

Scholarly deliberations have given rise to a delicate balancing act. On the one hand, Christians are opposed to holy war (military jihad). On the other hand, Christians affirm the role of a strong police and military whose purpose is to keep the peace.

On this issue, a passage of Scripture often cited among Christian theologians is Rom 13:1-5. In this passage the Apostle Paul explained that God established governments with the mandate to punish "those who do wrong" (v. 3). Paul added that the leader(s) of governments is "God's servant to do you good. But if you do wrong, be afraid, for he does not bear the sword for nothing. He is God's servant, an agent of wrath to bring punishment on the wrongdoer" (v. 4).

With this in mind, a fundamental insight has emerged and taken shape within the church. John R. W. Stott explains, "Whenever an evil aggressor threatens the security of the state, Christians are likely to polarize. Just-war theorists concentrate on the need to resist and punish evil, and tend to forget the other biblical injunction to 'overcome' it. Pacifists, on the other hand, concentrate on the need to overcome evil with good, and tend to forget that according to Scripture evil deserves to be punished. Can these two biblical emphases be reconciled? At least we should be able to agree with this: if a nation believes it is justified in going to war, in order to resist and punish evil, Christians will stress the need to look beyond the defeat and surrender of the national enemy to its repentance and rehabilitation. The punishment of evil is an essential part of God's moral government of the world. But retributive and reformative justice go hand in hand. The highest and noblest of all attitudes to evil is to seek to overcome it with good" (*A Christian Response to Good and Evil*, p. 55).

The Day Muhammad Almost Divorced All His Wives

I had been eager to ask Umar about the two ladies from among the wives of the Prophet regarding whom Allah said (in the Qur'an saying): If you two (wives of the Prophet namely Aisha and Hafsa) turn in repentance to Allah your hearts are indeed so inclined (to oppose what the Prophet likes) (66:4), till performed the Hajj along with Umar (and on our way back from Hajj) he went aside (to answer the call of nature) and I also went aside along with him carrying a tumbler of water. When he had answered the call of nature and returned, I poured water on his hands from the tumbler and he performed ablution. I said, "O Chief of the believers! Who were the two ladies from among the wives of the Prophet to whom Allah said:

> If you two return in repentance (66:4)? He said, "I am astonished at your question, O Ibn Abbas. They were Aisha and Hafsa.

Then Umar went on relating the narration and said, "I and an Ansari neighbor of mine from Bani Umaiya bin Zai who used to live in Awali Al-Medina, used to visit the Prophet in turns. He used to go one day, and I another day. When I went I would bring him the news of what had happened that day regarding the instructions and orders and when he went, he used to do the same for me. We, the people of Quraysh, used to have authority over women, but when we came to live with the Ansar, we noticed that the Ansari women had the upper hand over their men, so our women started acquiring the habits of the Ansari women. Once I shouted at my wife and she paid me back in my coin and I disliked that she should answer me back. She said,

> Why do you take it ill that I retort upon you? By Allah, the wives of the Prophet retort upon him, and some of them may not speak with him for the while day till night.

What she said scared me and I said to her, "Whoever amongst them does so, will be a great loser." Then I dressed myself and went to Hafsa and asked her,

> Does any of you keep Allah's Apostle angry all the daylong till night? She replied in the affirmative. I said, "She is a ruined losing person (and will never have success)! Doesn't she fear that Allah may get angry for the anger of Allah's Apostle and thus she will be ruined? Don't ask Allah's Apostle too many things, and don't retort upon him in any case, and don't desert him. Demand from me whatever you like, and don't be tempted to imitate your neighbor (i.e., Aisha) in her behavior towards the Prophet), for she (i.e., Aisha) is more beautiful than you, and more beloved to Allah's Apostle.

In those days it was rumored that Ghassan (a tribe living in Sham) was getting prepared their horses to invade us. My companion went (to the Prophet on the day of his turn, went and returned to us at night and knocked at my door violently, asking whether I was sleeping. I was scared (by the hard knocking) and came out to him. He said that a great thing had happened. I asked him, "What is it? Have Ghassan come?" He replied that it was worse and more serious than that, and added that Allah's Apostle had divorced all his wives. I said, "Hafsa is a ruined loser! I expected that would happen someday." So I dressed myself and offered the Fajr prayer with the Prophet. Then the Prophet entered an upper room and stayed there alone. I went to Hafsa and found her weeping. I asked her, "Why are you weeping? Didn't I warn you? Have Allah's Apostle divorced you all?" She replied, "I don't know. He is there in the upper room." I then went out and came to the pulpit and found a group of people around it and some of them were weeping. Then I sat with them for some time, but could not endure the situation.

So I went to the upper room where the Prophet was and requested to a black slave of his: "Will you get the permission of (Allah's Apostle) for Umar (to enter)?" The slave went in, talked to the Prophet about it and came out saying, "I mentioned you to him but he did not reply." So I went and sat with the people who were sitting by the pulpit, but I could not bear the situation, so I went to the slave again and said, "Will you get the permission for Umar?" He went in and brought the same reply as before. When I was leaving, behold, the slave called me saying, "Allah's Apostle has granted you permission." So, I entered upon the Prophet and saw him lying on a mat without wedding on it, and the mat had left its mark on the body of the Prophet, and he was leaning on a leather pillow stuffed with palm fires. I greeted him and while still standing, I said, "Have you divorced your wives?" He raised his eyes to me and replied in the negative. And then while still standing, I said chatting: "Will you heed what I say, O Allah's Apostle! We, the people of Quraysh used to have the upper hand over our women (wives), and when we came to the people whose women had the upper hand over them..."

Umar told the whole story (about his wife). "On that the Prophet smiled." Umar further said, "I then said, "I went to Hafsa and said to her: 'Do not be tempted to imitate your companion (Aisha) for she is more beautiful than you and more beloved to the Prophet.'"

The Prophet smiled again. When I saw him smiling, I sat down and cast a glance at the room, and by Allah, I couldn't see anything of importance but three hides. I said (to Allah's Apostle) "Invoke Allah to make your followers prosperous and given worldly luxuries, though they do not worship Allah?" The Prophet was leaning then (and on hearing my speech he sat straight) and said, "O Ibn Al-Khattab! Do you have any doubt (that the Hereafter is better than this world)? These people have been given rewards of their good deeds in this world only."

I asked the Prophet, "Please ask Allah's forgiveness for me. The Prophet did not go to his wives because of the secret which Hafsa had disclosed to Aisha [regarding Mary the Coptic Christian], and he said that he would not go to his wives for one month as he was angry with them when Allah admonished him (for his oath that he would not approach Mary).

When twenty-nine days had passed, the Prophet went to Aisha first of all. She said to him, "You took an oath that you would not come to us for one month, and today only twenty-nine days have passed, as I have been counting them day by day." The Prophet said, "The month is also of twenty-nine days." That month consisted of twenty-nine days. Aisha said, "When the Divine Revelation of Choice was revealed, the Prophet started with me, saying to me, "I am telling you something but you needn't hurry to give the reply till you can consult your parents." Aisha knew that her parents would not advise her to part with the Prophet. The Prophet said that Allah had said:

> O Prophet! Say to your wives: If you desire that the life of this world and its glitter,...then come! I will make a provision for you and wet you free in a handsome manner. But if you seek Allah and His Apostle, and the Home of the

> Hereafter, then verily, Allah has prepared for the good-doers amongst you. A great reward."
>
> Aisha said, "Am I to consult my parents about this? I need prefer Allah, His Apostle, and the Home and the Hereafter. After that the Prophet gave the choice to his other wives and they also gave the same reply as Aisha did.
>
> —*Sahih Burkari*, 3.43.648

Another sexual scandal threatened to disturb the domestic bliss of the Prophet's harem. To prevent sexual jealousy among his wives, Muhammad used to divide his time equally among them, spending one night with each of them in turn. On a day when it was his wife Hafsa's turn, she was out visiting her father. Returning unexpectedly, she surprised Muhammad in her bed with Mary the Coptic maid, his legal concubine. Hafsa was furious and reproached him bitterly; what is more, she threatened to expose him to others in the harem...As in the Zaynab affair, a divine revelation interposed to sort out his domestic problems. The heavenly message disallowed the earlier promise to keep away from the seductive maid and reprimanded the wives for their insubordination; it was even hinted that the Prophet would divorce all the wives in the whole harem and replace them with more submissive ones.

—David Goldmann, *Resurgent Islam and America*, pp. 34, 35

Muhammad's harem included a Coptic Christian concubine named Mary, "sent to him as a present," as Yusuf Ali writes, by a Christian community in Egypt. Mary was the mother of Muhammad's deeply lamented last son, Ibrahim, who died in infancy, just as Khadija's two sons had...When all was said and done, Muhammad liked women, especially strong, intelligent women..."Muhammad was one of those rare men who truly enjoy the company of women," as Karen Armstrong notes. "Some of his male companions were astonished by his leniency towards his wives and the way they stood up to him and answered him back."

—Edward Hotaling, *Islam without Illusions*, p. 42

According to custom and to be "fair" to women, Muhammad used to sleep every night with a different wife. One night when it was Hafza's turn, she was late getting back from her father's house. When she returned to her home she was surprised and angry to find Muhammad in her bed with his slave girl, Mary the Coptic. All hell broke lose...The scandal spread throughout the harem and Muhammad was shunned by all his wives. Just in time he had a divine revelation, which allowed him to negate his oath and threaten his wives with divorce if they did not behave.

—The Infidel, *A Letter to Muslims*, pp. 37, 38

of observation; but if they repent, and are steadfast in prayer, and give alms, then let them go their way; verily, God is forgiving and merciful.

6 And if any one of the idolaters ask thee for aid, then aid him, in order that he may hear the word of God; then let him reach his place of safety—that is, because they are a folk who do not know.

Justifications for Jihad

7 How can there be for the idolaters a treaty with God and with His Apostle, save those with whom ye have made a league at the Sacred Mosque! Then while they stand by you, stand ye by them; verily, God loves those who fear.

8 How!—if they prevail against you, they will not observe either ties of blood or ties of clientship; they please you with their mouths, but their hearts refuse; and most of them do work abomination.

9 They barter God's signs for a little price, and they turn folk from His way; verily, they—evil is that which they have done.

10 They will not observe in a believer ties of kindred nor ties of clientship; but they it is are the transgressors.

11 But if they repent and are steadfast in prayer and give alms, then they are your brethren in religion—we detail the signs unto a people that do know.

12 But if they break faith with you after their treaty, and taunt your religion, then fight the leaders of misbelief; verily, they have no faith, haply they may desist.

13 Will ye not fight a people who broke their oaths, and intended to expel the Apostle? They began with you at first, are ye afraid of them? God is more deserving that ye should fear Him!

14 If ye be believers, kill them! God will torment them by your hands, and disgrace them, and aid you against them, and heal the breasts of a people who believe;

15 and will remove rage from their hearts; for God turns unto Him

---

9.7 Muhammad noted that only those treaties with idolaters signed in the vicinity of the Ka'ba altar (the Sacred Mosque) in Mecca would be honored.

9.8-10 Treaties with idolaters were not honored (except those described in the previous verse) because their words could not be trusted.

9.11 As mentioned in v. 5, if the idolaters repented of their paganism and converted to Islam, they would be spared a military attack.

9.12 Treaties were not to be honored of those who had taunted the Islamic religion and opposed Muhammad as the Apostle of Allah.

9.14 *if ye be believers* — That is, if you be true believers in Allah. Muslim believers were sanctioned by Allah to torture, defile, and kill the infidels. The tone of the verse is that this mayhem was to be conducted with impunity. What is more, Allah would assist

whomsoever He pleases, and God is knowing, wise!

16 Did ye reckon that ye would be left, when God knows not as yet those of you who fought strenuously, and who did not take other than God and His Apostle, and the believers for an intimate friend? for God is well aware of what ye do.

Rewards and Punishments

17 It is not for idolaters to repair to the mosques of God, bearing witness against themselves to unbelief; they it is whose works are vain, and in the Fire shall they dwell for aye!

18 He only shall repair to the mosques of God who believes in God and the last day, and is steadfast in prayer, and gives the alms, and

fears only God—it may be that these will be of those who are guided.

19 Have ye made out the giving drink to the pilgrims and the repairing to the Sacred Mosque to be like being one who believes in God and in the last day, and is strenuous in the way of God?—they are not equal in God's sight, and God guides not an unjust people.

20 Those who believe and who have fled and been strenuous in the way of God, with their wealth and with their persons, are highest in rank with God, and these it is who are happy.

21 Their Lord gives them glad tidings of mercy from Himself, and goodwill; and gardens shall they have therein and lasting pleasure,

22 to dwell therein for aye! Verily, God,

them in this process.

9.16 *did ye think that ye would be left* — That is, did you think that Allah would spare you? Muhammad's point what the unless Muslims fought jihadistically (strenuously) against all who did not believe in Allah and His Apostle, they would not be spared divine judgment (see Q 3.32; 4.69, 79-80, 136; 5.80-81; 8.13, 20-23; 24.47, 48, 50-52, 54; 33.33, 71; 48.9-10; 57.19; 59.4; 72.22-23, 81.19-21 and 46.16, note).

9.17 *It is not for idolaters to repair to the mosques of God* — That is, idolaters were no longer permitted to visit any Islamic mosques (see v. 28).

9.18 Only faithful Muslims were permitted to visit mosques.

9.19 According to Muhammad, pagans who give water to Muslim pilgrims coming to the Ka'ba altar in Mecca is not equal to having placed one's faith in Allah. In spite of this gesture of good will, they are still an unjust people and will be judged accordingly.

9.20-22 According to Muhammad, Muslims of highest rank with Allah are those who: (a) emigrated from pagan lands to Muslim lands, (b) engaged in jihadistic activities in behalf of the Cause of Allah, and (c) sacrificed their wealth and their very selves in the Cause of Allah. These people are promised the gardens of Paradise. The implication is that Muslims of "the highest rank" will forego the examination at the Last Judgment and pass directly into Paradise.

9.23 Muslims were not to demonstrate loyalty to family members who were not de-

with Him is mighty here.

Question of loyalty

23   O ye who believe! take not your fathers and your brothers for patrons if they love misbelief rather than faith; for whosoever amongst you takes them for patrons these are the unjust.

24   Say, "If your fathers, and your sons, and your brethren, and your wives, and your clansmen, and the wealth which ye have gained, and the merchandise which ye fear may be slack, and the dwellings which ye love are dearer to you than God and His Apostle, and than fighting strenuously in His way—then wait awhile, until God brings His bidding, for God guides not a people

who work abomination!"

Battle of Honein

25   God has helped you in many a place, and on the day of "Honein when ye were so pleased with your numbers; but it did not serve you at all, and the road grew too strait for you, where it had been broad; and then ye turned your backs retreating;

26   then God sent down His shechina upon His Apostle and upon the believers; and sent down armies which ye could not see, and punished those who misbelieved; for that is the reward of the misbelievers,

27   then God turns after that to whom He will, for God is forgiving and

---

vout Muslims. Evidences of lack of devotion were an unwillingness to give of one's finances and possessions for the Cause of Allah and His Apostle and a refusal to engage in fighting strenuously in the way of Allah.

9.24 Muhammad believed that if a person possessed a deeper devotion to one's own family (parents, spouses, clansmen) than for Allah and Muhammad, that person is not worthy of Allah.

In contrast, Jesus said that such devotion should be given to Him. He said: "Anyone who loves his father or mother more than me is not worthy of me; anyone who loves his son or daughter more than me is not worthy of me; and anyone who does not take his cross and follow me is not worthy of me. Whoever finds his life will lose it, and whoever loses his life for my sake will

find it" (Matt 10:37-39).

9.25 Three weeks after the Conquest of Mecca on January 11, 630, the opponents of Muhammad staged a counterattack at Honein (Feb 1, 630). With an army of twelve thousand soldiers, Muhammad was again victorious in the battle. They took six thousand prisoners and acquired the spoils of twenty-four thousand camels (see map on p. 681).

9.26-27 During the battle, Muhammad explained, the Muslims were almost defeated. They began a retreat until Allah sent down his *shechina* (shekinah glory) upon his army and pushed back and defeated the enemy.

9.28 *they shall not approach the Sacred Mosque* — Muhammad denied non-Muslims entrance into Mecca since in its center was the sacred Ka'ba altar. This ordinance is in

Islamification

The Doctrine of Islamification, as defined in the Qur'an, is the gradual transformation of all the cultures of the world into that which recognizes the supremacy of Allah and submits to his laws. Moreover, since the Qur'an defines Islam as both a theology and a theocracy, the islamification of the world would necessarily impact both spheres of religion and politics. A mid-step in the islamification of the world is the practice of dhimmitude—that is, the accommodation of non-believers (infidels) in cultures that are officially Islamic. Such non-believers are recognized as second-class citizens with corresponding responsibilities and limitations of legal rights. The purpose of dhimmitude is to encourage non-believers to convert to Islam (see *Dhimmitude* on pp. 723-724).

The Doctrine of Jihad serves as an important methodology in advancing the islamification of the world. This is achieved at two levels: (a) through the use of Holy War, and (b) through cultural transformation. World history, specifically in the seventh through sixteenth centuries, and more recently in the twentieth and twenty-first centuries has given witness to the use of the first form, that of Holy War. The current efforts of Islamic terrorism clearly falls within this category (see *Jihad* on pp. 624-630). The second form, that of cultural transformation, has made important inroads in recent years via the methodology of *fatah*—that is, the infiltration of opposing cultural values with Muslim values. Western literature is a common breeding ground for the activities of *fatah*, particularly in widely read periodicals and school textbooks.

Non-Muslim Westerners have responded to the efforts of islamification in one of two ways. The first is to resist it openly and aggressively. These Westerners believe that society is seriously threatened by Islam due to its mandate to fundamentally transform society. The fact that many leaders of Hamas, for example, are college graduates from Western universities, with some having master's degrees, and yet are still committed to terrorism, speaks to Islam's power over Western values.[1]

Moreover, though most Muslims are not terrorists, the Qur'an (their sacred scripture) is "an all pervasive ideology that does not allow for theological subjugation into the private sphere"[2] of their minds. That is, the Qur'an demands that its values transform society. And since its fundamental values are opposed to fundamental Western values (e.g., democracy, freedom of speech, freedom of religion, and the tenets of secularism), these Westerners feel threatened that Muslims, if given the opportunity, will dismantle the West.

The second approach is to reach out and assimilate Islam. Westerners who embrace this approach believe that the power of islamification should be dismissed as an insignificant phenomenon—a tiger with no teeth. The founding fathers of Western sociology—Karl Marx, Max Weber, and Émile Durkheim—have left a legacy in Western academia where religion is understood to be a short term quietus and repose for people that tends to fade when their personal lives are stabilized and rationalized. In regards to Islam, as Muslims become immersed in Western secular culture, they will embrace Western values and either abandon their previously held Islamic beliefs or allow their beliefs to be restricted to a privatization deep within their minds. If this does not take place in their lives, it will certainly take place in the lives of their children and grandchildren. Moreover, that which will accelerate this transforming process is the undeniable and demonstrable failure of societies that are Islamic theocracies. Sam Harris writes, "If Muslim orthodoxy were as economically and technologically viable as Western liberalism, we would probably be doomed to witness the Islamification of the earth."[3] Yet, he insists, it is not.

The effectiveness of this second approach has formed a backlash among some Muslims living in the West. "They live in uniquely impenetrable, tightly knit networks of kinship" that hold together "even two generations down the line."[4]

---

[1] See Mosab Hassan Yousef, *Son of Hamas*, p. 220.
[2] Stephen Vertigans, *Islamic Roots and Resurgence in Turkey*, pp. 3, 4.
[3] Sam Harris, *The End of Faith*, p. 133.
[3] D. P. Sharma, *The New Terrorism*, p. 110.

Does the U.S. have a problem with Islam? Have the terrorist attacks of 9/11—and the other attempts since—permanently excluded Muslims from full assimilation into American life?…"Islamophobia has become the accepted form of racism in America," says Muslim American writer and commentator Arsalan Iftikhar. "You can always take a potshot at Muslims and get away with it."

—Bobby Ghosh, *Time*, p. 23

Throughout 2005 and early 2006, worldwide controversy escalated over the publication in Europe of political cartoons that depicted Islam's founder, Mohammad...A small group of Danish cartoonists had actually created the cartoons as a test of Europe's commitment to freedom of expression and freedom of the press in the face of what they saw as the growing "Islamification" of Europe.

—Rod Parsley, *Culturally Incorrect*, p. 117

Islamification was often state-led, but rarely state-initiated. By this I mean that the state often adopted the guise of Islam as a means of regime preservation.

—Beverley Milton-Edwards, *Islam and Politics in the Contemporary World*, p. 211

Europe may become a second front as the Islamification of Europe gathers speed. It has taken less than a generation for the face of Europe to change...High birth rates among first- and second-generation Muslims point to the prospect of Muslims constituting the majority of the population in many EU member states by the middle of the century.

—Michael Hart, *From Pride to Influence*, p. 105

It is likely that increasing Muslim populations and the "Islamification" of the Muslim world will impact on Western countries, including Australia...It is generally true to say that Australians know very little about Islam. Such knowledge of Islam as exists among the general public is mostly based on information provided in the media, often in the form of crude and inaccurate stereotypes. Accordingly, there is a great deal of scope for misunderstanding and misreading cross-cultural messages and concerns.

—Jamila Hussain, *Islam: Its law and Society*, p. 3

Much of the nervousness about "Islamification" arises from little more than the cultural disturbance caused, for example, by the subservient position of women or by religious practices which might seem strange to a larger secular or Christian society.

—Peter Stalker, *The Work of Strangers*, p. 80

American concerns about "Latinization" or French references to "Africanization" or "Islamification" are little more than new, often racist, names for "otherness."

—Jonathon Wayne Moses, *International Migration*, p. 179

merciful!

*Rules pertaining to
the Sacred Mosque*

28   O ye who believe! it is only the
     idolaters who are unclean; they
     shall not then approach the Sacred
     Mosque after this year. But if ye
     fear want then God will enrich you
     from His grace if He will; verily,
     God is knowing, wise!

Rules of Jihad

29   Fight those who believe not in God
     and in the last day, and who forbid

not what God and His Apostle have
forbidden, and who do not practice the religion of truth from
amongst those to whom the Book
has been brought, until they pay
the tribute by their hands and be
as little ones.

*Jewish and Christian
falsehoods*

30   The Jews say Ezra is the son of
     God; and the Christians say that
     the Messiah is the son of God; that
     is what they say with their
     mouths, imitating the sayings of
     those who misbelieved before—

force in our present times. Similarly, due to
the special significance of Medinah (Muhammad's home since his migration from Mecca—
the Hijrah—in 622), non-Muslims are prohibited entrance into this city, as well. Moreover, the restriction has expanded to any
mosque anywhere in the world.

In contrast, Judaism and Christianity has
made no such prohibitions. In ancient Israel, nonbelievers (Gentiles) were allowed entrance into the large section of the Temple
called the Courtyard of the Gentiles. It is
here where they could pray and worship.
In the modern era, the tradition of Conservative Judaism allows nonbelievers to attend
their worship services in synagogues, provided that male attendees wear a headcover-
ing (preferably a yarmulke). The tradition of
Reformed Judaism also allows nonbelievers
to attend their worship services in synagogues. They have no requirement of headcoverings.

Nonbelievers are also permitted to at-

tend Christian worship services (see 1 Cor
14:23). This is one of Christianity's principal
means of evangelism, with presentations of
the gospel often preached to attendees.

9.29a Muslims were instructed to wage war
against: (a) all who do not believe in Allah
and the Last Judgment, (b) all who permit
that which Allah and Muhammad had prohibited, (c) and do not practice the Islamic
faith.

9.29b *amongst those to whom the Book
has been brought* — That is, war is to be
waged against Jews and Christians (the
people of the Book), until they pay tribute
(*jizya*, the poll tax) and become as dependent "little ones" in the hands of the Muslims (see **Jihad** on pp. 616-622, and
Dhimmitude on pp. 716-717).

9.30a *The Jews say Ezra is the son of God*
— Curiously, no biblical or apocryphal documents exist to support this claim. Edward
Henry Palmer stated that "The Moslem tradition is that Ezra, after being dead 100

God fight them! how they lie!

31 They take their doctors and their monks for lords rather than God, and the Messiah the son of Mary; but they are bidden to worship but one God, there is no god but He; celebrated be His praise, from what they join with Him!

32 They desire to put out the light of God with their mouths, but God will not have it but that we should perfect His light, averse although

the misbelievers be!

33 He it is who sent His Apostle with guidance and the religion of truth, to make it prevail over every other religion, averse although idolaters may be!

34 O ye who believe! verily, many of the doctors and the monks devour the wealth of men openly, and turn folk from God's way; but those who store up gold and silver and expend it not in God's way—give

years, was raised to life, and dictated from memory the whole of the Jewish Scriptures which had been lost during the captivity, and that the Jews said he could not have done this unless he had been the son of God. There is no Jewish tradition in support of this interpretation of Muhammad, which probably was due to his own invention or to misinformation" (footnote to his translation of the Qur'an, Q 9.30.

9.30b *Christians say that the Messiah is the son of God* — This assertion by Muhammad is true. Throughout the New Testament Jesus is presented as the Son of God (see Lk 22:70; Jn 1:34, 49; 2 Cor 1:19; Gal 2:20; Eph 4:13; Heb 4:14; 1 Jn 3:8; 5:10). In addition, the Nicene-Constantinopolitan Creed states that Jesus is "begotten from the Father before all time, Light from Light, true God from true God, begotten not created, of the same essence as the Father, through whom all things came into being" (see **The Nicene-Constantinopolitan Creed** on p. 740).

9.31a *They take their doctors and their monks for lords* — Muhammad believed that Christians uncritically accepted the teachings of their theologians (doctors of theology and monks) rather than learning Scripture and

listening to God.

9.31c-32 *there is no god but He* — Muhammad insisted in an absolute monotheism which rejected the Hypostatic Union and the Doctrine of the Trinity (see **Definition of Chalcedon** on pp. 785-786 and **The Doctrine of the Trinity** on pp. 735-736). He therefore concluded that Christians desired "to put out the light of God with their mouths" (v. 32).

9.33 *make it prevail over every other religion* — This verse presents the essence of the notion of islamification. Muhammad believed that he was Allah's Apostle and that the Islamic religion is superior to all other religions. All other religions were averse (offensive) to Allah and subject to divine retribution.

9.34 Muhammad also believed that the leaders of the Church took much of the wealth of Christians for the Church's own purposes. This has resulted in a strange paradox: the church, with its vows of poverty, is enormously wealthy. This is a criticism that exists by both Christians and non-Christians alike. Yet, to its credit, the Church has used much of its wealth and investments for the betterment of mankind, exemplified by its many hospitals located around the world and its

35 them glad tidings of grievous woe!
On the day when it shall be heated
in the fire of hell, and their brows
shall be branded therewith, and
their sides and their backs!—"This
is what ye stored up for yourselves, taste then what ye stored
up!"

The four sacred months

36 Verily, the number of months with
God is twelve months in God's
Book, on the day when He created
the heavens and the earth; of these
are four that are sacred; that is the
subsisting religion. Then do not
wrong yourselves therein, but fight
the idolaters one and all, as they

fight you one and all, and know
that God is with those who fear.
37 Verily, putting off is but an increase
in misbelief to lead astray therewith those who misbelieve. They
make it lawful one year, but, they
make it unlawful another year, that
they may come to an understanding as to the number which God
has made sacred, and make lawful what God has prohibited.
Seemly to them are their evil
works, but God guides not a misbelieving people.

The call to fight
the Byzantines at Tabuk

38 O ye who believe! what ailed you

many ministries for the poor.

9.35 Muhammad believed that Christians will suffer the fires of Hell because of their false doctrines and accumulation of wealth.

9.36a *twelve months with God* — The Islamic tradition typically understands months as lunar months—not solar months. This causes the months, as understood in Islam, to migrate slowly through the four seasons of each year.

9.36b *God's Book* — That is, the decrees of Allah laid down at the beginning of time, when he created the heavens and the earth in six days.

9.36c *these are the four* — The four months set aside in Arabia for the cessation of hostility were: Muharram, Rajab, Dhu 'l -Qa'dah, and Dhu 'l-Hijjah.

9.36d *do not wrong yourselves therein* — In pre-Islamic Arabia, the tradition was to add a thirteenth month in every third, sixth,

and eighth year of every cycle of eight years as a way of stabilizing the lunar months with the solar months and eliminate the problem of the lunar months progressively migrating through the four seasons of each year. Muhammad claimed that the addition of these months was a man-made tradition that violated the original intent of Allah who established the twelve lunar months at the beginning of creation. The months of pilgrimage to the Ka'ba altar would be affected, causing people to observe the pilgrimage at the wrong times.

9.36e-37 If Muslims were to accept the man-made tradition of adding months periodically through an eight year cycle, it would result in putting off or a change in the months when warfare was permitted. Again, Muhammad was troubled by this, since it violated the prescribed time, determined by Allah at the time of creation, when warfare

when ye were told to march forth in God's way, that ye sank down heavily upon the earth? were ye content with the life of this world instead of the next? but the provision of this world's life is but a little to the next.

39 Unless ye march forth He will punish you with grievous woe, and will put in your stead a people other than you! ye cannot hurt Him at all, for God is mighty over all!

40 Unless ye help him—and God did help him, when those who misbelieved drove him forth the second of two. When they twain were in the cave; when he said to his comrade, "Grieve not, verily, God is with us;" and God sent down His shechina upon him, and aided him with hosts ye could not see, and made the word of those who misbelieved inferior, and the word of God superior; for God is mighty and wise.

41 March ye then, light and heavy, and fight strenuously with your wealth and persons in God's way; that is better for you if ye did but know!

42 Were there goods nigh at hand, and a moderate journey, they would have followed you; but the distance was too far for them; they will swear by God, "If we could, we would have gone forth with you." They destroy themselves, but God knows that they lie!

43 God forgive thee; why didst thou give them leave (to stay) until it was made manifest to thee who spake the truth—until thou mightest know the liars?

44 Those who believe in God and in the last day will not beg off from

---

was permitted.

9.38 Islamic scholars believe that this was a reference to the campaign to fight the Byzantines in northwest Arabia—the Expedition to Tabuk. The journey was long and arduous and many Muslims refused to go (see **The Expedition to Tabuk** on p. 862).

9.39 According to Muhammad, the Muslims who did not participate in a duly called Jihad were subject to divine punishment.

9.40 Muhammad attempted to motivate the Muslims to join the expedition by recounting the episode when he was banished from Mecca. He explained that only two people made that journey: himself and one other (possibly Abu Bakr). On this journey they spent time in a cave when Allah sent down upon them the *shechina* (that is, the shekinah

glory) along with a host of angels.

9.41 *fight strenuously with your wealth and persons in God's way* — That is, Muhammad admonished the Muslim people to fight jihadistically in the Cause of Allah. They were told to give of the wealth and even of their own lives in this Jihad (see Q 4.95; 5.35; 8.72, 74-75; 9.16, 44, 73, 81; 16.110; 22.78; 25.52; 29.6, 69; 47.31; 60.1; 66.9).

9.42 Muhammad claimed that Allah would not accept the excuse that the expedition to Tabuk was too long and therefore too costly.

9.43 Allah rebuked Muhammad for allowing Muslims to remain home and not fight.

9.44 *fighting strenuously with their wealth and person* — That is, engaging in Jihad jihadistically. Muhammad believed that those

fighting strenuously with their wealth and their persons; but God knows those who fear.

45 It is only those who believe not in God and in the last day who beg off from thee, and those whose hearts are in doubt, and in their doubt do hesitate.

46 Had they wished to go forth, they would have prepared for it a preparation; but God was averse from their starting off, and made them halt, and they were told to sit with those who sit.

47 Had they gone forth with you they would but have made you more trouble, and they would have hurried about amongst you craving a sedition; amongst you are some who would have listened to them; but God knows those who are unjust!

48 They used to crave sedition before and upset thy affairs; until the truth came, and God's bidding was made manifest, averse although they were.

49 Of them are some who say, "Per-

mit me, and do not try me!" Have they not fallen into the trial already, but hell shall encompass the misbelievers.

50 If good befall thee it seems ill to them; but if a calamity befall thee they say, "We had taken care for our affair before;" and they turn their backs and they are glad.

51 Say, "Nought shall befall us save what God has written down for us; He is our Lord, and upon God believers do rely!"

52 Say, "Do ye await for us aught but one of the two best things?" we too await for you that God will inflict on you torment from Himself, or by our hands. Wait then; and we with you are waiting too!

53 Say, "Expend ye in alms, whether ye will or no, it shall not be accepted from you; verily, ye are a people who do work abomination."

54 But nought hinders their alms-giving from being accepted save that they misbelieve in God and His Apostle, and perform not prayer save lazily, and expend not in alms

who fight jihadistically are motivated by the rewards given to them at the Last Judgment. They are willing to sacrifice their wealth as well as the lives (see Q 4.95; 5.35; 8.72, 74-75; 9.16, 41, 73, 81; 16.110; 22.78; 25.52; 29.6, 69; 47.31; 60.1; 66.9).
9.45 Muslims who were not convinced of the rewards of the Last Judgment were less inclined to fight jihadistically.
9.46-50 Allah did not want halfhearted soldiers participating in the military campaign.

Their lack of commitment would have jeopardized the success of the battle.
9.51 Muhammad reminded his Muslim soldiers of Allah's sovereign control. Only that which Allah decreed would befall them.
9.52 Muhammad addressed the Byzantine opponents, telling them that they would either be tortured by Allah himself, or tortured by Allah via the hands the Muslim jihadists marching towards them.
9.53-54 If the halfhearted Muslims, then,

save reluctantly.

55 Let not their wealth please you nor their children, God only wishes to torment them therewith in the life of this world, and that their souls may pass away while still they misbelieve.

56 They swear by God that, verily, they are of you; but they are not of you, and they are, a people who do stand aside in fear.

57 Could they but have found a refuge, or some caves, or a place in which to creep, they would have turned round in haste thereto.

Almsgiving

58 Of them are some who defame thee, with respect to alms; though if they are given a part thereof, they are content; and if they are

not given a part thereof, then are they in a rage.

59 Would that they were content with what God and His Apostle had brought them, and would say, "God is enough for us! God will bring us of His grace, and so will His Apostle; verily, unto God is our desire!"

60 Alms are only for the poor and needy, and those who work for them, and those whose hearts are reconciled, and those in captivity, and those in debt, and those who are on God's path, and for the wayfarer—an ordinance this from God, for God is knowing, wise.

Muhammad' critics

61 And of them are some who are by the ears with the prophet, and say,

should seek to recompense their lack of commitment with the giving of alms, they would receive no benefit.

9.55 Muhammad cursed the halfhearted Muslims and their children with torture. They would enter the afterlife as infidels, thereby assuring that they would suffer in the fires of Hell.

9.56-57 In spite of their confession of faith in Islam, Muhammad believed that they were not genuine believers.

9.58 Alms were given to Muhammad, who then distributed them according to the needs of the Muslim community. Some Muslims criticized Muhammad for the way in which he distributed the monies and goods.

9.59 Muhammad criticized them, in turn, saying that they lacked a thankful spirit.

9.60 Muhammad laid out the criteria for the eligibility of alms: (a) the poor, (b) the needy, (c) the officials entrusted in distributing alms, (d) for recent converts whose hearts have now been reconciled to Allah, (e) for the freeing of Muslims held in captivity by the enemy, (f) for those overburdened with debt, (g) for those engaged in the Cause of Allah—Jihad, and (h) for those on journeys. Islamic scholars are in general agreement that alms are to be given to needy Muslims. This explains why Islamic nations are reluctant to give financial aid to countries where major catastrophes occurred yet Muslims are not among the victims or the needy.

9.61a *He is all ear* — That is, Muhammad was gullible. He was criticized by other Mus-

"He is all ear." Say, "An ear of good for you!" he believes in God, and believes in those who do believe, and is a mercy unto such of you as believe; but those who are by the ears.

62 They swear by God to please you; but God and His Apostle are more worthy for them to please if they be believers.

63 Do they not know that whoso setteth himself against God and His Apostle, for him is the fire of hell, to dwell therein for aye? and that is mighty shame!

64 The hypocrites are cautious lest there be revealed against them a sûrah to inform them of what is in their hearts; say, "Mock ye! verily, God will bring forth that of which ye are so cautious!"

65 But if thou shouldst ask them, they will say, "We did but discuss and jest;" say, "Was it at God and His signs, and His Apostle, that ye mocked?"

66 Make no excuse! Ye have misbelieved after your faith; if we forgive one sect of you, we will torment another sect, for that they sinned!

67 The hypocrites, men and women, some of them follow others, bidding what is wrong and forbidding what is right, and they clench their hands. They forget God and He forgets them! Verily, the hypocrites, they are the doers of abomination!

68 God has promised unto the hypocrites, men and women, and unto the misbelievers, hell-fire, to dwell therein for aye; it is enough for them! God shall curse them, and theirs shall be enduring woe.

69 Ye are like those who were before

lims who noted that Muhammad believed whatever he heard.

9.61b Muhammad's response was that he was indeed trusting of his associates who share information with him.

9.62 The hypocrites swore by Allah that they had accurate information. Rather, said, Muhammad, he was more worthy than his critics.

9.63 Muhammad reminded his audience that all his opponents were destined for the fires of Hell. Their words of criticism, therefore, should not be heeded.

9.64 Muhammad also believed that his critics were worried that a surah from Allah would reveal the intentions of their hearts. Muhammad was therefore instructed to tell

them to keep on mocking him for a surah would surely be coming to denounce and condemn them.

9.65 *we did but discuss and jest* — That is, if questioned, Muhammad's critics would likely say that their criticisms of Muhammad were nothing more than idle talk. In this verse, Muhammad noted that he was not impressed with such an answer, believing the answer to be a serious discussion.

9.66-68 One of Muhammad's abiding problems were insincere Muslims within his own Islamic community. He claimed that Allah knew the intends of their hearts and would torture some (but not all). With this in mind, the hypocrites would suffer an "enduring woe" (the fires of Hell).

you. They were stronger than you and more abundant in wealth and children; they enjoyed their portion then, and ye enjoy your portion, as they enjoyed their portion before you; and ye discuss as they discussed. Their works are vain in this world and the next, and they it is who lose.

70 Did there not come to them the declaration of those who were before them? of the people of Noah and 'Âd and Thamûd, and of the people of Abraham, and the people of Midian? and of the overturned (cities)? Their apostles came to them with manifest signs; for God would not wrong them, but it was themselves they wronged.

*Characteristics
of the faithful*

71 And the believers, men and wo-

men, are some the patrons of others; they bid what is reasonable, and forbid what is wrong, and are steadfast in prayer, and give alms, and obey God and His Apostle. On these will God have mercy; verily, God is mighty, wise!

72 God has promised to believers, men and women, gardens beneath which rivers flow, to dwell therein for aye; and goodly places in the garden of Eden. But good will from God is the greatest of all! that is the mighty happiness!

*Call for Jihad against
apostate Muslims*

73 O thou prophet! strive strenuously against the misbelievers and the hypocrites, and be stern against them; for their resort is hell, and an ill journey shall it be.

74 They swear by God they did not

9.69-70 Muhammad compared the hypocrites (his opponents) to people of the distant past: (a) the people who lived in the days of Noah and perished in the Great Flood, (b) the people of Ad and Thamud who were destroyed by natural disasters, (c) the people who lived in the days of Abraham and were judged by God, (d) and the people of Midian who suffered a natural disaster (see **The Apostles** on pp. 396-398).
9.71 Muhammad contrasted his critics with those who were faithful Muslims. Faithful Muslims encouraged that which is reasonable, forbade that which was wrong, were steadfast in prayer, were generous in the giving of alms, and obeyed Allah and His Apostle.

9.72a *the garden of Eden* — That is, the gardens in Paradise (see Q 35.33, note).
9.72b *God is the greatest of all!* — In the Muslim world this phrase is called Takbir (*Allahu akbar*). See Q 34.23 note.
9.73a *strive strenuously against the misbelievers and the hypocrites* — That is, fight jihadistically against the infidels and apostates (see Q 4.95; 5.35; 8.72, 74-75; 9.16, 41, 44, 81; 16.110; 22.78; 25.52; 29.6, 69; 47.31; 60.1; 66.9).
9.73b *be stern against them* — That is, show them no mercy when fighting them.
9.74a The apostates denied speaking incorrectly. Yet, said Muhammad, by criticizing his apostleship they *de facto* spoke in-

The Expedition to Tabuk

October, 630

Following the Conquest of Mecca (January 11, 630), Muhammad heard rumors that the Byzantine Empire was planning a military campaign south into western Arabia with the intent of subduing the Muhammad and the growing Muslim threat. At the time, a large Byzantine army was protect-

ing the Palestine region against the Sassanid Empire (Persia) to the east.

According to the Ninth Surah, Muhammad organized a military expedition to travel north and meet the Byzantine challenge. He believed that the likely place of battle would be Tabuk, a small Arabian settlement in the northwestern frontiers of the Arabian Peninsula. He

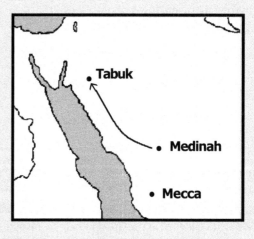

threatened any able bodied Muslim male with eternal condemnation in Hell, if he refused to participate in the expedition. As it turned out, many of Muhammad's Bedouin allies refused to go.

When the expedition reached Tabuk, Muhammad discovered, to his chagrin, that the Byzantines did not show up—and, hence, no battle took place. Some historians question the authenticity of this military campaign since Byzantine archives made no reference to the battle, or even a threat of a battle.

Tabuk was a well fourteen way stations' distance from Medinah. The settlement, which lay between Medinah and Damascus, took its name from this watering place. The Battle of Tabuk took place in the ninth year of the Hijra and it was to be the last raid in the Holy Prophet's lifetime.

—Hajjah Amina Adil, *Muhammad, the Messenger of Islam*, p. 533

When they arrived at Tabuk, they learnt that the Caesar and his allies had withdrawn their troops from the frontier and there was no enemy to fight with. Thus they won a moral victory that increased their prestige manifold and, that too, without shedding a drop of blood. In this connection, it is pertinent to point out that the general impression given by the historians of the campaigns of the Holy Prophet about the Campaign of Tabuk is not correct. They relate the event in a way as if the news of the mustering of the Roman armies near the Arabian frontier was itself false.

—Muhammad Saed Abul-Rahman,
The Meaning and Explanation of the Glorious Qur'an, p. 58

The Holy Prophet set on fire the house of Swailim, where the hypocrites used to gather for consultations in order to dissuade the people from joining the expedition to Tabuk. Likewise on his return from Tabuk, he ordered to pull down and burn the "Mosque" that had been built to serve as a cover for the hypocrites for hatching plots against the true Believers.

—Muhammad Saed Abdul-Radman, *Tafsir Ibn Kathir Juz 10*, p. 95

During the early era of Islam, a decisive campaign was led by Muhammad to Tabuk in 630 in order to challenge the Byzantines. Although no battle was fought, the expedition of some 30,000 helped to demonstrate the power of the Muslims, subjugate the local tribes, and include them into the Islamic realm.

—Sebastian Maisel and John A. Shoup,
Saudi Arabia and the Gulf Arab States Today, vol 1, p. 419

The army stayed for twenty days in Tabuk. It was evident that the rumors of danger from the Byzantines had been quite unfounded...Like the return from Badr, the return from Tabuk was fraught with sadness: another daughter of the Prophet, Umm Kulthum, had died during his absence; and this time her husband also had been absent. The Prophet prayed at her grave, and he said to Uthman that if he had had another unwedded daughter he would have given her to him in marriage.

—Martin Lings, *Muhammad*, pp. 333, 334

speak it, but they did speak the word of misbelief; and they disbelieved after they had embraced Islâm, and they designed what they could not attain and they only disapproved it because God and His Apostle had enriched them of His grace. If they turn again 'tis better for them; but if they turn their backs, God will torment them with mighty woe in this world and in the next, nor shall they have upon the earth a patron or protector.

75   And of them are some who make a treaty with God, that "If He bring us of His grace, we will give alms and we will surely be among the righteous."

76   But when He gave them of His grace they were niggardly thereof, and turned their backs and swerved aside.

77   So He caused hypocrisy to pursue them in their hearts unto the day when they shall meet Him—for that they did fail God in what they

promised Him, and for that they were liars!

78   Do they not know that God knows their secrets and their whisperings, and that God knows the unseen things?

79   Those who defame such of the believers as willingly give their alms, and such as can find nothing to give but their exertions, and who mock at them—God will mock at them, and for them is grievous woe!

80   Ask forgiveness for them or ask not forgiveness for them! if they shouldst ask forgiveness for them seventy times, yet would not God forgive them; that is because they disbelieved in God and His Apostle, for God guides not a people who work abomination.

Rebuke for half-heartedness

81   Those who were left behind rejoiced in staying behind the Apostle

correctly.

9.74b *if they turn again 'tis better for them* — That is, repentance and a return to the Apostle is better for them. If they do not repent, they would be tortured in this world as well as in the afterlife.

9.75-76 *make a treaty with God* — That is, make a commitment (a vow) with Allah. Muhammad believed that these apostates would only turn to Allah on the provision that Allah would grant them treasures from His bounty. Only then would they give alms. Yet, when Allah blessed them from His bounty, they remained committed to their

idols.

9.77-79 Muhammad warned the apostates that Allah knows all that they have done. He will therefore mock them at the Last Judgment and reward them with a "grievous woe"— the fires of Hell. This will be their fate no matter how often they plead for forgiveness.

9.80 According to Muhammad, anyone who failed to believe in Allah and Muhammad were an abomination and condemned to Hell (see Q 3.32; 4.69, 79-80, 136; 5.80-81; 8.13, 20-23; 24.47, 48, 50-52, 54; 33.33, 71; 48.9-10; 57.19; 59.4; 72.22-23, 81.19-21 and

of God, and were averse from fighting strenuously with their wealth and their persons in God's way, and said, "March not forth in the heat." Say, "The fire of hell is hotter still, if ye could but discern!"

82   Let them then laugh little, and let them weep much, as a recompense for that which they have earned!

83   But if God bring thee back to a sect of them, and they ask thee then for leave to sally forth; say, "Ye shall by no means ever sally forth with me, nor shall ye ever fight a foe with me! verily, ye were content to sit at home the first time, sit ye then now with those who stay behind."

84   Pray not for any one of them who dies, and stand not by his tomb; verily, they disbelieved in God and His Apostle and died workers of abomination!

85   Let not their wealth and their chil-

dren please you, God only wishes to torment them therewith in this world, and that their souls may pass away the while they misbelieve.

86   Whenever a sûrah is sent down to them, "Believe ye in God, and fight strenuously together with His Apostle," those of them who have the means will ask thee for leave to stay at home and say, "Let us be amongst those who stay behind."

87   They are content to be with those who are left behind. A stamp is set upon their hearts that they should not discern.

88   But the Apostle and those who believe with him are strenuous with their wealth and with their persons; these shall have good things, and these it is shall prosper.

89   God has prepared for them gardens beneath which rivers flow, to dwell therein for aye; that is the mighty

46.16, note).

9.81 *fighting strenuously with their wealth and their persons* — That is, fighting jihadistically with their wealth and their persons (see Q 4.95; 5.35; 8.72, 74-75; 9.16, 41, 44, 73; 16.110; 22.78; 25.52; 29.6, 69; 47.31; 60.1; 66.9). Muhammad believed that those who refused to join in the expedition to Tabuk (Q 9.38-57) sealed their fate to the fires of Hell.

9.83 Muhammad said that he would refuse to form an alliance and fight in any future skirmishes with anyone who refused to join the expedition to Tabuk.

9.84-85 Muhammad admonished faithful

Muslims to shun those who refused to join the expedition. He added that at the time of their deaths, they should not be honored at funeral gatherings. The reason for this treatment, he explained, is because Allah had condemned them. In the afterlife, they will suffer accordingly, "while they misbelieve" (v. 85).

9.87 *A stamp is set upon their hearts* — That is, Allah stamped the hearts of those who refused to join the expedition with unbelief, condemning them for the fires of Hell (see Q 4.155; 7.100-101; 9.93; 10.74; 16.108; 30.59; 40.35; 47.16; 63.3).

9.90 *certain desert Arabs* — Some of the

happiness!

Bedouin Arabs

90   There came certain desert Arabs that they might be excused; and those stayed behind who had called God and His Apostle liars. There shall befall those of them who misbelieved, a mighty woe.

91   For the weak, and the sick, and those who cannot find wherewith to expend in alms there is no hindrance, so they be only sincere towards God and His Apostle. There is no way against those who do well; for God is forgiving and merciful.

92   Nor against those to whom, when they came to thee that thou shouldst mount them, thou didst say, "I cannot find wherewith to

mount you," turned their backs while their eyes poured forth with tears, for grief that they could not find wherewith to expend.

93   Only is there a way against those who ask thee for leave to stay at home while they are rich; content to be with those who are left behind; on whose hearts God has set a stamp, so that they should not know.

94   They make excuses to you when ye return to them: say, "Make no excuse, we believe you not; God has informed us concerning you. God sees your works and His Apostle too!" Then shall ye be brought back unto Him who knows the unseen and the seen; and He shall inform you of that which ye have done.

95   They will adjure you by God when

Bedouin Arab tribesmen has asked Muhammad to be excused from the Tabuk campaign on the g rounds that their absence would leave their women and children defenseless in the face of attacks from enemy Bedouin Arabs. When Muham-mad rejected their explanation and demanded their participation in the campaign, they called Muhammad a liar (that is, not a spokesman for Allah). Muhammad's rejoinder was that they will suffer "a mighty woe" in the afterlife (the fires of Hell).

9.91 *the weak and the sick* — Muhammad had no criticism relegated against the weak and the sick, and those who had no means to purchase weapons for war. Provided that they remained committed to him as the Apostle of Allah, Muhammad remained com-

mitted to them.

9.92 *I cannot find wherewith to mount* — Muhammad also accepted the excuses of those who had no mounts (horses or camels) to not to participate in the campaign of Tabuk. They wept when they learned that they could not participate.

9.93-96 *God has set a stamp* — Everyone else, said Muhammad, had no legitimate excuse for not participating in the expedition. Allah placed stamps on their hearts, condemning them to unbelief and the fires of Hell. Muhammad described them as "a plague" and rejected them just as they had rejected him (see Q 4.155; 7.100-101; 9.87; 10.74; 16.108; 30.59; 40.35; 47.16; 63.3). Muhammad, however, made exceptions to this curse (see v. 118).

ye have come back to them, to turn aside from them; turn ye aside then from them; verily, they are a plague, and their resort is hell! a recompense for that which they have earned!

96 They will adjure you to be pleased with them; but if ye are pleased with them, God will not be pleased with a people who work abomination.

97 The Arabs of the desert are keener in misbelief and hypocrisy, and are more likely not to know the bounds which God has sent down to His Apostle; but God is knowing and wise.

98 And of the Arabs of the desert are some who take what they expend to be a forced loan, and they wait a turn of fortune against you; against them shall a turn of evil fortune be; for God both hears and knows.

99 And of the Arabs of the desert are some who believe in God and the last day, and who take what they expend in alms to be a means of approach to God and to the Apostle's prayers—is it not a means of approach for them? God will make them enter into His mercy; verily, God is forgiving and merciful.

100 As for the foremost in the race, the first of those who fled, and the helpers, and those who followed them in their kindness, God is well pleased with them, and they are well pleased with Him; He has prepared for them gardens beneath which rivers flow, to dwell therein for aye; that is the mighty happiness.

101 And of those who are round About you of the Arabs of the desert, some are hypocrites, and of the people of Medînah, some are stubborn in hypocrisy; thou dost not know them—we know them; we will torment them twice over; then shall they be sent off into mighty

9.97 *keener in misbelief and hypocrisy* — Muhammad rejected the excuses of most of the Bedouin Arabs.

9.98 *forced loans* — Some Bedouin Arabs believed their participation in the expedition to Tabuk was comparable to being forced to make a loan with their own monies with no hope of getting their investment returned to them.

9.99 *God will make them enter into His mercy* — Other Bedouin Arabs, however, remained faithful to Muhammad and joined the expedition. Muhammad remained grateful to them and promised them Paradise in the afterlife.

9.100 *As for the foremost in the race, the first of those who fled* — That is, those who were among the first to emigrate from Mecca to Medinah with Muhammad. Muhammad promised them Paradise in the afterlife.

9.101 Muhammad acknowledged that he was not aware of all the hypocrites in Medinah and among the Bedouin Arabs. Yet he was confident that Allah, who knows all, would bring upon them a double intensity of torture in the fires of Hell ("mighty woe") due

woe.

102 And others have confessed their sins—that they have mixed with a righteous action another evil action—haply it may be God will turn again to them; verily, God is forgiving and merciful.

103 Take from their wealth alms to cleanse and purify them thereby; and pray for them; verily, thy prayer is a repose for them; for God both hears and knows.

104 Do they not know that God accepts repentance from His servants, and takes alms; and that God is He who is easily turned and merciful.

105 And say, "Act ye;" and God and His Apostle and the believers shall see your acts, and ye shall be brought back to Him who knows

the seen and the unseen, and He shall inform you of that which ye have done.

106 And others are in hopes of God's bidding; whether He will torment them, or whether He turn again towards them; for God is knowing, wise.

The rival temple

107 And there are those who have taken to a mosque for mischief, and for misbelief, and to make a breach amongst the believers, and for an ambush for him who made war against God and His Apostle before; they surely swear, "We only wished for what was good;" but God bears witness that they are liars.

to their disloyalty.

9.102-106 Muhammad offered the blessings of Allah on all hypocrites who sincerely turned from their disloyalty and repented. True repentance would require the giving of alms. For all such people, Muhammad would pray that Allah would accept their change of heart and refrain from torturing them.

9.107 *and there are those who have taken a mosque for mischief* — The mosque of mischief was a rival religious temple (presumably Christian) built by Muhammad's enemies. Ever since his exodus from Mecca to (Yathrib) Medina Muhammad had been opposed by Abu Amir, a prominent member of the Khazraj tribe, who had embraced Christianity many years earlier and enjoyed a considerable reputation in Yathrib and among a

Christian community in Syria. He was known as "the Monk." From the very beginning of Muhammad's ministry in Yathrib, he allied himself with the Meccan and took part on their side in the Battle of Uhud.

Muhammad Asad writes, "Shortly thereafter he migrated to Syria and did all that he could to induce the Emperor of Byzantium, Heraclius, to invade Medinah and crush the Muslim community once and for all. In Medina itself, Abu Amir had some secret followers among the members of his tribe, with whom he remained in constant correspondence." In A.D. 631, he informed them that the Emperor Heraclius had agreed to send out an army against Medinah, and that large-scale preparations were being made to this effect. In anticipation of this invasion, Abu Amir asked his friends to build a church in the village of

108   Never stand up therein!—there is a mosque founded on piety from the first day: it is more right that thou shouldst stand therein—therein are men who love to be clean; for God doth love the clean.

109   Is he who has laid his foundation upon the fear of God and of His good-will better, or he who has laid his foundation upon a crumbling wall of sand, which crumbles away with him into the fire of hell?—but God guides not a people who do wrong.

110   The building which they have built will not cease to be a source of doubt in their hearts until their hearts are cut asunder; but God is knowing, wise.

Promise of Paradise

111   Verily, God hath bought of the believers their persons and their wealth, for the paradise they are to have; they shall fight in the way of God, and they shall slay and be slain: promised in truth, in the law and the gospel and the Qur'ân—and who is more faithful to His covenant than God? Be ye glad then in the covenant which ye have made with Him, for that is the mighty happiness!

Quba, in the immediate vicinity of Medinah. By doing this, they now had an alternative location in which to assemble for worship. It also obviated "the necessity of congregating in the mosque which the Prophet himself had built in the same village at the time of his arrival at Medinah" (*The Message of the Qur'an*, p. 315).

9.108 *Never stand up therein!* — Since this "mosque" was used for Christian worship, it is more correctly understood to be a church. Muhammad admonished all Muslims to never enter that mosque (church). Muslims should only enter into and worship in mosques that honored Allah and Muhammad, such as the one nearby the mosque that his opponents erected. Only then could they remain spiritually clean.

9.109 *the fires of hell* — Muhammad described the mosque (church) of his opponents as having a crumbling wall of sand and all who worshipped there as destined for the fires of Hell. He chose not to destroy the mosque (church) due to his standing conviction that any houses of worship, no matter the religion, should be honored and protected—provided that the religion be monotheistic in orientation (see Q 2.114, note).

9.110 *a source of doubt* — Muhammad looked upon this opposing mosque (church) as a source of doubt, undercutting genuine spirituality and a knowledge of Allah.

9.111a *slay and be slain* — Muhammad claimed that Paradise awaited all who fought "in the way of God." They shall slay and be slain, yet in either cause they are triumphant since they will be rewarded by Allah.

9.111b *in the law and the gospel and the Qur'an* — That is, in the Torah, the Gospel, and the Qur'an. Muhammad believed that his belief that all who fight and die in the cause of Allah shall enter Paradise is taught, not only in the Qur'an, but also in the Old and New Testaments.

Christian scholarship, however, rejects this assertion made by Muhammad. It main-

112   Those who repent, those who worship, those who praise, those who fast, those who bow down, those who adore, those who bid what is right and forbid what is wrong, and those who keep the bounds of God—glad tidings to those who believe!

Separation from idolaters

113   It is not for the prophet and those who believe to ask forgiveness for the idolaters, even though they be their kindred, after it has been made manifest to them that they are the fellows of hell.

114   Nor was Abraham's asking pardon for his father aught else but through a promise he had promised him; but when it was made manifest to him that he was an enemy to God, he cleansed himself of him; verily, Abraham was pitiful and clement.

115   Nor will God lead astray a people after He has guided them until that is made manifest to them which they have to fear; verily, God all things doth know.

116   Erily, God's is the kingdom of the heavens and the earth! He quickens and He kills! Nor have ye beside God a patron or protector.

Blessings

---

tains that such a teaching is foreign to both Old and New Testaments. In both, salvation and entrance into Heaven is consistently presented as a question of divine forgiveness based upon the rites of blood atonement. In the OT, these rites were associated with ritual animals sacrificed and their blood poured on the prescribed altar (see Lev 16, the ceremony of *Yom Kippur*). In the NT, Jesus Christ is understood as the fulfillment of Yom Kippur. The ritual of *Yom Kippur* was a mere figure pointing forward to Jesus Christ who served died on the cross and through His blood the salvation from sin is made possible (Rom 3:24-26; 5:1-11; Eph 2:13; Heb 9:14, 22; 1 Jn 1:7).

It is true, however, that in Church History, certain Christian leaders misunderstood the nature of salvation and adopted a teaching that reflected Muhammad's view. The period of the Crusades is a sad but accurate example of this. Pope Urban II proclaimed in his speech that launched the First Crusade: "All who die by the way, whether by land or by sea, or in battle against the pagans, shall have immediate remission of sins. This I grant them through the power of God with which I am invested" (speech at the Council of Clermont, 1095). As such, the pope proclaimed a false gospel.

9.112 Behavior that leads to eternal life includes: (a) repentance, (b) worship, (c) the offering of praise, (d) fasting, (e) prostrations, (f) adoration, (g) doing the right and forbidding the wrong, and (h) staying within the bounds of Allah.

9.113 Muhammad insisted that intercessory prayers on behalf of idolaters is a fruitless endeavor since they are already "the fellows of hell."

9.114 Muhammad used Abraham as an illustration of religious separation. When it was clear that his father would not turn away from idolatry, Abraham "cleansed himself from

117 God has now turned towards the prophet and those who fled with him, and towards the helpers who followed him in the hour of difficulty, after that the hearts of a part of them had well-nigh gone amiss. Then He turned unto them; verily to them He is kind and merciful:

118 —unto the three who were left behind, so that the earth with all its ample space was too strait for them, and their souls were straitened for them, and they thought that there was no refuge for them from God save unto Him. Then He turned again towards them that they might also turn; verily, God, He is easily turned and merciful!

Admonitions

119 O ye who believe! fear God and be with those who speak the truth.

120 It was not for the people of Medînah, and those around about them of the Arabs of the desert, to stay behind the Apostle of God and not

to prefer their souls to his: that is because neither thirst, nor toil, nor heat, nor hunger befell them on God's way. Nor do they stop to anger the misbelievers, nor do they get any (harm) from the enemy without a good work being written down to them; verily, God wastes not the hire of those who do well.

121 Nor do they expend in alms a small or great expense, nor do they cross a wady without it being written down to them; that God may reward them with better than that which they have done.

122 The believers should not march forth altogether; and if a troop of every division of them march not forth, it is only that they may study their religion and warn their people when they return to them, that haply they may beware.

123 O ye who believe! fight those who are near to you of the misbelievers, and let them find in you sternness; and know that God is with

---

him."

9.117 Muhammad believed that those who emigrated with him from Mecca to Medinah would be blessed by Allah since they helped him in the hour of difficulty. This stood in contrast to the many Muslims who refused to join the campaign to Tabuk.

9.118 *unto the three* — Most Islamic scholars believe that the three persons described in this verse were: Ka'b ibn Malik, Maranrah ibn ar-Rabi, and Hilal ibn Umayyah. All three abstained from the military campaign to Tabuk, which resulted in their ostracization

from Muhammad. Nevertheless, Muhammad stated that Allah forgave them their sin. The reason for their exception from the wrath of Allah, however, is not stated.

9.119-123 Muhammad reminded the Muslim people to learn the lesson of those who failed to join the military expedition to Tabuk. No matter how arduous the task, Muslims were to engage in Jihad when called upon. And when they did so, they were to fight the infidel without mercy.

9.124, 127 *whenever a surah is sent down* — Muhammad claimed that the surahs were

those who fear.

Qur'an

124   And whenever a sûrah is sent
       down, there are some of them who
       say, "Which of you has this in-
       creased in faith?" But as for those
       who believe, it does increase them
       in faith, and they shall rejoice:

125   but as for those in whose hearts is
       sickness, it only adds a plague to
       their plague, and they die misbe-
       lievers.

126   Do they not see that they are tried
       in every year once or twice? Yet
       they do not turn again, nor do they
       mind!

127   And whenever a sûrah is sent
       down, some of them look at the
       others—"Does any one see
       you?"—"When they turn away!
       God has turned their hearts, for
       that they are a people who do not
       discern.

Muhammad

128   There has come to you an apostle
       from amongst yourselves; hard for
       him to bear is it that ye commit
       iniquity; he is anxious over you
       after the believers, pitiful, compas-
       sionate.

129   But if they turn their backs, then
       say, "God is enough for me! there
       is no god but He! upon Him do I
       rely, for He is Lord of the mighty
       throne!"

Surah 49

*In the name of the merciful and compas-
sionate God.*

Reverence for Muhammad

1   O ye who believe! do not antici-
       pate God and His Apostle, but fear
       God; verily, God both hears and

"sent down" to him via the archangel Gabriel and then dictated to him (see ***The Perspicuous Book*** on pp. 178-179).

9.124-127 Muhammad believed that the
Qur'an effected people in one of two ways.
For people of faith, it would cause them to
increase in faith as they respond favorably
to the revelations. To people without faith,
it would cause them to become increasingly
hardened in their unbelief.

Surah 49. The title of this surah, *Inner
Chambers*, comes from v. 4. Its dominant
theme is social ethics, particularly the showing of due reverence and respect to Mu-

hammad. A secondary theme is the principle of loyalty that should characterize all
Muslims in their interactions with one another.

49.1, 2, 6, 11, 12 *O ye who believe* —
This phrase is mentioned five times in this
brief surah, making the point that its primary
audience was Muslim believers.

49.1 *do not anticipate God and His apostle*
— That is, do not allow your own desires to
take precedence over those of Allah and
Muhammad.

49.2-3 *raise not your voices above the voice
of the prophet* — Muhammad admonished
his Muslim followers to speak to him in a whis-

knows.

2 O ye who believe! raise not your voices above the voice of the prophet, and do not speak loud to him as ye speak loud to one another, lest your works become vain, while ye do not perceive.

3 Verily, those who lower their voice before the Apostle of God, they are those whose hearts God has proved for piety, for them is forgiveness and a mighty hire.

4 Verily, those who cry out to thee from behind the inner chambers, most of them have no sense;

5 but did they wait until thou come out to them, it were better for them—but God is forgiving, merciful.

Resolution of quarrels

6 O ye who believe! if there come to you a sinner with an information, then discriminate, lest ye fall upon a people in ignorance and on the morrow repent of what ye have done.

7 And know that among you is the Apostle of God; if he should obey you in many a matter ye would commit a sin; God has made faith beloved by you, and has made it seemly in your hearts, and has made misbelief and iniquity and rebellion hateful to you—These are the rightly directed

8 —grace from God and favour! and God is knowing, wise.

9 And if the two parties of the believers quarrel, then make peace between them; and if one of the twain outrages the other, then fight the party that has committed the outrage until it return to God's bidding; and if it do return then make

per or a muted voice. Such speaking, he claimed, demonstrated a proper sense of awe and reverence. In a related Hadith, he added: "None of you will have faith till he loves me more than his father, his children, and all mankind" (*Sahih Bukhari* 1.8.14).

49.4-5 *those who cry out to thee from behind the inner chambers* — Muhammad insisted that people were not to speak to him from across a wall while he was preoccupied in his inner chamber with one of this wives. They were to wait until he was finished and chose to come out. Anything less, he said, was an illustration of people having no sense and being disrespectful.

49.6 Muslims were not to believe in unsubstantiated gossip. The facts of the case must first be assessed. Otherwise, innocent people could be hurt or killed.

49.7 The concern was the wrongful identification of certain Muslims as apostates. If Muhammad were to join in and be part of an attack upon a people who were, in fact, innocent of wrongdoing, the sin would be greater still.

49.9-10 Muhammad admonished the Muslims who were quarreling with one another were to reconcile. Yet if reconciliation is not possible and one of the two parties is outraged by the other, then fighting is sanctioned until the erring Muslim returns "to God's bidding"—that is, authentic Islamic beliefs.

The first major test of this passage oc-

peace between them with equity, and be just; verily, God loves the just.

10   The believers are but brothers, so make peace between your two brethren and fear God, haply ye may obtain mercy!

Renouncement of ridicule and petty suspicions

11   O ye who believe! let not one class ridicule another who are perchance better than they; nor let women ridicule other women who are perchance better than they; and do not defame each other, nor call each other bad names—an ill name is iniquity after faith!

12   O ye who believe! carefully avoid suspicion; verily, some suspicion is a sin. And do not play the spy, nor backbite each other; would one of you like to eat his dead brother's flesh?—why! ye would abhor it! then fear God; verily, God is relentant, compassionate.

13   O ye folk! verily, we have created

curred approximately twenty years after the death of Muhammad. Uthman was the third caliph (successor of Muhammad) of Islam. Because he ruled unfairly—giving lucrative appointments to those in his own family and spending money for self-aggrandizement—unrest developed among those without power in the Muslim world, resulting in his assassination. Afterward, Ali ibn Talib—cousin and son-in-law to Muhammad—assumed the title as fourth caliph. But Muawiyah of the Umayyad clan also claimed the title as fourth caliph. A civil war erupted (656-661) with Ali and his Shi'ite army on one side and Muawiyah and his Sunni army on the other. The war came to an end when Ali was assassinated in 661. Muawiyah, now the undisputed fourth caliph, moved the capital of the empire to Damascus.

Upon Muawiyah's death in 680, the Shi'ite army sought revenge for Ali assassination and attempted to make Ali's son Husayn the fifth caliph. A second civil war broke out which continued for twelve years (680-692). It ended with the death of al-Husayn and, once again, the defeat of the Shi'ite army. These two civil wars left a lasting mark on the Muslim people (see **The Sunnis and the Shi'ites** on pp. 764-765). **49.11** Muhammad called for Muslims to avoid ridicule and defamation since such behavior is a sign of disrespect. This prohibition, of course, did not apply to Jews whom he called apes and pigs (see Q 2.65; 5.60; 7.165-166). **49.12** Muhammad also called for Muslims to avoid being suspicious of one another and thereby involving themselves in intrigues and espionage. Ironically, since the First Civil War and the subsequent divide of Sunnis from the Shi'ites, this prohibition of suspicion has largely gone unheeded (see Q 49.9-10, note). **49.13** Muhammad reminded the peoples of the world that their origin came from the creation of one male and female (Adam and Eve). He then made the peoples of the world into races and tribes. When placed in context with the preceding two verses, Muhammad's point was that the peoples of the world should not engage in ridicule or suspicion, based upon one's ethnic identity or tribal association.

you of male and female, and made you races and tribes that ye may know each other. Verily, the most honourable of you in the sight of God is the most pious of you; verily, God is knowing, aware!

Bedouin Arabs

14 The desert Arabs say, "We believe." Say, "Ye do not believe; but say, 'We have become Muslims;' for the faith has not entered into your hearts: but if ye obey God and His Apostle He will not defraud you of your works at all: verily, God is forgiving, compassionate!"

15 The believers are only those who believe in God and His Apostle, and then doubt not, but fight strenuously with their wealth and persons in God's cause—these are the truth-tellers!

16 Say, "Will ye teach God your religion?" when God knows what is in the heavens and what is in the earth, and God all things doth know!

17 They deem that they oblige thee by becoming Muslims. Say, "Nay! deem not that ye oblige me by your becoming Muslims! God obliges you, by directing you to the faith, if ye do speak the truth!"

18 Verily, God knows the unseen things of the heavens and the earth, and God on what ye do doth look.

49.14-15 Muhammad rejected the alleged faith of the Bedouin Arabs, claiming that they merely said that they were Muslims when, in fact, the Islamic faith had not entered their hearts. True faith, he explained, required that they obey Allah and Muhammad (see Q 3.32; 4.69, 79-80, 136; 5.80-81; 8.13, 20-23; 24.47, 48, 50-52, 54; 33.33, 71; 48.9-10; 57.19; 59.4; 72.22-23, 81.19-21 and 46.16, note), and fight strenuously (engage in jihad jihadistically) with their wealth and persons. This they had not done (e.g., the military campaign to Tabuk—Q 9.90-98; 48.11-13).

49.16-18 Muhammad was incredulous that the Bedouin Arabs believed that they could teach the true nature of God. Muhammad was also incredulous that they also believed that they did Muhammad a favor by becoming Muslims. Not so, said Muhammad.

Final Word

"**I** must say, it is as toilsome reading as I ever undertook. A wearisome confused jumble, crude, incondite; endless iterations, long-windedness, entanglement—insupportable stupidity, in short! Nothing but a sense of duty could carry any European through the Koran!"[1] So wrote Thomas Carlyle, a famous Scottish thinker of the nineteenth century.

Indeed, reading the Qur'an is a daunting task. Those who so venture typically put the book down after a few pages. It is neither arranged chronologically, in the order it was written, nor according to subject matter. Rather, with few exceptions, its one hundred fourteen surahs are organized in terms of size. It is like reading a long novel, such as *War and Peace*, with each of the chapters arranged with no internal logic other than that of size, from longest to shortest. Clearly, understanding such a novel would be an impossible undertaking.

Qur'an Revealed has been written to overcome this problem. The one hundred fourteen surahs were placed in chronological order, and supplemented with detailed notes, charts, maps and essays. With this arrangement, the Qur'an opens itself up. We are no longer dependent upon other books, radio and television news stories that offer their own interpretations. We can now think for ourselves. With this newly acquired knowledge, we can reach into at least three spheres of the Islamic faith and Muslim world.

Islam's many voices. Not all Muslims think or speak alike. Some are jihadistic; others are committed to peace. Some are eclectic, drawing from other worldviews and forming a hybrid Islam; others possess an unquestioned obedience to a pure Islam. Some have advanced degrees from Western universities and are seeking a synthesis between Islam and the West; others have similar advanced degrees yet remain opposed to the West. Some are at peace with their religion; others carry within themselves an angst of painful memories due to their previous involvement with fundamentalist Islam, an involvement that has left their souls scarred. On and on it goes.

Like the peoples of most cultures, Muslims do not march to the beat of a singular drummer. In his book *Arab Voices*, James Zogby asserts that one of the super myths associated with Islam is the assumption that all Muslims speak with one voice. If we don't hear them rightly, he adds, we will not know what they want or what they believe.

What does *Qur'an Revealed* offer? It provides a careful presentation of Islam's most sacred book, the Qur'an. It is a presentation that brings to light its historical inaccuracies and contradictions. These inaccuracies and contradictions include the way in which Abraham and Ishmael are presented, the founding of Mecca, and the early development of the Islamic religion. It also brings to light the overall theme of the Qur'an: that Allah is sovereign over the earth and will bring blessings to all who submit to him and judgment to all who refuse to submit to him. Moreover, this submission includes a reverent acknowledgement of Muhammad as the final prophet of Allah. It also clarifies its paramount vision—the islamification of the world, a struggle (a jihad) that demands great sacrifice and effort. This is not to say that the Qur'an does not contain some passages that are beautiful and sublime. Indeed it does. Still, when read in its entirety, the Qur'an presents itself as a timeless document that advocates violence and oppression upon all who refuse to submit to its demands. Knowing this helps give shape to our own voice when speaking of Islam.

Interfaith conversations. The West is committed to the practice of religious pluralism: the idea that no single religion should have a monopoly in a given culture. It has taken centuries to iron out this concept, with many wars fought in its wake. Yet, religious pluralism is a curious phenomenon. When rightly practiced, it encourages honest dialogues and inquiries between the devotees of differing religions. Honest and frank conversations are necessary, since without them suspicions and stereotypes take root and grow. Nothing is more counter-productive to the advancement of peace in a pluralistic society than to gloss over or ignore the questions people have of opposing religious traditions. In short, religious pluralism—rightly practiced—refuses to sacrifice *the pursuit of truth* on the altar of *keeping the peace*. Not only does it encourage dialogue, it welcomes people to proselytize and move from one religious tradition to another.

How does *Qur'an Revealed* contribute to our involvement in interfaith dialogues? It keeps our words centered on factual data: on the pursuit after truth. If we are to live in peace with Muslims—independent of suspicions and stereotypes—we must learn to speak courageously, honestly, and lovingly with them. In the West today, interfaith dialogues between Muslims and people of other faith traditions are not only desired, they are desperately needed. Douglas Pratt has rightly observed: "Although much has been written, and even more discussed, by both proponents of, and participants in, interreligious dialogue, yet relative to the history of interreligious encounters it could be said that the truly deep and searching dialogical task has hardly begun. And this is acutely the case with respect to the relationship between Islam and Christianity."[2]

Qur'an Revealed also helps us meet the Islamic challenge facing the West. It is no longer a secret that a large cadre of fundamentalist Muslims are committed to the islamification of the West. A senior member of the Muslim Brotherhood, for example, has written: "The *ikhwan* [Brotherhood] must understand that their work in America is a kind of grand Jihad in eliminating and destroying the Western civilization from within and 'sabotaging' its miserable house by their hands and the hands of the believers so that it is eliminated and God's religion is made victorious over all other religions."[3] We are in a culture war that may vastly redefine the West. Its challenge will only be effectively faced by a citizenry that is well informed. And, a well rounded knowledge of the Qur'an is vital to a well informed citizenry.

Evangelism. Though the Qur'an forbids Muslims from leaving Islam, with the warning of dire consequences for all who do, millions are questioning their faith and many have already set it aside. Some are public in their recantations of Islam. Most keep their apostasy private. In all cases, they are committed to the proposition that life rightly lived requires hard choices. An honest pursuit after truth demands no less.

In what respect does *Qur'an Revealed* equip us to help Muslims who are on such a spiritual journey? It is a resource, a clarification of the differences between Islam and Christianity. Muhammad opened the door to such an examination and comparison. In a number of his surahs, he made the case that the Islamic faith is superior (indeed, vastly superior) to the Christian faith. Since he opened this door, Muslims should feel free to walk through it, conduct their own examinations, and draw their own conclusions. After all, that is how we in the West address religious issues—with the freedom to rethink and reassess. When comparing Islam with Christianity, two issues come to the forefront:

- *Is Jesus, or is Jesus not, the Son of God?* Islam insists that God is one and cannot have a Son. Hence, Jesus must not be worshipped. Christianity insists that God is one, but is divided into Three Persons: God the Father, God the Son, and God the Holy Spirit. Hence, Jesus must be worshipped.

- *Is eternal salvation earned by good works, or is it offered as a free gift?* Islam insists that Paradise is the reward reserved for those who lived righteously on the earth. Hence, eternal salvation must be earned. Christianity insists that Heaven is offered to all who place their faith in Jesus Christ, the one who paid the penalty for all their sins on the cross. Hence, eternal salvation is a free gift.

Secularists, of course, could care less about such inquiries, regarding them as questions reserved for parlor games, or the like. Spiritually minded people think otherwise, that these inquiries are vastly important.

*   *   *

Speaking to his opponents, Jesus challenged them to have the courage to face the truth. The net result of such courage, he explained, is this: "Then you will know the truth, and the truth will set you free" (Jn 8:32). These provocative words from Jesus are timeless and are now directed to us. With Islam making its presence widely felt in the West, we are challenged to muster the courage to squarely face Islam—to be brought up to speed, so to speak, on its beliefs and practices. We can ill afford to remain in the dark, like ostriches with their heads buried in the sand. And, as we are brought up to speed, a groundwork will be laid for a meaningful dialogue. Our current world can only benefit from such a conversation.

---

[1] Thomas Carlyle, *On Heroes and Hero Worship*, p. 299.

[2] Douglas Pratt, *The Challenge of Islam*, p. 190.

[3] *On the General Strategic Goal for the Group in North America*, Government Exhibit 003-0085; 3:04-CR-240-G; United States of America *v.* Holy Land Foundation, et al., 2007.

Bibliography

Abd al-Qadir al-Jilani. *The Sublime Revelation,* transl. Muhtar Holland. Fort Lauderdale, Flor.: Al-Baz Publication, 1998.

Abdul-Radman, Muhammad Saed. *The Meaning and Explanation of the Glorious Qur'an.* MSA Publications, 2007.

_____. *Tasfir Ibn Kathir Juz 10.* Abdul-Radman, 2007.

Abu-Zahra, Nadia. *The Pure and Powerful: Studies in Contemporary Muslim Society.* Reading, Berkshire, UK: Ithaca Press, 1997.

Adang, Camilla. *Muslim Writers on Judaism and the Hebrew Bible.* New York: E. J. Brill, 1996.

Adil, Hajjah Amina. *Muhammad, the Messenger of Islam.* Washington, D.C.: Islamic Supreme Council of America, 2002.

Al-Ali, Ibrahim. *Filastin al-Muslimah,* London: Sept. 1996.

Al-Araby, Abdullah. *Islam: the Facade and the Facts.* Islam Review.com.

Al-Ghazali. *The Alchemy of Happiness,* transl. Claud Field. New Delhi: Kitabbhavan, 2004.

_____. *Inner Dimensions of Islamic Worship,* transl.: Muhtar Holland. Leicestershire, England: The Islamic Foundation, 1992.

_____. *Revival of Religious Learnings,* transl.: Al-Haj Maulana Fazal-ul-Karim. Lahore: Muhammad Ashraf Publishers, 2000.

Al-Ghazali, Sheikh Mohammed. *A Thematic Commentary on the Qur'an,* transl. by Ashur A. Shamis. Herndon, Virginia: International Institute of Islamic Thought, 2000.

Al-Ghazoli, Muhammad. *Christ, Muhammad and I*, transl. R. Winston Mazakis. Ontario, Calif.: Chick, 2007.

Al-Misri. *Reliance of the Traveller: A Classic Manual of Islamic Sacred Law*, ed. and transl. by Nuh Ha Mim Keller. Beltsville, Md. : Amana Publications, 1997.

Al-Qushayri, Abi Zayd. *Al Qushayri's Epistle on Sufism*, transl. Alexander D. Knysh. Reading, UK: Garnet Publishing Ltd. 2007.

Alasti, Sanaz. "Comparative Study of Stoning Punishment in the Religions of Islam and Judaism," *Justice Policy Journal*, No. 4.1, 2007.

Aldridge, Alan; Aldridge, Alan E. *Religion in the Contemporary World: a Sociological Introduction*. Malden, Mass.: Blackwell Publishers, 2000.

Ali, Ayaan Hirsi. *The Caged Virgin: An Emancipation Proclamation for Women and Islam*. New York: The Free Press, 2006.

_____. *Infidel*. New York: The Free Press, 2007.

Ali, Maulana Muhammad. *The Religion of Islam*. Dublin, Ohio: Ahmadiyya Anjuman Isha'at at Islam, 2005.

Ali, Abdullah Yusuf. *The Meaning of the Qur'an*. United Kingdom : Islamic Foundation, 2002

Alighieri, Dante. *Dante, the Divine Comedy*. New York: Cambridge University Press, 1987.

Amad, Ghulam; Saeed, Munawar Ahmed. *The Essence of Islam. The Light*, February 1990.

Amadasi, Maria Giulia; Schneider, Eugenia Equini. *Petra*. Chicago: Chicago University Press, 2002.

Amari, Rafat. *Islam: In Light of History*. Prospect Heights, Ill.: Religion Research Institute, 2004.

Anderson, Kerby. *Islam*. Eugene, Oregon: Harvest House, 2008.

Andræ, Tor. *In the Garden of Myrtles: Studies in Early Islamic Mysticism*. Albany, New York: State University of New York Press, 1987.

Armstrong, Karen. *Muhammad: A Biography of the Prophet*. San Francisco:

HarperSanFrancisco, 1992.

Asad, Muhammad. *The Message of the Qur'an*. Bristol, England: The Book Foundation, 2003.

Asbridge, Thomas. *The Crusades*. New York: HarperCollins, 2010.

Aslan, Resa. *No god but God: the Origins, Evolution, and Future of Islam*. New York: Random House, 2005.

Ata ur-Rahim, Muhammad. *Jesus, a Prophet of Islam*. London : MWH London Publishers, 1979.

Aziz, Zahid. *Islam, Peace and Tolerance*. Wembley, U.K.: Lahore Publications, 2007.

Baqir Al-Majlisi, Muhammad . *Hayat al-Qulub*. Qum: Ansariyan Publications, 2003.

Barber, Nicola. *Islamic Empires*. Chicago, Ill. : Raintree, 2005.

Baring-Gould, Sabine. *Legends of the Patriarchs and Prophets and Other Old Testament Characters*. New York: Holt & Williams, 1974.

Bell, Catherine. *Ritual: Perspectives and Dimensions*. New York: Oxford University Press, 2009.

Bell, Richard. "John of Damascus and the Controversy with Islam," *Transactions,* Glasgow University Oriental Society, 1926.

Ben-Shahar, Tal. *A Clash of Values: The Struggle for Universal Freedom*. New York: Writer's Showcase, 2002.

Beverley, James A. "Islam A Religion of Peace?" in *Christianity Today*, Jan 7, 2002.

Bianchi, Robert. *Guests of God: Pilgrimage and Politics in the Islamic World*. New York: Oxford University Press, 2004.

Boase, Abdelwahab. "Arabia" in *The Islamic Worldview*, July 1986.

Boice, James Montgomery. *Foundations of the Christian Faith*. Downers Grove, Ill.: InterVarsity Press, 1986.

Bostom, Andrew G. *The Legacy of Islamic Antisemitism: from Sacred Texts to Solemn History*.

Amherset, New York: Prometheus Books, 2008.

_____. *The Legacy of Jihad: Islamic Holy War and the Fate of Non-Muslims.* Amherset, New York: Prometheus Books, 2005.

Bowersock, Glen Warren. *Roman Arabia.* Cambridge: Harvard University Press, 1983.

Braswell, George W. *What You Need to Know About Islam and Muslims.* Nashville, Tenn.: Broadman & Holman, 2000.

Brown, Daniel W. *A New Introduction to Islam.* Malden, Mass.: Blackwell, 2004.

Burr, K. Millard and Collins, Robert O. *Alms for Jihad.* New York.: Cambridge University Press, 2006.

Busse, Heribert. *Islam, Judaism and Christianity*, transl. Allison Brown. Princeton, New Jersey: Markus Wiener Publishers, 1998.

Calvin, John. *Calvin's Commentaries: Hebrews, 1 Peter, 1 John, James, 2 Peter, and Jude.* Grand Rapids, Mich.: Baker Books, 1999.

_____. *Commentary on the Book of the Prophet Isaiah.* Grand Rapids, Mich.: Baker Books, 2003.

_____. *Commentary on the Book of Psalms.* Grand Rapids, Mich.: Eerdmans, 1949.

_____. *Commentary on Jeremiah.* Edinburgh: Banner of Truth Trust, 1989.

Caner, Emir Fethi; Caner, Ergun Mehmet. *More than a Prophet: An Insider's Response to Muslim Beliefs about Jesus and Christianity.* Grand Rapids: Kregel, 2003.

Caner, Ergun Mehmet; Caner, Emir Fethi; Land, Richard. *Unveiling Islam: An Insider's Look at Muslim Life and Beliefs.* Grand Rapids, Mich.: Kregel, 2002.

Chambers, Oswald. *Approved unto God.* London: Marshall Morgan and Scott, Ltd., 1962.

_____. *Biblical Ethics.* London: Simpkin Marshall, Ltd., 1941.

_____. *Conformed to His Image.* Newton Abbot: Oswald Chambers Publications Association, Ltd., 1991.

_____. *Disciples Indeed.* London: Marshall, Morgan & Scott, Ltd., 1955.

_____. *If Ye Shall Ask.* London: Marshall, Morgan & Scott Ltd., n.d.

_____. *The Pilgrim's Song Book.* London: Simpkin Marshall, Ltd. n.d.

_____. *Shade of His Hand.* London: Simpkin Marshall Hamilton Kent & Company, Ltd., 1924.

_____. *Studies in the Sermon on the Mount: God's Character and the Believer's Conduct.* Grand Rapids, Mich.: Discovery House Publishers, 1995.

Chayes, Sarah. *The Punishment of Virtue: Inside Afghanistan after the Taliban.* New York: Penguin Press, 2006.

Chejne, Anwar G. *The Arabic Language: Its Role in History.* Minneapolis: University of Minnesota Press, 1969.

Claus, Peter J.; Diamond, Sarah; Miller Margaret Ann. *South Asian Folklore: an Encyclopedia: Afghanistan, Bangladesh, India, Nepal, Pakistan, Sri Lanka.* New York: Routledge, 2003.

Colson, Charles; Vaughn, Ellen Santilli. *Kingdoms in Conflict.* Grand Rapids: Zondervan, 1987.

Cook, David, *Understanding Jihad.* Berkeley: University of California Press, 2005.

Corduan, Winfried. *Neighboring Faiths: A Christian Introduction to World Religions.* Downers Grove, Illinois: InterVarsity Press, 1998.

Cornell, Vincent J. *Voices of Islam.* Westport, Conn.: Praeger Publishers, 2007.

Cragg, Kenneth. *The Call of the Minaret.* New York: Oxford University Press, 1956.

_____. *Jesus and the Muslim: An Exploration.* London: G. Allen and Unwin, 1985.

Crandall, Richard. *Islam: the Enemy.* Longwood, Florida: Xulon Press, 2008.

Crone, Patricia. *Meccan Trade and the Rise of Islam.* Princeton: Princeton University Press, 1987.

Dakake, Maria Masse. "Human Contention and Divine Argument: Faith and Truth in the

Qur'anic Story of Abraham," in *Crisis, Call, and Leadership in the Abrahamic Traditions*, eds. Peter Ochs and William Stacy Johnson. New York: Palgrave Macmillan, 2009.

Darwish, Nonie. *Cruel and Usual Punishment*. Nashville: Thomas Nelson, 2008.

Dashti, Ali. *Twenty Three Years: A Study of the Prophetic Career of Mohammad*, transl.: F.R.C. Bagley. Boston.: G. Allen & Unwin, 1985.

Davidson, Linda Kay; Gitlitz, David Martin. *Pilgrimage and the Jews*. Westport, Conn.: Praeger Publishers, 2006.

Davis, Gregory M. *Religion of Peace?* Los Angeles, Calif.: World Ahead Publications, 2006.

De Pressense, "Letter dated Jan. 16, 1856," in *The Christian World: Magazine of the American and Foreign Christian Union*, 1856, vol. 7.

Denny, Frederick Mathewson. *An Introduction to Islam*. New York: Macmillan, 1993.

Dwight, Harrison Griswold. *Constantinople, Old and New*. London: Longmans, Green and Co., 1915.

El Fadel, Abou. *The Great Theft: Wrestling Islam from the Extremists*. New York: HarperOne, 2007.

Elias, Jamal J. *Islam*. Upper Saddle River, N.J.: Prentice-Hall, 1999.

El-Rouayheb, Khaled. *Before Homosexuality in the Arab-Islamic World: 1500-1800*. Chicago: University of Chicago Press, 2005.

Erickson, Millard. *Christian Theology*. Grand Rapids, Mich.: Baker Books, 1985.

Ernst, Carl W. *Words of Ecstasy in Sufism*. Albany, New York: State University of New York Press, 1985.

Espin, Orlando O.; Nickoloff, James. *An Introductory Dictionary Theology and Religious Studies*. Collegeville, Minn.: Liturgical Press, 2007.

Esposito, John. *The Islamic World: Past and Present*. New York: Oxford University Press, 2004.

_____. *What Everyone Needs to Know About Islam*. New York: Oxford University

Press, 2002.

Farah, Cesar E. *Islam: Beliefs and Observances*. Hauppauge, New York: Barron's Educational Series, 2000.

Farmer, Brian R. *Understanding Radical Islam: Medieval Ideology in the Twenty-first Century*. New York: Peter Lang, 2007.

Firestone, Reuven. *An Introduction of Islam for Jews*. Philadelphia: The Jewish Publication Society, 2008.

Flynn, Gabriel. *Yves Congar: Theologian of the Church*. Grand Rapids, Mich.: Eerdmans, 2005.

Forster, Charles. *The Historical Geography of Arabia*. London: Duncan and Malcom, 1844.

Freedman, David Noel; McClymond, Michael James. *The Rivers of Paradise: Moses, Buddha, Confucius, Jesus, and Muhammad as Religious Founders*. Grand Rapids: Eerdmans, 2001.

Fregosi, Paul. *Jihad in the West*. Amherst, New York: Prometheus Books, 1998.

Gabriel, Richard A. *Muhammad: Islam's First Great General*. Norman, Okla.: University of Oklahoma Press, 2007.

Gaiser, Adam R. *Muslim, Scholars, Soldiers: The Origin and Elaboration of the Ibadi Imamate Traditions*. New York: Oxford University Press, 2010.

Gätje, Helmut. *The Qur'an and its Exegesis: Selected Texts with Classical and Modern Muslim Interpretations*. Oxford: One World, 1996.

Geisler, Norman and Saleeb, Abdul. *Answering Islam*. Grand Rapids, Mich.: Baker Books, 2002.

George, Timothy. *Is the Father of Jesus the God of Muhammad? Understanding the Differences between Christianity and Islam*. Grand Rapids, Mich.: Zondervan, 2002.

Ghosh, Bobby. "Islamophobia: What's Behind the Protests Over Mosques?" in *Time*, Aug 30, 2010.

Glassé, Cyril. *The New Encyclopedia of Islam*. Walnut Creek, Calif.: Alta Mira Press, 2001.

Goldmann, David. *Resurgent Islam and America*. Longwood, Florida: Xulon Press, 2010.

Grady, Patrick. *Royal Canadian Jihad*. Ottawa: Global Economics, Ltd., 2005.

Graham, William A. and Kermani, Navid. "Recitation and Aesthetic Reception" in *The Cambridge Companion to the Qur'an*. New York: Cambridge University Press, 2006.

Greer, Thomas H. and Lewis, Gavin. *A Brief History of the Western World,* Belmont, Calif.: Wadsworth Thomson, 2005.

Guillaume, Alfred. *Islam*. New York: Penguin Books, 1956.

_____. *The Life of Muhammad: A Translation of Ibn Ishaq's Sirat rasul Allah*. New York: Oxford University Press, 2004.

Guthrie, Shirley C. *Christian Doctrine*. Louisville, Ken.: Westminster/John Knox Press, 1994.

Haddad, Yvonne; Esposito, John. *Islam, Gender and Social Change*. New York: Oxford University Press, 1998.

Hale, Edward Everett. *Knickerbocker Stories from the Old Dutch Days of New York*. New York: Newson & Company, 1897.

Hallaq, Wael B. *A History of Islamic Legal Theories*. New York: Cambridge University Press, 1997.

Hamlin, Christopher. *Cholera: The Biography*. New York: Oxford University Press, 2009.

Hanna, John U. *Cancer in America: the Enemy Within*. Oxford: Trafford, 2004.

Haneef, Suzanne. *What Everyone Should Know About Islam and Muslims*. Chicago: Library of Islam, 1996.

Harris, Sam. *The End of Faith: Religion, Terror, and the Future of Reason*. New York: W. W. Norton, 2004.

Hart, Michael. *From Pride to Influence: Towards a New Canadian Foreign Policy*. Vancouver: UBC Press, 2008.

Hazleton, Lesley. *After the Prophet: the Epic Story of the Shia-Sunni Split in Islam*. New York: Doubleday, 2009.

Hengel, Martin. "The Attitude of Paul to the Law in the Unknown Years between Damascus and

Antioch," in *Paul and the Mosaic Law*, ed. James D. G. Dunn. Grand Rapids, Mich.: Eerdmans, 2001.

Hesselgrave, David. *Communicating Christ Cross-Culturally.* Grand Rapids, Mich.: Zondervan, 1991.

Hewer, C. T. R. *Understanding Islam: An Introduction.* Minneapolis: Fortress Press, 2006.

Heyboer, Marvin W. *Journeys into the Heart and Heartland of Islam.* Pittsburgh, Penn.: Dorrance Publishers, 2009.

Hindson, Ed; Caner, Ergun. *The Popular Encyclopedia of Apologetics: Surveying the Evidence for the Truth of Christianity.* Eugene, Oregon: Harvest House, 2008.

Hitti, Philip Khuri. *The Origins of the Druze People and Religion.* New York: AMS Press, 1966.
_____. *Islam: A Way of Life.* Minneapolis: University of Minnesota Press, 1970.

Horne, Thomas Hartwell; John Ayre, Samuel Prideaux Tregelles. *An Introduction to the Critical Study and Knowledge of the Holy Scriptures.* London: Longman, Brown, Green, Longmans & Roberts, 1856.

Hotaling, Edward. *Islam without Illusions: Its Past, Its Present, and Its Challenges for the Future.* Syracuse, New York: Syracuse University Press, 2003.

Hudayl, Ibn. *L'Ornement des Ames*, transl. Louis Mercier, English transl. Michael J. Miller. Paris: 1939.

Hughes, Thomas Patrick. *Dictionary of Islam.* Chicago: KAZI Publications, 1994.

Hussain, Jamila. *Islam: Its law and Society.* Sydney, Australia: Federation Press, 2004.

Ibrahim, Farooq. *Answering Islam.* Http://www.answering-islam. org/Authors/Farooq_Ibrahim/ abrogation.htm.

Idriss, Mohammed; Abbinnet, Ross; Abbas, Tahir. *Honor, Violence, Women, and Islam.* New York: Routledge, 2010.

Ikeda, Daisaku; Tehranian, Majid. *Global Civilization: a Buddhistic-Islamic Dialogue.* London and New York: British Academic Press, 2003.

Infidel, The. *A Letter to Muslims: What We Don't Know About Islam.* New York: iUniverse, Inc.

2004.

Janin, Hunt. *Islamic Law: the Shari'a from Muhammad's Time to the Present.* Jefferson, N.C.: McFarland, 2007.

_____. *The Pursuit of Learning in the Islamic World: 610-2003.* Jefferson, N.C.: McFarland, 2005.

Jeffery, Arthur. *The Foreign Vocabulary of the Qur'an.* Leiden: Koninklijke Brill, 2007.

Johnson, William Stacy. *John Calvin: Reformer for the 21st Century.* Louisville, Ky: Westminster John Knox Press, 2009.

Jonnson, David J. *The Clash of Ideologies: the Making of the Christian and Islamic Worlds.* Longwood, Florida: Xulon Press, 2006.

Kathir, Ibn. *Tafsir ibn Kathir.* Riyadh: Darussalam, 2000.

Keating, Sandra Toenies; Takriti, Habib ibn Khidmah. *Defending the "People of Truth" in the Early Islamic Period: the Christian Apologies of Abu Raitah.* Boston: Brill, 2006.

Kelly, Marjorie. *Islam: the Religious and Political Life of a World Community.* New York: Praeger, 1984.

Kerry, Mark. *Tigers of the Tigris.* Indianapolis: Dog Ear Publications, 2008.

Khaldun, Ibn. *The Muqaddimah: An Introduction to History*, transl. Franz Rosenthal. Princeton: Princeton University Press, 1967.

Khan, Arshad. *Islam 101: Principles and Practice.* San Jose, Calif.: Khan Consulting and Publications, 2006.

_____. *Islam, Muslims, and America: Understanding the Basis of Their Conflict.* New York: Algora Publishers, 2003.

Khan, M. Q. "The Influence of Arabic Poetry on Dante's *The Divine Comedy,*" in *Widening Horizons: Essays in Honour of Professor Mohit K. Ray.* New Delhi: Sarup & Sons, 2005.

Khosrokhavar, Farhad. *Inside Jihadism: Understanding Jihadi Movements Worldwide.* Boulder, Colorado: Paradigm Publishers, 2009.

Kramer, Samuel Noah. *The Sumerians: Their History, Culture, and Character*. Chicago: The University of Chicago Press, 1971.

Küng, Hans. *Christianity and World Religions: Paths to Dialogue with Islam, Hinduism, and Buddhism*, transl. Peter Heinegg. New York: Maryknoll, 1993.

_____. *Islam: Past, Present & Future,* transl. John Bowden. Oxford: Oneworld Publications, 2007.

Kurkjian, Vahan M. *A History of Armenia*. New York: Armenian General Benevolent Union, 1958.

Lagassé, Paul, ed. *The Columbia Encyclopedia*, sixth ed. New York: Columbia University Press, 2000.

Lalljee, Yousuf N. *Know Your Islam*. Elmhurst, New York: Tahrike Tarsile, 1990.

Lammens, Henri. *Islam: Beliefs and Institutions,* New York: Routledge, 2008.

Lewis, Bernard. *The Crisis of Islam*. New York: The Modern Library, 2003.

Lewis, C. S. *Christian Reflections*. Ed. by Walter Hooper. Grand Rapids, Mich.: Eerdmans, 1967.

_____. *Letters of C. S. Lewis*. Ed. W. H. Lewis. New York: Harcourt Brace Jovanovich, 1966.

_____. *Letters of C. S. Lewis to Arthur Greeves (1914-1963)*. Ed. by Walter Hooper. New York: Collier/Macmillan, 1986.

_____. *Letters to Malcolm: Chiefly on Prayer.* New York: Harcourt Brace Jovanovich, 1964.

_____. *Mere Christianity*. New York: Macmillan, 1952.

_____. *Screwtape Letters*. New York: Macmillan, 1982.

_____. *The Weight of Glory and Other Addresses*, revised and expanded edition. New York; Macmillan, 1980.

Lings, Martin. *Muhammad: His Life Based Upon the Earliest Sources*. Rochester, Vermont:

Inner Traditions, 2006.

Livingstone, David M. *The Dying God: the Hidden History of Western Civilization.* Lincoln, Neb.: Writers Club Press, 2002.

Love, Rick. *Muslims, Magic, and the Kingdom of God: Church Planting Among Folk Muslims.* Pasadena, Calif.: William Carey Library, 2000.

Lutzer, Erwin. *Christ Among other gods.* Chicago: Moody Books, 1994.

MacLachlan, Ian. *Kill and Chill: Restructuring Canada's Beef Commodity Chain.* Toronto: University of Toronto Press, 2001.

Malik, S. K. *The Quranic Concept of War.* Lahore: Wajidalis, 1979.

Manji, Irshad. *The Trouble with Islam Today.* New York: St. Martin's Griffin, 2005.

Macmichael, Harold Alfred. *A History of the Arabs in the Sudan.* London: Cass, 1967.

Magda, Ksenija. *Paul's Territoriality and Mission Strategy: Searching for the Geographical Awareness Paradigm behind Romans.* Tübingen, Germany : Mohr Siebeck, 2009.

Maisel, Sebastian; Shoup, John A. *Saudi Arabia and the Gulf Arab States Today.* Westport, Conn.: Greenwood Press, 2009.

Mallouhi, Christine A. *Waging Peace on Islam.* Downers Grove, Illinois: InterVarsity Press, 2000.

Martin, Richard C. *Encyclopedia of Islam and the Muslim World.* Farmington Hills, Mich.: The Gale Group, 2003.

Maududi, Syed Abul. *Commentary on the Qur'an.* Http://www.islamicity.com/mosque/quran/maududi.

_____. "Fallacy of Rationalism," in *Modernist and Fundamentalist Debates in Islam: A Reader,* eds. Mansoor Moaddel and Kamran Talattof. New York: Palgrave Macmillan, 2002.

_____. *The Islamic Law and Constitution,* transl. Khurshid Ahwad. Lahore, Pakistan: Islamic Publications, Ltd., 1980.

McAuliffe, Jane Dammen, ed. *The Cambridge Companion to the Qur'an.* New York: Cambridge University Press, 2006.

_____. *The Encyclopedia of the Qur'an.* Boston: Koninklijke Brill, 2003.

McCullar, Michael. *A Christian's Guide to Islam.* Macon, Georgia: Smyth & Helwys, 2008.

McGrath, Alister E. *Christian Theology: An Introduction.* Cambridge, Mass.: Blackwell, 1995.

_____. *I Believe: Understanding and Applying the Apostles' Creed.* Grand Rapids, Mich.: Zondervan, 1991.

_____. *Understanding Jesus.* Grand Rapids, Mich.: Academie Books, 1990.

Mead, Larry; Sagar, David. *Fundamentals of Ethics.* Amsterdam: CIMA/Elsevier, 2006.

Michon, Jean-Louis. *Introduction to Traditional Islam Illustrated: Foundations, Art, and Spirituality.* Bloomington, Indiana: World Wisdom, 2008.

Migliore, Daniel L. *Faith Seeking Understanding: An Introduction to Christian Theology.* Grand Rapids, Mich.: Eerdmans, 1991.

Milton-Edwards, Beverley. *Islam and Politics in the Contemporary World.* Malden, Mass.: Polity Press, 2004.

Moghissi, Haideh. *Women and Islam: Criticial Concepts in Sociology.* Abingdon: Routledge, 2005.

Morgan, Diane. *Essential Islam: A Comprehensive Guide to Belief and Practice.* Santa Barbara, Calif.: Praeger, 2010.

Moses, Jonathon Wayne. *International Migration: Globalization's Last Frontier.* New York: Palgrave Macmillan, 2006.

Muir, William. *The Life of Mohammad from Original Sources.* Edinburgh: J. Grant, 1923.

Murata, Sachiko; Chittick, William C. *The Vision of Islam.* New York: Paragon House, 1994.

Musk, Bill A. *The Unseen Face of Islam: Sharing the Gospel with Ordinary Muslims at Street Level.* Grand Rapids, Mich.: Monarch Books, 2004.

Nadvi, Syed Muzaffar Uddin. *A Geographical History of the Qur'an*. Lahore: Ashraf, 1974.

Neall, Beatrice S. *Outreach to Judaism*. Http://www.outreachtojudaism.com/05.html.

Neuman, Jake. *God of Moral Perfection*. East Sussex: Gardner Books, 2009.

Neusner, Jacob; Sonn, Tamara. *Comparing Religions through Law: Judaism and Islam*. London: Routledge, 1999.

_____. *Judaism and Islam in Practice*. New York: Routledge, 2000.

Nieuwenhuijze, Christoffel. *The Lifestyles of Islam: Recourse to Classicism Need of Realism*. Leiden: E. J. Brill, 1985.

Nigosian, Solomon Alexander. *Islam: Its History, Teaching, and Practices*. Bloomington, Indiana: Indiana University Press, 2004.

Noll, Mark A. *Turning Points: Decisive Moments in the History of Christianity*. Grand Rapids: Baker Book House, 2000.

Nomani, Asra Q. *Standing Alone: An American Woman's Struggle for the Soul of Islam*. New York: HarperSanFrancisco, 2006.

Nydell, Margaret Kleffner. *Understanding Arabs*. Yarmouth, Maine: Intercultural Press, 1987.

Orwell, George. *Nineteen Eighty-Four*. New York: Harcourt Brace and Company, 1983.

Parsley, Rod. *Culturally Incorrect: How Clashing Worldviews Affect Your Future*. Nashville: Thomas Nelson, 2007.

Partner, Peter. *God of Battles: Holy Wars of Christianity and Islam*. Princeton, New Jersey: Princeton University Press, 1998.

Patterson, Margot. *Islam Considered: a Christian View*. Collegeville, Minn.: Liturgical Press, 2008.

Paz, Reuven. "Global Jihad and WMD" *in The Hudson Institute*. Sept. 12, 2005.

Perlmann, Moshe, ed. *The History of al-Tabari*. Albany, New York: State University of New York Press, 1987.

Peters, Dorothy M. *Noah Traditions in the Dead Sea Scrolls: Conversations and Controversies of Antiquity.* Atlanta: Society of Biblical Literature, 2008.

Peters, Francis E. *Mecca: A Literary History of the Muslim Holy Land.* Princeton: Princeton University Press, 1994.

_____. *Monotheists: the Peoples of God.* Princeton: Princeton University Press, 2003.

_____. *A Reader on Classical Islam.* Princeton: Princeton University Press, 1994.

Phares, Walid. *Future Jihad.* New York: Palgrave, 2005.

Phipps, William E. *Muhammad and Jesus: A Comparison of the Prophets and Their Teachings.* New York: Continuum, 1996.

Pinault, David. *The Shiites: Ritual and Popular Piety in a Muslim Community.* New York: St. Martin's Press, 1992.

Pratt, Douglas. *The Challenge of Islam: Encounters in Interfaith Dialogue.* Burlington, Vermont: Ashgate, 2005.

Rafiabadi, Hamid Naseem. *Challenges to Religions and Islam.* New Delhi: Sarup & Sons, 2007.

_____. *World Religions and Islam: A Critical Study.* New Delhi: Sarup & Sons, 2003.

Rahman, S. A. *Punishment of Apostasy in Islam.* Lahore: Institute of Islamic Culture, 1972.

Rawshandil, Jalil and Chadha, Sharon. *Jihad and International Security.* New York: Palgrave Macmillan, 2006.

Renan, Ernest. "Muhammad and the Origins of Islam," in *The Quest for the Historical Muhammad*, ed. Ibn Warraq. Amherst, N.Y.: Prometheus Books, 2000.

Renard, John. *Windows on the House of Islam: Muslim Sources on Spirituality and Religious Life.* Berkeley: University of California Press, 1998.

Rhodes, Ron. *The 10 Things You Need to Know About Islam.* Eugene, Oregon: Harvest House, 2007.

Rhouni, Raja. *Secular and Islamic Feminist Critiques in the Work of Fatima Mernissi.* Boston: Brill, 2010.

Ritmeyer, Leen; Ritmeyer, Kathleen. *Secrets of Jerusalem's Temple Mount*. Washington, D.C.: Biblical Archeology Society, 2006.

Robinson, Francis. *The Cambridge Illustrated History of the Islamic World*. New York: Cambridge University Press, 1996.

Rodinson, Maxime. *Muhammad: Prophet of Islam*. New York: I. B. Tauris, 2002.

Rosenberg, Joel. *Inside the Revolution*. Wheaton: Tyndale House, 2009.

Rubin, Uri. "Muhammad's Message in Mecca: Warnings, Signs, and Miracles," in *The Cambridge Companion to Muhammad*, ed. Jonathan E. Brockopp. New York: Cambridge University Press, 2010.

Rush, John A. *Failed God: Fractured Myth in a Fragile World*. Berkeley, Calif.: North Atlantic Books, 2008.

Ruthven, Malise. *Islam in the World*. New York: Oxford University Press, 2000.

Sa'd, Ibn. *Kitab Al-Tabaqat Al-Kabir*, transl. S. Moninul Haq. New Delhi, India: Kitab Bhavan, 1990.

Sadat, Jihan. *My Hope for Peace*. New York: Free Press, 2009.

Safi, Omid. *Memories of Muhammad: Why the Prophet Matters*. New York: HarperOne, 2010.

Sahas, Daniel J. *John of Damascus on Islam*. Leiden: Brill, 1972.

Salmi, Ralph H.; Majul, Cesar Adib; Tanham, George K. *Islam and Conflict Resolution*. Lanham, Maryland: University of America Press, 1998.

Sana, Ali. *Understanding Muhammad: A Psychobiography of Allah's Prophet*. Faith Freedom Publishing, 2008.

Santosuosso, Antonio. *Barbarians, Marauders, and Infidels: the Ways of Medieval Warfare*. Oxford: Westview Press, 2004.

Schenk, Richard. "Concluding Discussion..." *Progress, Apocalypse, and Completion of History and Life after Death of the Human Person in the World Religion*, ed. Peter Koslowski. Dordrecht: Kluwer Academic, 2002.

Schwartz, Stephen. *The Two Faces of Islam: The House of Sa'ud from Tradition to Terror.* New York: Doubleday, 2002.

Schweiker, William. *Blackwell Companion to Religious Ethics.* Malden, Mass.: Blackwell Publishing, 2005.

Schulewitz, Malka Hillel. *The Forgotten Millions: the Modern Jewish Exodus from Arab Lands.* New York: Cassell, 1999.

Shaltout, Mahmud. "Islamic Beliefs and Code of Law" in *Islam, the Straight Path: Islam Interpreted by Muslims*, ed. Kenneth W. Morgan. Delhi: Motilal Banarsidass, 1987.

Smith, Abdullah, *Genesis 1:26 Reinterpreted.* Http://www.answering-christianity.com.

Smith, George. *Short History of Christian Missions.* Edinburgh: T & T Clark, 1886.

Smith, Mark S. *The Memoirs of God: History, Memory, and the Experience of the Divine in Ancient Israel.* Minneapolis: Fortress Press, 2004.

Solomon, Sam. "Challenges from Islam" in *Beyond Opinion: Living the Faith We Defend*, ed. Ravi Zacharias. Nashville, Tenn.: Thomas Nelson, 2007.

Spaulding, Amy E. *The Wisdom of Storytelling in an Information Age.* Lanham, Md: Scarecrow Press, 2004.

Spencer, Robert. *Muhammad: Founder of the World's Most Intolerant Religion.* Washington, D.C.: Regnery Press, 2006.

_____. *Onward Muslim Soldiers.* Washington, D.C.: Regnery Press, 2003.

_____. *The Politically Incorrect Guide to Islam and the Crusades.* Washington, D.C. Regnery Publishing, 2005.

_____. *The Truth About Muhammad.* Washington, D.C.: Regnery Press, 2006.

Stalker, Peter. *The Work of Strangers: A Survey of International Labour Migration.* Geneva: International Labor Office, 1994.

Stannard, Russell. *God for the 21st Century.* Philadelphia: Templeton Foundation Press, 2000.

Stedman, Ray. *From Guilt to Glory.* Waco: Word Books, 1978.

Stobart, James William Hampson. *Islam and Its Founder*, New Dehli: Uppal, 1989.

Stoddard, Lothrop. *The New World of Islam.* East Sussex: Gardner Books, 2007.

Stott, John R. W. *The Authentic Jesus.* Downers Grove., Ill.: InterVarsity Press, 1985.

_____. *Baptism and Fullness.* Downers Grove., Ill.: InterVarsity Press, 1975.

_____. *Basic Christianity.* Grand Rapids, Mich.: Eerdmans, 1971.

_____. *Believing and Obeying Jesus Christ.* Downers Grove., Ill.: InterVarsity Press, 1980.

_____. *Between Two Worlds.* Grand Rapids, Mich.: Eerdmans, 1981.

_____. *Christ the Controversialist.* Downers Grove., Ill.: InterVarsity Press, 1970.

_____. *Christian Basics.* Grand Rapids, Mich.: Baker, 1991.

_____. *Christian Mission in the Modern World.* Downers Grove, Ill.: InterVarsity Press, 1975.

_____. "A Christian Response to Good and Evil" in *Perspectives on Peacemaking*, ed. J. A. Bernbaum. Ventura: Regal Books, 1984.

_____. *The Contemporary Christian.* Downers Grove, Ill.: InterVarsity Press, 1992.

_____. *The Cross of Christ.* Downers Grove, Ill.: InterVarsity Press, 1986.

_____. *Culture and the Bible.* Downers Grove, Ill.: InterVarsity Press, 1979.

_____. *The Letters of John.* Grand Rapids, Mich.: Eerdmans, 1988.

_____. *Our Guilty Silence.* Grand Rapids, Mich.: Eerdmans, 1969.

_____. *The Message of Ephesians.* Downers Grove, Ill.: InterVarsity Press, 1979.

_____. *The Message of Galatians.* Downers Grove, Ill.: InterVarsity Press, 1968.

_____. *The Message of the Sermon on the Mount.* Downers Grove., Ill.: InterVarsity Press, 1978.

_____. *Motives and Methods in Evangelism.* Downers Grove, Ill.: InterVarsity Press, 1967.

_____. *The Spirit, the Church, and the World.* Downers Grove., Ill.: InterVarsity Press, 1990.

_____. *The Uniqueness of Jesus Christ.* Chicago: Chicago Sunday Evening TV Club, 1978. Transcript of television broadcast.

Strauch, Samel. *Biography of the Prophet.* Riyadh: Darussalam, 2006.

Stetkevych, Suzanne Pinckney. *Early Islamic Poetry and Poetics.* Hampshire, England: Ashgate Variorum, 2009.

Swartley, Keith E. *Encountering the World of Islam.* Waynesboro, Georgia: Authentic Media, 2005.

Tabataba'i, Muhammad; al-Tabataba'i, Muhammad H.; Nasr, Seyyed Hossein. *Shi'ite Islam.* Albany, N.Y.: State University of New York Press, 1977.

Tabor, James D. *The Jesus Dynasty: the Hidden History of Jesus, His Royal Family, and the Birth of Christianity.* New York: Simon & Schuster, 2006.

Taylor, Jane. *Petra and the Lost Kingdom of the Nabataeans.* Cambridge: Harvard University Press, 2002.

Tisdall, William St. Clair. *The Original Sources of the Qur'an.* London: Society for Promoting Christian Knowledge, 1911.

Turner, Colin. *Islam: the Basics.* New York: Routledge, 2006.

_____. *Islam without Allah? The Rise of Religious Externalism in Safavid Iran.* Richmond, Surrey: Curzon, 2000.

Turner, Patricia and Coulter, Charles Russell. *Dictionary of Ancient Deities.* New York: Oxford University Press, 2001.

Uhlman, Kristine. "Overview of Shari'a and Prevalent Customs in Islamic Societies—Divorce and Child Custody," *California State Bar,* Winter 2004.

Vertigans, Stephen. *Islamic Roots and Resurgence in Turkey: Understanding and Explaining the Muslim Resurgence.* Westport, Conn.: Praeger Publishers, 2003.

Vuckovic, Brooke Olson. *Heavenly Journeys, Earthly Concerns: The Legacy of the Mir'raj in the Formation of Islam*. New York: Routledge, 2005.

Walsh, William Shepard. *Heroes and Heroines of Fiction*. Detroit: Gale Research Company, 1966.

Walvoord, John. "The Literal View" in *Four Views on Hell*, ed. William V. Crockett. Grand Rapids, Mich.: Zondervan, 1996.

Warraq, Ibn. *Leaving Islam: Apostates Speak Out*. Amherst, New York: Prometheus Books, 2003.

_____. *The Quest for the Historical Muhammad*. Amherst, New York: Prometheus Books, 2000.

Wario, Hussein Hajji. *Cracks in the Crescent*. Grandville, Mich.: Wario, 2009.

Weber, Max; Roth, Guenther; Wittich, Claus. *Economy and Society: an Outline of Interpretative Sociology*. New York: Bedminster Press, 1968.

Wensinck, Arent J. *The Muslim Creed: Its Genesis and Historical Development*. London: Frank Cass, 1965.

Werthmuller, Kurt J. *Coptic Identity and Ayyubid Politics in Egypt, 1218-1250*. New York: American University in Cairo Press, 2010.

West, Diana. *The Death of the Grown-Up: How America's Arrested Development is Bringing Down Western Civilization*. New York: St. Martin's Press, 2007.

Wherry, Elwood Morris; Sale, George. *A Comprehensive Commentary on the Qur'an*. New York: AMS Press, 1975.

Wigoder, Geoffrey, ed. *The New Standard Jewish Encyclopedia*. New York: Facts on File, 1992.

Wikan, Unni. *In Honor of Fadime: Murder and Shame*. Chicago: University of Chicago Press, 2008.

Williams, George; Willis, Robert. *The Holy City: Historical, Topographical, and Antiquarian Notices of Jerusalem*. London: J. W. Parker, 1849.

Wilson, Peter Lamborn. *Scandal: Essays in Islamic Heresies*. Brooklyn: Autonomedia, 1988.

Wolfe, Michael, ed. *Taking Back Islam: American Muslims Reclaim Their Faith.* Emmaus, Penn.: Rodale, 2002.

Yancey, Philip. *What's So Amazing About Grace?* Grand Rapids, Mich.: Zondervan, 1997.

Yazbeck, Yvonne; Esposito, John L. *Islam, Gender and Social Change.* New York: Oxford University Press, 1998.

Ye'or, Bat. *Islam and Dhimmitude: Where Civilizations Collide.* Madison, New Jersey: Fairleigh Dickinson University Press, 2002.

Yousef, Mosab Hassan. *Son of Hamas.* Wheaton: Salt River, 2010.

Zacharias, Ravi. *Beyond Opinion: Living the Faith We Defend.* Nashville: Thomas Nelson, 2007.

_____. *Jesus Among Other Gods: the Absolute Claims of the Christian Message.* Nashville: Word, 2000.

Zarrinkub, Abd al-Husain. "The Arab Conquest of Iran and Its Aftermath" in *The Cambridge History of Iran.* Cambridge: Cambridge University Press, 1991.

Zeitlin, Irving M. *The Historical Muhammad.* Cambridge, UK: Polity Press, 2007.

Zogby, James. *Arab Voices.* New York: Palgrave Macmillan, 2010.

Zwemer, Samuel Marinus. *The Influence of Animism on Islam: an Account of Popular Superstitions.* New York: Macmillan, 1920.

Ancient Literature

Al-Tirmidhi, Abu. *Jamil' at-Tirmidhi*, transl. Abu Khaliyl. Riyadh: Darussalam, 2007.

Ancient Christian Commentary: Old Testament—Psalm 51-150. Ed. Thomas C. Oden. Downers Grove, Ill.: InterVarsity Press, 2007.

The Ante-Nicene Fathers, "The Apocryphal New Testament," vol. 8, transl. Alexander Walker;

eds. Alexander Roberts, James Donaldson, and A. Cleveland Coxe. Buffalo, N.Y.: Christian Literature Publishing, Co., 1886; reprinted in 1999.

The Aramaic Bible, vol. 18, *The Two Targums of Esther,* transl. Bernard Grossfeld. Collegeville, Minn.: The Liturgical Press, 1987.

The Dead Sea Scrolls Bible, transl.: Martin Abegg, Jr., Peter Flint, and Eugene Ulrich. San Francisco: HarperSanFrancisco, 1999.

Epistle on Sufism. Ibn Abi Zayd al-Qushayri, transl. Alexander D. Knysh and Muhammad S. Eissa. Reading, UK: Garnet Publications, 2007.

Eratosthenes' Geography, fragments collected and translated by Duane W. Roller. Princeton, N.J.: Princeton University Press, 2010.

The Fathers of the Church, vol. 37, "The Writings of John of Damascus," transl.: Frederic H. Chase. New York: The Fathers of the Church Publications, 1958.

The Geography of Strabo, transl. Horace Leonard Jones. Cambridge, Mass.: Harvard University Press, 1969.

Gospel of Nicodemus, Willis Barnstone, ed., transl.: R. McL. Wilson in *The Other Bible*. San Francisco: HarperSanFrancisco, 2005.

Gregory of Tours: Glory of the Martyrs. transl. Raymond Van Dam. Liverpool: Liverpool University Press, 1988.

Herodotus. *The Histories*, ed. George Stade, transl. G. C. Macaulay. New York: Barnes & Noble Classics, 1991.

Jerusalem Talmud, transl.: Heinrich W Guggenheimer. Berlin: Walter DeGruyter, 2010.

Kitab al-Asnam. *The Book of Idols*, transl. Hisham ibn-al-Kalbi. Princeton University Press, 1952.

The Laws of Chametz and Matza, in the Mishnah Torah by Maimonides, transl. Eliyahu Touger. New York: Maznaim Publishers, 1987.

Leith, John H. *Creeds of the Churches: A Reader in Christian Doctrine, from the Bible to the Present.* Atlanta: John Knox Press, 1982.

Midrash Rabbah, transl.: H. Freedman and Maurice Simon. London: Soncino Press, 1939.

Midrash Tanhuma—Yelammedenu: an English Translation of Genesis and Exodus from the Printed Version of Tanuma—Yelammendenu with an Introduction, Notes, and Indexes. Samuel A. Berman. Hoboken, New Jersey: KTAV Publishing House, Inc. 1996.

The Mishnah, transl. Herbert Danby. New York: Oxford University Press. 1983.

The Old Testament Pseudepigrapha, ed. James H. Charlesworth. New York: Doubleday, 1985.

The Other Bible: Gnostic Gospels, Dead Sea Scrolls, Visionary Wisdom Texts, Christian Apocrypha, Jewish Pseudepigrapha, Kabbalah. Ed.: Willis Barnstone. San Francisco: HarperSanFrancisco, 2005.

The Periplus of the Erythraean Sea: Travel and Trade in the Indian Ocean by a Merchant of the First Century, ed. and transl. Wilfred H. Schoff. London: Longmans, Green, and Co., 1912.

Pliny the Elder. *Natural History*, ed. E. H. Warmington, transl. H. Rackham. Cambridge, Mass.: Harvard University Press, 1967.

The Romance of Alexander the Great, ed. Albert Murgrdich Wolohojian. New York: Columbia University Press, 1969.

Tractate Sanhedrin: Mishnah and Tosefta, transl. Herbert Danby. London: Society for Promoting Christian Knowledge, 1919.

Tafsir al-Jalalayn. Jalal al-Din Muhammad ibn Ahmad Mahalli, Suyuti, Feras Hamza, Mu'assasat Al al-Bayt lil-Fikr al-Islami. Louisville, Ky: Fons Vitae, 2008.

Index

Benayahu, son of Yehoyada 317

Benjamin, son of Jacob 375, 376

Beverley, James A. 727

Bianchi, Robert R. (1945-) 482

Big Dog Constellation (Canis Major) 140

Blessed Night, the 72, 214, 490

Boase, Abdelwahab 637

Boice, James Montgomery (1938-2000) 399, 427, 584

book in Allah's right hand 99, 121, 189, 499

book in Allah's left hand 189

booty 58, 676, 680, 681, 683, 692, 697, 796, 811, 829, 833, 834

Bostom, Andrew G. 566, 623, 717

Bouma, Gary D. 824

Bowersox, Gary W. 34

Braswell, Jr., George W. 117, 205, 670, 724

Buddha, the 595

Buraq, the 33, 489, 490, 502, 503

burning bush, the 166, 167, 233, 308, 350, 448, 449, 451

burqa(s) and *hijab(s)* 794, 816

Bush, George W. (1946-) 725, 727

Busse, Heribert 670

Byzantine Empire, the 27, 30, 34, 41, 66, 225, 227, 248, 276, 574, 619, 764, 842, 856, 857, 858, 862, 863

Caiaphas (Hebrew high priest) 285, 775

Cain 715, 719, 726

Calvin, John (1509-1562) 53, 139, 141, 264, 266, 349

Caner, Emir Fethi 286, 659, 727, 824

Caner, Ergun Mehmet (1966-) 286, 659, 727, 824

Cassiodorus (490-583) 561

cavalier disinterest 302, 349, 421, 422, 541

cave of Machpelah, the 33

Chambers, Oswald (1874-1917) 51, 157, 426, 537, 578, 669, 670

Chayes, Sarah (1962-) 772

Chejne, Anwar G. 153

Chittick, William C. 61, 171

Christians, cursed of Allah 604

Claus, Peter J. 125

clitoridectomy 611

Cockburn, Patrick (1950-) 766

concubine(s) 112, 457, 746, 750, 794, 815, 824, 839, 847

Congar, Yves (1904-1995) 741

Conquest of Mecca, the (630) 627, 819, 821, 828, 831, 835, 836, 842, 850, 862, **Summary Essay 835-836**

Constantine, Emperor (272-337) 276, 670

Cook, David (1966-) 54, 622

Cornell, Vincent J. 180

Council of Carthage, the (418) 160

Council of Chalcedon, the (451) 785, 786

Council of Constantinople, the (381) 740

Council of Ephesus, the (431) 160

Council of Florence (1438-1445) 650

Council of Nicaea (325) 740

Council of Trent (1545-1563) 650

cowardice 633, 634, 676, 683, 684, 758, 807, 833

Cragg, Kenneth (1913-) 57, 264, 266, 612, 670, 827

Crandall, Richard 71

Creed of the Wandering Aramean, the 59

Crone, Patricia (1945-) 32, 34

crucifixion, the practice of 353, 371, 557, 558, 592

crucifixion of Jesus 283, 657, 745, 777, 843

Crusades, Crusaders, the 53, 276, 397, 398, 622, 718, 870,

Damascus, city of 29, 151, 225, 247, 418, 423, 863, 874

Dante Alighieri (1265-1321) 65, 82

Dar al-Harb (the House of War) 574, 618, 619, 623

Dar al-Islam (the House of Peace) 574, 618, 717, 718

Robert Greer is available for speaking engagements and personal appearances. For more information contact:

Robert Greer
C/O Advantage Books
PO Box 160847
Altamonte Springs, FL 32779

info@ advbooks.com

To purchase additional copies of this book or other books published by Advantage Books call our toll free order number at:
1-888-383-3110 (Book Orders Only)

or online at: www.thequranrevealed.com

Longwood, Florida, USA
"we bring dreams to life" ™

Milton Keynes UK
Ingram Content Group UK Ltd.
UKHW051037251123
433129UK00023B/533